North India

Mark Honan
Joseph Bindloss   Joyce Connolly
Paul Greenway   Anthony Ham
Alan Murphy   Sarina Singh

LONELY PLANET PUBLICATIONS
Melbourne • Oakland • London • Paris

NORTH INDIA

KULLU
Follow the chariot of Rama as it is pulled through the streets during the colourful Dussehra festival

FATEHPUR SIKRI
Wander through Emperor Akbar's 'perfect city', built in honour of sufi mystic Shaikh Salim Chishti

KHAJURAHO
Admire the exquisite carved temples at this former Chandela capital

JAIPUR
Take an elephant ride up to the Amber Fort, a superb example of Rajput architecture

PALITANA
Climb up to the magnificent hill complex of Shatrunjaya, with its 863 Jain temples

SANCHI
Discover some of India's oldest and most spectacular stupas, built by Buddhism's most famous convert, Emperor Ashoka

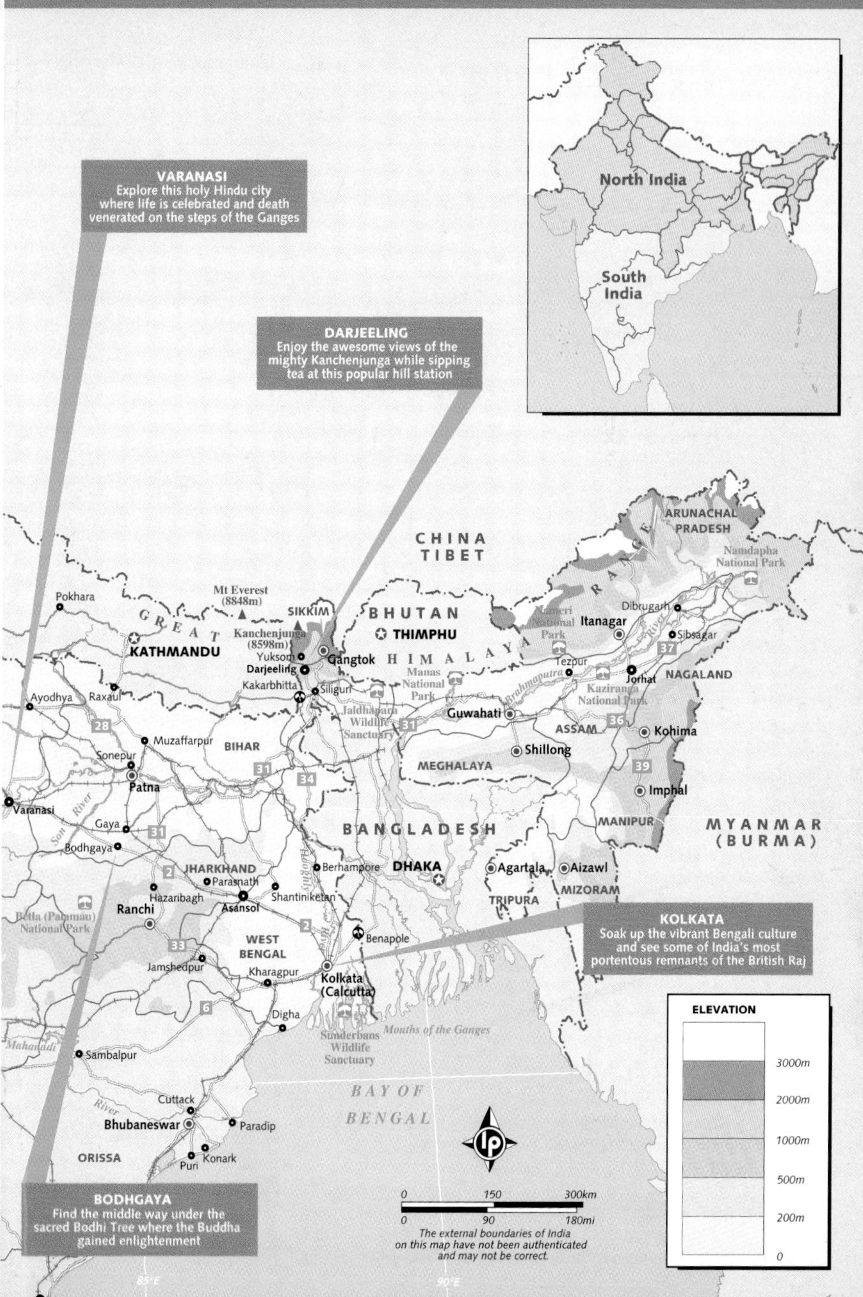
North India
South India
VARANASI
Explore this holy Hindu city where life is celebrated and death venerated on the steps of the Ganges
DARJEELING
Enjoy the awesome views of the mighty Kanchenjunga while sipping tea at this popular hill station
KOLKATA
Soak up the vibrant Bengali culture and see some of India's most portentous remnants of the British Raj
BODHGAYA
Find the middle way under the sacred Bodhi Tree where the Buddha gained enlightenment
CHINA
TIBET
BHUTAN
THIMPHU
ARUNACHAL PRADESH
Namdapha National Park
Mt Everest (8848m)
Kanchenjunga (8598m)
SIKKIM
Pokhara
KATHMANDU
GREAT HIMALAYA RANGE
Yuksom
Gangtok
Darjeeling
Kakarbhitta
Siliguri
Manas National Park
Jaldhapara Wildlife Sanctuary
Itanagar
Dibrugarh
Sibsagar
Tezpur
Jorhat
NAGALAND
Kaziranga National Park
Guwahati
ASSAM
Kohima
Shillong
MEGHALAYA
Imphal
MANIPUR
MYANMAR (BURMA)
Ayodhya
Raxaul
Muzaffarpur
BIHAR
Sonepur
Patna
Varanasi
Son River
Gaya
Bodhgaya
JHARKHAND
Parasnath
Hazaribagh
Ranchi
Asansol
Shantiniketan
Betla (Palamau) National Park
Berhampore
BANGLADESH
DHAKA
Agartala
Aizawl
TRIPURA
MIZORAM
WEST BENGAL
Benapole
Jamshedpur
Kharagpur
Kolkata (Calcutta)
Hooghly
Digha
Sunderbans Wildlife Sanctuary
Mouths of the Ganges
Mahanadi
Sambalpur
Cuttack
Bhubaneswar
Paradip
ORISSA
Puri
Konark
BAY OF BENGAL
Visakhapatnam
85°E
90°E
28
31
34
2
33
6
36
37
39
0 150 300km
0 90 180mi
The external boundaries of India on this map have not been authenticated and may not be correct.
ELEVATION
3000m
2000m
1000m
500m
200m
0

North India
1st edition – September 2001

Published by
Lonely Planet Publications Pty Ltd, ABN 36 005 607 983
90 Maribyrnong St, Footscray, Victoria 3011, Australia

Lonely Planet offices
Australia Locked Bag 1, Footscray, Victoria 3011
USA 150 Linden St, Oakland, CA 94607
UK 10a Spring Place, London NW5 3BH
France 1 rue du Dahomey, 75011 Paris

Photographs
Many of the images in this guide are available for licensing from Lonely Planet Images.
email: lpi@lonelyplanet.com.au

Front cover photograph
Bathing in the Ganges, Varanasi, Uttar Pradesh (Sara-Jane Cleland)

ISBN 1 86450 330 0

Printed by SNP SPrint (M) Sdn Bhd
Printed in Malaysia

Contents – Text

Contents – Maps

DELHI

PUNJAB & HARYANA

HIMACHAL PRADESH

JAMMU & KASHMIR

LADAKH & ZANSKAR

UTTAR PRADESH & UTTARANCHAL

BIHAR & JHARKHAND

KOLKATA (CALCUTTA)

WEST BENGAL

SIKKIM

NORTH-EASTERN REGION

RAJASTHAN

GUJARAT

MADHYA PRADESH & CHHATISGARH

The Authors

Mark Honan

Mark was the coordinating author of this book. After a university degree in philosophy opened up a glittering career as an office clerk, Mark decided that there was more to life than form-filling and data-entry. He set off on a two-year trip round the world, armed with a backpack and a vague intent to sell travel stories and pictures upon his return to England. Astonishingly, this barely formed plan succeeded and Mark became the travel correspondent to a London-based magazine. Since 1991, he has written Lonely Planet guidebooks to Vienna, Austria and Switzerland, updated the *Solomon Islands* guidebook and contributed to guides to Europe, Central America, Mexico and India, as well as to both volumes of *Lonely Planet Unpacked* (two books of travel horror stories) and *Out to Eat – London*. He is currently researching the new guide to Austria. Although more than happy not to be a clerk any more, he finds, curiously, that life as a travel writer still entails a good deal of form-filling and data-entry.

Joe Bindloss

Joe was born in Cyprus, grew up in England and has since lived and worked in several other countries. He currently calls London home. Joe gravitated towards journalism after a degree in biology eliminated science from his choice of future careers; he has also worked as a mural painter, book-maker and sculptor. Joe first developed wanderlust on family trips through the Mediterranean in an old VW Kombi. He has also worked on Lonely Planet guides to Australia, the Philippines and the Indian Ocean islands.

Joyce Connolly

Born in Scotland, Joyce has been on the road since an early age, including six years in Germany and the Netherlands where she developed a deep appreciation of beer. Fuelled by the travel bug, she studied to become a professional tourist, but instead stumbled into publishing. In 1995, she set off for Australia in pursuit of Jason Donovan, who obligingly moved house to become her neighbour. Having satisfied that urge she turned her attention to Lonely Planet; she updated part of the *Victoria* guide and has subsequently contributed to the *Zimbabwe*, *Morocco* and *India* guidebooks. Joyce has recently traded her *salwar kameez* for a bikini and was last spotted chasing cyclones in Western Australia.

Paul Greenway

Paul caught his first tropical disease in 1985 and has had the travel bug ever since. Gratefully plucked from the blandness and security of the Australian Public Service, he is now a full-time traveller and writer. Paul has contributed to several Lonely Planet guides, including South India and Indonesia, and has written guides to Mongolia, Iran and Bali & Lombok. During the rare times he is not travelling (or writing, reading or dreaming about it), Paul writes and records tuneless ditties, eats and breathes Australian Rules Football, and does anything else necessary to avoid settling down.

Anthony Ham

Anthony worked as a refugee lawyer for three years, during which time the people of the world visited him in his office. After tiring of daily battles with a mean-spirited Australian government, he set out to see the world and restore his faith in humanity. He has been travelling ever since, throughout Asia and Africa, all the while discovering unimagined uses for his masters degree in Middle Eastern politics. He is now based in Melbourne and works as a freelance writer and photographer. During his travels for Lonely Planet, Anthony has eaten rat in West Africa, been arrested in Iran, and found himself constantly overwhelmed by the many kindnesses from anything-but-ordinary people wherever he's travelled.

Alan Murphy

Born in Melbourne, Alan took off for a six-month stint around Europe and the Middle East in 1992. Four years later, after dipping his toes into the world of marketing and banking in between travel stints, he was back on home soil. Convinced of the need to avoid the 'corporate ladder' and peak-hour traffic, he returned to study in 1997. After completing a journalism course at Murdoch University he offered his services to Lonely Planet. Alan currently lives in Melbourne. He enjoys working strange hours and sniffing out new watering holes, and hopes one day to write a good pub guide. Alan has previously worked on Lonely Planet's *Southern Africa* and *Africa* guides.

Sarina Singh

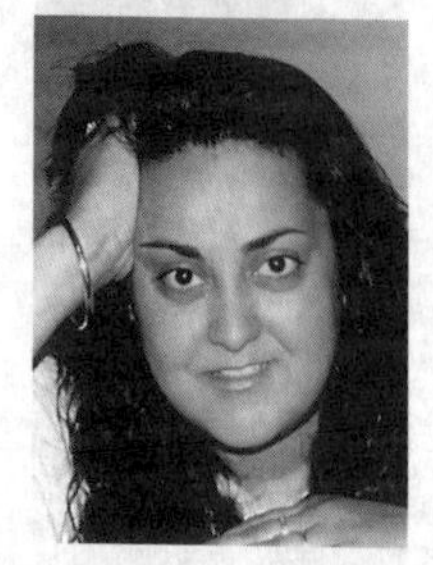

A passionate traveller ever since she can remember, Sarina bought a one-way ticket to Delhi after finishing a business degree in Melbourne. In India, Sarina completed a corporate traineeship with the Sheraton but later ditched hotels for newspapers, working as a freelance journalist and foreign correspondent. After four years in the subcontinent she returned to Australia, pursued postgraduate journalism qualifications and wrote two television documentary scripts. Other Lonely Planet books Sarina has worked on include *Aboriginal Australia & the Torres Strait Islands*, *India*, *Mauritius, Réunion & Seychelles*, *Africa on a shoestring*, *Sacred India*, two editions of *Rajasthan* and the *Out to Eat* restaurant guides to Melbourne and Sydney. She is also the author of *Polo in India* and has contributed to various international publications, including the *Sunday Times* and *National Geographic Traveler*.

FROM THE AUTHORS

Mark Honan

Many thanks to all my co-authors on this book, who willingly helped out with information when requested. Alan Murphy excelled himself in this regard, providing a range of useful snippets and recommendations. Special thanks also to Sarina Singh, whose fine work on the introductory chapters for the India guidebook provided a solid foundation for me to build on for the guidebook you're now holding. At the Lonely Planet head office, Hilary Ericksen was an amenable and efficient liaison.

Joe Bindloss

Thanks firstly to Rajinder Budhraja in Delhi for making the impossible possible. Thanks also to Ramesh Wadhwa in Agra for keeping me abreast of the Taj fee crisis. In Uttaranchal, thanks to the helpful staff of the GMVN and KMVN. This project could not have been completed without the help of the Tibetan Government in Exile in Dharamsala. And thanks to all the travellers who wrote in with advice, warnings and tips.

Joyce Connolly

Thanks to my mum and Reem Mina. Cheers to Rujendra Kumar, and also to Martin Hughes, Louari Ramouch and Isla James for a few unravelling sessions. Helpful people in Ladakh include: Tsering Dolang at LEDeG; Rebecca Norman, Aachan Dolma and Roxanna at Secmol; Dawa at Oriental Guest House; and Unchuck, the best driver in Ladakh. In Punjab, Prince Manyot Bubber made Amritsar fun, Manoj Sharma showed me Jalandhar and RC Yadar from the Punjab Department of Tourism helped me get there. Finally, I'd like to dedicate my contribution to Molly Blackford-Jennings – I'm doing it for you from now on.

Paul Greenway

Special plaudits to: Pema Gyaltsen Bhutia of the Khangchendzonga Conservation Committee in Yuksom; Bubu from Heritage Tours in Puri; and Amy Smith for being my drinking and travelling companion in Sikkim. At Lonely Planet, thanks to Geoff Stringer for sending me to all these weird and wonderful places; and apologies to all the long-suffering and unsung editors, cartographers and designers.

Anthony Ham

Special thanks must go to Ron, Jan, Lisa, Greg, Alex, Thomas, Tanya, Samantha and Damien for accepting my absences. Thanks also to Alan Paruit at STA Travel. Thanks in particular to Pankaj Shah of the KMVS in Bhuj; the staff at the SEWA Reception Centre in Ahmedabad; Mr Sorathia in Junagadh; Vinod Bhojak in Bikaner; Mukesh Mehta in Bundi; JD Khan at the Tourist Reception Centre in Ranthambore; Digvijay Singh Patan and his family; and Viro in Bharatpur. Special mention must be made of Shabir Ali Lalah – watch out for him at the Jaipur railway station (rickshaw registration RN 1406). Bhuwneshwari and Vishwa Vijay Singh taught me anew the magic of Udaipur and the hospitality of the Rajputs. Also in Udaipur, thank you to Meenu for her dignity and selflessness. Thank you to the travellers: Hamish and Anna, Matt and Bel, Laurent, Alpa and especially Carinae.

Alan Murphy

I would like to dedicate my portion of this book to my two beautiful nieces, Lauren Elise and Caitlin.

There were many people who helped make this project so enjoyable. Thanks to my partner, Justine Vaisutis, for her relentless research and, without whom, India would never have been so special. Also my appreciation to Jules at Flight Centre, a good friend and the best travel agent on the planet. In India, a special thanks to P Anbalagan (An-Bu) from Chennai for his skilful driving, his expertise with Hindi and most of all for being a good friend. His research assistance was invaluable. Also, thanks to: Mr Shaw at the Government of India Tourist Office in Varanasi; Dwarko Sundrani in Bodhgaya for helping me understand real charity and Mr Sunil Kumar Sinha for his wonderful hospitality; the gentleman in Patna for holding up the traffic and helping us to reverse out of a jam; Mr Ajay Awasthi at Global Village Development Organisation and the Government of India Tourist Office, both in Khajuraho; Mr D Karunanidhi at Welcome Tours and Travels; Rob and Michelle in Mandu for their company and some much needed R&R; and to all the friendly people who gave us directions, went out of their way to make us feel welcome and allowed us to briefly share their country with them. Lastly, to all the train station inquiry counters for helping me to understand bureaucracy and enlightening me as to the meaning of the phrase, 'like drawing blood out of a stone'.

Sarina Singh

In India I'm very grateful to the following people for so generously offering me their time and insights: to the remarkably knowledgable Bhaichand Patel for his perpetual assistance; to Mr and Mrs Neeraj Padhi for their help and wonderful company in Kolkata; to Arati Oberoi for her constant updates; to Tilottama Das (West Bengal Tourism Centre, Kolkata); and Satarupa Das and Ashok Banerjie (Government of India tourist office, Kolkata). For precious tips, thanks to Abisheik Khan, Priya Sharma, Rahul Bhatia, Ashok Roy, Shalini and Anand Krishnan, and Arvind Narayan. Special thanks to Patrick Moffat for casting an expert eye over the motorbike information and to Amit, Swati and Parth Jhaveri in Mumbai for their ongoing support and friendship.

This Book

Mark Honan was the coordinating author of this 1st edition of *North India*. He was responsible for the introductory chapters, with contributions from Sarina Singh and Richard Plunkett, and wrote the special sections 'The Way of the Buddha', 'North India's Pilgrimage Sites' and 'Islamic and Mughal Architecture'. Sarina Singh researched Kolkata (Calcutta) and the southern part of West Bengal. Joe Bindloss researched Himachal Pradesh, Uttaranchal and the Agra region of Uttar Pradesh. Joyce Connolly researched Delhi, Punjab, Haryana, Ladakh and Jammu & Kashmir. Paul Greenway researched the northern part of West Bengal, as well as Sikkim and the states of the north-eastern region. Anthony Ham researched Rajasthan and Gujarat. Alan Murphy researched central Uttar Pradesh and the Varanasi region, Bihar, Jharkhand, Madhya Pradesh and Chhatisgarh.

Garry Weare advised on trekking in the Himalaya and provided general information for chapters incorporating the Himalaya. Martin Hughes wrote the Food and Drinks sections in the Facts for the Visitor chapter and Michael Sklovsky wrote the Arts & Crafts section in the Facts about North India chapter. Bruce Evans provided specialist advice on Buddhism.

From the Publisher

John Hinman and Jody Whiteoak were the coordinating editor and coordinating designer, respectively. Kerryn Burgess, Yvonne Byron, Melanie Dankel, Janine Eberle, Bruce Evans, Susannah Farfor, Justin Flynn, Susan Holtham, Nancy Ianni, Evan Jones, Lynne Preston, Hilary Rogers, Kalya Ryan and Julia Taylor assisted with editing and proofing. Heath Comrie, Csanad Csutoros, Hunor Csutoros, Huw Fowles, Pablo Gastar, Birgit Jordan, Adrian Persoglia, Amanda Sierp and Rod Zandberg helped with mapping. Shahara Ahmed, Sarah Sloane and Maree Styles helped with both mapping and layout. Shahara Ahmed compiled the climate charts. Lara Morcombe compiled the index, with assistance from Joanne Newell. Matt King coordinated the illustrations and Annie Horner sourced the photographic images for the book. The cover was designed by Margaret Jung. Mark Germanchis provided expert Quark support through layout.

Thanks to Hilary Ericksen, senior editor, and Adriana Mammarella, senior designer, for valiantly overseeing the project.

Foreword

ABOUT LONELY PLANET GUIDEBOOKS

The story begins with a classic travel adventure: Tony and Maureen Wheeler's 1972 journey across Europe and Asia to Australia. Useful information about the overland trail did not exist at that time, so Tony and Maureen published the first Lonely Planet guidebook to meet a growing need.

From a kitchen table, then from a tiny office in Melbourne (Australia), Lonely Planet has become the largest independent travel publisher in the world, an international company with offices in Melbourne, Oakland (USA), London (UK) and Paris (France).

Today Lonely Planet guidebooks cover the globe. There is an ever-growing list of books and there's information in a variety of forms and media. Some things haven't changed. The main aim is still to help make it possible for adventurous travellers to get out there – to explore and better understand the world.

At Lonely Planet we believe travellers can make a positive contribution to the countries they visit – if they respect their host communities and spend their money wisely. Since 1986 a percentage of the income from each book has been donated to aid projects and human rights campaigns.

Updates Lonely Planet thoroughly updates each guidebook as often as possible. This usually means there are around two years between editions, although for more unusual or more stable destinations the gap can be longer. Check the imprint page (following the colour map at the beginning of the book) for publication dates.

Between editions up-to-date information is available in two free newsletters – the paper *Planet Talk* and email *Comet* (to subscribe, contact any Lonely Planet office) – and on our Web site at www.lonelyplanet.com. The *Upgrades* section of the Web site covers a number of important and volatile destinations and is regularly updated by Lonely Planet authors. *Scoop* covers news and current affairs relevant to travellers. And, lastly, the *Thorn Tree* bulletin board and *Postcards* section of the site carry unverified, but fascinating, reports from travellers.

Correspondence The process of creating new editions begins with the letters, postcards and emails received from travellers. This correspondence often includes suggestions, criticisms and comments about the current editions. Interesting excerpts are immediately passed on via newsletters and the Web site, and everything goes to our authors to be verified when they're researching on the road. We're keen to get more feedback from organisations or individuals who represent communities visited by travellers.

Lonely Planet gathers information for everyone who's curious about the planet – and especially for those who explore it first-hand. Through guidebooks, phrasebooks, activity guides, maps, literature, newsletters, image library, TV series and Web site we act as an information exchange for a worldwide community of travellers.

Research Authors aim to gather sufficient practical information to enable travellers to make informed choices and to make the mechanics of a journey run smoothly. They also research historical and cultural background to help enrich the travel experience and allow travellers to understand and respond appropriately to cultural and environmental issues.

Authors don't stay in every hotel because that would mean spending a couple of months in each medium-sized city and, no, they don't eat at every restaurant because that would mean stretching belts beyond capacity. They do visit hotels and restaurants to check standards and prices, but feedback based on readers' direct experiences can be very helpful.

Many of our authors work undercover, others aren't so secretive. None of them accept freebies in exchange for positive write-ups. And none of our guidebooks contain any advertising.

Production Authors submit their raw manuscripts and maps to offices in Australia, USA, UK or France. Editors and cartographers – all experienced travellers themselves – then begin the process of assembling the pieces. When the book finally hits the shops, some things are already out of date, we start getting feedback from readers and the process begins again…

WARNING & REQUEST

Things change – prices go up, schedules change, good places go bad and bad places go bankrupt – nothing stays the same. So, if you find things better or worse, recently opened or long since closed, please tell us and help make the next edition even more accurate and useful. We genuinely value all the feedback we receive. A well-travelled team reads and acknowledges every letter, postcard and email and ensures that every morsel of information finds its way to the appropriate authors, editors and cartographers for verification.

Everyone who writes to us will find their name in the next edition of the appropriate guidebook. They will also receive the latest issue of *Planet Talk*, our quarterly printed newsletter, or *Comet*, our monthly email newsletter. Subscriptions to both newsletters are free. The very best contributions will be rewarded with a free guidebook.

Excerpts from your correspondence may appear in new editions of Lonely Planet guidebooks, the Lonely Planet Web site, *Planet Talk* or *Comet*, so please let us know if you *don't* want your letter published or your name acknowledged.

Send all correspondence to the Lonely Planet office closest to you:

Australia: Locked Bag 1, Footscray, Victoria 3011
USA: 150 Linden St, Oakland, CA 94607
UK: 10A Spring Place, London NW5 3BH
France: 1 rue du Dahomey, 75011 Paris

Or email us at: talk2us@lonelyplanet.com.au

For news, views and updates see our Web site: www.lonelyplanet.com

HOW TO USE A LONELY PLANET GUIDEBOOK

The best way to use a Lonely Planet guidebook is any way you choose. At Lonely Planet we believe the most memorable travel experiences are often those that are unexpected, and the finest discoveries are those you make yourself. Guidebooks are not intended to be used as if they provide a detailed set of infallible instructions!

Contents All Lonely Planet guidebooks follow roughly the same format. The Facts about the Destination chapters or sections give background information ranging from history to weather. Facts for the Visitor gives practical information on issues like visas and health. Getting There & Away gives a brief starting point for researching travel to and from the destination. Getting Around gives an overview of the transport options when you arrive.

The peculiar demands of each destination determine how subsequent chapters are broken up, but some things remain constant. We always start with background, then proceed to sights, places to stay, places to eat, entertainment, getting there and away, and getting around information – in that order.

Heading Hierarchy Lonely Planet headings are used in a strict hierarchical structure that can be visualised as a set of Russian dolls. Each heading (and its following text) is encompassed by any preceding heading that is higher on the hierarchical ladder.

Entry Points We do not assume guidebooks will be read from beginning to end, but that people will dip into them. The traditional entry points are the list of contents and the index. In addition, however, some books have a complete list of maps and an index map illustrating map coverage.

There may also be a colour map that shows highlights. These highlights are dealt with in greater detail in the Facts for the Visitor chapter, along with planning questions and suggested itineraries. Each chapter covering a geographical region usually begins with a locator map and another list of highlights. Once you find something of interest in a list of highlights, turn to the index.

Maps Maps play a crucial role in Lonely Planet guidebooks and include a huge amount of information. A legend is printed on the back page. We seek to have complete consistency between maps and text, and to have every important place in the text captured on a map. Map key numbers usually start in the top left corner.

Although inclusion in a guidebook usually implies a recommendation we cannot list every good place. Exclusion does not necessarily imply criticism. In fact there are a number of reasons why we might exclude a place – sometimes it is simply inappropriate to encourage an influx of travellers.

Introduction

India is perhaps the ultimate travel destination, containing some of the most spectacular sights anywhere in the world. Yet to many visitors, India is an enigma. It can give you the best and worst of times – often in the same day. An extended visit will throw up plenty to surprise, plenty to amaze and plenty to frustrate. You won't be able to take everything in your stride, nor will you be able to take it all for granted. But you certainly won't be bored.

India is such a huge and diverse country that it almost impossible to take it all in at one visit. Whether you are a first-timer or an old hand, you're likely to find things more manageable if you concentrate on exploring one area. If that area is North India, you'll encounter most of the country's headline attractions – and a lot more besides.

You can see the world's highest and most impressive mountain range, some of the finest architectural creations ever fashioned, and even the odd beach or two. The so-called 'golden triangle' of travel in India is here in the north: It comprises the national capital, Delhi, with its Muslim monuments and top-notch shopping; Agra, in Uttar Pradesh, with the stupendous Taj Mahal mausoleum; and the remarkable 'pink city', Jaipur, in Rajasthan.

The daily routine of life in North India will make as big an impression as the main sightseeing goals. Things that would be astonishing elsewhere – a serene cow grazing in the middle of a busy city street, for example – are merely commonplace here. Not only will you see incredible sights, you will soon find that you live and breathe India.

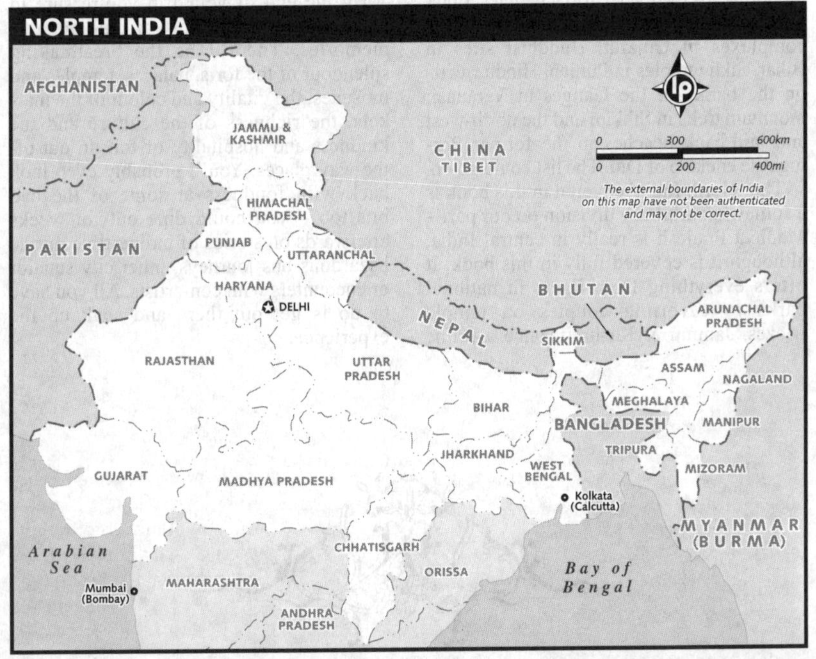

The multifarious aspects of life in the north will seep into your very pores.

Visitors will find North India a forward-looking and dynamic region, yet also a place with one foot seemingly stuck in the past. Rural North India remains much the same as it has for thousands of years, and life in the modern cities still moves very much according to the strictures of age-old verities, loyalties and obligations.

The north is not a homogenised region – far from it. It exhibits a range of customs and traditions that few countries in the world can match. A succession of invaders brought with them not only conflict, but a rich seam of ideas, skills and customs. Many reminders of these still exist for visitors to enjoy today, from the Mughal-built Taj Mahal to the remnants of the British Raj in Kolkata (Calcutta).

Both Himachal Pradesh and Ladakh have a distinctly Tibetan flavour, while Uttaranchal is influenced by Nepali culture and the far north-east by diverse tribal peoples. Look out also for palaces in Rajasthan, Jain hilltop complexes in Gujarat, Buddhist sites in Bihar, Sikh temples in Punjab, Hindu rituals on the banks of the Ganges at Varanasi, mountain treks in Sikkim and the north-west and laid-back beaches in the former Portuguese enclave of Diu. The list could go on.

The 'North India' covered in this book is a somewhat arbitrary division on our part – Madhya Pradesh is really in central India, although it is covered fully in this book. It offers everything from tigers in national parks to cavorting couples on temple friezes. Jammu & Kashmir, once a prime tourist destination in the far north, has been blighted by terrorist activity since the late 1980s. Although disruption has diminished of late, the region is not (yet) fully safe to visit, and is therefore covered only briefly. Every other northern Indian state is given the full treatment in this guidebook – we describe the main sights, pick out the best places to stay and eat, show you where to see traditional dances or grab a beer, and we pinpoint everything of importance on our customised maps.

India – some would say especially North India – is undeniably hard work. At times you'll feel you're simply helpless prey for every pseudo travel agent, scamming gem seller or commission-bent rickshaw-wallah that crosses your path. Such individuals will come up with every ingenious trick in the book (and a few not yet catalogued) to try to part you from your money. But despite the hassles, you'll find North India is well worth the effort.

By the end of your trip you're sure to leave with a whole host of unforgettable memories. There'll be the breathtaking splendour of the forts, palaces, temples and mosques, the vitality and colour of the markets, the richness of the culture and the kindness and hospitality of folk in out-of-the-way places. You'll probably even look back with fondness at some of the bad bits too – you could dine out for weeks afterwards on stories of indigestible meals, hazardous bus journeys, inner-city squalor or encounters with con-artists. All you have to do is get out there and soak up the experience.

Facts about North India

North India has had a long, sometimes turbulent history. Most of the invaders who arrived in India over the centuries approached by land, and therefore made their presence felt first (or only) in the north of the country. South India, although it has also suffered its share of conflicts, has generally had a more peaceful history; its contacts with the outside world have been forged through trade rather than by invasion.

The north also bore the brunt of the turmoil and bloodshed that occurred following the partition of the Indian subcontinent at the dawn of Independence. The consequences of those years are still being felt even now.

Yet the legions of invaders in the north did not have an entirely negative impact. Many left an enduring – and positive – mark on the culture and landscape. An unsurpassed diversity is the happy legacy for visitors to North India today.

The region has had its share of triumphs and achievements too. North India was the birthplace of two of the world's great religions (Hinduism and Buddhism) and one of its smallest (Jainism). Possibly no other country has its religions so intertwined with every aspect of life.

HISTORY

Indus Valley Civilisation

India's first major civilisation flourished around 2500 BC in the Indus River Valley, much of which lies within present-day Pakistan. This civilisation, which continued for 1000 years and is known as the Harappan culture, appears to have been the culmination of thousands of years of settlement. Excavation of different strata of Neolithic sites shows that the earliest inhabitants were nomadic tribespeople who began to cultivate the land and keep domestic animals. Considerable trade grew up, and by around 3500 BC an urban culture began to emerge. By 2500 BC the large cities of the Mature Harappa period were established.

The major cities such as Mohenjodaro and Harappa (discovered in the 1920s), and

The Gujarat Earthquake of 2001

On 26 January 2001, India's Republic Day, a massive earthquake hit the western state of Gujarat causing widespread damage and massive loss of life. The official death toll was close to 17,000 (including 15,000 in the Kutch (Kachchh) district of western Gujarat). Although some government ministers speculated that the number of people killed could reach as high as 100,000, the most likely figure was closer to 30,000. The exact figure will never be known, in part because the devastation was so widespread. Emergency relief efforts were so stretched and the potential for disease from unburied bodies was such that hundreds if not thousands of buildings had to be bulldozed without the bodies inside ever being accounted for. Up to 300,000 people were injured and over half a million left homeless. Centred on the isolated region of Kutch and measuring 7.9 on the Richter scale, the tremors were felt as far away as Chennai in the south and Nepal to the north-east.

In economic terms, the damage could have been much worse. Gujarat is one of India's most industrialised and hitherto wealthiest states, accounting for 13% of the country's industrial output and 11% of its income. Although there was much damage in Gujarat's economic capital of Ahmedabad, the state's industrial infrastructure remained largely intact. Of greater concern for Gujarat's, and hence India's, economic recovery was the significant damage suffered by Kandla port, which handles 17% of India's seagoing traffic. Not to mention the staggering social and economic cost of the reconstruction of shattered towns and communities.

For more on India's worst earthquake since Independence, see the Gujarat chapter.

Lothal near Ahmedabad in India, were carefully laid out with precise street plans. Several sites had a separate acropolis pointing to a clear religious function, and the great tank (reservoir) at Mohenjodaro may well have been used for ritual bathing purposes. The major cities were sizeable – estimates of the population of Mohenjodaro are as high as 40,000.

By the middle of the 3rd millennium BC the Indus Valley culture was the equal of other great cultures emerging at the time. The Harappans traded with Mesopotamia, and developed a system of weights and measures, a script (which remains undeciphered), and a developed art in the form of terracotta and bronze figurines. Recovered relics include models of bullock carts and jewellery, demonstrating an already distinctively Indian culture. Clay figurines found at these sites suggest that a Mother goddess (later personified as Kali) and a male three-faced god sitting in the attitude of a yogi attended by four animals (the prehistoric Shiva) were worshipped. Black stone pillars (associated with phallic worship of Shiva) and animal figures (the most prominent being the humped bull; later Shiva's mount) have also been discovered.

The decline of the culture, at the beginning of the 2nd millennium BC, was thought by some to have been caused by an Aryan invasion. Recently, however, historians have suggested several alternatives, one theory being that the decline was caused by the flooding of the Indus Valley; another possibility is that climatic changes led to decreased rainfall and the subsequent failure of agriculture.

Early Invasions & the Rise of Religions

It is important to note that some academics ardently dispute the 'colonial-missionary' Aryan invasion theory, claiming that there is no archaeological proof or evidence of an invasion in the ancient Indian texts. Some argue that the Aryans were in fact the original inhabitants of India and the invasion theory was actually devised by self-serving foreign conquerors. Others say that the arrival of Aryans was more of a gentle migration than an invasion.

Those who defend the invasion theory believe that from around 1500 BC onwards, Aryan (from a Sanskrit word meaning noble) tribes from Afghanistan and Central Asia began to filter into north-west India. Despite their martial superiority, their progress was gradual, with successive tribes fighting over territory and new arrivals pushing farther east into the Ganges plain. Eventually these tribes controlled the whole of northern India as far as the Vindhya Hills, and many of the original inhabitants, the Dravidians, were pushed south.

The invaders brought with them their nature gods, among whom the gods of fire (Agni) and battle (Indra) were predominant, as well as cattle-raising and meat-eating traditions. It was during this period of transition (1500–1200 BC) that the Hindu sacred scriptures, the Vedas, were written, and that the caste system became formalised, distinguishing between the Aryans and the indigenous Indians they were subduing. The Vedas justify caste by describing the natural creation of the system when the universe was formed:

> When they divided Purusha, how many portions did they make?
> What do they call his mouth, his arms? What do they call his thighs and feet?
> The Brahmin was his mouth, of both arms was the Rajanya Kshatriya made.
> His thighs became the Vaishya, from his feet the Shudra was produced.

As the Aryan tribes spread out across the Ganges plain, in the late 7th century BC, many of them became grouped together into 16 major kingdoms. The *asvamedha* or horse sacrifice was one aspect of an increasingly formal system of rule that prevailed. In this ritual a horse was allowed to roam freely, followed by a band of soldiers. If the horse's progress was impeded the king would fight for the land in question. At the end of the prescribed period, the entire area over which the horse had wandered was taken to be the king's unchallenged territory, and the horse was sacrificed. This ritual was still being performed centuries later by dynasties such as the Chalukyas of Badami to assert their unchallenged right to territory, and to demonstrate the ruler's complete control of his kingdom.

Gradually the 16 major kingdoms were amalgamated into four large states, with Kosala and Magadha emerging to be the most powerful during the 5th century BC. After a series of dynastic changes, the Nanda dynasty came to power in 364 BC, ruling over a huge area of North India.

During this period, the heartland narrowly avoided two other invasions from the west. The first was by the Persian king Darius (521–486 BC), who annexed Punjab and Sind (on either side of the modern India-Pakistan border). Alexander the Great marched to India from Greece in 326 BC, but his troops refused to go beyond the Beas River, in Himachal Pradesh. It was the easternmost extent of the Persian empire he conquered, and he turned back without extending his power into India itself. His most lasting legacy in the east was the development of Gandharan art, an intriguing mix of Grecian artistic ideals and the new religious beliefs of Buddhism.

Buddhism and Jainism arose around 500 BC, questioning the Vedas and condemning the caste system, though, unlike the Buddhists, the Jains never denied their Hindu heritage and their faith never extended beyond India.

SARAH JOLLY

The lotus is the national flower of India.

Buddhism, on the other hand, cut a radical swath through the spiritual and social body of Hinduism and experienced some spectacular growth after Emperor Ashoka embraced it in 262 BC and declared it the state religion. Nevertheless, it gradually lost touch with the masses and faded as Hinduism underwent a revival between AD 200 and 800. Yet such was the appeal of the Buddha that it could not be sidelined and forgotten. The Buddha was therefore incorporated into the Hindu pantheon as yet another of the avatars (manifestations) of Vishnu; a prime example of the way in which Hinduism has absorbed spiritual competitors and heretical ideologies.

The Mauryas & Emperor Ashoka

Chandragupta Maurya, the founder of the first great Indian empire, came to power in 321 BC, having seized the Magadha throne from the Nandas. He soon expanded the empire to include a huge area of the Indus Valley previously conquered by Alexander. According to an eyewitness account by an ambassador to the Mauryan court, Megasthenes, Chandragupta's capital at Pataliputra (modern-day Patna), was of an awesome size – 33.8km in circumference. If this is true, it would have been the largest city in the world at the time.

The Mauryan empire eventually spread across North India and as far south as modern-day Karnataka. The Mauryas set up a well-organised kingdom with an efficient bureaucracy, organised tiers of local government and a well-defined social order consisting of a rigid caste system. Security was maintained by an enormous standing army consisting, according to one account, of 9000 elephants, 30,000 cavalry and 600,000 infantry.

The empire reached its peak under Ashoka, who left pillars and rock-carved edicts which delineate the enormous span of his territory. Remnants of these can still be seen today in Delhi, Gujarat, Sarnath in Uttar Pradesh (on the spot where the Buddha delivered his first sermon expounding the Noble Eightfold Path, or middle way to enlightenment) and Sanchi in Madhya Pradesh.

Ashoka also sent missions abroad, and he is revered in Sri Lanka because he sent his son and daughter to carry Buddhism to the island. The development of art and sculpture also flourished during his rule, and his standard, which topped many pillars, is now the seal of modern-day India (four lions sitting back to back atop an abacus decorated with a frieze and the inscription 'truth alone triumphs'). The Republic of India, established on 26 January 1950, chose Ashoka's standard as its national emblem to reaffirm the ancient commitment to peace and goodwill. Under Ashoka, the Mauryan empire probably controlled more of India than any subsequent ruler before the Mughals or the British. Following Ashoka's death, in 232 BC, the empire rapidly disintegrated, finally collapsing in 184 BC.

An Interlude, Then the Guptas

A number of empires rose and fell following the collapse of the Mauryas. The Sungas ruled from 184 to 70 BC before being overcome by the short-lived Kanvas. In the north-west, the successors to Alexander's kingdoms expanded their power into Punjab, before being overrun by a new wave of invaders from Central Asia, including the Shakas. The Shakas were later relieved of power in North India (but not in the north-west and south) by the Kushanas, who briefly ruled over a massive area of North India and Central Asia. In central India the powerful Shatavahanas ruled the roost, and throughout the subcontinent small tribes and kingdoms held varying amounts of territory and influence.

Despite the lack of a central power, this was a period of intense development. Trade with the Roman empire (both overland and by sea through the southern ports) became substantial during the 1st century AD, and there was also overland trade with China. Buddhism flourished, despite experiencing a doctrinal split. Jainism's doctrine underwent a similar division, giving rise to the Digambara (sky clad) and Svetambara (white clad) sects.

In 319 AD, Chandragupta I, the third king of the little known Gupta tribe, came to prominence by a fortuitous marriage to the daughter of one of the most powerful tribes in the north, the Licchavis. The Gupta empire grew rapidly and under Chandragupta II (who ruled from AD 375 to 413) it achieved its greatest extent. The Chinese pilgrim Fa-hsien, visiting India at the time, described what he found:

> The people are rich and contented, the kings govern without recourse to capital punishment, but offenders are fined lightly or heavily according to the nature of their crime.

The arts flourished during this period. Towards the end of the Gupta period, however, Buddhism and Jainism both began to decline and Hinduism began to rise in popularity once more.

The invasions of the Huns at the beginning of the 6th century signalled the end of this era of history, and in 510 the Gupta army was defeated by the Hun leader Toramana. Subsequently, North India broke up into a number of separate Hindu kingdoms and was not really unified again until the arrival of the Muslims.

This power vacuum saw the rise of a number of important kingdoms based in central and southern India, among them the Shatavahanas, Kalingas, and Vakatakas. The Karnataka-based Chalukyas ruled mainly over the Deccan region of central India (from 550 to 753), although their power occasionally extended farther north. For more on these and other kingdoms, including the later Vijayanagar empire (which flourished from 1336 to 1565), refer to Lonely Planet's *South India*.

First Muslim Invasions

Following the demise of the Guptas, there was constant competition between rival northern states, though a power balance was maintained. At the very beginning of the 11th century, however, a new enemy threatened from the north-west.

Muslim power first made itself strongly felt on the subcontinent with the raids of Mahmud of Ghazni. Today, Ghazni is just a nondescript little town between Kabul and Kandahar in Afghanistan, but in the early years of the 2nd millennium, Mahmud turned it into one of the world's most glorious capital cities. The funds for this development were plundered from his neighbours' territories; from 1001 to 1025 Mahmud conducted 17 raids into India including one on the famous Shiva temple at Somnath in Gujarat. A Hindu force of 70,000 died in fierce fighting trying to defend the temple, which eventually fell in early 1026. In the aftermath of his victory Mahmud, unconcerned with acquiring territory, successfully transported a massive haul of gold and other booty back across the desert to his capital. These raids effectively shattered the balance of power in North India, allowing subsequent invaders to claim the territory for themselves.

Following Mahmud's death in 1033, Ghazni was seized by the Seljuqs and subsequently fell to the Ghurs, who originated in western Afghanistan. Their style of warfare was brutal – having taken Ghazni in 1150, they are reported to have spent seven days sacking the city, a feat which they achieved so thoroughly that the Ghur general Ala-ud-din was subsequently titled 'Burner of the World'.

In 1191, Mohammed of Ghur, who had been expanding his powers across Punjab, advanced into India and fought a major battle against a confederacy of Hindu rulers. He was defeated, but returned the following year and routed his enemies. One of his generals, Qutb-ud-din, captured Delhi and was appointed governor, while another continued east carving out a separate empire in Bengal. Within a short time almost the whole of North India was under Ghur control and following Mohammed's death in 1206, Qutb-ud-din became the first of the sultans of Delhi. His successor, Iltutmish, brought Bengal back under central control and defended the growing empire from an attempted invasion by the Mongols.

After a brief interlude in which his succession was fought over, Ala-ud-din Khilji came to power in 1296. Through a series of phenomenal campaigns, he pushed the borders of the empire south, while simultaneously fending off further attacks by the Mongols.

After Ala-ud-din's death in 1320, Mohammed Tughlaq, having murdered his father, ascended the throne in 1324. During Mohammed's reign the empire achieved its greatest extent and also, as a result of Mohammed's overreaching ambition, began to disintegrate. Unlike his forebears (including great rulers such as Ashoka), Mohammed dreamed not only of extending his indirect influence over South India, but of controlling it directly as part of his empire. After a series of successful campaigns he decided to move the capital from Delhi to a more central location. The new capital was called Daulatabad and was near Aurangabad in Maharashtra. In order to populate the city he forced every single inhabitant out of Delhi and marched them southwards, with great loss of life. After only a short period, however, he realised that this left the north undefended and so the entire capital was moved north again. Raising revenue to finance his huge armies was another problem; an attempt to introduce copper coinage had disastrous results and widespread counterfeiting soon buried the plan.

With the withdrawal from the south, several splinter kingdoms arose, including, in the Deccan, the Bahmani sultanate and the Hindu Vijayanagar empire. The last of the great sultans of Delhi, Firoz Shah, died in 1388 and the fate of the sultanate was sealed when Tamerlane (Timur) made a devastating raid from Samarkand into India in 1398. Tamerlane's sack of Delhi is supposed to have been truly merciless; some accounts say his soldiers slaughtered every Hindu inhabitant.

The Mughals

Although the Mughals' heyday was relatively brief, their empire was massive, covering, at its height, almost the entire subcontinent. Its significance was not only in its size, however. The Mughal emperors presided over a golden age of arts and literature and had a passion for building which resulted in some of the finest architecture in India. In particular, Shah Jahan's magnificent Taj Mahal ranks as one of the wonders of the world. The six great Mughals and the length of their reigns were:

Babur	1527–1530
Humayun	1530–1556
Akbar	1556–1605
Jehangir	1605–1627
Shah Jahan	1627–1658
Aurangzeb	1658–1707

The founder of the Mughal line, Babur, was a descendant of both Genghis Khan and Tamerlane. In 1525 he marched into Punjab from his capital at Kabul in Afghanistan. With revolutionary new knowledge of firearms, and consummate skill in employing artillery and cavalry together, Babur defeated the numerically superior armies of the Sultan of Delhi at the Battle of Panipat in 1526.

Despite this initial success, Babur's son Humayun was defeated by a powerful ruler of eastern India, Sher Shah, in 1539 and forced to withdraw to Iran. Following Sher Shah's death in 1545, Humayun returned to claim his kingdom, eventually conquering Delhi in 1555. He died the following year and was succeeded by his young son Akbar who, during his 49-year reign, managed to extend and consolidate the empire until he ruled over a huge area.

Akbar was probably the greatest of the Mughals, for he not only had the military ability required of a ruler at that time, but was also a man of culture and wisdom with a sense of fairness. He saw, as previous Muslim rulers had not, that the number of Hindus in India was too great to subjugate. Instead, he integrated them into his empire and used them as advisers, generals and administrators. Akbar also had a deep interest in religious matters, and spent many hours in discussion with religious experts of all persuasions, including Christians and Parsis. He eventually formulated a religion, Deen Ilahi, which combined the favoured parts of all of those he had studied.

SIMON BORG

The peacock is the national bird of India.

Jehangir ascended to the throne following Akbar's death in 1605. Despite several challenges to the authority of Jehangir himself, the empire remained in more or less the same form as Akbar had left it. In periods of stability Jehangir took the opportunity to spend time in his beloved Kashmir, eventually dying en route there in 1627. He was succeeded by his son, Shah Jahan, who secured his position as emperor by executing all male relatives of similar rank. During his reign, some of the most vivid and permanent reminders of the Mughals' glory were constructed.

The last of the great Mughals, Aurangzeb came to the throne in 1658, after a two-year struggle against his brothers and having imprisoned his father, Shah Jahan. Aurangzeb devoted his resources to extending the empire's boundaries, and fell into much the same trap that Mohammed Tughlaq had some 300 years earlier. He, too, tried moving his capital south (to Aurangabad) and imposed heavy taxes to fund his military. A combination of decaying court life and dissatisfaction among the Hindu population at inflated taxes and religious intolerance weakened the Mughal grip.

The empire faced serious challenges from several quarters – the Rajputs in Rajasthan and the Sikhs in Punjab as well as the Marathas in central India and, more significantly, the British in Bengal. With Aurangzeb's death in 1707, the empire's fortunes rapidly declined, and the sack of Delhi by Persia's Nadir Shah in 1739 served to confirm the empire's lack of real power. Mughal 'emperors' continued to rule right up to the Indian Uprising in 1857, but they were emperors without an empire.

The Rajputs & the Sikhs

Throughout the Mughal period, there were still strong Hindu powers, most notably the Rajputs. Centred in Rajasthan, the Rajputs were a proud warrior caste with a passionate belief in the dictates of chivalry, both in battle and in the conduct of state affairs. Their place in Indian history is much like that of the knights of medieval Europe. The Rajputs opposed every foreign incursion into their territory, but were never united or adequately organised to deal with superior forces on a long-term basis. When not battling foreign oppression they squandered their energies fighting each other. This eventually led to them becoming vassal states of the Mughal empire, but their prowess in battle was acknowledged, and some of the best military men in the emperors' armies were Rajputs.

Another emerging force were the Sikhs in Punjab. The Sikh religion was founded by Guru Nanak (1469–1539) in the late 15th century. Followers of Sikhism became bitter enemies of the Mughals, especially after Aurangzeb executed Sikh leaders when they refused to embrace Islam. To counteract threats from Hindus and Mughals, the Sikh religion became increasingly organised along military lines.

Expansion of British Power

The British were not the first European power to arrive in India, nor were they the last to leave – both those honours go to the Portuguese. In 1498, Vasco da Gama arrived on the coast of modern-day Kerala, and the Portuguese presence in India continued until 1961 (when they relinquished Goa, Diu and Daman). Generally, however, the Portuguese were quickly eclipsed after the arrival of the British, French and Dutch.

In 1600, Queen Elizabeth I granted a charter to a London trading company giving it a monopoly on British trade with India. In 1612, representatives of the East India Company (which was actually known by several other names until the 1830s, including the 'Company of Merchants') established the first trading post at Surat in Gujarat. Further British trading posts, administered and governed by representatives of the company, were established at Madras (now called Chennai) in 1640, Bengal in 1651 and Bombay (Mumbai) in 1668. Strange as it seems now, for nearly 250 years a commercial trading company and not the British government 'ruled' British India.

The British and Portuguese were not the only Europeans in India. The Danes and the Dutch also had trading posts: the former in Bengal, the latter in Surat from 1616 and on the Coromandel Coast in South India. In 1672 the French established themselves at Pondicherry, an enclave they would hold even after the British had departed. The stage was set for more than a century of rivalry between the British and French for control of Indian trade, which was largely resolved in favour of the British in 1750 when the directors of the French East India Company decided their representatives were playing too much politics and doing too little trading. French interests remained strong enough, however, for them to continue supporting various local rulers in their struggles against the British.

The transformation of the British from traders to governors began almost by accident. Having been granted a licence to trade in Bengal by the Great Mughal (the Muslim emperor in Delhi), and following the establishment of a new trading post (Calcutta, now called Kolkata) in 1690, business began to expand rapidly. Under the apprehensive gaze of the nawab (local ruler), British trading activities became extensive, and the 'factories' (trading stations) took on an increasingly permanent (and fortified) appearance.

Eventually the nawab decided that British power had grown far enough. In June 1756 he attacked Kolkata and, having taken the city, locked his British prisoners in a tiny cell. The space was so cramped and airless that many were dead by the following morning, and the cell infamously became known as the 'Black Hole of Kolkata'.

Six months later, Robert Clive led a relief expedition to retake Kolkata and entered into an agreement with one of the nawab's generals to overthrow the nawab himself. This he did in June 1757 at the Battle of Plassey (now called Palashi), and the general who had assisted him was placed on the throne. During the period that followed, with the British effectively in control of Bengal, the company's agents engaged in a period of unbridled profiteering. When a subsequent nawab finally took up arms to protect his own interests, he was defeated at the Battle of Baksar in 1764. This victory confirmed the British as the paramount power in east India. The following year, Clive returned to Kolkata to sort out the administrative chaos and profiteering that was prevailing.

In 1771 one of the greatest figures of the time, Warren Hastings, was made governor in Bengal and during his tenure the company greatly expanded its control. His astute statesmanship was aided by the fact that India at this time was in a state of flux – a power vacuum had been created by the disintegration of the Mughal empire. The Marathas were the only real Indian power to step into this gap and they themselves were divided. Hastings concluded a series of treaties with local rulers, including one with the main Maratha leader, thus removing a major threat (at least for the time being). This left only Punjab outside British control; that too fell in 1849 after the two Sikh wars.

The borders of Nepal were delineated following a brief series of battles between the British and the Gurkhas in 1814. The Gurkhas were initially victorious but, two years later, were forced to sue for peace as the British marched on Kathmandu. As part of the price of peace, the Nepalese were forced to cede the provinces of Kumaon and Shimla, but mutual respect for each other's military prowess prevented Nepal's incorporation into the Indian empire and led to the establishment of the Gurkha regiments that still exist in the British army today.

British India

By the early 19th century, India was effectively under British control. The country remained a patchwork of states, many nominally independent, and governed by their own rulers, the maharajas and nawabs. While these 'princely states' administered their own territories, a system of central government was developed. British organisation was replicated in the Indian government and civil service – a legacy that still exists today. From 1784 onwards, the British government in London began to take a more direct role in supervising affairs in India, although the territory was still notionally administered by the East India Company until 1858.

An overwhelming interest in trade and profit resulted in far-reaching changes. Iron and coal mining were developed and tea, coffee and cotton became key crops. A start was made on the vast rail network still in use today, irrigation projects were undertaken and the zamindar (landowner) system was encouraged. These absentee landlords eased the burden of administration and tax collection for the British, but contributed to an impoverished and landless peasantry.

The British also imposed English as the local language of administration. While this may have been useful in a country with so many different languages, and even today fulfils an important function in nationwide and international communication, it did keep the new rulers at arm's length from the Indians.

The Indian Uprising

In 1857, half a century after having established firm control of India, the British suffered a serious setback. To this day, the causes of the Uprising (known at the time as the 'Indian Mutiny' and subsequently labelled by nationalist historians as a 'War of Independence') are the subject of debate. The key factors included the influx of cheap goods, such as textiles, from Britain that destroyed many livelihoods, the dispossession of many rulers of their territories, and taxes imposed on landowners.

The incident that is popularly held to have sparked the Uprising, however, took place at an army barracks in Meerut in Uttar Pradesh on 10 May 1857. A rumour leaked out that a new type of bullet was greased with animal fat. In Hindu circles the rumour held that it was cow fat; in Muslim company the grease came from pigs. Pigs, of course, are unclean to Muslims, and cows are sacred to Hindus. Since the procedure for loading a rifle involved biting the end off the waxed cartridge, there was considerable unrest.

In Meerut, the situation was handled with a singular lack of judgement. The commanding officer lined up his soldiers and ordered them to bite off the ends of their issued bullets. Those who refused were immediately marched off to prison. The following morning the soldiers of the garrison rebelled, shot their officers and marched to Delhi. Of the 74 Indian battalions of the Bengal army, seven remained loyal (one of them Gurkhas), 20 were disarmed and the other 47 mutinied. The soldiers and peasants rallied around the ageing Great Mughal in Delhi, but there was never any clear idea of what they hoped to achieve. They held Delhi for four months and besieged the British Residency in Lucknow for five months, before they were finally suppressed. The incident left deep scars on both sides.

Almost immediately the East India Company was wound up and direct control of the country was assumed by the British government. The latter announced its support of the existing rulers of the princely states, claiming it would not interfere in local matters as long as the states remained loyal to Britain. A decision was wisely taken that there should be no public search for scapegoats.

Road to Independence

Opposition to British rule began to increase at the turn of the 20th century. The Indian National Congress (the country's oldest political party, known today as the Congress Party and Congress (I)) met for the first time in 1885 and soon began to push for a measure of participation in the government of the country. Progress was painfully slow, although there was movement after 1906 towards enfranchising a small proportion of Indian society. A highly unpopular attempt to partition Bengal in 1905 resulted in mass demonstrations and brought to light Hindu opposition to the division; the Muslim community formed its own league and campaigned for protected rights in any future political settlement. As pressure rose, a split emerged in Hindu circles between moderates and radicals, the latter resorting to violence to publicise their aims.

With the outbreak of WWI, the political situation eased. India contributed hugely to the war (more than one million Indian volunteers were enlisted and sent overseas, suffering more than 100,000 casualties). The contribution was sanctioned by Congress leaders, largely on the expectation that it would be rewarded after the war was over. Despite a number of hints and promises, no such rewards emerged and disillusion soon followed. Disturbances were particularly noticeable in Punjab, and in April 1919, following riots in Amritsar, a British army contingent was sent to quell the unrest. Under direct orders of the officer in charge they fired into a crowd of unarmed protesters attending a meeting. Firing continued for some 15 minutes, until there were well over 1000 casualties. News of the massacre spread rapidly throughout India and turned huge numbers of otherwise apolitical Indians into Congress supporters. (For more on this, see the boxed text 'Carnage at Jallianwala Bagh' in the Punjab & Haryana chapter.)

At this time, the Congress movement also found a new leader in Mohandas Gandhi. Gandhi, who subsequently became known as the Mahatma, or 'Great Soul', adopted a policy of passive resistance, known as satyagraha, to British rule. Not everyone involved in the struggle agreed with or followed Gandhi's policy of noncooperation and nonviolence, yet the Congress Party and Gandhi remained at the forefront of the push for Independence.

As political power sharing began to look increasingly likely, and the mass movement led by Gandhi gained momentum, the Muslim reaction was to look to their own interests. The large Muslim minority had realised that an independent India would also be a Hindu-dominated India, and despite Gandhi's fair-minded approach, others in the Congress Party would not be so willing to share power. By the 1930s Muslims were raising the possibility of a separate Muslim state.

Political events were partially disrupted by WWII, when large numbers of Congress supporters were jailed to prevent disruption to the war effort. During this time, support grew among Muslims for an independent state of their own.

Independence

The Labour Party victory in the British elections in July 1945 brought a new breed of political leader to power. The British realised that a solution to the Indian problem was imperative. Despite their willingness to grant Independence, there appeared to be no way to compromise between the wishes of the two major Indian parties. Mohammed Ali Jinnah, the leader of the Muslim League, declared that he wished to have 'India divided or India destroyed'. Meanwhile the Congress Party, led by Jawaharlal Nehru, campaigned for an independent greater India. Gandhi, the father figure of Congress, urged reconciliation, but his voice was drowned out by others.

Mahatma Gandhi

Mohandas Karamchand Gandhi was born on 2 October 1869 in Porbandar in Gujarat, where his father was chief minister. He was married at the age of 13. In 1888 he left India to train as a barrister in London, returning to India in 1891, but finding the legal profession oversubscribed, he accepted a contract to work in South Africa. On arrival in South Africa he experienced the discrimination directed at the Indian community and others. He soon became the spokesman for his community and championed equality for all. During these years he developed the concept of satyagraha, or passive resistance. Gandhi's mass mobilisation of the Indian workforce eventually forced the South African government to concede to many of his demands; concessions included recognition of Indian marriages and the abolition of a poll tax levied on Indians.

Gandhi returned to India in 1915 with many of his policies and beliefs in place. The doctrine of ahimsa (nonviolence) was central to his beliefs, as was his devotion to a simple and disciplined lifestyle. He set up an ashram in Ahmedabad (Gujarat) which was innovative for its admission of Untouchables, and for its economic and social activities, such as community spinning and weaving.

Gandhi initially felt his way cautiously around the Indian political scene, but within a year saw his first victory defending farmers in Bihar from exploitation. This was when he first received the title 'Mahatma' (Great Soul) from an admirer. The passage of the discriminatory *Rowlatt Acts* in 1919 spurred him to further action and he organised a national protest. In the days that followed this *hartal* (strike), feelings ran high throughout the country. In Amritsar, protesters at a peaceful meeting were massacred by soldiers and Gandhi, deeply shocked, called the movement off immediately.

By 1920 Gandhi was a key figure in the Indian National Congress, and he coordinated a national campaign of noncooperation. The effort was hugely successful in raising nationalist feelings, but once again led to violence. Gandhi called off the satyagraha and almost immediately afterwards he was imprisoned. He stayed behind bars until 1924.

Throughout the mid-1920s Gandhi kept a relatively low profile, and was dismissed by many as a

Each passing day increased the risks of intercommunity strife and bloodshed. In early 1946, a British mission failed to bring the two sides together and the country slid closer towards civil war. A 'Direct Action Day', called by the Muslim League in August 1946, led to the slaughter of Hindus in Kolkata, followed by reprisals against Muslims. Faced with a growing crisis, in February 1947 the British government made a momentous decision. The viceroy, Lord Wavell, would be replaced by Lord Louis Mountbatten and Independence would come by June 1948.

The new viceroy made a last-ditch attempt to convince the rival factions that a united India was a more sensible proposition, but they – Jinnah in particular – remained intransigent. The reluctant decision was then made to divide the country. Only Gandhi stood firmly against the division, preferring the possibility of a civil war to the chaos he so rightly expected. Faced with increasing civil violence, Mountbatten decided to follow a breakneck pace to Independence and announced that it would come on 14 August 1947. Once the decision had been made to divide the country, there were countless administrative decisions to be made, the most important being the actual location of the dividing line.

Neatly slicing the country in two proved to be an impossible task. Although some areas were clearly Hindu or Muslim, others had evenly mixed populations, and there were isolated 'islands' of communities in areas predominantly settled by other religions. Moreover, the two overwhelmingly Muslim regions were on opposite sides of the country and therefore Pakistan would inevitably have eastern and western halves divided by a hostile India. The instability of

Mahatma Gandhi

spent force. He returned to the struggle in 1927 and three years later captured the imagination of the country, and the world, with his most successful act of defiance against the British government. In early 1930 he led a march of several thousand followers from Ahmedabad to Dandi on the coast of Gujarat. On arrival, Gandhi ceremoniously made salt by evaporating sea water, thus publicly defying the hated salt tax; once again he was imprisoned. He was released in 1931 in order to represent the Indian National Congress at the second Round Table Conference in London where, despite winning over the hearts of the British people, he failed to gain many real concessions from the government.

Jailed again on his return to India, Gandhi immediately began a hunger strike, aimed at forcing his fellow Indians to accept the rights of the Untouchables. The country was seized with apprehension, and as Gandhi grew weaker, pressure on politicians mounted. Finally, just as it seemed that Gandhi was on the verge of death, an agreement was reached.

Emerging from jail, Gandhi found himself disillusioned with politics, believing the Congress leaders were ignoring his guidance. In 1934 he resigned his seat in Congress, and began to follow a personal policy of rural education, living among the villagers and attempting to improve their lot. He returned to the fray very publicly in 1942 with the Quit India campaign, in which he urged the British to leave India immediately. During the tension of WWII his actions were deemed subversive and he and most of the Congress leadership were imprisoned.

In the frantic bargaining that followed the end of the war, Gandhi was largely excluded, and he watched helplessly as plans were made to partition the country – a tragedy in his eyes. He toured the trouble spots of the country, using his own influence to calm intercommunity tensions and promote peace.

His work on behalf of members of all communities inevitably drew resentment from Hindu hardliners which led to his death. On his way to an evening prayer meeting on 30 January 1948, he was assassinated by a Hindu fanatic.

this arrangement was self-evident, but it was 25 years before the predestined split finally came and East Pakistan became Bangladesh.

Since a locally adjudicated dividing line was certain to bring recriminations from either side, an independent British referee was given the odious task of drawing the borders, knowing that the effects would be disastrous for countless people. The decisions were fraught with impossible dilemmas. In Bengal, Kolkata, with its Hindu majority, port facilities and jute mills, was divided from East Bengal, which had a Muslim majority, large-scale jute production, no mills and no port facilities. It has been estimated that one million Bengalis became refugees in the mass movement across the new border.

The problem was far worse in Punjab, where intercommunity antagonisms were already running at fever pitch. Punjab was one of the most fertile and affluent regions of the country, and had large Muslim, Hindu and Sikh communities. The Sikhs had already campaigned unsuccessfully for their own state, and now saw their homeland divided down the middle. The new border ran straight between Punjab's two major cities – Lahore and Amritsar. Before Independence, Lahore's total population of 1.2 million included approximately 500,000 Hindus and 100,000 Sikhs. When the dust had finally settled, Lahore had a Hindu and Sikh population of only 1000.

It was clear that Punjab contained all the ingredients for an epic disaster, but the resulting bloodshed was even worse than expected. Huge exchanges of population took place. Trains full of Muslims, fleeing westward, were held up and slaughtered by Hindu and Sikh mobs. Hindus and Sikhs fleeing to the east suffered the same fate. The army that was sent to maintain order proved totally inadequate and, at times, all too ready to join the partisan carnage. By the time the Punjab chaos had run its course, over 10 million people had changed sides and even the most conservative estimates calculated that 250,000 people had been slaughtered. The true figure may well have been over half a million.

The problems caused by Partition were by no means limited to border regions. Much of Delhi was torched and over 300,000 of the city's Muslim inhabitants abandoned their homes and fled, their places being taken by nearly half a million Hindu refugees, most of them from Lahore and other cities in present-day Pakistan. The incoming refugees had no choice but to set up camps wherever they could, and it took the Delhi government years to gradually sort out housing for the new arrivals (many ended up in the homes of the Muslim evacuees).

The provision of an independently adjudicated border between India and Pakistan failed to prevent disputes. The issue was complicated largely by the fact that the 'princely states' in British India were nominally independent. As part of the settlement process, local rulers were asked which country they wished to belong to – in all but three cases the matter was solved relatively simply. Kashmir, however, was a predominantly Muslim state with a Hindu maharaja who, by October 1948, had still not opted for India or Pakistan when a rag-tag Pathan army from North-West Frontier Province in the newly formed Pakistan crossed the border, intent on racing to Srinagar and annexing Kashmir without provoking a real India-Pakistan conflict. Unfortunately for the Pakistanis, the Pathans, inspired to mount their invasion by the promise of plunder, did so much plundering en route that India had time to rush troops to Srinagar and prevent the town's capture. The indecisive maharaja finally opted for India, provoking the first, albeit brief, India-Pakistan war.

The UN eventually stepped in to keep the two sides apart, but the issue of Kashmir has remained a central source of intense disagreement and conflict between the two countries ever since. With Kashmir's overwhelming Muslim majority and geographic links to Pakistan, many people were inclined to support Pakistan's claims to the region. To this day, India and Pakistan are divided in this region by a demarcation line (known as the Line of Actual Control), yet neither side agrees that this constitutes the official border.

The final stages of Independence had one last tragedy to be played out. On 30 January 1948, Mohandas Gandhi, deeply disheartened by Partition and the subsequent bloodshed, was assassinated by a Hindu zealot. Throughout the events leading up to Independence, he had stood almost alone in urging tolerance and the preservation of a single India. He argued that Jinnah should be given the leadership of a united India, if that was what it would take to prevent Partition. To some, whipped up by the events of the preceding months, this appeared to be tantamount to colluding with the enemy.

Post-Independence India

Since Independence, India has faced many problems and made considerable progress. The fact that it has not, like so many developing countries, succumbed to dictatorships, military rule or wholesale foreign invasion is a testament to the basic strength of the country's government and institutions. Economically, it has made major steps in improving agricultural output and is one of the world's top 10 industrial powers.

Jawaharlal Nehru, India's first prime minister, tried to follow a strict policy of nonalignment. Yet, despite maintaining generally cordial relations with Britain and electing to join the Commonwealth, India moved towards the former USSR – partly because of conflicts with China and US support for its archenemy Pakistan.

There were further clashes with Pakistan in 1965 and 1971, one over the intractable Kashmir dispute and another over Bangladesh. A border war with China in 1962 in Ladakh and the then North-East Frontier Area (NEFA; now the north-eastern region) resulted in the loss of Aksai Chin (in Ladakh) and smaller NEFA areas. India continues to dispute sovereignty over these.

These outside events tended to draw everyone's attention away from India's often very serious internal problems, especially its continual failure to address the rapid population growth.

Indira's India

Politically, India's major problem since Independence has been the personality cult that has developed around its leaders. There have only been three prime ministers of real stature – Nehru, his daughter Indira Gandhi (no relation to Mahatma Gandhi) and her son Rajiv Gandhi. Nehru personally led a series of five-year plans to improve output and managed to keep India nonaligned, thereby receiving aid from the then USSR, the USA and Europe. He died in 1964 and in 1966 Indira was elected as prime minister. In 1975 she faced serious opposition and unrest, which she countered by declaring a state of emergency (which became known as the Emergency) – a situation that in many other countries might have become a dictatorship.

During the Emergency, a mixed bag of good and bad policies were followed. Freed of many parliamentary constraints, Gandhi was able to control inflation remarkably well, boost the economy and decisively increase efficiency. On the negative side, political opponents often found themselves behind bars, India's judicial system was turned into a puppet theatre, the press was fettered and there was more than a hint of nepotism, particularly with her son Sanjay.

Indira Gandhi continued the dynasty which dominated Indian politics until the 1990s.

His disastrous program of forced sterilisations, in particular, caused much anger.

Despite murmurings of discontent, in 1977 Gandhi called a general election, believing the people were behind her. She was wrong. Her partially renamed Congress Party (Indira) or Congress (I) was bundled out of power in favour of the Janata People's Party. This party was founded by Jaya Prakash Narayan, 'JP', an ageing Gandhian socialist who established it to fight corruption and Indira's increasingly authoritarian rule. Many believe that without Narayan's moral stature and courage to stand up to Congress' monolithic rule, democracy might not have survived. A five-month jail term in 1975 severely debilitated his health, and he died in 1977.

Once victorious, it quickly became obvious that Janata had no other cohesive policies. Its leader, Morarji Desai, seemed more interested in protecting cows, banning alcohol and getting his daily glass of his own urine (high in vitamins and minerals) than coming to grips with the country's problems. With inflation soaring, unrest rising and the economy faltering, nobody was surprised when Janata fell apart in late 1979. The 1980 election brought Indira Gandhi back to power with a larger majority than ever.

India in the 1980s & 1990s

Indira Gandhi's political touch seemed to have faded as she grappled unsuccessfully with communal unrest in several areas, violent attacks on Dalits (the Scheduled Caste or Untouchables), numerous cases of police brutality and corruption, and the upheavals in the north-east and Punjab. Then her son and political heir, the unpopular Sanjay, was killed in a light aircraft accident in June 1980. In 1984, following the decision to send in the Indian army to flush out armed Sikh separatists (demanding a separate Sikh state, to be called Khalistan) from Amritsar's Golden Temple, Mrs Gandhi was assassinated by her Sikh bodyguards. Her highly controversial decision to desecrate the Sikhs' holiest temple was catastrophic, sparking bloody Hindu-Sikh riots which left more than 3000 people dead (mostly Sikhs who had been lynched). The quest for Khalistan has since been quashed.

Mrs Gandhi's son Rajiv, a former Indian Airlines pilot, become the next prime minister. However, after a brief golden reign, which included breaking India's protectionist stance on world trade, he was dogged with corruption scandals (most notably the notorious Bofors scandal) and also failed to quell unrest in Punjab, Kashmir and elsewhere. In 1991, during an election campaign tour in Tamil Nadu, Rajiv and others were killed by a bomb carried by a supporter of the Liberation Tigers of Tamil Eelam (LTTE; a Sri Lankan armed separatist group known as the 'Tamil Tigers').

Narasimha Rao assumed the leadership of the Congress Party and led it to victory at the polls in 1991. Rao shared Rajiv's determination to shove India into the economic realities of the 1990s. In 1992 the economy was given an enormous boost after the finance minister, Manmohan Singh, took the momentous step of partially floating the rupee against a basket of 'hard' currencies.

However, Rao inherited a number of intractable problems that tested the mettle of his government. His biggest headache was the festering issue of communalism, particularly between Hindus and Muslims, for which Ayodhya (revered by Hindus as the birthplace of Rama) in Uttar Pradesh became a hotbed. In December 1992, Hindu zealots, egged on by the staunchly Hindu revivalist Bharatiya Janata Party (BJP), destroyed a mosque, the Babri Masjid, which they claimed stood on the site of what was formerly the Rama Temple. Bloody rioting flared across the north; more than 250 people were killed and 1100 wounded following a series of bomb blasts in Mumbai.

The simmering unrest between India and neighbouring Pakistan took centre stage during the 1990s, with an alarming increase in guerrilla activities. India accused Pakistan of training and arming Kashmiri insurgents – of course Islamabad denied such claims, instead placing blame on the antagonistic Indian army. Foreign and Indian tourists were targeted by Kashmiri terrorists; a number of them were murdered.

A rise in Hindu nationalism, along with various corruption scandals plaguing the Rao government, spelt disaster for the Congress Party, which was defeated by the BJP in the 1996 general election. The government formed by the BJP lasted less than two weeks, and was replaced by a coalition of 13 parties called the United Front – this didn't last either. Just nine months later, in April 1997, it was voted out of office after Congress withdrew its support. Then, in 1998, the BJP and its allies emerged with the most seats of any single party, causing Congress president Sitaram Kesri to step aside to make way for Sonia Gandhi (Rajiv Gandhi's Italian-born widow). This move was vociferously condemned by some within the party (and beyond) who believed high positions (and the opportunity to become prime minister) should go to Indian-born members. Some party members were so disgusted they resigned in protest, creating turmoil in the party. But Sonia Gandhi stayed on; many believe she is keeping the political seat warm for her daughter Priyanka, cited as a future leader.

In 1998, the BJP, led by prime minister Atal Behari Vajpayee, took power and promptly blasted its way into world headlines by defiantly detonating five nuclear devices in the deserts of Rajasthan. This shattered any hopes of a peaceful resolution to the Kashmir crisis. Pakistan responded furiously to India by testing its own nuclear devices, igniting global concern about a nuclear arms race in South Asia. Despite international condemnation (translating to punitive economic sanctions by many nations), Vajpayee bagged the top job again, after the BJP won elections in October 1999. In these elections, only 43 women were elected. A bill to boost the number of women in key positions has been pledged by the government, but this is yet to be passed.

Although Vajpayee and his party are dubbed by many as intolerant Hindu chauvinists, they have so far proved to be more judicious administrators than the corruption-ridden Congress Party, despite the arms scandal allegations in March 2001.

India Beyond 2000

Over recent decades Indian politics has been plagued with corruption scandals. This very publicly came to the fore in October 2000, when one of the nation's most senior political figures, former Indian prime minister Narasimha Rao, was sentenced to three years' imprisonment. Rao, who held office from June 1991 to May 1996, was found guilty of paying bribes to garner support during a vital 1993 parliamentary vote. At the time of research he was on bail and appealing the decision.

In March 2001 dirty deals at high levels hit world headlines yet again when senior Indian government officials were implicated in an alleged arms bribery scandal that was first revealed via an Indian news Web site. To restore public confidence in the Vajpayee government, defence minister George Fernandes resigned soon after the scandal emerged, even though he claimed to have had no involvement. Despite vehement calls by opposition parties for the entire BJP-led coalition to resign, Vajpayee refused to step down. Instead, he promptly pledged to 'get to the bottom of the allegations' by ordering a high level judicial inquiry. The inquiry's findings were scheduled to be released at the time of publication of this book.

Political debate at the beginning of the new millennium has centred on the interminable dissension between India and Pakistan over the disputed territory of Kashmir (see the Jammu & Kashmir chapter for more information). Despite continuing vows by both countries to resume constructive dialogue, tensions between the South Asian neighbours remain exceptionally volatile.

GEOGRAPHY & GEOLOGY

India as a whole covers a total area of 3,287,263 sq km. This is divided into 29 states and six directly administered union territories. The states are further subdivided into districts.

This North India guidebook covers 22 states and four union territories; together these account for 2,270,696 sq km, or around 69% of India's total area.

The Himalaya

The north of the country is decisively bordered by the long sweep of the Himalaya, the world's highest mountains. They run from south-east to north-west, separating India from China, and form one of the youngest mountain ranges on earth. The evolution of the Himalaya can be traced to the Jurassic era (80 million years ago) when the world's land masses were split into two: Laurasia in the northern hemisphere and Gondwanaland in the southern hemisphere. The land mass that is now India broke away from Gondwanaland and floated across the earth's surface, eventually colliding with Laurasia. The hard volcanic rocks of India were thrust against the soft sedimentary crust of Laurasia, forcing it upwards to create the Himalaya. This continental collision still continues with the mountains rising by up to 8mm each year.

The Himalaya is not a single mountain range but a series of ranges with beautiful valleys wedged between them. The Kullu Valley in Himachal Pradesh and the Vale of Kashmir in Jammu and Kashmir are both Himalayan valleys, as is the Kathmandu Valley in Nepal. Kanchenjunga (8598m) is the highest mountain in India, although until Sikkim and Kanchenjunga were absorbed into India that honour went to Nanda Devi (7817m). Beyond the Himalaya stretches the high, dry and barren Tibetan plateau; Ladakh is a small part of this plateau actually lying within the boundaries of India.

The final southern range of the Himalaya, the Siwalik Hills, ends abruptly in the great northern plain of India.

The Northern Plain

In complete contrast to the soaring mountain peaks, the northern plain slopes so gradually that as it stretches east from Delhi to the Bay of Bengal it drops a total of only 200m. The mighty, sacred Ganges River rises in Gangotri and drains a large part of the northern plain before merging with the Brahmaputra River. In the north-west, the Indus River starts flowing through Ladakh in India but soon diverts into Pakistan to become that country's most important river. South of the northern plains, the land rises up into the high plateau of the Deccan.

The North-East

The north-east boundary of India is defined by the foothills of the Himalaya, separating it from Myanmar (Burma). It's here that India bends almost entirely around Bangladesh, almost meeting the sea on its eastern side.

The West

On the western side, India is separated from Pakistan by three distinct regions. In the north, in the disputed area of Kashmir, the boundary is formed by the Himalaya, which drops down to the plains of Punjab, merging into the Great Thar Desert in the western part of Rajasthan. This is an area of great natural beauty and is extremely barren. It's hard to imagine that it was once covered by thick forests. Discoveries made by palaeontologists in 1996 suggest that the area was inhabited by dinosaurs and their ancestors as long ago as 300 million years.

Finally, the Indian state of Gujarat is separated from the province of Sind in Pakistan

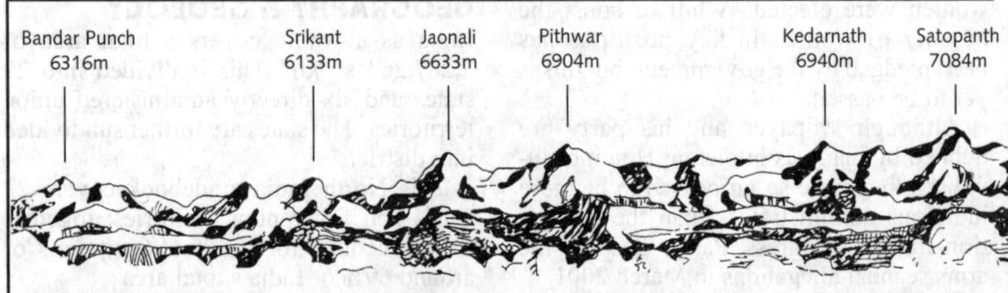

by the unusual marshland known as the Rann of Kutch. In the dry season (November to April), this marshland dries out, leaving many isolated salt islands perched on an expansive plain of hard, dried mud. In the wet season (June to August), the marshland floods, first with sea water, then by fresh river water, to become a vast inland sea.

CLIMATE

India has a three-season year – the hot, the wet and the cool. Generally the best time to visit is during the cool season (November to February) although there are regional variations (see the 'At a Glance' boxes at the start of each chapter for the best times to travel to each area). The hot broken by the wet of monsoonal deluges can make travelling an extreme challenge.

The Hot

The heat starts to build up on the northern plains of India from around February, and by April or May it becomes unbearable. In central India, temperatures of 45°C and above are commonplace. It's dry and dusty and everything is seen through a haze.

Later in May, the first signs of the monsoon are visible – high humidity, violent electrical storms, short rainstorms and dust storms that turn day into night. The hot and humid weather towards the end of the hot season can leave you frazzled.

The hot season is the time to leave the plains and retreat into the hills, and this is when Himalayan hill stations and states such as Sikkim are at their best (and busiest). By early June, the snow on the passes into Ladakh melts and the roads reopen.

The Wet

When the monsoon finally arrives, it does not just suddenly appear. After some advance warning, the rain comes in steadily, starting around 1 June in two areas: in the southern tip of South India and in the south of the north-eastern region (Tripura and Mizoram). It sweeps north-west to cover the whole country by early July. The monsoon doesn't really cool things off; at first hot, dry, dusty weather is simply traded for hot, humid, muddy conditions. Even so, it's a great relief, not least for farmers who face their busiest time of year as they prepare fields for planting. It doesn't rain solidly all day during the monsoon, but it certainly rains every day; the water tends to come down in buckets for a while followed by the sun, which can be quite pleasant.

Although the monsoon brings life to India, it also brings its share of death. Almost every year there are destructive floods and thousands of people are made homeless. Rivers rise and sweep away roads and railway lines, and many flight schedules are disrupted, making travel during this period uncertain.

The Cool

Finally, around October, the monsoon ends for most of the country, and this is when most tourists visit. It's not too hot and not too cool. The air is clear in the Himalaya, and the mountains are clearly visible, at least early in the day. Delhi and other northern cities become quite crisp at night in December and January. It becomes downright cold in the far north, but snow brings India's small skiing industry into action so a few places, such as the Kullu Valley, have a season too.

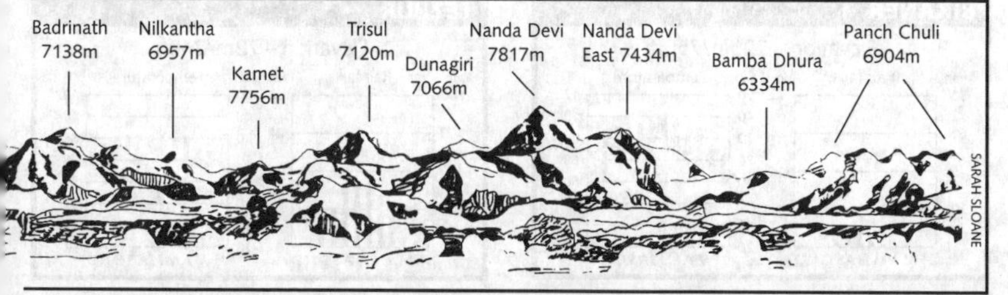

ECOLOGY & ENVIRONMENT

With more than one billion people, rapid industrialisation, poor infrastructure, ongoing deforestation and heavy reliance on chemical fertilisers, pesticides and herbicides, India's environment is under immense pressure. While there is no shortage of legislation designed to protect the environment, corruption and flagrant abuses of power are exacerbating India's environmental degradation. Another growing problem is the use of outdated factory equipment which does not meet new pollution control guidelines, resulting in serious cases of ongoing air and water pollution.

Some of the most positive and tenacious conservation efforts have emerged from within grassroots communities intent on saving their homes, livelihoods and traditions. For example, in environmentally

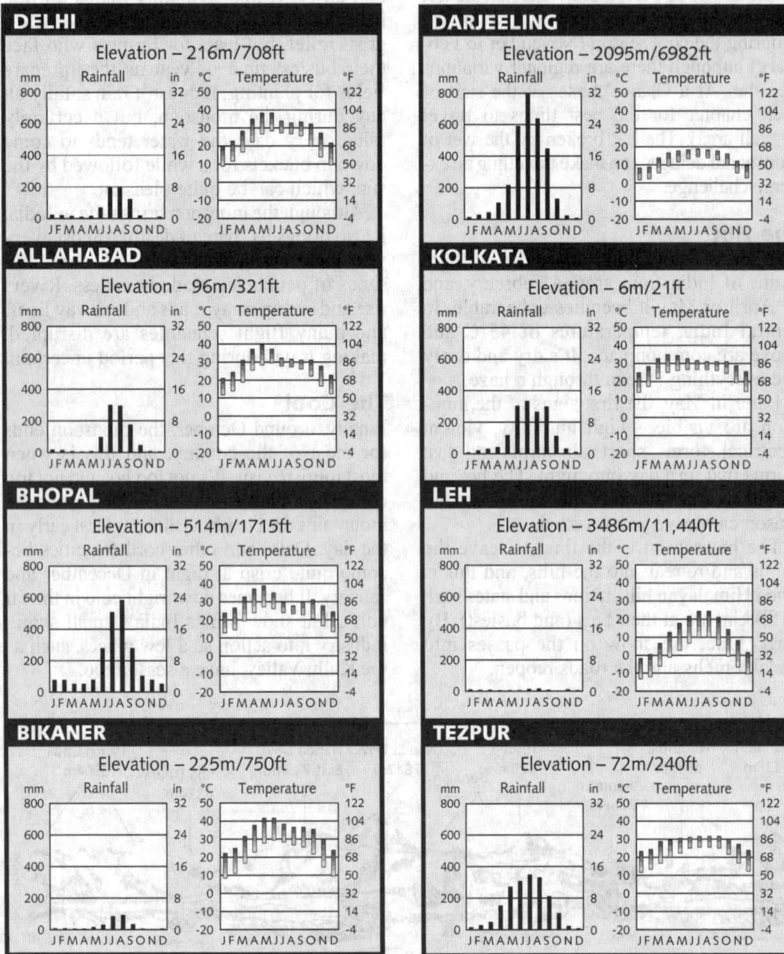

fragile Ladakh the locals are undertaking several initiatives, including energy-saving power and environmentally friendly tourism.

Of escalating concern nationwide is the level of discarded plastic (see Plastic Waste later in this section). Another problem is the neglect of public monuments: the Archaeological Survey of India (ASI) has the impossible task of trying to maintain 5000 monuments on a budget of only around US$7 million a year. Happily, there are signs that local businesses are beginning to shoulder some of the responsibility. (For more information on India's ecology and environment, see also Responsible Tourism in the Facts for the Visitor chapter.)

Conservation Contacts

The following organisations are working towards environmental protection and conservation in India and can offer information on conservation efforts nationwide. They may also be able to offer volunteer work.

Bombay Natural History Society (☎ 022-2821811, fax 2837615, ⓔ bnhs@bom4.vsnl.net.in) Hornbill House, Shaheed Bhagat Singh Rd, Mumbai 400023. One of the more renowned environmental groups in India and the largest nongovernmental organisation (NGO) on the subcontinent, it publishes an impressive list of books on India's flora, fauna and conservation issues.

Global Village Development Trust (☎ 07686-74237/72250) Chandra Prabha Gardens, Rajnagan Rd, Khajuraho, Madhya Pradesh. Launched by local residents in 2000 with the aim of empowering the local community to combat ecological devastation, the trust's major issues include polythene bags and other plastic waste, diminishing water sources, vehicle pollution and unhygienic garbage disposal practices. For more details contact Ajay Awasthi or Shailesh Singh.

Himalaya Trust (☎ 0135-773081, fax 620334, ⓔ ubcentre@del2.vsnl.net.in) 274/2 Vasant Vihar, Dehra Dun, Uttaranchal. The trust promotes the development of isolated mountain communities while safeguarding their environmental, cultural and spiritual heritage.

Himalayan Environment Trust (☎ 011-6215635, fax 6862374) Legend Inn, E-4 East of Kailash, New Delhi. This nonprofit trust raises public awareness about increasing ecological threats to the Himalaya.

Himalayan Foundation (☎ 0137-251268, fax 252367, ⓔ happrc@vsnl.com) Sartoli Village, PO Bagna, Nandprayag, Uttaranchal. Involved in large-scale afforestation in the Himalaya, with conservation projects covering 26,864 hectares in the Garhwal Himalaya.

Sankat Mochan Foundation (☎ 0542-313884, fax 314278, ⓔ vbmganga@satyam.net.in) Tulsi Ghat, Varanasi. This foundation established the Swatcha Ganga Environmental Education Centre, which runs environmental education courses with schools, local villages, Brahmin priests, pilgrims and boatmen regarding pollution problems in the Ganges River at Varanasi. Contact Professor Veer Bhadra Mishra.

Society for the Prevention of Cruelty to Animals *Bangalore:* (☎ 080-5540205) Kasturba Rd, near Queen's Circle, Bangalore 560001 *Kolkata*: (☎ 033-2370520, ☎/fax 2365592, ⓔ bdhar@caltiger.com) 276BB Ganguly St, 700012. Both branches are deeply involved in animal cruelty issues.

Traffic India (☎ 011-4698578, fax 4626837, ⓔ traffic@wwfind.ernet.in) 172B Lodi Estate, New Delhi 110003. Active in campaigns against the illegal wildlife trade.

Wildlife Institute of India (☎ 0135-620910, ⓔ wii.isnet@axcess.net.in) PO Box 18, Chandrabani, Dehra Dun, Uttaranchal. A leading authority on Indian fauna, the institute is involved in monitoring populations of Indian species.

Wildlife Preservation Society of India (no phone) 7 Astley Hall, Dehra Dun, Garhwal, Uttar Pradesh. The society promotes conservation awareness.

Wildlife Protection Society of India (☎ 011-213864, fax 3368729, ⓔ blue@giasdlol.vsnl.net.in) Thapara House, 124 Janpath, Delhi. This society runs wildlife projects throughout the country.

World Wide Fund for Nature (WWF; ☎ 011-4627586, fax 4626837) 172B Lodi Estate, Max Mueller Marg, New Delhi 11000. This is the Indian headquarters of the internationally established wildlife conservation pressure group.

Deforestation

India has a long tradition of venerating forests – trees have always had their defenders. In the 18th century hundreds of men and women from the Bishnoi cult in Rajasthan risked their lives to save the sacred khejri trees, which the authorities wanted in order to burn lime. This resulted in a ban on cutting any trees near a Bishnoi village. When the British commercialised forestry, protesters turned to Gandhian satyagraha to get their message across. In more recent times the Chipko movement has taken up the cause. Started as a localised protest in northern India in the mid-1970s, it has evolved into a much larger and more powerful force with women playing a leading role. When the authorities closed in to clear the protesters, women embraced the trees and refused to move. 'Soil, water and oxygen – not timber' is the Chipko catch cry, and this has echoed the length and breadth of India as communities fight to save their forest.

India's first Five-Year Plan in 1951 recognised the importance of forest cover for soil conservation, and the national forest policy supported the idea of increasing forest cover to at least 33%. But today about a third of dense forest cover remains and despite laws to protect it, more is lost every year.

There are many reasons why this has happened. Fuel wood, upon which millions of people depend, is being removed from forests at a rate of about 250 million tonnes a year – only a quarter of this can be extracted without permanent damage. As grazing lands shrink, domestic animals increasingly move into the forests causing damage. Denotification, a process whereby states may relax the ban on commercial exploitation of protected areas, is another factor. States are supposed to earmark an equivalent area for reafforestation, but conservationists say this isn't always happening or the land set aside often isn't suitable. Smuggling is another problem in some areas. Forest rangers are ill-equipped to deal with armed-to-the-teeth tree poachers. Natural disasters such as a series of landslides in northern Uttar Pradesh (now Uttaranchal) in 1998 (which killed 400 people and destroyed 12 villages) also contribute to deforestation. While plantation forest has increased in relative terms, critics point out that eucalyptus and other similarly exotic species are no substitute for native forest.

In the late 1990s the government took steps to increase reafforestation, largely calling for action at village level and more vigilant antipoaching measures. It is yet to be seen whether there will be marked improvements. The Arunachal Pradesh government has banned logging within its state.

Many of the organisations mentioned under Conservation Contacts, earlier, are involved in afforestation campaigns. The Web site www.greencleanindia.com is dedicated to planting more trees, ecological protection and increased public awareness of environmental issues.

Soil Degradation

An estimated 65% of India's land is degraded in some way, causing a rethink in the heavy use of chemicals encouraged during the Green Revolution of the 1960s when a quantum leap in agricultural output was achieved. India is the world's fourth-largest consumer of fertilisers, but with some 20 million more mouths to feed every year, fertiliser will continue to be dumped on agricultural land. Much of this runs off into surface water and leaches into ground water. The insecticides DDT and Benzene Hexachloride (BHC) were outlawed in 1992 and 1996 respectively. (Since Independence more than a million tonnes of DDT and BHC has been dumped on the land.)

Yet the demand for other chemicals seems unlikely to decline. Between 10% and 25% of annual produce is damaged by pests. Most of the damage, however, is caused by water erosion, which accounts for around 80% of degraded land. Water and wind erosion are largely caused by the loss of tree cover (see Deforestation earlier in this section). Unfortunately, policies aimed at helping agriculturalists, such as providing subsidies on irrigation and pesticides and bringing village water resources under government control, have added to the problem.

Recent reports indicate that constant cropping has caused severe mineral depletion from soils. This, coupled with the dumping of industrial effluents, explains the rise in various diseases, ranging from goitre to respiratory ailments.

Water Resources

Arguably the biggest threat to public health in India is inadequate access to clean drinking water and proper sanitation. Agriculture, which uses 85% of water, is expected to double its demand by 2025. Industry is similarly expected to double the amount it uses, and domestic use will triple. Already some parts of India, eg, northern Gujarat, are suffering serious shortages. More than 40% of Gujarat's electricity is expended on powering bore wells. And big cities such as Delhi cannot supply all their citizens' water needs; water tankers are a frequent sight in the suburbs that can afford to truck water in from other areas. Ground water (the source of 85% of rural drinking water and 55% of urban drinking water) is suffering from uncontrolled extraction and is extremely vulnerable to contamination from leaching. In West Bengal (and Bangladesh) ever-deeper tube wells contaminated with arsenic (which occurs naturally in pyrite bedrock) are poisoning tens of thousands of villagers. Much

The Dam Debate

Few projects highlight so tragically the dilemmas of development as the Narmada Valley Development Project. The ambitious and highly controversial US$6 billion project seeks to harness the waters of the river systems of the Narmada Valley and create 30 major, 135 medium and 3000 small dams.

Anyone who spends any time in the states of Gujarat, Madhya Pradesh and Rajasthan will understand the region's critical need for water. During the crippling drought of 1999–2000, some towns received piped water supplies only every three days and the failure of monsoonal rains ensured that the agricultural sector was destroyed. The Gujarat government claims that all available surface waters have been tapped, ground-water aquifers have contributed to a falling water table and problems with fluoride, nitrate and salinity, and 43% of Gujarat's energy is use to power borewells which go deeper every year. In contrast, exploiting the waters of the Narmada is said to provide reliable drinking water to 8215 villages and 135 urban centres, not to mention flow-on effects of stemming urban migration and slowing the process of desertification.

The human and environmental consequences of the project are similarly compelling. Critics of the project – the most prominent among them being Booker Prize-winning Indian author Arundhati Roy and the Narmada Bachao Andolan (Save the Narmada movement) – vehemently oppose it on the grounds that it will displace tens of thousands of Adivasis who have lived along and worshipped the waters of the Narmada River for generations and will significantly alter the ecology of an entire river basin. Such concerns were sufficient for the World Bank to withdraw its support for the project in 1993.

For now, the argument seems to have been won by the government and developers. On 18 December 2000 the Indian Supreme Court gave permission for the project to proceed and even allowed the dam to be raised to a height of 90m, above the minimum height supporters of the project were willing to accept. A minority judgement called for an environmental impact statement before proceeding.

The Gujarat government hailed the decision as ushering in 'a golden age in the history of Gujarat' and pointed to overwhelming popular support from the population because it will alleviate critical water shortages. The project's critics decried the decision as 'antipeople' and vowed to fight on to protect the rights of the soon-to-be-displaced villagers and to gain recognition for alternatives such as biomass and solar energy systems and rain-fed irrigation systems. In the meantime, the dam walls (and river levels) are slowly rising.

Of course, the environmental angle is complicated by the fact that hydroelectric power is much more environmentally friendly than the alternatives and will reduce pollution elsewhere in the country. The construction projects are providing some employment for local people but this will dry up quite rapidly once the plants are up and running. Many of the contracts for building and running the plants have gone to overseas contractors, bringing in an initial lump sum of foreign revenue, but reducing the long-term gains for the local area.

pumped water trickles away from leaky pipes – some estimate that nationwide the loss amounts to at least half of all water piped.

India's rivers suffer from runoff, industrial pollution and sewage contamination – the Sabarmati (which runs through Ahmedabad) and the Ganges are the most polluted rivers in India. Belatedly, some attempts are being made to address the problem of river pollution. Plans are afoot in Delhi to clean up the Yamuna River, which currently receives around 2000 million litres of effluent every day. Most of this is industrial waste containing dangerous chemicals; one of the measures proposed is to relocate industry out of the city and away from the river. See also the boxed text 'Helping the Great Mother to Breathe Again' in the Uttar Pradesh chapter, concerning efforts to clean up the Ganges.

Less than 20% of the newly formed Chhatisgarh state is irrigated and the region experiences frequent droughts. In 2000 more than 50% of landless labourers and marginal farmers migrated from the region because of droughts, which had the domino effect of preventing production from over half of the rice mills, rice being Chhatisgarh's main crop.

Air Pollution

There are currently around 45 million vehicles plying Indian roads. About 60% of them are two-stroke vehicles such as autorickshaws which, though economical to run and despite attempts to control their emissions, spew out pollutants. There's little incentive to move away from diesel, which is subsidised and relatively cheap.

Over the past decade, Delhi's vehicles have been a major source of air pollutants (see the boxed text 'Kicking the Habit' in the Delhi chapter). Happily, in recent years there has been a push to improve the situation: taxis, rickshaws and buses that are more than eight years old are now banned from Delhi and all taxis now use gas instead of diesel. The completion of the metro (currently under way) should further improve the situation.

Meanwhile in Agra, the 4km area surrounding the Taj Mahal was designated as a traffic-free zone in 1994. This was followed in 1999 by a Supreme Court ruling that ordered the closure of various polluting factories in the area. Illegal buildings within 500m of the Taj were also torn down under the ruling. Unfortunately, the legislation was sanctioned without any provision for the people affected by it. Many factories were forced to close without compensation, and others signed up to government relocation schemes only to find that the sites set aside for relocation were little more than plots in the desert, without water, power or roads. However, there have been positive developments in Agra, most notably the introduction of nonpolluting electric vehicles (many of which featured in the entourage during President Clinton's visit to the Taj in 2000); even cycle-rickshaws have been designed to lighten the load on the driver. Most of these schemes have been funded by American and European NGOs in collaboration with local hotels and Uttar Pradesh Tourism.

Despite ongoing government pledges and laws aimed at curtailing toxic emissions, industry accounts for significant levels of pollution around the nation, especially in the major cities.

One of the world's worst industrial disasters occurred in 1984 in Bhopal (see the boxed text 'The Bhopal Disaster – Curing an Outrage with Neglect' in the Madhya Pradesh & Chhatisgarh chapter).

Plastic Waste

Almost everywhere in India plastic bags and bottles clog drains, litter city streets, deserts and beaches and even stunt grass growth in the parks. Of growing concern is the number of cows, elephants and other creatures that consume plastic waste, resulting in a slow and painful death. The antiplastic lobby estimates that about 72% of plastics used are discarded within a week, and only 15% are recycled. It's up to individuals (including travellers) to restrict their use of plastic, and responsibly recycle bottles and bags. Fortunately there are more and more local initiatives to combat the plastic peril. For more information see Responsible Tourism in the Facts for the Visitor chapter.

Energy

Thermal plants account for about 75% of India's total power generation. Coal is the primary source of energy, accounting for 67% of the nation's commercial requirement. In 1976 oil was discovered off the shores of Maharashtra. Crude production grew at about 10% a year until the mid-1980s when it declined because of ageing fields and delays in finding new sources. The government has been forced to turn to imports to meet domestic demand.

Far less important, but much more controversial, are hydro and nuclear power. The benefits of hydro dams have been offset by environmental and social costs that critics claim cannot be justified in many cases (see the boxed text 'The Dam Debate'). Himachal Pradesh has recently begun a vast campaign to harness the hydroelectric potential of the state's major rivers. Construction is under way on a series of huge dams and power plants on the Sutlej, Baspa, Ravi and Parvati Rivers, all of which pass through areas of great natural beauty. The projects were conceived as a way to open up the rugged mountain country to economic development, but threaten both the local environment and the traditional mountain way of life.

Development of hydroelectric power schemes is also a priority of the government of the new state of Uttaranchal, thereby threatening to destroy the natural beauty of some areas before visitors ever get a chance to see them.

The installed power generation capacity of India has escalated from just 1400MW in 1947 to 92,864MW at the close of 1999. In 1999, nuclear power contributed less than 2000MW. Biomass (cow dung, agricultural residues, wood) is important in the noncommercial sector, especially for cooking. About three-quarters is consumed as firewood.

Renewable-energy installations include wind energy, solar energy and mini/micro hydro energy plants. India is the world's fourth-largest producer of wind energy (coming in behind Germany, the USA and Denmark).

FLORA & FAUNA

India's national animal is the tiger, its national bird is the peacock and the national flower is the lotus. This is just the tip of a teeming mass of life that's one of the world's richest natural heritages. India boasts 65,000 species of fauna, 350 of mammals (7.6% of the world's total), 408 of reptiles (6.2%), 197 of amphibians (4.4%), 1244 of birds (12.6%), 2546 of fish (11.7%) and 15,000 of flowering plants (6%). In addition there are some 16 major forest types which can be further subdivided into 221 minor types.

Sadly, all is not rosy, and some species are threatened with extinction (see the boxed text 'Creatures on the Critical List'). The one-horned rhino and the elephant, found in the northern grasslands, are among those in danger. Also under threat are many of the 2000 plant species used in traditional Ayurvedic medicine (a complex science of herbal remedies practised especially in southern India).

In the Himalaya, alpine, temperate and subtropical vegetation can be found. Above

The numbers of the heavily built and majestic tahrs have diminished over recent years.

the snowline hardy little plants such as anemones, edelweiss and gentian grow. Farther down, in the monsoon-soaked foothills, are mossy evergreen forests with cinnamon, chestnut, birch and plum. On the terai (plain), the dominant vegetation is usually sal *(Shorea robusta)*, a hardwood tree. The Indian banyan (fig) tree is dotted throughout India.

In the harsh extremes of India's hot deserts the khejri tree *(Prosopis Cineraria)* and various strains of acacia (scrubby, thorny plants well-adapted to the conditions) flourish. Any plant here needs to withstand temperatures of 50°C plus. Many have roots that can snake down deep into the soil to find water, and the leaves on most are small to minimise evaporation.

The Himalaya harbours a hardy range of creatures. Ladakh's freezing high altitudes are home to the yak, a shaggy, horned wild ox weighing around one tonne; the two-humped Bactrian camel which inhabits high-altitude dunes; a wild sheep called the Ladakh urial; the Tibetan antelope, the bharal (blue sheep); the kiang (Tibetan wild ass); the Himalayan ibex; and the Himalayan tahr. Other Himalayan inhabitants include black and brown bears (found in Kashmir), marmots, mouse-hares and musk deer. Musk deer are delicate creatures lacking antlers, but with harelike ears and canines that in males look like tusks. This animal, not a true deer at all, has been hunted mercilessly for its musk, which is used in perfume.

When it comes to mystique, none of these animals matches the snow leopard. It's so elusive that many myths have grown up around it; some believe it can appear and disappear at will. There are fewer than 5000

Creatures on the Critical List

The wellbeing of large animals, such as elephants, tigers and rhino, is often an early and highly noticeable indicator of things going wrong with the ecosystem. By that measure, India's natural world is looking less than robust. All three species are in danger of extinction.

Wildlife sanctuaries have existed since ancient times, but after Independence many more were created (see the major National Parks & Wildlife Sanctuaries boxed text, following). In 1972 the Wildlife Protection Act was introduced to stem the abuse of wildlife, followed by other conservation-oriented legislation such as the Forest Conservation Act and the Environment Protection Act. India is one of 143 signatories to the Convention on International Trade in Endangered Species of Fauna and Flora (CITES), brought into force in 1975 to regulate the trade in endangered wildlife. But huge pressure from a growing population hungry for land, a massive demand for animal body parts from the insatiable Chinese medicine market, and an international market for skins and furs are proving to be virtually insurmountable forces.

There are an estimated 65,000 animals belonging to about 645 different species in India's 230 zoos, most of which are run by state governments. The recent death of a dozen tigers (including eight rare white tigers) in Orissa's Nandankanan zoo highlighted the dire need for a review of the shoestring budgets of many of India's zoos, the cramped cages and the overall tardy management of animals in captivity.

India is one of 12 so-called megadiversity countries which together account for up to 70% of the world's biodiversity. It's the only country in the world that has both lions and tigers. But all across India many species are facing a perilous future, not least the tiger, India's national animal. According to the Environmental Investigation Agency (EIA), at least 100 tigers were slaughtered by poachers in 2000. With skins used as trophies and bones ground into virility potions, a whole tiger can fetch at least US$10,000. With over half the world's remaining tiger population in India, environmentalists are calling for the creation of a government agency to deal specifically with tiger poaching. While statistics for the tiger population are unclear, it is clear that as long as its natural habitats are decreasing and there is no government protection agency, the tiger's days are numbered.

snow leopards left in the world, and the number is dropping. They can still be found in Sikkim and Arunachal Pradesh.

The endearing but very rare red panda inhabits the bamboo thickets of the eastern Himalaya where it feeds on bamboo shoots, fruit, leaves and insects. The lakes and marshes of Kashmir provide temporary homes to migrating waterbirds, geese and ducks, many of which fly all the way from Siberia to winter here. Some species exhibit an extraordinary affinity with high-altitude travel; the red- and yellow-billed crow-like choughs are eminently capable of flying well above 5000m.

The Ganges and the Brahmaputra twist and turn their way for thousands of kilometres before merging and emptying into the Bay of Bengal, creating a delta of some 80,000 sq km. Within this delta are the swampy Sunderbans, home to a large population of tigers (estimated to number just under 300 in 2000), cleverly adapted aquatic reptiles, fish, crabs, wild boar, visiting sea turtles, snakes and chital, the spotted deer which have adapted to the environment's saltiness by acquiring the ability to secrete salt from glands. In the freshwater reaches of the Ganges live Gangetic dolphins, Shiva's mythical messengers; crocodiles (mugger or marsh crocs, plus the narrow-snouted antediluvian-looking gharial); scavenger crabs; and many species of fish.

The harsh deserts of Rajasthan and Gujarat are surprisingly well populated. The chinkara (Indian gazelle), the wild ass, the Indian wolf and the blackbuck have all adapted to the heat, salty soils and limited water resources of the region. The 1400 sq km Sasan Gir Wildlife Sanctuary in Gujarat

Creatures on the Critical List

The position of the one-horned rhinoceros is equally tenuous as it loses its natural grasslands habitat to sugar cane plantations and other cultivation. It's now found only in small pockets near the Nepalese border. Its horn, actually matted hair, is sought for its supposed medicinal properties, as are its urine, flesh and blood.

The tortoise has recently been declared an endangered species and its future also looks bleak unless adequate protectionist measures are implemented. In December 2000, Indian police seized 809 tortoises from smugglers, estimated to be worth around US$30,000 on the international market.

At present there are about 2500 Indian elephants in the wild and, inspired by efforts to save the tiger, conservationists have launched a major effort to ensure their numbers stay relatively stable. Project Elephant began in 1992 under the auspices of the Ministry of Environment & Forests, but with individual states contributing towards field costs and salaries. Eleven elephant reserves have been established, encompassing the four main elephant populations. The northern ones are in Uttar Pradesh, Uttaranchal, Bihar, Jharkhand, West Bengal, Arunachal Pradesh, Assam, Meghalaya and Nagaland. Overall, the project aims to protect elephants and elephant habitats. So far the project has improved the situation.

Trade in plants, animals and insects, both dead and alive, is monitored by a WWF division called Traffic India (see Conservation Contacts earlier in this chapter). It has targeted domestic consumers and overseas travellers in the hope of making them more aware of India's role in the insidious US$20 billion global wildlife market. Of particular concern is the trade in tiger bones, rhino horns, reptile skins, live mammals and reptiles, turtle shells and birds. A Delhi-based NGO called Friends of Butterflies has been instrumental in raising awareness of the trade in rare species, especially from the north-east (the 1972 Wildlife Protection Act specifically bans the trade in butterflies). The global butterfly trade is worth in excess of US$200 million, and the Himalayan mountains and foothills are the source of many rare species. Butterfly conservationists point out that the Atlas moth of the Khasi Hills is almost extinct because of poaching – this is an environmental catastrophe as this moth cross-pollinates many plants.

is the last refuge of the Asiatic lion; in May 2000 there were an estimated 325. These lions lack the impressive shaggy mane of their African relatives and they have an extra fold of skin on their bellies.

India's primates range from the extremely rare golden langur, found near the Bhutanese border, to more common species such as the bonnet macaque and its northern cousin, the rhesus macaque.

Distributed reasonably widely in peninsular India are dhole (wild dogs), jackals, and several species of deer and gazelle including the relatively common sambar. Barking deer and mouse deer are now quite rare. The snake-killing mongoose, immortalised by Kipling, is still hale and hearty.

Those averse to slithering creatures may prefer to ignore the fact that India has 238 species of snakes, 50 of them poisonous (including 20 species of sea snakes). Found widely in India, the cobra, king of the snakes, is the world's largest venomous snake, growing up to 5m in length. Its characteristic pose of arousal, hood spread, is an enduring image for anyone who's seen a snake charmer at work. Other poisonous snakes include the krait, Russel's viper and the saw-scaled viper. These four snakes together account for some 10,000 deaths each year, but on the whole it's rare for snakes and humans to come in contact. Harmless snakes include the rat snake, which looks disturbingly like a cobra, the bright green vine snake, the dark brown bronze-back tree snake, and the rock python.

National Parks & Sanctuaries

India has 84 national parks and 447 wildlife sanctuaries, which together constitute about 4.5% of the entire country. Added to this are 11 biosphere reserves, which have been established to conserve the diversity of various ecosystems and to promote research into ecological conservation.

Major National Parks & Wildlife Sanctuaries

name	location	features	best time to visit
Valley of Flowers National Park	25km from Badrinath, Uttaranchal	3500m above sea level: wildflowers & butterflies	June–Nov
Corbett National Park	50km from Ramnagar, Uttaranchal	sal forest & river plains: tigers, chitals, deer, elephants, leopards & sloth bears	Nov–June
Rajaji National Park	8km from Haridwar, Uttaranchal	forested hills: elephants, tigers, leopards, deer & sloth bears	Nov–June
Govind Wildlife Sanctuary& National Park	Saur-Sanki, Uttaranchal	mountain scenery: black & brown bears, snow leopards, deer & birdlife	June–Nov
Pin Valley National Park	Dhankar, Himachal Pradesh	pristine mountains: snow leopards, ibex, black bears, deer	June–Nov
Sunderbans Wildlife Sanctuary	southern West Bengal	mangrove forests: tigers, deer, monkeys & birdlife	Jan–Mar
Jaldhapara Wildlife Sanctuary	northern West Bengal	forest & grasslands: Indian rhinos, deer & elephants	Oct–May
Kaziranga National Park	Assam, North-Eastern Region	tall grasslands & swamp: rhinos, elephants, tigers & birdlife	Feb–Mar

Some of the most impressive national parks in India (indeed, in all Asia) are to be found in the north, particularly in the flat, alluvial plains of the Indus, Ganges and Brahmaputra Rivers. Here you will find India's first ever national park, the Corbett Tiger Reserve in the new state of Uttaranchal, established in 1936. Also in the north are the last remaining natural habitat of Asian lions (in Sasan Gir National Park in Gujarat), the best place to see Indian one-horned rhinos (in Kaziranga), and perhaps India's best national park for seeing a diverse range of wildlife (in Kanha). Flora fans can instead head for the Valley of Flowers in Uttar Pradesh.

Parks and sanctuaries are a major tourist drawcard. Whenever possible, book in advance for transport and accommodation and check whether a permit is required (see individual chapters for details). Various fees are charged for your visit (entrance, photography, etc) and these are often included in advance arrangements.

Most parks offer jeep or van tours and some offer boat trips or elephant safaris to approach wildlife more discreetly. Watchtowers and hides are sometimes available – they're great for observing wildlife close up.

See the regional chapters for details about the places listed in the Major National Parks & Wildlfe Sanctuaries table.

GOVERNMENT & POLITICS

National Politics

India is a constitutional democracy. There are 29 states and six union territories (which are administered by the president in Delhi, through an appointed administrator), and the constitution (which came into force on 26 January 1950) details the powers of the central and state governments as well as those powers that are shared. If the situation in a particular state is deemed to be

Major National Parks & Wildlife Sanctuaries

name	location	features	best time to visit
Sariska National Park	Sariska, Rajasthan	plains: tigers, chinkaras, sambars, nilgais & wild boars	Nov–June
Ranthambhore National Park	south of Jaipur, Rajasthan	around crocodile-filled lake: crocodiles & tigers	Oct–Apr
Keoladeo Ghana National Park	Bharatpur, Rajasthan	plains: Siberian cranes, herons, storks, geese & deer	Oct–late Feb
Sasan Gir Wildlife Sanctuary	Sasan Gir, Gujarat	oasis in desert: Asian lions, chowsinghas, leopards & crocodiles	Dec–Apr
Velavadar National Park	near Bhavnagar, Gujarat	grasslands in delta region: blackbucks	Oct–June
Little Rann of Kutch Wildlife Sanctuary	north-western Gujarat	desert region: Indian wild ass (khurs), wolves & caracals	Oct–June
Kanha National Park	Jabalpur, Madhya Pradesh	swamp: deer, tigers, chitals, gaurs, blackbucks, leopards & hyenas	Mar–June
Bandhavgarh National Park	Jabalpur, Madhya Pradesh	old fort on cliffs above plains: tigers	Nov–Apr

unmanageable the central government has the controversial right to assume power there. Known as President's Rule, this has been enforced in recent years, either because the law and order situation has deteriorated – notably in Punjab from 1985 to 1992, Kashmir in 1990 and Assam in 1991 – or because there is a political stalemate, such as occurred in Haryana and Meghalaya in 1991, and Nagaland in 1992.

Parliament is bicameral; the lower house is known as the Lok Sabha (House of the People) and the upper house is known as the Rajya Sabha (Council of States).

The Lok Sabha has 545 members, and elections (using the first-past-the-post system) are held every five years, unless the government calls an election earlier. All Indians over the age of 18 have the right to vote. Of the 545 seats, 125 are reserved for the Scheduled Castes and Tribes.

The upper house consists of 245 members; members are elected for six-year terms and one-third of the house is elected every two years. The president appoints 12 members and the rest are elected by state assemblies using a regional quota system. The president (whose duties are largely ceremonial) is elected by both houses and the state legislatures (the election is held every five years). The president must act on the advice of a council of ministers, chosen by the prime minister. The president may dissolve the lower house but not the upper.

It is generally accepted that North India has more political clout than South India. This is perhaps an inevitable consequence of the northern situation of Delhi, the national capital and the location of parliament, yet it is also helped along by the influence of highly populated states like Uttar Pradesh – which since Independence has managed to produce more prime ministers than the rest of the states put together.

The BJP forms the current government – see the History section for details.

Fighting to the Bitter End

Perhaps the most absurdly stubborn symbol of the troubles in Kashmir is India and Pakistan's 17-year military stalemate over the Siachen Glacier, dubbed 'the highest battlefield on earth'. Here at the northernmost point of Ladakh, not far from K2 and the border with China, around 20,000 Pakistani and Indian troops are dug in at altitudes between 6000m and 7000m. They are fighting over a 700-sq-km chunk of ice, at a cost of around US$2.5 million a day, in temperatures as low as minus 50°C. All for a useless, dangerous glacier of no strategic importance. Troops, who have been stationed here since 1984 (when India seized two-thirds of the glacier), can only get in or out via high-altitude helicopter. The air is so thin that mortar trajectories cannot be estimated accurately. The consequent ineffectiveness of mortars, allied to the incredibly inhospitable environment, means that around 80% of all fatalities are caused by cold, altitude or avalanches.

State Politics

At state level some legislatures are bicameral, and are run along the lines of the two houses of the national parliament. The chief minister is responsible to the legislature in the same way as the prime minister is responsible to parliament. Each state has a governor, who is appointed by the president and who may assume wide powers in times of crisis. At village level (where 75% of the population lives) there has been renewed interest in reviving the panchayat system of village councils, from where a number of volunteers are elected to represent the local people's interests.

Given North India's cultural and ethnic diversity, it's not surprising that state politics is often dominated by the plight and rights of significant minorities within those states. Some parts of North India, especially those on the geographical margins, have experienced years of lobbying by minorities seeking a greater degree of self-determination.

In November 2000, activists gained heart when three new states (Chhatisgarh, Jharkhand and Uttaranchal) were created out of existing states. Many analysts say that the creation of these new states will intensify campaigning by other secessionist groups seeking autonomy within India.

The independent state of Chhatisgarh emerged from the vast territory of Madhya Pradesh. The state split was first mooted in 1924, at which time it was argued that the area of Chhatisgarh was historically and culturally different from the rest of Madhya Pradesh.

The new state of Jharkhand was carved from Bihar, but not without a great deal of public and political opposition along the way. The push for the new state came largely from the Adivasis of the region, who felt they had been long overlooked by the government; agitation dates back to 1915. Jharkhand, comprising mineral-rich areas in the south of the old state, has a coalition government dominated by the BJP.

The BJP was the driving force behind the creation of Uttaranchal from northern Uttar Pradesh, which was largely populated by impoverished, under-represented but predominantly high-caste Hindus.

There are various other places in the north where secessionist groups are either active or biding their time. The north-east is a particularly unsettled region in this regard, with most of the states in this corner of India experiencing some sort of secessionist pressure. In Assam, for example, the Bodos are demanding a homeland separate from the rest of the state. Meanwhile in the Darjeeling region of West Bengal, Nepali-speaking groups are pressing for the creation of a separate state called Gorkhaland.

In the north-west, India and Pakistan have been squabbling over Jammu & Kashmir since Independence, and a significant faction in the region would like to see the back of both nations. Until the 1990s (when support dwindled) there was a movement among Sikhs in Punjab that sought to establish a separate state called Khalistan.

Ethnic skirmishes are sometimes settled without resort to partition. The Ladakhis are essentially a Buddhist minority within a Muslim state within a Hindu country. Violence between Buddhists and Muslims reared up in 1969, and simmered to a greater or lesser degree until 1995. In that year the creation of the Ladakh Autonomous Hill Development Council largely settled ethnic tensions in the region.

ECONOMY

In June 1991, India ended 40 years of central planning. Since Independence it had been so highly protectionist that its share of world trade had declined from 2% in the 1950s to under 0.5% in the 1980s. The reforms generated a huge increase in private investment, boosting exports and reducing the role of the public sector in many areas including heavy manufacturing, banking, telecommunications, power generation and distribution, ports and roads.

In 1999, exports grew by 6.1%. The 1999 budget concluded that the only way India could sustain and accelerate economic growth was by combining fiscal discipline with robust economic reforms. Time alone will tell if the government puts this into action.

India's exports comprise some 7500 commodities to almost 200 countries. Imports come from over 140 countries and cover around 6000 types of products. The country's main exports are gems and jewellery, cotton yarn and fabrics, handicrafts, cereals, marine products, ready-made garments and transport equipment. India's burgeoning software industry has recently emerged as a major foreign exchange earner.

The Indian government is facing escalating pressure to deregulate (a condition of World Bank and International Monetary Fund (IMF) monies) which could leave the Indian economy vulnerable. In particular, cheap Chinese imports have begun to flood local markets, and while Indian politicians promote this as an indication that India is indeed a truly free market, there are concerns as to whether Indian producers are adequately geared up to face such stiff competition.

India's current account deficit increased from US$4.04 billion in 1998–99 to US$4.16 billion in 1999–2000. Economic growth in 1999 was a healthy 6.8%; however, economists say that the economy will need further restructuring to achieve the 8% growth rate of the mid-1990s. Although the

Vajpayee government vows to improve the economic climate through greater privatisation, some potential foreign investors fear that inwards investment will remain hobbled by traditional bureaucratic procedures and constraints.

While Vajpayee may publicly champion growth, an Indian magazine reported recently that he is particularly worried about the 'digital divide between the IT (Information Technology) haves and have-nots' and the ramifications it could have for societal inequalities. IT developments are mostly in the south, which, together with the south-based movie industry, ensures that the political pre-eminence of the north over the south is not matched by economic superiority. In fact, with the southern states currently garnering the lion's share of new business investment, the north could soon be left far behind.

Agriculture

Agriculture contributes 27% of India's gross domestic product (GDP) and employs some 64% of the workforce. It is highly protected and subsidised.

Nearly all the states in North India are primarily agricultural – Uttar Pradesh and Uttaranchal together contribute a whopping 40% of India's total production. About one-third of India's cotton and one-sixth of its tobacco comes from Gujarat. Gujarat also weighs in with 30% of India's groundnut oil and 66% of its salt production. Uttar Pradesh is one of the most important states in India for sugar cane; so too are Madhya Pradesh and Chhatisgarh for soya beans. West Bengal is well known for its jute.

India is one of the world's most prolific producers of fruit, vegetables, milk, wheat, rice and sugar. Less than 1% of the raw commodities produced is processed and there are heavy restrictions on the import of processed foods. Food grains make up 63% of India's agricultural output (203 million tonnes in 1998–99), with the government expecting to produce 234 million tonnes in 2001–02. Sugar output was 16.5 million tonnes in 1999–2000, while oil-seed production was 21.6 million tonnes.

India leads the world in the production of bananas, mangoes, coconuts and cashews, as well as potatoes, tomatoes, onions and green peas. It is among the top 10 producers of citrus, pineapples and apples.

Punjab, the 'breadbasket of India', is one of the country's leading food producers – about 85% of Punjab's total land area is covered in crops, mainly wheat and rice. In fact, India is the world's second-largest producer of paddy rice and the fourth-largest wheat producer. India is also the world's number-one producer of tea, most of which is exported. The backbone of the industry is Assam, responsible for about 60% of India's tea production, though West Bengal (particularly the areas around Darjeeling) is also a major contributor.

India has the world's biggest livestock population, with 57% of the world's buffalo population and 15% of cattle. It is the largest milk producer on Earth, producing 73.5 million tonnes in 1998–99, and around one-third of this total comes from Punjab.

Industry

The state and central governments own and operate many of the enterprises that supply other producers with products such as fertiliser, machinery and chemicals. The private sector is made up of thousands of producers as well as a few large conglomerates (eg, the Tata Iron and Steel Company).

Kanpur in Uttar Pradesh is a major industrial town, with sugar refineries, chemical works, wool and leather industries, and mills producing cotton, flour and vegetable oil. West Bengal has engineering and electronics industries. Important sites for medium and heavy industries are scattered around Madhya Pradesh and Chhatisgarh, producing among other things steel, aluminium and paper.

Of India's big industry sectors, it's textile manufacturing – jute, cotton, wool, silk and synthetics – that employs the largest workforce (64.2 million in the mid-1990s, up from 39 million at the beginning of that decade). Textile exports currently account for more than one-third of India's total earnings. But by far the biggest overall employers in the manufacturing sector are the millions of small handicraft businesses, some of which service only their own village.

Manufacturing growth in the textile industry in 1999 was calculated at 6.7%, compared with 3.9% in the previous year. The rise was partly due to improved electricity infrastructure. The textile industry in India is a well-established one, with the first mill opened in 1854 in Mumbai. Textile production is Rajasthan's most important industrial earner, employing 50,000 people. The state is responsible for nearly half of India's output of polyester viscose yarn, worth about Rs 400 million.

In 1993–96 growth in India's industrial sector touched 9% per annum, but it slowed in the late 1990s and was 6.2% in the latter half of 1999, a result, it's claimed, of the high cost of credit and infrastructure

Only in India

India, with its 330 million Hindu gods and goddesses, is a land of inimitable records. While you're probably aware that India has the planet's biggest film industry, did you know that the 1982 epic *Gandhi* holds the world record for the most film extras (300,000 people)? When it comes to epics, India also bags the world record for the longest will (104,567 words) and the shortest one (two words: *sub beta* – everything to son). It also has the world's longest written constitution – it's been amended 79 times in 50 years.

Indians are credited with many mathematical records, including the invention of trigonometry (2 BC) and the earliest recorded decimal system (AD 6). The world's highest non-military airport is at Leh in Ladakh (3256m); the highest cricket pitch is at Chail, near Shimla (2250m); and the world's longest train platform (833m) is at Kharagpur in West Bengal. In fact, Indian Railways is the world's biggest employer, with 1.6 million staff on the payroll – but even this mind-numbing figure will be eclipsed by the estimated two million people who were roped in to compile India's 2001 census. Equally staggering is the estimate that 100 million people visited the 2001 Kumbh Mela in Allahabad – easily the world's biggest gathering (see the boxed text 'Kumbh Maha' in the Uttar Pradesh & Uttaranchal chapter).

There's little doubt that Kolkata's Howrah Bridge is the busiest bridge in the world, carrying daily as it does a continuous stream of some 100,000 vehicles, as well as pedestrians too numerous to count. Kolkata also boasts a 200-year-old banyan tree in its botanical gardens; it is claimed the tree has the second-largest canopy in the world (the largest is also in India, in the south in Andhra Pradesh). Trees of any size certainly flourish in the frequent rainfalls at Cherrapunjee, in Meghalaya in the north-eastern region – it's the wettest place in the world, once recording an annual rainfall of 26.46m.

Among India's luscious mix of other world records are the following: a Rajasthani septuagenarian wears the world's longest moustache (3.39m) – a record that may be in jeopardy if he ever encounters scissor-happy Ramzan Ali of Delhi, who holds the record for uninterrupted hairdressing (1200 customers in 102 hours). But it doesn't stop there. World records held by Indians include nonstop crawling (1400km), balancing on one foot (65 hours 50 minutes), handshaking (31,118 people in eight hours), belching (92 burps per minute) and vegetable chopping (964kg in 130 hours).

With ebullient talk of *more* records on the horizon, who better to document them all than India's Dinesh Pathak, the holder of the world record for continuous typing (210 hours).

MICK WELDON

impediments. In its latest budget, the BJP-led government remained committed to privatisation in certain public sector industries and pledged a 35% increase in outlay for power, communications and energy.

Mining

Coal is India's main source of energy, accounting for around 67% of the nation's commercial requirements. In 1998–99, 290 million tonnes of coal was produced. Since the 1970s, Indian coal production has grown at about 4% per annum. There are more than 500 coal mines (mostly state-owned) and India produces a small surplus. However, the quality is low. India also has rich reserves of limestone, iron ore, bauxite and manganese.

Madhya Pradesh and Chhatisgarh are rich in minerals and together are responsible for all of India's production of tin ore, as well as having the country's most important diamond mine (at Panna). Though an impoverished region overall, Bihar and the newly-created Jharkhand have large reserves of mineral wealth, including bauxite, copper and iron. They also contribute 50% of India's total mica production; India is one of the world's largest mica producers. Another mineral-rich state is Sikkim with deposits of coal, copper, garnet, gold, graphite, iron ore, lead, marble, pyrites, silver and zinc. The whole of India's output of emeralds comes from Rajasthan, as does about 94% of India's gypsum and 76% of its silver ore.

Oil (petroleum) production in the north is mostly centred in Gujarat and Assam (Asia's first oil refinery was established at Digboi). Mumbai also has offshore oil fields, though India can only meet about half its own petroleum requirements.

Fishing

Fishing takes place all along India's coastline and in the rivers and waterways of the interior. This is a growing industry in India; the commercial catch was 5.3 million tonnes in 1997–98 (marine and inland sources), compared with 4.6 million tonnes earlier that decade. Most boats are nonmechanised, although mechanisation is increasing, causing a detrimental effect on local fishing communities and on the marine environment.

Forestry

Commercial forestry, though not a large industry in India, is found in the western Himalaya and hilly areas of central India, as well as in South India (the Western Ghats). Forests in Madhya Pradesh and Chhatisgarh yield teak, sal and bamboo, as well as salai resin (used for incense and medicines). Forestry is also important in Himachal Pradesh and Assam.

Tourism

In 1999 there were an estimated 2.4 million visitors to India and this was expected to rise to 2.6 million in 2000–01. Tourism is a crucial foreign exchange earner for the country and it also stimulates the economy by boosting employment. Tourism officials claim that the lack of adequate flights to India, coupled with lacklustre marketing policies, is severely hindering tourism growth. Poor infrastructure within the country is another significant impediment.

In the late 1990s, most tourists to India came from the UK, followed by Germany, the USA and then (interestingly) Sri Lanka. Around one-third of foreign tourists take in the 'golden triangle' of Rajasthan, Delhi and Agra.

Although not a foreign-exchange earner, domestic tourism still has a positive effect on the economy. In 1999 around 160 million Indian people travelled within India, some 100 million for religious reasons.

Information Technology

In 1999–2000 Indian software exports earned about US$4 billion. By 2002, earnings are expected to touch US$6 billion, with the number of companies exporting software tipped to exceed 1000. The industry is pretty much based in South India as yet. However, India's pool of highly skilled (and relatively inexpensive) labour has been attracting a proliferating number of multinationals in recent years, which has prompted more Indian states to set up software development cities. But the information superhighway within

India is still surprisingly limited considering the one billion plus population: by mid-2001 the number of Indian Internet subscribers is expected to number only around 1.5 million.

POPULATION & PEOPLE

India has the world's second-largest population exceeded only by that of China. India crossed the billion mark in May 2000 and is tipped to be the planet's most populous nation in the next couple of decades. The Census of India (www.censusindia.net) has a population counter which rises by about 29 people per minute. The most populous state in India is Uttar Pradesh, with around 160 million people.

A population census is held once every 10 years – the most recent took place during 2001, too late for inclusion in this book. According to the last census, India's population was 846.3 million. Kolkata was the second-largest city (behind Mumbai) with 11 million and Delhi came third with 8.4 million.

The people of India are not homogenous. There are visual differences between various groups as well as a plethora of different customs, religions and languages. Hindus are mostly concentrated in the north – the influential Hindu upper castes comprise at least 20% of the population in the north, compared with only around 5% in South India.

The bias against India's female population continues (see Society & Conduct later in this chapter); more women than men die before the age of 35, and maternal mortality rates are high (forming 25% of the world's childbirth-related deaths). The proportion of females to males has declined over the years (it was 972:1000 in 1901; the 1991 census

Adivasis

At least 55 million people in India belong to tribal communities – the north-east is India's main tribal area, particularly Arunachal Pradesh. These Adivasis, as they are known in India, have origins which precede the Vedic Aryans and the Dravidians of the south. For thousands of years they lived more or less undisturbed in the hills and densely wooded regions regarded as unattractive by agriculturalists. Many still speak tribal languages not understood by the politically dominant Hindus, and follow customs foreign to both Hindus and Muslims.

Since Independence, with the burgeoning population putting pressure on land, many Adivasis have suffered hardship, exploitation and dispossession of their ancestral land. This has unfolded with the connivance and even encouragement of officialdom but the exploitation is something the government would prefer to forget and which it vehemently denies. Instead the government points to the millions of rupees said to have been sunk into schemes to improve the conditions of Adivasis. Although some of this has got through, corruption has gobbled a substantial portion of it.

In the north, Bihar and Madhya Pradesh have a poor record in their treatment of Adivasis. In Bihar, many areas inhabited by tribal people remain untouched by development, and the needs of these marginalised people have often been overlooked by politicians whose interests lie elsewhere. Such neglect has been instrumental in the development of the new state of Jharkhand, which is largely tribal. Though the Adivasis have welcomed the advent of the new state, whether or not they will actually be given a higher priority by the Jharkhand government is yet to be seen. The formation of the new state of Chhatisgarh (from Madhya Pradesh) was a result of consistent lobbying by people representing Adivasi interests for a new state and effective representation. See Government & Politics earlier for more on the creation of these new states.

Generally, it's unlikely that much genuine effort will be made to improve the lot of Adivasis, given the pressure for land. What is far more likely is that the erosion of their cultures and traditions will continue until they are close to being wiped out. For more on Adivasis tribes, see the regional chapters (eg, see the boxed text 'Adivasis' in the Rajasthan chapter).

figure was 927:1000). Chandigarh in Haryana has the lowest proportion – there are only 790 females for every 1000 males.

Improving the living standards of the poor has been a priority for governments since Independence. There have been encouraging results in places: Poverty alleviation programs in Uttar Pradesh have helped reduce the percentage of families in the state living below the poverty line from 56.3% in 1974 to 32% in 2000. However, poverty remains widespread. The gross national product (GNP) per capita is just US$360 per year. Punjab is India's most affluent state, enjoying a per capita income approximately double the national average; Bihar has the lowest average. Of India's children, half are undernourished. Preventable diseases such as TB, malaria, blindness and leprosy account for half of all reported illnesses. HIV/AIDS is a major cause for concern (see the boxed text 'AIDS in India' under Health in the Facts for the Visitor chapter).

Despite India's many large cities, the nation is still overwhelmingly rural. It is estimated that close to 75% of the population lives in the countryside.

EDUCATION

Under the Indian constitution, education is compulsory and free for all up to the age of 14. There are 688,000 primary and 110,000 secondary schools in India. In terms of tertiary institutions, there are 10,555 colleges and 221 universities nationwide (with 7,078,000 students currently enrolled). For the socially disadvantaged Scheduled Castes, government-subsidised tuition is offered to those wishing to take university entry exams. This scheme is currently implemented at 22 universities and 57 colleges.

In addition to state schools, there are many private (usually English-language) schools, very often run by church organisations, and places in these exclusive institutions are highly coveted among those who can afford them. Much investment has gone into higher education, although critics say the quality has declined, with many liberal arts graduates unable to find work. Many of India's brightest students go abroad to undertake their higher degrees and many never return.

Two-thirds of children are enrolled, including most children of primary school age. However, many don't attend school regularly and at least 33 million aren't enrolled at all. Girls are under-represented, especially in higher education. At least half of all students from rural areas drop out before completing school. In 1997–98, the national drop-out rate for secondary school students was 69%. There are an estimated 20 million disabled children attending primary and secondary schools; however, this represents only a fraction of India's total number. On top of that, the drop-out rate is high. Attempts to boost literacy among adults (especially women) have met with mixed success.

The state and union governments share responsibility for education, although the union government has been more active in promoting education for girls and other disadvantaged groups. The new state of Chhatisgarh is taking steps to improve education in the region by raising literacy rates and providing IT training for students.

According to the 1991 census, India's literacy rate was only 52.2%, with the rate for males almost double that of females. Kerala (in South India) recorded the highest literacy rate (89.81%) and Bihar the lowest (38.48%), with Rajasthan a close follower (38.55%).

Nevertheless, literacy rates generally improved during the 1990s, though the rate for women remains lower than that for men – usually between 50% and 20% lower in the north, depending on the state. Punjab shows the smallest gender gap, with a literacy rate of 50% for women and 64% for men. Himachal Pradesh shows the highest literacy figures overall for the north – 75% for men and 53% for women.

SCIENCE

The history of sciences such as mathematics, medicine and linguistics stretches back to Vedic times when the Aryan rituals were anthologised. It is claimed that the study of linguistics by the 4th century BC Sanskrit grammarian Panini was the first scientific analysis of an alphabet. Indian mathematics emerges from the 5th-century *Shulvasutras*, which examine geometry and algorithms. A theory of numbers also developed about this time, and included the concepts of zero, negative numbers, and simple algorithms using place-value notations. The concept of zero is in fact India's most important contribution to the world of mathematics and arrived in Europe via Arab traders. Instrumental in refining the concept was Brahmagupta, who was born in Gujarat in AD 598. He collected and edited a work on astronomy and mathematics which was used for several centuries.

The classic works on Ayurvedic medicine, the *Charak Samhita* and the *Sushrita*, were written in the 6th century BC. Surgeons such as Susruta were even experimenting with plastic surgery in this age.

In 1930, Sir Chandrasekhar Venkata Raman won the Nobel prize for physics for his work on how light changes when passing through transparent bodies (the Raman effect). Since Independence the government's emphasis has been on space technology, nuclear power and electronics. Electronics sowed the seeds for India's increasingly important software industry. But some argue that there has been not enough emphasis on 'social' sciences, a point reinforced in 1998, when Amartya Sen won the Nobel prize for economics for his contribution to the field of welfare economics. Sen developed concepts of capability and freedom and applied them to analyses of 'achievement inequality', deprivation and poverty in society. His work introduces a much needed ethical dimension to the often harsh logic of modern economics. Sen lives and works in the US but was born in India, where few of his ideas have been effectively put into practice.

PHILOSOPHY

In ancient India the Vedic religion permeated every aspect of the culture, including philosophy and the sciences. Through the Brahmin or priestly caste, Vedic knowledge has remained the central feature of Indian thought throughout its long history. Religion and philosophy don't compete; philosophical wisdom has the status of religious truth. Students had to gain a deep knowledge of the Vedic mantras and the correct Sanskrit phonetics before going on to participate in philosophical discussions at a *parisad* or academy. Orthodox schools of Hindu philosophy hold that the Vedic texts are the ultimate authority.

One of the great wellsprings of mystic philosophy is the Upanishads, the oldest of which are deemed to be Vedic. The Upanishads promote the notion of an all-pervading, universal One, in which there is no split between matter and spirit (non-dualism). But the Vedic texts and the Upanishads themselves offer more than one path: striving to make this life better, or renouncing society to seek enlightenment in solitude.

Buddhism rejected the concept of atman (soul), although it retained the notion of karma (justice for past deeds) and the goal of moksha (liberation from endless reincarnations). Jainism held to the concept of *naya*, the idea that there are many perspectives of reality, all of which are partially valid.

The challenges from Buddhism, and later from Islam, spurred a shift in Hindu thought. Shankaracharya (AD 788–820), looking to turn the tide, promoted non-dualism and *jnana* (the importance of knowledge) as a means to salvation. He argued that you should be free to pursue your own reasoning, as long as it doesn't contradict the Vedic scriptures. His view was challenged by the Tamil Brahmin Ramanuja, who, influenced by the southern bhakti cult (which prescribed devotion to a personal god and the rejection of Brahminic ritual), promoted the idea that while knowledge was one path to salvation, it wasn't the only path or even the most effective one.

While Islam and Hinduism are very different, Sufi mystics were important missionaries for Islam and used indigenous ideas such as yoga and fasting to spread the word.

In the 19th century the Bengali Ramakrishna and his disciple Vivekananda started a reform movement in Hinduism that acknowledged that other religions were striving towards the same goal as Hinduism.

Leading philosophers of the 20th century include Sri Aurobindo, who moved from political activism to the study of yoga, and Mahatma Gandhi, who took traditional ideas such as ahimsa (nonviolence) and remoulded them as weapons in the struggle against British rule.

Indian philosophy and science in the ancient era crossed paths frequently. In about 600 BC the philosopher Kanada proposed the existence of indivisible units of matter he called *parmanu* (atoms). He believed that different states of matter (fire, water, earth) had different parmanu, and that parmanu join to become a *dwinka* (molecule) with some of the properties of each.

ARTS

Dance

Dance is an ancient art form in India and is inextricably linked to mythology and classical literature. Dance can be divided into two main forms: classical and folk.

Classical dance is essentially based on well-defined traditional disciplines. There are seven different forms – Bharata Natyam, Kathakali, Kathak, Manipuri, Mohiniyattam, Kuchipudi and Odissi. Though some have their roots in the south, you may well come across them during your travels in the north.

SARAH JOLLY

Dance and mythology are combined in Shiva's cosmic dance.

Originally from the southern state of Tamil Nadu, Bharata Natyam has been widely embraced throughout India. Kathakali, which has its roots in Kerala, is often referred to as dance but essentially is not. It's actually a play (or drama) performed with words and gestures. Stories are usually based on the great Hindu epics; the striking make-up and costumes of the dancers leave a lasting impression. Kathak, which has Hindu and Islamic influences, was particularly popular with the Mughals, and dancers still wear costumes that hark back to the 17th century. Kuchipudi is a dance-drama that originated in the 17th century in the Andhra Pradesh village it's named after. Manipuri, which has a delicate, lyrical flavour, hails from Manipur, in the Assam Hills. It attracted a wider audience in the 1920s, when the Bengali poet Rabindranath Tagore invited one of its most revered exponents to teach at Shantiniketan, near Kolkata. Mohiniyattam is a graceful Keralan dance usually performed by women; the name means 'Dance of the Enchantress'. Odissi, claimed to be India's oldest classical dance form, was originally a temple art from Orissa, and was later also performed at royal courts.

India's second major dance form, folk, is widespread and varied. It ranges from the high-spirited Bhangra dance of Punjab, to the village *natti* dances of Himachal Pradesh, which are slow and measured at first, but quicken in tempo. In southern Rajasthan, the *ghoomer* is a type of ceremonial dance performed only by women on special occasions, such as festivals or weddings. Rajasthani men clash sticks together during the Holi festival in a dance known as the *gir*. From Uttar Pradesh and elsewhere, Chhau is a martial dance in which masks feature prominently. It is danced only by men, who use their bodies to create, project and develop moods to be conveyed in the dance. Themes in the dance range from mythology and aspects of nature, to everyday life or simply moods or emotion.

Kathak Comeback

Kathak is the best-known classical dance of North India. Originally, 'Kathaks' were storytellers who danced to depict their stories in the temples of North India. The advent of Muslim rule brought Kathak out of the temples and into the courts. The diversity among the Hindu courts of Rajasthan and the Muslim courts of Delhi, Agra and Lucknow saw Kathak develop into a much more stylised art, with an emphasis on solo performers and their virtuosity. It also enabled Kathak to become a fusion of Hindu and Muslim influences.

Two schools of Kathak emerged: the Jaipur Gharana and the Lucknow Gharana. The Jaipur Gharana focused on rhythmic movement, while the Lucknow Gharana focused on moods and emotions. Rhythm, timing and footwork are fundamental characteristics of Kathak. The dance is accompanied by the tabla and the sarangi, as well as the 200 bells on the dancers' feet.

Kathak suffered a period of notoriety when it moved from the courts into houses where *nautch* girls (dancing girls) tantalised audiences with renditions of the Krishna and Radha love story. It was restored as a serious art form in the early 20th century.

Variations of the dance are found in Bihar (where it's called *seraikella*) and West Bengal.

Pioneers of modern dance forms in India include Uday Shankar, older brother of sitar master Ravi, who once partnered Anna Pavlova. Tagore was another innovator who in 1901 set up a school at Shantiniketan (near Kolkata) that promoted the arts. A poet, playwright, philosopher, actor, painter and novelist, Tagore brought gurus from all over India to Shantiniketan, where a distinctive dance style evolved. Although this style was eventually criticised for its lack of technical precision, it is claimed the real achievement of the experiment lay in stimulating interest in dance within the wider public. (For more on Tagore, see the boxed text 'Rabindranath Tagore' in the Kolkata chapter.)

Music

Classical music in India traces its roots back to Vedic times, when religious poems chanted by priests were first collated in an anthology called the Rig-Veda. Over the millennia, classical music has been shaped by many influences, and the legacy today is Carnatic music (characteristic of South India) and Hindustani music (the classical style of North India). With common origins, both share a number of features. Both use the raga (the melodic shape of the music) and the *tala* (the rhythmic meter defined by the number of beats). *Tintal*, for example, has a tala of 16 beats. The audience follows the tala by clapping at the appropriate beat, which in tintal is at one, five and 13. There is no clap at the beat of nine since that is the *khali* (empty section), indicated by a wave of the hand. Both the raga and the tala are used as a basis for composition and improvisation.

Both Carnatic and Hindustani music are performed by small ensembles comprising about half a dozen musicians and both have many instruments in common. Neither style uses a change of key or harmonies; the drone establishes the raga's ground note (tonic) and usually its fifth as well. Hindustani has been more heavily influenced by Persian musical conventions (a result of Mughal rule); Carnatic music, as it developed in South India, cleaves more closely to theory and relies on a far greater use of voice. Hindustani music has more purely instrumental compositions. The most common vocal forms in Hindustani music today are the *khyal* and the *thumri;* the latter is a light classical style based on devotional literature about the Krishna and Radha love story.

Classical music is enjoyed by a relatively small section of society. Most people are more familiar with their own local, folk forms, popular during festivities and various village ceremonies, or with popular music. Wandering magicians, snake charmers and storytellers may also use song to entertain their audiences; the storyteller often sings the tales from the great epics. Radio, TV and cinema have played a major role in broadcasting popular music to the remote

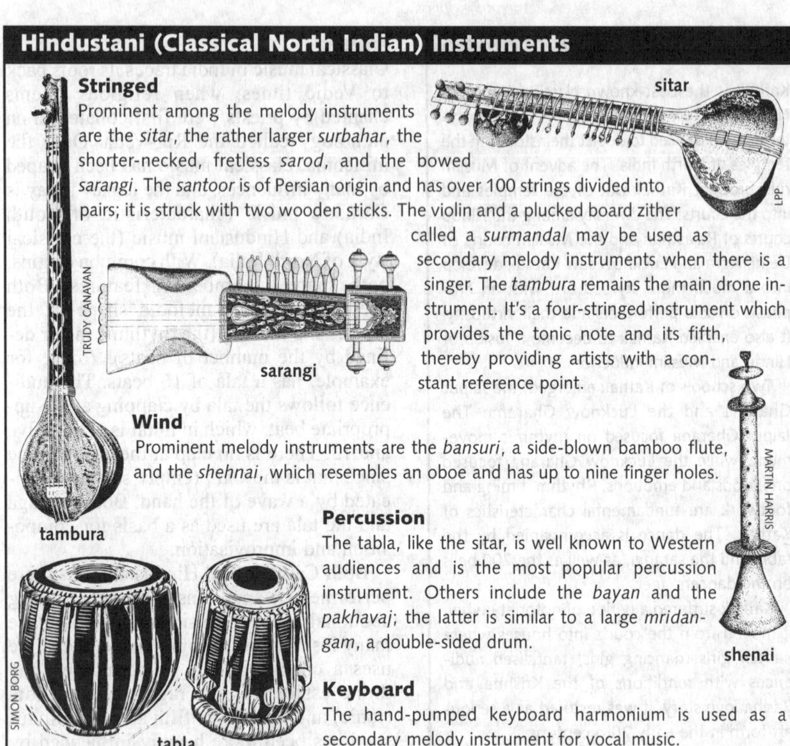

Hindustani (Classical North Indian) Instruments

Stringed

Prominent among the melody instruments are the *sitar*, the rather larger *surbahar*, the shorter-necked, fretless *sarod*, and the bowed *sarangi*. The *santoor* is of Persian origin and has over 100 strings divided into pairs; it is struck with two wooden sticks. The violin and a plucked board zither called a *surmandal* may be used as secondary melody instruments when there is a singer. The *tambura* remains the main drone instrument. It's a four-stringed instrument which provides the tonic note and its fifth, thereby providing artists with a constant reference point.

Wind

Prominent melody instruments are the *bansuri*, a side-blown bamboo flute, and the *shehnai*, which resembles an oboe and has up to nine finger holes.

Percussion

The tabla, like the sitar, is well known to Western audiences and is the most popular percussion instrument. Others include the *bayan* and the *pakhavaj*; the latter is similar to a large *mridangam*, a double-sided drum.

Keyboard

The hand-pumped keyboard harmonium is used as a secondary melody instrument for vocal music.

corners of India. Bollywood's latest musical offerings are never far away thanks to the proliferation of cassette players throughout the country.

Fusion music – an innovative blend of Eastern and Western influences – has become increasingly popular around the world. This style of music has featured in a number of Western blockbusters, including *Dead Man Walking*, which included some evocative fusion compilations by the renowned Nusrat Fateh Ali Khan.

Literature

India has a long tradition of Sanskrit literature, although works in the vernacular have contributed to a particularly rich legacy. In fact, it's claimed that there are as many literary traditions as there are written languages. For most visitors, only those works written in (or translated into) English are accessible. (See also Books in the Facts for the Visitor chapter.)

Khushwant Singh is one of India's most published contemporary authors and journalists, although as a prolific Sikh writer he seems to have as many detractors as fans. Among his multitude of books, he wrote on the holocaust of Partition in the harrowing *Train to Pakistan*. *My Bleeding Punjab* is about the Sikh campaign for a separate homeland. *Delhi* is about the history of Delhi from the first Mughal invasions to the fall of the British empire, as seen through the eyes of a series of poets, soldiers, sultans and ordinary people.

Salman Rushdie's *Midnight's Children*, which won the Booker Prize, tells of the children who were born, like modern India itself, at the stroke of midnight on that August night in 1947 and how the life of one particular midnight child is inextricably intertwined with events in India itself. Rushdie's follow-up, *Shame*, was set in modern Pakistan. *The Moor's Last Sigh* centres on a political party called Mumbai Axis.

Kolkata-born Vikram Seth's epic novel about post-Independence India, *A Suitable Boy*, centres on a Hindu mother's search for a suitable husband for her daughter. Seth's *An Equal Music* (set in London and Vienna) has also been highly acclaimed, and won an award in 1999 from the Indian bookshop Crossword as the best English-language novel. He has also had several collections of poetry published.

One of India's best-known writers, RK Narayan, died in 2001. He hailed from Mysore so it's not surprising that many of his stories were based in the south. His works include *Swami and Friends*, *The Financial Expert*, *The Guide*, *Waiting for the Mahatma*, *Malgudi Days* and *The World of Nagaraj*. Another southern author, Arundhati Roy, grabbed the headlines in 1997 by winning the Booker Prize for her novel *The God of Small Things*. In recent times Roy has been actively campaigning against the Narmada Dam project (see the boxed text 'The Dam Debate' earlier).

Shobha De's raunchy novels (Jackie Collins style) have been heralded by some critics as being extremely significant in their representation of Indian female sexuality, although others have condemned them as shameful trash. Nonetheless, she is the largest-selling Indian English-language author in India.

Neelam Saran Gour, from Allahabad, has received wide acclaim as an Indian female author. Her work tends to reflect everyday life in small towns of her native Uttar Pradesh. Both *Speaking of 62* and *Grey Pigeons and Other Stories* were very successful and well received by critics. *Winter Companions and Other Stories* did not enjoy similar reviews; many believed this work was somewhat simplistic and not a true reflection of her talent.

Pankaj Mishra's *The Romantics* is the story of Samar, a young graduate from Allahabad, who moves to the holy city of Benares (Varanasi) to escape the caste system and lack of opportunity in small-town India.

Vinod Kumar Shukla from Raipur (Chhatisgarh) has produced two works that have attracted considerable attention and acclaim: *There Used to be a Window in the Wall* and *The Servant's Shirt*. The latter is the story of a recently married junior clerk who struggles with the monotony of his office environment, and the hierarchical social structure in which he and his wife live. Shukla's use of symbolism in this work has been highly regarded.

Anita Desai has written widely on India; her works include *Cry*, *The Peacock*, *Fire on the Mountain*, and *In Custody* – which was filmed by Merchant Ivory. *Hullabaloo in the Guava Orchard*, by her daughter Kiran Desai, follows a bored post office clerk and dreamer who takes to the branches of a secluded guava tree in search of the contemplative life, only to be pursued by crowds of people seeking enlightenment.

A Matter of Time by Shashi Deshpande centres on the problems a middle-class family faces when the husband walks out. Deshpande (from Bangalore) writes powerful narratives on the relationships between men and women. *The Dark Holds No Terror* and *That Long Silence* are two of her most recent works.

Kaveri Nambisan, from Karnataka, writes eloquent historical novels that shed light on the colonial period. *The Scent of Peppers* and *Mango Coloured Fish* are worth reading.

Rabindranath Tagore was awarded the Nobel prize for literature in 1913 for *Gitanjali*, which he translated into English himself. (For more information, see the boxed text 'Rabindranath Tagore' in the Kolkata chapter.)

Mulk Raj Anand's work focuses on the downtrodden in works such as *Cooli*, and *Untouchable* – hailed as the first Dalit novel. Novelist Raja Rao penned *Kanthapura*,

Behind the Scenes of Indian Cinema

India's incredibly popular and successful film industry was born in 1897, when the first Indian-made motion picture, *Panorama of Kolkata*, was screened in the Star theatre in Kolkata (formerly Calcutta). It was made with foreign technicians and didn't have a story line. India's first feature film, *Raja Harishchandra*, was made in the silent era in 1913. It is from this film that Indian cinema traces its lineage. Between 1931 (when the talkies began) and 1999, India produced over 30,000 feature films, a world record by a long stretch.

India's film industry is the largest in the world, larger than Hollywood. And Mumbai (Bombay), the film capital, has earned itself the nickname 'Bollywood'. Other main film-producing centres are Chennai (Madras) and Hyderabad, both in South India. In 1999, 764 feature films were produced in 12 languages. Over 2.5 million people are employed in the film industry and India has around 13,000 theatres, including touring cinemas that go from village to village. For the poor, movies are the cheapest and most popular form of entertainment.

A visit to an Indian cinema can be quite rewarding if you don't mind the hustle and bustle. If the film has just opened and is a hit, filmgoers will probably have to buy their tickets at a premium price from a tout hanging in the alleys around the theatre. The transaction will be totally illegal but the police will look the other way because they are in cahoots. Still, this method of purchase is not recommended.

There are two categories of Indian films. For a cultural experience or, more likely, a culture shock, you should try what is known as the mainstream movie. You probably haven't seen anything quite like it. Three hours and still running, the blockbusters are 'multi-starrers' with up to three starring couples. You'll find rape, violence, a dream sequence, up to a dozen songs, an honest policeman with an evil brother who was probably lost in childhood or a car chase that doesn't take the plot anywhere.

It is all done with such verve, exuberance and sheer vitality that it carries the local audience along and leaves the foreigner dumbfounded. On the surface it may be Rambo, Romeo or Dirty Harry, but the subtext is likely to be the Mahabharata, dharma (doty) and social justice. These movies are heady, spicy stuff. Not for nothing do the locals call them masala (mixed spice) movies. They are pure fantasies. What the audience sees on the screen does not happen in the day-to-day lives of ordinary Indians. Technically, these days the films are as slick as anything made anywhere.

There is also a subgenre, the C-grade movie. These are truly awful. The story would have the heroine 'lose her honour' to the local feudal land owner. She becomes a vengeance-seeking dacoit

The Serpent and the Rope and *The Cat and Shakespeare*. Shashi Tharoor, whose work *The Great Indian Novel* received the Commonwealth Writers Prize, has also written *India: From Midnight to the Millennium*, which examines the successes and failures of independent India. Rohinton Mistry's *A Fine Balance* is a harrowing tale of the fate of two tailors and an insight into India's caste system. A widely translated novelist is Amitav Ghosh, whose work *The Circle of Reason* won the Prix Medici Etranger, one of France's top literary awards.

Poets include Nissam Ezekiel, an Indian Jew whose poetry largely explores aspects of Jewish identity in India, Kamala Das (one of the best-known women poets), AK Ramanujan *(The Striders, Relations)* and Arun Kolatkar, who won the Commonwealth Poetry Prize in 1977 for *Jejuri*, a collection of 31 poems in English.

Architecture

In ancient times Indian builders used wood (sometimes brick) to construct their temples. None has survived the vagaries of climate and today all that remains are Buddhist

Behind the Scenes of Indian Cinema

(outlaw). There are variations on this theme and a rape scene is obligatory. Not much acting skill is required, but the heroine must have an ample bosom and know how to ride a horse. These films cater to a male crowd that wants action and has no time for the love angle. Made on a shoestring, the films head straight for the flea-infested halls of smaller towns.

There are no explicit sex scenes in Indian films made for the local market. The censors are rigid on this score. Kissing has recently crept in but the established actresses refuse to be kissed on screen. The camera discreetly moves away at the crucial moment. However, lack of nudity is more than compensated for by heroines writhing to music in the rain in clinging wet saris. The front-benchers are delirious with contentment.

The big-budget films are often shot abroad. Switzerland is very popular – alpine peaks and lakes pass off as the Himalaya. The biggest box office hit of 2000, *Kaho Na Pyar Hai* (Say You Love Me), was largely shot in New Zealand. Australia and Eastern Europe are also becoming popular locations, the latter because it's cheaper.

Arthouse or 'parallel' cinema, on the other hand, takes Indian reality as its base. Its images are a faithful reproduction of what we see around us and the idiom in which it is presented is a Western one. Such films are, or at least are supposed to be, socially and politically relevant. Made on infinitely smaller budgets than their commercial cousins, these films win awards at film festivals abroad. Most of them make little money or sink without trace in the home market. If a film is any good, you can probably catch it back home at your local cinema.

Some of the better-known films in this category are the works of directors such as Satyajit Ray (*The Apu Trilogy, Charulata*), Mira Nair (*Salaam Bombay, Mississippi Masala, Kamasutra*) and Deepa Mehta (*Earth, Fire*). Mehta was to complete a trilogy with her third film, *Water*, but a few days into the shoot in Varanasi the unit was forced to pack up and leave. The script concerned the sorry plight of Hindu widows and the theme and treatment did not go down well with right-wing Hindu zealots. (See the boxed text 'Drowning in Conservatism' under Varanasi in the Uttar Pradesh chapter for more on this.)

Bhaichand Patel

Bhaichand Patel was formerly the director of the UN Information Centre for India. He now divides his time between New Delhi and New York and writes a column about the art scene for the *Hindustan Times* (New Delhi) and *Mid-Day* (Mumbai).

stupas. By the advent of the Guptas (4th to 6th centuries AD) sacred structures of a new type were being built, and these set the standard for temples for several hundred years (see Religion, later in this section). In northern temples the *sikara* (spire) is typically curvilinear, topped with a grooved disk on which sits a pot-shaped finial (South Indian temples have a characteristic stepped spire).

The Muslim invaders contributed their own architectural conventions – see the special section 'Islamic & Mughal Architecture'. Europeans left their mark in the churches of Daman and Diu, in the neoclassical-style buildings that were erected by the British in the 18th and 19th centuries (and of course the parliament complex of New Delhi), and in attempts to meld neo-Gothic and neo-Saracenic (Muslim) styles with local architectural traditions. Swiss architect Le Corbusier designed the entire city of Chandigarh in present-day Haryana in the early 1950s (see the boxed text 'Chandigarh – a Living City' in the Punjab & Haryana chapter for details).

Painting

The first significant style in the north came courtesy of the Jain lay community, thanks to its stake in trade and the patronage of local rulers sympathetic to the large community of Svetambara monks living in Gujarat. To attain spiritual merit, the Jains poured their money into lavish displays of temple building. After the Muslim conquest of Gujarat in 1299 they turned their attention to illustrated manuscripts, which could be hidden away and preserved. These manuscripts are the only form of Indian painting that managed to survive the Muslim conquest of North India. At first artists painted on palm leaves, but the availability of paper from the late 14th century allowed larger and more elaborate works, with gold-leaf script and lavish borders in blue, gold and red. Complex designs and luxurious materials testified to the wealth of the patron. Unlike the flowing Ajanta paintings of South India, dating from 200 BC to AD 650, the Jain style is angular, with deities and mortals depicted in profile, the eye projecting beyond the face.

The Indo-Persian style developed from Muslim royals, although the elongated eye is one convention that seems to have been retained from indigenous sources. The Persian influence flourished when artisans fled to India following the 1507 Uzbek attack on Herat (in present-day Afghanistan), and with trade and gift-swapping between the Persian city of Shiraz, an established centre for miniature production, and Indian provincial sultans. Soon after, the Mughals introduced their distinctive paintings to India (see the boxed text 'Mughal Masterpieces').

In Rajasthan, distinctive styles influenced by Mughal tastes and conventions developed, in part because local Rajput rulers were required to spend time at the

Mughal Masterpieces

The 1526 victory by Babur at the Battle of Panipat ushered in the era of the Mughals in India. Although Babur and his son Humayun were both patrons of the arts, it was Humayun's son Akbar who is generally credited with developing the characteristically Mughal style. Akbar recruited artists from far and wide to create an *atelier* (studio or workshop) that was, initially anyway, under the control of Persian artists. Artistic endeavour at first centred on the production of illustrated manuscripts (topics varied from history and romance to myth and legend), but later broadened into portraiture and the glorification of everyday events.

Akbar took a personal interest in the artists' work and rewarded those who pleased him. Within the atelier there emerged a high level of division of labour, which meant more work could be turned out in less time. Skilled designers sketched the outlines of the work. Colourists applied layer upon layer of pigment, burnishing each to achieve an enamel-like finish. Painters used squirrel- or camel-hair brushes to create the finest of lines. Artists of extraordinary talent, however, were allowed to do their own paintings and so display their mastery. European paintings influenced the artists, and occasionally reveal themselves in experiments with motifs and perspective.

Akbar's son Jehangir also patronised painting, but his tastes and interests were different. He preferred portraiture and his fascination with natural science resulted in a rich legacy of paintings of birds, flowers and animals. Style also took a distinctive turn under Jehangir. Despite its richness, there is nothing frivolous or wasteful about the paintings turned out by his atelier. The more formal ordering of figures reflects a penchant for strict etiquette in courtly life. Jehangir also saw portraiture as a useful tool for sizing up foreign rivals; he desired such paintings to reveal personality and requested them so that he might judge the subject's characteristics. Under Jehangir's son Shah Jahan, the Mughal style became less fluid, and although the colouring was bright and eye-catching, the paintings lacked the life and vigour of before. It was a trend that continued, hastened by the disintegration of the Mughal court in the 18th century. Mughal painting as such ended with the reign of Shah Alam II (1759–1806).

Mughal court. But Rajasthani painting had its own characteristics, marked by a poetic imagery evident in such popular themes as the *ragamala*, a depiction of musical modes, and the *nayakanayikabheda*, a classification of ideal types of lovers. The romanticism and eroticism they depict are in stark contrast to the strict morality that pervaded Rajput society. Portraiture was influenced by Mughal-trained artists recruited by Rajput rulers. But rather than being the revealing pictures favoured by Jehangir, these portraits lean more towards being idealised representations of individuals, whose weaknesses are well and truly disguised.

In the Himalayan foothills of north-west India a distinctive style of painting, dubbed Pahari, developed during the 17th and 18th centuries. This relatively small area (roughly between Jammu and Garhwal) was divided into 35 kingdoms. Pahari painting can be divided into two main schools: the Basohli school preceded the Kangra, which eclipsed it in the late 18th century. Basholi art is robust, bold and colourful. Kangra art is more subdued and fluid, probably testament to the influence of Mughal court painters migrating into the area at the time. The Kangra school survived until the late 19th century, but its best works are usually dated to around the late 18th and early 19th centuries.

By the 19th century, painting was often heavily influenced by Western styles (especially English watercolours), giving rise to what's been dubbed the Company School, which had its centre in Delhi.

Sculpture

For about 1500 years after the demise of the Indus Valley civilisation, sculpture in India seems to have vanished as an art form. Then, suddenly in the 3rd century BC, it reappeared in a new, technically accomplished style that flourished under the Mauryan rulers of central India.

It's a phenomenon that still puzzles scholars and art historians; some say Mauryan sculpture must have had its genesis abroad, possibly in Persia. But this has never been proved. The legacy of the Mauryan artists includes the burnished, sandstone columns erected by the Buddhist emperor Ashoka, the most famous of which, the lion-topped column at Sanchi, has become the state emblem of modern India.

Midway through the 2nd century BC a new format emerged, evident in the stupa railing of Bharut, Madhya Pradesh. Here can be seen the style and motifs that have since become an integral part of Indian sculpture. The ornamentation is symbolic of abundance (beauty and abundance are closely linked in Indian sculpture): the pot overflowing with flowers, the lotus, the trees, the elephants and the mythical *makara* (a protective crocodile-like creature). Here too are the *yakshas* and *yakshis*, male and female deities associated with ancient fertility cults and whose images provided the basis for Buddhist, Jain and Hindu iconography.

While there was an early reluctance to represent the Buddha in more than symbolic form, yaksha figures gradually became Buddha-like in the succeeding centuries, albeit devoid of their elaborate dress and ornamentation (deemed inappropriate in the light of Buddhism's monastic traditions). The Sarnath Buddha, for example, has a robe characteristically thrown over the left shoulder, the right hand raised in a *mudra* (gesture) signifying freedom from fear, the left resting on the waist, but empty handed. By the Gupta period in North India (4th to 6th centuries AD) the rather earthy and robust yaksha-style Buddha icons had been transformed into models of serene contemplation, eyes lowered, as befitted the compassionate Master of the Law.

Hindu and Jain iconography also began to evolve their distinctive forms at this time. Images sprouted multiple arms and heads (distinguishing them from mere mortals), and eventually adopted the serene expressions that have become associated with calm contemplation.

From the 10th century, sculpture and architecture were generally inseparable; temples were lavishly decorated with religious sculpture designed to impress and instruct. Much of this fabulous stonework survives today.

Theatre

The oldest form of classical theatre in India, Sanskrit theatre, shares a common ancestry with dance. Details on both were laid down in the *Natya Shastra* in ancient times. Sanskrit theatre, like dance, was divided into performances for the gods and those rendered for people's pleasure, and was further classified into naturalistic and stylised productions, notions reflected in the folk traditions of later times. After AD 1000, this type of theatre was largely eclipsed by folk theatre.

The many regions and languages of India provided fertile ground for folk theatre, which employs a few Sanskrit theatrical conventions, such as the opening prayer and the *vidushaka* (clown) – the hero's comic alter ego and the audience's ally. Folk theatre draws heavily from the Vedic epics, but also canvasses current political and social issues. Performances always take place outdoors and actors are invariably from castes where the art is passed from father to son; in rare cases women may also act. Troupes may tour for several months at a time and the more popular theatrical forms (secular rather than religious in nature) enjoy a very healthy following.

Puppetry has also enjoyed a good following in India, although most people are only familiar with Rajasthani *kathputhilis* (puppets) – wooden creations, dressed in colourful costumes and manipulated by the puppeteers (always male) using strings. Puppetry is losing its audience to competing attractions such as cinema and television and because puppeteers are reluctant to challenge the epic-based repertoire.

Modern theatre had its inception in Bengal in the 18th century. Exposed to Western theatrical and literary conventions earlier than most, Bengali artists combined Western staging techniques with folk and Sanskrit conventions. Their plays soon became vehicles for social and political comment and opposition to British rule. The touring Bombay Parsi theatre companies that developed in the north and west of India in the 19th century also used Western, classical and folk conventions to bring dramatic, lively entertainment in Hindi and Urdu to a wide audience.

Arts & Crafts

The depth of visual wonder makes travelling anywhere in India a wonderfully rich experience. Innumerable ethnic groups have produced an exuberant artistic heritage, rich in spirit, resourcefulness and cultural significance.

Arts and crafts encompass everything from vehicles decorated with folk craft to intricate pieces of jewellery. Natural materials such as wood, leather, bone, metal, stone, grass, papier-mache (a Kashmir speciality), cotton and wool are used.

Crafts are not always confined to the region of origin – you can come across a speciality Kashmir handicraft emporium or Tibetan shop anywhere.

See Shopping in the Facts for the Visitor chapter where you will find detailed information on products available as well as a range of prices.

Ceramics The potter's craft is steeped in mythology. The first humans are said to have been shaped from clay by Brahma, the creator. Indeed the name with which potters are most closely identified, *prajapati*, is one of Brahma's titles. Potters claim another link to the divine. It is said that when Shiva wished to marry Parvati, they lacked the water pot needed to carry auspicious ingredients required for the marriage ceremony, such as water and rice. So Shiva created a man and a woman from two beads plucked from his necklace. The man created the pot and together the man and woman created a lineage of potters. Today potters are also known as *kumbhar* or *kumbar*, a name shared with the ubiquitous water pot *(kumbh)*.

Despite the intrusion of plastic into the marketplace, the potter's craft is evident in every household and at shrines throughout the country. Smooth, round terracotta water pots are arguably the most commonly used household utensils in India; the narrow neck prevents spillage as women carry the pots on their heads from the well to home. The baked clay keeps the water pleasantly cool in a country where many households have no access to refrigeration. Potters also make

RICHARD I'ANSON

Ceramic pots are integral to everyday life.

a variety of cooking utensils; some say traditional dishes just don't taste the same prepared in metal pots and pans. Travellers will invariably come across the terracotta pots in which curd is sold and (in the south) the terracotta cups used by chai vendors at train stations.

Pots and storage jars of various kinds are created on the wheel (only men may use the wheel although women may decorate the pot after it has been removed); sometimes they are built up using slabs or coils. Plaster moulds are occasionally used.

The potter is also skilful in making chillums (clay smoking pipes), hookahs, beads and *jhanvan* (serrated palm-sized slabs) that can be used like pumice stone for smoothing rough skin on the feet.

Votive offerings also have a place in the potter's repertoire; these include terracotta horses, idols, and even replicas of human body parts (these offerings are placed before a shrine by those hoping for a miraculous recovery).

The Mughals manufactured coloured and patterned glazed tiles with which they decorated their mosques, forts and palaces.

Blue pottery (such as vases, plates, jewellery boxes, ashtrays, tiles and doorknobs) is largely produced for export, and hails from Jaipur and elsewhere. The plates and bowls are unsuitable for use with hot food because they contain high levels of lead. Blue pottery is distinctive for its hand-painted artwork and is fired only to a low temperature (750°C) to retain the brilliant colours.

Most village-produced work is low-fired and fragile. All glazed ceramic wares have been fired twice, with an initial bisque firing and a subsequent glaze firing. An easy way to tell if a piece is high- or low-fired is to tap the item – the higher the firing the higher the pitch. A cracked item can also be detected by this method. Both earthenware and stoneware are nonporous; however, some Indian earthenware is slightly underfired and not always fabulously glazed, so it is still a little porous.

Incense The smell of incense is common throughout India and its production is an ancient craft. It is associated with meditation and devotion and there are thousands of makers in India, particularly in Bangalore and Mysore.

Taxi, bus and truck drivers often burn incense in their vehicles before they set out on a journey, as a plea to the gods for safe passage. Similarly, many shopkeepers light incense and play bhajans (devotional songs) in the morning in the hope their shop will be blessed with a good day's business.

Incense from Auroville, an ashram near Pondicherry, is of high quality. Nag Champa is another very popular incense; it has a sandalwood base and is produced by devotees of Sai Baba.

Jewellery The wearing of jewellery is a sign of status and wealth. It is made from gold, silver and white metal, though

JANE SWEENEY

Jewellery is important for any special occasion.

cheaper metal may also be used and passed off as something more precious.

Gold is very expensive in India and is not really worth buying unless you find something with special Indian characteristics. Gold plating, with few exceptions, is done with little technology and is usually of low standard.

Traditional silver comes in many grades (including 0% white metal) and is rarely found to be above 84%, despite much information to the contrary. Sterling silver (92.5%) is sold by reputable jewellers, though you should ask to see a comparison with lower grades – you will soon be able to recognise the difference.

Many precious and semiprecious stones are mined and cut in India. It takes experience to recognise value in gemstones. Stone colour can be falsely heightened, raising an ordinary specimen to a rich, more highly prized hue, and many synthetic imitations are to be found. Nail polish remover, or a vigorous rub with a white cloth, will often reveal the deception. If stone colours are heightened by heating processes they cannot be 'rubbed off'.

Leather Sheep, goat and camel skin is used to make various qualities of leather. (Cow hide is generally not used by most Indians because of the religious significance of this animal.) Many styles of wallets, jackets and bags are available. Kolkata (Kolkata), Kanpur, Chennai (Madras) and Pondicherry all produce distinct styles. In Shantiniketan in West Bengal is produced the embossed, colourfully painted fine leather that is made into bags and wallets. The decorated shoes are called *jootis* and feature colourful embroidery that varies from region to region.

Tanning quality varies from the simple village preparation to sophisticated factory production for the Italian market. In a country where the cow is both common and sacred to the Hindu majority, it is the job of low-caste people to work with the skin of a fallen beast.

Traditional footwear is usually made from leather in a slip-on style. Highly decorative, some of the shoes feature a curled decorative front. Left and right shoes are the same and will mould to your foot shape; it's best to mark the inside so that you always wear them on the same foot.

Metal The versatility of metal craft can be seen in fine *qandeels* (hanging lamps with cut-out patterns), jewellery and the traditional water pipes for smoking.

Objects of devotion are traditionally made by the lost-wax method. The image is first made in wax, then dipped in clay to form a mould. Molten metal is poured in, melting and replacing the wax. The clay is then removed and the metalpolished in a time-consuming process requiring much skill; each mould is only used once. Consequently, ornaments or images made in this manner are often expensive. A machine-made multiuse mould is a much simpler and cheaper production method, but the lost-wax method is still quite widely used.

Tibetan communities in India produce distinctive metal crafts. Tibetan singing bowls, made from a secret mix of seven different metals, are a meditation device originating from the Bon religion of pre-Buddhist Tibet. These produce the 'disassociated' mystic hum when a playing stick is rotated around the outer edge of the bowl. Healing bowls should be partially filled with water and struck on the outer edge using a playing stick. Enlightenment may not always follow! Yak-butter lamps, horns and ornate teapots are other popular items.

Textiles This art has always played an important role in Indian society and trade (the Romans had textiles made to order in India). Fabulous brocade wedding saris, handloom rugs, *zari* (metal-thread brocade), block-print bedspreads, embroidered cushions, and festival tents erected in a city street for a wedding (a reminder of the days when maharajas and Mughals used tents for special occasions) are just a few examples of the spectacular textile art to be seen.

India is rightfully famous for hand-spun silk and cottons, including cheesecloth, voile and *khadi* (home-spun cloth). The promotion of khadi by Mahatma Gandhi was an important aspect of the struggle for Indian independence. Ousting foreign cotton from Manchester mills with khadi was such a significant political event that the spinning wheel still represents freedom and is the symbol on India's national flag.

Although the use of chemical dyes has been widespread for almost a century, there is also much use of natural dye products to produce colours including blue (indigo plant), red (madder root, poppy, tulip petals, rhubarb, rose roots, cherry skins, bark of the jujube tree), yellow (camomile, turmeric), orange (henna, plum bark), black (pomegranate peel, oak apples), tan/brown (acorn cups, walnut husks, naturally brown wool) and purple/violet (grape skin, cochineal).

Great textiles of wonderful variety are to be seen everywhere, with some particularly distinctive styles found in several centres, including Gujarat, Rajasthan and Kashmir.

Rugs Kashmir has a rich tradition of textiles that includes fine shawls, chain stitching and the embroidered felt rugs known as numdas. Numdas made with 50% or more wool in the felt are more durable. Nearly all styles of rug are made mostly from wool, including some in the Persian tradition, commonly blended with other fibres such as cotton and silk.

There are huge factories or workshops producing copies of Persian rugs. The use of child and bonded (some would say slave) labour is an ugly reality associated with some of these workshops and you should think twice before buying this type of product (see Be Shop Smart under Responsible Tourism in the Facts for the Visitor chapter).

Wherever you go in India you will find dealers in pile rugs and kilims (flat-weave tribal carpets). A myth of the rug world is that the durability of rugs depends on the number of knots per square inch. Although this is a factor, the type of wool used is more important. The wiry wool from local sheep makes an uncomfortable, itchy jumper but a wonderful long-lasting carpet.

Dhurries are flat-weave, chemically dyed rugs made from cotton or wool and are produced throughout India, though the northwest is the main base for commercial export. They may be striped in design or have different motifs, and come in an extensive range of colours.

Applique & Embroidery Applique (decoration of one material sewn to another) is particularly widespread in Rajasthani and Gujarati textile work and includes wall and door hangings. The motifs used in these pieces include colourful animals and tree-shaped patches sewn onto cotton cloth. Another style of door and wall hanging is called *toran* and features hand-embroidered cross-stitch patterns. Traditionally, a bridegroom upon reaching the home of his bride would pierce a toran over the doorway with his sword, thereby symbolically 'winning' his bride and gaining the right to enter the family home and claim her. This practice is still prevalent among the Rajputs and other Hindu clans.

Decorative crewel work (chain-stitched patterning) is used to make many wall hangings. This beautiful embroidery, sometimes incorporating mirrors, is used on caps, shawls and other clothing.

Shawls, often embroidered, are particularly striking and vary throughout the country. They are light to carry and may be worn in numerous ways, or used as curtains or wall hangings, or thrown over furniture. See Shopping in the Facts for the Visitor chapter for more information on shawls.

Saris These are worn by women all over the country, though especially in rural India. Much time, effort and expense is put into selecting the base fabric of a sari, the style of embroidery used to decorate it and the many choices of colour and thread available (ranging from synthetic right through to silver or gold, with beads, sequins, tassels and mirrors). The intricacies of the work all contribute to the final cost of the garment.

All sequined, beaded and *salma*-style (continuous spring threads) saris are handworked. The fabric is generally rayon, cotton, georgette, satin or silk and, measuring about 6m x 1m, can be used for other purposes such as cushions, curtains and fashion clothing.

Recycled saris are made into fashion garments for export as well as for street sale to tourists in places such as Rajasthan (especially Udaipur, Jaipur and Pushkar) and Delhi.

Woodwork Wood is used to great effect in all regions of India. In Kashmir it has been beautifully utilised in the local architecture and craft for many centuries. Many types of wood are used in carving in India, including teak, aromatic sandalwood, sheesham, walnut and other fruit trees and, in the north, Himalayan cedar. The most common wood used is sheesham plantation wood grown in North India, which has a dark stain. Mango wood is becoming a preferred alternative because of its affordability and quality. It is also a valuable use of natural resources given that the wood comes from old, less productive mango trees. In South India denser woods, which can be carved in more detail, are used.

Woodwork artisans often carve detailed works with great precision, while steadying the block with their feet. Jali work refers to the holes or spaces produced through carving.

Traditional doors are magnificent examples of wood artistry as most have intricate geometric designs. Unfortunately, most new housing has moved away from using this fixture. A wide range of household items and furniture are also created from wood, as are hand-carved ornamental pieces (figurines, masks and block-print blocks).

SOCIETY & CONDUCT

Marriage, Birth & Death

Ceremonies for important occasions, such as marriages, vary between the many religions found in the subcontinent, and each would need at least several pages to describe.

In Hindu-dominated India, although *samskaras* (rites of passage ceremonies) have been simplified over the centuries, they still hold great importance. One highly auspicious event is the marriage ceremony, which is an elaborate and expensive affair. Although 'love marriages' have increased in number in recent years, particularly in urban centres, most Hindu marriages are arranged (see also Women in Society later in this section). Discreet inquiries are made within the community, or, where the community isn't very close-knit (such as in big cities), advertisements may be placed in the local newspapers or on the Internet. Many non-resident Indians (NRIs) also advertise via newspapers or the Internet. They will make special trips to India to meet prospective applicants who have made it to the short list.

Horoscopes are checked, and if they match, a meeting between the two families usually takes place. Many potential matches are rejected purely on the basis that the astrological signs are not propitious. An astrologer is consulted again when it comes to fixing a wedding date. Dowry, although illegal, is still a key issue in many arranged marriages. In theory, the larger the dowry, the greater the bride's family's chances of securing a good match for their daughter.

[Continued on page 73]

The Way of the Buddha

Buddhism is the majority religion in many Asian nations, but in India it is very much a minority religion, with followers numbering around seven million. However, North India is rich in important Buddhist sites. Visiting some or all of these sites would make an interesting and rewarding tour for Buddhists and non-Buddhists alike. For information on the symbolism of statues of the Buddha see the boxed text 'Sculptural Symbolism' in the Bihar & Jharkhand chapter.

On the Trail of Enlightenment

The person who became known as the Buddha was born around 563 BC. His given name was Siddhartha Gautama, and in his early years he lived a life of privilege as the son of a Sakyan king of a minor kingdom. He married at 16, had a son and seemed destined to rule in his father's place. However, he became increasingly dissatisfied with the empty pleasures of courtly life and at age 29 he turned his back on earthly riches and took to the 'homeless life' of an itinerant ascetic seeking spiritual fulfilment. This action is known to Buddhists as 'The Great Renunciation'.

Thus began an austere life of wandering, meditation, yoga and asceticism. Six years of austerity and fasting brought him to the point of starvation, but no nearer to his spiritual goal. Deciding that extreme self-denial was not the answer, he formulated a philosophy of life that

JANE SWEENEY

Title page: Monks perform *puja* (prayers) at the annual Ningma Monlam gathering at Mahabodhi Temple, Bodhgaya (Photo by Richard I'Anson)

Inset: A wall detail from Labrang Gompa, Phodong, Sikkim (Photo by Richard I'Anson)

Bottom: The calm and illuminated visage of the Buddha at Mahabodhi Temple

BILL WASSMAN

RICHARD I'ANSON

BILL WASSMAN

sought a middle way between the sensual indulgences of normal living and the extreme self-denial and austerity espoused by Hindu ascetics. At this juncture he ended up in Bodhgaya in present-day Bihar. Here, while seated under a bo tree (a fig or pipal tree), he embarked on a lengthy spell of deep meditation, during which he resisted the worldly temptations proffered to him by the demon Mara. As his state of meditation deepened, he became aware of his previous lives and saw the comings and goings of other beings in their wanderings through samsara, the realm of rebirth. In the 'final watch' of the night he became aware of the cessation of all defilements in his mind and achieved true enlightenment, or nirvana (literally meaning 'cooled', but describing a pure clarity of mind). The bo tree became known as the Bodhi Tree, or tree of enlightenment. 'Buddha' means 'the awakened' or 'the enlightened' one.

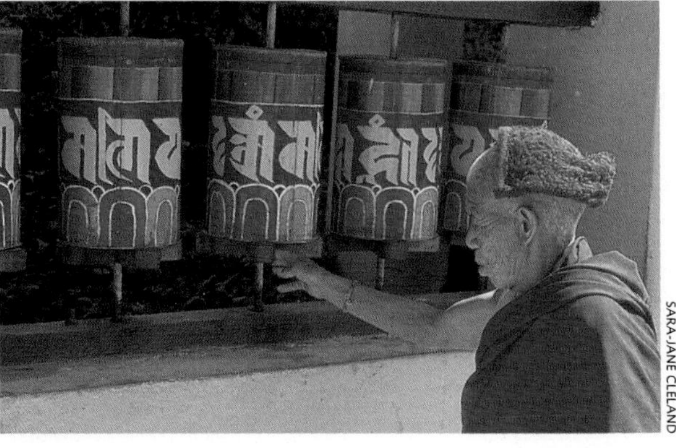

SARA-JANE CLELAND

Top: The Bodhi Tree at the Mahabodhi Temple. The tree is a descendant of the original bo tree under which the Buddha meditated.

Bottom: Prayer wheels at the official residence of the Dalai Lama in McLeod Ganj

The Buddha spent the next 45 years travelling around North India, preaching, building a following and living according to his own doctrine of the Noble Eightfold Path. He rejected the Hindu caste system, and founded monasteries in which all caste members were admitted. He died at the age of 80, having firmly established a monastic and lay following.

Buddhist Philosophy

The Buddha's teachings (*dharma*) were oral, though his disciples eventually recorded them in the Buddhist Canon (Tripitaka). Critical of the caste system, dependence upon Brahmin priests and the unthinking worship of gods, the Buddha urged his disciples to seek truth within their own experiences.

The Buddha taught that life is characterised by the Four Noble Truths: that life is rooted in *dukkha* (suffering); that suffering is caused by *tanha* (craving); that one can find release from *nirodha* (suffering) by eliminating craving; and that the *magga* (way) to eliminate craving is by following what he called the Noble Eightfold Path. This path consists of following the right understanding, right intention, right speech, right action, right livelihood, right effort, right awareness and right concentration. By successfully following the Noble Eightfold Path one can attain nirvana.

Inset: Commemorative Tibetan-style stupa, Kinnaur, Himachal Pradesh (Photo by Garry Weare)

Bottom: A novice monk at Rumtek Gompa, a large and wealthy monastery in East Sikkim

RICHARD I'ANSON

BILL WASSMAN

In the centuries after the Buddha's death, Buddhism split into two schools of thought: Theravada (Teaching of the Elders) and Mahayana (Greater Vehicle). Theravadins adhere to the teachings of the Pali Canon, which is generally considered to be an earlier version of the Buddha's teachings. For monks, the emphasis is on *vinaya,* or monastic discipline. Contrary to a popular notion, lay people are not excluded from this practice, and in traditional Theravadin countries they form a vital sector of the Buddhist community. According to the Theravadin tradition, each person's salvation is to be worked out individually.

Mahayana Buddhism adheres to the Bodhisattva ideal, which advocates renouncing final nirvana in order to help other beings along the way to salvation. Mahayanists consider their teaching to be more universal in application than other sects, such as Theravada, hence the term 'Greater Vehicle'. Unlike Theravada, the Mahayana also allows for later interpretations of the teachings.

Mahayana Buddhism is practised in China, Japan, South Korea and Tibet, hence it is also called Northern Buddhism. Theravada Buddhism, followed in Cambodia, Laos, Myanmar (Burma), Sri Lanka and Thailand, is also called Southern Buddhism. Buddhists in the Himalayan regions follow traditions similar to those in Tibet.

Top: The Great Stupa at Sanchi archaeological site has four superbly carved *toranas* (gateways), each an intricately carved 'book' on the life of the Buddha.

Inset: A stone-carved detail from Sanchi (Photo by Bill Wassman)

Sacred Sites

Stupas, which characterise Buddhist places of worship, essentially evolved from burial mounds. They were never designed to hold congregations, but were to serve as repositories for relics of the Buddha and, later, other venerated beings. A later development was the *chaitya*, or congregational hall, where devotees assembled for worship.

Shortly before his death the Buddha identified four locations that he considered should be sacred to his followers: Lumbini, Bodhgaya, Sarnath and Kushinagar. Devotion at these pilgrimage sites often takes the form of silent meditation or the chanting of Buddhist texts.

Lumbini (then known as Kapilavastu) is the Buddha's place of birth. It's in the Himalayan foothills, just across the border into Nepal, about 80km north of Gorakphur in Uttar Pradesh. A few Buddhist relics can be seen here, including a pillar erected by Emperor Ashoka. (Passport holders of most countries require a visa to visit Nepal, so it's probably not worth planning a visit to Lumbini unless you intend to explore Nepal further.)

Bodhgaya, in Bihar, is where the Buddha gained enlightenment. It's the most important Buddhist pilgrimage site in the world, and is probably the best place for non-Buddhists to find out more about Buddhist teachings. A descendent of the original bo tree stands at the exact spot where the Buddha attained nirvana. See the Bihar chapter for more information.

Sarnath, in Uttar Pradesh, is where the Buddha preached his first sermon, during which he expounded the doctrine of the Four Noble Truths and set in motion the Wheel of the Law (ie, the teaching leading to the transcendence of the round of rebirth). Sarnath is within easy reach of Varanasi and has some absorbing relics and a museum.

Kushinagar, also covered in the Uttar Pradesh chapter, is where the Buddha died, thereby attaining *parinirvana* (final passing away). Here there are numerous monasteries, and a large reclining Buddha statue. Like Lumbini and Bodhgaya, Kushinagar is particularly busy at full moon during Vaisakha (usually in May but sometimes in June), the date that marks the Buddha's birth, enlightenment and death.

Bottom: The pilgrimage site of Sanchi was close enough to the city of Vidisa to attract local pilgrims but far enough away to provide a place of peace and reflection for the monks and nuns who lived there.

KELLI HAMBLET

In addition to these four sites, there are a further four places sacred to Buddhists, each with an associated event which is often depicted in Buddhist works of art.

Rajgir, in Bihar, is where the Buddha stayed on several occasions and where he once tamed a wild elephant. Vaishali, also in Bihar, is where the Buddha preached his last sermon and where a monkey offered him honey. Shravasti, in Uttar Pradesh, is where the Buddha lived for a time and performed his 'great miracle' (multiplying himself a million times). Sankasya, also in Uttar Pradesh, is where the Buddha descended from heaven and where legend has it he spent one of his rains retreats.

Top: A monk lights candles in offering at the Mahabodhi Temple

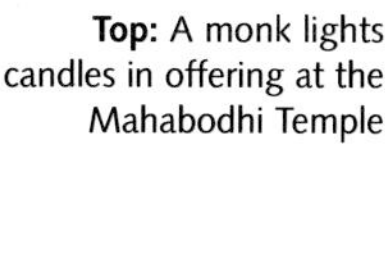

Of these four sites, Rajgir has the most to see. There are ruins, several temples, hot springs and the Vulture's Peak, from where the Buddha delivered many sermons. Vaishali is about 40km north of Patna and can be reached on a day trip from there. It has two Ashoka pillars and two stupas while Patna itself has the scruffy Patna Museum, displaying a collection of sculptures from Buddhist sites around Bihar. Shravasti, which has ruins of a stupa, is on the road between Bahraich and Balrampur (see Shravasti in the Uttar Pradesh chapter). Sankasya, where there are remains of an Ashoka pillar, is near Kannauj in central Uttar Pradesh.

There are further sites that were not visited by the Buddha during his lifetime but have since become important. In North India these include Sanchi and Nalanda. Sanchi, in Madhya Pradesh, is where the great Buddhist convert, Emperor Ashoka, built some immensely impressive stupas in the 3rd century BC. They are considered the finest examples of Buddhist art in India. (The Sanchi section in the Madhya Pradesh chapter contains explanations of the different symbols used in Buddhist art.) Nalanda, in Bihar, is the former site of one of the world's

RICHARD I'ANSON

greatest monastic universities, and now has an archaeological museum, a stupa and a Buddhist study centre.

The Tibetan Buddhist *gompas* (monasteries) found in Ladakh and Dharamsala are quite unlike anything else found on the subcontinent, embellished as they are with colourful, distinctly Tibetan motifs dedicated to the propagation of Mahayana Buddhist beliefs.

McLeod Ganj, in Himachal Pradesh, is the location of the Tibetan Government in Exile and home to the Dalai Lama, who is believed to be an incarnation of Avalokiteshvara (the Bodhisattva of Compassion). The Dalai Lama gives up to 12 public audiences each year, and Dharamsala and nearby McLeod Ganj have various Buddhist-related sites and institutes of learning.

Etiquette for Visitors You should remove your shoes and hat (and furl your umbrella) before entering the precincts of a stupa or gompa. You should also cover your legs and shoulders. Always walk around a stupa or gompa in a clockwise direction, and try not to turn your back on an image of the Buddha.

Getting There & Away A useful train for visiting Buddhist sites is the New Delhi to Barauni Vaishali Express, calling at Gorakphur (gateway to Kushinagar), Varanasi (for Sarnath) and Hajipur (for Vaishali). Gaya (the railhead for Bodhgaya), Rajgir and Nalanda are also on rail routes. The Indian Tourist Development Corporation runs a six-day train tour of Buddhist pilgrimage sites along the route from Kolkata (Calcutta) to Varanasi, which includes Gaya and Rajgir. See Organised Tours in the Getting Around chapter for agencies that offer 'Buddhist Circuit' tours.

Top: The impressive Tikse Gompa, Ladakh, is a busy monastery with continuous devotional chanting and music.

[Continued from page 64]

Families will often get into horrendous debt to raise the required cash and merchandise.

On the day of the wedding the bridegroom is escorted to his future in-laws' home (usually accompanied by an exuberant brass band and plenty of well-wishers) where offerings of roasted grain are tossed into the hearth fire. The ceremonies are officiated by a priest and the marriage is formalised when the bridegroom holds his bride's hand and they walk around the fire seven times.

The birth of a child is another momentous event, replete with its own set of ceremonies. These rituals centre on the casting of the child's first horoscope, name giving, feeding the first solid food, and hair cutting (performed on boys at around age five).

Divorce and remarriage are still generally frowned upon in India. Among the higher castes, widows are not expected to remarry, but are admonished to wear white and live pious, celibate lives. Traditionally widows have been excluded from religious ceremonies and festivals, and they are generally regarded as harbingers of bad luck.

Hindus cremate their dead, and funeral ceremonies are designed to purify and console both the living and the deceased. An important aspect of the proceedings is the *sharadda*, or paying respect to one's ancestors by offering water and rice cakes. It's an observance that's repeated at each anniversary of the death. After the cremation the ashes are collected, and 13 days after the death (when blood relatives are deemed ritually pure) a member of the family will usually scatter them in a holy river such as the Ganges, or in the ocean.

Pilgrimage

Devout Hindus are expected to go on *yatra* (pilgrimage); at least once a year is considered desirable. Pilgrimages are undertaken for various reasons, eg, to implore the gods to grant some wish, to take the ashes of a cremated relative to a holy river or to gain spiritual merit. There are thousands of holy pilgrimage sites throughout North India – see the special section 'North India's Pilgrimage Sites' for a selection. The elderly often make Varanasi their final goal, believing that dying here releases them from the cycle of rebirth. Despite the carnival-like atmosphere of some fairs, most festivals in India are rooted in religion and are thus a magnet for pilgrims.

The Caste System

Caste is the basic social structure of Hindu society. Living a righteous life and fulfilling your dharma (duty) will augment your chances of being born into a higher caste and thus better circumstances. Hindus are born into one of four varnas (castes): Brahmin (who were traditionally priests), Kshatriya (warriors), Vaishya (merchants) and Shudra (peasants). The Brahmins were said to have emerged from the mouth of Lord Brahma at the moment of creation. Kshatriyas were said to have come from his arms, the Vaishyas from his thighs and Shudras from his feet. Beneath the four main castes are the Dalits (formerly known as Untouchables). Their lives were the most menial of all, and even today sweepers and latrine cleaners are invariably drawn from their ranks. Within the varnas are thousands of caste *jatis*, or groups of 'families'.

Today the caste system, although weakened, still wields considerable power. The relationship between caste and politics is quite potent; those seeking power may look to certain caste jatis as potential vote banks. Tensions between the upper castes and the Dalits (Scheduled Castes) often turn violent. In an effort to improve the position of the Dalits, the government reserves significant numbers of public-sector jobs, parliamentary seats and university places for them. This has angered many well-educated people who miss out on jobs they would otherwise get on merit. In the 1990s there were serious protests against the raising of quotas – in 1991 at least 100 protesters immolated themselves – and the situation remains prickly. In 1999 the Indian Government admitted 242 caste jatis to the 'Other Backwards Classes' list. Castes on this list are eligible for special quotas representing 27% of positions in government employment. But this is still far less than the number proposed by the National Commission for Backward Classes (a body established by the Supreme Court), which recommended that an additional 110 caste jatis be added.

Women in Society

Although the professions are still very much male dominated, women are making inroads – in 1993, the first women were inducted into the armed forces, and they account for about 10% of all parliamentarians. Less visible to the public is women's influence in family affairs, especially when it comes to ceremonies.

For village women, it's much more difficult to get ahead, but groups such as the Self Employed Women's Association (SEWA) in Ahmedabad (Gujarat) have shown what's possible. Here, poor and low-caste women, many of whom work on the fringes of the economy, have been organised into unions, which offer at least some lobbying power against discriminatory and exploitative work practices (for further details see the boxed text 'SEWA' in the Gujarat chapter).

Traditionally, especially in the less affluent strata of Indian society, the desire to have male children is so strong that the government has had to pass legislation to prohibit the abortion of healthy foetuses, the modern equivalent of the age-old practice of female infanticide. 'Sex determination' clinics are also banned, but abortions, following

Glorifying the Burning Widow

In September 1987, India was plunged into controversy when an 18-year-old recently widowed woman, Roop Kanwar, burned to death on her husband's funeral pyre at the village of Deorala in Rajasthan. According to the dead girl's family and the entire village of Deorala, Roop Kanwar voluntarily ascended the funeral pyre and calmly recited prayers while she was consumed by flames. Sceptics have alleged that the young woman, who had only been married seven months, was drugged and forcibly thrown on the fire.

What is as shocking as the fact that a young woman should needlessly perish by fire, whether voluntarily or not, is that in the late 20th century the act of *sati* was glorified and the victim deified, not just by superstitious rural folk, but by hundreds of thousands of people around the country. Within one week of Roop Kanwar's death, Deorala had become a major pilgrimage site, attracting *half a million* pilgrims, most of whom left substantial donations for a temple to be built in her honour. Among the pilgrims who visited the site of the calamity were several members of both the state and central governments.

On 27 September, Prime Minister Rajiv Gandhi issued a statement declaring the circumstances of the death of Roop Kanwar 'utterly reprehensible and barbaric.' In December 1987 the central government passed a law banning sati, with family members of any person committing sati to be divested of their right to inherit her property. Persons charged with 'glorifying' sati would be prohibited from contesting elections. In addition, sati *melas* (fairs) were banned.

Despite these measures, the power of the sati continues to hold sway over large segments of the population, both educated and uneducated. Women reverently pay homage at shrines erected in honour of satis, believing that they have the power to make barren women fertile, or cure terminal illnesses.

In November 1999, a 55-year-old Dalit village woman in Satpurva (Uttar Pradesh) committed suicide on her husband's funeral pyre after her husband died from tuberculosis. Thousands of villagers quickly gathered to glorify the suicide and proclaim it as a sati death. Investigators concluded that it was not a true sati as the usual rituals (eg, wearing of a bridal dress) were not carried out, though the incident serves as a powerful reminder that sati as a concept is unlikely to go away any time soon.

examinations in illegal ultrasound clinics, continue. In poorer families, girls are often regarded as a liability to the family, not only because they leave the family when married (traditionally boys remain in their parents' house even after marriage), but also because usually a dowry must be supplied – an immense financial drain for many families.

Arranged marriages are still the norm rather than the exception. A village girl may well find herself married off while still in her early teens to a man she has never met. She then goes to live in his village, where she is expected not only to do manual labour (at perhaps half the wages that a man would receive for the same work), but also to raise children and keep house. This might involve a daily trek of several kilometres to fetch water, as much again to gather firewood, and a similar amount again to gather fodder for domestic animals. She has no property rights if her husband owns land, and domestic violence is not uncommon.

For the urban, middle-class woman, life is materially much more comfortable, but pressures still exist. She is much more likely to be given an education, but only because this will improve her marriage prospects. Once married, she is still expected to 'fit in' with her new in-laws, and to be a homemaker above all else. Like her village counterpart, if she fails to live up to expectations – even if it is just not being able to give her in-laws a grandson – the consequences can be dire, as demonstrated in the practice of 'bride burning.' It's claimed that for every reported case, some 320 go unreported and that less than 8% of the reported cases are actually pursued through the legal system.

A married woman faces even greater pressure if she wants to divorce her husband. Although the constitution allows for divorcees (and widows) to remarry, few are in a position to do so simply because they are considered outcasts from society – even a woman's own family will usually turn their back on her if she seeks divorce, and there is no social security provision. For many, another marriage also means another dowry has to be paid. A marriage in India is not so much a union based on love between two individuals, as a social contract joining two people and their families. It is then the responsibility of the couple to make the marriage work, whatever the obstacles; if the marriage fails, both husband and wife are tainted, but the fall-out for the woman is far worse. Divorce rates are, not surprisingly, low. The majority of divorces take place in the larger cities, where it is also generally more acceptable (although not particularly socially desirable) for women to pursue careers and independent lives.

Birth Control

With a population tipped to exceed China's in the coming decades, birth control is a perennial matter for concern. Moves to introduce birth control gained notoriety in the 1970s, especially during the Emergency when sterilisation squads moved into the countryside and terrorised villagers. In the 1980s, Rajiv Gandhi instituted an ambitious sterilisation target of 1.3 billion Indians by 2050. It met with mixed success, especially in the countryside, where children (especially male children) are regarded as security for one's old age. Widespread media coverage in support of birth control has promoted the ideal of the two-child family, and the use of contraceptives, especially condoms. However, families with more than two children are still common in rural India.

Indian Clothing

These days, in the larger cities (especially Delhi) it's not unusual to see young Indian women wearing jeans and T-shirts. However, the sari, which would have to be the world's most graceful attire, is still worn by most Indian women. In the upper echelons of society (among resident and nonresident Indians), the sari has become even more of a fashion statement, largely thanks to innovative contemporary designs by leading Indian fashion designers.

Buying a sari is an experience in itself. You'll be invited to sit, shoeless, on a spotless, white, cotton-covered mattress, and watch as the sari seller pulls out bolster after bolster of shiny fabric, tossing them on the mattress where they roll out to reveal brilliant colours and patterns. It's hard to say no. Many travellers use the fabric as home decoration or to make skirts or shirts.

The sari comes in a single piece (between 5m and 9m long and 1m wide) and is ingeniously tucked and pleated into place without the need for pins or buttons. Worn with the sari is a *choli* (tight-fitting blouse) and a cotton drawstring petticoat. The *palloo* is that part of the sari draped over the shoulder.

Young Indian women in particular tend to wear the *salwar kameez*, a loose tunic top (salwar) over drawstring trousers (kameez). This outfit is also popular with travellers (see Women Travellers in the Facts for the Visitor chapter). The salwar kameez is accompanied by a scarf-like length of matching fabric called a dupatta, which is usually draped across the neck at the front so that the two ends cascade down one's back. The dupatta is also used to cover one's head in temples, or in front of elders (especially in-laws) as a mark of respect.

Of course there are regional and religious variations in costume. For instance, you may see some Muslim women wearing the all-enveloping tent-like *burkha*.

Indian men generally wear Western-style trousers and shirts, although the *dhoti*, a loose white garment pulled up between the legs like a long loincloth, is also commonly worn. The lungi (similar to a sarong) is usually only seen in South India.

Dos & Don'ts

India is a country of time-honoured traditions and customs. While you are obviously not expected to get everything right, common sense and courtesy will take you a long way. If in doubt about how you should behave, watch what the locals do (eg, at a temple), or simply ask; people are generally happy to point you in the right direction and they'll appreciate your sensitivity.

Kissing and hugging in public is not on. Neither is full nudity, even if you're simply getting changed at a swimming pool. See Women Travellers in the Facts for the Visitor chapter for important tips on dress codes for women.

Lastly, watch where you're walking at night – any undefined, decent-sized shape is likely to be a sleeping human (especially in Kolkata and other large cities).

Religious Etiquette With so many spectacular and ancient religious shrines, most travellers to India will visit at least one. These places hold enormous spiritual significance, so don't blunder in as if it is your right. Getting it 'right' is not hard: Dress and behave appropriately – these are places of worship, so please be respectful in your conduct and the way you dress. Do not wear shorts or sleeveless tops (this applies to men and women) and don't smoke. Loud and intrusive behaviour isn't appreciated, and neither are public displays of affection, or kidding around. Before entering a holy place, remove your shoes (remember to tip the shoe minder a couple of rupees when you retrieve them). Photography is usually prohibited – check before taking photos. Never touch a carving or statue of a deity. In some places, such as mosques and some Hindu temples, you will be required to cover your head. For women, a dupatta is ideal (see Indian Clothing earlier). Many mosques do not admit non-Muslims, and some don't admit women. Always inquire to see if you are allowed into a particular mosque. Women are required to sit apart from men. Some Jain temples request the removal of leather items you may be wearing. They may also stipulate that menstruating women should not enter.

Religious etiquette entails not touching locals on the head, and not directing the soles of your feet at a person, religious shrine, or image of a deity, as this may cause offence. It is also offensive to touch someone with your feet.

Photographic Etiquette Exercise sensitivity when taking photos of people, especially women, who may find it embarrassing and offensive – always ask first. Taking photos inside a shrine, at a funeral, at a religious ceremony or of people bathing (in public baths or rivers) may cause offence. Flash photography should not be used in prayer rooms in *gompas* (monasteries) or to take pictures of murals. If in doubt, ask. See also Photography & Video in the Facts for the Visitor chapter.

Guest & Food Etiquette It's customary to use your right hand for eating and other social acts such as shaking hands; the left hand is used for less delicious matters like wiping your backside and removing grotty shoes. If you are drinking from a shared water container, hold the container a little above your mouth and pour (thus avoiding contact between your lips and the mouth of the container).

If you are invited to dine with a family, it's polite to take off your shoes if they do and wash your hands before taking your meal. The hearth is traditionally the sacred centre of the home, so it's best to approach it only if invited to do so. The same often applies for the kitchen (remove your shoes first). It's inappropriate to touch food or cooking utensils. At a meal, the etiquette is not to help yourself to food – wait to be served or invited to help yourself. If you are unsure about protocol, simply wait for your host to direct you.

Bathing Public nudity is completely taboo so if you fancy a cool dip, make sure you cover up (even in remote locations). Indian women invariably wear saris when bathing in a river or any place where they are in public view. For female travellers, a sarong is a great alternative for bathing – unless at a hotel swimming pool, when a swimsuit is acceptable. See also Women Travellers in the Facts for the Visitor chapter.

Taxi/Rickshaw Drivers If you hire a car and driver, keep in mind that many hotels (especially in tourist magnets like Rajasthan and Agra) do not permit taxi/rickshaw drivers onto their premises to dine, even if you are paying. That's because the commission racket has created all sorts of problems for many hotels and while your intentions may be warm-hearted, remember that the hotel owners are the ones who may face problems with demanding drivers long after you have departed India.

Although some places don't mind drivers joining guests at hotel restaurants, respect those that refuse entry – if in doubt, ask. If you want to stand your driver a meal, there are plenty of good, independent restaurants not attached to hotels that welcome one and all. And of course, if you are happy with your driver's services, a tip at the end of your trip goes down well. See also Car in the Getting Around chapter.

Treatment of Animals

India's ancient reverence for the natural world manifests itself in numerous ways: in myths, beliefs and cults that are an intrinsic part of the cultural fabric. But in a country where millions live below the poverty line, survival often comes before sentiment. In addition, big money is involved in the trade in animal parts for Chinese medicine, which has been a major factor in bringing India's national animal, the tiger, to the brink of extinction.

The World Society for the Protection of Animals (WSPA) is working to raise awareness of cases of cruelty and exploitation, with one recent campaign focusing on dancing bears. Endangered sloth bear cubs are captured from the wild, their muzzles are pierced so lead rope can be threaded through the hole, and their teeth are pulled out. For each bear successfully forced to 'dance', an average of four bears would have died during capture or training. The bears' nomadic handlers ply tourist traps in Agra (especially on the road to Fatehpur Sikri) and Jaipur. WSPA strongly urges visitors not to photograph the performances or give money, which is what inspired this cruelty in the first place. A WSPA report in 1999 also highlighted the extreme cruelty of the breaking-in process imposed on domestic elephants.

In 2000, captive snakes were the focus of animal rights activists, who claimed that their treatment in captivity was extremely cruel. According to the WWF, around 70,000 snakes (including the endangered king cobra) perish annually as a result of dreadful living conditions in captivity. There has recently been a crackdown on the vicious fights that are staged between snakes and mongooses. Snake charmers fear that the crackdown will end a time-honoured tradition in India and rob them of their livelihood.

RELIGION

From a postal worker performing *puja* (prayers) for the safe passage of a parcel, to a former car salesman who has renounced his material life and set off on the path to self-realisation, religion suffuses every aspect of life in India.

India's major religion, Hinduism, is practised by approximately 82% of the population and has the largest number of adherents of any religion in Asia. It is also (along with Buddhism, Jainism and Zoroastrianism) one of the oldest extant religions with firm roots extending back beyond 1000 BC. The Indus Valley civilisation seems to have developed a religion closely related to Hinduism, but it was the Veda scriptures that gave Hinduism its framework.

Buddhism and Jainism arose contemporaneously in the 6th century BC at a time of social and religious ferment. Both were reactions against the strictures of Brahminical Hinduism. Although more recent, Sikhism too has its roots in a protest movement, the bhakti (devotional) tradition of southern India. Islam swept into India from the north and was introduced to the south by Arab traders. Today it's the largest minority religion in the land. Christianity arrived in southern India with Syrian immigrants long before the first European ever dropped anchor in that part of the world. India is also home to one of the world's oldest Jewish communities.

For more information on religion, see the special sections 'The Way of the Buddha' and 'North India's Pilgrimage Sites'.

Hinduism

Hinduism defies attempts to define it. It has no founder, central authority or hierarchy. It is not a proselytising religion.

Essentially, Hindus believe in Brahman. Brahman is eternal, uncreated and infinite; everything that exists emanates from Brahman and will ultimately return to it. The

Hindu Signs & Times

One of Hinduism's most venerated signs is 'om'. Pronounced 'aum', it is an important mantra (sacred word or syllable). The '3' shape symbolises the creation, maintenance and destruction of the universe (and thus the Trimurti). The inverted chandra (crescent or half moon) represents the discursive mind and the bindu (dot) within it represents Brahman.

om

Buddhists believe that repeating 'om' often enough, with complete concentration, can lead to a state of emptiness.

ILLUSTRATIONS BY SIMON BORG

clockwise swastika

It's unfortunate that the swastika is now associated (at least in Western eyes) with Nazism. In fact, the swastika has long been a Hindu (and Buddhist) symbol, and the prongs can point in either direction. Essentially, it symbolises the wheel of time. A swastika where the prongs point clockwise (ie, the upwards prong bends to the right – the same direction as the Nazi symbol) represents things to come, and the anticlockwise swastika represents things that have been. The clockwise swastika is also associated with Ganesh and Vishnu, as well as with the sun, and is generally regarded as auspicious. The anticlockwise swastika is also associated with the destructive goddess Kali, the terrible incarnation of Devi.

Other Hindu signs and symbols include the lotus (signifying peace, purity and beauty) and various objects associated with the gods (eg, Shiva's trident).

anticlockwise swastika

multitude of gods and goddesses are merely manifestations – knowable aspects of this formless phenomenon – and the devotee may freely pick and choose from them.

Although beliefs and practices vary widely from region to region, there are several unifying factors. These include samsara (the endless cycle of birth, death and rebirth), karma (justice for past deeds) and dharma (appropriate behaviour for one's station in life), as well as the caste system (see Society & Conduct earlier in this chapter).

Hindus believe that earthly life is cyclical: you are born again and again, the quality of these rebirths being dependent upon your karma in previous lives. Living a righteous life and fulfilling your dharma will enhance your chances of being born into a higher caste and better circumstances. Alternatively, if enough bad karma has accumulated, your rebirth may take animal form. But it's only as a human that you can gain sufficient self-knowledge to escape the cycle of reincarnation and achieve moksha (liberation). Traditionally, women are unable to attain moksha. The best they can do is fulfil their dharma and hope for a male incarnation next time round.

Essentially there are three stages in life recognised under the *ashrama* system: *brahmachari* (chaste student); *grihastha* (householder who discharges their duty to their ancestors by having sons and making sacrifices to the gods); and *sanyasin* (wandering ascetic who has renounced worldly things). The disinterested discharge of your ritual and social obligations is known as *karma-marga* and is one path to liberation. But there are others, including *jnana-marga*, or the way of knowledge (the study and practise of yoga and meditation), and *bhakti-marga*, devotion to a personal god. The path of bhakti-marga is open to women and to members of the Shudra caste (a caste of labourers).

Sacred Texts Hindu sacred texts fall into two categories: *shruti,* meaning 'heard', or those that are believed to be the word of god; and *smriti*, meaning 'remembered', or those produced by people.

The Vedas, introduced to the subcontinent by the Aryans, are regarded as shruti knowledge and are considered the authoritative basis for Hinduism. The oldest of the Vedic texts, the Rig-Veda, was compiled more than 3000 years ago. Within its 1028 verses are prayers for prosperity and longevity as well as an explanation of the origins of the universe. The Upanishads, the last parts of the Vedas, reflect on the mystery of death and emphasise the oneness of the universe.

The oldest of the Vedic texts were written in Vedic Sanskrit, which is related to Old Persian. Later texts were composed in classical Sanskrit, but many have been translated into the vernacular.

The smriti texts comprise a large collection of literature spanning many centuries and include expositions on the proper performance of domestic ceremonies as well as proper pursuit of government, economics and religious law. Among the better known works contained within this body of literature are the Kamasutra, Ramayana, Mahabharata and Puranas, which expand on the epics and promote the notion of the Trimurti. Unlike the Vedas, the Puranas are not limited to initiated males of the higher castes and therefore have wider popular appeal. Also highly popular today are the Mahabharata and the Ramayana, which drew an estimated audience of 80 million when they were serialised by Indian state television in the 1980s.

The Mahabharata is thought to have been composed sometime around the 1st millennium BC and to have been the prerogative of the ruling and warrior classes, focusing as it did then on the exploits of their favourite deity, Krishna. By about 500 BC the Mahabharata had evolved into a far more complex creation, with substantial additions, including the Bhagavad Gita (where Krishna gives advice to Arjuna before a great battle). It is in fact the world's longest work of literature, eight times longer than the Greek epics the *Iliad* and the *Odyssey* combined.

The story centres on conflict between the gods – the heroes (Pandavas) and the demons

Gods & Goddesses

According to the scriptures, there are around 330 million deities in the Hindu pantheon. All are regarded as manifestations of Brahman, and the particular object of veneration and supplication is often a matter of personal choice or tradition at a local or caste level. Brahman is often described as having three main representations, the Trimurti: Brahma, Vishnu and Shiva.

Brahman

Brahman is the One; the ultimate reality. Brahman is formless, eternal and the source of all existence. Brahman is nirguna (without attributes), as opposed to all the other gods, who are manifestations of Brahman and therefore saguna (with attributes).

Brahma

Brahma only plays an active role during the creation of the universe. The rest of the time he is in meditation and is therefore regarded as an aloof figure, unlike the two other members of the Trimurti, Shiva and Vishnu. His consort is Saraswati, goddess of learning, and his vehicle is a swan. He is sometimes shown sitting on a lotus which rises from Vishnu's navel, symbolising the interdependence of the gods. He is generally depicted with four crowned and bearded heads, each turned towards one of the four points of the compass.

Brahma

Vishnu

The preserver or sustainer, Vishnu is associated with 'right action' and behaves as a lawful, devout Hindu. He protects and sustains all that is good in the world. He is usually depicted holding one item with each of his four arms: a lotus (the petals are symbolic of the unfolding of the universe); a conch shell (as it can be blown like a trumpet it symbolises the cosmic vibration from which all existence emanates); a discus; and a mace (a reward for conquering Indra, the god of battle). His consort is Lakshmi, the goddess of wealth. His vehicle is Garuda, a half bird, half beast creature, and he dwells in a heaven called Vaikuntha. The Ganges is said to flow from Vishnu's feet. Vishnu has 22 incarnations including Rama, Krishna and the Buddha. Vishnu is also known as Narayan; Lakshmi in turn is also known as Mohini.

Vishnu

Shiva

Shiva is the destroyer, but without him creation could not occur. Shiva's creative role is phallically symbolised by his representation as the frequently worshipped lingam. With 1008 names, Shiva takes many forms including Pashupati, champion of the animals, and Nataraja, lord of the *tandava* (cosmic dance), who paces out the creation and destruction of the cosmos.

Shiva is also characterised as the lord of yoga, a Himalaya-dwelling ascetic with matted hair and a naked, ash-smeared body; a third eye in his forehead symbolises wisdom. Sometimes Shiva has snakes draped around his neck and is shown holding a trident (representative of the Trimurti) as a weapon while riding Nandi, his bull. Nandi (literally, enjoyment) symbolises power and potency, justice and moral order. Shiva's consort, Parvati, is capable of taking many forms. Because of his generosity and reverence towards Parvati, women consider Shiva to be an ideal role model for a husband.

Shiva

Gods & Goddesses

Ganesh

The jolly, pot-bellied, elephant-headed Ganesh is held in great affection. He is the god of good fortune and patron of scribes (the broken tusk he holds is the very one he used to write down later sections of the Mahabharata). His animal mount is a rat-like creature. How Ganesh came to have the head of an elephant is a story with many variations. One legend says that Ganesh was born to Parvati in Shiva's absence – Ganesh grew up without knowing his father. One day as Ganesh stood guard while his mother bathed, Shiva returned and asked to be let into Parvati's presence. Ganesh refused him entry. Enraged, Shiva lopped off Ganesh's head, only to later discover that he had slaughtered his own son! He resolved to replace Ganesh's head with the head of the first live creature that he came across. This happened to be an elephant, so that's how Ganesh got an elephant's head.

Ganesh

Krishna

Krishna

Krishna is an incarnation of Vishnu sent to earth to fight for good and combat evil. Krishna is tremendously popular. His alliances with the gopis (milkmaids) and his love for Radha (a married woman) have inspired countless paintings and songs. Krishna is depicted as dark blue in colour and usually carries a flute.

Hanuman

Hanuman is the hero of the Ramayana and loyal ally of Rama. He embodies the concept of bhakti (devotion). Images of Rama and Sita are said to be emblazoned upon his heart. He is king of the monkeys, therefore assuring them refuge at temples across the country, but he is capable of taking on any form he chooses.

Murugan

Murugan is the son of Shiva and brother of Skanda. God of war, Murugan is extremely popular in South India. Some say Murugan and Skanda are one and the same. He is usually shown carrying a spear or trident.

Goddesses

Among the Shaivite (followers of the Shiva movement), Shakti – the goddess as mother and creator – is worshipped as a force in her own right. Those who follow her are known as shaktis.

The concept of shakti is embodied in the ancient goddess Devi (mother and fierce destroyer). In West Bengal she is known as Durga (a manifestation of Devi). The Durga puja (blessing) commemorates Parvati's return to Shiva, Parvati being the benign aspect of Devi. The Durga puja is tremendously popular in West Bengal. Durga's slaughter of the buffalo demon Mahishasura is a well-known Hindu myth and is frequently depicted in Hindu art as well as being the focus of the Dussehra festival held across India (see Public Holidays & Special Events in the Facts for the Visitor chapter).

Kali, the 'black one' with the red tongue, is the most fearsome of the Hindu deities. She is often depicted dancing on Shiva's 'corpse' and garlanded with human heads. She is bloodthirsty, hankering after battle and carnage, and she was appeased with human sacrifice until it was outlawed in the early 19th century.

Kali

Saraswati, goddess of learning, is the porcelain-skinned consort of Brahma and is widely considered to be the most beautiful goddess.

ALL ILLUSTRATIONS BY HIRA LAL DANGOL

Holy Creatures & Plants

Animals, particularly snakes and cows, have been worshipped since ancient times in India. The cow represents fertility and nurturing. The bull is more aggressive but its association with Shiva (as his mount, Nandi) accords it enormous respect. Cows and large white bulls roam freely in India, even in cities, where they repose beside busy roads (sometimes on traffic islands) seemingly unperturbed by the noisy, fume-belching vehicles surging around them.

Snakes, especially cobras, are also considered sacred. Naga stones (snake stones) serve the dual purpose of protecting humans from snakes and propitiating snake gods. Snakes are associated with fertility and welfare.

Some plants also have strong spiritual significance. The banyan tree *(Ficus benghalensis)* is so sacred that only in times of dire need would people pick its leaves or otherwise interfere with it. It symbolises the Trimurti and a pilgrimage to a sacred banyan is equal to 12 years of sacrifice. Its ashes are said to have the power to eradicate sin. The mango tree *(Mangifera indica)* is symbolic of love; Shiva is believed to have married Parvati under a mango tree and so mango leaves are often used to decorate marriage *pandals* (marquees).

TRUDY CANAVAN

A multiheaded cobra

(Kauravas). Krishna acts as charioteer for the Pandava hero Arjuna, who eventually triumphs in a great battle with the Kauravas.

The Ramayana was composed around the 3rd or 2nd century BC and is believed to be largely the work of one person, the poet Valmiki. Like the Mahabharata, it centres on conflict between the gods and demons. It particularly follows the exploits of Rama (an incarnation of Vishnu).

Sacred Places There are thousands of sacred sites in India, including groves, caves, mountains and other natural phenomena, or anything associated with the epics. For detailed information on the main sites, see the special section 'North India's Pilgrimage Sites'.

For Hindus the square is the perfect shape, and complex rules govern the location, design and building of each temple, based on numerology, astrology, astronomy and religious law. These are so complicated and important that it's customary for each temple to harbour its own particular sets of calculations as though they were religious texts.

Figuratively, a temple is a map of the universe. At the centre there is an unadorned space, the *garbhagriha* (inner shrine), which is symbolic of the 'womb-cave' from which the universe emerged. This provides a residence for the deity to whom the temple is dedicated. Above the shrine rises a superstructure known in North India as a sikara, which is representative of Mt Meru, the cosmic mountain that supports the heavens. Cave and mountain are linked by an axis that rises vertically from the shrine's icon to the finial atop the towering *vimana* (spire).

Because a temple provides a shelter for a deity it is sacred. Devotees acknowledge this by performing a *parkrama* (clockwise circumambulation) of it, a ritual that finds architectural expression in the passageways that track round the main shrine. Some temples also have a *mandapa* (hall) connected to the sanctum by vestibules. This mandapa may also contain vimanas or sikaras. Devotees ring brass bells upon entering the temple to attract the deity's attention.

Sadhus A sadhu is someone pursuing a spiritual search by means of meditation, devotion, the study of sacred texts, self-mortification and pilgrimage. A sadhu has surrendered all family and social responsibilities, as well as material possessions. Some even dispense with all clothing, while others wear simple, saffron-coloured robes.

Islam

Islam is the country's largest minority religion (around 12% of Indians are Muslims), and it was introduced to North India by invading armies. Islam as a religion was founded in Arabia by the Prophet Mohammed in the 7th century AD. The Arabic term *islam* means to surrender, and believers (Muslims) undertake to surrender to the will of Allah (God). The will of Allah is revealed in the Quran (sometimes spelt Koran). God revealed his will to Mohammed, who acted as his messenger.

Islam is monotheistic; God is unique and has no equal or partner. Everything is believed to be created by God and is deemed to have its own place and purpose within the universe. Only God is unlimited and self-sufficient. The purpose of all living things is submission to the divine will. Although God never speaks to humans directly, his word is conveyed through messengers who are charged with calling people back to God. However, prophets are never themselves divine; Mohammed is the most recent prophet.

In the years after Mohammed's death a succession dispute split the movement, and the legacy today is the Sunnis and the Shi'ias. The Sunnis, the majority, emphasise the 'well-trodden' path or the orthodox way. They look to tradition and the customs and views of the greater community. Shi'ias believe that only imams (exemplary leaders) are able to reveal the hidden and true meaning of the Quran. The orthodox view is that there have been 12 imams, the last of them being Mohammed. However, since then *mujtahids* (divines) have interpreted law and doctrine under the guidance of the imam, who will return at the end of time to spread truth and justice throughout the world. Most Muslims in India are Sunnis.

All Muslims, however, share a belief in the Five Pillars of Islam: the shahadah or declaration of faith ('there is no God but Allah; Mohammed is his prophet'), which must be recited aloud at least once in a believer's lifetime, with conviction and true understanding; prayer (ideally five times a day and on one's own if one can't make it to a mosque); the zakat (a tax) which today is usually a voluntary donation in the form of charity; fasting (during the month of Ramadan) for all except the sick, the very young, the elderly and those undertaking arduous journeys; and the haj (pilgrimage) to Mecca, which every Muslim aspires to do at least once.

One of the most striking differences between Hinduism and Islam is the absence from Islam of religious imagery. While Islamic art eschews any hint of idolatry or portrayal of god, it has evolved a rich heritage of calligraphic and decorative deigns.

The basic elements of a typical mosque are essentially the same worldwide. A large space or hall is dedicated to communal prayer. In the hall is a mihrab (niche), which marks the direction of Mecca. Outside the hall there is usually some sort of courtyard that has places where devotees may wash their feet and hands before prayers. Minarets are placed at the cardinal points and it's from here that the faithful are called to prayer.

Sikhism

There are some 18 million Sikhs in India, mostly from Punjab, where the Sikh religion was founded by Guru Nanak in the late 15th century. Sikhism began as a reaction against the caste system and the Brahmin domination of ritual. It was aimed at fusing the best of Islam and Hinduism. The Sikh's holy text, the Guru Granth Sahib, contains the teachings of the ten Sikh gurus among others. The text is read in its entirety, without a break (a devotion that takes three days to complete), at the start of Sikh

Gurupurabs – these are festivals that mark significant events in the lives of the gurus.

The first guru, Guru Nanak (1469–1539), honed his beliefs after decades of travelling across Asia. He taught that harmony with God depended upon one's thoughts and actions, and he identified three key elements to this: *naam* (meditation and repeating the name of God); *daan* (charity towards one's fellows); and *isnaan* (bathing). The third guru, Amar Das (1509–74), introduced the practice of communal worship in *gurdwaras* (Sikh temples). The fifth guru, Guru Arjan Dev (1563–1606), was the first to systematically collect together the teachings of all the gurus, thereby creating a definitive text that would evolve into the Guru Granth Sahib. His martyrdom (he was burnt at the stake by the Mughal ruler Jehangir) is one of the more important of the Sikh Gurupurabs. Another important Gurupurab marks the martyrdom of the ninth guru, Guru Tegh Bahadur (1622–75) – he was beheaded by the Mughal emperor Aurangzeb in Delhi.

Sikhs believe in one god and reject the worship of idols. Although Sikhs do not believe in idol worship, some have pictures of the ten gurus in their homes as a point of focus. Like Hindus and Buddhists, they accept karma and the cycle of birth, death and rebirth, as well as the notion that only a human birth offers the chance for salvation. There is no ascetic or monastic tradition ending the eternal cycles of death and rebirth in Sikhism.

Fundamental to Sikhism in the present day is the concept of *khalsa*. This was introduced by the 10th and last guru, Guru Gobind Singh (1666–1708). Khalsa is a belief in a chosen race of soldier-saints who abide by strict codes of moral conduct (abstaining from alcohol, tobacco and drugs) and engage in a crusade for *dharmayudha* (righteousness). There are five *kakkars* (emblems) denoting the Khalsa brotherhood: *kesh* (the unshaven beard and uncut hair that symbolises saintliness); *kangha* (a comb to maintain the ritually uncut hair); *kaccha* (loose underpants that symbolise modesty); *kirpan* (a sabre or sword which symbolises power and dignity); and *karra* (a steel bangle usually worn on the right wrist which symbolises fearlessness and strength).

A gurdwara invariably has a *langar* (community kitchen). These are open to all, and underline the Sikhs' rejection of the Hindu caste system. Gurdwaras usually also have a *nishan sahib* (flagpole) flying a triangular flag with the Sikh insignia. The Golden Temple in Amritsar (Punjab) is Sikhism's holiest shrine.

Buddhism

Some seven million people practise Buddhism in India, fewer than practise either Christianity or Sikhism. The Buddha (Awakened One) was a historical figure who is generally believed to have lived from about 563 to 483 BC. See the special section 'The Way of the Buddha' for an account of the life and teachings of the Buddha, and a description of the main Buddhist pilgrimage sites.

Buddhism had virtually died out in most of India by the turn of the 20th century. However, it enjoyed something of a revival from the 1950s onwards among intellectuals and Dalits (India's so-called Untouchables), who were disillusioned with the caste system. The number of followers has been further boosted with the influx of Tibetan refugees and the 1975 annexation of the previously independent kingdom of Sikkim.

Jainism

Jainism, which today has at least four million followers in India, was founded in the 6th century BC by Mahavira, a contemporary of the Buddha. Jains believe that only by achieving complete purity of the soul can one attain liberation. Purity means shedding all *karman*, matter generated by one's actions which binds itself to the soul. By following various austerities (eg, fasting, meditating, retreating to lonely places) one can shed karman and purify the soul. Right conduct is essential, and can really only be fully realised by monks as opposed to ordinary people. Fundamental to the right mode of conduct is ahimsa (nonviolence) in thought and in deed.

The religious disciplines of the laity are less severe than for monks. Some Jain monks go naked and use the palms of their hands as begging bowls. The slightly less ascetic maintain a bare minimum of possessions, but they keep a broom, with which they sweep the path before them to avoid stepping on any living thing, and a piece of cloth which is tied over their mouth to prevent the accidental inhalation of insects.

From the outside Jain temples resemble Hindu temples. But inside, Jain temples are a riot of sculptural ornamentation, the very opposite of ascetic austerity. This is partly explained by the Jain notion that beauty is found within. The Jain community, although small by Indian standards, is wealthy and believes in spending money to keep temples in immaculate condition.

Christianity

Christianity is said to have arrived in South India (specifically the Malabar Coast) with the Apostle St Thomas in 52 AD, though scholars date its arrival at around the 4th century. Today India has about 19 million Christians, though only around five million are in North India.

Churches in India reflect the fashions and trends of typically European ecclesiastical architecture. Gothic arches and flying buttresses, baroque ornamentation and elegant classical lines can all be found, many with Hindu decorative qualities by local artisans.

Zoroastrianism

Zoroastrianism, which was founded in Persia, was eclipsed there by the rise of Islam in the 7th century. Its followers suffered persecution, and in the 10th century some emigrated to India, where they became known as Parsis (Persians). These Parsis settled in Gujarat, becoming farmers and adopting the Gujarati language. When the British ruled India the Parsis moved into commerce and industry, forming a prosperous community in Mumbai. They adopted many British customs, including Western dress, and banned child marriages.

Zoroastrianism has a dualistic nature whereby good and evil are locked in continuous battle, with good always triumphing. Purity is achieved by avoiding contamination with dead matter and things pertaining to death. Unlike Christianity, Zoroastrianism entails no conflict between body and soul; both are united in the good-versus-evil struggle. Zoroastrianism therefore rejects such practices as fasting and celibacy except in purely ritualistic circumstances. Humanity, although mortal, has components such as the soul that are timeless. One's afterlife is enhanced by correct conduct and thoughts during one's earthly existence.

Sacred fire and sacrifice still play a fundamental role in Zoroastrian ritual. But perhaps the most famous practice involves the 'towers of silence'. The tower plays an important role in the rituals surrounding death. It is composed of three concentric circles (one each for men, women and children). The corpse is placed within, naked, and exposed to vultures, who pick the bones clean. The bones, once they have been dried by the sun, are swept into a central well. The fourth day of the death rites is the most important for it is on this day that the deceased's soul reaches the next world and presents itself before the deities for judgement.

Parsis only marry other Parsis, and there are an estimated 90,000 or so living in India today. Parsis remain economically and politically influential.

Tribal Religions

Tribal religions have so merged with Hinduism and other mainstream religions that few are now clearly identifiable. It is believed that some of the most basic tenets of Hinduism possibly originated from India's tribal cultures.

LANGUAGE

Although Hindi is India's national language, there are 18 official languages and more than a thousand dialects. Many North Indians speak several languages or dialects, including Hindi and some level of English.

Since Independence, states have been largely reorganised along linguistic lines.

You can probably guess in which states these languages are spoken: Gujarati, Punjabi, Kashmiri, Bengali and Assamese. Hindi predominates in the central north regions (eg, Uttar Pradesh, Rajasthan, Bihar and Madhya Pradesh). In the northern fringes of the Hindi heartland, Urdu is also fairly widely spoken, most particularly in Muslim areas. Urdu is the only one of these languages that is not classified as an Indic, or Indo-Aryan, language. For further information on the derivation of North India's languages, and for useful words and phrases in Hindi and Bengali, see the Language chapter and the Glossary near the back of this book.

Facts for the Visitor

HIGHLIGHTS

North India has so much to offer – extending from the heights of the Himalaya to the deserted beaches of Diu. The following themed highlights may help you prioritise your time, depending on your specific interests (see regional chapters for more details).

Temples, Tombs & Shrines

North India has numerous important religious sites, many of which are visited on pilgrimage. Some of these are places of breathtaking beauty. Others have great spiritual significance, but are less interesting for general sightseers. Sites that are special on both counts are: Sanchi (Madhya Pradesh), location of perhaps the finest Buddhist art in India; Varanasi (Uttar Pradesh), the Holy Hindu city on the Ganges; Amritsar (Punjab), home of the shimmering Golden Temple complex revered by Sikhs; and Shatrunjaya (at Palitana, Gujarat), a magnificent Jain hilltop complex comprising 863 temples. For a comprehensive coverage of pilgrimage sites, see the two special sections, 'North India's Pilgrimage Sites' and 'The Way of the Buddha'.

The temples at Khajuraho are famous for their artistic stonework, particularly the numerous erotic figures that embelish them.

The Mughal rulers left a legacy of tombs, beautifully carved and embellished in marble, in the north. Most famous of all is the Taj Mahal (Agra), a mausoleum built by Emperor Shah Jahan for his favourite wife Mumtaz. Also impressive are Humayun's Tomb and Nizam-ud-din's Shrine in Delhi.

Fabulous Forts

India's scores of mighty forts serve as stark reminders of the country's tumultuous history. The Red Fort in Delhi is one of the most striking, but Agra Fort is an equally massive remnant of Mughal power at its height. A short distance south is the huge, impregnable-looking Gwalior Fort.

The chivalrous Rajputs of Rajasthan were masters when it came to forts and they've got them in all shapes and sizes and with every imaginable tale to tell. Chittorgarh is tragic, Bundi and Kota forts are whimsical, Jodhpur's fort is massive, Amber Fort is simply beautiful and Jaisalmer is the essence of romance. Way out west in Gujarat are the impressive forts of Junagadh and Bhuj, built by the princely rulers of Saurashtra. In Central India there's Mandu, another grand fort and perhaps the best example of Afghan architecture in India; the fort has a chequered history and a spectacular setting.

Naturally the European invaders had their forts too; some are now largely in ruins, although the ruins also have a certain appeal. You can see fine Portuguese forts in Daman and Diu.

Some of these forts were in once-great cities that have since become all but deserted. The best example of this phenomenon is Fatehpur Sikri, near Agra; Akbar founded, built and left this impressive centre within a span of less than 20 years.

Festivals & Other Special Events

The bounty of festivals and fairs of North India, most of which have religious roots, are celebrated with inimitable zeal (see Public Holidays & Special Events later in this chapter). They kick off with the Republic Day Festival in Delhi each January – a procession and military might are the order of the day. Also early in the year are the Bikaner Camel Festival, the Nagaur Fair and the rather contrived Jaisalmer Desert Festival, all in festival-laden Rajasthan. Holi, the festival of colour marked by the exuberant throwing of coloured water and *gulal* (powder), heralds the onset of Spring and takes place nationwide in February/March. September/October is the time to head for the hills to see the delightful Festival of the Gods in Kullu. This is part of the Dussehra Festival which is celebrated in many places.

In November it's time for the famous Camel Festival at Pushkar in Rajasthan. Finally, at Christmas where else is there to be in North India than Darjeeling?

The Kumbh Mela swings around every three years, based at four different sites – Allahabad, Haridwar, Nasik and Ujjain (the next is in 2004 in Ujjain). The largest religious gathering in the world is the one at Allahabad, every 12th year, and it has something of a carnival atmosphere. See the boxed text 'Kumbh Mela' in the Uttar Pradesh chapter.

Kicking Back

Craving some time out from the rigours of travelling? Well, you're in luck. India has plenty of places where you can chill out with like-minded souls. Pushkar in Rajasthan has a semi-permanent traveller population

Fit for a King

If it's palaces and forts you want to see, North India is going to tickle your fancy big time. It boasts some of the world's most spectacular palaces and forts, some of which are still inhabited by the sons and daughters of former rulers. Rajasthan undoubtedly has the most diverse and breathtaking range. Indeed it was a Rajput ruler, Maharana Bhagwat Singh of Udaipur, who was largely responsible for putting Rajasthan (if not India) on the international tourist map, after he converted his summer abode (the Lake Palace) into an upmarket hotel in the 1960s. Nowadays most palace owners have a finger in the tourism pie, whether it be a palace-hotel/restaurant or a palace-museum. After all, they don't enjoy the financial privileges which their ancestors did (see the History section of the Facts about North India chapter).

Palaces traditionally had separate sections, with women generally having their own quarters (often known as a zenana), connected to the royal chambers by discreet tunnels.

Wherever possible, India's fort builders exploited natural barriers (to make invasion more difficult): water, such as lakes and the ocean; mountains and hills; forests; and desert. Deforestation has robbed some forts of their once notable impregnability, but some clearly reflect the strategic positioning, such as the mighty Meherangarh (fort) at Jodhpur, which looms high above the city on an unassailable rocky base. And of course, there was the man behind the Taj Mahal, Shah Jahan, who is also responsible for the Red Fort in Delhi – which demonstrates a marriage of practical considerations with aesthetic appeal.

MARK DAFFEY

The Lake Palace in Rajasthan, once a maharana's summer abode, now a luxury hotel

drawn by the enchanting (if somewhat commercial) atmosphere of this holy town. If you'd prefer more solitude, Rajasthan also has plenty of small royal abodes off the beaten track, which are now atmospheric hotels. The technicolour Tibetan outlook on life works well in Kathmandu, so why not in India – you'll find Dharamsala, McLeod Ganj and Manali, all in Himachal Pradesh, also have longer-term visitors. Leh, a remote and incredibly friendly outpost dubbed Little Tibet, is another travellers hangout; there's plenty of volunteer work available to those who can handle the climate and altitude.

To enjoy the pleasures of the beach and a laid-back pace of life, make for the ex-Portuguese island of Diu off the southern coast of Saurashtra (Gujarat).

Faded Touches of the Raj

Although the British left India more than 50 years ago, there are many places where you'd hardly know it. Much of India's government system, bureaucracy, communications, sports (the Indians are crazy over cricket) and media are British to the core, but you'll also find the British touch in more unusual, enjoyable and amusing ways.

Relax in true British style with afternoon tea at Glenary's tearooms in Darjeeling and later retire for a preprandial cocktail in front of the open fire in the lounge of the Windamere Hotel. There you can await the gong that summons you to dinner.

Many of the schools and churches built by the British in the hill stations are a wonderful reminder of days gone by. The schools are still run very much the way they were before Independence, right down to the immaculate uniforms and strict rules. Most schools welcome visitors.

The Tollygunge Club in Kolkata (Calcutta) is a Raj-era golf club and a luxurious hotel. Another particularly British institution is the Lutyens-designed secretariat buildings in Delhi. In Uttar Pradesh, the Nainital Boat Club is an old British club with a lakeside ballroom which was once the preserve of only true-blue Brits (the famous British hunter Jim Corbett, having been born in Nainital, was refused membership). The Gymkhana Club in Darjeeling still has its original snooker tables, Raj ghosts and cobwebs. Perhaps more nostalgic than all these is St Paul's Cathedral in Kolkata, which is stuffed with memorials to the Brits who didn't make it home, plus a Burne-Jones stained-glass window.

SUGGESTED ITINERARIES

North India offers such a tantalising smorgasbord of things to do and places to see that it can be difficult making choices in the time you have available.

Keep in mind that travelling here can be downright exhausting – some travellers squeeze too much into a day, leaving them completely frazzled at the end of their trip and in desperate need of a holiday upon returning home! Take some time to simply chill out.

Unless stated otherwise, the following itineraries assume you have a month to spend in India. For longer trips, simply combine two options; for shorter trips it's not too hard to chop away segments from the listed destinations. The itineraries take in the highlights of a region and assume that you don't want to spend the greater part of your time actually travelling between places.

If you have limited time, you may like to consider 'air packages' that will allow you to get to the main highlights across the whole region – see Air Passes in the Getting Around chapter. Another way you might be able to make the most of your travel time is by buying an 'open-jaw' air ticket to start and end your trip (see the Getting There & Away chapter), which will mean you don't have to loop back to your starting point. On this basis, you might find it easier to end up in Mumbai (Bombay) rather than returning to Delhi (eg, with the itineraries ending in Ahmedabad and Mandu). Mumbai is not covered in this book, though Lonely Planet does publish a *Mumbai* city guide.

For short visits of two weeks or less, especially if it's your first trip to North India, you might want to stick to the three headline cities – Delhi, Agra (for the Taj Mahal) and Jaipur – which tour operators often group together on an itinerary dubbed the 'golden triangle'. You could probably also squeeze in a visit to atmospheric Varanasi, one of the holiest cities in India. All four places are linked by rail.

To travel in style, note that there are a couple of luxury train services, including on-board accommodation, that visit sights in Rajasthan and Gujarat. Rajasthan also has some luxurious ex-palaces that are now hotels. You can also stay in former or current palaces elsewhere in North India, such as at Orchha and Bhopal (both in Madhya Pradesh) and Lucknow (Uttar Pradesh).

For details about the various travel options mentioned in this section, see the regional chapters.

Palaces, Temples & Holy Cities

Delhi – Jaipur – Agra – Jhansi – Khajuraho – Jabalpur – Kanha – Varanasi – Kolkata

This route gives you a taste of Rajasthan and includes the Taj Mahal. Jhansi is the station for the bus journey to the famous temples of Khajuraho, but it's worth stopping at Orchha, 18km from Jhansi, to see this well-preserved old city of palaces and temples. From Khajuraho, a three-hour bus journey brings you to Satna for trains to Jabalpur where a boat trip through the Marble Rocks is the main attraction. Next stop is Kanha National Park for tiger spotting, and then it's back to Jabalpur to catch a train to the holy city of Varanasi. The last stop is Kolkata, one of the most fascinating cities in the country due to its rich cultural background.

Mughals, Jains & the Portuguese

Delhi – Agra – Jaipur – Pushkar – Jodhpur – Ranakpur – Udaipur – Bhuj – Rajkot – Junagadh – Sasan Gir – Diu – Palitana – Ahmedabad

This route takes in the golden triangle's 'big three', prime tourist sites in Rajasthan, and also the best of lesser-visited Gujarat. Gujarat's hidden treasures include the tribal cultures of the Rann of Kutch in the far west; the fortified town of Junagadh; the magnificent Jain temples atop Girnar Hill, near Junagadh; Sasan Gir Wildlife Sanctuary – the last home of the Asiatic lion; Diu – the old Portuguese enclave with its beaches; Palitana – another town with hilltop Jain temples; and Ahmedabad – the busy city with its array of Indo-Saracenic architecture.

Hill Stations & the Himalaya

Delhi – Dalhousie – Dharamsala – Shimla – Manali – Leh – Delhi

This is a good route to follow if you're in North India during the summer, when the heat on the plains becomes unbearable – in fact the road from Manali to Leh is only open for a couple of months a year when the snow melts.

The hill stations of Shimla and Dalhousie hark back to an era that is rapidly being consigned to history; Dharamsala is a fascinating cultural centre, with nearby McLeod Ganj being the home of the exiled Dalai Lama; Manali in the Kullu Valley is simply one of the most beautiful places in the country; while Leh, high on the Tibetan plateau, is the capital of Ladakh and centre for another unique Himalayan culture.

Trekkers and adventure seekers are well catered for at various places on this route. From Manali there are literally dozens of treks, ranging from a couple of days to a couple of weeks, into places such as the remote Zanskar Valley. Leh, too, is a centre for trekkers.

With a little extra time, it would be easy on this itinerary to slot in a visit to Amritsar (Punjab) and/or Chandigarh (Haryana); both cities have bus connections to the Himalayan towns, as well as fast trains to/from Delhi.

Remote Retreats

Kolkata – Jorhat – Tezpur – Guwahati – Shillong – Agartala – Kolkata

If you want to escape other Westerners and get off the beaten track, the north-eastern is the place to do it. But be aware that not all places are safe (check the current political situation) and that some permits are required (see Restricted Area Permits under Visas & Documents later in this chapter).

Retreats from the Heat

RICHARD I'ANSON

The hill station of Shimla

Although they may take the credit for having popularised the concept of the hill station, the British cannot claim to have invented it. Almora, a hill station in Uttarakhand, was the capital of the Chand rajas of Kumaon way back in 1563. In the 16th and 17th centuries the Mughal emperors retreated into the Himalaya to avoid the searing heat of mid summer on the plains; their favourite spot was Kashmir.

In the 19th century, British troops exploring the country discovered that the incidence of disease was much lower in the cooler hills. In 1819 a hospital was opened in Shimla and the first British hill station was established. As the British presence in India grew, other hill stations were built and it became the custom to dispatch women and children to them for the summer months. They eventually developed into temporary capitals, with all the machinery of government decamping to the hills in the summer. Darjeeling was Kolkata's summer capital, and Shimla was Delhi's.

The cooler climate was certainly healthier but it seemed to infect most foreign residents with severe cases of nostalgia and they soon made their hill stations into little corners of England, building bungalows with names such as 'Earl's Court', 'Windamere' and 'Windsor Cottage'. During the summer season they were great social centres with balls, theatrical performances and an endless round of dinner parties. The main thoroughfare was almost always known as The Mall and closed to all but pedestrians – as long as they were not Indian.

Today, most hill stations have become holiday resorts for middle-class Indian tourists, especially for those on their honeymoon. Although they are dilapidated shadows of the elitist preserves they once were, they're nonetheless great fun to visit. The journey there can be interesting in itself, such as the ride on the 'toy train' up to Shimla or Darjeeling. Some hill stations are built around a lake, as at Naintal, and most have superb views and good walks along the surrounding ridges. For more on hill stations in Himachal Pradesh, see the boxed text 'A Home in the Hills' in that chapter.

Jorhat is the gateway to Upper Assam and the revered Majuli Island and the Kaziranga National Park (the best in the region). Tezpur has some colonial charm and is a base for a day trip (November to March) to Nameri National Park. From Tezpur, it's also possible to make a tiring detour to Tawang, featuring a majestic *gompa* (Tibetan Buddhist monastery). Most travellers end up in the uninspiring gateway of Guwahati, home to several temples and a decent zoo. It's also a base for enjoyable day trips to Hajo and Sualkachi. From Guwahati, buses (and even helicopters) regularly go to Shillong, a pleasant but wet hill station surrounded by exquisite waterfalls. Return to Guwahati, and fly to Agartala for a look around before flying back to Kolkata or going overland to Bangladesh.

Mughals & More (three to four weeks)

Delhi – Agra – Bharatpur – Jaipur – Shekhawati – Bikaner – Jaisalmer – Jodhpur – Pushkar – Bundi – Chittorgarh – Udaipur – Ahmedabad

This route gives you a taste of Mughal architecture, including, of course, the Taj Mahal; wildlife; the desert; Hindu temples; hippie hang-outs; Rajput exuberance; unusual Islamic architecture; and a chance to explore two very different major cities, Delhi and Ahmedabad.

Heading for India's Heartland (three to four weeks)

Delhi – Jaipur – Agra – Varanasi – Khajuraho – Jhansi – Sanchi – Mandu – Ahmedabad

This route starts with the classic tourist triangle – Delhi, Jaipur and Agra – before moving on to the holy city of Varanasi, and thereafter to central India and Madhya Pradesh. This lesser-visited state has a few top highlights: The erotic temples at Khajuraho are the big attraction, but Sanchi and Mandu between them have fine examples of Buddhist, Hindu and Afghan architecture. After Mandu you can head west to Ahmedabad (and then return to Delhi) or southwest to Mumbai.

Sikkim's Sights (two to three weeks)

Kolkata – Darjeeling – Pelling – Ravangla – Gangtok – Kolkata

From Kolkata, take the train to New Jalpaiguri (near Siliguri) and then a bus/train/jeep to Darjeeling. Most travellers do a circular route, starting/finishing in Darjeeling and Kalimpong. Pelling is the base for western Sikkim, and ideal for exploring major gompas. From there, visit the serene Khecheopari Lake, and then hike or use infrequent public transport to Yuksom. Return to Pelling, or Gezing or Legship, for a connection to Ravangla, with a Tibetan settlement and awesome views of Kanchenjunga. Gangtok is the base for eastern Sikkim, and day trips to places such as Phodong and Tsomgo Lake. With a few extra days, and the necessary permits, visit Fambong Lho Wildlife Sanctuary or the Kyongnosla Alpine Sanctuary, or go rafting. From Gangtok, buses go back to Siliguri and Darjeeling.

PLANNING

When to Go

Most foreign travellers visit India in the cooler winter months from November to March. For the Himalaya, though, it's too cold in winter; April to September is the season here, although there are regional variations according to the onset and departure of the monsoon. For more information about when to go where, see Climate in the Facts about North India chapter.

The timing of certain festivals and other special occasions may also influence when you want to go (see Public Holidays & Special Events later in this chapter). Incidentally, if your visit coincides with an election campaign, be prepared for transport delays, large crowds and other possible disruptions.

Maps

Lonely Planet's *India Travel Atlas* breaks the country down into more than 100 pages of maps, and gives unequalled coverage. Its format also makes it easy to refer to, even on jam-packed buses.

There is a dearth of reliable (and easily accessible) maps available on India – the Lascelles 1:4,000,000 map of *India, Pakistan, Nepal, Bangladesh & Sri Lanka* is probably the most useful general map of India. The Bartholomews map is similar. The Nelles Verlag series gives more detailed coverage, with each map homing on about one-fifth of the country, but these can be hard to get hold of.

When it comes to regional maps, be prepared to be disappointed. Probably the best (and most easily found in India) is the Discover India series, which has some useful state and city maps; prices range from Rs 35 to 50. The Indian Map Service (☎ 0291-740874), Sector G, Shastri Nagar, Jodhpur, Rajasthan 342003, produces a decent series of state road atlases (eg, covering Rajasthan or Gujarat) based on Survey of India maps.

The Survey of India produces some useful town maps for Himachal Pradesh and Uttaranchal, as well as cities in other areas, but many are permanently 'out of stock'. The trekking maps are fairly useless for anything apart from basic planning, and the marked distances are often wildly inaccurate. Nest and Wings also produce basic

Himalayan trekking maps with more accurate distances, but again the low level of detail means they are only really useful if used with the Nest & Wings trekking guides.

Throughout India, state government tourist offices stock local maps, which may at first glance appear pretty snazzy, but are usually dated and lacking essential detail.

What to Bring

No matter what kind of trip you're doing, the usual travellers' rule applies – bring as little as possible.

A suitcase is only a good option if you are travelling to a single destination, and all you have got to do is get it into the taxi and settle in at your hotel. Suitcases are

Dealing with Directions

You'll probably get lost more than once when you're in India – even the meticulously drawn maps in this book can't show every little alley and side street.

To save precious time, don't be shy about asking people on the street; they are usually happy to point you in the right direction. Having said that, there is an art to asking directions in India: You may well receive a fabricated answer (usually 'yes') if the person can't quite decipher your weird accent or simply didn't hear you properly. There is no malicious intent in this misinformation – they're just trying to be polite – after all, 'no' sounds so unsympathetic.

The key to getting useful directions lies in the phrasing of your question. For instance, it's best to ask 'Which way to the zoo?' rather than pointing and asking 'Is this the way to the zoo?' It's especially worth asking several people en route, just to ensure you're not going astray.

Sometimes you'll find that your questions are met with only a non-verbal response, such as a distinctive waggle of the head (which looks like they're shaking water out of their ears, according to Paul Theroux). Don't make the mistake of assuming this means yes – or even that it means no! Depending on the circumstances, it could mean either of those; or it could mean 'probably', or 'maybe', or 'who knows?' or (more likely) something along the lines of: 'I recognise you're asking me something, but sadly I don't quite understand what, so I'll just smile, stay silent and hope you can sort out the problem for yourself.' If you get this type of response, just ask other people – eventually someone will give you a non-ambiguous answer in English.

Note that even if you repeatedly ask for help, you may still go wrong, as the following extracts from travellers' letters illustrate:

> You have to ask at least four or five different people. Indians don't like to admit they don't know, so they may well tell you they know even if they don't (an Indian told me that). I experienced it one day when I asked three people where a particular place was. Even though they were all standing next to each other, each of them simultaneously pointed in a different direction! I thought I was in a Three Stooges movie.
>
> **Damon Veitch**

> Beware at the train stations. Upon being informed by six different sources that our train was departing from platform eight, we hurled our backpacks over to platform eight – only to discover there were no tracks at platform eight!
>
> **Dyan Mckie**

lockable, keep your clothes flat, and are less likely to get damaged by careless luggage handlers at the airport.

For others, a backpack is still the best carrying container. It's worth paying the money for a strong, good-quality, lockable pack, as it's much more likely to withstand the rigours of Indian travel. An alternative (unless you plan to do any trekking) is a large, soft, zip bag with a wide, securely fastened shoulder strap.

If you are spending time in the hill stations, especially during the cool season, bring along warm clothing for chilly nights. During winter, other parts of North India can also get surprisingly cold at night.

It's important to bring clothing that is culturally appropriate (see Society & Conduct in the Facts about North India chapter). A reasonable list would include:

- underwear and swimming gear
- one pair of cotton trousers
- one pair of shorts (men only)
- one long cotton skirt (women)
- a few T-shirts or lightweight shirts
- sweater or lightweight jacket for cool nights in the hills or North Indian winters
- one pair of sneakers or shoes
- sandals
- flip-flops (thongs) – handy when showering in shared bathrooms
- raincoat if you're visiting during the monsoon
- a set of 'dress up' clothes for that splurge meal or night at the disco
- a wide-brimmed hat – for protection from the sun; if you dislike sweaty hats, buy an umbrella in India (it provides shade plus air circulation)

If you are going camping or trekking you will need to take:

- walking boots – these must give good ankle support and have a sturdy but flexible sole. Ensure your boots are well broken in beforehand.
- warm jacket
- wool shirt or pullover
- breeches or shorts – but don't wear them in places where they may cause offence (eg, temples)
- shirts – T-shirts are OK, but shirts with collars and sleeves will give added protection against the sun
- socks – a mix of thick and thin pairs
- a sun hat
- a multi-fuel stove (optional)
- warm clothing for high altitude treks – it can get cold at night in the mountains, so take warm gloves, a warm hat and thermal underwear

Bedding A sleeping bag, although a bit of a bother to carry, can really come in handy. You can use it to spread over unsavoury-looking sheets in budget hotels, as a cushion on hard train seats, and as a seat for long waits on railway platforms. For hill treks, or overnight Rajasthan camel safaris during winter, a sleeping bag is essential. An inflatable pillow is also worth considering, especially if you are camping or staying in rock-bottom hotels, which usually have rock-hard pillows to match.

Toiletries Soap, toothpaste, shampoo and other toiletries are readily available in India, although hair conditioner often comes in the 'shampoo and conditioner in one' format. Astringent is useful for wiping away the grime at the end of the day and is available at most pharmacies. A nail brush and moisture-impregnated disposable tissues are also useful.

Tampons are not easily found (even in the larger cities), so it's certainly worth bringing your own stock. There's no need to bring sanitary pads – you'll find them in pharmacies at even the smallest towns. It's wise to bring your own condoms, as the quality of local brands is variable. Shower-caps can be hard to find (unless you're staying at a five-star hotel), so bring your own. A universal sink plug is useful, as few of the cheaper hotels have plugs. Women should consider bringing a lingerie bag to prevent delicate (and expensive) underwear from being battered or completely ruined by dhobis (washerpeople) and even hotel laundries.

Men can safely leave their shaving gear at home, as there are plenty of barber shops where you'll get the works for a nominal price. With India's HIV/AIDS problem, however, only choose those barber shops that look clean, and ensure that a fresh blade is used (you may like to bring your own).

Miscellaneous Items See Health later in this chapter for a medical kit check list. Some other items to stow away in your pack could include the following:

- a padlock, especially for budget travellers – most lower-priced hotels have doors locked by a flimsy latch and padlock. You'll find having your own sturdy lock on the door does wonders for your peace of mind. Some travellers bring a heavy-duty chain to secure their pack to the luggage racks of trains and buses.
- a knife (preferably Swiss Army) – it has a whole range of uses, such as peeling fruit
- a mini electric element – to boil water in a cup
- a sarong – can be used as a bed sheet, an item of clothing (recommended for bathing in public places), an emergency towel and a pillow
- insect repellent, a box of mosquito coils or an electric mosquito zapper – you can buy them in India (electric stuff is useless during power cuts, however). A mosquito net can be very useful – bring tape with you if it doesn't come with a portable frame.
- a torch (flashlight) and/or candles – power cuts (euphemistically known as 'load shedding') are not uncommon and there's little street lighting at night
- a voltage stabiliser – for those travellers who may be bringing sensitive electronic equipment
- a spare set of glasses and your spectacle prescription (although several travellers say good quality glasses are cheaply available in India, and that contact lens solution can be bought in cities at lower prices than at home)
- earplugs (to shut out the din in some hotels as well as outside traffic noise and barking dogs) and a sleeping mask
- sunglasses
- a water bottle – it should always be by your side. It's highly recommended that you use water-purification tablets or filters to avoid adding to India's alarming plastic waste problem (see Water Purification under Health, later in this chapter).
- high-factor sunscreen and lip balm – though becoming more widely available in India it's *expensive*!
- string – useful as a makeshift clothes line (double-strand nylon is good to secure your clothes if you have no pegs). You can buy small, inexpensive sachets of washing powder almost everywhere in India.
- women should consider bringing a sports bra if they intend doing a camel safari, as the trotting momentum can cause discomfort, even for just a few hours
- binoculars – if you plan to do bird-watching and wildlife-spotting
- a high-pitched whistle – some women carry these as a possible deterrent to would-be assailants

If you are motorcycling, remember that helmets are compulsory; bring a good one from home, as the quality in India can be variable. You should also bring good wet-weather gear, strong waterproof boots and thermal underwear if you plan to ride in the Himalaya (even in summer). For more details see Motorcycle in the Getting Around chapter.

RESPONSIBLE TOURISM

Responsible tourism involves not only behaving in a culturally appropriate manner (see Dos & Don'ts under Society & Conduct in the Facts about North India chapter), it also encompasses an awareness of the broader issues such as fair trade, child labour and economically sustainable tourism. Magazines such as *The New Internationalist* are useful sources of information; see also Conservation Contacts under Ecology & Environment in the Facts about North India chapter. Wherever you may travel in India, always think about the impact you may be having on the environment and its inhabitants.

There are a number of monuments in India that are suffering irreparable damage from tourism and government indifference. Arguably one of the most threatened is the Jaisalmer Fort in Rajasthan, which has been listed in the New York–based World Monuments Watch list of 100 endangered sites worldwide. Over the years, as tourism numbers have risen, so too have the number of shops, hotels and restaurants within the fort walls – to detrimental effect (see Jaisalmer in the Rajasthan chapter). Other monuments in dire need of protection include the Amber Fort, Jal Mahal and Hawa Mahal in Jaipur and the Champaner archaeological site in Gujarat.

At least in Agra continuing efforts *are* being made to reduce the impact of tourism on the Taj Mahal. In addition to the introduction of electric buses and auto-rickshaws

Responsible Trekking

Consider the following tips when trekking to help preserve the ecology of the Himalaya and elsewhere. See also Planning earlier in this chapter.

Rubbish

- Always carry out all your rubbish (including cigarette butts, sanitary napkins, tampons and condoms) and any rubbish you find.
- Never bury rubbish: Digging encourages erosion and buried rubbish may be dug up and consumed by animals (which can kill them).
- Take reusable containers or stuff sacks. Please don't buy plastic bottles (see Say No To Plastic later in the Responsible Tourism section).

Human Waste Disposal

- To prevent the spread of disease, use toilets where provided. If there aren't any, bury your waste. Dig a small hole at least 100m from any watercourse (bring a lightweight trowel) and adequately cover it with soil and a rock. Use minimal toilet paper (preferably none). In snow, make sure you dig the hole in the soil so it isn't exposed when the snow melts.
- If the area is inhabited, ask locals if they have any concerns about your chosen toilet site.
- Ensure that these guidelines are applied to a portable toilet tent if one is being used by a trekking party. All members (including porters) should use it.

Washing

- Don't use detergents or toothpaste in or near watercourses, even if they are biodegradable.
- For personal washing, use biodegradable soap and a water container at least 100m away from the watercourse. Disperse the waste water widely so the soil can adequately filter it.
- Wash cooking utensils 100m from watercourses using a scourer, sand or snow instead of detergent.

Appropriate Clothing, Fires & Low-Impact Cooking

- Many travellers aren't well prepared for the extreme cold of the mountains – comprehensively research the weather conditions in advance and seek professional advice on appropriate clothing. This will also reduce the need for fires for warmth.
- Cutting wood causes deforestation – a major problem in India – so avoid open fires and only stay at lodgings that don't use wood to cook or heat water.
- Use a lightweight kerosene, alcohol or Shellite (white-gas) stove and avoid those powered by disposable butane gas canisters.
- If you must light an open fire, use any existing fireplaces and only use dead, fallen wood. Always fully extinguish a fire; it's only truly safe to leave when you can comfortably place your hand in it.

Other Considerations

- Respect local cultural practices when interacting with communities. Observe any regulations in areas you visit and always seek permission from landowners if you intend entering private property.
- Always stick to existing tracks. Blazing new trails on slopes may turn them into watercourses, causing erosion. If an established track passes through a mud patch, walk in it: Walking around the edge increases the patch size.
- Hunting is illegal in India and even if locals encourage it, *never* agree.
- Refrain from feeding wildlife (don't leave food scraps behind either); this can lead to animals becoming dependent on hand-outs and increases their risk of disease. Place gear out of reach (possibly tie packs to rafters or trees).
- Despite the temptation, don't pick flowers or plants, and shut any gates you may open.

and the creation of a traffic exclusion zone, the recent hike in the admission fee to the Taj was partly devised to raise revenue for conservation purposes and also to limit visitor numbers to more manageable levels. Elsewhere in the north, private businesses have taken the lead by undertaking to fund the restoration of historic monuments, including the temples at Khajuraho and Delhi's Qutab Minar and Jantar Mantar observatory.

In Udaipur (Rajasthan), the large number of hotels around Lake Pichola has contributed to widespread pollution both within and around the lake. Travellers can help out by encouraging hotel management to dispose of rubbish in an environmentally friendly manner. You can apply similar pressure on the Rajasthan camel safari operators who dump rubbish in the desert during their tours. It's equally important to be responsible with rubbish in trekking regions. The authorities at Yuksom (the start of treks in Sikkim's Kanchenjunga National Park) are trying to implement a search of all trekkers' bags/packs going into the national park so that they can search again on the way out and identify the litter louts.

If you happen to be invited to stay with an Indian family, be aware that the cost of housing and feeding you can be a considerable financial drain to those families on small incomes; exercise judgement and help out by contributing to daily living expenses. Also, don't agree to post someone a copy of their photograph and then forget all about it. Finally, many Indians urge tourists not to hand out sweets, pens or money to children since it is positive reinforcement to beg. A donation to a charitable organisation (see Volunteer Work, later in this chapter), health centre or school is a more constructive way to help.

Following are other ways of doing your bit (regional chapters may contain further information).

Say No to Plastic

Many parts of once-pristine regions of India are vanishing under a sea of abandoned plastic mineral-water bottles (see also Ecology & Environment in the Facts about North India chapter). Travellers are largely responsible for plastic waste and can make a real difference by only purchasing products that use environmentally friendly packaging. Please avoid buying anything in plastic bags and bottles and if you must buy plastic, reuse it. Other ways of reducing India's plastic peril include: buying tea in terracotta cups at train stations instead of plastic; bringing along your own canteen and purifying your water rather than buying water in plastic bottles (see Water Purification under Health, later in this chapter); and buying soft drinks in (recyclable) glass bottles rather than in plastic bottles. If you really must buy bottled water and are staying put for a few days, get the largest size bottle and decant it into your personal water bottle as you need it.

Many travellers' refusal to buy plastic products has already sent a powerful message to tourism officials, though the response in some quarters has been mere words rather than actions. Nevertheless, some communities are independently taking action to fight plastic pollution. For instance, Leh (Ladakh) is a plastic-bag-free zone and all shops now use paper. In Delhi there are 'say no to plastic' signs all around the city (although shopkeepers still largely use plastic bags). In the same vein, the Sikkim government has banned the sale and use of plastic bags in that state.

Be Shop Smart

Tourists can put their money to excellent use by shopping at cooperatives. These have been set up to protect and promote the income of day labourers and handicraft producers at the grass-roots level. Prices are fixed and the quality of products is high. Gujarat has a number of cooperatives; the most prominent is the Self-Employed Women's Association (SEWA), and there are a couple of places in Kutch – see the Gujarat chapter for details. In neighbouring Rajasthan, the Urmul Trust supports and promotes handicrafts produced by rural artisans. Profits go directly back to these artisans.

In Himachal Pradesh, the Bhuttico (Bhutti weavers cooperative) program is a statewide enterprise with many shops; it employs village women to make shawls and caps, which are sold at fair prices with little sales pressure. In the same state, at McLeod Ganj, the Tibetan Office of Handicrafts and the Tibetan Handicrafts Cooperative employs newly arrived refugees who produce high-quality items at reasonable prices. Similarly, in Bodhgaya, Jabalpur and Gwalior, Tibetan refugee markets are a splendid opportunity for tourists to purchase woollen handicrafts, thereby supporting Tibetans in exile.

If you're on the hunt for a carpet, look out for the Smiling Carpet label; this is a UN/nongovernmental organisation (NGO) initiative to try to discourage the use of child labour in carpet manufacture.

As exotic and tempting as they may be, do not buy products that further endanger threatened species and habitats (see also the boxed text 'Creatures on the Critical List' in the Facts about North India chapter). And before you throw something away to lighten your backpack, think about donating it to a local charity.

For more information, see Shopping later in this chapter and Arts & Crafts in the Facts about North India chapter.

Child Prostitution

It goes without saying: Do not support this unpleasant industry. The Indian Penal Code and India's Immoral Traffic Act impose penalties for kidnapping and prostitution, and tourists can be prosecuted for child sex offences upon their return home. It is estimated that 7000 Nepalese girls (some as young as nine) are abducted from their homes annually and forced into a life of prostitution in India's major cities (particularly Mumbai and Kolkata).

TOURIST OFFICES

Local Tourist Offices

In addition to the national (Government of India) tourist office, each state also maintains its own tourist office. These state tourist offices vary widely in their efficiency and usefulness. While some are run by enthusiastic souls, others have grumpy staff who can be abrupt to the point of rudeness – you need to be persistent to get better than 'yes, no' responses from them. Many state governments also operate a chain of tourist bungalows, many of which house state tourist offices.

The overlap between national and state tourist offices often causes wasteful duplication. Both might produce a terrific brochure on place A, while neither has anything on place B. To add to the confusion, in many places there is also an office of the Indian Tourism Development Corporation (ITDC). The latter (which also operates hotels) is more an actual 'doing' organisation than a 'telling' one. For example, the ITDC will actually operate the tour bus for which the tourist office sells tickets.

For more details about tourist offices, see individual regional chapters.

Tourist Offices Abroad

The Government of India Department of Tourism (Web site: www.india-tourism.com) operates tourist offices, which include the following:

Australia
(☎ 02-9264 4855, fax 9264 4860, ⓔ indtour@ozemail.com.au) Level 2, Piccadilly, 210 Pitt St, Sydney NSW 2000

Canada
(☎ 416-962 3787, fax 962 6279, ⓔ india@istar.ca) 60 Bloor St West, Suite 1003, Toronto, Ontario M4N 3N6

France
(☎ 01 45 23 30 45, fax 01 23 33 45, ⓔ goitotar@aol.com) 1113 Blvd Haussmann, F-76009, Paris

Germany
(☎ 069-2429490, fax 2429497, ⓔ info@india-tourism.com) Baseler Strasse 48, D-60329, Frankfurt-am-Main 1

Italy
(☎ 02-8053505, fax 72021681) Via Albricci 9, Milan 21022

UK
(☎ 020-7437677, fax 4941048, ⓔ info@indiatouristoffice.org) 7 Cork St, London W1X 2AB

USA
New York: (☎ 212-586 4901, fax 582 3274) 30 Rockefeller Plaza, Suite 15, North Mezzanine, New York 10112
Los Angeles: (☎ 213-390 8855, fax 380 6111) 3550 Wiltshire Blvd, Suite 204, Los Angeles, CA 90010

VISAS & DOCUMENTS

Passport

You must have a passport with you all the time; it is the most basic travel document. Ensure that it will be valid for the entire period you intend to remain overseas. If your passport is lost or stolen, immediately contact your country's representative (see Embassies & Consulates later in this chapter).

Visas

Six-month multiple-entry visas (valid from the date of issue) are issued to most nationals regardless of whether you intend staying long or re-entering the country. Check visa options with your country's embassy as it may be possible to get longer-term visas. The six-month visas cost A$75 (an extra A$10 service fee applies at consulates) for Australians, US$65 for US citizens, UK£30 for Britons and 320FF for French passport holders.

A special People of Indian Origin (PIO) card is available to people of Indian descent (excluding those in Pakistan and Bangladesh) who hold a non-Indian passport and live abroad (maximum fourth generation). This card costs US$1000 and offers multiple-entry for 20 years. People of Indian origin can also apply for a five-year multiple-entry visa, which is about a quarter of the cost of the PIO card. Both are valid from the date of issue.

Visa Extensions Fifteen-day extensions may be possible (only under very exceptional circumstances, *not* as a matter of routine) from Foreigners' Registration Offices in the main Indian cities (see regional chapters). You can only get another six-month visa by leaving the country.

Restricted Area Permits

Even with a visa you are not allowed everywhere in India. Certain places require special additional permits. The permit requirements mentioned below are covered in detail in the respective regional chapters.

Gujarat In early 2001, to visit villages north and west of Bhuj required permission from local police – permits were issued on the spot (not on Sunday), but they were expensive.

Digging up Your Roots

Tourism officials in Uttar Pradesh have come up with a novel way of trying to increase its visitor numbers while assisting millions of people of Indian origin to trace their family roots.

Officials say that of the estimated 10 million ethnic Indians living overseas, the majority were born to migrant indentured labourers from eastern Uttar Pradesh who left in the 18th and 19th centuries for different parts of the planet. The officials are targeting groups in Mauritius, Fiji, Trinidad and Surinam, as well as in Europe, Canada and the USA. A substantial number of Indians living abroad have high disposable incomes, and a desired spin-off of the 'Discover Your Roots' scheme is to attract financial investment to the state.

Interested non-resident Indians should forward as much information as possible about their ancestry to Uttar Pradesh (UP) Tourism so officials can try to track down their ancestors' birthplace and possible relatives. The UP Tourism Web site (www.up-tourism.com) has more information, an application form and contact details. Good luck!

Himachal Pradesh & Uttaranchal Permits are required to enter some regions close to the India-Tibet border in Himachal Pradesh and Uttaranchal. For the crossing from Kinnaur to Spiti in Himachal Pradesh, tourists must obtain an Inner-Line Permit (currently free) that is valid for seven days. In theory you can get them from district offices in Shimla, Manali, Kullu, Keylong or Rampur, though in practice the magistrates there will normally tell you to apply in Kaza or Rekong Peo and pretend to be sorting through some papers until you leave the room.

The Milam glacier in northern Kumaon in Uttaranchal, which also falls under Indo-Tibetan Border Authority jurisdiction, is currently open to visitors at the discretion of the local police. Other areas around Nanda Devi are officially off-limits, but groups may succeed in getting the relevant

Inner-Line Permits from the district magistrate in Pithoragarh (☎ 05964-22202).

Ladakh You don't require a permit for most of Ladakh, however, you must fill out a Foreigners' Registration Form upon arrival at Leh airport or at a road checkpoint en route, and again at each hotel you stay in. Once in Leh you can apply for permits to the newly opened regions of Ladakh – you can either pay around Rs 100 for a travel agent to handle the bureaucratic formalities, or battle the red tape yourself.

North-Eastern Region Permits are no longer required for Assam, Meghalaya or Tripura. Separate permits are needed to visit the other four states in the north-east (Arunachal Pradesh, Manipur, Mizoram, Nagaland). Acquiring permits for yourself usually takes more than three weeks, or if you go on an organised tour your travel agent will take care of this (it might still take one to three weeks though). See the North-Eastern Region chapter for comprehensive details.

Sikkim A 15-day permit is required to enter Sikkim; permits are easy to obtain and extend. For details, see the Sikkim chapter.

West Bengal Foreigners need a permit (no charge) for the Sunderbans Wildlife Sanctuary and these are issued on the spot (on presentation of your passport) at the West Bengal Tourism Centre in Kolkata.

Onward Tickets

Many Indian embassies and consulates will not issue a visa to enter India unless you hold an onward ticket, which is taken as sufficient evidence that you intend to leave the country.

Travel Insurance

A travel insurance policy to cover theft, loss and medical problems is a good idea. There is a wide variety of policies available, so check the small print.

Some policies specifically exclude 'dangerous activities', which can include scuba diving, motorcycling, paragliding or even trekking. A locally acquired motorcycle licence is not valid under some policies.

You may prefer a policy that pays doctors or hospitals directly, rather than requiring you to pay on the spot and claim later. If you have to claim later make sure you keep all documentation. Some policies ask you to call back (reverse charges) to a centre in your home country where an immediate assessment of your problem is made.

Check that the policy covers ambulances or an emergency flight home.

Driving Licence

If you are planning to drive in India, get an International Driving Licence from your national motoring organisation. In some cities, such as Delhi, it's possible to hire and purchase motorcycles, and you will often need to produce a driving licence of some sort (see Motorcycle in the Getting Around chapter). An International Driving Licence can also come in handy for other identification purposes, such as plain old bicycle hire.

Other Documents

A health certificate, while not necessary in India, may well be required for onward travel. Student cards are virtually useless these days – many (though not all) student concessions have either been eliminated or replaced by 'youth fares' or similar age concessions. Similarly, a youth hostel (HI; Hostelling International) card is not generally required for India's many hostels, but you do pay slightly less at official youth hostels if you have one.

It's worth having a batch of passport photos for visa applications and for obtaining permits to remote regions. If you run out, Indian photo studios will do snappy portraits at pleasantly low prices.

Copies

All important travel or identity documents should be photocopied before you leave home. Leave one copy with someone at home and keep another with you, separate from the originals.

Travellers can securely store, via the Web, details of important travel information such as passports, visas, health information, banking details etc for free in the encrypted Travel Vault of Lonely Planet's eKno global communication service – a unique feature that was developed by Lonely Planet and will no doubt be copied by others soon.

EMBASSIES & CONSULATES

Indian Embassies & High Commissions

There are numerous Indian missions worldwide – the following list are just some of them (apart from an embassy, many countries also have consulates – inquire locally for details):

Australia *High Commission:* (☎ 02-6273 3999, fax 6273 3328) 3/5 Moonah Place, Yarralumla, ACT 2600
Bangladesh *High Commission:* (☎ 02-603717, fax 863662) 120 Road No 2, Dhanmondi Residential Area, Dhaka
Bhutan (☎ 09752-22162, fax 23195) India House Estate, Thimphu
Canada *High Commission:* (☎ 613-744 3751, fax 744 0913) 10 Springfield Rd, Ottawa, Ontario K1M 1C9
France (☎ 01 40 50 70 70, fax 01 40 50 09 96) 15 rue Alfred Dehodencq, 75016 Paris
Germany (☎ 030-257950, fax 25795102) Tiergartenstrasse 17, 10785 Berlin
Ireland (☎ 01-497 0843, fax 497 8074) 6 Leeson Park, Dublin 6
Israel (☎ 03-510 1431, fax 510 1434) 4 Kaufman St, Sharbat House, Tel Aviv 68012
Italy (☎ 06-488 4642, fax 481 9539) Via XX Settembre 5, 00187 Rome
Japan (☎ 03-3262 2391, fax 3234 4866) 2-2-11 Kudan Minami, Chiyoda-ku, Tokyo 102
Myanmar (Burma; ☎ 01-282550, fax 254086) 545–547 Merchant St, Yangon
Nepal (☎ 071-414940, fax 413132) Lain Chaur, PO Box 292, Kathmandu
The Netherlands (☎ 070-346 9771, fax 361 7072) Buitenrustweg 2, 2517 KD, The Hague
New Zealand *High Commission:* (☎ 04-473 6390, fax 499 0665) 180 Molesworth St, Wellington
Sri Lanka *High Commission:* (☎ 01-421605, fax 446403) 36–38 Galle Rd, Colombo 3
Thailand (☎ 02-258 0300, fax 258 4627) 46 Soi 23 (Prasarnmit), Sukhumvit Rd, Bangkok 10110
UK *High Commission:* (☎ 020-7838 8484, fax 7836 4331) India House, Aldwych, London WC2B 4NA
USA (☎ 202-939 9839, 939 9806, fax 265 7532) 2536 Massachusetts Ave NW, Washington, DC 20008
Web site: www.indianembassy.org

Embassies & Consulates in India

Most foreign diplomatic missions are based in the nation's capital, Delhi, but there are also quite a few consulates in Kolkata (and Mumbai).

If your country's mission is not listed below, that doesn't necessarily mean it is not represented in India – see the Indian phone directory to locate it, or call one of the below missions to find out contact details.

Australia
High Commission: (☎ 011-6888223, fax 6885199) 1/50G Shantipath, Chanakyapuri, Delhi
Consulate: (☎ 022-2181071, fax 2188189, e mumbai.immi@dfat.gov.au) 16th floor, Maker Tower, E Block, Cuffe Parade, Colaba, Mumbai
Austria
Embassy: (☎ 011-6889037, fax 6886929) EP13 Chandragupta Marg, Chanakyapuri, Delhi
(☎ 033-2822476) 10 Camac St, Kolkata
Bangladesh
High Commission: (☎ 011-6834065, fax 6839237) 56 Ring Rd, Lajpat Nagar III, Delhi
Consulate: (☎ 033-2475208) 9 Circus Ave, Kolkata
Consulate: (☎ 0381-225260) Palace Compound Rd, Agartala, Tripura
Bhutan
Embassy: (☎ 011-6889807, fax 6876710) Chandragupta Marg, Chanakyapuri, Delhi
Canada
High Commission: (☎ 011-6876500, fax 6876579) 7/8 Shantipath, Chanakyapuri, Delhi
China
Embassy: (☎ 011-6871585, fax 6885486) 50D Shantipath, Chanakyapuri, Delhi
France
Embassy: (☎ 011-6118790, fax 6872305) 2/50E Shantipath, Chanakyapuri, Delhi
Consulate: (☎ 022-4950918, fax 4950312, e consufra@bom3.vsnl.net.in) 2nd floor, Datta Prasad Bldg, 10 NG Cross Rd, off N Gamadia Marg, Cumballa Hill, Mumbai
Consulate: (☎ 0413-334058, fax 335594) Rue de la Marine, Pondicherry, Tamil Nadu

Germany
Embassy: (☎ 011-6871831, fax 6873117) 6/50G Shantipath, Chanakyapuri, Delhi
Consulate: (☎ 022-2832422, fax 2025493) 10th floor, Hoechst House, Vinayak K Shah Rd, Nariman Point, Mumbai
Consulate: (☎ 033-4792150, fax 4793029) 1 Hastings Park Rd, Kolkata
Consulate: (☎ 044-8271747) 49 Ethiraj Rd, Chennai
Consulate: (☎ 0832-235526, fax 223441) c/o Cosme Matias Menezes Group, Rua de Ourem, Panaji, Goa

Ireland
Embassy: (☎ 011-4626733, fax 4697053) 230 Jor Bagh Rd, Delhi
Consulate: (☎ 022-2024607, fax 2871087) 2nd floor, Royal Bombay Yacht Club, Shivaji Marg, Colaba, Mumbai

Israel
Embassy: (☎ 011-3013238, fax 3014298) 3 Aurangzeb Rd, Delhi
Consulate: (☎ 022-2819993, fax 2824676) 16th floor, Earnest House, Nariman Point, Mumbai
Consulate: (☎ 033-2800040, fax 2470561) 86C Topsia Rd (south), Kolkata

Italy
Embassy: (☎ 011-6114355, fax 6873889) 50E Chandragupta Marg, Chanakyapuri, Delhi
Consulate: (☎ 033-4792426, fax 4793892) 3 Raja Santosh Rd, Kolkata

Japan
Embassy: (☎ 011-6876581, fax 6885587) 4–5/50G Shantipath, Chanakyapuri, Delhi
Consulate: (☎ 022-4933843, fax 4932146) 1 ML Dahanukar Rd, Mumbai
Consulate: (☎ 033-4211970, fax 4211971) 55 MN Sen Lane, Tollygunge, Kolkata
Consulate: (☎ 044-8265594, fax 8278853) 60 Spur Tank Rd, Chetput, Chennai

Malaysia
Embassy: (☎ 011-6111291, fax 6881538) 50M Satya Marg, Chanyakyapuri, Delhi
Consulate: (☎ 044-4343048, fax 4343049) 6 Sri Ramnagar Nth St, Alwarpet, Chennai

Maldives
Embassy: (☎ 033-2485400, fax 2485750) 7C Kiron Shankar Roy Rd, Kolkata

Myanmar (Burma)
Embassy: (☎ 011-6889007, fax 6877942) 3/50F Nyaya Marg, Chanakyapuri, Delhi

Nepal
Embassy: (☎ 011-3328191, fax 3326857) Barakhamba Rd, Delhi
Consulate: (☎ 033-4791224, fax 4791410) 1 National Library Ave, Kolkata

Your Own Embassy

It's important to realise what your own embassy – the embassy of the country of which you are a citizen – can and can't do to help you if you get into trouble.

Generally speaking, it won't be much help in emergencies if the trouble you're in is remotely your own fault. Remember that you are bound by the laws of India. Your embassy will not be sympathetic if you end up in jail after committing a crime locally, even if such actions are legal in your own country.

In real emergencies you might get some assistance, but only as a last resort. For example, if you need to get home urgently, a free ticket is exceedingly unlikely – the embassy would expect you to have insurance. If all your money and documents are stolen, it might assist you get a new passport, but a loan for onward travel is out of the question.

The Netherlands
Embassy: (☎ 011-6884951, fax 6884956) 6/50F Shantipath, Chanakyapuri, Delhi

New Zealand
Embassy: (☎ 011-6883170, fax 6872317) 50N Nyaya Marg, Chanakyapuri, Delhi

Pakistan
Embassy: (☎ 011-4676004, fax 6872339) 2/50G Shantipath, Chanakyapuri, Delhi

Singapore
Embassy: (☎ 011-6877939, fax 6886798) E6 Chandragupta Marg, Chanakyapuri, Delhi
Consulate: (☎ 044-8415541, fax 8415544) West Minster, 108 Dr Radhakrishnan Salai, Chennai

South Africa
Embassy: (☎ 011-6149411, 6143605) B18 Vasant Marg, Vasant Vihar, Delhi

Sri Lanka
High Commission: (☎ 011-3010201, fax 3015295) 27 Kautilya Marg, Delhi
Consulate: (☎ 022-2045861, fax 2876132) 34 Homi Modi St, Fort, Mumbai
Consulate: (☎ 033-2485102, fax 2486414) Nicco House, 2 Hare St, Kolkata
Consulate: (☎ 044-4987896, fax 4987612) 196 TTK Rd Alwarpet, Chennai

Sweden
Embassy: (☎ 011-6875760, fax 6885401) Nyaya Marg, Chanakyapuri, Delhi

Consulate: (☎ 033-2807136) 9 Lala Lajpat Rai Sarani, Kolkata

Switzerland

Embassy: (☎ 011-6878372, fax 6873093) Nyaya Marg, Chanakyapuri, Delhi

Consulate: (☎ 033-2265557) 113 Park St, Kolkata

Thailand

Embassy: (☎ 011-6118103, fax 6872029) 56N Nyaya Marg, Chanakyapuri, Delhi

High Commission: (☎ 033-4407836, fax 4406251) 18B Mandeville Gardens, Kolkata

UAE

Embassy: (☎ 011-6872937, fax 6873272) EP-12 Chandragupta Mary, Chanakyapuri, Delhi

Consulate: (☎ 022-2183021, fax 2181162) Jolly Makers Apartment, No 1, Bungalow 7, Cuffe Parade, Colaba, Mumbai

UK

High Commission: (☎ 011-6872161, fax 6872882) 50 Shantipath, Chanakyapuri, Delhi

Consulate: (☎ 022-2830517, fax 2027940) 2nd floor, Maker Chambers IV, J Bajaj Marg, Nariman Point, Mumbai

Consulate: (☎ 033-2885171, fax 2883435) 1 Ho Chi Minh Sarani, Kolkata

Consulate: (☎ 044-8273136, 8273137, fax 8269004) 24 Anderson Rd, Chennai

Consulate: (☎ 0832-228571, fax 232828) Manguirish Bldg, 3rd floor, 18th June Rd, Panaji, Goa

USA

Embassy: (☎ 011-6889033) Shantipath, Chanakyapuri, Delhi

Consulate: (☎ 022-3633611, fax 3630350) Lincoln House, 78 Bhulabai Desai Rd, Cumballa Hill, Mumbai

Consulate: (☎ 033-2823611, fax 2822335) 5/1 Ho Chi Minh Sarani, Kolkata

Consulate: (☎ 044-8112000) Gemini Circle, 220 Anna Salai, Chennai

CUSTOMS

The usual duty-free regulations apply for India; that is, 1L of alcohol and 200 cigarettes or 50 cigars or 250g of tobacco.

You can bring in all sorts of Western technological gismos, but expensive items, such as video cameras and laptop computers, may be entered on a 'Tourist Baggage Re-export' form to ensure you take them out with you when you go (this is not always policed).

Technically you are supposed to declare any cash or travellers cheques over the value of US$10,000 on arrival. Regarding Indian currency, officially you are not supposed to take any into or out of India, however a number of travellers have been told that they can import a maximum of Rs 5000.

Note that if you are entering India from Nepal you cannot import anything duty free.

There are certain restrictions in what you can take out of India – see Antiques & Wildlife under Shopping, later in this chapter.

MONEY

Currency

The rupee (Rs) is divided into 100 paise (p). There are coins of five, 10, 20, 25 and 50 paise, and Rs 1, 2 and 5, and notes of Rs 10, 20, 50, 100 and 500. In 1996, the Reserve Bank of India decided to stop printing Rs 1, 2 and 5 notes, but there may still be a sprinkling of these in circulation. At the time of writing a new Rs 1000 note had been issued, but was in limited circulation.

When changing money, take your time and check each note even if the wad appears to have been stapled together. Don't accept any utterly filthy, ripped or disintegrating notes, as you'll have difficulty in having these accepted (you can change them at the Reserve Bank of India as a last resort). Also some bills look quite similar, so check them carefully.

It is often difficult to use large denomination notes because of a perpetual lack of change in shops, taxis etc so it's a good idea to maintain a constant stock of smaller notes.

Exchange Rates

To find out the latest exchange rates, visit the Web site www.oanda.com or ask at a bank. At the time of going to press, the exchange rates were:

country	unit		conversion
Australia	A$1	=	Rs 24.55
Canada	C$1	=	Rs 30.43
euro	€1	=	Rs 41.34
Japan	¥100	=	Rs 38.02
Nepal	Nep Rs 100	=	Rs 62.63
New Zealand	NZ$1	=	Rs 19.71
Pakistan	PakRs 100	=	Rs 76.40
Singapore	S$1	=	Rs 25.87
UK	UK£1	=	Rs 67.01
USA	US$1	=	Rs 47.05

Exchanging Money

Cash There's usually no problem changing money in capital cities and tourist centres. Moneychangers are widespread and generally open for longer than the banks, making them a convenient option. However, you many find it difficult or impossible changing money in smaller towns, especially in Gujarat, Ladakh, Bihar, Madhya Pradesh, the north-east region and parts of Uttar Pradesh. The currencies most widely accepted are US dollars or pounds sterling, and with these you may be able to organise an exchange in a shop if the banks fail you. Other currencies accepted at tourist centres include Australian dollars, German marks and French francs.

To avoid exchange problems, ensure you have an adequate stock of rupees before you deviate from the beaten track.

Travellers Cheques All major brands are accepted in India, though as with cash, you may have problems encashing travellers cheques in smaller towns. Also, a particular place may accept only some varieties (so consider taking more than one); American Express (AmEx) and Thomas Cook are the most widely traded. Pounds sterling and US dollars are the safest bet; yen, German marks and Australian dollars can be changed in the larger cities, but usually not at out-of-the-way places. It's probably wise to avoid euros until the currency is better established. Charges for changing travellers cheques vary from place to place and bank to bank.

For dealing with lost or stolen travellers cheques, see Dangers & Annoyances later in this chapter.

ATMs An increasing number of larger cities and tourist centres have ATMs (many 24 hour) that accept Cirrus, Maestro, MasterCard and Visa (but not always all cards). Such places include Ahmedabad, Amritsar, Chandigarh, Darjeeling, Delhi, Jaipur and Kolkata. Don't rely on ATM advances as your sole source of cash, as some ATMs don't accept foreign cards, and plenty of places don't have ATMs at all. Ladakh and Varanasi, for instance, do not currently have any ATMs. Check with your local bank before departing to confirm that your card can access international banking networks.

Credit Cards You can't rely entirely on credit cards – you'll need some ready cash too. MasterCard and Visa are the most widely accepted. Credit cards are accepted in most major cities and tourist centres, though rarely in budget hotels, restaurants and shops. Cash advances on major credit cards can be made at various banks (although not always in smaller towns). For details about whether you can access home accounts in India, inquire at your home bank before leaving.

Re-Exchange Before leaving India you'll probably want to change any leftover rupees back into foreign currency. To do so, you must produce encashment certificates (see Encashment Certificates later) that cover the rupee amount and are less than three months old. You'll also have to show your passport and airline ticket.

You can convert rupees back to major currencies at some city banks and moneychangers and at international airports, although if you want US dollars, some places will only allow you to re-exchange up to US$500 worth of rupees, and only within 48 hours of leaving the country.

International Transfers Money can be transferred instantly via the Thomas Cook's Moneygram service (charges are relatively high as it's only considered an emergency service), or the more competitively priced Western Union (via Sita Travels, ☎ 011-3311122, F12 Connaught Circus, Delhi, or DHL agencies). Western Union also has other agencies, including Nucleus Forex, which has branches in Delhi and Mumbai. Some private moneychangers, such as the Travellers Express Club in Kolkata, also offer money transfer facilities (see regional chapters for details). You need to bring along your passport when picking up money.

Black Market There's not much of a black market as the rupee is a convertible currency (ie, the exchange rate has been floated and is determined by market forces). If you come across it there's little risk involved (though it is illegal) and you might get a couple of rupees extra for your money – check on the spot that you have received the agreed amount.

Security

The safest place for your money and your passport is next to your skin, either in a moneybelt around your waist or in a pouch under your shirt or T-shirt. Never, ever carry these things in your luggage. You are also asking for trouble if you walk around with your valuables in a shoulder bag. Bum bags are not recommended as they virtually advertise that you have a stash of goodies; this could make you a target for a mugging. Never leave your valuable documents and travellers cheques in your hotel room. If the hotel is a reputable one, you should be able to use the hotel safe. It is wise to peel off a few hundred dollars and keep them stashed away separately from your main horde, just in case. Finally, try to separate your big notes from your small ones, so you don't publicly display large wads of cash when paying for minor services such as shoe polishing or when tipping.

Attracting attention to your valuables is asking for trouble.

Costs

Costs tend to vary depending on whether or not it's the tourist season. They also shoot up during festivals or other special events when it's not unusual for hotel rates to double. Be prepared to pay more in Delhi, Kolkata and other large cities, as well as at popular tourist destinations. There are also small variations depending on the state, eg, Gujarat is generally slightly cheaper than Rajasthan, Ladakh is slightly cheaper than Punjab. See the relevant chapters for specific hotel rates and other costs.

Costs also vary depending on whether you are travelling solo or in a group. It's more economical travelling with one or more people, as you can save money by sharing hotel rooms, taxis or rickshaws, and car hire.

Although some places are cheaper to stay than others, at rock bottom you can generally live on about US$8 per person per day, but expect to pay around US$10 to US$17 in larger cities such as Delhi, as well as at hill stations and tourist hot spots. The recent hike in admission charges at many tourist sites (see the boxed text 'Monumental Money') will make it hard to stick to these budgets if you're sightseeing intensively. To cut costs to the bone, use dormitories, public buses and cheap classes on trains, and take basic meals such as dhal and rice at streetside stalls. At the other extreme, big spenders can easily blow upwards of US$200 a night in a swanky palace hotel, and souvenirs, luxury meals and organised tours can gobble up many more dollars.

Most people will, of course, fall somewhere in the middle. To stay in mid-range hotels, eat at decent restaurants (with the occasional blowout) and largely travel by autorickshaw or taxi, you're looking at an average of between US$18 and US$35 a day (including the taxes that mid-range accommodation attracts). Again, the upper end of this scale pertains to the larger cities and tourist hotbeds.

Tipping, Baksheesh & Bargaining

In tourist restaurants or hotels, a 10% tip for service is the norm, and this will often be automatically tacked on to the bill. In basic

Monumental Money

Most tourist sites have an entry fee, as well as extra charges for cameras and videos (see regional chapters for details).

In late 2000 the Archaeological Survey of India (ASI) announced new entry fees for non-Indian tourists at 72 of India's national monuments. Entry to all World Heritage monuments – including the Taj Mahal, Agra Fort and Fatehpur Sikri – were set to be cranked up by a steep Rs 450 (US$10) or more. Entry to non–World Heritage monuments were pegged to increase by Rs 220 (US$5). The ASI has come under attack from the National Chamber of Commerce & Industries for the hard-hitting hike. Tourism officials have grave concerns that the sharp increase may result in a marked drop in visitor numbers.

Entry fees are often lower for Indian residents than for foreigners. (If you're a nonresident of Indian descent, the 'foreigners' rate officially applies – although you may escape detection or even be knowingly offered the lower local rate.)

In this book we have included the new beefed-up charges where available, even though not all price changes had been implemented at the time of writing. Just to complicate matters, there were rumours that the price hikes may actually be reversed because of the vehement protests by tourism operators. Some of the prices in this book may have changed by the time you read this, so it's best check the situation locally.

places, where tipping is optional, a few rupees is probably sufficient. Hotel and train porters expect about Rs 10 to carry bags and hotel staff expect around the same to provide services above and beyond the call of duty. It's not mandatory to tip taxi or autorickshaw drivers.

Baksheesh can be defined as a 'tip' and if you're going to be using a service repeatedly, an initial tip will ensure that standards are kept up. Baksheesh also refers to giving alms to beggars. Giving money to beggars is a matter of personal choice – but please don't hand out sweets, pens or money to children, since it encourages begging. Instead you may like to donate to a school or charitable organisation. See also Responsible Tourism, earlier in this chapter.

There are fixed-price stores in major cities, in bazaars and at markets specifically geared to tourists. Otherwise, you are generally expected to bargain. It helps if you have some idea of what you should be paying for any given article. You can find out by checking prices at fixed-priced stores (although these are often on the high side), asking other travellers what they have paid and shopping around before settling on a particular vendor. If all else fails, a general rule of thumb is to halve the original asking price, and then gradually meet the shopkeeper somewhere in the middle. You'll often find that the price drops if you start to head out of the shop saying you'll 'think about it'. Always keep in mind that haggling is a form of social interaction, not a vicious contest. Don't lose any sleep if you find you've paid a rupee or two more than someone else – you've probably still paid a good deal less than you would have at home.

Taxes

A tax or two (or even more) is usually whacked onto accommodation at mid-range and top-end hotels in India, as well as on food and beverages at upmarket restaurants. It usually starts at around 10%, but can be much more for air-con rooms and top-end hotels (eg, it's a hefty 30% on luxury hotels in Gujarat). Save yourself a nasty surprise when you get the bill by inquiring whether you will be taxed above the quoted price, and by how much before you check in. Budget places are usually exempt from hotel tax (or they simply decide not to levy it!), and you may even be able to persuade pricier hotels to waive the tax during slack periods.

The prices quoted under Places to Stay entries in this book are *without* tax, unless otherwise indicated. For more information on which taxes apply in which states, see the relevant chapters.

Encashment Certificates

Legally, all money should be changed at official banks or moneychangers, and you are supposed to be given an encashment certificate (money-exchange receipt) for each transaction – ask for it if you don't receive one. It is definitely worth getting them, especially if you want to re-exchange excess rupees for hard currency when you depart India.

Encashment certificates are also important if you stay in India longer than 180 days. In this instance you have to get a tax clearance certificate before leaving the country. This certificate supposedly proves that your time in India was financed with your own money, not by working in India or by selling things (tax clearance certificates are available from Foreigners' Registration Offices – see major cities in the regional chapters). You'll need to show your passport, visa extension form, any other appropriate paperwork and a handful of bank encashment certificates. Some shipping agents may also request these certificates.

POST & COMMUNICATIONS

Post

Indian postal and poste restante services are generally very good. Letters sent to/from India almost invariably reach their destination, although it may take several weeks. However, packages containing items of value have a higher chance of going astray. AmEx, in major city locations, offers an alternative to the poste restante system (for letters only). Some cities also have courier services (such as DHL Worldwide Express) that can arrange speedy and safe air freight around the world, though at markedly higher prices.

Sending Mail Sending aerograms and postcards worldwide costs Rs 8.50, airmail letters cost Rs 15.

Posting parcels is a somewhat convoluted process:

- Take the parcel to a tailor, or to a parcel-stitching wallah (occasionally found just outside post offices) and ask for your parcel to be stitched up in cheap linen. Negotiate the price first.
- At the post office, ask for the necessary customs declaration forms. Fill them in and glue one to the parcel. The other will be stitched onto it. To avoid duty at the delivery end it's best to specify that the contents are a 'gift'.
- Be careful how much you declare the contents to be worth. If you specify over Rs 1000, your parcel will not be accepted without a bank clearance certificate, which is a hassle to get.
- Have the parcel weighed and franked at the parcel counter.

Books or printed matter can go by bookpost, which is considerably cheaper than parcel post, but the package must be wrapped a certain way. Make sure it can be easily opened for inspection; alternatively, wrap it in brown paper or cardboard and tie it with string, with the contents visible at either end. To protect the books, wrap them in clear plastic first. No customs declaration form is necessary. Bookpost rates are about Rs 230 for 500g, Rs 455 for 1kg and Rs 1010 for 2kg.

Some shops offer to mail purchases to your home address, but exercise caution. Government emporiums are usually OK but in most other places it pays to do the posting yourself.

Receiving Mail Ask senders to address letters to you with your surname in capital letters and underlined, followed by 'poste restante, GPO', and the city or town in question. Many 'lost' letters are simply misfiled under given (first) names, so always check under both (or all) of your names. You'll need to show your passport to collect mail. Letters sent via poste restante are generally held for one month before being returned to the sender.

Telephone

Even in the smallest towns, you'll find private PCO/STD/ISD call booths with direct local, interstate and international dialling. They are usually found within shops or other businesses, and are invariably cheaper than direct dialing from hotel rooms. Many are open 24 hours. A nifty digital meter lets you keep an eye on what the call is costing, and gives you a printout at the end.

Throughout most of India, interstate calls from booths (not hotels) charge the full rate from around 9 am to 8 pm. After 8 pm the cost slides, with the cheapest time to call being between the unsociable hours of 11 pm and 6 am.

Direct international calls from call booths (not hotels) cost an average of Rs 100 per minute, depending on the country you are calling. There are often cheaper rates at certain times of the day – the cheapest times to make calls at the time of writing were: Europe (10 pm to 11 am), USA (11 am to 6 pm and midnight to 6 am), Australia (7 pm to 8 am). Some places also offer cheaper rates on Indian national holidays. To make an international call, you will need to dial 00 (the international access code from India), then the country code (of the country you are calling), the area code and then the local number.

In some centres PCO/STD/ISD booths may offer a 'call back' service – you ring your folks or friends, give them the phone number of the booth and wait for them to call you back. The booth operator will charge about Rs 5 per minute for this service, in addition to the cost of the preliminary call. Advise your caller how long you intend to wait at the booth in case they have trouble getting back to you – getting a line out of their country or one into India. The number your caller dials will be the caller's country international access code, then 91 (the international country code for India), the area code and then the local number (booth number).

The central telegraph offices in major towns are usually reasonably efficient and some remain open 24 hours.

Another option available to you is the Home Country Direct service, which gives you access to the international operator in your home country. For the price of a local call, you can then make reverse-charge (collect) or phonecard calls, although you may have trouble convincing the owner of the telephone you are using that they are not going to get charged for the call.

The countries in which this service is available and numbers to dial are:

country	number
Australia	☎ 0006117
Canada	☎ 000167
Germany	☎ 0004917
Italy	☎ 0003917
Japan	☎ 0008117
The Netherlands	☎ 0003117
New Zealand	☎ 0006417
Singapore	☎ 0006517
Spain	☎ 0003417
Taiwan	☎ 00088617
Thailand	☎ 0006617
UK	☎ 0004417
USA	☎ 000117

India's Yellow Pages can be found at (www.indiayellowpages.com) and can be very useful. For those who may be trying to locate a long lost friend, you could try your luck at the Welcome to 1 Billion Indians Web site (www.1billionindians.com), affectionately dubbed as 'India's People Finder'.

Fax

Many of the PCO/STD/ISD booths also have a fax machine for public use. The going rate for international faxes ranges from Rs 125 to 155 per A4 page. The cost of receiving faxes can range from Rs 10 to 30 per page.

Email & Internet Access

Internet outlets in India are expanding rapidly, though some bureaus have poor connections and can be excruciatingly slow. Connections and speed are usually superior in the morning and early afternoon (peak demand seems to fall between 5 and 9 pm making this a slow period). Places to surf the Internet are widespread in the larger cities, as well as in travellers haunts such as Dharamsala and Pushkar.

Costs are usually somewhere between Rs 30 and 60 per hour, though a few places may charge more (particularly in Himachal Pradesh and Uttaranchal), while other locations are cheaper (notably Paharganj in Delhi). See the regional chapters for details. With bureaus spreading like chatroom gossip, charges in pricier regions should tumble.

INTERNET RESOURCES

The World Wide Web is a rich resource for travellers. You can research your trip, hunt down bargain air fares, book hotels, check on weather conditions or chat with locals and other travellers about the best places to visit (or avoid!).

There's no better place to start your Web explorations than the Lonely Planet Web site (www.lonelyplanet.com). Here you'll find succinct summaries on travelling to most places on earth, postcards from other travellers and the Thorn Tree bulletin board, where you can ask questions before you go or dispense advice when you get back. You can also find travel news and updates to many of our most popular guidebooks, and the subWWWay section links you to many useful travel resources elsewhere on the Web.

There are many Web sites relating to India, but they can come and go with some frequency. You will find that more than a few sites are nothing more than glossy (often inaccurate) PR puff, though most of the state tourist offices have sites that are worth an exploratory click (see regional chapters for addresses). Many newspapers and magazines have useful sites and these include: www.expressindia.com, www.hindustantimes.com, www.india-today.com, www.india-today.com. and www.timesofindia.com.

Some good portals and search engines include: Khoj (www.khoj.com); 123 India (www.123india.com); and Rediff On The Net (www.rediff.com).

The Web site www.mapsofindia.com has various interactive maps, and also gives brief profiles on specific states, including the three new states of Chhatisgarh, Jharkhand and Uttaranchal.

And for those of you seeking the perfect Indian name for your unborn child, you may be interested in checking out www.indiaexpress.com/special/babynames – good luck!

BOOKS

India is one of the world's largest publishers of books in English. You'll find a treasure trove of interesting, affordable books about India by Indian publishers, which are generally not available in the west. Recently published Western books also reach Indian bookshops remarkably fast (to forestall possible pirates) and with very low mark-ups.

Most books are published in different editions by different publishers in different countries. As a result, a book might be a hardcover rarity in one country while it's readily available in paperback in another. Fortunately, bookshops and libraries search by title or author, so your local bookshop or library is best placed to advise you on the availability of the following recommendations.

There are numerous books that deal with India – the following is just a small selection. See Literature under Arts in the Facts about North India chapter for profiles of prominent Indian authors and some of their works of fiction.

Lonely Planet

Lonely Planet publishes a range of detailed guides to North India's regions and cities: there's *Delhi*, *Rajasthan*, *Indian Himalaya* and *Trekking in the Indian Himalaya*. If you want to explore the south, there's *South India*, *Mumbai*, *Goa* and *Kerala*, as well as the prize-winning general *India* guidebook. We also comprehensively cover the region with guides to *Pakistan*, *Nepal*, *Bangladesh*, *Sri Lanka*, *Bhutan* and more.

Lonely Planet also publishes a handy *Hindi/Urdu* phrasebook, *Healthy Travel Asia & India* and *Read This First: Asia & India*.

In Rajasthan, by Royina Grewal, is an insider's view of this enthralling state, and is one of many titles in Lonely Planet's travel literature series, Journeys.

Lonely Planet also has some lavishly illustrated offerings, including *Chasing Rickshaws*, a tribute to cycle-powered vehicles and their drivers by photographer Richard I'Anson and Tony Wheeler – see the Kolkata chapter for an excerpt. There's also *Sacred India*, another full-colour book with stunning images of India's diverse religious culture written by Lonely Planet staff and authors. Buddhist *Stupas in Asia: The Shape of Perfection* is a full-colour hardback pictorial that explores the spread of Buddhism and stupa-building across India and Asia.

Specialist Guidebooks

You'll find a range of guidebooks at most Indian bookshops. *From Here to Nirvana,* by Anne Cushman & Jerry Jones, is a popular guide to India's many and varied ashrams and gurus. It provides useful practical information that will help you figure out which place suits your particular needs and aspirations. It also provides useful tips on how to spot dodgy operators.

An excellent specialist guide about the painted *havelis* (ornate merchants' mansions) in Rajasthan is *The Guide to the Painted Towns of Shekhawati* by Ilay Cooper, which provides information about the buildings accompanied by some fine sketch maps.

Benaras – The Sacred City by EB Havell describes the people and city of Varanasi from around the 15th century to the 20th century (it was written in 1905), and includes information on Hinduism, Buddha and the Jains. There are also chapters on the temples and Ghats in the city.

Travel Writing

Karma Cola by Gita Mehta amusingly and cynically describes the collision between India looking to the West for technology and modern methods, and the West descending upon India in search of wisdom and enlightenment.

Ved Mehta has written a number of interesting personal views of India. *Walking the Indian Streets* is a slim and highly readable account of the culture shock he went through on returning to India after a long period abroad. *Portrait of India* is by the same author.

Ronald Segal's *The Crisis of India* is written by a South African Indian on the premise that spirituality is not always more important than a full stomach.

The Gunny Sack by MG Vasanji explores a similar theme, this time from the point of view of a group of Gujarati families that migrated to East Africa in Raj times but retained their connections with India.

Subtitled *A Year in Delhi,* William Dalrymple's acclaimed *City of Djinns* delves into this city's fascinating history. He turns up a few surprises in his wanderings around Delhi, and the book is written in a light style that makes in accessible to a broad readership. Dalrymple is also the author of *The Age of Kali* – a compilation of insights gleaned from 10 years of travelling the subcontinent.

Slowly Down the Ganges by Eric Newby is an entertaining boat-trip tale, bordering, at times, on sheer masochism.

A Season in Heaven: True Tales from the Road to Kathmandu is an enticing and historic narrative from travellers who took the 'hippie trail' to India and Nepal in the 1960s and 1970s.

Chasing the Monsoon by Alexander Frater is an Englishman's account of a journey panning out around the monsoon as it moves north across the country.

Robyn Davidson's *Desert Places* is about the author's journey, as a solo woman, by camel with the nomadic Rabari of Rajasthan.

Scoop-wallah by Justine Hardy is an account of the author's time spent as a journalist for *The Indian Express* in Delhi.

Finally, no survey of personal insights into India can ignore VS Naipaul's two controversial books *An Area of Darkness* and *India – A Wounded Civilisation*. Born in Trinidad of Indian descent, Naipaul tells in the first book of how India, unseen and unvisited, haunted him and of the impact upon him when he eventually made his pilgrimage to the motherland. In the second book he writes of India's unsuccessful search for a new purpose and meaning for its civilisation. His *A Million Mutinies Now* is also evocative reading.

History & Politics

A Traveller's History of India by Sinharaja Tammita-Delgoda expounds on Indian history in one handy volume, and includes useful maps, lists and a gazetteer. For a more thorough read there's the two-volume

A History of India. Volume one by Romila Thapar takes the story to the coming of the Mughals in the 16th century; volume two by Percival Spear continues from there. For even more detail, turn to the *Oxford History of India* by Vincent Smith.

The Wonder That Was India by AL Basham has detailed descriptions of the Indian civilisations, major religions, origins of the caste system and social customs.

The Nehrus and the Gandhis by Tariq Ali is a very readable account of the history of these families and hence of India in the 20th century.

Plain Tales from the Raj edited by Charles Allen consists of a series of interviews with people who took part in British India on both sides of the table.

Freedom at Midnight by Larry Collins and Dominique Lapierre is an enthralling account of events that led up to Independence in 1947.

Former BBC correspondent Mark Tully has written widely on India. His works include *Amritsar*, *From Raj to Rajiv* and *No Full Stops in India*.

Nayantara Sahgal's *Prison and Chocolate Cake* is the author's account of growing up in Allahabad when Mahatma Gandhi was campaigning for an independent India.

The Proudest Day – India's Long Road to Independence by Anthony Read & David Fisher is an engaging account of India's pre-independence period.

Pavan K Varma's *The Great Indian Middle Class* is a powerful and often cutting social history of India's most influential socio-economic group and its descent into cynicism and materialism.

The scholarly *Tribes of India – the Struggle for Survival* by Christoph von Fürer-Haimendorf documents the sometimes shocking treatment of India's tribal peoples.

Lucknow, Memories of a City, edited by Violette Graff, is a collection of pieces detailing the history of Lucknow over the last 150 years.

Women

A Princess Remembers by Gayatri Devi & Santha Rama Rau contains the memoirs of the maharani of Jaipur, Gayatri Devi, the glamorous wife of the last maharaja, Man Singh II. It provides a vivid insight into the bygone days of India's royalty.

India's Bandit Queen by Mala Sen is the biography of the remarkable Phoolan Devi (now a politician). It portrays her struggle with the caste system in rural India and the atrocities she endured as a consequence. The book also describes her life as a bandit and her eventual surrender to the authorities. The story also been made into a film.

May You Be the Mother of One Hundred Sons by Elisabeth Bumiller offers some interesting insights into the plight of women, especially with regard to arranged marriages, dowry deaths, *sati* – the ritual immolation of a widow on her husband's funeral pyre – and female infanticide.

Difficult Daughters by Manju Kapor, which is set at the time of Partition, provides an insight into the conflict between love and duty from the point of view of a young woman from Amritsar.

Caste as Woman by Vrinda Nabar looks at what feminism really means in India in a variety of contexts.

There is a plethora of books about the late Mother Teresa, including *The Joy In Loving* complied by Jaya Chaliha & Edward Le Joly, *Mother Teresa: A Life For God* by Lavonne Neff, *Mother Teresa* by Navin Chawla and *Mother Teresa: Beyond the Image* by Anne Sebba.

Religion & Spirituality

There are often booklets available at temples and other shrines throughout India that provide excellent religious insights.

Two of the Hindu holy books, The Upanishads and The Bhagavad Gita, are available in translations.

Hindu Mythology, edited by Wendy O'Flaherty, is an interesting annotated collection of extracts from the Hindu holy books. The Ramayana is easily digestible in DS Sarma's summary written for children.

Hinduism, an Introduction by Shakunthala Jagannathan seeks to explain what Hinduism is all about – if you have no prior knowledge of the subject matter, this book is a good starting point.

Am I a Hindu? edited by Viswanathan attempts to explore and explain the fundamental tenets of Hinduism through a discourse of questions and answers.

Why I Am not a Hindu by Kancha Ilaiah is an insightful and provocative analysis of the caste system in modern India.

The Riddle of Ganesha by Rankorath Karunakaran is a beautifully illustrated and informative book that explains some of the nuances and complexities of the many sides of this popular elephant-headed god.

A Classical Dictionary of Hindu Mythology & Religion by John Dowson is in dictionary format and can help unravel who's who in Hinduism.

A Handbook of Living Religions edited by John R Hinnewls provides a succinct and readable summary of India's religions, including Judaism.

There are various titles by his Holiness the 14th Dalai Lama, including *The Way to Enlightenment*, a personal discourse on the nature of Buddhism, and *Transforming the Mind*, a commentary on the *lojong* texts written by the 11th-century Buddhist philosopher Langri Thangpa. Both provide an excellent starting point for anyone interested in Tibetan Buddhism. Also scintillating is the Dalai Lama's autobiography *Freedom in Exile*.

Gautama Buddha: His Life and His Teaching is a very readable account by Walter Henry Nelson.

Vicki MacKenzie's *A Cave in the Snow* is the autobiography of a British woman who converted to Buddhism and spent 12 years meditating in a cave above Keylong in Himachal Pradesh.

Environment & Wildlife

The World Wide Fund for Nature (WWF) in Delhi and other cities usually has a bookshop that stocks a decent collection of books about wildlife and the environment.

The Book of Indian Animals by SH Prater was first written in 1948 but remains one of the best overviews of India's wildlife and includes colour illustrations.

The Insight Guide *Indian Wildlife* provides a solid background and plenty of colour illustrations.

The magnificent lammergeier, or bearded vulture, can be seen high in the Himalaya.

Cheetal Walk: Living in the Wilderness by ERC Davidar describes the author's life among the elephants of the south and looks at how they can be saved from extinction.

Bird-watchers may find the *Collins Handguide to the Birds of the Indian Subcontinent* useful.

There are numerous glossy coffee-table books on Indian wildlife. Among the best are: *In Danger: Indian Wildlife & Habitat* by Paola Mandredi; *India's Wild Wonders* by Rajesh Bedi; *Through the Tiger's Eyes: A Chronicle of India's Wildlife* by Stanley Breeden & Belinda Wright; *In Search of Wild India* by Charlie Pye-Smith; and *Wild India: The Wildlife & Scenery of India and Nepal* by Cubitt & Mountfire and the WWF. The book from the BBC series of the same name, *Land of the Tiger*, by one of India's foremost wildlife experts, Valmik Thapar, is beautifully illustrated with plenty of interesting facts, figures and background.

This Fissured Land – An Ecological History of India by Madhav Gadgil & Ramachandra Guha provides a good overview of ecological issues.

Architecture, Arts & Crafts

The Archaeological Survey of India publishes a series of booklets on major sites and works (eg, *Chola Temples*), which are inexpensive and available in India.

The History of Architecture in India: From the Dawn of Civilisation to the End of the Raj by Christopher Tadgell provides a good overview and has plenty of illustrations.

The Royal Palaces of India, with text by George Michell and photographs by Antonio Martinelli, is a comprehensive guide to the forts and palaces of India. In addition to the photographs, there are some excellent archaeological maps.

Arts and Crafts of India by Ilay Cooper & John Gillow examines India's wealth of handicrafts, their manufacture and significance.

Woodcut Prints of Nineteenth Century Calcutta edited by Ashit Paul is a collection of woodcut prints covering mythology, social scenes, book illustrations and advertising from 1816 to the early 20th century. Four essays focus on this short-lived but vital urban art form.

Novels

Ruskin Bond, a respected and widely published author in India, has a number of terrific publications including *Collected Fiction*, which is a compilation of short stories.

English, August by Upamanyu Chatterjee is the cynical, funny tale of a dope-smoking civil servant sent to Madna, one of India's dreariest towns. Chatterjee has also written the darkly humorous *The Last Burden,* which examines a dysfunctional family.

Adib Khan's *The Storyteller* is set in the backstreets of Delhi and centres around an outcast dwarf with a skill for storytelling who shares Delhi's darker side with the pimps, pickpockets and *hijras* (eunuchs).

The Burning Ghats by Paul Mann concerns a chemical spill in the Ganges in Varanasi, which kills and injures thousands of people. This book has the winning ingredients for a mystery, including death, intrigue, corruption in high places and danger.

William Sutcliffe's *Are You Experienced?* is a hilarious tale of a first-time backpacker who accompanies his best friend's girlfriend to India in an attempt to seduce her. The story follows him as he gets the girl (sort of), suffers Delhi-belly and 'experiences' India.

A Passage to India by EM Forster is an absorbing account of a collision of British and Indian outlooks; *The Nightrunners of Bengal* by John Masters has a similar theme, with the 1857 Indian Uprising as a backdrop. Look out also for *Heat & Dust* by Ruth Prawer Jhabwala and *The Far Pavilions* by MM Kaye.

And of course, there are the golden oldies, such as Rudyard Kipling's Victorian-era stories *Kim*, *Plain Tales from the Hills* and *The Jungle Books*.

General

Autobiography of an Unknown Indian and *Thy Hand, Great Anarch!: India 1921–1952* are two autobiographical books by one of India's most prominent contemporary writers, Nirad Chaudhuri. They are a superb account of the history and culture of modern India.

Traditional rural roles are dissected in *Social Structures of Indian Villages – A Study of Rural Bihar* by Hetuka Jha.

For a perceptive examination of India as it is today, get hold of *The Idea of India* by Sunil Khilnani.

The Vintage Book of Indian Writing 1947–97 is a collection of essays and short stories edited by Salman Rushdie & Elizabeth West. It's one of the many books published in celebration of India's 50 years of independence and contains some brilliant writing by such acclaimed authors as Jawaharlal Nehru, Nayantara Sahgal, Anita Desai, Vikram Seth and Arundhati Roy.

The Garden of Life – An Introduction to the Healing Plants of India by Naveen Patnaik is a magnificently illustrated book on an intriguing subject. The text is interspersed with fine drawings and some glorious poetry.

The Anger of Aubergines by Bubul Sharma is subtitled *Stories of Women and Food.* It's an amusing and unique culinary analysis of social relationships, interspersed with mouthwatering recipes.

MN Srinivas, one of India's most distinguished sociologists, has written several books including *Religion and Society Among the Coorgs of South India*, *The Remembered Village* and *Social Change in Modern India*.

The Namaste Book of Indian Short Stories edited by Monisha Mukanda provides a delightful cross-section of voices and styles from contemporary Indian writing.

FILMS

Numerous foreign films have been made about India over the years. Prominent among them are *Gandhi*, *Heat & Dust*, *A Passage to India* and *The Far Pavilions*. Recent films include *Holy Smoke* and *City of Joy*.

India itself makes more movies than any other nation. For information on Indian movies, see the boxed text 'Behind the Scenes of Indian Cinema' in the Facts about North India chapter.

NEWSPAPERS & MAGAZINES

English-language dailies include the *Times of India*, the *Hindustan Times*, *The Statesman*, *The Pioneer*, the *Asian Age*, *The Hindu* and the *Indian Express*; many rate the *Express* as the pick of the bunch. The *Economic Times* is for those interested in business and economic analysis. There are also various city and regional English-language dailies such as the *Bihar Times* and *Garha Chronicle*.

Popular news magazines include *Frontline*, *India Today*, *Sunday*, *Rashtriya Sahara*, *Outlook*, *The Week* and the *Illustrated Weekly*. They're widely available at bookshops and newspaper stands.

Major city bookshops and top-end hotels usually stock a healthy collection of international publications, though they can be dated and are pricey by local standards. These include *The Economist*, *Time*, *Newsweek*, *The International Herald-Tribune* and *Der Spiegel*.

Popular women's magazines include *Femina*, *Savvy* and *Gladrags*, as well as Indian versions of *Elle* and *Cosmopolitan*. To get the lowdown on who's who and who's doing what to whom in Bollywood, grab a copy of *Stardust*, *Cineblitz* or *Filmfare*.

There are also other English-language magazines specialising in everything from sports to information technology.

TV & RADIO

Television viewing was once dominated by the rather dreary national broadcaster, Doordarshan. Following the arrival of satellite and cable TV in the early 1990s India fast became one of the world's most avid channel-surfing nations. Cable is available at all top-end hotels, most mid-range ones and even a handful of budget places. Check local newspapers for program details.

Running 24 hours, cable offers over 50 channels with plenty of Hindi-language ones, including the immensely popular Zee TV. Bollywood buffs are well catered for with multiple movie channels churning out blockbuster after blockbuster. Meanwhile, those in need of spiritual sustenance can switch to the Maharishi Mahesh Yogi's channel, which offers a devout diet of holy images, bhajans (devotional songs) and overall positive vibes. There are also some Indian regional channels that broadcast in various local languages.

English-language channels include the BBC, CNN, Discovery and National Geographic Channels, as well as Star TV's offerings, including Star Movies (for Hollywood blockbusters), Star Plus (for American sitcoms, soapies and more), Star Sports and Star News; the latter two broadcast in Hindi and English. Also in English, Nickelodeon rolls out various sitcoms, while AXN and HBO screen movies (including some choice golden oldies). MTV and Channel V are the premier music channels, with everything from *bhangra* (Punjabi disco) to American rap.

Radio programs can be heard on All India Radio (AIR), which broadcasts various interviews, music, sports and news features. In 1999 the government announced that FM broadcasting licences would be opened up to private operators via a bidding process. Frequency allocation had not been completed at the time of research, so check local newspapers for the latest offerings. Several that were up-and-running during the research for this book include 102.6FM (Delhi) and FM107 (Kolkata), which both broadcast local event information, news and classical Indian/regional music. Details on programs and frequencies are listed in all the major English-language dailies throughout India.

Some radio stations broadcast late-night talkback in English, which can be highly amusing and enlightening. However, you need to scan the dial to find these programs as they tend to jump about.

PHOTOGRAPHY & VIDEO

Lonely Planet's *Travel Photography* by renowned travel photographer Richard I'Anson offers professional, practical tips for improving the quality of your photographs. The following are some handy hints for taking better photos:

- The quality of your photos depends on the quality of light you shoot under. Light is best when the sun is low in the sky – around sunrise and sunset.
- Don't buy cheap equipment, but don't load yourself down with expensive equipment you don't know how to use properly either.
- A good SLR camera is advisable, but be aware that the quality of your lenses is the most important thing. Zoom lenses are heavier than fixed focal length lenses and the quality isn't as good. An alternative to the zoom is a teleconverter which fits over your lens and doubles the focal length.
- Always carry a skylight or UV filter. A polarising filter can create dramatic effects and cut glare, but don't fit it over a UV filter.
- Take a tripod and faster film (at least 400ASA) rather than a flash. Flash creates harsh shadows. A cable release is useful for shooting with a tripod.
- Settle on a brand of film and assess how it works with your camera's automatic exposure settings *before* you head off.
- Keep your film in a cool dark place if possible, before and after exposure.
- Expose for the main component of a scene and fill the frame with what you are taking.
- Previsualise – it's one of the most important elements in photographic vision. You must 'see' your picture clearly before you take it.

Video in India uses the VHS format, although it is possible to convert to and from PAL and NTSC in the larger cities.

Film & Cartridges

Colour print film processing facilities are readily available in major cities and larger towns. Film is relatively cheap (eg, Rs 95 for a 36-exposure roll) and the quality is usually (but not always) good. Same-day processing is often available. Colour slide film is less widely available than print film. You'll generally only find it in the major cities and tourist traps. Colour slides can be processed (usually in two to three days; specify whether you want them mounted or not) in major cities including Delhi, Kolkata, Bhopal and Jaipur, but most travellers prefer to get it developed back home.

Always check the use-by date on local film and slide stock. Make sure you get a sealed packet and ensure you're not handed a roll that's been sitting in a glass cabinet in the sunshine for the last few months. Heat and humidity can play havoc with film, even if the use-by date hasn't been exceeded. A tip: Be wary of street hawkers in India. Some travellers report that old, useless film is loaded into new-looking canisters. The hapless tourist only discovers the trick when the film is developed back home. The best advice is to avoid street vendors and only buy film from reputable stores – and preferably film that's been refrigerated.

Video users can get cartridges (including digital, VHS, Super 8 and Betacam) in major cities such as Delhi, Jaipur, Ahmedabad and Kolkata. Cartridges cost from Rs 220 (Super 8) up to Rs 750 (digital).

Restrictions & Photographing People

Be careful what you photograph. India is touchy about places of military importance – this can include train stations, bridges, airports, military installations and sensitive border regions. Temples may prohibit photography in the *mandapam* (forechamber of a temple) and inner sanctum. If in doubt, ask. Some temples, and numerous sites such as museums and forts, levy a camera and video fee that you must pay upfront (see regional chapters for exact costs).

Some people are more than happy to be photographed, but care should be taken in pointing cameras at women. Again, if in doubt, ask. A zoom is a less intrusive means of taking portraits – even when you've obtained permission to take a portrait, shoving a lens in your subject's face can be disconcerting. A reasonable distance between you and your subject will help to reduce your subject's discomfort, and will result in more natural shots.

Protecting Your Camera & Film

Film manufacturers warn that, once it's been exposed, film should be developed as quickly as possible; in practice the film seems to last, even in India's summer heat, without deterioration for months. Try to keep your film cool, and protect it in sealed containers if you're travelling during the monsoon. Silica gel sachets distributed around your gear will help to absorb moisture. It's worth bringing along a camera-cleaning kit as the dust, sand and general grime in India can be prolific.

Some travellers invest in a lead-lined bag, as repeated exposure to X-ray (even so-called 'film proof' X-ray) can damage film. Never put your film in baggage that will be placed in the cargo holds of aeroplanes, as it may be subjected to large doses of X-ray, which will ruin it. Some professional photographers never take film through any X-ray machine, but prefer to pack it in see-through plastic containers and carry them by hand through customs. Just be aware that some customs officers may wish to open every single canister before you're allowed through.

TIME

India is 5½ hours ahead of GMT/UTC, 4½ hours behind Australian Eastern Standard Time (EST) and 10½ hours ahead of American EST. It is officially known as IST (Indian Standard Time), although many affectionately dub it as 'Indian Stretchable Time'.

ELECTRICITY

The electric current is 230-240V AC, 50 Hz. Electricity is widely available, but power cuts are not uncommon – keep a torch (flashlight) or candle handy. Breakdowns and blackouts ('load shedding') lasting from several minutes to several hours are common, especially in the hotter months when demand outstrips supply. If you are bringing any sensitive electrical equipment (eg, a laptop computer), you'll require a voltage stabiliser to safeguard it from the power fluctuations.

Sockets are the three round-pin variety, similar (but not identical) to European sockets. European round-pin plugs will go into the sockets, but as the pins on Indian plugs are somewhat thicker, the fit is loose and connection is not always guaranteed.

You can purchase small immersion elements, perfect for boiling water for tea or coffee, for around Rs 55. For about Rs 75 you can buy electric mosquito zappers. These take chemical tablets that melt and emit deadly vapours (deadly for the mozzie, that is). They're widely available in various brands, with delightful names such as Good Knight.

WEIGHTS & MEASURES

Although officially India is metricated, imperial weights and measures are still used in some areas of commerce. A metric conversion chart is included on the inside back cover of this book. You will often hear people referring to lakhs (one lakh = 100,000) and crore (one crore = 10 million) of people, money, camels or whatever. A *tola* is 11.6g.

LAUNDRY

Getting your sweaty, crumpled clothes washed and ironed in India is a breeze. Unless the hotel has its own in-house laundry your clothes will be washed by a dhobi-wallah at the dhobi ghats (see the boxed text 'India's Washing Wizards'). If you don't think they will stand up to being beaten clean, then hand-wash them yourself. Washing powder can be bought very cheaply in small sachets almost anywhere, and hotels are usually happy to lend you a bucket.

At budget and mid-range hotels, clothes are usually washed by a dhobi (inquire at reception). You simply hand over your dirty clothes in the morning and you'll usually get them back washed and pressed that same evening for around Rs 10 per item (often a little more in touristy places). Most, if not all, upmarket hotels have an in-house laundry with upmarket charges to match. Many crank up the price for same-day service.

India's Washing Wizards

Thanks to India's dhobi-wallahs (washer-people) you hardly need more than one change of clothes. You simply give them your dirty clothes in the morning and hey presto, they come back freshly washed and crisply ironed later that very day. And all for a minimal price. But what happened to your clothes between their departure and return?

Well, they certainly did not get anywhere near a washing machine. First of all they're taken to the dhobi ghat – a series of steps near a lake or river where the dhobi-wallahs ply their trade. Upon arrival at the ghat the clothes are separated – all the white T-shirts are washed together, all the burgundy socks, all the blue jeans. Your clothes are soaked in soapy water for a few hours, following which the dirt is literally belted out of them. No newfangled washing machine can wash as clean as a determined dhobi, although admittedly after a few visits to the Indian laundry your clothes do look distinctly thinner and faded. Buttons also tend to get shattered, so bring some spares. Zips, lace, bras and flimsy panties sometimes fare likewise. Once clean, the clothes are dried in the glorious Indian sun, then they're pressed with primitive-looking irons – even your underwear will come back with knife-edge creases.

Even though hundreds, even thousands, of items are washed at the same place each day, the deft dhobi-wallah's secret system of marking means your clothes won't get mistakenly bundled into another dhobi's load. Apparently criminals have even been tracked down by these tell tale 'dhobi marks'.

Women should consider bringing a lingerie bag to protect delicate bras and underpants if they intend handing them over to either a dhobi-wallah or a hotel laundry. Make sure you explain how the bag is actually used or else your precious lingerie will promptly be taken out and thrashed like regular clothes.

TOILETS

All top-end and most mid-range hotels have sit-down flush toilets with toilet paper supplied. Some mid-range and most budget hotels usually have a choice of squat and sit-down toilets (see 'The Inside Story on Bathrooms' boxed text under Accommodation, later in this chapter). In the real rock-bottom category and in places well off the tourist circuit, squat toilets are the norm (and are actually a more hygienic option than the sit-down variety) and toilet paper is rarely provided.

Most upmarket restaurants have sit-down flush toilets, while most budget eateries will make you work those calf muscles.

When it comes to effluent etiquette, it's customary to use your left hand and water, not toilet paper. A strategically placed tap (usually with a little plastic jug nearby) is available in most bathrooms. If you can't get used to the Indian method, bring your own paper (widely available in cities and towns). But remember, stuffing paper, sanitary napkins and tampons down the toilet is going to further clog an already overloaded sewerage system. Often a bin is provided for used toilet paper etc – please use it.

HEALTH

Travel health depends on your predeparture preparations, your daily health care while travelling and how you handle any medical problem that does develop. While the potential dangers can seem quite frightening, in reality few travellers experience anything more than an upset stomach.

In some northern cities, especially Kolkata and Delhi, the air pollution from vehicles can be particularly problematic for people with asthma or any form of respiratory ailment – bring along appropriate medication. Also be aware that cerebral malaria is a problem in Bihar, and that India accounts for four out of 10 polio cases in the world (most of these cases occur in Bihar and Uttar Pradesh).

In even the smallest Indian town you'll find at least one well-stocked pharmacy (selling everything from malaria medication to nail polish). Many are open until late, or even round-the-clock. Many pharmaceuticals sold in India are manufactured under license from multinational companies, so you'll probably be familiar with many brand names. Always check expiry dates.

There are plenty of English-speaking doctors and pharmacists in urban centres, fewer in rural areas. Most hotels have a doctor on call; if you're staying at a budget hotel and they can't help you, try contacting an upmarket hotel to find out which doctor they use. If you're seriously ill, contact your country's embassy (see Embassies & Consulates, earlier), which usually has a list of recommended doctors and dentists.

Treatment at public hospitals is generally reliable, though private clinics do offer the advantage of shorter queues. However, there have been reports that some private clinics have bumped up the level of treatment than is necessary to procure larger medical insurance claims (see Dangers & Annoyances, later in this chapter).

Finally, many Indian towns have both Ayurvedic and Western clinics; if it's not obvious which philosophy the clinic follows, ask at the outset.

Predeparture Planning

Immunisations Plan ahead for getting your vaccinations: Some of them require more than one injection, while some vaccinations should not be given together. Note that some vaccinations should not be given during pregnancy or in people with allergies – discuss with your doctor.

Medical Kit Check List

Following is a list of items you should consider including in your medical kit – consult your pharmacist for brands available in your country.

- ☐ **Aspirin or paracetamol (acetaminophen in the USA)** – for pain or fever
- ☐ **Antihistamine** – for allergies, eg, hay fever; to ease the itch from insect bites or stings; and to prevent motion sickness
- ☐ **Cold and flu tablets, throat lozenges and nasal decongestant**
- ☐ **Multivitamins** – consider for long trips, when dietary vitamin intake may be inadequate
- ☐ **Antibiotics** – consider including these if you're travelling well off the beaten track; see your doctor, as they must be prescribed, and carry the prescription with you
- ☐ **Loperamide or diphenoxylate** – 'blockers' for diarrhoea
- ☐ **Prochlorperazine or metaclopramide** – for nausea and vomiting
- ☐ **Rehydration mixture** – to prevent dehydration, which may occur, for example, during bouts of diarrhoea; particularly important when travelling with children
- ☐ **Insect repellent, sunscreen, lip balm and eye drops**
- ☐ **Calamine lotion, sting relief spray or aloe vera** – to ease irritation from sunburn and insect bites or stings
- ☐ **Antifungal cream or powder** – for fungal skin infections and thrush
- ☐ **Antiseptic (such as povidone-iodine)** – for cuts and grazes
- ☐ **Bandages, elastic plasters and other wound dressings**
- ☐ **Water purification tablets or iodine**
- ☐ **Scissors, tweezers and a thermometer** – note that mercury thermometers are prohibited by airlines
- ☐ **Sterile kit** – in case you need injections in a country with medical hygiene problems; discuss with your doctor

It is recommended that you seek medical advice at least six weeks before you travel. It is importatnt to remember that there is often a greater risk of disease with children and during pregnancy.

Discuss your requirements with your doctor, but vaccinations you should consider for this trip include the following (for more details about the diseases themselves, see the individual disease entries later in this section). Carry proof of your vaccinations, especially yellow fever, as this is sometimes needed to enter some countries.

Diphtheria & Tetanus Vaccinations for these two diseases are usually combined and are recommended for everyone. After an initial course of three injections (usually given in childhood), boosters are necessary every 10 years.

Hepatitis A The vacine for Hepatitis A (eg, Avaxim, Havrix 1440 or VAQTA) provides long-term immunity (possibly more than 10 years) after an initial injection and a booster at six to 12 months. Alternatively, an injection of gamma globulin can provide short-term protection against hepatitis A – two to six months, depending on the dose given. It is not a vaccine, but is ready-made antibody collected from blood donations. It is reasonably effective and, unlike the vaccine, it is protective immediately, but because it is a blood product, there are current concerns about its long-term safety. Hepatitis A vaccine is also available in a combined form, Twinrix, with hepatitis B vaccine. Three injections over a six-month period are required, the first two providing substantial protection against hepatitis A.

Hepatitis B Travellers who should consider vaccination against hepatitis B include those on a long trip, as well as those visiting countries (including India) where there are high levels of hepatitis B infection, where blood transfusions may not be adequately screened or where sexual contact or needle sharing is a possibility. Vaccination involves three injections, with a booster at 12 months. More rapid courses are available if necessary.

Japanese B Encephalitis Consider vaccination against this disease if spending a month or longer in high risk areas in India, making repeated trips to a risk area or visiting during an epidemic. It involves three injections over 30 days.

Meningococcal Meningitis Vaccination is recommended for travellers to certain parts of India. A single injection gives good protection against the major epidemic forms of the disease for three years. Protection may be less effective in children under two years.

Polio Everyone should keep up to date with this vaccination, which is normally given in childhood. A booster every 10 years maintains immunity.

Rabies Vaccination should be considered by those who will spend a month or longer in India where rabies is common, especially if they are cycling, handling animals, caving or travelling to remote areas, and for children (who may not report a bite). Pretravel rabies vaccination involves having three injections over 21 to 28 days. If someone who has been vaccinated is bitten or scratched by an animal, they will require two booster injections of vaccine; those not vaccinated require more.

Tuberculosis The risk of TB to travellers is usually very low, unless you will be living with or closely associated with local people in high risk areas in India. Vaccination against TB (BCG) is recommended for children and young adults living in these areas for three months or more.

Typhoid Vaccination against typhoid may be required if you are travelling for more than a couple of weeks in India. It is now available either as an injection or as capsules to be taken orally. A combined hepatitis A/typhoid vaccine was launched recently but its availability is still limited - check with your doctor to find out its status in your country.

Yellow Fever A yellow-fever vaccine is required if coming from an infected area such as Central Africa and parts of South America. You may have to go to a special yellow-fever vaccination centre.

Malaria Medication Malaria occurs in most parts of India. Antimalarial drugs do not prevent you from being infected but kill the malaria parasites during a stage in their development and significantly reduce the risk of becoming very ill or dying. Expert advice on medication should be sought, as there are many factors to consider, including the area to be visited, the risk of exposure to malaria-carrying mosquitoes, the side effects of medication, your medical history and whether you are a child or an adult or pregnant. Travellers to isolated area in high risk countries may like to carry a treatment dose of medication for use if symptoms occur.

Health Insurance Make sure that you have adequate health insurance. See Travel Insurance under Visas & Documents earlier in this chapter.

Travel Health Guides *Healthy Travel Asia & India*, published by Lonely Planet, is a handy pocket-sized guide to staying healthy on your trip. *Travel with Children*, also from Lonely Planet, includes advice on travel health for younger children.

There are also a number of excellent travel health sites on the Internet. From the Lonely Planet home page there are links at www.lonelyplanet.com/weblinks/wlheal.htm to the World Health Organisation and the US Centers for Disease Control & Prevention.

Other Preparations Make sure you're healthy before you start travelling. If you are going on a long trip make sure your teeth are OK. If you wear glasses take a spare pair and your prescription. (See also What to Bring under planning earlier in this chapter).

If you require a particular medication take an adequate supply, as it may not be available locally. Take part of the packaging showing the generic name rather than the brand, which will make getting replacements easier. It's a good idea to have a legible prescription or letter from your doctor to show that you legally use the medication to avoid any problems.

Basic Rules

Food Although care should be taken as to what you eat and drink, don't become paranoid – sampling the local cuisine is a highlight of travel after all and India has some phenomenal culinary offerings. It's sensible to modify your diet gradually, so resist that urge to feast on pakoras (deep-fried vegetable fritters) the moment you arrive.

Vegetables and fruit should be washed with purified water or peeled where possible. Beware of ice cream that is sold in the street or anywhere it might have been melted and refrozen; if there's any doubt (eg, a power cut in the last day or two), steer well clear. Shellfish such as mussels, oysters and clams should be avoided as well as undercooked meat, particularly in the form of mince. Steaming does not make shellfish safe for eating.

If a place looks clean and well run and the vendor also looks clean and healthy, then the food is probably safe. In general, places that are packed with travellers or locals will be fine, while empty restaurants are questionable. The food in busy restaurants is cooked and eaten quite quickly with little standing around and is probably not reheated. Although street stalls may look unappetising, the big plus is that you can usually see your food being freshly cooked in front of your eyes.

Water The number one rule is *be careful of the water* and especially ice. If you don't know for certain that the water is safe, assume the worst. Reputable brands of bottled

Nutrition

If your diet is poor or limited in variety, if you're travelling hard and fast and therefore missing meals or if you simply lose your appetite, you can soon start to lose weight and place your health at risk.

Make sure your diet is well balanced. Cooked eggs, tofu, beans, lentils (dhal in India) and nuts are all safe ways to get protein. Fruit you can peel is usually safe and a good source of vitamins. Melons can harbour bacteria in their flesh and are best avoided. Try to eat plenty of grains (including rice) and bread. Remember that although food is generally safer if it is cooked well, overcooked food loses much of its nutritional value. If your diet isn't well balanced or if your food intake is insufficient, it's a good idea to take multivitamin tablets.

In hot climates make sure you drink enough – don't rely on feeling thirsty to indicate when you should drink. Not needing to urinate or voiding small amounts of very dark yellow urine is a danger sign. Always carry a water bottle with you on long trips. Excessive sweating can lead to loss of salt and therefore muscle cramping. Salt tablets are not a good idea as a preventative, but in places where salt is not used much, adding salt to food can help.

water or soft drinks are generally fine, although in some places bottles may be refilled with tap water. Only use water from containers with a serrated seal – not tops or corks. Take care with fruit juice, particularly if water may have been added. Milk should be treated with suspicion as it is often unpasteurised, though boiled milk is fine if it is kept hygienically. Tea or coffee should also be OK, since the water should have been boiled.

Water Purification The simplest way of purifying water is to boil it thoroughly. Vigorous boiling should be satisfactory; however, at high altitude water boils at a lower temperature, so germs are less likely to be killed. Boil it for longer in these environments.

Consider purchasing a water filter for a long trip. There are two main kinds of filter. Total filters take out all parasites, bacteria and viruses and make water safe to drink. They are often expensive, but they can be more cost effective than buying bottled water. Simple filters (which can even be a nylon mesh bag) take out dirt and larger foreign bodies from the water so that chemical solutions work much more effectively; if water is dirty, chemical solutions may not work at all. It's very important when buying a filter to read the specifications, so that you know exactly what it removes from the water and what it doesn't. Simple filtering will not remove all dangerous organisms, so if you cannot boil water it should be treated chemically. Chlorine tablets will kill many pathogens, but not some parasites such as giardia and amoebic cysts. Iodine is more effective in purifying water and is available in tablet form. Follow the directions carefully and remember that too much iodine can be harmful.

Be aware that relying on some method of water purification helps the environment, as it stops you adding to India's rubbish mountain of used plastic bottles – see Responsible Tourism earlier in this chapter. Note that some hotels provide filtered water.

Medical Problems & Treatment

Self-diagnosis and treatment can be risky, so you should always seek medical help. An embassy, consulate or five-star hotel can usually recommend a local doctor or clinic. Although we do give drug dosages in this section, they are for emergency use only. Correct diagnosis is vital. In this section we have used the generic names for medications – check with a pharmacist for brands available locally.

Note that antibiotics should ideally be administered only under medical supervision. Take only the recommended dose at the prescribed intervals and use the whole course, even if the illness seems to be cured earlier. Stop immediately if there are any serious reactions and don't use the antibiotic at all if you are unsure that you have the correct one. Some people are allergic to commonly prescribed antibiotics such as penicillin; carry this information (eg, on a bracelet) when travelling.

Environmental Hazards

Altitude Sickness Lack of oxygen at high altitudes (over 2500m) affects most people to some extent, so take care in the Himalaya region. The effect may be mild or severe and occurs because less oxygen reaches the muscles and the brain at high altitude, requiring the heart and lungs to compensate by working harder. Symptoms of Acute Mountain Sickness (AMS) usually develop during the first 24 hours at altitude but may be delayed up to three weeks. Mild symptoms include headache, lethargy, dizziness, difficulty sleeping and loss of appetite. AMS may become more severe without warning and can be fatal. Severe symptoms include breathlessness, a dry, irritative cough (which may progress to the production of pink, frothy sputum), severe headache, lack of coordination and balance, confusion, irrational behaviour, vomiting, drowsiness and unconsciousness. There is no hard-and-fast rule as to what is too high: AMS has been fatal at 3000m, although 3500m to 4500m is the usual range.

Treat mild symptoms by resting at the same altitude until recovery, usually a day or two. Paracetamol or aspirin can be taken for headaches. If symptoms persist or become worse, however, *immediate descent is necessary*; even 500m can help. Drug treatments should never be used to avoid descent or to enable further ascent.

The drugs acetazolamide and dexamethasone are recommended by some doctors for the prevention of AMS; however, their use is controversial. They can reduce the symptoms, but they may also mask warning signs; severe and fatal AMS has occurred in people taking these drugs. In general we do not recommend them for travellers.

To reduce the chances of getting acute mountain sickness:

- Ascend slowly – have frequent rest days, spending two to three nights at each rise of 1000m. If you reach a high altitude by trekking, acclimatisation takes place gradually and you are less likely to be affected than if you fly directly to high altitude.
- It is always wise to sleep at a lower altitude than the greatest height reached during the day if possible. Also, once above 3000m, care should be taken not to increase the sleeping altitude by more than 300m per day.
- Drink extra fluids. The mountain air is dry and cold and moisture is lost as you breathe. Evaporation of sweat may occur unnoticed and result in dehydration.
- Eat light, high-carbohydrate meals for more energy.
- Avoid alcohol as it may increase the risk of dehydration.
- Avoid sedatives.

Everyday Health

Normal body temperature is up to 37°C (98.6°F); more than 2°C (4°F) higher indicates a high fever. The normal adult pulse rate is 60 to 100 per minute (children 80 to 100, babies 100 to 140). As a general rule the pulse increases about 20 beats per minute for each 1°C (2°F) rise in fever.

Respiration (breathing) rate is also an indicator of illness. Count the number of breaths per minute; between 12 and 20 is normal for adults and older children (up to 30 for younger children, 40 for babies). People with a high fever or serious respiratory illness breathe more quickly than normal. More than 40 shallow breaths a minute may indicate pneumonia.

The Himalayan First Aid & Survival Manual by Jim Duff & Peter Gormly has practical advice to diagnose and treat ailments associated with high altitudes. All profits from the publication go to the Kathmandu Environmental Education Project. It's available from Dr J Duff, PO Box 53, Repton, NSW 2454, Australia and KEEP, PO Box 9178, Jyathu, Kathmandu, Nepal.

Heat Exhaustion Dehydration and salt deficiency can cause heat exhaustion. Take time to acclimatise to high temperatures, drink sufficient liquids and do not do anything too physically demanding.

Salt deficiency is characterised by fatigue, lethargy, headaches, giddiness and muscle cramps; salt tablets may help, but adding extra salt to your food is better.

Anhidrotic heat exhaustion is a rare form of heat exhaustion that is caused by an inability to sweat. It tends to affect people who have been in a hot climate for some time, rather than newcomers. It can progress to heatstroke. Treatment involves removal to a cooler climate.

Heatstroke This serious, occasionally fatal, condition can occur if the body's heat-regulating mechanism breaks down and the body temperature rises to dangerous levels. Long, continuous periods of exposure to high temperatures and insufficient fluids can leave you vulnerable to heatstroke.

The symptoms are feeling unwell, not sweating very much (or at all) and a high body temperature (39°C to 41°C or 102°F to 106°F). Where sweating has ceased, the skin becomes flushed and red. Severe, throbbing headaches and lack of coordination will also occur, and the sufferer may be confused or aggressive. Eventually the victim will become delirious or convulse. Hospitalisation is essential, but in the interim get victims out of the sun, remove their clothing, cover them with a wet sheet or towel and then fan continually. Give fluids if they are conscious.

Hypothermia Too much cold can be just as dangerous as too much heat. If you are trekking at high altitudes or simply taking a long bus trip over mountains, particularly at night, be prepared.

Hypothermia occurs when the body loses heat faster than it can produce it and the core temperature of the body falls. It is surprisingly easy to progress from very cold to dangerously cold due to a combination of wind, wet clothing, fatigue and hunger, even if the air temperature is above freezing. It is best to dress in layers; silk, wool and some of the new artificial fibres are all good insulating materials. A hat is important, as a lot of heat is lost through the head. A strong, waterproof outer layer (and a 'space' blanket for emergencies) is essential. Carry basic supplies, including food containing simple sugars to generate heat quickly and fluid to drink.

Symptoms of hypothermia are exhaustion, numb skin (particularly toes and fingers), shivering, slurred speech, irrational or violent behaviour, lethargy, stumbling, dizzy spells, muscle cramps and violent bursts of energy. Irrationality may take the form of sufferers claiming they are warm and trying to take off their clothes.

To treat mild hypothermia, first get the person out of the wind and/or rain, remove their clothing if it's wet and replace it with dry, warm clothing. Give them hot liquids – not alcohol – and some high-kilojoule, easily digestible food. Do not rub victims: Instead, allow them to slowly warm themselves. This should be enough to treat the early stages of hypothermia. The early recognition and treatment of mild hypothermia is the only way to prevent severe hypothermia, which is a critical condition.

Jet Lag When a person travels by air across more than three time zones (each time zone usually represents a one-hour time difference) jet lag is experienced . It occurs because many of the functions of the human body (such as temperature, pulse rate and emptying of the bladder and bowels) are regulated by internal 24-hour cycles. When we travel long distances rapidly, our bodies take time to adjust to the 'new time' of our destination, and we may experience fatigue, disorientation, insomnia, anxiety, impaired concentration and loss of appetite. These effects will usually be gone within three days of arrival, but to minimise the impact of jet lag:

- Rest for a couple of days prior to departure.
- Try to select flight schedules that minimise sleep deprivation; arriving late in the day means you can go to sleep soon after you arrive. For very long flights, try to organise a stopover.
- Avoid excessive eating (which bloats the stomach) and alcohol (which causes dehydration) during the flight. Instead, drink plenty of non-carbonated, nonalcoholic drinks such as fruit juice or water.
- Avoid smoking.
- Make yourself comfortable by wearing loose-fitting clothes and perhaps bringing an eye mask and ear plugs to help you sleep.
- Try to sleep at the appropriate time for the time zone you are travelling to.

Motion Sickness Eating lightly before and during a trip will reduce the chances of motion sickness. If you are prone to motion sickness try to find a place that minimises movement – near the wing on aircraft, close to midships on boats, near the centre on buses. Fresh air usually helps; reading and cigarette smoke don't. Commercial motion-sickness preparations, which can cause drowsiness, have to be taken before the trip commences. Ginger (available in capsule form) and peppermint (including mint-flavoured sweets) are natural preventatives.

Prickly Heat Excessive perspiration trapped under the skin causes an itchy rash called prickly heat. It usually strikes people who have just arrived in a hot climate. Keeping cool, bathing often, drying the skin and using a mild talcum or prickly heat powder or resorting to air-conditioning may help.

Sunburn In the tropics, the desert or at high altitude you can get sunburnt surprisingly quickly, even through cloud. Use a sunscreen, a hat, and a barrier cream for your nose and lips. Calamine lotion or a commercial after sun preparation are good for mild sunburn. Protect your eyes with good quality sunglasses, particularly if you will be near water, sand or snow.

Infectious Diseases

Diarrhoea Simple things such as a change of water, food or climate can all cause a mild bout of diarrhoea, but a few rushed toilet trips with no other symptoms is not indicative of a major problem.

Dehydration is the main danger with any diarrhoea, particularly in children or the elderly as dehydration can occur quite quickly. Under all circumstances *fluid replacement* (at least equal to the volume being lost) is the most important thing to remember. Weak black tea with a little sugar, soda water, or soft drinks allowed to go flat and diluted 50% with clean water are all good. With severe diarrhoea a rehydrating solution is preferable to replace minerals and salts lost. Commercially available oral rehydration salts (ORS) are very useful; add them to boiled or bottled water. In an emergency you can make up a solution of six teaspoons of sugar and a half teaspoon of salt to a litre of boiled or bottled water. You need to drink at least the same volume of fluid that you are losing in bowel movements and vomiting. Urine is the best guide to the adequacy of replacement – if you have small amounts of concentrated urine, you need to drink more. Keep drinking small amounts often. Stick to a bland fat-free diet as you recover.

Gut-paralysing drugs such as loperamide or diphenoxylate can be used to bring relief from the symptoms, although they do not actually cure the problem. Only use these drugs if you do not have access to toilets, eg, if you *must* travel. Note that these drugs are not recommended for children under 12 years.

In certain situations antibiotics may be required: diarrhoea with blood or mucus (dysentery), any diarrhoea with fever, profuse watery diarrhoea, persistent diarrhoea not improving after 48 hours and severe diarrhoea. These suggest a more serious cause of diarrhoea and in these situations gut-paralysing drugs should be avoided.

In these situations, a stool test may be necessary to diagnose what bug is causing your diarrhoea, so you should seek medical help urgently. Where this is not possible the recommended drugs for bacterial diarrhoea (the most likely cause of severe diarrhoea for travellers) are norfloxacin 400mg twice daily for three days or ciprofloxacin 500mg twice daily for five days. These are certainly not recommended for children or pregnant women. The drug of choice for children would be co-trimoxazole with the dosage dependent on the child's weight. A five-day course is given. Ampicillin or amoxycillin may be given in pregnancy, but medical care is necessary.

Two other causes of persistent diarrhoea in travellers are giardiasis and amoebic dysentery.

Giardiasis is caused by a common parasite, *Giardia lamblia*. Symptoms include stomach cramps, nausea, a bloated stomach, watery, foul-smelling diarrhoea and frequent gas. Giardiasis can appear several weeks after you have been exposed to the parasite. The symptoms may disappear for a few days and then return; this can go on for several weeks.

Amoebic dysentery, caused by the protozoan *Entamoeba histolytica*, is characterised by a gradual onset of low-grade diarrhoea, often with blood and mucus. Cramping abdominal pain and vomiting are less likely than in other types of diarrhoea, and fever may not be present. It will persist until treated and can recur and cause other health problems.

You should seek medical advice if you think you have giardiasis or amoebic dysentery, but where this is not possible, tinidazole or metronidazole are the recommended drugs. Treatment is a 2g single dose of tinidazole or 250mg of metronidazole three times daily for five to 10 days.

Fungal Infections These occur more commonly in hot weather and are usually found on the scalp, between the toes (athlete's foot) or fingers, in the groin and on the body (ringworm). You get ringworm (which is a fungal infection, not a worm) from infected animals or other people. Moisture encourages these infections.

To prevent fungal infections wear loose, comfortable clothes, avoid artificial fibres, wash frequently and dry yourself carefully. If you do get an infection, wash the infected area at least daily with a disinfectant or medicated soap and water, and rinse and dry well. Apply an antifungal cream or powder such as tolnaftate. Try to expose the infected area to air or sunlight as much as possible and wash all towels and underwear in hot water, change them often and let them dry in the sun.

Hepatitis This is a general term for inflammation of the liver. It is a common disease in India and worldwide. There are several different viruses that cause hepatitis, and they differ in the way that they are transmitted. The symptoms are similar in all forms of the illness, and include fever, chills, headache, fatigue, feelings of weakness and aches and pains, followed by loss of appetite, nausea, vomiting, abdominal pain, dark urine, light-coloured faeces, jaundiced (yellow) skin and yellowing of the whites of the eyes. People who have had hepatitis should avoid alcohol for some time after the illness, as the liver needs time to recover.

Hepatitis A is transmitted by contaminated food and drinking water. You should seek medical advice, but there is not much you can do apart from resting, drinking lots of fluids, eating lightly and avoiding fatty foods. Hepatitis E is transmitted in the same way as hepatitis A; it can be particularly serious in pregnant women.

There are almost 300 million chronic carriers of hepatitis B in the world. It is spread through contact with infected blood, blood products or body fluids, for example through sexual contact, unsterilised needles and blood transfusions, or contact with blood via small breaks in the skin. Other risk situations include having a shave, tattoo or body piercing with contaminated equipment. The symptoms of hepatitis B may be more severe than type A and the disease can lead to long term problems such as chronic liver damage, liver cancer or a long term carrier state. Hepatitis C and D are spread in the same way as hepatitis B and can also lead to long term complications.

There are vaccines against hepatitis A and B, but there are currently no vaccines against the other types. Following the basic rules about food and water (hepatitis A and E) and avoiding risk situations (hepatitis B, C and D) are important preventative measures.

HIV & AIDS Infection with the human immunodeficiency virus (HIV) may lead to acquired immune deficiency syndrome (AIDS), which is a fatal disease. Any exposure to blood, blood products or body fluids may put the individual at risk. The disease is often transmitted through sexual contact or dirty needles – vaccinations, acupuncture, tattooing and body piercing can be potentially as dangerous as intravenous drug use. HIV/AIDS can also be spread through infected blood transfusions. Although India does have the resources to screen blood donations, extreme care should still be taken, as not all laboratories have adequate controls implemented to ensure this is done thoroughly.

If you do need an injection, ask to see the syringe unwrapped in front of you, or take a needle and syringe pack with you.

Fear of HIV infection should never preclude treatment for serious medical conditions.

AIDS in India

In 2000 India recorded the highest number of HIV infections on the planet, with 3.7 million reported cases of HIV – a figure believed to be artificially low as most AIDS cases and deaths go unreported. Mumbai has the highest rate of infection in India. In this city an estimated 72% of sex workers (who service an average of 50 clients each per day) are believed to be HIV-positive. Apart from sex workers, truck drivers (nationwide) also fall into the high-risk category.

In a country of more than one billion people, some health officials warn that unless there are dedicated educational programs and increased condom use throughout India, the number of HIV-positive cases could swell to a staggering 31 million by 2010.

Intestinal Worms These parasites are most common in rural, tropical areas. The different worms have different ways of infecting people. Some (eg, tapeworms) may be ingested on food such as undercooked meat and some (eg, hookworms) enter through your skin. Infestations may not show up for some time, and although they are generally not serious, if left untreated some can cause severe health problems later. Consider having a stool test when you return home to check for these and determine the appropriate treatment.

Meningococcal Meningitis This serious disease can be fatal. There are recurring epidemics in North India and Nepal.

A fever, severe headache, sensitivity to light and neck stiffness which prevents forward bending of the head are the first symptoms. There may also be purple patches on the skin. Death can occur within a few hours, so urgent medical treatment is required.

Trekkers to rural areas of Nepal should be particularly careful, as the disease is spread by close contact with people who carry it in their throats and noses and spread it through coughs and sneezes; they may not be aware that they are carriers. Lodges in the hills where travellers spend the night are prime spots for the spread of infection.

Treatment is large doses of penicillin given intravenously, or chloramphenicol injections.

Sexually Transmitted Infections HIV/AIDS and hepatitis B can be transmitted through sexual contact – see the relevant entries earlier for more details. Other STIs include gonorrhoea, herpes and syphilis; sores, blisters or rashes around the genitals and discharges or pain when urinating are common symptoms. In some STIs, such as wart virus or chlamydia, symptoms may be less marked or not observed at all, especially in women. Chlamydia infection can cause infertility in men and women before any symptoms have been noticed. Syphilis symptoms eventually disappear completely but the disease continues and can cause severe problems in later years. While abstinence from sexual contact is the only 100% effective prevention, using condoms is also effective. The treatment of gonorrhoea and syphilis is with antibiotics. The different sexually transmitted diseases each require specific antibiotics.

Travellers to India should consider bringing along condoms from their home country, which may be more reliable than local brands.

Typhoid This fever is a dangerous gut infection caused by contaminated water and food. Medical help must be sought.

In its early stages sufferers may feel they have a bad cold or flu on the way, as early symptoms are a headache, body aches and a fever which rises a little each day until it is around 40°C (104°F) or more. The victim's pulse is often slow relative to the degree of fever present – unlike a normal fever where the pulse increases. There may also be vomiting, abdominal pain, diarrhoea or constipation.

In the second week the high fever and slow pulse continue and a few pink spots may appear on the body; trembling, delirium, weakness, weight loss and dehydration may occur. Complications such as pneumonia, perforated bowel or meningitis may occur.

Insect-Borne Diseases

Filariasis, leishmaniasis, Lyme disease and typhus are all insect-borne diseases, but they do not pose a great risk to travellers. For more information on them see Less Common Diseases at the end of this Health section.

Travellers are advised to prevent mosquito bites at all times. The main messages are:

- Wear light-coloured clothing.
- Wear long trousers and long-sleeved shirts.
- Use mosquito repellents containing the compound DEET on exposed areas (prolonged overuse of DEET may be harmful, especially to children, but its use is considered preferable to being bitten by disease-transmitting mosquitoes).
- Avoid perfumes or aftershave.
- Use a mosquito net impregnated with mosquito repellent (permethrin) – it may be worth taking your own.
- Impregnating clothes with permethrin effectively deters mosquitoes and other insects.

Dengue Fever This viral disease is transmitted by mosquitoes and fast becoming one of the top public health problems in the tropical world. Unlike the malaria mosquito, the *Aedes aegypti* mosquito, which transmits the dengue virus, is most active during the day, and is found mainly in urban areas, in and around human dwellings.

Signs and symptoms of dengue fever include a sudden onset of high fever, headache, joint and muscle pains (hence its old name, 'breakbone fever') and nausea and vomiting. A rash of small red spots sometimes appears three to four days after the onset of fever. In the early phase of illness, dengue may be mistaken for other infectious diseases, including malaria and influenza. Minor bleeding such as nose bleeds may occur in the course of the illness, but this does not necessarily mean that you have progressed to the potentially fatal dengue haemorrhagic fever (DHF). This is a severe illness, characterised by heavy bleeding, which is thought to be a result of second infection due to a different strain (there are four major strains) and usually affects residents of the country rather than travellers. Recovery even from simple dengue fever may be prolonged, with tiredness lasting for several weeks.

You should seek medical attention as soon as possible if you think you may be infected. A blood test can exclude malaria and indicate the possibility of dengue fever. There is no specific treatment for dengue. Aspirin should be avoided, as it increases the risk of haemorrhaging. There is no vaccine against dengue fever. The best prevention is to avoid mosquito bites at all times by covering up, using insect repellents containing the compound DEET and mosquito nets – see the advise on avoiding mosquito bites earlier in this section.

Japanese B Encephalitis This viral infection of the brain is transmitted by mosquitoes. Most cases occur in rural areas as the virus exists in pigs and wading birds. Symptoms include fever, headache and alteration in consciousness. Hospitalisation is needed for correct diagnosis and treatment. There is a high mortality rate among those who have symptoms; of those who survive many are intellectually disabled.

Malaria This serious and potentially fatal disease is spread by mosquito bites. If you are travelling in endemic areas it is extremely important to avoid mosquito bites and to take tablets to prevent this disease. Symptoms range from fever, chills and sweating, headache, diarrhoea and abdominal pains to a vague feeling of ill-health. Seek medical help immediately if malaria is suspected. Without treatment malaria can rapidly become more serious and can be fatal.

If medical care is not available, malaria tablets can be used for treatment. You need to use a malaria tablet that is different from the one you were taking when you contracted malaria. The standard treatment dose of mefloquine is two 250mg tablets and a further two six hours later. For Fansidar, it's a single dose of three tablets. If you were previously taking mefloquine and cannot obtain Fansidar, then other alternatives are Malarone (atovaquone-proguanil; four tablets once daily for three days), halofantrine (three doses of two 250mg tablets every six hours) or quinine sulphate (600mg every six hours). There is a greater risk of side effects with these dosages than in normal use if used with mefloquine, so medical advice is preferable. Be aware also that halofantrine is no longer recommended by the WHO as emergency standby treatment, because of side effects, and should only be used if no other drugs are available.

Cuts, Bites & Stings

See Less Common Diseases later in this section for details of rabies, which is passed through animal bites.

Cuts & Scratches Wash well and treat any cut with an antiseptic such as povidone-iodine. Where possible avoid bandages and elastic plasters, which can keep wounds wet. Coral cuts are notoriously slow to heal and if they are not adequately cleaned, small pieces of coral can become embedded in the wound.

Bedbugs & Lice Bedbugs live in various places, but particularly in dirty mattresses and bedding, evidenced by spots of blood on bedclothes or on the wall. They can be a real problem at rock-bottom hotels in India. Bedbugs leave itchy bites in neat rows. Calamine lotion or a sting relief spray may help.

All lice cause itching and discomfort. They make themselves at home in your hair (head lice), your clothing (body lice) or in your pubic hair (crabs). You catch lice through direct contact with infected people or by sharing combs, clothing and the like. Powder or shampoo treatment will kill the lice and infected clothing should then be washed in very hot, soapy water and left in the sun to dry.

Bites & Stings Bee and wasp stings are usually painful rather than dangerous. However, in people who are allergic to them severe breathing difficulties may occur and require urgent medical care. Calamine lotion or a sting relief spray will give relief and ice packs will reduce the pain and swelling. There are some spiders with dangerous bites but antivenins are usually available. Scorpion stings are notoriously painful and can actually be fatal. Scorpions often shelter in shoes or clothing.

There are various fish and other sea creatures that can sting or bite dangerously or which are dangerous to eat – seek local advice.

Jellyfish Avoid contact with these sea creatures, which have stinging tentacles – seek local advice. Dousing in vinegar will deactivate any stingers which have not 'fired'.

Calamine lotion, antihistamines and analgesics may reduce the reaction and relieve the pain.

Leeches & Ticks Leeches may be present in damp rainforest conditions; they attach themselves to your skin to suck your blood. Trekkers often get them on their legs or in their boots. Salt or a lighted cigarette end will make them fall off. Do not pull them off, as the bite is then more likely to become infected. Clean and apply pressure if the point of attachment is bleeding. An insect repellent may keep them away.

You should always check all over your body if you have been walking through a potentially tick-infested area as ticks can cause skin infections and other more serious diseases. If a tick is found attached, press down around the tick's head with tweezers, grab the head and gently pull upwards. Avoid pulling the rear of the body as this may squeeze the tick's gut contents through the attached mouth parts into the skin, increasing the risk of infection and disease. Smearing chemicals on the tick will not make it let go and is not recommended.

Snakes To minimise your chances of being bitten always wear boots, socks and long trousers when walking through undergrowth where snakes may be present. Don't put your hands into holes and crevices, and be careful when collecting firewood.

Snake bites do not cause instantaneous death and antivenins are usually available. Immediately wrap the bitten limb tightly, as you would for a sprained ankle, and then attach a splint to immobilise it. Keep the victim still and seek medical help, if possible with the dead snake for identification. Don't attempt to catch the snake if there is a possibility of being bitten again. Tourniquets and sucking out the poison are now comprehensively discredited.

Women's Health

Gynaecological Problems Antibiotic use, synthetic underwear, sweating and contraceptive pills can lead to fungal vaginal infections, especially when travelling in hot climates. Thrush or vaginal candidiasis is characterised by a rash, itch and discharge. Nystatin, miconazole or clotrimazole pessaries are the usual treatment, but some people use a more traditional remedy involving vinegar or lemon-juice douches, or yogurt. Maintaining good personal hygiene and wearing loose-fitting clothes and cotton underwear may help prevent these infections.

Sexually transmitted diseases are a major cause of vaginal problems. Symptoms include a smelly discharge, painful intercourse and sometimes a burning sensation when urinating. Medical attention should be sought and male sexual partners must also be treated. For more details see under Sexually Transmitted Infections earlier. Besides abstinence, the best thing is to practise safer sex using condoms.

Pregnancy It is not advisable to travel to some places while pregnant as some vaccinations used to prevent serious dieases are not advisable during pregnancy (eg, yellow fever and cholera). In addition, some diseases are much more serious for pregnant women (eg, malaria and hepatitis E), and may increase the risk of a stillborn child.

Most miscarriages occur during the first three months of pregnancy. Miscarriage is not uncommon and can occasionally lead to severe bleeding. The last three months should also be spent within reasonable distance of good medical care. A baby born as early as 24 weeks stands a chance of survival, but only in a good modern hospital. Pregnant women should avoid all unnecessary medication, although vaccinations and malarial prophylactics should still be taken where needed. Additional care should be taken to prevent illness and particular attention should be paid to diet and nutrition. Alcohol and nicotine, for example, should be avoided.

Less Common Diseases

The following diseases pose a small risk to travellers, and so are only mentioned in passing. Seek medical advice if you think you may have any of these diseases.

Cholera This is one of the worst types of diarrhoea and medical help should be sought. Outbreaks of cholera are generally widely reported, so you can avoid such problem areas. *Fluid replacement is the most vital treatment* – the risk of dehydration is severe as you may lose up to 20L a day. If there is a delay in getting to hospital, then begin taking tetracycline. The adult dose is 250mg four times daily. It is not recommended for children under nine years nor for pregnant women. Tetracycline may help shorten the illness, but adequate fluids are required to save lives.

Filariasis This is a mosquito-transmitted parasitic infection found in various countries including India. Possible symptoms include fever, pain and swelling of the lymph glands; inflammation of lymph drainage areas; swelling of a limb or the scrotum; skin rashes; and blindness. Treatment is available to eliminate the parasites from the body, but some of the damage already caused may not be reversible. Medical advice should be obtained promptly if the infection is suspected.

Leishmaniasis This is a group of parasitic diseases transmitted by sandflies, which are found in India and other parts of the world. Cutaneous leishmaniasis affects the skin tissue causing ulceration and disfigurement, and visceral leishmaniasis affects the internal organs. Seek medical advice, as laboratory testing is required for diagnosis and correct treatment. Avoiding sandfly bites is the best precaution. Bites are usually painless, itchy and yet another reason to cover up and apply repellent.

Lyme Disease This is a tick-transmitted infection that may be acquired in India. The illness usually begins with a spreading rash at the site of the tick bite and is accompanied by fever, headache, extreme fatigue, aching joints and muscles and mild neck stiffness. If untreated, these symptoms usually resolve over several weeks but over subsequent weeks or months disorders of the nervous system, heart and joints may develop. Treatment works best early in the illness. Medical help should be sought.

Rabies This fatal viral infection is found in many countries, including India. Many animals can be infected (such as dogs, cats, bats and monkeys) and it is their saliva which is infectious. Any bite, scratch or even lick from an animal should be cleaned immediately and thoroughly. Scrub with soap and running water, and then apply alcohol or iodine solution. Medical help should be sought promptly to receive a course of injections to prevent the onset of symptoms and death.

Tetanus This disease is caused by a germ that lives in soil and in the faeces of horses and other animals. It enters the body via breaks in the skin. The first symptom may be discomfort in swallowing, or stiffening of the jaw and neck; this is followed by painful convulsions of the jaw and whole body. The disease can be fatal. It can be prevented by vaccination.

Tuberculosis Tuberculosis (TB) is a bacterial infection usually transmitted from person to person by coughing but which may be transmitted through consumption of unpasteurised milk. Milk that has been boiled is safe to drink, and the souring of milk to make yogurt or cheese also kills the bacilli. Travellers are usually not at great risk as close household contact with the infected person is usually required before the disease is passed on. You may need to have a TB test before you travel as this can help diagnose the disease later if you become ill.

Typhus This disease is spread by ticks, mites or lice. It begins with fever, chills, headache and muscle pains followed a few days later by a body rash. There is often a large painful sore at the site of the bite and nearby lymph nodes are swollen and painful. Typhus can be treated under medical supervision. Seek local advice on areas where ticks pose a danger and always check your skin carefully for ticks after walking in a danger area such as a tropical forest. An insect repellent can help, and walkers in tick-infested areas should consider having their boots and trousers impregnated with benzyl benzoate and dibutylphthalate.

WOMEN TRAVELLERS

India is generally perfectly safe for women travellers, including those travelling alone. Although foreign women (including those of Indian descent) have been hassled, being ogled (incessantly) is the most you'll probably encounter. The tips provided in this section are intended to cut the hassles, not to alarm you. See the boxed text 'Sexual Harassment' for more information.

Women travelling with a male partner are less likely to be harassed. However, a foreign woman of Indian descent travelling with a non-Indian male may cop disapproving stares; having a non-Indian partner is still not condoned in many parts of India.

Being a woman has some advantages. Women can usually queue-jump without consequence, use ladies-only carriages on trains, and sometimes get free entry into nightclubs. There are even special ladies' sections in some cinemas, restaurants and other public places.

What to Wear

Staying safe is a matter of common sense and culturally appropriate behaviour. Close attention to standards of dress will go a long way to minimising problems for female travellers (see also Society & Conduct in the Facts about North India chapter). Refrain from wearing sleeveless blouses, shorts, skimpy or tight-fitting clothing and, of course, the bra-less look. Women who publicly flash ample flesh are not only making themselves an easy target for sexual harassment, they're also making it hard for fellow travellers by painting a poor image of foreign women in general.

Wearing Indian dress, when done properly, makes a positive impression. However, going into public wearing a *choli* (small tight blouse worn under a sari) or a sari petticoat (which many foreign women mistake for a skirt) is rather like strutting around half dressed – don't do it. On the other hand, the *salwar kameez* (traditional Punjabi long shirt and trouser combination) is considered to be respectable attire and has become increasingly popular among female travellers. It's practical, comfortable, attractive and comes in a range of prices. A cotton salwar kameez is also surprisingly cool in the hot weather and keeps the burning sun off your skin. The *dupatta* (scarf) that is worn with this outfit is handy if you visit a shrine that requires your head to be covered.

Staying Safe

Getting constantly stared at is something you'll simply have to get used to. Don't allow it to get the better of you. Just walk confidently and refrain from returning male stares, as this may be considered a come-on; dark glasses can help. A good way to block out stares in restaurants is to take along a book or letters to write home.

Whenever you wish to keep conversations short (especially when dealing with male service staff at hotels) get to the point as quickly and politely as possible. Getting involved in inane conversations with men can be considered a turn-on. Questions such as 'did you know your eyes are like the sunset?' or 'do you have a boyfriend?' are strong indicators that the conversation is getting too steamy. Some women prepare in advance by wearing a pseudo wedding ring, or by announcing early on in the conversation that they are married or engaged (regardless of whether they are or not!). This is a highly effective way of keeping interactions 'lust free'. If you still get the uncomfortable feeling that he's encroaching on your space, the chances are that he is. A firm request to keep away is usually enough to take control of the situation – especially if it's loud enough to draw the attention of passers-by.

On trains and buses, don't hesitate to return any errant limbs, put some item of luggage in between you and, if all else fails, find a new spot. You're also within your rights to tell him to shove off! It's wise to arrive in towns before it gets dark and, of course, avoid walking alone at night especially in isolated areas.

Other harassment women travellers have encountered includes lewd comments, provocative gestures, jeering, getting 'accidentally' bumped into on the street, and being groped. There have been several reported cases of rape among foreign women. Exuberant special events (such as the Holi festival) can pose problems for women (see Dangers & Annoyances later in this chapter).

Sexual Harassment

Foreign women are not alone when it comes to unwanted male attention. In recent years there have been more and more reports of Indian women being subjected to what is locally dubbed as 'Eve-teasing' (a euphemistic term for what is invariably sexual harassment). One recent newspaper report went so far to say that up to 80% of city women are subjected to 'this disgusting experience once in awhile', predominantly at college campuses and bazaars. According to authorities, most Eve-teasers are groups of lusty teenagers and university students, many the sons of wealthy families.

Good-intentioned authorities have made laudable attempts to deal with the problem. For instance, in Indore (Madhya Pradesh) police launched 'Operation Rangeen' aimed at stamping out Eve-teasing; regrettably the campaign failed to yield adequate results and was promptly shelved. Meanwhile, in some Indian police stations, special 'We Care for You' units have been set up with the sole intent of encouraging women to report sexual harassment. However, the response to this has also been disappointing. Many women have said they're too ashamed to file reports. Some have openly declared that they have no faith in the system because they've been harassed by men of the law in the past. Other women have simply been too afraid to lodge complaints after receiving brutal threats from their perpetrators if they 'blab to the cops'.

GAY & LESBIAN TRAVELLERS

Although the more liberal sections of certain cities (predominantly the larger centres such as Delhi and Kolkata) are becoming more tolerant of homosexuality, generally gay life is still largely suppressed in India. You may see Indian men holding hands with each other or engaged in other public affectionate behaviour, but don't instantly assume they are gay; this is an accepted expression of non-sexual friendship.

Since marriage is still very highly regarded in India, most gay people stay in the closet or risk being disowned by their families and society.

As with relations between heterosexual Western couples travelling in India – both married and unmarried – gay and lesbian travellers should exercise discretion and refrain from displaying overt affection towards each other in public.

India's most visible nonheterosexual group are the hijras – a caste of transvestites and eunuchs who dress in women's clothing. Some are gay, some are hermaphrodites, and some were unfortunate enough to be kidnapped and castrated. As it is traditionally unacceptable to live openly as a gay man, hijras get around this by becoming, in effect, a sort of third sex. They work mainly as uninvited entertainers at weddings and celebrations of the birth of male children, and as prostitutes.

Legal Status

Homosexual relations for men are illegal in India. Section 377 of the national legislation forbids 'carnal intercourse against the order of nature' (that is, anal intercourse). The penalties for transgression can be up to life imprisonment. There is no law against lesbian relations.

Publications & Internet Resources

The Mumbai publication *Bombay Dost* is a popular gay and lesbian magazine available at a number of bookshops and news stands in various Indian cities.

Delhi's gay magazine, *Darpan*, is published by the gay group Humrahi and can be found at city bookshops and pavement stalls.

For more information about India's gay scene, some excellent Web sites include: Gay Delhi (www.members.tripod.com/gaydelhi), Bombay Dost (www.bombay-dost.com); Gay Bombay (www.gaybombay.com); Humrahi (www.geocities.com/West Hollywood/Heights/7258); and also Humsafar (www.humsafar.org).

DISABLED TRAVELLERS

Travelling in India can entail some fairly rigorous challenges, even for the able-bodied traveller – long bus trips in crowded vehicles between remote villages, the crush of people in larger towns and the steep staircases in some budget and mid-range hotels can test even the hardiest traveller. If you can't walk, these challenges are increased many-fold. Very few buildings have access for wheelchairs (the Taj Mahal has, though); toilets have certainly not been designed to accommodate wheelchairs; and footpaths, where they exist (only in larger towns), are generally riddled with holes, littered with debris and packed with pedestrians, severely restricting mobility.

Nevertheless, seeing the mobility-impaired locals whiz through city traffic at breakneck speed in modified bicycles may serve as inspiration! Also, there are faint stirrings that the needs of disabled people are being addressed; eg, in Sanchi (Madhya Pradesh), there's now a wheelchair ramp at the Buddhist site, and information on the monuments is available in Braille.

If your mobility is restricted you will need a strong, able-bodied companion to accompany you, and it would be well worth considering hiring a private vehicle and driver.

Organisations that may be able to assist with information on travel practicalities in India for disabled people include:

Holiday Care Service (☎ 01293-77 4535), 2nd floor, Imperial Buildings, Victoria Rd, Horley, Surrey, RH6 7PZ
Web site: www.holidaycare.org.uk

The Royal Association for Disability and Rehabilitation (Radar; ☎ 020-7250 3222, fax 7250 0212, e radar@radar.org.uk), 12 City Forum, 250 City Rd, London EC1V 8AF, UK
Web site: www.radar.org.uk

Society for Accessible Travel & Hospitality (☎ 212-447 7284, e sathtravel@aol.com), 347 5th Ave, Suite 610, New York, NY 10016, USA
Web site: www.sath.org

Wheelchair Travel (☎ 1800-674 468, e sales@travelability.com), 29 Ranelagh Dr, Mount Eliza, VIC 3930, Australia
Web site: www.travelability.com

SENIOR TRAVELLERS

Unless your mobility or vision is impaired or you're incapacitated in any other way, there is absolutely no reason why the senior traveller should not consider North India as a potential holiday destination.

It's worth keeping in mind that travelling in India can be downright exhausting (even for the most effervescent young traveller), so don't make the mistake of cramming too much sightseeing into a day. In fact, it's not a bad idea to set aside several intermittent days devoted purely to doing absolutely nothing – a tremendous way to recharge your batteries.

If you like your creature comforts, opt for top-end or mid-range hotels (although some mid-range places are far from luxurious) and consider incorporating some organised tours into your trip (see regional chapters for details). Tour buses tend to let you off in more convenient locations than public buses. Alternatively, many senior travellers hire a car and driver, which allows greater flexibility (and comfort) in moving around than does public transport (see Car in the Getting Around chapter). No matter what you plan to do in India, it's wise to discuss your proposed trip with your local GP (see also Health, earlier in this chapter).

TRAVEL WITH CHILDREN

India is a very child-friendly destination, not so much because of facilities available for kids, but rather in the way children are accepted being seen and heard. Indeed children can often enhance your encounters with local people, as they possess little of the self-consciousness and sense of the cultural differences that can inhibit interaction between adults.

Being a family-oriented society, children are heartily welcomed at most hotels and restaurants. A number of hotels have 'family rooms' or will happily provide an extra bed. Some upmarket hotels also offer babysitting services.

When it comes to meals, although few restaurants offer a special children's menu, many will happily whip up simple requests. Staff don't usually get snooty if your little angels treat the dining area a bit like a playroom (please take the initiative to ensure they don't ruin it for other diners though).

It's worth bringing along some favourite books, toys and hand-held video games to keep the children occupied when you need some quiet time. If you're staying in a hotel with cable TV, there are several English-language children's channels, including the Cartoon Network.

Despite the acceptance of children, travelling with kids in India can be hard work and, ideally, the burden needs to be shared between two adults. Although caution should be exercised at all times, be especially careful near roads, as Indian traffic can be erratic, even in smaller towns. Any long-distance road travel undertaken should include adequate stops, as rough road conditions can make travel more tiring than usual, especially for little ones. Train travel is usually a more comfortable mode of transport. Remember to bring enough sunscreen and a wide-brimmed hat, as the midday sun can really pack a punch (even during winter). Always carry sufficient drinking water.

Standard baby products such as nappies (diapers) are available in big cities and even in smaller towns; the larger cities often stock some Western brands too, but they can be expensive. To give you an idea of costs, Nestle baby food costs Rs 77 (400g), locally made diapers are Rs 160 (pack of 10), and Lactogen milk powder is Rs 236 (1kg tin). It's wise to bring along any special items, such as medication or baby food if your child is fussy, from home, just in case you can't locate them in India. Travellers have also recommended that parents bring a washable changing mat, which comes in handy for covering dirty surfaces.

For details about attractions for children (such as zoos, amusement parks, sound-and-light shows, guided horse rides in the hill stations) see the regional chapters.

See Health earlier in this chapter for important tips, and get hold of a copy of Lonely Planet's *Travel with Children* by Maureen Wheeler. A good Web site for a personal account of travelling in India with children is www.southwest.com.au/~lockley. Lonely Planet's Thorn Tree Web site (www.lonelyplanet.com.au) has a subdirectory on travelling with children.

DANGERS & ANNOYANCES

Tourists (and residents) can get robbed, duped or scammed anywhere and everywhere in the world. Although we provide warnings about current scams and other potential dangers in this section, there's no need to be suspicious to the point of paranoia. We certainly don't intend to paint a negative picture of India or its people. It would be a shame if an overriding preoccupation with the potential problems inhibited you from participating in activities and meeting Indian people. India is renowned for its hospitality to visitors, so don't go jeopardising potential friendships by prematurely jumping to the conclusion that *everyone* is out to get you. They're not. Yes, there are hassles and yes, the touts and tricksters can wear you down at times, but you achieve nothing taking out your frustrations on ordinary people. A regrettable consequence of touts and others who pester tourists is that many paranoid foreigners are getting a reputation for rudeness towards genuinely friendly Indian people, especially in places such as Delhi and parts of Rajasthan. Consider this advice culled from the many readers letters LP receives every week:

Relax! Trust the people. Use the usual cautions but apart from that there is no need to be paranoid. Indians are great people, a bit curious but that's all, be patient and give them a chance. There is no point seeing India through a stained window of an air-con bus.

Kosta Matejic

In my experience India was very safe and the Indians I met were, almost without exception, warm, friendly and charming; even the hustlers hustle you with good humour. India's bad rep does deter Westerners from visiting and it may partially explain (although not justify) the appalling rudeness, aggression and hostility I witnessed from some of my fellow travellers towards Indians.

Frank Curran

Like anywhere else, common sense and reasonable caution are your best weapons against theft or worse. The tips we offer are intended to alert you to possible risks in India; most are based on travellers reports. During your trip, it's worth taking the time to chat with other travellers, hotel staff, tour operators etc, in order to stay abreast of the latest potential hazards.

Theft

Never leave those most-important valuables (passport, tickets, money) in your room; you should be keep them with you at all times (see Security under Money earlier). When travelling on trains, keep your all gear near you; padlocking a bag to a luggage rack can be useful, and some of the newer trains have loops under the seats which you can chain things to. Never walk around with valuables casually slung over your shoulder. Take extra care on crowded public transport.

Thieves are particularly prevalent on train routes where there are lots of tourists. The Delhi to Agra *Shatabdi Express* service is particularly notorious; no matter which train you are travelling on, exercise caution at all times. Train departure time, when the confusion and crowds are at their worst, is the time to be most careful. Just as the train is about to leave, someone may attempt to distract you while their accomplice is stealing your bag from by your feet. Airports are another place to be careful, especially when international arrivals take place in the middle of the night, when you are unlikely to be at your most alert.

From time to time there are also drugging episodes. Travellers meet somebody on a train or bus or in a town, start talking and are then offered a chai or something similar. Hours later they wake up with a headache and all their gear gone, the tea having been full of sleeping pills. Be cautious about accepting drinks or food from strangers, particularly if you're on your own.

Beware also of your fellow travellers. Unhappily, there are enough backpackers who make their money go a little bit further by helping themselves to other people's.

Keep in mind that backpacks are very easy to rifle through. Never leave valuables in them, especially during flights. Remember also that something may be of little or no value to a thief, but to lose it would be a real heartbreak to you – such as used film or your journal.

A good travel insurance policy is essential. If you do have something stolen, you're going to have to report it to the police.

You'll also need a statement proving you have done so if you want to make an insurance claim. Insurance companies, despite their rosy promises of full protection and speedy settlement of claims, are just as disbelieving as the Indian police and will often attempt every trick in the book to avoid paying out on a baggage claim. Note that some policies specify that you must report an item stolen to the police within a certain amount of time after you observe that it is missing.

Travellers Cheques If you're unlucky enough to have things stolen, some precautions can ease the pain. All travellers cheques are replaceable, although this does you little immediate good if you have to go home and apply to your bank. What you want is instant replacement. Furthermore, what do you do if you lose your cheques and money and have a day or more to travel to the replacement office? The answer is to keep an emergency cash stash in a totally separate place. In that same place you should keep a record of the cheques' serial numbers, proof of purchase slips, encashment vouchers and your passport number.

AmEx and others tend to make considerable noise about 'instant replacement' of their cheques but a lot of people find out, to their cost, that without a number of precautions 'instantly' can take longer than you think. If you don't have the receipt you were given when you bought the cheques, rapid replacement will be difficult. Obviously the receipt should be kept separate from the cheques, and a photocopy in yet another location doesn't hurt either.

To replace lost AmEx travellers cheques, you need a photocopy of the police report and one photo, as well as the proof-of-purchase slip and the numbers of the missing cheques. If you don't have the latter they will contact the place where you bought them. If you've had the lot stolen, AmEx is empowered to give you limited funds while all this is going on. For lost or stolen cheques, it has a 24-hour number in Delhi (☎ 011-6145151), which you must ring within 24 hours.

Holi Festival

The Hindu festival of Holi (see Public Holidays & Special Events later in this chapter) is usually loads of fun, but some merrymakers can go too far. Celebrated in late February or early March, the last day is marked with the exuberant and excessive throwing of coloured powder and water. Some travellers have been doused with toxic substances mixed in water, leaving them with painful and disfiguring scars.

On the last day of Holi there is an unwritten tradition of guzzling alcohol and consuming cannabis-derived *bhang* in the form of lassis (yogurt drink), pakoras and cookies. Female travellers have reported being indecently assaulted by spaced-out men – particularly in tourist traps such as Rajasthan. It's advisable for women to avoid venturing onto the streets alone on the last day of Holi when this festival reaches its (often unruly) climax.

Contaminated Food & Drink

Sometimes microbes aren't the sole, or main, risk when it comes to eating and drinking. In Rajasthan and other places bhang lassis can pack more of a punch than the hapless traveller would expect (see Drinks, later in this chapter).

There have been reports of scams at some private clinics that provide more treatment than is necessary for stomach upsets in order to procure larger medical insurance claims – get several opinions where possible. Worse still, a serious food scare broke out in northern India in 1998, principally in Agra and Varanasi, when numerous travellers became sick (three died) after eating at local establishments. The scam, which was arranged to get travellers to seek medical assistance from particular doctors, seems to have been quashed, but keep alert (see the boxed text 'Diarrhoea with Your Meal, Sir?' in the Uttar Pradesh chapter).

Water can also be a potential problem. Always ensure the seal is intact on bought mineral water and also check that the bottom of the bottle has not been tampered with. A traveller has reported that he was sold drugged mineral water. Crush plastic bottles after use to eradicate the possibility of them being resold with contaminated water. Better still, avoid bottled water altogether and purify your own (see Responsible Tourism earlier in this chapter for a discussion of the environmental issues involved).

Risky Regions

In the past few years close to two dozen foreigners have vanished or been murdered in the Kullu region. You're advised to trek in an organised group and steer clear of drugs (see Legal Matters later in this chapter). Trekkers should also make a point of telling people where they are going and when they will be back. See the boxed text 'Fatal Vacations' in the Himachal Pradesh chapter for details.

Some sensitive border areas, particularly strife-torn Jammu & Kashmir are subject to terrorist activities including kidnappings. Although you may be cajoled by smooth-talking touts trying to get you to these areas (especially in Delhi), seek the latest advice from your embassy.

Regional chapters have further important warnings relating to specific areas.

Racism

It's not unusual for black travellers to encounter outright racism in India. African students in India will often tell of racist attitudes towards them, ranging from name calling to being refused admission to certain restaurants and nightclubs.

Although skin colour is not always related to caste in India, lighter shades of brown are considered more attractive than dark skin – just have a look at the matrimonial pages in Indian newspapers and you'll see that being 'fair' is often a prerequisite for a potential spouse.

Although not all black travellers encounter racism during their time in India, at the very least they should be prepared for even more incessant (often disapproving) stares than lighter-skinned travellers.

Natural Disasters

Every year monsoonal floods sweep through parts of the north as rivers break their banks. There are always some deaths and some buildings washed away, so be sure to keep abreast of weather reports if you're travelling at this time. In September 2000 the worst floods for 25 years hit West Bengal, claiming 1500 lives and leaving 12 million people homeless.

India is not a high-risk earthquake area, but in 2001 a quake killed over 30,000 people (some estimates put the number at as many as 100,000), injured 300,000 and made half a million homeless. It hit on 26 January, and was measured at 7.9 on the Richter scale. The force unleashed was 30,000 times greater than that generated by the atomic bombs dropped on Japan in WWII. The epicentre was near Bhuj, in Gujarat, though the shockwaves of India's worst earthquake for 50 years were felt as far away as Delhi and Mumbai. Some villages in the vicinity of the Gulf of Kutch suffered the destruction of 90% of their buildings, and some historical monuments in Jaisalmer in Rajasthan were also damaged. See the boxed text 'The Gujarat Earthquake of 2001' in the Facts about North India chapter.

A professor at Delhi's Jawaharlal Nehru University, who correctly forecast the earthquake a year earlier, has warned that tremors could rock Delhi and Jabalpur (Madhya Pradesh) in the near future. Saumitra Mukherjee of the Center for Environmental Studies said he based his calculations on sun spots and the emission of large quantities of energy from the outer regions of the sun.

Other Important Warnings

Several women have reported being molested by masseurs and other therapists in McLeod Ganj (Himachal Pradesh). No matter where you are, it's always wise to check the reputation of any teacher or therapist before going along to a solo session. If at any time you feel uneasy, simply leave.

Many travellers have reported being hoodwinked by fake gurus, sometimes resulting in theft, injury or worse – see the boxed text 'Gurus, Ashrams & Your Spiritual Journey', later in this chapter.

For important information about current cons, including notorious gem rackets, see

Carbon Monoxide Poisoning

Fires – charcoal burners in particular – are not recommended as a means of heating in hotel rooms, because a number of deaths from carbon monoxide poisoning occur each year.

If you're cold, and unsure of the ventilation in the room, take a tip from trekkers who fill their drinking bottles with boiling water at night to use as a hot-water bottle (covered with a sock to prevent burning). In the morning, the water can be drunk because it's been purified. Some hotels even provide hot-water bottles. At all costs, *never* use a charcoal burner.

the boxed text 'Buyer Beware!' in the Shopping section, later in this chapter. The boxed text 'Choose Carefully' has tips on assessing adventure activity operators. Meanwhile, the boxed text 'About Touts' under Accommodation later in this chapter, has details about the hotel commission racket.

Indian beaches can have dangerous rips and currents and many people drown on them each year. Don't assume there'll be warning signs erected. Exercise caution and always ask around locally before swimming anywhere in the sea.

For information about *bandhs* (strikes), see the North-Eastern Region chapter. Finally, all travellers should read the boxed text 'Carbon Monoxide Poisoning' for crucial advice about heating rooms.

EMERGENCIES

Hospitals and other emergency services are listed in the regional chapters. Throughout many parts of India, local emergency numbers are:

ambulance	☎ 102
fire	☎ 101
police	☎ 100

LEGAL MATTERS

If you find yourself in a sticky legal predicament, immediately contact your embassy (see Embassies & Consulates earlier in this chapter). Foreign travellers are subject to Indian laws and in the Indian justice system it can often seem that the burden of proof is on the accused.

You should carry your passport with you at all times and the less you have to do with local police the better.

Drugs

India has long been known for its smorgasbord of illegal drugs (mostly grass and hashish), but would-be users should be aware of the severe risks. Apart from opening yourself up to being taken advantage of (see the boxed text 'Beware Of Those Bhang Lassis!' under Drinks later in this chapter), the penalties for possession, use and trafficking in illegal drugs are enforced and Westerners have been jailed. If convicted on a drugs-related charge, sentences are a *minimum* of 10 years for trafficking and at least a year for possession. In addition, there's usually a hefty monetary fine. Court appearances can be slow – in early 2000 there were an estimated 25 million cases waiting to be heard in courts around India! Places where drugs are widespread (eg, Manali) are often the riskiest places to get involved in drug deals.

BUSINESS HOURS

Official business hours are generally 9.30 am to 5.30 pm Monday to Friday. Unofficially they tend to be more 10 am to 5 pm. Government offices particularly seem to have lengthy lunch hours which are sacrosanct and can last from noon to late into the afternoon.

Most banks are open from 10 am to 2 pm on weekdays, and 10 am to noon on Saturday – there are variations, so it pays to check. Travellers cheque transactions usually cease 30 minutes before the official bank closing time. In some tourist centres there may be foreign exchange offices that stay open longer (eg, Thomas Cook is open 9.30 am to 6 pm Monday to Saturday).

In the state capitals, the main post office is generally open from 10 am to 5 pm weekdays and on Saturday morning. Many public institutions such as museums and galleries close at least one day during the week (see regional chapters for details).

Shop hours vary from state to state, but most tend to open from around 10 am to late afternoon daily (except Sunday). It's wise to check locally.

PUBLIC HOLIDAYS & SPECIAL EVENTS

Rich in religions and traditions, India has scores of vibrant holidays and festivals. Many festivals occur during Purnima (full moon) which traditionally is considered to be auspicious. Some Web sites with information on festivals in India include: www.hindunet.org/festivals and www.indiatimes.com/.

The 'wedding season' generally falls between the cooler months of November and late March (although dates still revolve around the most auspicious dates as set by astrologers). If you visit during this period, you're likely to see at least one wedding procession on the streets of cities, towns or villages – a merry mix of singing and dancing, and a loud brass band.

Most holidays and festivals follow either the Indian lunar calendar (a complex system determined chiefly by astrologers) or the Islamic calendar (which falls about 11 days earlier each year; 12 days earlier in leap years), and therefore changes from year to year according to the strictures of the Gregorian calendar.

The India-wide holidays and festivals listed below are arranged according to the Indian lunar (and Gregorian) calendar that starts in Chaitra (March or April) – contact local tourist offices for the exact dates (especially for Muslim festivals, which have particularly variable dates). The Sikhs used to use the lunar calendar, but in 1999 adopted their own Nanakshahi calendar, which takes as its starting point the birth of Nanak Dev, the first Guru, in 1469. Though the months have different names, dates are fixed relative to the Gregorian calendar.

See the Festivals table at the start of each regional chapter for regional festivities, Special Events headings in regional chapters and Festivals & Other Special Events under Highlights at the beginning of this chapter.

Chaitra (Mar/Apr)

Mahavir Jayanti This Jain festival commemorates the birth of Mahavira, the founder of Jainism.

Ramanavami Hindu temples all over India celebrate the birth of Rama. In the week leading up to Ramanavami, the Ramayana is widely read and performed.

Easter This Christian holiday marks the crucifixion and resurrection of Christ.

Vaisakha (Apr/May)

Muharram This 10-day Muslim festival commemorates the martyrdom of Mohammed's grandson, Imam Hussain.

Buddha Jayanti This 'triple blessed festival' falls on the full moon and celebrates the Buddha's birth, enlightenment and attainment of final nirvana. Processions of monks carrying sacred scriptures pass through the streets of Gangtok (Sikkim) and other towns. In Himalaya regions it is called Saga Darwa. The Buddha Jayanti usually falls in May, though it can also fall in late April or early June – see the Varanasi festivals boxed text in the Uttar Pradesh chapter for dates over the next few years.

Jyaistha (May/June)

Milad-un-Nabi This Muslim festival celebrates the birth of Mohammed.

Asadha (Jun/July)

Martyrdom of Guru Arjan Dev This Sikh festival is in memory of the fifth Guru, who was burnt to death at the stake. It falls on 16 June (the 2nd day of Harh), and includes the offering of lassi to passers-by.

Sravana (July/Aug)

Naag Panchami This Hindu festival is dedicated to Ananta, the serpent upon whose coils Vishnu rested between universes. Offerings are made to snake images, and snake charmers do a roaring trade. Snakes are supposed to have power over the monsoon rainfall and keep evil from homes.

Raksha Bandhan (Narial Purnima) On the full-moon day girls fix amulets known as *rakhis* to their brothers' (not necessarily blood related) wrists to protect them in the coming year. The brothers reciprocate with gifts. Some people also worship the Vedic sea-god deity Varuna on this day.

Bhadra (Aug/Sept)

Independence Day This public holiday on 15 August celebrates the anniversary of India's independence from Britain in 1947. The prime minister delivers an address from the ramparts of Delhi's Red Fort.

Drukpa Teshi This festival celebrates the first teaching given by the Buddha.

Ganesh Chaturthi This joyful festival celebrates the birth of the popular elephant-headed god, Ganesh. It is widely celebrated across India. Firecrackers explode at all hours and families buy clay idols of Ganesh, the god of good fortune. On the last day of the festival the idols are paraded through the streets before being ceremoniously dunked in a river, sea or tank.

Janmashthami The anniversary of Krishna's birth is celebrated with happy abandon – in tune with Krishna's own mischievous moods. Devotees fast all day until midnight. In Mathura (Krishna's birthplace) the festivities last for an entire month and involve the ritual of *ghata* where temples are entirely decked out in a single colour (including the roof and the idols), accompanied by vast amounts of singing and dancing.

Shravan Purnima On this day of fasting, high-caste Hindus replace the sacred thread, which they always wear looped over their left shoulder.

Pateti Parsis celebrate their new year at this time.

Asvina (Sept/Oct)

Dussehra The popular festival celebrates Durga's victory over the buffalo-headed demon Mahishasura. In many places it culminates with the burning of huge images of the demon king Ravana and his accomplices, symbolic of the triumph of good over evil. In Delhi it is known as Ram Lila (Life story of Rama) and celebrated with fireworks and re-enactments of the Ramayana. In West Bengal the festival is known as Durga Puja and in Gujarat it's Navratri (Festival of Nine Nights). In Kullu, the festival begins a week later than elsewhere.

Gandhi Jayanti This public holiday is a solemn celebration of Gandhi's birthday on 2 October with prayer meetings at the Raj Ghat in Delhi where he was cremated.

Kartika (Oct/Nov)

Diwali (Deepavali) This is the happiest (and noisiest) festival of the Hindu calendar, celebrated on the 15th day of Kartika. At night decorative oil lamps are lit to show Rama the way home from his period of exile. The festival is also dedicated to Lakshmi and (in Kolkata) to Kali. In all, the festival lasts five days. On the first day, houses are thoroughly cleaned and doorsteps are decorated with intricate *rangolis* (chalk designs). Day two is dedicated to Krishna's victory over Narakasura, a legendary tyrant. Day three is spent worshipping Lakshmi, the goddess of wealth. Traditionally, this is the beginning of the new financial year for companies. Day four commemorates the visit of the friendly demon Bali whom Vishnu put in his place. On the fifth day men visit their sisters to have a tikka put on their forehead. Diwali has also become the 'festival of sweets'. Giving sweets has become as much a part of the tradition as the lighting of oil lamps and firecrackers.

Govardhana Puja A Hindu festival dedicated to that holiest of animals, the cow.

Aghan (Nov/Dec)

Nanak Jayanti The birthday of Guru Nanak, the founder of Sikhism, is celebrated with prayer readings and processions.

Ramadan This 30-day dawn-to-dusk fast is the most auspicious Muslim festival. It was during this month that the Prophet Mohammed had the Quran revealed to him in Mecca. This festival generally occurs between November and December, but can also fall in early January.

Eid-ul-Fitr This is a day of feasting to celebrate the end of Ramadan.

Pausa (Dec/Jan)

Christmas Day Christians celebrate the anniversary of the birth of Christ on 25 December.

Magha (Jan/Feb)

Republic Day This public holiday on 26 January celebrates the anniversary of India's establishment as a republic in 1950; there are activities in all state capitals but most spectacularly in Delhi, where there is a colourful military parade along Rajpath. As part of the same celebration, three days later a 'Beating of the Retreat' ceremony takes place near Delhi's Rashtrapati Bhavan, the residence of the Indian president.

Vasant Panchami It is traditional to dress in yellow to celebrate this Hindu festival, held on the 5th day of Magha. In some places, especially West Bengal, Saraswati, the goddess of learning, is honoured. Books, musical instruments and other objects related to the arts and scholarship are placed in front of the goddess to receive her blessing.

Phalguna (Feb/Mar)

Holi This is one of the most exuberant Hindu festivals, when people celebrate the end of winter by throwing coloured water and *gulal* (powder) at one another. In tourist places it might be seen as an opportunity to take liberties with foreigners, especially women (see Dangers & Annoyances earlier in this chapter); don't wear good clothes on this day, and be ready to duck. On the night before Holi, bonfires are built to symbolise the destruction of the evil demon Holika. In Barsana near Mathura, women not only douse men in coloured powder, they also get the pleasure of beating them with sticks, reliving the routing of the *gopas* by the *gopis*.

Shivaratri This day of Hindu fasting is dedicated to Shiva, who danced the *tandava* (cosmic dance) on this day. Temple processions are followed by the chanting of mantras and anointing of lingams.

Eid-ul-Zuhara This Muslim festival commemorates Abraham's attempt to sacrifice his son.

ACTIVITIES

Whether it's plodding through the desert atop a sleepy-eyed camel, or swooshing down snowy mountains, North India has no shortage of activities for the adventurous and not-so-adventurous. The following offers a whiff of possibilities – see the regional chapters for more details (and for more gentle pastimes such as ten-pin bowling and billiards). If you prefer someone else to do the activity on your behalf, opt for a massage, steam bath and Ayurvedic treatment in Khajuraho (see the Madhya Pradesh chapter).

Camel, Horse & Jeep Safaris

Camel safaris have taken off in Rajasthan, especially around Jaisalmer. You can opt for an afternoon trot or take longer jaunts lasting a few days or longer. If Jaisalmer is too much of a scene, you could try Bikaner or Shekhawati. Camel safaris are also possible through the dunes at Hunder (Ladakh) on native double-humped Bactrian camels.

Horse safaris are offered in many tourist areas, particularly Rajasthan, the hill stations and the Himalaya. You may be required to bring your own riding boots (inquire when booking). You can get polo lessons at tiny Dundlod (see the Rajasthan chapter).

There are plenty of jeep safaris around, especially in tourist-laden Rajasthan; one-day jeep village safaris to the Bishnoi villages around Jodhpur are especially popular.

Biking & Boating

There are some excellent organised bicycle or motorcycle tours, or you can arrange your own rental (usually available on an hourly, daily or weekly basis). For more details, see under Bicycle and also Motorcycle in the Getting Around chapter. Boat trips include shared rowboats to the impressive Marble Rocks (see the Madhya Pradesh chapter). Boat trips on the Ganges are very popular in Varanasi (Uttar Pradesh).

Kayaking & River Rafting

India's mountain rivers are ideal for rafting, with grades of white-water to suit all levels of experience. In Himachal Pradesh, rafting is possible on the Beas, Ganges, Indus, Spiti and Kanskar Rivers, all of which are accessible from Manali. The best time for rafting is April to July, when the rivers are swelled by monsoon rain, but Ganges trips are possible from September to October. In Uttaranchal, Rishikesh is the starting point for one-day river-rafting trips on the Ganges. River-rafting expeditions are also possible in other regions, including the Indus and Zanskar Rivers in Ladakh and Zanskar and on the Teesta and Rangeet rivers in the West Bengal hills.

Mountaineering

Those planning mountaineering expeditions on peaks over 6000m need to obtain clearance from the International Mountaineering Foundation (IMF; ☎ 011-4677935, fax 6883412), Benito Juarez Marg, Anand Niketan, New Delhi 110021.

For information on mountaineering expeditions to less lofty heights in Uttaranchal, contact the Trekking & Mountaineering division of the Garhwal Mandal Vikas Nigam (GMVN; ☎ 01364-32648, fax 30372), Kailash Gate, Muni-ki-Reti, Rishikesh. It offers an extensive range of organised trips and can also arrange guides, porters and equipment for independent groups.

In Himachal Pradesh, mountaineering trips can be organised by tour operators in Manali or through the Institute of Mountaineering and Allied Sports in Manali (☎ 01902-52342) or Bharmour (☎ 01090-25036). Also useful is the Regional Mountaineering Centre in McLeod Ganj (☎ 01892-21787).

See the boxed text 'Responsible Trekking' earlier in this chapter.

Looking for Mr Good Guide

If you fancy a ramble around the hills or elsewhere, strolls lasting a couple of hours can usually be completed without a guide. Other walks can be more challenging and may take a full day or even longer – these walks require local experience and knowledge and are best undertaken with the help of a professional guide. The problem is, how do you know a good guide when you see one? Well, there is no sure-fire answer. Some places in India have a flood of touts claiming to be professional guides. Certainly some guides who offer their services are highly professional and will probably make your outing far more rewarding than if you did it independently. Others may have little knowledge and will take you for a ride rather than a walk.

The first thing to do is ascertain exactly what type of walk you wish to do as well as your capability. Are you looking for something leisurely or strenuous? Do you want to return before nightfall or are you keen to get out there for a few days?

Seek specific recommendations from other travellers, and if you are engaged in negotiations with a potential guide, the following questions are worth asking:

- Do you have any written testimonials? (These, of course, are easy to fabricate but they can give you a sense of who you may be talking with.)
- Can you give us an idea of the route we'll take, including the distances, grades and the type of terrain involved?
- Can you identify any potential obstacles we may encounter: river crossings, wild animals etc?
- If we are walking for more than a day, how many hours a day will we need to walk to complete the trek?
- If we are trekking into tribal areas do you speak the language? Know the customs?
- What time can we expect to return?
- Do you have a torch (flashlight) and first-aid equipment? (Trekkers should always have their own, but a good guide will also have some.)
- If the guide (or the booking company) is going to supply camping equipment, can we inspect the equipment before we agree to the deal?
- If the trek includes a cook, what's on the menu and who supplies the food?
- Will there be places along the way to replenish water?
- Is the price quoted per person, group, day, hour or some combination of these? Does it include meals?

It is preferable to travel with even a small group rather than setting out alone with a guide, and of course you should ensure that you have adequate clothing (including footwear) for variable weather. It's also wise to let someone know where you will be and when you expect to return.

Always thoroughly question your potential guide.

Paragliding & Hang-gliding

For a breathtaking view of the Himalaya, tandem hang-gliding and paragliding (using a parachute instead of a hang-glider) is possible at Solang Nullah, just north of Manali, and at Billing, in the hills north-east of Mandi. Himachal Tourism conducts the Himalayan Hang-gliding Rally in Billing every May.

Excursion flights usually operate from February to June and September to November, and cost about Rs 1500 for 30 minutes. Unfortunately safety standards are variable (see the boxed text 'Choose Carefully', following). Reliable organisations include North Face Adventure Tours (☎ 01902-52441) and Himalayan Journeys (☎ 01902-52365) in Manali. Based in Delhi, Himalayan Adventure Club International (☎ 011-7178870) E15, Plot No 144–145, Sector 8, Rohini, offers excursion flights and training courses at various locations throughout the Himalaya. Nainital in Uttaranchal is also emerging as a future paragliding destination.

Skiing

India's premier ski resort is at Auli, near Joshimath in Uttaranchal. The GMVN (☎ 0135-46817, fax 744408) 74/1 Rajpur Rd, Dehra Dun, runs very competitively priced ski packages, which include ski hire, tows, lessons and accommodation. The Auli season runs from early January to late March.

There are less-developed resorts in Himachal Pradesh at Solang Nullah, north of Manali, and Kufri and Narkanda, near Shimla. Ski packages at both resorts are run by Himachal Tourism; offices are conveniently located in Shimla (☎ 0177-214311, fax 212591) and Manali (☎ 01902-52175). Most travellers report that the residential packages to Solang Nullah offered by private tour operators in Manali are superior.

Trekking

With some of the highest mountains in the world, it's hardly surprising that North India has some breathtaking trekking regions, although the trekking industry is not as developed as it is in Nepal. The main areas are Uttaranchal, Himachal Pradesh, Ladakh, the Darjeeling area (West Bengal) and Sikkim.

Organised trekking packages in Uttaranchal are provided by GMVN (☎ 01364-430372, fax 43178) in Rishikesh and the Kumaon Mandal Vikas Nigam (KMVN; ☎ 05942-36209) in Nainital. In Himachal Pradesh, try the Institute of Mountaineering & Allied Sports in Manali (☎ 01902-52342) or the Regional Mountaineering Centre in McLeod Ganj (☎ 01892-21787).

(See Lonely Planet's *Trekking in the Indian Himalaya* for more detailed information and the boxed text 'Responsible Trekking' earlier in this chapter.)

Wildlife Safaris

Various major wildlife sanctuaries, including Rajaji and Corbett National Parks in Uttaranchal, offer sensational elephant-back safaris, which are generally a better way of getting closer to wildlife than passenger jeeps. Expect to pay about Rs 100 for a two-hour trip. Other places where short elephant safaris are possible include the Jaldhapara Wildlife Sanctuary in West Bengal, as well as some of Madhya Pradesh's national parks.

Wildlife safaris by jeep are more widely available and although not as romantic as those on a pachyderm, are still worthwhile. Options include Rajasthan's Sariska and Ranthambhore National Parks, Gujarat's Sasan Gir Wildlife Sanctuary, and the Kanha and Bandhavgarh National Parks in Madhya Pradesh.

Choose Carefully

While India has some world-class adventure activities on offer – and there are numerous good, reputable and trustworthy operators around – it's worth noting that the level of experience and equipment available is not always up to scratch. When undertaking potentially dangerous sports and activities in India, you should always exercise good judgement (much the same as you would at home) and carefully scrutinise operators before committing yourself to their operation.

Over the years Lonely Planet has received numerous reports of dodgy operators taking naive tourists into dangerous situations, often resulting in serious injury and even death. Always check safety equipment before you set out and make sure it is included in the price quoted. If you're not comfortable with the operator's standards, inform them; if they refuse to replace equipment or improve their standards, refuse to use them and file a report with the local tourism authorities.

Once you have found an operator you are satisfied with, ensure you have adequate insurance should something go wrong; many travel insurance policies won't cover dangerous activities – including trekking!

Adventure Tour Operators

Local tour operators are listed in regional chapters. The following trek and tour outfits are all based in Delhi:

Amber Tours Pty Ltd (☎ 011-3312773, fax 3312984) Flat 2, Dwarka Sadan, C42 Connaught Place. Amber Tours offers yoga and mystic tours, river rafting, trekking, fishing for mahseer, and private jet or helicopter flights over the Himalaya.

Himalayan River Runners (☎ 011-615736) 188A Jor Bagh. This outfit has a range of rafting expeditions in the western Himalaya.

Mercury Himalayan Explorations (☎ 011-312008) Jeevan Tara Bldg, Parliament St. Mercury specialises in organised treks in the western Himalaya.

Shikhar Travels (☎ 011-3312444, fax 3323660) S209 Competent House, 14 Middle Circle, Connaught Circus. This company specialises in trekking and mountaineering tours and can also organise mountaineering expeditions for beginners.

World Expeditions (☎ 011-6983358, fax 698 3357), ground floor, MG Bhawan-1, 7 Local Shopping Centre, Madangir. World Expeditions has operated world-class Himalayan tours and treks since 1975.

COURSES

You may like to mesh your holiday with a course – the regional chapters give more options and details. Varanasi in particular is a place with an abundance of courses (see the Uttar Pradesh chapter).

Language

From February to December, the Landour Language School, near Mussoorie in northern Uttar Pradesh, offers three-month beginners' courses in Hindi, as well as more advanced courses. In Varanasi, Hindi courses tailored for travellers are available at Bhasha Bharati (the length of the course is flexible). At McLeod Ganj (Himachal Pradesh) it is possible to learn Tibetan either at the Library of Tibetan Works and Archives or from private teachers. Private Hindi lessons are also available. In Darjeeling, beginners' courses in Tibetan are available at the Manjushree Centre of Tibetan Culture.

Meditation, Reiki, Yoga & Philosophy

Most North Indian cities and towns have at least one place where you can pursue courses in meditation, yoga and philosophy.

Courses in aspects of Tibetan Buddhism and culture, including meditation and Buddhist philosophy, are offered in McLeod Ganj, Darjeeling, Choglamsar (near Leh) and Leh. McLeod Ganj (Himachal Pradesh) also has a formal study centre for Indian Early Buddhism and various private centres for yoga, reiki and other alternative therapies.

Rishikesh in Uttaranchal is the undisputed yoga capital of India with literally dozens of ashrams and yoga centres offering courses in Hatha and other disciplines of yoga. Some places are free, some expect a donation, and others charge a flat rate of Rs 100 per day. Many of the more reputable centres only accept long-term students and have strict rituals of daily prayer and meditation.

Yoga courses have also proliferated in Varanasi. The Malaviya Bhavan at Benares Hindu University offers courses in yoga and Hindu philosophy. The International Yoga Clinic & Meditation Centre has also been strongly recommended. For the less

SARAH JOLLY

Stretch mind and body with a yoga course

Gurus, Ashrams & Your Spiritual Journey

India has long attracted travellers from around the globe in search of spiritual guidance, including some who weren't actually aware that they were looking for it when they arrived. Travellers who come to India on a spiritual quest are many and varied and India offers an equally varied array of gurus and ashrams.

A guru is a spiritual guide. The word guru means 'the dispeller of darkness' or 'heavy with wisdom'. Most gurus live in an ashram, a spiritual community or retreat, which is usually established when a guru stays in one place and disciples congregate around them. Many ashrams are the legacies of deceased gurus. The atmosphere surrounding the ashram can have a profound and deeply moving effect on visitors, however some ashrams are more reputable than others.

Lonely Planet has received numerous reports from travellers who have been conned, drugged (then robbed), or worse by people falsely claiming to be gurus. While there are plenty of genuine gurus and ashrams, sadly, some self-styled spiritual impersonators are not as sincere in their motives: Always exercise common sense and talk to locals and other travellers before rushing into a decision as to which guru and ashram is likely to best suit you. If you don't feel comfortable with a guru or ashram, don't stay.

Many ashrams have codes of conduct; most are vegetarian and you may also be asked to abstain from eggs, tobacco and alcohol. Some ashrams may request that you wear white; others aren't so specific. Many ashrams don't require notice of your arrival, but it's wise to check in advance. Keep in mind that some gurus often move from place to place without much notice, so check first to avoid disappointment.

For details of ashrams around North India, see the regional chapters.

committed, various places in the old city (including hotels) run yoga classes.

In Bodhgaya (Bihar) you can also learn meditation or go on a retreat; for example, meditation courses are run by the Burmese and Tibetan monasteries, and the Dhammabodhi Vipassana Meditation Centre, the latter focussing on a very strict regime. More informal courses in Bodhgaya are run by the International Meditation Centre, where students can start and finish any time they choose.

Other Courses

Scores of arts and crafts centres enable you to learn everything from miniature painting to pottery. For traditional Tibetan woodcarving, there's the Tibetan Refugee Self-Help Centre in Darjeeling (West Bengal).

In Pushkar (Rajasthan) the Saraswati Music School offers lessons in classical tabla (drums) and singing. In the same state, at Udaipur, you can take sitar (an Indian stringed instrument), tabla and flute lessons at Prem Musical Instruments. In Varanasi, the Triveni Music Centre provides lessons for most classical Indian instruments including the tabla and sitar. Also in Varanasi, Jnana-Pravaha run a number of short courses including Indian culture, art, music and philosophy.

Kali Travel Home conducts a two-week food and cultural tour in Kolkata, during which you get to see the city, dine at various restaurants and learn to cook Bengali food under the tutelage of local Bengali women. Shorter cooking courses are also possible. In McLeod Ganj (Himachal Pradesh), Tibetan refugees offer private classes in Tibetan cooking, including lessons on how to make the perfect *momo* (dumpling).

VOLUNTEER WORK

Numerous charities and international aid agencies have branches in India and, although they're mostly staffed by locals, there are some opportunities for foreigners. Don't assume it's your right to just turn up and volunteer your services at any place. You are more use to the charity concerned if you write in advance and, if you're needed, if you stay for long enough to be of help. A week on a hospital ward may go a little way towards salving your own conscience, but you may actually do not much more than get in the way of the people who work there long-term.

Flexibility in what you are prepared to do is also vital. Some charities are inundated with foreign volunteers to help care for babies in an orphanage for instance, but few are willing to work with adults with physical or mental disabilities.

Overseas Volunteer Placement Agencies

For information on specific charities in India, contact the main branches in your own country. For long-term posts, the following organisations may be able to help or offer advice and further contacts:

Australian Volunteers International (☎ 03-9279 1788, fax 9419 4280, ⓔ ozvol@ozvol.org.au) PO Box 350, Fitzroy VIC 3065, Australia
Web site: www.ozvol.org.au

Co-ordinating Committee for International Voluntary Service (☎ 01 45 68 49 36, fax 01 42 73 05 21, ⓔ ccivs@zcc.net) Unesco House, 1 rue Miollis, 75732 Paris Cedex 15, France
Web site: www.unesco.org/ccivs

Global Volunteers (☎ 800-487 1073, fax 651-482 0915, ⓔ email@globalvolunteers.org) 375 East Little Canada Rd, St Paul, MN 55117-1627, USA
Web site: www.globalvolunteers.org

Voluntary Service Overseas (VSO; ☎ 020-8780 7200, fax 8780 7300, ⓔ enquiry@vso.org.uk) 317 Putney Bridge Rd, London SW15 2PN, UK

Volunteer Work Information Service (VWIS; ☎/fax 01273-470015, ⓔ info@workingabroad.com) PO Box 2759, Lewes, BN7 1WU, East Sussex, UK
Web site: www.workingabroad.com

Aid Programs in India

As mentioned earlier, it's best to contact these organisations in advance and discuss volunteer possibilities. Child Relief and You (CRY; ☎ 022-306651, ⓔ crymum@bom3.vsnl.net.in), 189A Anand Estate, Sane Guruji Marg, Mumbai, is an independent trust organising fundraising for more than 300 projects India-wide. You'll find further information on some of the following places within the regional chapters.

Bihar The Sujata Charitable Society (☎ 0631-400463) in Bodhgaya runs a school that provides free education to illiterate children and adults. There are also plans to make free medical services available for people in Bihar. Also in Bodhgaya, the Samanway Ashram may offer voluntary work on social development projects in the area, and volunteers receive tuition in Indian spirituality.

Himachal Pradesh Long-term visitors at McLeod Ganj are always welcome to teach English and computer skills to newly-arrived Tibetan refugees. Ask at the Library of Tibetan Works and Archives in Gangchen Kyishong or check out local noticeboards and the classified section of *Contact* magazine. Volunteers are also considered at the Tibetan Youth Congress, Tibetan Welfare Office, Tibetan Children's Village, Tibetan Women's Association and Refugee Reception Centre. Medical practitioners may be able to volunteer at the Delek Hospital (☎ 01892-22053).

Ladakh Mahabodhi International Meditation Centre (PO Box 22, Leh, Ladakh, 194101 Jammu & Kashmir) operates a residential school for poor children and accepts volunteers to assist with teaching and secretarial work. Contact the centre at the above address, or through its head office (☎ 0812-260684, fax 260292) at 14 Kalidas Rd, Gandhinagar, Bangalore 560009.

Organisations in Leh that are involved in educational and environmental aid are the Ladakh Ecological Development Group (LEDeG), the Child Welfare Society and the Student's Educational & Cultural Movement of Ladakh (Secmol).

Madhya Pradesh Voluntary work may be possible at the Global Village Development Trust in Khajuraho (see Conservation Contacts under Ecology & Environment in the Facts about North India chapter).

Rajasthan SOS Worldwide runs more than 30 programs across India. The society looks after orphaned, destitute and abandoned children, who are cared for by unmarried women, abandoned wives and widows. In Jaipur, SOS has a fine property surrounded by gardens, and cares for more than 150 children and young adults. Volunteers are welcome at the centre to teach English, help the children with their homework and simply to join in their games. For more information contact SOS Children's Village (☎ 0141-202393, fax 200140), opposite Pital Factory, Jhotwara Rd, Jaipur 302016.

The Urmul Trust provides primary health care and education to the people of remote villages in Rajasthan; raises awareness among the women of the desert of their rights and privileges in society; and promotes the handicrafts of rural artisans with profits going directly back to them artisans. There is volunteer work available in social welfare, teaching English, health care, and other projects. Even if you don't have skills in these areas, Urmul may have positions in implementation and overseeing of projects. Contact the secretary at the Urmul Trust (☎/fax 0151-523093), inside Urmul Dairy, Ganganagar Rd, Bikaner (next to the bus station).

Les Amis du Shekhawati is one of a number of charities whose aim is to safeguard and preserve India's crumbling but rich architectural heritage – in this case the havelis (ornate traditional mansions) and paintings of the Shekhawati region in Rajasthan. Ramesh Jangid, the association president, welcomes volunteers who are keen to preserve the paintings of Shekhawati and can be contacted at Ramesh Jangid's Tourist Pension (☎ 01594-24060, fax 24061) in Nawalgarh.

Help in Suffering (☎ 0141-760803, fax 761544, ⓔ hisjpr@datainfosys.net), an animal hospital based in Jaipur, is doing excellent work. It's funded by the World Society for the Protection of Animals (WSPA) and Animaux Secours, Arthaz, France. Qualified vets interested in volunteering should write to Help in Suffering, Maharani Farm, Durgapura, Jaipur, 302018, Rajasthan.

Uttaranchal In the Garwhal region is the International Society For Alternative Medicine (ISAM; ☎ 0135-653709, ⓔ arawal@nde.vsnl.net.in), Rawal Nursing Home, 35/1 East Canal Road, Dehra Dun. This charitable organisation provides health care to disabled and impoverished local people, using alternative and traditional medicines. ISAM welcomes volunteers and can help arrange accommodation.

West Bengal Mother Teresa's Missionaries of Charity headquarters, the 'Motherhouse' (☎ 033-2447115) is at 54 AJC Bose Rd, Kolkata 700016. Volunteers can work in a number of homes including Nirmal Hriday (Home for the Dying), Prem Dan (for the sick and mentally ill) and Shishu Bhavan (the children's orphanage). There are also opportunities to work with the sisters in rural areas. If you're in Kolkata, you can visit the Motherhouse for placement information at 3 pm on Monday, Wednesday and Friday. See the Kolkata chapter for information about the late Mother Teresa.

For those with the time to give a medium to long-term commitment, especially if you have any medical background, Calcutta Rescue, started in 1979 by Dr J Preger, now encompasses several different clinics. Dr Jack's, as it's affectionately known, caters to the medical, nutritional and educational needs of the destitute and socially disadvantaged of Kolkata and rural West Bengal. Postal inquiries should be directed to Calcutta Rescue, PO Box 9253, Middleton Row PO, Kolkata 700071. In Kolkata, you can visit the administrative office at 85 Collins St (☎/fax 033-2175675, 2461520, ⓔ calres@cal.vsnl.net.in).

The Calcutta Society for the Prevention of Cruelty to Animals (CSPCA) is doing a truly admirable job to help the animals of this city. Established in 1861, this organisation helps the many street dogs and other sick or injured animals of Kolkata. It desperately needs volunteers and donations. Anyone who loves animals is welcome to volunteer, but qualified vets are especially needed (a minimum of one month is requested). To arrange volunteer work, contact the president of the CSPCA (☎ 033-2370520, ☎/fax 2365592, ⓔ bdhar@caltiger.com). Donations can be forwarded to the CSPCA, 276BB Ganguly St, Kolkata 700012. Signing up as a life member costs Rs 1000.

Volunteer work may be available at the following places in Darjeeling. The Nepali Girls' Social Service Centre (☎ 0354-2985), Gandhi Rd, undertakes projects to protect the environment, and to promote the empowerment of women, child survival and development. Volunteers are welcome on an informal basis to teach English, art or music.

Hayden Hall is a Christian-based organisation which can arrange volunteer work in medicine, teaching, handicrafts and counselling, but volunteers must be prepared to commit themselves for at least six months. For more information you cancontact the staff (ⓔ hayden@cal.vsnl.net.in) at 42 Laden La Rd.

The Tibetan Refugee Self-Help Centre has openings for volunteer teachers (of children and adults), medical staff and geriatric and child care workers. For more information, contact its head office (☎ 0354-52346) at 65 Gandhi Rd.

In Kalimpong, volunteers can help out at Dr Graham's home (an orphanage and school).

ACCOMMODATION

India has a mixed bag of places to stay, ranging from remarkably cheap (but very basic) guesthouses for shoestringers, to incredibly ritzy top-end hotels for those with cash to flash. Some hotels operate on a 24-hour system (ie, your time starts when you check in). Others have fixed check-out times (from an ungenerous 9 am to a more civilised 1 pm), so it pays to ask before checking in. Some hotels even offer a handy half-day rate – ideal for breaking long journeys.

Credit cards are accepted at most top-end hotels, some mid-range ones, and very few budget hotels. Some hotels may request an upfront payment based on your estimated length of stay. If your expenses don't match the prepaid amount you'll receive a refund at the time of checkout. You may be asked to sign a blank impression of your credit card, which will be reportedly destroyed when you pay your bill at the end of your stay. This should be avoided. If a hotel does demand an impression of your card you should refuse to sign it. If they still insist, then write in an amount that will be less than your estimated expenditure.

Although rare, some of the ultra-cheap under-staffed lodgings refuse to accept foreigners because of the hassle of the foreign registration 'C forms' (these must be submitted to the local police station within 24 hours of a foreigner checking in).

During the peak tourist season and during some festivals, hotel tariffs can really shoot up and it can be difficult finding a bed, especially in tourist hot spots. Advance reservations are advisable.

Although most prices quoted in this book are for single and double rooms, many hotels will put an extra bed in a room to make a triple for about an extra 25%.

Even budget rooms usually have a ceiling fan. 'Air-cooled' is considered the next step up – this means you'll get a large (usually noisy) fan built into a frame within a wall. It is a water-filled cooling system, which is less effective during the humid monsoon months. At some places you may have to fill the air-cooler with water yourself, though usually you can expect the staff to do it. Air-conditioning is the most efficient method of keeping cool, and is offered in many mid-price places and all top-end hotels. However, you probably won't find air-con necessary during the winter, or at any time of the year in mountain regions.

Budget Hotels

India has no shortage of cheap hotels, ranging from squalid dives at rock bottom prices to well-kept mid-range places at pleasantly moderate charges. Many cheap hotels come with mozzie zappers or possibly even nets. Most rooms have ceiling fans but be careful when adjusting mosquito nets on your bed, as low ceilings mean low ceiling fans – a dangerous combination if the fan is switched on at full speed!

Don't expect cheap hotels to be completely flawless – even if budget or mid-range hotels

The Inside Story on Bathrooms

You'll probably develop an intimate relationship with Indian bathrooms, especially if you experience the likely (but by no means inevitable) bowel troubles. Back home, you might find yourself dining out on your toilet tales (lovely image!) for weeks afterwards. For instance, how could we forget the beach toilet block we visited, where the lavatory outflow pipe fed directly into a pig trough – at which several hungry piglets were eagerly lapping up the contents!

Certain terminology is commonly used in the places to stay sections throughout this book. Unless squat toilets are specifically mentioned, bathrooms have sit-down flush toilets. Keep in mind that in North India some hoteliers refer to squat toilets as 'Indian-style' and sit-down flush toilets as 'Western-style'. In some places you may come across the curious hybrid toilet, which is basically a sit-down flush toilet with footpads on the edge of the bowl! See also Toilets, earlier in this chapter.

'Shared bathroom' or 'without bathroom' means shared/communal bathroom facilities. 'Private bathroom' or 'with bathroom' indicates that the room has its very own bathroom, which means you can belt out your favourite tune in the shower or make urgent and unlimited diarrhoea trips without being snickered at over the breakfast table.

'Running' or 'constant' water indicates that there is water available around the clock (theoretically – it's not always the case in practice). 'Bucket water' means that water is, as the name suggests, available in buckets. Many hotels only have running cold water in guest bathrooms but can provide hot water in buckets (sometimes only between certain hours and sometimes at a small charge).

Hotels that advertise 'room with shower' can sometimes be misleading. Even if a bathroom does indeed have a shower, it's a good idea to actually check that it works before accepting the room. Some hotels surreptitiously disconnect showers to save costs, while the showers at other places render a mere trickle of water.

A geyser is a small hot-water tank, usually found in cheaper hotels. Some geysers need to be switched on an hour or so before use.

in this book are described as 'clean', they're unlikely to be absolutely spotless. Indeed, even in some respectable mid-range hotels it's usual for rooms to have minor imperfections, and in some places you may even find yourself sharing the room with cockroaches or other creepy crawlies.

Throughout India, you may hear locals categorise hotels as 'Western' or 'Indian'. The latter are usually more modestly furnished and thus cheaper. Most also have squat toilets (not only because they are cost-effective, but also because they are generally considered to be more hygenic). 'Western' hotels invariably have a sit-down flush toilet and may be more fancy inside. However, don't instantly assume that the 'Western' hotels are necessarily superior; you can often find modern, well-maintained 'Indian' hotels and disheveled, poorly run 'Western' hotels.

Some cheap hotels (particularly in parts of Rajasthan) allow guests to sleep on the rooftop (which resembles a flat balcony) for a nominal charge. This should include a pillow, sheet or blanket, and use of a shared bathroom.

Some of the cheaper hotels in India lock their gates at night and remain unmanned on the outside, so let the appropriate staff member know if you intend coming back late.

Note that some hotel rooms have a master switch on the *outside* of each room (usually near the door). If you return to your room to find that the lights, TV, geyser etc don't work, make sure you check that your master switch has not been turned off. If you make a hasty assumption that there's a general power cut, you'll be waiting an awfully long time to see the light (excuse the pun).

Expensive Hotels

India boasts some exquisite hotels, from world-renowned hotel chains such as the Oberoi, Taj and Welcomgroup (affiliated to

Sheraton) to lusciously romantic palace-hotels in exotic settings. You'll generally only find top-end hotels in the bigger cities and major tourist centres.

The government-operated ITDC (Indian Tourism Development Corporation) hotels can be found nationwide and often fall into the top-end price category. Although they're often cheaper than other upmarket hotels, most lack attention to detail and get poor reports from travellers.

If you're interested in staying at a top-end hotel, it's sometimes cheaper to book them through a travel agent in your home country.

Government Accommodation & Tourist Bungalows

Back in the days of the British Raj, a string of government-run accommodation units were set up with labels such as Rest Houses, Dak Bungalows, Circuit Houses, PWD (Public Works Department) Bungalows, Forest Rest Houses and so on. Today most of these are reserved for government officials, although in some places they may still be available for tourists if there is room (except Circuit Houses, which are strictly for travelling VIPs).

'Tourist Bungalows' are usually run by the state government and often serve as replacements for the older (often decrepit) government-run accommodation. Their facilities and level of service vary enormously; the majority are below average. For shoestringers, some offer cheap dorm beds. Most have a restaurant (commonly called the 'dining hall'), which generally has good food at reasonable prices. Some also have a nondescript bar. The local branch of the state government tourist office is often on the premises of these Tourist Bungalows.

Homestays & Paying Guest House Scheme

Staying with an Indian family can be an enriching experience and a refreshing change from dealing strictly with tourist-oriented people. This Paying Guest House Scheme is particularly popular in tourist-laden Rajasthan, but is also available elsewhere in India, such as Varanasi (Uttar Pradesh) – see regional chapters.

About Touts

Hordes of accommodation touts operate in many Indian towns – Agra, Jaipur and Varanasi in particular. They're usually most prevalent at airport terminals and bus/train stations. Very often they are the *rickshaw-wallahs*. Their technique is simple – they take you to hotel A and pocket a commission for taking you there rather than to hotel B. The problem with this procedure is that you may well end up not at the place you want to go to but at the place that pays the best commission. Some very good cheap hotels simply refuse to pay the touts and you'll then hear lots of stories about the hotel you want being 'full', 'closed for repairs', 'no good any more' or even 'burnt down'. Nine chances out of 10 they will be just that – stories.

Think twice before agreeing to stay in a hotel recommended by touts or rickshaw-wallahs, as some travellers have warned that they stayed in such hotels only to be subsequently badgered to take part in rip-off insurance and import schemes or to accept the sightseeing services of a particular taxi or rickshaw driver.

Realise that the question 'first time in India?' is a way for an unscrupulous tout to work out if they can manipulate you; instead of answering 'yes' you might want to say something like 'no, I've been here many times'.

Touts do have a use though – if you arrive in a town when some big festival is on, or during peak season, finding a place to stay can be almost impossible. Hop into a rickshaw, tell the driver in what price range you want a hotel, and off you go. The driver will know which places have rooms available and unless the search is a long one you shouldn't have to pay the driver too much. Remember that he will be getting a commission from the hotel too.

If you're interested, state tourist offices have details about the scheme. Expect to pay upwards of Rs 100.

Railway Retiring Rooms

Important train stations have retiring rooms, which may be either dormitories or private rooms. These are just like regular hotels or dormitories except that to stay here you are technically supposed to have a train ticket or Indrail Pass (any cheap, unreserved ticket bought specially for this reason would do!). The rooms are, of course, extremely handy if you have an early train departure, although they can be noisy if it is a busy station. Nonetheless, in some places they're the most convenient option and can be super value. They vary in quality, but at best they're very cheap and can even be ruthlessly clean. Most are let on a 24-hour basis.

Other Possibilities

There are YMCAs and YWCAs in many of the big cities – the quality varies, but some are in good shape and cost about the same as a mid-range hotel. There are a few camping places around India, but travellers with their own vehicles can almost always find hotels with gardens where they can park and camp (sometimes for a nominal charge which includes shared bathroom facilities).

Indian youth hostels (HI – Hostelling International) can be very cheap but the fabric and service is variable. You are not usually required to be a YHA (HI) member (as in other countries) to use the hostels, although your YHA/HI card will generally get you a lower rate.

Accommodation (for a donation) is available at some *gurdwaras* (Sikh temples) and *dharamsalas* (pilgrims' lodgings). These simple places are essentially designed to cater for pilgrims so please exercise judgement about the appropriateness of staying. If you are welcome, abide by any protocols (eg, Jain places usually don't allow leather articles inside) and behave with respect at all times.

Taxes & Service Charges

Most state governments slap a variety of taxes on hotel accommodation (and restaurants). At most rock-bottom budget places you won't have to pay any taxes. Once you get into the highest echelon of budget places, and certainly for mid-range accommodation, you will have to pay something (usually 10%), and top-end places can stack on all sorts of taxes. Taxes vary from state to state – see regional chapters for details.

Another common tax, in addition to the basic tax, is a service charge, which is usually pegged at 10%. In some hotels, this is only levied on room service and telephone use, not on the accommodation costs. At others, it's levied on the total bill. If that's the case and you're trying to keep costs down, don't clock up room service to your room bill and keep telephone use to a minimum.

Many hotels raise their tariffs on an annual basis, so expect increments on the room rates quoted in this book. Rates quoted in the regional chapters of this book exclude tax unless otherwise indicated.

Seasonal Variations

In popular tourist hangouts (hill stations, beaches and the Delhi-Agra-Rajasthan triangle), most hoteliers crank up their high-season prices by two to three times the low-season price.

The definition of the high and low seasons obviously varies depending on location. For the beaches and the Delhi-Agra-Rajasthan triangle it's basically a month before and two months after Christmas. In the hill stations, it's usually April to July when the lowlands are unbearably hot. In some locations and at some hotels, there are even higher rates for the brief Christmas/New Year period, or over major festivals such as Diwali, Dussehra and the Pushkar Camel Fair.

Conversely, in the low season(s), prices at even normally expensive hotels can be surprisingly affordable.

FOOD

Perhaps the best way of cutting to the heart of this extraordinary culture is by exploring its protean gastronomy. Dining in Indian restaurants abroad cannot prepare you for the experience of eating Indian food in India as the food is inextricably particular to place and is not easily exported. It reflects the multilayered culture that fascinates every visitor, and it changes shape as you move between each neighbourhood, town and state.

Amazingly, many travellers 'do' India *despite* the food, treating the cuisine as something suspect, to be tolerated or even avoided. Do this and you'll be like a pebble skimming across the cultural surface. You might get splashed every now and then but you'll never be immersed in it. Yes, you stand a good chance of getting a dose of the runs at some stage, but – with equal measures of good sense and adventure – a few desperate dashes to the toilet will seem like a trifling inconvenience compared with the culinary rewards and cultural insight you will glean.

The basis of any Indian meal is a grain – rice in the south, and wheat in the form of roti (bread) in the north. These are generally eaten with dhal (lentils), *sabzi* (curried vegetables) and *chatni* (chutney). Depending on circumstances, fish and meat may be added. Beyond these familiar staples, the diversity and potential of Indian food knows no bounds and is limited only by the geography of the region and the imagination of each cook.

Spices

Walk into any Indian home at meal time and you will be enveloped in a waft of exotic aromas that will make your taste buds stand to attention.

Christopher Columbus was actually looking for the black pepper of Kerala's Malabar Coast when he stumbled upon America. The region still grows the finest quality of the world's favourite spice, and it is integral to most savoury dishes. Turmeric is the essence of every Indian curry but coriander seeds are the most widely used spice and lend flavour and body to just about every savoury dish, while most Indian 'wet' dishes – curries as they're known in the West – begin with the crackle of cumin seeds in hot oil. Tamarind is sometimes known as the 'Indian date' and is a popular souring agent in the south. The green cardamom of Kerala's Western Ghats is regarded as the world's best, and you'll find it in savouries, desserts and, warming winter chai (tea). It is also a mouth-refreshing digestive.

Saffron evokes images of wealth and rarity unparalleled in the culinary lexicon. It is the dried stigmas of a crocus grown in Kashmir, and is made up of fine, orange-red coloured threads that are so light that it takes more than 1500 hand-plucked flowers to yield just 1g of saffron. It is worth its weight in gold and makes a wonderful gift to bring home. Because of the prices it can fetch, it is frequently adulterated, usually with safflower, dubbed – no doubt by disgruntled tourists – as 'bastard saffron'.

Indian Food Fallacies

What most of us know as Indian cuisine – think dhal, tandoori chicken, naan, aloo gobi, lassi, chicken tikka etc – can all be found in one of India's states, Punjab. When the state was carved up during Partition, millions of displaced Punjabis scattered around India and beyond. Some opened restaurants that popularised their favourite dishes and Punjabi fare came to represent Indian cuisine the world over.

There is no such thing as a 'curry' in India, and the word – an Anglicised derivative of the Tamil word *kari* (black pepper) – was used by gentlemen of the British empire as an all-encompassing term for any dish that included spices. Similarly, curry powder was invented purely for export to the nostalgic former residents of the Raj in Britain, and no self-respecting Indian cook would dream of using the same masala (combination of spices) in multiple dishes.

Similarly the word balti, which is used in balti houses all over England, was created as a marketing ploy by entrepreneurial restaurateurs. Balti is a north-west England name for the common Indian wok, better known as a *kadhai*. In the better balti houses of Birmingham, the term generally refers to dishes of Punjab and the north-western frontier.

Rice

Rice is the most important staple and, in a place where food and spirituality are inseparable, it is commonly used as a symbol of purity and fertility. It turns up in virtually every meal in the south, east and west, and the average Indian eats 2kg of it each week. Long-grain white rices are the most common but, between Assam's sticky rice and Kerala's red grains, you will find innumerable local varieties. Many are indistinguishable to the visiting palate, although one stands out above all. *Basmati* gets its name from the Hindi 'queen of fragrance', and its scent is well known around the world. The grains are white, long and silky and its aroma is reminiscent of the uncluttered freshness of the Himalayan foothills from where the best variety comes.

Roti (Bread)

A meal is not a meal in North India unless it comes with roti. The irresistible chapati, made with whole wheat flour and water, is cooked on a concave hotplate known as a *tawa*. *Puris* are wholewheat discs of stiff dough that, when deep-fried, puff up into soft crispy balloons and are eaten with various stewed meats and vegetables. *Kachoris* are similar only the dough is pepped up with lentils, corn or split peas. Flaky *parathas*, combined with any typical northern sauce, make for a delicious snack and nothing beats a naan fresh from the tandoor (clay oven).

Dhal (Lentils)

While the staples divide north and south, the whole of India goes doolally for dhal, a dish of stewed pulses and spices. Where we refer to our basic living as our 'bread and butter', Indians refer to dhal roti (dhal and bread) as all they need to survive. From the thin sambars of the south to the thick mung (pronounced moong) dhals of the north, you may encounter up to 60 different pulses including lentils, dried beans and peas, which are eaten with most meals.

Meat

While India probably has more vegetarians than the rest of the world put together, it still has an extensive repertoire of carnivorous fare largely lapped up by the Muslim and Christian communities. Goat (known as 'mutton' since the days of the Raj), lamb and chicken are the mainstays because religious taboos forbid Hindus from eating beef and Muslims from pigging out on pork.

Fish & Seafood

Blessed with rich waters surrounding three sides of the Indian subcontinent, fish and seafood are important staples. Freshwater fish is the mainstay in West Bengal, where it is commonly curried in nose-tingling mustard.

Fruit & Vegetables

Indian fruit and vegetable markets are mesmerising, a feast for the eyes and foreplay for the touring taste buds. With its climatic range, India grows more fruit and vegetables than most countries. You'll find different species of familiar vegetables as well as truly exotic ones, such as gourds that look more like props from the *X-Files* than edibles. Visit the market to get your culinary bearings. Indians are also fond of *saag* (leafy greens), which include mustard, spinach, fenugreek and white radish.

India is a paradise for those who like fruit. Whatever time of year, there's always something to entice you, set your heart racing, and make your vitamin count surge. If you're mad about mango you might consider migrating here; Indians enjoy more than 500 varieties of what they regard as the king of fruit.

Citrus fruits (oranges that are actually yellow-green, tangerines, pink and white grapefruits, kumquats, and sweet limes) grow throughout the country. Himachal Pradesh produces delicious apples in autumn. Juicy and flavoursome strawberries abound in Kashmir during summer. Labour-intensive pomegranates, with their leathery jackets and sweet seeds encased in an inedible membrane, are winter favourites. Reach for a gorgeous guava to slake your thirst or, if you're game, have a juice made from sweet lime from the ubiquitous juice cart.

Pickles, Chutneys & Relishes

No Indian meal is complete without one, and often all, of the above. The most well-known relish is *raita* (plain yogurt combined with vegetables or fruit, and served chilled), which makes a delicious and refreshing counter to even the most fiery meal. There is a litany of 'little bits' that can go a long way to changing the flavour of your meal, but proceed with caution before polishing off that pickled speck on your thali; it'll quite possibly be the hottest thing you've ever tasted and usually the smaller the speck, the bigger the smash.

Oils

Just as each state uses different ingredients, different cooking mediums are used to give dishes their characteristic regional flavours. Peanut (groundnut) oil is the most common, and is especially important around Maharashtra and Gujarat. It is high in protein and has a neutral flavour and taste. Strong, pungent mustard oil is the preferred medium along the east coast, particularly West Bengal and Bihar as well as in parts of Punjab and in Jammu & Kashmir. Discerning cooks in the south use light sesame oil, which imparts a nutty nuance to the food and has a high boiling point, making it ideal for frying. In the south and west, where coconuts grow so abundantly, coconut oil is widely used. To the uninitiated, the flavour coconut oil imparts in many dishes can be strong and unpleasant. Many out-of-state Indians don't dig coconut oil either, and there's no problem asking the cook to use something else. On your travels, you may also find rapeseed oil – the poor man's oil – but never olive oil.

Platform Food

One of the thrills of travelling by rail is the culinary circus that greets you at every station. As the train arrives the platform springs into a frenzy. Roving vendors accost the trains yelling and scampering up and down the carriages; bananas, omelettes and nuts are offered through the grilles on the windows; and platform chefs try to lure you from the train with the sizzle of fresh samosas. Frequent rail travellers know which station is famous for which food item, and plan their appetites accordingly. Agra is famous for *peitha* (crystallised gourd), and Dhaund near Delhi for its biryani.

Dairy

The cow wasn't deemed sacred because of its grace, athleticism and good looks; it was protected because, to the Indian diet, it is worth a lot more alive than dangling from a hook. Holding up traffic or sitting right in your way in a narrow lane, for Hindus the cow is also venerated because it represents fertility and nurturing.

Milk and milk products make a staggering contribution to Indian cuisine: *dahi* (curds) are served with most meals and are handy for countering heat; *paneer* (unfermented cheese) is a godsend for the vegetarian majority; the popular lassi is just one in a host of nourishing sweet and savoury drinks; ghee (clarified butter) is the traditional and pure cooking medium (although not used nearly as much in India as in Indian restaurants abroad); and the best sweets are made with milk.

Desserts & Ice cream

Kheer – called *payasam* in the south – is a rice pudding and India's favourite dessert. It might be flavoured with cardamom, saffron, pistachios, flaked almonds, cashews or dried fruit. You can bet your sweet tooth that all communal gatherings will conclude with delicious, creamy payasam served in earthenware cups or bowls. Vermicelli – yes, the Italian pasta – is another common dessert, popularly made into a milk pudding or fried in ghee with raisins, flaked almonds and sugar in a sweet, dry treat. *Gulab jamun* are deep-fried balls of *khoya* (reduced milk) dough soaked in rose-flavoured syrup, and are eaten both as a snack and at the end of a meal. *Kulfi* is a delicious firm-textured Indian ice cream made with reduced milk and flavoured with any number of nuts, fruits and berries.

Street Food

It is on the streets that you'll find India at its vital best and revolting worst, its most colourful and drab, joyful and depressing. India is laid bare in the theatre of its thoroughfares and the streets are a banquet for the senses. You won't like some of the courses but the tastes, smells, sights, rhythm and atmosphere of street cooking will be an experience you will never forget.

Whatever the time of day, people are boiling, frying, roasting, peeling, juicing, simmering, mixing or baking some class of food and drink to lure passers-by. It can be as simple as puffed rice or peanuts roasted in hot sand, as unexpected as a fried-egg sandwich, or as complex as the riot of different flavours known as *chaat* (any snack seasoned with the popular spice blend chaat masala – the closest approximation in the West would be salad). It will be served in biodegradable bowls made of roughly stitched sal leaves or yesterday's newspaper. Deep-fried fare is the staple of the boulevards, and you'll find samosas, *aloo tikkis* and bondas (both mashed potato patties), pakora and *bhaji* (vegetable fritters) in varying degrees of spiciness. In season, cobs of roasted corn are hard to resist and you can't visit Mumbai without sampling *pao-bhaji* (spiced vegetables with bread) and *bhelpuri* on Chowpatty Beach. Popular 'modern' items include omelettes, hard-boiled eggs, and even regular old sandwiches (tomato, cucumber and green chutney).

GREG ELMS

Roti is part of almost every meal

Paan

Meals are polished off with paan, a sweet, spicy and fragrant mixture of betel nut, also called areca nut, lime paste, spices and condiments wrapped up in an edible betel leaf (from a different plant) and eaten as a digestive and mouth freshener. The betel nut is mildly narcotic and some aficionados eat them the same way heavy smokers consume cigarettes. If you chew a lot of paan, over many years the betel nut will rot your teeth red and black, which accounts for the number of people you'll encounter who look like they had their faces kicked in the night before.

There are two basic types: *mitha* (sweet) and *saadha* (with tobacco). Avoid the foul tobacco version, but a parcel of mitha paan is an excellent way to finish a satisfying meal without any harm. You'll soon find yourself walking out of restaurants and immediately heading for the nearest paan-wallah, whom you'll find in a jiffy, for they are as common as bumpy roads. Pop the whole parcel in your mouth and chew slowly, letting the juices secrete around your gob. When you've chewed the flavour out, spit the remains out onto the street (there really is no point in trying to be discreet).

To give somebody paan is a mark of great respect. Shah Jahan, who built the Taj Mahal, once caught his daughter with a man he didn't care for. He smiled and offered the unapproved beau a betel leaf. The betel leaf was packed with poisonous ingredients but the beau could not risk offending the emperor, thanked him, started to chew and commenced dying.

Thali

Don't be disappointed if the waiter tells you there is no menu, 'only meals'. In this case you'll have the choice of veg or nonveg thalis, delicious and inexpensive all-you-can-eat lunches. The thali is named after the dish in which it is traditionally served, usually a plate with bowl-shaped indentations known as *katori*. It is a wonderful way to explore regional variations and always features dry and wet vegetable preparations, chapati, pappadam, rice, pickle, curd, a sweet and a meat if that's what you're after. As soon as you've put a dent in any of the dishes, the waiter will come around and top you up (usually when you've got your mouth full).

In South India, and for communal feasts, thalis are usually served on banana leaves. The form originated in Gujarat and although a thali provides a great opportunity to explore regional differences, don't leave India until you've sampled a lightly spiced and sweet Gujarati one. Even if you can't make it to Gandhi's original stomping ground, you'll find Gujarati thalis in neighbouring states and major towns.

Northern Specialities

The cauldron of Indian cuisine overflows with dishes that vary so immensely, that no Indian would be able to taste them all in a lifetime. It is a fascinating kaleidoscope of different regional influences, as varied as those of Europe, and you should seek out the regional specialities wherever you go.

Mughlai cuisine is popular in the north, particularly in the cities of Delhi and Lucknow where you'll find rich *pulous*, known as pilaus in the West, and biryanis infused with nuts, dried fruits, spices and meat. Kebabs are another popular Muslim staple and come in two basic varieties; sheekh (skewered) and *shami* (wrapped). Kakori kebabs are a delicacy named after the town near Lucknow. The meat is pounded into a fine paste, which is then spiced, wrapped around a skewer and quickly charred until crispy on the outside and almost creamy within. Speciality Muslim breakfasts include *nihari* (a rich broth made by simmering goat's trotters overnight on low embers and eaten with warm bread) and *harissa* (wheat porridge with lamb also slowly cooked over embers).

From Punjab's tandoors emerge *tangri* (plump chicken drumsticks), *boti* (spicy bits of bite-sized boneless lamb), chicken tikka (succulent pieces of marinated chicken on a skewer) and, of course, the ubiquitous tandoori chicken. Tandoori dishes get their characteristic flavour from the charcoal used in the oven and from the blend of spices used in the marinade, known as tandoori masala. It consists of cumin, coriander seeds, chilli, ginger, turmeric and a flavourless red colouring that gives the food its distinctive red tinge. *Palak paneer* (soft, unfermented cheese in a spicy gravy of pureed spinach) is a popular Punjabi vegetarian alternative.

Cereals form the backbone of Rajasthani food. *Bati* (baked balls of wholemeal flour) is the state's most remarkable dish, broken up by hand, soaked in ghee and mixed with a spicy dhal. *Besan* (chickpea flour) is another staple, and is used to make pakora, *sev* (savoury nibbles) and other salted snacks known as *farsan*. Another distinctive dish is *besan gate*, where spiced besan dough is rolled into 'snakes' – there's a better description but you might not appreciate the imagery – and steamed and curried in spicy gravy.

Freshwater fish is the food closest to the heart of Bengalis. Hilsa, a relative of the

Celebrating with Sweets

Food is a medium for joy and celebration and you could hardly make it through a week here without getting caught up in the excitement of some looming festival, which will be marked with special feasts and specific dishes.

Mithai (sweets) are the most luxurious foods and vast quantities are made, exchanged and consumed during festivals. Most are sickeningly sweet to Western tastes although the milk-based concoctions of West Bengal, particularly *rasgullas* (balls of soft, unfermented cheese in syrup), are a glorious exception. Visit during a festival and you'll be smothered with sweet offerings. The main categories are *barfi* (a fudge-like sweet made from milk), *halwa* (soft sweetmeats that can be made with vegetables, cereals, lentils, nuts or fruit) and *ladoo* (sweetmeat balls made with gram flour, semolina and umpteen other ingredients). Many sweets come shimmering in a foil you might presume to discard; this is actually edible silver.

The Meaning of Vegetarian

There are now multitudes of restaurants – or 'hotels' – all over India and their signage will identify them as either 'veg', 'pure veg' or 'nonveg'. Pure veg indicates that no eggs are used and that there is no risk of the food being contaminated with meat. Most mid-range restaurants serve one of two basic genres; South Indian (which in restaurants means the vegetarian food of Tamil Nadu and Karnataka) and North Indian (which comprises Punjabi food with Mughlai touches). You will also find the cuisines of neighbouring regions and states. Indians frequently migrate in search of work and these restaurants cater to the large communities seeking the familiar tastes of home, as well as locals.

herring, is the most popular and is made into a spicy *jhaal* (a curry made with ground mustard seeds and chillies).

In Bihar *sattu* (roasted yellow gram, ground to a fine flour) is the unifying theme and is enjoyed by all classes. There are few more tempting smells than sattu being roasted in earthenware pots over coals.

Tenga, the favourite Assamese fish stew, is made of pieces of sweet-tasting *rohu* (a type of carp), lightly sauteed with onions and simmered in a watery gravy, zested with lots of lemon juice. And if you venture as far as Kashmir you can taste an authentic *rogan josh*, the fiery lamb curry.

DRINKS

Tea

Chai is the beverage of the nation but you won't find many porcelain cups and dainty pinkies here. Chai is made with more milk than water, more sugar than you'd care to think about, and spiced with cardamom in winter and ginger in summer. It is served from street stalls dotted all over the country and wherever people gather. It won't be for everyone, but if you immerse yourself in its culture you'll experience the very essence of this mad and magical country.

A glass of steaming sweet milky and frothy chai is the perfect antidote to the heat and stress of Indian travel and is a tonic for body and soul. The disembodied voice droning 'chai, chai garam' (hot tea) down the carriageway of your train will become one of the most familiar and welcome sounds of your trip. You can have a 'boy' bring it to even the most basic hotel room – whether he's 10 or 80, if he fetches tea or carries your bag, he's still called the boy.

If chai's not your cuppa, you'll be able to find the familiar formula of black tea, milk and lumps of sugar in multistarred hotels and in the planters clubs of tea-growing regions. You can order 'tray' or 'separate' tea just about anywhere, but if it's not the establishment's usual offering, you'll wish you hadn't.

The fragrant, light and sweet tea produced in Darjeeling will be familiar to even amateur connoisseurs. However, how many of us have actually tasted it before? While there are 12 million kilograms of tea produced in Darjeeling per annum, more than 60 million kilograms of 'Darjeeling Tea' are sold around the world each year! (See Darjeeling in the West Bengal chapter). Assam and Nilgiri Hills are India's other tea-growing regions.

Coffee

While chai is the choice of the nation, South Indians in particular share their loyalty with coffee, although it's sometimes made with so much milk and sugar that you couldn't tell them apart. In the more discerning establishments, you'll be pleasantly surprised with Indian coffee, most notably beans such as Mysore Nuggets and the enchantingly named Monsooned Malabar.

Other Drinks

Coca-Cola and Pepsi are bombarding India with advertising and young 'hip' locals are lapping up their sickly sweet concoctions. These – and local brands such as Thums Up and Campa Cola – are generally safe to drink as long as you're not diabetic. '*Masala soda*' is the quintessentially Indian soft drink available at all drinks stalls. It is a freshly opened bottle of soda pepped up with a lime, spices, salt and sugar.

There's a mind-boggling range of fruit, most of which is blended into juice at some

Beware of Those Bhang Lassis!

Although rarely printed in menus, some restaurants in certain parts of India (predominantly the tourist hotbeds such as Rajasthan) clandestinely whip up *bhang lassi*, a yogurt and iced-water beverage laced with bhang, a derivative of marijuana. Usually called 'special lassi', this often potent concoction does not agree with everyone. Some travellers have been stuck in bed for several miserable days after drinking it; others have been robbed while lying in a state of delirium.

And why do they call it Bhang again?
MICK WELDON

stage. Restaurants think nothing of adding salt and sugar to intensify the flavours but if you just want vitamins, tell the waiter to leave the additives out. The most popular street juices are made from sweet lemon, and sugar cane, which is pressed in front of you by a mechanised wheel complete with jingling bells.

Jal Jeera is the most therapeutic and refreshing indigenous drink. It's made with lime juice, cumin, mint and rock salt. It is sold in large earthenware pots by street vendors as well as in restaurants. The juice from the green tender coconut is safe and refreshing, and you'll find it sold from carts all over the country. Watching the machete-wielding wallah whop the coconut into a drink is half the fun. After you've drunk the juice, he'll whop the coconut some more and give the remains back to you as chunks of tasty coconut meat.

Sweet and savoury lassis (yogurt drinks) are popular throughout, although the best are in Varanasi and Punjab. *Faluda* is a rose-flavoured Muslim speciality made with milk, cream, nuts and strands of vermicelli. Hot or cold *milk badam*, flavoured with saffron and almonds, is an invigorating morning drink.

Alcoholic Drinks

Indian drinkers come in two categories; the hoi polloi who drink to get blotto and the hoity-toity who sip Indian and imported spirits. The common man quaffs 'country liquor' such as the notorious arak of the south, which comes with quaint names such as Amanush (Inhuman) and Asha (Hope) in the north. It is cheap, gives an instant high and tastes ghastly. If you feel compelled to sample some, make sure you drink the government-distilled variety. Each year, hundreds of people are killed or blinded by the methyl (wood) alcohol in illegal arak.

Most Indian spirits are made of rectified spirit and flavouring, and taste vaguely familiar yet unpleasant. Peter Scott, Antiquity and Solan No 1 – in that order – are the best legal whiskies.

The best-known drink is a clear spirit with a heady pungent flavour called *mahua*, which is distilled from the flower of the mahua tree. It is brewed in makeshift village stalls all over central India during March and April, when these trees bloom. It's safe to drink as long as it comes from a trustworthy source.

Toddy, the sap from the palm tree, is drunk in coastal areas. Wherever you hear the rhythmic tapping of buffalo bone against the palm bud (in the morning and evening), look for the toddy tapper and beg him for a sample of this mildly alcoholic natural wonder.

Feni is the primo Indian spirit, and the preserve of laid-back Goa but not often found in the north. Coconut and cashew are the two main varieties. Coconut feni is light and unexceptional but the much more popular cashew feni – made from the fruit of the cashew tree – is worth taking home.

Most travellers look forward to a beer at the end of a hot, dusty day, although the quality generally isn't worthy of your thirst.

Most brands are straightforward pilsners around the 5% alcohol mark, and have glycerine as an emulsifier. Outside the cities and tourist centres, you'll struggle to find a beer cold enough to quench your thirst. Make sure you feel the bottle first before letting the waiter open it; beer is expensive and the only thing worse than drinking lukewarm Indian beer is blowing your budget in the process.

Most travellers champion Kingfisher, which is available nationwide. Royal Challenge, Dansberg, Golden Eagle, London Pilsner and Sandpiper are our favourite national brands. Solan, from Himachal Pradesh and the highest brewery in the world at 2400m, is also a reasonable choice.

ENTERTAINMENT

If you confine your expectations of entertainment to bars, nightclubs and other activities you may take for granted at home, you're going to miss out on an awful lot. Check the regional chapters for specific recommendations.

Although many of the bigger cities do have independent bars and nightclubs, the majority of upmarket ones tend to be found in top-end hotels. Here, you'll get the chance to rub shoulders with the local Indian yuppies (if that's your thing). However, many hotel discos restrict admission to members and hotel guests; couples have a better chance of being admitted. Plus they're *expensive* – once you've shelled out the hefty door charge, which ranges from Rs 200 to 400 per couple, a pricey drinks menu awaits inside.

Unlike discos and pubs, one thing you're likely to find in most towns is cinemas. There are many thousands of cinemas all over the country and entry is nominal. If you're passing through Jaipur in Rajasthan, the Raj Mandir cinema is highly recommended (see Jaipur in the Rajasthan chapter for details).

If you've never seen a Bollywood blockbuster, it's worth making the time to see at least one. The audience reactions during a show are often just as entertaining as the film itself. For more on the cinema-going experience, see the boxed text 'Behind the Scenes of Indian Cinema' in the Facts about North India chapter.

Vibrant traditional regional music and dance performances are usually held at major hotels and other venues (see regional chapters for details). At some festivals, such as Pushkar's Camel Fair in Rajasthan, you may be treated to impromptu performances by livestock traders around a campfire. *Kathputlis* (traditional puppeteers) are another attraction of Rajasthan. Many major cities, such as Delhi, Khajuraho and Kolkata, have a spectacular sound-and-light show which is an atmospheric way of absorbing culture and history.

North India is a glorious place to simply sit back and watch the day unfold. 'People watching' arguably rivals any form of contrived entertainment. Not only is it a veritable feast for the eyes and mind, it's also absolutely free! Varanasi's bathing ghats are unbeatable in this respect. Sitting in the lobby of a five-star hotel can be fascinating way of 'accessing' the local high society; you'll see a cross-section of people, from elegant Indian women decked out in traditional saris, to glam young things sporting the latest Western designer labels. At the other end of the social spectrum, there's the inimitable (and highly inspirational) scene of everyday life on the streets – from the indefatigable traffic police zealously trying to tame the wild traffic, to mobile street vendors selling everything from bulky plastic rubbish bins to quaintly decorated plastic bangles.

Board games have a long tradition in India. Chess, for example, is thought to have originated in India in the 6th century AD. Carrom, although its origins are obscure, is a traditional game that has survived over time and has its fans to this very day (it's also played in Sri Lanka). Carrom centres on a square wooden board and allows a maximum of four players. In the centre of the board are nine black and nine white coins plus one pink coin called a queen. On each corner of the board are pockets and the goal is to use a striker to send the coins (black or white depending on which you have drawn) into one of the pockets.

Traditional sports which still enjoy a healthy following in India include *kho-kho* and *kabaddi*, both of which are essentially elaborate games of tag, but which require great skill and stamina.

SPECTATOR SPORTS

India's national sport (obsession almost) is cricket. During the cricket season, if an international side is touring India and there is a test match on, you'll see crowds outside shops with TVs, and people walking down the street with a pocket radio pressed to their ear. Test matches with Pakistan have a particularly strong following as the rivalry is intense. One thing you can count on is that most Indians will know the names of the entire touring cricket team, and, if the team's from your home country, they'll be surprised if you can't demonstrate similar knowledge. If you do have an interest in cricket, the atmosphere in India is phenomenal and always a sure-fire way of igniting passionate conversations.

International cricket matches are played at several major centres in India, mainly during winter. Renowned cricket centres in North India include those at Ahmedabad (Sardar Patel Stadium and Modhara Stadium), Kolkata (Ranji Stadium, Eden Gardens), Delhi (Feroz Shah Kotla Stadium), and the Mohali (PCA Stadium) in Chandigarh. The Ranji Stadium in Kolkata holds more than 100,000 people and has one of the best atmospheres of any cricket ground in the world. Ticket prices are around Rs 25 for state matches, Rs 150 for one day internationals and Rs 500 for the full five days of a test match. Tickets for cricket matches are usually advertised in the press a few weeks in advance; it's obviously preferable to buy a ticket well ahead, although some travellers claim they have been able to get tickets from the stadium on the same day a match is being played.

India is also one of the world leaders in hockey, and has several Olympic gold medals to its credit – although none since 1980. In the 2000 Olympics at Sydney, the one billion-strong nation only bagged one medal, a bronze for weightlifting, won by

Cricketing Woes

Cricket, which is followed religiously by many Indians, has a particular area of conflict with the majority religion, Hinduism. Despite the sacred status of the cow, cow hide has been used for many years to make cricket balls – it is estimated that annually around 1125 cows are killed for this purpose in India. In 1999 a high-ranking Hindu priest, Swami Nischalananda Saraswati, started a campaign to ban the use of leather in cricket balls. In this important domestic contest – Hindu icon versus cricket – cricket won decisively. Saraswati's efforts were met with minimal support and much derision.

More recently, Indian cricket fans have been rocked by allegations of match-fixing scandals involving Indian bookmakers and several international teams. A number of Indian cricketers have been implicated following international investigations. When former Indian captain Mohammed Azharuddin was first accused of match-fixing, infuriated Indian cricket fans publicly burnt effigies of him and the other players accused (as they were considered to be traitors to their nation). Azharuddin and ex-Test player Ajay Sharma were found guilty of match fixing in late 2000 and banned for life. Manoj Prabhakar and Ajay Jadeja have been punished with a five-year ban for their involvement with Indian bookmakers.

Allegations that Indian idol Kapil Dev was also involved in wrongdoing have still not been proven. However, the *Indian Express* revealed in January 2001 that a tax investigation uncovered a bank account held by Kapil Dev that contained around US$500,000 in undeclared income. Prabhakar and Jadeja apparently had similar sums stashed away, while Sharma and the bowler Nikhil Chopra reputedly had around US$150,000 each.

Karnam Malleswari. India's dismal performance at the Olympics sparked heated debate in India, with bitter accusations of corruption and mismanagement aimed at Indian officials, and complaints that the team didn't receive sufficient funding.

When it comes to tennis, India traces its links to Wimbledon right back to 1908 when Sadar Nihal Singh was the first Indian to ever compete there. However, the first Indian to bag a major award was Ramanathan Krishnan, who became the junior Wimbledon champion in 1954. In the 1970s, India's Vijay Amritraj reached the quarterfinals at both Wimbledon and the US Open. However, the biggest success stories are Leander Paes and Mahesh Bhupathi who won Wimbledon's prestigious men's doubles title in 1999 – the first Indians to ever do so.

Horse polo is particularly popular among elite circles. Emperor Akbar was believed to have been the first person to introduce rules to the game, and the sport flourished during the years of the British Raj. One of the world's oldest polo clubs, established back in 1862, is in Kolkata. After Independence its popularity declined (it's expensive to play and stage), though today there is a renewed interest in the game, largely due to beefed up sponsorship commitment. You can see it being played during the winter months at various centres including Delhi, Jaipur and Kolkata – check local newspapers for current venues and timings. Polo, along with archery, is also popular in Ladakh – see the boxed text 'Polo & Archery' in the Ladakh & Zanskar chapter.

SHOPPING

India is bursting with beautiful things to buy. The cardinal rule when purchasing handicrafts is to bargain and bargain hard. You can get a good idea of what is reasonable (in terms of quality and price) by visiting the various state emporiums and the Central Cottage Industries Emporiums, which can be found in major cities. At these places, you can inspect items from all over the country. Because prices are fixed (albeit often quite high), you can get an idea of how hard to bargain when you purchase similar items from regular vendors. In the tourist traps, the offerings at craft emporiums is almost identical – expect to find Kashmiri carpets, papier-mâché, sandalwood elephants, Rajasthani textiles, Tibetan trinkets, imitation Mughal miniature paintings and Benares silk. For information about cooperatives see Responsible Tourism, earlier in this chapter.

Be careful when buying items that include delivery to your home country. You may be told that the price includes home delivery and all customs and handling charges. Often this is not the case, and you may find yourself having to collect the item yourself from your country's main port or airport, pay customs charges (which could be as much as 20% of the item's value) and handling charges levied by the airline or shipping company (up to 10% of the value). If you can't collect the item promptly, or get someone to do it on your behalf, exorbitant storage charges may also be charged.

Opening hours for shops differ (Sunday seems to be a holiday for most), so check this out locally to ensure you don't leave all your shopping to your last day in India only to discover that they're all shut!

South India produces some excellent items, which you'll see for sale in the north. Sandalwood carving (mainly images of the gods) is one of Karnataka's specialities, while Kerala is noted for its rosewood carving (usually of animals – particularly elephants). In Maharashtra, Aurangabad is known for Himroo shawls, sheets and saris, and Paithan produces exquisite (and expensive) silk and gold thread saris. Also in the south, delightful small images of the gods (especially Shiva as dancing Nataraja) are made by the age-old lost-wax process. For more information on these products and others, see the *South India* guidebook. For more details about the northern specialities mentioned below, see Arts & Crafts in the Facts about North India chapter or the regional chapters.

Carpets

In Kashmir, where India's finest carpets are produced, the carpet-making techniques and styles were brought from Persia even before the Mughal era. The art flourished under the Mughals and today Kashmir is packed with small carpet producers. Persian motifs have been much embellished on Kashmiri carpets, which come in a variety of sizes – 0.9m x 1.5m, 1.2m x 1.8m and so on. They are either made of pure wool, wool with a small percentage of silk to give a sheen (known as 'silk touch') or pure silk. The latter are more for decoration than hard wear. Expect to pay at least Rs 7000 for a good-quality 1.2m x 1.8m (4ft x 6ft) carpet and don't be surprised if the price is more than twice as high. Other carpet-making areas include Badhoi and Mirzapur in Uttar Pradesh.

In Kashmir and Rajasthan, the coarsely woven woollen *numdas* are made. These are more primitive and folksy, and consequently cheaper, than the fine carpets. Around the Himalaya and Uttar Pradesh *dhurries*, flat-weave cotton warp-and-weft rugs are woven. In Kashmir *gabbas* are applique-like rugs. The numerous Tibetan refugees in India have brought their craft of making superbly colourful Tibetan rugs with them. A Tibetan rug with 48 knots per square inch will cost around Rs 2300 per square metre. Good places to buy Tibetan rugs are Darjeeling, Gangtok and McLeod Ganj, which is also a good place to pick up Kashmiri souvenirs.

Unless you're an expert it's best to get advice or buy from a reputable dealer if you're spending large amounts of money on carpets. Check prices back home too; many Western carpet dealers sell at prices you would have difficulty matching even at the source. Also look out for the Smiling Carpet label; this is a UN/NGO initiative to try and discourage the use of child labour in carpet manufacture.

Textiles

This is still India's major industry and 40% of the total production is at the village level where it is known as *khadi*. There are government khadi emporiums (known as Khadi Gramodyog) around the country, and these are good places to buy handmade items of homespun cloth, such as the popular 'Nehru jackets' and the kurta pyjama. Bedspreads, tablecloths, cushion covers or material for clothes are other popular khadi purchases.

There is an amazing variety of cloth styles, types and techniques around the region.

Punjab is known for its *phulkari* bedspreads or wall hangings, while Barmer (Rajasthan) is famous for its embroidery. Indeed Rajasthan is noted for its wonderfully vibrant textiles – Jaipur probably has the widest range.

Batik is a fairly recent introduction from Indonesia but already widespread; *kalamkari* cloth from Gujarat is an associated but far older craft. Also in Gujarat is the mirrored embroidery of Kutch, which usually sports geometric designs and is best bought in Bhuj, the villages of the Rann of Kutch, or Ahmedabad.

Markets in some of the larger cities, especially Delhi, stock decent Western fashions at competitive prices.

Shawls, Silk & Saris

Traditional wool shawls from the Kullu Valley are one of the most popular souvenirs from the Himalaya and are excellent value for money. Most are produced on traditional wooden handlooms by cooperatives of village weavers and prices range from about Rs 200 for a simple wool shawl to Rs 6000 for a stylish pashmina or angora shawl. The heavy embroidered shawls worn by many women in the mountain villages can cost as much as Rs 10,000. One excellent organisation is Bhuttico (the Bhutti Weavers Cooperative), with fixed-price shops in many towns in Himachal Pradesh. Also popular are the traditional caps worn by men and women from the mountain tribes, which range from Rs 30 for a thin but colourful Kullu cap to Rs 200 for a warm woollen Kinnaur cap. Ladakh is also known for its beautiful pashmina shawls – for more on these, see the boxed text 'Pashmina and Shatoosh' in the Ladakh & Zanskar chapter.

The 'silk capital' is Kanchipuram in Tamil Nadu, although Varanasi is also popular, especially for silk saris. In Varanasi expect to pay at least Rs 150 per metre. It costs about Rs 125 to 140 for a tailor to make you a long

Buyer Beware!

In popular travellers' hangouts (particularly Agra, Jaipur and other parts of Rajasthan, Varanasi, Delhi and Kolkata) take extreme care with the commission merchants. These incredibly tenacious fellows hang around waiting to pick you up and cart you off to their favourite dealers where whatever you pay will have a hefty margin built into it to pay their commission. Stories about 'my family's place', 'my brother's shop' and 'special deal at my friend's place' are just that – stories and nothing more.

Whatever you might be told, if you are taken by a rickshaw driver or tout to a place, be it a hotel, craft shop, market or even restaurant, the price you pay will be inflated. This can be by as much as 50% (even more), so try to visit these places independently – no matter how persistent the touts are.

Another trap that many travellers fall into occurs when using a credit card. You may well be told that if you buy the goods, the merchant won't forward the credit slip for payment until you have received the goods, even if it is in three months' time. This is total bullshit. No trader will be sending you as much as a postcard until they have received the money, in full, for the goods you are buying. What you'll find in fact is that within 48 hours of you signing the credit slip, the merchant has contacted the bank in Delhi and the money will have been credited to their account.

Also beware of any shop that takes your credit card out the back and comes back with the slip for you to sign. Sometimes while out of sight, the vendor will imprint a few more forms, forge your signature, and you'll be billed for items you haven't purchased. Have the slip filled out right in front of you.

If you believe any stories about buying anything in India to later sell at a profit elsewhere, you'll simply be proving (once again) that old adage about separating fools from their money. Precious stones and carpets are favourites for this game, particularly in Jaipur and Agra. Operators who

sleeve shirt or knee-length dress. Kolkata is also known for its fine hand-woven cotton and silk saris, which are widely displayed in city shops and markets. Sualkuchi in Assam is another silk-weaving centre.

For more on Varanasi silk, see the boxed text 'Benares Silk' under Varanasi in the Uttar Pradesh chapter.

Jewellery

Many Indian women put a large chunk of their wealth into jewellery, so it is no wonder that so much of it is available. However, for Western tastes it's the heavy folk-art jewellery that has particular appeal – you'll find it all over the country, but particularly in Rajasthan. You'll also find Tibetan jewellery, which is even chunkier and more folk-like.

If you're looking for fine jewellery as opposed to folk jewellery, you may well find that much of what is produced in India is too ornate for your liking.

In Rajasthan, Jaipur is especially renowned for its precious and semi-precious gems (see the boxed text 'Buyer Beware!' for important information about gem scams).

Some of the jewellery pieces on offer in Tibetan centres such as McLeod Ganj and Darjeeling are genuine antiques carried in by refugees, but most are actually reproductions made locally and artificially 'aged'. Loose beads of agate, turquoise, carnelian and silver are also available if you feel like stringing your own necklace. Buddhist rosaries made of gems, wood or inlaid bone make great souvenirs; prices range from around Rs 20 for wooden beads to Rs 500 for an amber rosary.

Leatherwork

Indian leatherwork is not usually made from cow-hide but from buffalo-hide, camel, goat or some other substitute. Kanpur in Uttar Pradesh is the country's major centre for leatherwork.

Chappals, those basic leather sandals found all over India, are a particularly popular purchase. In Rajasthan you can buy the

Buyer Beware!

practise such schemes are very good at luring trusting souls – they are invariably very friendly – often taking travellers to their homes and insisting on paying for meals etc. They'll often tell you hard-luck stories about an inability to obtain an export licence, hoping to garner your sympathy. It's all part of the con – do *not* fall for it. Merchants will tell you that you can sell the items in Australia, Europe or the USA for several times the purchase price, and will even give you the (often imaginary) addresses of dealers who will buy them. You'll also be shown written statements, supposedly from other travellers, documenting the money they have supposedly made – it's all a sophisticated scam. The stones or carpets you buy will be worth only a fraction of what you pay (or if you agreed to have them sent, they probably won't even arrive).

An alternative ploy used by some gem merchants is to tell you that if *they* export gems, they'll pay tax, but if *you* carry them with you, you can export them free of tax. They'll offer you a fat fee for your trouble, although (and here's where the warning bells should start ringing) you'll first have to fill out a credit card slip as security. The merchant will tell you that their agent will pick up the goods in your home town, and pay you your fee upon receipt. Forget it – no agent will turn up and you'll be lumbered with unwanted jewels that are worth much less than the value of the credit card transaction (which, of course, the vendor has long-since cashed in).

Don't let your desire for a quick buck cloud your judgement. Despite our warnings over many editions, we inevitably receive a clutch of reports from distressed travellers with tales of woe concerning the very scams we warn about.

While it is certainly a minority of traders who are actually involved in dishonest schemes, virtually all are involved in the commission racket, so you need to shop with care – take your time, be firm, bargain hard and don't hesitate to say no.

delightful traditional leather shoes – jootis; those for men often have curled up toes.

At craft shops in Delhi you'll find well-made leather bags, handbags and other items. Kashmiri leather shoes and boots, often of reasonably good quality, are widely found, along with coats and jackets of often abysmally low quality.

Paintings

Reproductions of the beautiful old miniatures are painted in many places, but beware of paintings purported to be antique – it's highly unlikely that they are. Also note that quality can vary widely; low prices often mean low quality, and if you buy before you've had a chance to look at a lot of miniatures (thus developing some knowledge about them) you'll inevitably find you bought unwisely. Udaipur (Rajasthan) has some good shops specialising in modern reproductions on silk and paper; they cost anything from Rs 10 for a small square to Rs 2000 for large pieces. In the same state, Jaipur has several shops with brilliant contemporary paintings by local artists (prices range from Rs 200 to 50,000).

The murals of Shantiniketan (West Bengal) hail from the town that they are named after, which also happens to be famous for its association with Nobel Prize winning author Rabindranath Tagore.

Bihar's unique folk art is the sublime Mithila or Madhubani paintings, created by the women of Madhubani (see the boxed text 'Mithila Paintings' in the Bihar & Jharkhand chapter). They're most easily found in Patna.

Papier-Mâché

This is probably the most characteristic Kashmiri craft. The basic papier-mâché article is made in a mould, then painted and polished in successive layers until the final intricate design is produced. Prices depend upon the complexity and quality of the painted design and the amount of gold leaf used. Items include bowls, cups, containers, jewellery boxes, letter holders, tables, lamps, coasters, trays and more. A small bowl might cost only Rs 40, whereas a large, well-made item might approach Rs 1000.

Rajasthan (especially Jaipur and Jaisalmer) is *the* place to buy colourful papier-mâché puppets – they make wonderful gifts (prices range from around Rs 200 to 1000).

Bronze Figures, Pottery & Terracotta

Jaipur (Rajasthan) specialises in blue-glazed pottery that usually features floral and geometric motifs.

Kolkata is known for its terracotta ware, from simple little bowls to large decorative figurines. Terracotta images of gods and children's toys are also made in Bihar.

Woodcarving

Carved wooden furniture and other household items, either in natural finish or lacquered, are made in various locations. In Kashmir, intricately carved wooden screens, tables, jewellery boxes and trays are carved from Indian walnut. They have a similar pattern to the decorative trim of houseboats.

Wood-inlay work is one of Bihar's oldest craft industries and you'll find wooden wall hangings, tabletops, trays, boxes etc decorated with inlaid metals and ivory.

The carved wooden massage wheels and rollers available at many Hindu pilgrimage sites make great gifts – they're cheap and light to carry.

Metalwork & Marble

Copper and brass items are popular throughout India. Candle-holders, trays, bowls, tankards and ashtrays are made in Mumbai and other centres. In Rajasthan and Uttar Pradesh the brass is inlaid with exquisite designs in red, green and blue enamel. Bihar is also good for enamelled trinkets and religious images. *Bidri* emanates from northern Karnataka; silver is inlaid into gunmetal to create hookah pipes, lamp bases and jewellery boxes. Many Tibetan religious objects are made using a similar technique, inlaying silver into copper. Prayer wheels, ceremonial horns and document cases are all popular and inexpensive purchases. Painted cast-metal statues of Tibetan deities are heavier but will look stunning back home. Prices start at Rs 350 for small figurines.

A sizeable cottage industry has sprung up in Agra – marble souvenirs inlaid with semi-precious stones. The inspiration for most pieces comes from the *pietra dura* marble inlays found on the Taj Mahal and other monuments; items on offer range from complete miniature Tajs to bulky chess sets. Expect to pay about Rs 200 for a jewellery box and Rs 1000 upwards for a detailed wall plaque.

Musical Instruments

Indian musical instruments have long been an attraction for travellers and are predominantly available in the larger towns (including Delhi, Kolkata and Jaipur), some with beautiful inlay work. Make sure you shop around to find the highest quality items at the most competitive prices.

In Delhi the best place to buy instruments is Netaji Suhash Marg. The cost of a *tabla* and *doogi* (drums are traditionally paired – the tabla is the long drum with tuning blocks and the doogi is the broader metal drum) is upwards of Rs 950. Ornamental souvenir drums cost as little as Rs 100, but the quality of fabric and sound are inferior. Good-quality sitars range from Rs 3000 to 16,000, but they can cost up to Rs 30,000. Kolkata also offers some fine Indian instruments at competitive prices.

In Varanasi, you can buy musical instruments at the Triveni Music Centre.

Note that certain types of wood with which some sitars are made, may warp in certain climates, adversely affecting the sound of the instrument.

Odds & Sods

Throughout India, books are an absolutely brilliant buy. There's a wide range of titles at prices likely to be far cheaper than you'd pay back home. You can easily whittle away several hours simply browsing through bookshops and it's a perfect way to spend a lazy afternoon.

Darjeeling and Kalimpong (West Bengal) are splendid places to pick up aromatic tea. Also in West Bengal, in Siliguri, caneware does a roaring trade. You can get everything from small letter racks to bulky lounge furniture.

An interesting speciality of Bihar is the tapper mats of the Palamau district. Tapper is a durable material derived from the sun hemp plant – bags made from the fibre were once used to transport grains and other heavy loads. Nowadays, tapper yarn is dyed in various colours and available in various forms, such as handbags.

Meanwhile, in Bhopal, *jari* shoulder bags are a speciality. Made of cotton, they sport colourful designs and can be purchased for as little as Rs 35. Meghalaya, in India's north-eastern region, is particularly noted for its beautiful hand-woven baskets.

Antiques & Wildlife Restrictions

Articles over 100 years old are not allowed to be exported from India without an export clearance certificate (which is not easy to obtain anyway). If you have doubts about any item and think it could be defined as an antique, you can check with regional branches of the Archaeological Survey of India (☎ 011-3019451 in Delhi).

The Indian Wildlife Protection Act bans any form of wildlife trade. Don't buy any products that further endanger threatened species and habitats – the consequences of doing so may result in heavy fines and even imprisonment.

Getting There & Away

> **Warning**
>
> The information in this chapter is particularly vulnerable to change. Prices for international travel are volatile, routes are introduced and cancelled, schedules change, special deals come and go, and rules and visa requirements are amended. Airlines and governments seem to take a perverse pleasure in making price structures and regulations as complicated as possible. You should check directly with the airline or a travel agency to make sure you understand how a fare (and ticket you may buy) works. In addition, the travel industry is highly competitive and there are many lurks and perks.
>
> The upshot of this is that you should always get opinions, quotes and advice from as many airlines and travel agencies as possible before parting with your hard-earned cash. The details in this chapter should be regarded as pointers and are not a substitute for your own careful, up-to-date research.

AIR

Airports & Airlines

Mumbai (formerly Bombay), Delhi, Kolkata (formerly Calcutta) and Chennai (formerly Madras) are India's main gateways for international flights. For visiting the north, Delhi or Kolkata are your best bets, though Mumbai is also reasonably convenient (see the 'Getting to North India from Mumbai' boxed text later in this chapter). It's worth noting that thick fog can sometimes play havoc with flight schedules in Delhi during winter, particularly in December and January. Ahmedabad in Gujarat also has some international services.

In addition to the above airports (see Tickets in India later), the airport at Amritsar (Punjab) has some Air India flights to/from the Middle East. There are also plans to upgrade the airport at Guwahati (north-eastern region) to receive international flights, though it's unlikely anything will be done within the next two years.

India's national carrier is Air India (www.airindia.com), which also carries passengers on some domestic sectors of international routes (see also Air in the Getting Around chapter). Indian Airlines, the country's major domestic carrier, offers flights to some 16 neighbouring countries (for specific destinations see the Web site at www.indian-airlines.nic.in).

Buying Tickets

World aviation has never been so competitive, making air travel better value than ever. But you have to research the options carefully to make sure you get the best deal. The Internet is an increasingly useful resource for checking air fares.

Full-time students and people under 26 years (under 30 depending on the country/airline) have access to better deals than other travellers. You have to show a document proving your date of birth or a valid International Student Identity Card (ISIC) when buying your ticket and possibly also when boarding the plane.

Generally, there is nothing to be gained by buying a ticket direct from the airline. Discounted tickets are released to selected travel agencies and specialist discount agencies, and these are usually the cheapest deals going.

One exception to this rule is the expanding number of 'no-frills' carriers, which mostly only sell direct to travellers. Another exception is booking on the Internet. Many airlines offer some excellent fares to Web surfers. They may sell seats by auction or simply cut prices to reflect the reduced cost of electronic selling.

Many travel agencies around the world have Web sites, which can make the Internet a quick and easy way to compare prices. There is also an increasing number of online agents which operate only on the Internet.

Online ticket sales work well if you are doing a simple one-way or return trip on

Air Travel Glossary

Alliances Many of the world's leading airlines are now intimately involved with each other, sharing everything from reservations systems and check-in to aircraft and frequent-flyer schemes. Opponents say that alliances restrict competition. Whatever the arguments, there is no doubt that big alliances are the way of the future.

Courier Fares Businesses often need to send urgent documents or freight securely and quickly. Courier companies hire people to accompany the package through customs and, in return, offer a discount ticket which is sometimes a bargain. However, you may have to surrender all your baggage allowance and take only carry-on luggage.

Fares Airlines traditionally offer 1st-class (coded F), business-class (coded J) and economy-class (coded Y) tickets. These days there are so many promotional and discounted fares available that few passengers pay full fare.

Lost Tickets If you lose your airline ticket, an airline will usually treat it like a travellers cheque and, after inquiries, issue you with another one. Legally, however, an airline is entitled to treat it like cash and if you lose it then it's gone forever. Take very good care of your tickets.

Onward Tickets An entry requirement for many countries is that you have a ticket out of the country. If you're unsure of your next move, the easiest solution is to buy the cheapest onward ticket to a neighbouring country or a ticket from a reliable airline which can later be refunded if you do not use it.

Open-Jaw Tickets These are return tickets where you fly out to one place but return from another. If available, this can save you backtracking to your arrival point.

Overbooking Since every flight has some passengers who fail to show up, airlines often book more passengers than they have seats. Usually excess passengers make up for the no-shows, but occasionally somebody gets 'bumped' onto the next available flight. Guess who it is most likely to be? The passengers who check in late. If you do get 'bumped', you are normally offered some form of compensation.

Reconfirmation Some airlines require you to reconfirm your flight at least 72 hours prior to departure. Check your travel documents to see if this is the case

Restrictions Discounted tickets often have various restrictions on them – such as needing to be paid for in advance and incurring a penalty to be altered or cancelled. Others are restrictions on the minimum and maximum period you must be away.

Round-the-World Tickets RTW tickets give you a limited period (usually a year) in which to circumnavigate the globe. You can go anywhere the carrying airlines go, as long as you stay within the set mileage/number of stops and, with some tickets, don't backtrack. The number of stopovers or total number of separate flights is decided before you set off and they usually cost a bit more than a basic return flight.

Ticketless Travel Airlines are gradually waking up to the realisation that paper tickets are unnecessary encumbrances. On simple one-way or return trips, reservations details can be held on computer and the passenger merely shows ID to claim their seat.

Transferred Tickets Airline tickets cannot be transferred. Travellers sometimes try to sell the return half of their ticket, but officials can ask you to prove that you are the person named on the ticket. On an international flight, tickets are compared with passports.

specified dates. However, online superfast fare generators are no substitute for a travel agent who knows all about special deals, has strategies for avoiding layovers and can offer advice on everything from which airline has the best vegetarian food to the best travel insurance to bundle with your ticket.

You may find the cheapest flights are advertised by obscure agencies. Most such firms are honest and solvent, but there are some rogue fly-by-night outfits around. Paying by credit card generally offers protection, as most card issuers provide refunds if you can prove you didn't get what you paid for. Similar protection can be obtained by buying a ticket from a bonded agency, such as one covered by the Air Travel Organiser's Licence (ATOL) scheme in the UK (more details available at its Web site: www.atol.org.uk). Agencies that only accept cash should hand over the tickets straight away and not tell you to 'come back tomorrow'. After you've made a booking or paid your deposit, call the airline and confirm that the booking was made. It's generally not advisable to send money (even cheques) through the post unless the agency is very well established – some travellers have reported being ripped off by fly-by-night mail-order ticket agencies.

If you purchase a ticket and later want to make changes to your route or get a refund, you need to contact the original travel agency. Airlines only issue refunds to the purchaser of a ticket – usually the travel agent who bought the ticket on your behalf. Many travellers change their routes halfway through their trips, so think carefully before you buy a ticket that is not easily refunded.

Return flights don't necessarily have to go into and out of the same city – an 'open jaw' return (eg, flying into Mumbai and departing from Delhi) might not be more expensive.

Travellers with Special Needs

If they're warned early enough, airlines can often make special arrangements for travellers, such as wheelchair assistance at airports or vegetarian meals on the flight. Children under two years travel for 10% of the standard fare (or free on some airlines) as long as they don't occupy a seat. They don't get a baggage allowance. 'Skycots', baby food and nappies (diapers) should be provided by the airline if requested in advance. Children aged between two and 12 can usually occupy a seat for half to two-thirds of the full fare, and do get a baggage allowance.

The disability-friendly Web site www.everybody.co.uk has an airline directory that provides information on facilities offered by various airlines.

Departing India

It's important to reconfirm international tickets at least 72 hours before departure; some travellers have reported having their seat cancelled for not doing so.

Airlines recommend travellers check in three hours prior to international flight departures; allow time for getting stuck in India's often congested traffic, especially during peak hours. Most Indian airports have free luggage trolleys, but you'll probably be accosted by porters eagerly offering to lug your load for a tip (Rs 10 is fine). Once inside the airport, you'll be required to have your check-in baggage screened and sealed by security tape before proceeding to check-in. Don't forget to fill out an embarkation card before heading for the customs gate.

Departure Tax The departure tax of Rs 500 (Rs 150 for Bangladesh, Bhutan, Nepal, Pakistan, Maldives and Sri Lanka) is included in the price of virtually all airline tickets – check with your travel agent. Some travellers have reported inadvertently paying it for a second time at the airport.

Tickets in India

Although you can get international tickets in Mumbai and Kolkata, it is in Delhi where the real wheeling and dealing goes on. There are a number of bucket shops – unbonded travel agencies specialising in discount airline tickets – around Connaught Place, but inquire with other travellers about their current trustworthiness. And if you use a bucket shop, double check with the airline itself that the booking has been made.

Fares from India

from	to	one-way fare
Delhi	Auckland	Rs 26,800
	Bangkok	Rs 11,000
	Belfast	Rs 22,500
	Dubai	Rs 7700
	Karachi	Rs 7800
	Kathmandu	US$142
	Kuala Lumpur	Rs 18,000
	Lahore	Rs 5880
	London	Rs 16,650–23,000
	Moscow	Rs 13,800
	Singapore	Rs 18,000
	Sydney	Rs 20,280
	Tel Aviv	Rs 17,000
	Toronto	Rs 29,500
	Vancouver	Rs 36,000
Mumbai	Bangkok	Rs 15,000
	Colombo	Rs 13,350
	Dhaka	Rs 9975
	Hong Kong	Rs 24,000
	Kathmandu	US$217
	London	Rs 16,500–26,500
	Los Angeles	Rs 22,000–28,500
	Nairobi	Rs 19,300
	New York	Rs 31,000
	Paris	Rs 25,700
	Singapore	Rs 21,550
	Sydney	Rs 29,000
Kolkata	Bangkok	Rs 5300-7300
	Dhaka	Rs 2560
	Geneva	Rs 21,000
	Hong Kong	Rs 11,800
	Kathmandu	US$96
	London	Rs 18,000
	Los Angeles	Rs 32,000
	New York	Rs 23,700
	Paris	Rs 21,000
	Rome	Rs 19,000
	Singapore	Rs 7100
	Toronto	Rs 33,300
	Yangon	Rs 5775
Ahmedabad	Chicago	Rs 27,000
	Kuwait City	Rs 12,500
	London	Rs 22,000
	Muscat	Rs 10,300
	New York	Rs 27,000
	Sharjah	Rs 10,300

To give you an idea of costs, the following list shows fares from Indian international departure points (flights from other countries *to* India are provided under country headings later in this chapter). The following list is not exhaustive – many more international destinations are serviced from India (check with travel agencies). Note that fares here are one-way and given in the currency (rupees or US dollars) in which they are quoted in India.

The USA

Discount travel agencies in the USA are known as consolidators (although you won't see a sign on the door saying 'Consolidator'). San Francisco is the ticket consolidator capital of the USA, although good deals can be found in Los Angeles, New York and other big cities. Consolidators can be found through the *Yellow Pages*, the Internet or major daily newspapers.

For students or travellers under 26 years, popular travel agencies in the USA include: Council Travel (☎ 800-2COUNCIL), which has a Web site at www.ciee.org and its head office at 205 E 42 St, New York, NY 10017; and STA Travel (☎ 800 777 0112), which has offices in Boston, Chicago, Miami, New York, Philadelphia, San Francisco and other major cities. For more information see its Web site (www.statravel.com). Ticket Planet is a leading ticket consolidator in the USA and is recommended. Visit its Web site at www.ticketplanet.com.

The high season for flights from the USA to India is June to August and December to January. Low season runs from March to around mid-May and September to November.

From the USA's east coast most flights to India are via Europe. Prices quoted are for return fares. Low-season fares to Mumbai start from around US$1480, with Air India via London and American Airlines via Zurich. Fares to Delhi start from around US$1270 with Singapore Airlines via Frankfurt or Air India via London. Ahmedabad can be reached from New York five times weekly, and from Chicago twice weekly; these are Air India flights going

Getting to North India from Mumbai

Mumbai is the main international gateway to India. It also has the busiest network of domestic flights. It may work out cheaper and more convenient to fly to Mumbai and to head to North India from there.

Mumbai is a reasonably convenient option for North India, especially if you're visiting Madhya Pradesh or Gujarat. However, if you're thinking of hiring a car to drive up the coast, think again. The route north, highway 8, is one of the most congested roads in the country; you'll be lucky to make the 150km trip to Daman (the first worthwhile destination in Gujarat) inside six hours.

Though there are long-distance buses (private buses depart from Dr Anadrao Nair Rd, near Mumbai Central train station), the best way to transfer to the north is probably to fly or take the train.

In this section we've included details on major flights and train routes to North India, from Mumbai.

Air

The international and domestic airports are both north of Mumbai – 30km and 26km respectively.

The international terminal (officially called CST, but still better known as Sahar) is about 4km away from the domestic terminal, Santa Cruz.

Sahar's arrival hall has a duty-free shop, several foreign-exchange counters offering reasonable rates, Government of India tourist office, hotel reservation counter and a prepaid taxi booth – all open 24 hours. There's a left-luggage shed in the car park, about 200m left of the arrivals hall exit.

Mumbai's Santa Cruz domestic airport has two terminals, a couple of minutes' walk apart. Terminal A handles Indian Airlines flights, while terminal B caters to Jet Airways and Sahara Airlines. Planes start departing and arriving around dawn and stop around midnight. You're advised to check in one hour before departure.

Both terminals have foreign-exchange bureaus, ticketing counters and a restaurant-bar. The 24-hour left-luggage facility is midway between the two terminals. Note that flights on domestic sectors of Air India routes depart from the international airport.

Mumbai: This Fortnight has a list of major international airline offices in Mumbai, or consult the *Yellow Pages* for a more comprehensive list. Travel agents are a better bet for booking international flights, and will reconfirm your flight for a small fee.

The 1½- to two-hour taxi trip downtown from Sahar airport should cost Rs 260 (Rs 325 from midnight to 5 am) if you use the prepaid taxi booth. Don't take an autorickshaw, as they can't enter downtown so you'll end up stranded a few kilometres short of the train stations. If you're going north, you might be able to take a taxi or autorickshaw to one of the suburban stations north of the city (eg, Bandra) instead of tracking all the way down to the terminus, Mumbai Central. However, you'll need to be sure that the train you intend to catch does stop at the suburban station concerned – call Western Railways (☎ 131).

At the domestic airport there's no prepaid taxi counter, so make sure the driver uses the meter. Expect to pay around Rs 250 for the one- to 1½-hour trip. A free shuttle bus goes between the airports for people with connecting flights.

Tickets for domestic airlines bought overseas need to be reconfirmed and the usual 72-hour rule applies. For Indian Airlines and Air India you may have to visit one of their offices to reconfirm. You can buy tickets to North India from any of the many travel agencies or you can buy them from the following airline offices:

Indian Airlines (☎ 2023031, fax 2830832) Air India Bldg, Nariman Point. The national 24-hour reservation number is ☎ 141.
Jet Airways (☎ 2837555, fax 2855694) Amarchand Mansion, Madame Cama Rd
Sahara Airlines (☎ 2835671, fax 2870076) 7 Tulsiani Chambers, Free Press Journal Marg, Nariman Point

Getting to North India from Mumbai

There are direct flights to several North Indian cities from Mumbai:

destination	flights per day	fare (US$)
Ahmedabad	2	75
Aurangabad	2	75
Bangalore	14	140
Delhi	20	175
Jaipur	3	155
Kolkata	7	230
Lucknow	2	250
Udaipur	1	125

Train

Two train systems operate out of Mumbai. Central Railways (☎ 134 for inquiries) handles services to the east and south, plus a few trains to the north. It operates from Chhatrapati Shivaji Terminus (CST), still better known locally as Victoria Terminus (VT). The reservation centre is at the back of the station where the taxis gather and is open from 8 am to 8 pm Monday to Saturday, and until 2 pm on Sunday. Tourist-quota tickets (which can be fully booked several weeks in advance during the high season) and Indrail passes can be bought at counter No 7 (closed Sunday).

The other train system is Western Railways (☎ 131), which has services to the north (including Rajasthan) from Mumbai Central (MC) train station (still usually called Bombay Central). The easiest place to make bookings for Western Railways trains is at the crowded reservation centre opposite Churchgate train station, open from 8 am to 8 pm Monday to Saturday, from 8 am to 8 pm Sunday. The foreign tourist-quota counter (open 9.30 am to 4.30 pm weekdays and until 2 pm on Saturday) is upstairs next to the Government of India tourist office, but tourist-quota tickets are only sold 24 hours before departure and you must pay in foreign currency. There's a reservation centre adjacent to Mumbai Central, but it doesn't sell tourist-quota tickets. Following are the major trains from Mumbai

destination	train No & name	departures	distance (km)	duration (hrs)	fare (Rs)
Agra	2137 *Punjab Mail*	7.10 pm CST	1344	21½	326/945
Ahmedabad	2009 *Shatabdi Exp*	6.25 am MC	492	7	630/1270
	2901 *Gujarat Mail*	9.50 pm MC	492	9	165/477
Bhopal	2137 *Punjab Mail*	7.10 pm CST	831	14	244/707
Kolkata	2859 *Gitanjali Exp*	6.00 am CST	1968	33½	393/1139
	8001 *Howrah Mail*	8.15 pm CST	1968	36	393/1139
Delhi	2951 *Rajdhani Exp*	4.55 pm MC	1384	17	1485/2405
	2925 *Paschim Exp*	11.35 am MC	1384	23	329/954
	2137 *Punjab Mail*	5.10 pm CST	1538	25¼	343/995
Hyderabad	7001 *Hussainsagar Exp*	9.55 pm CST	790	15¼	235/680
Indore	2961 *Avantika Exp*	7.25 pm MC	829	14½	244/707
Jaipur	2955 *Jaipur Exp*	7.05 pm MC	1200	17½	304/882
Varanasi	1065 *Gorakhpur Exp*	6.35 am D	1490	30¼	340/986

Abbreviations for train stations: CST – Chhatrapati Shivaji Terminus (Victory Terminus), MC – Mumbai Central, D – Dadar

Note: Fares are for sleeper/air-con 3-tier sleeper on overnight trips (2-tier if there are no 3-tier carriages), except for *Shatabdi Express* and *Rajdhani Express* (air-con chair with meals included).

via London, and prices start at around US$1400.

From the USA's west coast to Mumbai or Delhi, Aeroflot has the best bargain fares. Expect to pay around US$1000 for a low-season fare via Moscow. Another good deal to Delhi is with Korean Airlines or Asiania Airlines, both via Seoul; return fares start from around US$1200.

Other fares include Cathay Pacific Airway to Mumbai via Hong Kong from around US$1396 and US$1581 with El Al Israeli Airlines via Tel Aviv.

Canada

Fares from Canada are similar to fares from the USA. Travel CUTS (☎ 800-667 2887) is Canada's national student travel agency and has offices in all major cities. Its Web site is www.travelcuts.com.

From Canada most flights to India are via Europe but there are options for travel via the USA or Asia.

Low-season return fares from Vancouver to Delhi or Mumbai start from around C$2500, flying Northwest via Hong Kong or Singapore or Air France via Paris.

Return fares from Montreal or Toronto to Mumbai or Delhi in the low season start from C$2117 with Air France via Paris or C$2340 via Frankfurt with Lufthansa.

Australia

Two well-known internation agencies for cheap fares are STA Travel and Flight Centre. STA Travel (☎ 03-9349 2411) has its main office in Melbourne, at 224 Faraday St, Carlton, VIC 3053, and offices in all major cities and on many university campuses. Call ☎ 131 776 Australia-wide for the location of your nearest branch or visit its Web site (wwwstatravel.com.au). Flight Centre (☎ 131 600 Australia-wide) has a central office at 82 Elizabeth St, Sydney, NSW 2000, and there are dozens of offices throughout Australia. Its Web site is www.flightcentre.com.au.

From Australia, low-season return fares to Delhi start at A$1290 with Air India/Qantas via Singapore. Malaysia Airlines, SriLankan Airlines and Gulf Air all have return fares starting at around A$1345 to Mumbai and Delhi. Low-season return fares to Kolkata start from around A$1500.

New Zealand

As in Australia, STA Travel and Flight Centre International are popular travel agencies. Flight Centre (☎ 09-309 6171) has a large central office in Auckland at National Bank Towers (on the corner of Queen and Darby Sts) and many branches throughout the country. Its Web site is at www.flightcentre.co.nz. STA Travel (☎ 09-309 0458) has its main office at 10 High St, Auckland, and has other offices in Auckland as well as in Hamilton, Palmerston North, Wellington, Christchurch and Dunedin. The Web site is www.statravel.co.nz.

There are no direct flights either to or from New Zealand so several airlines offer stopovers in Asia. Low-season return fares to Delhi from Auckland start at NZ$1799 with Malaysia Airlines, via Kuala Lumpur or NZ$1940 with Air New Zealand, flying via Singapore.

The UK & Ireland

Discount air travel is big business in London. Advertisements for many travel agencies appear in the travel pages of the weekend broadsheet newspapers, in *Time Out*, the *Evening Standard* and in the free magazine *TNT*.

For students or travellers under 26 years, or for anybody else looking for a budget fare, popular travel agencies in the UK include: STA Travel (☎ 020-7361 6262), 86 Old Brompton Rd, London SW7, with a Web site at www.statravel.co.uk, and Usit Campus (☎ 0870-240 1010), 52 Grosvenor Gardens, London SW1, with a Web site at www.usitcampus.co.uk. Both agencies have branches throughout the UK.

Other recommended travel agencies for all age groups include:

Bridge the World (☎ 020-734 7447) 4 Regent Place, London W1
Web site: www.b-t-w.co.uk

Flightbookers (☎ 020-7757 2000) 177–178 Tottenham Court Rd, London W1
Web site: www.ebookers.com

Quest Travel (☎ 020-8547 3123) 10 Richmond Rd, Kingston-upon-Thames, Surrey KT2 5HL
Web site: www.questtravel.co.uk
Trailfinders (☎ 020-7938 3939) 194 Kensington High St, London W8
Web site: www.trailfinders.co.uk

From London to Delhi, Aeroflot has low-season return fares (via Moscow), starting at UK£380. British Airways has direct flights to Delhi starting at UK£580, direct Virgin Atlantic flights are around UK£481 in the low season. London-Kolkata return fares start from UK£430, London-Mumbai from UK£348, and London-Ahmedabad from about UK£380.

Return fares from Belfast to Mumbai or Delhi start from around UK£694 with British Airways.

Continental Europe

In the Netherlands, recommended agencies include NBBS Reizen (☎ 020-620 50 71) 66 Rokin, Amsterdam, plus branches in most cities. Check out its Web site (www.nbbs.nl). An NBBS subsidiary, Budget Air (☎ 020 627 1251), 34 Rokin, Amsterdam, is another agency worth trying and shares the same Web site address.

Agencies in Germany include STA Travel (☎ 030-311 0950), Goethestrasse 73, 10625 Berlin (www.statravel.com/de) and Usit Campus (☎ 01805-788336) with its Web site at www.usitcampus.de. Both these popular travel agencies have a number of branches throughout Germany.

Travel agencies in France include Usit Connect Voyages (☎ 01 42 44 14 00), 14 rue de Vaugirard, 75006 Paris (www.usitconnect.fr/newsite/index.asp) and OTU Voyages (☎ 01 40 29 12 12), 39 ave Georges-Bernanos, 75005 (www.otu.fr). Like Usit Voyages, this agency specialises in student and young people's travel. Nouvelles Frontiéres (01 45 68 70 00) 87 blvd de Grenelle, 75015 Paris, also has many branches both in Paris and throughout France. See its Web site (www.nouvelles-frontieres.fr) for more information.

Some return fares from Europe are: Frankfurt-Delhi (DM1758), Amsterdam-Delhi (f1350) and Paris to Delhi (4040FF).

Africa

There are plenty of flights between East Africa and Mumbai due to the large Indian population living in Kenya. Typical one-way fares from Nairobi to Mumbai are US$399. You can get an Air India return flight from Nairobi to Delhi from about US$820 plus taxes.

Bangladesh

There are Indian Airlines flights between Kolkata in West Bengal and several Bangladeshi centres, including Dhaka (US$52) and Chittagong (US$67).

Malaysia

As Thailand has more – and cheaper – flight options, most travellers in South-East Asia choose to depart for India from Bangkok, rather than Kuala Lumpur. The one-way economy fare from Kuala Lumpur to Delhi is US$230.

Myanmar (Burma)

There are no land crossing points between Myanmar and India (or between Myanmar and any other country), so your only choice from India is to fly there. Indian Airlines flies from Yangon (Rangoon) to Kolkata (US$152 one way).

Nepal

Royal Nepal Airlines Corporation (RNAC) and Indian Airlines share routes between India and Kathmandu. Druk Air also has flights which continue on to Bhutan. RNAC and Indian Airlines have one-way flights from Kathmandu to Delhi (US$102), Mumbai (US$151) and Kolkata (US$96).

Pakistan

Pakistan International Airlines (PIA) has one-way Karachi to Delhi flights, via Lahore, for US$107 and from Lahore to Delhi for US$70.

Singapore

The full-price one-way economy fare from Singapore to Delhi is US$670, with either Singapore Airlines or Thai Airways International (via Bangkok).

Sri Lanka

One-way flights from Colombo cost about US$210 to Mumbai and US$255 to Delhi with SriLankan Airlines or Indian Airlines.

Thailand

Bangkok is the most popular departure point from South-East Asia into India. Flights are available from Bangkok to major Indian cities, including Kolkata for US$159 and Delhi for US$203, both one way. Thai Airways International and Indian Airlines also fly via Yangon in Myanmar to Kolkata for around US$410 return.

LAND

Bangladesh

To the immense delight of locals and travellers alike, a direct bus service between Kolkata (India) and Dhaka (Bangladesh) was introduced in 1999, making the once complex task of crossing the border far more straightforward. Although there are also minor crossing points from India, the new bus service between Kolkata and Dhaka (see Kolkata to Dhaka, following) is by far the most convenient option, as minor (lesser-used) routes are variable and thus uncertain.

If you're travelling from Bangladesh to India, no exit permit is required to leave Bangladesh, but if you enter Bangladesh by air and leave via a land crossing, a road permit is officially required. This can be obtained in Dhaka at the Immigration & Passport office (☎ 02-9556020), 127 New Eskaton Rd, Mogh Bazar. It's open 10 am to noon Saturday to Thursday. For further details about Bangladesh, get hold of Lonely Planet's *Bangladesh*.

Kolkata to Dhaka The direct bus to Dhaka departs Kolkata at 7 am daily, arriving in Dhaka at about 8 am the next morning. A return ticket costs Rs 1000. You can purchase the Kolkata-Dhaka bus ticket from Shyamoli Paribahan (☎ 033-2290345, fax 2293715) at 51 Mirza Ghalib St (Free School St; near the Hotel VIP International) in Kolkata. At the time of writing, buses departed from the International Bus Depot out at Salt Lake (double check in case a more convenient departure point has since commenced). A taxi from the Sudder St area (where most tourists stay) to Salt Lake should cost around Rs 40.

You need a visa for Bangladesh and these are available at the Bangladesh foreign missions (see Embassies & Consulates in the Facts for the Visitor chapter). In Kolkata, the Bangladesh consulate processes visas from 9 am to noon Monday to Friday, ready for collection on the same afternoon (between 3 and 5 pm). You'll need to supply your passport and three passport photos (for places to get snapshots, see Photography in the Kolkata chapter). Visas are a maximum of one month, however you can extend these at the Immigration & Passport office in Dhaka (see Bangladesh, earlier, for contact details). Visa costs vary depending on nationality: US$21 for Australians, Rs 2900 for Britons and US$45 for Americans.

Siliguri to Bhurungamari This northern border crossing is rarely used by travellers. Getting to the Indian border town of Chengrabandha from Siliguri is relatively straightforward. There are buses every hour between 6 am and 1 pm. The 70km trip costs Rs 35 and takes about 3½ hours. The Indian immigration office opens at 9 am daily, except Sunday. You can take buses direct to Rangpur (5½ hours), Bogra (eight hours) or Dhaka (15 hours).

New Jalpaiguri to Chilahati Take a train from New Jalpaiguri (northern West Bengal) to Haldibari, the Indian border checkpoint (Rs 20, two hours). From here it's a 7km walk along a disused railway line to the Bangladesh border point at Chilahati, where there's a train station.

Shillong-Sylhet The border crossing is at Dawki, 70km from Shillong and accessible by daily buses. From Dawki in Meghalaya, it's a 1.5km walk to Tamabil, from where it's a 15-minute walk to the bus station and about 2½ hours by bus to Sylhet.

Agartala-Dhaka This border is close to Dhaka, along Akhaura Rd, 4km west of

Agartala in Tripura. From the Bangladeshi side, plenty of transport goes to Akhaura, 5km away.

From Akhaura, a train to Dhaka (2½ hours) leaves at 12.15 pm Bangladeshi time. Alternatively, more comfortable buses (four hours) leave when there's enough demand. The border is open 8 am to 6 pm daily.

Nepal

Political and weather conditions permitting, there are three main land entry points into Nepal. The most popular crossing points from India are Sonauli/Bhairawa (south of Pokhara), Raxaul Bazaar/Birganj (south of Kathmandu) and Kakarbhitta (near Siliguri in the far east). If you are travelling to or from Delhi or elsewhere in western India the route through Sonauli/Bhairawa is the most convenient. An ordinary bus to Sonauli from Varanasi costs Rs 140 (10 hours). In Varanasi you can get through tickets to Kathmandu or Pokhara for Rs 400, though as you change buses at the border anyway you're probably better off buying two separate tickets (it's cheaper and more flexible). When crossing the border, remember that Nepal is 15 minutes ahead of India (ie, GMT/UTC plus 5¾ hours).

From Delhi, private buses to Kathmandu leave at 1.30 pm on Monday and Thursday, arriving around 6 or 7 am two days later. The journey requires a six-hour wait at the border where you must change buses. The fare is Rs 800. Most travellers seem to find that it's a lot more comfortable and better value to do the trip by train to Gorakhpur (Uttar Pradesh), and then take buses from there.

You can also enter via the little-used border crossing from Banbassa in Uttaranchal to Mahendrenagar in western Nepal. Despite its proximity to Delhi, this is probably the slowest route to Kathmandu or Pokhara, but it does provide a chance to explore western Nepal en route. Buses to Banbassa leave Delhi's Anand Vihar bus stand hourly from 7 am to 9 pm (Rs 138, 10 hours). Visas are available at the border (US$30, two passport photos required), but only from 9 am to 4 pm. The border crossing itself is open 7 am to 7 pm. It's a short rickshaw ride from Banbassa to the border. Buses wait on the far side to transfer you to the old bus stand in Mahendrenagar, from where there are daily buses to Kathmandu at around 2 pm which take a bum-numbing 24 hours. Alternatively you can take a bus from Mahendrenagar's new bus stand to Nepalganj (nine hours) and pick up a bus to Kathmandu or Pokhara from there (15 hours). You can forget about rail connections to Banbassa; this is really a dry-season only route as the road on from Mahendrenagar is prone to flooding in the monsoon.

From Kolkata, Patna or most of eastern India, Raxaul Bazaar to Birganj is the best entry point. From Kolkata to Raxaul, catch the *Mithilla Express* which departs Kolkata at 4 pm daily and arrives the next morning at 7.30 am (be warned that it's notorious for arriving two to three hours late). The ticket costs Rs 245 (2nd class) or Rs 1085 (two-tier air-con). From Raxaul, get an autorickshaw to Birganj for about Rs 10. From Birganj to Kathmandu it's about 350km and there are frequent buses (Rs 156, about eight hours). To Pokhara, it's about 255km and there are hourly buses (Rs 125, about 5½ hours).

A visa is required to enter Nepal (see Embassies & Consulates in the Facts for the Visitor chapter). You'll need a passport photo and visas are usually ready in 24 hours (except Friday when you should apply in the morning and your visa will be ready later that afternoon). In Delhi, the embassy is open for visa processing 9 am to noon Tuesday to Friday. A multiple-entry 60-day visa costs Rs 1410. It's also

Warning

Many travellers have complained about scams involving ticket packages to India, especially out of Pokhara – bookings fail to materialise or are for lower-quality services than were paid for. The package usually involves coordination between at least three different companies so the potential for an honest cock-up is at least as high as the potential for a deliberate rip-off.

possible to get a visa at the airport or at the border (US$30).

In Sikkim, foreigners are not allowed to go anywhere near the Tibetan or Nepalese borders, so obviously you can't exit the country from there.

Pakistan

Currently, due to the continuing unstable political situation between India and Pakistan, there's only one border crossing open (see following entry) and that remains hostage to volatile Pakistan-India relations.

A visa is required for Pakistan. One- and two-month single-entry visas are available from the Pakistani embassy in Delhi (see Embassies & Consulates in the Facts for the Visitor chapter). Applications are accepted between 8.30 and 11.30 am Monday to Friday and visas are issued the next working day. The cost depends on your nationality, ranging from Rs 120 for Swiss nationals to Rs 2975 for Canadians.

Delhi to Lahore There is a direct bus linking Delhi with Lahore in Pakistan. Buses leave the Dr Ambedkar Bus Terminal near Delhi Gate at 6 am each Tuesday, Wednesday, Friday and Saturday. The journey takes 12 hours and costs Rs 800 (including meals).

Amritsar to Lahore The only legal overland crossing between India and Pakistan is at Wagah, just east of Lahore (Attari on the India side), by rail and road (there are buses or you can drive your own vehicle). On each side you clear immigration, customs and further security checks. The border is open 9 am to 3 pm daily (9.30 am to 3.30 pm India time). Daily express trains link Lahore with Amritsar. There are slower Lahore-Wagah trains daily. Buses are quicker and more frequent, but the trip still takes nearly half a day.

Ultimately, the most convenient and straightforward option is the recently introduced direct bus between Delhi and Lahore (described earlier).

Bhutan

For a full rundown on travelling to, and within Bhutan, see Lonely Planet's *Bhutan*.

Siliguri to Phuentsholing It's a 169km trip between Siliguri (West Bengal) to Phuentsholing (Bhutan). From Siliguri, buses from the Bhutan bus stand on Burdwan Rd leave at 8 and 11 am and 2 and 3 pm daily (Rs 60, 3½ hours). From Phuentsholing to Thimphu, there are various buses ranging from Rs 107 to 149. The trip takes around six to seven hours.

Although no permits are currently required for Phuentsholing, you *must* get a visa (at least 15 days before your trip) from a registered travel agency listed under the Tourism Authority of Bhutan (TAB).

Europe

A trickle of people drive their own motorcycles or vehicles overland from Europe. There are some interesting, though difficult, routes to the subcontinent through Eastern Europe and the republics that were once a part of the USSR. An international carnet is required. Many people combine travel to the subcontinent with the Middle East by flying from India or Pakistan to Amman in Jordan or one of the Gulf States. A number of the London-based overland companies operate bus or truck trips across Asia (see Organised Tours later in this chapter for some possibilities).

For more detail on the overland route see the Lonely Planet guides to *Pakistan, Iran, Turkey* and *Istanbul to Kathmandu*.

South-East Asia

In contrast to the difficulties of travelling overland in Central Asia, the South-East Asian overland trip is still wide open. From Australia the first step is to Indonesia, particularly Timor, Bali or Jakarta. Most people fly from an east-coast city or Perth to Bali, but there are also other options such as Darwin (inquire at local travel agencies).

From Bali you head north through Java to Jakarta, from where you either travel by ship or fly to Singapore or continue north through Sumatra and then cross to Penang in Malaysia. After travelling around Malaysia you can fly from Penang to Chennai or, more popularly, continue north to Thailand and eventually fly out from

Bangkok to India, perhaps with a stopover in Myanmar. Unfortunately, crossing by land from Myanmar to India (or indeed to any other country) is forbidden by the Myanmar government.

An interesting alternative route is to travel from Australia to Papua New Guinea and from there cross to Irian Jaya, then to Sulawesi in Indonesia. There are all sorts of travel variations possible in South-East Asia; the region is a delight to travel through and heartily recommended. For full details see Lonely Planet's *South-East Asia*.

SEA

Basically, this isn't an option for North India. The shipping services between Africa and India only carry freight (including vehicles), not passengers.

ORGANISED TOURS

In addition to companies that provide more standard tours, there are numerous foreign eco, leisure and adventure-travel companies which can provide unusual and interesting trips to India, such as the yoga tours (accompanied by a yoga teacher) organised from Australia by Maharani Travel Tours. There are too many companies to include them all here – the following are just a selection.

The USA

Adventure Center (☎ 800-227 8747) 1311 63rd St, Suite 200, Emeryville, CA 94608
Web site: www.adventure-center.com

Asian Pacific Adventures (☎ 800-825 1680) 826 Sierra Bonita Ave, Los Angeles, CA 90036
Web site: www.asianpacificadventures.com

Geographic Expeditions (☎ 415-922 0448, fax 346 5535) 2627 Lombard St, San Francisco, CA 94123
Web site: www.geoex.com

Nature Exhibitions International (☎ 800-869 0639) 7860 Peters Rd, Plantation, FL 33324
Web site: www.naturexp.com

Sacred India Tours (☎ 310-834 9843) 350 West Pacific Coast Highway, Wilmington, CA 70744
Web site: www.sacredindia.com

Australia & New Zealand

Community Aid Abroad Tours (☎ 08-8232 2727) PO Box 34 Rundle Mall, Adelaide, SA 5000
Web site: www.caa.org.au

Maharani Travel Tours (☎ 08-9335 1512) 28 Market St, Fremantle, WA 6160

Peregrine Adventures (☎ 03-9663 8611) 258 Lonsdale St, Melbourne, VIC 3000 (also has offices in Sydney, Brisbane, Adelaide, Perth and Hobart)
Web site: www.peregrine.net.au

World Expeditions (☎ 02-9264 3366) 3rd floor, 441 Kent St, Sydney, NSW 2000; (☎ 09-522 9161) 21 Reumera Rd, New Market, Auckland
Web site: www.worldexpeditions.com.au

The UK

Encounter Overland (☎ 020-7370 6845) 267 Old Brompton Rd, London SW5 9JA
Web site: www.encounter-overland.com

Essential India (☎ 01225-868544) Upper Westwood, Bradford on Avon, Wiltshire, BA15 2DS
Web site: www.essential-india.co.uk

Exodus Expeditions (☎ 020-8673 0859) 9 Weir Rd, London SW12 0LT
Web site: www.exodustravels.co.uk

Imaginative Traveller (☎ 020-8742 3113) 14 Barley Mow Passage, Chiswick, London W4 4PH
Web site: www.imaginative-traveller.com

Indian Encounters (☎ 01929-481421) Creech Barrow, East Creech, Wareham, Dorset, BH20 5AP
Web site: www.indianencounters.com

Getting Around

AIR

Domestic Air Services

India's aviation industry is booming, with services to more than 70 airports nationwide. Indian Airlines (www.indian-airlines.nic.in) and its subsidiary, Alliance Air, have the most extensive services (59 destinations). Some of its fleet is ageing and checking in can be slow. Although it has a reputation for being unreliable, Indian Airlines is being partially privatised and will not be under government management after 2001, which will hopefully lead to improvements.

The international carrier, Air India, also flies on several domestic routes. Note that most of these flights leave from international terminals (check ahead).

Jet Airways (www.jetairways.com) flies to 38 cities nationwide and is rated as the country's best airline, with efficient staff and a modern fleet. The third biggest carrier is Sahara Airlines (www.saharaairline.com), which flies to 14 major destinations.

Fares are practically identical between the major carriers.

There is also a handful of small regional airlines, such as Jagson Airlines (serving Himachal Pradesh), but services can be erratic so it's best to check the current situation with a travel agent.

Reservations

The main airlines have computerised booking and there are thousands of computerised travel agencies. Phone numbers for city offices are given in the regional chapters. All the airlines require a telephone number and address when booking. The major airlines don't require reconfirmation unless your ticket was bought outside India, in which case the usual 72-hour rule applies.

Tickets can be paid for with rupees, foreign currency and, in most cases, with credit cards. Change is given in rupees. A lost ticket is very bad news – airlines may issue a replacement ticket at their discretion, but a refund is almost impossible.

Indian Airlines offers a 25% discount for students as well as for those aged between 12 and 30.

Air Passes

Indian Airlines' 'Discover India' pass costs US$500/700 for 15/21 days. It allows unlimited travel with one restriction – you can't go to the same place twice unless to take a connecting flight. Many flights are routed through Delhi, and you'll need to research schedules carefully to make sure your proposed itinerary is viable. Note that there's a risk of losing some days due to Delhi's fog problems during December and January. Also compare the pass price against the cost of buying individual tickets; an east-west trip taking in Kolkata (Calcutta)-Guwahati-Delhi-Jaipur-Ahmedabad would cost US$450 if you bought four separate tickets.

Jet Airways' offers 'Visit India' passes which cost US$300/550/800 for 7/15/21 days, less 50% for kids under 12. Jet Airways also offers discounts in luxury hotels, mostly in North India. The same restriction (as for the 'Discover India' pass) applies on visiting a city twice.

There's also Indian Airlines 'India Wonder' fare, which costs US$300 for one week's unlimited travel within any one of four regions. Three regions are relevant to the scope of this guidebook:

Northern Agra, Amritsar, Bhopal, Chandigarh, Delhi, Gwalior, Indore, Jaipur, Jammu, Jodhpur, Khajuraho, Leh, Lucknow, Raipur, Srinagar, Udaipur, Varanasi

Western Ahmedabad, Aurangabad, Bhavnagar, Bhuj, Goa, Indore, Jamnagar, Jodhpur, Kozhikode, Mangalore, Mumbai, Nagpur, Rajkot, Udaipur, Vadodara

Eastern Agartala, Bhubaneswar, Dibrugarh, Guwahati, Imphal, Jorhat, Kolkata, Lucknow, Patna, Ranchi, Silchar, Tezpur, Vadodara, Varanasi, Visakhapatnam

Discounts don't apply to either of Indian Airlines' passes.

Air Routes

from	to	duration (hrs)	frequency	one-way (US$)
Delhi	Agra	¾	1d	55
	Ahmedabad	1½	2d	135
	Amritsar	1	5w	100
	Khajuraho	1¾	1d	100
	Kolkata	2	4d	200
	Leh	1¼	1d	105
	Shimla	1	6w	100
	Varanasi	1¼	1d	125
Kolkata	Agartala	1	2d	50
	Guwahati	1¼	4d	70
	Patna	1	1d	100
Jaipur	Ahmedabad	1	3w	105
	Kolkata	2¼	1d	220

Frequency abbreviations: d – daily, w – weekly

Check-In

Check-in is one hour before departure. An extra 15 minutes is needed on flights to and from Leh, Jammu and Srinagar.

The baggage allowance is 20kg in economy class and 30kg in business. Some flights have security measures such as having to identify your baggage on the tarmac just before boarding (ask if this is required when checking in), and comprehensive clothing and baggage searches. You have to take out all batteries, even cells used for camera flashguns, and put them into checked luggage. Any batteries discovered by security personnel on your person or in cabin luggage will be confiscated. This is so no-one detonates anything once aboard.

If you've got hand luggage, remember to get a tag for it when you check in, or you may later be sent back to the check-in counter to get one (as the tag must be stamped when you clear security).

BUS

Although India has a comprehensive bus network, most travellers prefer to travel by train, as it's generally more comfortable and lacks the nerve-wracking zigzagging of road travel. Nonetheless, bus travel can make a refreshing change from trains, even though the journey can be a lot slower (involving frequent stops to pick-up/drop off passengers) or, alternatively, frighteningly fast. On top of that, many buses are in an advanced state of decrepitude. You'll usually have a choice of buses run by the state government or private companies (see the regional chapters for details).

The big advantage of buses over trains is that they travel more frequently and getting one involves comparatively little predeparture hassle. A drawback is that it can be difficult to know if you're on the right bus, particularly if (as in Gujarat) destination names and platform numbers are written only in local script. Buses are best suited to short journeys – if you've got a long trip (particularly overnight) opt for a train if there's a choice.

It's worth taking earplugs (or a Walkman) on bus trips, as some drivers love their Hindi pop and have no qualms about pumping up the volume. Some of the more expensive bus services have videos, which are also usually turned up at full volume for hours on end. If you're travelling overnight by bus and hope to get some shut-eye, avoid video coaches.

India's Mechanical Monsters

MICK WELDON

Local city buses in India, particularly in the big cities such as Kolkata and Delhi, are generally fume-belching, human-stuffed, mechanical rattletraps which travel at breakneck speed (except when they are stuck in traffic). Little time is given for disembarkation and there are daily reports of injury and death caused by buses. This is largely due to the immense pressure placed on bus drivers to rake in as much cash as possible.

Bus drivers are often paid by the number of passengers they carry, and may even be fined for each minute they are late. Naturally, this leads to dangerous and cut-throat competition among bus drivers. Those drivers who are caught for dangerous driving are given bail and immediately return to work, content in the knowledge that their case won't come to court for years; by that time any witnesses have disappeared or have little memory of the incident. According to newspaper reports, four out of five drivers are simply fined, never tried.

Many drivers openly admit they are 'forced' to adopt 'techniques' such as intentionally blocking the way of rival buses, or taking risky measures to overtake them, all at the peril of innocent pedestrians and fellow road users. According to drivers, in off-peak times they initially drive slowly to scoop up the maximum number of passengers, then wildly accelerate towards the end of the journey to make up time.

The moral is, when crossing a road don't even entertain the notion of stepping out in front of an oncoming bus. Moreover, don't even weave through a group of buses at a stop, as another, faster moving bus may be obscured by the first one!

When you reach your destination town on a long-distance bus, always confirm with some fellow passengers where you should get off. Sometimes touts will board buses on the outskirts of town (eg, in Agra) and shout down the aisle that this is the town centre. The few unwitting foreigners who get off at this point are then at the mercy of the waiting taxi and autorickshaw drivers.

Classes

The quality and choice of buses can vary wildly from state to state (see regional chapters for options and fares). In some states there is a choice of state-run buses plying the main routes, including ordinary, express and deluxe. Additionally, private buses operate in some regions, and apart from often being a quicker and more comfortable option (some have 'luxuries' such as tinted windows and reclining seats), the booking procedure is usually much simpler than for state-run buses. However, unlike state-operated bus companies, private operators are exceptionally eager to maximise their profits and unfortunately this can mean maintenance is less and drivers speed more – a dangerous combination. Another downside of some private companies is that they will change schedules at the last minute to get as many dhotis/saris on seats as possible. As the standard of private operators is so variable, it's best to seek advice from fellow travellers, tour operators etc, so you can ascertain which companies have a good reputation at the time of your visit.

Two common bus types are: 'ordinary' and 'express'. 'Ordinary' buses generally have five seats across – three on one side of the aisle, two on the other – although if there are only five people sitting in them consider yourself lucky! Aisles are often crammed with baggage and in some more remote places there will be people travelling 'upper class' (ie, on the roof).

'Express' buses are a big improvement in that they stop less often – they're still usually crowded, but at least you feel as if you're getting somewhere. The fare is usually a bit more than on an ordinary bus – well worth the extra. Most states also offer some more upmarket services which go by various names – inquire locally.

Reservations

For the cheaper bus services it pays to have a strategy. If there are two of you, one of you can guard luggage while the other storms the bus in search of a seat. The other accepted method is to pass a book or article of clothing through the open window and place it on an empty seat, or ask a passenger to do it for you. Having made your 'reservation' you can then board the bus after things have simmered down. This method rarely fails.

You can, however, often make advance reservations (sometimes for a small additional fee), but this usually only applies to the more upmarket services such as express and deluxe. Private buses should always be booked in advance.

Many bus stations have a separate women's queue, although this is not always obvious because the relevant sign (where it exists at all) is not often in English and there may not be any women queuing. More often than not, the same ticket window will handle the male and the female queue (don't be surprised if you get stories to the contrary from queuing males!). Despite the evil glares (or even refusal to shift by men in the queue), female travellers should simply sharpen their elbows and confidently make their way to the front, where they will get almost immediate service.

Baggage

Some companies charge a few rupees to store your luggage in an enclosed compartment at the back of the bus (make sure the people who demand money for this actually work for the bus company). Alternatively, baggage is sometimes carried for free on the roof and if this is the case, it's worthwhile taking some precautions: make sure it's tied on securely and that nobody dumps a heavy tin trunk on top of your gear. If someone lugs your bag onto the roof, make sure you pay a few rupees for their service. Theft can be a problem so keep an eye on your bags during any stops en route (which are an ideal time to stretch your legs anyway).

Toilet Stops

On long-distance bus trips, chai stops can be far too frequent or, conversely, agonisingly infrequent. Long-distance trips can be a real hassle for women travellers as toilet facilities are generally inadequate to say the least. For stops in the middle of nowhere, forget about modesty and do what the local women do – wander a few metres off to find a convenient bush.

TRAIN

India has the world's biggest train network under one management, totalling over 60,000km of track spans. Indian Railways (www.indianrailway.com) also has 1.6 million staff, which makes it the world's biggest employer, moving 11 million passengers daily to any of 7085 stations. It's certainly a ride in India's mainstream. At first the railways can seem as complicated as India itself – trains range from inter-city Shatabdi ('arrow') expresses to country passenger services on narrow gauge tracks, with 10 classes from air-con executive chair to ordinary wooden benches, and separate reservation offices or chaotic queues. Yet it's straightforward enough once you get used to it. While sometimes slower than buses, train journeys can be relaxing, fascinating and even a little romantic. And for overnight journeys they are much preferred to buses.

There are tourist quotas for many express trains, and special offices or counters for foreigners in major cities and destinations (you must bring a money-changing receipt or ATM slip when paying in rupees). We've listed important trains but there are many, many more. The national *Trains at a Glance* (Rs 25) has 200 pages of trains, and there are timetables covering each regional zone. Check at station newsstands.

Despite a seemingly alarming rate of accidents it's a secure way to travel, though not always fast. Kolkata to Delhi takes 17 to 24 hours by train, or two hours if you fly. In the monsoon, floods and high rivers cause havoc with tracks and bridges, particularly in North India's Ganges basin and coastal deltas.

Several cities have suburban train networks, which are usually comfortable during the day but overcrowded in peak hours. These trains might stop only briefly at a station; if it's crowded, you have to edge your way to the door in preparation.

Classes

Shatabdi express trains are same-day services between major and regional cities of between three and eight hours. These are the fastest and most expensive trains, with only two classes: air-con executive chair and air-con chair. Shatabdis are comfortable, but the glass windows cut the views considerably compared to nonair-con classes on slower trains, which have barred windows and fresh air.

Rajdhani express trains are long-distance express services between Delhi and state capitals, and offer air-con 1st class (1A), two-tier air-con (2A), three-tier air-con (3A) and 2nd class. Two-tier means there are two levels of bunks in each compartment, which are a little wider and longer than their counterparts in three-tier. Two- and three-tier air-con cost respectively a half and one-third as much as air-con 1st class, and are perfectly adequate for an overnight trip.

Other express trains and mail trains have two-tier air-con coaches, chair car (if it runs only during the day), nonair-con sleeper (bring your own bedding), nonair-con 2nd class, and finally unreserved tickets. Sleeper costs only one-quarter as much as two-tier air-con. Some trains also have three-tier air-con and nonair-con 1st class, but the latter is being phased out. Mail and express trains carry some fine titles (*Flying Mail, Himalayan Queen,* or *Black Diamond Express*) which don't necessarily tell you the destination. You can search through *Trains at a Glance*, or big stations often have English-speaking staff at inquiry counters, who can be helpful with picking the best train. At a smaller station mid-level officials such as the deputy station master usually speak English.

Aficionados of 2nd class can seek out the one-class-only *Janata* (People) express trains, which cost as little as Rs 174 (US$4) to go 1000km. Travel on 2nd-class passenger trains is even cheaper, about 60% less than 2nd class on express trains. In the cheaper classes the squat toilet is usually cleaner than the sit-down flush toilet. Passenger trains do slow local routes, stopping at each tiny country station. These are best on a quiet day, when you can feel the breeze through the windows and listen to local itinerant singers at a leisurely pace.

Reservations

To make a reservation you must fill out a form giving which class you need and the

Express Train Fares in Rupees

distance (km)	1st-class air-con (1A)	2-tier air-con (2A)	3-tier air-con (3A)	chair car (CC)	sleeper (SL)	second (II)
100	542	322	158	114	84	32
200	778	430	243	171	84	54
300	1052	543	329	231	114	73
400	1296	653	405	277	140	90
500	1541	771	482	323	166	107
1000	2506	1253	783	522	270	174
1500	3154	1577	986	658	340	219
2000	3644	1841	1139	800	393	253

train's name and number. For overnight journeys it's best to reserve your place a couple of days in advance, particularly if it's a holiday period. If there is no special counter or office at the station for foreigners (sometimes classed with other minorities such as 'Freedom Fighters'), you have to adopt local queuing practices. These range from reasonably orderly lines to milling scrums. As with buses, there are sometimes separate 'Ladies' Queues' but usually the same window handles men and women each at a time. So women can go to the front of the queue, next to the first male at the window, and get served almost immediately.

If this is too much, many travel agencies and hotels are in the business of purchasing train tickets for a small commission. This can be a major time and hassle-saver, and should be a safe option at well-established outlets and higher-quality hotels, but do ask around before committing yourself. Also watch out for small-fry travel agents who promise express train tickets and deliver tickets for obscure mail or passenger trains. Only leave a small deposit, if any, and check the tickets before paying.

Reserved tickets show your berth and carriage number. The efficient railway staff also stick lists of names and berths on each reserved carriage, as well as the carriage number in chalk. Air-con carriages tend to be towards the front of trains.

If you can't buy a reserved seat you can ask if there is a waiting list, or try your luck by getting on anyway. Unless it's a popular express train or it's a busy holiday it usually works out. You can get on without a ticket but it is more polite to buy an unreserved ticket, which go on sale one hour before departure, and try to upgrade it. Find a reserved-class carriage and a spare seat of your choice, and wait for the conductor (officially the TTE or Travelling Ticket Examiner) to find you. Explain you could only buy an unreserved ticket and ask about vacancies. With luck, the conductor is happy to oblige. You pay the difference between the ordinary fare and the fare of whichever class you're in, plus a small excess charge of around Rs 25. It's a hassle if you don't have enough change, as conductors usually don't either. You might have to wait until he can collect it.

Costs

Fares are calculated by distance, but vary greatly depending on the train and the seat. To go between Delhi and Kolkata on the fastest train costs (including meals) Rs 4270 in air-con 1st class (1A), Rs 2470 for a two-tier air-con berth (2A) or Rs 1500 for a three-tier air-con berth (3A); the same journey on a slower, nonair-con express train costs Rs 1119 in 1st class, Rs 213 in 2nd class. Reserved tickets attract extra fees of around Rs 50. If your journey is longer than 500km, you can take a day's break en route but you must have your ticket endorsed by the station master or ticket collector at the station where you disembark. If you want to get from A to B via C, inquire about circular train tickets, as these can be cheaper than buying tickets for separate segments.

Bedding is free in air-con classes, and costs Rs 20 in nonair-con 1st class. Meals are free on express Rajdhani and Shatabdi trains, and cheap meals are available on other trains.

'Bringing People Together'

Indian Railway sees itself not just as a train operator but as a force for national unity, where people of all communities and castes meet as equals. But more than this, it reaches out to many groups with discounts, from the worthy to the unfortunate. These include a 50% discount for cadets of marine engineering, senior citizens, amateur performers, professional circus parties, unemployed youth and deaf people, and a 75% cut for leprosy patients (noninfectious at least), blind people, war widows and cancer sufferers. Freedom fighters, a range of award winners and parents accompanying child winners of the National Bravery Award are also granted concessions. Unfortunately, even if you are a deaf amateur acrobat studying marine engineering, foreigners are not eligible.

Important stations have retiring rooms, available if you have a valid ticket (any cheap, unreserved ticket bought specially for this reason would do). They vary in quality, but at best they're very cheap and can even be ruthlessly clean, with either dormitories or private rooms (see also Accommodation in the Facts for the Visitor chapter).

Refunds Tickets are refundable but fees apply. If you present unused tickets more than a day in advance, a fee of up to Rs 50 applies. Steeper charges apply with less than four hours to departure, but you can get some sort of refund as late as 12 hours afterwards.

When refunding your ticket you officially have a magic pass to go to the front of the queue, as the next person might require the spot you're surrendering.

Indrail Passes

Indrail passes permit unlimited travel for the period of their validity, but they are expensive and they don't get you to the front of the queue. To get full value out of them you'd need to travel about 300km every single day. However, some people find them useful for journeys soon after they arrive in India. Most Western countries have travel agencies which arrange or sell Indrail passes, and they're sold at railway offices in 20 Indian cities.

Children between five and 12 pay half fare. There is no refund for lost or partially used tickets.

Special Trains

The *Palace on Wheels* makes an eight-day circuit of Rajasthan, and you stay in the 'fit for a maharaja' carriages (see the Rajasthan chapter for details). In the opulent saloon cars of *The Royal Orient*, you travel predominantly through Gujarat, but also take in some of Rajasthan (see the Gujarat chapter).

Indrail Pass Prices (US Dollars)

days	1st-class air-con	2-tier air-con	nonair-con
1	57	26	11
2	95	47	19
7	270	135	80
15	370	185	90
30	495	248	125
60	800	400	185
90	1060	530	235

Left Luggage

Most stations have left-luggage rooms which cost a couple of rupees per day for one bag. It's useful if you want to visit but not stay in a town, or to hunt for accommodation unencumbered.

CAR

Few people bring their own vehicles to India. If you do decide to bring a car or motorcycle to India it must be brought in under a carnet, a customs document guaranteeing its removal at the end of your stay. Failing to do so will be very expensive.

Rental

Self-Drive Self-drive car rental in India is a possibility – by Western standards the cost is quite low, but given India's hair-raising driving conditions it's much better and more economical to hire a car and driver.

If you're still interested in self-drive, expect to pay around Rs 1500 per day (with a two-day minimum). Insurance is extra (around Rs 45 per day) and you usually have to leave a deposit (refundable) of Rs 10,000. Budget, Euro Car, Hertz and several other companies maintain offices in the major cities. You officially need either a valid international driving licence or regular licence from your home country.

Private Car & Driver Hire Long-distance car hire with driver is becoming an increasingly popular way to get around parts of India. Spread among say, four people, it's not overly expensive and you have the flexibility to go where you want when you want. Rental rates increase in line with hikes in petrol prices.

Almost any local taxi will quite happily set off on a long-distance trip in India. Inquiring at a taxi rank is the easiest way to find a car – you can also ask your hotel to book one for you, although this will usually cost more.

Most trips are officially based on a minimum of 250km a day (about Rs 4 per km); there is an additional charge per kilometre if you cover more than 250km a day. If you're hiring for at least several days, try to negotiate a daily rate, as this works out cheaper. If you're only taking a day trip, remember that a one-way fare is more expensive per kilometre because it is based on the assumption that the driver will return empty to the starting point. An air-con car will cost about twice as much as a nonair-con vehicle. Note that there is sometimes an entry fee into other states.

The usual quote for a nonair-con Ambassador car and driver in Delhi is around Rs 1300 per day, but you should be able to barter this down if you intend hiring for a few days. In the hills, the charge starts at Rs 800 per day, though a specific trip to a destination one hour's drive away would cost around Rs 400 one way, or Rs 600 return (including up to two hours' waiting time). Journeys are usually priced by the farthest point reached. If you want to detour off the most direct route to this farthest point, the side trips will be priced as extra journeys and added to the total cost for the trip.

Share-Jeeps & Taxis Supplementing the bus service in many parts of the Himalaya, share-jeeps are particularly useful for getting to the trail-heads for trekking routes, as few buses run out to the smaller villages.

Jeeps generally run between transport hubs, usually the junctions of major roads with connections to towns and villages in the local area. For many destinations in the Himalaya there is often only one bus a day, but you can almost always complete the same route in several stages by share-jeep. Jeeps leave when full from well-established 'passenger stations' on the outskirts of towns and villages; locals should be able to

Driving the Best Bargain

If you hire a car and driver for an extended period of time, try to get a driver who speaks at least some English and who is knowledgeable about the region(s) you intend visiting. It's wise to shop around before deciding so that you have a fair idea of costs and won't be easily hoodwinked.

More than a few travellers have paid well over the odds, stumping up for the driver's accommodation and meals (even booze!), completely unaware that his lodging/meal cost has already been factored into the fee. Make sure you understand the accommodation/meal arrangement for the driver *before* paying the car hire company and ensure this is made clear to the driver before you set off (usually it *is* already included).

When it comes to where the driver stays overnight, this is for him to decide and should never be your headache – many choose to sleep in the back seat of the car thus pocketing their accommodation allowance. Some hotels, especially in remote areas, will provide free (or minimal cost) accommodation for drivers, as there is nowhere else to stay.

In the cities and towns, many hotels in tourist hot spots do not permit drivers to stay or eat in guest areas, even if you insist on paying – for more details see 'Dos and Don'ts' under Society & Conduct in the Facts about North India chapter.

Finally, and very importantly, it is imperative you set the ground rules from day one. Many travellers have complained of having their holiday completely dictated by their driver (eg, being bullied into accepting meal times and hotel choices that suited the driver, not the passengers). Your holiday is going to be much more pleasant if you don't have prickly relations with your driver. The way to achieve this is by politely, but firmly, letting him know at the outset that you are the boss.

At the end of your trip, a tip is the best way of showing your appreciation. About Rs 50 per day is considered fair, but if you are really chuffed with your driver's service, anything above that is going to get a big smile.

Some Indian Rules of the Road

Drive on the Left

Theoretically vehicles keep to the left in India – as in Japan, Britain or Australia. In practice most vehicles keep to the middle of the road on the basis that there are fewer potholes in the middle than on the sides. When any other vehicle is encountered the lesser vehicle should cower to the side. Misunderstandings as to status can have unfortunate consequences.

Overtaking

When overtaking a truck, you first sound your horn to let him know you're there. After that the truck driver should lean out the window and indicate whether or not the road is clear for overtaking (he has a much better view). If it's OK he gestures with a repeated upward gesture, if it's not it's a downward gesture. You then sound the horn to let him know you're actually going to overtake. Smaller vehicles unexpectedly encountered in mid-manoeuvre can be expected to swerve apologetically out of the way. If a larger vehicle is encountered it is to be hoped that the overtakee will slow, pull off or otherwise make room for the overtaker.

Driving at Night

It is a matter of courtesy to turn your headlights off as you approach blind corners – so as not to bedazzle anyone coming the other way. How the oncoming driver is supposed to be aware of your presence around the blind corner is another matter altogether.

point you in the right direction. The average fare for a one-hour trip is around Rs 50.

Some share-jeeps can really pack in the passengers to make as much money as possible (despite maximum passenger regulations) – some travellers may find them too claustrophobic for longer trips.

Though buses are more frequent in other parts of the north, share taxis are available in many locations for travel between towns. In Madhya Pradesh, for example, you can expect to pay about Rs 5/10 per kilometre for nonair-con/air-con.

Purchase

Buying a car is expensive and not worth the effort unless you intend to stay in India for many months.

On the Road

Because of the extreme congestion in the cities and the narrow, bumpy roads in the country, driving is often a slow, stop-start process – hard on you, the car and fuel economy. Roads are particularly potholed in Bihar and parts of Madhya Pradesh (eg, between Khajuraho and Bhopal), where you'll probably average only about 30km to 40km per hour. Petrol prices are around Rs 19 per litre.

Service is so-so in India, and parts and tyres are not always easy to obtain, though there are plenty of puncture-repair places. All in all, driving is not all that pleasurable (especially for longer trips) except in rural areas where there's little traffic.

MOTORCYCLE

Travelling by motorcycle is exhilarating and offers the freedom to go when and where you like. Sure you'll probably get a sore backside and receive misleading directions on the way (see the 'Dealing with Directions' boxed text in the Facts for the Visitor chapter), but you'll also have priceless experiences not available to travellers who rely on public transport. These days, there are a number of excellent motorcycle tours on offer (see Organised Motorcycle Tours later in this section).

There is an array of books about motorcycle travel in India including *Bullet up the Grand Trunk Road* by Jonathan Gregson, which is the author's account of his journey through northern India on a classic Enfield motorcycle. Bill Aitken's *Divining the Deccan* and *Riding the Ranges* are also accounts of motorcycle journeys across some interesting parts of India.

Equipment

You must have either an International Driving Licence or regular licence from your home country to motorcycle in India.

It's definitely worthwhile bringing along your own helmet, as even though Indian helmets may be cheaper, it can be tough finding one that fits well; plus, the quality is variable. Leathers, gloves, boots, driving goggles, waterproofs and other protective gear should also be brought from your home country.

Organised tours often have a vehicle which transports luggage, but if you're travelling independently, make sure you have a pack that is easy to carry.

Rental

Organised tours (described later) provide motorcycles, but if you are planning an independent trip, bikes can be rented in several places in India, such as Delhi, at negotiable prices. Expect to pay upwards of Rs 400/10,000 per day/month for a 500cc bike, including insurance. You'll probably have to leave a cash deposit (refundable) and/or your return air ticket.

Purchase

Before buying, canvass as many opinions as you can to get an idea of the latest machines on the market and their costs. To buy a new bike, you officially have to have a local address and be a resident foreign national. When buying second-hand, all you need to do is give an address.

Purchasing a second-hand machine is a matter of asking around and a perfect place to start is with mechanics, who can usually also offer advice about insurance options. Old bikes are obviously cheaper, but you are far more open to getting gypped, either by paying too much or by getting a dud bike; also you run a greater risk of breaking down once on the road.

In Delhi the area around Hari Singh Nalwa St in Karol Bagh is full of places buying, selling and renting motorcycles. Two places recommended by travellers are:

Inder Motors (☎ 011-572 8579, fax 5781052) 1744/55 Hari Singh Nalwa St, Karol Bagh
Madaan Motors (☎ 011-573 5801, fax 7235684, ⓔ madaanmotors@yahoo.com) 1767/53 Naiwala St, Karol Bagh

Prices for new bikes include:

Enfield 500cc	Rs 69,000
Enfield 350cc	Rs 54,000 (standard)
	Rs 58,000 (deluxe)
Rajdoot 175cc	US$800

Inder and Madaan Motors can ship a bike for around Rs 13,500 including the crate, packing and insurance. Second-hand bikes (two to three years old) cost about US$1000 for a 500cc. Transferring ownership costs Rs 1000 to 1500.

When the time comes to sell the bike, try not to appear too anxious to get rid of it. If you get a reasonable offer, grab it.

Ownership Papers An obvious tip perhaps, but do not part with your money until you have the ownership papers, receipt and affidavit signed by a magistrate authorising the owner (as recorded in the ownership papers) to sell the machine – not to mention the keys to the bike and the bike itself! Each state often has a different set of ownership transfer formalities – inquire locally to find out the latest requirements.

On the Road

Local driving habits and road conditions make motorcycling a reasonably hazardous endeavour, and one ideally undertaken by experienced riders. Hazards range from goats crossing the road to defunct trucks which have been abandoned in the middle of the highway. Added to that are the perpetual potholes and unmarked speed humps. Rural roads sometimes have various grain crops laid out on roads to be threshed by passing vehicles – it can be a real hazard for bikers.

The risk of bike theft is minimal. The worst you're likely to experience is the way people seem to treat parked motorcycles as public utilities – handy for sitting on, using

Beep or Be Beeped

Bald tyres and dodgy brakes hardly raise an eyebrow in India, but a vehicle without a horn is considered almost as asinine as chai without sugar. Surveys by Lonely Planet authors have revealed that the average driver uses the horn 10 to 20 times per kilometre, so a 100km trip can involve a mind-blowing 2000 blasts of the trusty beeper! The horn can be very loud, especially if you sit in the front of buses, so have earplugs handy. There's rarely any respite. Road signs prohibiting use of horns are more likely to be answered by a rebellious 'toot' than by meek compliance.

the mirror to comb their hair, fiddling with the switches – none of which is usually intended to do any damage. You'll just have to turn all the switches off and re-adjust the mirrors when you get back on.

Avoid covering too much territory in one day. As so much energy is spent simply concentrating on the road, long days are exhausting and potentially dangerous. On the busy national highways expect to average 50km/h without stops; on smaller roads, where driving conditions are worse, 10km/h is not an unrealistic average. On the whole, on good roads you can easily expect to cover a minimum of 100km a day (up to 300km with minimal stops).

Night driving should be avoided at all costs. If you think driving in daylight is difficult, imagine the extra dangers at night when you factor in the likelihood of half the vehicles being inadequately lit (or not lit at all).

For really long hauls, putting the bike on a train can be a convenient option. You'll generally pay about as much as the 2nd-class passenger fare for the bike. The fuel tank must be empty, and there should be a tag in an obvious place detailing name, destination, passport number and train details. When you pack the bike, it's wise to remove the mirrors and loosen the handlebars to prevent damage.

Repairs & Maintenance

Original spare parts bought from an 'authorised dealer' can be rather expensive compared to the copies available from your spare-parts wallah. Delhi's Karol Bagh is a good place to go for spare parts for all Indian and imported bikes. If you're going to remote regions, take basic spares with you (valves, piston rings etc) as they may not be readily available.

For all machines (particularly older ones), make sure you regularly check and tighten all nuts and bolts, as Indian roads and engine vibration tend to work things loose quite quickly. Check the engine and gearbox oil level regularly – with the quality of oil it is advisable to change it and clean the oil filter every 2000km.

Given the condition of many Indian roads, chances are you'll make constant visits to a puncture-wallah. These phenomenal fix-it men are found almost everywhere, but it's obviously good to have the tools to at least remove your own wheel. Indeed, given the hassles of constant flat tyres, it's worth lashing out on new tyres if you buy a second-hand motorcycle with worn tyres. A new rear tyre for an Enfield costs around Rs 600 to 700.

Organised Motorcycle Tours

Motorcycle tours are a superb (no hassles) way of seeing India. They usually operate with a minimum number of people and some can even be tailor-made to suit a groups' wishes. Contact operators directly for prices and other details.

Asia Safari (☎/fax 011-6136752) 491 Sector A, Pocket C, Vasant Kunj, New Delhi. Offers tours of Kumaon, Garwhal, Lahaul, Spiti and Kinnaur. Web site: www.asiasafari.com

Classic Bike Adventure (☎ 0832-262076, fax 276124, 277343), Casa Tres Amigos, Socol Vado No 425, Assagao, Bardez, Goa, is a German company that organises bike tours to various destinations in North India lasting several weeks. Web site: www.classic-bike-india.de

Ferris Wheels (☎/fax 02-9904 7419, ⓔ safari @ferriswheels.com.au) Box 743, Crows Nest, NSW 2065, Australia. Organises tours through the Himalaya and Rajasthan on classic Enfields. Web site www.ferriswheels.com.au

Himalayan Motorcycle Tours (☎/fax 1256-771773, ⓔ patrickmoffat@yahoo.com) 16 High St, Overton, Hants R625 3HA, UK. Run by an easy-going American expat, Patrick Moffat. Patrick conducts upmarket tours of Himachal Pradesh, Sikkim, Ladakh and Rajasthan. Web site: www.himalayanmotorcycles.com

Himalayan Roadrunners (☎ 908-236 8970, fax 236 8972) Box 538, Lebanon, New Jersey, 08833 USA; (☎/fax 01233-733001) Charles House, Ham St, Ashford, Kent, TN26 2HJ, UK. This is the largest motorcycle touring outfit on the subcontinent, with a large fleet of motorcycles and a choice of itineraries. Web site: www.ridehigh.com

Indian Motorcycle Adventures (☎ 09-372 7550, ⓔ gumby@ihug.co.nz) 40 O'Brien Rd, Rocky Bay, Waiheke Island, New Zealand. Offers 20-day tours of Rajasthan.

BICYCLE

India offers an immense array of experiences and challenges for a long-distance cyclist: there are high-altitude passes and rocky dirt tracks; smooth-surfaced highways; coastal routes through lush coconut palms; and meandering country roads through picturesque tea plantations. Hills, plains, plateaus, deserts – you name it, North India's got it!

Nevertheless, long-distance cycling is not for the faint of heart or weak of knee. You'll need physical endurance to cope with the roads, traffic and climate.

Before you set out, it's a good idea to do some reading. Cycling magazines provide useful information including listings for bicycle tour operators and the addresses of spare-parts suppliers. For a taste of bike touring, there are various options including Dervla Murphy's *Full Tilt – From Dunkirk to Delhi on a Bicycle*, Lloyd Sumner's *The Long Ride* and Bettina Selby's *Riding the Mountains Down* – 'A Journey by Bicycle to Kathmandu'. Your local cycling club may also be able to help with information and advice.

If you're a serious cyclist or amateur racer and want to contact counterparts while in India, there's the Cycle Federation of India; contact the secretary, Yamun Velodrome, New Delhi. If you're after anything bike related in Delhi head for Jhandwalan market, near Karol Bagh, which has imported and domestic new and second-hand bikes and spare parts.

In the summer, UP Tourism offers five-day mountain-bike tours of Kumaon (see the Uttar Pradesh chapter). More informal mountain biking tours are offered by Yogi's Uttaranchal Cycle Tours, based at the Uttarakhand Tourist Lodge, Kausani (☎ 059628 84112). Natural Exposure Adventure Travel (☎ 08-9389 1971, ⓔ sfneat@starwon.com.au) PO Box 592, Nedlands, WA 6909, Australia, organises mountain-bike expeditions in Ladakh and the Himalaya.

Using Your Own Bike

It may be hard to find parts, especially wheels, for touring bikes with 700cc wheels. Parts for bicycles with 26-inch wheels are available but of variable standards.

Carry a good lock and use it. Consider wrapping your bicycle frame in used inner tubes – this not only hides fancy paint jobs, but protects them from knocks and scrapes. If planning to buy a bike in India, consider bringing you own saddle, rack and good-quality panniers.

Rental & Purchase

Even in the smallest towns there is usually at least one outlet that rents bikes. In tourist areas (eg, hill stations, Rajasthan) there are a handful of places, but the rates are cranked up (see regional chapters for details). Himachal Pradesh and Uttaranchal are prime sites for mountain-biking, but few places offer bike hire.

Surviving the Roads

In 1951 the number of motorised vehicles on India's roads totalled 300,000. The figure had climbed to 5.4 million by 1981 and swelled to an estimated 45 million by 2001. Road deaths have risen in line with vehicle numbers and are now the highest in the world – an estimated 80,000 people each year! According to the Central Road Research Institute, about 10% of road fatalities are pedestrians and cyclists in the major cities. A big problem are the footpaths, which are often in a state of severe disrepair, tiny or nonexistent, therefore tempting pedestrians to jaywalk – with deadly results.

The reasons for the high road toll in India are numerous, and many of them fairly obvious. Firstly, there's road congestion and vehicle overcrowding – when a bus runs off the road there are plenty of people stuffed inside to get injured, and it's unlikely too many of them will be able to escape in a hurry.

Secondly, there is India's unwritten 'might is right' road law which means that vehicles always have the right of way over pedestrians and bigger vehicles always have the right of way over smaller ones. It's not surprising that so many pedestrians are killed in hit-and-run accidents (the propensity to disappear after the incident is not wholly surprising, however, since lynch mobs can assemble remarkably quickly, even when the driver is not at fault).

A substantial number of accidents involve trucks. Being the biggest, heaviest and mightiest vehicles on the road, you either get out of their way or get mowed down. Also, as with so many Indian vehicles, they're likely to be grossly overloaded and not in the best of condition. Trucks invariably carry considerably more than the maximum recommended by the manufacturer. It's a real eye-opener to see the number of trucks crumpled by the sides of the national highways, and these aren't old accidents, but ones that have obviously happened in the last 24 hours or so.

If you are driving, you need to be alert at all times. At night there are unilluminated cars and ox carts, and in the daytime there are zigzagging cyclists and hordes of pedestrians. Day and night there are the fearless truck drivers to contend with. The other thing you have to endure at night is the eccentric way in which headlights are used – a combination of full beam and totally off (dipped beams are virtually unheard of). A loud horn definitely helps since the normal driving technique is to put your hand firmly on the horn, close your eyes and plough through regardless. Considering the hazards of night driving, it's best to avoid it altogether.

Even though Indian roads can be a nail-biting experience, it may help if you take solace in the Indian karma theory – accidents are less to do with the vehicles that may collide with you than with the events of your previous life catching up with you.

You may want to buy a bike while you're in India and your best bet is to shop around to get a feel for brands and prices – new bicycles cost from around Rs 1500 to 3000 in Delhi's cycle market. There are many brands of Indian clunkers, including Hero, Atlas, BSA and Raleigh. Raleigh is considered the finest quality, followed by BSA, which has a big line of models including some nice sporty jobs. Hero mountain-style bicycles are on sale in the larger towns.

Once you've decided on a bike you have a choice of luggage carriers – mostly the rat-trap type varying only in size, price and strength. There's a plethora of saddles available but all are equally bum-breaking. It's probably a good idea to get a machine fitted with a stand and bell.

Reselling is usually a breeze. Count on getting about 60% to 70% of what you originally paid if it was a new bike. A local cycle-hire shop will probably be interested, or simply ask around to find potential buyers.

Most travellers prefer to buy a bicycle in India, but by all means consider bringing your own. Mountain bikes are especially suited to India – their sturdier construction makes them more manoeuvrable, less prone to damage and allows you to tackle rocky, muddy roads unsuitable for lighter machines.

Inquire in your home country about air transport and custom formalities.

Transporting Your Bike

Remove pedals, all luggage and accessories, turn the handlebars, cover the chain and let the tyres down a bit.

On the Road

It's safer and more pleasurable to ride on more quiet roads – avoid big cities where the chaotic traffic can be a real hazard for cyclists. National highways can also be a nightmare, with speeding trucks and buses yielding no ground to vulnerable cyclists. Always make inquiries before venturing off road.

If you've never cycled long distances, start with 20km to 40km a day and increase this as you gain stamina and confidence. For an eight-hour pedal a serious cyclist and interested tourist will probably average 90km to 130km a day on undulating plains, or 70km to 100km in mountainous areas.

Be warned that asking directions can send you on a wild goose chase (see the 'Dealing with Directions' boxed text in the Facts for the Visitor chapter).

Avoid leaving anything on your bike that can easily be removed when it's unattended. You may like to bring along a padlock and chain. But don't be paranoid – your bike is probably safer in India than in Western cities.

Repairs & Maintenance

For Indian bikes, there are plenty of repair 'shops' (some consisting only of a puncture-wallah with his box of tools under a tree) which makes maintenance delightfully straightforward. Puncture-wallahs will patch tubes for a nominal cost.

If you bring your own bicycle to India, you'll need to be prepared for the contingencies of part replacement or repair. Several travellers warn that it is not at all easy locating foreign parts, though another traveller reported that if you have a bike with 26-inch wheels you'll find the spares situation much less of a problem. Ensure you have a working knowledge of your machine. Bring all necessary tools with you as well as a compact bike manual with diagrams – Indian mechanics can work wonders and illustrations help overcome the language barrier. Roads don't often have paved shoulders and are very dusty, so keep your chain lubricated.

HITCHING

Hitching is never entirely safe in any country in the world, and we don't recommend it. Travellers who decide to hitch should understand that they are taking a small but potentially serious risk. People who do choose to hitch will be safer if they travel in pairs and let someone know where they are planning to go.

Hitching in India is not a realistic option. There are not that many private cars passing by so you are likely to be on board trucks. You are then stuck with the old quandaries of: 'Do they understand what I am doing?', 'Should I be paying for this?', 'Will the driver expect to be paid?', 'Will they be unhappy if I don't offer to pay?', 'Will they be unhappy if I offer or will they simply want too much?'. The only place where hitching is quite common for travellers is in Ladakh and even there, there is no definite procedure. The old rule applies – make sure you know if it's a free ride or you're expected to be a paying passenger before you go.

It is a very bad idea for women to hitch. A woman in the cabin of a truck on a lonely road is perhaps tempting fate.

BOAT

There is a possibility that passenger boats may start up on the Ganges soon, with services connecting Varanasi and Kolkata. The river is already being deepened in parts in preparation. Other than this, there are ferries across many northern rivers.

LOCAL TRANSPORT

Although there are comprehensive local bus networks in most major towns, unless you have time to familiarise yourself with the routes you're better off sticking to taxis, autorickshaws, cycle-rickshaws and hiring bicycles. The buses are often so hopelessly overcrowded that you can only really use them if you get on at the starting point and get off at the terminus.

A basic ground rule applies to any form of transport where the fare is not ticketed or fixed (unlike a bus or train), or calculated by a meter: agree on the fare beforehand. If you fail to do that you can expect enormous arguments and hassles when you get to your destination. And agree on the fare clearly – if there is more than one of you make sure it covers all of you. If a cycle-rickshaw-wallah holds up five fingers, establish at the outset that this means Rs 5 and not Rs 50 (even if Rs 50 would be ridiculous!). If you have baggage, clarify whether there's an additional charge (some drivers charge a few rupees extra for this). If a driver refuses to use the meter, or insists on an extortionate rate, simply walk away – if he really wants the job the price will drop. If you can't agree on a reasonable fare, find another driver. Don't put up with any nonsense, but also don't waste half your trip fighting over every last rupee; in some places (eg, Varanasi) it is considered 'fair' that foreigners should pay more than locals. Also bear in mind that fares are often steeper (as much as double the day fare) at night.

There are a few more points to consider when catching taxis/rickshaws. Always have enough small change, as drivers rarely do and this can be a real hassle at night when shops/banks (where you can get change) are closed. If you are staying or dining at a top-range venue, try walking a few hundred metres down the road to avoid the drivers who hang outside assuming you're a cash cow. Finally, it's a good idea to carry around a business card of the hotel where you are staying, as your pronunciation of streets, hotel names etc, may be incomprehensible to drivers. Some hotel cards even have a nifty little sketch map clearly indicating their location.

Many autorickshaw drivers are into the commission racket – see Touts under Accommodation in the Facts for the Visitor chapter.

To/From the Airport

There are official buses, operated by the government, Indian Airlines or some local cooperative, to a number of airports in India. Where there aren't any, there will be taxis or autorickshaws. There are some airports close enough to town to get to by cycle-rickshaw.

When arriving at an airport anywhere in India, the first thing to do is find out if there's a prepaid taxi booth inside the arrival hall. If there is, pay for one there. If you don't do this and simply walk outside to negotiate your own price, you'll invariably pay more and also have to go through the hassle of negotiating. Taxi drivers are notorious for refusing to use the meter outside airport terminals. Obviously some taxi drivers don't like the prepaid system (as there's no scope for rip-offs), so it's a good idea not to present the voucher until you have arrived at your destination.

For more information about arriving at destinations, see the regional chapters; eg, the 'Dodgy Delhi' boxed text in the Delhi chapter has useful information about how to get to downtown from the airport, especially for first-time visitors to India.

Taxi

There are taxis in most towns in India, and most of them (certainly in the major cities) are metered. Getting a metered fare is a different situation. First of all the meter may be 'broken'. Threatening to get another taxi will usually fix it immediately, except during rush hours. It's best to get a prepaid taxi if it's available (described in the previous To/From the Airport section).

Secondly the meter will almost certainly be out of date. Fares are adjusted upwards so much faster and more frequently than meters are recalibrated that drivers almost always have 'fare adjustment cards' indicating what you should pay compared to what the meter indicates. This is, of course, wide open to abuse. You have no idea if you're being shown the right card or if the taxi's meter has actually been recalibrated and you're being shown the card anyway. In states where the numbers are written differently (such as Gujarat) it's not much use asking for the chart if you can't read it.

The only answer to all this is to try to get an idea of what the fare should be before departure (ask information desks at the airport or at your hotel). You'll soon begin to develop a feel for what the meter says, what the cards say and what the two together should indicate. Guideline fares are given in the regional chapters.

In various regions, particularly in the hills of Himachal Pradesh and Uttaranchal, taxi operators have organised themselves into unions and offer fixed rates to common destinations, often with some local sightseeing tours thrown in. Generally, these rates cannot be bargained down, although drivers may approach you away from the union office and offer lower fares. Taxi union offices can be found at the bus stands in major towns.

Autorickshaw

An autorickshaw is a noisy three-wheel device powered by a two-stroke motorcycle engine with a driver up front and seats for two (or sometimes more) passengers behind. They don't have doors and have just a canvas top. They are also known as scooters or autos. Although many are made by Bajaj, there is an amazing variety of models and designs. Many display artistic devotional images, while others are almost completely covered with glossy pictures of the driver's favourite Bollywood stars.

They're generally about half the price of a taxi, usually metered and follow the same ground rules as taxis (see the previous entry).

Because of their size, autorickshaws are often faster than taxis for short trips and their drivers are decidedly more aggressive road users – hair-raising near-misses are guaranteed and glancing-blow collisions are not infrequent; thrillseekers will love it!

In busy towns you'll find that, when stopped at traffic lights, the height you are sitting at is the same as most bus and truck exhaust pipes – copping dirty great lungfuls of diesel fumes is part of the autorickshaw experience. Also, their small wheel size and rock-hard suspension makes them supremely uncomfortable; even the slightest bump will have you instantly airborne.

Tempo

Somewhat like a large autorickshaw, these ungainly looking three-wheel devices operate like minibuses or share taxis on fixed routes. Unless you are spending large amounts of time in one city, it's not really worth working out the routes. You'll find it much easier and more convenient to go by autorickshaw.

Cycle-Rickshaw

This is effectively a three-wheeler bicycle with a seat for two passengers behind the rider. Although they no longer operate in most of the big cities, except in the old part of Delhi and parts of Kolkata, they are still in all the smaller cities and towns, where they're the basic means of transport. You'll have a quieter ride than in an autorickshaw, and you won't be contributing to air pollution.

As with taxis and autorickshaws, fares must always be agreed on in advance. Avoid situations where the driver says something like: 'As you like'. He's hoping you are not well acquainted with the correct fares and will overpay. But invariably, no matter what you pay in situations such as this, it will be deemed too little and a very unpleasant situation can quickly develop. This is especially the case in heavily touristed places, such as Agra and Jaipur – simply settle on the price before you get moving to avoid prickly arguments. A typical ride in a cycle-rickshaw is generally between 1km and 3km and will cost between Rs 15 and Rs 30. The ride is extremely strenuous work for the driver, so a tip is much appreciated.

It's quite feasible to hire a rickshaw-wallah by time, not just for a trip. Hiring one for a day or several days can make good financial sense for both you and the rickshaw-wallah.

Other Transport

People-drawn rickshaws still operate in parts of Kolkata – see the Kolkata chapter for more information. Kolkata also has a large tram network and India's first underground railway system (metro). Delhi has suburban trains. In a handful of places, such as Bharatpur and Ujjain, tongas (horse-drawn two-wheelers) still run.

ORGANISED TOURS

At almost any place of tourist interest, and quite a few places which aren't, there will be tours operated either by the Government of India tourist office, the state tourist office or the local transport company – sometimes all three. There is also a growing number of private operators. Tours are usually very good value, particularly in places where the sights are spread out. You probably couldn't get around Delhi on public transport as cheaply as you can on a tour for instance.

These tours are not purely aimed at foreign tourists; you will almost always find yourself outnumbered by local tourists. Despite this, the tours are usually in English (ask when booking). One major drawback of many tours is that they try to cram far too much into too short a period of time. If a tour looks too hectic, you're better off doing it yourself at a more appropriate pace – or you could go on it with the intention of finding out which places you'd like to visit on your own at a later time.

If you're interested in a tour of Buddhist sites, Potala Tours & Travels (☎ 3723284/3722552, ⓔ potala@vsnl.com) in Delhi organises a 'Buddhist circuit' trip from 10 to 15 days for most budgets. Check out its Web site at www.potalatours.com/buddhist. In Bihar, try Buddha Travel Corporation (☎ 662443, fax 674589), Bhattacharya Rd, Patna.

Delhi

Delhi is the capital of India, its third-largest city and North India's industrial hub. Old Delhi was the capital of Muslim India between the 17th and 19th centuries, and a legacy of mosques, monuments and forts testifies to this. New Delhi was built as the imperial capital of India by the British. It is a spacious, open city and contains embassies and government buildings. The newer, wealthy suburbs are mostly to the south of New Delhi, and an ever-growing belt of poorer suburbs and *jhuggis* (slums) stretches in all directions.

In addition to its historic interest and role as the government centre, Delhi is a major travel gateway. It is one of India's busiest entrance points for overseas airlines, the hub of the North Indian travel network, and a stop on the overland route across Asia. The city of Delhi covers most of Delhi state.

Few travellers have much that is good to say about India's fastest growing city; the intense air pollution and persistent touts often make it an unsettling experience for newcomers. It does, however, have a long and fascinating history and there's a tangible energy and confidence that only comes with a history as rich and varied as Delhi's.

There is no smoking in public, especially around monuments and religious sites, but it's acceptable in restaurants and bars. Most sights are open sunrise to sunset, although following the dramatic price hikes of 2000, many have become poor value.

Delhi at a Glance

Population: 13.8 million
Area: 1483 sq km
Main Languages: Hindi, Urdu, English & Punjabi
Telephone Area Code: 011
When to Go: Oct to Mar

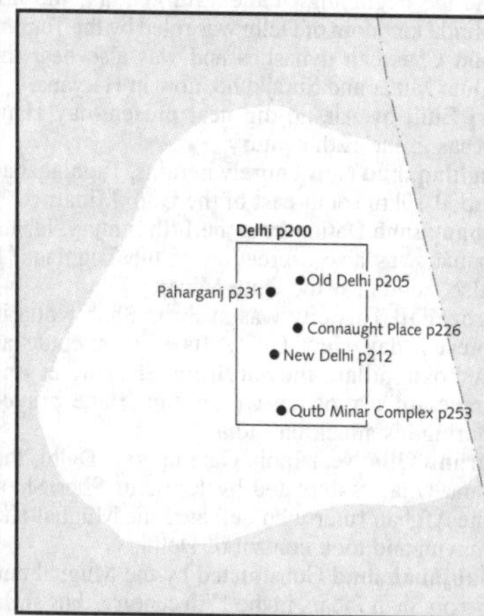

- Wander at leisure around the Red Fort, Delhi's extraordinary Mughal-era fort
- See Qutb Minar, a massive tower built to proclaim the arrival of Islam in India
- Discover Jama Masjid, the largest mosque in India and built by Shah Jahan, who built the Taj Mahal
- Explore Connaught Place, the thriving heart of New Delhi
- Visit Humayun's tomb, a fine example of early Mughal architecture
- Peruse and purchase arts and crafts at Janpath's Central Cottage Industries Emporium or Dilli Haat
- Marvel at the lotus-shaped Bahai Temple, the symbol of the unity of all religions

HISTORY

Delhi hasn't always been the capital of India, but it has played an important role in Indian history. The settlement of Indraprastha, which featured in the epic Mahabharata over 3000 years ago, was approximately on the site of present-day Delhi. Over 2000 years ago, Pataliputra (near modern-day Patna) was the capital of Ashoka's empire. The Mughal emperors made Agra the capital during the 16th and 17th centuries. Under the British, Kolkata

(Calcutta) was the capital until the inauguration of New Delhi in 1931.

There have been at least eight cities around modern Delhi, and the old saying that whoever founds a new city in Delhi will lose it has come true every time – most recently for the British who lasted only 16 years. The first four cities were to the south, around the area where the Qutb Minar stands.

Indraprastha The earliest known Delhi, Indraprastha was centred near present-day Purana Qila. At the beginning of the 12th century, the last Hindu kingdom of Delhi was ruled by the Tomara and Chauthan dynasties and was also near the Qutb Minar and Surajkund, now in Haryana.
Siri Built by Ala-ud-din near present-day Hauz Khas in the 12th century.
Tughlaqabad Now entirely in ruins, Tughlaqabad stood 10km south-east of the Qutb Minar.
Jahanpanah Dating from the 14th century, Jahanpanah was also a creation of the Tughlaqs. It also stood near the Qutb Minar.
Firozabad This city was at Firoz Shah Kotla in present-day New Delhi. Its ruins include an Ashoka pillar, moved from elsewhere, and traces of a mosque where Tamerlane prayed during his attack on India.
Purana Qila Near India Gate in New Delhi, Purana Qila was created by Emperor Sher Shah, the Afghan ruler who defeated the Mughal Humayun and took control of Delhi.
Shahjahanabad Constructed by the Mughal emperor, Shah Jahan, in the 17th century, thus shifting the Mughal capital from Agra to Delhi; Shahjahanabad roughly corresponds to Old Delhi today and is largely preserved, including the Red Fort and the majestic Jama Masjid.
New Delhi Constructed by the British. The move from Kolkata (Calcutta) to New Delhi was announced in 1911 but construction was not completed, and the city officially inaugurated, until 1931.

Delhi has seen many invaders through the ages. Tamerlane plundered it in the 14th century; the Afghan Babur occupied it in the 16th century; and in 1739 the Persian emperor, Nadir Shah, sacked the city and carted the Kohinoor Diamond (now part of the British royal family's crown jewels) and the famous Peacock Throne off to Iran. The British captured Delhi in 1803, but during the Indian Uprising of 1857 it was a centre of resistance to the British. Prior to Partition, Delhi had a very large Muslim population and Urdu was the main language. In 1947, it became the capital of truncated India, and Hindu and Sikh refugees poured in from Pakistan. Now Hindu Punjabis have replaced many of the Muslims, and Hindi predominates.

William Dalrymple's excellent *City of Djinns* is a wonderfully entertaining introduction to Delhi's past and present.

ORIENTATION

Delhi is a relatively easy city to find your way around, although it is very spread out. The section of interest to visitors is on the west bank of the Yamuna River and is divided into two basic parts – the tightly packed streets of Old Delhi and the spacious, planned areas of New Delhi.

Old Delhi is the 17th-century walled city of Shahjahanabad, with city gates, narrow alleys, constant traffic jams and terrible air pollution, the enormous Red Fort and Jama Masjid, temples, mosques, bazaars and the famous street known as Chandni Chowk. Here you will find the Old Delhi train station and, a little farther north, the main Inter State Bus Terminal (ISBT) near Kashmiri Gate. Near New Delhi train station, and acting as a sort of buffer zone between the old and new cities, is the crowded market area of Paharganj. This has become the budget travellers' hang-out, and there are many popular cheap hotels and restaurants in this area.

New Delhi is a planned city of wide, tree-lined streets, parks and fountains, but still has the Indian touches of doe-eyed cows calmly ignoring the traffic and squatter hovels on waste land. It can be subdivided into the business and residential areas around Connaught Place to the north and the government areas around Rajpath to the south. At the eastern end of Rajpath is the India Gate memorial and at the west end is Rashtrapati Bhavan, the residence of the Indian president.

The hub of New Delhi is the great circle of Connaught Place and the streets that radiate from it. Here you will find most of the airline offices, banks, travel agents, state and national tourist offices, more budget accommodation and several of the big hotels. The Regal Cinema, at the south side of the circle, and the Plaza Cinema, at the north, are two important landmarks and are useful for telling taxi or autorickshaw drivers where you want to go.

Janpath and Sansad Marg (Parliament St) are the two main streets running off Connaught Place, here you'll find more tourist offices, hotels, airlines and a number of other useful addresses.

South of the New Delhi government areas are Delhi's more expensive residential areas, with names such as Defence Colony, South Extension, Lodi Colony, Greater Kailash and Vasant Vihar. Many of the better (and more expensive) cinemas and shopping centres are found here. The Indira Gandhi International Airport is to the south-west of the city, and about halfway between the airport and Connaught Place is Chanakyapuri, the diplomatic enclave. Most of Delhi's embassies (and the prime minister's house) are concentrated in this strikingly tidy area and there are several major hotels here.

Across the Yamuna River (heavily polluted for the nine months of the year that the monsoon is not flushing it) lie many new industrial and residential areas, as well as some of the grimmest slum areas.

The 250-page *Eicher City Map* (Rs 270) includes 174 area maps, and is a good reference if you are venturing farther into the Delhi environs. It's available at most larger bookshops and modern fuel stations.

INFORMATION

Tourist Offices

The Government of India tourist office (☎ 3320005) at 88 Janpath is open from 9 am to 6 pm Monday to Friday and 9 am to 2 pm Saturday. The office has a lot of information and brochures on destinations all over India, but you have to ask for it. It has a good give away map of the city, and the staff can also help with accommodation. Some have been known to try to sell overpriced taxi tours.

There are tourist offices in the arrivals halls of the international (☎ 5694229) and domestic (☎ 5665296) airports that are open around the clock. Here, too, staff can help you find accommodation although, like many other Indian tourist offices, they may tell you the hotel you choose is 'full' and steer you somewhere else.

There is a Delhi Tourism Corporation office (☎ 3313637) in N-Block, Connaught Place, open from 7 am to 9 pm Monday to Friday, and another (with a pleasant coffee shop and garden) near the state emporiums on Baba Kharak Singh Marg. There are also counters at New Delhi, Old Delhi and Nizamuddin train stations, as well as at the ISBT at Kashmiri Gate.

Official guides are available at the major sites (around Rs 100 for half a day) and through the above tourist offices. Unofficial guides will also offer their services.

There are several city guides available from newsstands – *Delhi City Guide, Delhi this Fortnight* and *Delhi Diary* among them. *First City* (Rs 30) is a monthly magazine with gossip on what the city's upper-class 'tiger ladies' are up to, but also has good listings and reviews of cultural events and restaurants. Try www.delhigate.com for information about the city, and www.delhi123.com has news, events, venues, weather and more.

Most of the state governments have information centres in Delhi, staffed by a mix of helpful people and surly *babus* (bureaucratic bureaucrats):

Andaman & Nicobar Islands (☎ 6871443) 12 Chanakyapuri
Andhra Pradesh (☎ 3382031) Andhra Bhavan, 1 Ashoka Rd
Arunachal Pradesh (☎ 3013956) Arunachal Bldg, Kautilya Marg, Chanakyapuri
Assam (☎ 3342064) B1 Baba Kharak Singh Marg
Bihar (☎ 3368371) 216–217 Kanishka Shopping Plaza, Ashoka Rd
Goa (☎ 4629967) 18 Amrita Shergil Marg
Gujarat (☎ 3734015) A6 Baba Kharak Singh Marg
Haryana (☎ 3324910) Chandralok Bldg, 36 Janpath
Himachal Pradesh (☎ 3325320) Chandralok Bldg, 36 Janpath
Jammu & Kashmir (☎ 3345373) Kanishka Shopping Plaza, Ashoka Rd
Karnataka (☎ 3363862) Karnataka State Emporium, Baba Kharak Singh Marg
Kerala (☎ 3368541) Kanishka Shopping Plaza, Ashoka Rd

Madhya Pradesh (☎ 3341187) Kanishka Shopping Plaza, Ashoka Rd
Maharashtra (☎ 3363773) A8 Baba Kharak Singh Marg
Manipur (☎ 3344026) State Emporium Bldg, Baba Kharak Singh Marg
Meghalaya (☎ 3014417) 9 Aurangzeb Rd
Mizoram (☎ 3012331) Mizoram State Government House, Circular Rd, Chanakyapuri
Nagaland (☎ 3343161) Nagaland Emporium, Baba Kharak Singh Marg
Orissa (☎ 3364580) B4 Baba Kharak Singh Marg
Punjab Kanishka Shopping Plaza, Ashoka Rd
Rajasthan (☎ 3383837) Bikaner House, Pandara Rd
Sikkim (☎ 6115346) New Sikkim House, 14 Panchsheel Marg, Chanakyapuri
Tamil Nadu (☎ 3735427) State Emporium Bldg, Baba Kharak Singh Marg
Tripura (☎ 3793827) Tripura Bhavan, off Kautilya Marg, Chanakyapuri
Uttar Pradesh (☎ 3322251) Chandralok Bldg, 36 Janpath
West Bengal (☎ 3732840) A2 Baba Kharak Singh Marg

Money

The major offices of all the Indian and foreign banks operating in India can be found in Delhi, where it's possible to get cash around the clock. If you do need to change money outside regular banking hours, Citibank and Standard Chartered Grindlays have 24-hour branches in Connaught Place and Thomas Cook also has 24-hour branches at New Delhi train station and at the airport. There are also plenty of ATMs dotted around.

At other times there's plenty of choice. In Paharganj, Chequepoint foreign exchange on Main Bazaar exchanges cash and travellers cheques without commission between 9.30 am and 8 pm daily.

American Express (AmEx; ☎ 3324119) has its office in A-Block, Connaught Place, and is open from 9 am to 7 pm daily. Thomas Cook has more branches in C-Block, Connaught Place and at The Imperial hotel, which is open from 9.30 am to 6 pm.

Other banks (most with ATMs) include:

Bank of America (☎ 3722332) DCM Bldg, Barakhamba Rd
Banque Nationale de Paris (☎ 3314848) 2nd floor, Hansalya Bldg, Barakhamba Rd
Citibank (☎ 3712484) Jeevan Bharati Bldg, Outer Circle, Connaught Place
Deutsche Bank (☎ 3712028) 15 Tolstoy House, Tolstoy Marg
HongKong & Shanghai Bank (☎ 3314355) ECE House, Kasturba Gandhi Marg
Standard Chartered Grindlays (☎ 3721242) 10 H-Block, Connaught Place; (☎ 3732260) 17 Sansard Marg, Connaught Place

Post & Communications

There are small post offices in Paharganj and A-Block, Connaught Place, but the main post office is on the roundabout on Baba Kharak Singh Marg, 500m south-west of Connaught Place. Poste restante mail can be collected here from 10 am to 4.30 pm Monday to Saturday. Ensure mail is addressed to New Delhi, otherwise it will go to the Old Delhi post office. Mail can also be sent to the Government of India tourist office on Janpath.

There are plenty of private STD/ISD call offices around the city, many of which also have fax and email facilities. The telecom centre in the Arunachal Building, Barakhamba Rd has fax and phone facilities, and the central telegraph office at Eastern Court has multimedia facilities. Both are open from 10 am to 7 pm Monday to Saturday.

Internet access around Connaught Place tends to be more expensive than elsewhere. Hub Internet Centre in B-Block is modern and has plenty of terminals for Rs 30 per hour (minimum time). DSIDC Cyber Cafe, next to Delhi Tourism Corporation in N-Block, is smaller and more expensive, charging Rs 30/50 per half hour/hour, but you get a free drink. It's open from 9 am to 8 pm. There are a couple of smaller places around Ringo Guest House that also charge Rs 30/50.

In Paharganj a few guesthouses have 24-hour Internet access at around Rs 20 per hour, and there's a whole heap of other places on Main Bazaar and in the lanes running off it. If your guesthouse doesn't have Internet access, you can enjoy a beer while you surf the Web at Hotel Gold Regency. Internet access costs Rs 20 per hour but the system is electronically timed and can cut off half way through sending a message. To the west along Main Bazaar down the small lane east of Khosla Cafe is a really good place open 24 hours. It's a bit pricier at Rs 30 per hour but access is fast. There's another good place with fast access opposite the Malhotra restaurants that is open until 9 pm.

Internet Resources

Following are some useful Internet resources for Delhi:

delhigate City listings site with a query page. www.delhigate.com
delhi123 City listings site with news, events, venues, weather and more. www.delhi123.com

Visa Extensions & Other Permits

You will find the Foreigners' Regional Registration Office (FRRO; ☎ 3319489) in Hans Bhavan, near the Tilak Bridge train station. Come here to get permits for restricted areas such as Mizoram in the north-eastern region. The office is open from 9.30 am to 1.30 pm and 2 to 4 pm Monday to Friday.

The FRRO can issue 15-day visa extensions for free if you just need a few extra days before you leave the country. To apply for a maximum one-month extension on a six-month visa is more complicated. First you need a very good reason, then you must collect the long-term visa extension form from the Ministry of Home Affairs at Lok Nayak Bhavan in Khan Market (☎ 4693334), on Subramania Bharati Rd. The office is open from 10 am to noon Monday to Friday. It's a typical Indian government office, so be prepared to wait. Once you've collected the form, you then need to take it, along with four photos, to the FRRO, which is about a Rs 20 rickshaw ride away. A one-month extension costs US$30. When (or if) the extension is authorised, the authorisation has to be taken *back* to the Ministry of Home Affairs, where the actual visa extension is issued.

Since it's difficult to get an extension on a six-month visa, you may be approached by people offering to forge your visa for a longer stay. Don't fall for this one – the authorities will check your details carefully against their computer records when you leave India. There are heavy fines if you're caught and you won't be allowed to visit India again.

If you need a tax clearance certificate before departure, the Foreign Section of the Income Tax Department (☎ 3317826) is at Indraprastha Estate. Bring exchange certificates with you, though it's entirely likely nobody will ask for your clearance certificate when you leave the country. The office is closed from 1 to 2 pm.

Export of any object over 100 years old requires a permit. If in doubt, contact the Director, Antiquities, Archaeological Survey of India (☎ 3017220), on Janpath, next to the National Museum.

Travel Agencies

In the ITDC Hotel Janpath, the Student Travel Information Centre (☎ 3327582) is used by many travellers and is the place to renew or obtain student cards (Rs 200), although their tickets are not usually as cheap as elsewhere.

Some of the ticket discounters around Paharganj and Connaught Place are real fly-by-night operations, so take care. Those that have been recommended by readers include the following:

Aa Bee Travels (☎ 3510172, ⓔ aabee@mail.com) Hare Rama Guest House, Paharganj
Cozy Travels (☎ 3312873) BMC House, 1 N-Block, Connaught Place
Don't Pass Me By Travels (☎ 3352942) 1st floor, Ringo Guest House
VINstring Holidays (☎ 3368717) YWCA International Guest House, Sansad Marg
Vin Tours (☎ 3348571) YWCA Blue Triangle Family Hostel, Ashoka Rd
Y Tours & Travel (☎ 3711662) YMCA, Ashoka Rd

Hotel Namaskar (☎ 3621234), just off Main Bazaar, Paharganj, and the travel agency at the Hotel Ajanta (☎ 3620927), Arakashan Rd, have also been recommended (see Places to Stay later in this chapter).

For more upmarket travel arrangements, both within India and for foreign travel, there are a number of agencies that are mostly located around Connaught Place. These include Cox & Kings (☎ 3320067) in H-Block and Sita World Travels (☎ 331-1133) in F-Block.

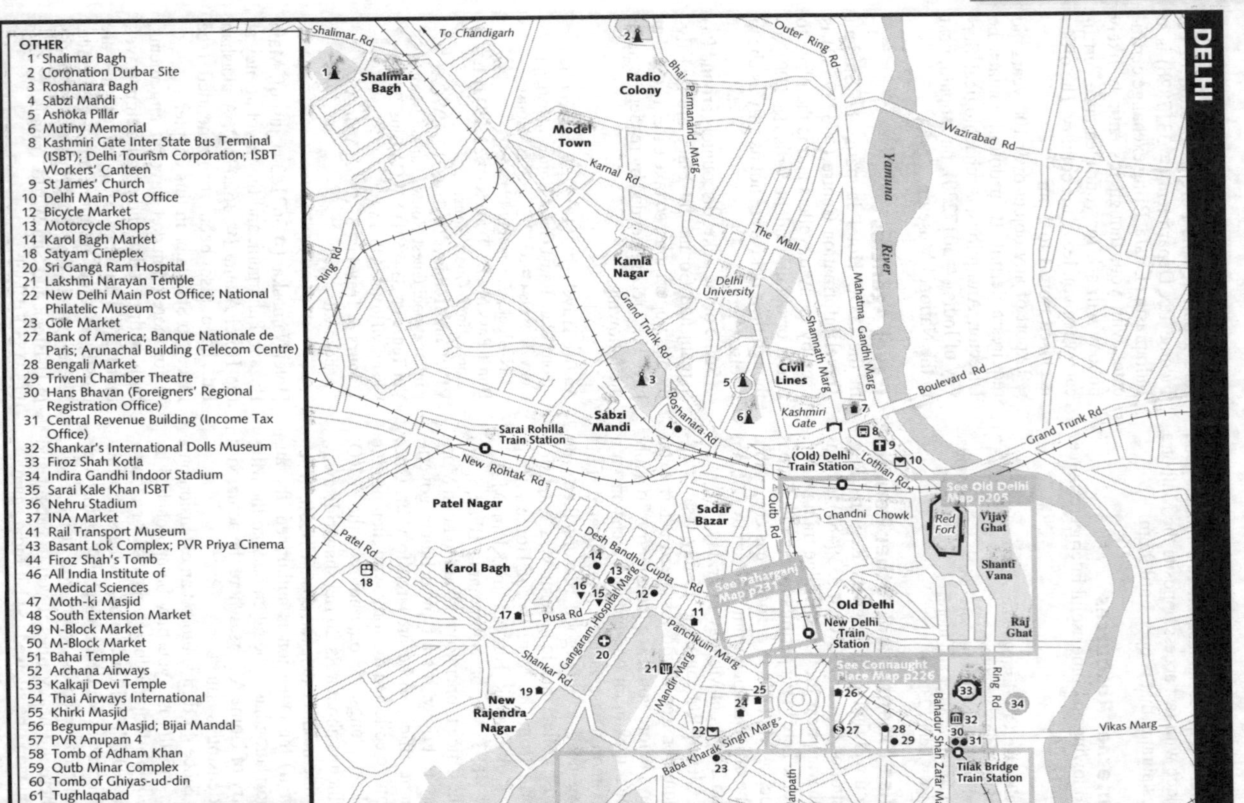
DELHI
DELHI
OTHER
1 Shalimar Bagh
2 Coronation Durbar Site
3 Roshanara Bagh
4 Sabzi Mandi
5 Ashoka Pillar
6 Mutiny Memorial
8 Kashmiri Gate Inter State Bus Terminal (ISBT); Delhi Tourism Corporation; ISBT Workers' Canteen
9 St James' Church
10 Delhi Main Post Office
12 Bicycle Market
13 Motorcycle Shops
14 Karol Bagh Market
18 Satyam Cineplex
20 Sri Ganga Ram Hospital
21 Lakshmi Narayan Temple
22 New Delhi Main Post Office; National Philatelic Museum
23 Gole Market
27 Bank of America; Banque Nationale de Paris; Arunachal Building (Telecom Centre)
28 Bengali Market
29 Triveni Chamber Theatre
30 Hans Bhavan (Foreigners' Regional Registration Office)
31 Central Revenue Building (Income Tax Office)
32 Shankar's International Dolls Museum
33 Firoz Shah Kotla
34 Indira Gandhi Indoor Stadium
35 Sarai Kale Khan ISBT
36 Nehru Stadium
37 INA Market
41 Rail Transport Museum
43 Basant Lok Complex; PVR Priya Cinema
44 Firoz Shah's Tomb
46 All India Institute of Medical Sciences
47 Moth-ki Masjid
48 South Extension Market
49 N-Block Market
50 M-Block Market
51 Bahai Temple
52 Archana Airways
53 Kalkaji Devi Temple
54 Thai Airways International
55 Khirki Masjid
56 Begumpur Masjid; Bijai Mandal
57 PVR Anupam 4
58 Tomb of Adham Khan
59 Qutb Minar Complex
60 Tomb of Ghiyas-ud-din
61 Tughlaqabad
Shalimar Rd
To Chandigarh
Shalimar Bagh
Radio Colony
Outer Ring Rd
Bhai Parmanand Marg
Model Town
Wazirabad Rd
Karnal Rd
Yamuna River
The Mall
Ring Rd
Kamla Nagar
Delhi University
Grand Trunk Rd
Mahatma Gandhi Marg
Shamnath Marg
Civil Lines
Boulevard Rd
Kashmiri Gate
Sabzi Mandi
Roshanara Rd
Sarai Rohilla Train Station
(Old) Delhi Train Station
Lothian Rd
New Rohtak Rd
See Old Delhi Map p205
Patel Nagar
Sadar Bazar
Qutb Rd
Chandni Chowk
Red Fort
Vijay Ghat
Shanti Vana
Patel Rd
Desh Bandhu Gupta Rd
Karol Bagh
Gangaram Hospital Marg
See Paharganj Map p231
Old Delhi
Pusa Rd
Panchkuin Marg
New Delhi Train Station
Raj Ghat
Shankar Rd
Mandir Marg
See Connaught Place Map p226
Ring Rd
New Rajendra Nagar
Baba Kharak Singh Marg
Bahadur Shah Zafar Marg
Vikas Marg
Janpath
Tilak Bridge Train Station

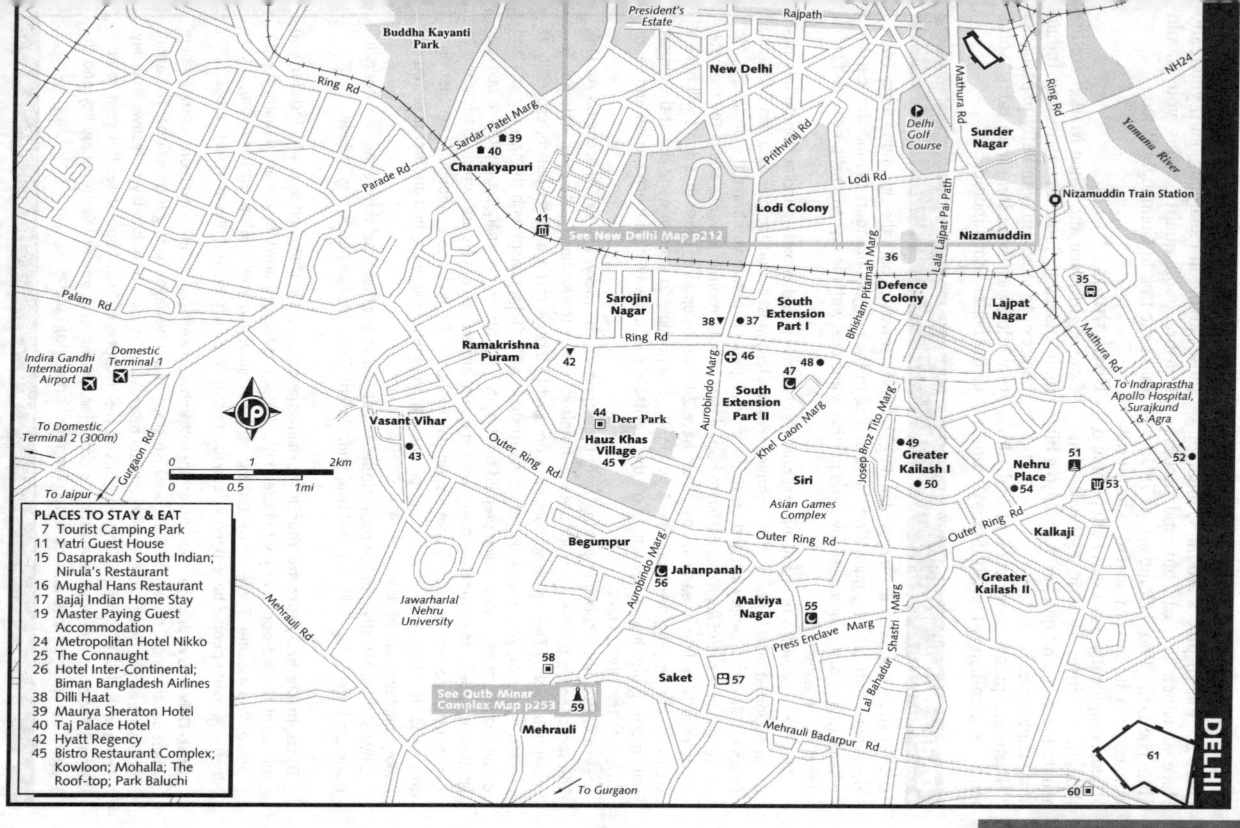
DELHI
PLACES TO STAY & EAT
7 Tourist Camping Park
11 Yatri Guest House
15 Dasaprakash South Indian; Nirula's Restaurant
16 Mughal Hans Restaurant
17 Bajaj Indian Home Stay
19 Master Paying Guest Accommodation
24 Metropolitan Hotel Nikko
25 The Connaught
26 Hotel Inter-Continental; Biman Bangladesh Airlines
38 Dilli Haat
39 Maurya Sheraton Hotel
40 Taj Palace Hotel
42 Hyatt Regency
45 Bistro Restaurant Complex; Kowloon; Mohalla; The Roof-top; Park Baluchi
0 1 2km
0 0.5 1mi
President's Estate
Rajpath
Buddha Kayanti Park
New Delhi
Ring Rd
Sardar Patel Marg
Chanakyapuri
Parade Rd
Prithviraj Rd
Lodi Rd
Lodi Colony
Delhi Golf Course
Mathura Rd
Sunder Nagar
NH24
Yamuna River
Nizamuddin Train Station
Nizamuddin
Lala Lajpat Pai Path
See New Delhi Map p212
Bhisham Pitamah Marg
Defence Colony
Lajpat Nagar
Sarojini Nagar
South Extension Part I
Ring Rd
Palam Rd
Ramakrishna Puram
Aurobindo Marg
South Extension Part II
Khel Gaon Marg
Josep Broz Tito Marg
To Indraprastha Apollo Hospital, Surajkund & Agra
Indira Gandhi International Airport
Domestic Terminal 1
Vasant Vihar
Deer Park
Hauz Khas Village
Outer Ring Rd
Greater Kailash I
Nehru Place
Siri
Asian Games Complex
To Domestic Terminal 2 (300m)
Gurgaon Rd
To Jaipur
Begumpur
Outer Ring Rd
Kalkaji
Jahanpanah
Greater Kailash II
Jawarharlal Nehru University
Mehrauli Rd
Malviya Nagar
Press Enclave Marg
Lal Bahadur Shastri Marg
Saket
See Qutb Minar Complex Map p253
Mehrauli
Mehrauli Badarpur Rd
To Gurgaon
DELHI

Photography

There are lots of places around Connaught Place at which you can buy and process film. The Delhi Photo Company, at 78 Janpath, close to the Government of India tourist office, competently processes both print and slide film. Kinsey Bros in A-Block, Connaught Place is a bit quicker but is also a bit more expensive.

There are plenty more camera and film shops for snap-happy tourists. Sanjay Studio next to Diamond Cafe is convenient for those staying in Paharganj, but if you really treasure good quality snaps you should make the trek to Connaught Place.

Bookshops

Connaught Place and Khan Market are the main places to look for interesting Indian books or to stock up with hefty paperbacks to while away those long train rides. Some of the better shops include:

Dodgy Delhi

Delhi is an assault on all the senses, daunting most new arrivals to both the city and to India. Frazzled from a long journey, many find the hounding of the beggars and touts too much, especially when trying to manoeuvre past cows and rickshaws and deal with the myriad smells, noise and pollution at the same time.

This is compounded by many international flights arriving and departing Indira Gandhi International Airport at terrible hours of the morning. Fortunately, most airport facilities are open 24 hours, so it's possible to change cash and make travel arrangements before you brave the onslaught. No matter the time of arrival, it's advisable to book a decent hotel room in advance and notify the hotel if you're arriving late or early. Many places have 24-hour receptions; those that don't will have a staff member sleeping nearby to check you in. It's also possible to sleep or hang out at the airport until morning but this is only putting off the inevitable and, anyway, it's a much quicker and easier drive into the city at night.

Even with a hotel booking, getting from the airport can be tricky. The Ex-Servicemen's Air Link Transport Service (EATS) bus stops at large hotels as well as the Kashmiri Gate Inter State Bus Terminal (ISBT), New Delhi train station and Connaught Place. A taxi is a better option, especially at night; if you're on your own look for others to share with. Get a receipt with the taxi number and destination from the traffic police prepaid taxi booth – the others overcharge. Despite the taxi registration number and destination being written down, airport taxi drivers are notorious for scams to get tourists into expensive and commission-paying hotels. Be firm and confident – don't let on if this is your first visit; if the driver is not prepared to go where you want, find another taxi. You can make complaints about drivers on ☎ 6101197.

Drivers' most effective and popular stories to get you to another hotel during the wee hours include the hotel being 'full', 'burnt down' and 'closed'. Two other scenarios may include:

Riots-in-Delhi Syndrome Your driver claims there are riots in Delhi and as you're insisting you still want to be dropped at your chosen hotel the taxi is flagged down by a man in uniform – the police, you assume. There's a heated exchange in Hindi and you're informed the rioting is very bad and many people have been killed. You end up in an expensive hotel in a 'safe' area.

Lost-Driver Syndrome Your driver doesn't know where your hotel is (everyone knows where Main Bazaar and Connaught Place are), so stops at a travel agency to get directions. The agent offers a free phone call to check your hotel reservation as it's a busy holiday or festival that day. The agent dials the number and you talk to the 'receptionist' who apologises but your room is double-booked and your reservation is cancelled. Fortunately, you're in a travel agency and the agent can get you into a much better (commission-paying) place.

Bahri & Sons Khan Market
The Bookshop Khan Market, Subramania Bharati Rd
Bookworm 29B Radial Rd No 4, Connaught Place
English Book Store 17L Radial Road No 5, Connaught Place
New Book Depot 18 B-Block, Connaught Place

There are plenty of pavement stalls in various places around Connaught Place, particularly on Sansad Marg, near the Kwality Restaurant, and in Paharganj. Most stalls have a good range of cheap paperback books, and will often buy them back from you if they are returned in a reasonable condition. Almost next door to the Kwality Restaurant is People Tree, which sells books about the environment as well as eco-friendly crafts.

Prabhu Book Service in Hauz Khas Village has an interesting selection of second-hand and rare books. Bookshops in deluxe

Dodgy Delhi

Many decide that Delhi (and therefore India) is just too much and book the next flight home. Hang on in there if you start feeling this way – it's really not that bad. Take a few days to chill out and acclimatise to the Indian surroundings. Don't hide away in the tourist ghettos – explore some of Delhi's more relaxed sights such as the gardens, the Red Fort, Humayun's tomb, the National Museum and Raj Ghat. If you're really suffering, head for Connaught Place where air-con and familiar brands of beer and pizza can help transport you home for a while. Avoid chaotic Old Delhi until you're more relaxed and are ready to appreciate the city's colourful history and vibrant personality – who knows, you may even start to like the place.

If you're still determined to leave, there are plenty of calmer places easily accessible from Delhi by various modes of transport (see also the Getting There & Away section later in this chapter):

Train One of the easiest and most comfortable ways out, there are special foreigner railway reservation offices at central locations. Beware of touts outside New Delhi train station who redirect travellers to their travel agencies (generally across the road) on the pretext that the reservation office is closed, has moved or spontaneously combusted the day before.

Bus Public and private buses ply popular routes. Private buses, booked through accommodation and travel agencies, are generally the more comfortable and direct option.

Tours If you prefer minimum hassle then tours are good. The Delhi-Jaipur-Agra triangle is popular. Tourist offices and accommodation have details. Beware of travel agents and touts dedicated to helping confused tourists – Lonely Planet receives hundreds of complaints about these guys (see Travel Agencies in this chapter for recommended operators). Kashmiris around Connaught Place and Paharganj in particular do the hard sell on their economically crippled yet beautiful homeland. There is a good reason they tout so hard – it's a war zone (see the Jammu & Kashmir chapter for details).

Taxi It's possible to hire the use of a taxi and driver for around US$30 per day (based on two people sharing an all-inclusive tour around North India) through accommodation and travel agencies. Airport transfers and Delhi sightseeing tours are usually 'thrown-in' on longer trips.

hotels are more expensive but have a good selection of novels, glossy art books and historical works.

Libraries & Cultural Centres

Delhi has a fair selection of libraries and cultural centres, including Delhi Public Library, opposite the (Old) Delhi Train Station on SP Mukherjee Marg, open 8.30 am to 8.30 pm daily, except Sunday. Others include:

Alliance Française (☎ 6258128) D-13 South Extension Part II

American Center (☎ 3316841) 24 Kasturba Gandhi Marg, Connaught Place. Open 10 am to 6 pm Thursday to Saturday and Monday to Tuesday.

British Council Library (☎ 3711401) 17 Kasturba Gandhi Marg, Connaught Place. Open 10 am to 6 pm Tuesday to Saturday. This is better than the US equivalent, but officially you have to join to get in.

India International Centre (☎ 4619431) Near the Lodi tombs. The centre has weekly lectures on art, economics and other contemporary issues by Indian and foreign experts.

World Wide Fund for Nature India (☎ 469-3744) 172-B Lodi Estate. This organisation has excellent computerised environmental records, a good library, and an ecoshop selling handicrafts and books. It's open 9.30 am to 5.30 pm Monday to Friday.

For Sangeet Natak Akademi, a performing arts centre with substantial archive material, Lalit Kala Akademi, the academy of fine arts and sculpture, and Sahitya Akademi, the literature academy, see Museums & Galleries later in this chapter.

Laundry

Most hotels and guest houses have a laundry service. You'll save a bit of cash by taking your laundry to the parcel office next door to Hare Rama Guest House, where t-shirts/trousers are machine washed for around Rs 5/10 per garment. There are several other laundries around Connaught Place and the suburbs; most of these will also do dry-cleaning.

Left Luggage

Most hotels will store baggage for a nominal fee or for free. Otherwise gear can be safely stored at The Luggage Room (☎ 3618971), in a lane east of Hare Rama Guest House in Paharganj, for Rs 4 per day. It won't store cash, cameras or walkmans and you'll need your passport for both deposit and collection, which is possible between 8 am and 8 pm daily. Shota Tours and Travel above Diamond Cafe charges a rupee or two more for the same service.

Medical Services & Emergency

The Indraprastha Apollo Hospital (☎ 692 5858), Sarita Vihar, Mathura Rd, is one of the best hospitals in Delhi, if not India. The East West Medical Centre (☎ 4623738, 4699229), near Delhi Golf Course, at 38 Golf Links Rd, is popular with travellers. All rickshaw-wallahs know where these hospitals are.

Reputable government hospitals include Dr Ram Manohar Lohia Hospital (☎ 336 5525), Baba Kharak Singh Marg, and the All India Institute of Medical Sciences (☎ 6561123), Ansari Nagar. Embassies have lists of recommended doctors and dentists.

There is a 24-hour pharmacy (☎ 3310163, ext 180) at Super Bazaar in Connaught Place. The ambulance service can be reached on ☎ 102.

OLD DELHI

When Shah Jahan built his new capital of Shahjahanabad here in the 17th century, one of the key elements was a high red-brick wall, pierced by 14 gates. The British then strengthened and repaired it with stone, and added a number of bastions for increased protection. Only three of the original gates remain today – **Ajmeri, Turkman** and **Delhi** – all on the southern side. The **Kashmiri Gate** was built by the British in 1835 and was the scene of desperate fighting when the British retook Delhi during the 1857 Uprising. Lahore Gate has been demolished (this is not the Lahore Gate of Red Fort, but the Lahore Gate of Old Delhi).

It's possible to walk along the only remaining stretch of wall running west of Delhi Gate towards Turkman Gate. West of Kashmiri Gate, near Sabzi Mandi, is the British-erected **Mutiny Memorial**, to the soldiers who lost their lives during the Uprising.

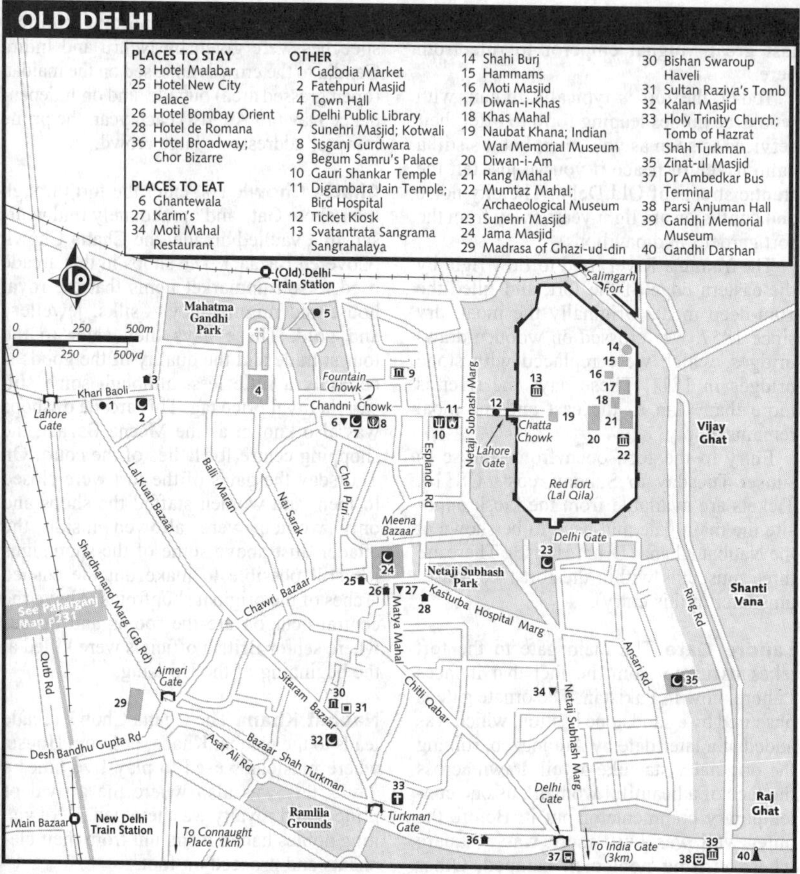

Near the monument is an **Ashoka pillar** which, like the one in Firoz Shah Kotla, was brought here by Firoz Shah.

A novel and relatively stress-free way of exploring crowded Old Delhi, where walking 10m can take close to 10 minutes, is to hire a cycle-rickshaw for a few hours.

Red Fort

The red sandstone walls of the Lal Qila, or Red Fort, extend for 2km. Marking out an irregular octagon, the walls vary in height from 18m on the river side to 33m on the city side. Shah Jahan began construction of the massive fort in 1638, and it was completed in 1648. He never completely moved his capital from Agra to his new city of Shahjahanabad in Delhi because he was deposed and imprisoned in Agra Fort by his son, Aurangzeb.

The Red Fort dates from the very peak of Mughal power, when it was known as the Qila-e-Mu'alla (Auspicious Fort); the name Lal Qila dates from the British era. When the emperor rode out on an elephant into the streets of Old Delhi it was a display of pomp and power at its most magnificent. The Mughal reign from Delhi was a short one, however; Aurangzeb was the first and last great Mughal emperor to rule from here.

Today, the fort is typically Indian, with would-be guides leaping forth to offer their services as soon as you enter, but it's still a calm haven of peace if you've just left the frantic streets of Old Delhi. The city noise and confusion are light years away from the fort gardens and pavilions.

The Yamuna River used to flow right by the eastern edge of the fort, and filled the 10m-deep moat. Originally the moat, dry since 1857, was crossed on wooden drawbridges, which were replaced with stone bridges in 1811. These days the river is more than 1km to the east and the moat remains empty.

Entry to the fort, open from sunrise to sunset Tuesday to Sunday, costs US$10. Tickets are available from the kiosk opposite the main gate and need to be shown at the Naubat Khana (Drum House). There are three museums within the fort (see Museums later in this entry).

Lahore Gate The main gate to the fort takes its name from the fact that it faces Lahore, now in Pakistan. The ornate gate is obscured by a sandstone bastion, which was added at a later date by Aurangzeb, ruining the original vista 'like a veil drawn across the face of a beautiful woman', as one contemporary commentator put it. Before the outer wall was built there was a square where visiting noblemen camped. Other more recent modifications include the installation of a sandstone tower that houses a lift, and the filling in of the gate-tower windows with sandstone during the 1980s; it was thought they would make a great perch for a sniper trying to knock off the prime minister during the Independence Day speech.

If one spot could be said to be the emotional and symbolic heart of the modern Indian nation, the Lahore Gate of the Red Fort is probably it. During the struggle for independence, one of the nationalists' declarations was that they would see the Indian flag flying over the Red Fort in Delhi. After Independence, many important political speeches were given by Nehru and Indira Gandhi to the crowds amassed on the maidan (open grassed area) outside, and on Independence Day (15 August) each year, the prime minister addresses a huge crowd.

Chatta Chowk You enter the fort through the Lahore Gate and immediately find yourself in a vaulted arcade, the Chatta Chowk (Covered Bazaar). The shops in this arcade used to sell upmarket items that the royal household might fancy – silks, jewellery and gold. These days they cater to the tourist trade and the quality of the goods is certainly a little less, although some still carry a royal price tag. This arcade of shops was also known as the Meena Bazaar, the shopping centre for ladies of the court. On Thursday the gates of the fort were closed to men, and women staffed the shops and only women were allowed inside the citadel. Just above some of the shop signs it's still possible to make out the cusped arches of the original shopfronts. Above the central octagon are the rooms and offices where senior British officials were killed at the beginning of the Uprising.

Naubat Khana The Chatta Chowk arcade leads to the Naubat Khana, or Drum House, where musicians used to play five times a day – this was also where the arrival of princes and royalty was heralded. Here visiting nobles had to dismount from their elephants and proceed on foot.

The grassed open courtyard beyond the Naubat Khana formerly had galleries along either side and a central tank, but these were removed by the British Army when the fort was used as their headquarters. Around the tank over 50 Europeans were executed on 16 June 1857. Another intrusive reminder of the British presence is the huge, conspicuous, three-storey barrack block section north of the courtyard.

Diwan-i-Am The Hall of Public Audiences was where the emperor would sit to hear complaints or disputes from his subjects, until Aurangzeb abolished the custom.

The alcove in the wall was panelled with marble and set with precious stones, many of which were looted following the Uprising. This elegant hall was restored as a result of a directive by Lord Curzon, Viceroy of India between 1898 and 1905. The marble panels behind the throne canopy are thought to have been designed in Italy.

The marble table below the throne is where the *wazir,* or chief minister, used to sit; he would listen to the petitioners and relay the complaints to the emperor. Justice was also rapidly dispensed here, with the convicted being put to death using various methods – poisonous snakes, the stomp of an elephant's foot or beheading. By the door in the walls to the right of the throne, two eunuchs would guard the entrance to the **Imtiaz Mahal**, which was reserved for women. Although the hall is in good condition, it would have created a vastly different impression when it was in use. Not only were the walls and pillars completely covered with white plaster, but the floor was strewn with rugs and rich crimson awnings shaded the interior.

This was as far into the palace as most nobles could ever hope to go.

Diwan-i-Khas The Hall of Private Audiences, built of white marble, was the luxurious inner sanctum where the emperor would hold private meetings. The corners of the building are topped with marble *chhatris* (small domed canopies). This is where Bahadur Shah was proclaimed emperor at the height of the Uprising. The centrepiece of the hall was the magnificent Peacock Throne, until Nadir Shah carted it off to Iran in 1739. The solid gold throne had figures of peacocks standing behind it, their beautiful colours resulting from countless inlaid precious stones. Between them was the figure of a parrot carved out of a single emerald. This masterpiece in precious metals, sapphires,

The Adventures of the Kohinoor Diamond

The Kohinoor diamond has enjoyed an extensive travel itinerary over the last 600 or so years. The well-travelled diamond moved from India to Persia and back again before finishing up in the UK as part of the crown jewels.

The Hindu maharajas believed that whoever owned the Kohinoor diamond would rule the world. It is suggested that the Kohinoor may have been discovered 5000 years ago near Masulipatnam. One story states that it was found by a child along the banks of the Godavari River in Andhra Pradesh in 57 BC. Another story dates the Kohinoor centuries earlier to the time of Karna, the Raja of Anga, who is said to have worn it as a sacred talisman. Originally, the fabled stone was named Semantik Mani, 'the Prince and Leader of All Gemstones', but when it was captured by Nadir Shah, he renamed it Kohinoor, meaning 'Mountain of Light'. When Nadir Shah captured Delhi he was unable to locate the diamond, but a spy told him it was hidden in the turban of the defeated Emperor Mohammad Shah, so the crafty Nadir Shah held a banquet for his Mughal foe, and in a traditional gesture of Eastern friendship insisted that they swap turbans at the end of the feast. Later that night he unwrapped the turban and found his prize.

In 1813 the Kohinoor found its way back to India in the possession of Shah Shuja, who was deposed from the Persian throne by his brother Mohammed, a previous holder of the throne. Shuja subsequently lost the diamond to the Sikh king Ranjit Singh. When Britain annexed the state of Punjab, the Kohinoor became the property of the British East India Company, which presented it to Queen Victoria. Since then, it has taken up residence in the Tower of London as part of the crown jewels. There is a legend that the diamond will bring misfortune to whichever man owns it, so a superstitious Queen Victoria decreed in her will that the Kohinoor should henceforth be the possession of the wife of the King. In 1911 it was incorporated into the design of Queen Mary's crown, and in 1937 it was removed from Mary's crown and placed in that of the wife of King George VI, Queen Elizabeth (the present Queen Mother).

rubies, emeralds and pearls was broken into pieces, and the so-called Peacock Throne displayed in Teheran today is constructed from various bits of the original. The throne was said to have taken seven years to make, and it was 3m long, 2.2m wide and 4.5m high. The famous Kohinoor Diamond, taken from the throne, is now on display in the Tower of London, set in a crown belonging to the Queen Mother (see boxed text 'The Adventures of the Kohinoor Diamond'). The marble pedestal on which it used to sit is all that remains of the Peacock Throne in Delhi.

In 1760, the Marathas also removed the silver ceiling from the hall; the gilt work on the ceiling dates to the time of the Coronation Durbar (see the Coronation Durbar Site section in this chapter) of 1903. Inscribed in gold on the walls of the Diwan-i-Khas is that famous Persian couplet, attributed to Shah Jahan's wazir, Saadullah Khan:

Agar firdaus bar rue zamin ast
Hamin ast o hamin ast o hamin ast.

If there is a paradise on earth
it is this, it is this, it is this.

Royal Hammam Just north of the Diwan-i-Khas are the *hammams* (baths) – three large rooms surmounted by domes, with a fountain in the centre – one of which was set up as a sauna. The eastern chamber, used as a dressing room, featured a fountain which sprayed scented rose-water. The floors used to be inlaid with *pietra dura* 'inlaid marble', work (for more on pietra dura, see the Taj Mahal entry in the Uttar Pradesh & Uttaranchal chapter), and the rooms were illuminated through panels of coloured glass in the roof. The baths are closed to the public.

Moti Masjid Built in 1659 by the ever-paranoid Aurangzeb for his personal use, the small and totally enclosed Pearl Mosque – made of marble – is next to the baths. Curiously, the mosque's outer walls are oriented to be in exact symmetry with the rest of the fort, while the inner walls are aligned at a different angle, so that the mosque inside has the correct orientation with Mecca.

Shahi Burj This modest, three-storey octagonal tower at the north-eastern edge of the fort was once Shah Jahan's private working area and was also a favourite place for the emperors to hold their private conclaves. From here the **Nahr-i-Bhisht** (Stream of Paradise) water channel used to flow through the Royal Baths, the Diwan-i-Khas, the Khas Mahal and the Rang Mahal. These days the channel is now largely overgrown and it's difficult to imagine what it must have looked like when it was flowing. Like the baths, the tower is closed to the public but was undergoing renovation at the time of research.

Khas Mahal The small Khas Mahal, south of the Diwan-i-Khas, was the emperor's private palace, divided into rooms for worship, sleeping and living. Today its most outstanding feature is the fine *jali* (inlaid marble screen), which spans the Nahr-i-Bhisht. The screen shows the sun, moon and stars, as well as the scales of justice.

A small balcony protrudes out over what was the river bank, and from here the emperor used to give a morning audience. If for some reason he didn't appear, nervous speculation would rapidly mount as to his wellbeing.

Below the Khas Mahal is the gate through which the emperor and senior nobles would enter the Rang Mahal.

Rang Mahal The Rang Mahal (Palace of Colour) pavilion took its name from the painted interior that is now sadly gone. The building was badly defaced after the Uprising, when it was used as an officers' barracks. This was once the residence of the emperor's chief wife. On the floor in the centre is a beautifully carved marble lotus, and the water flowing along the channel from the Shahi Burj used to flow into here. Originally there was a fountain made of ivory in the centre, and the ceiling was silver. In the rooms at either end it is still possible to see the inlaid mirrorwork on the ceilings.

In an effort to alleviate the heat of Delhi's fierce summers, many people built underground rooms. This is the case with the

Rang Mahal, although you can only peer in through the sandstone grilles that line the building below the raised platform that serves as its floor.

Mumtaz Mahal Still farther south along the eastern wall is the last of the remaining pavilions, the Mumtaz Mahal. It was formerly the residence of one of the Mughal court's greatest women, Jahanara Begum, Shah Jahan's favourite daughter and overseer of the royal harem. Today this building houses a small and tatty, but interesting, archaeological museum.

Gardens Between all the exquisite buildings were highly formal Persian gardens, complete with fountains, pools and small pavilions. Sadly, while the general outline and some of the pavilions are still in place, the gardens were all uprooted by the British and replaced with sterile, featureless lawns.

Museums There's a dusty **Indian War Memorial museum**, displaying armoury and uniforms upstairs in the Naubat Khana. In the Mumtaz Mahal, the **archaeological museum** displays weapons as well as carpets, textiles and scenes of courtly life. It's well worth a look, although most visitors seem to rush through the Red Fort, bypassing the museum.

Another museum worth seeing is the **Svatantrata Sangrama Sangrahalaya** (Museum of the Independence Movement), to the left before the Naubat Khana, among the army buildings. The independence movement is charted with newspaper cuttings, letters, photos and several impressive dioramas. Did the Rani of Jhansi really ride into battle with a baby strapped to her back?

Tickets to all three museums (Rs 2 each), open from 9 am to 5 pm Saturday to Thursday, are available from the booth by the Naubat Khana.

Sound-and-Light Show Each evening an entertaining sound-and-light show re-creates events of India's history, particularly those connected with the Red Fort. Shows are in English and Hindi, and tickets are available from the fort (Rs 30). The English sessions start at 7.30 pm from November to January, at 8.30 pm from February to April and September to October, and at 9 pm from May to August. It's well worth making the effort to see this show, which degenerates into a comedy at stages, but make sure you are well equipped with plenty of mosquito repellent.

Chandni Chowk

The main street of Old Delhi is the colourful shopping bazaar known as Chandni Chowk (Silver St). It's hopelessly congested (and polluted) day and night, in very sharp contrast to the open, spacious streets of New Delhi and the street Shah Jahan knew. During his reign it was lined with mansions and gardens and an ornamental canal ran down the centre. One of the only mansions left today is **Begum Samru's Palace** north of Chandni Chowk. Unfortunately, the building is all but obliterated by hoardings.

At the eastern (Red Fort) end of Chandni Chowk there is a **Digambar Jain Temple**, with a small marble courtyard surrounded by a colonnade. There's also an interesting **bird hospital** for injured pigeons, run by the Jains; entry is free but donations are gratefully accepted. The entrance is about 50m south of Chandni Chowk.

Next door, behind all the marigold garlands, is the 800-year-plus **Gauri Shankar Temple** dedicated to the Hindu god Shiva. The marble chair in the courtyard is where the saint Bhagwat Swaroup Brachmachari spent more than 50 years. It's his photo and sandals on the chair.

Opposite the Victorian-era **Fountain Chowk** is the Sikh **Sisganj Gurdwara**, built on the site where the ninth Sikh guru, Tegh Bahadur, was executed by Aurangzeb. There is a kitchen and accommodation here.

Next to the old *kotwali* (police station) is the **Sunehri Masjid**. In 1739, Nadir Shah, the Persian invader who carried off the Peacock Throne, stood on the roof of this mosque and watched while his soldiers conducted a bloody massacre of Delhi's inhabitants.

The western end of Chandni Chowk is marked by the **Fatehpuri Masjid**, which was erected in 1650 by one of Shah Jahan's wives. The building ceased to function as a mosque after the Uprising, when Muslims were driven out of Old Delhi. On their return they found a Hindu family had bought and were living in the courtyard. The British had to buy the family out – by offering them four Hindu villages – in order to return it to the Muslims.

The street running west from the mosque is **Khari Baoli**, where Gadodia Market, Delhi's bustling wholesale spice market, is situated. Things have changed very little over the decades in this atmospheric area, where huge sacks of goods are brought here on long narrow barrows heaved by wiry labourers. In the morning it gets hectic as literally hundreds of barrow boys jostle for position. Other goods for sale include giant jars of chutneys and pickles, nuts, lentils, tea and soap (see also the boxed text 'Shopping Spots' later in this chapter).

Jama Masjid

Jama Masjid literally means 'Friday Mosque'. A jama masjid is the main mosque of an area, and holds the Juma prayer service on Friday afternoons (Juma, or Friday, is the holy day of the Muslim week, the equivalent of Sunday in the Christian week). The Jama Masjid of Delhi, built by a team of around 5000 workers, is the largest mosque in India and was the final architectural extravagance of Shah Jahan. Designed by the architect Ustad Khalil, the process of its construction began in 1644 and was not completed until 1658. It has three great gateways, four angle towers and two minarets standing 40m high and constructed of alternating vertical strips of red sandstone and white marble.

Broad flights of steps lead up to the imposing gateways. The eastern gateway was originally only opened for the emperor, and is now only open on Friday and on Muslim festival days. The general public can enter by either the north or south gates (Rs 10). Shoes must be removed, and those considered unsuitably dressed (bare legs for either men or women) can hire robes at the northern gate.

In the north-east corner is a small pavilion containing relics of the Prophet. Pilgrims come here from all over India. In 1766 there was a vision here of the Prophet in paradise, and legend has it that the Prophet will appear here on Judgement Day.

For Rs 5 (Rs 10 with a camera) it's possible to climb the southern minaret, but women should be accompanied by a male as unaccompanied women have reported being hassled at the top. The views in all directions are superb – Old Delhi, the Red Fort and the polluting factories beyond it across the river, and New Delhi to the south. You can also see one of the features that the architect Lutyens incorporated into his design of New Delhi – the Jama Masjid, Connaught Place and Sansad Bhavan (Parliament House) are in a direct line. There's also a fine view of the Red Fort from the east side of the mosque.

Raj Ghat

North-east of Firoz Shah Kotla, on the banks of the Yamuna River, a simple square platform of black marble marks the spot where Mahatma Gandhi was cremated following his assassination in 1948. A commemorative ceremony takes place each Friday, the day he was killed.

Jawaharlal Nehru, the first Indian prime minister, was cremated just to the north at Shanti Vana (Forest of Peace) in 1964. His daughter, Indira Gandhi, who was killed in 1984, and grandsons Sanjay and Rajiv were also cremated in this vicinity (in 1980 and 1991 respectively).

The park is a beautiful and tranquil place to wander and is also the venue for prayers on the anniversaries of Gandhi's birth and death in October and January.

Gandhi Darshan & Gandhi Memorial Museum

Across the road from Raj Ghat, the Gandhi Darshan (☎ 3319001) is a poorly patronised display of paintings and photos about the Mahatma's life and deeds. It is open from 10 am to 5.30 pm Monday to Saturday; admission is free.

On the opposite corner is the Gandhi Memorial Museum (☎ 3310168), with yet more memorabilia, including photos, the bamboo staff Gandhi carried on the Salt March in Gujarat, the bullet which killed him and even two of his lower teeth, which were extracted in 1936. The museum is open from 10 am to 5.30 pm Tuesday to Sunday; admission is free and there is a library.

NEW DELHI

New Delhi, the latest and perhaps last imperial city ever, combines 20th-century architecture with a monumental 17th-century vision, and features one of the biggest palaces in the world, Rashtrapati Bhavan.

The main architects of New Delhi were Sir Edward Lutyens and Sir Herbert Baker, though assistants such as Robert Tor Russell were responsible for much of the detail, including the government bungalows, hospitals, police stations, lesser official buildings and Connaught Place. The complex geometrical city plan owes something to other imperial British regional capitals such as Pretoria, Canberra and Ottawa. Baker and Lutyens initially rejected Indian styles of architecture – Lutyens in particular could be brutally dismissive of Indians and Indian culture in general – but the final result shows many Indian elements melded with Classical design.

Connaught Place

At the north end of New Delhi, Connaught Place is the business and tourist centre. It's a vast traffic circle with a uniform series of colonnaded buildings around the edge, mainly devoted to shops, banks, restaurants and airline offices. It's spacious but busy, and you'll be continually approached by people willing to provide you with everything imaginable, from an airline ticket for Timbuktu to having your fortune read.

Be careful when walking around Connaught Place as shoeshiners have developed a sneaky technique whereby they surreptitiously chuck a lump of shit on your shoe, draw your attention to it then kindly offer to clean it off for a fee. It's also not a good idea to put anything smaller than your elbow in your ear so try to ignore the glowing testimonials the ear-cleaning brigade show you.

In 1995 the inner and outer circle were renamed Rajiv Chowk and Indira Chowk respectively (the son within the mother), but everyone still calls it CP (Connaught Place) despite the signs. The outer circle is known as Connaught Circus.

Hanuman Mandir

This mandir (temple) built by Maharaja Jai Singh II, and dedicated to the Ramayana hero, is opposite the state emporiums on Baba Kharak Singh Marg. Surrounded by *lac* (plastic) bangle and religious offering stalls, and women touting *mehndi* (temporary henna tattoos), it is extremely popular and always busy. It is even more hectic on Tuesday when there is a market, and during festivals when devotees dressed as Hanuman leap and jump around the place.

Jantar Mantar

Only a short stroll down Sansad Marg (Parliament St) from Connaught Place, this strange collection of salmon-coloured structures is one of Maharaja Jai Singh II's observatories. Surrounded by new office buildings it has an almost futuristic look, and is in harmony with its modern surroundings. The ruler from Jaipur constructed this observatory in 1710, and it is dominated by a huge sundial, the **Samrat Yantra**, or Supreme Instrument.

Just south of the Samrat Yantra is the **Jai Prakash**, an instrument designed by Jai Singh (hence the name, which means Invention of Jai) consisting of two concave hemispherical structures which together ascertain the position of the sun and other heavenly bodies.

South again are two circular buildings which together form the **Ram Yantra**. Each has a central metal pole, and the shadow cast falls upon markings on the walls and floor, thus making it possible to determine the azimuth and altitude of the sun.

Other instruments include the **Misra Yantra**, or Mixed Instrument, which stands to the right of the garden as you enter. This ingenious device makes it possible to tell the time in four other places in the world when it is noon in Delhi.

NEW DELHI

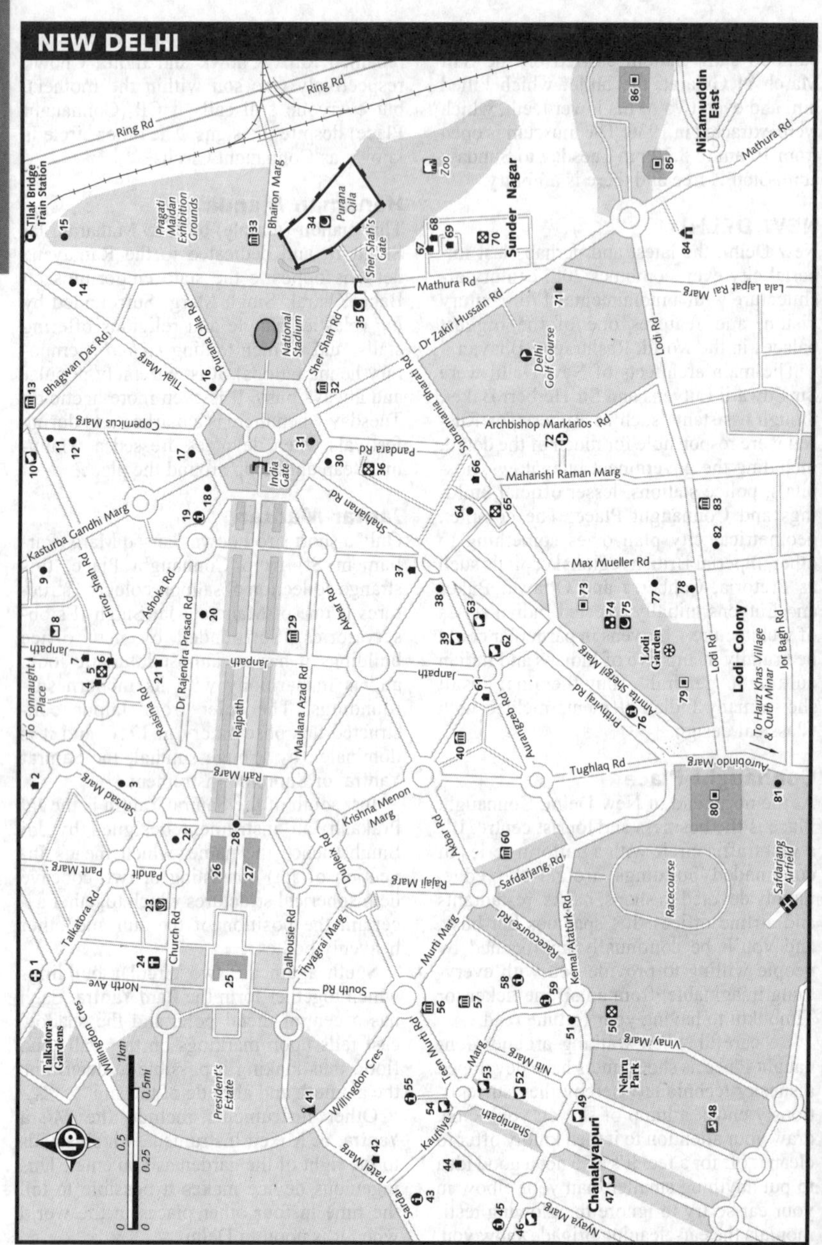
Ring Rd
Tilak Bridge Train Station
Pragati Maidan Exhibition Grounds
Bhairon Marg
Purana Qila
Zoo
Nizamuddin East
Mathura Rd
Sunder Nagar
Sher Shah's Gate
National Stadium
Sher Shah Rd
Purana Qila Rd
Bhagwan Das Rd
Tilak Marg
Copernicus Marg
Pandara Rd
India Gate
Dr Zakir Hussain Rd
Delhi Golf Course
Lala Lajpat Rai Marg
Lodi Rd
Archbishop Markarios Rd
Subramania Bharati Rd
Maharishi Raman Marg
Shahjahan Rd
Kasturba Gandhi Marg
Firoz Shah Rd
Ashoka Rd
Max Mueller Rd
Akbar Rd
Janpath
To Connaught Place
Dr Rajendra Prasad Rd
Raisina Rd
Rajpath
Maulana Azad Rd
Lodi Garden
Lodi Colony
Amrita Shergil Marg
Prithviraj Rd
Aurangzeb Rd
To Hauz Khas Village & Qutb Minar
Jor Bagh Rd
Aurobindo Marg
Tughlaq Rd
Sansad Marg
Rafi Marg
Krishna Menon Marg
Duplex Rd
Pant Marg
Pandit
Talkatora Rd
Church Rd
Dalhousie Rd
Thyagaraj Marg
Rajaji Marg
Safdarjang Rd
Racecourse Rd
Racecourse
Safdarjang Airfield
Kemal Atatürk Rd
Murti Marg
North Ave
South Rd
Talkatora Gardens
Willingdon Cres
President's Estate
Teen Murti Rd
Niti Marg
Vinay Marg
Nehru Park
Kautilya Marg
Shantipath
Chanakyapuri
Nyaya Marg
Sardar Patel Marg
1km
0.5mi

NEW DELHI

PLACES TO STAY

2 YWCA Blue Triangle Family Hostel; Vin Tours
4 ITDC Hotel Indraprastha; Coconut Grove
6 ITDC Hotel Kanishka; Kanishka Shopping Plaza; Bihar Tourist Office; Jammu & Kashmir Tourist Office; Kerala Tourist Office; Madhya Pradesh Tourist Office
7 ITDC Hotel Janpath; Sri Lankan Airlines; Virgin Airways; Student Travel Information Centre; Kazakhstan Airlines
21 Le Meridien
37 Taj Mahal Hotel
42 Hotel Diplomat
44 Youth Hostel
61 The Claridges
66 The Ambassador Hotel
67 Maharani Guest House
68 La Sagrita Tourist Home; Kailash Inn
69 Jukaso Inn
71 The Oberoi

OTHER

1 Dr Ram Manohar Lohia Hospital
3 Indian Airlines
5 Kanishka Shopping Plaza
8 Eastern Court; Central Telegraph Office
9 Max Mueller Bhavan
10 Nepalese Embassy
11 Rabindra Bhavan; Sangeet Natak Akademi; Lalit Kala Akademi; Shahitya Akademi
12 Kamani Auditorium
13 National Musuem of Natural History
14 Supreme Court
15 Appu Ghar
16 Patiala House
17 Baroda House
18 Hyderabad House
19 Andhra Pradesh Tourist Office
20 Indira Gandhi National Centre for the Arts
22 Sansad Bhavan (Parliament House)
23 Gurdwara Rakab Ganj
24 Cathedral Church of the Redemption
25 Rashtrapati Bhavan
26 Secretariat (North Block)
27 Secretariat (South Block)
28 Vijay Chowk
29 National Museum; Archaeological Survey of India
30 Bikaner House
31 India Gate's Children's Park
32 National Gallery of Modern Art
33 Crafts Museum
34 Qila-i-Kihna Masjid
35 Khairu'l Manzil Masjid
36 Pandara Market; Ichiban; Pindi; Chicken Inn
38 French Information Resource Centre
39 Brazilian Embassy
40 Gandhi Smriti
41 Gandhi Salt March Sculpture
43 Andaman & Nicobar Tourist Office
45 New Sikkim House; Sikkim Tourist Office
46 US Embassy
47 French Embassy
48 NDMC Swimming Pool; Tamura
49 Australian Embassy
50 Santushti Shopping Centre; Basil & Thyme
51 Iran Air
52 UK Embassy
53 Norwegian Embassy
54 Sri Lankan High Commission
55 Mizoram Tourist Office
56 Nehru Planetarium
57 Nehru Memorial Museum
58 Tripura Tourist Office
59 Arunachal Pradesh Tourist Office
60 Indira Gandhi Memorial Museum
62 Danish Embassy; Meghalaya Tourist Board
63 Israeli Embassy
64 Lok Nayak Bhavan (Ministry of Home Affairs)
65 Khan Market: The Bookshop; Bahri & Sons; China Garden; China Fare; Ministry of Home Affairs
70 Sunder Nagar Market; Sweets Corner; Nathu
72 East West Medical Centre
73 Sikander Lodi's Tomb
74 Sheesh Gumbad
75 Bara Gumbad Masjid
76 Goa Tourist Office
77 India International Centre
78 World Wide Fund for Nature India
79 Mohammed Shah's Tomb
80 Safdarjang's Tomb
81 Indian Airlines (24 Hours)
82 Indian International Centre; Habitat World
83 Tibet House
84 Nizam-ud-din's Shrine
85 Isa Khan's Tomb
86 Humayun's Tomb

Once the site of political protests, Jantar Mantar has now been fenced in. The US$5 entry fee is not really justified as you can see most of the instruments from outside.

Lakshmi Narayan Mandir

West of Connaught Place, this Orissan-style temple was erected by the industrialist BD Birla in 1938. Dedicated to Narayan (Vishnu the Preserver) and his wife Lakshmi, the goddess of wealth, it's commonly known as Birla Mandir.

The temple is faced with red sandstone and is surrounded by gardens filled with man-made caves, waterways and gaudy creatures. There are a couple of cafes and you can even get a novelty souvenir photo taken.

Bangla Sahib Gurdwara

This large temple complex is the main Sikh place of worship in Delhi. With the customary tank and temple as well as an information office, kitchen and library it offers those not venturing into Punjab the opportunity to experience the amazing hospitality and tranquility of the Sikh faith. Don't forget to cover your head, remove your shoes and wash your feet before entering.

Rajpath

The Rajpath (Kingsway) is another focus of Lutyens' New Delhi. It is immensely broad and is flanked on either side by ornamental ponds. At the eastern end of Rajpath lies the India Gate, while at the western end lies Rashtrapati Bhavan, now the president's residence, but built originally for the viceroy. It is flanked by the two large Secretariat buildings, and these three buildings sit upon a small rise, known as Raisina Hill.

The Republic Day parade is held here every 26 January, and millions of people gather to enjoy the spectacle. Three days later at **Vijay Chowk**, the open intersection at the foot of the Secretariat Buildings, the Beating Retreat, a much smaller parade followed by fireworks, takes place. During the construction of New Delhi, this was where the narrow-gauge Imperial Delhi Railway terminated. It was constructed specifically to transport the buff sandstone from Dholpur, red sandstone from Bharatpur and marble from Rajasthan. In the early 1920s there were over 3500 Indian stonemasons working on the site. The names of the architects and builders who worked on the buildings are inscribed in the sandstone walls that line the rise from here up to the Secretariat buildings.

India Gate

The 42m-high stone arch of triumph stands at the eastern end of Rajpath. Officially known as the All India War Memorial, it bears the names of 90,000 Indian Army soldiers who died in the campaigns of WWI, the North-West Frontier operations of the same time and the 1919 Afghan fiasco. In the 1970s an eternal flame, flanked by uniformed soldiers, was established in the arch to honour the Unknown Soldier, though the shallow bowl on top of the arch was originally going to be filled with burning oil for ceremonial occasions.

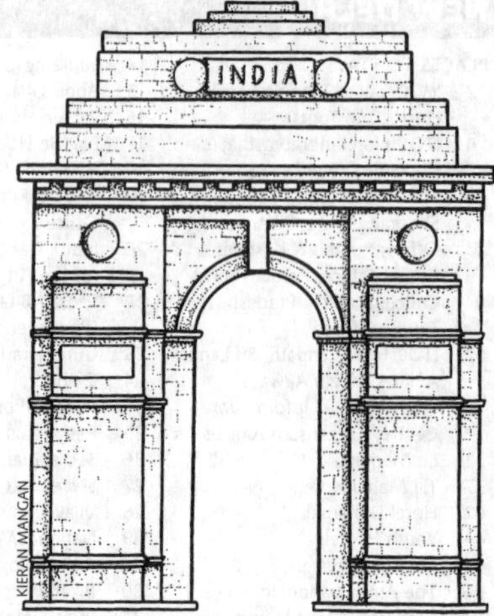

India Gate, a symbol of national freedom

Facing the arch is an open cupola which once contained the statue of King-Emperor George V, which now languishes in the Coronation Durbar Park. Despite plans to put a statue of Mahatma Gandhi in its place it has so far remained empty; some say this symbolises India's freedom better than any new statue could.

The best time to visit India Gate is at sunset, when it is illuminated and large numbers of Delhiites come out for an evening promenade. The place takes on a real carnival atmosphere, complete with the usual gaggle of hawkers and hangers-on that always seem to materialise whenever there's a crowd about. As darkness falls, it seems as though every secluded spot in the surrounding paths and lawns is occupied by a canoodling couple.

Rashtrapati Bhavan

Prior to Independence, this imposing building at the opposite end of the Rajpath from India Gate was the viceroy's residence. Following Independence it became the official residence of the president of India. Completed in 1929, the palace-like building is an interesting blend of Mughal and Western architectural styles, the most obvious Indian feature being the huge copper dome which was camouflaged with black paint during the war years. It is the centrepiece of New Delhi, a huge, grandiose building (larger than Versailles) designed and positioned to assert the dominance of the British empire, despite the fact that by the time of its construction the British were already facing an increasingly effective Indian Nationalist movement. The building is dramatically illuminated during Republic Day celebrations in January.

To the west of the building is a Mughal garden that occupies 130 hectares. This garden is only open to the public in February; book through the Government of India tourist office on Janpath. At the time of Mountbatten, India's last viceroy, the number of servants needed to maintain the building's 340 rooms and its extensive gardens was enormous. There were 418 gardeners alone, 50 of them boys whose sole job was to chase away birds!

Secretariat Buildings

Designed by Herbert Baker and closely resembling his government buildings in Pretoria in South Africa, the North Block and South Block secretariat buildings lie either side of Rajpath on Raisina Hill. These imposing two-tone sandstone buildings are a skilful blend of classical and Mughal styles, and the baroque, cathedral-like central domes, decorated with lotus motifs and elephants, are surrounded by Mughal chhatris. The two red sandstone columns at the front of each block together represent the four dominions of empire – Australia, Canada, New Zealand and South Africa – and each is topped by a tarnished bronze model of a sailing vessel. Above the great gateway to North Block is the rather patronising inscription 'Liberty will not descend to a people: a people must raise themselves to liberty. It is a blessing which must be earned before it can be enjoyed'.

On the eastern face of each building are the foundation stones of New Delhi, originally laid by King George V and Queen Mary at the Coronation Durbar in 1911, when the move of the capital from Kolkata to New Delhi was formally announced. The stones were moved here at a later date once construction was under way (see Coronation Durbar Site later in this chapter).

The North Block now houses the ministries of home affairs and finance; the South Block houses the external affairs ministry.

Sansad Bhavan

Although it is another large and imposing building, Sansad Bhavan, the Indian parliament building, stands almost hidden and virtually unnoticed at the end of Sansad Marg, just north of Rajpath. The building is a circular colonnaded structure 171m in diameter, the foundation stone for which was laid by the Duke of Connaught in 1921. It was opened in 1927. Originally the parliamentary building was going to be an annexe on Rashtrapati Bhavan. After the Montague-Chelmsford reforms of 1919, which created a large assembly, the present site was chosen. There are three main chambers inside the structure: the Lok Sabha (lower house of parliament), the Rajya Sabha (upper house of parliament) and the library. The red sandstone boundary wall has carved blocks that evoke jali (carved marble lattice) screens.

Although it's an impressive building, its relative physical insignificance in the grand scheme of New Delhi shows how the focus of power has shifted from the viceroy's residence, which was given pride of place during the time of the British Raj when New Delhi was conceived.

Permits to visit the parliament so you can sit in the often-entertaining public gallery and view sessions in the public gallery are available from the reception office on Raisina Rd, but you'll need a letter of introduction from your embassy.

Purana Qila

Just south-east of India Gate and about 2km north of Humayun's tomb is the Purana Qila (Old Fort). This is the supposed site of Indraprastha, the original city of Delhi. The Afghan ruler Sher Shah, who briefly interrupted the Mughal sovereignty by defeating Humayun, completed the fort during his reign from 1538 to 1545, before Humayun regained control of India. The fort has massive walls and three large gateways.

Entering from the south gate you'll see the small octagonal red sandstone tower, the Sher Mandal, later used by Humayun as a library. It was while descending the stairs of this tower one day in 1556 that he slipped, fell and received injuries from which he later died.

Just beyond it is the **Qila-i-Kuhna Masjid**, or Mosque of Sher Shah, which, unlike the fort itself, is in fairly reasonable condition. This building is Delhi's finest example of the Lodi style of architecture, which blended Hindu elements, such as square pillars, with Muslim arches and domes to create the first genuinely Indian architectural style.

There's a small archaeological museum just inside the main gate, the top of which has good views of New Delhi. It's open from sunrise to sunset, and entry costs US$5.

A sound-and-light show, (☎ 4603178) (using poor-quality loudspeakers) is held each evening and costs Rs 25. English sessions start at 7.30 pm from November to January, 8.30 pm from February to April and September to October and 9 pm from May to August. Tickets are available on site or from the tourist office.

Just across the road is the **Khairu'l Manzil Masjid**, a 16th-century mosque built by Akbar's influential wet nurse and mother of Adham Khan, Maham Anga. The double-storeyed cloisters were used as a madrasa (Islamic college). Almost next to the mosque is the imposing **Sher Shah's Gate**, one of the gates into his city which lay west of the Purana Qila.

Humayun's Tomb

Built in the mid-16th century by Haji Begum, the Persian-born senior wife of Humayun, the second Mughal emperor, this is a wonderful early example of Mughal architecture. The elements in its design – a squat building, high arched entrances that let in light, topped by a bulbous dome and surrounded by formal gardens – were to be refined over the years to the magnificence of the Taj Mahal in Agra. This earlier tomb is thus of great interest for its relation to the later Taj.

The tomb itself sits on a red sandstone platform, a practice that became a key feature of Mughal tombs. The walls of the platform are marked by arched openings leading into small cells. In these are many unmarked tombs, the graves of members of the Mughal royal family.

The main tomb is built with red sandstone skilfully inlaid with black and white marble. The central octagonal chamber contains the tombstone of Humayun but, as is the case at the Taj Mahal, the real tomb is some 6m under the floor on the lower level. (It's possible to enter the lower level, but you'll need a torch and a strong constitution – the smell of bat droppings is overpowering. The entrance is through the first arch to the right of the southern steps.) In each of the four chambers at the corners of the main tomb lie other important Mughal tombs. On the stone platform outside the tomb are yet more Mughal tombs bearing Persian inscriptions; one of these contains the headless remains of Dara Shikoh, Shah Jahan's favoured son and heir.

The 38m-high marble dome on the roof is one of the earliest examples of a full dome in India, although it was in use in Persia from the 13th century. (A 'full' dome is a complete hemisphere; up until this time domes in India had only been half hemispheres.) The chhatris on the roof serve to blend the curves of the dome with the angles of the rest of the structure.

The gardens surrounding the tomb are laid out in the typically formal Mughal pattern, and still contain the watercourses which divided the garden into 32 small squares around the main platform. It is probably the most complete garden of its type remaining in India.

Entry to Humayun's tomb is US$10 (and Rs 25 for video cameras). An excellent view can be obtained over the surrounding area from the terraces of the tomb.

Isa Khan's Tomb As you enter the tomb area, and before you have to pay, a crumbling stone gateway on the right leads into the octagonal enclosure which contains the tomb of Isa Khan, a nobleman at the court of Sher Shah. With its octagonal form, small overhanging *chajja* (eaves) and chhatris on the roof, it's a good example of Lodi architecture. A few small patches of blue tilework give a tantalising hint as to how it may have looked when first built. A small mosque stands at the western edge of the enclosure.

Bu Halima's Garden The next feature is the stone gateway that marks the entrance to Bu Halima's Garden, although when approaching it from this side it's actually the exit. Bu Halima was a Mughal noble, and the stone structure in the garden on the left is believed to be her tomb.

Arab Serai Once through the main gateway (where you must pay the entry fee), today the main entrance to Humayun's tomb lies straight ahead, but it's worth making a detour to the Arab Serai, the northern gate of which is the impressive soaring structure to the right of the path.

The serai was built by Haji Begum, Humayun's widow, in the mid-16th century, supposedly to house 300 Arabs she brought back from Mecca. It is unclear whether these men were actually Arab clerics or Persian artisans brought in to work on the construction of Humayun's tomb.

Inside the serai is the **Afsarwala Mosque & Tomb**, but it is not known who was the *afsar* (officer) responsible for these buildings.

Most visitors to Humayun's tomb spare these buildings barely a passing glance, and virtually no-one crosses the somewhat overgrown serai enclosure to visit the impressive **eastern gate** of the serai, which still has some of its enamelled tilework in place. An inscription over the gateway indicates it was built by Mihr Banu, a wet nurse of Jehangir. The gateway gives on to a ruined mandi (market).

While you're here, if you leave the serai enclosure via the eastern gate and walk along the road for about 100m, you'll come to what was the main entrance to Humayun's tomb, the **southern gate**.

Return along the gravel path that runs alongside the western wall of the main tomb enclosure, and enter the formal garden surrounding the tomb through the western gate.

Other Attractions In the south-eastern corner of the garden is the square, twin-domed **Tomb of the Barber**, so-called because it is said to be that of Humayun's barber. Outside the enclosure in this corner is the **Nila Gumbad** (Blue Dome), an octagonal tomb with an impressive blue-tiled dome, thought to date from 1625. The domed tomb on the traffic circle on Mathura Rd is known as the **Sabz Burj** (Green Dome) and dates from the 17th century. The blue tiles are courtesy of the Archaeological Survey of India in the 1980s; the green, blue and yellow tiles below the dome are original.

Nizam-ud-din's Shrine

Across the road from Humayun's tomb is the shrine of the Muslim Sufi saint, Nizam-ud-din Chishti, who died in 1325, aged 92. His shrine, with its large tank, is one of several interesting tombs here. The construction of Nizam-ud-din's tank caused a dispute between the saint and the constructor of Tughlaqabad, to the south of Delhi (see Tughlaqabad in the Greater Delhi section later in this chapter).

Other tombs include the later grave of Jahanara, the daughter of Shah Jahan, who stayed with her father during his imprisonment by Aurangzeb in Agra's Red Fort. Amir Khusru, a renowned Urdu poet, also has his tomb here, as does Atgah Khan, a favourite of Humayun and his son Akbar. Atgah Khan was murdered by Adham Khan in Agra. In turn Akbar had Adham Khan killed; his grave is near the Qutb Minar.

The village itself, which sprang up around the shrine, predates New Delhi and is unique in the city. It has narrow, crowded lanes which are only passable on foot, and it is possessed of an almost medieval atmosphere. You'll know when you're getting close as beggars will appear and others will be hassling you to look after your shoes, which must be removed before entering the shrine complex.

Always a hive of activity, the shrine is particularly worth visiting around sunset on Thursday, a popular time for worship when qawwali (Sufi devotional singing) follows evening prayers. This is one of Delhi's most important pilgrimage sites, so dress appropriately and be prepared for lots of beggars.

Safdarjang's Tomb

Beside the small Safdarjang airport in New Delhi, this tomb was built in 1753–54 by the Nawab of Avadh for his father, Safdarjang, and is one of the last examples of Mughal architecture before the final remnants of the great empire collapsed. The tomb stands on a high terrace surrounded by an extensive walled garden. It makes a pleasant retreat from the urban bustle, and there is a cool garden cafe nearby.

The tomb is open from 6.30 am to 5.30 pm daily, and entry is US$5. It's a short walk from Lodi Gardens.

Parks & Gardens

Nehru Park in Chanakyapuri is one of Delhi's major lungs. Extensively landscaped with material from the nearby Ridge, it has Indian classical music concerts and an artists' corner on Sunday mornings.

Buddha Jayanti Park occupies a major section of the 650-hectare Southern Ridge, west of Rajpath, and commemorates the Buddha's attainment of nirvana. The park has been planted with trees and shrubs associated with the life of the Buddha, including, of course, a bodhi tree sapling.

Talkatora Gardens, on Baba Kharak Singh Marg, were once a walled tank (*tal* means tank and *katora* means cup), and it was here that the Marathas fought an unsuccessful battle against the Mughals in 1738. These days it's far more peaceful, and is also the site of a major indoor stadium, Talkatora Stadium.

To the north of Pragati Maidan on Mathura Rd is **Appu Ghar**, an amusement park with roller coasters and whizzy things and Oysters water park. The entrance is dominated by a large Shaktimaan (India's 'superman'), perhaps on hand should one of the rides malfunction. Entry costs Rs 10/20 for kids/adults and there are extra charges for the rides. It's open from 1 to 9 pm daily.

More traditional (and free) kids' entertainment can be found at **India Gate's Children's Park**, which has slides, monkey bars and swings within gardens.

Lodi Gardens About 3km to the west of Humayun's tomb and adjoining the India International Centre are the Lodi Gardens. In these well-kept gardens are the tombs of the Sayyid and Lodi rulers. Mohammed Shah's tomb (1450) was a prototype for the later Mughal-style tomb of Humayun, a design that would eventually develop into the Taj Mahal. Other tombs include those of his predecessor, Mubarak Shah (1433), as well as Ibrahim Lodi (1526) and Sikander Lodi (1517). The latter is within a peaceful and overgrown walled enclosure, and there is the Tulaq-era Athpula (eight-tiered) stone bridge.

The **Bara Gumbad Masjid** is entered through a Lodi tomb, although just who it belongs to is unclear. The mosque itself displays fine plaster decoration. To the north is the Sheesh Gumbad, with the remains of the dazzling blue tilework that once covered it.

The gardens are incredibly popular with members of Delhi's expat community and middle-class joggers. With its ponds, footpaths and shady trees, it also attracts young couples sneaking in a few quiet moments away from the prying eyes of the family.

An autorickshaw should cost about Rs 30 one way from Connaught Place.

GREG ELMS

Ibrahim Lodi's tomb in the Lodi Gardens

Museums & Galleries

National Museum On Janpath, just south of Rajpath, the National Museum (☎ 301 9272) has a good collection of Indian bronzes, terracotta and wood sculptures dating back to the Mauryan period (3rd–2nd century BC), exhibits from the Vijayanagar period in South India, miniature and mural paintings, Mughal clothes, tapestries, ornaments and manuscripts, costumes of the various tribal peoples and a wide array of musical instruments.

The ground floor features the prehistoric age, with a gallery dedicated to prehistory and the Indus Valley civilisation. This includes the famous bronze dancing girl statue from Mohenjodaro, the important archaeological site located in modern-day Pakistan, the discovery of which proved that there was a civilisation developing in that region simultaneously with civilisations in Egypt, China and Sumer (in present-day Iraq).

The next four ground-floor galleries are filled with sculpture and jewellery, including pieces from the Greek-influenced Gandhara period (3rd–2nd century BC) such as Buddhas dressed in togas are much more sensuous in form than the terracotta figures from the Gupta period (6th–4th century AD), including images of the river goddesses Ganga and Yamuna.

Some of the treasures on the first floor include miniature paintings from Rajasthan and Uttarakhand, Tanjore paintings on glass, illustrated manuscripts, Central Asian Buddhist antiquities and the autographed memoirs of the Mughal Emperor Jehangir.

The 2nd-floor galleries include a wonderful collection of weapons (deadly but beautiful) and musical instruments, and a section devoted to tribal arts and artefacts.

The museum, open from 10 am to 5 pm Tuesday to Sunday, offers free guided tours at 10.30 and 11.30 am, noon and 2 pm and is definitely worth visiting. Admission is Rs 5/150 for Indians/foreigners. There are films shown on weekends.

Next door is the Archaeological Survey of India office. Publications available here cover all the main sites in India, many of which are not available at the particular sites themselves. The office is open from 9 am to 1 pm and 3.30 to 5 pm Monday to Friday.

National Gallery of Modern Art This gallery (☎ 3382835) is near India Gate at the eastern end of Rajpath, and was formerly the Delhi residence of the Maharaja of Jaipur. It houses an excellent collection of works by both Indian, colonial and international artists, and has a reference library.

It is open from 10 am to 5 pm Tuesday to Sunday, and admission is Rs 5/150 for Indians/foreigners, although you can wander through the sculpture garden for free.

National Museum of Natural History The natural history museum (☎ 3314849) is opposite the Nepali embassy on Barakhamba Rd. Fronted by a large model dinosaur, it has a collection of fossils, stuffed animals and birds, and a 'hands-on' discovery room for children. It's open from 10 am to 5 pm Tuesday to Sunday.

Nehru Memorial Museum & Planetarium On Teen Murti Rd near Chanakyapuri, the residence of Jawaharlal Nehru, Teen Murti Bhavan, has been converted into a museum. Photographs and newspaper clippings on display give a fascinating insight into the history of the independence movement. The museum is open from 10 am to 5 pm Tuesday to Sunday. Admission is free.

There's also a planetarium in the grounds (40-minute shows in English at 11.30 am and 3 pm, Rs 10), above which is a small cafe.

The monument on the mound by the planetarium is the **Kushk Mahal**, thought to have been a hunting lodge during the reign of Firoz Shah.

Tibet House This museum (☎ 4611515) in New Delhi has a small but fascinating collection of ceremonial items brought out of Tibet when the Dalai Lama fled following the Chinese occupation. There are a couple of shops selling a wide range of Tibetan handicrafts and literature, and there are often lectures and discussion sessions held here. The museum, on Lodi Rd, is open from 10 am to 1 pm and 2 to 5.30 pm

Monday to Friday. Admission to the museum is Rs 5.

Exhibition Grounds There are a few museums and exhibitions at Pragati Maidan on Mathura Rd. The **Crafts Museum** (☎ 337 1817) contains a collection of traditional Indian crafts in textiles, metal, wood and ceramics, and in many cases you can see the artisans at work. The museum is part of a 'village life' complex where you can visit rural India without leaving Delhi – there are recreations of rural huts found throughout the country. There's also a pretty reasonable crafts shop.

Opening hours are from 10 am to 5.30 pm Tuesday to Sunday, and admission is free. The museum is accessible through Pragati Maidan or from Bhairon Marg, opposite Purana Qila.

Other exhibits include the **National Science Centre** (☎ 3371873), Nehru Pavilion, the Son of India (Sanjay Gandhi), Defence and Atomic Energy.

Gandhi Smriti This house on Tees January Marg was the former home of the well-known industrialist BD Birla, and is where Mahatma Gandhi used to stay during his many visits to Delhi. It was during one of these visits that he was assassinated by a Hindu fanatic in 1948.

These days it's another museum dedicated to Gandhi (☎ 3014849). There is memorabilia tracing Gandhi's life and dioramas of major events in the Independence struggle. A small pillar in the back garden marks the spot where Gandhi was shot, and bizarre concrete footprints trace his last walk from the house to the garden. The house is open from 10 am to 5 pm Tuesday to Sunday. Admission is free and there is a *khadi* (homespun cloth) shop and a book shop.

Indira Gandhi Memorial Museum The former residence of Indira Gandhi at 1 Safdarjang Rd has also been converted into a museum (☎ 3010094). On show are some of her personal effects, including the sari she was wearing at the time of her assassination (complete with blood stains). The crystal plaque in the garden, flanked constantly by two soldiers, protects a few brown spots of Mrs Gandhi's blood where she fell after being shot by two of her Sikh bodyguards in December 1984.

Opening hours are from 9.30 am to 4.45 pm Tuesday to Sunday, but it's a good idea to avoid weekends when hordes of Indian tourists are herded through. Admission is free. You're not allowed to take food or water in.

Sangeet Natak Akademi A major performing arts centre with substantial archival material, Sangeet Natak Akademi (☎ 338 7248) is at 35 Firoz Shah Rd, Rabindra Bhavan. The academy of fine arts and sculpture, Lalit Kala Akademi and the literature academy, Shahitya Akademi, are also here in separate wings.

The academy has a large archive of audio and video footage, a library and an exhibition of musical instruments and costumes. It is open from 9 am to 6 pm Monday to Friday; entry is free.

Shankar's International Dolls Museum In Nehru House on Bahadur Shah Zafar Marg, this museum (☎ 3316970) displays 6000 dolls from 85 countries. More that one-third of them are from India and one exhibit comprises 500 dolls in the costumes worn all over India. The museum is open from 10 am to 5.30 pm Tuesday to Sunday. Admission is free and there is also a children's library.

National Philatelic Museum The National Philatelic Museum (☎ 3710154), hidden in the post office at Dak Bhavan, Sardar Patel Chowk on Sansad Marg, has an extensive collection. It's open from 9.30 am to 4.30 pm Monday to Friday.

OTHER ATTRACTIONS

Coronation Durbar Site

This is a sobering sight for people interested in the Raj. In a desolate field stands a lone obelisk, where, in 1877 and 1903, the great theatrical durbars featuring the Indian army and the full set of Indian rulers paid homage to the British monarch. This was also where, in 1911, King George V was declared emperor of India. New Delhi was originally to be constructed in this neighbourhood, until the architects Lutyens and Baker chose a new site that was less at risk of flooding, and one night quietly moved the foundation stone to Raisina Hill, where Rashtrapati Bhavan stands today.

Close by there's a shabby walled garden complete with a rogues' gallery of marble statues of former imperial dignitaries, languishing like disgraced schoolboys out of the public eye. Mysteriously there are many more plinths than statues these days. Pride of place would have to go to a 15m-high statue of the King-Emperor George V which rises ghost-like above the acacia trees. It was placed here after being removed from the canopy midway along Rajpath, between India Gate and Rashtrapati Bhavan, soon after Independence. The place it was taken from remains empty, supposedly signifying the freedom of India (see India Gate earlier in this chapter).

These days this lonely yet historic bit of spare ground lies forgotten on the outskirts of the city, a reminder of recent ceremonies of lavish proportions that today seem distant and irrelevant.

Coronation Durbar Site is north of Old Delhi and is best reached by autorickshaw (about Rs 120 return from Paharganj) or by taxi. However, very few drivers are aware of the existence of this place. Ask for Radio Colony – the site is just north of the radio masts near the Outer Ring Rd.

Firoz Shah Kotla

Despite the fact that there were already at least three existing palaces in Delhi at the time (Siri, Bijai Mandal and the Qutb at Mehrauli), Firoz Shah decided to build a new one on the banks of the Yamuna River in 1354. This became Firozabad, the fifth city of Delhi. The city is thought to have extended from the Ridge north of Old Delhi to Hauz Khas to the south-west.

The ruins of this city can be found at Firoz Shah Kotla, east of Connaught Place by the Ring Rd, although not a great deal remains of the fortress-palace today, as most of the materials were pinched for the construction of Shahjahanabad.

The high stone walls enclose a peaceful garden, in stark contrast to the mayhem of Bahadur Shah Zafar Marg right outside. The main structure is the remains of the royal apartment, atop of which is a 13m-high sandstone **Ashokan Pillar** dating back to the 3rd century BC. The pillar was erected by Emperor Ashoka in Ambala and was brought to Delhi by Firoz Shah after he took a liking to it. It is similar to the one on the Ridge north of Old Delhi, but it is in much finer condition. The Brahmi inscription on the pillar was first deciphered in 1837; it details Ashoka's edicts to his subjects. Like other Ashokan Pillars, this one exhorts his people to follow the Buddhist faith by observing the moral code of dharma – virtue, social cohesion and piety. It also mentions a more modern concern – taxation.

Next to the apartment building are the remains of what was once another fine **Jama Masjid**, built on a series of ground floor cells. Only the rear (western) wall remains. It is said that Timur prayed here when he sacked Delhi in 1398. As the mosque is still in use today, you should remove your shoes before entering.

The large circular construction in the middle of the garden is a **baoli**, or step-well, which includes subterranean apartments. The door into the baoli is usually open, but be careful getting down the steps as they're very dark.

In the dividing strip on Bahadur Shah Zafar Marg, right outside Firoz Shah Kotla is the **Khuni Darwaza**, or Bloody Gate, a survivor of Sher Shah's 16th-century city some distance to the south. Its popular name dates from the time of the Uprising, as it was here in 1857 that the sons of the last Mughal emperor, Bahadur Shah, were shot by a British officer, Captain Hodson, and put on public display. Local stories speak of blood dripping from the gateway's ceiling.

The surrounding area has a distinct Islamic atmosphere and is worth a little wander. Entry to the fort, which is open sunrise to sunset, costs US$5.

Rail Transport Museum

This museum (☎ 6881816) at Chanakyapuri is for anyone fascinated by India's exotic collection of railway engines. The exhibit includes an 1855 steam engine, still in working order, and a large number of oddities such as the skull of an elephant that charged a mail train in 1894, and lost. There are also a number of lavish carriages that were used by British royalty, though the best is the Maharaja of Mysore's carriage, complete with rosewood bed and decorated with teak, gold and ivory.

There are a number of model displays with buttons to push, and displays on every aspect of rail transport you could possibly think of; there's even a Braille exhibit for the blind. A toy train chugs around the grounds throughout the day according to demand (Rs 5/10 for kids/adults).

The museum is open from 9.30 am to 5.30 pm (until 7.30 pm from April to September) Tuesday to Sunday; admission costs Rs 3/5.

Hauz Khas Village

Midway between Safdarjang's tomb and the Qutb Minar, this urban village surrounded by parkland was once the reservoir for the second city of Delhi – Siri – which lies slightly to the east. Interesting sights here include **Firoz Shah's tomb** (1398) and the remains of an ancient college. It was around here that Tamerlane defeated the forces of Mohammed Shah Tughlaq in 1398. Hauz Khas is now one of the more chic places in Delhi; there are some excellent (if pricey) restaurants and shops here.

Also part of the old city of Siri is the **Moth-ki Masjid**, which lies some distance to the east of Hauz Khas. It is said to be the finest mosque in the Lodi style. Count on about Rs 70 for an autorickshaw from Connaught Place.

Bahai Temple

Lying to the east of Siri, this building is shaped like a lotus flower. Completed in 1986, it is set among pools and gardens, and adherents of any faith are free to visit the temple and pray or meditate silently according to their own religion.

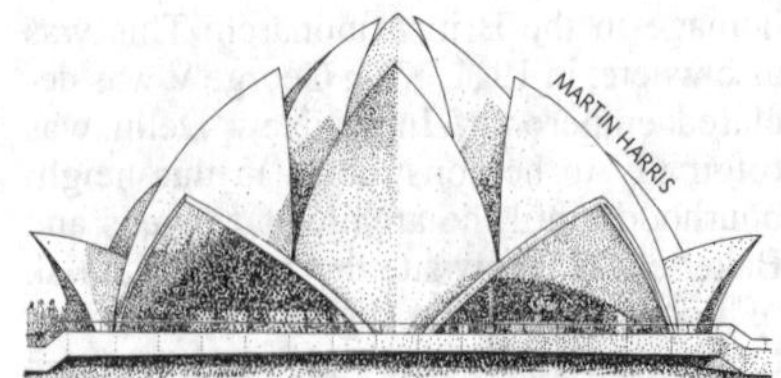

The Bahai Temple, a place all religions meet

The lotus was chosen as a symbol common to Hinduism, Buddhism, Jainism and Islam: 'the lotus is part of the dream of all cultures'. The 35m-high petals are made of Korean concrete (later clad with white marble), which had to be cooled at the right temperature; during summer it was mixed with ice. From the exterior, the temple itself appears to float on nine pools of water, which create natural air-conditioning within. Attendants ensure there is no talking within the building; a reverential atmosphere of quiet prayer prevails. Those praying towards the heavens can appreciate the interlocking ribs of the 'petals' that are clearly visible on the interior of the dome.

The temple looks spectacular when floodlit at dusk, particularly from the air, but is rather disappointing close up. Open from 9.30 am to 5.30 pm daily October to March and 9 am to 7 pm April to September, the temple is just inside the Outer Ring Road, 12km south-east of the city centre. An autorickshaw should be around Rs 70 one way.

Urusvati Museum of Folklore

Urusvati Museum of Folklore (☎ 6149385) in Vasant Vihar displays arts and crafts from North India. It is open from 10 am to 6.30 pm daily and entry is free.

ACTIVITIES

The range of sporting facilities in Delhi is impressive, although many of the clubs are the playgrounds of the city's elite, with restricted membership and astronomical fees.

Delhi Tourism Corporation (☎ 3363607) on Baba Kharak Singh Marg has an adventure tourism division if you fancy a bit of rock climbing, rafting or other adrenaline-pumping activity while in Delhi.

The main public **swimming pool** is in the Talkatora Gardens, but it has a reputation for being less than 100% clean. Most luxury hotels offer access to their swimming pools and health clubs, although whether or not you are let in rather depends on the whim of the management. You'll be charged from Rs 200 to 500, but in summer it can be a lifesaver. Most pools are empty over winter.

It's possible to hire **dinghies** and go for a paddle in the ornamental ponds that line Rajpath. These cost just a few rupees and are available throughout the day from the north side of Rajpath, near the intersection with Rafi Marg.

The old moat at Purana Qila is also put into use for **boating**. Although it's little more than a large, stagnant pool, the pedal boats here are a popular source of amusement among locals. The boats are available from 10 am to 6 pm daily, and cost Rs 30 per half hour.

The Delhi Development Authority sports complexes in Siri Fort (☎ 6497482) and Saket (☎ 6965742) hire out **tennis courts**. The Delhi Lawn Tennis Association (☎ 617 6140) on Africa Ave in the Safdarjang Enclave, just north of Hauz Khas, might interest long-term visitors and residents. The main centre court stadium has a capacity of 3000 spectators.

Delhi Golf Club (☎ 4362768), Dr Zakir Hussain Marg, charges foreigners in foreign currency – US$35 on weekdays and US$40 on weekends. Still, this 27-hole course is the best in Delhi and hosts PGA tournaments. Plus it offers the slightly vandalistic thrill of accidentally hitting the ball into one of the Mughal monuments scattered around the course. Abundant birdlife and ancient trees add to the atmosphere.

COURSES

Yoga & Meditation

Longing to relieve some of the city tensions? Yoga and meditation centres offer classes; **Sivanda Yoga Vedanta Centre** (☎ 6480869) at 41 Kailash Colony has daily 'drop in' yoga sessions at 10 am, and other daily classes include gentle yoga for pensioners or kids yoga. In south Delhi, **Sri Aurobindo Ashram** (☎ 6569225) on Sri Aurobindo Marg has yoga and meditation from Monday to Saturday.

ORGANISED TOURS

Delhi is very spread out, so taking a city tour makes a lot of sense. Two major organisations arrange Delhi tours (beware agents offering cut-price tours). The Indian Tourism Development Corporation (ITDC), operating under the name Ashok Travels & Tours (☎ 3322336), has tours that include guides and a luxury coach. Their office is in L-Block, Connaught Place, near Nirula's Hotel, but you can also book at the Government of India tourist office on Janpath or at the major hotels. Delhi Tourism Corporation (☎ 3313637) arranges similar tours; their office is in N-Block, Middle Circle.

A five-hour morning tour of New Delhi costs Rs 147 with Delhi Tourism. Starting at 8 am, the tour includes the Bahai Temple, Qutb Minar, Humayun's Tomb, India Gate, the Jantar Mantar and the Lakshmi Narayan Temple. The afternoon Old Delhi tour for Rs 126 starts at 2.15 pm and covers the Red Fort, Jama Masjid, Raj Ghat, Shanti Vana and Firoz Shah Kotla, finishing at 5 pm. If you take both tours on the same day it costs Rs 231. These tours don't include entry fees, which on a full-day tour would total US$35. Similar tours are run by operators in Paharganj from around Rs 150.

It's also possible to arrange tours outside Delhi. A one-day trip to Agra costs from Rs 250 to 1500. This doesn't include entry to the Taj Mahal, and tour operators often include Agra Fort on the itinerary only to whiz by, pointing it out through the window. Other day trips visit Jaipur and Amber Fort, prices start at Rs 275. A three-day Delhi-Agra-Jaipur tour should cost around Rs 3000. There are many more tours including areas such as Manali, Rajasthan, Kathmandu and pilgrimage sites. If you're interested in a 'Buddhist circuit' tour, Potala Tours & Travels (☎ 3723284, 3722552, ⓔ potala@vsnl.com), 1011 Antriksh Bhavan, 22, KG Marg, New Delhi, organises a trip from 10 to 15 days with prices for most budgets. Check out its Web site at www.potalatours.com.

Hotel Broadway, near Delhi Gate, has gastronomic walking tours of Old Delhi for Rs 450. After a guided wander through historical bazaars and alleys, participants get to digest it all over a meal at the hotel's excellent restaurant.

The India Habitat Centre (☎ 4682222) has a walkers' group with regular guided walks to monuments, parks, wetlands and museums with relevant experts. The centre's Web site at www.habitatworld.com has details of forthcoming walks.

SPECIAL EVENTS

Delhi hosts a number of festivals, including.

Lori Citywide, January. Features bonfires, singing and dancing.
Delhi Horse Show Below Red Fort, January.
Delhi Flower Show Citywide, January.
Kite flying festival Connaught Place, January.
Republic Day Rajpath, 26 January. Features a military parade.
Beating Retreat Vijay Chowk, 29 January. Features a ceremony near Delhi's Rashtrapati Bhavan, the president's residence, with a parade and fireworks.
Martyr's Day Raj Ghat, 30 January. Anniversary of Gandhi's death.
Vasant Panchami Citywide, 2 February. Spring festival.
Garden Tourism Festival Citywide, February. Flower & garden show.
Surajkund Crafts Fair Surajkund, February. Indian states exhibiting crafts.
Amir Khusrau's Birthday Nizzamudin, April. Pilgrimage.
National Drama Festival Rabindra Bhavan, April. Features drama performances.
Mango Festival Talkatora Stadium, July. Features tastings and cultural events.
Independence Day Red Fort, 15 August. Prime minister addresses the nation.
Phoolwalonki Sair Old Delhi, 30 September. Ancient flower vendors' festival.
Gandhi Jayanti Raj Ghat, 2 October. Gandhi's birthday.
Dussehra Sudhash Maidan & Ramlila Grounds, October. Features drama, fireworks and a fair.
Qutb Festival Qutb Minar, October/November. Features singing & dancing.
Indian Trade Fair Pragati Maidan, Mathura Rd, November. Features trade fair with state representatives.

PLACES TO STAY

If Delhi is your first stop in India, it's probably a good idea to book a room in advance from home – reasonable places fill up quickly, leaving new arrivals easy prey for the commission sharks. This is especially true if you're arriving in the middle of the night (see the boxed text 'Dodgy Delhi' near the beginning of this chapter). Fortunately many places, including budget hotels, have 24-hour receptions allowing for late arrivals.

Prices given here don't include luxury tax, which ranges from 10% to 22.5% in mid-range to top-end places; budget places generally don't charge tax. During summer (May to August) discounts of up to 50% are often available, and it's always worth asking for a discount if you're staying more than a couple of days.

Unless stated otherwise checkout is at noon – although if you check in between 6 am and noon most places will apply a 24-hour checkout – and rooms have fans and/or air coolers. There is little need for air-con out of the hot sticky summer months, especially as Delhi Central Government forbids the use of it between 6.30 and 9.30 pm. Unless stated otherwise toilets are sit-down flush toilets and hot water is available 24 hours.

PLACES TO STAY – BUDGET

While most budget rooms may not be much to write home about, facilities such as 24-hour room service, TV, baggage storage, travel arrangements, airport pick-ups and laundry services make them good value and convenient places to stay.

Camping

Delhi's main camp ground closed in 2000 after some drug-related issues with the police. It may well reopen, but in the meantime it is possible to pitch a tent at the ***Tourist Camping Park** (☎ 3973121)*, opposite the ISBT in Old Delhi. It's possible to camp in the small lawned area right next to the very busy main road for Rs 30 per person. It also has some very basic rooms for Rs 140/175 a single/double, and a few with bathroom for Rs 250. The toilet and shower blocks are reasonably clean and have hot water.

Connaught Place

The ***Youth Hostel*** *(☎ 6116285, fax 6113469, ⓔ yhoste@del2.vsnl.net.in, 5 Nyaya Marg)* is in serene Chanakyapuri, but you have to be a member to stay (membership costs Rs 250). Beds in single-sex dorms without air-con cost Rs 50 and Rs 250 with air-con. Doubles with shared bathroom start at Rs 300/650 – prices go up after five days and there's no smoking or alcohol allowed. Open 24 hours (although check-in is at 11 am and checkout is at noon), this place has a cafe, bank, garden and recreation centre.

Down a side street near the Government of India tourist office, ***Ringo Guest House*** *(☎ 3310605)* is an ageing travellers' institution with its fair share of detractors as well as fans. Small, basic and gloomy rooms around a central open courtyard restaurant cost Rs 125/250 for a single/double with shared bathroom and from Rs 350 to 400 for a double with bathroom (squat toilets and 24-hour hot water). Dorm beds cost Rs 90.

Nearby and very similar, ***Sunny Guest House*** *(☎ 3312909)* is marginally better than Ringo Guest House. Rooms with shared bathroom that are not quite so dark cost Rs 125/250 and from Rs 350 to 450 for doubles with bathroom, again around a central courtyard restaurant. Dorm beds are available for Rs 90. Both places are reasonably clean and friendly, with a shabby charm, and are good for swapping travellers' tales and storing luggage (Rs 8 per day). However, they can be pretty awful when it's very hot (in July) or very cold (rainy February nights), and unless you specifically want to be near Connaught Circus you can find much better deals in Paharganj.

Hotel Blue *(☎ 3322222, ⓔ hotel-blue@yahoo.com)* is an older 3rd-floor place with a fair amount of character. Decent-sized rooms with phone, TV and shared bathroom cost Rs 300/500; those with bathroom are Rs 500/800. Tax is added. It has a large balcony terrace and small open courtyard.

Hotel Bright *(☎ 3323456, fax 3736049)*, directly below, is of a similar style without the terrace, so it's not quite as nice. Rooms without bathroom cost Rs 350/550; Rs 575/1100 with private bathroom.

Central Court Hotel *(☎ 3315013, N-Block)* has a bit of character and has old-style rooms with bath, fireplace and separate lounge area for Rs 800/1150. The fact that they're accessed from the terrace almost makes up for them having no windows. Rooms with shared bathroom cost Rs 600/800 and all have air-con, TV, fridge and phone. The hotel has a coffee shop and two restaurants.

Paharganj

Hotel Navrang *(☎ 521965)* on Baoli Chowk is popular with the grungy crowd and serves a selection of Japanese dishes in its secluded terrace cafe. Rooms with private bathroom (squat toilets and bucket hot water that costs Rs 10) cost Rs 80/100/150 for a single/double/triple – the more you pay the bigger they get. Try for one on the block overlooking the cafe as these get more light and have small terrace areas outside.

Hotel Bajrang *(☎ 3551730)* is a basic but friendly place with doubles around an open courtyard for Rs 100 with shared bathroom and Rs 150 with private bathroom (geyser hot water). There's a very cheap canteen for food and drink in the courtyard and Internet access is available for Rs 12 per hour.

The very funky ***Camran Lodge*** *(☎ 352 6053, fax 3621030, ⓔ camranlodge@id.eth.net)* is basic but has a lot of character. It's the unmistakable old red building on Main Bazaar, with onion domes and a disused mosque on the roof – a great place to catch the sunset. Blue and green rooms have windows onto Main Bazaar; the 2nd-floor rooms, created by metal partitions, can get a bit hot. Singles/doubles with shared bathroom cost Rs 80/160 and Rs 100/180 with private bathroom (bucket hot water and squat toilets). The front door closes at midnight.

Hotel Namaskar *(☎ 3621234, fax 362 2233, ⓔ namaskarhotel@yahoo.com)* gets good reports and the brothers who own it thrive on helping out travellers. Airy pink and green rooms, most with windows, cost Rs 200/250 with shared bathroom and from Rs 300 to 400 with bathroom (bucket hot water and both squat and sit-down flush toilets); air-con rooms cost Rs 450. One of the few places where the owners also manage

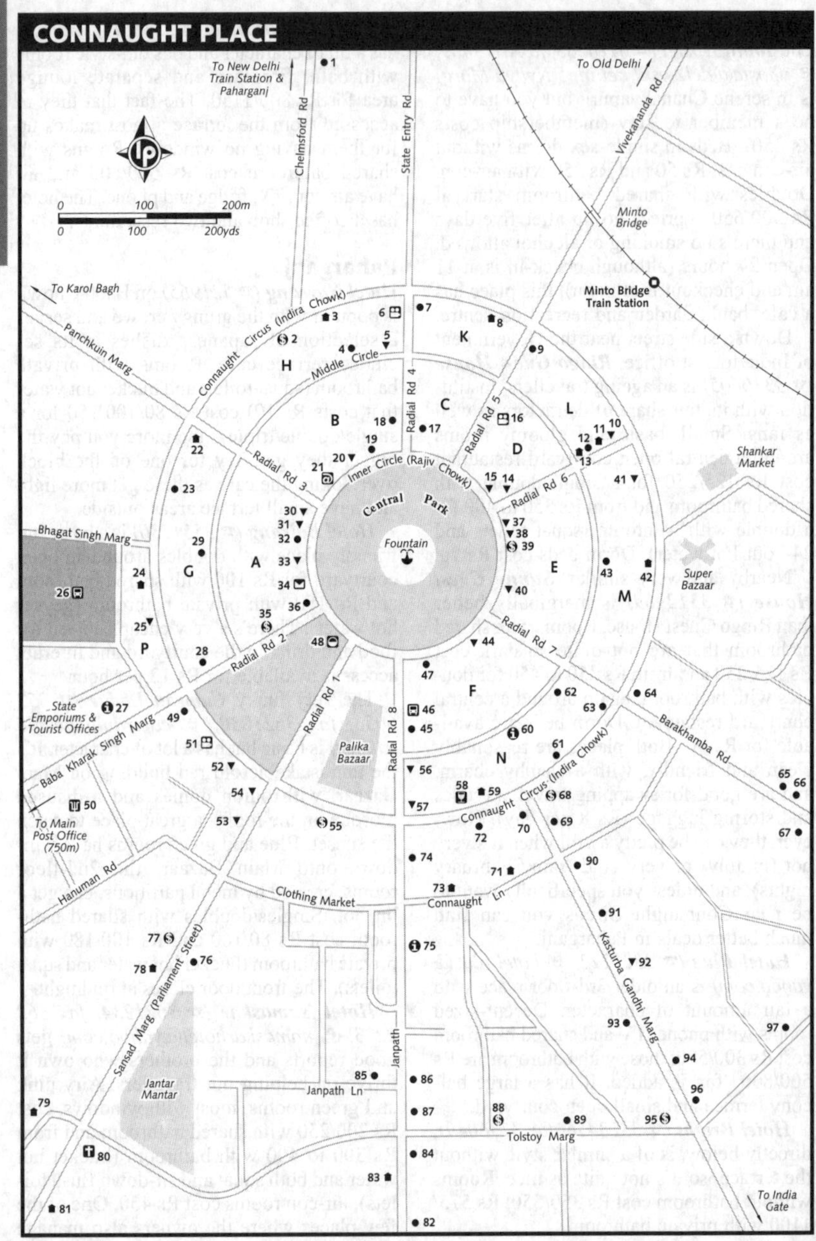
CONNAUGHT PLACE
To New Delhi Train Station & Paharganj
To Old Delhi
Chelmsford Rd
State Entry Rd
Vivekananda Rd
Minto Bridge
Minto Bridge Train Station
To Karol Bagh
Panchkuin Marg
Connaught Circus (Indira Chowk)
Middle Circle
Radial Rd 4
Radial Rd 5
Radial Rd 3
Inner Circle (Rajiv Chowk)
Radial Rd 6
Central Park
Fountain
Shankar Market
Bhagat Singh Marg
Super Bazaar
Radial Rd 2
Radial Rd 7
Radial Rd 1
Radial Rd 8
State Emporiums & Tourist Offices
Baba Kharak Singh Marg
Palika Bazaar
Barakhamba Rd
To Main Post Office (750m)
Hanuman Rd
Clothing Market
Connaught Ln
Sansad Marg (Parliament Street)
Kasturba Gandhi Marg
Janpath
Janpath Ln
Jantar Mantar
Tolstoy Marg
To India Gate
0 100 200m
0 100 200yds

CONNAUGHT PLACE

PLACES TO STAY
- 3 Hotel 55
- 8 York Hotel
- 11 Nirula's Hotel
- 13 Hotel Jukaso Inn Downtown
- 22 Hotel Marina
- 24 Hotel Alka; Vega
- 42 Hotel Blue; Hotel Bright
- 59 Central Court Hotel
- 71 Sunny Guest House
- 73 Ringo Guest House; Don't Pass Me By Cafe; Don't Pass Me By Travels
- 78 The Park
- 79 YMCA Tourist Hotel; Y Tours & Travels
- 81 YWCA International Guest House; VINstring Holidays
- 83 The Imperial; Thomas Cook

PLACES TO EAT
- 5 Nizam Katri Kebab
- 10 Nirula's Complex; Pegasus
- 14 The Embassy
- 15 Pizza Express
- 20 Cafe 100
- 25 McDonald's
- 30 Keventers
- 31 Wenger's
- 33 Rodeo
- 37 Kovil; Pizza Hut
- 38 Berco's
- 40 United Coffee House; Ruby Tuesday's
- 41 Domino's Pizza
- 44 The Host
- 52 Gaylord
- 53 Kwality; People Tree
- 54 DV8
- 56 Nirula's
- 57 Wimpy
- 92 Parikrama; Tarom

OTHER
- 1 Railway Booking Office
- 2 Standard Chartered Grindlays Bank
- 4 Cox & Kings
- 6 Plaza Cinema
- 7 Alcohol Shop
- 9 English Book Store
- 12 Ashok Travels & Tours
- 16 Odeon Cinema
- 17 Thomas Cook
- 18 Bookworm
- 19 New Book Depot
- 21 Hub Internet Centre
- 23 Gulf Air
- 26 Local Bus Station
- 27 Delhi Tourism Corporation
- 28 Malaysia Airlines; Royal Jordanian
- 29 Alcohol Shop
- 32 American Express
- 34 Post Office
- 35 American Express Bank (ATM)
- 36 Kinsey Bros
- 39 24-Hour Standard Chartered Grindlays Bank (ATM)
- 43 Singapore Airlines
- 45 Indian Airlines
- 46 EATS Airport Bus
- 47 Sita World Travels
- 48 Prepaid Autorickshaw Kiosk
- 49 Khadi Gramodyog Bhavan
- 50 Hanuman Mandir
- 51 Regal Cinema
- 55 24-Hour Citibank (ATM); Air India
- 58 The Blues Bar
- 60 Delhi Tourism Corporation; DSIDC Cyber Cafe
- 61 Jet Airways; Sahara Airlines
- 62 Aeroflot
- 63 Cozy Travels
- 64 British Airways; Qantas
- 65 Emirates
- 66 Kuwait Airways
- 67 Saudi Arabian Airlines
- 68 Hong Kong & Shanghai Bank (ATM)
- 69 Air Canada
- 70 Air France
- 72 Delhi Transport Corporation
- 74 Air India; Budget Car Rental
- 75 Government of India Tourist Office; Delhi Photo Company
- 76 Swissair
- 77 Standard Chartered Grindlays Bank (ATM)
- 80 Free Church
- 82 Chandralok Building: Haryana, Himachal Pradesh & Uttar Pradesh Tourist Offices; Delta Airlines; Druk Air; Japan Airlines
- 84 Central Industries Emporium
- 85 Map Sales Office
- 86 Lufthansa Airlines; Budget Car Rental
- 87 Royal Nepal Airlines Corporation (RNAC)
- 88 Deutsche Bank (ATM)
- 89 Jagson Airlines
- 90 Pakistan International Airlines (PIA)
- 91 American Center
- 93 British Council
- 94 Asiana Airlines; Ethiopian Airlines; Kuwait Airways
- 95 Credit Lyonnaise
- 96 Ambadeep Building: United Airlines; Sahara India; Scandinavian Airlines (SAS)
- 97 KLM-Royal Dutch Airlines; Northwest Airlines; El Al Israel Airlines; Uzbekistan Airways

the hotel, it is a good source of information and offers free luggage storage.

Smyle Inn *(☎ 3559107, ⓔ smyleinn@hotmail.com)*, nearby, has rooms with private bathroom, TV and phone for Rs 150/200.

Major's Den *(☎ 3629599)* has few of the facilities of its competitors (there is no restaurant or Internet connection) but remains a popular and safe haven for those looking for respite from Main Bazaar. It has a terrace, travel service and clean rooms with bathroom and windows start at Rs 250/300. The major who lives downstairs with his wife and daughter is both a businessman and a pukka (proper) chap who can help in times of need. The doors close at midnight.

Traveller Guest House Inn *(☎ 3544849)* is a popular choice especially as it's one of the first places reached when coming from the station. Clean rooms with private bathroom and TV start at Rs 240; not all rooms have windows.

Hotel Victoria *(☎ 3524413)* is a very friendly place in a quiet area, east of Rajguru Rd. The large rooms with TV and private bathroom (both sit-down flush and squat toilet) have equally as large windows covered in plastic which gives everything a lovely pink hue. They start at Rs 222/250.

Hotel Payal *(☎ 3520867)* has good-sized and clean rooms with private bathroom (geyser hot water) and window for Rs 200/250; rooms with shared bathroom start at Rs 150.

Royal Guest House *(☎ 7535880, fax 3625538)* is a very friendly place with windows looking onto Main Bazaar. Rooms with private bathroom cost Rs 225 and Rs 450/490 with air-con.

Hotel Sweet Dream *(☎ 3629801)* offers rooms with bathroom (some with balcony) for Rs 175/200. A 10% service charge is added to room prices.

Ajay Guest House *(☎ 35431253, fax 3540656, e sent@ndf.vsnl.net.in)* has average doubles without window/with onto the stairwell, as well as phone and private bathroom with geyser hot water, for Rs 260/270; a couple of larger air-con rooms (Rs 400) have small balconies. There is a rooftop cafe (with great views), a travel agency and an Internet centre. The best thing about this place is the bakery on the ground floor which has good coffee and tasty cakes, pizzas and rolls as well as a couple of pool tables. Checkout is 24 hours.

Hare Rama Guest House *(☎ 3521413, fax 7532795, e harerama@ndf.vsnl.net.in)*, opposite, has similar rooms around a covered courtyard, with a mix of sit-down flush and squat toilets and the addition of a fridge and TV, for Rs 250/320. It, too, has a 24-hour rooftop restaurant (with TV) on its treetop-flanked terrace. Catering to a large Israeli clientele, it also has a travel agency, Internet centre, art shop and luggage storage. Checkout for this place, which attracts louder late-night crowds, is 24 hours.

Anoop Hotel *(☎ 3521451, fax 7532942, e anoophotel@hotmail.com)* is almost next door to Hare Krishna and has marble-lined singles/doubles with phone and private bathroom (geyser hot water) for Rs 220/ 280, and Rs 150/220 with shared bathroom. These two places share a good 24-hour Thai restaurant on their large rooftops and Internet facilities on the ground floor of the Anoop. Checkout for both is 24 hours.

Hare Krishna Guest House *(☎ 3521467, e anoophotel@hotmail.com)*, under the same management, on Main Bazaar has rooms with phone for Rs 220 with shared bathroom and from Rs 230 to 250 with private bathroom (geyser hot water). Checkout is 24 hours.

Vivek Hotel *(☎ 3512900, fax 7537103, e vivekhotel@mailcity.com)* has bright rooms with a few windows around an open courtyard for Rs 200/250 with private bathroom and Rs 150/200 with shared bathroom. Leema Restaurant is on the 1st floor but it's worth risking the elevator to get up to the much nicer rooftop terrace restaurant complete with a tiny lawned area.

Hotel Vishal *(☎ 3526314)* has a couple of good restaurants downstairs, but the rooms are a bit cell-like and most lack windows. Rooms with bathroom and phone cost Rs 200/250.

Hotel Fortuna *(☎ 3614211)*, with an arcade on the ground floor, is recently painted and has with rooms with TV, phone and private bathroom for Rs 200/250. Those at the front have balconies.

Hotel Satyam *(☎ 3525200)* has rooms with TV, phone, bathroom (both squat and sit-down flush toilets and geyser hot water) and grubby sheets for Rs 250/300. There's a long rooftop terrace and balconies overlooking Rajguru Rd.

Hotel Star View *(☎ 3556300, fax 3554220, e starview@vsnl.com)*, next door, has the same views down Rajguru Rd from its terrace, the back section of which is a restaurant. Comfortable doubles with TV, phone, velour-covered furniture and private bathroom (geyser hot water) cost Rs 300 (Rs 500 with air-con).

Hotel Rak International *(☎ 3550478, e hotelrak@yahoo.com)* on Baoli Chowk has rooms with TV, phone, sofa and private bathroom (both sit-down flush and squat toilets and geyser hot water) for Rs 250/ 350. A 24-hour terrace restaurant overlooks the square and temple below.

Shivlok Palace *(☎ 3511270)* has a bit of character, with sofas on its rooftop terrace and circular beds. Rooms with phone, TV and bathroom start at a negotiable Rs 350/400 (plus 10% service charge).

There are a couple of options on Arakashan Rd, across an incredibly busy and hard-to-cross road from Main Bazaar, although you'll be paying more for less here. ***Hotel Soma DX*** *(☎ 3621002, fax 3552634)* has good front rooms with big windows. Rooms with TV, phone and bathroom (squat toilets and hot water in the morning and evening) start at Rs 250/300; it has a lift.

Old Delhi

Staying in Old Delhi ensures that you're right in the thick of things. The area has a colourful atmosphere, and there are not too many other tourists around – the clientele in the area is predominantly Indian males.

The railway retiring rooms, at the high-rise ***Rail Yatri Niwas*** *(☎ 3313484)*, on the Ajmeri Gate side of New Delhi train station (on the Paharganj map), are available for those in transit. Bona fide rail travellers with tickets for distances over 500km can stay in singles/doubles with shared bathroom for Rs 150/210; Rs 250 with private bathroom and Rs 500 with private bathroom and air-con. There are also dorm beds for Rs 70. Check-in is from 9 am and the maximum stay is three days.

Hotel New City Palace *(☎ 3279548, fax 3289923)* makes the most of its position overlooking the Jama Masjid with plenty of balconies and a roof terrace with restaurant. The rooms with phone and bathroom (squat toilet and 24-hour hot water) for Rs 450 are less impressive and somewhat contradict the hotel's self-promotion as a 'home for palatial comfort' – try to get a room at the front. Checkout is 24 hours.

Hotel de Romana *(☎ 3266031, fax 328 6635, ⓔ de-romana@hotmail.com)*, in a lane behind the Jagat Cinema, is a better deal with 'every damn thing' (except a view), including OK rooms with TV, phone, private bathroom (sit-down flush toilet and 24-hour hot water) and air-con for Rs 330/400. Checkout is by noon.

Hotel Bombay Orient *(☎ 3286253)*, on a main lane leading away from Jama Masjid, is another reasonable choice. Rooms with private bathroom (sit-down flush toilet and 24-hour hot water) cost Rs 250/350.

Hotel Malabar *(☎ 3956669)*, at the end of Chandni Chowk, is for those who prefer to really be in the heart of Old Delhi. Basic rooms with private bathroom are Rs 150/250.

PLACES TO STAY – MID-RANGE

Connaught Place

The YMCA/YWCA has a large complex, about a 10-minute walk south-west of Connaught Place, with three accommodation options. They all have a religious institution air and aren't that great a deal, although they are clean and central and good places to meet other travellers. Check-in and checkout for all is at noon, and rates, which are subject to tax and service charge (except dorms), include breakfast.

YMCA Tourist Hostel *(☎ 3361915, fax 3746032, ⓔ ymcath@ndf.vsnl.net.in, Jai Singh Rd)* is closest to Connaught Place and the largest of the bunch with a laundry, swimming pool (open from April to October), fitness centre, restaurant, travel agency and Internet access. Singles/doubles with shared bathroom cost Rs 415/725 rising to 800/1350 with air-con, TV, phone and bathroom, plus a Rs 30 temporary membership fee. It's open 24 hours, and accepts credit cards.

YWCA International Guest House *(☎ 3361561, fax 3341765, ⓔ ywcaind@del3.vsnl.net.in, 10 Sansad Marg)* is surrounded by a small garden and has a 24-hour cafe and a travel agency. Rooms cost Rs 800/1000, and it accepts AmEx cards.

ITDC Hotel Indraprastha *(☎ 3344511, fax 3368153, 19 Ashok Rd)* is a high-rise popular with Indian holiday makers. With a very institutionalised atmosphere, rooms are a reasonable size but you might want to have a look at a few. They cost Rs 600/750/1000 for one/two/three people in a standard room or Rs 750/850/1100 in a deluxe (plus 12.5% tax for both). There's a bar and a characterless 24-hour self-service restaurant and cafe.

Places directly on Connaught Circus are housed in colonial era buildings and therefore have a modicum of character.

Hotel Alka *(☎ 3344328, fax 3732796, ⓔ hotelalka@vsnl.com, P-Block, Connaught Circus)* has a mad mirrored corridor, a good vegetarian restaurant and a bar, and a terrace overlooking the local bus station. Rooms start at Rs 1800/2900 for a single/double and Hotel Alka accepts credit cards.

Hotel Marina *(☎ 3324658, fax 3328609, ⓔ marina@nde.vsnl.net.in)* is quite swish, with a bar, restaurant, 24-hour coffee shop and resident dentist. It has rooms starting at Rs 2600/3200, including breakfast, and credit cards are accepted. Incidentally, this is the place at which Gandhi's assassin stayed the night before the horrific act.

Nirula's Hotel *(☎ 3322419, fax 3353957, L-Block)*, right by the restaurant of the same name, has good rooms with phone, fridge and TV for Rs 1995/3500. Children under 12 stay free.

York Hotel *(☎ 3323769, fax 3352419, K-Block, Connaught Circus)* has clean and cool rooms with fridge and TV for Rs 1800/2950. The rooms at the back of the hotel are quietest.

Hotel Jukaso Inn Downtown *(☎ 3324451, fax 3324448, ⓔ jukaso@vsnl.com, L-Block, Radial Rd 6)* has a terrace and a cosy 24-hour coffee shop, and although the rooms are small, most have windows (Rs 1650/2200). Children under six can stay free.

Hotel 55 *(☎ 3321244, fax 3320769, ⓔ hotelfiftyfive@hotmail.com, 55 H-Block, Connaught Circus)* is well designed with air-con throughout, but the rooms are on the small side. Rooms with balcony and private bathroom cost Rs 1100/1600.

Paharganj

Prince Polonia *(☎ 3511930, fax 3557646)*, near the Imperial Cinema, has a small clean poolon its rooftop terrace (nonguests can use it for two hours for Rs 100). Double deluxe rooms/superdeluxe rooms/suites, most with balcony and all with TV, fridge, solar-heated hot water and air-con cost Rs 935/1155/1320. There are also another couple of terraces to relax on and a lift to get you up to them.

Metropolis Tourist Home *(☎ 7531782, ⓔ metravel@bom9.vsnl.net.in)* has basic but clean air-con singles/doubles with phone, TV and bathroom (geyser hot water) for Rs 600/675. There is a cheerless ground-floor licensed restaurant, and a pleasant roof terrace restaurant with tablecloths and atmosphere. There is also foreign exchange and a travel agency.

Hotel Relax *(☎ 3681030, ⓔ vidur109@hotmail.com)* is a shiny new place on Ramdwara Rd south of Nehru Bazaar. The management is very enthusiastic and clean rooms come with phone, TV, fridge and air-con for Rs 800/1000. There's a good balcony from where you can watch the masses below while eating.

Vinn Inn *(☎ 3677705, fax 3621398)* is a modern and nicely furnished place away from the madness of Main Bazaar off Rajguru Rd. Cleanish rooms with windows are Rs 500/700.

Yatri Guest House *(☎ 3625563, ⓔ yatri@nde.vsnl.net.in, 3/4 Punchkuin Marg)* is actually in a small lane off Punchkuin Marg, opposite the junction with Mandir Marg. It's small, calm and secure with a lawn out front and a couple of small, open courtyards at the back. Spotless, fan-cooled doubles with big beds and private bathrooms (geyser hot water) cost Rs 1250, including tax. There are meals and snacks as well as all-inclusive taxi tours starting at US$28 per day.

There is an array of places north of Paharganj on and around Arakashan Rd. With less hassle than Main Bazaar, these places are modern and prices are open to negotiation. The only issue is that a few are run by those who grab newcomers at the airport, pressuring them into paying over the odds.

Hotel Ajanta *(☎ 3620927, fax 3620228, ⓔ ccity@nda.vsnl.net.in)* is one of the best places, providing a good service to travellers. There's a restaurant and a reputable travel service, as well as Internet access. Rooms are on the small side but are very clean and those at the front have balconies. Prices start at Rs 425/525 for singles/doubles.

Hotel Syal *(☎ 3610091, fax 3514290, ⓔ nomex@vsnl.com)*, nearby, is a centrally

PAHARGANJ

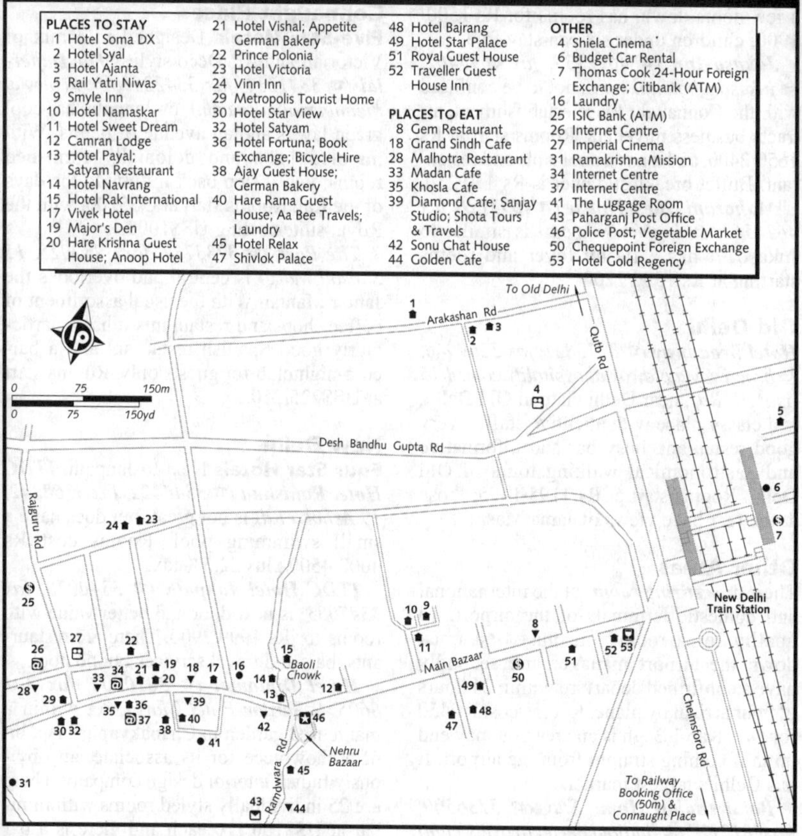

PLACES TO STAY
1 Hotel Soma DX
2 Hotel Syal
3 Hotel Ajanta
5 Rail Yatri Niwas
9 Smyle Inn
10 Hotel Namaskar
11 Hotel Sweet Dream
12 Camran Lodge
13 Hotel Payal; Satyam Restaurant
14 Hotel Navrang
15 Hotel Rak International
17 Vivek Hotel
19 Major's Den
20 Hare Krishna Guest House; Anoop Hotel
21 Hotel Vishal; Appetite German Bakery
22 Prince Polonia
23 Hotel Victoria
24 Vinn Inn
29 Metropolis Tourist Home
30 Hotel Star View
32 Hotel Satyam
36 Hotel Fortuna; Book Exchange; Bicycle Hire
38 Ajay Guest House; German Bakery
40 Hare Rama Guest House; Aa Bee Travels; Laundry
45 Hotel Relax
47 Shivlok Palace
48 Hotel Bajrang
49 Hotel Star Palace
51 Royal Guest House
52 Traveller Guest House Inn

PLACES TO EAT
8 Gem Restaurant
18 Grand Sindh Cafe
28 Malhotra Restaurant
33 Madan Cafe
35 Khosla Cafe
39 Diamond Cafe; Sanjay Studio; Shota Tours & Travels
42 Sonu Chat House
44 Golden Cafe

OTHER
4 Shiela Cinema
6 Budget Car Rental
7 Thomas Cook 24-Hour Foreign Exchange; Citibank (ATM)
16 Laundry
25 ISIC Bank (ATM)
26 Internet Centre
27 Imperial Cinema
31 Ramakrishna Mission
34 Internet Centre
37 Internet Centre
41 The Luggage Room
43 Paharganj Post Office
46 Police Post; Vegetable Market
50 Chequepoint Foreign Exchange
53 Hotel Gold Regency

air-conditioned place used by tour groups. Rooms, some with balcony, start at Rs 450. It has a roof terrace and a good restaurant.

New Delhi

YWCA Blue Triangle Family Hostel *(☎ 3360133, fax 3360202, ⓔ ywcadel@vsnl.net, Ashoka Rd)* has a restaurant, TV lounge and Internet facility. Rooms with phone start at Rs 575/1035 and range to Rs 2875 for a two-bedroom suite with kitchen/lounge room (no service charge). There are also dorm beds for Rs 185 (Rs 275 with air-con). You need to become a temporary member for Rs 20 to stay here. Children under five stay free.

There are a few places in the Sunder Nagar, conveniently located between Purana Qila and Humayun's tomb. This area has some antique shops, a couple of reasonable restaurants and lots of greenery. The air-con hotels are all set within lawned gardens offering clean comfort in relative tranquillity.

La Sagrita Tourist Home *(☎ 4694541, fax 4636956, ⓔ lasagrit@del3.vsnl.net.in)* is the pick of the bunch with very comfortable rooms starting at Rs 1490/2090.

Kailash Inn *(☎ 4623634, fax 4617401)*, a few doors down, has rooms for Rs 1500/1900; children under six can stay free.

Jukaso Inn *(☎ 4692137, fax 4694402, ⓔ jukaso@hotmail.com)*, not to be confused with the Connaught Place establishment, attracts business travellers. Rooms start at Rs 1650/2400, and it has a pool table and restaurant. Buffet breakfast/dinner is Rs 150/250.

Maharani Guest House *(☎ 4693128, fax 4624562, ⓔ mgh@vsnl.com)* is similar to Jukaso. It has a flashy foyer and rooms starting at Rs 1500/2200.

Old Delhi

Hotel Broadway *(☎ 3273821, fax 3269966, ⓔ broadway@oldworldhospitality.com, 4/15 Asaf Ali Rd)*, near Delhi Gate in Old Delhi, is a classy place with attentive staff, a very good restaurant, busy bar and informative and gastronomical walking tours of Old Delhi. Rooms start at Rs 1195/1495; those at the rear have views of Jama Masjid .

Other Areas

There are ***retiring rooms*** at the international and domestic terminals of the airport. To qualify for a room you must first track down the airport manager and secondly have a confirmed departure within 24 hours of your arrival by plane. Rooms cost Rs 450 for two. Karol Bagh is an area you may end up in if coming straight from the airport. It has Delhi's largest market.

Bajaj Indian Home Stay *(☎ 5736509, fax 5812127, ⓔ india@perfecttravels.com)* is a modern attempt at a *haveli* (traditional ornately decorated residence). The effect isn't too bad and the owners are friendly and intent on providing good service. Singles/doubles with minibar start at Rs 1365/1785, including buffet breakfast.

En route to the airport, ***Master Paying Guest Accommodation*** *(☎ 5741089, R-500 New Rajinder Nagar)* is a cool little place in a residential area away from the action. Rooms with classic furniture and French windows are full of character and cost Rs 500/600 with shared bathroom (including tax). Breakfast, drinks and snacks are served in the homely lounge or shady roof terrace.

PLACES TO STAY – TOP END

Connaught Place

Five-Star Hotels Designed in a mix of Victorian and Art Deco styles, ***The Imperial*** *(☎ 3341234, fax 3342255, ⓔ luxury@theimperialindia.com)*, on Janpath, has cool green lawns and an avenue of palms. With marbled halls and colonially furnished rooms, you'll step back in time to the days of the Raj. Rooms start at US$200, with the Royal suite costing US$1000.

The Park *(☎ 3733737, fax 3732025, 15 Sansad Marg)* is central and overlooks the Jantar Mantar. With the usual assortment of coffee shops and restaurants it has a particularly good Spanish restaurant and a bar-cum-nightclub for guests only. Rooms start at US$225/250.

New Delhi

Four-Star Hotels Next to Janpath, ***ITDC Hotel Kanishka*** *(☎ 3344422, fax 3368242, 19 Ashoka Rd)* is not great, but does have a small swimming pool. Rooms cost Rs 4000/4500 plus 22.5% tax.

ITDC Hotel Janpath *(☎ 3340070, fax 3347083)* is next door and better value with rooms for Rs 1999/2900. There are restaurants, bars and travel services but no pool.

Hotel Diplomat *(☎ 3010204, fax 301 8605, 9 Sardar Patel Marg)*, set within a manicured garden in Chanakyapuri, is a bit of a showpiece for its associate, an obviously Indian interior design company. There are 25 individually styled rooms with minibar at US$100/110 each and there is a bar and restaurant.

Five-Star Hotels The grandly named ***The Claridges*** *☎ 3010211, fax 3010625, ⓔ Claridges.hotel@gems.vsnl.net.in, 12 Aurangzeb Rd)* has a European package holiday look from the outside and an Art Deco-style marbled interior. It has four restaurants (see Places to Eat – International Hotels), a bakery, a bar overlooking the lawn, a swimming pool, a health club and parking. It's a good choice in this category, with rooms for a negotiable US$175/200.

The Oberoi *(☎ 4363030, fax 4360484, ⓔ reservations@oberoidel.com, Dr Zakir*

Hussain Marg), on the edge of the Delhi Golf Course, is a member of the World's Leading Hotels. A very swish place it has a tempting pool, bars, and restaurants with renowned chefs. Rooms start at US$295/320.

Le Meridien *(☎ 3710101, fax 3714545, e info@lemeridien-newdelhi.com)* is a modern and fairly characterless place on Janpath. Inside is an opulent atrium and the usual five-star facilities, including a health club, are provided. Rooms are less opulent, but they do have good views; they start at US$220/240.

The Ambassador Hotel *(☎ 4632600, fax 4632252, e ambassador.delhi@tajhotels.com, Cornwallis Rd)* is a recently renovated Raj-era place. Rooms start at US$135/145 and there's a 'trying to be trendy' bar.

Five-Star Deluxe A rather luxurious place with business facilities, ***Taj Mahal Hotel*** *(☎ 3026162, fax 3026070, e tmhfo.del@tajhotels.com)* is central yet quiet. Rooms start at US$275/295.

Other Areas

Four-Star Hotels A modern place with good restaurants, ***The Connaught*** *(☎ 336 4225, fax 3340757, e prominent.hotels@gems.vsnl.net.in, 37 Panchkuin Marg)* has a travel agency, 24-hour coffee shop, boutiques and an astropalmist. Rooms cost US$120/130, including breakfast.

Five-Star Hotels A good hotel for business travellers, the very plush Maurya Sheraton Hotel (☎ *6112233, fax 6113333, e maurya@cyber-club.com, Sardar Patel Marg)* has a whole eight floors designed to cater to every good businessperson's whim. It also has a few renowned restaurants, the usual bar, nightclub, swimming pool etc, and the not so usual Internet cafe and indoor golf. Rooms start at Rs 7000/7500.

Five-Star Deluxe Large and modern, ***Hotel Inter-Continental*** *(☎ 3320101, fax 3325335, e newdelhi@interconti.com, Barakhamba Ave)* has a marbled foyer combining Indian and colonial styles. With all you would expect, including a 3rd-floor outdoor swimming pool and business lounges (with one catering specifically to legal executives), rooms start at US$220/245 – nonsmoking rooms are available.

The Metropolitan Hotel Nikko *(☎ 334 2000, fax 3343000, e reservations@hotelnikkodelhi.com)* is a swish new place, with some good dining options and a more intimate feel than some of its competitors. Rooms start at US$210/240, which includes perks such as a welcome drink, mineral water, use of the health spa and a special souvenir on departure. Executive rooms, at US$330/360, also include transfers, access to an exclusive lounge and use of a car, butler and boardroom, plus more. Nonsmoking rooms are available.

PLACES TO EAT

Delhi has an excellent array of places in which to eat – from *dhabas* (snack bars), with dishes from Rs 15, to top-of-the-range restaurants where a meal for two can easily top Rs 3500.

Connaught Place

There are many fast food places – Western and Indian – around Connaught Place. Here you will find ***McDonald's*** along with ***Wimpy***, ***Kwality***, ***Pizza Hut*** *(☎ 3738626)* and ***Dominoes Pizza*** *(☎ 1600-111123)*. ***Nirula's*** *(☎ 331 6694)*, a Delhi-based chain, is very good and has Indian, burgers, pizzas and ice cream (the best in Delhi, and you can try before you buy). The advantage of this area is that the establishments are clean and they serve good food at reasonable prices. However, most have nowhere to sit – it's stand, eat and run. More upmarket chains such as ***TGI Friday's*** and ***Pizza Express*** are also appearing.

Cafe 100 *(B-Block, Connaught Place)* is a very popular semi self-service place that's giving Nirula's a run for its money. There are Indian snacks, burgers, a wide range of ice creams and an excellent buffet upstairs (open from noon to 3 pm and 7 to 11 pm).

There are ***dhabas*** opposite L-Block on the Outer Circle, above Palika Bazaar and near Ringo Guest House. ***Nizam Katri Kabab*** in H-Block is the place to head if you fancy a quick meat-on-a-stick fix.

Berco's is one of Delhi's most popular places serving Chinese and Japanese for about Rs 150 per dish. Don't be surprised if you have to queue.

DV8 *(☎ 3361444)* on the corner of Connaught Circus and Sansad Marg is a place that keeps re-creating itself to attract the 'in-crowd'. The scene of Delhi's first disco (now closed) back in the 1960s, today it is a welcoming place to chill out while enjoying a drink or some pretty good fusion food. Upstairs you have the opportunity for fine dining, while downstairs the mood is more relaxed with leather couches, a library and pool table (Rs 125 per 30 minutes). The menu, with a large and varied choice, is the same in both and a meal for two will cost around Rs 800. If that's beyond your budget, but you can afford Rs 70/150 for a coffee/pitcher of beer, take the time to linger and enjoy some cool tunes while reading the paper. It's open from 11 am until late and sometimes has live music (cover charge).

Rodeo *(A-Block, Connaught Place)* is a lively restaurant serving good Tex-Mex and Indian food; it's worth visiting just for the sight of waiters in cowboy suits. Dinner for two will set you back about Rs 400. After 8.30 pm a Rs 175 cover charge is applied, unless you are dining, and there's a singing and organ-playing duo to entertain. It has cocktails and Mexican beers.

Gaylord *(Connaught Circus)* is one of the priciest, plushest restaurants on Connaught Place, with big mirrors, chandeliers and excellent Indian food. Main dishes are around Rs 200, but the high quality of the ingredients makes this a worthwhile splurge.

Parikrama *(Kasturba Gandhi Marg)*, a revolving restaurant, is an interesting place to eat. Unlike many places of this ilk, where the 1st-class views are supposed to distract you from decidedly 2nd-class food, the fare here is excellent but pricey. Main dishes are around Rs 150. It's open daily for lunch and dinner, and for drinks from 3 to 7 pm.

The Embassy *(D-Block, Connaught Place)* has excellent veg and nonveg food. It's popular among office workers; meals for two cost about Rs 350.

Kovil *(E-Block)* is one of the best places for South Indian vegetarian food, costing about Rs 150 per person.

Coconut Grove in ITDC Hotel Indraprastha is good for more of a splurge – don't be put off by the hotel's rather depressing institutionalised appearance.

Vega, at the Hotel Alka, specialises in vegetarian food cooked Delhi style (in pure ghee but without onion and garlic) for about Rs 200 per person.

United Coffee House *(E-Block, Connaught Place)* is quite plush with a pleasantly relaxed atmosphere, good food and some of the best coffee in Delhi for about Rs 100.

The Host *(F-Block, Connaught Place)* serves excellent Indian and Chinese food. It's extremely popular with well-heeled Indians, but it isn't cheap.

Keventers on the corner of Connaught Place and Radial Rd No 3 is a small milk bar around the corner from AmEx that has good fresh milk.

Wenger's *(A-Block, Connaught Place)* is a cake shop with a range of little cakes that management will put in a cardboard box and tie up with a bow so you can self-consciously carry them back to your hotel room for private consumption.

Paharganj

There is a whole band of similarly styled restaurants catering to the hungry traveller along Main Bazaar. The menus are a fairly standard mix of Indian, Chinese and continental fare with the odd Israeli, Japanese and Korean specialty thrown in. Service is conducive to lingering and you can eat pretty well for around Rs 50 to 100. Some places will even serve beer if you're discreet about it. Most travellers' cafes have a subsidiary service such as a travel agency, bookshop, clothing shop or baggage store attached.

Diamond Cafe and ***Grand Sindh Cafe*** have cassettes and CDs for sale – great places to relax and sip coffee while picking out some souvenir tunes.

Khosla Cafe and ***Madan Cafe*** on Main Bazaar have pavement seating, which can be either pleasant or a nightmare depending on the time of day you're there. Sitting in the mid-morning or late afternoon you're going to be pestered by beggars, hawkers, dogs and who knows what else.

If you want the fresh air but without the hassle try ***Satyam*** next to Hotel Payal, which has a rooftop terrace overlooking the vegetable market.

The place for South Indian food is ***Sonu Chat House*** – it's very popular with locals but also caters to travellers' tastes with banana chocolate dosas.

Appetite German Bakery, next to Hotel Vishal, has a small selection of tempting cakes accompanied by new age music, chess and a small library.

Gem Restaurant is a new, and therefore clean, place with fluorescent lighting and large 1st-floor windows – goldfish would feel at home here.

Golden Cafe at Nehru Bazaar offers a change of scene with some outside seating, and dishes that include Korean specialties.

If you want a really good feed and don't mind paying a few rupees more than normal, ***Malhotra Restaurant***, behind the Metropolis Tourist Home, is the place to go. Popular with tourists and locals alike, it rarely disappoints.

Those in need of a vitamin C burst should stop at one of the ***juice shops*** dotted around; those close to Diamond Cafe are popular.

Many guesthouses and hotels have their own restaurants, some of which are on rooftop terraces (see Places to Stay for details). There are alcohol shops on Desh Bandhu Gupta Rd and at Gole Market.

Old Delhi

The ***ISBT Workers' Canteen***, in the Kashmiri Gate Inter State Bus Terminal, has good food at reasonable prices.

Karim's, down a lane across from the south gate of the Jama Masjid, is very well known among Delhi-wallahs for its excellent nonveg food. In this large restaurant there's everything from kebabs to the richest Mughlai dishes, and prices are reasonable.

Moti Mahal Restaurant *(Netaji Subhash Marg, Daryaganj)* is a licensed open-air place with live qawwali (devotional chants). It's particularly noted for its tandoori dishes.

Chor Bizarre in the Hotel Broadway serves tasty Kashmiri and Indian fare in quirky surrounds. Bizarre features include a vintage car, still in working condition, that serves as a salad bar, and for those planning a romantic liaison, there's a four-poster bed table. The menu makes great reading and not just for the excellent dishes; it recommends you go for a *thali* (meal), which gives you a good range of tasty dishes for Rs 225/295 for veg/nonveg). If you can get eight people together, take advantage of the Kashmiri feast eaten on the floor around a large platter (Rs 585 each).

Ghantewala *(Chandni Chowk)*, near the Sisganj Gurdwara, is reputed to have some of the best Indian sweets in Delhi. The ***stalls*** along the road in front of the Jama Masjid are very cheap.

New Delhi

There are some good eating options in the area south of Connaught Place, but you'll need a taxi or transport to get to most of them.

At Pandara Market, which is a shopping centre near Bikaner House, are some good-value mid-range places such as ***Ichiban***, ***Pindi*** and ***Chicken Inn***, plus several others popular with middle-class Delhiites. They all cost around Rs 300 to 400 for two.

Khan Market also has some good restaurants, including ***China Garden*** and ***China Fare***, for a little less than the Pandara Market places.

At Sunder Nagar Market, ***Sweets Corner*** has tasty pure veg food, including South Indian, and has outdoor seating. Next door, ***Nathu*** has more of a fast-food slant.

Dilli Haat *(Aurobindo Marg)*, opposite the INA Market, is a great place to sample food from all over India – many of the stalls devoted to particular states have restaurants, and for around Rs 50 per person they offer cheap value. This may be your one chance to try Naga or Mizo food (from the north-eastern region). There is a Rs 7 entry fee.

There are lots of restaurants in Hauz Khas Village, nearly all of them mid-range places that charge around Rs 250 per person. The licensed ***Bistro Restaurant Complex*** includes the ***Kowloon*** (Chinese restaurant), ***Mohalla*** (curries in gravy) and ***The Roof-top*** (Indian barbecue plus live music and dance) and is very popular. ***Park Baluchi***, within the nearby Deep Park, specialises in Afghan cuisine such as tandoori chicken wrapped around a sword.

Tamura, at the NDMC swimming pool in Nehru Park, is a licensed Japanese restaurant where most customers are Japanese. It has Japanese newspapers and the Japanese equivalent of thali; a meal for two should cost around Rs 700.

Basil & Thyme *(Chanakyapuri)*, in the nearby swish Santushti Shopping Centre, has good continental food and excellent service. Meals for two cost about Rs 500 and it opens for lunch Monday to Saturday only.

Karol Bagh has some good choices for hungry shoppers or bikies. ***Dasaprakash South Indian*** does a good selection of dosas for around Rs 80 per person in clean and modern surrounds.

Mughal Hans Restaurant, opposite, is good for a more diverse range of dishes.

International Hotels

Many Delhi residents reckon the best food is at the major hotels.

The restaurants at The Claridges are very good value and they're interesting places to eat. ***Dhaba*** offers 'rugged roadside' cuisine, and is set up like a typical roadside cafe; ***Jade Garden*** serves Chinese food in a bamboo-grove setting; Pickwicks offers Western food, and the decor is 19th-century England; while outdoor ***Corbetts*** gets its inspiration from Jim Corbett of tiger hunting fame, complete with recorded jungle sounds. As might be expected, meat features prominently on the menu. All these restaurants are moderately priced – most main dishes cost under Rs 200.

Hotel Inter-Continental has a range of restaurants, including the Indian ***Baluchi***, offering a biryani buffet on Sunday for Rs 500 (including beer), and the ***Blue Elephant*** on the rooftop, with Thai buffet lunches on Wednesday, Thursday and Sunday for Rs 550 (including wine and soft drinks).

At Hyatt Regency, ***Delhi Ka Angan*** specialises in very rich Punjabi and Mughlai food. ***La Piazza*** has Italian food and possibly Delhi's best Italian wine list. ***TK's*** has Japanese and Mongolian buffet lunches. All places charge about Rs 1000 for two.

The Imperial is a great place for an alfresco breakfast in the pleasant garden. ***Spice Route*** offers mainly spicy Thai and Keralan dishes; it's very popular and very expensive (Rs 1800 for two). The decor includes a 'wealth section' with 24 carat gold leaves on the walls. At the ***Tavern Restaurant*** main dishes cost around Rs 200. Prices at the less formal ***Garden Party*** are 10% lower.

One of the best restaurants in the city is ***Bukhara*** at Maurya Sheraton . It has many Central Asian specialities, including tandoori cooking and dishes from the Peshawar region in north-west Pakistan. The dhal here is so popular they have started selling it in cans for Rs 150. Also at Maurya ***Bali Hi*** is a Chinese restaurant, and ***West View*** a European one. All three restaurants cost around Rs 1000 per person. Another restaurant here is the ***Dum Pukht***, named after the cuisine championed by the nawabs of Avadh (Lucknow) around 300 years ago. The dishes are covered by a pastry cap while cooking, so the food is steamed as much as anything else. It's quite distinctive and absolutely superb, and is a little cheaper than the others at Rs 1200 for two.

Metropolitan Hotel Nikko's ***Sakura Japanese restaurant*** uses ingredients from Japan and has a 24-hour patio with fresh international fare.

Probably the best Thai restaurant in Delhi is ***Baan Thai*** at the Oberoi. Count on Rs 1100 for two; weekday lunch buffets cost Rs 550 and Mongolian barbeques start at Rs 475. It also offers the choice of dining by the pool.

Las Meninas at the Park is India's first Spanish restaurant. Dinner for one/two will cost around Rs 850/1200. Las Meninas is only open for dinner.

ENTERTAINMENT

Bars & Nightclubs

Most bars and discos are at the five-star hotels and are wildly expensive. The discos especially are quite exclusive and entry is usually restricted to members and hotel guests; couples and women stand a better chance of being admitted than unaccompanied men. Once inside, you'll find the music is invariably a blend of European and Indian pop. Frequented by the Indian middle and upper classes these nightclubs offer some good opportunities to meet young Indian professionals.

Alcohol is served in some restaurants (which usually have no problem with you drinking only) and the more expensive hotel bars; pretty pricey to start with it's then taxed another 30% – expect to pay between Rs 60 and Rs 200 for a beer before tax. Fortunately, many places have happy hours, which are mainly from mid-afternoon to early evening. You don't have to worry too much about completely breaking the bank, though, as most places stop the alcohol flowing at 10.30 pm, curtailing serious drinking sessions. Drinking in public places is prohibited.

There are a few options for a beer in Paharganj. Some backpacker restaurants will serve you beer in a teacup if you're discreet about it, otherwise ***Hotel Gold Regency*** is very sociable. Its licensed restaurant has a bit of a beer hall feel and is usually full of Indians and foreigners in equal numbers, swapping info and stories and no doubt a few dodgy deals. It also has a bar area, which sometimes doubles as a dance and gay venue, although it's had problems with Russian prostitutes in the past. Buy two beers or one whisky and get one free until 10 pm.

In Connaught Place, ***The Blues Bar***, ***DV8***, ***Pizza Express*** and ***Rodeo*** are good for drinks while listening to live or recorded music, although the latter applies a Rs 175 cover charge after 8.30 pm if you're not dining (see also Places to Eat earlier). ***Pegasus*** bar at Nirula's tries hard to re-create an English pub, but doesn't quite pull it off. There are also plenty of other restaurants to choose from; look for the happy hours or drink offers in their windows.

Most trendy drinking action takes place in south Delhi. The ***Top of the Village*** in the Village Bistro Complex in Hauz Khas village and ***Mezz*** at 17 Community Centre in New Friends Colony are popular.

If you feel like a bit of a sing-song, ***Ruby Tuesday's*** has karaoke on a Tuesday night. It also has stuff for kids on a Sunday lunch time and a ventriloquist and magician the same evening for adults. It's a licensed restaurant that serves up burgers, grills, baked spuds and salads and attracts a wacky, fun-seeking crowd.

Cinemas

In 2000, following some tragic cinema fires, Delhi police reported that only six of all Delhi cinemas were safe, however they wouldn't name which these were.

If you're willing to risk it, a number of cinemas around Connaught Place screen typically Hindi mass-appeal movies; seats range from Rs 25 to 50. Bookings are required for popular movies, sometimes up to a week in advance.

Delhi's better cinemas are mostly in the southern suburbs, and they include the ***PVR Priya Cinema*** *(☎ 6140048)*, at 61 Basant Lok, Vasant Vihar, ***PVR Anupam 4*** *(☎ 6865999)*, in the Saket Community Centre, Saket, and the ***Satyam Cineplex*** *(☎ 5797387)*, Patel Nagar on Patel Road, west of Karol Bagh. These cinemas show the Hollywood blockbusters that are tame enough to sneak past the Indian censors. However, they are usually jointly billed with Hindi flicks.

GREG ELMS

The Indian movie industry is the most prolific in the world.

For something a little more cerebral, the ***British Council*** *(☎ 3710111),* on Kasturba Gandhi Marg, often screen foreign films as do other cultural institutes. Habitat World also has a cinema featuring Indian documentaries and art-house films.

Cultural Programs

Delhi is renowned for its dance and visual arts scene. Each month there are debates, plays, exhibitions, dance and live music. Tickets range from around Rs 50 to 200. Check out the listings guides, such as *First City*, for what's going on.

Major dance and live music venues include the following: ***Habitat World*** *(☎ 4682222)* on Lodi Rd, Web site www.habitatworld.com; ***India International Centre*** *(☎ 4619431)* near Habitat World; ***Kamani Auditorium*** *(☎ 3388084)* Copernicus Marg, near Rabindra Bhavan; and ***Triveni Chamber Theatre*** *(☎ 3718833)* 205 Tansen Marg, at Triveni Kala Sangam, near Rabindra Bhavan.

For over 25 years there have been nightly performances of Dances of India at ***Parsi Anjuman Hall*** *(☎ 6234689)*, near Delhi Gate, at 7 pm. Classical and folk dances, such as Kathakali, Bhangra and Manipuri, are showcased; entry costs Rs 130.

Sound-and-Light Shows

These light-hearted introductions to the history of Delhi take place in the atmospheric surrounds of the Red Fort and Purana Qila (see those individual entries). The shows have the added bonus of offering a reasonable opportunity to get into Red Fort and Purana Qila without paying the inflated day-time tourist prices.

Along the same lines, with illuminations after sunset, is a series of musical fountains. The biggest is in the ***Ajmal Khan Park*** *(☎ 524834)* in Karol Bagh.

SHOPPING

Good buys include silk products, precious stones, leather and woodwork, but the most important thing about Delhi is that you can find almost anything from anywhere in the whole country. If this is your first stop in India, and you intend to buy something while you are here, then it's a chance to compare what is available from all over the country. If this is your last stop and there was something you missed elsewhere in your travels, Delhi provides a chance to find it.

Two good places to start are in New Delhi, near Connaught Place. The Central Cottage Industries Emporium is on Janpath. In this building you will find items from all over India, generally of good quality and reasonably priced. Whether it's woodcarvings, brassware, paintings, clothes, textiles or furniture, you'll find it here. It's open from 10 am to 7 pm Monday to Saturday. Along Baba Kharak Singh Marg, two streets around (clockwise) from Janpath, are the emporiums, run by state governments. Each of them displays and sells handicrafts from their state from 10 am to 6.30 pm Monday to Saturday. There are plenty of touts who will try and convince you that their emporium is run by the government when it isn't – the price of goods will invariably include a fat commission for your guide.

Another good place for India-wide crafts is Delhi Tourism's Dilli Haat. Artisans from different states come here to sell their wares for a fortnight at a time. Open from 11 am to 10 pm daily (Rs 7 entry), it is pleasantly laid out with cheap food stalls specialising in regional cuisines – great for an alfresco lunch or dinner. It also has a small open-air theatre with regular cultural performances.

There are many other shops around Connaught Place, Janpath and Main Bazaar in Paharganj catering largely to foreign tourists, with clothing and arts and crafts from all over India. Connaught Place also has stores catering to middle-class Delhiites and has pavement book stalls. By The Imperial hotel are a number of stalls and small shops run by Tibetan refugees and rapacious Kashmiris selling carpets, jewellery and many (often instant) antiques. These areas have huddles of Rajasthani women selling brightly embroidered and mirrorworked wall hangings and pillowcases. Main Bazaar in Paharganj has household goods and material shops in among the tie-dyed clothes and leather-goods shops. It also has an interesting variety of perfumes, oils, soaps and incense at two places (both signposted), one near Vivek Hotel and another near Camran Lodge. Take advantage of all the free testers. Monday is the official weekly holiday for the shops in Main Bazaar and Connaught Place, and many places are closed on that day, although a surprising number remain open seven days a week.

In recent years Karol Bagh Market, Delhi's largest market, 3km west of Connaught Place along Panchkuin Marg (Radial Rd No 3), has become popular.

In Old Delhi, Chandni Chowk is the city's most famous (and crowded) shopping street. In a series of convoluted back alleys you'll find an array of goods from carpets and jewellery to religious posters and wedding decorations.

Shops in the major international hotels often have high-quality items at equally high prices. If you have a bit of time there are plenty of classy shopping areas where it's possible to dig out a unique craft or antique, although you will still have to pay handsomely for it. The newer suburbs of south Delhi are good for boutiques, furniture shops, Western foods and anything else the trendy set yearns for.

Santushti Shopping Centre in Chanakyapuri has a string of small upmarket boutiques set around a lawn. Run by officers' wives, the centre is within the grounds of Willingdon air force base and is the place to be seen shopping.

North of the Outer Ring Rd, the M-Block Market in Greater Kailash I is one of the

Shopping Spots

While old villages have been swallowed up by urban sprawl, their essence lingers on in the weekly *haat* (market). Traditionally held for the sale of goods such as farming implements and food, today practically every suburb has a haat selling contemporary goods needed by the city dweller. The largest is the Monday haat at Karol Bagh.

There are also many specialised shops and markets dedicated to particular products or trades. Generally concentrated in specific areas, they can be complete marketplaces or a string of shops which create intense competition and low prices.

The following places are open seven days unless otherwise indicated:

market/shop	product
Sunder Nagar (Mon–Sat),	antiques & brassware
Hauz Khas (Mon–Sat)	antiques & brassware
Paharganj	clothing
Nehru Place	computers
Chandni Chowk	decorations
Shankar Market, Paharganj	fabrics
INA Market (Tues–Sun)	food
Panchkuin Rd	furniture
Kaori Baoli	herbs & spices
Chandni Chowk	homeopathic medicine
Sadar Bazaar, Paharganj	household goods
Karol Bagh, Khan Market,	imported goods
Palika Bazaar (Mon–Sat)	imported goods
Chandni Chowk	jewellery
Karol Bagh, Jama Masjid	motor parts
Chandni Chowk	musical instruments
Meena Bazaar	Muslim goods
Jama Masjid, Chor Bazaar (Thieves Market; Sun)	second-hand goods
Karol Bagh, Sadar Bazaar	shoes

biggest upper- and middle-class shopping centres in Delhi. The N-Block Market nearby has a similar collection, including the famous clothing, fabric and furnishings store Fab India (younger Indian parliamentarians are sometimes referred to as the Fab India gang).

GETTING THERE & AWAY

Delhi is a major international gateway to India; for details on arriving from overseas see the introductory Getting There & Away chapter. At certain times of the year international flights out of Delhi can be heavily booked so it's wise to make reservations as early as possible. This particularly applies to some of the heavily discounted airlines operating out of Europe – check and double-check your reservations and make sure you reconfirm your flight.

Delhi is also a major centre for domestic travel, with extensive bus, train and air connections. Delhi airport is prone to fog in 'the cool' – December and January – and during these months flights in and out can be severely delayed.

Air

The domestic terminals (Terminals IA and IB of the Indira Gandhi International Airport) are 12km from the centre, and the international terminal (Terminal II) is a farther 5km. There's a free IAAI bus between the two terminals every 20 minutes, or you can use the Ex-Servicemen's Air Link Transport Service (EATS; see Getting Around later in this chapter).

If you're arriving at the airport from overseas, there's 24-hour State Bank of

Domestic Flights from Delhi

destination	duration (hrs)	airline	freq	fare (US$)
Ahmedabad	1¼	IC	2d	135
		9W	1d	
Amritsar	1	IC	5w	100
Bagdogra	1½	IC	3w	185
		9W	1d	
Bangalore	2½	S2	2d	255
		IC	3d	
Bhopal	½	CD	1d	120
Chandigarh	¾	CD	2w	75
		9W	1d	
Chennai	2½	S2	1d	260
	1½	IC	2d	
Dehra Dun	1	IC	3w	100
Dharamsala	1½	IC	3w	145
Dibrugarh	3½	S2	1d	254
Guwahati	3¼	S2	1d	210
	2¼	IC	1d	
		9W	1d	
Gwalior	¾	IC	5w	70
Imphal	3¾	IC	2w	240
Indore	2¼	CD	1d	135
		9W	1d	
Jaipur	¾	CD	1d	55
		9W	1d	
Jodhpur	1½	CD	1d	105
Kolkata	3½	S2	4w	200
	2	IC	3d	

destination	duration (hrs)	airline	freq	fare (US$)
Kullu	1¾	IC	3w	145
Leh	1¼	CD	4w	105
Lucknow	1	S2	1d	90
		IC	17w	
		9W	1d	
Mumbai	2	S2	2d	175
		IC	7d	
		CD	5w	
		9W	8d	131
Patna	1½	S2	1d	145
	2¼	IC	2d	
Shimla	1	IC	3w	110
Udaipur	3	CD	1d	105
		9W	1d	
Varanasi	2½	S2	1d	125
		IC	1d	
		9W	1d	

Airline codes:

CD	Alliance Air (Indian Airlines)
IC	Indian Airlines
S2	Sahara Airlines
9W	Jet Airways

Frequency abbreviations:

d	daily
w	weekly

India and Thomas Cook foreign-exchange counters in the arrivals hall, after customs and immigration. Once you've left the arrivals hall you won't be allowed back in.

Several airlines now require you to have the baggage you're checking in X-rayed and sealed; do this at the machines just inside the departure hall before you queue to check in. Nearly all airline tickets include the departure tax in the price; if not included, you must pay at the State Bank counter in the departures hall, also before check-in.

Facilities at the international terminal include a snack bar, bookshop and banks. Once inside the departure lounge there are a few duty-free shops with the usual inflated prices, and another snack bar where you have the privilege of paying in US dollars.

Indian Airlines The Malhotra Building office (☎ 3310517), in F-Block, Connaught Place, is probably the most convenient of the Indian Airline offices, although it is busy at most times. It's open 10 am to 5 pm daily except Sunday.

There's another office in the PTI Building (☎ 3719168) on Sansad Marg in New Delhi, open 10 am to 5 pm daily except Sunday.

At Safdarjang airfield on Aurobindo Marg there's a 24-hour office (☎ 141), which can be a quick place to make bookings.

Business-class passengers can check in by telephone on ☎ 5665166. Prerecorded flight departure information is available on ☎ 142.

Indian Airlines flights depart from Delhi to all the major Indian centres – see the table 'Domestic Flights from Delhi'. Check-in at the airport is 1¼ hours before departure. Note that if you have just arrived and have an onward connection to another city in India, it may be with Air India, the country's international carrier, rather than the domestic carrier, Indian Airlines. If that is the case, you must check in at the international terminal (Terminal II) rather than the domestic terminal.

Other Domestic Airlines As well as the offices listed following, private airlines have offices at the airport's domestic terminal:

Archana Airways (☎ 6842001, 5665768) 41A Friends Colony East, Mathura Rd
Jagson Airlines (☎ 3721594) 12E Vandana Bldg, 11 Tolstoy Marg
Jet Airways (☎ 6853700) 40 N-Block, Connaught Circus
Sahara Airlines (☎ 3326851) Ambadeep Bldg, Kasturba Gandhi Marg

International Airlines Offices for many international airlines can be found in Delhi, these include:

Aeroflot (☎ 3312843) BMC House, 1st floor, 1 N-Block, Connaught Place
Air Canada (☎ 3720014) ALPs Bldg, 56 Janpath
Air France (☎ 3738004) 7 Atma Ram Mansion, Connaught Circus
Air India (☎ 3311225) 2nd floor, Jeevan Bharati Bldg, Sansad Marg
Asiana Airlines (☎ 3315631) Ansal Bhavan, 16 Kasturba Gandhi Marg
Biman Bangladesh Airlines (☎ 3354401) World Trade Centre, Babar Rd, Connaught Place
British Airways (☎ 5652077) 11th floor, Gopal Das Bhawan, Barakhamba Rd
Delta Airlines (☎ 3325222) Chandralok Bldg, 36 Janpath
Druk Air (☎ 3310990) Chandralok Bldg, 36 Janpath
El Al Israel Airlines (☎ 3357965) Prakash Deep Bldg, 7 Tolstoy Marg
Emirates (☎ 3324665) Kanchenjunga Bldg, 18 Barakhamba Rd
Ethiopian Airlines (☎ 3312302) Ansal Bhavan, 16 Kasturba Gandhi Marg
Gulf Air (☎ 3324922) 12 G-Block, Connaught Circus
Iran Air (☎ 6889123) Ashok Hotel, Chanakyapuri
Japan Airlines (☎ 3324922) Chandralok Bldg, 36 Janpath
Kazakhstan Airlines (☎ 3367889) ITDC Hotel Janpath
KLM-Royal Dutch Airlines (☎ 3721141) Prakash Deep Bldg, 7 Tolstoy Marg
Kuwait Airways (☎ 3359711) Ansal Bhavan, 16 Kasturba Gandhi Marg
Lufthansa Airlines (☎ 3323310) 56 Janpath
Malaysia Airlines (☎ 3324308) G-55 Connaught Place
Northwest Airlines (☎ 3721141) Prakash Deep Bldg, 7 Tolstoy Marg
Pakistan International Airlines (PIA; ☎ 3313161) Kailash Bldg, Kasturba Gandhi Marg
Qantas Airways (☎ 3329027) Barakhamba Rd

Royal Jordanian (☎ 3320635) 56 G-Block, Connaught Place
Royal Nepal Airlines Corporation (RNAC; ☎ 3321164) 44 Janpath, Connaught Place
Saudi Arabian Airlines (☎ 3310466) DCM Bldg, 16 Barakhamba Rd
Scandinavian Airlines (SAS; ☎ 3352299) Ambadeep Bldg, Kasturba Gandhi Marg
Singapore Airlines (☎ 3329036) Ashoka Estate Bldg, Barakhamba Rd
SriLankan Airlines (☎ 3326843) Room 1, ITDC Hotel Janpath
Swissair (☎ 3325511) DLF Bldg, Sansad Marg
Tarom (☎ 3354422) 22 Kasturba Gandhi Marg
Thai Airways International (☎ 6239988) Park Royal Hotel, America Plaza, Nehru Place
United Airlines (☎ 3353377) Ambadeep Bldg, Kasturba Gandhi Marg
Uzbekistan Airways (☎ 3357939) Prakash Deep Bldg, 7 Tolstoy Marg

Bus

All the main roads leading out of Delhi are heavily congested and more than a little scary. It's best to leave early in the morning. The main bus station is the ISBT at Kashmiri Gate, north of the (Old) Delhi train station. It has 24-hour left-luggage facilities, a State Bank of India branch, post office, pharmacy and restaurant. City buses depart from here to locations all around Delhi. State government bus companies (and the counter they operate from) are:

Delhi Transport Corporation (☎ 3354518) Counter 34
Haryana Roadways (☎ 2961262) Counter 35
Himachal Roadways (☎ 2968694) Counter 40
Punjab Roadways (☎ 2967842) Counter 37
Rajasthan Roadways (☎ 2961246) Central block; bookings can also be made at Bikaner House, south of Rajpath
Uttar Pradesh Roadways (☎ 2968709) Central block

Rajasthan Bikaner House, near India Gate, is the place to head for more comfortable state-operated buses to Rajasthan. Daily buses leave for Ajmer (Rs 269, nine hours, 7, 10 and 11.40 pm), Jaipur (Rs 206/331 deluxe/air-con, six hours, between 6 am and 12.30 am), Jodhpur (Rs 364, 14 hours, 10 pm) and Udaipur (Rs 404, 15 hours, 7 pm). There are more buses from the ISBT to Ajmer (Rs 174) at 11 pm, Jaipur (Rs 113) between 6 am and 5 pm, Jodhpur (Rs 364) and Udaipur (Rs 404) at 6.15 pm.

North of Delhi For Himalayan destinations it's a much better option to take a train as far as Pathankot or Shimla then transfer to a bus. Should you prefer to take the bus the whole way you can opt for the public buses that leave the ISBT or a private bus from Paharganj or Connaught Place. The public buses are generally run by the state that your destination is in.

Private buses usually leave in the evening. Prices fluctuate according to the season and price wars; the fares given in our bus tables are the average cost.

South of Delhi From the Sarai Kale Khan ISBT (☎ 4643259), close to Nizamuddin train station, there are frequent departures for Agra (Rs 75 to 100 depending on class, five hours), Mathura and Gwalior. It's generally quicker to go by train to all these places, though. There's a city bus link between this station and Kashmiri Gate ISBT.

Nepal Private buses travelling Kathmandu (Rs 800) leave at 1.30 pm Monday and

Private Buses

destination	fare (Rs)
Agra (tour coach)	200
Ajmer (for Pushkar)	250
Amritsar	250
Dehra Dun	200/300*
Dharamsala	300
Haridwar	200/300*
Jaipur	200
Jodhpur	250
Manali	300
Mussoorie	200/300*
Nainital	200/300*
Rishikesh	200/300*
Shimla	350
Udaipur	275

* ordinary/air-con

Public Buses

destination	duration (hrs)	departures	fare (Rs)
Amritsar	11	6.30 pm	430
Chandigarh	5	half-hourly	205/215 *
Dehra Dun	7	7.15 am–9.30 pm ◆	120/163 *
Dharamsala	13	6.30 am–11 pm	240/340 *
Haridwar	6	5.45 am–5 pm ◆	95/129 *
Kullu	13	6.40 am–8 pm ◆	266/452 *
Manali	16	11.30 am–10.15 pm ◆	322
Mandi	16	5.40 am	222
McLeod Ganj	14	5.30 pm	246
Rekong Peo	20	8 pm	351
Rishikesh	7	8 am; 8–10 pm	96/108 *
Shimla	10	5 am–10 pm	182/360 *

* ordinary/deluxe ◆ six departures

Thursday, arriving around 6 or 7 am two days later. The journey requires a six-hour wait at the border, where you must change buses. Most travellers seem to find that it is a lot more comfortable and is better value to do the trip by train to Gorakhpur (Uttar Pradesh), and then to take buses from there.

Buses to the northern Uttar Pradesh village of Banbassa (for the border with Nepali) leave Delhi's Anand Vihar bus stand hourly from 7 am to 9 pm (Rs 138, 10 hours). There are daily buses to this village from New Delhi. See the Uttar Pradesh & Uttaranchal chapter for more details.

Train

Delhi is an important rail centre and an excellent place to make bookings. The best place is the special foreign tourist booking office upstairs in New Delhi train station, open from 7.30 am to 5 pm Monday to Saturday and 8 am to 2 pm Sunday. Ignore the touts lurking around the station who may try to lead you astray. This is the place to go if you want a tourist-quota allocation, are the holder of an Indrail Pass or want to buy an Indrail Pass. The office gets very busy, and it can take up to an hour to be served. If you make bookings here tickets must be paid for in rupees backed up by bank exchange certificates, or in US dollars and pounds sterling with any change given in rupees.

Other foreigner reservation offices include one at the airport (open 24 hours) and another at the Delhi Tourism Corporation in N-Block, Connaught Place (open from 7.30 am to 5 pm Monday to Saturday).

The main ticket office is on Chelmsford Rd, between New Delhi train station and Connaught Place. This place is well organised, but can get chaotic – the women-only queues are much shorter.

It's best to arrive first thing in the morning, or when all counters reopen after lunch. The office is open from 8 am to 8 pm Monday to Saturday and 8 am to 2pm Sunday.

Remember that there are two main stations in Delhi – Delhi train station in Old Delhi, and New Delhi train station at Paharganj. New Delhi is much closer to Connaught Place; if you're departing from the Old Delhi train station you should allow adequate time (up to an hour in peak times) to wind your way through Old Delhi's traffic snarls. Between the Old Delhi and New Delhi stations you can take the No 6 bus. At New Delhi station, reservations can be made between 2 hours and 45 minutes before train departure from the less crowded current reservations office to the right of the main entrance.

There's also the Nizamuddin train station south of the New Delhi area, where some trains start or finish. It's worth getting off here if you are staying in Chanakyapuri or anywhere else south of Connaught Place.

Kicking the Habit

During the 1990s the number of vehicles whizzing around Delhi's roads tripled. Their uncontrolled emissions, together with foul smoke belching forth from factories, were poisoning the air. Vehicles standing at traffic intersections, carbon monoxide pouring from exhaust pipes bearing stickers that read 'Pollution Under Control', contributed to emissions as high as 5000mg per cubic metre – 50 times the World Health Organization (WHO) standard. On windless days a dark veil hung over the city.

In 1997 Delhi council took the dramatic step of banning smoking in public places. Given that simply to breathe Delhi's foul air was equivalent to smoking 20 cigarettes a day (40 a day in traffic) it seemed a small step. Pressure to improve on this, including a supreme court directive to clean up Delhi, led to on-the-spot fines for littering and spitting, the banning of commercial vehicles over eight years old, the conversion of all taxis to gas instead of diesel, improvements in public transport and the banning of trucks from the city during peak hours (24 hours in Connaught Place). Proposals for further improvements, such as moving all industry to outside the city limits (helping the Yamuna River, which is estimated to receive more than two billion litres of waste per day), continue to be acted upon.

At the same time many slums are being bulldozed, one has to wonder where the current 320,000 slum dwellers are going to live, especially as Delhi's homeless already numbers 23,000.

While there has been a noticeable improvement, Delhi remains heavily polluted, especially during the humid summer months, and you're still likely to be on a pack a day. If you're asthmatic don't stay too long.

Some trains between Delhi and Jaipur, Jodhpur and Udaipur operate to and from Sarai Rohilla train station rather than Old Delhi – it's about 3.5km north-west of Connaught Place on Guru Govind Singh Marg.

There are inquiries counters at the train stations, but it's much easier to telephone for the latest train information:

General inquiries	☎ 131
Northern departures	☎ 1336
Eastern departures	☎ 1337
Western departures	☎ 1338
Southern departures	☎ 1339
Reservation status	☎ 1335

GETTING AROUND

Delhi is large and congested, and the buses get hopelessly crowded. The alternative is a taxi, an autorickshaw or, for the truly brave, a bicycle. At the time of research, the first phase of construction of a metro system had commenced; the system is due for completion in 2005.

To/From the Airport

Although there are a number of options, airport-to-city transport is not as straightforward as it should be due to predatory taxi and autorickshaw drivers who target unwary first-time visitors.

Bus The Ex-Servicemen's Air Link Transport Service (EATS; ☎ 3316530) has a regular bus service between the airport (both terminals) and its office near Indian Airlines in F-Block, Connaught Place, between 4 am and 11 pm. The fare is Rs 50 plus Rs 5 per large piece of luggage, and it will drop you off at most of the major hotels, and the Ajmeri Gate entrance to New Delhi train station (for Paharganj) en route.

When leaving the international terminal, the counter for the EATS bus is just to the right as you exit the building. This is probably the best, although not the quickest, way into the city if you arrive late at night (see the boxed text 'Dodgy Delhi' earlier in this chapter).

Taxi What you want from the airport is not just a prepaid taxi, but the right prepaid taxi. Look for the Delhi Traffic Police Prepaid Taxi Booth outside the terminal entrance, where you'll get the lowest prices (Rs 170 to Paharganj). The others will try for much more. You will be given a voucher that you should give to the driver at your destination.

At the domestic terminal, the taxi booking desk is just inside the terminal and charges Rs 120 to Paharganj, plus Rs 5 per bag. The taxi-wallahs outside will try for much more.

Most accommodation and travel agencies can also arrange airport pick-ups and drop-offs although they charge a minimum of Rs 200 for the service. If you need to get to the airport in the early hours of the morning, arrange this the day before – get a receipt and ensure you know exactly where your pick-up point is.

Bus

Avoid buses during rush hour. Whenever possible try to board (and leave) at a starting or finishing point, such as the Regal and Plaza Cinemas in Connaught Place, as there is more chance of a seat. There are some seats reserved for women on the left-hand side of the bus. The Delhi Transport Corporation runs some buses, others are privately owned, but all operate along the same set routes. Western embassies generally advise their staff not to take buses; the White Line and Green Line buses are slightly more expensive and are thus a little less crowded. Private buses and minibuses also run on these routes. A short bus ride

Major Trains from Delhi

destination	train No & name	departures	distance (km)	approx duration (hrs)	fare (Rs) (2nd/1st)
Agra	2180 *Taj Exp*	7.15 am HN	199	2½	53/279
	2002 *Shatabdi Exp*	6 am ND		2	390/760 *
Ajmer	2015 *Shatabdi Exp*	6.15 am ND		4½	630/1250 *
Amritsar	2013 *Shatabdi Exp*	4.30 pm ND	447	5½	610/1220 *
Bangalore	2430 *Rajdhani Exp*	8.50 pm HN	2444	34	2205/3470/6385 ◆
	2628 *Karnataka Exp*	9.15 pm ND	2434	41	278/1659
Bhopal	*Shatabdi Exp*	6.15 am ND		8	850/1800 *
Chandigarh	2011 *Shatabdi Exp*	7.40 am		3¼	435/8651
Chennai	2434 *Rajdhani Exp*	3.30 pm HN	2194	28	2045/3335/5965 ◆
	2622 *Tamil Nadu Exp*	10.30 pm ND		33	1524/2664
Haridwar	2017 *Shatabdi Exp*	7 am ND	320	4½	60/910 *
Jaipur	2413 *Delhi Jaipur Intercity Exp*	5.15 am OD	308	5¾	77/405
	2015 *Shatabdi Exp*	6.15 am ND		4½	495/985 *
Kolkata	2302 *Rajdhani Exp*	5.15 pm ND	1441	17½	1500/2470/4270 ◆
	2304 *Poorva Exp*	4.15 pm ND		24	213/1119
Lucknow	4230 *Lucknow Mail*	2.20 pm ND	487	17½	105/552
	2004 *Shatabdi Exp*	6.20 am ND		6	
640/1320	*				
Mumbai	2952 *Rajdhani Exp*	4 pm ND	1388	16½	485/2405/4180 ◆
	2926 *Paschim Exp*	4.30 pm ND		23	210/1103
Patna	2310 *Rajdhani Exp*	5 pm	992	12½	1230/1885/3605 ◆
Shimla	4095 *Himalayan Queen*	6 am ND	364	4	84/441
Udaipur	9615 *Chetak Exp*	8.35 am SR	739	21	145/762
Varanasi	2382 *Poorva Exp*	4.15 pm ND	764	12½	149/783

Abbreviations for train stations: ND – New Delhi, OD – Old Delhi, HN – Hazrat Nizamuddin, SR – Sarai Rohilla

* Air-con chair/air-con executive class (fare includes meals and drinks)

DELHI

(such as Connaught Place to Red Fort) is only about Rs 2.

Useful buses include the following:

Bus No 505 Super Bazaar or Janpath (from opposite The Imperial hotel) to the Qutb Minar
Bus No 101 Kashmiri Gate Inter State Bus Terminal to Connaught Place
Bus Nos 620 & 630 Connaught Place (from outside the Jantar Mantar) to Chanakyapuri
Bus Nos 101, 104 & 139 Regal Cinema bus stand to the Red Fort

Car

Given Delhi's mind-boggling traffic (six road deaths per day on average), it's better to not drive.

If you must rent a self-drive car, try Avis (☎ 4304027, e crs@avisdel.com) in The Oberoi on Dr Zakir Hussain Marg, or Budget (☎ 3354772, e bracindia@hotmail.com) at 82 Janpath and the New Delhi train station (☎ 3232725).

Motorcycle

If you are in the market for a shiny new Enfield motorcycle or anything else bike related, go to Karol Bagh. Try either Madaan Motors (☎ 5735801, fax 5755812, e madaanmotors@yahoo.com) at 1767/53 Naiwala Gali, Har Kishan Das Rd, or Inder Motors (☎ 5728579, fax 5781052, e lalli@ndf.vsnl.net.in), 1740/55 Hari Singh Nalwa St. Both also hire bikes from Rs 200 to 400 per day.

Taxi & Autorickshaw

All taxis and autorickshaws are metered but the meters are invariably out of date, allegedly 'not working' or the drivers will simply refuse to use them.

If you're anywhere near Connaught Place and need an autorickshaw, pick one up from the very useful prepaid booth near Palika Bazaar. Otherwise, you'll need to negotiate a price before you set out and this will always be more than it should be.

At the end of a metered journey you will have to pay according to a perversely complicated scale of revised charges (there are separate charts for recalibrated and unrecalibrated meters). Drivers are supposed to carry conversion cards but if you demand to see one, strangely enough they won't be able to find it. At the time of research the formula to work out metered fares for taxis was to multiply the metered fare by five then add Rs 3.50; for autorickshaws multiply by 2.5 then add Rs 3. The fare charts are printed in the *Delhi City Guide* (Rs 15, available from newsagents). If you have a chart, pay what you think is the right price and leave it at that. Rest assured that no one is going to be out of pocket, except yourself, despite hurt or angry protestations to the contrary.

Rickshaws, both auto- and pedal-powered, navigate Old Delhi's Chandni Chowk.

Connaught Place to the Red Fort should cost around Rs 60 by taxi or Rs 30 by autorickshaw, although the traffic jams can make this a long trip. From Connaught Place to Paharganj should cost about Rs 15 according to the meter system, but Rs 30 seems to be the standard minimum fare for foreigners. About Rs 30 is fair for an autorickshaw from Connaught Place to Humayun's tomb.

From 11 pm to 5 am there is a 20% surcharge for autorickshaws and 25% for taxis.

[Continued on page 251]

ISLAMIC & MUGHAL ARCHITECTURE

The Muslim invaders who poured in from the west changed the face of North India. Their architectural legacy survives to this day, providing some of the top sightseeing attractions the region has to offer – just think of the Red Fort and Jama Masjid in Delhi, the 'ghost city' of Fatehpur Sikri, and of course the jewel of them all, the Taj Mahal in Agra.

The newcomers introduced standard motifs of Islamic architecture, particularly arches, mosaics, geometric patterns, Kufic (Quranic) calligraphic inscriptions, minarets and domes. They quickly learned to combine these innovations with existing characteristics of Indian architecture, such as courtyards, colonnades and extensive ornamentation. The resultant Indo-Islamic architectural style began appearing from around the 13th century, but reached its most distinctive and impressive phase under the Mughals from the 16th to the 18th centuries. The Mughals, in turn, influenced the Rajput architecture found in Rajasthan.

The Muslim architects not only borrowed from Hindu design concepts, they also sometimes borrowed the actual Hindu masonry. Many Hindu temples were destroyed by the invading warriors, and the Muslim builders were sometimes able to salvage materials from these temples to reuse in their new creations. Unfortunately, they occasionally rebuilt their Islamic temples on the actual site of the old Hindu temples. Certain sites are now deemed sacred by both religions, giving rise for much tension and argument to this day. The most famous

KELLI HAMBLET

Inset: The domes of the Jama Masjid silhouetted at sunset. (Photo by Richard I'Anson)

Right: Delhi's Jama Masjid, the largest mosque in India, was built by Shah Jahan, the Mughal emperor who commissioned the Taj Mahal.

example is Ayodhya, one of seven holy Hindu cities. In the 15th century, the Mughals constructed a mosque on what is believed to be the site of Rama's birthplace, and this was torn down by Hindu fundamentalists in 1992. In its place they erected a very crude Hindu shrine. Recently, it has even been suggested that the Taj Mahal was built around a Hindu temple devoted to Shiva (a theory expounded by PN Oak in *Taj Mahal – The True Story*).

Early Indo-Islamic Architecture

From the early 13th century, much of North India was under the control of the Muslim invaders from Turkey and Afghanistan. The pure Islamic style of architecture they initially brought with them was somewhat austere, and largely devoid of the ornamentation that characterised later Islamic design.

The earliest examples of Indo-Islamic architecture are in what is called the Sultanate (or Pathan) styles. They reflect the innovations of Islamic architecture defined through the centralised power of the five Delhi dynasties. Although borrowing heavily from Hindu styles, they usually incorporate arches and minarets. A good example is the Qutb Minar in Delhi, which illustrates three key elements of Islamic design: the pointed arch, the dome and geometric design. The first storey was built in 1210, and two further storeys were added in 1368. The Quwwat-ul-Islam mosque, also in Delhi, was the first mosque built in India (1192), and was built on the site of Delhi's largest temple in order to commemorate the victory of Islam over Hinduism. It uses the square pillars that are usually favoured by Hindu builders.

Regional architects soon experimented with variations on the design conventions established by the Delhi sultanate to come up with the next architectural phase, usually dubbed the provincial style. Gujarat experienced a succession of rulers until the Mughal emperor, Akbar, exerted his authority over the region in 1572, and each of the subsequent Muslim dynasties left its architectural mark. The state has many examples of regional architectural adaptations. In particular, Ahmedabad boasts some impressive mosques from the 15th century, including the unique Jama Masjid (1423), which features 300 Hindu-style pillars, and includes a sanctuary that is based on the characteristic *mandapam* (pillared hall) of Hindu temples.

CHRIS MELLOR

Left: Delhi's Qutb Minar soars 73m skyward.

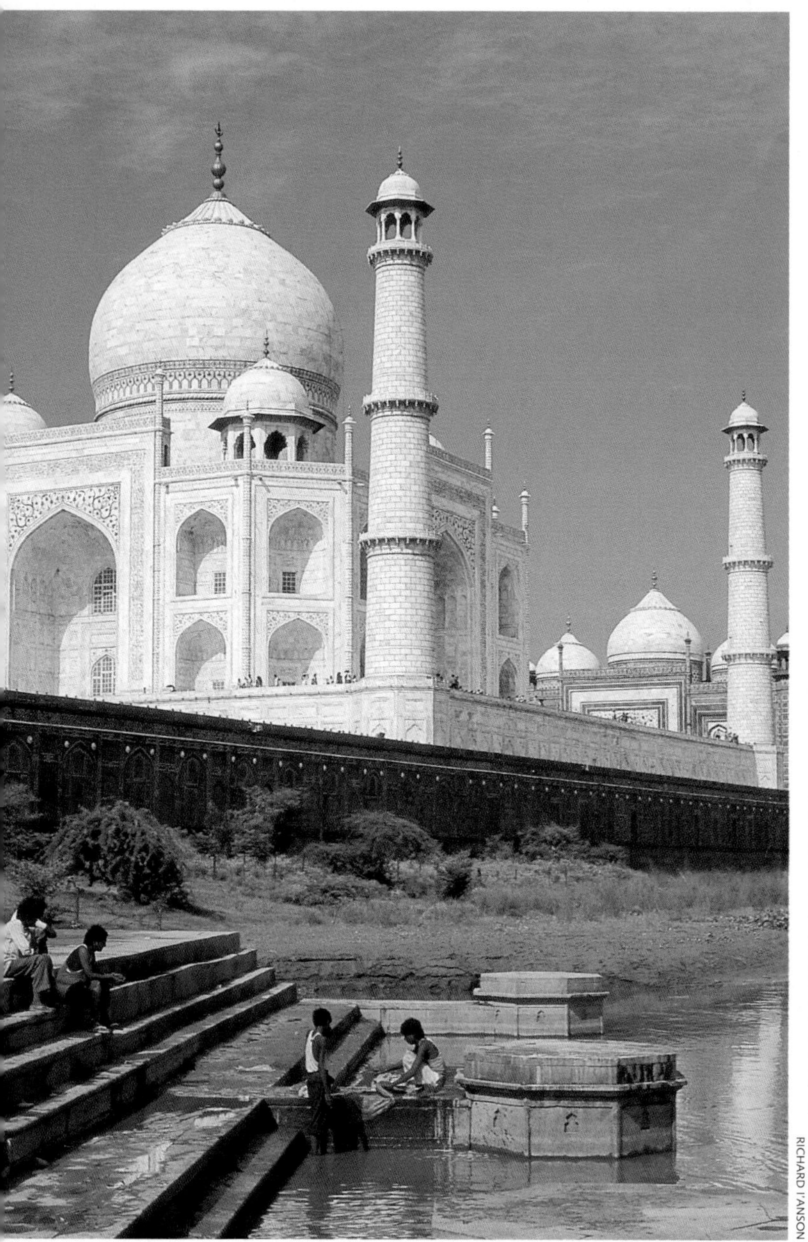

RICHARD I'ANSON

Everyday life continues in the shadow of Agra's Taj Mahal. Craftsmen were brought from as far afield as Venice and Bordeaux to build this astonishing tribute to romantic love. Construction is said to have cost three million rupees, the equivalent of about US$60 million today.

ALL PHOTOGRAPHS BY CHRIS MELLOR

Delhi has many fine examples of Mughal architecture: Humayun's tomb, a model for the Taj (top); Qutb Minar dates from early Muslim rule (centre right); Safdarjang's elegant tomb was built in 1753–54 (bottom right); the Red Fort was the home of emperors then the barracks of British troops (bottom left)

Mughal Architecture

Many of the most impressive structures in North India today are those built by the Mughals. They were simply so much wealthier than any previous rulers and were able to lavish vast sums of money on the finest materials (particularly marble) and could afford to employ the most experienced and talented artisans. Persian, Indian and provincial styles were successfully melded to create works of great refinement and quality.

The Mughals appeared on the scene in 1526 and within a few years ran an empire extending across a large swathe of North India, including almost everything north of a line running from Jodhpur in Rajasthan to Gaur in West Bengal. By 1605 they had added Gujarat and most of Madhya Pradesh and Orissa to their empire.

The Early Mughal Period

During the early Mughal period buildings were made of red sandstone with marble details. Emperor Akbar (r. 1556–1605), grandfather of Shah Jahan, was an avid builder. He created Fatehpur Sikri, a complete, beautifully preserved city of red sandstone. Akbar's mausoleum in Sikandra, near Agra, is an extremely impressive example of the fusion of red standstone and marble, and the design shows clear hints of the style that was to reach its apotheosis in the Taj Mahal.

A characteristic of Mughal tombs is that they were built on high, square platforms. Typically, the platform would be surrounded by a formal Persian-style garden, which was intended to portray the Islamic ideal of the Gardens of Paradise. The style was known as *charbagh*, literally 'four gardens' – the huge courtyard surrounding the tomb was quartered by watercourses, and these quarters were then divided by smaller channels. The tombs themselves had marble domes

RICHARD I'ANSON

Right: A detail of Uttar Pradesh's Fatephur Sikri, the deserted Mughal city that has been carefully preserved.

surrounded by small *chhatris* (umbrella-like structures). Humayun's tomb, built in the mid-16th century, is a superb example of Mughal tomb architecture and one of the finest buildings in Delhi. The garden here is one of the very few to still have its original watercourses intact, although they remain empty most of the time. This style continued into the middle and late periods – the Taj Mahal also has a charbagh garden.

The Middle & Late Periods

During the middle period, much more use was made of marble, and buildings had more bulbous domes and towering minarets. Jama Masjid and Fatehpuri Masjid (both in Delhi) are good examples, but the supreme building from this period is, of course, the Taj Mahal in Agra. The Taj was commissioned by Shah Jahan (r. 1627–58), who has made the most enduring mark on North India's architectural history. The Taj is the tomb for his queen Mumtaz Mahal. Shah Jahan was also responsible for several other fine buildings in Agra, as well as the Red Fort in Delhi.

An essential element of much Mughal architecture is the ornamentation added to the basic structure, and the Taj Mahal is a superb example of this. Close up, the most impressive feature of the Taj is the patterns created by using semiprecious stones inlaid into the marble. The process is known as *pietra dura*, which is a technique used in various other Mughal creations, such as the Itimad-ud-Daulah tomb, also in Agra. Completed in 1622, it was the first Mughal building to make extensive use of pietra dura. In the Taj, 43 different precious stones were used, including amethyst, coral, crystal, jade, lapis lazuli, mother-of-pearl, onyx and turquoise, which were gathered from sources as far away as China, Persia and Russia. Also impressive are the Taj's delicate lattice screens, carved from white marble.

In the late Mughal period the style became over-elaborate and the materials used were inferior as money became scarcer; good examples of this decadent period are the Sunehri Masjid on Chandni Chowk in Old Delhi and Safdarjang's tomb in New Delhi, one of the last notable Mughal buildings.

RICHARD I'ANSON

Left: A detail from the Taj Mahal, in Agra, showing meticulously worked pietra dura, or marble-inlay work.

[Continued from page 246]

If you're on your own at night make a show of writing down the licence plate number before setting off.

You will no doubt be asked if you want to go shopping (the driver will insist that 'just looking' is OK), as drivers get paid (Rs 200 is standard) just for taking foreigners to stores – even if you don't purchase anything. You could arrange with your driver to make a show of looking around a few shops and in return get your sightseeing for free, although the hard-sell tactics at the shops can wear you down. To hire a taxi for eight hours should cost around Rs 450, though the driver will expect a tip (around Rs 100).

Bicycle & Cycle-Rickshaw

Although traffic and pollution are dreadful in Old Delhi and around Connaught Place, the bicycle is one way of getting around the sights to the south, though cyclists are an oppressed caste on Delhi's roads. There are very few places to hire bikes. In Paharganj, there's a small cycle hire shop near Rajguru Rd. Jhandewallan Market in Karol Bagh is India's largest bicycle market, however, with domestic and international bikes and spares for sale.

Cycle-rickshaws are banned from the Connaught Place area and New Delhi itself, but they can be handy for travelling between Connaught Circus and Paharganj, for around Rs 10.

Greater Delhi

JAHANPANAH

Jahanpanah (Refuge of the World) was the fourth city of Delhi, built by Mohammed Shah Tughlaq in the 14th century by enclosing the inhabited but unprotected area between the first two cities of Delhi – Siri to the north and Qila Rai Pithora to the south.

The remains of the city today lie in the village of Begumpur, which has been engulfed by the modern housing developments of the suburb of Panchshila Park South. The easiest access is from a small road which heads east off Aurobindo Marg between the Outer Ring Rd and the Qutb Minar Complex, right next to the Aurobindo Ashram.

Bijai Mandal

The remains of Mohammed Tughlaq's palace, the Bijai Mandal, are impressive, despite being in an advanced state of decay. The whole complex was known as the Thousand-Pillared Palace, the central feature of which was a massive, squat tower built on a high platform. It was from here that Mohammed Shah is said to have reviewed his troops. As there are very few visitors to the site, it's still possible to climb the tower for a great view over southern Delhi.

Adjoining the tower on the platform are the ruins of Mohammed Shah's private apartment and the hall where he gave audiences.

Begumpur Masjid

Close to the Bijai Mandal, and visible from the tower, is the rubble-built Begumpur Masjid with its large courtyard and multiplicity of domes. This was one of the seven mosques built by Firoz Shah's prime minister, Khan Jahan. The mosque consists of a large paved courtyard, enclosed on three sides by arched cloisters, while the fourth contains the prayer hall, the large central arch of which is flanked by tapering minarets. Decoration is minimal, but the overall effect is powerful.

As at the Bijai Mandal, it's possible to climb the minarets for a sweeping view of the Qutb Minar to the south-west, the distinctive lotus shape of the Bahai Temple to the east, and if there's not too much smog you can make out the white marble dome of Humayun's tomb to the north-east (to the right of the striped shopping complex tower in the middle distance); in the far distance, just to the right of the Bijai Mandal, is the dome of Rashtrapati Bhavan.

Khirki Masjid

This interesting mosque with its four open courts dates from 1380 and is another of

Khan Jahan's constructions. In each of its four corners stands a massive bastion that makes the mosque look much more like a fort. The main entrance is the eastern gate, although only the southern gate is unlocked these days. The mosque and nearby village take their names from the *khirkis* (latticed windows) that appear on the upper level of the mosque's exterior wall.

Although still in pretty good condition, this mosque has very few visitors and consequently the area immediately surrounding it is in danger of becoming a garbage dump. It is just off Press Enclave Marg, which heads east from Aurobindo Marg, about 1km north-east of the Qutb Minar.

Moth-ki Masjid

This 16th-century mosque lies hidden deep in the modern suburb of South Extension Part II, south of the Ring Rd and west of Ashwamegh Gram Rd, but it's well worth seeking out. The mosque stands on a raised platform in a walled enclosure, entered through an impressive red sandstone gateway on its eastern side. It was built in the time of Sikander Lodi (1488–1517) and, despite its present-day obscurity, is one of the finest mosques of this period in Delhi. Its five-arched, triple-domed form, the high level of ornamentation of the mihrab (niche indicating the direction of Mecca) and the arches (particularly the central one) are innovative features which made this mosque an important step towards the fine ornamentation of the later Mughal mosques.

The mosque takes its name from the *moth* (lentil) seed, picked up by Sikander Lodi and used by his wazir, Miyan Bhuwa, to produce more seed and eventually raise a crop large enough to finance the construction of the mosque.

TUGHLAQABAD

The massively strong walls of Tughlaqabad, the third city of Delhi, are east of the Qutb Minar. The walled city and fort which has 13 gateways was built by Ghiyas-ud-din Tughlaq. Its construction involved a legendary quarrel with the saint Nizam-ud-din – when the Tughlaq ruler took the workers Nizam-ud-din wanted for work on his shrine, the saint cursed the king, warning that his city would be inhabited only by shepherds. Today that is indeed the situation.

The dispute between king and saint did not end with curse and counter-curse. When the king prepared to take vengeance on the saint, Nizam-ud-din calmly told his followers (in a saying that is just as current in India today): 'Delhi is a long way off'. Indeed it was, for the king was murdered on his way from Delhi in 1325.

The fort walls are constructed of massive blocks and outside the south wall of the city is an artificial lake with the king's tomb in its centre. A long causeway connects the tomb to the fort, both of which have walls that slope inward.

Getting There & Away

The easiest way to visit Tughlaqabad is to combine it with a visit to the Qutb Minar. It is a long trip by autorickshaw, so a taxi is preferable. It will cost Rs 150.

QUTB MINAR COMPLEX

The buildings in this complex, 15km south of Delhi, date from the onset of Muslim rule in India and are fine examples of early-Afghan architecture. It's open from sunrise to sunset; entry is US$5.

The Qutb Minar itself is a soaring tower of victory that was started in 1193, immediately after the defeat of the last Hindu kingdom in Delhi. It is nearly 73m high and tapers from a 15m diameter base to just 2.5m at the top.

The tower has five distinct storeys, each marked by a projecting balcony. The first three storeys are made of red sandstone, the fourth and fifth of marble and sandstone. Although Qutb-ud-din began construction of the tower, he only got to the first storey. His successors completed it and, in 1368, Firoz Shah rebuilt the top storeys and added a cupola. An earthquake brought the cupola down in 1803 and an Englishman replaced it with another in 1829. However, that dome was deemed inappropriate and was removed some years later.

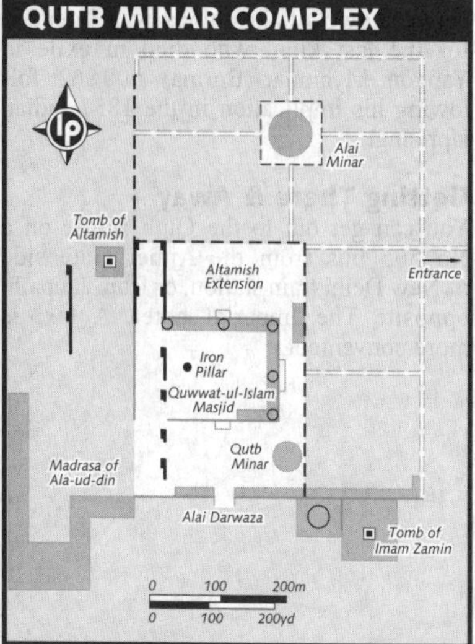

Today, this impressively ornate tower has a slight tilt, but otherwise has worn the centuries remarkably well. It is no longer possible to climb the tower, which is illuminated each evening. The Qutb festival in October/November has evening song and dance recitals.

Quwwat-ul-Islam Masjid

At the foot of the Qutb Minar stands the first mosque to be built in India, the Might of Islam Mosque. Qutb-ud-din began construction of the mosque in 1193, but it has had a number of additions and extensions over the centuries. The original mosque was built on the foundations of a Hindu temple, and an inscription over the east gate states that it was built with materials obtained from demolishing '27 idolatrous temples'. Many of the elements in the mosque's construction indicate their Hindu or Jain origins.

Altamish, Qutb-ud-din's son-in-law, surrounded the original mosque with a cloistered court built between 1210 and 1220. Ala-ud-din added a court to the east and the magnificent Alai Darwaza gateway at the beginning of the 14th century.

Iron Pillar This 7m-high pillar stands in the courtyard of the mosque and has been there since long before the mosque's construction. A six-line Sanskrit inscription indicates that it was initially erected outside a Vishnu temple, possibly in Bihar, and was raised in memory of Chandragupta Vikramaditya, the Gupta king who ruled from AD 375 to 413.

What the inscription does not tell is how it was made, for the iron in the pillar is of quite exceptional purity. Scientists have never discovered how this iron, which is of such purity that it has not rusted after 2000 years, could be cast with the technology of the time. It was said that if you can stand with your back to the pillar and encircle it with your arms your wish will be granted; however, you won't now have any chance to try – the pillar is now protected by a fence.

Alai Minar

At the time Ala-ud-din made his additions to the mosque he also conceived a far more ambitious construction program. He would build a second tower of victory, exactly like the Qutb Minar, except it would be twice as high! By the time of his death the tower had reached 27m and no-one proved willing to continue his overambitious project. This incomplete tower stands to the north of the Qutb Minar and the mosque.

Other Features

Ala-ud-din's **Alai Darwaza** gateway is the main entrance to the whole complex. It was built of red sandstone in 1310 and stands just south-west of the Qutb Minar. The **tomb of Imam Zamin** stands beside the gateway, while the **tomb of Altamish**, who died in 1235, is by the north-western corner of the mosque. The largely ruined **madrasa of Ala-ud-din** stands at the rear of the complex.

A short distance west of the enclosure, in Mehrauli Village, is the **tomb of Adham Khan** (see Nizam-ud-din's Shrine in the New Delhi section earlier in this chapter), who murdered his rival Atgah Khan, who like him was related to a wet nurse of the

Emperor Akbar. When Akbar learned of the murder, Adham Khan ended up being heaved off a terrace in the Agra Fort, not once but twice. Also in Mehrauli, a large new Shakti Pitha temple complex is under construction.

South of the enclosure is the Jain Ahimsa Sthal, and an impressive 4m statue in pink granite of Mahavir. There are some summer palaces in the area as well as the tombs of the last kings of Delhi, who succeeded the Mughals. An empty space between two of the tombs was intended for the last king, who died in exile in Yangon, Myanmar (Burma), in 1862, following his implication in the 1857 Indian Uprising.

Getting There & Away

You can get out to the Qutb Minar on a No 505 bus from the Ajmer Gate side of New Delhi train station, or from Janpath, opposite The Imperial hotel. A taxi is more convenient.

Punjab & Haryana

'The Land of Five Rivers', Punjab was probably the part of India that suffered the most destruction and damage at the time of Partition, yet today it is far and away the most affluent state in India. No natural resource or advantage gave the predominantly Sikh Punjabis this enviable position; it was sheer hard work.

Although Punjab is first and foremost an agricultural state, supplying a large proportion of India's rice, dairy and wheat, it also has a thriving industrial base including Hero Bicycles, India's (and the world's) biggest bicycle manufacturer.

Amritsar and its Golden Temple is Punjab's only well-known attraction yet the state has many other impressive *gurdwaras* (Sikh temples), and the Grand Trunk Rd (GT Rd), one of the busiest roads in India, has many caravanserais and Mughal monuments straddling it as it cuts through Punjab to Lahore, Pakistan.

A predominantly Hindu state created from the partition of Punjab, Haryana surrounds Delhi; if you are heading to almost any major attraction in North India – such as Jaipur, Agra, or Amritsar – you will need to go through Haryana. Close to Chandigarh, the capital, are a few resort-type places popular with Delhi-wallahs for their cheap alcohol (Haryana's taxes are much lower than Delhi's). With a slightly raffish atmosphere, they still offer a pleasant escape from the city.

Chandigarh, the capital of both states, lies along the main route to Shimla and is worthy of a stop if only to see the bizarre rock garden and the immaculate Mughal gardens at Pinjore.

History

Before Partition, Punjab extended across both sides of what is now the India-Pakistan border, and what was its capital, Lahore, is now the capital of the Pakistani state of Punjab.

Evidence of settlement in Punjab dates from 3000 BC and it's from here that the

Punjab & Haryana at a Glance

PUNJAB
Population: 21.4 million
Area: 50,362 sq km
Capital: Chandigarh
Main Language: Punjabi
When to Go: Oct to Mar

HARYANA
Population: 17.8 million
Area: 44,212 sq km
Capital: Chandigarh
Main Language: Hindi
When to Go: Oct to Mar

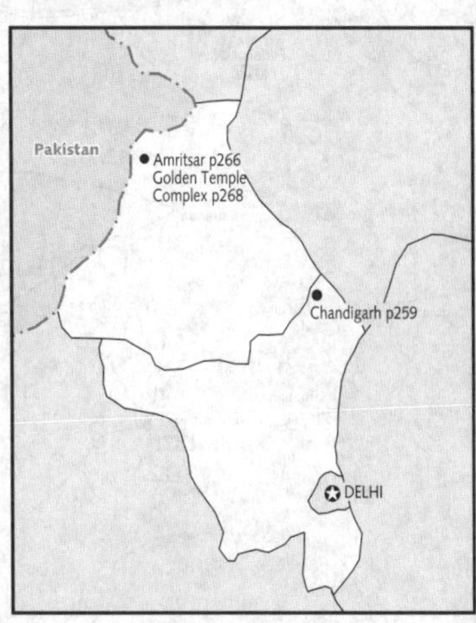

- Admire Amritsar's beautiful Golden Temple, Sikhism's most sacred site
- Visit Le Corbusier's planned city of Chandigarh and see the rock garden, where the city's discarded junk has been recycled into bizarre human and animal sculptures
- Savour Sikh hospitality at a *gurdwara* (Sikh temple): Tuck into a meal, stay the night, or join volunteers in peeling potatoes and cleaning marble floors

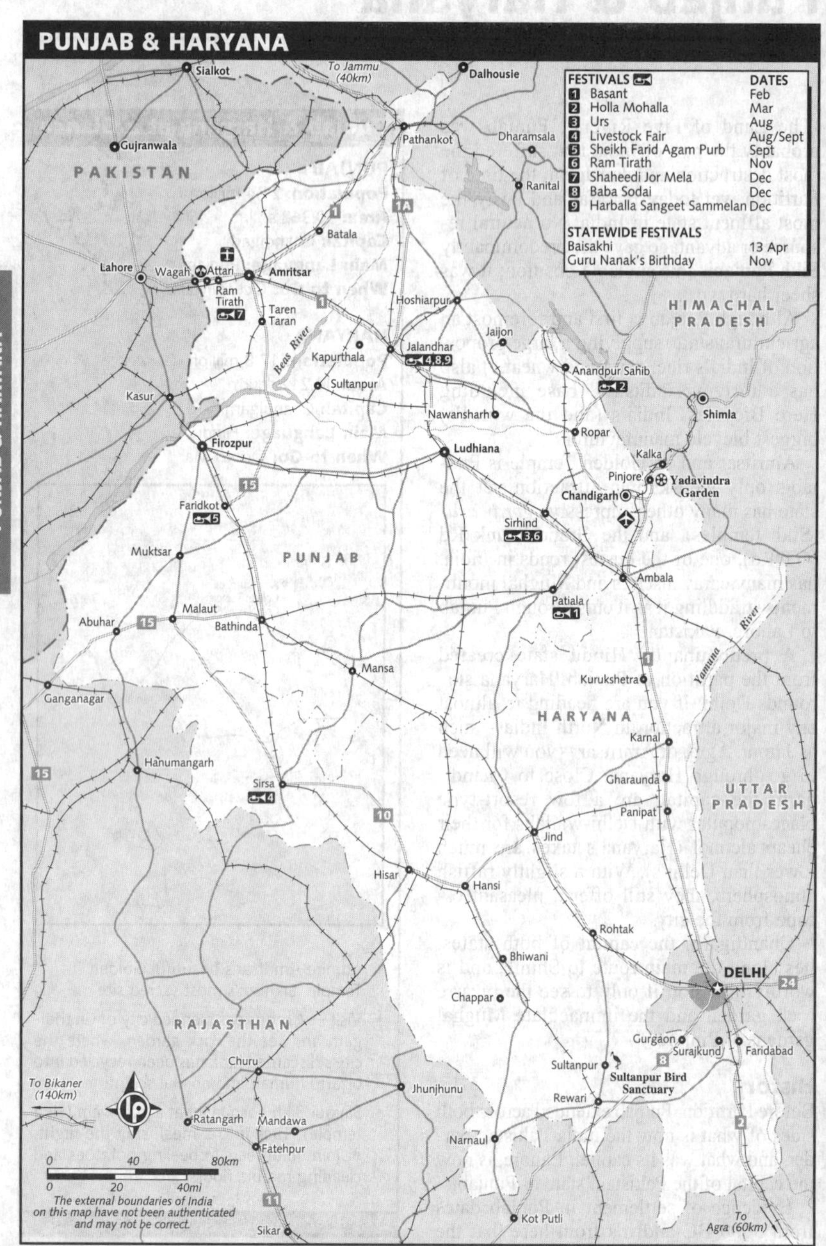
PUNJAB & HARYANA
FESTIVALS DATES
1 Basant Feb
2 Holla Mohalla Mar
3 Urs Aug
4 Livestock Fair Aug/Sept
5 Sheikh Farid Agam Purb Sept
6 Ram Tirath Nov
7 Shaheedi Jor Mela Dec
8 Baba Sodai Dec
9 Harballa Sangeet Sammelan Dec
STATEWIDE FESTIVALS
Baisakhi 13 Apr
Guru Nanak's Birthday Nov
To Jammu (40km)
Sialkot
Dalhousie
Pathankot
Dharamsala
Ranital
Gujranwala
PAKISTAN
Batala
Lahore
Wagah
Attari
Amritsar
Ram Tirath
Taren Taran
Hoshiarpur
HIMACHAL PRADESH
Jaijon
Beas River
Kapurthala
Jalandhar
Anandpur Sahib
Sultanpur
Kasur
Nawanshahr
Shimla
Ropar
Firozpur
Ludhiana
Kalka
Pinjore
Yadavindra Garden
Chandigarh
Faridkot
Sirhind
Muktsar
PUNJAB
Ambala
Patiala
Malaut
Abuhar
Bathinda
Yamuna River
Mansa
Kurukshetra
Ganganagar
HARYANA
Karnal
Hanumangarh
Gharaunda
UTTAR PRADESH
Sirsa
Panipat
Jind
Hisar
Hansi
Rohtak
Bhiwani
DELHI
Chappar
RAJASTHAN
Gurgaon
Surajkund
Faridabad
Churu
Sultanpur
Sultanpur Bird Sanctuary
To Bikaner (140km)
Jhunjhunu
Rewari
Ratangarh
Mandawa
Fatehpur
Narnaul
0 40 80km
0 20 40mi
The external boundaries of India on this map have not been authenticated and may not be correct.
Kot Putli
To Agra (60km)
Sikar

Harappan civilisation emerged. The Aryan invasion in 1700 BC brought about bloody times, and many battles recorded in the Mahabharata have been embraced by Hindu mythology. (Punjabis, and Sikhs in particular, are still famed for their fearless fighting skills; impressive demonstrations of this remain a feature of many festivals and fairs.)

The Aryans were only the first invaders. Punjab became a strategic barrier between treasure-hungry Mughals and the wealth that India had to offer. The Mughals gained power and controlled the region until the demise of their empire in the 18th century.

The first Sikh guru, Guru Nanak, was born in 1469. Reacting against the harsh caste system and social unrest of the time, he established the foundations of the Sikh movement. Fusing Hindu and Muslim practices into a religiously tolerant and egalitarian faith, the Sikhs became a target for persecution by the Mughals – whole galleries of martyrs testify to this.

The tenth guru, Guru Gobind Singh, reformed the religion with the Khalsa brotherhood. It consolidated the basic Sikh principles, denouncing *purdah* (the seclusion of women) and encouraging Sikhs to throw off their caste names in favour of Singh (Lion; for the men) and Kaur (Lioness; for the women). It also introduced some of the features associated with Sikhism such as uncut hair and the *kirpan* (sabre or sword) allowed for use when 'all else has failed'.

The Sikhs filled the void left by the defeated Mughals until they became the servants of the British, filling many of the Indian army's ranks. After the Jallianwala Bagh massacre the Sikhs joined the rebellion against the British and the tradition of martyrdom continued (see the boxed text 'Carnage at Jallianwala Bagh' later in this chapter for more details).

The fight for Independence was won but the grim logic of Partition sliced the population of Punjab into a Muslim region and a Sikh and Hindu region. As millions of Sikhs and Hindus fled eastward and equal numbers of Muslims fled west, there were atrocities and killings on both sides. Punjab's major city, Amritsar (the holy city of the Sikhs), only 24km from the new Pakistan border, saw some of the worst atrocities.

Even after the dust had settled, it was thought wise to build a safer capital farther within India. At first Shimla, the old imperial summer capital, was chosen, but Chandigarh, a new planned city, was conceived and built in the 1950s to serve as capital of the new state.

During the 1960s the Green Revolution transformed Punjab's farming industry and the state prospered. However, Sikh political demands racked the state and militants demanded the creation of an independent Sikh state, to be called Khalistan (Land of the Pure). In 1966 Punjab underwent another split. This time it was divided along predominantly linguistic lines: between the mostly Sikh, Punjabi-speaking state of Punjab and the majority Hindi-speaking state of Haryana.

Unfortunately, this further partition did not have the desired effect of appeasing the Sikh separatists. At the same time some of the northern parts of Punjab were hived off to Himachal Pradesh. Chandigarh, on the border of Punjab and Haryana, remained the capital of both of the states. The separatist movement gained ground in 1973 when Sikh leaders listed their religious, political and economic demands in the Anandpur Sahib resolution.

In 1984, following a terror campaign, extremists occupied the Golden Temple in Amritsar and were evicted only after a bloody battle with the Indian army. Punjab was considered by central government to be in a state of emergency and was placed under President's Rule from 1985 to 1992.

'Supercop', KPS Gill, was sent in to stamp out militancy in the state. He did this very effectively and by 1992 most militants were either dead or in prison. Gill left behind a legacy of police brutality and human rights issues which are still being contested today.

For more information on the events of the 1980s, Sikh demands and the response of the Indian state, the following books are two good options: *My Bleeding Punjab* by Khushwant Singh, and *Amritsar: Mrs Gandhi's Last Battle* by Mark Tully and Satish Jacob.

In 1986 the government announced that Chandigarh would be handed over to Punjab in an attempt to placate the Sikhs. However, with the continued violence in Punjab this didn't take place, although eventually it will. In the meantime, Chandigarh remains the capital of the two states, yet is itself administered as a Union Territory from Delhi.

The Sikhs still dream of Khalistan but the memories of the past violence are still raw enough for them to seek a peaceful resolution. In the meantime the state prospers economically and is a calm, friendly and peaceful place to visit.

Special Events

Baisakhi, on 13 April, is celebrated by Hindus as new year's day and by Sikhs as the foundation day of the Khalsa. Spilling over into Delhi and other states it is characterised by men and women swirling their way through the *bhangra* and *giddah* dances.

All of the **Sikh gurus' birthdays** are celebrated. Guru Nanak's (November) and Guru Gobind Singh's (October/November) are the largest. In towns and villages volunteers sweep the streets ahead of processions carrying the Guru Granth Sahib. Fireworks are lit and Sikh warriors show off their combat skills to the accompaniment of brass bands.

Haryana

Shah Jahan built *kos minars* (milestones) along the road from Delhi to Lahore and serais at longer intervals. Most of the kos minars still stand but there is little left of the serais. The Haryanans have, however, built a series of 'service centres' along the main roads – complexes with motels, restaurants and service stations, all named after birds found in the state – that can make travelling through the area more enjoyable.

Typically the complexes have a camping ground, camper huts (usually for around Rs 350) and rooms (in the Rs 500 to Rs 800 range if they have air-con, and cheaper without). Some places also have dormitories and camping spots. All have restaurants, and some serve fast food.

For details pick up a pamphlet from the Haryana Government Tourist Bureau (☎ 3324910), at the Chandralok Building, 36 Janpath, Delhi, or from the tourist office in Chandigarh, Sector 17B.

CHANDIGARH

☎ 0172 • pop 750,000

Chandigarh was conceived and born in the 1950s and was the master plan of the European modernist architect Le Corbusier. No other Indian city feels quite like this one. Indians are very proud of it and it's the cleanest and healthiest city in the country.

Orientation

Chandigarh is on the edge of the Siwalik Hills, the outermost edge of the Himalaya. Divided into 91 sectors, it's separated by broad avenues. Each sector is quartered into four zones, A to D, and each building within them has a unique number. Despite this logical breakdown, orientation can be tricky without a map, as only the broad separating avenues have street names. 'SCO' in business addresses stands for 'shop-cum-office'. The bus station, the modern town centre and many of the restaurants are in Sector 17. As the train station is 8km out of Chandigarh, buses are much more convenient than trains.

Information

Tourist Offices The Chandigarh tourist office (☎ 703839, ⓔ htcchd@ch1.vsnl.net.in), upstairs in the bus station, is open 9 am to 5 pm Monday to Friday and to 1 pm Saturday. Open much the same hours and located next door are Himachal Tourism (☎ 708569) and, one floor up, Punjab Tourism (☎ 711878) and UP Tourism (☎ 707-649). Haryana Tourism (☎ 702955), in Sector 17B, SCO 17–19, is open weekdays.

Money Major institutions for foreign exchange are in Sector 9, including branches of Punjab National Bank, with ATMs that accept Mastercard, Maestro and Cirrus cards; and ICIC Bank with an ATM accepting Visa. There is a Dresdner Bank behind them and a branch of Thomas Cook that is open 9.30 am to 6 pm Monday to Saturday.

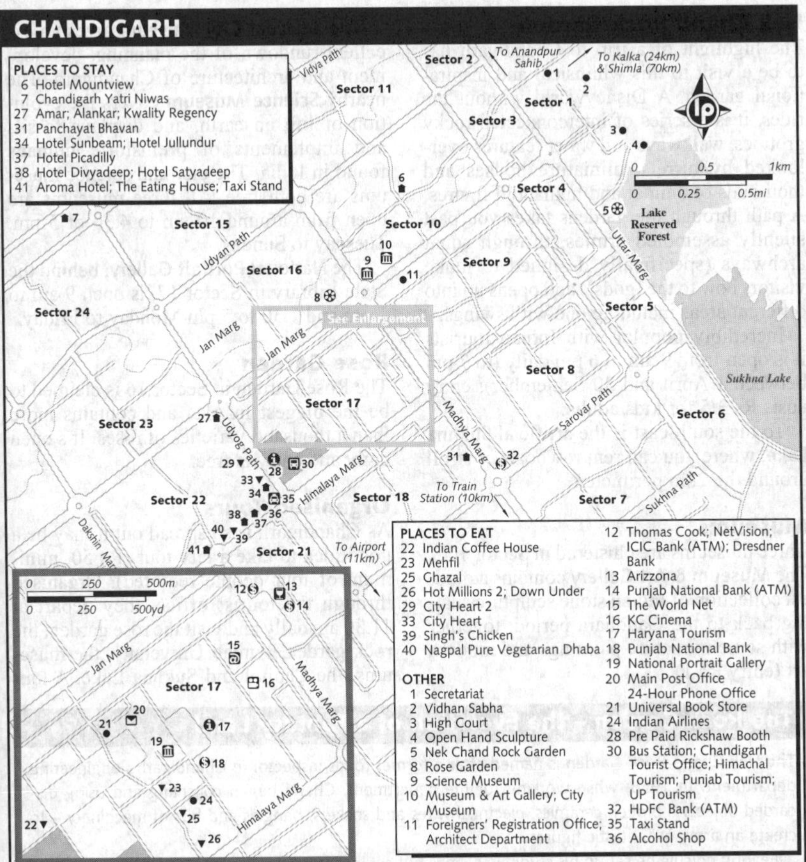

Post & Communications The main post office and 24-hour phone office is in Sector 17. For Internet access, try The World Net in Sector 17, which charges Rs 35 per hour, or NetVision near the banks in Sector 9.

Photography There are camera and film shops along Udyog Path opposite the bus station.

Government Buildings

The Secretariat and the Vidhan Sabha (Legislative Assembly) buildings are in Sector 1. The roof garden at the top of the Secretariat yields an excellent view over Chandigarh, but the building is less accessible since the chief minister of Punjab was assassinated here in 1995. Nearby is a huge, revolving open hand sculpture, conceived as a symbol of unity, and the colourful High Court with its double roof.

It's possible to visit some of the government buildings, including the industrial-looking Vidhan Sabha, with prior permission from the friendly Architect Department on the second floor of the UD Secretariat in Sector 9 – the tourist office can help arrange this.

Nek Chand Rock Garden

The highlight of a trip to Chandigarh has to be a visit to this whimsical and inspirational garden. A Disneyworld without the rides, it is a series of interconnected rocky grottoes, walkways and water features overlooked by turrets, miniature houses and thousands of animal and humanoid figures. A path through the gardens takes you past silently assembled armies, through squat archways (specifically designed to make visitors bow to the 'gods') and opens up into different areas including one with swings.

Incredibly popular with Indian tourists it is open from 9 am to 6 pm daily (to 7 pm between 1 April and 30 September); entry costs Rs 3/5 for kids/adults.

To the south-east is the artificial **Sukhna Lake**, where you can rent rowboats or stroll around the 2km perimeter.

Museums

Three museums are clustered in Sector 10C. The **Museum & Art Gallery** contains a modest collection of Indian stone sculptures dating back to the Gandhara period, together with some miniature paintings and modern art (entry Rs 1).

The adjacent **City Museum** gives an excellent rundown of the planning, development and architecture of Chandigarh. The nearby **Science Museum** covers the evolution of life on earth, and displays fossils and implements of prehistoric humans found in India. The city and science museums are both free. All three museums are open from around 10 am to 4.30 or 5 pm, Tuesday to Sunday.

The **National Portrait Gallery**, behind the State Library in Sector 17, is open 9 am to 1 pm and 1.30 to 5 pm Monday to Friday.

Rose Garden

The Rose Garden in Sector 16 is claimed to be the biggest in Asia and contains more than a thousand varieties of roses. It's open daily and entry is free.

Organised Tours

As Chandigarh is so spread out it may be a good idea to take a city tour (Rs 50, minimum of four people required). Organised through the tourist office, they depart at 11.30 am daily and visit the rose garden, the rock garden, Punjab University, the museums, the Capitol and Sukhna Lake. A tour

The Rock Garden – the Evolution of a Fantasy Land

The Nek Chand Rock Garden is named after a former roads inspector in Chandigarh's engineering department. In 1958, while working for the department, Chand began collecting and using discarded objects – broken ceramics, electrical wires and sockets, bangles and bits of machinery – to create an array of fantastic figures.

Fearing ridicule he set up his studio in a small hut set in a forest far away from the prying eyes of the embryonic city – even his wife initially had no idea what he was up to. So began a routine of scouring the city for materials by day and transforming them into art under the light of burning tyres by night.

In 1972 disaster loomed when workmen clearing space for the expanding city stumbled upon Chand's secret. Occupying government land, the garden was immediately slated for destruction. But the garden's discovery soon became the talk of the town and the authorities relented. In fact they went one step further and Chand was given a salary and workforce to continue and extend his garden. Soon the work was acclaimed internationally, with invites to exhibit abroad, and Chand was lauded as a key exponent of 'outsider' art.

Chand is often to be found in the garden which now covers 4 hectares and is still growing. Already some 5000 sculptures populate the garden, which is visited by a similar number of visitors daily. A self-effacing chap, Chand is generally happy to speak to visitors and modestly describes his work as 'engineering rather than art'.

to Pinjore Gardens, just outside Chandigarh, will cost Rs 80.

Places to Stay

Chandigarh has scant budget accommodation, and hotels are often full. There are some cheap guesthouses but the government is trying to close these and you will be told that they 'aren't registered to take foreigners'. It's still worth checking them out to see if the situation has changed; there are a couple on the street behind Hotel Jullundur.

Most places add a 10% luxury tax. All places listed have private bathrooms (with sit-down flush toilets and hot water), and checkout is at noon unless otherwise stated.

Places to Stay – Budget

Panchayat Bhavan *(☎ 780701, Sector 18)* has the cheapest options in an institutional block with a hostel atmosphere. Dorm beds cost Rs 24 or there are large, bare doubles with TV for Rs 200 (Rs 500 with air-con).

Hotel Divyadeep *(☎ 705191, Sector 22B)* has simple single/double rooms with fan for Rs 250/300, rising to Rs 450/500 with air-con. ***Hotel Satyadeep*** *(☎ 703103)* is just along the road and gives an almost identical deal, except rooms are Rs 50 cheaper and it only has singles at the lowest price. The first place has a good veg restaurant below it, and the second has a sweet shop. Checkout for both is 24 hours.

Chandigarh Yatri Niwas *(☎ 706038, Sector 24B)* is a bit far out but has clean rooms with TV and phone for Rs 500/750 with air-cooler/air-con. It also has dorms for eight people for Rs 800. There is a cheap restaurant here and it has free bike hire.

Places to Stay – Mid-Range

Hotel Jullundur *(☎ 706777, ⓔ info@jullundurhotel.com, Sector 22B)* is right opposite the bus station. Standard single/double rooms with TV and air-con start at Rs 300/ 550; the single is really small. It has a licensed restaurant and room service.

About 500m north-west of the bus station there are a few hotels with ground-floor restaurants and bars side by side on Udyog Path in Sector 22A.

Amar *(☎ 704638)* charges Rs 300/400 for small and plain rooms with TV; air-con rooms start at Rs 600.

Alankar *(☎ 708802)* has rooms with air-cooler and TV for Rs 500/600; air-con rooms cost Rs 800.

Kwality Regency *(☎ 720205, fax 720 206)* is nearly top-end quality with 12 stylish, air-con 'designer rooms' starting at Rs 1295/1425. It also has business facilities.

Aroma Hotel *(☎ 700045, fax 700051, ⓔ hotelaroma@glide.net.in, Sector 22C)* out along Himalaya Marg is similarly swish but on a slightly larger scale. Rooms start at Rs 1145/1395. It has business facilities, a courtyard restaurant with waterfall feature, a bar and a 24-hour coffee shop and bakery.

Hotel Sunbeam *(☎ 708101, fax 708900, Udyog Path, Sector 22B)* is opposite the bus station. Pleasant air-con rooms with fridge start at Rs 1095/1495. It has a restaurant, a 24-hour coffee shop and a bar with live music.

Places to Stay – Top End

Hotel Piccadilly *(☎ 707571, fax 705692, Sector 22B)* is central and popular with businesspeople. It charges Rs 1838/2165 for singles/doubles and has a restaurant and bar.

Hotel Mountview *(☎ 740544, fax 742 220, ⓔ citci10@ch1.dot.net.in, Sector 10)* is set in peaceful gardens. It has air-con rooms with balcony for Rs 1950/2450, a restaurant, 24-hour coffee shop, swimming pool, health club and bar with live music. It also has free bike hire.

Places to Eat

Chandigarh has many modern places to eat offering a variety that ranges from Western-style fast food to Chinese and Indian regional dishes, usually found within the same venue.

City Heart *(Udyog Path)*, near the bus station, serves cheap Indian veg food. Nearby, ***City Heart 2*** is nonveg and more expensive; it also serves beer.

Singh's Chicken *(Sector 22, Himalaya Marg)* has a good range of chicken dishes for about Rs 25 to 50. Its sign makes the confusing claim that it's the 'Winner

PUNJAB & HARYANA

Chandigarh – a Living City

Chandigarh is unlike any other city in India. On the positive side, it is orderly and regulated. It has a wonderful feeling of space, with modern concrete buildings broken up by broad boulevards and many open, green parks and lawns. It has an air of prosperity, with more private vehicles than one normally finds in India. Footpath dwellers, street side cobblers and vendors, and bedraggled beggars are scarce. Also – almost unique in India – no cows or other livestock roam the streets. On the negative side, it is too spread out; some of the open stretches are rather barren, and it takes a long time to get anywhere, especially by cycle-rickshaw. Likened to Milton Keynes, a grim planned town in the UK, it lacks the vibrant life and colour of other Indian cities.

Most of these differences stem from the fact that it is a planned city. The government of Punjab appointed American town planner Albert Mayer and Polish architect Matthew Nowicki to create their new capital. But in the early days of the project Nowicki died in a plane crash, prompting Mayer to withdraw.

The Swiss-born architect Le Corbusier was appointed to take over the project. Le Corbusier was known for his functional concrete-and-steel buildings and he completely revised Nowicki and Mayer's plans. Le Corbusier wanted Chandigarh to facilitate four basic functions: living, working, circulation, and care of body and spirit. He conceived of the city as a unified entity, like a living organism, with the administrative buildings in Sector 1 forming the head, the city centre (Sector 17) forming the heart, cultural institutions the intellect, and the roads the circulatory system.

Had Nowicki survived to complete his commission Chandigarh would undoubtedly have looked very different. He commented that the 'dream of some modern planners depends entirely on…a way of life alien to that of India'. Did Le Corbusier take notice of these sentiments? Judge for yourself.

PUNJAB & HARYANA

of Lonely Planet Book of UK World Tourism Guide'.

Along the road, ***Nagpal Pure Vegetarian Dhaba*** is popular for Indian veg dishes for less than Rs 40.

There are lots of places to eat in the Sector 17 shopping district. ***Hot Millions 2*** *(SCO 74–75, Sector 17D)* serves fast food (pizzas, Tex-Mex and Indian) on three different and loud levels and is very popular with families.

Indian Coffee House is more subdued and serves cheap Indian fare until 9.30 pm.

Mehfil *(SCO 185, Sector 17C)* and, across the road, ***Ghazal*** *(SCO 189–91)* are Chandigarh's top restaurants. Their menus are the standard mix of continental, Chinese and Indian, with main courses around Rs 100 (half portions are available). Mehfil has live music nightly, except Monday, and both have bars.

The open-air ***restaurant*** attached to the rock garden is a good place to stop before or after visiting the main attraction; it serves meals, snacks and beer.

A couple of the hotels have 24-hour coffee shops which also serve food should you have the midnight munchies. ***The Eating House*** at Aroma Hotel is one with particularly good cakes and ice cream.

Food stalls set up each evening along Udyog Path, where there are cheap beer shops. You'll also find beer shops along Himalaya Marg.

Entertainment

Down Under, in the basement of Hot Millions 2, is an Aussie-themed pub with pool table, very loud music and food.

Arizzona is a licensed dance venue that is open 1 to 6 pm on Saturday and Thursday afternoons. Popular with a younger crowd it's dark and loud.

KC Cinema, near Haryana Tourism, shows the latest US and Bollywood movie releases.

Shopping

Woollen sweaters and shawls from Punjab are good buys, especially in the government emporiums. Most of these are in Sector 17, which probably has the most extensive range of shops in India.

Getting There & Away

Air Indian Airlines (☎ 704539), SCO 170, Sector 17C, is open 10 am to 5 pm. It has flights on Wednesday and Saturday to both Delhi (US$65) and Amritsar (US$55) and one flight on Wednesday to Leh (US$70).

Bus Chandigarh's huge and noisy bus station is in Sector 17, alongside the local bus terminal. There are phone offices, a post office, a luggage store, a restaurant and a prepaid rickshaw booth. Buses generally depart between 7 am and midnight.

Train The train station is inconveniently located 8km south-east of the centre; however, reservations can be made at the office (☎ 708573) upstairs in the bus station, open 8 am to 8 pm Monday to Saturday (until 2 pm on Sunday). Local bus No 37 runs between the bus and train stations to coincide with train arrivals and departures.

It is 245km from Delhi to Chandigarh, which the twice-daily *Shatabdi Express* covers in around three hours. The fare is Rs 400/790 in an air-con chair car/executive class. There is also a slower overnight train (Rs 97/489 in normal/air-con sleeper, six hours).

There are daily trains to Kalka (Rs 5, one hour), just 24km up the line, from where four daily trains rattle up the narrow-gauge mountain railway to Shimla (Rs 31, five hours).

Getting Around

To/From the Airport The airport is 11km south of Sector 17. Fares are Rs 250 by taxi or Rs 57 by autorickshaw.

Local Transport Chandigarh is far too spread out to walk around. The extensive bus network is the cheapest option. Bus No 13 runs by the Aroma Hotel as far as the government buildings in Sector 1, and bus No 37 connects the train and bus stations.

If you're planning a longer trip across the city consider taking a blue autorickshaw. There is a prepaid autorickshaw stand behind the bus station. Rickshaw-wallahs may offer lower rates when business is slack. From the bus station it should cost Rs 34 to the train station or Rs 20 to the rock garden.

Bicycle is the best form of transport; a couple of hotels have free bike hire (see Places to Stay) and the tourist office can also help out with rentals. There are 24-hour taxi stands near the larger hotels; rates are Rs 250 for local two-hour runs, Rs 400 for Pinjore and Rs 800 for Anandpur Sahib return.

AROUND CHANDIGARH

Pinjore

Chronicled in the Mahabharata, the Mughal **Yadavindra Gardens** at Pinjore were designed by Fidai Khan, Aurangzeb's foster

PUNJAB & HARYANA

Buses from Chandigarh

destination	platform No	departures	duration (hrs)	fare (Rs) ordinary/deluxe
Amritsar	29 & 34	hourly	6	196/–
Anandpur Sahib	29 *	hourly	2 ½	50/–
Delhi	12 & 13/11	½ hourly/every 5 mins	5 ½	108/215
Dharamsala	9	1.30 pm	10	140/–
Haridwar/Rishikesh	16	½ hourly	6	95/–
Manali	–	5.50, 6.40 & 7.30 pm	10	155/–
Pinjore	7 ◆	every 10 mins	1	15/–
Sirhind	26	two hourly	2	29/–

* between 10 am and 4 pm buses depart from the bus station in Sector 43
◆ from local bus stand

brother, who also designed the Badshahi Mosque in Lahore, Pakistan. Situated 20km from Chandigarh, near Kalka, the terraced gardens feature the Rajasthani Mughal-style Shish Mahal with mirror ceiling, the Rang Mahal (an arched pavilion), the cubical Jal Mahal and a series of fountains and waterfalls. The gardens, open 7 am to 10 pm daily, are colourfully illuminated at night. Entry costs Rs 5. There is a **mini-zoo,** which also has an otter house, near the gardens.

The ***Golden Oriole*** restaurant and bar and ***Budgerigar Motel*** *(☎ 01733-20177)* are both within the gardens. Rooms cost Rs 400 (Rs 600 with air-con). You can also stay and eat in town.

Buses from Chandigarh (Rs 15, one hour) stop at the entrance to the gardens every 10 minutes or so.

CHANDIGARH TO DELHI

Kurukshetra

South of Chandigarh, Kurukshetra is known as Brahmavarta (Land of Brahma) and is the site of the battle where Arjuna learned about dharma as told in the Mahabharata. It has become a place of pilgrimage.

The **Kurukshetra tank** attracts as many as a million pilgrims during eclipses of the sun, when the water is believed to come from all of India's sacred tanks making it especially purifying.

Neelkhanthi Krishna Dham Yatri Niwas *(☎ 01744-21615)* is a government-run place with dorms for Rs 75 and rooms for Rs 500. Set within lawns, it has a restaurant and lockers.

Karnal

Karnal, mentioned in the Mahabharata, is the place from where in 1739 Nadir Shah, the Persian who took the Peacock Throne from Delhi, defeated the Mughal emperor Mohammed Shah. The British, in turn, built a cantonment here but were forced out by malaria. There is an artificial lake nearby.

Panipat

Panipat, 92km north of Delhi, is the site of three great battles of the Mughal era. In 1526 Ibrahim Lodi, the Delhi Sultan, was defeated by the first Mughal emperor, Akbar. The next battle, in 1556, saw another Akbar (the son of Humayun) defeat an Afghan invasion. For the third battle in 1761 the Mughals sent the Marathas to battle for them against invading Afghans. The Marathas lost but the Afghan army mutinied over lack of pay and the region remained in limbo for years afterwards. Today the town is peaceful – apart from the swish of the 30,000 textile looms churning out carpets and fabrics.

Panipat is also famous for being one of the most fly-infested places in India – because, it is said, of a Muslim saint buried here. Abu Ali Kalandar is supposed to have totally rid Panipat of flies, but when the people complained that he had done too good a job he gave them all the flies back, multiplied by a thousand.

Kala Amb *(☎ 01742-46242)*, 7km outside Panipat, has lawns and rooms for Rs 400. In town, hotels can be found along GT Rd.

SURAJKUND

Surajkund, only 10km south of Delhi, was founded by the Rajputs who built the Sun Temple found here.

The **Surajkund Crafts Mela**, one of Haryana's highlights, takes place in the first two weeks of February. It showcases crafts from a different state each year, and you can buy direct from the craftspeople. Quality is very high and prices are lower than in the state emporiums.

Accompanying the fair is an army of acrobats, magicians and other roving entertainers. During the fair, Haryana Tourism has a 30-minute bus service (Rs 5) from its state emporium on Baba Kharak Singh Marg in Delhi.

SULTANPUR

☎ 0124

There are many birds, including flamingos, at Sultanpur's bird sanctuary, 46km south-west of Delhi. September to March is the best time to visit, and you can stay at Haryana Tourism's ***Rosy Pelican*** *(☎ 6375242)*. Rooms start at Rs 400.

At the time of research, public transport to the lake from Delhi didn't really justify a trip out here, although Haryana Tourism is planning a rail link in the very near future. To get here, take a blue Haryana bus from Dhaula Khan in Delhi to Gurgaon, and then a Chandu bus to Sultanpur. The trip takes about half a day by bus, but will eventually be easier by train.

ROHTAK

An alternative railway route to Amritsar runs 70km north-west of Delhi to Rohtak, which was once a border town between the Sikhs' and Marathas' regions, and was the subject of frequent clashes. Archaeological digs around the area have uncovered finds from pre-Harappan civilisations.

HANSI

Hansi, north-west of Rohtak, is where Colonel Skinner died. Skinner's Horse, the private cavalry regiment he founded in the 1790s, was responsible for the conquest of large areas of North India for the East India Company.

SIRSA

Sirsa, in the far west of Haryana, is an ancient city; there is believed to have been a settlement here since 1500 BC. Apart from the city walls little evidence of its past glories remain. It comes alive in August/September when there is a livestock fair.

Punjab

Despite centuries of persecution and conflict, Punjab, with double the average income per capita and the highest consumption of alcohol in India, is a prosperous state. Many of its sights, sounds and smells are often strangely familiar to Westerners who have sampled Indian culture at home and the turbaned Sikhs have unwittingly become a symbol of India.

This is partly a result of the number of Punjabis who have migrated to or studied in the West. You're just as likely to hear a broad Brummie, Canadian or Australian accent as you are Punjabi here – thousands of nonresident Punjabis visit family and make the pilgrimage 'home' each year. Add the Mughal-influenced food, especially popular after a skinful of beer in Indian restaurants throughout the world, and the increasingly popular Punjabi-influenced music, and at times you certainly could be in one of Europe's larger cities.

Punjabis are justifiably proud of their state, and all denominations rave about the Golden Temple where the Sikh ideologies of harmony and hospitality are most evident.

AMRITSAR

☎ 0183 • pop 1 million

Founded in 1577 by Ram Das, the fourth guru of the Sikhs, Amritsar is both the centre of the Sikh religion and the major city of Punjab state. The name means 'Pool of Nectar', referring to the sacred tank around which the Sikhs' Golden Temple is built. Although Amritsar is just another dusty Indian city, the Golden Temple is an exceptionally beautiful and peaceful place.

The original site for the city was granted by the Mughal emperor Akbar, but in 1761 Ahmad Shah Durani sacked the town and destroyed the temple. The temple was rebuilt in 1764; in 1802 it was roofed over with copper-gilded plates by Ranjit Singh and became known as the Golden Temple. During the turmoil of the Partition of India in 1948, Amritsar was a flash point for the terrible events that shook Punjab.

During unrest in the early 1980s, Amritsar's Golden Temple was occupied by Sikh extremists who were intent on expelling non-Sikhs from the state and creating a Sikh homeland. They were finally evicted, under the orders of Indira Gandhi, by the Indian army in 1984 in a military action that resulted in hundreds of Sikh deaths. Later that year Indira Gandhi was assassinated by her Sikh bodyguards.

The temple was again occupied by extremists in 1988. The damage wrought on the Golden Temple by the tanks of the Indian army has now been repaired, and following a few years of unrest things are quiet again.

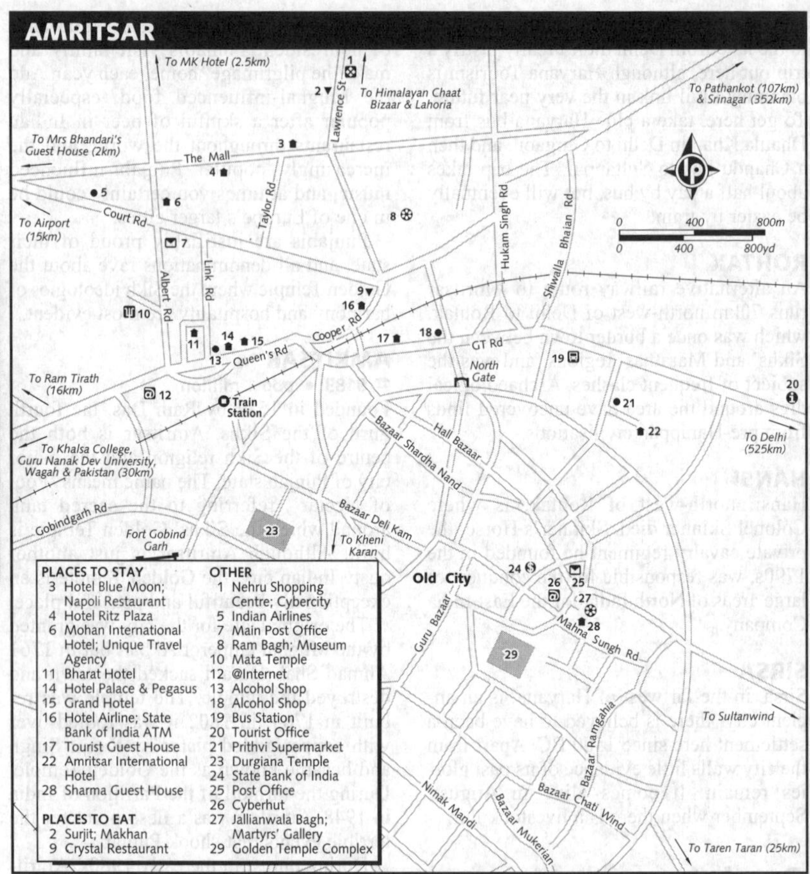

Orientation

The old city is south-east of the main train station and is surrounded by a circular road that used to contain the massive city walls. There are 18 gates still in existence but only the north gate facing the Ram Bagh gardens is original. The Golden Temple and the narrow alleys of the bazaar area are in the old city.

Modern Amritsar is north of the train line, station and Queen's Rd, where you will find most of the hotels. The bus station is 2km east of the train station on the road to Delhi.

Information

Tourist Offices The tourist office (☎ 231452) is in the former youth hostel, 1km east of the bus station, and is fairly helpful. It's open 9 am to 5 pm Monday to Saturday. The information office at the Golden Temple is open 8 am to 1 pm and 2.30 to 8 pm daily, and staff, who offer free guided tours, are very helpful. There is another tourist office at the airport.

Money There are moneychangers on Link Rd, opposite the train station and near the Golden Temple; rates are marginally worse than at banks. There is a Bank of Punjab at the Golden Temple that changes US dollars only and has an ATM accepting Mastercard. The State Bank of India in the old city changes dollars and sterling. The branch near Hotel Airline has an ATM but doesn't offer foreign exchange.

Post & Communications A post office at the Golden Temple sells stamps (open 9 am to 6.30 pm Monday to Saturday). The main post office is on Court Rd north-west of the train station (9 am to 5 pm Monday to Saturday). There are a few Internet places around town charging Rs 30 per hour. Cybercity in the Nehru Shopping Centre is open 24 hours. @Internet near the train station is open 8.30 am to 10 pm, as is Cyberhut near the Golden Temple.

Golden Temple Complex

The holiest shrine of the Sikh religion is in the centre of the old part of Amritsar. The temple itself, also known as the Hari Mandir (or Darbar Sahib), is surrounded by the pool Amrit Sarovar, which gave the town its name, and is reached by a causeway. Open to all denominations, it's a beautiful place, especially early in the morning, at sunset or during Diwali when the temple is brightly illuminated.

At most times the grounds are filled with tourists and pilgrims. Hundreds of *sewas* (volunteers) enthusiastically wash down the marble walkways, dispense advice, clean shoes or peel potatoes – Sikhs consider it an honour to serve in this way. Others assemble for meals in the kitchen or settle into the pilgrim accommodation provided free to all (donations are expected). Around the tank, bathers perform their ablutions, children play next to devotees in silent prayer and a constant stream of the faithful patiently cross the Gurus' Bridge to pay homage at the temple.

All visitors must remove their shoes, wash their feet and cover their heads before entering the precincts (you can borrow headscarves). No smoking is allowed and photography is only permitted from the Parkarma, the marble walkway that surrounds the sacred pool. An English-speaking guide is available at the information office near the main entrance; the office also has a number of interesting free publications.

Standing in the middle of the sacred pool, the Hari Mandir is a two-storey marble structure. The lower parts of the marble walls are decorated with inlaid flower and animal motifs in the *pietra dura* style of the Taj Mahal (a style that entails creating patterns with semiprecious stones inlaid into marble). Once inside the temple, pilgrims offer sweet doughy *prasad* (food offerings) to the attendants, who take half to distribute to everyone as they leave the temple.

The architecture of the Hari Mandir is a blend of Hindu and Muslim styles. The golden dome (said to be gilded with 100kg of pure gold) is supposed to represent an inverted lotus flower. It is inverted, turning back to the earth, to symbolise the Sikhs' concern with the problems of this world.

Guru Granth Sahib Four priests at key positions around the temple keep up a continuous reading in Punjabi from the Sikhs' holy book. More like singing or chanting, it is broadcast by loudspeaker which adds to the overall atmosphere. The original copy of the Guru Granth Sahib is kept under a pink shroud in the Hari Mandir during the day; at around 10 pm each night it is ceremoniously returned to the Akal Takht (Sikh Parliament) building. The morning processional ceremony takes place at 4 am in summer, 5 am in winter.

Sikh Museum The Sikh Museum is upstairs in the clock tower and comprises a gallery of often gruesome paintings telling the story of the Sikhs and their martyrs. It's open 7 am to 7 pm daily.

Akal Takht The Shiromani Gurdwara Parbandhak Committee, or Sikh Parliament, meets in this building, which is why it was a target for the Indian army in 1984. It has since been completely rebuilt. If you're really interested, you could ask to see inside.

Gurdwaras It was the egalitarian Guru Nanak who introduced the idea of all people

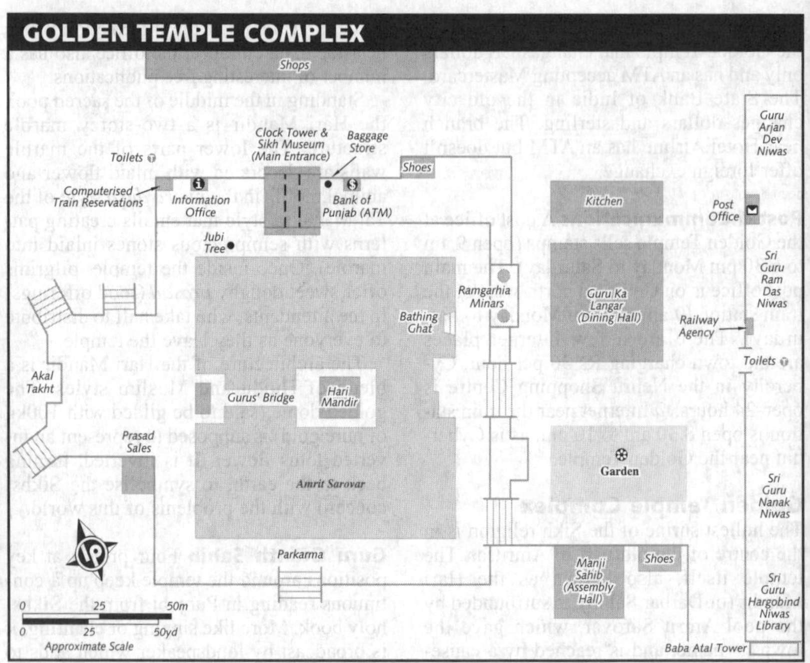

irrespective of class, creed or colour 'breaking bread' together. He said:

> Work hard, recite the name of God, and share with the less fortunate.

Today his legacy continues with community kitchens in all Sikh temples, and in this one alone volunteers prepare free meals for around 35,000 people every day. The food is very basic – chapatis and lentils – and is prepared and dished out in an orderly fashion. Take a plate, sit on the rush matting and wait for the prayers to be completed before tucking in.

Nearby are the gurdwaras, offering free accommodation to all.

The temple uses all donations to maintain the temple and help the poor and infirm, so don't forget to leave a donation, especially as pilgrims are so well provided for with a good library, post office, bank and railway booking agent.

Jubi Tree Over 400 years old, this tree is believed to have been the shaded resting place of the first priest of the temple. The first priest, between carrying out his fair share of volunteering, would rest here and monitor progress. Today it is more commonly surrounded by women, eager to give birth to sons, busy arranging colourful threads from its branches. Marriages are also arranged and blessed here.

Other Buildings To the south-east of the temple enclosure is the nine-storey (30m) **Baba Atal Tower**, built in 1784. The tall **Ramgarhia Minars**, scarred by tank fire, stand outside the temple enclosure.

The Old City

A 15-minute walk from the Golden Temple through the narrow alleys of the old city brings you to the Hindu **Durgiana Temple**. This small temple, dedicated to the goddess Durga, dates back to the 16th century.

A larger temple, also built in the centre of a lake, is dedicated to the Hindu deities Lakshmi and Narayan (Vishnu).

There are a number of mosques in the old city, including the mosque of **Mohammed Jan**, with three white domes and slender minarets.

Mata Temple

North-west of the train station, this Hindu temple commemorates a bespectacled 20th-century female saint, Lal Devi, and is a scaled-down version of the cave temple found near Jammu. Women wishing to have children pray here. It's notable for a Disneyesque series of grottoes and shrines featuring Hindu deities (take the stairs on the left), and a circumnavigation involves crawling through a tunnel and wading through a stream.

Jallianwala Bagh

This tree- and flower-filled park commemorates the 2000 Indians who were killed or wounded here, shot indiscriminately by the British in 1919. This appalling massacre was one of the major events in India's struggle for independence movingly re-created in the film *Gandhi* (see the boxed text 'Carnage at Jallianwala Bagh').

The park is a five-minute walk from the Golden Temple and is open 6 am to 7 pm in summer and 7 am to 6 pm in winter. A section of wall with visible bullet marks is preserved, as is the well that some people jumped into to escape; 120 bodies were recovered from it. Portraits and potted histories of some of those involved appear in the **Martyrs' Gallery**, open 9 am to 5 pm in summer, 10 am to 4 pm in winter.

Ram Bagh

This park in the new part of town has a **museum** in the small palace built by the Sikh maharaja Ranjit Singh. The museum contains weapons dating back to Mughal times and some portraits of the ruling houses of Punjab. It's open 10 am to 4.45 pm Tuesday to Sunday (entry Rs 5).

Khalsa College & Guru Nanak Dev University

Founded in 1892, Khalsa College is an imposing seat of learning which has produced many leading Indian figures. The colonial building surrounded by cool lawns certainly has an essentially colonial and academic air. Guru Nanak Dev University is a modern addition specialising in sport.

Carnage at Jallianwala Bagh

Unrest in Amritsar was sparked by the Rowlatt Act (1919), which gave the British authorities emergency powers to imprison without trial Indians suspected of sedition. Hartals (one-day strikes) were organised in protest. The lieutenant governor of Punjab, Sir Michael O'Dwyer ('a reactionary with contempt for educated Indians', according to text in the Martyrs' Gallery), adopted a hard line, and an Indian leader was arrested. Further Indian protests followed, which escalated into rioting and looting after the British fired upon the protesters.

General Dyer was called upon to return order to the city. He and 150 troops arrived at a peaceful demonstration on 13 April 1919 in Jallianwala Bagh, attended by 20,000 Indians. Dyer ordered the crowd to disperse – tricky seeing that the meeting space was surrounded by high walls, and he and his men were ranged in front of the very narrow and only entrance. Without further warning the British opened fire. Some six minutes later the toll of Indian deaths numbered 337 men, 41 boys and one baby. A further 1500 men and boys lay wounded. Some were shot as they tried to escape over the wall.

Although there was an international outcry over this massacre, O'Dwyer and Dyer were not considered culpable by the British; on the contrary, some thought them heroes. Meanwhile, in response, Gandhi instigated his program of civil disobedience and announced that 'cooperation in any shape or form with this satanic government is sinful'.

Dyer died in 1927 from a fall. O'Dwyer met his end in 1940, assassinated by a Sikh volunteer who had been serving water at the 1919 meeting.

Taren Taran

This is an important Sikh tank about 25km south of Amritsar. The temple predates Amritsar, and there's a tower on the eastern side of the tank, which was constructed by Ranjit Singh. It's said that any leper who can swim across the tank will be miraculously cured. Buses run every five minutes from Amritsar bus station (Rs 9, one hour).

Ram Tirath

Only 16km west of Amritsar, Ram Tirath commemorates Maharishi Balmik Ji's hermitage and is the site of a four-day mela during November's full moon.

Places to Stay – Budget

Tourist Guest House *(☎ 553830, 1355 Grand Trunk Rd)* has some clean and lovely old rooms with lots of character. With bathroom (geyser hot water) they cost Rs 150/200 per single/double, without bathroom Rs 100. There is a nice, small lawn and a good terrace; the only drawback is the smell of animal hides from the nearby market. It also has evening Internet access and is staffed 24 hours.

Bharat Hotel *(☎ 227536)* near the train station is a friendly place with reasonable, clean rooms with TV, phone and bathroom (geyser hot water) for Rs 150 to Rs 250.

Hotel Palace & Pegasus *(☎ 565111, Queen's Rd)* is more basic but closer to the station. Rooms with bathroom (squat toilets and bucket hot water) start at Rs 150/250.

There are a few cheap places around the Golden Temple. ***Sharma Guest House*** *(☎ 551657)* is very friendly and has a restaurant. Rooms are Rs 150/200 with shared bathroom and Rs 250 with private bathroom.

Many enjoy the camaraderie at the pilgrim accommodation at the ***Golden Temple***, open 24 hours although checkout is noon. To stay more than one night you will need to get special permission. A Rs 50 refundable deposit is required and a donation should be given.

Places to Stay – Mid-Range

Mrs Bhandari's Guest House *(☎ 228509, fax 222390, e payal@mol.net.in, 10 Cantonment)* is set in a large, peaceful garden with a swimming pool. Clean rooms with fireplaces vary in size and start at Rs 750/950 for a single/double. Camping in the garden costs Rs 150 per person. Meals are available to residents (Rs 250), who are also welcome to have a nose around Mrs Bhandari's house; it has a fantastic Art Deco interior.

Grand Hotel *(☎ 562424, fax 229677, e grand@jla.vsnl.net.in)*, opposite the train station, is a good choice with rooms around a grassy, flowered (no plucking) garden. With TV, phone and bathroom (geyser hot water) they cost Rs 395/500, or Rs 675/775 with air-con; credit cards are accepted. There's also a good bar and restaurant here and a pool table (Rs 100 per hour) on the patio.

Hotel Airline *(☎ 564848, Cooper Rd)* has rooms with interesting features such as cushioned swings and bathtubs and a central courtyard patio. They also have TV and phone and cost Rs 350/450, or Rs 600/750 with air-con. At the time of research a new restaurant was being built.

Run by Punjab Tourism, ***Amritsar International Hotel*** *(☎ 555991)* is a typical high-rise government hotel with a small lawn area, a restaurant and parking. Rooms with bathroom start at Rs 475/550 and the staff are helpful.

Hotel Blue Moon *(☎ 220416, fax 22180, e bluemoon@jla.vsnl.net.in)* on The Mall is a reasonable place surrounded by lawns. Single rooms with TV, phone and bathroom cost Rs 695 to 745; doubles cost Rs 990 to 1080. The more expensive rooms are modern and brighter.

Places to Stay – Top End

Mohan International Hotel *(☎ 227801, fax 226520, Albert Rd)* is a central top-end hotel. It has a swimming pool and the Unique Travel agency. Rooms start at Rs 1500/2500.

Amritsar's newest hotel, ***MK Hotel*** *(☎ 504610, fax 507910, e mkhotel@mol.net.in, Ranjit Ave)*, is a sparkling place quite a way out of town. It has a 1st-floor terrace courtyard pool and a restaurant with music. Rooms start at Rs 1600/2500.

Hotel Ritz Plaza *(☎ 562836, 226657, e itz@del3.vsnl.net.in, 45 The Mall)* is another posh place with good service. It too has a pool, a sophisticated lounge bar and a restaurant. Rooms with balconies start at Rs 1650/2200 and meals cost Rs 275.

Places to Eat

Lawrence St, with lots of interesting *dhabas* (snack bars), is the place to head for excellent and cheap food. Recommendations include ***Surjit***, the most famous tandoori chicken shop in Punjab, and ***Makhan***, an open-air tandoori fish place which sells out within a couple of hours but refuses to cook more. Other good spots include the ***Himalayan Chaat Bizaar*** and the ***Lahoria*** sweet shop.

The popular ***Crystal Restaurant*** *(☎ 225 555)* serves a tasty range of Indian, Chinese and continental cuisine in swish air-con surrounds for around Rs 60 to 120 per dish. It's licensed. Another of Amritsar's better restaurants is ***Napoli*** at the Hotel Blue Moon which is also licensed.

Amritsar is renowned for its lassis, and shops selling them can be found all over the old town. There are ***alcohol shops*** around the train station. ***Prithvi supermarket*** near the bus stand is the place to stock up on food and toiletries.

Shopping

Woollen blankets, shawls and sweaters are supposed to be cheaper in Amritsar than in other places, as they are locally manufactured – look around Guru Vihar near the Hari Mandir. Tea and silver are other good buys and Katra Jaimal Singh, near the telephone exchange in the old city, has good shopping.

Getting There & Away

Air Air India (☎ 546122) operates international flights to and from Amritsar airport mainly to the Middle East. The Indian Airlines office (☎ 503780) is at 39A Court Rd. Flights link Amritsar to Delhi (US$90, one hour, five weekly) and Lucknow (Rs 4565, 1½ hours, two weekly).

Bus Local buses leave the bus station frequently for Delhi (Rs 160, 10 hours), Chandigarh (Rs 90, five hours, counter 15), Jammu (Rs 70, five hours, counter 15), Taren Taran (Rs 9, one hour, counters 1 to 4) and Wagah (Rs 13, one hour, counters 2 and 3). There are also buses to Dehra Dun at 7 am (Rs 167, 10 hours, counters 13 and 14), Dalhousie at 9.20 am (Rs 90, 10 hours, counter 8) and Dharamsala at 11 am (Rs 93, 10 hours, counters 13 and 14); it's easier to get a train as far as Pathankot then change to a bus there. For bus inquiries call ☎ 551734.

Private buses leave from in front of the train station and tickets are available at agencies there.

To/From Pakistan Hourly buses run from Amritsar to Attari (Rs 13, one hour) until about 3 pm, but not all continue on to Wagah. It is easy to get a rickshaw between Attari and Wagah. Taxis from Amritsar cost Rs 300 to Rs 400, or look for minibuses by the train station (Rs 60).

Neem Chameli Tourist Complex *(☎ 231 452)*, operated by Punjab Tourism at Wagah, has dorm beds and cheap doubles, and there are cafes for eating or changing money.

Train In addition to the one at the train station, there is a train reservation service at the Golden Temple open 8 am to 2 pm and 2.15 to 8 pm Monday to Saturday and 8 am to 2 pm Sunday.

There are direct rail links to Delhi (Rs 99/520 in 2nd/1st class, eight to 10 hours, 447km) but the daily *Shatabdi Express* does the journey in only 5½ hours (Rs 610/1220 in chair car/executive class). For other destinations, the 3006 *Amritsar-Howrah Mail* links Amritsar with Lucknow (Rs 158/830 in 2nd/1st class, 17 hours, 850km), Varanasi (Rs 201/1056, 23 hours, 1251km) and Calcutta (Kolkata; Rs 245/1336, 38 hours, 1829km).

To/From Pakistan The rail crossing point is at Attari, 26km from Amritsar, and the 4607 *Indo-Pak Express* leaves Amritsar at 7 am, reaching Lahore in Pakistan at 4.15 pm. However, it only goes on Monday and Thursday (returning Tuesday and Friday) and spends hours at the border.

The road crossing at Wagah, about 4km beyond Attari, is quicker. The border is open 9 am to 3.30 pm (winter) or 4 pm (summer) daily, and most people walk

Border Displays

Relations between India and Pakistan are rarely tranquil – each country seems determined to outdo the other at every opportunity, whether on the cricket pitch or, more worryingly, in the field of nuclear armaments. A harmless but entertaining manifestation of this long-standing rivalry can be witnessed daily at the Wagah border, the only road crossing between the two countries.

About 30 minutes before sunrise and sunset, the guards on each side of the border assemble to parade and preen themselves in an immaculately turned out display of synchronised marching and bellowed military commands. The flag of each country is then carefully raised or lowered and the gates are opened or slammed shut.

Crowds congregate on both sides of the border, but the Indians seem to have the upper hand with a concrete stand which has been specially built for the event, and guards with whistles ensure everyone gets a good view. The total number of spectators is amazing, around 5000 each evening, all of whom are there to cheer on the efforts of their own guards and deride those of the opposition. At the end of the ceremony the crowds are encouraged to surge forward to the gates for some serious fist-shaking – don't get caught waving or being friendly to the opposition or you'll be severely whistled at by a vexed border guard.

across because vehicles are delayed. There is a Punjab Tourism office at the border.

Getting Around

The airport is 15km from the city centre; the trip costs Rs 100 by autorickshaw or Rs 400 by taxi.

A trip from the train station to the Golden Temple should cost about Rs 15 by cycle-rickshaw or Rs 30 by autorickshaw. Both forms of transport run all over town.

KAPURTHALA

Named after its founder, Nawab Kapur Singh, this town 19km from Jalandhar has a couple of attractions. A prominent feature is the **mosque** modelled on the Moorish Koutoubia mosque in Morocco.

The **Shalimar Garden** is a small garden with pool and library. A few kilometres outside Kapurthala, **Kanjli wetland** is filled with migratory birds during winter.

JALANDHAR

☎ 0181

Jalandhar, once the capital of an ancient Hindu kingdom, survived a sacking nearly 1000 years ago by Mahmud of Ghazni and later became an important Mughal city. It is now a major crossroads and an important commercial centre famous for the production of sporting goods and hand tools.

Most facilities can be found on or near GT Rd which runs straight through the city. These include the bus stand, hotels, banks with ATMs, Thomas Cook, airline offices and restaurants. The main train station (Jalandhar City) is north of the main bazaar area.

There isn't that much to see in Jalandhar, although if you yearn for a genuine Indian cricket bat and ball or an Aussie Rules footy you can visit one of the **sporting goods factories** which supply gear worldwide and are happy to show visitors around for free. These places aren't touristy, but a rickshaw-wallah will be able to take you to one.

Desh-Bhagat Memorial Hall chronicles the fight for Independence and the martyrs who died in the struggle (many of whom came from Jalandhar).

The **Catholic cathedral** in the cantonment, merging Punjab and Classic designs, is unique and there is the usual scattering of temples, gurdwaras and mosques.

Harballah Sangeet Sammelan in December is a music festival attracting world-class performers from all over India. Popular for some time now, it was attended by Mahatma Gandhi in 1929. **Baba Sodai** is another festival held in December.

Places to Stay & Eat

Accommodation is largely aimed at the business traveller although cheap guest houses can be found around the main train and bus stations.

In the bazaar area, ***Amar Guest House*** *(☎ 55290)* is a nicely terraced place with lots of balcony areas. Basic single/double rooms with TV, phone and bathroom (bucket hot water) cost Rs 175/250.

Hotel International *(☎ 223846, fax 225505)*, 200m east of the bus station, is a convenient choice with bar and restaurant. Rooms with TV, phone, bathrooms and cosy quilts cost Rs 300/350, or Rs 495/595 with air-con.

Just off GT Rd, ***Hotel Kamal Palace*** *(☎ 58462, fax 239826)* is an upmarket place with roof lawn, Punjab's only glass elevator, restaurants and a bar done out like a train. Rooms with TV, phone and safes start at Rs 1500/2300 (including tax).

Dhabas, some serving beer, can be found all over town, including a string of them overlooking the grassy areas outside the bus stand and along the road directly in front of and heading away from the city train station. The local speciality is fried fish from the surrounding waterways.

Restaurants along GT Rd include ***Moti Mahal*** which does a good thali and ***The Clocktower*** which has pool tables; both serve Indian, Chinese and continental fare for around Rs 100 per person and are licensed. Sweet tooths should visit ***Kaypee Confectionery*** *(GT Rd)* which makes absolutely delicious cream puffs during the cooler months and good almond biscuits year-round.

Getting There & Away

There are at least hourly bus services between Jalandhar and Amritsar, Chandigarh, Delhi, Pathankot and beyond. There is also a private coach service (☎ 55425) between Hotel International and Delhi airport (Rs 550) five times daily.

There are two train stations. Jalandhar City station is more central and convenient. The *Shatabdi Express* stops in Jalandhar. Tickets to Amritsar cost Rs 230/455 in 2nd/1st class; tickets to Delhi cost Rs 530/1075. Mail trains and other express trains also stop here.

ANANDPUR SAHIB

☎ 01881

One of Sikhism's holiest sites with a number of historic gurdwaras, Anandpur Sahib (City of Bliss) has been a pilgrimage site for over 300 years. It was here in 1699 that Guru Gobind Singh baptised five of his followers who came from different castes and founded the Khalsa (Pure) – a sacred military brotherhood. He made them drink *amrit* (nectar) from a common bowl and gave them the surname of Singh.

The tercentenary of the Khalsa's founding in 1999 saw a huge influx of pilgrims to Anandpur Sahib. To cater for that event new infrastructure was put in place which is assisting the tourist authorities in their drive to attract visitors. There's a tourist information office as you enter town, and facilities such as foreign exchange, restaurants and top-end accommodation should soon be in place. The bus and train stations are about 200m apart on the main road through town.

Gurdwara Kesgarh Sahib is a large gurdwara and the spot where the Khalsa was born. Inside the shrine devotees sing devotional songs and weapons are displayed. There is an information office, accommodation and a kitchen.

The day after Holi (usually in March) the birth of the movement is commemorated with the festival of **Holla Mohalla.** Founded after Holi had degenerated into a time to settle old scores it has become a time for reflection and celebration. Hordes of pilgrims gather on the ground below the gurdwara to watch armies of Nihangs (colourful Sikh warriors) re-enact the bloody scenes from the religion's history. It is also a time for prayer and a reaffirmation of faith. Essentially though it's a time for festivity with lots of singing and bravado.

Back on the hill and facing Kesgarh Sahib is **Gurdwara Anandgarh Sahib**. Distinguishable by its small fort, below which a series of steps lead to a well with healing waters, the gurdwara is the scene of a nightly sound-and-light show.

Places to Stay & Eat

At the time of research accommodation in Anandpur Sahib was limited to the gurdwaras and ***Champa Tourist Huts*** on the main road below the gurdwaras. There are snack stands, and of course you can always get a meal at the gurdwara kitchens.

Getting There & Away

Anandpur Sahib, which lies 75km north-west of Chandigarh, can be reached by bus or train. Buses leave for Sector 43 in Chandigarh hourly (Rs 29, 2½ hours), but it's probably easier to get a more regular bus to Ropar and change for Chandigarh (or elsewhere) there.

Trains for Ambala (Rs 25, 3½ hours), from where it's possible to connect to Delhi trains, leave four times daily.

A taxi for a day trip from Chandigarh should cost around Rs 800.

LUDHIANA

The textiles centre of India, Ludhiana was the site of great battles during the First Sikh War. Founded by Lodi princes (hence the name), it has a **fort** with a shrine that attracts thousands of Hindu and Muslim pilgrims annually.

There are a few educational institutions, including the **Agricultural University**, which helped make Punjab India's largest food producer.

The archaic, bureaucratic muddle of the offices of the old **law courts** (the Purana Karcharia) is worth a look.

SIRHIND

☎ 0173

Sirhind, 72km south-east of Ludhiana, was once a very important frontier town (Sir-i-Hind literally means 'Frontier of India') and the capital of the Pathan Sur dynasty. It is an important site of pilgrimage for Sikhs and Sunni Muslims. About 2.5km from the town centre and just off GT Rd is **Aam Khas Bagh**, a large Mughal serai constructed for the use of royalty and riff-raff equally. Started by Babar it was completed by Emperor Shah Jahan and today the gardens and tank continue to make a good stopover.

At the eastern end of the garden is a large, walled enclosure with a tank and a mirrored palace. Beyond are more walled enclosures of the emperor's private domain. Today they are overgrown or have been cultivated for agriculture. The Archaeological Survey has an office here with pictures and information on other significant sites in Punjab.

At the other end of the garden walkway, past orchards, fountains, flowerbeds and a playground, are some slightly more dilapidated monuments. The main structure, the Daulat Khana, was the emperor's residence and remnants of the decoration that once covered the walls can just be made out. More visible is the decor in the *hammam*, the circular building enclosing the well to the left of the Daulat Khana. Elephants were used to pull water up from the well; it was then pumped to bathing pools and through a series of channels to supply air-conditioning and irrigation.

In the north-east of town on the road to Ropar, the **Fategarh Sahib Gurdwara** commemorates the martyrdom of the two young sons of the tenth Sikh guru, Gobind Singh, who were completely sealed within a brick chamber as punishment for not converting to Islam. Their shrine is in the basement of the main temple next to the boys' grandmother's tomb; she died from the shock of their martyrdom. A two-day Urs (death anniversary) festival, **Shaheedi Jor Mela,** takes place at the gurdwara in December.

About 500m beyond the gurdwara, **Rauza Sharif** is a small 14th-century mausoleum with a mosque and several tombstones. It is venerated as a second Mecca, and Sunni Muslims flock here to pay homage in August from places as far afield as Indonesia.

Places to Stay & Eat

It's possible to stay next to Aam Khas Bagh at the ***Red Rose Tourist Complex*** *(☎ 22250)*. Sadly characterless rooms with bathroom and phone cost Rs 500; there is a restaurant. Outside town, but still on GT Rd heading towards Amritsar, ***Bougainvillea Tourist Complex*** *(☎ 22170)* has similarly priced rooms, camping and a floating restaurant. Ask to be dropped here if coming by bus.

Getting There & Away

The train station is a few kilometres south of the town centre. Most trains between Delhi and Amritsar stop here. Buses between Delhi and Amritsar stop on the GT Rd. Frequent local buses depart to statewide destinations throughout the day.

PATIALA

About 35km south of Sirhind is Patiala, which was once the capital of an independent Sikh state. Off the main tourist route, it is a city of palaces and gardens. **Qila Mubarak**, an 18th-century fort built by Maharaja Amar Singh and surrounded by a moat, dominates the town. Within the fort is another, **Qila Androon**, with an ornate lime-plastered gateway. The fort has been declared a national monument on account of its well-preserved frescoes depicting Hindu and Sikh scenes – over 75% of the originals remain. There is a museum displaying chandeliers and weapons.

One of the largest palaces in Asia, **Motibagh Palace** is a mish-mash of European, Mughal and Hindu styles surrounded by lawns and gardens. Within the grounds is a museum and art gallery (housing the world's largest collection of medals) and the National Institute of Sports.

The **Punjab Government Archives** in the Baradari complex has a rich collection of manuscripts. The palace is at the south end of Mall Rd.

Good buys in Patiala are unique, gold-embroidered *jootis* (decorated shoes).

There are hotels and restaurants in the town centre and local buses link Patiala with local towns and train stations.

Patiala is the site of the Basant festival held each year in February.

BATHINDA

The railway line from Delhi passes through Bathinda, which was an important town of the Pathan Sur dynasty but is now focused on industry.

During Baisakhi, the Talwadi Sabo, which has been recognised as a national fair, has dancing and martial arts displays. The city is important to Sikhs as Guru Gobind Singh recomposed the Guru Granth Sahib here.

FARIDKOT

Faridkot is named after a famous Sufi mystic, Baba Farid, whose work appears in the Guru Granth Sahib. Some 350km north-west of Delhi, close to the Pakistan border, it was once the capital of a Sikh state of the same name and has a 700-year-old **fort** famous for its mirrorwork and murals. Faridkot also has many fine buildings, the best of which is the Secretariat. It is the site of the **Sheikh Farid Agam Purb** festival in September.

FIROZPUR

Firozpur, almost on the border, is 382km north-west of Delhi; before Partition the train line continued to Lahore, now in Pakistan. (The only remaining railway crossing into Pakistan is at Wagah.)

The **Shaheed Bhagat Singh Memorial** honours those martyred for plotting a revolution against the British. Each year on 23 March thousands gather to pay homage here.

Another war-related site is the **Saragarhi Memorial Gurdwara** commemorating an 1897 battle in which 31 Sikhs fought to the last man against a greater tribal force. Thousands pay homage to the heroes on 12 September.

The **Anglo-Sikh War Memorial** founded in 1976 has war-themed paintings and weapons.

PATHANKOT

☎ 0186 • pop 150,000

Pathankot (pronounced Pattan-cot), in the extreme north of Punjab, is an important railhead for those travelling to Dharamsala and Dalhousie. There is a helpful Himachal Pradesh tourist office, open 10 am to 5 pm Monday to Saturday, opposite the Pathankot train station entrance. Regular buses mean you probably won't have to stay in this uninspiring town too long; should you find yourself here for a while you can spend time chatting to the locals at a dhaba, wandering the bazaar or exploring the nearby River Beas.

The Bank of India and the main post office are along the left fork in Gurdaspur Rd – the main road in from Delhi. There's also an Internet cafe here.

Places to Stay

Most hotels are along Gurdaspur Rd, which makes the front-facing rooms noisy. Unless stated otherwise all have noon checkout, sit-down flush toilets and geyser hot water.

Closest to the train station is ***Green Hotel*** with rooms off a side balcony with TV, phone and bathroom for Rs 250. There's a 1st-floor restaurant and a ground-floor bar.

Near the fork in Gurdaspur Rd, ***Hotel Tourist*** is the best of the cheapies with rooms around a open courtyard. Those on the terrace with squat toilets are light and Rs 90/ 100; those on the first two floors with full bathroom (squat toilets) are Rs 220/ 225. There are plenty of rooms, all of which haveTV and phone. According to a sign, there's even a sex, venereal disease and skin doctor on the 1st floor, should you need one.

North-east of the post office, ***Hotel Airlines*** *(☎ 20505)* is a bit quieter than those on Gurdaspur Rd and has a licensed restaurant with 1960s decor. Rooms around a covered courtyard cost Rs 150 with squat toilet, Rs 250 with bathroom and balcony; they all have phone and TV.

About 100m beyond the bus station towards Delhi, ***Hotel Parag*** *(☎ 25672)* has large, cleanish rooms with TV, phone and bathroom for Rs 250 to Rs 350 with air-cooler, and Rs 500 with air-con.

Places to Eat

There are heaps of ***dhabas*** along Gurdaspur Rd and the hotels all have their own reasonable restaurants, the best of which is ***Vitaka*** at Hotel Parag.

Kalotra Coffee House, east of the post office, has good coffee and mango shakes, but unmarried couples are only allowed a maximum of 20 minutes to enjoy them.

Getting There & Away

Gurdaspur Rd is where you'll find the bus station and, about 400m farther towards town, Pathankot train station. From Chowkibank train station you can cover the 3km between the two by cycle-rickshaw for Rs 25.

Several daily trains leave here for Delhi (Rs 105/552 in 2nd/1st class). There are also trains to Amritsar (Rs 20/173, 2½ hours) and Jammu (Rs 32/173, three hours). The station's computer reservation office is open daily.

Buses to Dalhousie (Rs 45, three hours), Chamba (Rs 70, five hours), Dharamsala (Rs 60, four hours) and Mcleod Ganj (Rs 90, 4½ hours) leave every hour or so between 5 am and 5 pm. Buses to Manali leave between 4.30 and 8 am, and between 5 and 8 pm (Rs 225, 13 hours). Buses to Chandigarh leave every five minutes or so (Rs 48, three hours).

You can do the same journeys by taxi slightly more quickly but for much more cash – around Rs 800 to Dalhousie or Dharamsala. The 24-hour taxi stand is next to the Himachal Pradesh tourist office.

Himachal Pradesh

Himachal Pradesh at a Glance

Population: 6.13 million
Area: 55,673 sq km
Capital: Shimla
Main Languages: Hindi & Pahari
When to Go: mid-May to mid-Oct (trekking); late Dec to Mar (winter sports)

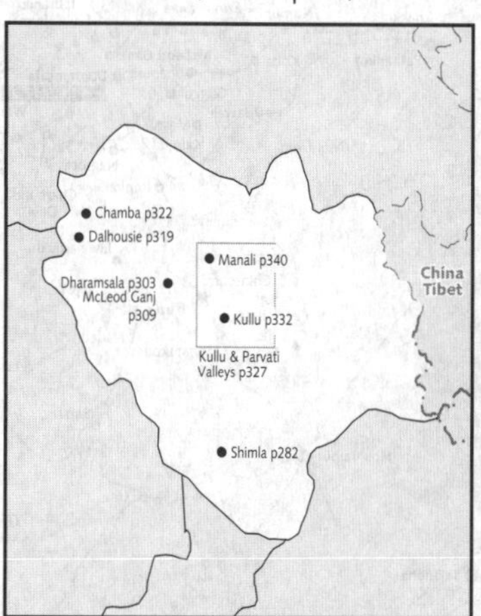

- Hop aboard the toy train to Shimla and bask in the faded grandeur of the Raj
- Study Buddhism in the Dalai Lama's home of exile, or volunteer to help Tibetan refugees at McLeod Ganj
- Explore the wild frontier of Kinnaur in the far east
- Take in the ancient temples and stunning mountain scenery of the Chamba Valley
- Brave the skiing, rafting or paragliding at Manali, Himachal's adventure playground

Himachal Pradesh – the land of eternal snow peaks – takes in the transition zone from the plains to the high Himalaya and, in the trans-Himalayan region of Lahaul and Spiti, actually crosses that mighty barrier to the Tibetan plateau.

The Kullu Valley, with its developed and tourist-oriented economy, can be considered the backbone of the state, though commercialism has eroded some of the charm that first drew travellers here back in the 1960s. Off to the east is the Parvati Valley, popular with long-stay visitors. Few make it farther north to the splendid Chamba Valley, with its rugged scenery, hill stations and beautiful temple complexes. The Kangra Valley is best known as the home of the Tibetan Government in Exile, with its headquarters in Dharamsala and the residence of His Holiness the Dalai Lama in McLeod Ganj, a few kilometres away.

For untouched mountain scenery, head for the bleak, high-altitude districts of Lahaul, Spiti and Kinnaur. Closed to foreigners until as late as 1992, the region lies in the rain shadow of the Himalaya and has more in common with nearby Tibet than the rest of India. The area has been profoundly influenced by Tibetan Buddhism and, following the ravages of the Cultural Revolution across the border in China and Tibet, the spectacular *gompas* (monasteries) here are some of the best remaining examples of Tibetan religious architecture. Permits (easily obtained) are necessary to visit the sensitive area that links Spiti and Kinnaur.

See Lonely Planet's *Trekking in the Indian Himalaya* and *Indian Himalaya* for details on trekking in this region.

History

The regions that today comprise Himachal were, in ancient times, crossed by trade routes to Tibet (over the Shipki La) and Central Asia (via the Baralacha La and Leh) and also commanded the Sach La that led to Kashmir. Rajas, Ranas and Thakurs ran their rival *rahuns* and *thakurais*, making Himachal a patchwork quilt of tiny states. Only Kangra and Kullu (and later Chamba)

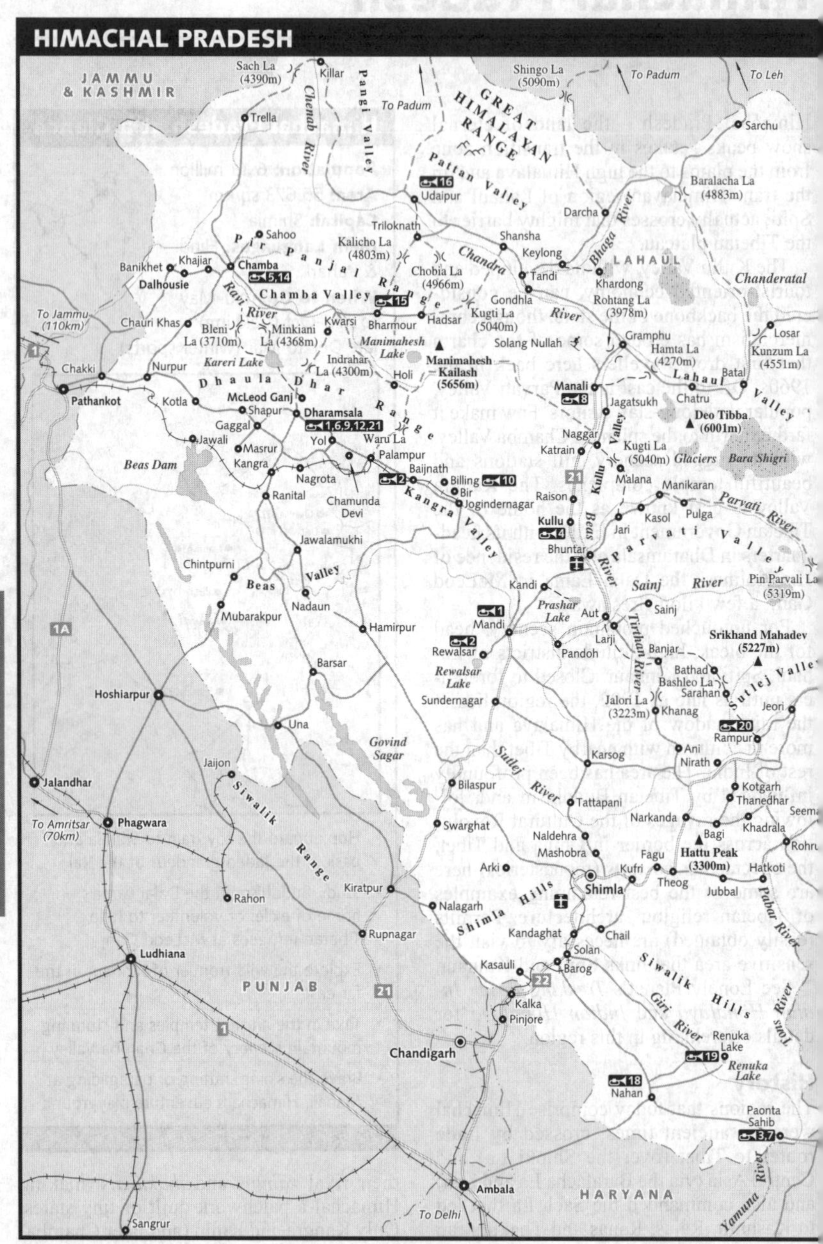

HIMACHAL PRADESH

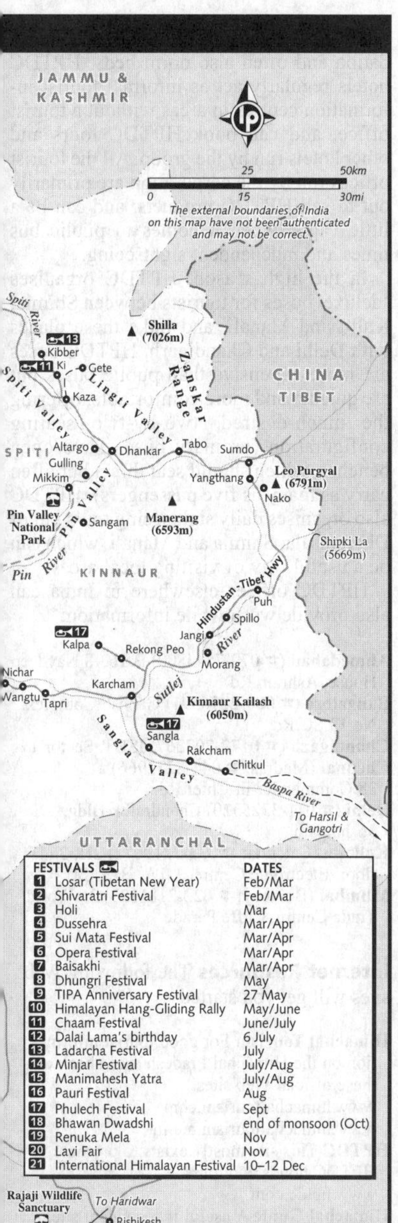

had the power to break out of the petty feuding system.

Several Himachal states had kings from Bengal; the best known of these states is Mandi, which was founded in 1527. With the exception of the bigger states, most of the later hill states were founded by Rajput adventurers from the plains in the early medieval period. During the colonial period, many Rajas cast in their lot with the British, only to lose their kingdoms and titles when India became independent.

The first Westerners to visit the region were Jesuit missionaries in search of the legendary kingdom of Prester John. The British 'discovered' Himachal after their wars with the Sikhs and the Gurkhas. Little bits of England were created at Shimla, Dalhousie and Dharamsala by homesick British during the 19th century. Apple cultivation was introduced to Himachal by the American missionary, the Reverend NS Stokes, who developed the Kotgarh apple orchards. In the early part of the 20th century a railway was built to Shimla and another was laid through the Kangra Valley. In the interior, however, feudal conditions remained: Men were forced to work without pay and women were regarded as chattels.

The state of Himachal Pradesh was formed in 1948. By 1966, the Pahari-speaking parts under Punjab administration, including Kangra, Kullu, Lahaul and Spiti, were added. Full statehood was achieved in 1971. The area is politically stable, but the influx of refugees from war-torn Kashmir has added to the poverty in the state.

Geography

Himachal Pradesh is dominated by mountains, which rise steeply from the Punjabi plains, and their associated rivers and valleys. The tallest peaks here are Leo Purgyal (6791m), near Nako in Kinnaur; Deo Tibba (6001m), not far from Manali; and Kinnaur Kailash (6050m), which dominates the views from Rekong Peo and Kalpa in Kinnaur.

Himachal is made up of several culturally distinct regions, separated by high mountain ridges. Even today, the only links between communities are high mountain passes such as the Rohtang La (3978m), Baralacha La (4883m) and Kunzum La (4551m) – 'la' is a Tibetan word meaning pass – which are frequently blocked by snow in winter. Some parts of Lahaul and Spiti can be cut off completely for several months of the year.

The topography of Himachal was carved by the rivers that drain the Tibetan plateau. The Chandra and Bhaga Valleys of Lahaul were formed by the Chandra River, which becomes the Chenab River, before flowing west into Kashmir. Farther east, the Spiti River joins the Sutlej River in Kinnaur and flows all the way to Punjab. The Kullu Valley is drained by the Beas River (pronounced '**bee**-ahs') and stretches from Mandi to Manali. The Parvati River flows down the valley of the same name to the east, joining the Beas near Bhuntar.

Just north of Mandi, where the Beas turns towards Punjab, lies the peaceful Kangra Valley, separated by the snow-capped Dhaula Dhar Range from the wonderfully rugged Chamba Valley. The Ravi River flows through Chamba and on to Lahore in northern Pakistan. Beyond the Chamba Valley is the remote Pattan Valley (upper Chenab river valley) isolated from the rest of the state by the Pir Panjal Range.

Economy

Much of Himachal's income comes from tourism, agriculture and the textile industry. The Himachal government is now hoping to add hydroelectric power to that base with the construction of huge dams across many of the state's rivers, which are believed to hold 25% of India's hydroelectric potential.

A large part of the revenue from tourism is generated by the 10% luxury tax, which all but the cheapest hotels slap onto the bill at the end of each stay. Rates quoted for accommodation in this chapter do not include tax.

Information

Tourist Offices The Himachal Pradesh Tourist Development Corporation (HPTDC) offers local information and maps, runs local tours and manages a number of mid-range hotels in the state, which offer reliable, if slightly institutional, accommodation and often also dorm beds. HPTDC hotels regularly act as informal tourist information centres in areas without a tourist office, and can book HPTDC tours and other hotels run by the group. All the tourist offices run by the corporation are primarily out to sell HPTDC products, and can be a little vague when it comes to public bus times and independent sightseeing.

In the high season, HPTDC organises 'deluxe' buses for tourists between Shimla, Kullu and Manali, and links these places with Delhi and Chandigarh. HPTDC buses are more expensive than public buses but are quicker and more comfortable, offering the much-desired, two-by-two seating configuration (ordinary buses have open benches, which should seat three, but often carry as many as five passengers). HPTDC also organises daily sightseeing tours out of Dharamsala, Shimla and Manali, which can be a useful way of visiting local areas.

HPTDC offices elsewhere in India can also provide worthwhile information:

Ahmedabad (☎ 079-7544800) B/163/8 Navdeep House, Ashram Rd
Bangalore (☎ 080-2876591) Ganesh Complex, No 13 SC Rd
Chandigarh (☎ 0172-707267) ISBT, Sector 17
Chennai (Madras; ☎ 044-8272966) 28 Commander-in-Chief Rd
Delhi (☎ 011-3325320) Chandralok Bldg, 36 Janpath
Kolkata (Calcutta; ☎ 033-2219072) 2H, 2nd floor, Electronic Centre, 1-1A, BAC St
Mumbai (Bombay; ☎ 022-2181123) 36 World Trade Centre, Cuffe Parade

Internet Resources The following Web sites will get you started:

Himachal Tourism For good tourist information on the Himachal Pradesh area check out these official Web sites.
www.himachaltourism.com
www.himachaltourism.nic.in
HPTDC This site mostly exists to promote HPTDC hotels and tours.
www.hptdc.com
Himachal Guide A useful independent site.
www.himachalguide.com

GREG ELMS

Snack sellers assail passengers at every stop.

RICHARD I'ANSON

All aboard the family sedan!

GREG ELMS

Morning light streams into an alley off Chandni Chowk, Delhi, where vendors ply their wares.

GARRY WEARE

Fording rivers in the Spiti Valley presents few problems for the well prepared and well equipped.

PAUL BEINSSEN

Shiva, whose third eye represents wisdom

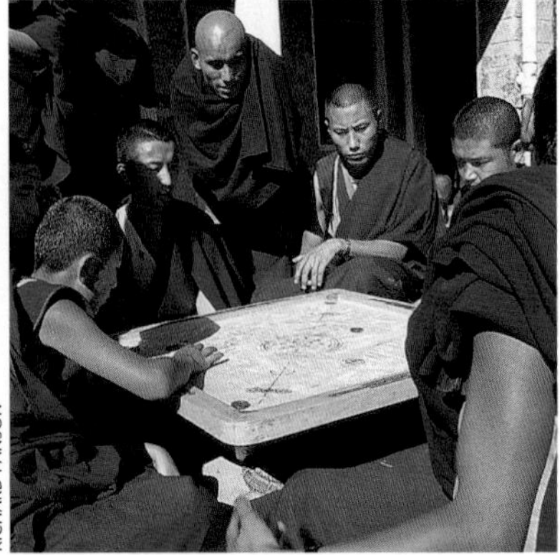

RICHARD I'ANSON

Monks enjoy a game of *carrum* in Dharamsala.

GARRY WEARE

The Himalaya stretches skyward in Kullu Valley.

Permits The region surrounding the Tibetan border is politically sensitive, and inner line permits are required for some areas of Spiti and Kinnaur. However, regulations and their implementation have been noticeably relaxed in recent years, though authorities are holding out on the region around Tabo, which lies between Kinnaur and Spiti in the far north-east of the state. If you want to cross from Kaza in Spiti to Rekong Peo in Kinnaur, you'll need an inner line permit, best obtained from the subdivisional magistrates' (SDM) offices at Kaza and Rekong Peo in Kinnaur (see this heading under the Kinnaur and the Lahaul & Spiti sections later in this chapter for more details). Currently the application process is just a formality, but any rise in Indian-Chinese tension could result in a tightening of restrictions so check the current regulations before visiting the area.

Special Events

The most important Hindu festival in Himachal is **Dussehra**, which is celebrated with great aplomb – and more than a little bloodlust – in March or April at Kullu and as part of the Astomi festival at Sarahan. The festival commemorates Rama's victory over Ravana, the demon king of Lanka, and features dancing and sacrifices of buffalo and other animals.

Other important festivals in Himachal Pradesh are Buddhist in origin. **Losar**, the Tibetan New Year, was introduced to the area by Tibetan Buddhists and is celebrated with great pomp and circumstance in February or March in Dharamsala, McLeod Ganj and in Rewalsar Lake, as well as the remote, high-altitude regions of Lahaul and Spiti.

The festival actually dates back to the primitive Bon religion, which preceded Buddhism in the area. Many regional Buddhist festivals are celebrated with Chaam rituals, in which lamas dance in colourful masks representing heroes and demons from Tibetan legends. The most common story is the victory of Guru Rinpoche over the forces of evil.

Shimla

☎ 0177 • pop 123,000 • elevation 2205m

Shimla was once part of the Nepalese kingdom and called Shyamala, another name for the goddess Kali, but saw few visitors until it was 'discovered' by British seeking respite from the baking plains in 1819. Three years later, the first 'British' house was erected, and in 1864 Shimla became the summer capital of India.

Right up until 1939, the whole government of India would pack its bags and migrate almost 2000km from the sweltering heat of Kolkata or Delhi to the cool heights of Shimla for the summer. The construction of the Kalka-Shimla railway line in 1903 allowed easy access for Raj families who couldn't bear to be completely cut off from the plains, and many built opulent mansions here, some of which are still used as government offices. Following Independence, Shimla was initially the capital of Punjab, then became the capital of Himachal Pradesh in 1966.

Set among cool pine-clad hills with plenty of crumbling colonial charm, for many people Shimla is the archetypal hill station. Some buildings, such as the mock-Tudor municipality building at Scandal Point, are plucked straight from 19th-century England. There are stunning views all the way to the Himalaya and some good places to stay and eat, although it can be hard to find reasonably priced accommodation in the high season. However, Shimla certainly attracts the crowds and some travellers find the place a little 'touristy' compared with other hill towns in the region.

High season is mid-April to mid-July, mid-September to late October and mid-December to mid-January. The best time to visit is mid-September to late November. The first snows at Shimla usually begin in January.

Orientation

The main road in Shimla is known as The Mall, and runs east-west along the top of the

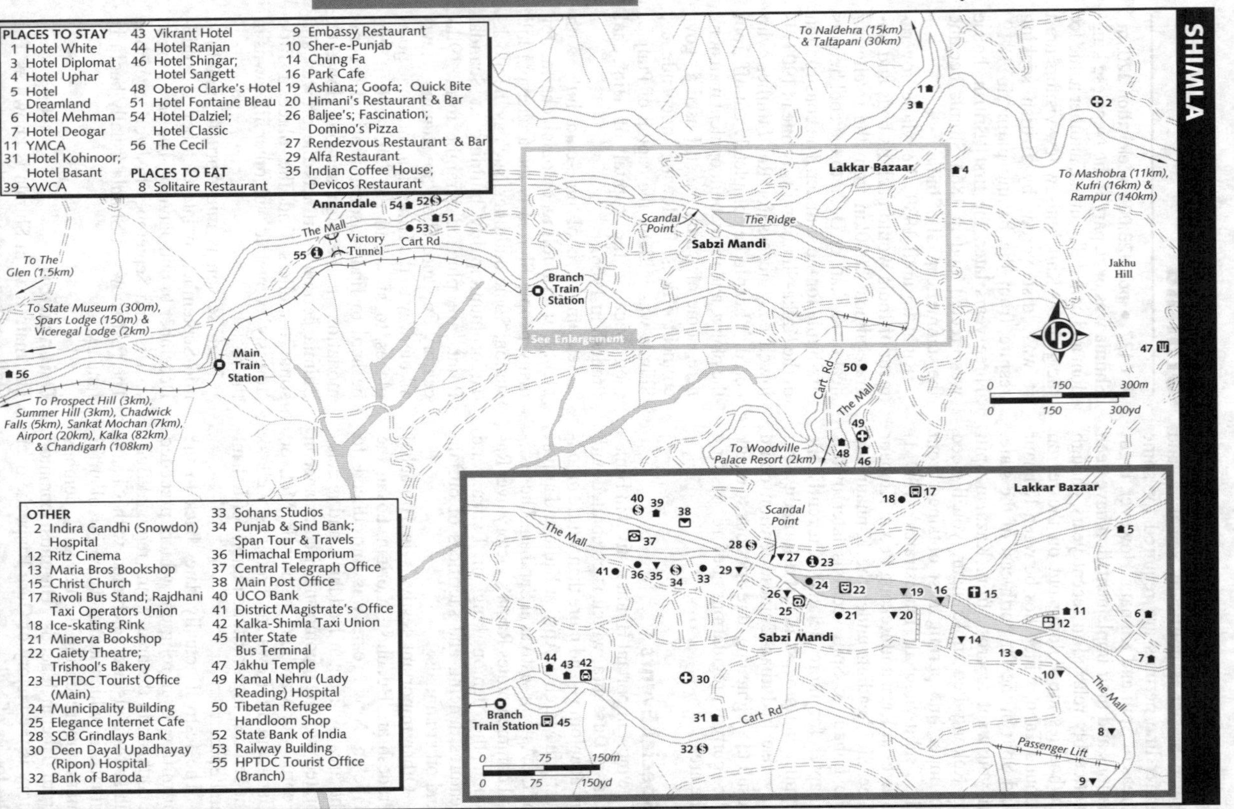
SHIMLA
HIMACHAL PRADESH
PLACES TO STAY
1 Hotel White
3 Hotel Diplomat
4 Hotel Uphar
5 Hotel Dreamland
6 Hotel Mehman
7 Hotel Deogar
11 YMCA
31 Hotel Kohinoor; Hotel Basant
39 YWCA
43 Vikrant Hotel
44 Hotel Ranjan
46 Hotel Shingar; Hotel Sangett
48 Oberoi Clarke's Hotel
51 Hotel Fontaine Bleau
54 Hotel Dalziel; Hotel Classic
56 The Cecil
PLACES TO EAT
8 Solitaire Restaurant
9 Embassy Restaurant
10 Sher-e-Punjab
14 Chung Fa
16 Park Cafe
19 Ashiana; Goofa; Quick Bite
20 Himani's Restaurant & Bar
26 Baljee's; Fascination; Domino's Pizza
27 Rendezvous Restaurant & Bar
29 Alfa Restaurant
35 Indian Coffee House; Devicos Restaurant
OTHER
2 Indira Gandhi (Snowdon) Hospital
12 Ritz Cinema
13 Maria Bros Bookshop
15 Christ Church
17 Rivoli Bus Stand; Rajdhani Taxi Operators Union
18 Ice-skating Rink
21 Minerva Bookshop
22 Gaiety Theatre; Trishool's Bakery
23 HPTDC Tourist Office (Main)
24 Municipality Building
25 Elegance Internet Cafe
28 SCB Grindlays Bank
30 Deen Dayal Upadhayay (Ripon) Hospital
32 Bank of Baroda
33 Sohans Studios
34 Punjab & Sind Bank; Span Tour & Travels
36 Himachal Emporium
37 Central Telegraph Office
38 Main Post Office
40 UCO Bank
41 District Magistrate's Office
42 Kalka-Shimla Taxi Union
45 Inter State Bus Terminal
47 Jakhu Temple
49 Kamal Nehru (Lady Reading) Hospital
50 Tibetan Refugee Handloom Shop
52 State Bank of India
53 Railway Building
55 HPTDC Tourist Office (Branch)
To Naldehra (15km) & Taltapani (30km)
To Mashobra (11km), Kufri (16km) & Rampur (140km)
Lakkar Bazaar
The Ridge
Scandal Point
Sabzi Mandi
Jakhu Hill
Branch Train Station
See Enlargement
Annandale
The Mall
Victory Tunnel
Cart Rd
To The Glen (1.5km)
To State Museum (300m), Spars Lodge (150m) & Viceregal Lodge (2km)
Main Train Station
To Prospect Hill (3km), Summer Hill (3km), Chadwick Falls (5km), Sankat Mochan (7km), Airport (20km), Kalka (82km) & Chandigarh (108km)
To Woodville Palace Resort (2km)
0 150 300m
0 150 300yd
Passenger Lift
0 75 150m
0 75 150yd

Scandal

The enigmatic Scandal Point is named after one of the biggest scandals to rock British India. During the late 19th century, the British commander in chief's daughter, who was married to a British gentleman, had a passionate affair with the dashing Bhupinder Singh, the Maharaja of Patiala. Their tryst continued for some time before news of their indiscretion reached the ears of the young woman's father, who promptly exiled the maharaja from Shimla, but not before the story had done the rounds of all the gossips in Shimla.

Bhupinder Singh returned the compliment by creating a whole new summer capital of his own at nearby Chail, and later went on to lead the first all-Indian cricket tour to England in 1911. Scandal Point picked up the nickname from the promenaders who passed the gossip of Shimla back and forth on their evening strolls.

ridge, reaching its highest point at Scandal Point (or Scandal Corner), the de facto centre of town. The open area known as The Ridge lies between Scandal Point and Christ Church and is a popular spot for strolling.

Down the hill, Cart Rd circles the southern part of Shimla, and is where you'll find the bus and taxi stands and train station. It's a steep trek uphill from here to almost everywhere else as traffic is banned from The Ridge. Numerous alleyways and lively bazaars zigzag up and down between Cart Rd and The Mall. There is also a passenger lift connecting Cart Rd to The Mall, emerging near the Solitaire Restaurant.

At the bus and train stations you will be besieged by porters who will offer to carry your luggage for Rs 10 to 30. Most hotels are a strenuous trek uphill so a porter is not a bad idea. In practice, most are hotel touts, and hotels will automatically double your room tariff to cover their commission. The only way to be sure you are paying fair rates is to turn up to your hotel unaccompanied – get your porter to drop you and your bags at a prominent landmark on The Mall (say at Christ Church) and then walk from there.

Information

Tourist Offices The HPTDC tourist office (☎ 252561) at Scandal Point primarily exists to take bookings for HPTDC buses, hotels and local tours, but has a small amount of information on the local area. It's open 9 am to 8 pm daily in the high season and 9 am to 6 pm in the low season. There's a small satellite office by Victory Tunnel, 1km west of Scandal Point.

Money The State Bank of India, at the western end of The Mall only exchanges Thomas Cook or American Express (AmEx) cheques in US dollars and UK pounds. Visa and AmEx cheques in US dollars or UK pounds are accepted at the Punjab and Sind Bank on The Mall. The UCO Bank only changes cash in US dollars or UK pounds, but there's no fee. SCB Grindlays Bank at Scandal Point charges an outrageous Rs 200 to change travellers cheques but accepts most major cheques in UK pounds and US and Australian dollars. Cash advances on Visa and MasterCard cost Rs 100. The Bank of Baroda, down on Cart Rd, gives cash advances on Visa and MasterCard. If you are headed to Kinnaur it's worth changing extra money in Shimla as there are no exchange facilities at all in Kinnaur, Spiti or Lahaul.

Post & Communications The main post office, housed in a mock-Tudor building not far from Scandal Point, is open 10 am to 5 pm Monday to Saturday. There's a reliable poste restante service here. The central telegraph office (fax 202598), west of Scandal Point, is open 24 hours and is the cheapest place to make telephone calls and to send and receive faxes. There's also a small, unreliable, Internet cafe (Rs 65 per hour). Slightly more reliable Internet access is available at Elegance Internet cafe, just off The Mall below Scandal Point (Rs 60 per hour).

Bookshops The well-stocked Maria Bros and Minerva bookshops on The Mall have good stocks of novels, plus maps and glossy books on Himachal.

Photography If you're heading farther north to the devastatingly photogenic regions of Kinnaur, Spiti and Lahaul, Shimla is your last chance to stock up on slide film. Processing of print film is available for Rs 20 plus Rs 3.50 per print. Try Sohans Studios on The Mall.

Medical Services & Emergency If you have medical problems there are several good hospitals in Shimla, including the Indira Gandhi (formerly Snowdon) Hospital (☎ 254092) east of The Ridge, the Deen Dayal Upadhayay (Ripon) Hospital (☎ 254 097) in the Sabzi Mandi area and the Kamal Nehru (formerly Lady Reading) Hospital (☎ 225097) near the Oberoi Clarke's Hotel.

The main police station (☎ 212344) is based in the rather splendid municipality building near The Ridge. For emergencies call ☎ 100.

Himachal State Museum & Library

About 2.5km west of Scandal Point, near the communications mast, the state museum has a good collection of statues, miniatures, coins, photos and other items from around Himachal Pradesh and is worth a visit. Entry is free and the museum is open 10 am to 5 pm daily (closed Monday and public holidays). Photography is strictly prohibited.

Viceregal Lodge

The Viceregal Lodge, also known as Rashtrapati Niwas, was formerly the residence of the British Viceroy Lord Dufferin, and is now the home of the Indian Institute of Advanced Study. This appealing colonial structure was where many decisions affecting the destiny of the subcontinent were made. Incredibly, every brick of the six-storey building was transported from the plains around Delhi by mule (the railway wasn't built at that time). The lodge was eventually finished in 1888.

You can take a guided tour of the lodge between 9 am and 5.30 pm daily (except Monday) for only Rs 10. While you're here, take time to explore the magnificent lawns and **botanical gardens**. The lodge is a pleasant 2km walk west of the museum – about 4.5km from Scandal Point – and there's a small cafe where you can get a well-earned cup of hot coffee.

Next to the lodge is a small **aviary** featuring, among other birds, the Monal pheasant (Himachal's state bird). The aviary is open 10 am to 5 pm daily (closed Monday). Entry is Rs 5, but use of a camera/video camera costs an extra Rs 25/100.

Christ Church

The second oldest church in northern India (the oldest is in Ambala), Christ Church was built between 1846 and 1857. None of the clocks now works, but the church is one of Shimla's major landmarks and is renowned for its stained glass windows. You can attend English-language services every Sunday morning during the tourist season.

Jakhu Temple

Dedicated to the monkey god, Hanuman, Jakhu Temple is east of the town centre near the highest point of the Shimla ridge (2455m). The temple itself isn't particularly noteworthy, but it offers a fine view over the surrounding valleys out to the snow-capped peaks, and over Shimla itself. Appropriately, there are many monkeys around the temple. It's a steep 45-minute walk from Scandal Point. Take the footpath that heads east past the Hotel Dreamland.

Walks

In addition to a promenade along The Mall and the walk to the Jakhu Temple, there are a great number of interesting walks around Shimla. For information on places farther afield, see the Around Shimla section later in this chapter.

The Glen, about 4km west of Scandal Point, is one of the former playgrounds of rich British colonialists. The turn-off is on the way to the state museum and goes through **Annandale**, another lovely area. This was the site of a famous racecourse, and cricket and polo are still played there.

Summer Hill is 5km away, on the Shimla-Kalka railway line, and has pleasant, shady walks. It's also famous because Mahatma Gandhi once stayed at the Raj Kumari Amrit Kaur mansion here. In the same direction, **Chadwick Falls** (67m high) are 2km farther west, but only really worth visiting during or just after the monsoon (July to October).

There's a Kamna Devi Temple at **Prospect Hill** and some excellent views. It is about 5km west of Shimla, and a 15-minute climb from Boileauganj. There are also great views from the Hanuman Temple at **Sankat Mochan**, 7km from Shimla, and the Tara Devi Temple, perched on a hilltop 10km from Shimla. Take a taxi from Shimla or walk the 3km from Tara Devi train station.

Organised Tours

The HPTDC organises daily sightseeing tours in the high season, which leave from the Rivoli bus stand between 10.30 and 11 am, and drop off at the end of the day at the bottom of the lift on Cart Rd:

- Chail via Kufri (Rs 172)
- Fagu, Theog & Narkanda (Rs 168)
- Kufri, Fagu, Mashobra & Naldehra (Rs 151)
- Naldehra & Tattapani hot springs (Rs 172)

Kalka-Shimla Taxi Union (☎ 258225), on Cart Rd just east of the Inter State Bus Terminal (ISBT), and the Rajdhani Taxi Operators Union (☎ 208654) also offer one-day sightseeing tours to the following places:

- Chail via Kufri (Rs 810)
- Naldehra via Mashobra (Rs 460)
- Narkanda via Fagu & Theog (Rs 810)
- Tattapani via Mashobra & Naldehra (Rs 810)

In the high season the HPTDC also offers an interesting heritage walk, which takes in many of the historic buildings around town, including the Viceregal Lodge. The walk costs Rs 50.

A Home in the Hills

Whether it was homesickness or the heat of the plains that drove the British to the hills, they certainly made their presence felt, creating miniature versions of England at Shimla, Dalhousie, Mussoorie and Nainital (to name just a few locations). To complete the illusion of home, the hill stations featured quaint stone churches, ballrooms, cricket pitches, summer houses and teas on the lawn.

Most of the hill stations owe their existence to British explorers, who built holiday homes at scenic spots that reminded them of home. As the hill station phenomenon took off, whole towns of summer houses sprung up in the hills, attracting vast crowds of homesick British every summer.

Even the colonial government in Delhi and Kolkata (Calcutta) packed up its bags and retreated to Shimla, which was declared the 'summer capital' of India. A special railway line was constructed to help move all the documents and officials required to run the nation from the hills. In fact, the British were continuing a centuries-old local tradition; the ancient rulers of Himachal Pradesh and Uttaranchal also headed for the hills during the hot season, creating their own summer capitals such as Almora in the Kumaon highlands.

Many maharajas built opulent summer palaces in the hill stations to hobnob with the snooty British gentry, and all manner of affairs went on under the noses of the British establishment. However, the experience of most Indians was less glamorous. Every summer, hundreds of coolies and porters had to physically haul the British and their belongings up into the hills.

After Independence, the hill stations were finally reclaimed by ordinary Indians, and they found a new role as the honeymoon capitals of India. These days, tens of thousands of newlyweds flock to the hills every summer to have honeymoon portraits taken among the crumbling British houses and Himalayan peaks.

Places to Stay

Accommodation in Shimla is expensive, particularly during the high season. But in the low season, or when business is quiet, prices drop substantially, sometimes by as much as half. Unless otherwise stated, prices given below are for the high season, and do not include the luxury tax.

Places to Stay – Budget

If you're on a low budget, the cheapest accommodation is around the ISBT, and along Cart Rd heading east.

The ***YMCA*** (☎ *250021, fax 211016*) accepts men and women and is probably the best budget choice in the high season, when it can be booked out (reservations are taken by phone). It's a big, old institutional place, with singles/doubles for Rs 133/173 with breakfast and shared bathroom with hot water (available 7 pm to 9 am). Nonmembers will need to pay Rs 40 for a seven-day temporary membership. Doubles with private bathroom cost Rs 250 with breakfast. It's not far behind Christ Church, up the lane beside the Ritz cinema.

The ***YWCA*** *(☎ 203081)*, also for men and women, beyond the main post office, isn't quite as good value but it's a convenient, friendly old place with great views. Small rooms with private bathroom cost Rs 150/200 in the low/high season. There is a Rs 20 temporary membership charge.

Near the ISBT bus stand, but a hike away from The Mall are the cheap ***Hotel Ranjan*** *(☎ 252818)*, with large doubles with private bathroom starting at Rs 300 (Rs 150 low season), and the ***Vikrant Hotel*** *(☎ 253 602)*, which charges the same and also has a dorm for Rs 73.

Hotel Basant *(☎ 258341)*, farther east along busy Cart Rd, is a cheap option in the high season, but you can get more for your money elsewhere at other times of year. Singles with shared bathroom cost Rs 110; doubles with private bathroom start at Rs 220. Hot water comes by the bucket.

Hotel Kohinoor *(☎ 202008)*, next door, is more expensive but much nicer. Rooms with private bathroom and running hot water cost from Rs 200 to 350.

Around the Lakkar Bazaar area, a steep climb past The Ridge, are several reasonably priced places. ***Hotel Dreamland*** *(☎ 206897)* has rooms ranging from Rs 250/400 for a single/double to Rs 650 for a deluxe double. Credit cards are accepted.

The nearby ***Hotel Uphar*** *(☎ 257670)* is used to backpackers and has adequate doubles with hot shower and TV for Rs 275, or Rs 400 with a view and small balcony.

Those in search of old-world charm should head for the quaint, family-run ***Hotel Fontaine Bleau*** *(☎ 23549)*, just downhill from the State Bank of India, at the western end of The Mall. Large doubles in this old house start at Rs 250, with hot shower.

Places to Stay – Mid-Range

The majority of rooms in this range will usually include cable TV and a bathroom with hot water. They are particularly good value in the low season; at most hotels the rate for a double drops to about Rs 200.

Just off The Mall, about 500m up from the train station, is the friendly and comfortable ***Hotel Classic*** *(☎ 253078)*, with tacky singles for Rs 300 and decent doubles with good views from Rs 400 to 500. A few doors down, ***Hotel Dalziel*** *(☎ 252691)* is also good value, with rooms from Rs 350 to 600, all with carpets and geysers. All rates drop by 50% in the winter.

North of The Ridge, and around the Lakkar Bazaar area, are several good places, though they are a long trek from the bus or train stations. Options here include ***Hotel Diplomat*** *(☎ 252001)*, with reasonable doubles from Rs 1000 to 1600 (less 50% in low season), and the good-value ***Hotel White*** *(☎ 255276)*, with comfortable doubles for Rs 425 or Rs 500 with good views; superior rooms with superior views cost Rs 700 upwards.

A couple of minutes' walk east of Christ Church, ***Hotel Doegar*** *(☎ 208527)* is a good choice, with flexibly priced doubles from Rs 650 to 950 (Rs 250 to 300 in low season). The pricier rooms have fantastic views over Shimla.

Just uphill, the modern ***Hotel Mehman*** *(☎ 213692)* has spotlessly clean carpeted

Monkey Business

Shimla's monkeys may look appealing but they certainly aren't tame. Remember that these are wild animals and may become aggressive if they feel threatened, particularly if they have young. Room raids by errant apes are common, so beware of leaving your window or balcony door open if you go out. During the Raj, the British police in Shimla had a special folder for 'Monkey Incidents' to rule out a simian hand in thefts in the city. In 1996, a cheeky rhesus macaque seized a bag containing the takings of a Shimla shopowner and scattered the money to the delighted crowds!

rooms and bathrooms. Comfortable rooms range from Rs 550 to 1000, depending on the views, with a 50% discount in the low season.

There are two good places across from Oberoi Clarke's Hotel, at the south-eastern end of The Mall. ***Hotel Shingar*** *(☎ 252881, fax 252998)* has rooms for Rs 900, or Rs 1100 with a view (less 30% out of season). Nearby, ***Hotel Sangeet*** *(☎ 202506, fax 255823)* has good-value rooms from Rs 700 to 900, discounted in the low season.

For a quiet stay on the colonial edges of Shimla try the ***Spars Lodge*** *(☎ 257908, fax 213435)*, 2km west of Shimla centre, near the state museum. Pleasant, homey singles/doubles with clean, bright bathrooms cost Rs 600/900. Spars Lodge also serves good food.

Places to Stay – Top End

Oberoi Clarke's Hotel *(☎ 251010, fax 211321)*, at the south-eastern end of The Mall, is one of Shimla's earliest hotels. The luxurious singles/doubles start at US$70/125 (plus 10% tax), including a compulsory three-meal 'American Plan'.

Woodville Palace Resort *(☎ 223919, fax 223098)*, 2km south of the Oberoi Clarke's Hotel, is an ivy-covered building constructed in 1938 by Raja Rana Sir Bhagat Chandra, the ruler of the former princely state of Jubbal. It's a small place, set among very pleasant gardens. Doubles are Rs 2000, and suites start at Rs 3000. Bookings are recommended.

The rather spectacular hotel ***The Cecil*** *(☎ 204848, fax 211024, ⓔ reservations@thececil.com)*, at the western end of The Mall, is easily the classiest place in town. The hotel is part of the Oberoi Group and luxurious singles/doubles, arranged around a central atrium start at Rs 6075/7875, even in the low season. Rudyard Kipling stayed here for a season in 1885.

Places to Eat

Indian Most Indian restaurants in Shimla serve primarily southern Indian food.

Baljee's, on The Mall close to the main tourist office, has a delicious range of Indian and Western food, and the service is good. However, prices can be a little high at around Rs 100 for a meat dish. ***Fascination***, the associated restaurant upstairs, is similarly priced and just as popular.

Alfa Restaurant, near Scandal Point, is about the same standard, price and popularity as Baljee's.

Himani's Restaurant & Bar, just downhill from the Municipality Building on The Mall, does tasty southern Indian snacks and meals for Rs 70 to 150, and has a popular and relaxed bar.

The dingy ***Rendezvous Restaurant & Bar***, right on Scandal Point, offers Indian and Thai food from Rs 65 and has a bar, but the service is slow.

Sher-e-Punjab, along The Mall just east of Scandal Point, is an excellent cheap option, offering Indian fast-food standards such as *channa* (curried chickpeas) from just Rs 50.

Farther downhill, the ***Solitaire Restaurant*** serves a good selection of Indian dishes from Rs 70, in a big dining room overlooking the valley.

The absurdly popular ***Indian Coffee House***, along The Mall, is run by a cooperative of workers in the coffee industry. Above-average Indian coffee and southern Indian snacks are served up by waiters in fading cummerbunds.

Western & Chinese The no-smoking ***Embassy Restaurant***, not far from the top of the lift on The Mall, is a canteen-style place with great individual pizzas and hamburgers, as well as Indian and Chinese food for around Rs 40.

Devicos Restaurant, on The Mall near Scandal Point, is a clean, trendy place that does good fast food starting at Rs 50, but it's a little overpriced.

The cosy ***Park Cafe***, below Scandal Point and up some steps from The Mall, is popular with both backpackers and local students alike. It's an interesting, bohemian spot serving good pizza (Rs 60 to 80), milkshakes and breakfasts, and with laid-back, late-evening music.

If you're craving a taste of home (your home or someone else's), ***Domino's Pizza*** serves American-style pizzas at American-style prices.

HPTDC has a building on The Ridge with three places to eat, but the service is extremely slow. ***Ashiana*** is about the best for decor and speed, and is also the most expensive. Expect to pay around Rs 150 for a meal. ***Goofa*** downstairs is nowhere near as classy, but serves a reasonable (and early) breakfast. In the same complex, the ***Quick Bite*** has cheap pizzas and Indian food.

Chung Fa, down some steps just off The Mall, is the best place for cheap Chinese food. There's a good range of noodles, dumplings and main dishes, all for less than Rs 40 a dish.

Oberoi Clarke's Hotel is good for a splurge in some pleasantly luxurious surroundings; expect to pay around Rs 250 for a meal.

For a quick snack, ***Trishool's***, next to the Gaiety Theatre, is recommended for its cakes and pastries. ***Baljee's*** has a bakery counter at the front, and it's a great place to enjoy either morning or afternoon tea.

Entertainment

Probably the most popular entertainment is to stroll along The Mall and The Ridge and watch everyone watching everyone else. There are stunning sunsets over the Himalaya in the evenings.

The ice-skating rink by the Rivoli bus stand is open in winter (Rs 50/30 adults/children, including skate hire) – follow the signs from Scandal Point.

The lovely old ***Gaiety Theatre*** (☎ 205 639) occasionally has shows or recitals, particularly in summer. The ***Ritz*** cinema near Christ Church screens all-singing, all-dancing Indian blockbusters.

The bar at ***Himani's***, just downhill from the Municipality Building, is a popular and upbeat place. ***Rendezvous*** on Scandal Point also has a bar, but it is pretty dingy and unwelcoming. The expensive hotels usually serve alcohol.

Shopping

The Himachal Emporium on The Mall near The Ridge has a reasonable collection of local handicrafts and, inexplicably, pottery dogs. The Tibetan Refugee Handloom Shop, at the other end of The Mall, is the showroom for a local development project and it sells carpets, clothing and other Tibetan crafts.

North of The Ridge is the small, bustling Lakkar Bazaar, Shimla's main souvenir market area, though most of the offerings are firmly aimed at Indian tourists. Wooden massage wheels and rollers make cheap and lightweight mementoes or easily transported presents.

For fruit, vegetables and just about anything else, head for the bustling Sabzi Mandi (Vegetable Market), between the

Ridge and Cart Rd. The kinetic chaos of the market streets is a welcome and refreshingly riotous contrast to the genteel, British-influenced Mall.

Getting There & Away

Air Shimla airport is about 23km south at Jubbarhatti and is served by small aircraft from Delhi. Indian Airlines flies from Delhi to Shimla (US$110, one hour) at 9 am on Monday, Wednesday and Friday, continuing on to Kullu/Manali (US$100, 30 minutes) at 10.20 am. From Kullu, the plane returns directly to Delhi.

Jagson Airlines has a flight from Delhi to Shimla (US$100) at 8 am daily except Sunday, continuing on to Kullu (US$85) at 9.20 am. To get to Delhi from Shimla, you'll have to fly via Kullu.

Airline bookings can be made with travel agents on The Mall – Span Tour & Travels (☎ 260850) is reliable. There is no bus to the airport, so you'll have to take a taxi for a flat rate of Rs 410.

Bus The large and chaotic ISBT on Cart Rd is set up on the reasonable assumption that most foreigners take the train or a tourist bus. However, there is a very handy private computer-booking booth (Counter 9), where the employees speak English, and you can book a ticket on any public bus up to a month ahead.

Buses to destinations east of Shimla depart from the Rivoli bus station, on the northern side of the main ridge, below the HPTDC office. For Tattapani, Kasauli and local destinations en route to Kalka or Narkanda, such as Kufri and Theog, catch one of the regular local buses along Cart Rd.

To Manali (11 hours) there are buses at 4.40, 8 and 9.15 am (Rs 160) and a night bus at 7 pm (Rs 207). All Manali buses stop in Kullu. There are buses to Dharamsala every few hours from 4.40 am to 10.30 pm (Rs 152/190 day/night, 10 hours). Buses leave frequently until late in the evening for Mandi (Rs 90, six hours) and Chandigarh (Rs 70, 4 hours).

Deluxe buses to Delhi (Rs 360) leave every few hours from 8.25 am to 9.45 pm and offer your best chance of sleeping en route. Ordinary buses (Rs 182) leave every hour. Buses depart at 5.10 am and 5.40 and 6.30 pm for Haridwar (Rs 171, 10 hours), via Paonta Sahib (Rs 110) and Dehra Dun (Rs 137, nine hours).

From the Rivoli bus station, there are hourly buses to Rekong Peo (in Kinnaur; Rs 143, 10 hours) from 5 to 11.30 am, via Narkanda (Rs 38, three hours) and Rampur (Rs 78, six hours). There is one bus at 7.30 am direct to Sangla (Rs 143), or you can change to a local bus or jeep at Karcham. At the time of research the road had been destroyed between Karcham and Rekong Peo, requiring a 5km trek, but may be repaired by the time you read this. There are buses to Sarahan (Rs 104, 7½ hours) at 3.30, 9.45

Toy Train

The train journey from Delhi to Shimla involves a change from broad to narrow gauge at Kalka, a little north of Chandigarh, where the Shimla toy train begins its tortuous ascent into the hills. The tiny railway was built in 1903 to ferry the colonial government to the hill stations, and it passes through a staggering 103 tunnels as it snakes its way up to Shimla. Unsurprisingly, it's a scenic trip, and even more so if you can afford the special Rail Car service (Rs 340), which runs during the high season and offers luxury seats in a special glass-sided carriage.

For lesser mortals, there are three more conventional classes: 2nd class (Rs 16), chair car (Rs 140) and 1st class (Rs 170). Trains run uphill from Kalka at 4, 5.30, 6.30 and 11.55 am, heading back down to Kalka from the main station in Shimla at 10.35 am and 2.25, 5.30 and 5.45 pm. In the high season, there are three extra trains in each direction. Ask at the station for details.

See Train in this section for more information on travelling from Delhi to Shimla by train.

and 10.10 am. There are also local buses to Mashobra, Naldehra and Tattapani.

Travel agencies along The Mall offer private, overnight 'deluxe' buses (two-by-two seating) to Manali (Rs 275) and Delhi (Rs 300). Prices and timings change according to demand and the season. In the high season, HPTDC also offers daily deluxe buses to Manali (Rs 338, 10 hours) at 8.30 am and 8 pm and a night bus to Delhi (Rs 339, 10 hours) at 8 pm via Chandigarh. Book at the main tourist office (buses depart from the satellite office at Victory Tunnel).

Train There are two train stations in Shimla, but most trains arrive and depart from the main train station on the western edge of town. The train reservation office (☎ 252 915) at the main station can arrange bookings for the Kalka and Delhi line and, in theory, for other trips in northern India. It's open 10 am to 1.30 pm and 2 to 5 pm Monday to Saturday, 10 am to 2 pm Sunday.

To travel from Delhi to Shimla by train in one trip, the best and most reliable way is to catch the *Himalayan Queen* from New Delhi station at 6 am, arriving in Kalka at 11.40 am. You then cross to another platform to take the 11.55 am toy train (see the boxed text 'Toy Train' earlier in this section), which arrives in Shimla at 5.20 pm. Reservations can be made all the way to Shimla and the fare is Rs 400 for air-con chair car (with seats like those in an airplane). Some travellers have found their ticket or reservation is valid only to Kalka, so check this when you buy it.

The only way to do the reverse trip (Shimla-Delhi) in one day is to catch the 10.35 am train from Shimla, which connects with the *Himalayan Queen* at Kalka and arrives in New Delhi at 10.30 pm. The best overnight connection is the *Shivalik Express*, which leaves Shimla at 5.30 pm to connect with the *Kalka-Howrah Mail*, arriving in Delhi at 6.25 am. Fares are Rs 140/589 sleeper/two-tier air-con.

From Kalka there are also trains to Amritsar at 4.15 pm (Rs 151 sleeper) and several trains daily to Chandigarh (Rs 104/347 sleeper/two-tier air-con).

Taxi There are taxi unions close by both the ISBT and Rivoli bus stands, and the set rates are almost impossible to bargain down, even in the low season. The Kalka-Shimla Taxi Union (☎ 258225) is on Cart Rd, east of the ISBT bus station. At the Rivoli bus stand, talk to the Rajdhani Taxi Operators Union (☎ 208654). The cheapest taxis are 'multivans' that take three passengers plus the driver. More comfortable and spacious Sumo or Maruti jeeps and Ambassador taxis cost about 10% more than the prices that follow.

Examples of one-way taxi fares from Shimla are:

destination	cost (Rs)
Chandigarh	910
Dehra Dun	2550
Delhi	2850
Dharamsala	2450
Kalka	610
Kalpa via Rekong Peo	2650
Kullu	1850
Manali	2450
Rampur	1450

Getting Around

To/From the Airport The fixed price for a taxi ride between the airport and Shimla is Rs 410. Local buses headed to Nalagarh pass close to the airport but they're hopelessly crowded.

Passenger Lift To save you lugging your bags uphill there is a lift that goes up to the eastern end of The Mall (Rs 5) from Cart Rd, a short walk east from the bus station. It runs 8 am to 9 pm.

Around Shimla

There are several interesting villages and towns in the area that can be visited as day or overnight trips from Shimla. It's best not to be over-ambitious when planning day trips; transport on these mountain roads is slow and you'll be lucky to cover more than 30km per hour by taxi or bus.

There are several areas of interest to the east of Shimla, on or around the highway that links Himachal Pradesh and Uttaranchal. It's possible to break the journey between Dehra Dun and Shimla at the Sikh pilgrimage centre of Paonta Sahib or Nahan, or the ancient town of Nahan, which is handy to the nearby Renuka Lake.

MASHOBRA

About 11km north of Shimla, the small village of Mashobra has some pleasant walks, including one to Sipi, where there is a fair every May and a wooden **temple** dedicated to Shiva.

The only place to stay in Mashobra is the ***Gables Resorts*** *(☎ 0177-480169)*, which offers rural luxury from Rs 2200, and a dining room with views of the mountains. The village has one or two ***dhabas*** (snack bars).

About 3km from Mashobra, along a lovely trail, is the resort of **Craignano** – the path leads downhill from the temple in the middle of Mashobra. You can book a room at the ***Municipal Rest House*** *(☎ 0177-224850)* in Craignano through HPTDC in Shimla.

At Charabra, 2km from Mashobra, **Wildflower Hall** was built as the residence of the then British commander in chief, Lord Kitchener, and was run as a hotel before it was gutted by fire in 1993. It's now being renovated by the Oberoi hotel chain and should open in the year 2001 – call the Oberoi Clarke's Hotel in Shimla (☎ 0177-251010) for more information.

NALDEHRA

Fifteen kilometres north of Mashobra, at an altitude of 2050m, the village of Naldehra is known mostly for its golf course, which is one of the oldest and highest in the world. It's a pleasant spot and the park surrounding the course is popular for picnics, with the inevitable horse rides on offer. Most popular is the trip up to the **Mahunag Mandir** in the middle of the golf course (Rs 250). There's a Rs 5 entry fee to the park.

The golf course is only open from March to November and green fees are US$10 (Rs 100 for Indians) for 18 holes (twice around the course), plus US$5 for club hire and Rs 60 for a caddy. During the high season, the course is open 7 am to 7 pm daily.

HPTDC runs the ***Hotel Golf Glade*** *(☎ 0177-487739)*, with six luxurious log cabins from Rs 1100 to 4000, and better-value rooms from Rs 800 to 1000, plus a restaurant that functions as an informal clubhouse. Occasional buses run here for Rs 31, or it's a Rs 700 return taxi ride from Shimla.

TATTAPANI

About 30km beyond Naldehra, this peaceful village was known for its hot sulphurous springs, but the Sutlej River burst its banks in August 2000 and washed away the baths as well as half the village. The ruins are an impressive testament to the power of the river, but in its current state, Tattapani isn't really worth the long journey out here. It's worth checking with the HPTDC in Shimla to see whether the baths have been redeveloped.

If you do feel like making the trip, the road passes through some impressive scenery and there are a few places to stay, including the ***HPTDC Tourist Inn*** with basic rooms from Rs 250, which replaces an older hotel destroyed by the floods (take the path uphill just beyond the bridge). Local buses run here from Shimla or you can take a return taxi for Rs 800.

CHAIL

The hilltop village of Chail (2250m), 65km south of Shimla, was created by the Maharaja of Patiala as a summer capital after he was expelled from Shimla. The town is built on three hills – one is topped by the Chail Palace, one by the village itself and the other by the Snowview mansion.

Three kilometres from the village is the world's highest **cricket ground** (2444m), built in 1893. There is also a **wildlife sanctuary** 3km from Chail with a limited number of deer and birds. There are plenty of interesting treks in the surrounding hills. Taxis are the easiest way to see sights around Chail.

Places to Stay & Eat

The ***HPTDC Palace Hotel*** *(☎ 01792-48141, fax 48142)* has a range of suites, cottages, log huts and rooms set among 30 hectares of lawns. Modest luxury starts at Rs 1000 for a log hut or Rs 1200 for a regular room, and moves up to Rs 6000 for the four bed 'maharaja suite'. There is a top-class restaurant, cafe and bar.

HPTDC Hotel Himneel *(☎ 01792-48337)* has more modest rooms with private bathroom for Rs 600 a double.

Hotel Deodar *(☎ 01792-48318)* has doubles with private bathroom and TV from Rs 250 to 350 and the ***Pine View Tourist Lodge*** *(☎ 01792-48349)* has rooms from Rs 150 with shared bathroom and Rs 200 to 500 with private bathroom.

Getting There & Away

Chail can be reached from the Shimla-Kalka road via Kandaghat or, more commonly, via the turn-off south from Kufri. A one-way/return taxi from Shimla, via Kufri, costs Rs 600/800. There are occasional buses (more in the high season) to Chail from Shimla and Chandigarh.

KASAULI

About 75km from Shimla and 12km from the road to Kalka, Kasauli (1850m) is a charming village surrounded by pines; it makes a popular day trip from Shimla. There are several Raj-era buildings in town, and numerous peaceful walks around Kasauli, including one to **Sanawar**, another picturesque hill town, and the location of a famous colonial college. The 4km walk to **Monkey Point** lies on Indian air force land and has great views, but no monkeys. You'll need to get permission from the gatehouse before you set out.

The upmarket ***Alasia Hotel*** *(☎ 01792-72008)* has rooms from Rs 1500 with good views. More humble accommodation is available at ***Anchal Guest House*** *(☎ 01792-72052)*, starting at Rs 350 for a double. ***HPTDC Hotel Ros Common*** *(☎ 01792-72005)* has rooms with TV from Rs 800 to 1300 and a pleasant location. All have a private bathroom.

Local buses run between Shimla and Kausali. A one-way/return taxi from Shimla to Kasauli costs about Rs 750/1000.

NAHAN

The historical town of Nahan, founded in 1621, has an interesting bazaar, packed with crumbling temples, and is a springboard to nearby Renuka Lake, but most tourists just pass through on the bus between Shimla and Dehra Dun. Nahan hosts a festival called **Bhawan Dwadshi** at the end of the monsoon, when over 50 idols of Hindu gods are led through the streets and ceremonially bathed in picturesque Ranital (Rani Lake) in the centre of town. The most appealing structure here is the old **Raja Mahal** palace, but it's closed to visitors.

There are several cheap and cheerful hotels in Nahan, including the ***Hotel Hill View*** *(☎ 01702-22338)* by the bus station, with decent singles/doubles for Rs 200/450, and the ***Hotel Regency*** *(☎ 01702-23302)* with good-value rooms from Rs 275 to 495 with balcony and hot-water bathroom. The pleasant ***Milan Restaurant*** here serves the best food in town.

Nahan is served by regular buses from Shimla (Rs 85) and Dehra Dun (Rs 52). For Renuka Lake, there are hourly buses to Dadahu (Rs 20).

RENUKA LAKE

About an hour by bus from Nahan is lovely Renuka Lake (Renukaji), the largest natural lake in Himachal Pradesh. It's a growing centre for water sports, but unless you come on an organised tour, you'll probably be restricted to hiring a pedal boat from the Hotel Renuka.

There are several temples here, including the 18th-century **Renuka Temple**, and some attractive walks, including the 3km trek past the ashram and down to the **wildlife park**, which has Asiatic lions, barking deer and Himalayan black bear. Parshuramtal, the artificial lake next to Renukaji, has a small **temple** of the same name. If you're feeling more energetic, trek the 8km up to **Jamu peak** for great views.

Special Events

The week-long **Renuka Mela** is held in November in honour of Renukaji, wife of the *rishi* (poet) Jamdagni, who is said to have been killed and miraculously brought back to life on this spot. During the celebrations, the image of the god Pashuram is carried on a throne down from Jamu peak to meet his mother, Renukaji, at the lake. Thousands of pilgrims join in the festivities, which include ritual bathing in the lake, dancing and general merrymaking.

Places to Stay & Eat

The ***HPTDC Hotel Renuka*** *(☎ 01702-67339)* has spacious, comfortable rooms in secluded gardens from Rs 450 to 900, all with bathroom. There are also dorm beds for Rs 75, and a good restaurant.

Hotel Himlok, 4km away in the village of Dadahu, is the only other place to stay. Rooms cost Rs 200 to 400.

Getting There & Away

A bus from Nahan goes to Dadahu roughly every hour, from where you can walk 40 minutes to the lake (though some buses do continue on to the lake). There are private buses from the lake direct to Paonta Sahib (Rs 30, two hours) every few hours.

PAONTA SAHIB

On the Uttaranchal border is the town of Paonta Sahib, which isn't hugely interesting in its own right, but is home to an impressive **gurdwara** (temple) dedicated to the 10th Sikh guru, Gobind Singh, who lived there between the ages of 16 and 20.

Inside the gurdwara (see Special Events following) is a small **museum** housing the personal weapons and other relics of Gobind Singh. You'll need to cover your head (coverings can be borrowed at the entrance), take off your shoes and wash your feet before entering.

Special Events

The gurdwara is in an attractive spot on the banks of the holy Yamuna River and overflows with pilgrims during **Holi** (which commemorates the burning of the murderous princess Holika by Lord Vishnu and celebrates the victory of good over evil) and **Baisakhi** (which commemorates the creation of the five symbols of Sikh purity and the ritual of *amrit*, or baptism, by the tenth Sikh guru Gobind Rai) festivals in March and April.

Places to Stay & Eat

The ***HPTDC Hotel Yamuna (☎ 01704-22341)***, on the riverside about 100m from the entrance to the temple, is the best option. Nice doubles cost from Rs 450 to 1200, the latter with air-con, and there's a good restaurant and bar. It's worth the splurge as the alternatives are fairly poor.

Getting There & Away

Hourly buses go to Shimla (Rs 110) till 1 pm, Dehra Dun (Rs 27, 1½ hours) and Nahan (Rs 25, two hours). There are three morning buses to Delhi (Rs 110, seven hours).

KUFRI

Kufri (2510m) is a nondescript little highway village, but the nearby countryside offers some good hiking, including a trek to nearby Mahasu peak. Above Kufri on the road to Chail is the **Himalayan Nature Park** which has a collection of animals and birds unique to Himachal Pradesh, but you won't see much unless you have your own vehicle or you're on a tour. There is a Rs 10 entry fee, plus Rs 30/100 extra for a camera/video camera; the park is open 10 am to 5 pm daily.

Nearby is the little **Indira Tourist Park**, run by the HPTDC (entry is Rs 5), which has great views and the friendly ***Cafe Lalit***, serving good vegetarian and nonveg food for Rs 40 upwards. On the road to the park, you can have your photo taken with a yak for Rs 5, or take a horse ride to Mahasu peak for good views over the forest (Rs 160).

Kufri is promoted for its skiing (December to February), but the infrastructure is limited and the snow doesn't always show up on time. Tobogganing is a popular and cheaper alternative.

Places to Stay & Eat

Hotel Snow Shelter *(☎ 0177-480135)*, on the main road in the village, has cosy rooms, great views and private bathroom with hot water at a reasonable Rs 275/440 a single/double.

Next door, ***Kufri Holiday Inn*** *(☎ 0177-480341)* has upmarket rooms from Rs 400 to 1250 (the pricier rooms have great views) and ***Honey Dew***, the best restaurant in town.

Uphill on the way to the nature park, ***Kufri Holiday Resort*** *(☎ 0177-480300)* is a posh place with luxurious rooms for Rs 2550 upwards, two restaurants and a bar. Staff can organise winter sports, including skiing, during the high season. Call ahead to be picked up from Shimla for Rs 300.

On the main road at the start of the village are the ***Deluxe Food Corner*** and ***Himgiri Bhojanalya***, which serve reasonable *dhaba* (snack) food.

Getting There & Away

Kufri is a stop on any of the regular bus routes between Shimla, Narkanda and Rampur. The bus to Chail also passes through Kufri. A one-way taxi from Shimla to Kufri costs about Rs 350.

HATKOTI

Few travellers make it to the hilltop **Temple of Hatkoti** in the village of the same name, 115km from Shimla. The shrine is dedicated to a legendary squabble between Shiva and his wife in her wrathful form as Durga, and is set in a pretty area of terraced fields and orchards. ***HPTDC Hotel Pabbar*** *(☎ 017815-8269)* has great-value dorms for Rs 75 and pleasant doubles for Rs 400, plus a small restaurant.

NARKANDA

Halfway between Shimla and Rampur, Narkanda (2708m) is basically a truck-stop town, but the surrounding hills are popular place for **skiing** in winter. The ski season lasts from January to mid-April, but Narkanda is not as well set up for skiing as Solang Nullah, north of Manali, and nowhere near the standard of Auli in Uttaranchal. There is no ski lift, so you'll have to trek back up to the top of the slopes after each run, but good opportunities exist for cross-country skiing if you have the equipment and experience.

Out of season, the ski-slopes become the setting for some interesting treks, including the trek up to **Hattu peak** (3300m), 8km to the east.

Skiing Tours

The HPTDC in Shimla (☎ 0177-252561) offers seven-day skiing packages for Rs 3900, including board, lodging, equipment and tuition. You may also be able to ski here with the Institute of Mountain-eering & Allied Sports (☎ 01902-52342) in Manali; both organisations offer mainly fixed-date packages. Locally, Highland Travel and Adventures (☎ 01782-8444) can organise ski hire and trekking.

Places to Stay & Eat

On the main road, ***Hotel Mahamaya Palace*** *(☎ 01782-8448)* has lovely large rooms with private bathroom and hot water, balcony and views for Rs 400 to 800. There's a good restaurant and the hotel should offer discounts in low season.

Perched above the village, ***Himalayan Hotel*** *(☎ 01782-8440)* has slightly ramshackle but not unpleasant doubles with private bathroom for Rs 250 to 300; amazing views and friendly staff make the place tolerable. Take the steps behind the bus stand (the hotel is the big white building on top of the hill).

The secluded ***HPTDC Hotel Hatu*** *(☎ 01782-8430)* is 250m up a track east of the main road (look for the sign). Good doubles with private bathroom cost Rs 600 to 900 in the high season (discounts are possible at other times).

There are many basic, friendly ***dhabas*** in Narkanda town centre. If you prefer eating with cutlery try the ***restaurants*** at Hotel Hatu or Hotel Mahamaya Palace, where staples such as tandoori chicken cost around Rs 75.

Getting There & Away

Narkanda is served by regular buses on the Shimla to Rampur route – you shouldn't have to wait more than 30 minutes in either direction. A taxi from Shimla will cost about Rs 700.

Sutlej Valley

The Sutlej River flows through a narrow gorge providing the southern access to Kinnaur. The road that runs along the gorge was constructed by Lord Dalhousie in 1850, and originally ran to Tibet (providing a sneaky access route for the British invasion of Tibet in 1904). But foreigners are only allowed as far north as Sumdo in Kinnaur, where the road to Spiti and Lahaul branches off. The string of resorts established by the British finishes at Narkanda and settlements farther north owe their existence to the Bushahr maharajas who once ruled over all of Kinnaur. Perhaps the most interesting is Sarahan, home to the famous Bhimakali Temple, which once played host to human sacrifices.

RAMPUR

Rampur (924m) was once on the ancient trade route between India and Tibet, and is a former centre of the mighty Bushahr empire, which spread deep into Kinnaur. These days Rampur is a fairly typical medium-sized hill town, with a bustling bazaar, an imposing palace and some ancient temples down by the river. If you are heading on to Kinnaur, you should ask about the current condition of the road here.

Orientation & Information

Rampur consists of a network of narrow lanes, squeezed between the highway and the river. All the places to stay are downhill from the highway. For the main bazaar and most of the temples, follow the steps downhill, across from the bus stand.

Things to See & Do

The **Padam Palace**, built in 1925, is along the main road, and once belonged to the Maharaja of Bushahr. You can't go inside, but there are lovely gardens that you can wander around. The most impressive temple in Rampur is the ancient stone **Raghunath Temple**, in a compound opposite the bus stand. Nearby is a Buddhist gompa housing a vast prayer wheel. Also interesting are the old stone **Purohit Mandir** and the colourful stucco **Sri Sat Narain Temple**, built in 1926, both down by the river on the main bazaar.

It's possible to **trek** from Rampur to the Kullu Valley via the Bashleo La (3277m) in about four days, passing through the villages of Sarahan (not to be confused with the more important Sarahan across the valley) and Bathad, which both have ancient wooden temples.

Special Events

The ancient **Lavi Fair** is held in Rampur every year in the second week of November. People from the remote regions of Lahaul, Spiti and Kinnaur congregate in the town to trade local produce and horses, and it's a great place to buy handicrafts from the hills.

Places to Stay & Eat

Rampur is a popular alcohol stop for truck drivers so the hotels here can be a little rowdy.

One of the best options is the popular *Hotel Bhagwati (☎ 01782-33117)*, just off the main bazaar at the bottom of town (follow the signs from the bus stand). Comfortable doubles with private bathroom start at Rs 110 (Rs 165 with TV), deluxe rooms cost Rs 385.

A short walk uphill from the bus station, *Narindera Hotel (☎ 01782-33155)* has decent doubles with private bathroom and hot water from Rs 150 to 275. Air-con rooms are Rs 500. There's a good restaurant here.

There are dozens of cheap dosshouses in Rampur. Most have noisy bars and spartan rooms from Rs 75 to 200. Better options include *Hotel Paradise (☎ 01782-33334)* on the main bazaar, and *Highway Home (☎ 01782-33063)*, downhill from the bus stand along the highway.

The HPTDC *Cafe Sutlej* is worth the 1km walk from the palace towards Shimla for views and good food. The old town has plenty of *dhabas* – the best is just down the steps opposite the bus stand on the right-hand side.

Getting There & Away

Rampur is a major transport hub, so is well connected by (crowded) buses. There are buses every 30 minutes between 4.30 am to 6.30 pm to Narkanda (Rs 38, two hours) and then on to Shimla (Rs 78, six hours). The road to Rekong Peo was destroyed in August 2000; at the time of research buses only ran as far as Karcham (Rs 45, 3½ hours), at the junction to the Sangla Valley, from where it's a 5km trek and 20-minute jeep or local bus ride on to Rekong Peo. Buses to Sarahan depart every two hours or so from 7.30 am to 4.30 pm (Rs 25, one hour). A one-way taxi from Shimla to Rampur will cost Rs 1450.

SARAHAN

The former summer capital of the Bushahr empire, which rose to power in the 6th century, Sarahan is a wonderful little village set high above the valley floor. Sarahan is best known for the ancient Bhimakali Temple, but it's also a good base for treks to nearby villages such as Ranwin and the towering Bashal peak. The flamboyant palace of the last Maharaja of Bushahr is just behind the Bhimakali Temple. There are spectacular views of Srikhand Mahadev (5227m) from almost everywhere in the village.

Bhimakali Temple Complex

This ancient temple complex is regarded as one of the finest examples of Himachal architecture. The two main temples are built in the form of towers with elaborately carved, overhanging upper storeys. As with many Himachal buildings, alternating layers of timber and stone were used to enable the temples to withstand earthquakes.

The right-hand temple is around 800-years-old but is no longer structurally sound. Visitors can climb the newer left-hand temple, which dates from the 1920s. Stairs ascend to the 2nd floor where the main statue of Bhimakali (a local version of the blood-thirsty goddess Kali) is housed, surrounded by images including Parvati, Buddha and Annapurna, all under a beautiful filigree silver canopy. On the first floor there is a statue of Parvati, wife of Shiva. As you enter the compound, notice the finely decorated silver doors.

The temple is open 9 am to 7 pm daily and there are some quite strict entry rules. Visitors must wear a cap (which can be borrowed from inside the temple), leather goods such as belts and wallets must be left with the guards (putting any valuables in your pockets), photography is only allowed outside the two main temples, and shoes must be removed.

In the far right of the courtyard is a small display of ancient ceremonial lamps and weapons. Also in the compound is the squat **Lankra Vir Temple** where, up until the 19th century, human sacrifices were performed to appease Bhimakali. The tradition lives on in the form of the bizarre **Astomi** ritual during Dussehra. There are a couple of other temples in the complex dedicated to Narsingh (Narasimha) and Raghunath.

Places to Stay & Eat

The excellent ***guesthouse*** *(☎ 01782-74248)*, inside the temple complex, is the best budget bet. It offers a handful of clean, quiet rooms with private bathroom for Rs 150, Rs 200 or Rs 300, plus some extremely basic dorms for Rs 25.

Close to the temple gates, the ***Bushahr Guest House*** *(☎ 01782-74238)* charges

Calming Kali

The Lankra Vir Temple in the Bhimakali compound was once the scene of grisly human sacrifices. Once every decade, a man was ceremonially killed before the shrine and his blood dripped on the tongue of the statue of Kali enshrined within. Once the goddess was satiated, the lifeless bodies were thrown into the adjacent well. The British stamped out the practice in the 1800s, persuading the priests to take up animal sacrifices instead.

These days, the goddess is appeased with the annual slaughter of a bizarre combination of animals at the blood-thirsty Astomi ritual, held two days before the end of Dussehra. Vast crowds gather to watch the sacrifice of a hapless buffalo-calf, a goat, a sheep, chickens, fish and even, legend has it, a spider, all of which are laid before the effigy of the murderous goddess.

Rs 150 for clean, cosy doubles with private bathroom and hot water.

Right by the bus stand, the ***Snow View Hotel*** *(☎ 01782-74383)*, has seen better days. Ramshackle doubles with private bathroom cost Rs 100 or Rs 200 with a view.

Nearby, the distinctive ***Hotel Srikhand*** *(☎ 01782-74234)* is run by the HPTDC and offers large, comfortable rooms with TV, private bathroom and hot water, as well as views over the valley from Rs 600 to 1100. Dorm beds cost Rs 75 when available. The restaurant here is excellent.

Better restaurants in Sarahan include ***Ribal***, for Chinese food, and ***Ajay*** for both Tibetan and Indian offerings.

Getting There & Away

There are three direct buses daily from Shimla to Sarahan (Rs 105) but it's easier to get a through bus to the junction at Jeori and wait for a local bus (every hour or two) up the steep 17km road to Sarahan. Buses run between Rampur and Sarahan every few hours for Rs 25. A taxi from Rampur to Sarahan is pricey at around Rs 500, but will save a lot of time; from Jeori to Sarahan a taxi costs about Rs 200. Heading back down the valley, it's best to leave by lunch time, as the number of buses drops off rapidly in the afternoon.

Kinnaur

Kinnaur is a remote mountainous district between Shimla and the Tibetan border. The region was derestricted in 1991 and travel to and around Kinnaur is now possible with easy-to-obtain permits.

Kinnaur is bound to the north by the formidable Zanskar Range, which forms the border with Tibet, and follows the valley of the Sutlej River, which flows from the sacred Tibetan peak of Mt Kailash. To the east, there are spectacular views of Kinnaur Kailash (6050m), particularly from Kalpa, the former capital, and nearby Rekong Peo, the current capital of Kinnaur. Both towns are reached by a side road from the Hindustan-Tibet Hwy.

South of Kinnaur Kailash is the beautiful Sangla Valley, described as one of the most scenic places in the entire Himalaya.

Kinnaur is home to the Kinnauri tribal group, an Aryan people who have always regarded themselves as distinct from other Indians. Ancient Hindu texts refer to them as the Chinas (Kinners), believed to be halfway between humans and gods. Most Kinnauris follow a mixture of Hinduism and Tibetan Buddhism, and villages often have both Hindu and Buddhist temples side by side, along with shrines to numerous local deities. The Kinnauris were traditionally known as 'celestial musicians', a tradition kept alive in the open-sided 'music chambers' which are found in most Kinnauri temple complexes.

Probably the most distinctive part of the Kinnauris' dress is the grey woollen *thepang* (cap) worn by men and women. It is curled up at one side, and edged with green felt strips. Kinnauri women often wear exquisitely embroidered shawls. Polyandry is still common in Kinnaur.

Barley and wheat are the dominant crops, but apples, apricots and walnuts are often grown. Tradition forbids Kinnauris to consume chicken but they enjoy alcohol, such as *angoori* grape wine and arak, made from fermented barley.

The peaceful existence of the Kinnauris is being eroded somewhat by the Himachal government's hydroelectric program. Huge dams have been constructed on the Sutlej River and the Baspa River in the Sangla Valley, but most of the wealth, like the electricity, ends up down the valley in Shimla.

Kinnauri (often called Homskad) is the major indigenous language and it has about 12 different dialects. One of these is called Sangnaur, and is only spoken in the village of the same name near Puh, close to the border with Tibet. Most Kinnauris also have an excellent grasp of English, a legacy of the days when they were pressed into *begar* (forced labour) by the British to help build the Hindustan-Tibet Hwy.

The roads in upper Kinnaur rank as some of the most spectacular in the Himalaya. The epic, all-weather Hindustan-Tibet Hwy links upper Kinnaur and Spiti, passing through some of the most breathtaking scenery in the region. The road celebrated its 150th anniversary in June 2000 (construction began in 1850 under Lord Dalhousie) and was promptly washed away in August 2000 by the flooding Sutlej River. At the time of research, several sections could only be negotiated on foot. Check the status of the road before travelling in the north of Kinnaur.

Permits

From the Shimla region, you can get as far as Rekong Peo, Kalpa and the Sangla Valley without a permit. For travel to northern Kinnaur, past Jangi to Tabo in Spiti, you currently need an inner line permit, which will satisfy the Indo-Tibetan border police that you aren't going to make a run for the border. The policy is a hangover from the 1962 conflict between India and China, but is still strictly enforced, so you'll need to visit the SDM office in Rekong Peo before you go any farther.

Fortunately, getting hold of a permit is relatively easy, providing the SDM in Rekong Peo is 'in station' (it's worth calling ahead on ☎ 01786-22252 to make sure). In theory, tourists must be in a group of four and be booked on an official tour to get a permit, but this is rarely enforced. The permit is valid for seven days and is normally issued the same day on production of three passport photos and photocopies of the identity pages and Indian visa from your passport. In theory, permits are also available from the SDM in Rampur and the divisional magistrate in Shimla. If you come here on a tour, the travel agent will usually arrange the permit for you.

Despite what may be written on the permit, you can stay in any village and camp anywhere along the main road between Kaza and Rekong Peo; you can travel on any form of public or private transport; and you can travel alone or in a group of any size. The form states that photography and maps are forbidden, but this is rarely enforced.

Checkpoints between Rekong Peo and Kaza are at Jangi, Chango and Sumdo. Never wander too far from the main road as this is frontier territory, and the Indo-Tibetan border patrols are not to be messed with.

Coming from Lahaul and Spiti, permits are best obtained from the SDM office in Kaza (☎ 01906-22302), though the magistrate's office in Manali, Kullu or Keylong may also be willing to fill in the paperwork. The rule about groups of four is much more likely to be enforced at these offices. At the time of research there were rumours of a US$30 fee being introduced for this permit.

REKONG PEO

☎ 01786 • elevation 2290m

The modern settlement of Rekong Peo is an important transport and administrative hub and has good views of Kinnaur Kailash, but it lacks the charm of nearby Kalpa. You'll need to come here to apply for an inner line permit if you're heading north to Spiti.

Orientation & Information

Most places to stay are grouped around the intersection of the road to Kalpa and the pedestrian main bazaar, which also provides a handy shortcut to the bus stand at the top of the hill.

Inner line permits can be obtained from the SDM office (☎ 22252) in the administrative complex at the bottom of town (look for the red turrets on the roof). There is nowhere to change money in Rekong Peo.

Across the road are several places to make photocopies of permits and passports, and stock up on some necessities (mineral water is hard to find outside of Rekong Peo). Several tailors here sell Kinnauri caps and shawls.

A brightly coloured gompa, the **Kinnaur Kalachakra Celestial Palace** (Mahabodhi Gompa), is a 20-minute, steep walk above the village, just behind the radio station. Also here is a huge standing Buddha statue, staring contemplatively towards Kinnaur Kailash.

Places to Stay & Eat

Fairyland Guest House (☎ 22477), 200m from the bus stop, has a restaurant and decent rooms with hot water for Rs 200;

an extra Rs 50 gives you fantastic views of Kinnaur Kailash without having to get out of bed.

Shivling View Hotel & Restaurant *(☎ 22421)* is a short walk downhill from the bus stand. Pleasant doubles with private bathroom and hot water cost Rs 300 to 500.

Right in the centre, ***Hotel Snow View*** *(☎ 22048)* has Rs 220 doubles with private bathroom and an OK restaurant. Similar rooms at similar prices can be found at ***Hotel Rangin*** *(☎ 22246)* in the main bazaar and ***Shambhala Hotel*** *(☎ 22852)*, a 10-minute walk uphill from the bus station.

Manish Bhojnalya restaurant, right in the centre of town, serves excellent Tibetan *thugpa* (noodle soup) and *momos* (dumplings). ***Vijay Bhojnalya*** next door is good for Indian food.

Getting There & Away

Most arriving buses let passengers off in the centre of town but officially depart from the new bus station, a five-minute walk uphill from the centre (follow the bazaar opposite Hotel Snow View and bear right at the police station – it's farther along the highway). Most buses are through buses, so departure times and seat bookings are a little unpredictable.

There are buses uphill to Kalpa via Pangi (Rs 5) at 7.30 and 9 am and 1, 3.30 and 5 pm. The last trip downhill is at 6 pm. Taxis charge a steep Rs 250 one way for the journey.

There are daily buses to Kaza (Rs 120, 12 hours) at 7.30 am, returning from Kaza at the same time. To Sangla you'll have to take a jeep downhill and trek back to Karcham, where there are several buses daily to Sangla village and Chitkul (unless the road has been repaired, in which case there may be direct buses). Buses to Shimla (Rs 45) leave from Karcham every hour or so, or there are numerous public and private buses to Rampur.

KALPA

☎ 01786 • elevation 2960m

Known as Chini back in the days when it was the regional capital, the spectacular village of Kalpa has changed little in the last 500 years. This is the legendary winter home of Shiva, who is said to retire here each winter for some hashish-inspired meditation. Kalpa's narrow alleyways are crowded with traditional slate-roofed wooden homes and ancient temples, and many villagers still wear traditional Kinnaur costume. Most visitors opt to stay in the homely guesthouses here rather than the modern concrete places down in Rekong Peo.

The views across to Kinnaur Kailash are some of the most spectacular in the Himalaya. You can get a full panorama from the school playground behind the *chorten* (Tibetan pagoda) at the top of the hill. The temple next door houses a huge prayer wheel.

Just downhill, the **Narayan-Nagini** temple complex includes shrines to Hindu, Buddhist and local deities. The wooden shrines here are carved with images of deities and animals and the slate roofs are edged with dangling wooden pegs that rattle atmospherically in the wind. Look out for the open-sided 'music chamber' among the carved wooden temples. In September, villagers offer wildflowers to local deities as part of the colourful **Phulech Festival**.

Places to Stay & Eat

You can make reservations for ***Forest Rest Houses*** (including the one at Sangla) with the District Forest Officer *(☎* 22252, 25207) in Kalpa.

Right in the centre is the modern and bland ***Hotel Blue Lotus*** *(☎ 26001)*, with expensive rooms for Rs 500 upwards, but a decent restaurant.

On the road above the village, the ***HPTDC Kinner Kailash Cottage*** *(☎ 26159)* was being redeveloped at the time of research but should be re-opened by the time you read this. The new units are designed to blend in with the village houses and rates are tipped to start at around Rs 700 a double. The hotel is just off the metalled road at the top of the village.

Across the road is the modern but friendly ***Shivalik Guest House*** *(☎ 26158)*, which has good doubles with hot shower for Rs 300 to 500 (Rs 200 in winter).

A five-minute walk north-east along the same road will bring you to the homely ***Auktong Guest House*** *(☎ 26019)*, set in a pleasant apple orchard overlooking the valley. The simple but comfortable rooms have great views across to the mountains and cost Rs 100 with shared bathroom.

Timberline Trekking Camps *(in Delhi ☎ 011-6984049 for details)*, on the outskirts of the village, offers luxury tents (with hot water) in a pleasant location for Rs 1250 a double. The whole place packs up and goes back to Delhi from October to May.

Getting There & Away

It's a pleasant 45-minute walk downhill from Kalpa to Rekong Peo – follow the short cuts rather than the winding road. Don't even think about doing it uphill.

There are somewhat unreliable buses from Kalpa to Rekong Peo (Rs 5, one hour) at 8.30 and 10 am and 2, 4.30 and 6 pm daily. Most buses continue on from Rekong Peo to other destinations farther south. Taxis to Rekong Peo cost a steep Rs 250/400 one way/return.

HINDUSTAN-TIBET HWY

Inner line permits are required for the section of the road from Rekong Peo (Kinnaur) to Tabo (Spiti). **Jangi**, 31km past the turn off to Rekong Peo, is the first checkpoint, and the last point you can reach without a permit.

The only private accommodation between Rekong Peo and Tabo is in the village of **Nako**, 7km uphill from Yangthang (share-jeeps cost Rs 40). This remote village has a beautiful setting beside bewitching Nako Lake and an 11th-century gompa, with four small temples. Legend has it that Padmasambhava, the progenitor of Tibetan Buddhism, created the lake by throwing a boulder here. You can trek from Nako to the peak of Purgyal and the ancient gompas at Tashigang (5 hours) and Somang (7 hours), but a guide is probably advisable.

The yellow ***guesthouse*** by the bus stop is one of several places offering rooms for around Rs 100 (ask for directions). It's an easy downhill walk to the highway if you miss the bus.

As an alternative, there are ***Public Works Department (PWD) Rest Houses*** at Morang, Jangi, Puh and Yangthang, which may offer you a bed if they aren't full; book ahead with the PWD in Kaza (☎ 01906-2252) or Kalpa (☎ 01785-26027).

Other sights along the road include the small gompas at **Khanum**, near Spillo, and at **Morang**. The road to Spiti branches off at **Sumdo**, 120km north of Rekong Peo, while the *very* out-of-bounds road to Tibet continues 19km east to the border. The Hindustan-Tibet Hwy is frequently blocked by landslides, particularly around Milling, to add to the problems caused by the Sutlej floods south of Rekong Peo. At the time of research the road was impassable at several points requiring travellers to trek between the stretches that are open to buses. Loitering porters will carry your bags for a fee.

See also Around Kaza at the end of this chapter for destinations at the end of this route.

Sangla Valley

The Sangla, or Baspa, Valley has been called 'the most beautiful valley in the Himalaya' and for once this is more than just marketing jargon. Strung out along the valley floor are a number of ancient villages with traditional stone and timber architecture, friendly people and magnificent mountain scenery on all sides. The mouth of the valley is marred somewhat by the construction site for yet another hydroelectric plant, but it soon vanishes from sight as you climb up the gorge. The road into the valley must be one of the most hair-raising in the Himalaya.

The Sangla Valley is best visited in spring (April to May) or autumn (September to early November). In the summer the monsoon makes for long, damp days, and roads are regularly blocked by snow in winter.

SANGLA

☎ 017869 • elevation 2680m

This wonderful village is the largest in the valley. Traditional slate-roofed houses are seemingly stacked on top of each other and there are awe-inspiring views of Kinnaur Kailash (6050m) from almost everywhere in town. The ancient carving on some of the wooden houses is spectacular.

Things to See & Do

Among the interesting temples here are the **Bering Nag Temple**, sacred to the local deity Nagas, and the **Mahavan Buddha Temple**, just downhill from the bus stand, with a vast prayer wheel and small shrines to Shiva and Vishnu. There are some interesting old murals in the Buddhist temple on the next spur of land. During the **Phulech Festival**, locals pile wildflowers at the Bering Nag Temple, filling the air with a (literally) intoxicating perfume that inspires much merrymaking.

It's a short walk through orchards to nearby Kamru, with its **ancient fort** – follow the road behind the Public Works Department.

More intensive treks lead to the Har-ki-Dun Valley in Garhwal (Uttaranchal) and Karcham via the Shivaling La (3980m), taking in many remote villages. Some of these walks may require an inner line permit – inquire at the SDM office in Rekong Peo (☎ 01786-22252). Trekmount Adventures, above the Robert Photo Studio, can organise guides and porters. (The Birma and Sunder tailor nearby sells warm thepangs for Rs 200.)

Places to Stay & Eat

A short walk down the highway from the bus stand, ***Baspa Guesthouse*** *(☎ 42206)* has rooms for Rs 165, or Rs 275 with private bathroom.

Farther downhill and up a road to the right is ***Mount Kailash Guest House*** *(☎ 42527)*, with good doubles with private bathroom upstairs for Rs 380 (Rs 300 downstairs), and a dorm for Rs 75 per head.

On the next corner is ***Highland Guest House*** *(☎ 42285)* with basic rooms for Rs 150 and Rs 200. In the summer ***Banjara Camps*** *(in Delhi ☎ 011-6855153)* offers accommodation in luxury tents on the far side of the river at Batseri.

The lovely old ***Forest Rest House*** nearby must be reserved with the Divisional Forest Office (DFO; ☎ 01786-22252, 25207) in Kalpa.

Monal Reception restaurant in the centre of town is a good place for Indian and Chinese food and breakfast.

Getting There & Away

There are buses uphill to Chitkul (Rs 15) at noon and 4 pm, but both return at 6 am the next morning. For a day trip, you'll have to take one of the infrequent share-jeeps (Rs 50) or a taxi for Rs 600 return. Buses head downhill to Rampur (Rs 12) at 7, 8 and 10 am and 3 pm. If the road is repaired there may also be buses to Rekong Peo. Share-jeeps run down to Karcham at the mouth of the valley, where you can pick up frequent buses to Shimla and Rampur.

KAMRU

Clinging to a narrow rocky spur 2km above Sangla, the village of **Kamru** (2600m) was the former capital of the Bushahr empire which once ruled Kinnaur. Kamru is dominated by the fort-like **Kamakhya Devi Temple**, which can be visited from 8 to 9 am and 7 to 8 pm only (a hat is required and shoes must be removed). There are several wooden Buddhist and Hindu temples just downhill.

A sealed road runs through apple orchards from Sangla to a stone gateway, from where it's a steep climb to the village proper. By the gate is a cairn of carved *mani* stones (stones carved with the Tibetan Buddhist mantra *'Om mani padme hum'*) and a Buddha image said to prevent people smuggling in ghosts and other evil spirits.

RAKCHAM & CHITKUL

High above Sangla are the remote villages of Rakcham (3050m), 14km from Sangla, and Chitkul (3450m), right at the end of the 44km-long valley road. Chitkul has three 500-year-old wooden **temples** and a small gompa, and both villages offer great views, traditional architecture and friendly people. It's possible to make an adventurous trek from Chitkul over the high Lamkhaga La (5284m) to Harsil in Garhwal on the road to

Gangotri, but you'll need an inner line permit from Rekong Peo. This is definitely one time you'll need a local guide.

There is nowhere to stay in Rakcham, but Chitkul has several guesthouses. Easiest to find is the friendly ***Anwar House,*** with doubles at Rs 100 and with home-cooked meals. Buses run uphill from Sangla (Rs 15) at noon and 4 pm, returning at 6 am. A share-taxi from Sangla costs Rs 30 to Rakcham and Rs 50 to Chitkul, or it's Rs 600 to charter a taxi.

Kangra Valley

The beautiful Kangra Valley starts near Mandi, runs north, then bends west and extends to Shapur on the road to Pathankot. To the north the valley is flanked by the Dhaula Dhar Range, to the side of which clings Dharamsala. There are a number of places of interest along the valley, including McLeod Ganj, home of the Dalai Lama and headquarters of the Tibetan Government in Exile.

The main Pathankot to Mandi road runs through the valley, and there is a narrow-gauge railway line from Pathankot as far as Jogindernagar. The Kangra school of painting developed in this valley.

DHARAMSALA

☎ 01892 • pop 19,200

While Dharamsala is synonymous with the Tibetan Government in Exile, the actual headquarters is about 4km above Dharamsala at Gangchen Kyishong, and most travellers hang out at McLeod Ganj, which stretches along a high ridge 10km by road above Dharamsala.

Dharamsala itself is of little interest to travellers, although Kotwali Bazaar, at the foot of the roads leading up to McLeod Ganj, is a colourful market, and you can visit the Kangra Art Museum.

To the right of the bus terminal building is a steep staircase that leads up to the vegetable market at Kotwali Bazaar.

Information

The HPTDC tourist office (☎ 24212) is friendly and provides better than average local information as it doesn't offer its own tours. The office is open 10 am to 5 pm Monday to Saturday.

The computerised branch of the State Bank of India accepts most travellers cheques and cash in US dollars and UK pounds; the Punjab National Bank just accepts travellers cheques. The Bank of Baroda, nearby, can give cash advances on Visa cards within 24 hours (you can call ahead to reserve on ☎ 23175 and pick up your money the next day).

The DFO (☎ 24887) opposite the main post office is the place to book Forest Rest Houses on the trekking routes above McLeod Ganj.

Kangra Art Museum

This museum, a few minutes' walk south of the tourist office, has miniature paintings from the Kangra school of painting, which flourished in the Kangra Valley during the 17th century. It also has elaborately embroidered, traditional costumes of Kangra people, woodcarvings and tribal jewellery. It's open 10 am to 5 pm Tuesday to Sunday. Entry is free.

Places to Stay & Eat

Sood Guest House *(☎ 24269, Cantt Rd, Kotwali Bazaar)* has reasonable rooms with private bathroom that can function as singles/doubles/triples for Rs 75/100/125.

B Mehra Hotel *(☎ 23582)*, a few doors up on the opposite side of the road, has scruffy doubles (with brilliant views!) for Rs 250 with private bathroom and hot water. Singles with shared bathroom are Rs 125.

The ***HPTDC Hotel Dhauladhar*** *(☎ 249 26)* has standard rooms with private bathroom for Rs 500 in the annexe and Rs 800 to 1500 in the main building. The restaurant and bar have excellent sunset views.

Uphill towards Gangchen Kyishong is ***Surbhi Guest House*** *(☎ 24677)*, with comfortable rooms with hot shower and TV for Rs 250 and Rs 350.

Cloud's End Villa *(☎ 24904)* is the residence of the Raja of Lambagraon-Kangra. Although inconveniently located halfway between Dharamsala and Gangchen

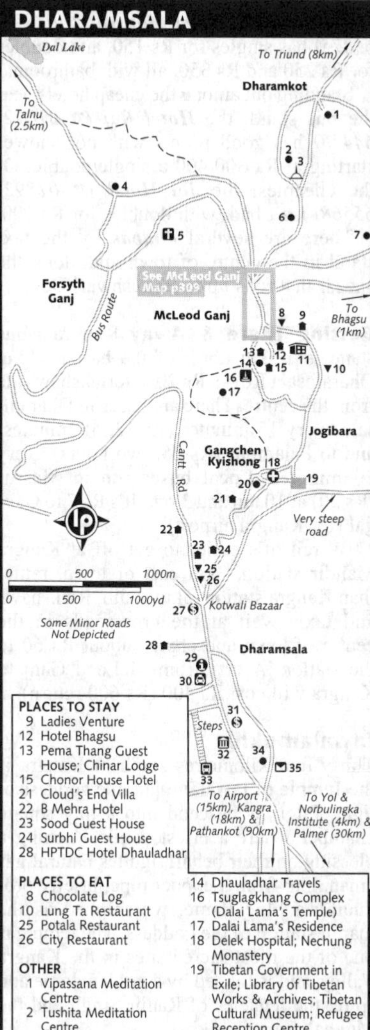

Kyishong, it's a great place for a splurge. The five rooms range from Rs 770 to 1250 and have all the classic colonial trappings.

In Dharamsala, ***City Restaurant*** is popular and serves up a bit of everything. ***Potala Restaurant***, up a narrow flight of stairs opposite, has good vegetarian and nonveg Tibetan and Chinese cuisine.

Getting There & Away

Buses to McLeod Ganj (Rs 6, 30 minutes) depart every half hour. The easiest place to catch one is at the top (southern) end of Kotwali Bazaar. Cramped passenger jeeps also run a shuttle service for the same price. A Maruti van taxi, from the stand on the main thoroughfare, should cost Rs 100.

There are buses to Pathankot (Rs 55, 3½ hours) every hour or so between 5 am and 5 pm; to Mandi (Rs 80, six hours) at 5 and 11 am and 6 pm; and to Manali (Rs 190, 12½ hours) at 4 am and 6 and 8.30 pm via Kullu (Rs 120, 10 hours). There are four daily services to Dalhousie (Rs 85, six hours); the 8.30 am service continues on to Chamba (Rs 125, eight hours) and is probably the most convenient.

There are three morning and three evening buses to Shimla (Rs 185 to 225, 10½ hours); a single bus at 3 pm to Haridwar (Rs 237, 12 hours); and a 9 pm bus to Dehra Dun (Rs 231, 11 hours) – both in Uttaranchal. To Delhi, there are ordinary services (Rs 237, 13 hours) at 5 and 7 am and 4.30, 5.30, 7.30 and 8 pm, and a single deluxe bus (Rs 340) at 8 pm.

There are regular local buses to Gaggal (for Dharamsala airport), Yol (for Norbulingka), Kangra and Jawalamukhi, plus occasional services to Masrur. For Baijnath and Palampur, take any bus to Mandi or Manali.

AROUND DHARAMSALA

Masrur

South-west of Dharamsala, via Gaggal, is the small settlement of Masrur, which has 15 Indo-Aryan style rock-cut temples that were hewn from the sandstone cliffs in the 10th century. The temples were devastated by the earthquake of 1905 (which also put paid to McLeod Ganj) but among the rubble, it's still possible to see the resemblance between these temples and the better-known and much larger temples at Ellora in Maharashtra. The Archaeological Survey of India has slapped a whopping US$5 entry fee on the temples, which is quite steep considering their condition.

There are buses to Masrur from Kangra, but from Dharamsala you'll probably have to change at Gaggal. The ruins are at the top of the hill. A taxi from McLeod Ganj will cost around Rs 800 one way (Rs 1200 return).

Kangra

At one time this ancient town, some 18km south of Dharamsala, was the seat of the Chand dynasty, which ruled over the princely state of Kangra. The famous **Bajreshwari Devi Temple** was of such legendary wealth that every invader worth their salt took time to sack it. Mahmud of Ghazni carted off a fabulous fortune in gold, silver and jewellery in 1009. In 1360 it was plundered once again by Tughlaq but it was still able to recover and, in Jehangir's reign, was paved in plates of pure silver.

These days, the temple worth visiting more for the atmosphere than the actual building. It is in the bazaar above the crossroads in the middle of town, at the end of a labyrinthine series of alleyways flanked with stalls selling *prasad* (food offerings that are used in religious ceremonies).

The British took possession of the ancient fort of **Nagar Kot**, 2.5km south of modern Kangra, and established a garrison. The disastrous earthquake that shook the valley in 1905 destroyed the fort and the temple, though the latter has since been rebuilt. The ruins are perched high on a windswept ridge overlooking the confluence of the Manjhi and Baner Rivers, and can be reached from Kangra by autorickshaw (Rs 40). The Archaeological Survey of India levies a steep US$5 entry fee for foreign tourists.

Places to Stay Close to the centre on Dharamsala Rd, ***Hotel Royal*** *(☎ 01892-65013)* has spotless doubles with hot shower for Rs 300 and Rs 350. Farther down Dharamsala Rd, ***Hotel Maurya*** *(☎ 01892-65875)* has singles for Rs 150, and doubles for Rs 250 and Rs 350, all with bathroom.

Standing out among the cheap hotels near the bus stand, the ***Hotel Raj*** *(☎ 01892-64478)* has good rooms with hot shower starting at Rs 300/400 a single/double. Of the cheapies, the ***Jai Hotel*** *(☎ 01892-65568)* isn't bad, with doubles for Rs 100.

There are several ***dhabas*** by the taxi stand in the centre of town and along the bazaar that runs up to Bajreshwari Devi.

Getting There & Away Kangra's bus stand is 1.5km north of the bazaar along Dharamsala Rd – a Rs 20 autorickshaw ride from the centre. There are buses to Dharamsala every 15 minutes (Rs 12, 45 minutes) and to Palampur (Rs 25, two hours) every 20 minutes. Local buses run to Masrur (Rs 20) at 10 am and 3 pm. It's Rs 7 to Gaggal (for Kangra airport).

By rail, it's easier to get off at Kangra Mandir station, 3km east of town, rather than Kangra station, 5km south. Rickshaws and taxis wait at the crossroads in the centre of town and charge about Rs 60 to the station. A taxi from McLeod Ganj to Kangra will cost Rs 400 (Rs 600 return).

Jawalamukhi

Thirty-four kilometres south of Kangra is the **Temple of Jawalamukhi**, the goddess of light. Pilgrims descend into a tiny square chamber where a priest, while intoning a blessing on their behalf, ignites natural gas emanating from a copper pipe, briefly producing a blue flame, worshipped as the manifestation of the goddess. The temple is one of the most sacred sites in the Kangra Valley, and is topped by a golden dome and spire, the legacies of Ranjit Singh and the Mughal emperor Akbar.

The ***HPTDC Hotel Jawalaji*** *(☎ 01970-22280)* has doubles with private bathroom from Rs 450 to 1000. Dorm beds are Rs 75. There's a 30% low-season discount.

Buses to Dharamsala (Rs 35) leave throughout the day from the stand below the road to the temple. From McLeod Ganj taxis cost Rs 700/1000 one way/return.

Nurpur

Only 24km from Pathankot, on Dharamsala Rd, this town was named by Jehangir in honour of his wife Nurjahan. **Nurpur Fort** is now in ruins, but still has some finely carved reliefs. A ruined temple dedicated to Krishna, also finely carved, stands within the fort, which looms over the main road.

The ***PWD Rest House*** *(☎ 01893-2009)* with large, very clean doubles for Rs 100.

Norbulingka Institute

This educational complex, 14km from McLeod Ganj and 4km from Dharamsala, was established to teach and preserve traditional Tibetan art, such as woodcarving, *thangka* (cloth) painting, goldsmithing and embroidery. Work by Norbulingka artists is available from the Institute or from the Norling Designs shop in McLeod Ganj. Norbulingka itself is set amid Japanese-influenced gardens with shady paths, wooden bridges across small streams and tiny waterfalls, and makes a pleasant side trip from McLeod Ganj. Visit its Web site at www.norbulingkainstitute.org for more information on the Norbulingka Institute.

Nearby is the **Dolmaling Nunnery**, site of the Women's Higher Studies Institute, offering nuns courses at advanced levels in Buddhist philosophy.

The friendly ***Norling Guest House*** *(☎ 01892-22664)* in the Institute gardens has good singles/doubles from Rs 1000/1150. Meals can be ordered or you can eat at the nearby ***Norling Cafe***.

To get here, catch a Yol-bound bus and ask to be let off at Sidhpur, near the Sacred Heart School, from where it's a 20-minute walk. A taxi from McLeod will cost Rs 200.

Chamunda Devi Temple

Midway between Dharamsala and Palampur, and 10km to the west, the colourful Chamunda Devi Temple complex sits on the bank of the Baner River. Chamunda is a particularly wrathful form of Durga, and the idol is completely hidden beneath a red cloth.

The ***HPTDC Yatri Niwas*** *(☎ 01892-36065)* has doubles with bathroom for Rs 400 and Rs 550, and dorm beds for Rs 50.

Nearby, ***Chaumunda*** *(☎ 01892-52241)* and ***Vatika*** *(☎ 01892-52247)* hotels both have rooms from Rs 300 to 600.

Buses between Dharamsala and Palampur will drop you at the Chamunda Devi Temple, or for Rs 300/500 take a one-way/return taxi.

Palampur

☎ 01894 • elevation 1260m

A pleasant little town surrounded by tea plantations, Palampur is 30km south-east of Dharamsala. A four-day trek takes you from Palampur to **Holi** via the Waru La, or on a shorter walk, you can visit the **Bundla chasm**, just outside of town, where a waterfall drops into the Bundla stream through a 305m cleft in the rock. If you are planning on trekking from Palampur to Holi bear in mind that you must make the necessary arrangements in McLeod Ganj.

Places to Stay & Eat The ***HPTDC Hotel T-Bud*** *(☎ 31298)*, 1km north of Main Bazaar, has doubles with bathroom from Rs 550 to 800 (Rs 330 to 450 in low season).

Hotel Highland Regency *(☎ 31222)*, just next to the new bus station, has pleasant rooms and clean bathrooms for Rs 275, Rs 400 or Rs 550. It also has a good restaurant. ***Hotel Chandan Palace*** *(☎ 34837)* next door has similar rooms for similar prices.

In town, ***Hotel Sawhney*** *(☎ 30888)* has basic doubles from Rs 165 to Rs 275 with TV.

Pine's Hotel *(☎ 32633)*, down near the old bus station, has singles from Rs 110 to 140, and doubles from Rs 175 to 250.

Joy Restaurant, near the Hotel Sawhney, has cheap fare, including hybrid dosas with North Indian fillings. ***Sapan Restaurant***, opposite the post office in Main Bazaar, serves Indian and Chinese cuisine. There's also a ***restaurant*** at the Hotel T-Bud.

Getting There & Away The new bus station is 1km south of Main Bazaar; a taxi costs a steep Rs 50. Buses leave all day for Dharamsala (Rs 20, two hours); Mandi (Rs 57, four hours) and Pathankot (Rs 70, four hours; last bus at 2.15 pm). A taxi from Dharamsala costs Rs 500 (Rs 700 return).

Maranda, 2km west of Palampur, is on the narrow-gauge train line between Pathankot and Jogindernagar. There are six passenger trains daily between Maranda and Kangra to the west (for Dharamsala), or the end of the line at Jogindernagar, to the east.

Tashijong & Taragarh

The friendly Tashijong Gompa, 5km north-west of Baijnath, is the focus of a small Drukpa Kagyud community of 150 Tibetan monks and 400 refugees. The monastery complex has several colourful prayer halls and there's a carpet-making, woodcarving and thangka-painting cooperative.

Tashijong village is a 2km walk north from the main Palampur to Baijnath Rd. Ask the bus to let you off near the Tashijong turn-off. Alternatively, you can take a taxi from Dharamsala for around Rs 600/750 one way/return.

It's possible to stay at the ***Monastery Guesthouse***, where doubles cost from Rs 100 to 150. There is a second, cheaper ***guesthouse*** above the village clinic.

Two kilometres south of Tashijong, at Taragarh, is the extraordinary ***Palace Hotel*** *(☎ 01894-63034)*, the summer palace of the last maharaja of Jammu & Kashmir, now run as a hotel by his son, Dr Karan Singh. Portraits of the royal family are displayed throughout the hotel, which has the usual assortment of tiger skins and colonial furnishings. Doubles range from Rs 950 to 2000; the beautifully furnished suites cost up to Rs 2500. The hotel does take reservations from nonguests for breakfast, lunch or dinner.

Baijnath

The small town of Baijnath (1010m), 46km south-east of Dharamsala, is an important pilgrimage place due to its ancient stone **Baidyanath Temple**, sacred to Shiva in his incarnation as Vaidyanath, Lord of the Physicians. It is said to date from AD 804, although according to tradition it was built by the Pandavas, the heroes of the Mahabharata. The temple features intricate carvings on the exterior walls, including some stunning figures set into alcoves, and the inner sanctum enshrines one of India's 12 *jyoti linga* (linga of light), believed to be a source of divine power, or *shakti*. Large numbers of pilgrimscome here for the **Shivaratri Festival** in late February/early March.

HIMACHAL PRADESH

Exiles

In May 1949, the newly established communist government of China signed a treaty extending Chinese sovereignty to Tibet, based on the premise that both nations were once part of the Mughal empire. The Chinese People's Army marched into Lhasa the same year, beginning a brutal regime that has left some 1.2 million Tibetans dead and countless others imprisoned in forced-labour camps.

In the years since 1949, some 90% of the nation's religious institutions have been destroyed. Fearing for his life and the lives of his people, the spiritual leader of Tibet, His Holiness the 14th Dalai Lama, Tenzin Gyatso, made the difficult decision to lead his people into exile in 1959.

Accompanied by a small entourage, the Dalai Lama arrived in India, on foot, after trekking for weeks across the Himalaya. Since then, some 292,000 Tibetans have followed in his footsteps, settling in Dharamsala, Darjeeling and other mountain communities. The exiled Tibetan government was granted political asylum in Gangchen Kyishong below McLeod Ganj, which has become the headquarters for a 40-year struggle for liberation. Tenzin Gyatso was awarded the Nobel Peace Prize in 1989 for his efforts to find a peaceful solution for the liberation of Tibet.

China has resisted all attempts at dialogue over the Tibet issue. With Western nations relaxing their restrictions on China, many now fear for the future of the Free Tibet Movement. The Tibet Museum at Namgyal Gompa in the Tsuglagkhang Complex has extensive displays telling the tragic story of the Chinese occupation.

Baijnath itself is a chaotic and ramshackle town, although the Dhaula Dhar Range provides a fine backdrop. There are several places to stay, including ***Hotel Shanker View*** *(☎ 01894-63036)*, 300m out of town on the road to Mandi, with singles/doubles from Rs 150/250; hot water by the bucket is Rs 10.

The best place to eat here is the ***HPTDC Cafe Bhairav***, beside the road downhill from town, with great views and the usual HPTDC offerings from Rs 60 to 150.

All buses from Dharamsala to Palampur and destinations farther south pass through town. The narrow-gauge railway passes through Baijnath on its way to Pathankot (six hours) and Jogindernagar (three hours); the station is at Paprola, 1km west of the main bus stand. A taxi from Dharamsala costs Rs 700 (Rs 1000 return).

Bir & Billing

About 9km south of Baijnath and 4km uphill from the highway is the little Tibetan settlement of Bir, perched at 2080m. There's a beautiful **gompa** belonging to the Tibetan Nyingmapa order here, which is reached by a path to the west of the main village.

Hang-Gliding & Paragliding Far above Bir at 2600m, Billing is the launching site for some of the most impressive hang-gliding and paragliding in India. Every May/June, HPTDC organises the Himalayan Hang Gliding Rally, which attracts participants from all over the world. A tent village is provided for accommodation; contact HPDTC in Shimla (☎ 0177-252561) or Delhi (☎ 011-3325320) for more information.

At other times of year, you may be able to book paragliding trips with tour operators in McLeod Ganj or Manali. Based in Delhi, Himalayan Adventure Club International (☎ 011-7178870) E15, Plot No 144-145, Sector 8, Rohini, offers excursion flights and training courses at Billing during the summer. Billing Adventures (☎ 01894-68541) in Bir is the only local operator.

Getting There & Away There is one daily bus from Jogindernagar to Bir, or you can catch any bus between Baijnath and Jogindernagar and walk up from the junction. A day trip by taxi from Dharamsala will cost around Rs 1200; from Jogindernagar, expect to pay around Rs 700.

McLEOD GANJ

☎ 01892 • elevation 1770m

About 4km by foot above Dharamsala (10km by a winding road), McLeod Ganj is the headquarters of the Tibetan Government in Exile and the home of His Holiness the 14th Dalai Lama, as well as being the main traveller hang-out in the Kangra Valley. Here you'll find friendly Tibetan monks, budget hotels, trekking companies, Western food, video movies and wall-to-wall shops selling Tibetan souvenirs.

The town was established in the mid-1850s as a British garrison and became an important administrative centre for the Kangra region until a disastrous earthquake in 1905 forced the British to move down into the valley. Things were fairly quiet until 1959 when the Dalai Lama and his entourage claimed asylum here following the Chinese invasion of Tibet (see the boxed text 'Exiles').

The curious name comes from the Lieutenant Governor of Punjab, David McLeod and *ganj*, the Hindi word for market. Before the arrival of the British, Upper Dharamsala was home to the seminomadic Gaddi people and there is still a sizable Gaddi population in the surrounding villages.

Orientation

The heart of McLeod Ganj is the bus stand. From here roads radiate out to various points around the township, including the main road back to Dharamsala, which passes the church of St John in the Wilderness and the cantonment area of Forsyth Ganj. Other roads lead to the villages of Dharamkot and Bhagsu.

Temple Rd leads to the Tsuglagkhang Temple, about 800m to the south. From there you can take a short cut down to the administrative area of Gangchen Kyishong, where after a walk of some 20 minutes you'll find the Library of Tibetan Works & Archives. The other road through the bazaar, Jogibara Rd, also wends its way down to Gangchen Kyishong via the village of Jogibara.

HIMACHAL PRADESH

Cleaning Up McLeod

After growing concern about the piles of garbage around McLeod Ganj, the Tibetan Welfare Office and foreign volunteers have established one of the first green garbage collection services in India. The scheme consists of four 'green workers' – generally new arrivals from Tibet – who collect about 40kg to 50kg of recyclable goods from homes and businesses around McLeod each day, which are then sold to scrap merchants down in the valley.

Another initiative under the welfare office is the Green Shop, on Bhagsu Rd, which was established in response to the shocking numbers of plastic drinking water bottles mounting up around McLeod. In the low season, 25 to 30 bottles of water are sold each day, rising to a staggering 100 to 120 bottles per day in the high season. If you have your own canteen or even an empty mineral water bottle, you can buy inexpensive boiled and filtered mountain water for a few rupees. Also on offer are rechargeable batteries and natural cosmetics.

The Green Shop has a small environmental museum and distributes posters on environmental issues, in Hindi, to surrounding villages, as yet with only limited Indian government support.

Encouraging local businesses to recycle and using your own canteen or recycled mineral water bottle may help create the environment for change.

Information

Tourist Offices The new HPTDC office, opposite Bookworm, is open 10 am to 1.30 pm and 2 to 5 pm daily, and sells maps and guides to the area, as well as providing train information.

Money The Punjab National Bank on Temple Road can change US dollar and UK pounds travellers cheques but not cash. Fortunately, most travel agencies in Dharamsala can change both cash and travellers cheques at close to or better than government rates. Summit Adventures is reliable and displays a noticeboard with the daily exchange rates. Several places offer Western Union money transfers; try Paul Merchants Ltd in the arcade opposite the bus stand.

Post The post office is on Jogibara Rd, just past the State Bank of India. To post parcels you need to complete a customs form (in triplicate!), which you can get at the Office of Tibetan Handicrafts. It costs Rs 3 and is not required for book postage. There are several places that offer a parcel packing service on Jogibara Rd. Letters sent 'c/o poste restante, GPO McLeod Ganj' are held for one month.

Telephone & Fax The telecom office (fax 21528) is up a flight of stairs behind the bus stand. You can make international calls and send and receive faxes at government rates (the fax machine is not on at night). The office is open 10 am to 6 pm Monday to Saturday. Most hotels charge around Rs 3 per minute to receive incoming international calls.

Email & Internet Access McLeod Ganj has the best Internet facilities in the Himalaya with fast connections and reasonable prices (Rs 60 per hour is the going rate). Probably the most popular place is the Green Cyber Cafe at the Green Hotel, which has loads of PCs and funky mandala screen savers. The nearby Himalayan Bamboo Hut Cafe and Aroma Cybercafe on Jogibara Rd also charge Rs 60 per hour.

Travel Agencies There are numerous travel agencies in McLeod Ganj. The following are reliable and offer deluxe bus and train booking and tours:

Himachal Travels (☎ 21428, fax 21528, ⓔ himachaltravels@vsnl.com) Jogibara Rd

Potala Tours & Travels (☎ 21378, fax 21427, ⓔ potala@vsnl.net.in) opposite the Hotel Tibet; can book air, train and bus tickets, as well as arrange tours

Summit Adventures (☎ 21679, fax 21681, ⓔ summit65@yahoo.com) Jogibara Rd

Tibet Tours & Travels (☎ 21966, fax 21528) Temple Rd

HIMACHAL PRADESH

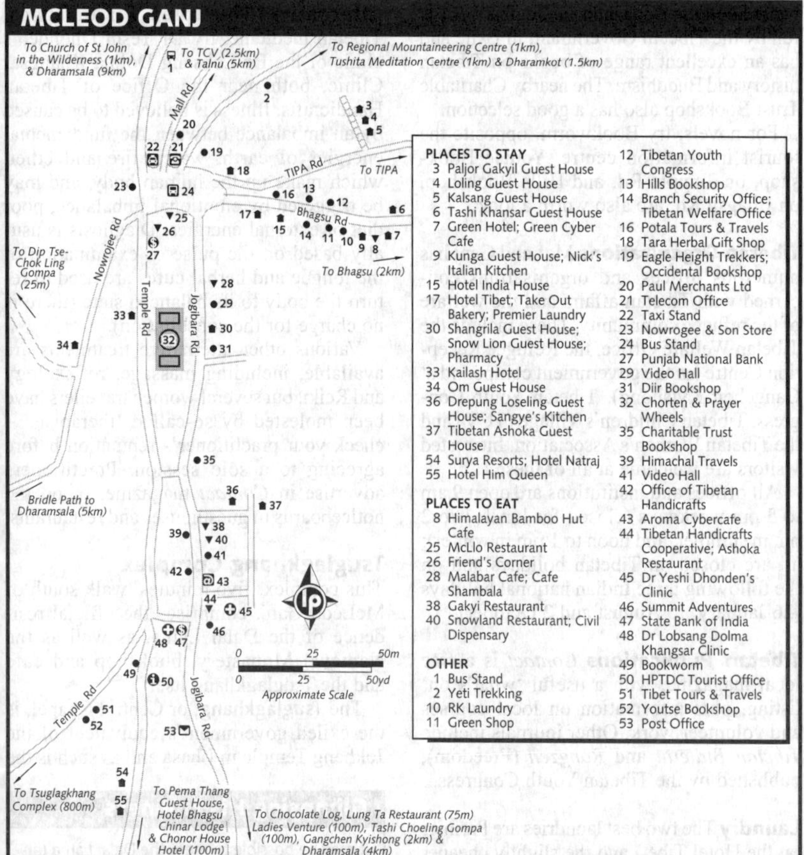

Trekking Organisations In the Occidental Bookshop, Eagle Height Trekkers (☎ 21 330) can organise trekking for US$40 per day, including porters and guides. It's possible to trek from here to the Kullu, Chamba, Lahaul and Spiti Valleys and Ladakh.

At the Regional Mountaineering Centre (☎ 21787), above McLeod on the road to Dharamkot, you can get advice on treks and mountaineering in the Chamba and Kangra Valleys, and it has a useful list of registered local guides and porters. It's a good idea to advise the centre if you are planning an independent trek.

Summit Adventures (☎ 21679) is a well-run place that offers four-day trips to Indrahar La and Kareri Lake (Rs 3600) from May to November, and local trips at other times.

Yeti Trekking (☎ 21060) arranges tailor-made treks to most areas, with accommodation en route in huts and houses. It can be found in a fine old building reached through a gate off the road to Dharamkot. Rates start at around Rs 800 per day.

Bookshops McLeod has numerous bookshops specialising in Buddhist literature, usually with an excellent range of novels as well. The Diir Bookshop on Jogibara Rd is run by the Tibetan Government in Exile and has an excellent range of books on Tibetan history and Buddhism. The nearby Charitable Trust Bookshop also has a good selection.

For novels, try Bookworm, opposite the tourist information centre. Youtse Bookshop, on Temple Rd, and Hills Bookshop, on Bhagsu Rd, are also worth a look.

Tibetan Organisations McLeod Ganj has numerous offices and organisations concerned with Tibetan affairs and the welfare of the refugee community. These include the Tibetan Welfare Office, the Refugee Reception Centre (in the government compound at Gangchen Kyishong), Tibetan Youth Congress, Tibetan Children's Village (TCV) and the Tibetan Women's Association. Interested visitors are welcome at all of these.

All offices and institutions are open 9 am to 5 pm weekdays (closed for lunch 1 to 2 pm in summer, and noon to 1 pm in winter); all are closed on Tibetan holidays and on the following three Indian national holidays (26 January, 15 August and 2 October).

Tibetan Publications *Contact* is a free local magazine, with a useful 'what's on' listing, plus information on local courses and volunteer work. Other journals include *Tibetan Bulletin* and *Rangzen* (Freedom), published by the Tibetan Youth Congress.

Laundry The two best laundries are Premier (at the Hotel Tibet) and the slightly cheaper RK Laundry down the road. Expect to pay Rs 10 to 20 for each pair of trousers, shirt or T-shirt. Same-day service may be available if you can drop off your laundry before 10 am.

Medical Services The Delek Hospital (☎ 22053) in Gangchen Kyishong is a charitable hospital for refugees that has open consultation sessions on weekday mornings. The official charge is Rs 5, but any donation over this will go towards the treatment of refugees. In McLeod you could try the Civil Dispensary on Jogibara Road. Reliable chemists include the Snow Lion pharmacy near the guest house of the same name.

Alternative Therapies For traditional Tibetan medicine, try Dr Yeshi Dhonden's clinic or the Dr Lobsang Dolma Khangsar Clinic, both near the Office of Tibetan Handicrafts. Illness is believed to be caused by an imbalance between the fundamental energies of earth, water, fire and ether, which make up the human body, and may be triggered by emotional imbalance, poor diet or external energies. Diagnosis is usually based on the pulse or examination of the tongue and herbal cures are used to return the body to its balanced state (there is no charge for the consultation).

Various other alternative treatments are available, including massage, reflexology and Reiki, but several women travellers have been molested by so-called 'therapists' – check your practitioner's reputation before agreeing to a solo session. Practitioners advertise in *Contact* magazine, or on the noticeboards in guesthouses and restaurants.

Tsuglagkhang Complex

This complex, five minutes' walk south of McLeod Ganj, comprises the official residence of the Dalai Lama, as well as the Namgyal Monastery, bookshop and cafe and the Tsuglagkhang itself.

The **Tsuglagkhang**, or Central Chapel, is the exiled government's equivalent of the Jokhang Temple in Lhasa and as such is the

Glimpsing His Holiness

It may be possible to meet the Dalai Lama (albeit briefly) at one of the occasional public audiences held in Dharamsala. Contact the Office of His Holiness the Dalai Lama (☎ 01892-21343) for details.

Requests for private audiences should be made in writing four months in advance to: The Office of His Holiness the Dalai Lama, Thekchen Choeling, PO McLeod Ganj, Dharamsala 176219, India. There are many Tibetans with more urgent need to see the Dalai Lama, so don't be surprised if you receive a polite rejection or written advice instead of an invitation.

most important Buddhist monument in McLeod Ganj. Although a relatively modest structure, it enshrines three magnificent images, including an enormous 3m-high gilt statue of Sakyamuni Buddha. To the left, facing Tibet, are statues of Avalokiteshvara (Chenrezig in Tibetan), the Tibetan deity of compassion, of whom the Dalai Lama is considered an incarnation, and Padmasambhava (Guru Rinpoche in Tibetan), the Indian scholar who introduced Buddhism and Tantric teachings to Tibet in the 8th century. Inside the Avalokitesvara statue are several relics rescued from the Jokhang Temple during the Cultural Revolution.

Also housed in the temple is a collection of sacred texts known as the Kangyur, which are based on the teachings of the Buddha, and the Tangyur texts of important Buddhist philosophical debates. The mural to the side depicts the trio of ancient Tibetan kings who oversaw the introduction of Buddhism into Tibet.

Next to the Tsuglagkhang is the **Kalachakra Temple**. Built in 1992, it houses a stunning mural of the Kalachakra (Wheel of Time) mandala. Sand mandalas are created here annually on the 5th day of the third Tibetan month. Photography is allowed in the Tsuglagkhang, but not the Kalachakra Temple.

The remaining buildings form the **Namgyal Gompa**, where it is possible to watch monks debate most afternoons, sealing points of logic with a great flourish and a clap of the hands. The bookshop at the monastery has a good selection of Buddhist texts and bundles of prayer flags. Nearby is the excellent **Tibet Museum**, which uses photos and video clips to tell the tragic story of the Tibetan struggle. It's open 10 am to 6 pm daily except Monday; entry is Rs 5.

Most Tibetan pilgrims make a *kora* (ritual circuit) of the Tsuglagkhang Complex. Take the road to the left, past the entrance to the temple, and after a few minutes a small path leads off to the right, eventually looping all the way around the Dalai Lama's residence back to the entrance to the temple. The path is flanked by colourful mani stones and prayer flags, and at one section there is a series of small prayer wheels. The kora should be made in a clockwise direction only.

Dip Tse-Chok Ling Gompa

This beautiful little gompa is at the bottom of a steep track, which leads off the lane past the Om Guest House. The main *dukhang* (prayer hall) houses an image of Sakyamuni, and two enormous goat-skin drums made by monks at the gompa. Also here are some superb butter sculptures, made during Losar and destroyed the following year. Fine and detailed sand mandalas are also made here.

Tibetan Institute of Performing Arts (TIPA)

TIPA promotes the study and practice of Tibetan performing arts to ensure the preservation of Tibet's cultural heritage. The most important of the arts taught and practised at the institute is traditional *lhamo* (Tibetan opera), which features vividly colourful costumes and traditional Tibetan music, and retells stories from the ancient Buddhist texts. The best time to see lhamo is at the annual festivals organised by TIPA (see Special Events later in this section).

Library of Tibetan Works & Archives

Many of Tibet's ancient texts were destroyed when the Cultural Revolution came to Tibet, but what was saved (representing some 40% of the nation's sacred literature) was brought here. The library is housed in the government compound at Gangchen Kyishong and includes translations of many Buddhist texts into English and other European languages.

To access the collection you must become a temporary member (Rs 15 per month); bring your passport as ID when you apply. The library is open 9 am to 5.30 pm weekdays only (till 5 pm in winter).

There's also a **Tibetan Cultural Museum** on the first floor, with some excellent exhibits, including fine statues, rare Tibetan stamps and a medal from the Younghusband mission to Lhasa. Entry costs Rs 10.

Also worth a visit near the library complex is the **Nechung Monastery**, home to the Tibetan state oracle. Taxis run up to McLeod Ganj from here for Rs 50.

Tibetan Medical & Astrological Institute

This institute is at Gangchen Kyishong, about five minutes' walk below the main entrance to the library area. There's a museum, library and a college at which Tibetan medicine and astrology is taught. It's possible to have a life horoscope prepared for around US$30.

Also here is the fascinating **Men Tsee-Khang Museum** devoted to traditional Tibetan medicine. The well-labelled exhibits cover all manner of plants and minerals used in Tibetan medicine, including such oddities as the mysterious 'Great Precious Hot Compound'. Don't miss the medical books and doctors' tools downstairs. The museum is open 9 am to 1 pm and 2 to 5 pm daily; entry is Rs 5.

St John in the Wilderness

Almost the only trace of the British presence in Dharamsala is the pretty church of St John in the Wilderness, just north of McLeod on the main road to Dharamsala. In a half-hearted attempt to keep up with the eastern religions, meditation classes are held here from time to time.

Walks

Interesting short walks around McLeod include the 2km stroll east to **Bhagsu**, where there is a temple and waterfall, and the 3km walk north-east to the little village of **Dharamkot**, where there are fine views. From Dharamkot, you can continue east down to Bhagsu and walk back to McLeod along the main Bhagsu road. See the boxed text 'Trekking in the Dhaula Dhar' later in this section for information on longer walks in the area.

Courses

Buddhist Philosophy Courses About 20 minutes' walk above McLeod is the Tushita Meditation Centre. Follow the road towards Dharamkot and take the steps uphill behind the small white chorten. The centre has facilities for retreats, as well as offering eight- and 10-day, fixed-date introductory courses in Buddhist philosophy led by Western and Tibetan teachers. There is a small library at Tushita, which is open to students and non-students. The courses cost Rs 2560 for eight days and Rs 3200 for 10 days. The office (☎ 21866) is open 9.30 to 11.30 am and 1 to 4.30 pm Monday to Saturday, but registration is only accepted between 1.30 and 3.30 pm.

Behind Tushita is the new Dhamma Sikhara Vipassana Meditation Centre (☎ 21 309), which offers 10-day courses in Theravada insight meditation. The centre is open from April to November.

Down at the library (☎ 22467) in Gangchen Kyishong, classes in specific aspects of Buddhist philosophy are led by Tibetan lamas and translated into English. Subjects are divided into two-week chunks, take place at 9 and 11 am weekdays and cost Rs 100 per month, plus Rs 50 registration.

Tibetan Language Courses The best place to study the Tibetan language is the Library of Tibetan Works & Archives in Gangchen Kyishong. Classes are held at 10 am on weekdays from April to November. Beginner and advanced courses both cost Rs 200 per month, plus Rs 50 registration. Call ☎ 22467 for more information.

Many local people also offer lessons – check the noticeboards in town or *Contact* magazine for details.

Tibetan Cooking Courses Several refugees have started up Tibetan cooking courses in the evenings, which will teach you how to make the perfect momo, among other things. Options include Sangye's Kitchen near Drepung Loesling Guest House and Lhamo's Kitchen at the Tashi Choeling Gompa on Jogibara Rd. Classes for both courses run three times a week at 11 am and 5 pm and cost Rs 100 per day.

Voluntary Work

If you're interested in teaching English or computer skills to newly arrived refugees, check noticeboards at the Library of Tibetan Works & Archives, as well as looking in *Contact* magazine. Or you could offer your services in person at any of the Tibetan organisations listed in the Information section earlier.

Special Events

From 27 March to 4 April, TIPA convenes an **opera festival**, which includes folk dancing and performances of traditional folk operas. There is also a three-day **TIPA Anniversary Festival** from 27 May, celebrating the foundation of the institute. Details of these and other performances are posted around McLeod Ganj.

Losar (Tibetan New Year) in February/March is a great time to be in McLeod Ganj, when the Dalai Lama gives week-long teachings and there are also Buddhist pilgrimages.

From the 10 to 12 December, McLeod Ganj is home to the **International Himalayan Festival**, featuring cultural events from all the Himalayan nations.

Another good time to be in McLeod Ganj is 6 July, when Buddhists celebrate the **Dalai Lama's birthday**.

Organised Tours

Local operators have devised the following fixed-rate taxi tours to points of interest around McLeod Ganj and in the Kangra Valley:

- Bhagsunath Temple, Tsuglagkhang, Dal Lake, Church of St John and Talnu (Rs 300, three hours)
- Norbulinka, Chinmaya Ashram at Tapovan, Chamunda Devi, Kangra and Jawalamukhi Temple (Rs 1600, eight hours)
- Norbulinka, Tapovan, Chamunda Devi, Palampur and Baijnath (Rs 1000, eight hours)

Places to Stay – Budget

There are dozens of budget options in McLeod Ganj but accommodation can be tight during Losar, the Dalai Lama's birthday (6 July) and other Tibetan festivals.

Kalsang Guest House *(☎ 21709)* is the first of several places up some steep steps

Trekking in the Dhaula Dhar

There are plenty of demanding treks around McLeod Ganj, and the beauty of trekking in the Dhaula Dhar is that you can be right up among the snow-covered peaks on the first day. Forest resthouses can be booked through the Divisional Forest Office in Dharamsala (☎ 24887).

Starting from McLeod, it's an easy 8km to **Triund** (2827m), a flat green area at the foot of the Dhaula Dhar, from where it feels like you could reach out and touch the peaks. The path veers off to the right across scree just beyond Dharamkot. From Triund, it's another 5km to the snow line at **Ilaqa** where there's a forest resthouse.

In summer, it's possible to trek from Ilaqa all the way to Bharmour in the Chamba Valley over the **Indrahar La** (4300m). Trekkers normally spend the first night in **Lahesh Cave** below the pass (6km), cross the pass the following day and camp at **Chata Parao** (7km) that evening. From here, it's a tough 14km to **Kwarsi**, where you can stop at the forest resthouse. The final descent passes through Lamu to Choli, where you can pick up buses to Chamba or Bharmour.

You can also trek from McLeod to Chamba via **Kareri Lake** (3200m), continuing over the **Minkiani La** (63km, five days) via a series of high-altitude lakes. A third alternative is the gentle crossing over the **Bleni La** (3710m), which takes four or five days, finishing at Dunali, which has buses to Chamba.

Because of the high passes, most of the trails are only passable from May to June and from September to October. Eagle Height Trekkers (☎ 21330), Yeti Trekking (☎ 21060) and Summit Adventures (☎ 21679) can arrange guides and all-inclusive treks. You can purchase Survey of India trekking maps (Rs 45) and the paperback *Treks & Passes of Dhauladhar & Pir Panjal* (Rs 150) from shops in McLeod Ganj. See also Lonely Planet's *Trekking in the Indian Himalaya* for more information on these and other treks.

above the TIPA road. It's cheap and deservedly popular, with tiny singles with shared bathroom for Rs 50 and doubles with bathroom for Rs 150 to 275 (the more expensive rooms have great views).

Farther up the same set of stairs ***Loling Guest House*** *(☎ 21072)* is run by the Drepung Gompa and offers clean rooms for Rs 50/75 with shared bathroom and Rs 150 with private bathroom.

Paljor Gakyil Guest House *(☎ 21443)*, above the Loling, has doubles with cold shower for Rs 110, and better doubles with hot shower ranging from Rs 155 to 275 (pricier rooms have a view), plus a small dorm for Rs 25 a head.

Green Hotel *(☎ 21200)*, on Bhagsu Rd, is a long-time favourite with travellers. Small spartan rooms with shared bathroom cost Rs 80, or Rs 175/250 with private bathroom and cold/hot water. Some rooms have great valley views, and there's a good restaurant here.

Tashi Khansar Guest House, opposite the Green, has basic singles with shared bathroom for Rs 70, and doubles with private hot shower for Rs 165, some with excellent views.

Back towards the bus stand is the ***Kunga Guest House*** *(☎ 21180)*, above Nick's Italian Kitchen, where clean but plain doubles with shared bathroom cost Rs 100 and doubles with private bathroom are Rs 200.

Kailash Hotel *(☎ 21044)*, opposite the chorten, has rudimentary doubles for Rs 100, all with shared bathroom (24-hour hot water). Rooms at the back have good views.

Om Guest House *(☎ 24313)*, on a path leading down from the bus stand, is a very good option. Pleasant rooms with shared bathroom cost Rs 160/180 for a single/ double and nicer upper-floor rooms with private bathroom cost Rs 225 and Rs 250. Views from the restaurant terrace are marvellous.

Shangrila Guest House *(☎ 21661)*, on the other side of the chorten, has doubles with shared bathroom (bucket hot water) for Rs 70.

Snow Lion Guest House *(☎ 21289)*, next door, is a friendly place with clean and well-maintained rooms with private bathroom and hot water for Rs 175, or Rs 200 with private balcony and good views.

Drepung Loseling Guest House *(☎ 23 187)*, down an alley off Jogibara Rd, is popular with long-term volunteers. Singles with shared bathroom cost Rs 75, while doubles with private bathroom range from Rs 125 to 200.

Tibetan Ashoka Guest House *(☎ 21763)*, opposite, is similar but plainer, with doubles with share bathroom for Rs 90, and brighter rooms with private bathroom for Rs 275 and Rs 330.

Ladies Venture *(☎ 21559)*, opposite the Geden Choeling nunnery down Jogibara Rd, is a very quiet and friendly place. Singles with private bathroom are Rs 100 or big doubles cost Rs 150 with shared bathroom and Rs 250 with private bathroom and a view. Dorms cost Rs 40 but are often full.

Places to Stay – Mid-Range & Top End

Hotel Tibet *(☎ 21587, fax 21327)*, a few steps from the bus stand on Bhagsu Rd, has standard doubles for Rs 500, semideluxe doubles for Rs 600, and deluxe rooms for Rs 900. All rooms are carpeted and have cable TV and private bathroom. There's a very good restaurant and bar here.

Hotel India House *(☎ 21144)* is bright, comfortable and a good option, though it lacks the Tibetan touch. Rooms cost Rs 600/800 a single/double (Rs 1100/1500 for deluxe rooms) and most have a balcony with excellent views.

There are a few other large Indian-run hotels on the road past the tourist office but the service in some of these places leaves a little to be desired. Better places include ***Surya Resorts*** *(☎ 21418)*, which has smart rooms from Rs 1400 to 2200, the ***Hotel Him Queen*** *(☎ 21861)*, with good doubles from Rs 750 to 1600, and the ***Hotel Natraj*** *(☎ 21529)*, with doubles for Rs 600 on the ground floor and Rs 800 upstairs.

Farther along is the pleasant ***Pema Thang Guest House*** *(☎ 21871)*, which has a nice restaurant (the Sunday vegetarian buffet lunch is good value) and tasteful rooms with wooden trim for Rs 600 downstairs and Rs 700 upstairs.

Opposite Pema Thang is the HPTDC ***Hotel Bhagsu*** *(☎ 21091)*, which has a range of good doubles from Rs 700 to 1500 (half this in low season).

Nearby, the homey ***Chinar Lodge*** *(☎ 21767)* offers carpeted rooms with plenty of space for Rs 600 on the top floor and Rs 500 downstairs, all with TV and hot shower.

The most stylish place to stay in McLeod Ganj is the splendid ***Chonor House Hotel*** *(☎ 21006, fax 21468)*, owned by the Norbulingka Institute. Doubles range from Rs 1900 to 2800 (with Rs 300 discount for singles) and are beautifully decorated with traditional Tibetan artefacts. There's also a good Tibetan restaurant and bakery here. Bookings are recommended.

Places to Eat

Green Hotel has a very popular restaurant, with a range of excellent home-made cakes (the carrot cake is recommended), as well as vegetarian dishes such as spinach quiche. Most dishes cost around Rs 50. It's also a good place for breakfast.

The nearby ***Himalayan Bamboo Hut Cafe*** also has good food and a wonderful rooftop balcony with views over the plains, though the service is very slow.

Nick's Italian Kitchen nearby is renowned for it's vegetarian Italian food, including excellent home-made spinach and cheese ravioli. Meals cost around Rs 40 to 50 and there are also great cakes and coffee.

Hotel Tibet has probably the best restaurant in town and features Tibetan, Chinese and Indian cuisine. There's also a convivial bar here. Prices reflect the classier surroundings, starting at Rs 65.

McLlo Restaurant, right above the bus stand, has an extensive menu, good food and a bar, though it's a little overpriced. The kitchen is open till 10.30 pm. Dishes such as chilli chicken cost around Rs 90.

Friend's Corner, nearby, serves excellent Chinese food and prices are reasonable for the large portions.

Malabar Cafe, north of the chorten on Jogibara Rd, is a pleasant little place serving good Indian, Chinese and continental cuisine. The nearby ***Cafe Shambhala*** is also popular, with a standard East-meets-West menu.

Gakyi Restaurant, farther down Jogibara Rd, serves the best muesli in town and has a good range of healthy vegetarian food such as tofu and brown rice. The nearby ***Snowland Restaurant*** is recommended for cheap and tasty vegetarian Tibetan food. Both have Tibetan vegetarian food for around Rs 40.

For nonveg Tibetan food, you can't beat the ***Snow Lion Restaurant*** at the guesthouse of same name. Its mutton momos are strongly recommended and there's also real coffee. Most dishes are around Rs 45.

Ashoka Restaurant, on Jogibara Rd, has the best Indian food in town. The tandoori chicken (Rs 70 for a half portion) and chicken Mughlai (Rs 100) are excellent and there are also continental dishes such as pizza and spaghetti.

Another popular place is the ***restaurant*** at Om Guest House, which serves plenty of good cheap vegetarian options. There's also a sound system, plus spectacular sunset views.

The ***restaurant*** at Hotel Bhagsu is pricier but has very good food and cold beers. On sunny days, tables are set up in the gardens, and you can eat outside.

McLeod Ganj is a godsend for anyone with a longing for Western pastries and cakes. ***Take Out Bakery*** is a place beneath the Hotel Tibet where you can buy freshly baked bread, cakes and doughnuts. The ***Chocolate Log***, a few minutes' walk down past the post office on Jogibara Rd, is an old favourite serving various types of cakes and snacks on its sunny verandah (closed on Tuesday).

In the same area is the ***Lung Ta Restaurant*** with good cheap Japanese food.

Nowrogee & Son is the best-stocked provisions store for self-caterers and campers.

Entertainment

There are several ***video halls*** in the town centre on Jogibara Rd. They show new releases and documentaries on Tibet all day and evening, with the program posted out the front. Tickets are Rs 10.

At the end of an evening most visitors end up in the ***bar*** at the McLlo Restaurant, which serves cold beer and food till late.

Shopping

Tibetan textiles such as bags, *chubas* (dresses worn by Tibetan women), hats and trousers can be found at the Office of Tibetan Handicrafts, just north of the State Bank of India. Here you can have a chuba made to order with your own fabric (Rs 100 stitching charge) or some of theirs (Rs 650). Stitches of Time, farther downhill on Temple Rd, is run by the Tibetan Women's Association, and also makes chubas and other clothes to order.

Across the road is the Tibetan Handicrafts Cooperative, which employs about 145 people, many of them newly arrived refugees, in the weaving of Tibetan carpets. Fine New Zealand–wool carpets, with 48 knots per square inch are Rs 2603 per square metre. The cooperative can pack and post purchases home, and visitors are welcome to watch the carpet makers at work on traditional looms.

There are dozens of other shops selling Tibetan artefacts. Interesting purchases include inlaid metal prayer wheels, prayer flags (a bargain at Rs 20 a bundle), gemstone rosary beads, traditional silver jewellery and figurines of Tibetan gods. See Shopping in the Facts for the Visitor chapter for more information. The Tibetans have a very different attitude to Indians when it comes to haggling and the prices quoted are usually fair from the outset, though a little bargaining is acceptable.

Haggling is obligatory at the numerous shops selling Kashmiri handicrafts, such as papier mache boxes and *gabbas* (applique rugs), though with a bit of bargaining savvy, you can pay very reasonable prices. Tara Herbal Gift Shop, near the bus stand, has traditional Tibetan herbal incense and books on Tibetan medicine.

Getting There & Away

Air Kangra airport is 15km south of Dharamsala at Gaggal (it used to be called Gaggal airport). Indian Airlines flies from Delhi to Kangra (US$145, 1 hour 25 minutes) at 1.15 pm on Monday, Wednesday and Friday, returning to Delhi at 3 pm the same day. Competition for the 18 seats on each flight is fierce so book *well* ahead. Dhauladhar Travels (☎ 21158, fax 21246) on Temple Rd is the agent for Indian Airlines in Dharamsala.

Bus All the roads in McLeod radiate out from the bus stand, where you'll find the Himachal Roadways Transport Corporation (HRTC) booking office. Here you can book seats on the daily buses to Delhi, Dehra Dun and Pathankot.

Ordinary Delhi buses leave at 4.30, 6.15 and 7.30 pm (Rs 247, 12 hours), but you're better off taking the super deluxe bus at 7pm (Rs 346). Buses leave for Pathankot at 10, 11.20 and 11.50 am and 3 and 4 pm (Rs 60, four hours). There's also a daily bus to Dehra Dun (Rs 260, 12 hours) at 8 pm. For other services you'll have to head down to Dharamsala.

Various travel agents in town offer deluxe (two-by-two seating) buses to Delhi, which leave at around 6 pm just downhill from McLeod Ganj on Dharamsala Rd. Other destinations include Dehra Dun (Rs 280, 7 pm) and Manali (Rs 250, 9 am). See Travel Agencies under Information earlier in this section for a list of reliable operators. When booking a bus to Delhi take care to check that it goes to Connaught Place and/or Parharganj, not just the ISBT at Kashmir Gate.

There are also buses for the 40-minute trip down to Dharamsala (Rs 6), departing every 30 minutes between 4.15 am and 8.30 pm. Cramped passenger jeeps also run when full for the same price.

Train Many travel agencies will book train tickets for services that leave from Pathankot, down on the plains in Punjab (see Pathankot in the Punjab & Haryana chapter). It's worth booking as early as possible, preferably a week in advance. Generally, a Rs 75 to 100 booking fee is levied (which pays for a staff member to take the bus down to Pathankot and make the reservation).

The most convenient rail station for McLeod is at Kangra (Kangra Mandir station), about 20km south of Dharamsala, which sits on the narrow-gauge line from Pathankot to Jogindernagar. The best train on the line is the *Kangra Queen*, which leaves Pathankot at 8.20 am, arriving in Kangra around 11 am (Rs 155/245 chair/sleeper class). There are at least four other daily trains that take five hours to reach Kangra but only cost Rs 20 a seat. All trains continue to Palampur and some go all the way to Jogindernagar, 58km from Mandi.

Taxi McLeod's taxi stand (☎ 21034) is next to the bus station. A taxi to Pathankot is around Rs 900. See the individual destination entries in this section for more taxi fares from McLeod. To hire a taxi for the day, covering less than 80km, costs Rs 800.

Short hops include Gangchen Kyishong (Rs 70), Dharamsala's Kotwali Bazaar (Rs 90) and Dharamsala bus station (Rs 100).

Autorickshaw Because of the steep roads, autorickshaws are only really useful for getting to Bhagsu (Rs 30) and Gangchen Kyishong (Rs 70).

AROUND McLEOD GANJ

Bhagsu

If you find McLeod too much of a scene, there is quieter accommodation available in the village of Bhagsu, 2km east, also known as Bhagsunag. The village has a cold spring with **baths** and a small **Shiva temple** built by the Raja of Kangra in the 16th century. There's an attractive **waterfall** a short walk beyond the temple.

You can change money and check email (Rs 60 per hour) at the Oasis Cybercafe, uphill from the Pink Guest House.

Places to Stay & Eat On the left as you enter Bhagsu, ***Hotel Triund*** *(☎ 21122)* is a fairly typical mid-range Indian hotel, with deluxe carpeted rooms with hot water and TV ranging from Rs 700 to 995.

At the other end of the village, ***Hotel Meghavan*** *(☎ 21277)* is another big hotel catering largely to Indian tourists; rooms with private bathroom cost from Rs 750 to 950.

Opposite, ***Pink White Guest House*** *(☎ 21917)* has good singles/doubles with private bathroom, balcony and views from Rs 150/200. The nearby ***Oak View*** has good value rooms with private bathroom for Rs 250 and Rs 350.

If you take the path leading uphill from the main bus stop you come to three guesthouses aimed squarely at Western backpackers. ***Samgyal Guest House*** has rooms with shared/private bathroom for Rs 150/250 and ***Seven Seas Lodge*** *(☎ 23359)* has clean and spacious marble-clad rooms for Rs 150 (ground floor) and Rs 200 (1st floor). Farther uphill is the ***Omni Guest House*** *(☎ 21576)* with lots of murals, a decent restaurant and basic rooms with shared hot shower for Rs 80.

Trimurti Restaurant has good, cheap vegetarian food such as *aloo ghobi* (potato and cauliflower) for around Rs 40. There's also a noticeboard detailing local yoga and massage courses.

The ***HPTDC Cafe Jaldhara*** nearby offers southern Indian dishes such as *dosa* (lentil pancakes) for about Rs 50. ***Shiva Cafe***, above the waterfall in Bhagsu, is a good spot for a *chai* (spicy milk tea).

Dharamkot & Dusallan

Many long-term visitors rent rooms from villagers in Dharamkot, a 2km trek uphill from Dharamsala, or at Dusallan, below the Bhagsu road (from McLeod, take the path beside the Green Hotel). Both villages are home to very informal ***guesthouses***, where you can rent rooms from Rs 50 to 150. Guesthouses aren't marked so you'll have to ask around.

Chamba Valley

Separated from the Kangra Valley to the south by the high Dhaula Dhar Range and the remote Pattan Valley to the north by the Pir Panjal Range is the beautiful Chamba Valley, through which flows the Ravi River. For over 1000 years this region formed the princely state of Chamba, the most ancient state in northern India.

Few travellers find their way here, and of those that do, even fewer continue down the valley beyond the hill station of Dalhousie. The valley is renowned for its fine *sikhara* temples, which feature ornate curvilinear stone towers topped by an *amalaka*, imitating a segmented gourd. There are excellent examples in the beautiful town of Chamba, 56km from Dalhousie, and at the ancient capital of Bharmour, 65km farther down the valley to the south-east. Bharmour is also the starting point for some fine treks, including that to the sacred lake of Manimahesh, 28km away.

DALHOUSIE

☎ 01899 • pop 10,100 • elevation 2036m

Sprawling over five hills, Dalhousie was a sort of 'second-string' hill station during the British era, mainly used by people who lived in Lahore. It was acquired from the Raja of Chamba by the British and was named after Lord Dalhousie, then viceroy of India, by David McLeod (after whom McLeod Ganj was named). These days, Dalhousie is best known for its public schools.

The main reason to come to Dalhousie is for the views (which are stupendous) or to stay in one of the old Raj-era hotels. Dalhousie is also noticeably cheaper than other hill stations, though finding accommodation during the early summer and peak Indian holiday periods can be difficult. The high season runs from mid-April to mid-July, mid-September to mid-November and mid-December to early January. Rates quotes are for the high season; at other times expect to pay half or even a third of these rates.

Orientation

Dalhousie is quite spread out, but the British managed to build a number of fairly level roads linking the various parts of town, so getting around can be quite a pleasant experience. The bus stand and several of the poshest hotels are about 1km downhill from the rest of town, past the Tibetan market.

The settlements of Subhash Chowk and Gandhi Chowk up on the ridge are linked by the peaceful and forested Mall, which is actually two roads. The higher of the two is closed to traffic and is known as Garam Sarak (Hot Rd) as it receives more sunshine. The other road is known as Thandi Sarak (Cold Rd). The steep Air Force Rd connects the two areas over the top of the ridge.

There are many registered porters around the bus stand. In the low season, they charge Rs 20 from the bus stand to Gandhi Chowk, and Rs 10 to Subhash Chowk.

Information

Tourist Offices The tourist office (☎ 421 36) is on the top floor of the telegraph office, just below the bus stand. It's open 10 am to 5 pm Monday to Saturday (plus Sunday during the tourist season).

Money The State Bank of India, near the bus stand, changes US dollar travellers cheques issued by AmEx, Thomas Cook or Citicorp. The Punjab National Bank, a five-minute walk south of the St Francis Church, can exchange cash and travellers cheques in US dollars and UK pounds, except on Wednesday.

Travel Agencies Span Tours & Travels (☎ 40281, fax 40341) can book luxury coaches to Delhi, Manali and Dharamsala, and can also make train and air reservations. Trek-n-Travels (☎ 40277, fax 40476), nearby, can arrange treks in the local area for Rs 300 to 600 per day, depending on the duration and route of the trek.

Things to See & Do

There are some pleasant strolls around Dalhousie. If you walk along Garam Sarak between Gandhi and Subhash Chowks, you'll pass brightly painted **low-relief pictures** of Tibetan deities, including Padmasambhava and Avalokiteshvara, as well as Tibetan script bearing the sacred mantra 'Om mani padme hum'. Closer to Gandhi Chowk is a **rock painting** of Tara Devi. Also worth a look is the small **Tibetan market** near the bus stand.

The **Kalatope Wildlife Sanctuary** is 8.5km from Gandhi Chowk and is home to a variety of species, including black bear and barking deer, as well as an abundant

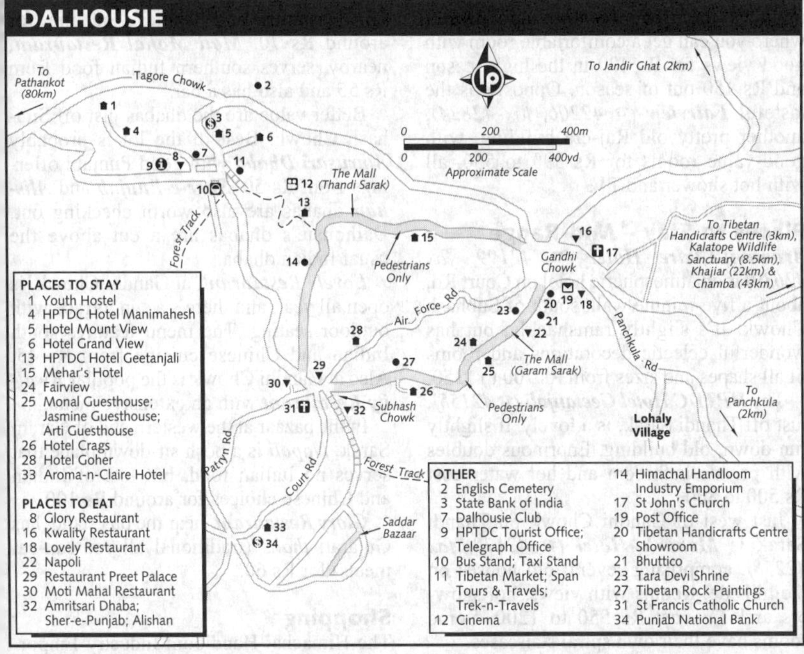

birdlife. There's a checkpoint at **Lakkar Mandi**, on the perimeter of the sanctuary, which has fine mountain views. It's possible to get a taxi to here (Rs 150 return), and walk 3km into the sanctuary. To take a vehicle into the sanctuary, you require a permit from the DFO in Chamba (☎ 01899-22239). The ***Forest Rest House*** here must be reserved with the same person.

One leisurely stroll can take you from Subash Chowk down Court Rd, and back via Patryn Rd. A more rigorous walk is the Upper Bakrota Round, about 5km from Gandhi Chowk.

Places to Stay – Budget

Dalhousie has over 50 hotels, although a fair number of them have a run-down, left-by-the-Raj feel to them. Prices given below are for high season but remember that most give a 50% discount whenever business is quiet.

The ***Youth Hostel*** *(☎ 42189)* is rather run-down but friendly, and a five-minute walk from the bus stand. Rates remain constant all year at Rs 20 (Rs 40 for nonmembers). This doesn't get you bedding, but pillows, sheets and blankets can be hired for Rs 2, and quilts for Rs 6. The hostel is closed between 10 am and 5 pm. Every December, the hostel stages a six-day, winter trek into the Pir Panjal.

Hotel Goher *(☎ 42253)*, just off Subhash Chowk, is the most reasonably priced of the hotels on Air Force Rd. Doubles cost from Rs 600 in the high season; at other times they drop to Rs 200.

Hotel Crags *(☎ 42124)* is a five-minute walk along Garam Sarak, just below the road. It has various doubles for Rs 350 to 550, but rarely charges the full rate. All rooms have private bathroom and hot water. It's a somewhat dilapidated place, but the peaceful location and the spectacular terrace overlooking the valley more than make up for it.

Farther around Garam Sarak, near Gandhi Chowk, is a cluster of guesthouses that includes the ***Arti***, ***Jasmine*** and ***Monal*** where you can get a comfortable room with good views for Rs 400 in the high season and Rs 150 out of season. Opposite is the tasteful ***Fairview*** *(☎ 42206, fax 42824)*, another pretty old Raj-era building, with good-value rooms for Rs 390 to 550, all with hot shower and TV.

Places to Stay – Mid-Range

Aroma-n-Claire Hotel *(☎ 42199, fax 42639)* is an atmospheric hotel on Court Rd, about a five-minute walk south of Subhash Chowk. It's slightly ramshackle, but has wonderful eclectic decorations and rooms of all shapes and sizes from Rs 700 to 1350.

The ***HPTDC Hotel Geetanjali*** *(☎ 42155)*, just off Thandi Sarak, is a lovely, if slightly run-down, old building. Enormous doubles with private bathroom and hot water cost Rs 500 to 800.

Just west of Gandhi Chowk on Thandi Sarak is ***Mehar's Hotel*** *(☎ 42179, fax 42258)*, comprising several old houses on the hillside. Rooms with views, hot showers and TV cost Rs 550 to 1200. Some rooms have their own spiral staircases.

Hotel Grand View *(☎ 40760, fax 40609)*, just above the bus stand, has doubles from Rs 1350 to 1800 and double suites for Rs 1950. This is a beautifully maintained place and better value than other hotels in the same price category. The Himalaya seem within touching distance from the garden terrace.

Nearby, is the ***Hotel Mount View*** *(☎ 421 20, fax 40741)*, which bills itself as a heritage hotel, but is a bit chintzy. Doubles range from Rs 1000 to 1400 (30% less in the low season).

The new ***HPTDC Hotel Manimahesh***, near the youth hostel, offers a range of very good rooms for Rs 800 to 1500.

There's a ***Forest Rest House*** in the Kalatope Wildlife Sanctuary (see earlier); to reserve a room you'll need to contact the DFO in Chamba (☎ 01899-22239).

Places to Eat

Restaurant Preet Palace, on Subhash Chowk, features reasonably priced Mughlai, Kashmiri and Chinese cuisine for around Rs 70. ***Moti Mahal Restaurant***, nearby, serves southern Indian food from Rs 55 and also has a bar.

Better value are the dhabas just off Subhash Chowk. Best of the lot is probably ***Amritsari Dhaba*** with good Punjabi offerings from Rs 50. ***Sher-e-Punjab*** and ***Alishan*** dhabas are also worth checking out. Dalhousie's dhabas are a cut above the usual Indian dhaba.

Lovely Restaurant, at Gandhi Chowk, is open all year, and there's a sun terrace with outdoor seating. The menu features south Indian and Chinese cuisine from Rs 45. Also at Gandhi Chowk is the popular ***Kwality Restaurant*** with an extensive menu.

In the bazaar at the western end of Garam Sarak, ***Napoli*** is a posh sit-down place that serves no Italian food, but lots of Indian and Chinese choices for around Rs 100.

Glory Restaurant, near the bus stand, has Gujarati *thalis* (traditional all-you-can-eat meals) for Rs 60.

Shopping

The Himachal Handloom Industry Emporium on Thandi Sarak has a good selection of Kullu shawls. Bhuttico has a branch on the bazaar on Garam Sarak with a wide selection of shawls and fair prices.

At the Tibetan Handicrafts Centre (☎ 42119), 3km from Gandhi Chowk along the Khajiar road, you can have Tibetan carpets made to order. There are over 180 traditional designs to choose from. You can buy carpets, bags and purses from the Tibetan Handicrafts Centre Showroom, on Garam Sarak. The shops nearby sell a range of goods, including Kashmiri shawls.

Getting There & Away

The booking office at the bus stand is open 9 am to 2 pm and 3 to 5 pm daily. There are hourly buses to Pathankot (Rs 45, four hours), and at least four buses to Dharamsala (Rs 85, six hours) between 7.30 am and 2.15 pm. You can also take a Pathankot bus and change at Chakki. There is a single daily bus to Shimla at 12.45 pm (Rs 210, 12 hours) and one to Manali at 1.30 pm (Rs 260, 17 hours).

Buses to Chamba leave every hour or so from 7 am to 4.30 pm (Rs 34, three hours). The 9.30 and 10.10 am and 4.30 pm buses go via Khajiar (Rs 15, 1½ hours). In the high season, there's a 9 am government sightseeing bus from Dalhousie to Chamba (Rs 100) with a one-hour stop in Khajiar, returning directly to Dalhousie. At least one private bus covers the same route at 10.10 am (Rs 80).

Rates quoted at the taxi stand (☎ 40220) include fares to Pathankot (Rs 920 one way), Chamba (Rs 720/920 one way/return), Khajiar (Rs 460 return), Bharmour (Rs 1650 one way), Kalatope (Rs 360 return) and Dharamsala (Rs 1550 one way).

Getting Around

From the bus stand to Gandhi Chowk or Subhash Chowk is Rs 50 by taxi.

KHAJIAR

This grassy *marg*, or meadow, is 22km from Dalhousie towards Chamba, and you can get here by bus (1½ hours) or in a day's walk. Over 1km long and nearly 1km wide, it is ringed by pine trees with a pond in the middle. The 12th-century **Khajjinag Temple** has fine woodcarving on the cornices, and some crude carvings of the five Pandavas, the heroes of the Mahabharata, installed by the Raja of Chamba in the 16th century.

It's possible to do a circuit of the marg on horseback (Rs 50).

Places to Stay & Eat

The ***HPTDC Hotel Devdar*** (☎ 01899-36333) has cottages right on the edge of the marg for Rs 750 to 1100 a double, plus dorm beds for Rs 75. There are more dorm beds for Rs 75 in the HPTDC basic ***Khajiar Cottage*** on the northern side of the marg.

Parul Guest House *(☎ 01899-36344)*, behind the temple, has pleasant rooms overlooking the marg for Rs 400.

Gautam Guest House *(☎ 01899-36355)*, a couple of minutes' walk east of the marg, is the best budget choice. Clean and bright rooms with private bathroom and hot water cost Rs 250 (Rs 150 in the low season) and there's a nice sitting area.

There are several ***restaurants*** on the marg.

Getting There & Away

Buses from Dalhousie to Khajiar (Rs 13, 1½ hours) leave at 9.30 and 10.10 am and 4.30 pm. In the reverse direction most buses skip Khajiar; the only reliable service is at 3.30 pm. To Chamba (Rs 15, 1½ hours) they should depart at 11 am, 12.30 pm and 5.30 pm. Tourist buses to Chamba stop at Khajiar for an hour. A taxi from Khajiar to Chamba is around Rs 400.

CHAMBA

☎ 01899 • pop 19,000 • elevation 996m

Chamba is perched on a ledge flanking the Ravi River. It has often been compared to a medieval Italian village, with its narrow streets and ancient temples. For 1000 years prior to Independence, Chamba was the headquarters of a district of the same name, and was ruled by a single dynasty of maharajas. The town was founded by Raja Sahil Varman, who shifted the capital here from Bharmour and named it after his daughter Champavati. Its altitude is lower than Dalhousie's so it's warmer in summer.

Chamba has a grassy promenade known as the Chowgan, which is the focus for the Minjar and Sui Mata Festivals (see Special Events later in this section). It's a beautiful, if somewhat hair-raising, 56km trip from Dalhousie to Chamba via Khajiar (43km). The views down over the terraced fields are spectacular, with tiny villages clinging to the sheer slopes of the valley.

Information

The tourist office (☎ 24002) is in the interesting beige building next to the Hotel Iravati on Court Rd. It's open 10 am to 5 pm daily except Sunday.

The only place to change money is the Punjab National Bank on Hospital Rd, which fortunately changes all travellers cheques in US dollars or UK pounds.

The friendly family-run Mani Mahesh Travels (☎ 22507), close to the Lakshmi Narayan Temple complex, can arrange treks with guides and porters for Rs 700 to 900 per day (Rs 1400 over the high mountain passes). The owner's son can provide a commentary on Chamba's beautiful

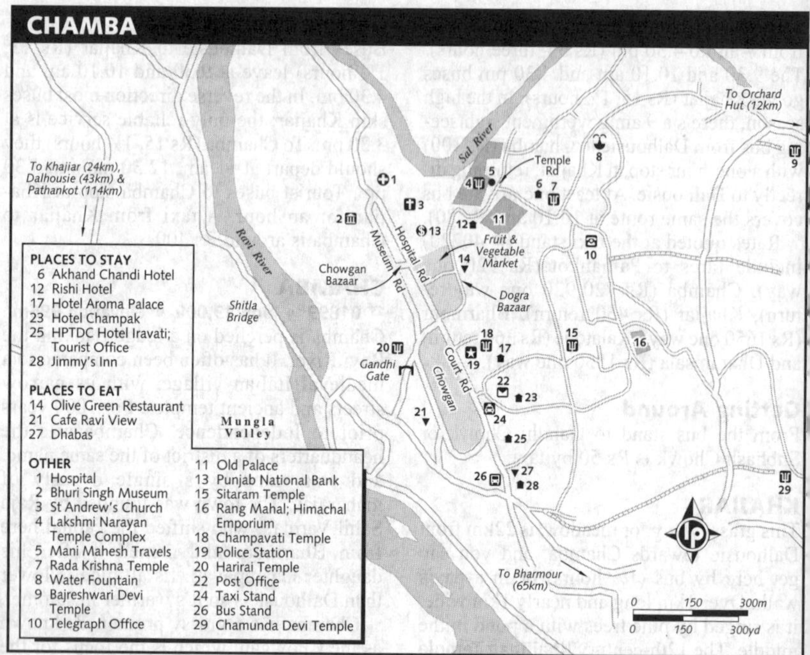

temples (Rs 300) and his daughter acts as a guide for female trekkers when required.

You can send/receive faxes at the telegraph office (fax 25333), hidden in the backstreets not far from the Rishi Hotel.

Lakshmi Narayan Temple Complex

The six temples in this complex, all featuring exquisite sculpture, are representative of the shikhara style, although they also share characteristics distinctive to the Chamba Valley. Three of the temples are dedicated to Vishnu, and three to Shiva. The largest (and oldest) temple in the group is that of Lakshmi Narayan (Vishnu) and is directly opposite the entrance to the complex. According to tradition, it was built during the reign of the founder of Chamba, Raja Sahil Varman, in the 10th century. It was extensively renovated in the 16th century by Raja Partap Singh Varna. The image of Lakshmi Narayan enshrined in the temple dates from the temple's foundation. A small niche at the back harbours a beautiful sculpture of a goddess churning the ocean with Sheshnag, the snake of Vishnu, to bring the poison up from the bottom.

The fourth temple on the right, the Gauri Shankar Temple, is the most interesting of the other shrines here. It's dedicated to Shiva and features fine stone carvings of the Ganges and Yamuna Rivers personified as goddesses on either side of the door frame.

Bajreshwari Devi Temple

A further five-minute walk leads up to the ancient Bajreshwari Devi Temple. The temple conforms to the shikhara style, and is topped by a wooden *amalaka* (a flourish shaped like a fluted medallion). The sanctum enshrines an image of Bajreshwari (a form of Durga), although it is difficult to make it out beneath its garlands of flowers. The entire surface of the temple is elaborately carved, and a form of ancient script called *takri* can be seen crudely incised on the right column, and on other spots around the temple. At the rear of the temple, Durga can be seen slaying the giant Mahishasura and his buffalo vehicle. On either side of the door jambs, the Yamuna and Ganges Rivers are personified as goddesses holding pitchers of water.

Chamunda Devi Temple

A terrace before this hilltop temple gives an excellent view of Chamba with its slate-roof houses (some of them up to 300-years-old), the Ravi River and the surrounding countryside. It's a steep 30-minute climb along a path that begins above the bus stand, passing a small rock outcrop sacred to the goddess of the forest, Banasti. When you reach the road, you can either proceed up the steep staircase, or follow the road to the left.

The temple is dedicated to Durga in her wrathful aspect as Chamunda Devi. Almost the entire wooden ceiling of the *mandapa* (forechamber) is richly carved, with animal and floral motifs, and depictions of various deities. There are suspended numerous brass bells, offered to the goddess by devotees.

Harirai Temple

This fine stone sikhara-style temple on the north-western side of the Chowgan is from the 11th century. It is dedicated to Vishnu and enshrines a fine triple-headed image of Vaikuntha Vishnu. In April 1971, the statue was stolen from the inner sanctum, but fortunately Interpol intercepted the statue on a ship destined for the USA seconds before the boat was to sail. At the rear of the temple is a fine sculpture of Vishnu astride six horses.

Other Temples

Several other temples lie hidden within Chamba's maze of backstreets. Places to seek out include the **Rada Krishna Temple**, also known as the Bhansi Gopal, the **Sitaram Temple**, devoted to Rama, and the **Champavati Temple**, dedicated to the daughter of Raja Sahil Varman.

Rang Mahal

The Rang Mahal, or Old Palace, now houses several government offices and the **Himachal Emporium**. Here you can purchase *rumals* (small cloths featuring very fine embroidery in silk). The reverse side of the cloth features a mirror image of the front and there is no evidence of knots or loose threads.

A finely stitched rumal can take up to a month to complete, and cost from Rs 300. Also available are the inevitable shawls (you can visit the handloom workshop upstairs) and repoussé brass plates. The emporium is open 10 am to 5 pm Monday to Saturday.

Bhuri Singh Museum

This museum has an interesting collection representing the art and culture of the region – particularly the miniature paintings of the Basohli and Kangra schools. It also houses some of the murals that were recovered from the Rang Mahal after it was damaged by fire. The museum is open 10 am to 5 pm daily except Monday. Entry is free.

Special Events

The four-day **Sui Mata Festival** is held in March/April on the Chowgan. Sui Mata, the daughter of an ancient raja, gave her life to save the inhabitants of her father's kingdom. She is particularly revered by Chamba women, who carry her image from the Old Palace up to her small shrine, accompanied by singing and dancing.

The **Minjar Festival** is celebrated in late July/early August, coinciding with the end of the maize harvest. The festival dates back to the victory of Chamba's founder Raja Sahil Varman over the Raja of Kangra in 935, but also doubles as a harvest festival. Silk tassels representing *minjars* (sheaves of maize), are distributed to the crowds during the festival. The festival culminates with a colourful procession headed by a palanquin bearing an image of Raghuvira (incarnation of Rama). The procession proceeds to the banks of the Ravi River, where the minjars are thrown into the water. The festival attracts many Gaddi, Churachi, Bhatti and Gujar people from surrounding villages.

Places to Stay

The ***HPTDC Hotel Iravati*** *(☎ 222671, fax 2565)*, a few minutes' walk from the bus stand on Court Rd, has slightly old doubles with private bathroom from Rs 500 to 1000 (25% less in low season).

A better mid-range option is the ***Hotel Aroma Palace*** *(☎ 25177)*, towards the Sitaram Temple, with welcoming singles/doubles with TV and bathroom starting at Rs 400/700.

Hotel Champak *(☎ 22774)*, behind the post office, is also run by HPTDC and has large doubles with shared/private bathroom for Rs 200/250. Dorm beds are Rs 75.

Jimmy's Inn *(☎ 24748)*, opposite the bus stand, has an eclectic collection of rooms with private bathroom from Rs 100 to 300 (all rooms are clean and more expensive rooms have hot water and TV).

Rishi Hotel *(☎ 24343)*, on Temple Rd, close to the Lakshmi Narayan Temple complex, has ordinary doubles with above average views for Rs 200 and Rs 300 with hot showers, and gloomy rooms at the back with cold water for Rs 100.

The old stone ***Akhand Chandi Hotel*** *(☎ 24 072)*, in the shadow of the Rada Krishna Temple, is in a beautiful courtyard and has clean, carpeted rooms with private bathroom and hot water for Rs 300 and Rs 400.

Orchard Hut *(☎ 22607)* is in a lovely tranquil spot in the Saal Valley, 12km from Chamba. It's owned by the same family as Mani Mahesh Travels and rooms range from Rs 350 with breakfast and dinner, to Rs 650 for three superior meals. When you arrive in Chamba, go to Mani Mahesh Travels first to arrange transfers.

Manimahesh Yatra

In July/August thousands of pilgrims from all over northern India converge on Bharmour for Manimahesh Yatra to commence the pilgrimage to the sacred lake of Manimahesh, 28km away and below the peak of Manimahesh Kailash (5656m). Fifteen days prior to the pilgrimage, a week-long fair is held at Bharmour, followed by wrestling competitions and folk dances by pilgrims from distant villages. At the end of the celebrations, the pilgrims are led by priests up the steep trail to Manimahesh.

Parents blessed with a male child during the preceding year take the infant on the pilgrimage, during which time the child's hair is ceremonially cut by the priests. The destination for the yatra is an ancient and very beautiful temple on the lakeshore, dedicated to Lakshmi Devi in her form as slayer of the buffalo demon (Mahishasuramardini). Pilgrims finish the pilgrimage by honouring the enshrined image, which dates from the 7th century AD.

Places to Eat

Chamba is known for its *chukh* – a chilli sauce consisting of red and green peppers, lemon juice, mustard oil and salt – but sadly not its restaurants.

HPTDC runs the little ***Cafe Ravi View*** on the edge of the Chowgan area, which serves the standard HPTDC range of Indian and Chinese dishes from around Rs 50.

A better choice is the restaurant at the ***Hotel Iravati***, also run by the HPTDC, with good vegetarian and nonveg options for about Rs 75.

Worth a visit is the ***Olive Green Restaurant***, upstairs on Temple Rd. There is a good range of reasonably priced vegetarian and nonveg dishes, including the local speciality *Chamba madhra* (kidney beans with curd and ghee). Dishes costs around Rs 50.

There are a few basic ***dhabas*** by the bus station.

Getting There & Away

There are six buses daily for the somewhat nerve-shattering trip to Bharmour (Rs 38, 3½ hours). To Dharamsala (Rs 100 to 135, 10 hours) there are buses at 6 and 11.30 am and 4 and 9.30 pm. From Dharamsala, the best bus is probably the 8.30 am service (Rs 125). To Khajiar, buses leave at 7.30 am and 2 and 5 pm (Rs 15, 1½ hours). Buses to Dalhousie depart every few hours from 6 am to 6 pm (Rs 34, three hours). There are hourly services to Pathankot (Rs 67, six hours). If there are no buses to Dalhousie at the time you want to leave, you could also take a Pathankot bus, and change to a local bus in Banikhet (7km below Dalhousie).

One-way/return taxi fares include Rs 400/600 to Khajiar, Rs 800/1000 to Bharmour and 800/1050 to Dalhousie.

BHARMOUR

Sixty-four kilometres south-east of Chamba is the ancient slate-roofed village of Bharmour (2195m), reached by a spectacular trip along a fairly precarious road up the Ravi river valley. Rocky peaks crowd in on all sides and tiny villages cling to the valley walls, though the lower stretches are marred by yet another hydroelectric project.

Before Raja Sahil Varman founded the new capital at Chamba in AD 920, Bharmour was the ancient capital of the princely state of Chamba for over 400 years. The **chaurasi temples** are testament to the town's wealth and are dedicated to several deities, though Shiva dominates (just look at all the Shiva linga in the courtyard!). The legend goes that Shiva visited the site accompanied by 84 saints and neglected to honour the resident deity Brahmani Devi. In retaliation, the goddess turned the saints into stone linga, which formed the basis of the group (*chaurasi* means 84).

The largest temple in the group is the central sikhara-style **Manimahesh Temple**, dedicated to Shiva, faced by a huge bronze Nandi statue. Farther back is the smaller sikhara-style **Harsingh Temple** dedicated to Vishnu in his lion form. Next to the Manimahesh Temple is the older **Laskna Devi Temple** from AD 700, featuring a truly wonderful carved doorway, topped by a 12-armed Vishnu riding Garuda.

Trekking in the Pir Panjal

North of the Chamba Valley is the untouched Pir Panjal Range, which divides the Chamba Valley from the isolated Pattan Valley west of Keylong. There are numerous treks across the Pir Panjal to this little-visited region.

Bharmour, at the western end of the valley, is the main departure point for treks, including the popular 28km trek to sacred **Manimahesh Lake** (4115m) at the foot of Kailash peak (5656m), which is the destination for an important pilgrimage in July/August. The trail begins at Hadsar, a 13km jeep ride from Bharmour.

Hadsar is also the departure point for the trek over the **Kugti La** (5040m) into Lahaul. Kugti translates roughly to 'that which makes one miserable to reach it'. In fact the trek is anything but miserable, though the steep gradient and high altitude mean it is only for experienced trekkers. The destination for the trek is Shansha in the Pattan Valley (59km), which can be reached in five strenuous days, continuing on to Keylong by bus.

An alternative route from Hadsar to Lahaul crosses the **Chobia La** (4966m) to Udaipur (64km), which is also connected by bus to Keylong. It's also possible to cross to Udaipur from Bharmour via the **Kalichho La** (4990m, 80km). The pass is sacred to Kali and traditionally the first person to cross the pass sacrifices a goat to dissuade the goddess from taking a member of the trekking party as a sacrifice.

From Chamba, buses run north-west to Trella from where you can trek over the **Sach La** (4390m) to Udaipur. It's a testing 130km trek, but the gradients are lower than many other treks in the Pir Panjal. Some travellers hire ponies for the trip.

Because of the high passes, most of the trails are only passable from May to June and from September to October, and acute mountain sickness is a real risk (see under Health in the Facts for the Visitor chapter). The best way to go is with an organised group, which can be arranged in Chamba, Bharmour or McLeod Ganj. If you must go it alone, hire a local guide and be sure to make stops to adjust to the significant changes in altitude. See Lonely Planet's *Trekking in the Indian Himalaya* for more information on trekking in this region.

Bharmour is a centre for the seminomadic Gaddis, pastoralists who move their flocks up to alpine pastures during the summer, and descend to Kangra, Mandi and Bilaspur in winter. There are some fine treks that commence from Bharmour, including the pilgrimage to the sacred lake of Manimahesh; see the boxed text 'Manimahesh Yatra' for more details.

Places to Stay & Eat

On the road up to the temple compound, the ***Amit Guest House*** *(☎ 01090-25104)* has over-priced doubles with private bathroom and hot water for Rs 350.

Better value is the ***PWD Rest House*** on the lower of the two roads leading up from the bus stand, which charges Rs 250 per night for a double with private bathroom.

Just downhill is the friendly ***Chamunda Guest House*** *(☎ 25056)*. Simple rooms with shared bathroom cost Rs 150 (Rs 100 at quiet times).

Another cheap option is the ***Krishna Lodge*** by the old bus stand (ask for directions), with basic rooms for around Rs 50.

There are several ***dhabas*** just downhill from the Chaurasi temples.

Getting There & Away

There are buses to Chamba every two hours from 6.30 am to 5.30 pm (Rs 38, 3½ hours). Taxis charge Rs 800/1000 one way/return from Chamba. The road here is particularly prone to landslides.

Kullu & Parvati Valleys

The Kullu Valley and, to a lesser extent, the Parvati Valley, have always been popular places to hang out and take in mountain scenery. Recent tourist spillover from the political violence in Kashmir, however, has had a profound effect on the valleys and Manali, in particular, has developed rapidly, threatening the peaceful atmosphere.

Originally known as Kulanthapitha (End of the Habitable World), the first recorded inhabitants of the Kullu Valley date back to the first century AD. The capital was first at Jagatsukh, then moved to Naggar before the British moved it to Kullu town. The Kullu Valley, about 80km long and often less than 2km wide, rises northward from Mandi at 760m to the Rohtang La at 3978m, the gateway to Lahaul and Spiti.

The Kullu and Parvati Valleys, from Mandi to Manali, are serviced by the airport at Bhuntar, 10km south of Kullu town.

The high season is mid-April to mid-June, mid-September to early November, Christmas and New Year.

MANDI

☎ 01905 • pop 26,000

Formerly an important junction on the salt route to Tibet, Mandi is the gateway to the Kullu Valley, and also the junction of roads from Kullu, Kangra and Shimla. The town is more Punjabi than Himalayan in atmosphere, with a large Sikh community and around 81 temples of varying ages dotted around the hillsides. It's a pleasant place to break the journey between Shimla and the Kullu Valley and there are some interesting detours into the surrounding hills, including the holy lakes at Rewalsar and Prashar.

Orientation & Information

The centre of Mandi is the town square, dominated by a sunken multilevel shopping complex called the Indira Market. Most of the hotels and places to eat are around or very near the square. Over the river, to the east, is the bus station, a 15-minute walk away.

The only place to change money is the Evening Plaza Hotel in the main square, which also changes AmEx travellers cheques for a 1% commission. Below town on the way to Rewalsar, the Bank of Baroda gives cash advances on Visa and MasterCard.

Things to See & Do

For a cool respite from town, take an autorickshaw up the very steep 4km or 5km to **Tarna Hill** (about Rs 30 return). At the summit, the Rani Amrit Kaur Park (opened by the Dalai Lama in 1957) has superb views and a nice cafe. In the park, the

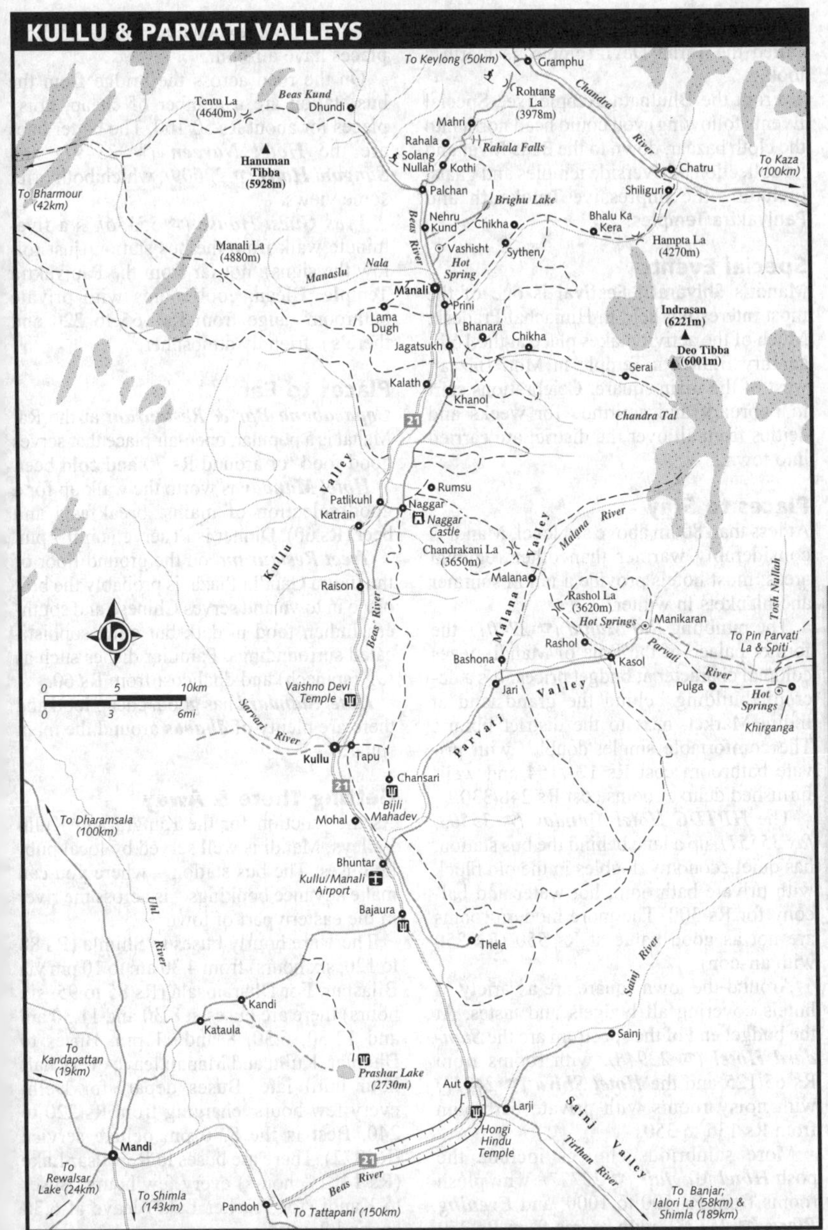
KULLU & PARVATI VALLEYS
To Keylong (50km)
Gramphu
Rohtang La (3978m)
Chandra River
Tentu La (4640m)
Beas Kund
Dhundi
Mahri
Rahala
Rahala Falls
Solang Nullah
Kothi
Hanuman Tibba (5928m)
Chatru
To Kaza (100km)
To Bharmour (42km)
Palchan
Shiliguri
Brighu Lake
Nehru Kund
Chikha
Bhalu Ka Kera
Beas River
Hampta La (4270m)
Vashisht
Sythen
Manali La (4880m)
Nala
Hot Spring
Manaslu
Manali
Prini
Lama Dugh
Indrasan (6221m)
Bhanara
Chikha
Jagatsukh
Deo Tibba (6001m)
Serai
Kalath
Khanol
Chandra Tal
21
Rumsu
Patlikuhl
Naggar
Katrain
Naggar Castle
Malana River
Kullu Valley
Chandrakani La (3650m)
Malana Valley
Malana
Raison
Rashol La (3620m)
Tosh Nullah
Beas River
Hot Springs
Manikaran
To Pin Parvati La & Spiti
Rashol
Parvati River
Kasol
Bashona
Pulga
Hot Springs
Jari
Parvati Valley
Khirganga
0 5 10km
0 3 6mi
Vaishno Devi Temple
Sarvari River
Kullu
Tapu
21
Chansari
Bijli Mahadev
To Dharamsala (100km)
Mohal
Bhuntar
Kullu/Manali Airport
Uhl River
Bajaura
Thela
Sainj River
Kandi
Kataula
Sainj
To Kandapattan (19km)
Prashar Lake (2730m)
Aut
Larji
Sainj Valley
Hongi Hindu Temple
Mandi
21
Tirthan River
Beas River
To Rewalsar Lake (24km)
To Shimla (143km)
Pandoh
To Tattapani (150km)
To Banjar; Jalori La (58km) & Shimla (189km)

17th-century Hindu **Syamakali Temple**, also called the Tarna Devi Temple, is worth a look.

From the Bhutnath Temple (see Special Events following) you could head north into the cloth bazaar, down to the **Beas River** and its collection of riverside temples and ghats, including the impressive **Triloknath** and **Panjvaktra Temples**.

Special Events

Mandi's **Shivaratri Festival** is one of the most interesting held in Himachal Pradesh. Much of the activity takes place at the 16th-century Bhutnath Temple in Moti Bazaar, west of the main square. Celebrations start in February and continue for weeks and deities from all over the district are carried into town.

Places to Stay

At less than 800m above sea level, Mandi is considerably warmer than other regional areas; most hotels provide a fan in summer and blankets in winter.

The rambling ***Raj Mahal*** *(☎ 22401)*, the former palace of the Raja of Mandi, oozes colonial character at budget prices. It's a decrepit building behind the grandstand at Indira Market, next to the district library. The comfortable singles/doubles with private bathroom cost Rs 121/154 and well-furnished deluxe rooms cost Rs 248/330.

The ***HPTDC Hotel Mandav*** *(☎ 35503, fax 35551)*, up a lane behind the bus station, has quiet economy doubles in the old block with private bathroom, hot water and balcony for Rs 300. The more modern rooms are not as good value at Rs 550 (Rs 850 with air-con).

Around the town square are a variety of hotels covering all budgets and tastes. At the budget end of the spectrum are the ***Standard Hotel*** *(☎ 22948)*, with rooms from Rs 65/125 and the ***Hotel Shiva*** *(☎ 24211)* with noisy rooms with private bathroom from Rs 135 to 350.

More salubrious choices include the posh ***Hotel Mayfair*** *(☎ 22777)*, with plush rooms from Rs 500 to 1000, and ***Evening Plaza*** *(☎ 25123)*, with rooms from Rs 250 to 800. More expensive rooms in both places have air-con.

On the road across the bridge from the bus station are a number of cheap, noisy places for about Rs 50/100. The better ones are the ***Hotel Naveen*** *(☎ 23491)* and ***Sangam Hotel*** *(☎ 22009)*, which both offer some views.

Vyas Guest House *(☎ 35556)* is a five-minute walk from the bus station (just follow the signs), not far from the Panjvaktra Temple. Clean, cool rooms with private bathroom range from Rs 165 to 220 and there's a friendly atmosphere.

Places to Eat

Copacabana Bar & Restaurant at the Raj Mahal is a popular, open-air place that serves good food for around Rs 70 and cold beer.

Hotel Mandav is worth the walk up for a good selection of mains, breakfasts and beer (Rs 60). Dinner isn't served until 7 pm.

Treet Restaurant, on the ground floor of the Indira Gandhi Plaza, is probably the best place in town and serves Chinese and southern Indian food in dark but quite sophisticated surroundings. Familiar dishes such as *sag* (spinach) and dhal cost from Rs 60.

Hotel Standard has good, cheap food and there are plenty of ***dhabas*** around the main square.

Getting There & Away

As the junction for the Kangra and Kullu Valleys, Mandi is well served by local public buses. The bus station – where you can make advance bookings – is across the river in the eastern part of town.

There are hourly buses to Shimla (Rs 88 to 120, six hours) from 4.30 am to 10 pm via Bilaspur. For Dharamsala (Rs 85 to 95, six hours) there are buses at 8.30 and 11.30 am and 12.30, 6.30, 8 and 11 pm. Buses to Bhuntar, Kullu and Manali leave every half hour until late. Buses depart for Delhi every few hours, charging from Rs 220 to 240. Best is the 8.30 pm deluxe service (Rs 372). There are buses to Rewalsar Lake (Rs 14, 1½ hours) every few hours. Buses to Kandi (for Prasher Lake) leave at 6.30 am and 2 pm.

Taxis congregate outside the bus station, and at a stand on the eastern side of the town square. A one-way trip by taxi from Mandi to Kullu costs Rs 700 (Rs 600 to Bhuntar).

AROUND MANDI

Rewalsar Lake

Rewalsar Lake (1350m), high up in the hills, 24km south-west of Mandi, is an important Tibetan Buddhist centre. The 8th-century monk Padmasambhava departed from here to spread the faith to Tibet, and there are several gompas sacred to the Nyingmapa sect. Every year, shortly after the Tibetan New Year in February/March, many Buddhists make a pilgrimage here from Dharamsala.

As you enter the lake area, the **Drigung Kagyud Gompa**, immediately on the right, has friendly monks who will show you around. Off to the left is a small chorten and a vast pile of engraved mani stones. Just beyond is the **Tso-Pema Ogyen Heru-kai Nyingmapa Gompa & Institute** (usually just called Nyingmapa), which was built in the 19th century, and houses a vast prayer wheel. The beautiful new murals here were painted in 2000 by a team of traditionally trained artists from Spiti. The **Zigar Gompa** uphill also features some of their work.

Hindus also revere the lake because it was where the sage Rishi Lomas did his penance as a dedication to Shiva, who, in return, gave Rishi the seven lakes in the vicinity, including Rewalsar. The Sikhs have the huge **Guru Gobind Singh Gurdwara**. It was built in 1930 by Raja Joginder Sen, and dedicated to Gobind Singh, who stayed at Rewalsar for a month.

Around the lake, there are three **Hindu temples** dedicated to Rishi Lomas, Shiva and Krishna. A steep 30-minute trek above the lake is a huge Buddha image in a cave; head for the prayer flags at the top of the hill.

Places to Stay & Eat The ***HPTDC Tourist Inn*** *(☎ 01905-80252)* has dorm beds for Rs 75, and nice doubles/triples for Rs 200/300 in the old building and Rs 300/350 in the new building. The hotel restaurant serves a good mix of Indian and Chinese food.

The Drikung Kagyud Gompa offers cosy rooms in its ***Peace Memorial Inn*** which cost Rs 65/150 with shared/private bathroom.

The ***guesthouse*** at the Nyingmapa Gompa has basic rooms on the lakeside for Rs 25/50 and deluxe rooms for Rs 100/150 with private bathroom and hot water. It's popular with Western Buddhists.

The Zigar Gompa ***guesthouse*** has rooms with bathroom for about Rs 50 and the friendly ***Tibetan Food Corner*** restaurant.

Nearby are the ***Mentok*** and ***Choesang*** restaurants, which serve good momos and thugpa.

Getting There & Away Rewalsar isn't actually on the way to anywhere, so you will have to travel via Mandi. Buses from Mandi go to Rewalsar village (Rs 14, one hour) every 1½ hours, making it an easy day trip along a pretty, but fairly rough, road. A taxi from Mandi costs about Rs 300/450 one way/return.

MANDI TO KULLU

Twenty kilometres from Mandi, the road passes the huge **Pandoh Dam**, which diverts water from the Beas River through two 12km-long tunnels. Eight kilometres past the dam is the **Hongi Hindu Temple**, where your driver will probably offer thankful prayers for a safe passage.

A few kilometres farther is **Aut**, the turn-off for the undeveloped Sainj Valley. With a fishing licence from Kullu, you can fish for trout at **Larji**, at the pretty junction of the Sainj and Tirthan Rivers. South-east of Larji on the road to Narkanda, **Banjar** is the home of the attractive **Shringa Rishikesh Temple**, which combines features of pagoda and pahari architecture. The shrine is sacred to a mystical stone that, legend has it, demanded of passers-by that it be installed in a temple.

Fifteen kilometres south of Kullu in the village of Bajaura is the **Basheshar Mahadev**, the largest stone temple in the Kullu Valley. Built in the 8th century from carved stone blocks, the temple has extremely fine carvings and sculptures.There is a carving of Durga standing on a crocodile and tortoise, slaying Mahishasuramardini, the buffalo demon. The temple is reached by a 200m trail leading from the main road (look for the sign marked 'Indo Italian Fruit Dev').

Prashar Lake

Hidden away in the hills between Mandi and Bajaura is spectacular Prashar Lake at 2730m. This ancient pilgrimage site has magnificent views of the Himalaya and is sacred to the Hindu sage Prashar Rishikesh. A splendid 14th-century temple to the guru sits on the lakeshore. You can stay at the Forest Inspection Hut, which can be booked through the DFO in Mandi (☎ 01905-22160).

The lake is a steep 8km trek from Baggi (just off the hill road from Mandi to Bajaura). Buses run to Kandi (Rs 20), where you can walk or pick up a local jeep for the 6km to Baggi. A taxi from Kullu or Mandi will charge around Rs 700 one way, but may take you most of the way uphill.

Bhuntar

This unremarkable junction town only warrants a mention for its airport, which serves all of the Kullu Valley, and its position as the turn-off to the Parvati Valley on the other side of the Beas. Bhuntar is only 10km from Kullu but, if you have an early departure or a late arrival, it might be handy to stay here.

Jagson Airlines (☎ 01902-65222) has an office next to the airport and there are several travel agencies around the village.

Places to Stay & Eat Best of a bad bunch near the airport/bus station is ***Hotel Airport-End*** *(☎ 01902-65130)*, with clean but noisy rooms with private bathroom for a negotiable Rs 250 to 350.

About 500m north of the airport, towards Kullu, are some mid-range places. All give a 50% discount in the low season. ***Hotel Sunbeam*** *(☎ 01902-65790)* has reasonable rooms with hot shower for Rs 200 to 550. ***Hotel Amit*** *(☎ 01902-65123)*, next door, has doubles for Rs 450 to 850.

Around the bus station, several ***dhabas*** serve basic Indian and Chinese food; the ***Malabar Restaurant*** opposite the airport entrance is probably the best of the lot. ***Lazeez Restaurant*** at the Sunbeam and the ***Havemore*** restaurant at the Amit Hotel have both good food and ambience.

Getting There & Away Bhuntar is well served by buses, which leave from the bus stand outside the airport entrance. Most buses go to Kullu (Rs 5), where you may have to change for destinations farther north. All buses between Manali and anywhere south of Kullu stop at, or very near, Bhuntar.

Bhuntar is the main hub for buses to Manikaran and other destinations in the Parvati Valley. Regular buses run to Manikaran (Rs 20) via Jari (Rs 17) and Kasol (Rs 17).

Taxis charge Rs 125 to Kullu, Rs 650 to Manali, Rs 500 to Manikaran and Rs 700 to Mandi; the Hill Taxi Operators Union is by the bus stand.

For details of flights from Bhuntar see Getting There & Away under Kullu.

KULLU

☎ 01902 • pop 16,000 • elevation 1200m

The busy town of Kullu is the district headquarters of the valley but is not the main tourist centre – that honour goes to Manali. Kullu is reasonably set up with hotels and other facilities, and is not a bad place (especially around Dhalpur), but most visitors head straight for the travellers centres dotted around the valleys.

Orientation

Kullu is divided in two by the Sarvari River. The *maidan* (field) area at Dhalpur (the setting for Kullu's festivals) is on the south bank, where you'll find the taxi stand and the tourist office, as well as many of Kullu's better hotels. The bus station and Raghunath Temple are both on the north bank; it's quicker to take the footpath next to the Hotel Shobla than the road. The main shopping district is farther north at Akhara Bazaar, which is a good place to buy Kullu shawls and other handicrafts.

Information

Tourist Offices The HPTDC tourist office (☎ 22349) is by the maidan at Dhalpur. It's

HIMACHAL PRADESH

Shopping for Shawls

The Kullu Valley is known as the Valley of Apples, but Valley of Shawls might be more appropriate. From Bhuntar to Manali, the road is lined with literally hundreds of shops selling traditional Kullu shawls, which are woven on wooden handlooms, and are light and remarkably warm.

Originally a cottage industry, the shawl business now employs hundreds of village women in the valley. As well as countless emporiums, there are dozens of places where you can see weaving in action. It's even possible to visit the farms where the pashmina goats and angora rabbits are raised. With this much competition, the sales pressure in most places can be fairly overbearing, though prices are often surprisingly low.

For high quality without the hard sell, you should head for Bhuttico, the Bhutti Weavers' Cooperative. Established in 1944 by a group of village women, Bhuttico has outlets in major towns throughout Himachal Pradesh. The cheapest shawls are made of lambswool, but for a good-quality shawl made of angora or pashmina wool, you should be prepared to pay at least Rs 1000. The embroidered shawls worn by village women take months to produce and cost upwards of Rs 6000.

open 10 am to 7 pm daily in summer (10 am to 5 pm in winter) but is only really useful for booking HPTDC buses, which leave from outside the office.

Money The only place that changes money is the State Bank of Patiala, at the northern end of Akhara Bazaar, a five-minute walk from the Central Hotel. It's open 10.45 am to 2 pm Monday to Friday. This branch accepts most travellers cheques (except Citicorp) but doesn't change cash.

Post & Communications The main post office is uphill from the taxi stand; you may have to wait, the service is a bit slow. You can send (and receive) faxes at government rates from the telegraph office (fax 22720) in Akhara Bazaar. The Madhu Chandrika Guest House offers Internet access for Rs 100 per hour.

Temples

The **Raghunath Temple** (AD 1660), in the north of town, is dedicated to the principal god in the valley. Although it's the most important temple in the area, it's not terribly interesting and is only open before 9 am and after 5 pm.

Only three kilometres from Kullu, in the village of Bhekhli, is the **Jagannathi Devi Temple** (also known as the Bhekhli Temple). It's a stiff 1½-hour climb, but from the temple there are great views over Kullu. Take the path off the main road to Akhara Bazaar after crossing the bridge. A taxi will charge Rs 200/300 one way/return, or there are a few unreliable public buses.

Another curious shrine is the **Bijli Mandev Temple**, 14km north-east of Kullu, which features a huge metal staff that acts as a lightning conductor. Periodically lightning strikes the pole and shatters the Shiva lingam inside the temple, which is considered a hugely auspicious event. The pieces are then rejoined with butter, accompanied by much celebration. The temple is a 2km trek from Chansari, which can be reached by bus, or a Rs 600 return taxi trip from Kullu.

The cave temple of **Vaishno Devi**, 3km from Kullu on the way to Manali, is only really worth a visit for the free reflexology (healing massage of the feet) that is practised here.

Special Events

Kullu holds one of the most colourful **Dussehra** festivals in India. During the festival Rama is worshipped in his form as Raghunath and the image from the temple is borne through the streets on a wheeled *rath* (chariot) pulled by pilgrims, ending up at the Dhalpur maidan. Following the procession, villagers dance in traditional dress and buffaloes are slaughtered before the gigantic structure is hauled back to Raghunath temple. The festival is quite spectacular, but it is becoming increasingly commercialised and finding transport and accommodation in the Kullu area during the festival can be a real problem.

Organised Tours

The Kullu Taxi Operators' Union (☎ 22332), just north of the Dhalpur maidan, offers a variety of sightseeing tours. Options include:

- Bhekhli Temple, Vaishno Devi Temple, Raghunath Temple, shawl factory and Bajaura (Rs 550, five hours)
- Kasol and Manikaran (Rs 700, six hours)
- Rewalsar Lake (Rs 1300, eight hours)
- Vaishno Devi Temple, Naggar Castle and Roerich Gallery (Rs 550, five hours)
- Larji, Banjar and Jalori La (Rs 1500, 10 hours)

Shopping

The best places to buy Kullu Shawls are Bhuttico and the Himachal Emporium, both on the highway in Aakhara Bazaar (you may pass the huge Bhuttico headquarters on the bus when travelling south to Mandi). See the boxed text 'Shopping for Shawls' earlier in this chapter.

Places to Stay – Budget

Dhalpur The popular ***Hotel Bijleshwar View*** *(☎ 22677)*, behind the tourist office, has quiet rooms with hot-water bathroom which start at Rs 350 to 500 (discounts are given in the low season).

In the same area, the ***Hotel Daulat*** *(☎ 22358)* has slightly overpriced rooms with a balcony for Rs 300 to 350.

Hotel New Vikrant *(☎ 22756)*, is on an alley behind the taxi stand and has an excellent range of rooms from Rs 150 to 375 and some nice communal sitting areas.

Nearby is the large ***Hotel Ramneek*** *(☎ 25588)*, which offers good rooms with hot showers, TV and carpets from Rs 350.

Across the other (eastern) side of the maidan, ***Hotel Fancy*** *(☎ 22681)* isn't bad at Rs 125 to 250 for rooms with private bathroom and hot water.

Hotel Rock-n-River *(☎ 24214)* has a somewhat inconvenient but pleasant location on the banks of the Sarvari River. Clean and bright rooms are good value at Rs 300 to 700 (with a tub).

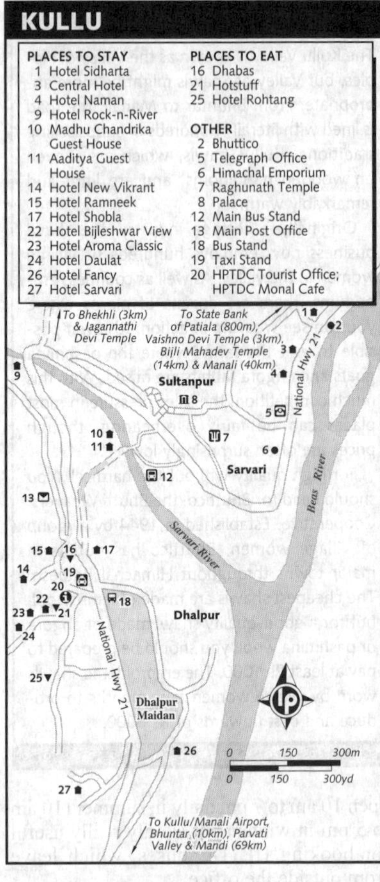

Akhara Bazaar Area There are several choices just across the river from the bus stand. Closest is ***Aaditya Guest House*** *(☎ 24263)*, right by the bridge, with bright doubles with shared/private bathroom and hot water for Rs 100/200.

Nearby, ***Madhu Chandrika Guest House*** *(☎ 24395)* charges Rs 100/150 with/without bathroom, and has a small dorm for Rs 40. There's also an Internet cafe.

The friendly ***Central Hotel*** *(☎ 22482)* is the oldest hotel in Kullu, with an almost infinite range of slightly threadbare rooms ranging from Rs 50 to 200.

Not far away, the ageing ***Hotel Naman*** *(☎ 22667)* has a similarly diverse range of rooms, costing from Rs 80 for musty singles to Rs 300 for the best double in the house.

Places to Stay – Mid-Range

Hotel Shobla *(☎ 22800)*, in the centre of town, has luxury rooms for Rs 550 to 950. Packages including meals and accommodation are available.

HPTDC Hotel Sarvari *(☎ 22471)* is a little south of the maidan, and a short walk off the main road. It's a well-run place with clean, bright doubles in the old block for Rs 450, rooms in the new block for Rs 800 upwards, and dorm beds for Rs 75.

Hotel Aroma Classic *(☎ 23075)* is another well-run place with rooms from Rs 500 to 750 and a good restaurant.

Hotel Sidharta *(☎ 24243)* is the best hotel in Akhara Bazaar, with clean but smallish rooms for Rs 400, Rs 500 and Rs 650.

Places to Eat

The ***HPTDC Monal Cafe***, by the tourist office, serves good meals and snacks. ***Hotstuff***, nearby, is a good fast-food place that serves up pizzas, soup and just about everything else.

There are numerous ***dhabas*** north of the taxi stand and around the bus stand.

Hotel Rohtang has nice views of Dhalpur maidan, a good food selection and reasonable prices; breakfast is good.

Hotel Aroma Classic looks expensive, but isn't – the setting, service and selection make it a good option.

Hotel Shobla has the best views, all the service you would expect and good food at fair prices (dishes start at Rs 40).

Getting There & Away

Air Jagson Airlines flies between Delhi and Kullu/Manali airport (Bhuntar) daily for US$145, with a stop in Shimla. The flight leaves Delhi at 8 am and returning directly to Delhi at 10.10 am. Indian Airlines flies the exact same route at 9 am on Monday, Wednesday and Friday (US$145) and returning directly to Delhi at 11.10 am. Both airlines use small turboprops for this flight.

Jagson Airlines has an office (☎ 65222) opposite the airport in Bhuntar; Indian Airlines can be booked through Ambassador Travels (☎ 25286) in Kullu. Tickets are most easily booked through travel agencies in Kullu.

Bus Kullu has a large, busy bus station; timetables are displayed in English, and there's an advance booking system. The bus stop at the Dhalpur maidan is only good if you're going to Bhuntar or the Parvati Valley, but these buses may be full by the time they get to Dhalpur from the main Kullu bus station.

Buses pass through Kullu on their way to Mandi every 30 minutes from 4 am to 8.15 pm (Rs 44, two hours), also stopping in Bhuntar (Rs 5, 15 minutes). There are buses to Shimla (Rs 132, eight hours) every three hours from 4.30 am to 7.45 pm. Buses leave for Manikaran (Rs 27) hourly; alternatively, change at Bhuntar. There is a bus every 15 or 20 minutes between Kullu and Manali (Rs 24, two hours). To Naggar, buses leave at 3.30 and 5.30 pm. It's easier to take a Manali-bound bus to Patlikuhl (Rs 13) and change there.

There are public buses to Dharamsala (Rs 135 to 160, eight hours) at 9.50 am and 5 and 8 pm. Public express buses go to Delhi (Rs 270 to 290, 14 hours) hourly all afternoon. All services go via Chandigarh. For local sights, there are hourly buses to Bajaura (Rs 10, one hour) and buses to Bhekhli (Rs 7, 45 minutes) at 9 am and 2.30 and 5.30 pm. Buses to Kandi (for Prasher Lake; Rs 21) leave at 6.30 am and 2 pm.

HPTDC buses from Manali stop at the tourist office in Kullu and bookings can be made in advance there. Buses run daily in the high season to Shimla (Rs 337) at 9.15 am, Delhi (Rs 521) at 6.30 pm, and Chandigarh (Rs 312) at 8.15 am.

Travel agencies in Kullu sell tickets for deluxe private buses 'from Kullu', but these are really just part of the trips from Manali organised by bus companies. In the high season, overnight buses go to Delhi (Rs 350); Dharamsala (Rs 250); to Leh, with a connection in Manali (Rs 1000); and to Shimla (Rs 250).

Taxi From Kullu to Manali, a taxi costs Rs 550 via National Highway 21 (on the western side of the river), or Rs 700 if you take the slower but more scenic route via Naggar.

Fixed taxi fares include Naggar (Rs 400/550 one way/return), Manikaran (Rs 450/600), Katrain (Rs 225/325), Mandi (Rs 800 one way), Dharamsala (Rs 1900) and Shimla (Rs 1900). The set price to the airport at Bhuntar is Rs 125.

Getting Around

An autorickshaw is handy to get around, particularly if you have heavy gear, or want to visit the nearby temples. From Dhalpur to the bus station should cost about Rs 15, or to the airport at Bhuntar, Rs 60.

JARI

☎ 01902 • elevation 1524m

Jari is halfway along the Parvati Valley – about 19km from Bhuntar. Like Kasol, it has become something of a traveller resort, though on a much smaller scale. Several of the best places to stay are located in the hamlets above Jari. The views and tranquillity of Jari have been marred slightly by the new Parvati River hydroelectric project.

Across the river from Jari is the interesting Malana Valley. The village of **Malana** (2652m) can be reached in a full day trek from Jari. Legend has it that was this was where Jamlu, the main deity of the area, opened a casket containing the gods of the Parvati Valley, who were distributed around the valley by the breeze. There are about 500 people in Malana and they speak a peculiar dialect with strong Tibetan elements. It's an isolated village with its own system of government and a caste structure so rigid that it's forbidden for visitors to touch either the people or any of their possessions. It's very important to respect this custom; wait at the edge of the village for an invitation to enter. From here, you can also continue to Naggar. Organised treks are the way to go; talk to Negi's Himalayan Adventures (☎ 73619) in Jari.

Places to Stay & Eat

Just above the bus stand, the huge white ***Dharma Family Guest House*** has OK rooms for Rs 60.

On the main road are the pleasant ***Om Shiva Guest House*** *(☎ 73202)*, which has singles/doubles for Rs 50/100, and the ***Roman Guest House*** *(☎ 73641)*, with rooms from Rs 100.

Golden Rays Hotel *(☎ 73210)* is the best bet on the main road, with clean, spacious doubles with shared/private bathroom for Rs 100/165.

Village Guest House *(☎ 73570)*, a 10-minute uphill trek from the village centre, is a peaceful, well-run place with decent rooms for Rs 50 or Rs 75. This is the place to get away from it all, though you may think twice if you have heavy luggage.

Also high above the village is the ***Thakur Family Guest House*** *(☎ 73354)*, with rooms for Rs 50 with shared bathroom.

Deepak Restaurant on the main road is a popular place with locals for food.

Om Shiva Guest House has the ***Rooftop Cafe*** with great views.

Getting There & Away

Parvati Valley buses go to Manikaran (Rs 7), Bhuntar (Rs 12) and Kullu (Rs 20). A one-way taxi from Kullu to Jari is around Rs 350.

KASOL

Kasol (1565m) is another tiny village that has developed (some would say overdeveloped) into a travellers centre. The village has a lovely setting among pines and streams, but has seen a spate of guesthouse building in recent years. The prettier part of the village, known as 'Old Kasol', is on the Bhuntar side of the bridge. Charmless 'New Kasol' is on the Manikaran side.

Places to Stay & Eat

In a modern building in the centre of New Kasol are the ***Rainbow Cafe & Guest House*** *(☎ 01902-73714)* and ***Parvati River View Guest House*** *(01902-73716)*, which both offer reasonable rooms from Rs 100 to 150 with shared bathroom (Rainbow also

Warning – Fatal Vacations

Between 1996 and 2000 more than 17 foreign tourists have disappeared or been murdered in the Kullu Valley. Most were reported missing from the travellers centres of Naggar, Malana, Manali, Manikaran and Kasol after setting off on unaccompanied treks into the Kullu hills. Until recently, Indian police put most of the disappearances down to accidents while trekking, but following the brutal murders of a German tourist in July 2000 and a Spanish woman and her child in August 2000, it seems likely that many of the others who disappeared have met a similar fate.

The area is a major centre for *charas* (marijuana) production – many travellers come here for just this reason – and drugs are believed to have played a part in many of the disappearances. If you go to the area we recommend that you avoid trekking alone, stay clear of drugs and tell your hotel or guesthouse where you are going before you set out on any walk. Be extremely cautious of befriending sadhus (spiritual men) and other people wandering in the hills.

If you have any information about any of the people who have disappeared, a Foreign Missing Persons Bureau has been set up in Delhi and can be contacted through the British High Commission (☎ 011-6872161).

has doubles with private bathroom for Rs 200). Nearby are several Italian and Israeli restaurants.

Two of the nicest places to stay in Old Kasol are ***Yerpa's Guest House*** *(☎ 01902-73763)* on the main drag, and the ***Alpine Guest House***, tucked away in the woods. Both have clean rooms with shared bathroom and hot water for Rs 100 to 150 and more expensive deluxe rooms, as well as pleasant restaurants.

High above Old Kasol in an old village house is the friendly ***White House Guest House***, which has great views from its restaurant and spartan but spotless rooms with shared bathroom. Follow the signs from the village.

Near the bridge are the ***Deep Forest Cafe*** and ***Moon Dance***, which both offer Western food and groovy tunes.

MANIKARAN

☎ 01902 • elevation 1737m

Famous for its hot springs, which are hot enough to boil rice and apparently cure anything from rheumatism to bronchitis, Manikaran is another place from which many foreigners have forgotten to leave. Manikaran means 'Jewel from the Ear' in Sanskrit. According to the local legend, a giant snake took earrings from Parvati while she was bathing and then snorted them through its nose to create spaces where the hot springs spewed forth.

The clouds of steam spewing out from the baths and temples make Manikaran quite atmospheric, but once the sun leaves the valley (early in the afternoon), it can be dank and chilly. The town is revered by both Hindus and Sikhs and is chock-a-block with sadhus, pilgrims and religious souvenir shops.

In the light of the murders of foreigners in the surrounding countryside, this is not the place to befriend *chillum* (hashish pipe) smokers or go off wandering by yourself in the hills.

Things to See & Do

At the start of the village is the monumental but dilapidated **Sri Guru Nanak Dev Ji Sikh** gurdwara. Interesting temples here include the Hindu **Raghunath Temple** by the public baths and the **Rama Temple**, tucked away in a courtyard off the main square.

Diluted to a bearable heat, there are **baths** where you can sample the beneficial effects of the waters at the Sikh temple beneath the gurdwara; there are separate facilities for men and women. Alternatively there is a public bath in the town centre, which is used for washing clothes and is probably not that hygienic. For a more private 20-minute bath, the Hotel Parvati charges Rs 25 for one person, or Rs 40 for two, or there are baths in most local guesthouses.

As part of an organised trek, it's possible to visit the atmospheric **hot springs** at

HIMACHAL PRADESH

Khirganga, 25km above Manikaran, where Shiva sat and meditated for 2000 years, or even continue on to the Pin Valley in Spiti via the Pin Parvati La (5319m). Porters and guides can be hired in Manikaran – ask at any guesthouse or restaurant.

Orientation & Information

The more appealing old town on the north bank of the roaring Parvati River has most of the guesthouses, places to eat and temples. Across the pedestrian-only suspension bridge, the south bank of the river is home to the grubby bus stand and a few mediocre mid-range hotels. Moneychangers at the bus stand can exchange cash only.

Places to Stay

Like the rest of the region, prices vary according to demand.

Sharma Guest House (☎ *73742)* is the first place you come to after crossing the footbridge. It has decent doubles for Rs 75 to 125.

Sharma Sadan (☎ *73703)* is a good choice, with its fine location next to the Rama Temple on the main square and nice rooms from Rs 125 (low season) to Rs 400 (June/July).

Just off the square are the ***Padha Family Guest House*** (☎ *73728)* and ***Kailash Guest House*** (☎ *73717)*, which both offer naturally hot spa-baths and courtyard rooms from Rs 75 to 300.

The ***HPTDC Hotel Parvati*** (☎ *73735)* has clean doubles at Rs 450 (Rs 200 in low season), which is not particularly good value around here.

By the bus stand are the dingy ***Hotel Amar Palace*** (☎ *73740)* and better ***Hotel Sharda Classic*** (☎ *73851)*, with OK rooms for around Rs 500 (Rs 200 in low season).

Shivalik Hotel (☎ *73817)* is farther down the valley and offers reasonable rooms from Rs 350. Nearby, the ***Hotel Dev Bhoomi*** (☎ *73781)* has rooms by the river for Rs 200.

Places to Eat

At the eastern end of the village, ***Hot Springs Restaurant*** serves delicious pizzas.

Holy Palace has an impressive carved wooden frontage and reasonable Italian and Israeli food for around Rs 40 a dish.

Nearby, overlooking the river, is the similar ***O-Rest*** with international dishes for around Rs 45.

Shiva Restaurant, near the gurdwara, caters to pilgrims as well as travellers with a menu of thalis and Italian standards.

Getting There & Away

Buses between Kullu and Manikaran (Rs 27, 2½ hours) leave every 30 minutes or so until 1.15 pm. For Manali, take any of the Kullu or Bhuntar buses heading downhill and change (Rs 20, two hours). The last trip to Bhuntar leaves Manikaran at 5.45 pm. Another option is a day trip from Manali on a tourist bus for Rs 197, which stops at Kasol for a quick look on the way.

A return taxi from Manali to Manikaran will cost Rs 1100. A fixed-price taxi from the stand at the bus station in Manikaran will cost Rs 500 to Bhuntar (one way), and Rs 600 to Kullu.

KULLU TO MANALI

There are two roads between Kullu and Manali; the main highway runs along the west bank of the Beas, while the rougher but more scenic road goes along the east bank, through Naggar.

None of the settlements on this side of the valley stands out. **Raison**, 13km from Kullu, is home to the ***HPTDC Adventure Resort*** (☎ *01902-40516)*, which offers kayaking and other activities on the Beas. A hut with two bedrooms costs Rs 650 (less in the low season).

Fishing enthusiasts may be interested in **Katrain**, 6km north, which has good trout stocks and the ***HPTDC Anglers Bungalow*** (☎ *01902-40136)*, with doubles from Rs 250 to 300. The cheap, family-run ***Nangdraj Guest House*** is also OK.

Patlikuhl is about halfway between Kullu and Manali, and has good trout fishing, but nearby Naggar is a far nicer place to stay. There is a fisheries office at the northern edge of town where you can buy trout and get a fishing licence.

NAGGAR

☎ 01902 • elevation 1760m

The lovely little village of Naggar is known for its castle, its ancient temples and its Russian art gallery. There are also pleasant treks in the surrounding forests, including the two-day trek to Jari over the Chandrakhani La (3650m). Tour arrangements can be made at the Ragini, Snow View and Poonam Lodge hotels for around US$30 per day. Many people visit Naggar as part of a day tour, but there's plenty here to warrant an overnight stop.

The main settlement of Naggar lies on the eastern Kullu to Manali road, but the gallery, temples and hotels are grouped around the castle at the top of a steep 2km road. To get here get off the bus at Patlikhul village, on the main road, and walk up, or take one of the taxis or autorickshaws milling around.

Naggar Castle

Naggar was capital of the Kullu Valley for nearly 1500 years and the castle was built by the Raja Sidh Singh about 500 years ago. The castle is built around a courtyard, containing the tiny **Jagtipath Temple** – which houses a slab of stone said to have been carried there by wild bees – and a small **museum**. Surrounding the castle is a fortified verandah offering stupendous views of the Beas Valley. The living quarters were converted into a hotel in 1978 when the raja fell on hard times. The castle is open 7 am to 10 pm daily for a Rs 10 entry fee, but it's free if you're staying here or dining at the restaurant.

Temples

The grey sandstone Shiva **Temple of Gauri Shankar** is at the foot of the small bazaar below the castle and dates from the 11th or 12th century. Almost opposite the front of the castle is the curious little **Chatar Bhuj Temple** dedicated to Vishnu. Near the Snow View Guest House is the pagoda-like **Tripura Sundari Devi Temple**, with some ornate wooden carvings. High up on the ridge above Naggar, near the village of Thawa, is the **Murlidhar Krishna Temple**, reached by a woodland path beyond the Roerich Gallery.

Art Venues

One kilometre past the castle is the interesting **Roerich Gallery**, a fine old house displaying the artwork of the eccentric Russian painter Nikolai Roerich, who died in Naggar in 1947, and his son, Svetoslav Roerich, who died in Bangalore in 1993. It's open 9 am to 5 pm daily (10 am to 5 pm in winter); entry is Rs 10. Leave your shoes at the front door.

A five-minute trek uphill from the gallery is **Urusvati Himalayan Folk & Art Museum,**

Roerich – Painter, Mystic, Spy

Born in St Petersburg in 1874, the Russian painter Professor Nikolai Roerich was a curious eccentric who came to India in search of the mystical Shambhala, the Northern Paradise described in the ancient Tibetan Buddhist texts. While painting his distinctive pictures of the Himalaya – which fall somewhere between surrealism and Russian icon painting – Roerich became convinced that a secret valley lay hidden somewhere among the peaks, and within it lay paradise on earth.

When not pursuing the esoteric, Roerich campaigned to protect the great architectural treasures of the world from wartime shelling, culminating in the historic Roerich Act, signed at the White House in Washington in 1935. Roerich also made several dramatic expeditions into Turkestan, Siberia, Mongolia and China, earning the immediate distrust of the British, American and Chinese governments. He didn't help matters by handing over his diaries of the expeditions to the Russian consul upon his return! Some American statesmen even claimed he won supporters for the Roerich Act through mystical powers.

Roerich was not without a sense of humour. At the height of the spy rumours, he gave the Soviet Commissar of Education a painting of a huge head looming over the world and looking east, with the title *The Time Has Come*. Roerich never found the hidden valley, but he created his own version of Shambhala at Naggar, where many of his paintings can still be seen.

which houses a collection of embroidery and folk art. Upstairs is a modern art gallery that sells postcards and copies of Roerich's paintings.

Places to Stay

Housed in the castle, the ***HPTDC Castle Hotel*** *(☎ 47816)* is reputedly haunted and is certainly one of the more interesting heritage places. Basic rooms with shared bathroom cost Rs 250 and much better doubles with private bathroom range from Rs 600 to 1500. Dorm beds cost Rs 75, but are often booked out.

Poonam Mountain Lodge & Restaurant *(☎ 47747)* is down the alley behind the castle. Good singles/doubles with private bathroom and hot water cost Rs 150/200; the helpful owner rents trekking gear.

The well-run ***Hotel Ragini*** *(☎ 47855)* is a mid-range place with nice wooden decor and excellent rooms for from Rs 350 to 500 with TV, hot shower and balcony (heaters are an extra Rs 50).

Sheetal Guest House *(☎ 47719)*, next door, is less impressive, with tired-looking rooms from Rs 200 to 500 with private bathroom (Rs 150 with shared bathroom with hot water).

Closer to the Roerich Museum, the ***Snow View Guest House*** *(☎ 47325)*, has dark but OK doubles with private bathroom from Rs 100 to 200 and small singles with shared bathroom for Rs 50 and Rs 70.

Alliance Guest House *(☎ 47763)* is simple but clean, friendly and comfortable. It's run by an expat French man and offers rooms with shared bathroom and hot water for Rs 100 and a few doubles with private bathroom for Rs 200 to 300. In winter, you'll want to avail yourself of a heater for Rs 50.

Places to Eat

Castle Hotel provides the best views, certainly the best atmosphere in the village, and the food is pretty good, too. Nonveg dishes such as tandoori chicken costs around Rs 75.

Kailash Rooftop Restaurant at the Hotel Ragini and ***Cinderella Restaurant*** at the Sheetal Guest House are both worth a try.

Poonam Restaurant has vegetarian food and a great location in the shadow of the Vishnu temple. Next door, the ***Rollick Restaurant*** is a tiny pure-veg place.

La Purezza Italian Restaurant, in the village on the main road, at the start of the road up to the castle, serves authentic pasta dishes for around Rs 70.

Getting There & Away

Buses go directly between the village of Naggar (on the main road) and Manali six times a day (Rs 11, one hour).

An option is to get the bus to Patlikuhl (there are more buses along the western side of the river) from either Manali or Kullu, then take a taxi (Rs 100) from Patlikuhl to Naggar Castle (you could walk, but it's steep).

A one-way/return taxi from Manali to Naggar Castle will cost Rs 300/400; a return taxi from Kullu is Rs 400. A Kullu to Manali taxi (Rs 550) will probably charge an extra Rs 150 for a quick stopover in Naggar.

JAGATSUKH

Like Naggar, Jagatsukh was also once capital of the Kullu Valley, and is home to many ancient temples including the 8th-century **Gauri Shankar Temple**. There is another ancient temple in the nearby village of Shooru. Jagatsukh is the starting point for the difficult five-day trek to the eerie Chandrata (4800m), set at the foot of Deo Tibba peak (6001m).

The only place worth staying in Jagatsukh is the ***Rishi Guest House***, which has ordinary rooms for Rs 150. Buses from Manali to Naggar pass through or you can walk the 6km from Manali along the eastern bank of the Beas.

MANALI

☎ 01902 • pop 4200 • elevation 2050m

At the northern end of the Kullu Valley, the popular resort of Manali is the last major settlement in the Kullu Valley. When it was first discovered by travellers during the 1960s, Manali was something of a mountain Shangri-la, with old stone houses and peaceful alpine scenery. The last of the views vanished behind hotel buildings sometime in the 1980s and today Manali looks like any other modern resort, with wall-to-wall souvenir shops, travel agents and dozens of hotels.

During the 1970s and 1980s, Manali picked up a reputation as a kind of Amsterdam of the Himalaya because of the charas produced in the local area. These days, the dope scene has died down considerably and most tourists come here to take advantage of the good skiing and other adventure sports in the surrounding hills or, in the case of Indian tourists, to celebrate their honeymoon.

Although there are plenty of activities on offer, Manali is a fairly charmless town. It lacks the colonial history of Shimla and the culture and spectacular setting in Lahaul, Spiti and Kinnaur. Recent years have seen an explosion of hotel building to cater to the honeymoon market. However, a few traces of Manali's ancient history remain in surrounding hills, and the markets are a great place to browse for handicrafts produced by local villagers and the refugee Tibetan community.

Legend has it that Manu, Hinduism's Noah, stepped off a boat in Manali to recreate human life after floods had devastated the world – Manali means Home of Manu. From mid-April to late June, mid-September to early November, Christmas and New Year it can seem like all of humanity has descended on Manali. The outlying settlements of Old Manali, Dhungri and Vashisht attract large numbers of travellers in the summer, but close down almost entirely in the winter.

Orientation

Manali is based around one street, The Mall, a continuation of the highway into town. North of the main town and across the Manalsu Nala River is Old Manali, with much more character, and the pretty village of Vashisht due east of Old Manali, high above the Beas on the eastern side of the valley.

Information

Tourist Offices For tourist information try Himachal Pradesh Tourism Reception Centre (☎ 52175), the small white hut under the Hotel Kunzam. It's open 10 am to 5 pm Monday to Saturday (daily in summer). Don't confuse this place with the larger HPTDC Tourism Marketing Office (☎ 52116) next door, which sells bus tickets for HPTDC buses and makes reservations for the skiing courses and hotels, but doesn't have local information. It's open 8 am to 7 pm daily.

Money The UCO Bank opposite the tourist offices can change most travellers cheques in US dollars and UK pounds but not cash, and is open seven days a week (only till noon on Saturday). The State Bank of India is south of Hotel Ibex on The Mall and changes cash and most travellers cheques in US, Australian and Canadian dollars, Swiss francs and UK pounds. Numerous moneychangers and travel agents also offer exchange facilities.

It's important to remember if you're headed north of Manali, change some extra money here as there are no exchange facilities in Lahaul, Spiti or Kinnaur!

Post & Communications The main post office, in Model Town, is open 9 am to 5 pm Monday to Saturday. The poste restante here is reliable. The central telegraph office (fax 52404), a block north, is the cheapest place to send/receive faxes (Rs 100/10 per page).

There are several good Internet cafes. In the centre, try Himalayan Quest, above Chopsticks restaurant, or Himalaya Internet, next to the post office; both charge Rs 60 per hour. Below Old Manali, Nirvana Travels has lots of PCs and charges Rs 60 per hour.

Adventure Tour Operators The following locally run places are reliable, long established, organise their own tours and activities and have high safety standards:

Antrek Tours (☎ 52292, fax 52786, ⓔ naushad_kaludi@yahoo.com) Manu Market
Himalayan Adventures (☎ 52750, fax 52182, ⓔ roopu@nde.vsnl.net.in) The Mall (next to the UCO Bank)
Himalayan Journeys (☎ 52365, fax 53065, ⓔ himjourn@del3.vsnl.net.in) The Mall (opposite Nehru Park)
North Face Adventure Tours (☎ 52441, fax 52694, ⓔ northface_adventures@usa.net) The Mall (near Mount View Restaurant)
Institute of Mountaineering & Allied Sports (☎ 52342), opposite the Ram Regency Honeymoon Hotel (2km from the centre)

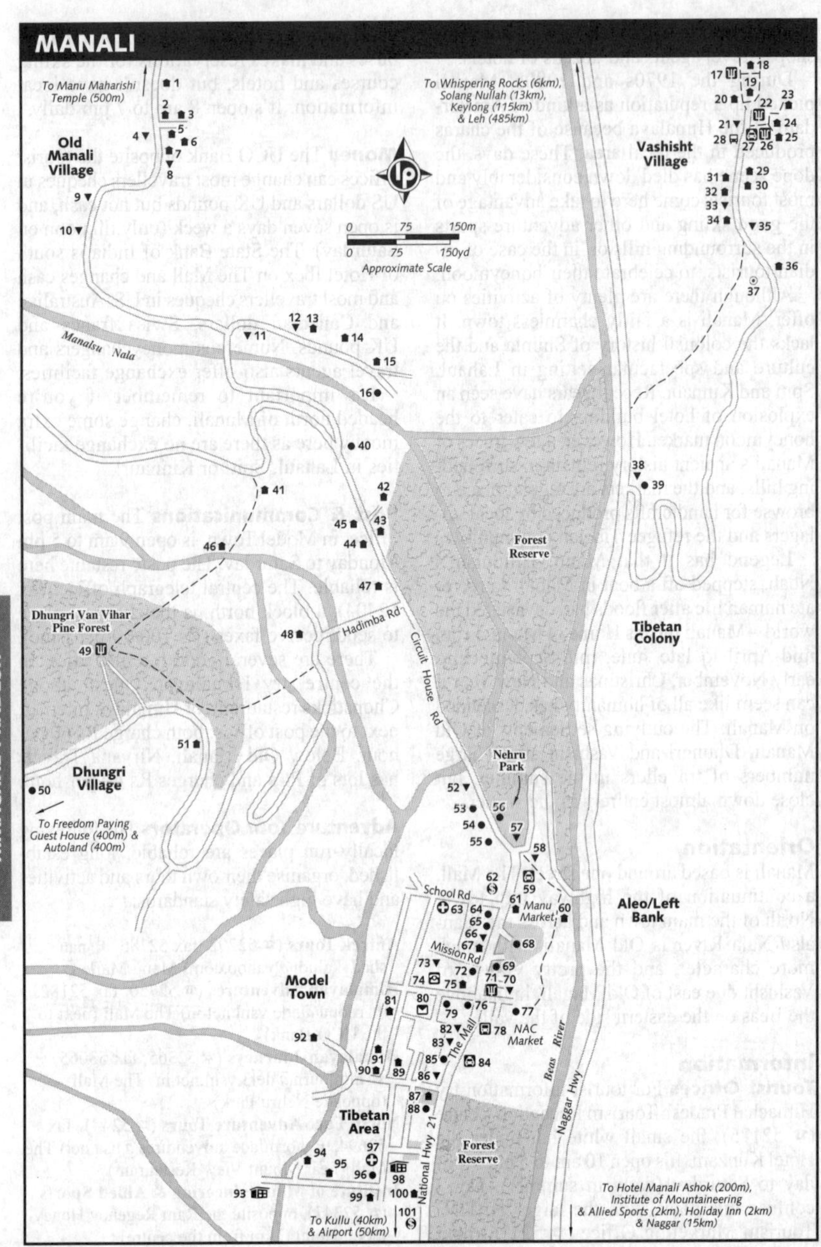
MANALI
To Manu Maharishi Temple (500m)
Old Manali Village
To Whispering Rocks (6km), Solang Nullah (13km), Keylong (115km) & Leh (485km)
Vashisht Village
0 75 150m
0 75 150yd
Approximate Scale
Manalsu Nala
Forest Reserve
Dhungri Van Vihar Pine Forest
Hadimba Rd
Circuit House Rd
Tibetan Colony
Nehru Park
Dhungri Village
To Freedom Paying Guest House (400m) & Autoland (400m)
School Rd
Manu Market
Aleo/Left Bank
Mission Rd
Model Town
NAC Market
The Mall
Beas River
Naggar Hwy
National Hwy 21
Tibetan Area
Forest Reserve
To Kullu (40km) & Airport (50km)
To Hotel Manali Ashok (200m), Institute of Mountaineering & Allied Sports (2km), Holiday Inn (2km) & Naggar (15km)

MANALI

PLACES TO STAY

1 Krishna Guest House
2 Diplomat Guest House
3 Dragon Guest House
5 Tourist Nest
6 Veer Paying Guest House
7 Kishoor Guest House
13 Hotel Riverbank; Hotel Him View
14 Rising Moon; Riverside; Hema Guest House; Mamta Paying Guest House
15 Jungle Bungalow
18 Bodh Guest House
19 Dolath Guest House
20 Negi Guest House
23 Guest House Dharma; Amrit
24 Kalptaru
25 New Dharma
29 Anand Hotel; Travel Assistance Centre
30 Sonan; Prem
31 Surabhi Guest House & World Peace Cafe
32 Janta; Ganga
34 Hotel Valley View; Hotel Bhrigu; Basho Restaurant
36 Sita Cottage
41 Hotel Kalpana
42 Pinewood Hotel
43 Hotel Mayflower
44 Banon Resorts
45 Sunshine Guest House
46 Hotel Chetna
47 John Banon's Hotel
48 Hotel Rohtang Manalsu
51 Hotel Shrinagar Regency
60 Hotel Beas
61 HPTDC Hotel Kunzam; HPTDC Tourism Reception Centre; HPTDC Tourism Marketing Office
67 Hotel Renuka
75 Su-Khiran Guest House
81 Mona Lisa
87 Hotel Ibex; Ibex Travels; Hotel Snow View; Underground Market; Tibetan Market
89 Premier Hotel
90 Hotel Diamond
91 Hotel Shishar; Lhasa Hotel
92 Mount View Hotel
94 Potala Hotel
95 Sunflower
99 Hotel Snow Drop
100 Samrat Hotel

PLACES TO EAT

4 Mount View Cafe
8 Little Tibet Cafe; Shiva Garden Cafe
9 Ish Cafe
10 Moon Dance Garden
11 River Music Cafe
12 Tibet Kitchen
21 Super Bake; Zodiac Cafe; Ranu Rooftop Cafe
33 Freedom Cafe
35 Rose Garden Inn
38 Phuntsok Coffee House
52 Johnson's Cafe
57 Sa-Ba
58 Juniper; Chandertal
66 Sher-e-Punjab
70 Mona Lisa
73 Swamiji's Madras Cafe; Sangam; Neel Kamal
82 Mount View Restaurant; Chopsticks; Himalayan Quest
83 Kamal Dhaba; Himalaya Dhaba
86 Gozy Restaurant

OTHER

16 HPTDC Club House
17 Two-storey Temple
22 Vashisht Temple
26 Rama Temple; Public Baths; Rainbow Cafe
27 Taxi Stand
28 Bus Stand
37 HPTDC Hot Baths Complex
39 The Enfield Club
40 Nirvana Travels
49 Dhungri Temple & Shrine
50 Utopia Complex; Handicraft Museum
53 Ambassador Travels (Indian Airlines)
54 Himalayan Journeys
55 Jagson Airlines
56 Himachal Emporium
59 Him-Aanchal Taxi Stand
62 UCO Bank
63 Mission Hospital
64 Himalayan Adventures; Bhuttico
65 Charitrust Tibetan Handicraft Emporium
68 Antrek Tours
69 Bhuttico
71 Temple
72 Swagtam Tours
74 Central Telegraph Office
76 Harison Travels
77 Bookworm
78 Bus Station
79 Delightful Things; Tibetan Food Corner
80 Main Post Office; Himalaya Internet
84 Him-Aanchal Taxi Stand
85 North Face Adventure Tours
88 Tibetan Market
93 Gadhan Thekchokling Gompa
96 Inder Motors
97 Mentsikhang Clinic
98 Himalayan Nyingmapa Gompa
101 State Bank of India

HIMACHAL PRADESH

Bookshops The best choice in town is at Bookworm, 16 NAC Market, behind the bus station, with a great selection of imported novels and books on India.

Dangers & Annoyances Although marijuana is widely available in the outlying villages, travellers should remember that drugs are still illegal in Manali. Over the last decade, 140 foreigners have been arrested for drug-related offences and drugs are believed to have played a part in many of the disappearances and murders of foreigners in the Kullu Valley.

Dhungri Temple & Shrine

The Dhungri or Hadimba Temple is a four-storey wooden building in the middle of a

Outdoor Activities in Manali

Fishing

The Himachal Pradesh Tourism Reception Centre in Manali (☎ 52175) issues one-day fishing permits for Rs 100. The season is from March to June and July to November. You can also get permits at the fisheries office in Patlikuhl. The best angling in the Kullu Valley is said to be at Larji, Katrain and Kasol.

Hiking

There are several good day treks from Manali. The 12km trek up the western side of the Beas River to the Solang Valley is a nice alternative to the bus. Lama Dugh meadow is a 6km trek up the Manalsu Nala, west of Manali town and makes a nice day trip. For longer expeditions, book onto an organised trip; there are other less risky, more beautiful areas for hiking by yourself. See the boxed text 'Fatal Vacations'.

Popular options include Beas Kund (three days), the Hamta La (4270m, five days) and the village of Malana in the Parvati Valley (five days). Another interesting route takes you to Naggar via the Chandrakhani La. Rates with Himalayan Journeys and other operators range from US$30 to US$45 a day, including guides, porters, meals and good camping gear.

Mountain Biking

Himalayan Journeys will rent you a bike and helmet and drop you up at the Rohtang La for around Rs 900 (minimum four people). It can also arrange biking tours.

Mountaineering

The Institute of Mountaineering & Allied Sports offers fixed-date, basic and advanced mountaineering courses lasting 25 days, with food, gear, training and (dormitory) accommodation included, but not transport. Prices range from Rs 700 to 1000 per day. Himalayan Journeys offers weekly courses for beginners for Rs 7000 (you'll need your own boots).

Paragliding

In summer, several travel agencies organise paragliding on the slopes of Solang Nullah, north of Manali. Himalayan Journeys and North Face Adventure Tours both offer two-minute tandem 'joy rides' for Rs 400, or 10- to 15-minute 'high rides' for Rs 1500. For more extensive flights, you'll have to head up to Gullubah on the way to the Rhotang La (Rs 2500, 30 minutes to one-hour flight). Courses are offered but don't lead to any internationally recognised qualification. Seven days' flying is Rs 7000. The paragliding scene at Solang closes down in April/May when everyone in the business heads to Billing in the Kangra Valley for the Himalayan Hang-Gliding Rally (see Bir & Billing in the Kangra Valley section earlier).

Rafting

Basic rafting is available along the Beas River from April to July and, depending on the monsoon, from mid-September to mid-October. Trips generally start at Pirdi and continue 16km down to Jhiri. Prices depend on the number of passengers and your bargaining power but are around Rs 900 for the day, including transport, equipment, lunch and a guide. More interesting (and expensive) trips are possible to the Spiti, Zanskar and Indus Rivers. Contact Himalayan Adventures or Himalayan Journeys for more details.

Skiing

Skiing for beginners is possible at Solang Nullah from January to March – the later the better, because January is very cold. For details, see Solang Nullah in the Manali section later in this chapter. Skiing in summer (April to June) is possible on virgin snow (experienced skiers only) at the Rohtang La, north of Manali. North Face offers skiing day trips to Mahri, near the pass, for around Rs 1000. For about US$900 a day you can try heli-skiing on any of the deep snowfields around the region. Himalayan Journeys can organise this if you have the money and experience.

lovely forested park, known as the Dhungri Van Vihar. Erected in 1553, the temple is dedicated to the goddess Hadimba and features intricate wooden carvings of dancers and characters from various Hindu stories; horns of bulls and other animals decorate the walls. Every May, there is a major **festival** at the temple, when sacrifices are carried out in honour of Hadimba.

Across the road, near the Utopia complex is an **ancient pine tree** venerated as a shrine to local deity Ghatotakach. Villagers make offerings of knives here as thanks for answered prayers. The entrance to the park is 20-minute walk or a five-minute taxi or autorickshaw ride (Rs 20).

Utopia Complex

The Utopia Complex (☎ 53846) is a new leisure centre near the Dhungri Temple, which offers a fairly pedestrian vision of utopia in the form of snooker tables, steam baths, a gymnasium (Rs 25 per session) and boardgames, plus a restaurant and small museum.

The **Handicraft Museum** in the complex is worth a quick visit. The curator has spent years collecting folk art and handicrafts from surrounding villages to protect the traditions of the Kullu Valley. There's a reasonable entry fee of Rs 5.

Gompas

Built by Tibetan refugees in the late 1960s, the **Gadhan Thekchokling Gompa** has some brightly coloured frescoes and a central statue of Sakyamuni Buddha and dominates the Tibetan area at the bottom of The Mall. It's open 6 am to 7 pm and there's a Rs 2 charge for photography.

Nearby and also worth a quick look is the modern **Himalayan Nyingmapa Gompa**.

Old Manali

The original settlement of Manali is about 2.5km north-west of 'new' Manali. It's a pleasant (but rapidly developing) area of old guesthouses and orchards. The modern but tasteful **Manu Maharishi Temple** is built on the site where Manu meditated after he arrived in the area. Old Manali is uphill from The Mall on the far side of the Manalsu Nala. Follow the road to the left at the top of The Mall.

HPTDC Club House

Over the bridge to Old Manali, this place offers one-day temporary membership (Rs 5), allowing access to the nice, but pricey, bar and restaurant, and a library where you can read (but not borrow) English-language books. Table tennis and snooker can be played for a few extra rupees.

Organised Tours

Tours are organised by the HPTDC Tourism Marketing Office and local private bus companies (see Bus under Getting There & Away later in this section). They may be touristy, but are often the cheapest and easiest way to visit local places, especially if you're on your own and you can't share the cost of a taxi.

The HPTDC offers the following tours:

- Rohtang La (3978m), Nehru Kund (lake), Kothi, Rahala Falls and Marrhi (Rs 172)
- Parvati Valley, Vaishno Temple and Manikaran (Rs 197)
- Solang Nullah and Naggar Castle (high season only; Rs 146)

Private travel agents and taxis offer the same tours plus a trip to Naggar Castle, Roerich Gallery and the Jagatsukh temples (Rs 400).

Places to Stay

Prices listed in hotel receptions are the authorised *maximum* prices and most places will quickly offer a 'low-season discount' of up to 50% – even during high season if things are quiet. The high season is from May to July and from mid-December to mid-January, though some places also up their rates in October. Prices quoted are for the high season.

Note that few hotels in Manali have heating or insulation. Even in some mid-range places, be prepared to dive under four or five blankets to stay warm. All places in this section have private bathrooms unless otherwise stated.

Places to Stay – Budget

While there aren't many cheap places in Manali itself, budget accommodation can be easily found in the nearby villages of Old Manali, Vashisht (see under Around Manali later in this section) and Dhungri.

Manali The ***Su-Khiran Guest House*** *(☎ 52178)* behind The Mall is one of the best-value places in Manali. Basic doubles are Rs 125 with shared bathroom; dorms are Rs 25.

Hotel Renuka *(☎ 53294)* is central but can be noisy and rooms are a little pricey at Rs 450 with hot water and balcony.

Mount View Hotel (☎ 52465), in Model Town, has decent doubles with TV for around Rs 450, plus good low-season discounts and recommended food.

Samrat Hotel *(☎ 52356)*, on the main highway past the Hotel Ibex, is slightly gloomy but has good-value doubles in low season from Rs 250 (Rs 330 in high season).

Hotel Snow Drop *(☎ 52883)* in the Tibetan area, offers clean, airy rooms from Rs 150 to 350, depending on the season.

Potala Hotel *(☎ 52950)*, nearby, has clean and comfortable rooms for Rs 425 to 625 (Rs 250 to 300 in low season).

Sunflower *(☎ 52419)* is cheaper, doubles are Rs 275 and Rs 450, and big triples start at Rs 325. All rooms have TV. Low-season rates drop to a very reasonable Rs 100.

Uphill from the turn-off to Old Manali are several reasonable places. ***Hotel Chetna*** *(☎ 52245)* and ***Hotel Kalpana*** *(☎ 52413)* both have lovely views of the pine forest and rooms which start at Rs 450 (Rs 200 in the low season).

Old Manali This overgrown village offers numerous hotels firmly aimed at backpackers, but it's not as atmospheric as nearby Vashisht. Most places are downhill from the old village on the road to new Manali. Most of Old Manali closes down for the winter.

Tourist Nest *(☎ 56520)*, in the village itself, is new with clean bright doubles with hot water for Rs 200 to 300. There's a travel agent; the new wing should be finished by the time you read this.

The family-run ***Dragon Guest House*** *(☎ 52790)*, opposite, is a thriving concern with big, modern rooms for Rs 250 and Rs 300 fronting onto an orchard.

Down a path behind the Tourist Nest, the old wooden ***Veer Paying Guest House*** and the concrete ***Kishoor Guest House*** have nice settings and charge about Rs 150 for clean rooms.

Farther uphill, the ***Diplomat Guest House*** and ***Krishna Guest House*** are modern buildings with rooms for around Rs 200 a double.

Various ***village houses*** offer basic rooms for Rs 50 – ask around the village when you arrive.

Downhill, in a less appealing area by the bridge and the HPTDC Club House are several basic guesthouses including the ***Rising Moon*** (☎ 52731), ***Riverside***, ***Mamta Paying Guest House*** and ***Jungle Bungalow***, all of which have doubles for about Rs 150 and fairly poor travellers cafes. Slightly posher places include the ***Hotel Riverbank*** (☎ 53004), ***Hotel Him View*** (☎ 53074) and the ***Hema Guest House*** (☎ 52285), with rooms from around Rs 200 to 400.

Dhungri The village of Dhungri attracts a certain kind of traveller, but there's not much reason to be here unless you have a special herbal interest in the area. Old village family homes have been converted to guesthouses with cheap ultrabasic rooms and shared bathroom, and the owners walk around the place soliciting for guests.

Places include the ***Freedom Paying Guest House*** *(☎ 53673)* with rooms for Rs 50 and ***Autoland*** *(☎ 53673)* with OK rooms for Rs 150. Villagers offer ***rooms*** for Rs 50.

Places to Stay – Mid-Range

A lot of the mid-range places are new concrete hotels all lined up in the charmless, uninspiring 'suburb' called Model Town, one block west of The Mall. Each hotel offers almost identical facilities – usually including TV and private bathroom with hot water – for an almost identical price of around Rs 450 for a double (high season) and Rs 250 (low season). Some of the better hotels (close to the post office) are: ***Mona Lisa*** *(☎ 52447)*,

HIMACHAL PRADESH

Hotel Shishar *(☎ 52745)*, ***Lhasa Hotel*** *(☎ 52134)*, ***Premier Hotel*** *(☎ 52473)* and ***Hotel Diamond*** *(☎ 53825)* the latter; also rents motorcycles.

There are some much more attractive options on the main road between Manali and Old Manali, catering mainly for the Indian family and honeymoon market. Quite a few are housed in old colonial houses and offer TV, hot showers, gardens and (a rare luxury!) fireplaces.

John Banon's Hotel *(☎ 52335)* is an old Raj-era building with clean, large old-fashioned rooms for Rs 550 a double.

Just uphill, ***Pinewood Hotel*** *(☎ 52118)* is another old colonial-style place run by the Banon family. Doubles in this rambling building cost Rs 650.

Across the road, the ***Sunshine Guest House*** *(☎ 52320)* is yet another old-style place with a nice lawn and good rooms with fireplace from Rs 350 to 600.

Farther uphill is the excellent ***Hotel Mayflower*** *(☎ 52104, fax 53923)*, a brand-new hotel with lovely pine-furnished rooms for Rs 600 to 700, and great suites for Rs 1400.

HPTDC runs several places. Bookings can be arranged at the HPTDC Tourism Marketing Office on The Mall. ***Hotel Beas*** *(☎ 52832)*, on the eastern side of The Mall, has great views of the river, and rooms from Rs 250 to 650. ***Hotel Rohtang Manalsu*** *(☎ 52332)*, on the road to the Dhungri Temple, is a pleasant place with good views across the valley. Doubles cost Rs 500, or Rs 700 in the new block.

At the upper end of the price bracket are the ***Hotel Ibex*** *(☎ 52480)* and ***Hotel Snow View*** *(☎ 52684)*, both at the southern end of The Mall. Good rooms cost around Rs 900 in the high season and Rs 450 at other times.

Places to Stay – Top End

Top-end prices in Manali won't necessarily get you top-end service, but it will guarantee you central heating and working geysers.

The ***HPTDC Hotel Kunzam*** *(☎ 53197)*, at the top of The Mall, has good rooms from Rs 1000 to 1600 (30% less in low season).

Hotel Shrinagar Regency *(☎ 52251)*, en route to Dhungri village, is more central and has doubles from Rs 1650.

On the road to Old Manali is the splendid ***Banon Resorts*** *(☎ 53026, fax 52378)* with luxurious rooms, a plush restaurant, a terrace cafe and a bar. Rates start at Rs 1400 (Rs 900 in the low season).

Holiday Inn *(☎ 52262, fax 52263)* has all the luxury you would expect, but is about 2km south of town. Rooms cost from Rs 2650, including meals.

Hotel Manali Ashok *(☎ 52331, fax 53108)*, just south of Manali on the left bank of the Beas, has luxurious rooms with views from Rs 1700 to 2150.

Halfway to Solang Nullah, the excellent ***Whispering Rocks*** *(☎ 56680, fax 56622)* has a splendidly isolated location, attractive gardens, a restaurant and an outdoor swimming pool. Well-appointed rooms range from Rs 1200 to 2000.

Places to Eat

Manali The ***Sa-Ba*** in Nehru Park, at the top of The Mall, has good Western food, such as hamburgers, pizzas (from Rs 35) and milkshakes.

HPTDC has a complex right near the bridge containing the ***Juniper*** and ***Chandertal*** restaurants. Each offers a vast selection of dishes served in a nice setting; prices start at Rs 65 for mains.

Sher-e-Punjab, on The Mall, has a sterile setting, but its Indian food (as well as pizza and pasta) is recommended. There's another (unassociated) restaurant with the same name just down the road, but it's often empty.

Gozy Restaurant, at the southern end of The Mall, is where many people end up at the end of an evening. There's a great selection of authentic Punjabi and Gujarati food at reasonable prices and good service. A meal shouldn't cost more than Rs 120.

Swamiji's Madras Cafe, farther along The Mall, has large thalis for Rs 35. The nearby ***Sangam*** is also worth a try.

Mount View Restaurant and ***Chopsticks***, next door, are cosy, friendly places where you can order authentic Chinese food, Tibetan momos or Japanese sukiyaki (thinly sliced meat) from Rs 45.

The ***Tibetan Food Corner***, above the Delightful Things Tibetan souvenir shop, also does good momos.

Mona Lisa, opposite the bus station, is another congenial place that serves Indian and Western food at reasonable prices, but it closes in winter.

The ***Himalaya*** and ***Kamal*** dhabas offer good-value Indian food.

Johnson's Cafe is farther uphill and a bit more upmarket. The pleasant open-air garden cafe serves good pasta and pizza (Rs 100), excellent desserts (creme caramel!) and cold beer.

Phuntsok Coffee House, at the junction of the Naggar Hwy and the road to Vashisht, is a Tibetan-run place that serves up great traveller-oriented breakfasts and the standard Tibetan fare.

Old Manali There are various traveller-oriented options up in Old Manali, uphill from most of the places to stay. Most food caters to the visiting crowds, so there's plenty of Italian and Israeli food, but not much Indian fare. Few places charge more than Rs 65 for a dish.

Moon Dance Garden, just over the bridge, is a typical laid-back, outdoor place with one of the many local 'German bakeries'.

Ish Cafe, farther up, is deservedly popular for its laid-back atmosphere and good, if Westernised, food. Close to Ish is the ***Little Tibet Cafe***, which serves wholesome, cheap Tibetan food.

Also nearby, the ***Shiva Garden Cafe*** has good Italian food, and serves Israeli cuisine. A bit farther up, the ***Mount View Cafe*** is worth a visit for its wonderful seclusion.

Back by the bridge, the ***Tibet Kitchen*** is the best bet, with an excellent range of hearty Tibetan noodles and Western delicacies. The funky ***River Music Cafe*** has good music and food.

Shopping

The shawl industry that has been building up all along the Kullu Valley comes to a head in Manali, with literally dozens of shawl emporiums vying for your custom. Most of the shops along the mall have moved to a fixed-price system (some even proudly announce 'No Discount!'), which certainly provides for a more relaxing shopping experience, though you may pay slightly more. You can always take your chances at the numerous market stalls, where you may get a bargain. A good place to start your search is Bhuttico, with outlets on The Mall and near Himalayan Adventures, which employs women from mountain villages and won't try to sell you wool as pashmina. The Himachal Emporium farther north also and offers high quality at reasonable prices.

The main market areas are the Underground Market, under the Ibex Hotel, and the NAC Market behind the bus stand. See the boxed text 'Shopping for Shawls' in the Kullu section earlier in this chapter for more information on what to look for in a shawl.

There are also a few Tibetan refugee shops selling jewellery and other Tibetan handicrafts. The Charitrust Tibetan Handicraft Emporium on The Mall, and Delightful Things on the road behind the post office both sell good quality thangkas and other crafts. The Tibetan Market, spread around the back of the Hotel Ibex, sells mainly modern knick-knacks.

Getting There & Away

Air Kullu/Manali airport is actually 52km south of Manali and 10km south of Kullu in Bhuntar. See Getting There & Away under Kullu in the previous section for details on flights. You can make bookings at the Jagson Airlines office (☎ 52843) in the north of Manali new town (Visa cards accepted), and at most travel agencies. Ambassador Travels (☎ 52110), at the northern end of The Mall, is the agent for Indian Airlines.

Bus At the main bus stand are two booths, open 9 am to noon and 2 to 5 pm, which provide computerised booking services. You can book a ticket up to a month in advance, which is a good idea on the popular routes to Leh, Dharamsala and Delhi.

Long-distance bus companies from Manali (and local sightseeing tour operators) are:

Harison Travels (☎ 53319) The Mall
Ibex Travels (☎ 53180) Hotel Ibex, The Mall
Swagtam Tours (☎ 52390) Mission Rd

Leh Several daily deluxe and public buses connect Manali with Leh from about June to mid-September – private buses run a few weeks later according to the weather and demand. This long, truly spectacular ride takes two days, with a stopover in a tent.

HPTDC runs a daily bus (originating in Delhi) for Rs 1100, including an overnight camp at Sarchu, dinner and breakfast. Private agencies charge around Rs 1000 without food or accommodation and buses depart at 5 am. The daily public bus leaves Manali at noon and costs Rs 405, with an overnight stop at Keylong. Take some food, water and warm clothes and try not to sit at the back of the bus.

For details about the route, see Leh to Manali in the Ladakh & Zanskar chapter.

Spiti, Lahaul & Kinnaur All roads between Manali and Spiti cross over high mountain passes and are only open from April to October. In the high season, there are regular buses to Keylong (Rs 72, six hours) between 4.30 am and 3 pm. For Spiti catch the 4.30 am departure to Tabo (Rs 160, 15 hours) or the 6 am bus to Kaza (Rs 135, 12 hours).

Kullu & Parvati Valleys Public buses shuttle between Manali and Kullu town (Rs 24, 1½ hours) every 30 minutes, continuing on to Mandi (Rs 71, four hours). All these buses pass close to the airport in Bhuntar (Rs 31). To Naggar (Rs 11, one hour) there are six daily buses from Manali between 7 am and 5.30 pm.

For the Parvati Valley, you'll have to take a bus to Bhuntar (Kullu buses leave Manali every 15 minutes and pass through Bhuntar), from where there are frequent connections uphill until 6 pm.

Other Destinations To Delhi (16 hours), there is one public 'deluxe' bus at 5 pm (Rs 492) and at least six ordinary buses (Rs 305). Considering the length of the journey, it's probably worth splashing out for a private 'two-by-two' bus on this route. The same luxury coaches can be booked through travel agencies in Paharganj in Delhi, but make sure you get a two-by-two bus when you book; more than a few travellers have paid luxury prices only to be dumped on a very ordinary village bus.

HPTDC has one overnight bus to Delhi at 5 pm (Rs 521) or you can book a trip with any of the private bus companies in town for Rs 350 to 450. All buses leave around 3.30 pm and pass through Chandigarh (Rs 300, 10 hours).

In the high season, there are also private and HPTDC buses to Shimla (Rs 250 to 275, 10 hours) and Dharamsala (Rs 250 to 275, 10 hours) at around 7 pm.

Public buses to Dharamsala (Rs 157 day, Rs 190 night) leave at 8 and 9 am and 6 pm. There are also five daily buses to Shimla (Rs 160). For Uttaranchal, there are buses to Haridwar (Rs 280, 16 hours) at 10 am and 12.40 pm and Dehra Dun (Rs 305, 15 hours) at 5.15 pm.

Taxi Long-distance taxis are available from the two Him-Aanchal Taxi Operators' Union stands (☎ 52120) on The Mall. A one-way/return taxi from Manali to Kullu is Rs 550/700 (Rs 800 returning via Naggar). One way/return to Naggar is Rs 300/400. Other one-way fares include Bhuntar (Rs 650), Dharamsala (Rs 2500) and Leh (Rs 13,000 for three days, two nights).

Getting Around

Motorcycle There are several places that hire motorcycles in Old Manali and Vashisht. Nirvana Travels (☎ 53222), in north Manali, hires Enfields and smaller Japanese bikes for Rs 300 per 24 hours, including third-party insurance. The Hotel Diamond also charges Rs 300 per day. For bike repairs or a tune-up before heading up to Leh, try Inder Motors in Manali's Tibetan area or The Enfield Club by the turn-off to Vashisht.

Autorickshaw Known locally as three-wheelers, these can take you, and your heavy luggage, to Dhungri, Old Manali and Vashisht, but not much farther, for a negotiable Rs 30 to 60.

AROUND MANALI

Vashisht

Vashisht is a lovely little village, about 4km by road up the hillside from The Mall, with plenty of old stone houses and some ancient temples, but it's definitely a 'scene'.

Vashisht remains a very popular place for long-term budget travellers attracted by its cheap facilities, great setting and the herbal attractions of the hills.

Orientation & Information Buses and taxis stop in the centre of the village near Super Bake, from where pedestrian-only footpaths radiate through the village. The path uphill to the right leads to the Vashisht Temple, public baths, the Rainbow Restaurant and the New Dharma, Amrit and Kalptaru guesthouses. The other guesthouses are located in the lower village, in the vicinity of the two-storey Bhimakali-style temple.

Try the Travel Assistance Centre or the World Peace Cafe for Internet access.

Travel agents by the bus stand can book places on luxury buses out of Manali.

Travellers should note that many places to stay and eat are closed in winter.

Things to See & Do Indian pilgrims come to Vashisht to ceremonially bathe in the hot springs at the **Vashisht Temple**, which is sacred to the sage Vashisht Muni. There are several other old temples in the village that are dedicated to the sage and to the god Rama.

The footpath and road to Vashisht go straight past the HPTDC **Vashisht Hot Baths Complex**, open 8 am to 8 pm every day (but often closed by industrial action). A 30-minute soak in the regular baths costs Rs 40 for one person, Rs 60 for two; a splash-out in the deluxe baths costs Rs 80/100 for two people. The common **public baths** (separate areas for men and women) in Vashisht village are free, but don't look very hygienic (open 9 am to 5 pm).

Several video houses screen foreign **movies** for about Rs 10.

Places to Stay Budget places include the ***Dharma*** *(☎ 01902-52354)*, ***Amrit*** and ***Kalptaru*** guesthouses, behind the Vashisht Temple, and the ***Bodh***, ***Negi***, and ***Dolath*** guesthouses, downhill from the bus stand. All offer very similar, no-frills rooms in the heart of the village with shared bathrooms. Rates vary from Rs 50 to 100.

New Dharma *(☎ 01902-52354)*, a big white building on the hilltop, behind the Kalptaru guesthouse, charges Rs 200 for a double with private bathroom.

Downhill, ***Anand Hotel*** *(☎ 01902-54153)* has cleaner, spacious rooms with private bathroom for Rs 100 to 150.

Nearby, the ***Surabhi Guest House & World Peace Cafe*** *(☎ 01902-52796)* is a well-maintained modern building overlooking the valley with rooms for Rs 200 to 350 with bathroom (hot shower). There's an Internet cafe and a good restaurant.

Downhill are the very similar ***Sonan***, ***Prem***, ***Ganga*** and ***Janta*** guesthouses with cafes and rooms for Rs 50 to 80.

Farther towards Manali, ***Hotel Bhrigu*** *(☎ 01902-53414)* has reasonable, slightly pricey rooms starting at Rs 400. ***Hotel Valley View*** *(☎ 01902-53420)* next door, offers good rooms and great views from Rs 200 to 500.

The best option in Vashisht is the lovely ***Sita Cottage*** *(☎ 01902-52164)* near the HTPDC baths, which has good rooms with all mod-cons for Rs 500 upwards, and a very stylish restaurant.

Places to Eat The ***cafe*** at the HPTDC Hot Baths Complex serves hot and cold drinks, and a selection of good Chinese and Indian food.

Rose Garden Inn, over the road, has pricey but delicious Italian and other continental food.

Just uphill the ***restaurant*** at Sita Cottage may be the best in town. ***Basho Restaurant*** at Hotel Bhrigu is also an upmarket choice, with daily specials and good views.

Freedom Cafe, along the road a little, has a great outdoor setting and serves good

HIMACHAL PRADESH

Western breakfasts and Israeli food, though it's a bit more expensive than other options.

Super Bake, in the village centre, serves wonderful baked goodies. At the bus stand, ***Ranu Rooftop Cafe*** and the ***Zodiac Cafe*** are both good places to hang out. Uphill by the town baths is the ***Rainbow Cafe*** with a broad traveller menu.

Getting There & Away Vashisht is connected by a good road, so a three-wheeler can take you there for around Rs 50 (a good idea if you have loads of gear). On foot, it's quicker to take the unmarked trail that begins about 150m past the turn-off to Vashisht and goes all the way to the Hotel Valley View via the HPTDC Hot Baths Complex.

Solang Nullah

Some of Himachal Pradesh's best ski slopes are at Solang Nullah, about 13km northwest of Manali. There are 2.5km of runs, with black, red and blue routes mainly for beginners, but only one 300m ski lift. A longer lift is still in the planning stages. The slopes are a steep climb above the village.

February and March are the best months to ski; January is bitterly cold, and Christmas can be busy with Indian tourists. Don't disregard Solang if it isn't snowing as the area is very pretty in spring and summer and offers great treks.

Skiing Courses Several options for skiing courses exist. Prices quoted are a guide – final prices will depend on group size, type of accommodation and level of service provided. The following companies offer ski-course packages:

Antrek Tours Seven- to 10-day packages, including accommodation, all meals, equipment and instruction, cost around Rs 1500 per day.

Himalayan Adventures A basic seven-day course (minimum five people) costs Rs 6000; a 15-day advanced package costs Rs 12,000, all inclusive.

Himalayan Journeys A week-long course starts at Rs 7000 for small groups; a two-week course costs Rs 14,000. Prices include accommodation and meals in Solang, as well as lessons and equipment.

HPTDC A seven-day skiing package from Manali, including accommodation in Manali, food, lessons and some sightseeing, costs Rs 3900 per person. Some travellers have written complaining about poor tuition and service.

Mountaineering Institute & Allied Sports Basic, intermediate and advanced 15-day courses cost US$220, including equipment, food and dorm accommodation near the slopes, but not transport.

North Face Adventure Tours A week's skiing costs Rs 7770 and a week's snowboarding costs Rs 8880, including accommodation at North Face's Patalsu lodge in Solang. The lodge offers single-day classes for Rs 500 with gear; ski-hire costs Rs 200 (Rs 400 for snowboards).

Places to Stay & Eat By the bus stop, ***Friendship Guest House*** *(☎ 56510)* has large rooms for Rs 300 and smaller rooms with shared bathroom for Rs 250. ***Friendship Fastfood Corner*** serves good food.

Raju Paying Guest House *(☎ 56575)* has large doubles with attractive wood panelling for Rs 200, or four-bed rooms for Rs 300, all with private bathroom.

Downhill is the grey-stone ***Hotel Patalsu Heights*** *(☎ 56509)* with simple rooms for Rs 100/200 (shared/private bathroom), which is home to the North Face ski school and is often booked up with skiers on courses. Farther downhill are the ***Snow Nest Paying Guest House*** and the ***Hotel Iceland*** *(☎ 56508)*, which both offer comfortable rooms with geysers and electric heaters for Rs 250.

All the hotels have dining rooms with cosy fireplaces where you can warm yourself with vegetarian meals and hot cups of chai. The funkiest private restaurant is the brand new ***Snowboard Cafe***, which you'll find by the bus stand.

Getting There & Away Buses leave Manali at 8 am and 2 and 4 pm every day for Solang Nullah (Rs 8). Another option is to take the bus to Palchan, the turn-off to Solang Nullah from the main road, and then walk for about an hour to Solang through gorgeous countryside. Taxis cost Rs 300 one way from Manali. Roads may be blocked by snow in January and February.

Lahaul & Spiti

Lahaul and Spiti, the largest district in Himachal Pradesh, is an area of high mountains and narrow valleys bounded by Ladakh to the north, Tibet to the east, Kinnaur to the south-east and the Kullu Valley to the south. Lahaul and Spiti fall in the rain shadow of the Himalaya, creating a bleak high-altitude desert that inspired Rudyard Kipling to proclaim, 'Surely the gods live here; this is no place for men'.

Centred on Keylong, Lahaul is often regarded as a midway point en route to Leh and the Indus Valley, but there are several ancient gompas in the surrounding hills. To the east, linking Lahaul to Kinnaur, Spiti was only opened to foreign tourists in 1991, and is still regarded as a frontier territory, with basic facilities and limited transport links. Travellers are rewarded for their effort by seeing ancient villages and a spectacular, uncompromising landscape.

Most people in Spiti are Buddhists, and colourful gompas dominate the villages and village life. In Lahaul, about half of the population is Buddhist, while the other half is Hindu, but, as in Kinnaur, it's not unusual to see idols from both religions side by side in temples and homes. Traditionally, polyandry has been common, but this has changed recently.

This region has a paucity of agricultural land, and farms, which are usually inherited by the eldest son, rely solely on natural springs or complicated irrigation systems for crop growth. The main crops are *no* (barley), *do* (wheat), *alu* (potatoes) and hops (Lahaul and Spiti is the only area in India where hops are grown). *Kuth*, a herb reputedly endowed with medicinal powers, is exported to Europe.

The main indigenous language of the area is Bhoti, which is very similar to Tibetan; there are several distinct, but mutually comprehensible, dialects. The very handy word *jule*, which in Ladakhi means hello, goodbye, please and thank you, is also used in Lahaul and Spiti.

Both Lahaul and Spiti are cut off from the Kullu Valley by heavy snow for up to eight months of the year. The Rohtang La to Lahaul is normally closed between mid-November and mid-June and the Kunzum La to Spiti is normally closed from mid-October to mid-July. In theory, the road from the Sutlej Valley to Kaza is open year-round, but landslides and flooding frequently block the route, requiring travellers to trek some of the way. At the time of research, the road had been severely damaged south of Rekong Peo and north of Kharu, requiring travellers to trek 7km in total (until the road is repaired, there is no access to Lahaul and Spiti for motorcycles via this route).

The best time to visit Lahaul is mid-June to late October, and for Spiti it's August to October. Beware of the power of the sun in this region – you can get burnt very easily even on cold days.

History

In the 10th century, upper Lahaul was united with Spiti and Zanskar as part of the vast Guge kingdom of western Tibet. After Ladakh's defeat by the Mongol-Tibetan armies in the 18th century, Lahaul was split into two regions. Upper Lahaul came under the influence of the Kullu raja, while lower Lahaul, across to the district of Pangi, came under the influence of the courts of Chamba. The more geographically isolated Spiti remained part of Ladakh.

In 1847, Kullu and Lahaul came under British administration as a division of the Kangra state; Spiti was added two years later. In reality power rested with the Nonos, hereditary rulers of Spiti, and the region was far too remote for the British to enforce their paper rule.

With the Chinese occupation of Tibet in 1949, the region's cultural links were severed but there has been a resurgence in the cultural and religious life of Spiti following the creation of the Tibetan Government in Exile by the Dalai Lama. Much work has been done to preserve the ancient Buddhist art in the region's gompas, which are now even more priceless since the destruction of Tibetan monasteries during the Cultural Revolution in China. At the same time, improved communications have seen a rapid integration with the rest of India and a tentative entry into the modern world.

Permits

Inner line permits are not necessary for travel from Lahaul to Spiti and you are now permitted to go as far down the valley as Tabo. A permit is only necessary if you're travelling between Tabo and Rekong Peo, the capital of Kinnaur. For more information, see Permits in the Kinnaur section earlier in this chapter.

MANALI TO KEYLONG

Heading north from Manali, buses first cross the **Rohtang La** (3978m), which takes its name from the Tibetan for Pile of Corpses, a reference to the many travellers who have frozen to death here over the centuries. The pass is a popular chai stop for buses and offers wonderful views over the **Sonapani Glacier**, plus the first taste of the Himalayan snows.

About 5km beyond the junction town of **Gramphu**, where the road to Kaza branches east, **Khoksar** is a bleak, cold spot with a police checkpoint where you'll need to get out and sign the register. Single women travellers have reported harassment here so be on your toes, especially at night or if you smell alcohol on anyone's breath.

The road continues on to Gondhla, site of the seven-storey **castle** of the Thakur of Gondhla and the starting point for a visit to the **Guru Ghantal Gompa** at the village of Tupchiling, a steep 4km away. Founded about 800 years ago, but repaired extensively about 30 years ago, the gompa is linked to the one at Stakna, in Ladakh, and belongs to the Drukpa order. You can also trek to Tupchiling from **Tandi**, where the Bhaga and Chandra Rivers join to form the Chenab.

KEYLONG

☎ 019002 • pop 1797 • elevation 3350m

In the fertile Bhaga Valley, Keylong, the capital of the region of Lahaul and Spiti, is a reasonable place to break the journey from Manali to Leh (although you're just out of Manali), or to base yourself for day trips to nearby gompas.

The bus station is on the main Manali to Leh road, from where it's a short walk down a series of steps to the town itself. There's a telegraph office in the north of town but nowhere to change money. Drilbu Adventures (☎ 22207), next to the Gyespa Hotel, is a new travel agency and can help arrange porters and transport to Leh.

Places to Stay & Eat

***Lamayuru Hotel** (☎ 22279)* is a good budget bet; spacious, but damp rooms with bathroom and hot water are Rs 100.

***Gyespa Hotel** (☎ 22207)* has dreary singles/doubles for Rs 100/150 and is an emergency option only. However, it has a good restaurant.

Hotel Dubchen Keylong is better, with doubles starting at Rs 200.

***Hotel Snowland** (☎ 22219)*, a two-minute walk uphill from the Lamayuru, has comfortable rooms with nice bathrooms from Rs 300 to 500.

The ***HPTDC Tourist Bungalow** (☎ 22247)* has a few overpriced doubles at Rs 350, and some dorm beds (six in a room) for Rs 50.

***Hotel Dekyid** (☎ 22217)* and ***Tashi Deleg** (☎ 22450)* are mid-range places offering clean rooms with private bathroom for around Rs 300. Tashi Deleg has a good restaurant.

About 18km north of Keylong in the village of Jispa is the posh ***Hotel Ibex-Jispa** (☎ 019003-33204)* with luxury rooms from Rs 800 to 1200, plus a dorm for Rs 100.

Getting There & Away

Six daily buses travel between Keylong and Manali (Rs 72, six hours); book your ticket in advance at the ticket office. To Kaza (Rs 115) there's a direct bus at 6 am; otherwise change at Gramphu (Rs 30).

From 15 July to 15 September the daily, long-distance deluxe HPTDC buses between Leh and Manali stop in Keylong, but it's very hard to get a confirmed seat. You may have to book the ticket from Manali to Leh and pay the full fare (about Rs 1000). The public bus leaves Keylong at 4 am. Plenty of trucks ply the busy road and offer a good alternative. (See Leh to Manali in the Ladakh & Zanskar chapter for more details.)

AROUND KEYLONG

Khardong Gompa

The 900-year-old gompa at Khardong, formerly a capital of Lahaul, lies directly across the Bhaga Valley from Keylong. This Drukpa Kagyud monastery is the largest in the area with about 30 lamas and *chomos* (nuns). There are excellent frescoes, but you'll have to track down a nun to open the doors for you. The prayer wheel here is reputed to contain one million strips of paper bearing the mantra: 'Om mani padme hum'.

To get to the monastery, head through the bazaar, follow the stepped path down to the hospital and take the bridge over the Bhaga River, from where it's 4km up to Khardong.

Shashur Gompa

Three kilometres from Keylong is the Shashur Gompa. Dedicated to the Zanskari lama Deva Gyatsho, it was built in the 16th century and is of the Gelukpa order. The 5m **thangka** (Tibetan cloth painting) is famous in the region. Look out for the statue of Deva Gyatsho, which is reputed to contain the heart of the lama, which refused to burn when he was cremated. The annual **Chaam Festival**, held every June/July (depending on the Tibetan calendar) is renowned for the mask dances performed by the lamas.

Pattan Valley

Very few tourists pass through the secluded western reaches of the Chenab or Pattan Valley. However, the town of **Udaipur**, 45km north-west of Keylong, is a growing destination for treks across the Pir Panjal from the Chamba Valley. Udaipur is home to the 15th-century Markula Devi temple, but most trekkers head straight for the relative comfort of Keylong.

About 16km south of Udaipur and 4km from the highway is the **Temple of Triloknath**, which was originally Hindu and became a Buddhist shrine in the days of Ashoka, but is now sacred to both religions. Thousands of pilgrims flock here every August for the three-day **Pauri Festival**. Several buses a day run up the valley from Keylong to Udaipur, passing the turn-off to Triloknath.

KEYLONG TO KAZA

There are several interesting detours between Keylong and Kaza. About 17km east of the Gramphu junction, the village of **Chatru** is the starting or finishing point for treks over the Hamta La (4268m) to Manali. From **Batal**, 24km farther on, you can trek up to the huge **Bara Shigri** (Big Glacier), which is one of the longest in the world at 10km long by 1km wide.

Just beyond here, the road switches back over the **Kunzam La** (closed from October to July) where everyone piles off the bus to do a kora of the flag-draped Geypan Temple. A path runs 9km north from the pass to the hauntingly beautiful **Chandratal** (Moon Lake), set at 4250m, and continues on to the Baralacha La (4830m) on the road to Leh.

About 60km short of Kaza is the pretty village of **Losar**, at 4079m, which has a couple of cheap guesthouses and a modern but tasteful gompa.

KAZA

☎ 01906 • elevation 3640m

The low-rise mountain town of Kaza is the administrative centre and transport hub of Spiti subdistrict, and is surrounded by inspirational scenery. Kaza's 'old town', around the new bus stand, is a maze of little shops, hotels and whitewashed houses. The 'new town', across the creek, is a collection of tin-roofed government buildings, including the SDM office (look for the Indian flag). There are one or two photo shops in Kaza who should be able to rustle up some passport photos for the inner line permit application. The State Bank of India doesn't change money, though some shopkeepers might exchange small-denomination US dollar notes. It's an easy-going place in which to spend a few days resting from an arduous bus trip, visiting some stunning monasteries or waiting for your permit if you're heading on to Kinnaur.

About 13km east of Kaza and 7km from Gete (which, at 4270m, may actually be the highest village in the world), is the secluded

Thang Yud Gompa, which belongs to the Sakyapa order and can be reached by a steep three-hour trek.

Places to Stay & Eat

Mahabauda Guest House, on the main road right up at the top end of the old town, is a family-run place offering cosy rooms with share bathroom for Rs 150. ***Snow Lion Hotel and Restaurant***, next door, is also friendly and good value.

Travellers have recommended the ***Hotel Snow View*** and ***Hotel Moonlight***, which both offer doubles from Rs 100 to 250.

The accommodating ***Milaraepa Guesthouse***, across the creek, has good-value rooms with clean sheets for Rs 175.

Sakya's Abode (☎ *22254*), next door, is a favourite of tour groups and has a lovely garden. Good rooms cost from Rs 250 to 500, while gloomy singles cost Rs 100. It has a dining hall serving good Spitian food.

The ***HPTDC Tourist Lodge***, in the new town, isn't a bad choice, with five comfortable rooms with private bathroom and hot water for Rs 400.

Layul Cafe serves huge bowls of excellent *kiyu* (square noodles, potato, tomato and onion stew). Other places for food include the Tibetan-style ***Himalaya Hotel*** and ***Il Pomo d'Oro***, run by an Italian expat and serving good, but pricey Italian food.

Getting There & Away

The new bus stand is on the southern edge of town. A bus to Rekong Peo (Rs 105, 12 hours) leaves Kaza at 7 am. There are one or two daily buses both to/from Manali (Rs 100, 12 hours) around 6 am and one to Kullu (Rs 145) at about 4.30 am. There are also irregular buses between Kaza and Keylong (Rs 115, eight hours); alternatively, take a Manali-bound bus to Gramphu (Rs 85) and change there. For Tabo (Rs 30, two hours) take any east-bound bus.

There's an informal taxi stand in front of the Zambala Guest House, but minivans also hang around the old town centre. Fares are high because of the lack of competition and high petrol transportation costs. A taxi to Manali costs a pricey Rs 4000.

AROUND KAZA

Ki Gompa & Kibber

Ki (pronounced 'key'), the oldest and largest gompa in Spiti, is in a spectacular location (4116m) 14km from Kaza and surrounded by high-altitude desert. It was built by the famous Tibetan translator, Ringchen Zangpo, and belongs to the Gelukpa order. The gompa was invaded three times in the 19th century by Ladakhis, Dogras and Sikhs, and later partially destroyed by an earthquake in 1975, but a priceless collection of ancient thangkas has survived these various assaults. No photos are allowed inside the gompa. While you're here, you may hear the deep bass tones of the 3m-long monastery horns that used to warn of impending danger.

Repairing the damage caused by the 1975 earthquake, the restoration of the gompa was completed in 2000, just in time for the visit of the Dalai Lama, who performed an auspicious *kaalchakra* (wheel of time) ritual here, intended to promote harmony throughout the world. Ki has a **Chaam Festival** in June/July, and one of the most popular Losar Festivals in February/March. Also here is the **reliquary chorten** of Lotsawa Rinpoche, the reincarnation of Ringchen Zangpo.

About 11km from Ki village is the small village of **Kibber**, also known as Khyipur. Kibber was once part of the overland salt trade, and has a dramatic, if desolate location. At 4205m, Kibber used to claim to be the highest village in the world, but now only claims to be the highest village in the world with a motorable road and electricity. The **Ladarcha Festival**, held near Kibber each July, attracts Buddhists from all over the region.

Places to Stay & Eat It is normally possible to stay at Ki Gompa for a donation, otherwise the friendly ***Samdup Tashi Khangsar Hotel & Restaurant*** in Ki village has nice rooms for around Rs 50.

Kibber has three small guesthouses. ***Sargaung Guest House*** and ***Hotel Rainbow*** rent out no-frills rooms for Rs 50 and offer basic food. ***Resang Hotel & Restaurant***, at the entrance to the village, has carpeted rooms with bathroom for Rs 150.

Getting There & Away In summer, a bus leaves Kaza every day at 2 pm for Ki and Kibber (Rs 10). This will allow you time to see Ki Gompa while the bus continues on to Kibber, but you won't be able to see both Ki and Kibber in one day. A return taxi from Kaza to Ki will cost about Rs 350. If you want to combine both Ki and Kibber, a taxi will charge about Rs 400/500 one way/return.

Some travellers have attempted to walk to both Ki and Kibber from Kaza in one day, but it is a very long walk (about 22km from Kaza to Kibber). Perhaps a better option is to get the bus to Kibber, walk down to Ki and stay the night there.

Dhankar Gompa

Built nearly 1000 years ago, Dhankar Gompa has a spectacular rocky setting. Once the site of the capital of Spiti, and then a jail, the gompa still has some interesting sculptures and frescoes. Approach the monks at the new gompa below Dhankar for a guide to the old monastery. Herbs growing here are claimed to cure lung and heart complaints. Dhankar holds a **Chaam Festival** in November. A testing 15km trek from Dhankar will take you to **Lhalung Gompa**, which is over 1000-years-old and has some impressive woodcarvings.

From Kaza to Dhankar, take any bus headed down the valley and get off just before the village of Sichling, from where there is a steep 8km walk (including an altitude increase of about 600m). Jeeps may occasionally run up here from Sichling. A return taxi from Kaza to Dhankar Gompa costs Rs 800.

Pin Valley National Park

The Pin Valley, south of Dhankar, has been declared a national park and is famous for its wildlife – tourist agencies refer to it as the 'land of ibex and snow leopard' – but the animals here are *very* elusive. You stand the best chance of seeing ibex from October to December, when the animals gather for the annual mating rut. Your chances of seeing a snow leopard are virtually nil.

This beautiful valley is the only area in Spiti in which Nyingmapa Buddhism is practiced. The most important gompa in the valley is the 600-year-old **Kungri Gompa**, 2km off the main road near Gulling. With a guide and a vast amount of energy, it's possible to trek from the Pin Valley all the way to the Parvati Valley via the Pin Parvati La (5319m).

This is trekking and camping country. Accommodation is limited to the ***Hotel Himalaya*** at Gulling (Rs 120) and the ***Ibex*** and ***Narzang*** guesthouses at Sagnam (Rs 50). Sangam is the best starting point for treks and guesthouse owners here should be able to fix you up with a guide.

Public transport goes only to Mikkim, though a road to Mud has been under construction for years. There's a single morning bus from Kaza to Mikkim (Rs 25) at around 5 am. If you're coming from the east, wait for it at Attargo, at the junction with the main road just west of Dhankar. A one-way taxi from Kaza to Mikkim costs Rs 800.

Tabo Gompa

Tabo Gompa is one of the most important monasteries in the Tibetan Buddhist world, and is planned as the place where the current Dalai Lama will retire. It was built in AD 996 by the Great Translator, Ringchen Zangpo, who brought artists from Kashmir to decorate the gompa. Tabo celebrated its 1000-year anniversary in 1996. Along with Alchi in Ladakh and Tholing in western Tibet, Tabo has some of the best preserved Indo-Tibetan art in the world (most examples in Tibet having been destroyed during the Cultural Revolution).

The nine temples in the complex (collectively known as the *choskhor*) are all at ground level and date from the 10th to the 16th centuries. The main assembly hall of the **Tsuglhakhang Tsuglha** is surrounded by 33 raised Bodhisattva statues, which form a 3D mandala, and houses a four-sided statue of Sarvarvid Vairocana, one of the five Dhyani Buddhas.

To the left of the Tsuglhakhang is the **Lhakang Chenmo**, featuring a central Sakyamuni Buddha and eight Medicine Buddhas. Farther left is the **Serkhang** (Golden Chapel), with several statues of Tibetan gods. The statue of Tara is particularly beautiful, showing the same fluid lines and coloured *dhoti* (loincloth) seen in Ladakh's Alchi Gompa.

Around the back of the main complex is the **Kyil Khor** (Mystic Mandala Temple), with some beautiful but faded mandalas. The last two chapels to the north are the **Dromton Lhakhang**, particularly notable for its Kashmiri-influenced wooden door frame and the **Maitreya Chapel**, with a 6m statue of Maitreya (Jampa in Tibetan).

On the other side of the road, opposite Tabo village, there are some **caves** known locally as Pho Gompa, with some faded ancient murals – bring a torch. Photography is prohibited inside the temples.

The excellent **library** in the monastery guesthouse, open to all, is an excellent place to learn about Tibetan Buddhism. There is also a **thangka painting school** nearby, founded by the Dalai Lama. The impressive **Chaam Festival** in October is known for its mask dances.

Places to Stay & Eat The ***gompa guesthouse*** has good rooms with bathrooms around a central atrium for Rs 200. If they aren't being used by monks, dorms may be available for around Rs 50.

Himalayan Ajanta Hotel has peaceful, carpeted rooms for Rs 100 to 150.

Another possibility is the ***Forest Rest House***, which must be reserved at the DFO in Keylong (☎ 01902-22235).

The best food is at the ***Tenzin Restaurant*** and ***Millennium Monastery Restaurant*** at the back of the gompa guesthouse.

Getting There & Away From Kaza to Tabo (Rs 35, two hours), you should take the 7 am bus, which goes on to Rekong Peo. Buses returning to Kaza pass through Tabo in the afternoon. A bus to Kullu departs around 5.30 am daily and a taxi from Kaza costs Rs 1200.

Jammu & Kashmir

The state known in India as Jammu & Kashmir (J&K) incorporates the regions of Ladakh and Zanskar which are covered in the Ladakh & Zanskar chapter. Srinagar is J&K's summer capital, while the city of Jammu, farther south on the plains, is the winter capital. The regions of Jammu and Kashmir (as distinct from Ladakh) have been subject to political unrest since the late 1980s and the following information is intended as background reading only.

Warning

Lonely Planet strongly advises against travelling to Jammu & Kashmir. While the Indian government has not placed restrictions on visitors, it is foolhardy to go. There are hundreds of militant groups in the state and the risk of being kidnapped is very real – four of the six Westerners taken hostage in the Lidder Valley near Pahalgam in 1995 have never been accounted for. Bomb blasts and shootings are common on the streets of Jammu and Srinagar, and foreigners have been robbed at gunpoint. Buses and trains en route to Jammu have also come under attack and areas near the Pakistani border (eg, near Drass heading towards Kargil) are often shelled.

Ignore the Kashmiri touts in Delhi who will very convincingly tell you that it's perfectly safe to visit. They will have photos and reports from other travellers who have had a 'fantastic' time. Some who have fallen for this (and have usually paid well over the odds for it, too) have found that once in Kashmir the conflict is used to hold them a virtual prisoner with little opportunity to explore independently.

Peace talks continue, but tensions, especially since the nuclear tests of 1998, are still running high. The Indian army's Web site (armyinkashmir.org) gives their perspective on the conflict with biased details of the latest violence; www.kashmirnews.com gives a slightly more balanced view. If you are determined to go, personally check the latest information with your embassy in Delhi beforehand.

Jammu & Kashmir at a Glance

Population: 10.1 million
Area: 222,236 sq km
Capital: Srinagar (summer), Jammu (winter)
Main Languages: Kashmiri, Dogri, Urdu & Ladakhi
When to Go: May to Sept

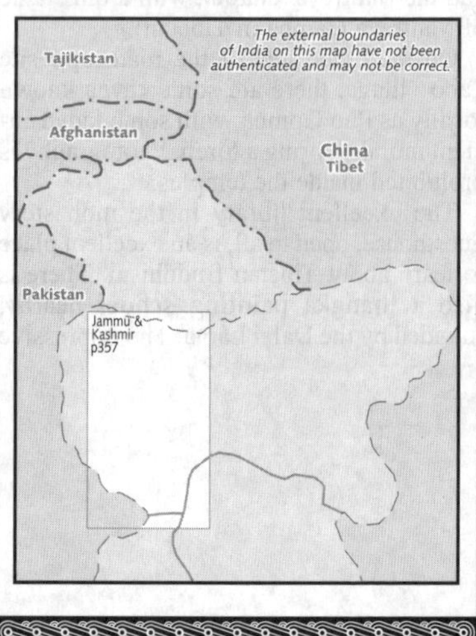

There are strong cultural and geographical contrasts in J&K. The Kashmir Valley, or Vale of Kashmir, is a fertile, verdant region enclosed by the high snowcapped ridges of the Pir Panjal range to the west and south, and the main Himalaya range to the east. Its population is over 60% Muslim (the only Indian state with a Muslim majority), with a rich Islamic history that can be traced back to the 14th century. South of the Kashmir Valley is the region of Jammu. It includes the city of Jammu, situated on the North Indian plains, a short distance from the rolling Siwalik Hills. North of the Siwaliks, the rest of the Jammu region is drained by the Chenab River whose vast catchment area

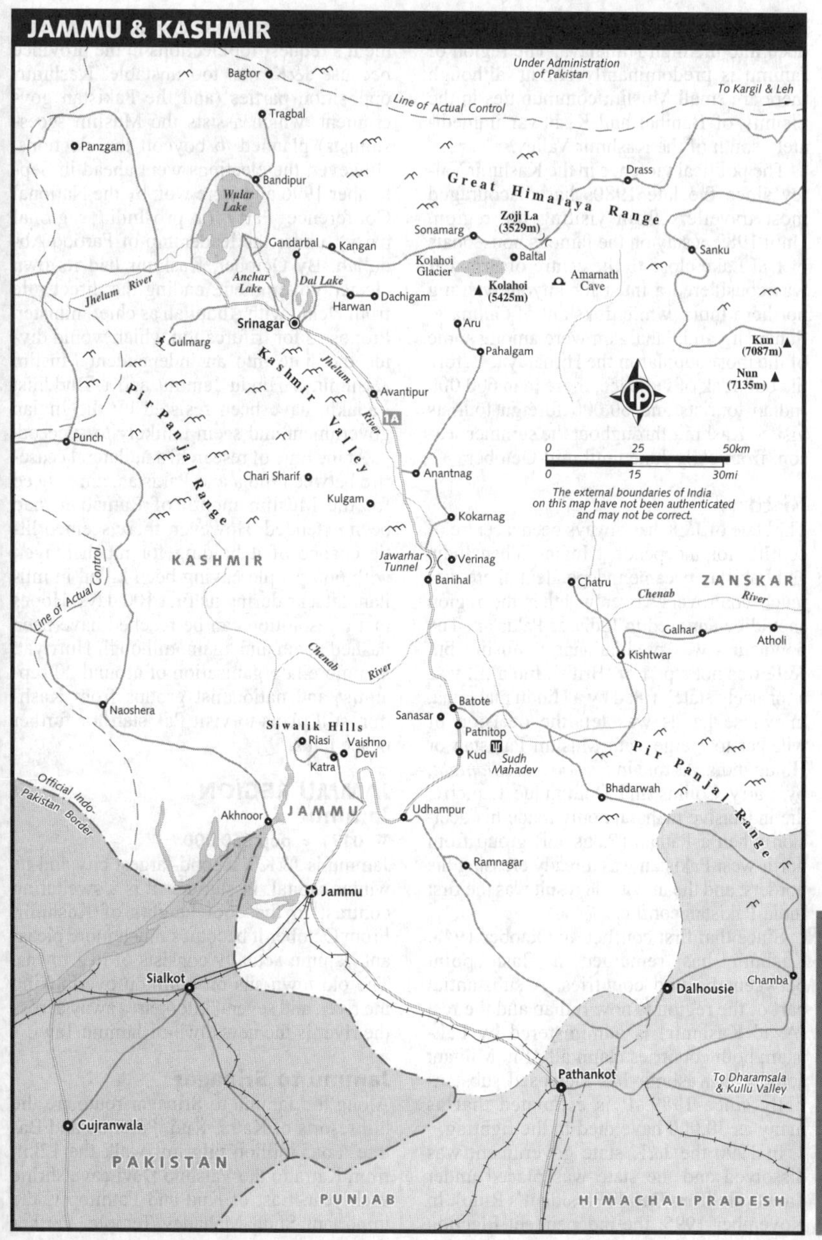
JAMMU & KASHMIR
Under Administration of Pakistan
To Kargil & Leh
Line of Actual Control
Bagtor
Tragbal
Panzgam
Bandipur
Wular Lake
Drass
Great Himalaya Range
Zoji La (3529m)
Sonamarg
Gandarbal
Kangan
Baltal
Sanku
Kolahoi Glacier
Amarnath Cave
Jhelum River
Anchar Lake
Dal Lake
Harwan
Dachigam
Kolahoi (5425m)
Srinagar
Aru
Gulmarg
Pahalgam
Kun (7087m)
Nun (7135m)
Kashmir Valley
Jhelum River
Avantipur
Pir Panjal Range
1A
Punch
Anantnag
Chari Sharif
Kulgam
Kokarnag
0 25 50km
0 15 30mi
The external boundaries of India on this map have not been authenticated and may not be correct.
KASHMIR
Jawarhar Tunnel
Verinag
Banihal
Chatru
ZANSKAR
Chenab River
Line of Actual Control
Galhar
Atholi
Kishtwar
Chenab River
Naoshera
Batote
Sanasar
Patnitop
Siwalik Hills
Riasi
Vaishno Devi
Katra
Kud
Sudh Mahadev
Pir Panjal Range
Official Indo-Pakistan Border
Bhadarwah
Akhnoor
JAMMU
Udhampur
Ramnagar
Jammu
Sialkot
Chamba
Dalhousie
Pathankot
To Dharamsala & Kullu Valley
Gujranwala
PAKISTAN
PUNJAB
HIMACHAL PRADESH

includes several narrow valleys that extend deep into the high Himalaya. The region of Jammu is predominantly Hindu, although there are small Muslim communities in the vicinity of Banihal and Kishtwar immediately south of the Kashmir Valley.

The political violence in the Kashmir Valley since the late 1980s has discouraged most travellers from visiting the region. Until 1989, a stay on the famous houseboats of Dal Lake close to the centre of Srinagar was considered a must for anyone visiting northern India, while treks out of Gulmarg, Sonamarg and Pahalgam were among some of the most popular in the Himalaya. Before the outbreak of violence, more than 600,000 Indian tourists and 60,000 foreign tourists visited Kashmir throughout the summer season, from early June until mid-October.

History

The state of J&K has always been a centre of conflict for independent India. When India and Pakistan became independent, there was much controversy over whether the region should be annexed to India or Pakistan. The population was predominantly Muslim but J&K was not a part of 'British India'. It was a 'princely state', ruled by a Hindu maharaja, in whose hands was left the decision of whether to merge with Muslim Pakistan or Hindu India. As told in *Freedom at Midnight*, by Larry Collins and Dominique Lapierre, the indecisive maharaja only made his decision when a Pathan (Pakistani) group from north-west Pakistan was already crossing his borders, and the inevitable result was the first India-Pakistan conflict.

Since that first conflict, in October 1948, Kashmir has remained a flash point between the two countries. A substantial part of the region is now Indian and the rest (Azad Kashmir) is administered by Pakistan; both countries claim all of it. Militant activity in Kashmir has increased substantially since 1989. It is estimated that as many as 30,000 have died in the fighting.

In 1990 the J&K state government was dissolved and the state was placed under direct rule from Delhi (President's Rule). In November 1995, the independent Election Commission rejected the Indian Government's request for elections in the province because J&K was too unstable. Kashmiri opposition parties (and the Pakistan government, which assists the Muslim secessionists) planned to boycott the elections. However, the elections went ahead in September 1996 and were won by the National Conference Party (a pro-India regional party), under the leadership of Farooq Abdullah. By October, Kashmir had its own elected government, ending the direct rule from Delhi, with Abdullah as chief minister. Proposals for trifurcation which would divide the state into an independent Muslim Kashmir, a Hindu Jammu and a Buddhist Ladakh, have been resisted by the Indian government and seem unlikely to succeed.

At the time of research, a unilateral ceasefire between India and Pakistan, announced for the Muslim month of Ramadan, had been extended. However, there seemed little chance of it holding for much longer, with 666 people having been killed in militant attacks during its first 100 days. Hopes that a resolution can be reached have been dashed again and again, although Hurriyat, an umbrella organisation of around 20 separatist and nationalist groups from Kashmir, still plans to visit Pakistan for further peace talks.

JAMMU REGION

Jammu

☎ 0191 • pop 260,000

Jammu is J&K's second-largest city and its winter capital. In summer it is a sweltering contrast to the cool heights of Kashmir. From October it becomes much more pleasant. Jammu actually consists of two towns. The old town sits on a hilltop overlooking the river, and several kilometres away across the river is the new town of Jammu Tawi.

Jammu to Srinagar

Along the Jammu to Srinagar route are the hill resorts of Katra, Kud, Patnitop and Batote. Four million pilgrims walk the 12km from Katra to the Vaishno Devi cave shrine each year. East of Kud and Patnitop is the important Sudh Mahadev Temple. Farther along, Sanasar is a beautiful valley where Gujar shepherds gather each summer.

Before the completion of the Jawarhar tunnel, Srinagar was often cut off from the rest of India. The 2.5km-long tunnel is 200km from Jammu and 93km from Srinagar and has two separate passages; inside it's very damp and full of fumes. From Banihal, 17km south of the tunnel, the Kashmiri region begins and people speak Kashmiri as well as Dogri. At the northern end of the tunnel is the lush Kashmir Vally.

KASHMIR VALLEY

This is one of the most beautiful regions of India, but since 1989 it has been racked by political violence.

The Mughal rulers of India were always happy to retreat from the heat of the plains to the cool green heights of Kashmir. Jehangir's last words, when he died in 1627 en route to the 'happy valley', were a simple request for 'only Kashmir'. It is here that the Mughals developed their art of formal gardens to its greatest heights.

Among Kashmir's greatest attractions were the Dal Lake **houseboats**. During the Raj period Kashmir's ruler would not permit the British (who were as fond of Kashmir's cool climate as the Mughals) to own property here. So the British adopted the brilliant solution of building houseboats – each one a little bit of England afloat on Dal Lake. A visit to Kashmir, it was often said, was not complete until you had stayed on a houseboat.

Srinagar

☎ 0194 • pop 725,000

Srinagar, the summer capital of Kashmir, stands on Dal Lake and the picturesque Jhelum River.

It is a city that seems to have a distinctly Central Asian flavour. Heading south from Srinagar is always referred to as 'returning to India'.

The old city is in the vicinity of Hari Parbat Hill and includes the labyrinth of alleyways, mosques and houses that constitute the commercial heart of the city. The more modern part of the city is farther up the Jhelum River (above its famous seven bridges), which sweeps through Srinagar.

East of the city is Dal Lake, much of it a maze of intricate waterways. Dal comprises a series of lakes, including Nagin Lake some 8km from the city centre. Most of the more modern houseboats are on these lakes. The famous Mughal gardens, including the Shalimar Bagh and Nishat Bagh, are on the far (east) side of Dal Lake.

Pahalgam

Pahalgam is about 95km east of Srinagar, at an altitude of 2130m. At the junction of the East and West Lidder Rivers, Pahalgam was a popular trekking base before the present troubles. Each year in July/August the Sri Amarnath *yatra* (pilgrimage) attracts thousands of Hindu pilgrims, who approach the Amarnath Cave from this area.

Gulmarg

This large meadow is 52km south-west of Srinagar at 2730m. The name means 'Meadow of Flowers' and in spring it's just that. Once a popular trekking base, Gulmarg used to be India's premier skiing resort.

Srinagar to Kargil

At 2740m, **Sonamarg** is the last major town before Ladakh and, until the terrorist activity began, it was an excellent base for trekking. Its name means 'Meadow of Gold'.

Baltal, an army camp, is right at the foot of the Zoji La (3529m). **Zoji La** is the watershed between Kashmir and Ladakh – on one side you have the green, lush scenery of Kashmir while on the other side everything is barren and dry. **Drass** is the first main village after the pass. From here it's another 56km to Kargil (see the Ladakh & Zanskar chapter).

Ladakh & Zanskar

Ladakh – the land of high passes – marks the boundary between the peaks of the western Himalaya and the vast Tibetan plateau. Opened up to tourism in 1974, it has been variously described as 'the Moonland', 'Little Tibet' and even 'the last Shangri-la'. Whatever the description, it is one of the most remote regions of India.

As Ladakh has always had close cultural and trading connections with Tibet, its predominant culture stems from Buddhism. This history is particularly evident in the most populated region of Leh and the Indus Valley, with its many whitewashed *gompas* (monasteries) and forts perched on top of sugarloaf mountains.

Padum, the regional administration centre of the more remote Zanskar, shares this Buddhist heritage. Kargil and the Suru Valley, the third main region of Ladakh, is predominantly Shi'ia Muslim and shares a cultural affinity with Baltistan (across the border in Pakistan since the Partition in 1947). This area is very close to the de facto border areas of India and Pakistan.

Today, Ladakh and Zanskar remain part of the disputed state of Jammu & Kashmir, albeit now under the control of the Ladakh Autonomous Hill Development Council (LAHDC).

The region is a particularly good destination if you wish to avoid the monsoons the rest of India suffers – June to September is the best time to visit. Winter is extreme.

You do not need a permit to travel to Zanskar, Leh or anywhere along the major routes to Srinagar and Manali. However, permits are required for other remote areas and no-one should ever stray too close to sensitive border areas. The Kargil to Srinagar road can be closed to foreigners when relations with Pakistan get heated.

Money-changing facilities are poor, to say the least; Leh is the only place to change money between Manali and Kargil. Don't rely on credit cards – take cash or travellers cheques.

Ladakh & Zanskar at a Glance

Population: 170,000
Area: approx 96,701 sq km
Capital: Leh
Main Languages: Ladakhi, Purig, Tibetan & English
When to Go: June to Sept
Trekking Areas: Padum to Darcha, Lamayuru & Leh; Spituk to Markha Valley & Hemis; Lamayuru to Chiling; Likir to Temisgam

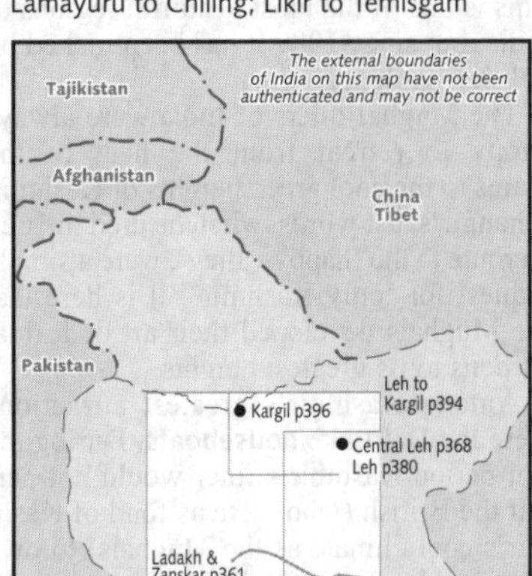

- Explore the labyrinthine alleyways of Leh's old town and wander up to Leh Palace, Ladakh's 'mini Potala'
- Witness the extraordinary ceremonies performed by the monks at Matho Gompa's annual festival
- Stand in awe before some of the finest artwork in the Buddhist world at Alchi, Hemis and Tikse
- Visit one of Ladakh's most stunningly located gompas, Lamayuru
- Trek across the high mountain passes of the isolated region of Zanskar

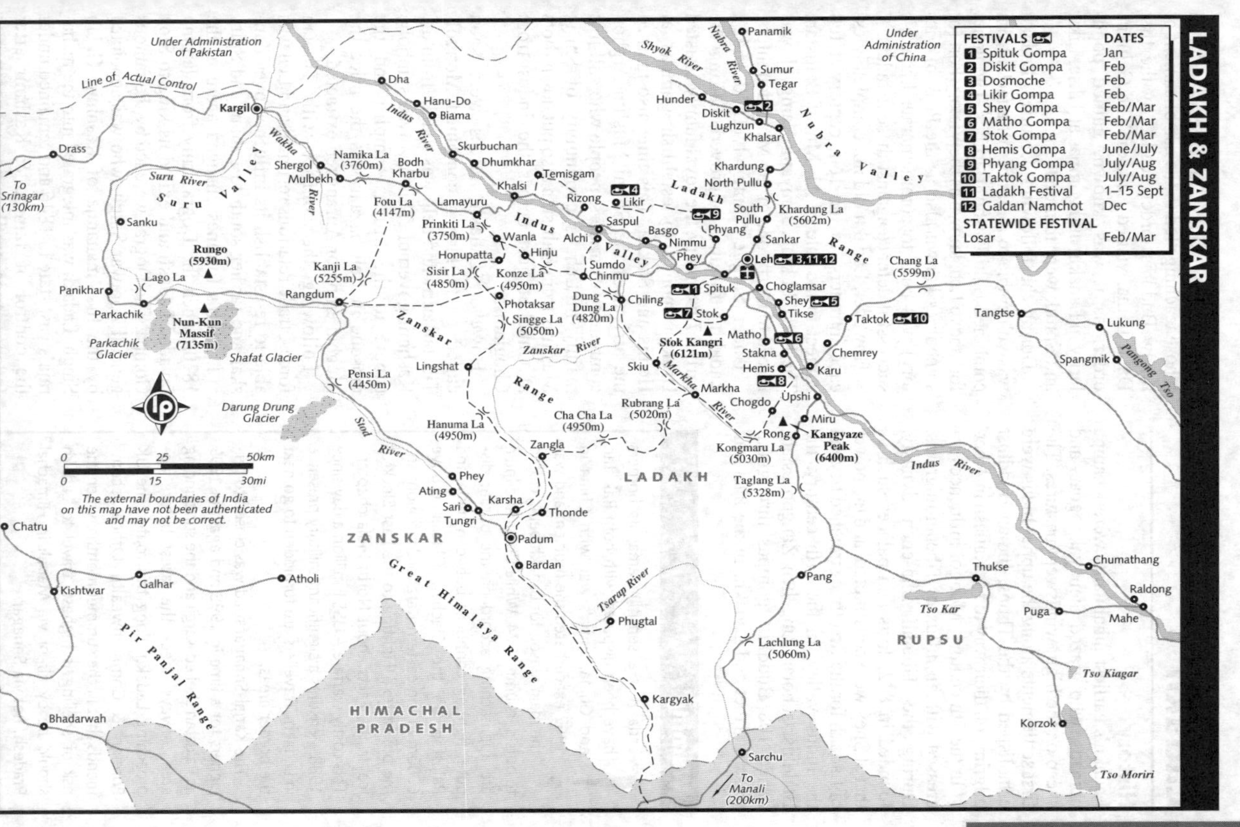
LADAKH & ZANSKAR
FESTIVALS
1 Spituk Gompa Jan
2 Diskit Gompa Feb
3 Dosmoche Feb
4 Likir Gompa Feb
5 Shey Gompa Feb/Mar
6 Matho Gompa Feb/Mar
7 Stok Gompa Feb/Mar
8 Hemis Gompa June/July
9 Phyang Gompa July/Aug
10 Taktok Gompa July/Aug
11 Ladakh Festival 1–15 Sept
12 Galdan Namchot Dec
STATEWIDE FESTIVAL
Losar Feb/Mar
DATES
Under Administration of Pakistan
Line of Actual Control
Under Administration of China
Kargil
Drass
To Srinagar (130km)
Dha
Hanu-Do
Biama
Indus River
Skurbuchan
Dhumkhar
Wakha River
Suru River
Suru Valley
Shergol
Mulbekh
Namika La (3760m)
Bodh Kharbu
Fotu La (4147m)
Lamayuru
Khalsi
Temisgam
Rizong
Likir
Saspul
Alchi
Basgo
Nimmu
Phyang
Phey
Leh
Spituk
Choglamsar
Shey
Tikse
Stok
Matho
Stakna
Hemis
Karu
Chemrey
Taktok
Chang La (5599m)
Tangtse
Lukung
Spangmik
Pangong Tso
Panamik
Shyok River
Nubra River
Nubra Valley
Sumur
Tegar
Hunder
Diskit
Lughzun
Khalsar
Khardung
North Pullu
South Pullu
Khardung La (5602m)
Sankar
Ladakh Range
Indus Valley
Prinkiti La (3750m)
Wanla
Hinju
Honupatta
Sisir La (4850m)
Konze La (4950m)
Sumdo
Chinmu
Dung Dung La (4820m)
Chiling
Photaksar
Singge La (5050m)
Zanskar Range
Zanskar River
Stok Kangri (6121m)
Skiu
Markha
Markha River
Rubrang La (5020m)
Cha Cha La (4950m)
Chogdo
Upshi
Miru
Rong
Kangyaze Peak (6400m)
Kongmaru La (5030m)
Taglang La (5328m)
LADAKH
Rungo (5930m)
Sanku
Lago La
Panikhar
Parkachik
Nun-Kun Massif (7135m)
Parkachik Glacier
Shafat Glacier
Kanji La (5255m)
Rangdum
Lingshat
Pensi La (4450m)
Darung Drung Glacier
Stod River
Hanuma La (4950m)
Zangla
Phey
Ating
Sani
Tungri
Karsha
Thonde
Padum
Bardan
ZANSKAR
Great Himalaya Range
Tsarap River
Phugtal
Kargyak
HIMACHAL PRADESH
Sarchu
To Manali (200km)
Lachlung La (5060m)
Pang
Thukse
Tso Kar
RUPSU
Puga
Mahe
Chumathang
Raldong
Indus River
Tso Kiagar
Korzok
Tso Moriri
Chatru
Kishtwar
Galhar
Atholi
Pir Panjal Range
Bhadarwah
0 25 50km
0 15 30mi
The external boundaries of India on this map have not been authenticated and may not be correct.

Ladakh

History

Ladakh's earliest inhabitants were Khampa nomads, who grazed their yaks, goats and sheep on the high, windswept pastures. The first settlements along the upper Indus were established by the Thons, Indian Buddhist pilgrims on their way to Mt Kailash in Tibet.

In the 7th century, Mongol influences increased with an influx of Tibetan migrants. During the Tibetan Lha-chen dynasty, founded in 842, forts and palaces such as that at Shey were constructed, and the power of Ladakh for the first time stretched beyond the Indus Valley. In the 11th century, the Buddhist scholar Ringchen Zangpo established 108 Buddhist gompas throughout western Tibet and Ladakh. In the late 14th century, Tsongkhapa, a Tibetan pilgrim whose teachings led to the establishment of a new Buddhist order headed by the first Dalai Lama, visited Ladakh. The Gelukpa order, as it was known, gained popularity in Ladakh, and gompas at Tikse, Likir and Spituk were founded.

During the following centuries, Ladakh was vulnerable to a number of attacks from combined Balti-Kashmir armies. The upper fort above Leh, known as the Victory Fort (or sometimes known also as the Peak of Victory) was built to commemorate Ladakh's successful defence against these invaders.

However, Ladakh did not completely escape intruders. In the 16th century it fell subject to the rule of Ali Mir of Baltistan. The Ladakhi king, Jamyang Namgyal, was forced to marry one of the Mir's daughters.

Under Singge Namgyal (1570–1642), Ladakh's fortunes improved. During the early 17th century, the royal family assisted Drukpa monks to establish gompas at Hemis and Stakna. This time also marked the arrival of the Sunni Muslim Arghon community of traders, people who still live mainly in Leh. A community of Shi'ia Muslims from Baltistan also put down roots at Chuchot, just across the Indus from Choglamsar.

However, Ladakhi forces were soon called on to face a combined Mongol-Tibetan army and help was sought from the Kashmir governor. This involved symbolic tribute to the Mughal empire and the mosque in Leh bazaar was the price the Mughal emperor Aurangzeb extracted.

Following the conflict with Tibetan forces, trade relations resumed and Leh was able to re-establish its influence over Zanskar and farther south to Lahaul and Spiti.

Ladakh's fortunes changed again in the 1830s when the Dogra army from Jammu invaded Ladakh and exiled its king to Stok Gompa. The Dogras were led by the famous general Zorawar Singh, who was appointed by the first maharaja of Kashmir, Gulab Singh. Ladakh was integrated into the maharaja's vast state in 1846 and remained under the control of Jammu & Kashmir after Independence, until some autonomy was

Warning

Ladakh is a sensitive area; its borders have been disputed with both Pakistan and China. India's war with China in 1962 exacerbated the problem and was the main reason for Ladakh being closed to outsiders until 1974. While China and India are approaching accord on the border dispute, fighting continues between India and Pakistan on the Siachen Glacier (above 6000m in the eastern Karakoram region; see the boxed text 'Fighting to the Last Block of Ice' in the Facts about North India chapter). This costly warfare – US$1 million a day since 1988 – ensures a significant military presence in Ladakh. Travellers are forbidden to go near the border areas.

The Kargil-Srinagar road was closed to foreigners for a time in 1998 and again in 1999 as Pakistan shelled Kargil and the surrounding area. Always check the latest before approaching Ladakh along this route. The UK Foreign & Commonwealth Office recommends that in the summer months, when the risk of shelling is highest, travel to Ladakh should be by air or via Manali in Himachal Pradesh, not via Srinagar.

granted in 1995, following several years of political and social unrest.

Geography

Ladakh is part of the Trans-Himalaya, a vast, complex mountain region between the main Himalaya range and the Tibetan plateau. This region receives only minimal rainfall each year, which is diverted along irrigation canals. Barley fields and lines of poplar trees in the depths of the valleys contrast with the barren ridges and mountains that define the region's geographical character.

Ladakh is bordered to the south-west by the Great Himalaya Range, including the impressive snowcapped peaks of Nun (7135m) and Kun (7087m), the highest peaks in the Kashmir Himalaya, forming the Nun-Kun Massif. North and parallel to the Himalaya is the Zanskar Range, the main range between the Himalaya and the Indus Valley. The region is drained by the Zanskar River, which flows into the Indus River just to the west of Leh, and the Suru River which flows into the Indus upstream of Dha.

The Stok Range, immediately south of Leh and north of the Zanskar Range, is an impressive outlier; north of Leh is the snow-capped Ladakh Range. Farther north, the Nubra and Shyok Rivers drain the huge peaks of the eastern Karakoram including Rimo 1 (7385m) and Teram Kangri 1 (7464m), which define Ladakh's northern border.

In the east of Ladakh are several scintillating *tsos* (lakes), including Pangong Tso forming the border with Tibet, and Tso Moriri and Tso Kar set in a high-altitude desert characteristic of the Tibetan plateau.

Climate

The temperatures in Ladakh are extreme. Some claim it's the only place where it's possible to sit in the sun with your feet in the shade and catch sunstroke and frostbite at the same time. The sun, which shines for 300 days of the year, is deceptively strong at this high altitude; make sure you bring sun screen.

Over the past few years the climate has been changing with more rain and snow fall creating problems for inhabitants of a traditionally desert region, where average precipitation should be six inches per year. Average summer (June to September) and winter (October to May) temperatures are:

region	summer	winter
Dha-Hanu	-3–29°C	-15–15°C
Leh	-9–30°C	-20–17°C
Nubra Valley	-3–28°C	-15–15°C
Pangong Tso	-12–18°C	-25–18°C
Tso Moriri	-10–17°C	-22– 6°C

Polyandry & Primogeniture

In the tough farming environments of Ladakh, Zanskar and Spiti the land can only physically support a limited population. For this reason family fields are rarely divided. The eldest son traditionally inherits the land and house when he has children old enough to help in the fields. At that point the father either moves into a smaller home, or builds a new one.

Less common these days but still prevalent among the older generations, is the system of polyandry, where a woman marries two brothers. Both husbands are regarded as the fathers of any offspring. Equally, a man might have two sisters as wives if his first wife was unable to have children. The basis of the system was to have only one marriage per household in each generation. If another couple wished to marry, they had to set up their own house and had no claim on the family property. Men and women who didn't marry always had the option of joining a monastery or nunnery. Otherwise the only option was a life without a partner working the family fields.

Permits

Permits are not required for Leh. However, you must fill out a Foreigners' Registration Form at the airport (at Upshi or Drass if coming by road) on arrival and departure, and again at your hotel.

All foreigners (including non-Ladakhi and non-Zanskari Indians) require permits for the restricted areas of the Nubra Valley, Pangong Tso, Tso Moriri and Dha-Hanu. You are allowed to travel by public or private transport, alone or in a group of up to

Winter in Ladakh

To visit Ladakh in winter you either have to be a bit mad or seriously tough. Although it is sunny during the day, night-time temperatures drop drastically and you'll find yourself wrapping up as soon as the sun goes down. Hot water is supplied in buckets but getting your clothes off to have a wash is torturous. Many guesthouses and restaurants close, tourist attractions and services all but disappear and home comforts such as heating become a distant and longed-for luxury.

Despite all the hardship, this is still a great time to visit. Tourist numbers are low and you feel a certain satisfaction to hear just how crowded Ladakh becomes during summer when Western faces far outnumber the locals. This is most apparent during festivals, which have traditionally been held in winter but are increasingly being moved to the summer tourist season. In winter it's much easier to participate in and appreciate the centuries-old rituals being re-enacted without having to wrestle with busloads of tourists.

The sense of isolation provides another buzz – you feel truly intrepid knowing that the road routes are cut off. For those flying out it's easy to worry about being stranded here for longer than planned; many travellers spend their last few days nervously scanning the skies for the dreaded clouds that will trap them here.

Perhaps the best thing is the opportunity to interact more with the hardy Ladakhis. It's impossible not to respect those who endure this hardship year after year with their ever-smiling faces and an unfalteringly generous disposition.

four, as long as there are four names and passport details on the permit.

Available through travel agencies, permits cost Rs 100 to 200, are issued the same day, and are valid for seven days. Four people must apply for a permit together, although they are not actually required to travel together. Travel agencies usually have old photocopies of other passports to help 'fill up' the required numbers for 'groups'. List every place you may visit and carry the original and photocopies of the permit; every one of the several checkpoints requires a copy.

Don't even think about setting off without a permit, going to forbidden areas or overstaying your allotted seven days. If you get caught breaking the rules, a visit to an Indian jail is not unlikely, and your travel agency will be severely penalised.

What to Bring

Even at the height of summer, temperatures in some valleys can be extremely cold. A sleeping bag and warm clothes are vital in all areas. The days can be hot, causing dry skin and sunburn, so a hat, sun screen and so on are important, as is paracetamol for headaches brought on by the change in altitude. Other items worth considering are a torch (flashlight) and candles – electricity, if there is any, is unreliable, with an official cut-off time of 10 pm. Binoculars might be handy for admiring the wildlife, which is guaranteed to disappear as soon as you get close.

Dangers & Annoyances

Over the past few years Pakistan has sporadically shelled the area in and around Kargil (see the boxed text 'Warning' at the start of this chapter). Then in 2000, further violence erupted when Buddhist monks clashed with the police in Leh, causing shops and businesses to close. (See the boxed text 'Buddhists, Muslims & Christians' later in this chapter.) The area was calm at the time of research, but it's always prudent to check with your embassy in Delhi or consulate elsewhere before visiting this potentially volatile area.

Coming to an altitude of 3505m, visitors to Leh invariably suffer some symptoms of acute mountain sickness (see Environmental Hazards under Health in the Facts for the Visitor chapter). Allow for this by ensuring full rest in the first 24 hours after arrival and drinking lots of water. If you plan to fly one way, fly into Leh and take the bus out; the altitude effects on the Leh to Manali journey will not be so great as travelling in the other direction. Many people coming from Manali spend an uncomfortable night at Sarchu, where the altitude is around 4100m.

Travellers have reported that when using a non-Ladakhi vehicle to visit gompas on the tourist circuit from Leh, they've been fined Rs 500 for not having a 'gompa ticket' (Rs 20), supposedly available from the taxi union in Leh. No-one there knows anything about it, suggesting it's yet another scam.

Special Events

Now that tourism is flourishing in the region, the annual **Ladakh Festival** has been extended and is held in the first two weeks of September in a blatant attempt to prolong the tourist season. Nevertheless, the festival should not be missed. Regular large, colourful displays of dancing, sports, ceremonies and exhibitions are held throughout Ladakh. Leh is the main venue, with other smaller, associated festivals in Tangtse, near Pangong Tso; Shey; Basgo; Korzok, on Tso Moriri; and Biama, in Dha-Hanu.

The festival starts with a spectacular march through Leh's main streets. People from all over Ladakh – monks in yellow and orange robes, polo and archery troupes and Tibetan refugees from Choglamsar, wearing *perak* (tall, bright hats) and *papu* (curled shoes) – walk proudly in traditional costume. The march culminates in a day-long cultural display at Leh polo ground. For the best view on the first day, ignore the march and get to the polo ground early.

Other activities during the two weeks include mask dances, which are serious and hypnotic when performed by monks, or cheeky and frivolous when performed by small children. There are also archery and polo competitions, concerts and other cultural programs throughout Ladakh.

The Nubra Valley isn't as crowded with gompas as the area around Leh, so festivals there tend to be less religious and more sports oriented. During the Ladakh Festival in the valley, events not be missed include a camel safari between Diskit and Hunder, 'warfare demonstrations' (not quite as violent as they sound), ibex and peacock dances, traditional marriage ceremonies, sword dancing from Baltistan, flower displays and archery competitions. Activities are generally centred in the main villages of Diskit and Sumur.

Festivals still held in winter include those at New Year – Galdan Namchot, Dosmoche and Losar. In December, **Galdan Namchot** celebrates the birthday of Tsongkhapa, the founder of the Gelukpa school. Buildings throughout the region are illuminated.

During **Dosmoche**, also known as the 'Festival of the Scapegoat', a large wooden mast is erected outside Leh and dough figures are cast into the desert or burnt, thus carrying away the evil spirits of old year.

Losar is a month-long celebration of the New Year, held every December/January.

Visiting Gompas

Mahayana Buddhist Tibetan *gompas* (monasteries) dominate the Ladakhi landscape; they are still active places of worship and teaching. Colourfully clad with flags and wheels relaying prayers through the breeze, they've become popular tourist attractions with their shrines and stupas embellished with superb ancient frescoes. Gompas usually have a caretaker monk on site who finds visitors and shows them around for a donation of Rs 10 to 20. Some gompas provide cheap accommodation for serious students of Buddhism. Always show respect by adhering to the following guidelines when visiting a gompa:

- Your arms and legs should be covered.
- Remove your shoes before entering a shrine.
- Don't drink, smoke or spit.
- Never touch religious objects.
- Don't disturb monks during prayers, including festival ceremonies.
- Never use a camera flash – the frescoes are very fragile.
- Always pass *chortens* (Tibetan for stupa), *mani* walls (Tibetan stone walls with sacred inscriptions) and prayer wheels in a clockwise direction, keeping them to your right.

Offerings are made to the gods, friends and family visit each other in their traditional dress and children receive money for a party at the end of the festival. Meto processions, with their burning torches and chanting in the evening, are designed to chase away evil spirits but participants put a bit more energy into partying afterwards.

In Dha-Hanu the Drokpas celebrate the harvest every three years with the **Bono-na Festival**. Singing and dancing commemorates their migration here and keeps their cultural links distinct from the rest of Ladakh.

There are individual festivals held at gompas throughout the year which feature religious ceremonies, music and dance.

Gompa festivals are traditionally held to solemnise major events in Tibetan Buddhism such as saints' birthdays. Thousands crowd courtyards to see the monks perform *chaams* (sacred mask dances) in theatrical robes. They are worth attending not only for the spectacle, but also because those witnessing the ceremonies are protected from evil, sickness and untimely death while gaining prosperity and longevity.

Volunteer Work

Nongovernmental organisations (NGOs) are constantly attracted to Ladakh, perhaps because it is so active itself in retaining Tibetan Buddhist culture and the delicate balance of its fragile ecosystem. One target has been the poor education record; 90% of Ladakhi Year 10 students fail their exams, with only 1200 per year (85% of whom are female) advancing to further education in Jammu, Chandigarh or Delhi. The main problem has been language. Until Year 8, lessons have been in Urdu, followed by two years of lessons in English, in which the exams are set.

Various groups have campaigned to change lessons to English from the start and to produce locally relevant books (ie, picture books with yaks instead of elephants). These organisations run summer and winter schools, pay and train teachers and provide medicine and materials. They are very keen for volunteers to help students with English and provide a cross-cultural experience while helping to preserve Ladakhi culture. Volunteers with teaching or trade skills are most useful, but almost anyone who simply wants to interact with and help local kids is welcome. Work is generally only available in summer, but those with specialised skills can get work through winter too. It's easiest to arrange work through Leh offices upon arrival.

Ecologists, permaculturists and engineers should have no problem finding voluntary work here. All organisations listed below would welcome assistance in construction and research into new technologies. There are usually strict rules regarding smoking, drugs and alcohol.

Child Welfare Society of Ladakh (☎/fax 53308) Fort Rd. This society provides aid to students in remote areas of Ladakh and Zanskar. Held in Leh, it takes volunteers during winter school, December to February, to teach English, provide administration and generally hang out with the students. Its office is open 10 am to 1 pm and 2 to 5 pm Monday to Saturday and they always have a cuppa for visitors.

Ladakh Ecological Development Group (LEDeG; ☎ 52646) Karzoo. LEDeG initiates and promotes ecological and sustainable development which blends with the traditional culture. With an emphasis on training, they accept skilled volunteers for research and development and teaching.

The Students Educational & Cultural Movement of Ladakh (Secmol; ☎ 53012, fax 53561) Founded by returning Ladakhi graduates, Secmol runs courses for students and teachers. It also produces teaching aids, encourages the arts and is working as part of Operation New Hope to overhaul the education system in Ladakh. Based at Phey, 18km from Leh, you can drop into their Leh office, on the road to the polo ground. A maximum of eight volunteers pay Rs 100 per day for a bed in a solar-heated dorm (bring a sleeping bag) and veg food. Your English doesn't need to be perfect; illustrators are needed year-round.

Language

Ladakhi is the most common language used in Ladakh and Zanskar. Once similar to Tibetan, Ladakhi has now changed considerably. If you only remember one word, it will be the all-purpose *jule* (pronounced **joo**-lay), which means 'hello', 'goodbye', 'please' and 'thank you'. Urdu is spoken in Kargil and the Suru Valley; it has been the language used in primary schooling. English too has been used in education and is the main language used in tourist areas and for administration purposes.

Activities

Ladakh is an adventure playground, with an increasing number of adrenaline-pumping activities on offer. Safety standards are reasonable and in the case of an emergency, the Indian army will helicopter casualties out – make sure you have adequate insurance.

There are a heap of agencies in Leh and Delhi that can organise trips. Ensure your choice has environmentally friendly policies in place (see Responsible Tourism in the Facts for the Visitor chapter). The best time for most activities is from June to September. The Ladakh Adventure Sports Institute (fax 1982-52735) in Leh can help with local advice on the following activities plus more.

White-Water Rafting Several agencies offer white-water rafting trips on the Indus and Zanskar Rivers. Rafting is not especially popular as the rivers aren't particularly reliable and the season only lasts from about early July to mid-September. A three-hour, calm trip from Hemis to Choglamsar or Phey to Nimmu costs Rs 1000 per person. Nimmu to Alchi costs Rs 2000 and full moon overnight trips cost Rs 2000. Longer, customised rafting trips for the adventurous cost about US$70 per day, including all transport, gear, food and a guide.

Two of the better travel agencies in Leh that handle rafting trips are Indus Himalayan Explorers (☎ 52788), in the Shamshu Complex opposite the taxi stand in Fort Rd, and Rimo Expeditions (☎ 53257) at Hotel Kamglachan.

Camel Safaris Just to prove Ladakh is a desert, it has camels. It's possible to trek 8km across the sand dunes at Hunder on one of these shaggy double-humped beasts. One-day all-inclusive jeep trips from Leh cost around Rs 1000, or you can organise it yourself through a guesthouse in Hunder and Diskit.

Mountaineering Unsurprisingly, Ladakh is a mountaineering and climbing paradise. Popular climbs include Stok Kangri (6121m) in the Zanskar Range south of Leh as well as Kangyaze Peak (6400m) south-east of Leh and the Nun-Kun Massif (7135m) accessible from the Kargil-Padum road.

Groups wishing to climb in the region should first obtain permission from the International Mountaineering Foundation (see Mountaineering under Activities in the Facts for the Visitor chapter). Agencies in Leh also arrange expeditions for around US$60 per day (based on a four- to five-day expedition).

Trekking Trekking trips cost US$30 to US$40 per day all inclusive (minimum of four people required). See Trekking in Ladakh later in this chapter.

LEH

☎ 01982 • pop 15,000

Leh is nestled in a side valley just to the north of the Indus Valley. Until 1947 it had close trading relations with Central Asia; yak trains would set off from the Leh bazaar to complete stages over Karakoram La to Yarkand and Kashgar. Today Leh is an important strategic centre for the military, which has a large presence here and is a reminder that the region is along India's sensitive borders with Pakistan and China.

Leh's character changed when Ladakh was opened up to foreign tourists in 1974. Since then, more than 100 hotels have been established and many of the shops on Main Bazaar Rd have been converted to sell arts and crafts. Leh is dominated by the dilapidated nine-storey Leh Palace, home of the Ladakhi royal family before it was exiled to Stok Gompa in the 1830s. Above the palace at the top of Namgyal Hill is the Victory Fort, built to commemorate Ladakh's victory over the Balti-Kashmir armies in the 16th century.

The old town of Leh, situated at the base of Namgyal Hill, is a labyrinth of alleyways and houses stacked with dry wood and dung,

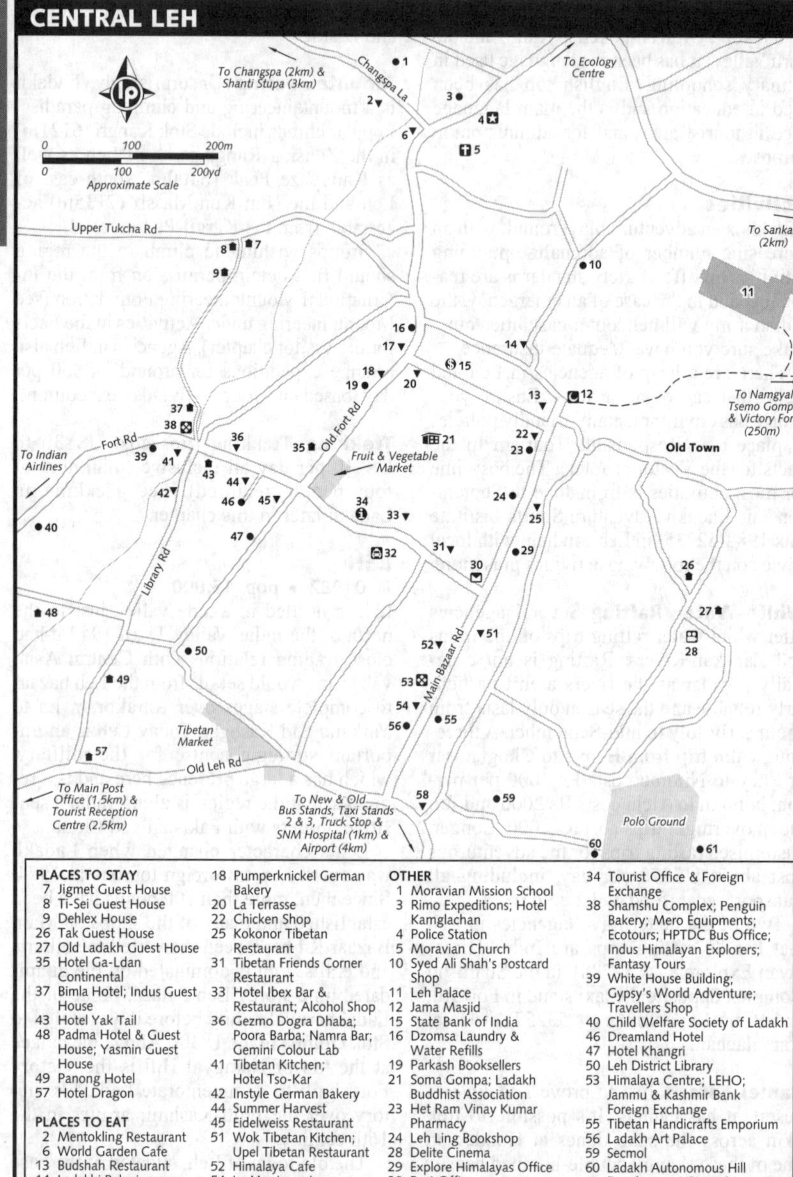
CENTRAL LEH
0
100
200m
0
100
200yd
Approximate Scale
To Changspa (2km) & Shanti Stupa (3km)
Changspa La
To Ecology Centre
To Sankar (2km)
Upper Tukcha Rd
To Namgyal Tsemo Gompa & Victory Fort (250m)
Old Town
Fort Rd
To Indian Airlines
Old Fort Rd
Fruit & Vegetable Market
Library Rd
Main Bazaar Rd
Tibetan Market
Old Leh Rd
Polo Ground
To Main Post Office (1.5km) & Tourist Reception Centre (2.5km)
To New & Old Bus Stands, Taxi Stands 2 & 3, Truck Stop & SNM Hospital (1km) & Airport (4km)
PLACES TO STAY
7 Jigmet Guest House
8 Ti-Sei Guest House
9 Dehlex House
26 Tak Guest House
27 Old Ladakh Guest House
35 Hotel Ga-Ldan Continental
37 Bimla Hotel; Indus Guest House
43 Hotel Yak Tail
48 Padma Hotel & Guest House; Yasmin Guest House
49 Panong Hotel
57 Hotel Dragon
PLACES TO EAT
2 Mentokling Restaurant
6 World Garden Cafe
13 Budshah Restaurant
14 Ladakhi Bakeries
17 Tibetan Cafe
18 Pumperknickel German Bakery
20 La Terrasse
22 Chicken Shop
25 Kokonor Tibetan Restaurant
31 Tibetan Friends Corner Restaurant
33 Hotel Ibex Bar & Restaurant; Alcohol Shop
36 Gezmo Dogra Dhaba; Poora Barba; Namra Bar; Gemini Colour Lab
41 Tibetan Kitchen; Hotel Tso-Kar
42 Instyle German Bakery
44 Summer Harvest
45 Eidelweiss Restaurant
51 Wok Tibetan Kitchen; Upel Tibetan Restaurant
52 Himalaya Cafe
54 La Montessori
58 Iqra Restaurant
OTHER
1 Moravian Mission School
3 Rimo Expeditions; Hotel Kamglachan
4 Police Station
5 Moravian Church
10 Syed Ali Shah's Postcard Shop
11 Leh Palace
12 Jama Masjid
15 State Bank of India
16 Dzomsa Laundry & Water Refills
19 Parkash Booksellers
21 Soma Gompa; Ladakh Buddhist Association
23 Het Ram Vinay Kumar Pharmacy
24 Leh Ling Bookshop
28 Delite Cinema
29 Explore Himalayas Office
30 Post Office
32 Taxi Stand 1; Union Office
34 Tourist Office & Foreign Exchange
38 Shamshu Complex; Penguin Bakery; Mero Equipments; Ecotours; HPTDC Bus Office; Indus Himalayan Explorers; Fantasy Tours
39 White House Building; Gypsy's World Adventure; Travellers Shop
40 Child Welfare Society of Ladakh
46 Dreamland Hotel
47 Hotel Khangri
50 Leh District Library
53 Himalaya Centre; LEHO; Jammu & Kashmir Bank Foreign Exchange
55 Tibetan Handicrafts Emporium
56 Ladakh Art Palace
59 Secmol
60 Ladakh Autonomous Hill Development Council
61 District Magistrates Office

which is collected to use as fuel to withstand the long winter months. To the south of the old town is the polo ground (see Spectator Sports later in this chapter). The mosque at the head of Main Bazaar Rd was commissioned by the Mughal emperor Aurangzeb.

In Changspa, an outlying village 2km north-west of Leh, there are important Buddhist carvings dating back to the 8th and 9th centuries when Ladakh was converted to Buddhism. Sankar, another outlying village of Leh, is the site of a modern gompa that serves much of the Leh Valley. The gompa is attended by some 15 to 20 monks from the gompa at Spituk. Leh's main Buddhist place of worship is the Soma Gompa, close to the Jama Masjid.

Orientation

Leh is small enough to find your way around easily. The road from the airport goes past the new and old bus stands, then turns into the main street, Main Bazaar Rd, where there are plenty of shops and restaurants. South-west of the Leh Palace, around Fort Rd, is the most popular area for places to eat, sleep and spend money. Changspa, just 2km away, has many guesthouses and long-term visitors. A similar distance north-east, Sankar also has many family-run guesthouses.

Information

Tourist Offices The Tourist Reception Centre (☎ 52297) is 3km south of the town

Buddhists, Muslims & Christians

Relations between the Buddhist and Muslim communities of Leh have improved vastly since the social conflicts of the early 1990s, but tensions remain. One unmistakable sign is the war of the loudspeakers between the Jama Masjid and the Soma Gompa, the headquarters of the Ladakh Buddhist Association. Some days when the mosque broadcasts the *azan*, the Muslim call to prayer ('Allah-o-Akbar' – God is Great), the nearby gompa sees fit to retaliate with a high-volume broadcast of Buddhist choral singing with flutes. As one Muslim leader put it, there's a cold war going on.

Traditionally, relations between Buddhists and the Muslim Arghon community were very close, and intermarriages were common. Even today there aren't many people in Leh who don't have both Muslim and Buddhist relatives. This began to change when an uprising started in Kashmir in the 1980s. The Buddhists of Ladakh began agitating to separate from Muslim-majority Jammu & Kashmir and become a Union Territory. As the number of tourists slumped and the economy faltered because of the conflict in Kashmir, tensions grew. In 1989 the Ladakh Buddhist Association ordered and enforced a social boycott of Muslims. Suddenly neighbours didn't speak to each other, families were split and even violence erupted on occasion.

Eventually the government in Delhi banged enough heads together to work out a compromise; Ladakh's Buddhists could be a majority in their own Ladakh Autonomous Hill Development Council, as long as the social boycott ended. The boycott was called off in 1993 and the new administration was set up in 1995.

Other causes of dispute linger. Buddhists resent that many intermarriages result in a Buddhist girl becoming Muslim, while Muslims feel unhappy that Buddhists, who own much of the land, receive the bulk of income from tourists. Muslims, traditionally traders, themselves feel encroached upon by the mainly Kashmiri businessmen who arrive every year for the tourist season. Things came to a head once more in 2000. Following an attack on a monk, the police and Buddhists clashed. This led to riots and the closing of shops in Leh's Main Bazaar Rd for two hours.

Leh's tiny Christian community of 30 or so families, which began with the arrival of the German Moravian mission in 1885, seems to get on with both sides. Every Christian family has relatives belonging to another religion. The Moravian Mission School in Changspa Lane is regarded as the best in Leh and children of all faiths attend.

centre, on the road to the airport. For general inquiries the small office on Fort Rd is far handier. Both tourist offices are open 10 am to 4 pm Monday to Saturday. There is a small tourist information counter at the airport open for flight arrivals to handle Foreigners' Registration Forms and distribute maps.

Money Money and travellers cheques can be exchanged at the State Bank of India and Jammu & Kashmir Bank foreign exchange offices around Main Bazaar Rd. The first is open 10.30 am to 4 pm, and the second from 10.30 am to 2.30 pm, Monday to Friday; both are open 10.30 am to noon on Saturday. Expect long queues in high season.

Hotel Khangri and Yasmin Guest House also change money at slightly lower rates; some people prefer to change US dollars in cash at a slightly better rate with the shopkeepers on Fort Rd.

Post & Communications The main post office is open from 10 am to 1 pm and 2 to 5 pm Monday to Saturday and is hopelessly inconvenient, more than 2km south of the centre of Leh. The smaller post office on the corner of Fort and Main Bazaar Rds is open 10 am to 1 pm and 2 to 5 pm, Monday to Saturday. Poste restante at the main post office is unreliable.

All around Leh you'll find small phone booths with long-distance facilities. Calls within India cost Rs 30 to 40 per minute; to Australia/New Zealand and Europe, Rs 70; and to USA/Canada, Rs 80. However, connections are poor, especially in the evening. Faxes are more expensive and unreliable (Rs 3 per second for international faxes), but machines are available.

You can receive/send emails through Gypsy's World Adventure in the White House building on Fort Rd for Rs 30/50 per message; you can also access the Internet but the connection is relayed through Srinagar so is very slow and, at Rs 5 per minute, expensive. At similar prices, you can also try Cyberia at the Hotel Tashi Dalek.

Travel Agencies Many travel agencies operate in Leh in the summer. Almost all agencies work on a commission basis, selling tickets for other agencies' buses and tours to Ladakh's restricted areas. Travel agencies recommended by readers include:

Ecotours (☎ 52918) Shamshu Complex, Fort Rd
Explore Himalayas (☎ 52727, fax 53354) Main Bazaar Rd
Fantasy Tours (☎ 53124) Fort Rd
Gypsy's World Adventure (☎ 53659, fax 52735) White House, Fort Rd
Oriental Trek & Tour (☎ 53153, fax 52414, e orientalleh@hotmail.com) Oriental Guest House, Changspa
Paradise Trek & Tour (☎ 52640) Fort Rd
Rimo Expeditions (☎ 53257) Hotel Kamglachan

Photography Several places along Fort Rd and Main Bazaar Rd sell print and slide film, but always check the expiry date. The Gemini Colour Lab on Fort Rd, opposite the Hotel Yak Tail, does a pretty good job of developing print (not slide) film and Jullay Colour Lab in the Moti Market does repairs. You can also buy film, and wonderful prints of photos of old Ladakh, from Syed Ali Shah's Postcard Shop behind the mosque.

Equipment Hire Some travel agencies rent sleeping bags, tents and so on, but the gear can be of low quality and poorly maintained, plus they demand a hefty deposit for each item. Check the gear carefully before you take it.

Places that rent gear, including mountaineering equipment, are the Travellers Shop (☎ 52248) in the White House, Mero Equipments (☎ 53070) across the road in the Shamshu Complex, and the tourist office. Approximate rental prices per day are: Rs 100 for a two-person tent; Rs 70 for a sleeping bag and Rs 30 for a gas stove. A deposit on a tent can be as high as Rs 3000.

Bookshops & Libraries Leh Ling Bookshop has a great selection of books on Ladakh and Tibet, as well as novels. The Tibetan Handicrafts Emporium, on Main Bazaar Rd, is also good for Tibetan literature. Next to the Hotel Bijoo, the small Leh District Library has (mainly old) books about Ladakh, along with recent issues of

English-language newspapers and magazines. It is open 10 am to 4 pm, Monday to Saturday. The Ecology Centre runs a good library with books on local issues and ecological matters. For books on Buddhism and Tibet, try the Tibetan library in Choglamsar, or the library at the Mahabodhi Meditation Centre in Changspa Lane.

Newspapers & Magazines Copies of Indian English language newspapers and magazines can be obtained a day or two after publication at Parkash Booksellers on Old Fort Rd. The bilingual (English and Ladakhi) quarterly magazine *Ladags Melong* (Rs 20) is an interesting source of information on Ladakhi culture, education, history and so on. It is sold at bookshops.

Laundry Dzomsa Laundry & Water Refills is an environmentally friendly laundry that washes clothes away from streams to avoid contaminating the precious water supply. It charges Rs 15 for pants and Rs 10 for shirts, and does an excellent job. Dzomsa also refills water bottles with pressure-boiled water for Rs 7, which spares Leh yet more plastic rubbish. Unfortunately it closes for winter. There are plenty of other laundries.

Medical Services & Emergency If you suspect you are suffering from the symptoms of AMS, medical advice is available (☎ 52113 from 10 am to 4 pm, ☎ 52014 all hours). For more information on AMS, see Environmental Hazards under Health in the Facts for the Visitor chapter.

Leh has several clinics and pharmacies that dispense advice and medicines for low-level complaints. For anything serious the public Sonam Norbu Memorial (SNM) Hospital (☎ 52360) is about 2km south of town.

There are also a few *amchi* (traditional Tibetan medicine) clinics around town, including one with English-speaking doctors between 9 am and 3 pm on Sunday at the Ecology Centre. All proceeds go towards developing the practice further. You will need to make an appointment one day in advance. Lectures on amchi are held the same day at 10 am.

Het Ram Vinay Kumar near the mosque on Main Bazaar Rd sells medicines and Western toiletries, including tampons.

The number for the police is ☎ 52018; if you need an ambulance call ☎ 53629.

Leh Palace

The Potala in Lhasa, Tibet, is said to be based on this deserted and dilapidated palace, built in the 17th century. The Archaeological Survey of India has moved in to do restoration work at their legendary pace, meaning it's no longer possible to catch the view from the roof.

Entry is Rs 10, including a look at the central prayer room. It's open 7 am to 9 pm daily. Watch out for holes in the floor.

Namgyal Tsemo Gompa

The Tsemo (Red) Gompa contains a fine three-storey-high Maitreya Buddha (Future Buddha) image and ancient manuscripts and frescoes. It's open in the morning and evening when a monk from Sankar Gompa comes to tend the butter lamps.

The red-walled *gonkhang* (chapel of protector deities) nearby has an unusual portrait in a court-scene fresco just to the left of the door, thought to be the great Ladakhi King Tashi Namgyal. He built the gonkhang in the 16th century, as well as a now ruined **fort** farther up this steep crag (where the views of Leh are superb). However, women aren't traditionally allowed to enter gonkhangs.

The steep path starts from the road to the Leh Palace by the mosque, or a taxi costs Rs 150 return. All taxis and buses leave from bus or taxi stations in Leh. It's a killer climb if you've just flown in.

Soma Gompa

Leh's 'new gompa' is over 40 years old and serves as the headquarters of the Ladakh Buddhist Association. A 2m-high statue of Shakyamuni is flanked by a modern Buddha on the left and Padmasambhava on the right. Puja (ritual offerings or prayers) are held at 9.30 am and 4.30 pm and there is a library and noticeboard displaying articles on local Buddhist issues. This is the place from where the chanting that competes with the mosque's call to prayer emanates. Look for the large ornate wooden gates opposite the State Bank of India.

Sankar Gompa

It's an easy 25-minute stroll to the 150-year-old Sankar Gompa, north of the town centre. The gompa has electric lighting so an evening visit is worthwhile. Upstairs is an impressive representation of Avalokitesvara, the Bodhisattva of Compassion, complete with 1000 arms and 1000 heads. Also upstairs is a library and great views from the roof. Sankar is home to Ladakh's most senior Gelukpa monk, the Kushok Bakula, who is also head of Spituk Gompa; the *rinpoche* (revered lama) has an apartment above the main building.

This interesting little gompa is only open from 7 to 10 am and 5 to 7 pm. A donation of Rs 10 is requested. A return taxi from Leh costs Rs 135.

Shanti Stupa

Looming impressively, especially at night when it is lit up, this stupa (Buddhist religious monument) was built by a Japanese order with the intention of spreading the word of Buddhism by building temples throughout the world. With some financial assistance from the Japanese government, it was opened by the Dalai Lama in 1985.

The stupa is 3km away, out by Changspa. If on foot, be warned that there is a very steep set of steps – not to be attempted if you have just arrived in Leh. By taxi (Rs 135 return) or with your own transport, a longish, winding (but less steep) road goes straight to the top, from where there are great views.

Jama Masjid

Leh's charming Friday Mosque is more impressive from the outside than the inside, although the dusty, carpeted prayer hall has some distinctly Ladakhi features that make it unique, such as the carved roof beams and the curling edges of the mihrab (niche indicating the direction of Mecca). The ground floor of the building is occupied by shops, a sign of the Arghon community's roots in trade. The mosque was built in about 1666.

Try not to visit during prayer times, especially Friday's noon prayers. It's respectful to cover your head before entering. For more information on religious etiquette, see Dos & Don'ts under Society & Conduct in the Facts about North India chapter.

Ecology Centre

Known as the Ecology Centre, Ladakh Ecological Development Group (LEDeG, founded 1983) 'initiates and promotes ecological and sustainable development which harmonises with and builds on the traditional culture'. This includes environmental and health education, strengthening the tradition of organic farming, and publishing local-language books. The centre has had great success with its simple design for greenhouses, which you'll see all over Ladakh. (See also Volunteer Work earlier in this chapter). The small library is very good; the handicraft shop has a good, if a little pricey (it is nonprofit), selection of locally made goods, and there's an amchi clinic each Sunday.

The centre is open 10 am to 4.30 pm, April 1 to October 30; 10.30 am to 1.30 pm and 2 to 4 pm the rest of the year.

Sauna & Massage

To help unwind after a trek, Ladakh Sauna & Massage in Changspa offers a sauna for Rs 100 and a massage for Rs 300 with one day's advance notice.

Courses

Buddhist study centres have been set up in both Leh and nearby Choglamsar. In summer, the Mahabodhi Meditation Centre (☎ 44025) on Changspa Lane has yoga between 3.15 and 4.45 pm and one-hour group meditation sessions at 5 pm Monday to Friday. The centre also holds study camps that last for upwards of five days, and has a bookshop and library.

Organised Tours

Organised jeep and taxi trips to the sights around Leh can be booked through travel agencies. The quality of vehicle, tent accommodation, food, destination and guide, as well as demand, all affect the price, but expect to pay around Rs 5985 for a three-day trip to Diskit and Panamik, and US$140 for four days including Stok. Ensure you don't just get a local taxi-driver-cum-guide which can be organised for far less at the taxi-stand. Unionised fares are listed in Getting There & Away later in this chapter.

Places to Stay

Unless stated otherwise, the hotels and guesthouses listed here close down during winter. The exact time of closure depends on demand, but generally they start shutting shop any time from 15 September, reopening from March onwards. Within this time it's still worth checking out your first choice, but be aware that many will have turned off their hot and cold water supplies to avoid broken pipes. At these times hot and cold water are available in buckets and the rates given here become highly negotiable. Many mid-range to top-end places will also charge an arbitrary 'service tax' of about 10%.

Although very few places have heating, most rooms are designed with large windows, which allows them to be heated by the daytime sun. Their biggest bonus, when it's warm enough, comes with leaving the curtains open at night to enjoy the sunrise over the mountains from the comfort of bed. At any time of the year inquire how regular hot water is before paying extra for it. Leh's electricity supply is spasmodic, so a torch (flashlight) and candles may be needed.

There are literally hundreds of guesthouses in and around Leh, and the following is only a small selection; from June to September it's advisable to book accommodation in advance, especially if you intend to be here for the Ladakh Festival in September.

Places to Stay – Budget

Leh The ***Old Ladakh Guest House*** *(☎ 52951)*, which has remained open every single day since 1974, is a wonderful place and full of character north of the polo ground. It has cosy, individually styled rooms which start at Rs 180/250 without/with bathroom and creaky wooden stairs rise from its small tree-filled courtyard up to its terrace. Almost directly opposite, ***Tak Guest House*** is much simpler, with shared squat toilets and bathrooms. Dark rooms downstairs are Rs 100; but the upstairs rooms for Rs 150 are bigger, brighter and better.

North of Fort Rd is a cluster of reasonable places. ***Jigmet Guest House*** *(☎ 53563)* has large rooms, one of which doubles as a library, for Rs 150/300 without/with bathroom.

Ti-Sei Guest House *(☎ 52404)* has a nice garden and a Ladakhi kitchen. Singles/doubles cost Rs 150/200.

Dehlex Guest House has a large garden, and singles/doubles with shared bathroom cost Rs 100/200.

Changspa The ***Oriental Guest House*** *(☎ 53153, fax 52414, ⓔ orientalleh@hotmail.com)*, in a garden below Shanti Stupa, is a friendly family-run place that has good local information. Singles/doubles with shared bathroom in the old section of the house are Rs 80/120, while those in the new section with private bathroom and heating are Rs 250/300. There is solar-heated water year-round and a large cushioned dining area where breakfast (Rs 35) and dinner (Rs 45) are served. It stays open in winter and organises eco-friendly tours in collaboration with an NGO.

Goba Guest House is similar, but surrounded by more fields. Simple rooms with shared bathroom are Rs 80/150 and meals can be enjoyed with the family in the kitchen. One traveller likes it so much they've been here for the last three years, ensuring it stays open during winter.

Shanti Guest House *(☎ 53084)* is another popular farmhouse. Below the Shanti Stupa, it too has been recommended as friendly. Rooms cost Rs 100/200. It stays open for winter. Behind it, closer to Shanti Stupa, ***LEDeG Hostel*** *(☎ 52918)* is a non-smoking eco-friendly hostel with rooms for those with a particular interest in LEDeG projects. Solar-heated rooms with hot water cost Rs 100/160.

Asia Guest House *(☎ 53403)* is an old favourite, with a good terrace restaurant overlooking a large garden. Rooms cost Rs 150.

Eagle Guest House *(☎ 53074, fax 52107)* has rooms starting at Rs 100/250 and a terrace overlooking the surrounding fields.

Stumpa Guest House is a family home with rustic rooms which start at Rs 60/160. ***Greenland Guest House*** *(☎ 53156)* is similar with a small garden and large rooms for Rs 100/160.

Places to Stay – Mid-Range

Bimla Hotel *(☎ 52754)*, just off Fort Rd and surrounded by trees, has singles/doubles with big windows and private bathroom for Rs 200/300. Some rooms have verandas and there are views from the roof over to the palace and fort as well as a downstairs lounge. ***Indus Guest House*** *(☎ 52502)*, next door, is similar. Views can be enjoyed from its rooms with private bathroom, which cost Rs 250/350. Both are open during winter.

Padma Hotel & Guest House *(☎ 52630, fax 51019)* offers the best of both worlds and remains open in winter. Large, cosy rooms in the original farmhouse cost Rs 150/300 and those in the spotless new section cost Rs 900/1500 with meals. Meals can be taken on the roof terrace, or in the garden or kitchen, and it remains open for winter.

Yasmin Guest House *(☎ 52405)* is a two-storey modern place with a sunny courtyard garden. Good doubles with hot water cost Rs 400/500 without/with bathroom.

Panong Hotel *(☎ 52300)* is a modern place used by Indian Airlines to accommodate passengers when flights are delayed by bad weather, so it remains open in winter when rooms cost from Rs 200 to 500.

Hotel Saser *(☎ 52654, fax 52575)*, near the Ecology Centre in Changspa, is modern with traditional features. Singles/doubles around a garden courtyard cost Rs 800/900.

Silver Cloud Guest House *(☎ 53128, fax 52659)*, away from the crowds in Sankar, has been repeatedly recommended by travellers. Rooms, some with balcony, start at Rs 300/400 with private bathroom and Rs 150/300 with shared bathroom.

Places to Stay – Top End

Places in this category generally don't offer much more comfort than the cheapies, although hot water will generally be running when the others have resorted to sloshing it into buckets.

Hotel Yak Tail *(☎/fax 52118, Fort Rd)* is a large central place with a pleasant courtyard, restaurant and money exchange. The largish rooms with private bathroom also have TV and some even have an attached sitting room. Full-board rates are Rs 1600/2070 a single/double; room only is Rs 1000/1300. This place has nightly entertainment during the summer.

One of the few actually worthy of being in this range is ***Hotel Dragon*** *(☎ 52139, fax 52720, ⓔ advnorth@vsnl.com)*. Bright and nicely decorated rooms start at Rs 850/1200. There are a few balcony terraces around the central courtyard and plenty of traditional woodcarvings to admire. It also has a large dining room and travel agency.

Hotel Ga-Idan Continental *(☎ 52173, fax 52414, Old Fort Rd)* is central. Rooms cost Rs 1595/1895 and some have TV.

Hotel Lasermo *(☎ 52313)*, in Changspa, has rooms for Rs 1890/2270 including meals in its Ladakhi style dining room. It remains open during winter.

Gypsy's Panorama Hotel *(☎ 52660, fax 52735, ⓔ matin@vsnl.com)*, in Changspa, has central heating and so remains open year-round. Rooms are still quite basic, but when you're freezing, the heating and meals are well worth the Rs 1800/2277 charged. Rooms without heating are available for Rs 800.

Places to Eat

Most hotels have restaurants that offer a good range of dishes. They are likely to be closed during winter unless they consider their guest register to be full enough to justify staying open. Bakeries are usually restaurants, so there are licensed bakeries too. Guesthouses with their cosy Ladakhi kitchens, with warm stoves and shelves of copper pots, are still likely to offer wholesome meals (usually made from organically home-grown vegetables) regardless of the number of guests.

Leh has a sizable Tibetan refugee population, which naturally has influenced the cuisine and increased the number of Tibetan (and therefore vegetarian) restaurants. There are plenty to chose from and a handful remain open during winter to cater to hardy tourists and to locals. Unless stated otherwise, the following are open year-round serving a range of Tibetan, Chinese and Western-oriented dishes. You'll need to be seated before 8.30/7.30 pm in summer/ winter to guarantee a feed. Some of the hotel restaurants may charge 10% service.

Main Bazaar Area Along Main Bazaar Rd, mostly on the buildings' 2nd or 3rd floors, are several good, cheap (and well-signed) places with large windows looking onto the activity below. Popular choices for Tibetan fare include the ***Himalaya Cafe***, which has Leh's most ambient lighting and music, ***Kokonor Tibetan Restaurant***, ***Wok Tibetan Kitchen***, also with Japanese fare, ***La Montessori*** and ***Upel Tibetan Restaurant***. Near the Soma Gompa, ***La Terrasse*** has a pleasant upstairs terrace with umbrellas, though it is better for breakfast or snacks than main meals. It closes during winter.

Budshah Inn, close to the mosque, has pretty good Kashmiri dishes for about Rs 100 per person – it's a good place if you're craving meat. ***Iqra Restaurant***, at the other end of Main Bazaar Rd, serves a much more limited range of basic Kashmiri meat dishes, but has good views. ***Tibetan Cafe*** on Old Fort Rd is good for tea and snacks.

There's a ***spit-roasted chicken shop*** on Main Bazaar Rd. A full chicken – great for a picnic – costs Rs 100.

Hot, fresh Indian and Tibetan-style bread can be bought from the ***Ladakhi bakeries*** in the street just behind the mosque. They bake throughout the day and you can watch them make your loaf – it's great with locally made jam.

Fort Road Opposite the Hotel Yak Tail, ***Gezmo Dogra Dhaba***, is the place for no-frills Indian food, such as filling vegetable curries and rice. It has a useful noticeboard. Nearby, ***Poora Barba*** is good for a cuppa.

Tibetan Kitchen, in Hotel Tso-Kar, is the best restaurant in town and charges accordingly – it's around Rs 250 for dinner. For the uninitiated, the varieties of Tibetan cuisine are explained on the menus. It will do a famous *gyarhcee* (Tibetan hotpot) for at least four people with a day's notice. Unfortunately, it closes for winter.

Tibetan Friends Corner Restaurant, lacking views as it's down a side entrance opposite the taxi stand, is an established favourite with the locals who love *thugkpa* (Tibetan noodle soup).

Summer Harvest, upstairs on Fort Rd near the Hotel Yak Tail, is very popular, and deservedly so. It closes for winter.

Instyle German Bakery just off Fort Rd is a great place for a cup of coffee and a cake, sandwiches and breakfast, including piping-hot porridge. ***Pumperknickel German Bakery***, at the top of Old Fort Rd, is very popular; specialities include lasagne and a big set-price breakfast (Rs 40). Both bakeries close for winter.

If you fancy a beer with you meal, try ***Eidelweiss Restaurant***, down a driveway next to Summer Harvest, ***Penguin Bakery*** or ***Ibex Bar & Restaurant***. The first two close for winter. There is a ***fruit and vegetable market*** on the corner of Fort and Old Fort Rds.

Changspa The places to eat here are open during summer only. If you're based here you'll be restricted to your own guesthouse's fare unless you fancy a dark and cold walk or can arrange a taxi into Leh.

Shelden Green Restaurant serves beer rather more quickly than it serves the usual mix of Western, Chinese and Indian meals, but the shady garden is pleasant. ***Mentokling Restaurant,*** near the Moravian Mission School, is another open-air place selling beer. The ***World Garden Cafe***, in pleasant gardens, is good for chilling out.

The open-air ***Mona Lisa Bar & Restaurant***, west of the Ecology Centre, is very relaxing and serves beer, pizzas and Ladakhi bread with falafel for about Rs 60, and it has Western popular music.

If you run out of wind on the walk into town, ***Rainbow Cafe*** makes a good drink stop and it's open during winter.

Entertainment

Bars If you're desperate for a bottle of Turbo Extra Strong Lager, there are one or two bars and licensed restaurants (see Places to Eat). It should cost around Rs 60. *Chang* (Tibetan rice or millet beer) is hard to find; ask your hotel if it can acquire some for you. ***Namra Bar***, opposite Hotel Yak Tail, is Leh's best bar, with dark lighting and music. It also serves food, but is more of a drinking venue.

There is a ***shop*** selling bottles of Indian beer and whisky at the Hotel Ibex complex, slightly ominously situated just across from where the taxi stand drivers are. Another can be found at the Moti Market.

Cinemas Fans of old Hindi musicals with gory fight scenes can get their fix at the ***Delite Cinema*** in the old town. The video *Ancient Futures – Learning from Ladakh* is shown at the Ecology Centre; usually at 4.30 pm Monday to Saturday depending on demand. It's worth seeing for an insight into Ladakh, and the problems associated with tourism. An earnest discussion group follows the video. The Tibetan Environment Network in Choglamsar also screens movies with a Tibetan theme at 4.30 pm every Monday and Friday.

Cultural Performances In summer only, the ***Cultural & Traditional Society*** (CATS) puts on a cultural show behind the Shamshu Complex at 6 pm; tickets cost Rs 50. In competition with this, the ***Ladakh Artists' Society of Leh*** also puts on a show of Ladakhi songs and dances at 5.30 pm daily outside the Leh Palace, costing Rs 70. It's an entertaining show at a great location. Bring a torch (flashlight) for the walk back.

While they *are* set up for tourists, these shows are likely to be the closest you'll get to traditional singing and dancing, and to try (if you dare) some Ladakhi *gur-gur* (butter tea). It's a good idea to avoid the front rows unless you want to become part of the spectacle at the end of the show.

Spectator Sports

Weekly polo matches are contested between Leh and outlying villages in the Indus Valley at the polo ground south of the old town. During winter the locals play ice hockey on the pond outside the Ecology Centre.

Polo & Archery

During the last century, polo games were played in the bazaar and main street of Leh. Nowadays, on Tuesday and Saturday in summer, they are often held at the Leh polo ground (although on Thursday the ground is reserved for a serious football game), with regular matches and competitions during the Ladakh Festival.

Historically, the game has always been more popular in the Muslim regions near Kargil than in Buddhist areas. In Leh, the two goals are placed about 100m apart, although in some villages more than a dozen players in both teams may use fields more than 350m long. Normally, a team consists of six men on horses (normally tough little Zanskari ponies), with one player defending the goal. One local rule stipulates that the team changes ends after each goal, so when a goal is scored defenders make an immediate dash to the opposite goal. The game is played at a frantic pace in 20-minute halves. (Beware, it can be hazardous sitting in the first row at the Leh polo ground!)

Archery competitions are usually held between two teams in the villages, or more often at the National Archery Stadium in Leh. The team with the most arrows closest to the target – often just a lump of sand with a painted round symbol – wins. Archery is not particularly exciting to watch, but it's a great excuse for local people to dress up in their finest traditional clothing and party. During a match, there is plenty of dancing, singing and drinking of *chang* (Tibetan rice or millet beer) – and some archery in between it all. Not surprisingly, the standard of archery is much higher in Kargil, where Islam forbids drinking.

Shopping

Local specialities include Tibetan handicrafts, *pashminas* (cashmere shawls), woolly socks and organic apricots. Prices can be high; you may find exactly the same item on sale for less in Delhi, Dharamsala or Nepal.

The Tibetan Market, off Old Leh Rd, sells Western products and is a good place to look for coats, bags and sunglasses for trekking trips. Moti Market, en route to the bus stands, has a more interesting selection of items including local crafts and jewellery. Other good places are the shops in the old town behind Main Bazaar Rd, including Ladakh Art Palace and the Tibetan Handicrafts Emporium, the Ecology Centre and the Cottage Industries Exposition in Changspa. At the time of the Ladakh Festival Leh has good exhibitions and stalls selling handicrafts and clothes. Stovepipe hats and other traditional Ladakhi/Tibetan garb are also available in and around Main Bazaar Rd.

Ladakh Environment & Health Organisation (LEHO; ☎ 53691) is training local women in the traditional production of pashminas. It organises for shoppers to visit its village cooperative 20km outside Leh, where they can watch the women at work before making a purchase. Shawls range from Rs 50 to 4500, although they're not quite up to Kashmiri standards.

Getting There & Away

Air Indian Airlines is currently the only airline flying to Leh, as compensation for the loss-making flights it must maintain during the winter. It warns passengers it cannot depart Leh with more than 60 to 75 passengers because of the altitude, climatic conditions and short runway. So, at peak periods, flights can be heavily booked. To avoid this, book well ahead and be prepared for disappointment. If you can't get a booking in economy class, it's worth trying for 1st class. Another option is to go on the waiting list – even if you're number 100, there is still a good chance you will get on a flight, especially as an improvement in conditions can increase the passenger load. Don't book your Delhi flight and flight

Pashmina & Shatoosh

Unique to the north of India, *pashminas* (cashmere shawls) are made from the very fine hair of the cashmere goat and are soft, light, warm, comfortable and available at a fraction of the cost you'd pay back home.

Not that we need to sell them to you – there are plenty of enthusiastic seasonal Kashmiri traders to do that, and they will at every opportunity. Naturally there are pitfalls to watch out for. Not every shawl you're shown will be pashmina; many are blended with wool or synthetic materials and even so-called experts can't tell the difference between the genuine and a clever fake. One test is to burn a small thread; burning wool has a distinctive smell and synthetic materials will melt. Many pashminas have embroidery and the quality of the shawl can often be verified by the quality of the hand-stitching.

You can learn much by shopping around and doing some research first. Ladakh, the traditional home of pashmina wool, has cooperatives where it's possible to see the authentic stuff being woven, but in the end it's down to whether you like a particular shawl and if it feels good.

Even more luxurious than pashmina are *shatoosh*, also known as ring shawls because the wool, at three-quarters the width of cashmere and one-fifth that of human hair, produces a shawl so fine it's possible to pass the whole thing through a ring. Shatoosh are woven from the fine underbelly hair of the Tibetan antelope *(Pantholpos hodgsonii)*, found in the Himalaya and locally known as chiru. The sale of shatoosh is strictly prohibited under the Wildlife Protection Act 1972, as at least five animals must be slaughtered for each shawl. The 'Say No to Shatoosh' campaign launched in 1999 aims to protect the chiru, which fell from a population of one million in 1900 to fewer than 75,000 in 1975. As the shatoosh is something of a status symbol, it is unlikely you will be offered the genuine article, but if you are, report it to the authorities.

home for the same day; allow a couple of days for bad weather. If flights from Leh are delayed, Indian Airlines will pay for passengers' overnight accommodation.

When flying into the world's highest commercial airport (☎ 52255) at Leh it is important to be aware that the altitude is likely to have a severe effect – always allow at least two days for your body to adjust before setting out on proper exploration of the area. It's a great excuse to spend at least the first 24 hours doing absolutely nothing.

The Indian Airlines office (☎ 52076) is on the extension of Fort Rd, in a small white building about 4km out of town, and is open 10 am to 1 pm and 2 to 5 pm Monday to Saturday and 10 am to noon on Sunday. The competition for seats is savage during high season – some people even resort to bribery. It is worth getting to the office early.

From June to September Indian Airlines has daily flights between Leh and Delhi (US$105), via Chandigarh (US$70) on Wednesday. From October to May the Delhi-Leh flight goes four times weekly, but this depends greatly on weather conditions.

There are year-round direct flights on Sunday from Leh to Srinagar (US$55), and twice a week to Jammu (US$65). They can be a useful, indirect, way of getting out of Leh if the Delhi flights are overbooked.

Bus There is a good local bus and minibus network to take visitors to the main sights and farther afield. Buses leave from the new bus stand, south of town.

There are only two overland routes across the Himalaya to Leh – the road from Srinagar, and the road from Manali in Himachal Pradesh. A complication when trying to leave Leh for Srinagar or Manali is that you may not be able to buy tickets on the local buses (or private buses at the end of the high season) until the evening before departure, because buses may not turn up from either of these places. Thus you can't be certain you will be leaving until the last moment. Try to book ahead, if possible, especially in the high season, at the new bus stand in Leh, from where the public buses leave, or through travel agencies.

To/From Srinagar The Leh to Srinagar road is usually open from the beginning of June to October, but in practice the opening date can be variable. In recent years the road from Kargil to Srinagar has been closed to foreigners because of Pakistani shelling; check at the tourist office for more information. The trip takes two days (about 12 hours travel each day), with an overnight halt at Kargil. There are two classes of public bus, but you may not get the class you want on the day you want. Jammu & Kashmir State Transport Corporation (J&KSTC; ☎ 52085) buses to Kargil/Srinagar cost Rs 145/285 (air-con) or Rs 110/220 (general). Deluxe buses to Srinagar cost Rs 460. They all leave the new bus stand in Leh at 3.30 am daily in high season.

To/From Manali The Leh-Manali road is open for a shorter period, usually from July to mid-September, and never after 15 October; again, the opening and closing dates can be variable depending on climatic conditions. There is a good selection of private and public buses for this route. As the road climbs to 5328m at its highest point, most people suffer the effects of altitude (headaches, nausea), unless they have spent time acclimatising elsewhere. There are three types of buses which travel between Leh and Manali, all of which generally run daily during the high season, more often if there is demand. Late in the high season, the availability of buses from Leh depends on the demand for passengers travelling from Manali to Leh. All the buses leave from the new bus station south of town.

The most comfortable Himachal Pradesh Tourist Development Corporation (HPTDC) bus departs at 6 am from the Shamshu Complex on Fort Rd in Leh, and the HPTDC Marketing Office (☎ 01902-2116) on The Mall, Manali. Tickets, available from travel agencies and at the new bus stand, cost Rs 750 and Rs 1000 including a tent, dinner and breakfast in Sarchu. You can stay in the same tent and order the same meals yourself in Sarchu for less.

Privately owned (mostly by Manali travel agencies) buses offer an alternative. They all leave around 3.30 am and cost about Rs 800, plus accommodation and food in Sarchu or Darcha – the price is subject to change according to demand. In Leh, you can buy your tickets from any travel agency, which means you probably won't know what bus you have a ticket for until you get on. In Manali, bookings can be made directly with the bus agencies or travel agencies. See Getting There & Away under Manali in the Himachal Pradesh chapter for details.

The third alternative is the least comfortable and generally slower – but certainly cheaper – public bus. These buses leave from Leh at about 5 am daily. Tickets, which should be bought at least one day in advance from the new bus stand, cost Rs 400.

Truck These are a worthy, and acceptable, method of travelling to Manali or Srinagar or to places on the way. However, trucks may not stop overnight, but instead drive through – not a great idea; or they may stop anywhere alongside the road – not much fun. They can be more comfortable if there are only a couple of people in the cabin and are faster and cheaper (around Rs 300) than the bus. Plenty of trucks travel this route in season. Talk to drivers at the old bus stand in Leh the day before you want to travel.

Jeep & Taxi These are an expensive, but useful alternative to the bus, and they allow for stops to take photos and visit villages. 'Indian jeeps' take five passengers, while 'Japanese jeeps' and Ambassador taxis take four. Taxis can be hired through accommodation, or at three designated stands. Taxi stand No 1 (☎ 52723) is on Fort Rd and is open 7 am to 7 pm. Additional taxis hang around Fort Rd in the very early morning. Stand No 2 is at the old bus stand, where a few old taxis loiter and No 3 is at the new bus stand, but fewer taxis hang around here. If planning a long trip or tour, try to get a driver who speaks English and knows the area – this can be arranged the day before.

Unionised fares are listed at the stands (discounts of up to 40% are negotiable in low season). Return trips to nearby gompas cost:

Sankar, Spituk, Phyang	Rs 580
Shey, Tikse, Stok	Rs 685
Stakna, Matho	Rs 785
Two-day trip from Leh to Manali (including an overnight stop)	Rs 10,130

Extra charges are Rs 250 if staying overnight, and waiting time for the second and third hour (the first is free) is Rs 115 per hour. For fares to other gompas, see individual entries.

Motorcycle Riding a motorcycle is just about the perfect way of getting to and travelling around Ladakh. There are no villages between Keylong and Leh, so you have to take all your spare parts, particularly spare chains and tubes. There are petrol stations at Tandi and Keylong, and tent sites may sell limited (sometimes diluted) petrol at twice Leh or Manali prices. Always wear cold- and wet-weather gear, including boots, because the road is always substandard, muddy, wet and/or dusty.

For local exploration, World Adventure (☎ 53373) on Main Bazaar Rd, and Peaks and Lamas, on Fort Rd, hire bikes for about Rs 500 per day, plus petrol. Ensure that you have comprehensive insurance that covers you in an accident in which either yourself or a local person is injured.

Getting Around

To/From the Airport There is an erratic bus service from the airport but it's much easier to take a taxi to Leh/Changspa for Rs 80/125. Some of the 'taxi drivers' awaiting arrivals are actually hotel touts, but they don't pressure you too much if you insist on being taken straight to your chosen hotel.

Bicycle There are many sights within cycling distance of Leh. Dreamland Hotel and Wisdom Travels, both on Fort Rd, hire out mountain bikes for around Rs 250 per day.

AROUND LEH

Beautiful gompas and villages make good day trips from Leh, as well as areas which have recently been opened to travellers (with permits) by the Indian authorities. Some, such as Pangong Tso and Tso Moriri,

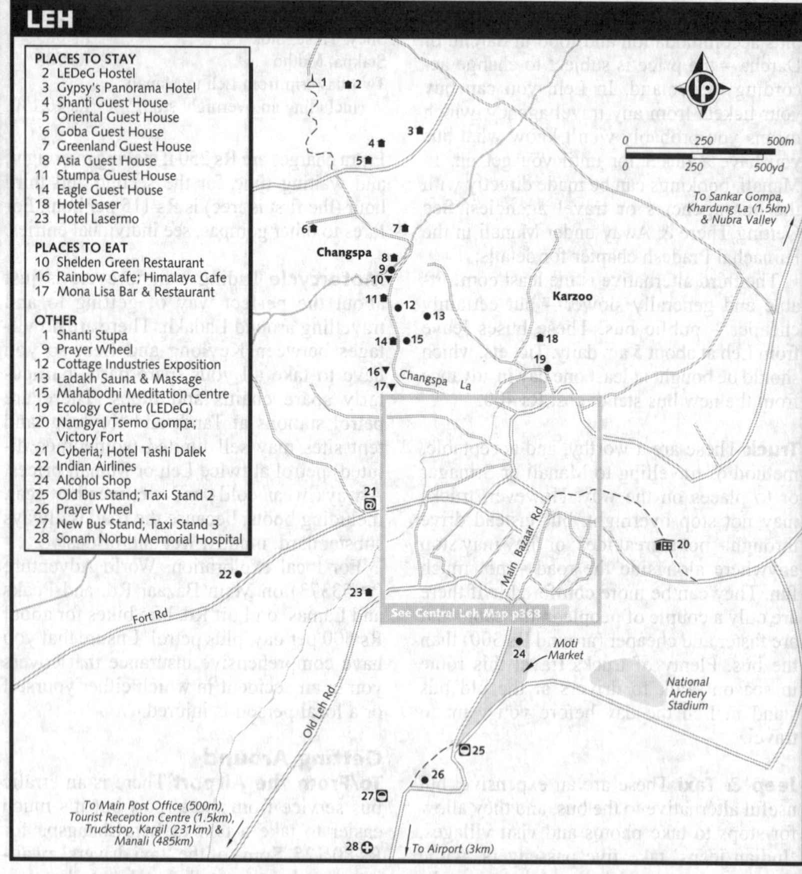

have no guesthouses or shops to sell supplies (although this may change soon). You must take your own food, as well as sleeping and cooking equipment (which can be hired in Leh). In the more populated areas with guesthouses and shops you still might want to bring canned meat and fresh vegetables from Leh to liven up a boring plate of dhal and rice or to share with the locals.

Spituk Gompa

On a hilltop above the Indus River and only 8km from Leh, this gompa was built in the 15th century under the Gelukpa order. It has an ugly view of the airport at the front, but the back looks onto the pretty local village.

The two prayer rooms have some nice Buddha statues, only unveiled once a year during the January festival. There are also good *thangkas* (Tibetan rectangular cloth paintings) and ceremonial masks on display. The red-walled gonkhang at the top of the hill is particularly spooky. There is a strongly worded warning, aimed at visiting Hindus, that the fearsome guardian deities are not to be worshipped as the goddess Kali.

Spituk has nowhere to stay or eat. From Leh to Spituk is a long, hot walk. Instead, you could take one of the minibuses (Rs 4.50) which leave Leh every 30 minutes. Taxis from Leh cost Rs 225 return.

Phyang

Not far past Spituk, a long, roughish track off the main road leads to the pretty village of Phyang. **Mani walls** (stone walls with sacred inscriptions) lead to the little-visited gompa, which was built around the 16th century by King Tashi Namgyal and is today home to about 45 monks of the Kagyupa order. An elaborate thangka is unveiled at the annual festival in July/August.

Minibuses leave Leh for Phyang (Rs 9) at 8 am and return at 10 am, buses leave daily at 7.30 am, 1.30 and 4.30 pm (Rs 11.50). Taxis from Leh cost Rs 495 return.

Likir

The magnificent gompa at Likir, known as the **Klu-kkhyil Gompa** (Klu-kkhyil means water spirits), was founded in the 14th century, and was the first in Ladakh known to have been built under the direction of Tibetan monks. The present gompa was rebuilt in the 18th century, rededicated to the Gelukpa order, and is now inhabited by almost 150 monks, who offer free tea and guided tours to visitors.

There is a small museum upstairs, with an impressive collection of thangkas up to 500 years old, as well as some interesting Buddha figures. Unfortunately, the wall paintings have suffered much water damage. There is no entrance fee, but there's a donation box for voluntary contributions. Among other things, the monks ask that visitors do not engage in 'smooching or hugging'.

To stay in Likir, return to the village, about a 30-minute walk across the fields. The pleasant ***Norboo Guest House*** has a large, authentic Ladakhi kitchen and a thangka studio. Rooms here, including all meals, are good value at Rs 150 per person. ***Gaph-Chow Guest House & Camping*** has rooms for Rs 200 and a big kitchen. Camping costs Rs 60.

Leh to Likir minibuses (Rs 26.50) leave at 3.30 pm daily, returning at 7 am. A one-way/return taxi from Leh costs Rs 795/890.

Nimmu

Nimmu is a pleasant place to stop for tea. About 8km east, towards Leh and easily seen from the road, is the junction of the differently coloured Indus and Zanskar Rivers. If you can, get out and admire this really spectacular sight. A direct minibus leaves Leh for Nimmu (Rs 16) at 3.30 pm, returning at 7 am; a one-way/return taxi from Leh costs Rs 577/715.

Basgo

Basgo was the capital of lower Ladakh before the Ladakh kingdom was united at Leh. Listed as one of the top 100 endangered World Heritage Sites in 2000, the 400-year-old mud-brick **gompa** is up winding, steep tracks. The prayer room in the **Ser Zung Temple** has great frescoes; another temple has an enormous gold-and-copper statue of the Maitreya Buddha (Future Buddha), and some elaborate roof and wall frescoes. The Basgo Welfare Committee of Volunteers are working to restore the gompa as best it can. In 2000, after three months of hard work, a wall that the volunteers had just completed promptly fell down.

There are a couple of options for staying in ***family homes*** just below the gompa. Daily buses from Leh to Alchi pass Basgo. A one-way/return taxi from Leh costs Rs 660/825.

Saspul

Saspul is a village on the main road, over the river from Alchi. There is a small white-and-red **cave temple** to the left of the gompa.

The ***Chakzoth Guest House***, on the main road in Saspul, has small rooms for Rs 50. ***Hotel Duke*** *(☎ 194106-27021)* is a decent mid-range place with Ladakhi murals and carved doors; it has comfortable doubles for Rs 500, and dinner for Rs 120.

Minibuses to Saspul (Rs 27.50) leave Leh at 3.30 pm, returning at 7 am.

Alchi

Alchi is a busy village with an ancient gompa and several good places to stay and eat. It is a pretty place, especially at the end of summer when villagers are harvesting. There's also a lovely walk down to the

Indus River. It's worth staying here to break up the long haul between Leh and Kargil or Srinagar, or as a base for exploring places such as Likir, Basgo and Rizong. This is mainly a summer tourist village; come winter many residents pack up and head to Leh.

Alchi Gompa Abandoned as a place of worship centuries ago, the *chos-kor* (religious enclave) at Alchi is one of the great art treasures of the Buddhist world, one of the very few remaining examples of Indian Buddhist art from the 11th century. This collection of five small temples has a miraculously preserved series of statues and frescoes in a style quite different from the rest of Ladakh's gompas, but which has been likened to those at the Ajanta Caves in Maharashtra. The finest of the temples is the **sumtsek** (three-storey temple), with ornate wooden carvings at the entrance and three remarkable Buddha statues inside. Take a torch (flashlight) to examine the miniature paintings on the robes of the Buddhas, but don't use a camera flash as it will damage the art currently under restoration.

In the niche on the left is a statue of Avalokitesvara, with scenes of court life painted on its clothing. The statue of Manjushri on the right has images of pilgrimages and palaces, while Maitreya, the central statue in the niche at the rear has figures in Tantric positions. The three statues protrude into the upper storey, which can be reached by a rickety ladder. Around the walls are numerous mandalas.

The nearby **dukhang** (main prayer room) is the oldest building in Alchi and has six beautiful mandalas and a stunning statue of the Vairocana Buddha, one of the five 'transcendental Buddhas' used as themes for meditative reflection and ritual in Mahayana Buddhism. The courtyard is partially open to the sky but you'll need a torch to properly examine the Vairocana statue in the niche at the back of the inner hall. Behind the gilded statue and on either side there are some interesting friezes of fierce deities, royalty and ancient armies.

The small temple next to the dukhang contains an image of **Ringchen Zangpo**, who founded the gompa in the 11th century on his return from India, which accounts for the Indian and, particularly, Kashmiri, influences. The **Lhakhang Soma** or 'new' temple to the left of the sumtsek is painted with incidents from the life of the Buddha.

One of the more enjoyable aspects of this gompa is that it is the only one in the Ladakhi region on flat ground, so no knee-breaking climbing is involved.

Places to Stay & Eat Alchi's accommodation is mainly grouped around the gompa and car park (with a tea stand and small grocery shop), both of which are at the end of the road into the village. As this is primarily a summer tourist resort virtually everything here closes in winter. During the rest of the year, guesthouses operate restaurants.

Choskor Guest House, to the left as you enter Alchi, is a cosy traditional house with singles/doubles for Rs 80/100.

Lotsava has basic but clean and comfortable rooms for Rs 100/150. Most of the bathrooms are outside, within the small garden.

Samdup Ling Guest House has rooms with private bathroom for Rs 150 and a garden restaurant.

Alchi Resort, in a fairly ugly compound, has two-room huts with bath and solar-heated hot water for Rs 500. There is a bit of a courtyard, which helps the ambience a little.

Getting There & Away There is one daily minibus to Alchi (Rs 32), leaving Leh at 3.30 pm, returning at 7 am. Otherwise, take a bus to Khalsi or beyond and walk the fairly easy 3km from the bridge about 2km past Saspul. A one-way/return taxi from Leh costs Rs 935/1155.

Rizong

About 6km along a steep, rocky track north of the main road is the start of the isolated area containing **Julichen Nunnery** and **Rizong Gompa**. Reaching the gompa, belonging to the Gelukpa order, entails a very steep climb. Founded just over 100 years ago, it is less notably artistic than others, but is known for its frescoes. The lamas and *chomos* (nuns) follow a strict lifestyle.

There is no village at Rizong, but you may be able to stay at the gompa (men only) or the nunnery (women only); bring your own supplies. Alternatively, near the turn-off to Rizong, about 200m towards Alchi on the main road, is the pricey ***Uley Tokpo Camping Ground*** *(☎ 01982-53640, fax 52735)* with mildly luxurious tents set among apricot trees for Rs 2280 a double including meals.

There is no direct bus to Rizong from Leh, so it is a matter of getting a bus bound for Kargil. If coming from Alchi, it is not difficult to hitch a ride on a truck or bus for 20 minutes between the turn-offs for Alchi and Rizong. As an alternative, a taxi one way from Leh to the bottom of the walk up to the gompa will set you back Rs 1330.

Temisgam

Once capital of Ladakh, Temisgam is 92km north-west from Leh. A popular trekking village, it is dominated by Temisgam Palace which is encircled by a defence wall.

Namra Guest House has dorm beds for Rs 100, and singles/doubles for Rs 200/300. It also has a restaurant.

Buses from Leh (Rs 42) leave at 1 pm, returning at 9 am.

Khalsi

There has been a bridge over the Indus River, at the turn off to Dha-Hanu, for many centuries, the latest of which was being constructed at the time of research. This is a major military area, where your passport will be checked regardless of where you are going, and your permit checked if you're going to Dha-Hanu. There are ***food stalls*** and unsavoury ***accommodation*** options on the road through town.

Choglamsar

This is an important centre for Tibetan Buddhism and the study of Tibetan culture and history. Around the refugee camp, off the main road from Leh, is a Tibetan library and the Central Institute of Buddhist Studies, with its own library open Monday to Saturday. Both have books on Buddhism, Tibet and Ladakh. There is also a medical centre, handicraft shops, study centre, bookshops, plenty of restaurants and the Dalai Lama's prayer ground, Jiva-tsal.

Choglamsar buses leave the new bus stand in Leh every 15 minutes (Rs 4); a one-way taxi costs Rs 130. There are a couple of crummy ***guesthouses*** along the very noisy main road, but it's close enough to Leh that you can avoid these.

Shey Gompa

Shey, 15km south of Leh, was the former summer palace of the kings of Ladakh. The gompa, still partially used, is being restored. There's a small library, a collection of thangkas, and some stupas and **mani walls** nearby.

The 12m **Sakyamuni Buddha statue**, made of copper but gold-plated, is the largest in the region, built by King Singge Namgyal's son. More crumbling **chortens** (Tibetan for stupas) are scattered around the nearby fields. About 1km towards Leh, where the road sweeps around a rocky spur, there is an ancient carving of the five Buddhas of meditation; the images are thought to date from the 8th century.

Oracles offer advice here free of charge (a donation may be expected) during the annual **festival** in February/March.

Shey is easy to reach and can be combined with a visit to Tikse. Minibuses to Shey (Rs 8) leave every 30 minutes; by taxi it costs Rs 265 return. The only place to stay is the pleasant and large ***Shilkhar Hotel & Restaurant***, near the road up to the gompa. Rooms with bathroom cost Rs 150/200.

Tikse Gompa

About 17km south of Leh, this beautiful gompa, part of the Gelukpa order, is a fine example of how donations have been put to good use through extensive restoration work. It is a bit garish, and some may feel it has a slightly oppressive feudal atmosphere, but the setting is absolutely stupendous. Beside the car park you are able to see the small **Zan-La Temple**.

The gompa has an important collection of Tibetan books in its library, some excellent artwork and a new Maitreya temple. It's a busy place, with almost incessant chanting and music, and there is a good chance to witness a puja. Go to the roof for great views of the valleys and villages. There is even a small (and welcome) cafe and shop. The gompa is open 7.30 am to 6 pm daily. Permission is required to use video cameras.

The only place to stay in Tikse is the ***Skalzang Chamba Hotel*** *(☎ 47004)*, at the start of the road leading to the gompa. It is a well-run, pleasant place with a small garden. It costs Rs 200 per room and there is a restaurant. Serious students (male only) of Buddhism, but not ordinary backpackers, may possibly be able to stay at the gompa.

A bus from Leh to Tikse (Rs 8) leaves every 15 minutes. From the bus stop, it is a fair walk up to the gompa. A return taxi from Leh will cost Rs 400.

Chemrey Gompa

Chemrey village has a well-maintained and quiet gompa that sees few tourists because it is a little difficult to get to. Built to commemorate the death of King Singge Namgyal in 1645, the gompa belongs to the Drukpa order, and is where invading Dogras defeated a Tibetan army in the 1840s. The friendly monks can show you the impressive ancient library, and lovely Buddhist images on the wall of the prayer room. Nearby is a **cave gompa**.

To get to Chemrey, catch the bus to Taktok, get off at Chemrey village, and be prepared for a long (about an hour) and steep walk (it's steeper than that to Tikse Gompa). By car, you can take a road to the top, but it is very narrow and windy. From Leh, return taxis cost Rs 860, or you could try to arrange a side trip to Chemrey and Taktok if you're going on to Pangong Tso. There is nowhere to stay in Chemrey, but plenty of camping spots. However, before setting up your tent, check with the villagers as to the correct places to camp.

Taktok Gompa

With at least five different spellings, Taktok is the only gompa in the upper Indus Valley belonging to the Nyingmapa order. Built around a cave above the village of Sakti, the actual date of construction varies depending on who you talk to, but there have been some recent additions. The frescoes have been damaged over the years but there are some intricate rugs and paintings to see.

Taktok is a little difficult to get to, and not on the usual 'gompa trail'. Tourists are not common, so you may have to find a monk to open the prayer rooms for you. Two **festivals** are held each year, from the ninth to 11th days of the sixth month (July/August), and from the 26th to 29th days of the ninth month (around November) of the Tibetan calendar.

The ***J&KTDC Tourist Bungalow***, opposite the gompa, has doubles for Rs 35 but no running water and only meagre food. However, there are excellent camping sites everywhere. One or two early-morning daily buses go past Taktok from Leh, but departure times change regularly, so check at the tourist offices in Leh. There is at least one late afternoon bus back from Taktok to Leh every day. A return taxi from Leh costs Rs 980.

Stok Gompa & Museum

Over the bridge from Choglamsar, the Stok Gompa is where the last king of Ladakh died in 1974. Built in 1814, it is popular because it is so easy to get to. There are over 80 rooms, but only a few are open to the public. It also has some fine masks and frescoes.

The museum, in front of the gompa, has a unique display of rare ornaments from the royal family plus thangkas, traditional clothing and jewellery. Entry is Rs 20 and it's open 8 am to 7 pm in summer. Photography is not permitted. Oracles hold court here during the annual **festival** in February/March.

The only nearby place to stay is the elegant ***Hotel Highland*** *(☎ 3783)*, just under the museum, with doubles for Rs 600. There are other smaller places to stay towards the main road. Direct buses (Rs 7) leave Leh at 1, 4 and 4.30 pm, returning at 8 and 8.30 am and 2 pm. A return taxi from Leh will cost Rs 370.

Matho Gompa

Built in the early 16th century, but virtually destroyed in subsequent wars, the gompa at

Matho belongs to the Sakyapa order. A 5km walking trail links Matho and Stakna Gompa. There are some impressive thangkas in the very old library, and a rather tacky museum (which includes a stuffed yak). It is a busy place, with a school for 30 children, and the 20 or so monks can be seen making intricate silver and gold decorations for stupas. From the roof are staggering views of the dry, rocky 'moonscapes' of Ladakh.

The **festival** here, along with those at Shey and Stok, is famous for its oracles. Two monks meditate in complete isolation during the month leading up to the festival, held in February/March. Emerging in a trance-like state, they are able to invoke deities' spirits and dish out advice and perform ceremonies to ensure good luck. Some of the oracles get into such a state they inflict wounds on themselves that miraculously don't draw blood or, if they do, appear to heal immediately.

The minibus from Leh to Matho (Rs 12) leaves Leh at 7.30 am and 4.30 pm, returning at 6.30 am. A taxi to Stakna and Matho from Leh costs about Rs 785. There is no accommodation in Matho, but it's possible to camp.

Stakna Gompa

The gompa at Stakna – meaning 'Tiger's Nose' – is another gompa set spectacularly on the Hemis side of the Indus. Built by King Singge Namgyal's stepbrother, as part of the Brokpa order, it is accessible from, and can be combined with a trip to, Matho.

A brightly restored courtyard leads to several new and old prayer rooms, one of which has a lovely silver chorten. From the roof are some of the best views to be had of Ladakh.

To get there, take the 7.30 am minibus from Leh (Rs 12) and get off at the sign by the road to the gompa. Cross the bridge and walk for 30 minutes across the shadeless fields and up the steep path. A return taxi from Leh costs Rs 630. There is no guesthouse in the village, but it's possible to camp near the Indus.

Hemis Gompa

Also known as Chang-Chub-Sam-Ling (Lone Place of the Compassionate Person), Hemis Gompa, 45km south of Leh, belongs to the Drukpa order and was founded in the early 17th century.

Now it is one of the most accessible, famous and, therefore, most touristy gompas. Cradled in a lovely valley, surrounded by streams and fronted by long mani stone walls, it is certainly worth a visit. The gompa is also important for Ladakhi Buddists, who are meant to visit it once in their lifetime.

The gompa has an excellent library, well-preserved frescoes showing some Kashmiri influence, and good Buddha figures and the largest thangka in Ladakh, over 12m long. The famous annual **festival** commemorating the birth of the renowned Indian sage, Padmasambhava, is held on the ninth to 11th days of the fifth Tibetan month, in June/July. Every 12 years, during the Year of the Monkey, the festival is the scene for the unfurling of the thangka. It's next on display in 2004.

Hemis is worth staying over for a night so you can explore the Gotsang Hermitage Gompa, along a trail for an hour behind the Hemis gompa. There are also some caves nearby.

There are no guesthouses near the gompa, but the ***East West Guesthouse*** in the village, a long walk away, has doubles for Rs 150. Several places near the gompa allow camping; you can set up your own tent next to the gompa for Rs 35, or rent a preset two-person tent for Rs 50. Book at the nice ***outdoor restaurant*** next to the gompa entrance, which serves unexciting but welcome Chinese food, tea and beer. A daily minibus (Rs 20) leaves Leh for Hemis at 9.45 am and 4 pm, returning to Leh at 7 am and noon. A bus also leaves Leh at 1.30 pm returning at 9 am. Return taxis from Leh cost Rs 860.

NUBRA VALLEY

☎ 01982

The Nubra Valley – *nubra* means 'green' – used to be on the trading route connecting Tibet with Turkistan, and was the envy of Turkistan, which invaded it several times. Also known as the Valley of Flowers, Nubra has always been well cultivated and fertile, with the best climate in Ladakh, so grains and fruits, such as apples and apricots, have always been plentiful. Ninety per cent of the Nubra's population is Buddhist.

The valley is a wonderful area to visit, dominated by an incredible broad, empty floodplain through which the Nubra and Shyok Rivers pass. There are pretty, small villages, dense forests and some wildlife – camels are common on the sand dunes near Hunder – but inevitably the area is slowly becoming more affected by the increasing number of travellers who make the effort to visit. Your permit only allows you to travel as far as Hunder along the southern valley, and to Panamik in the northern valley.

All places in the valley provide meals and electricity until 10 pm but are very basic. Most close in winter and the only place where you will find accommodation at this time is in Diskit, during which time hot water is provided in buckets. Unless stated otherwise, toilets are sit-down flush style and bathrooms are private.

Getting There & Away

The road to the Nubra Valley, along the highest motorable road in the world, is officially open year-round. Trucks and buses are only allowed across the pass in each direction between 10 am and noon on alternate days: Tuesday, Thursday and Saturday towards Nubra and Monday, Wednesday, Friday and Sunday towards Leh. Taxis, private vehicles and the military can travel at any time.

Bus Buses travel to both sides of the Nubra Valley from Leh every few days. The buses are slow and crowded, as to be expected in this region, but fun. Buses between Leh and Diskit travel on Thursday (Rs 57.50, six hours); they leave Leh at 5.30 am. A bus to Sumur and Panamik (Rs 79, 10 hours), leaves Leh at 5.30 am on Tuesday and Saturday.

Truck Lifts on trucks, even military ones – in fact, anything travelling along the roads to and around the Nubra Valley – is quite acceptable for tourists and locals alike. As usual, negotiate a fare (around the cost of the bus fare) the day before, and prepare yourself for a rough old ride.

Taxi Hiring jeeps or taxis may be the only option, and for groups it's often a good one. A one-way/return taxi to Diskit from Leh will cost Rs 3355/4425. A taxi from Leh to Panamik costs Rs 3520 one-way, or Rs 4700 return. A return trip from Leh visiting Diskit, Hunder, Sumur and Panamik for three days will cost about Rs 8000 per taxi.

Getting Around

In the valley there is a limited public bus service for exploration purposes. From Diskit, buses to Panamik (Rs 28, three hours) via Sumur (Rs 16, 1¼ hours) leave at 4 pm Monday and Wednesday, returning the next day at 8.30 am. If there are taxis around Diskit, they will offer full-day tours around the valley's southern side for Rs 950; Rs 1250 including both sides. One-way/return fares from Diskit to Panamik are Rs 1155/1490 and from Diskit to Sumur Rs 770/970.

Khardung La

The road to the Nubra Valley goes through the highest motorable pass in the world at Khardung La (5602m). The pass is almost permanently covered in fog and snow, and is likely to be bitterly cold at the top regardless of the time of year. The pass is occupied by a grubby military camp, the highest temple in the world, a free tea stand and stacks of oil drums. In summer, you may see one of the world's highest traffic jams of trucks and buses. The road between Leh and Khalsar is reasonable, except between the miserable road-building camps of South Pullu and North Pullu, just before and after Khardung La, where the road is atrocious. The camps have toilets, tea shops and food, and there are many places to stop for views near the pass, such as India Gate.

Beyond the pass is Khardung village, with one very basic shop and an unused government resthouse.

Khalsar

The Nubra Valley really starts at the village of Khalsar (3018m), where there are several teahouses and a lot of discarded army equipment. The road divides just before the village of Lughzun – the left fork going to Hunder and beyond following the Shyok River, and the right heading north to Panamik and beyond, following the Nubra River.

Diskit

The turn off to Diskit (3144m) stretches about 3km along an awesome, wide and dry riverbed before climbing and clinging to the hillside for another 13km.

Diskit Gompa, with about 70 monks, is the oldest (over 350 years old) and the biggest of its kind in the Nubra Valley, and shouldn't be missed. It is particularly famous for its murals, and the view from the roof is wonderful. According to legend, there is a statue in the gompa that has the head and arm of an invader from over five centuries ago. There are three prayer rooms on different levels, as well as a library, some very old frescoes, and a few nice thangkas. If you want to see the heads of the statues uncovered you'll have to visit at festival time (February).

From the village, the gompa is a 40-minute walk. It is slightly hidden, up the hill, and can be confusing to find. If in doubt, keep asking locals for directions.

Between Diskit and Hunder is an area of **sand dunes**, not unlike the Sahara Desert (if you can ignore the snowcapped mountains in the background!).

Places to Stay & Eat The guesthouses in Diskit almost run in a line from below the gompa to the village centre.

The first you'll spot is ***Olthang Guest House*** *(☎ 20025)*, which has nicely furnished singles/doubles with private bathroom (squat toilets) for Rs 150/200. At the time of research a couple of other rooms with sit-down flush toilets were being built next to the main building. There's a comfortable lounge area, a sun room and a large garden with car parking, and it's open in winter. On the opposite side of the road as you head down to the right of Olthang is ***Sunrise Guest House*** *(☎ 20011)*. In a nice garden, it has sunny rooms with good views and bathrooms (sit-down flush and squat toilets) for Rs 100/200, and a cosy Ladakhi kitchen.

On the same side of the road, through an archway with a stupa on top, is ***Karakuram Guest House*** *(☎ 20024)*. Quite basic singles/doubles around a 1st-floor terrace with the choice of private or shared squat toilets are Rs 50/100. It's also possible to camp here for Rs 25 per tent and it's open in winter.

Next up, and open all year, is ***Khangsar Guest House*** *(☎ 20014)*, a farmhouse which you enter through a yard full of cows. It has even more basic rooms, again around a 1st-floor terrace, but it's quite homey, with rooms with shared squat toilets for Rs 50/100.

Opposite the hospital in an overgrown garden is ***Sangum Guest House*** *(☎ 20016)*, made of concrete but with an Australian weatherboard house appearance. Clean rooms with bathroom (squat and sit-down flush toilets), homey furniture and good views are Rs 200/300; it is open all year.

In the centre near a couple of roadside ***restaurants*** and the bus stand, and set within a scruffy garden, is ***Sand Dune Guest House***. Spacious rooms are Rs 150/200 with private bathroom (sit-down flush toilets).

Hunder

Hunder is a pretty village, set among lots of trees and gurgling streams. It is nicer than Diskit, but Diskit, the bigger village of the two, has slightly better facilities. Some enjoy the 8km walk between the villages, either along the main road or across the sand dunes (watch out for wild camels!). Alternatively you can ride a tame camel across for around Rs 200 – guesthouses can organise this. Native to the region, the hardy, shaggy Bactrian camels were used to carry supplies along trade routes.

The **gompa** at Hunder is about a 2km walk above the village, including a short, steep, rocky climb. It is completely deserted and quite eerie. There is only a small Buddha statue and some damaged frescoes, but the climb is worth it for the views and atmosphere. Don't wander too far up the road – there's a heavy military presence.

Places to Stay Hunder is quite a sprawl, so you'll probably need to ask directions to the following places, which are both central but a bit of a trek north of the dunes. They offer the same facilities as those in Diskit.

Moon Land Guest House is a big, sign-posted, brick place in a pleasant and large garden, with a nice Ladakhi kitchen. Large rooms with private bathroom (sit-down flush toilets) are Rs 100/150 a single/double and it stays open in winter.

Snow Leopard Guest House, also in a nice garden, has biggish rooms with bathroom (sit-down flush toilets) for Rs 200.

At the time of research a new place was being built opposite Moon Land.

Sumur

Sumur (3096m), a major village along the Nubra River side of the valley, is a pretty place worth exploring.

The **Samstemling Gompa**, over 150 years old, is a large complex with seven temples. Inaugurated by the Dalai Lama in 1962, it is a busy, friendly place with about 45 children chanting, or cultivating apples and apricots. The prayer rooms open to the public house an impressive collection of thangkas and restored frescoes. Strict rules apply here, including one that forbids females entry to the gompa between sunset and sunrise.

By road, it is a fair distance from Sumur village to the gompa: about 3km south towards the village of Tegar, from where a 3km road to the gompa starts. It's far quicker on foot, as you can go up the hill from the village to avoid the road, but you will have to ask directions. It can be confusing because the gompa near the start of the road to the Samstemling Gompa is actually the Tegar Gompa. The Samstemling Gompa is the more colourful one closer to Sumur.

On the opposite side of the river to Sumur is Charasa, easily identifiable atop a hillock. Facing Samstemling, the valley's most important gompa, it served as the palace of Nubra's royalty until the region came under the direct control of Leh.

Places to Stay & Eat Just by the turn-off into the centre and near the shops, ***Twesang Jorgais Guest House***, in a big garden, has rooms on the 1st floor of the family house for Rs 100/150 a single/double.

Farther down the same road, ***Tashi Khangsar Guest House*** is a concrete-block place, but the rooms, for Rs 100/150, are comfortable enough.

Continuing farther down the lane, ***LP Guest House*** has rooms within a farmyard for Rs 100/150. Although the toilets are sit-down flush style, you have to go outside to get to them.

Probably the nicest place, with basic rooms within a traditional farmhouse for Rs 100/200, is ***Largyal Guest House***. Prices include meals served in the Ladakhi kitchen. Camping is also available here.

There are a couple of upmarket options. ***Hotel Yarabtso*** (☎ 20008) is a big place in Tegar village just south of Sumur. Rooms with private bathroom are Rs 1200/1750 including all meals.

Back in Sumur, down by the river, ***Lharimo North Camp*** (☎ 52177) charges Rs 1650/200, including all meals.

Panamik

Panamik (3183m) is another small village, famous for centuries for its **hot springs**, and as the first or last stop along the ancient trade route between Ladakh and Central Asia. Farther north lies the high altitude battlefield of the Siachen Glacier. Don't come specifically for the springs – you'll be disappointed. Do come for the satisfaction of reaching the end of the road, and to appreciate the natural beauty of this isolated spot.

The spring water, rumoured to cure rheumatism and other ailments, is pumped in from the Nubra River, about 2km away. There is a dark, double-chambered hut for bathing but it's male-dominated and none too clean. Despite the signs stating it's prohibited, many soldiers use the springs to do their laundry.

The 250-year-old **Ensa Gompa** is a fair trek from the village – a couple of hours at least. It is farther than it seems. If you do want to get there, walk about 5km to Hargam, then cross the bridge for some more walking. Strictly speaking, this means going beyond the permit zone, so the soldiers might insist you go back. Some have tried to cross the river by swimming or wading, and many have nearly come to a tragic end. Be sensible and take the bridge.

Overlooking the river and Ensa Gompa, ***Silk Route Guest House*** is in a large garden with large well-furnished rooms with squat toilets for Rs 100/200. Although it's open during summer only, one room and the dining room have heaters.

RUPSU VALLEY

This is an area of nomadic people, known as Khampas, who can often be seen taking advantage of the summer months to move herds of goats, cows and yaks from one grazing spot to another. Khampas live in large, movable family tents or in solid winter-proof brick huts, and are referred to as Chinese cowboys. Another great aspect of this region is the amount of wildlife – the best (accessible) place in Ladakh for it. Commonly seen are wild asses (known as *kiangs*), foxes and cuddly marmots busy waking up from their last hibernation, or preparing for the next. On the lakes, you may see large flocks of endangered black-necked geese; the best times for spotting birds are July and August.

There are currently no hotels in the region, though this may change as demand increases. You must bring your own tent and all equipment. There are preset tents at the astronomical price of Rs 800 per two-person tent at Tso Moriri Village; these are set up for upmarket, organised tour groups.

There are also no restaurants in the region so, again, bring your own food and cooking equipment. This is a very fragile environment, so make sure you take out everything you bring in – cans, bottles, papers, *everything*!

Getting There & Away

There are two ways that your 4WD jeep is physically able, and permitted, to enter or leave the region. The first route takes you over the Mahe Bridge (near Raldong, at the south-eastern end of the Indus Valley road) through Puga, and then to one or both lakes. The other route is the road south from Upshi, over Taglang La, then a detour to Thukse – look out for the yellow sign.

No public transport goes even remotely near the lakes. The area has no signposts, and quality maps of the area are nonexistent, so motorcycles are not recommended unless you have a guide (you could easily burn out the clutch in the sand drifts as well). There will be very few people around to give you directions – the marmots around here outnumber humans by about 50 to one.

A round taxi trip will cost about Rs 9000 from Leh to Tso Moriri over three days via Tso Kar and Taglang La; the shorter, more direct way is Rs 7500. From Leh, a two-day round trip just to Tso Kar will be Rs 6500. Travel agencies in Leh can organise a three-day 'jeep safari' from Rs 7500 to 10,000 per vehicle, including meals and tent accommodation, depending on which way you go.

Tso Moriri

Known as 'Mountain Lake', Tso Moriri (4400m) is about 140km (but a rough-and-tumble six or so hours by jeep) from Leh. This saltwater lake is about 28km long and 8km at its widest. Surrounded by barren hills, which are backed by snow-covered mountains, Tso Moriri is a good place to relax, visit nearby **gompas** and do some walking.

Note, the small collection of huts on the shore of Tso Moriri is also called Tso Moriri. Here you must register and show your permit. You can pitch your tent here (there's a toilet), but there is nothing stopping you from camping anywhere else.

Korzok

A path at the back of the Tso Moriri huts leads for a kilometre or so to the delightful village of Korzok. The **gompa** here is quite unusual because it is inhabited predominantly by women, who often spend their days making beautiful garments which are not for sale (or not yet). The gompa was built in about 1850, replacing one destroyed during a Dogra invasion.

Tso Kar

Tso Kar (White Lake), 6km north-west of Tso Moriri, has a small **gompa** at the village of Thukse, a collection of solid brick huts set up for the dramatic winters. You will have to find a monk to let you in. On a slight, and legal, detour off the track linking Tso Kar and Tso Moriri is the smaller lake of **Tso Kiagar**.

PANGONG TSO

The salty Pangong Tso – *pangong* means 'hollow' – is the highest lake in Ladakh (at an altitude of 4250m), and is flanked by massive peaks over 6500m high. The lake is 150km long, but is only 4km at its widest point, and extends almost in a straight line, way into Tibet – only a quarter of the lake is in India.

Unfortunately, visitors are usually only allowed to spend an hour or two at the lake itself, and some travellers have reported that the army make it clear they would prefer you didn't visit at all. Many visitors find the long trip and quick turnaround a waste of time and money. Permits allow travel from Leh to Pangong Tso via Karu, Chang La (5599m), Durbuk, Tangtse, Lukung and only as far as **Spangmik**, the first village you come to on the southern side of the lake.

The area around **Tangtse**, on the way to the lake, is of historical significance, as it was an important stop on the old trade routes. There is a small **gompa** and, nearby, some **inscriptions**, possibly 1000 years old, on some hard-to-find rocks.

Places to Stay & Eat

There are no guesthouses in the villages except for a ***government resthouse*** in Tangtse, which is not strictly for tourists, so all visitors will have to bring their own tents and all their own supplies. Foreigners are no longer permitted to pitch their tents by the lake.

Official camping sites are at Durbuk, Tangtse and Lukung; otherwise, just take your pick of any unofficial spot in the countryside. Lukung is about the best area for camping. There are several little villages along the lake, and on the way to it, but they offer little, if anything, in the way of supplies.

Getting There & Away

From Leh, the road is reasonable to the military town of Karu, it then goes over the Chang La (5599m) and becomes terrible down to Tangtse, another military site. It alternates between bad and barely adequate until Lukung, and then Spangmik, which is as far as your permit will allow. A 4WD vehicle is necessary for this section.

By Indian or Japanese jeep from Leh the one-way/return fare to Tangtse is Rs 2915/3630. A more leisurely two-day trip, which is about all you may need, will cost Rs 5250 per vehicle from Leh. You may be able to fit in a side trip to the gompas at Tikse and Chemrey on the way to Tangtse.

There are occasional buses from Leh to Tangtse, but taking one will severely limit your ability to explore the area, as there is no local public transport.

DHA-HANU

Dha-Hanu consists of a handful of villages along the road leading north-west from Khalsi. The steep bare walls of the Indus give the terraced fields more light and heat than other parts of Ladakh, which, combined with the lower altitude, enables rich crops of vegetables and fruits (especially apricots) to grow here.

It is a small region and doesn't get many visitors, which is not a bad reason to visit. The definite pluses are its accessibility by bus (along a reasonable road), the charming villages and the people, who have different traditions and appearances to the rest of the population of Ladakh. Currently, permits will allow you to go only as far as Dha and Biama villages.

The area is probably most famous for its inhabitants, known as Dards or Brokpas, 'People of the Land', an ancient Indo-Iranian people with Mediterranean features and bacchanalian fertility festivals. Despite their proximity to Pakistan and other Islamic regions, they are traditionally not Muslims (though there are a few mosques in the area), but retain their own Buddhist traditions and beliefs.

The Brokpas often wear traditional clothes. Men wear coats similar to those worn in Leh, and some are made from goatskin. Women often wear caps (rather than the *gondas* (stovepipe hats) found in Leh) adorned with jewellery, flowers and peacock feathers. They also wear long, ornate chains, heavy earrings, and have their hair long.

Places to Stay & Eat

There are a handful of basic guesthouses in the village of Dha. ***Skyababa Guesthouse*** at the Leh end of the village has basic doubles for Rs 100, and the family is friendly. In the heart of the village, ***Chunu Guesthouse*** has very rustic double rooms for Rs 60. Nearby, ***Lhariemo Shamo Guesthouse*** is similar, but charges Rs 100 for a double.

There are recognised camping sites at the villages of Dhumkhar, Skurbuchan, Biama, Hanu-Do and Dha, and plenty of other legal, but unofficial, places along the way. The one or two shops at Dha and Skurbuchan offer little in the way of food, but guesthouses usually provide basic meals.

Getting There & Away

Daily buses between Leh and Dha (Rs 72) leave in each direction at 9 am; another daily bus from Leh to Skurbuchan leaves at 10 am, returning at 9 am. A taxi to Dha from Leh costs Rs 2486/3393 one-way/return over two days.

LEH TO MANALI

Since opening to foreigners in 1989, this road has become a popular way into and out of Leh. (The only other road to Leh goes through Kashmir and along a stretch between Drass and Kargil made more hazardous than usual by Pakistani artillery, and there is often difficulty in getting flights into and out of Leh.) There is nothing to see along the road in the way of villages or gompas; it is the raw high-altitude scenery that will certainly impress, and is reason enough for travelling this way.

The road to Manali is the world's second-highest motorable road, reaching 5328m at Taglang La. As only about half of the total distance of 485km between Leh and Manali is paved, it can be a rough journey. For much of the way the only inhabitants of the high plateaus are Khampa nomads, soldiers and teams of tar-covered workers from Bihar and Nepal struggling to keep this strategic road open. Whatever form of transport you choose, the trip will take at least two days, with an overnight stop at a tent camp, probably in Sarchu in Himachal Pradesh.

Sudden changes in weather are common, even in the mid-summer month of August, and can cause delays of several days. It is worth having some cold- and wet-weather gear with you in the bus because the weather, especially around the highest passes, can be

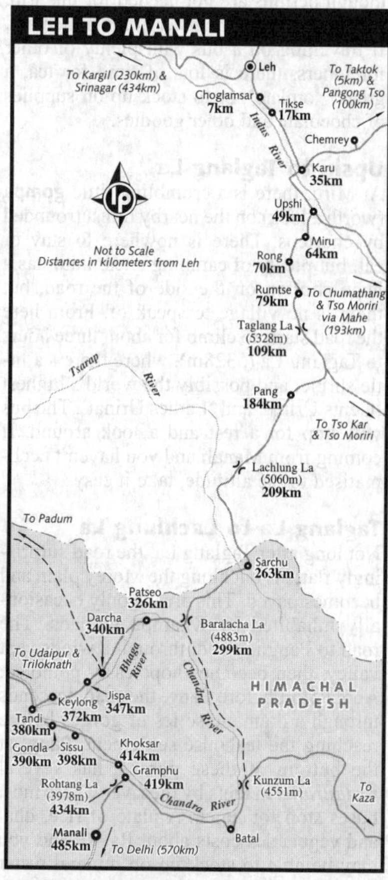

very cold and wet. The road is usually open between early June and mid-October.

Leh to Upshi

Leaving Leh, from the main road you will get your last glimpse (or your first, of course, if coming from Manali) of the magnificent gompas at Shey, Tikse and Stok. For an hour or so before Upshi, along a paved but dusty road, there are plenty of ugly military sites, such as Karu, the turn-off to the Pangong Tso area and to the gompas at Chemrey and Taktok. The first checkpoint of Upshi is the turn-off south to Manali. Although permits are not needed for this trip, foreigners have to register at the police hut. If travelling on a bus with plenty of other foreigners, there is lots of time for tea, a greasy 'omlate', or to stock up on supplies of chocolate and other goodies.

Upshi to Taglang La

At Miru, there is a crumbling little **gompa** (worth a look) on the nearby hill surrounded by chortens. There is nowhere to stay or eat, but plenty of camping sites. Lato has a huge **chorten** on the side of the road, but there is no village to speak of. From here the road starts to climb for about three hours to Taglang La (5328m), where there's a little shrine, and possibly the world's highest 'Gents Urinal' and 'Ladies Urinal'. The bus will stop for a rest and a look around. If coming from Manali and you haven't acclimatised to the altitude, take it easy.

Taglang La to Lachlung La

Not long after Taglang La, the road surprisingly flattens out along the Morey plain and becomes paved. This area is only occasionally inhabited by Khampa nomads. The road to Pang is good, through a windswept valley, then becomes hopelessly potholed. About 5km before Pang, the road descends through a dramatic series of **gorges** before reaching the teahouse settlement. **Pang**, at the bottom of these gorges, has several ***restaurants*** in tents by the river where most buses stop for lunch. A plate of rice, dhal and vegetables costs about Rs 30, and you may be able to stock up on mineral water and biscuits. Most tents have a mattress where you can unroll your sleeping bag for around Rs 50 per night. There are some rather grim toilets.

At 5060m, Lachlung La is the second-highest pass on the Leh to Manali road. Nearby, there is an incredible 20km of switchback roads, which includes the spine-tingling 21 Gata Loops, or hairpin bends, on one side of one mountain.

Sarchu

Sarchu (4100m) is just inside Himachal Pradesh and is where most buses stop overnight. It is just a collection of tents, dotted over a length of 15km or so, which are all packed up for eight months of the year (ie, October to May). Just opposite the striped HPTDC tent camps, you must register, again, with the police. Your driver may collect passports and do it himself, but it still involves a lot of waiting.

HPTDC buses stop at its own ***tent camps***. They are the best of the lot; clean two-person tents with camp beds and lots of blankets are Rs 115 per person. A ***tent kitchen*** has dhal and rice for dinner, and omelettes for breakfast, for about Rs 40.

Public and other private bus drivers seem to have some sort of 'arrangement' with other tent-site owners, so you may have little choice but to stay in a tent camp not even remotely as good as the HPTDC site, but for around the same price. Travellers on buses arriving late at the camps suffer the most. Although the driver may try to dissuade you, you can sleep on the bus for free, where it will be warmer. There are plenty of places to put your own tent.

Just over the bridge from the HPTDC camp are several ***tent restaurants*** that serve dhal and rice, tea, omelettes, curried noodles, and, for those long cold evenings, a shot of whisky or chang (take it easy; alcohol is more powerful at high altitude).

Baralacha La

It's only a short climb to this 4883m pass Baralacha La (Crossroads Pass) – it is a double pass linking both the upper Chandra and Bhaga Valleys with the Lingti Valley and vast Lingti plains around Sarchu. About an hour farther on is the police checkpoint at Patseo. Here the road begins to hug the Bhaga River to Tandi, where it meets the Chandra River.

Darcha

Darcha is the other major tent site on this road. Faster buses from Leh, or slower ones from Manali, may stay here, depending on the time and the state of the road around Baralacha La. Like Sarchu, Darcha is just a temporary place, with some crummy tents for hire (Rs 50) and a few ***tent restaurants***. Shortly after Darcha, you pass through Jispa, where there is still yet another large army camp.

Darcha is the start of a popular trekking option to get into Padum in Zanskar, and in winter it is the only way. From here, you can also trek into places such as Hemis (about 11 days). If you have your own transport, try to get to the little lake of **Deepak Tal** about 16km from Darcha. It is a great spot for camping and exploring.

Keylong To Manali

Keylong is the first town of any size on the journey from Leh to Manali, and the administrative centre of Lahaul and Spiti. From Keylong, it isn't far to the T-junction at Tandi. From here there is a road that goes sharply to the north-west along the Chenab River to the little-visited parts of Himachal Pradesh towards Udaipur and the famous temple site of Triloknath (see under Mandi in the Himachal Pradesh chapter for details).

The road to Manali heads south-east, and climbs steadily past Gondla, Sissu and Khoksar. There are ***Public Works Department (PWD) resthouses*** that you may be able to use, in all three places, but nothing much else. At Sissu, there is a nice **waterfall** nearby, set under spectacular peaks. Farther on, at Gramphu, the road continues south to Manali – if instead you want to go to Kaza, get off at Gramphu or at Keylong. From Gramphu the road to Kaza climbs along Lahaul and Spiti.

Rohtang La (3978m) – not high, but treacherous all the same – marks the start of the descent into Manali. See the Himachal Pradesh chapter for more details on Keylong and Manali.

LEH TO KARGIL

This section refers to places on, or near, the main road from Leh to Kargil. A number of buses ply the 231km road to Kargil. Trucks are also a good option for a lift between villages. Taxi fares may seem outrageous, but with a group sharing the cost you can visit several gompas on the way. There are tourist bungalows along the route, but these must be booked in advance through the Leh or Kargil tourist offices.

Lamayuru

After you've explored other villages in the area, Lamayuru (3390m) will seem a relatively scruffy little place. But it is completely overshadowed by one of the most famous and spectacularly set gompas in Ladakh.

The **gompa**, part of the Kagyupa order, is not as interesting as many others. Here it's the location – perched above a drained lake on an eroded crag overlooked by massive mountains – that makes it special. The oldest known gompa in Ladakh, dating back beyond the 10th century, it has been destroyed and restored several times over the centuries. The gompa got its name after Arahat Nimagung made a prophecy that a monastery would develop on this spot. He then made corn offerings to the *naga* (serpent) spirits which moulded with the earth into the shape of a swastika.

The gompa has renowned collections of carpets, thangkas and frescoes. Criminals were once granted asylum here (not any more, you'll be glad to know!), which explains another name for the gompa: Tharpa Ling or 'Place of Freedom'. Get there early to witness a mesmerising puja.

While you are here make sure you wander through the wonderful stone passages and courtyards of the lower part of the complex to the **Singge Gang lhakhang**, an Alchi-era temple with guardian deities in an adjacent chamber. It's hard to spot – look for the red-and-white walls.

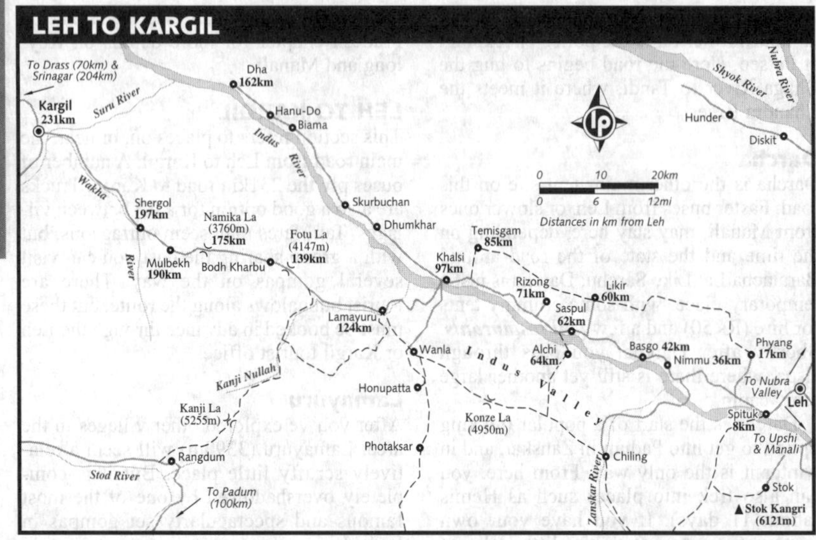

Several kilometres south-east of the village of Lamayuru is the small **Wanla Gompa**, set on the popular trekking route to Padum in Zanskar.

Places to Stay & Eat There are few choices in Lamayuru; bathrooms are shared and hot water comes in a bucket. ***Hotel Shangri-La***, on the main road through the village, is a bit run-down but the views from its Rs 150 rooms are good. It also has a restaurant, but the whole place closes down for winter.

In the village, and signposted from the tracks up to the gompa, are two family-run places with a bit more character that are more likely to be open during the colder months. ***Hotel Dragon*** has pleasantly decorated rooms for Rs 100 and prepares meals on request. ***Hotel Moonland*** is also good, and has the bonus of a restaurant. At the time of research the ***gompa*** accommodation was a dubious choice, but a new building which promises to be much more salubrious was being constructed.

Getting There & Away There are no buses from Leh or Kargil directly to Lamayuru, so take the Leh to Kargil/Srinagar bus and get off at the truck stop at the top of Lamayuru. A better option is a ride on one of the many trucks that stop overnight, leaving Lamayuru early in the morning. A one-way taxi from Leh costs Rs 1952.

Mulbekh

From Lamayuru the road passes Fotu La (4147m), the route's highest pass, then Namika La (3760m), before turning into a fertile valley. Mulbekh is the last sign of Buddhism before heading into Muslim-dominated regions near Kargil and beyond.

Mulbekh's main claim to fame is the impressive 8m-high **Maitreya statue**, an image of a Future Buddha, cut into the rock face and dating back to about AD 700. Unfortunately, all buses stop for food and a rest at the village of Wakha, 2km from Mulbekh, so this gives you no opportunity to inspect the statue on the way, but you can see it from the bus window.

There are also two gompas, **Serdung** and **Gandentse**, offering great views of the valley. As in other smaller villages, it is wise to inquire if the gompa is open before making the ascent.

Paradise Hotel and Restaurant, directly opposite the statue, costs Rs 80 per room. ***Namchung Hotel*** is similar. Another option is ***Jammu & Kashmir Tourism Development Corporation (J&KTDC) Tourist Bungalow***, on the Leh side of the statue, with rooms for Rs 40 per person.

From Leh take the Kargil/Srinagar bus. Mulbekh makes a decent day trip from Kargil. A couple of buses leave Kargil for Mulbekh daily. A return taxi from Kargil plus an hour in Mulbekh will cost Rs 800.

Shergol

About 7km farther on towards Kargil, along a fertile valley, is the small village of Shergol. Meaning 'Lord of the Morning Star', Shergol is set on the opening of the Wakha River, and has a tiny **cave gompa** perched halfway up the steep, eastern slope of the mountain. It is almost deserted, and is really for those who can't get enough of gompas and stiff walks up mountains. The view, of course, is magnificent. Below the gompa is a **nunnery**, home to a dozen or so chomos.

KARGIL

☎ 01985 • elevation 2817m

Administering the valleys of Suru, Drass (said to be the second coldest place on earth after Siberia), Wakha and Bodh Kharbu, Kargil lies midway between the alpine valleys of Kashmir and the fertile reaches of the Indus Valley and Ladakh. The region is politically part of India, ethnically part of Baltistan, and geographically an integral part of Ladakh. It is the only region of India with a Shi'ia Muslim majority.

The earliest settlers of these isolated Indus tributaries were the Dards. According to the historian AH Franke, the Dards were already acquainted with Buddhist teachings prevalent in north-west India, and had absorbed them into their culture some time before AD500. Later, as Tibetan forces invaded Ladakh, much of Dardic culture was abandoned, although isolated pockets of their heritage remain significantly intact, notably at Drass.

The full cultural shift came much later, in the 15th century, shortly after the Kashmiris were converted to Islam. Most Dardic groups were also converted, including the people of Drass, who may have appeared to convert but actually retained their own beliefs. Dardic groups still exist today, distinct from the Baltis in both language and religion – the Dards are Sunni Muslims, and the Baltis are Shi'ia. To complete this cultural patchwork, there are some isolated Dardic communities, in the Dha-Hanu region below Khalsi, who are still Buddhist.

In the Suru, Wakha and Bodh Kharbu Valleys, the cultural similarities with Baltistan are more apparent. Trade links were also strong between Gilgit (Pakistan) and Kargil, so the region's attention focused along the Indus Valley. Isolated Buddhist communities still remain at Mulbekh in the Wakha Valley, and in the tiny kingdom of Heniskot in the upper Bodh Kharbu Valley.

The regions of Dardistan and Baltistan maintained a degree of independence from both the Mughal armies that held Kashmir, and the Mongol-Tibetan armies intent on taking Ladakh. In the 1830s, however, the Suru Valley was invaded by the army of Jammu's Dogra general Zorawar Singh, who was intent on invading Ladakh. As a result of the Dogra forays, Ladakh and Baltistan came under the influence of Jammu, and in 1846 became an integral part of the maharaja's state of Jammu & Kashmir. A century later the region was divided, and the ceasefire line between Pakistan and India was drawn across the state of Jammu & Kashmir just north of Kargil, though in the war of 1971 the frontier moved back about 12km from the town. As a consequence, the regions down the valley from Kargil are strictly no-go areas for foreigners.

Continuing political problems in Kashmir have seriously affected the number of visitors to Kargil and the hotels survive at present from the handful of visitors travelling from Leh to Padum and the Zanskar Valley.

The people of Kargil are mostly Shi'ia Muslims: Arabic script is found everywhere and men and mosques dominate the town that has been shelled by the Pakistani army several times. When artillery duels flare up, the town is declared off limits.

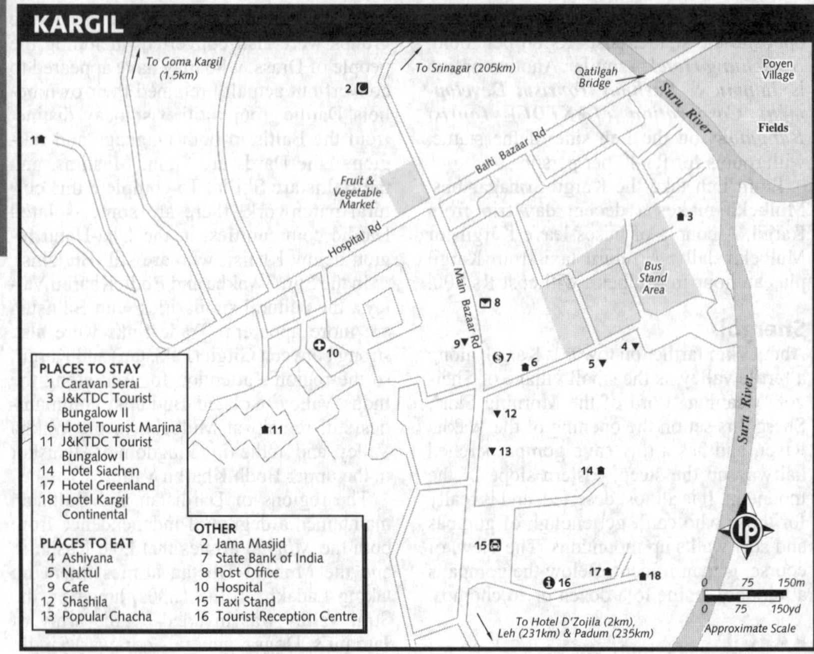

Orientation & Information

Kargil, by the roaring Suru River, is the second-largest town in Ladakh, but little more than one long main road called Main Bazaar Rd, with lots of little lanes jutting off (watch out for wide trucks). Along this road are plenty of places with long-distance/international telephone facilities, the post office and State Bank of India (with foreign exchange), open 10 am to 2 pm weekdays.

If you have time, walk up Hospital Rd for some decent views of the area. There are also nice fields and villages across the Qatilgah Bridge, at the end of Balti Bazaar Rd.

The Tourist Reception Centre (☎ 2228) is near the taxi stand, just off Main Bazaar Rd. Open 10 am to 4 pm on normal working days, it has no great information on local areas, or on Zanskar. It does, however, rent out trekking gear: tents are Rs 40 per day and sleeping bags are Rs 16 per day. The best place to arrange trekking and travel is through the Greenland and Siachen hotels.

The phone number for the police is ☎ 2210, ☎ 2382 for an ambulance and for the hospital call ☎ 2216.

Places to Stay

Catering mainly to those on an overnight stop en route between Leh and Srinagar, Kargil has a few good choices close to the transport hubs. Hotel staff are generally helpful and friendly, and where hot water is limited they will provide you with bucket hot water.

You will find two ***J&KTDC Tourist Bungalows** (☎ 2328)* in town. The first, up the hill behind the hospital, has a variety of singles/doubles/triples for Rs 200/300/400 but they really don't warrant the climb. Much more convenient and cheaper, the second, right next to the bus station, has rooms for Rs 45 per person.

***Hotel Tourist Marjina** (☎ 33085)* has basic rooms with private bathroom for Rs 150/200/250 on the ground/1st/2nd floor,

The Shi'ias of Ladakh

Kargil, including the Suru Valley, is the only region of India where the majority of the population are Shi'ia Muslims. Isolated from both their Sunni Muslim neighbours in Kashmir and the Buddhists of the Indus Valley, the Shi'ias look far afield, to Iran and the city of Lucknow in Uttar Pradesh, the centre of Shi'ia India. Books and other religious materials come from Lucknow, while the area's religious leaders study in Iran (the great Shi'ia centres in Iraq are off limits for now). Religious students from Iran regularly visit Kargil and hold public lectures.

Shi'ia Islam broke away from the majority Sunni school over the successor to Mohammed, or Imam. Shi'ias hold that the Imamate rightfully belonged to Mohammed's cousin Ali and his descendants, including Ali's martyred son Hussein. The major Shi'ia festival in Kargil is during the Islamic month of Muharram, commemorating the battle of Karbala in modern-day Iraq when Hussein was killed.

Shi'ism also differs from Sunni Islam with its hierarchy of clerics; currently the highest authority is the Supreme Leader of Iran, Ayatollah Khamenei, although a dispute over self-flagellation has led to a split that has reached even Kargil. During the Muharram processions it is customary for men to whip themselves in mourning for Hussein. Ayatollah Khamenei says the custom should be stopped and that it would be better to give blood to a blood bank, but Ayatollah Shirazi, a senior Iranian cleric, argues the custom should continue. You can sometimes tell which side of the debate a Kargil shopkeeper stands on by portraits stuck on the wall; some are of the rather jolly looking white-bearded Ayatollah Shirazi, others show the bespectacled Ayatollah Khamenei.

The spiritual leaders of Kargil's Shi'ias are known as Aghas, descended from the missionaries who started converting the population, apparently peacefully, in the 15th century. Many of those missionaries were Syeds, direct descendants of the Prophet Mohammed. The Syeds are recognisable by their black turbans. Shi'ia clerics who are not Syeds wear white turbans.

The Shi'ias of Ladakh have lagged behind their Buddhist neighbours economically; perhaps because Islam doesn't have the same exotic appeal to foreign tourists as Buddhism, the Shi'ias have received only a tiny share of the tourist dollar. Nevertheless, relations between the two communities are quite good; the Shi'ias have never taken part in the Islamic extremism that has racked Kashmir.

A new generation of mullahs (Islamic clerics) in Kargil has gradually lifted many of the old prohibitions, in particular on music, polo, female education and learning English. One of the old mullahs ordered that people wishing to learn another language should learn Arabic, to prepare them for paradise, where only Arabic is spoken. Increased literacy has changed the relationship between mullahs and lay Shi'ias; people are now encouraged to study their faith themselves and to ask their mullahs questions on law, theology and ethics, while in turn the mullahs are expected to be knowledgeable in all aspects of the faith.

Nevertheless, the Suru Valley is still a conservative area without the familiarity that people in Leh have with foreigners; taking photos of women is not appreciated and non-Muslim visitors to the Jama Masjid (Friday Mosque) aren't really welcome.

set around a pleasant garden and you enter the hotel through the (decent) restaurant.

Hotel Kargil Continental *(☎ 2304)* has large singles/doubles with private bathroom and warm bedding for a negotiable Rs 200/400. The rooms at the back look onto the river and there is parking and a restaurant.

If everything else in the budget range is full you could try ***Hotel Greenland*** *(☎ 2324)*, which has grubby ground-floor rooms with private bathroom for Rs 50/100. Try for the upper floors which have verandas and cost Rs 150/300.

Hotel Siachen *(☎ 2221)* has excellent rooms with verandas and hot water for Rs 350/500. They are on three floors set around a garden and there's a travel agency, restaurant and parking.

The classiest place in town, ***Caravan Serai*** *(☎ 2278)* is on a hill overlooking town.

It has good rooms with hot water and views for Rs 1500/2000, including breakfast. Catering primarily for upmarket trekking parties, it closes during winter.

About 2km out of town on the Padum road, ***Hotel D'Zojila*** *(☎/fax 2227)* is not really worth the effort unless you specifically want river views and running hot water. The rooms with private bathroom are large, basic and overpriced at Rs 1200/1500. They would rather you take an all-inclusive package with meals in their restaurant for Rs 2064/2484.

Places to Eat

There is not much to recommend the restaurants in Kargil – it really isn't set up for long-term visitors. The choice is limited to Kashmiri and Chinese food and hotels usually do omelettes and bread for breakfast. On and near Main Bazaar Rd are some bearable small restaurants: ***Ashiyana***, ***Naktul***, ***Shashila*** and ***Popular Chacha***. One of a few open for breakfast is the ***cafe*** across the road from the bank.

The ***restaurants*** at the Siachen and Greenland hotels are quite adequate and they'll discreetly serve a bottle of beer for Rs 125 in the evening (alcohol is prohibited in Kargil, hence the price). There is a ***fruit and vegetable market*** on the corner of Hospital Rd and Main Bazaar Rd, and plenty of shops to pick up other picnic supplies.

Getting There & Away

Bus Daily buses leave for Leh at 5.30 am (Rs 140/200 ordinary/air-con, 12 hours) and Srinagar at 4.30 am (Rs 160/200 ordinary/air-con, 12 hours). The road to Srinagar has been closed to foreigners in the past during periods of Pakistani shelling – check locally for the latest information. Towards Leh, there are also two daily buses to Mulbekh and one to Shergol; towards Srinagar, there are regular daily buses to Drass.

There are at least two daily buses to nearby Panikhar and Parkachik. To Padum, in Zanskar, there is a 4.30 am bus on alternate days (Rs 150/220 B/A class, 15 hours).

The Kargil bus stand is just off Main Bazaar Rd. Book tickets one day ahead. Buses often have their destinations in Ara bic script, so go by the bus number.

Taxi In one day, a taxi from Leh can get yo to Kargil for Rs 3355, or from Kargil t Srinagar for Rs 3100. A taxi from Kargil t Padum is not a bad alternative to the bu but the trip will cost a hefty Rs 7000 on way or Rs 12,000 return. The Kargil ta stand is on Main Bazaar Rd.

KARGIL TO PADUM

Sanku

The road from Kargil heads south-wes away from Padum, following the Suru Va ley. It's still predominantly inhabited b Muslims, who converted to Islam in th 15th century; a **Muslim shrine**, dedicated t Sayed Mir Hashim, is located in Karpc Khar near Sanku. Sanku can also be reache from Drass, west of Kargil on the road t Srinagar, on a two- to three-day trek.

Sanku accommodation is limited to th ***Government Rest House*** and ***J&KTD Tourist Bungalow***. At the time of researc the latter was barely operational but cost onl Rs 40 per person. There's a daily bus fro Kargil to Sanku at 3 pm (Rs 18). One-wa return taxis from Kargil cost Rs 700/1050.

Panikhar & Parkachik

Farther down the Suru Valley, Panikhar an Parkachik are the places to get off and ad mire, or even get closer to, the twin mou tains of **Nun** (7135m) and **Kun** (7087m). is a lovely area in summer, often full flowers and is popular with mountaineers

It's a four-hour walk to and from Lag La, from where there is a breathtaking vie of the Nun-Kun Massif. Walk about 3km u the road towards Padum, cross the suspe sion bridge over the Suru River, walk dow the valley for about 1km and then head u the foot trail to the pass. The last part quite tough, but the view justifies the effor From the top you can walk down the oth side to Parkachik and head back along th road; it's quicker to return the way yo came. A few kilometres beyond Parkachi the **Parkachik Glacier** sticks a great tongu of ice out towards the Suru River.

In Panikhar, the best accommodation option is a room at the comfortable ***J&KTDC Tourist Bungalow*** for Rs 150 per person. There is a second ***J&KTDC Tourist Bungalow*** in Parkachik.

Between Panikhar and Kargil, buses cost Rs 35, and leave twice daily in the morning; or take the Kargil to Padum bus, which leaves at 5.30 am on alternate days. One-way/return taxis cost Rs 1200/1800.

Rangdum

About halfway in travel time, but not distance, between Kargil and Padum, is Rangdum, where taxis and trucks (but not buses) may stop for the night. You can visit the 18th-century **Rangdum Gompa**, which serves as a base for about 35 monks and many novices. The ***J&KTDC Tourist Complex*** has basic facilities for Rs 40 per person. Several village ***teahouses*** offer unexciting food. From Rangdum, there is another good trek, north-east through the Kanji La (5255m) which links up to the Leh to Kargil road.

The road from Rangdum heads in a more southerly direction and crosses Pensi La (4450m). Farther on is Ating, from where you can visit the **Zongkul Gompa**. As you approach Padum, the valley becomes more populated, with plenty of small villages such as Tungri, Phey and Sani.

TREKKING IN LADAKH

The following information is an overview for travellers wishing to experience a trek. Serious trekkers might consider buying Lonely Planet's *Trekking in the Indian Himalaya*.

Treks out of Leh and the Indus Valley include the popular trek from Spituk just below Leh to the Markha Valley and Hemis Gompa, and the trek from Lamayuru Gompa to Chiling village alongside the Zanskar River. Treks can be completed from the end of June until the middle of October, when the first of the winter snow settles on the high passes. Proper acclimatisation is also necessary as many of the passes have an altitude in the vicinity of 5000m. Indeed, a few days resting in Leh (3505m) is highly recommended before commencing your trek.

There are many trekking agencies in Leh offering inclusive treks with a guide, packhorses, food and supplies. Allow a minimum of US$40 per day for an all-inclusive trek. If you are making your own arrangements, packhorses can be hired from Spituk or Lamayuru for around Rs 250 to 300 per horse per day. It is recommended that all camping gear, including a sleeping bag and tent, are brought with you even on *inclusive* treks, as the gear provided may not be adequate. Food supplies should also be carried with you from Leh as village lodges and teahouses are not available on all stages of the treks.

The British and Australian foreign affairs departments advise trekkers to travel in groups, engage local guides and register with the local police before commencing a trek. In 2000, there were several attacks on trekkers, including a murder, in the mountain areas of Himachal Pradesh and Ladakh.

Spituk to Markha Valley & Hemis via Kongmaru La

The trek from Spituk Gompa follows the Jingchen Valley to Ganda La (4920m). At least one rest day should be included before crossing the pass. It is then a steady descent to the Markha Valley and the village of Skiu. It is a further stage to Markha village, before ascending to the yak pastures at Nimaling. Above the camp is the impressive peak of Kangyaze (6400m). Kongmaru La (5030m), the highest pass on the trek, affords great views south to the Zanskar Range and north to the Ladakh Range. After crossing the pass there is one further camp site at the village of Chogdo before reaching Hemis Gompa. From Hemis there is a daily bus back to Leh.

stage	route	duration (hrs)
1	Spituk to Rumbak	6–7
2	Rumbak to Yurutse and camp	4–5
3	Yurutse to Skiu via Ganda La	6–7
4	Skiu to Markha	7–8
5	Markha to Nimaling	7–8
6	Nimaling to Chogdo via Kongmaru La	6
7	Chogdo to Hemis	4–5

Lamayuru to Chiling via Konze La & Dung Dung La

From Lamayuru the trek crosses Prinkiti La (3750m) to the ancient gompa and village at Wanla. It is a further stage to the village of Hinju at the base of Konze La (4950m) where an additional day is recommended for acclimatisation before crossing the pass. From Konze La there are impressive views of the East Karakoram Range before a short descent to the village of Sumdo Chinmu. The following day's climb to Dung Dung La (4820m) is rewarded with views of the Zanskar Range and a bird's-eye view of the swirling Zanskar River before a long and tiring descent to the village of Chiling.

From Chiling you can either return to Leh or continue to the Markha Valley. The stage from Chiling to the village of Skiu in the Markha Valley can be completed in three hours. It's an interesting stage that includes crossing the Zanskar River by a pulley bridge; the bridge is maintained and operated by villagers from Chiling, who charge Rs 100 per crossing.

stage	route	duration (hrs)
1	Lamayuru to Wanla via Prinkiti La	3–4
2	Wanla to Hinju	4–5
3	Hinju to Sumdo Chinmu via Konze La	6
4	Sumdo Chinmu to Dung Dung La base camp	3
5	Base camp to Chiling via Dung Dung La	6

Likir to Temisgam

This trek can be completed in a day if you are fit. From the Klu-kkhyil Gompa at Likir the trail crosses a small pass to the village of Yantang a short distance from Rizong Gompa. Stage 2 leads to the village of Hemis-Shukpachu. It is a further short stage over two minor passes to the roadhead at Temisgam. The trek can be completed throughout the year. Horses can be hired from Likir, while supplies and a tent must be brought from Leh. Road building will eventually render this trek obsolete. Until then there is a daily bus service to Likir and another from Temisgam back to Leh.

stage	route	duration (hrs)
1	Likir to Yangtang	4–5
2	Yangtang to Hemis-Shukpachu	3
3	Hemis-Shukpachu to Temisgam	3–4

Zanskar

The isolated region of Zanskar is composed of a number of small mountain-locked valleys to the south of Ladakh. The valleys are bounded to the north by the Zanskar Range, and to the south by the Great Himalaya Range. To the east and west, high ridges linking the Himalaya and Zanskar Ranges ensure that there is no easy connection between Zanskar and the outside world.

Zanskar essentially comprises the Stod Valley in the west and the Lunak Valley in the east, which converge at Padum, the administrative centre of the region. The fertile region of Padum and its outlying villages and gompas form the nucleus of Zanskar. The area's uninterrupted Buddhist heritage has been principally due to its isolation.

PADUM

Padum is the administrative headquarters of the Zanskar region, but was once an ancient capital. It is not a particularly attractive place, with incongruous government buildings that were constructed when the road from Kargil was completed in 1981. This has resulted in the town gaining a character similar to roadheads everywhere – vehicles are repaired, diesel cans are discarded and much that is not used is disposed of here. The main camp site and the small hotel area is close to the newly constructed mosque (the only one in the Zanskar region) that serves the Sunni Muslim community. The only telephone office is at the Hotel Ibex.

Padum is also the starting point for a number of demanding treks.

Places to Stay & Eat

There's a limited choice of basic guesthouses and one more comfortable option.

RICHARD I'ANSON

RICHARD I'ANSON

SARA-JANE CLELAND

Culturally and spiritually Ladakh is a 'Little Tibet': monks at morning puja *(prayer)* at Tikse Gompa (top); festivals provide a reason for donning traditional dress in Leh (bottom right); masked dancers perform during the Hemis Gompa festival (bottom left)

RICHARD I'ANSON

GARRY WEARE

RICHARD I'ANSON

GARRY WEARE

Buddhist monasteries compete with the majesty of the Ladakhi Himalaya: the sound of conch shells calls monks to prayer at Tikse Gompa (top); a lama makes ceremonial cakes (centre right); spectacular Victory Fort at Leh (bottom right); Wanla Gompa perched high in the Zanskar Range (bottom left)

Hotel Shapodok-la, in the centre of town, has cheap dorm beds. The ***Hotel Haftal View***, by the bus stand, is a bit grubby, with singles/doubles for Rs 100/150. The ***Hotel Chorala*** nearby is somewhat better, also with doubles for Rs 150.

Hotel Snowland is one of the better choices, with a nice garden and rooms for Rs 100/150. It is set in the fields about 100m behind the Hotel Chorala.

J&KTDC Tourist Bungalow has fairly big rooms with bath (cold water only) for Rs 50 per person. ***Hotel Ibex*** *(☎ 01983-45012)* is the best in town, with decent doubles set around a sheltered courtyard for Rs 300 (no discount for singles).

There is little to say about eating in Padum. The least worst place is the ***restaurant*** at the Hotel Ibex. ***Lhasa Tibetan restaurant*** across the road from the Ibex is OK, as is ***Hotel Chorala*** and the ***Tibetan restaurant*** at the bus stand under the Campa Cola sign.

Getting There & Away

The Kargil to Padum trip is spectacular, even impressing jaded travellers who thought that they had seen it all along the Leh to Kargil road. But as usual in this part of the world, the road is narrow, winding and slow. It is only open from July to early October and is impassable the rest of the year, effectively isolating the Zanskari people.

Bus In season, a bus runs between Padum and Kargil every alternate day (check with local bus stations for up-to-date information), departing at about 4.30 am. The cost of the bus between Kargil and Padum is Rs 150/220 for B/A class (it depends which bus shows up), and the trip usually takes about 15 hours, but can take a lot longer.

You can and should book your ticket the day before in Padum or Kargil. You can get off anywhere you want on the road between Kargil and Padum, but you may have to then wait a day or so for another bus, or rely on hitching a lift on an infrequent truck.

Taxi By taxi, it costs Rs 7000 one way and Rs 12,000 return from Kargil to Padum, but with a group to cut costs, this is a great way to really admire the amazing scenery. This trip can be done in one long day with about 12 hours driving, or you can stop at Rangdum, Parkachik or Panikhar.

Truck Trucks go along this route, but less often than on the Kargil to Leh road, because so few people live in and around Zanskar. Nevertheless, hitching a ride on a truck, if you can find one, is normal practice, and most drivers will take you for a negotiable fee, maybe about the same as the bus fare.

Getting Around

The Padum Taxi Union office opposite Hotel Haftal View charges exorbitant rates: Rs 650 return to Sani Gompa, Rs 800 return to Karsha Gompa, and Rs 5500/7000 one way/return to Rangdum. Few visitors use taxis; most choose to trek.

TREKKING IN ZANSKAR

Treks in the Zanskar area include the popular treks from Padum over Shingo La (5090m) to Darcha and Manali, and over Singge La (5050m) to Lamayuru and Leh. There is also a remote trek north over Cha Cha La (4950m) and Rubrang La (5020m) to the Markha Valley and Leh.

These treks can be undertaken from the end of June, when the snows begin to melt on the high passes, to the middle of October, before the first of the winter snows. There are of course exceptions to this as heavy storms blowing up from the Indian plains occasionally interrupt itineraries in August and September. River crossings are also a problem, particularly on the trek from Padum to the Markha Valley; it is advisable not to undertake this trek until the middle of August, when waters subside. It is also important to note that all of these treks involve high-pass crossings of around 5000m so proper acclimatisation is essential.

If making your own arrangements, packhorses can be hired from Padum or Karsha for around Rs 200 a day, although this can increase during the harvest period in late August to early September. A local guide is also a valuable asset, particularly on the trek from Padum to the Markha Valley.

Camping gear including a tent and sleeping bag must be brought with you, as there are a number of stages on these treks where there are no villages to stay. Food supplies must also be brought from Leh.

Padum to Darcha via Shingo La

This trek follows the well-defined route up the Tsarap Valley for the first three stages before diverting to Phugtal Monastery, one of the oldest monasteries in Zanskar. The trek continues through a number of villages to the highest settlement at Kargyak. From here it is another stage to the base of Shingo La (5090m) before crossing the Great Himalaya Range. A final stage brings you to the roadhead at Darcha in Himachal Pradesh and your onward transport to Leh or Manali.

stage	route	duration (hrs)
1	Padum to Mune	6
2	Mune to Purne	8
3	Purne to Phugtal Monastery and Tetha	6
4	Tetha to Kargyak	7
5	Kargyak to Lakong	6–7
6	Lakong to Rumjak via Shingo La	6–7
7	Rumjak to Darcha	6–7

Padum to Lamayuru via Singge La

This trek may commence from either Padum or from Karsha Gompa, the largest in the Zanskar region. The trek follows the true left bank of the Zanskar River for two stages before diverting towards the Hanuma La (4950m) and Lingshat Monastery. It is a further stage to the base of the Singge La (5050m) before crossing the Zanskar Range. From the pass there are dramatic views of the Zanskar Gorges, while to the south are the peaks of the Great Himalaya Range. Singge La is not a demanding pass crossing and the gradual descent to the village of Photaksar can be completed in one stage.

From Photaksar the trail crosses Sisir La (4850m) to the village of Honupatta. It is a further stage to the ancient monastery at Wanla before finally crossing Prinkiti La (3750m) to Lamayuru Gompa and onward transport by bus or truck to Leh.

stage	route	duration (hrs)
1	Padum to Karsha	2
2	Karsha to Pishu	4–5
3	Pishu to Hanumil	4–5
4	Hanumil to Snertse	5
5	Snertse to Lingshet via Hanuma La	5–6
6	Lingshet to Singge La base camp	5–6
7	Singge La base camp to Photaksar via Singge La	5–6
8	Photaksar to Honupatta via Sisir La	6
9	Honupatta to Wanla	5
10	Wanla to Lamayuru via Prinkiti La	3–4

Padum to Leh via Cha Cha La, Rubrang La & the Markha Valley

This challenging trek is followed by only a handful of trekkers each season. From Padum the trail heads north to the village of Zangla before diverting from the Zanskar Valley to Cha Cha La (4950m).

From the pass there are great views south towards the Great Himalaya Range. Heading north, the trail enters a series of dramatic gorges that support rare wildlife including brown bears, bharal (wild Himalayan sheep) and snow leopards. It takes a minimum of two stages to reach Rubrang La (5020m) and the Zanskar Range crest before a steady descent to the villages of the Markha Valley. From Markha Village it takes a further three stages to cross Kongmaru La (5030m) to Hemis Gompa and the Indus Valley.

stage	route	duration (hrs)
1	Padum to Zangla	7
2	Zangla to Cha Cha La base camp	3
3	Base camp to Gorge camp via Cha Cha La	6
4	Gorge camp to Tilat Sumdo	6
5	Tilat Sumdo to Rubrang La base camp	5–6
6	Base camp to Markha via Rubrang La	6
7	Markha to Nimaling	7–8
8	Nimaling to Chogdo via Kongmaru La	6
9	Chogdo to Hemis	4–5

Uttar Pradesh & Uttaranchal

Uttar Pradesh used to stretch from the Ganges plain all the way up to the Tibetan border, but the vast territory was chopped down to size with the creation of the new state of Uttaranchal in November 2000. Uttar Pradesh still covers a large area of the plains, including Agra, Varanasi and the state capital of Lucknow.

Uttar Pradesh & Uttaranchal at a Glance

Population: 166.1 million (Uttar Pradesh), 8.5 million (Uttaranchal)

Area: 231,254 sq km (Uttar Pradesh), 63,157 sq km (Uttaranchal)

Capital: Lucknow (Uttar Pradesh), Dehra Dun (Uttaranchal)

Main Language: Hindi

When to Go: Oct to Mar

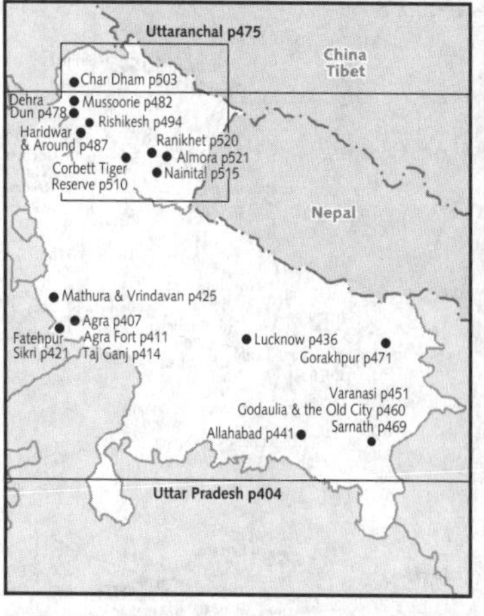

- Visit the Taj Mahal at sunrise and deserted Fatehpur Sikri at sunset
- Follow in the footsteps of Krishna in Mathura and Vrindavan
- Take a dawn boat ride on the Ganges at Varanasi
- Meditate at the Buddhist shrine of Sarnath
- Scout for tigers in Corbett Tiger Reserve
- Practise yoga on the banks of the Ganges in Rishikesh
- Trek to remote lakes and glaciers in Garhwal and Kumaon

Uttar Pradesh

Often referred to as the 'cow belt' or 'Hindi belt', Uttar Pradesh has dominated Indian politics and culture since Independence, producing over half of India's prime ministers. This is partly because it's the nation's most populous state – it has as many inhabitants as Brazil – and partly because of the central role the state plays in the religious landscape of Hinduism. The Ganges, which forms the backbone of Uttar Pradesh, is the sacred river of Hinduism, and four of the religion's seven holy towns are in the state, including the holiest, Varanasi. Uttar Pradesh is also a place of major importance to Buddhists; the Buddha first preached his message of 'the middle way' at Sarnath, outside Varanasi.

The people of Uttar Pradesh are predominantly poorly educated farmers, who stand in stark contrast to the wealthy urbanites who control the state's political and economic destiny. Aside from its religious centres, Uttar Pradesh is best known as the home of India's most famous monument, the Taj Mahal. Fans of Mughal architecture can find numerous other fine examples of this effusive style dotted around the state.

Except in the very cheapest hotels, you can expect a 5% luxury tax to be added to your hotel bill in Uttar Pradesh. Rates quoted for accommodation in this chapter do not include tax.

History

Over 2000 years ago the area that became Uttar Pradesh was part of Ashoka's great

Buddhist empire. Muslim raids from the north-west began in the 11th century, and by the 16th century the region was part of the famed Mughal empire whose capital was for some time at Agra and Fatehpur Sikri.

Following the decline of the Mughal empire, Persian invaders stepped in briefly before the nawabs of Avadh rose to prominence in the central part of the region. The nawabs were responsible for turning Lucknow into a flourishing centre for the arts but their empire came to a dramatic end when the British East India Company deposed the last nawab, triggering the Uprising of 1857. Agra was later merged with Avadh and the state became known as United Province. It was renamed Uttar Pradesh (Northern State) after Independence, and is often known simply as UP.

In recent times Uttar Pradesh has become the main support base for the ruling Hindu fundamentalist Bharatiya Janata Party (BJP). During the early 1990s, the desecration of Hindu temples by Mughal invaders was used as a rallying cry by the BJP, leading to tension between Hindus and Muslims in many key cities. Things came to a flash-point in 1992 in the town of Ayodhya,

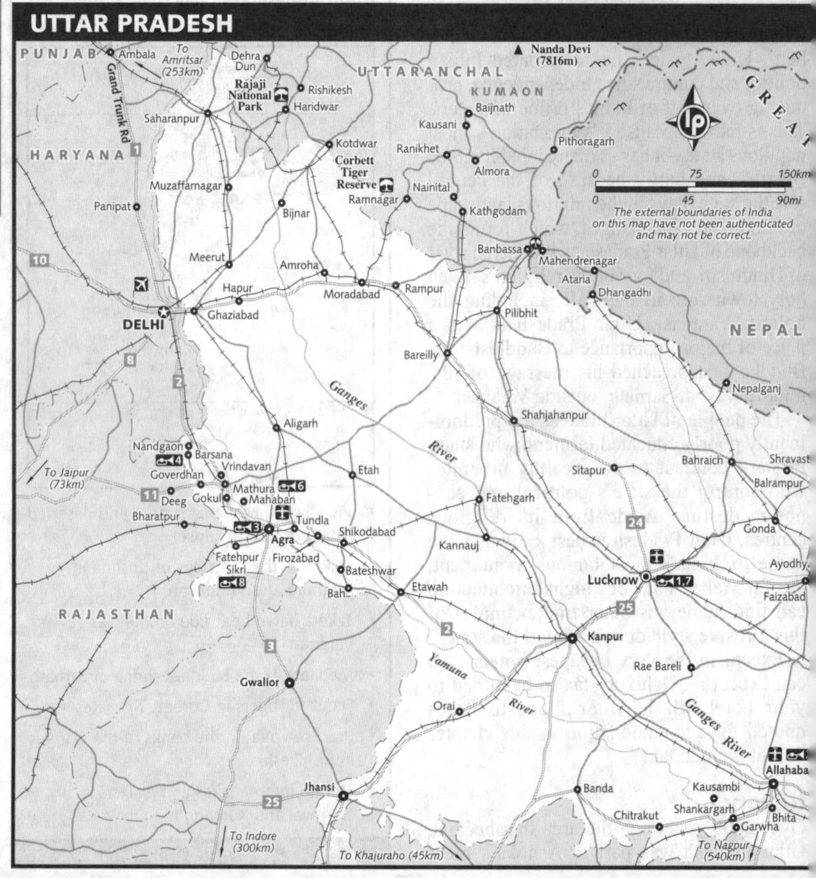

when rioting Hindus tore down a mosque built by the Mughals over the temple of Rama. After wide-spread riots and killings around India, things quietened down, but several other potential trouble spots now have a 24-hour armed guard, including the mosque built over Krishna's birthplace in Mathura and the mosque built over the original Vishwanath Temple in Varanasi. The recent discovery of Jain ruins under the Mughal city of Fatehpur Sikri, near Agra, has caused some ominous rumblings.

In late 1996 the state was placed under direct rule from Delhi when elections resulted in a hung assembly. After five months of political stalemate the BJP, which won the most seats, formed a coalition government with the Bahujan Samaj Party (BSP), an anticaste, secular party at the opposite end of the political spectrum. The coalition has since seen several changes; the Congress Party was also briefly included, before both it and the BSP were replaced by the UP Loktrantrik Congress and Jantantrik Bahujan Samaj parties. Currently, the BJP is facing struggles from within and a number of party members have resigned in protest at the 'autocratic' political style of UP Chief Minister Kalyan Singh.

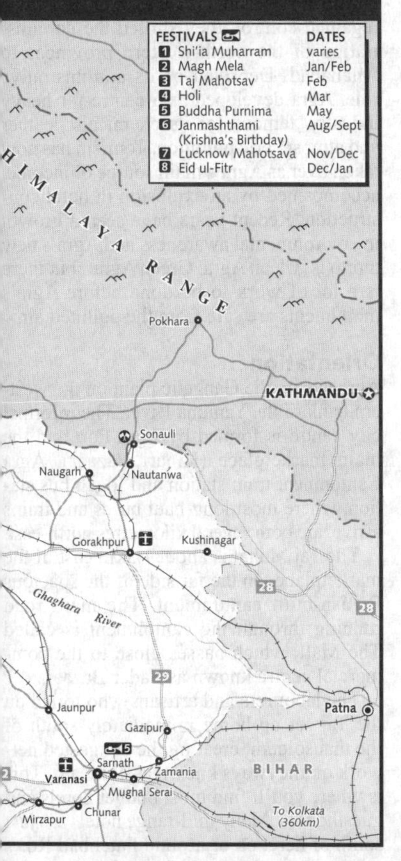

Information

Tourist Offices UP Tourism offices can be found in the major Indian cities:

Ahmedabad (☎ 079-6560752) 303 Ashwamedh House, 5 Smriti Kunj, Navrangpura
Chandigarh (☎ 0172-707649) SCO 1046-47, 1st floor, Sector 22B
Chennai (Madras; ☎ 044-8283276) 28 Commander-in-Chief Rd
Delhi (☎ 011-3322251, fax 3711296) Chandralok Bldg, 36 Janpath
Kolkata (Calcutta; ☎ 033-2207855) 12A Netaji Subashi Rd
Lucknow (☎ 0522-2233632, fax 221776, e upstdc@lw1.vsnl.net.in) Chitrahar Bldg, 3 Naval Kishor Rd
Mumbai (Bombay; ☎ 022-2185458) 38 World Trade Centre, Cuffe Parade, Colaba

Internet Resources For useful information, the following sites are a good place to start; see also Internet Resources in the Uttaranchal section.

UP Tourism A thorough and independent site dedicated to Uttar Pradesh and helping you visit 'the land of Taj'.
www.up-tourism.com
Uttar Pradesh gateway site Presents 'Uttar Pradesh on a platter', with hotel listings; also covers Uttaranchal.
www.upportal.com

AGRA

☎ 0562 • pop 1,118,800

This sprawling industrial town, 204km from Delhi, is synonymous with the Taj Mahal, India's most famous building, which sits on the banks of the Yamuna River east of the town. The Mughal emperor Babur established his capital here in 1526 and for the next hundred years, Agra witnessed a remarkable spate of architectural activity as monarch after monarch tried to outdo the grandiose monuments built by his predecessor. Many of these imposing structures still remain, including a magnificent fort and several sandstone mausoleums, as well as the famous Taj.

Choking these ancient monuments is the hectic and polluted modern city of Agra. There is a lively *chowk* (market) and a wide range of places to stay and eat, but for most visitors Agra is more a place to endure than enjoy. Much of the blame falls on local rickshaw-wallahs, touts and souvenir vendors, who stop at nothing in their efforts to separate tourists from their cash. The polluted atmosphere further reduces the town's charm. Former US president Bill Clinton's visit in 2000 highlighted the damage that air-pollution is causing Agra's monuments.

Following the controversial price hikes at the Taj Mahal and other Mughal sites, many tourists are choosing to visit Agra on whistle-stop day trips from Delhi and there's an excellent train service making this eminently practicable. However, it would be a shame to miss Agra's other attractions if you can afford the entry fees. The Taj certainly deserves more than a single visit if you want to appreciate how its appearance changes under different light. Agra Fort, Itimad-ud-Daulah and Akbar's Mausoleum and the nearby deserted city of Fatehpur Sikri make for several days of sightseeing.

History

Agra is believed to have been founded on the site of an ancient Hindu kingdom, which was utterly destroyed by the Afghan Mahmud of Ghazni in about AD 1022. Raja Badal Singh built a fort on the site of the present Agra Fort in 1475, but Agra didn't really come into its own until 1501, when Sultan Sikander Lodi built his capital on the opposite bank of the Yamuna.

The city fell into Mughal hands in 1526, when Babur defeated the last Lodi sultan at Panipat, 80km north of Delhi. The much fought-over city reached the peak of its magnificence between the mid-16th and mid-17th centuries under the reigns of Akbar, Jehangir and Shah Jahan. It was during this period that the fort, Taj Mahal and Agra's major tombs were built. In 1638 Shah Jahan built a new city in Delhi, and his son Aurangzeb moved the capital there 10 years later, imprisoning his father in the fort.

In 1761 Agra fell to the Jats, who looted its monuments, including the Taj Mahal. Next in line were the Marathas, who seized power in 1770, before the British finally wrested control in 1803.

There was heavy fighting around the fort during the Uprising of 1857; after the British regained control, they shifted the administration of the north-western provinces to Allahabad. Deprived of its administrative role, Agra developed as a centre for heavy industry, famous for its chemicals, leather and atmospheric pollution. Tourism has now taken over as Agra's main source of income, accompanied by an explosion in hotel construction. Recent years have seen a growth in environmental awareness and Agra's new motto is 'Clean Agra; Green Agra', but there is a lot of work to be done before Agra's monuments are safe from the polluted air.

Orientation

Agra sits on the Gangetic plain on the western bank of the Yamuna River. The informal city centre is formed by Agra Fort and the main marketplace (Kinari Bazaar). Agra Cantonment train station and Idgah bus station, where most long-haul buses and trains arrive, are both several kilometres north-east.

The Taj Mahal is about 1.5km east of the marketplace, on the far side of the spacious British-built cantonment. The main road running through the cantonment is called The Mall, which passes close to the commercial centre known as Sadar Bazaar.

The labourers and artisans who toiled on the Taj set up home immediately south of the mausoleum, creating the congested network of alleyways known as Taj Ganj. This is where you'll find most budget hotels and guesthouses. Many mid-range hotels are just south of here, on or around Fatehbad Rd.

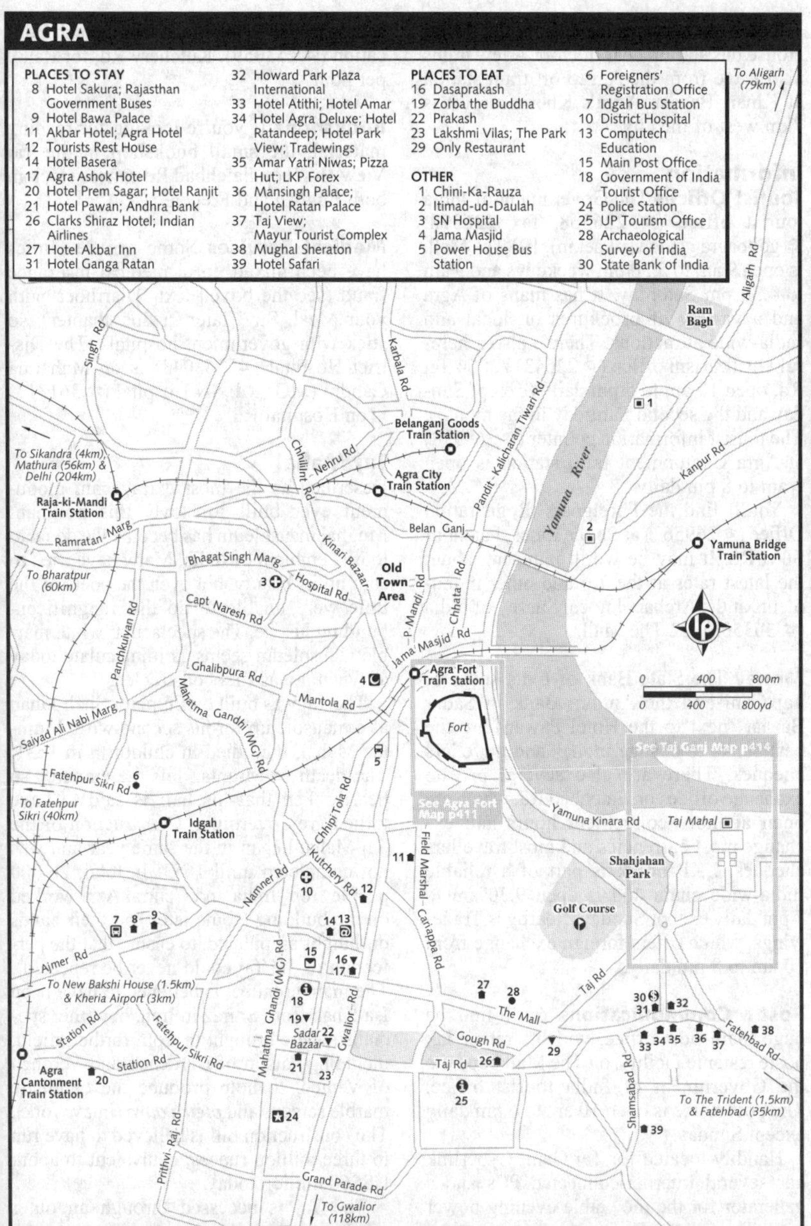
AGRA
PLACES TO STAY
8 Hotel Sakura; Rajasthan Government Buses
9 Hotel Bawa Palace
11 Akbar Hotel; Agra Hotel
12 Tourists Rest House
14 Hotel Basera
17 Agra Ashok Hotel
20 Hotel Prem Sagar; Hotel Ranjit
21 Hotel Pawan; Andhra Bank
26 Clarks Shiraz Hotel; Indian Airlines
27 Hotel Akbar Inn
31 Hotel Ganga Ratan
32 Howard Park Plaza International
33 Hotel Atithi; Hotel Amar
34 Hotel Agra Deluxe; Hotel Ratandeep; Hotel Park View; Tradewings
35 Amar Yatri Niwas; Pizza Hut; LKP Forex
36 Mansingh Palace; Hotel Ratan Palace
37 Taj View; Mayur Tourist Complex
38 Mughal Sheraton
39 Hotel Safari
PLACES TO EAT
16 Dasaprakash
19 Zorba the Buddha
22 Prakash
23 Lakshmi Vilas; The Park
29 Only Restaurant
OTHER
1 Chini-Ka-Rauza
2 Itimad-ud-Daulah
3 SN Hospital
4 Jama Masjid
5 Power House Bus Station
6 Foreigners' Registration Office
7 Idgah Bus Station
10 District Hospital
13 Computech Education
15 Main Post Office
18 Government of India Tourist Office
24 Police Station
25 UP Tourism Office
28 Archaeological Survey of India
30 State Bank of India
To Aligarh (79km)
Aligarh Rd
Ram Bagh
Singh Rd
Karbala Rd
Pandit Kalicharan Tiwari Rd
Yamuna River
Kanpur Rd
Belanganj Goods Train Station
Chhilint Rd
Nehru Rd
Agra City Train Station
To Sikandra (4km), Mathura (56km) & Delhi (204km)
Raja-ki-Mandi Train Station
Ramratan Marg
Belan Ganj
Yamuna Bridge Train Station
Kinari Bazaar
Bhagat Singh Marg
To Bharatpur (60km)
Hospital Rd
Old Town Area
Capt Naresh Rd
P Mandi Rd
Chhata Rd
Panchkuiyan Rd
Jama Masjid Rd
Agra Fort Train Station
Ghalibpura Rd
0 400 800m
0 400 800yd
Mantola Rd
Mahatma Gandhi (MG) Rd
Fort
Saiyad Ali Nabi Marg
See Taj Ganj Map p414
Fatehpur Sikri Rd
To Fatehpur Sikri (40km)
Chhipi Tola Rd
See Agra Fort Map p411
Yamuna Kinara Rd
Taj Mahal
Idgah Train Station
Field Marshal Cariappa Rd
Shahjahan Park
Kutchery Rd
Namner Rd
Golf Course
Ajmer Rd
To New Bakshi House (1.5km) & Kheria Airport (3km)
Taj Rd
The Mall
Station Rd
Sadar Bazaar
Gough Rd
Fatehbad Rd
Gwalior Rd
Agra Cantonment Train Station
Taj Rd
Shamsabad Rd
To The Trident (1.5km) & Fatehbad (35km)
Prithvi Raj Rd
Grand Parade Rd
To Gwalior (118km)

Local bus services leave from the Power House bus station near the fort. A few trains also leave from the Agra Fort train station at Kinari Bazaar. Agra's Kheria airport is 7km west of the city.

Information

Tourist Offices The Government of India tourist office (☎ 226368, fax 226378, e goitoagra@nde.vsnl.net.in), 191 The Mall, is open 9 am to 5.30 pm weekdays and 9 am to 4.30 pm Saturday. It has maps of Agra and a variety of brochures on local and India-wide attractions. There's also a helpful UP Tourism office (☎ 226431) at 64 Taj Rd, open 10 am to 5 pm daily (except Sunday and the second Saturday in the month). The tourist information counter (☎ 368598) at Agra Cantonment train station is open 8 am to 8 pm daily.

You'll find the Foreigners' Registration Office (☎ 269563) at Police Lines, Fatehpur Sikri Rd. It may be worth inquiring about the latest rates at the Taj and other monuments at the Archaeological Survey of India (☎ 363506), 22 The Mall.

Money The State Bank of India south of Taj Ganj and the Andhra Bank in Sadar Bazaar (next to the Hotel Pawan) are the best banks to change money and travellers cheques. There are also several private exchange offices on Fatehbad Rd, which are open at more convenient hours and exchange most currencies and most travellers cheques. LKP Forex is part of a reliable India-wide chain and is open 9.30 am to 7 pm daily except Sunday. Nearby is Tradewings, which offers foreign exchange from 10 am to 8 pm daily.

Post & Communications You'll find the huge main post office, with its rather lax poste restante facility, on The Mall opposite the Government of India tourist office. The post office is open 10 am to 6 pm daily except Sunday.

Handily located for Taj Ganj, Cyberlink has several Internet-connected PCs and a generator for the inevitable evening power cuts. The rate is Rs 90 per hour. Internet access is also available at Computech Education (☎ 253059), Kutchery Rd, for Rs 80 per hour.

Bookshops If you're looking for reading material, the small bookshop in the Taj View Hotel on Fatehbad Rd carries stock in both English and French.

Medical Services Some private clinics have been mixed up in medical insurance fraud (see the boxed text 'Diarrhoea with your Meal, Sir?' later in this chapter), so stick with government hospitals. The District Hospital (☎ 363043) is on Mahatma Gandhi (MG) Rd; SN Hospital (☎ 361313) is on Hospital Rd.

Taj Mahal

Described as the most extravagant monument ever built for love, this poignant Mughal mausoleum has become the de facto tourist emblem of India. Many have tried to sum up its beauty, but even the poets of the time were unable to do this magnificent building justice. The spectacular white marble mausoleum seems as immaculate today as when it was first constructed.

The Taj was built by Emperor Shah Jahan as a mausoleum for his second wife, Mumtaz Mahal, who died in childbirth in 1631. The death of Mumtaz left the emperor so heartbroken that his hair is said to have turned grey overnight. Construction of the Taj Mahal began in the same year and was not completed until 1653. In total, 20,000 people from India and Central Asia worked on the building (some later had their hands or thumbs amputated, to ensure that the perfection of the Taj could never be repeated). The main architect is believed to have been Isa Khan from Shiraz in Iran, but other specialists were brought in from further afield, including Austin of Bordeaux and Veroneo of Venice, to help produce the exquisite marble screens and *pietra dura* (inlay work). The construction bill is believed to have run to three million rupees, equivalent to about US$60 million today.

The Taj is accessed through an outer courtyard, which has gates facing west, south and east (most tourists enter from the west gate, which is closest to the car park). You enter the inner compound through a vast red sandstone gateway on the south side of the forecourt, inscribed with verses from the Quran. Beside the gateway is the ticket office and a small cloakroom where prohibited items must be deposited, including food, tobacco, matches, mobile phones, camera tripods, and *paan* (betel nut; prohibited to keep the Taj free of unsightly red blotches). The guards will search your bags thoroughly, so anything you don't feel comfortable leaving in the cloakroom should be left at your hotel.

Cameras are permitted, and there's no problem taking photos of the outside of the Taj, though guards will prevent you from taking photographs inside the mausoleum. The chances are that you won't immediately be able to see the Taj through the crowds of tourists taking *the* shot of the Taj reflected in the watercourse that runs through the gardens. You can bring in your video recorder for Rs 25, but the guards won't let you take it beyond the gateway steps (thereafter it must be left in a locker until you return).

Paths leading from the gateway to the Taj are divided by a long cruciform **watercourse**, which sometimes reflects the Taj, but is more often disturbed by splashing children. The ornamental gardens are set out along classical Mughal *charbagh* lines – a square quartered by watercourses, with an ornamental marble plinth at the centre.

To the west is a small **museum**, open 10 am to 5 pm daily except Monday and Friday. It houses original architectural drawings of the Taj, information on the semiprecious stones used in its construction, and some nifty celadon plates, said to split into pieces or change colour if the food served on them contains poison (handy for those dodgy Taj Ganj meals!). Entry to the museum is free.

The Taj Mahal itself stands on a raised marble platform at the northern end of the gardens. Purely decorative white **minarets** grace each corner of the platform, but are never used for prayer. The red sandstone mosque to the west of the main structure is an important gathering place for Agra Muslims. The identical building to the east is purely for symmetry (it can't be used as a mosque because it faces in the wrong direction).

The central Taj structure is constructed of semitranslucent white marble, carved with flowers and inlaid with thousands of semiprecious stones in beautiful patterns using a process known as pietra dura. The geometry of the building is spectacular; the four identical faces of the Taj feature vast vaulted arches embellished with pietra dura scrollwork and quotations from the Quran. The whole structure is topped off by four small domes surrounding the famous bulbous central dome.

Below the main dome is the **Cenotaph of Mumtaz Mahal**, an elaborate false tomb surrounded by an exquisite perforated screen inlaid with some 43 different types of semiprecious stones. Beside it, offsetting the perfect symmetry of the Taj, is the **Cenotaph of Shah Jahan**, who despite his ambitions for a matching black mausoleum, was interred beside his wife with little ceremony

Price Hikes at the Taj

After decades of charging only a few rupees, the Archaeological Survey of India has upped the entry fee for the Taj Mahal to a whopping Rs 960. The rate hike only applies to foreign visitors – Indians pay only Rs 20 – and was conceived as a way to reduce tourist numbers (which currently threaten to cause structural damage to the monument) and to provide much-needed income for conservation.

However, the majority of visitors to the Taj are Indian, and many overseas visitors feel the price hike amounts to an arbitrary tax on foreigners. The long-standing tradition of free entry on Friday has also been abandoned, triggering violent demonstrations by local Muslims who were temporarily charged to enter the Taj to pray! Negotiations are currently under way to find an intermediate fee that addresses the differential wealth of Indian and foreign visitors, without placing an unfair burden on international travellers.

by Aurangzeb in 1666. Light is admitted into the central chamber by finely cut marble screens, and the vaulted roof produces impressive echoes. The physical **tombs** of Mumtaz Mahal and Shah Jahan are in a locked basement room below the main chamber.

In recent years, there has been growing concern about the damage that atmospheric pollution is causing to the Taj. Acid rain, produced by sulphur dioxide from vehicle emissions, is discolouring the famous white marble and eroding the fine carving and inlays. In an attempt to reduce pollution, new industrial developments were banned from a 10,400-sq-km exclusion zone around the Taj Mahal in 1994, and motor vehicles are now prohibited from the 4km area surrounding the monument.

Sunset is an extremely impressive time to see the Taj as the white marble first takes on a rich golden sheen, then slowly turns pink, red and finally blue with the changing light. In winter, it's not really worth getting up early for the sunrise as it's invariably cold, hazy and foggy.

As of October 2000, the entry fee for the Taj was raised to a staggering Rs 960 for foreigners, while Indians continue to pay Rs 20, or Rs 110 before 7 am or after 5 pm. For more information on the rate hike controversy, see the boxed text 'Price Hikes at the Taj' earlier in this section. The Taj is open from sunrise to 7 pm daily except Friday (there is no longer a free entry day). The local tourist industry is campaigning to have a free day reinstated and entry rates lowered; ask about the current situation when you arrive in Agra.

Agra Fort

Construction of the massive red sandstone Agra Fort on the bank of the Yamuna River was begun by Emperor Akbar in 1565, though additions were made up until the rule of his grandson, Shah Jahan. The fort was built primarily as a military structure, but during Shah Jahan's reign it was upgraded to a palace, and finally became a prison (albeit a gilded one) for Shah Jahan after his son Aurangzeb seized power in 1658.

Mysteries of the Taj

Academic research indicates that the Taj was intended as more than an elaborate mausoleum. Analysis of the extensive passages from the Quran inscribed on the walls suggests that this perfect exercise in symmetry was also designed to be a symbolic replica of the throne of God. The official story of the Taj's construction has never been universally accepted, however. The British deluded themselves for some time that such an exquisite building must certainly have been designed by the Europeans on the project!

Recently, a new Hindu fundamentalist conspiracy theory has claimed that the Taj was built atop a Hindu temple called Tejo Mahalaya, predating Shah Jahan by several centuries. There is some evidence to support this: The European traveller Johan Mandelslo wrote extensively about Agra in his 1638 memoirs, but makes no mention of the construction of the Taj. Supporters of the theory cite the fact that Mumtaz Mahal is referred to in historic texts only as Mumtaz-ul-Zamani as evidence that the monument was not named for Shah Jahan's wife. Whatever the truth, the myth that decapitated Shiva statues are locked in the rooms below the cenotaph is pure propaganda.

One unusual story about the Taj that may actually be true is the legend that Shah Jahan intended to build two Taj Mahals. Excavations across the Yamuna River have uncovered Mughal gardens and building foundations that are in alignment with the Taj, fitting in with the story that Shah Jahan intended to build a second Taj in black marble as his own tomb, a negative image of the white Taj of his wife. In fact, such a building would have been prohibitively expensive, even for the vast treasuries of the Mughals, and Shah Jahan was rapidly deposed by his son, Aurangzeb, spending his final days imprisoned in Agra Fort, looking across to the final resting place of his wife.

The auricular fort's colossal double walls rise over 20m in height and measure 2.5km in circumference. They are encircled by a fetid moat and contain a maze of buildings that form a small city within a city. Unfortunately many of the structures here were severely damaged over the years by Nadir Shah, the Marhattas, the Jats and finally the British during the Uprising of 1857. The most impressive building to survive is the legendary white marble **Moti Masjid** (Pearl Mosque), regarded by some as the most beautiful mosque in India, but sadly it's not open to visitors.

The Amar Singh Gate to the south is the sole entry point to the fort, and is open from sunrise to sunset daily; entry is Rs 510 for foreigners and Rs 20 for Indians. Having paid the steep entry fee, it's worth hiring a guide to get the most out of your visit as there's a lot to see in the fort. Keep an eye out for monkeys and vivid green parakeets as you walk around the fort.

Diwan-i-Am & Nagina Masjid The Hall of Public Audiences was built by Shah Jahan and replaced an earlier wooden structure. The throne room, with its typical inlaid marble work, indisputably bears Shah Jahan's stamp. This is where the emperor met officials and listened to petitioners.

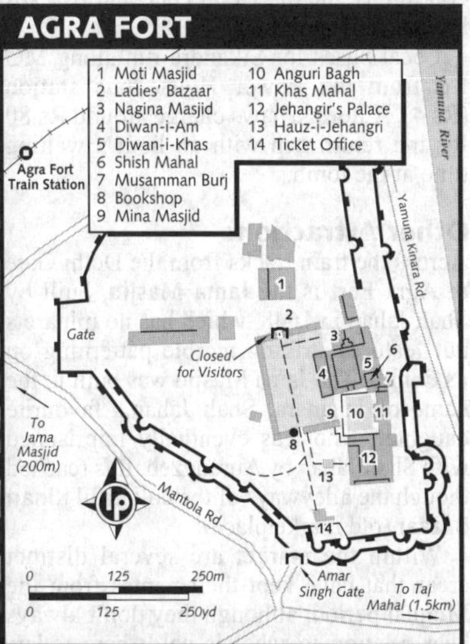

Beside the Diwan-i-Am is the small **Nagina Masjid**, or Gem Mosque. A door leads from here into the **Ladies' Bazaar**, where female merchants came to sell goods to the ladies of the Mughal court. No males were allowed to enter the bazaar except Akbar, though according to one apocryphal story he still enjoyed visiting in female disguise.

Diwan-i-Khas The Hall of Private Audiences was also built by Shah Jahan, between 1636 and 1637. It's where the emperor received important dignitaries or foreign ambassadors. The hall consists of two rooms connected by three arches. The famous Peacock Throne was kept here before being moved to Delhi by Aurangzeb. It was later carted off to Iran and its remains are now in Tehran.

Musamman Burj The exquisite Musamman Burj (Octagonal Tower) stands close to the Diwan-i-Khas. Shah Jahan died here after seven years imprisonment in the fort. The tower poignantly looks out over the Yamuna towards the Taj Mahal, but Agra's pollution is now so thick that it's hard to see. The Mina Masjid was Shah Jahan's private mosque during his imprisonment. Between the Musamman Burj and the Diwan-i-Khas are the ornate Royal Baths, an ingenious piece of Mughal plumbing.

Jehangir's Palace Akbar is believed to have built this palace for his son. It was the largest private residence in the fort and indicates the changing emphasis from military to luxurious living quarters. The palace displays an interesting blend of Hindu and Central Asian architectural styles.

Other Buildings Shah Jahan's **Khas Mahal** is a beautiful white marble structure that was used as a private palace. The rooms underneath it were intended as a cool retreat from the summer heat. The **Shish Mahal** or Mirror Palace is reputed to have been the harem dressing room and its walls are inlaid with tiny mirrors. The **Anguri Bagh** or Grape Garden probably never had any grapevines but was simply a small, formal Mughal garden.

In front of Jehangir's Palace is the **Hauz-i-Jehangri**, a huge bowl beautifully carved out of a single block of stone. According to one traditional story, Jehangir's wife, Nur Jahan, made *attar* (perfumed essential oil) of roses in the bowl.

The **Amar Singh Gate** takes its name from a maharaja of Jodhpur who slew the imperial treasurer in the Diwan-i-Am in 1644 and, in a bid to escape, reputedly rode his horse over the fort wall near here. The unlucky horse perished, though it is now immortalised in stone. Amar Singh survived the fall but he didn't survive Shah Jahan's wrath and was thrown from the walls a second time, this time fatally.

Itimad-ud-Daulah

On the opposite bank of the Yamuna, north of the fort, is the exquisite Itimad-ud-Daulah – the tomb of Mirza Ghiyas Beg. This Persian gentleman was Jehangir's *wazir* (chief minister), and his beautiful daughter, Nur Jahan, later married the emperor. Nur Jahan constructed the tomb between 1622 and 1628 in a style similar to the tomb she built for Jehangir near Lahore in Pakistan.

Although much less elaborate, many of the Itimad-ud-Daulah's design elements foreshadow the Taj, earning it the nickname 'Baby Taj'. The Itimad-ud-Daulah was the first Mughal structure totally built from marble and the first to make extensive use of pietra dura, the marble inlay work which is so characteristic of the Taj. The mausoleum features extremely fine marble lattice-work passages, admitting decorative shafts of light to the interior, and the beautifully patterned surface of the tomb is superb.

The Itimad-ud-Daulah is open from sunrise to sunset daily and carries the usual royal price tag of Rs 235 for foreigners and Rs 15 for Indians (free on Friday). Video cameras require a Rs 25 permit.

Akbar's Mausoleum

The sandstone and marble tomb of Akbar, the greatest of the Mughal emperors, lies in the centre of a peaceful garden grazed by deer at Sikandra, 4km north-west of Agra. Akbar started its construction himself, blending Islamic, Hindu, Buddhist, Jain and Christian motifs and styles, much like the syncretic religious philosophy he developed. When Akbar died, the mausoleum was completed by his son, Jehangir, who significantly modified the original plans, which accounts for its somewhat cluttered architectural lines.

Like Humayun's tomb in Delhi, it's an interesting place to study the gradual evolution in design that culminated in the Taj Mahal. Langur monkeys hang out on the walkway waiting to be fed. The stunning southern gateway is the most impressive part of the complex. It has three-storey minarets at each corner and is built of red sandstone strikingly inlaid with white marble abstract patterns. The ticket office is here, to the left of the entrance. The mausoleum is open from sunrise to sunset and entry is Rs 235 for foreigners, Rs 15 for Indians and free on Friday. A video camera permit costs Rs 25.

Sikandra is named after Sikander Lodi, the Delhi sultan who ruled from 1488 to 1517, immediately preceding the rise of Mughal power on the subcontinent. He built the **Baradi Palace**, in the mausoleum gardens. Between Sikandra and Agra are several tombs, the old Delhi Gate and two *kos minars* (milestones).

Local buses for Sikandra run along MG Rd from the Power House bus station (Rs 4). Autorickshaws charge around Rs 80 for the return trip with an hour's waiting time at the tomb.

Other Attractions

Across the train tracks from the Delhi Gate of Agra Fort is the **Jama Masjid**, built by Shah Jahan in 1648, which has no minarets but features striking marble patterning on its domes. The Jama Masjid was built in the name of Jahanara, Shah Jahan's favourite daughter, who was eventually imprisoned with Shah Jahan by Aurangzeb. It is reached though the alleyways of the colourful **Kinari Bazaar** (old marketplace).

Within the market are several distinct areas that have kept their names from the Mughal period, although they don't always bear relation to what is sold there today.

The **Loha Mandi** (Iron Market) and **Sabji Mandi** (Vegetable Market) are still operational, but the **Nai-ki-Mandi** (Barber's Market) is now famous for textiles.

The squat **Chini-ka-Rauza** (China Tomb), 1km north of the Itimad-ud-Daulah, is the mausoleum of Afzal Khan, a poet and high official in the court of Shah Jahan. Over the centuries the mausoleum has lost most of its brightly coloured enamelled tiles, but you can still get an impression of the building's former glory. Entry is free.

Ram Bagh, about 500m north, the earliest of India's Mughal gardens, is also forlorn and doesn't really warrant the Rs 225 entry fee (Rs 5 for Indians). You'll need to use a lot of imagination to picture how it must have looked in 1528 when it was constructed by Babur. The gardens are open from sunrise to sunset daily.

Swimming

The following hotels allow nonguests to use their pools for a fee: Agra Ashok Hotel (Rs 200), Hotel Atithi (Rs 250) and the Clarks Shiraz Hotel (Rs 300). Ashok has the best pool.

Organised Tours

Guided tours of Agra's main sights depart from the Government of India tourist office at 9.30 am for Agra Cantonment train station to pick up passengers arriving from Delhi on the *Taj Express*, which pulls in at 9.47 am. The tours include the Taj Mahal, Agra Fort and a rather hasty visit to Fatehpur Sikri, returning to the station by 6 pm so day trippers can catch the *Taj Express* back to Delhi at 6.35 pm. The tour costs Rs 2100 for foreigners and Rs 250 for Indians. You can just take the Fatehpur Sikri part of the tour for Rs 650 (Rs 175 Indians) and finish up at the eastern gate to the Taj Mahal at 1.30 pm. Tickets must be bought from the tourist information counter at the train station (you can board the bus at the Government of India tourist office before buying).

Special Events

From 18 to 27 February every year, the **Taj Mahotsav Festival** is held in Shilpgram, a crafts village and open-air emporium about a kilometre along the road running from the eastern gate of the Taj. The festival features live performances of music and dance.

Places to Stay – Budget

Intermittently, Agra operates a paying guest scheme, where travellers can stay with local families for between Rs 200 and Rs 500. Ask at the tourist information counter at the train station when you arrive to see if the scheme is currently running.

The cheapest rooms can be found in Taj Ganj, but there are better options, which only cost a little more in the Sadar Bazaar and Fatehbad Rd areas. Unless stated otherwise, rooms mentioned have private bathroom and checkout time is 10 am. Expect to pay double the quoted rates if you arrive with a rickshaw-wallah in tow.

Taj Ganj Area There are plenty of remarkably cheap hotels in this compact area immediately south of the Taj, all of which claim to offer rooftop views of the Taj and promise 'cheap and best' rooms. Usually this translates to an interrupted and distant view of the famous onion dome and basic rooms with thin mattresses and leaky plumbing. But they're cheap and you'll bump into plenty of other travellers who are scrimping and saving in order to cover the hefty entrance fee at the Taj.

The central ***Hotel Kamal*** *(☎ 330126, ⓔ hotelkamal@hotmail.com)* receives consistently good reports from travellers and boasts a clear view of the Taj from the pleasant eating area on the roof. The staff are helpful and OK singles/doubles cost Rs 120/150; Rs 150/200 with hot water.

A few doors down, ***Shanti Lodge*** *(☎ 330 900)* gets mixed reviews, but offers a decent view of the Taj from its rooftop eating area. Slightly cramped rooms start at Rs 80/100, or Rs 150 for doubles with views of the Taj through a fly screen and a grubby window.

Hotel Host *(☎ 331010)*, not far from the Taj's western gate, has small, plain rooms for Rs 100/150 and better doubles with balcony for Rs 200. All rooms have hot water and there's an OK view from the roof.

Close by, ***Hotel Sidhartha*** *(☎ 331238)* is a clean, spacious place built motel-style around a garden courtyard and the rooms have decent-sized windows. Rooms with bucket hot water cost Rs 100/150, or Rs 200/300 for big rooms with hot water on tap.

By the south gate to the Taj you'll find the large ***Hotel Raj*** *(☎ 331314)*, which was once quite upmarket for the area, but has fallen in line with everyone else over the years. Clean rooms with hot water start at Rs 100/150.

Across the road, the basic ***Hotel Sikander*** *(☎ 330279)* offers simple rooms with hot water for Rs 80/100.

Hotel Noorjahan *(☎ 333034)*, next door, is similar to Hotel Sikander but cheaper, with plain rooms for Rs 75 with private bathroom and Rs 50 without.

On the other side of the Hotel Sikander is the tiny ***Indo Guest House***, a clean, basic, family run affair where rooms with hot water start at Rs 80/100.

Near the police station, ***Hotel Shahjahan*** *(☎ 331159)* has rather ordinary rooms with shared bathroom for Rs 60/100 and nicer rooms with private bathrooms and hot water for Rs 150. There's a free luggage room for guests.

Hotel Sheela *(☎ 331194)* is well located near the Taj's eastern gate within the non-traffic zone, and has a variety of rooms set around a peaceful garden. Smaller doubles cost Rs 200 and the larger rooms cost Rs 300 to 350 (with cavernous bathrooms). This place is highly recommended and is often full so book ahead.

Sadar Bazaar Area One of the best options in Agra is the ***Tourists Rest House*** *(☎ 363961, ⓔ trh@vsnl.com, Kutchery Rd)*. Set in a quiet location with a peaceful garden dining area, this homely guesthouse gets good reports from travellers year after year. The friendly owners can make train/air reservations, provide good local information and also run tours to Rajasthan. Comfortable, spotless, air-cooled singles/doubles are Rs 75/120 with shared hot shower; Rs 150/200 with hot water on tap (toiletries and towels are provided). Decent vegetarian food is served in the candle-lit courtyard or in the rooftop restaurant. Rickshaw-wallahs may try to steer you away as the guesthouse doesn't give commissions. Don't confuse this place with the nearby (and inferior) Kapoor Tourist Rest House on Fatehpur Sikri Rd or the Tourist Guest House near Agra Fort bus stand.

Midway between Sadar Bazaar and Taj Ganj, the quiet ***Hotel Akbar Inn*** *(☎ 226836, 21 The Mall)* has a relaxed atmosphere, which makes up somewhat for the ageing facilities. Simple rooms with shared bathroom are a bargain at Rs 60, while fan-cooled doubles cost from Rs 150 to 200.

Agra Hotel *(☎ 363331, Field Marshall Cariappa Rd)* is housed in an ageing cantonment building and is a popular wedding venue so it is often booked out. Singles with fan and bathroom cost Rs 150 and doubles with hot shower are Rs 250 to 450. Air-con is sometimes available in summer.

Akbar Hotel *(☎ 363312, 196 Field Marshal Cariappa Rd)*, next door, is quieter and

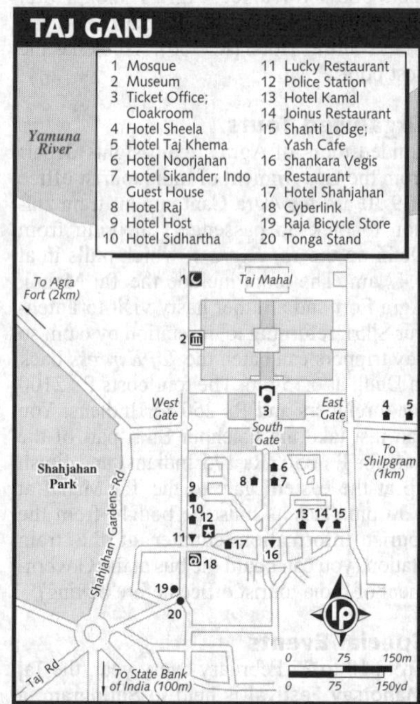

offers doubles with cold shower for Rs 150 and rooms with hot shower for Rs 300 to 450. A new block of ultrabasic 'student' rooms is under construction; it remains to be seen whether the proposed rates of Rs 25/50 a single/double materialise.

Well located for the restaurants at Sadar Bazaar, ***Hotel Pawan*** *(☎ 225506, fax 225 604, 3 Taj Rd)* is a passable mid-range hotel with hot water in all the rooms. Singles/doubles with fan start at Rs 240/350 while much better air-con rooms with phone and TV start at Rs 500/600. Checkout is noon.

West of Sadar Bazaar There are several hotels right by the Idgah bus station, though the noise levels here are correspondingly high. Pick of the bunch is ***Hotel Sakura*** *(☎ 369961, Ajmer Rd)* which is also the departure point for deluxe buses to Jaipur. Clean fan-cooled singles/doubles are Rs 200/250 with hot shower. Slightly chintzy air-con rooms with TV and a 'Mughal' theme cost Rs 450/600.

Hotel Bawa Palace *(☎ 265681, Ajmer Rd)*, nearby, is more upmarket, with carpets, TV and hot water throughout. Rooms cost Rs 550/700 with fan; Rs 800/1000 with air-con.

Hotel Basera *(☎ 262128, 19 Ajmer Rd)* is a good choice. Clean, tidy rooms with TV and hot showers cost Rs 400/500 with fan; Rs 500/700 with air-con.

Hotel Prem Sagar *(☎ 267408, 264 Station Rd)* is one of the better mid-range places with friendly staff and a bright, airy building. Spacious and clean doubles/triples with fan and hot water cost Rs 275/325.

Next door, ***Hotel Ranjit*** *(☎ 364446, 263 Station Rd)* offers good-value fan-cooled rooms with hot shower for Rs 250/400 a single/double; Rs 330/480 with TV, phone and air-con.

The ***retiring rooms*** at Agra Cantonment station have dorms for Rs 50, and singles/doubles for Rs 150/200; Rs 300/400 with air-con.

Fatehbad Road Area Set back from Fatehbad Rd, ***Hotel Ratan Palace*** *(☎ 333400)* offers value for money. Adequate singles/doubles with bathroom cost Rs 250/300 with fan and doubles with air-con are Rs 500.

South of Fatehbad Rd, the friendly ***Hotel Safari*** *(☎ 333029, Shamsabad Rd)* is run by the same owners as the Tourists Rest House. It is popular; clean and good-value air-cooled singles/doubles with hot water and bathtub cost Rs 175/250 (plus Rs 100 for air-con). Rooms with shower only cost Rs 120/200. All rooms are supplied with towel, soap and toilet roll.

Places to Stay – Mid-Range

Most mid-range places are around Fatehbad Rd and offer hot water, TV, phone and air-con. A 5% luxury tax is usually charged on top of the tariffs below.

Close to the eastern gate of the Taj, ***Hotel Taj Khema*** *(☎ 330140)* is a ramshackle UP Tourism hotel. It's main claim to fame is that former US president Bill Clinton delivered his environmental address from the hummock in the garden. There are good views of the Taj from this point, but the rooms are expensive for what you get. Fan-cooled singles/doubles start at Rs 600/700, while air-con rooms are Rs 800/900. From April to September, rates drop by 20%.

There are several OK mid-range places along Fatehbad Rd, which offer passable carpeted rooms with TV. Rates start at Rs 400/600 for a single/double with fan; and Rs 500/700 with air-con. Options include ***Hotel Agra Deluxe*** *(☎ 330110, fax 331330)*, ***Hotel Park View*** *(☎ 331139)* and ***Hotel Ratandeep*** *(☎ 331074, fax 334920)*.

By the Pizza Hut on Fatehbad Rd, ***Amar Yatri Niwas*** *(☎ 333800, fax 333805)* isn't much to look at from the outside, but the rooms are above average. Tidy and well-maintained rooms with air-con, TV and phone start at Rs 900/1100.

Near the State Bank of India, the ***Hotel Ganga Ratan*** *(☎ 330329, fax 330193, Fatehbad Rd)* is a no-nonsense mid-range hotel with good facilities and a professional attitude. All rooms have air-con; rooms with TV and hot shower start at Rs 900/1020.

Hotel Atithi *(☎ 330879, fax 330878, Fatehbad Rd)* has good-sized, well-equipped air-con rooms starting at Rs 1175/1425, plus a swimming pool and restaurants. Rates are usually negotiable.

Hotel Amar *(☎ 331885, fax 330299)*, next door, is another upmarket place with a pool, prices start at Rs 1300/1550 for rooms with TV, carpet and bathroom.

Mayur Tourist Complex *(☎ 332302, fax 332907, Fatehbad Rd)* is also run by UP Tourism, but it's certainly seen better days. The rooms are arranged around a lawn and there's a pretty good restaurant and a pool that is often closed for cleaning. Air-cooled singles/doubles cost Rs 900/1050 and air-con rooms start at Rs 1000/1200.

New Bakshi House *(☎ 302176, fax 301 448, 5 Laxman Nagar)* is between the train station and the airport. It's effectively a private home, and you can use the family's lounge. Comfortable doubles in this clean place range from Rs 850 to 1250, some with air-con.

Places to Stay – Top End

All top-end hotels have air-con and swimming pools and most are on Fatehbad Rd.

Midway from Agra Cantonment to the Taj, ***Agra Ashok Hotel*** *(☎ 361223, fax 361620, 6B The Mall)* is a well-managed, pleasant place. It's not cheap, though; doubles cost Rs 2000 from April to September and Rs 2500 from October to March (inexplicably, singles cost Rs 1995 year-round).

The curiously named ***Clarks Shiraz Hotel*** *(☎ 226121, fax 282001, 54 Taj Rd* e *clarkraz@nde.vsnl.net.in)* is a long-standing Agra landmark (Shiraz was the home of the architect of the Taj). Singles/doubles cost US$45/90 and have the expected comforts, including a fridge.

Built using local red sandstone, the splendid ***Mansingh Palace*** *(☎ 331771, fax 330202,* e *mansingh.agra@mailcity.com, Fatehbad Rd)* is stylishly themed with lots of Mughal details and has attentive staff. Such luxury doesn't come cheap; sophisticated rooms start at Rs 1995/3000.

The efficient ***Howard Park Plaza International*** *(☎ 331870, fax 330408,* e *hppi@nde.vsnl.net.in)*, nearby, is well run and has some luxurious touches. Air-con rooms with all mod-cons cost US$45/75.

Taj View *(☎ 331841, fax 331860)* is a five-star member of the Taj group hotels and has all the usual luxury trimmings. You'll pay US$105/115 a single/double for the view of the Taj; similar rooms without the view cost US$90/95.

Mughal Sheraton *(☎ 331701, fax 331730)* is arguably Agra's top hotel. The award-winning red-brick building fails to win over all visitors, but the hotel boasts an impressive range of luxury facilities and has standard rooms from US$110/120, or US$175/185 with a medium-range view of the Taj Mahal.

Nearby, ***The Trident*** *(☎ 331818, fax 331 827)* is a low-rise Mughal-style hotel with a garden and restaurant. Luxury rooms are excellent value at US$44/88, but it's set in a fairly unappealing area.

Places to Eat

Agra offers a wide range of prices and standards of dining. Taj Ganj is the cheapest place to eat, but for more flavoursome cuisine, you will have to head to the Sadar Bazaar area or the restaurants at some of the luxury hotels. If you're walking around the Kinari Bazaar, don't forget to try the local speciality, *peitha* (ultrasweet candied pumpkin).

Taj Ganj Area In the Taj Ganj area there is a huge number of rooftop eateries catering to budget travellers. All offer almost identical menus of Indian and international favourites, and these days most will refrain from adding bacteria to your meal (see the boxed text 'Diarrhoea with your Meal, Sir?' opposite), though you should still be wary of eating in empty restaurants. None are licensed but beer can usually be 'arranged' if you ask. The popularity of specific restaurants waxes and wanes with the seasons; take a stroll around and see which places are currently drawing a crowd.

Close to the Hotel Kamal, ***Joinus Restaurant*** has the best rooftop vantage point and turns out a passable range of curries, Western dishes and breakfasts for less than Rs 50, accompanied by good music. On clear days, there are good views of the Taj.

Across the road, ***Shankara Vegis Restaurant*** is another rooftop place that tries its hand at everything from *murg masala* (chicken curry) to beef schnitzel. Meals cost roughly Rs 30 to 55.

Yash Cafe, close to the Shanti Lodge, is on a terrace rather than a rooftop. It's a good place to unwind, with Western music, games and comfy chairs. There is a wide range of Western food, but usually not beer.

Back at street level, ***Lucky Restaurant*** has the usual have-a-go-at-everything menu but it's one of the more convivial places to hang out. There are a also a few tables on the roof with views of the Taj.

Elsewhere Run by devotees of the late guru Osho, ***Zorba the Buddha*** *(☎ 225055, Sadar Bazaar)* offers truly excellent vegetarian food in a pleasant nonsmoking environment. The naan bread made from yogurt dough is magnificent. Main dishes cost from Rs 70 to 80. This place is very popular with travellers, so it's wise to book in the evening. The restaurant is closed each year in May and June.

Around the corner on Taj Rd, ***Lakshmi Vilas*** is a cheap South Indian vegetarian restaurant serving 23 varieties of *dosas* (lentil pancakes) for around Rs 30.

Nearby, ***The Park*** is an upmarket restaurant serving Indian and Chinese food in stylish surroundings. Dishes range from Rs 70 to 130.

Across the road, ***Prakash*** is dingy but popular, with great value vegetarian thalis for Rs 38.

Upstairs in the Meher Cinema complex near the Agra Ashok Hotel, ***Dasaprakash*** serves tasty and highly regarded South Indian food in the Rs 45 to 100 range and is open late into the evening.

Only Restaurant, at the Taj Ganj end of The Mall, is highly rated by locals, though the food is fairly bland. There's often live Indian music in the evening.

For those craving Western familiarity there's a ***Pizza Hut*** on Fatehbad Rd, next to Amar Yatri Niwas, but it's rather pricey.

There is top-end dining at top-end prices at the restaurants in most luxury hotels. Try the ***Clarks Shiraz Hotel*** and the ***Mughal Sheraton*** for a splurge.

Diarrhoea with your Meal, Sir?

CLINT CURÉ

During the late 1990s, Agra became the centre for a food-poisoning scam of monstrous proportions. Over several years, hundreds of travellers were given adulterated food by restaurants in Taj Ganj and taken to private clinics where doctors treated them for severe food poisoning. In the process foreign insurance companies were billed for thousands of dollars worth of phoney treatments.

Mercifully, there were no fatalities in Agra, but two Irish backpackers died in 1998, apparently due to a similar scam in Varanasi. The insurance companies soon got wise and sent in their own investigators, leading to the arrest of several doctors and restaurant staff. There were no new cases at the time of writing, but many of the clinics and restaurants involved are still in business, so the scheme could resurface at any time. In this edition, we haven't recommended any establishment known to be linked to the scam.

Shopping

Agra is well known for marble items inlaid with coloured stones, similar to the pietra dura work on the Taj. Sadar Bazaar and the area south of Taj Ganj are full of emporiums of one kind or another, but prices here are more expensive than in the bazaars of the old part of the city. Expect to pay around Rs 200 for an inlaid jewellery box and Rs 1000 for a richly inlaid wall plaque. Shops are known to swap marble items for cheaper soapstone pieces when they pack up purchases, so make sure you see your purchase go into the box!

Other popular buys include rugs, leather and gemstones, though the latter are imported from Rajasthan and can be bought much more cheaply in Jaipur. Gem shops are also some of the worst offenders when in comes to credit-card fraud and other scams (see the boxed text 'Agra-Phobia').

About a kilometre along the road running from the eastern gate of the Taj is Shilpgram, a crafts village and open-air emporium. Electric shuttle buses run here from Agra Fort and the eastern gate to the Taj and you can pick up good-quality crafts from all over the country, though prices are aimed at the package-tour bracket.

Getting There & Away

Air Agra is a stop on the extremely popular tourist shuttle route from Delhi to Agra, Khajuraho and Varanasi with Indian Airlines. The 40-minute flight leaves Delhi at 11.30 am, continuing on from Agra to Khajuraho and Varanasi at 12.35 pm. The return flight to Delhi leaves at 5.20 pm. Fares from Agra are US$55 to Delhi, US$80 to Khajuraho and US$160 to Varanasi. Indian Airlines has an office (☎ 360948) at the Clarks Shiraz Hotel, open 10 am to 1.15 pm and 2 to 5 pm daily.

Bus Most long-haul buses leave from the Idgah bus station (☎ 363588) near the train station. Buses to Delhi's Sarai Kale Khan bus station (Rs 92, five hours) leave hourly from 4 am to 11.30 pm. There are also hourly services to Jaipur (Rs 103, six hours) and Mathura (Rs 28, 1½ hours). Buses to Fatehpur Sikri (Rs 17, 1½ hours) leave every 30 minutes from 6.30 am to 7 pm. There is one bus to Khajuraho (Rs 140, 10 hours) at 5 am.

The smaller Power House bus station (also known as Agra Fort bus station) in the old city has regular slow buses to Mathura (Rs 23, two hours). For Bateshwar, you're best off taking a bus to Bah and changing there. City buses to Sikandra stop outside the bus station and cost Rs 4.

Rajasthan government buses depart from a small booth outside the Hotel Sakura, close to the Idgah bus station. Air-con buses depart every hour for Jaipur (Rs 201, six hours) from 6.30 am to midnight, but you should book a day in advance.

Train Agra Cantonment train station is an important stop on the main Delhi-Mumbai line with several trains daily from both New Delhi train station and Nizamuddin. The fastest train to Delhi is the daily air-con *Shatabdi Express* (Rs 125/390, sleeper class/air-con chair class, two hours). It leaves Delhi at 6 am and departs from Agra for the return trip at 8.18 pm, making it ideal for day-tripping.

A much cheaper alternative is the daily *Taj Express* (2½ hours). It leaves Delhi's Nizamuddin station at 7.15 am and departs from Agra for the return trip at 6.35 pm. This gives you less time in Agra but it conveniently connects with the organised tour (see Organised Tours earlier in this section). There are at least four other express trains from New Delhi train station daily. Be doubly cautious with your baggage on this route; a chain and padlock (obtainable from vendors on the platform) isn't a bad idea.

Agra-Phobia

With its many and varied scams and persistent touts and rickshaw-wallahs, Agra can leave travellers on the verge of hysteria. The many pitfalls can be negotiated, but you'll need to be on your toes. Be wary of anyone who offers to make things easier for you. A cheap or free ride will inevitably lead you straight to a craft shop. If you accept assistance with train bookings, don't be surprised if the service you want suddenly turns out to be full in all classes, necessitating an expensive private bus or taxi ride. Anyone turning up to the steps of a hotel with a rickshaw-wallah in tow is likely to pay a 100% mark-up on the rate for their room.

If you accept any of the detours to gem and souvenir shops offered by rickshaw drivers, you will inevitably pay elevated prices to cover the drivers' commission. Some shops may take advantage of the fact that you will be unable to find them again to pull a variety of stunts, from substituting marble souvenirs for soapstone to the grandmaster of all Agra scams, the 'gem import scam' (see the boxed text 'Buyer Beware!' under Shopping in the Facts for the Visitor chapter).

Agra has several daily trains to Howrah (in Kolkata; Rs 337, sleeper class) but none of these pass via Varanasi. The best option is the daily *Marudhar Express* which leaves Agra Cantonment at 8.45 pm, reaching Varanasi (Rs 208) between 8 and 9.30 am the next morning. Alternatively, there are trains to Mughal Serai, a short bus ride from Varanasi.

There are daily trains to Mumbai (Rs 315, 23 to 29 hours) at 8.30 am, 12.30 and 12.45 pm. For Goa (Rs 329, 24 hours) there are trains to Pune at 1.47 and 5.30 pm. The daily train to Chennai (Rs 393, 33 hours) leaves at 9.30 pm and the daily *Kerala Express* bound for Thiruvananthapuram (formerly Trivandrum; Rs 489 two days) leaves at 2.10 pm.

If you're bound for Rajasthan, the daily *Marudhar Express* leaves Agra Cantonment at 7.15 am, reaching Jaipur (Rs 123) at 2 pm and Jodhpur (Rs 205) at 8.50 pm. For Khajuraho, take any train to Jhansi (Rs 95, three hours) and change to a bus there.

Getting Around

To/From the Airport Agra's Kheria airport is 7km from the centre of town and 3km west of Idgah bus station. From Taj Ganj, taxis charge around Rs 100 and autorickshaws Rs 60, but try to bargain.

Taxi & Autorickshaw Although they are some of the biggest offenders for atmospheric pollution – and you'd be doing the city a favour taking a cycle-rickshaw – taxis and autorickshaws are convenient and useful for longer trips such as to Sikandra and Fatehpur Sikri. Both taxis and autorickshaws are unmetered so be prepared to haggle if you pick up a lift in the street.

Prepaid taxis and autorickshaws can be booked at a booth in Agra Cantonment train station. From the station to Taj Ganj costs Rs 40/150 by autorickshaw/taxi. A four-hour sight-seeing trip to the Taj Mahal and Agra Fort costs Rs 250/350. For more extensive sightseeing, a prepaid taxi will charge Rs 500 for eight hours (Rs 650 if you include Fatehpur Sikri). Expect to pay 25% more for air-con. Unfortunately, the prepaid rates aren't actually displayed, so if no-one is in the booth, it's back to bargaining.

Cycle-Rickshaw This nonpolluting form of transport is probably the best way to get around Agra, if you don't mind the endless offers of lifts from cycle-rickshaw-wallahs. Try to keep your patience, agree a price before setting out and don't take any nonsense from rickshaw-wallahs who offer to take you from A to B via a few marble or jewellery shops.

From Taj Ganj to Sadar Bazaar should be Rs 15 or less, and all other trips in Agra shouldn't cost more than Rs 20. Few drivers will accept less than Rs 30 from Taj Ganj to Agra Cantonment train station.

Reinventing the Rickshaw

In an effort to promote increased use of environmentally friendly cycle-rickshaws by tourists, the Institute for Transportation and Development Policy and foreign charities have joined together to create a new breed of cycle-rickshaws, which are more comfortable for passengers, and considerably easier to ride for drivers.

The new rickshaws are based on rickshaws being used in many European cities, which feature lightweight materials and multiple gears – a radical step for Indian bicycles – allowing rickshaw-wallahs to cycle uphill for the first time. It is hoped that the scheme will reverse the trend towards polluting autorickshaws. A recent study revealed that if all the cycle-rickshaws in Agra used two-stroke engines instead of pedal power, they would produce more than 11 tonnes of extra lead in the atmosphere every year!

The scheme also aims to improve the lot of Agra's rickshaw-wallahs, who are traditionally at the bottom of the poverty ladder. Most rickshaws in Agra are leased and operated by teams of three drivers, who take shifts in the saddle and earn only a few hundred rupees a day. The big Agra hotels (including the Sheraton, Taj View and Ashok) are now offering the new rickshaws to their guests for day-tours, providing a reasonable wage for the drivers and a taste of rickshaw transport in style for visitors.

Several big hotels offer special cycle-rickshaws, which have been designed to be more comfortable for passengers and drivers (see the boxed text 'Reinventing the Rickshaw' earlier).

Bicycle The simple solution to Agra's transport problem is to hire a bicycle, though most of the bikes on offer are of the Indian bone-shaker variety. The Taj, Agra Fort and even Itimad-ud-Daulah and Sikandra are all within a 5km radius. Try Raja Bicycle Store, on the way out of Taj Ganj towards the cantonment; bicycles cost Rs 50 for a full day. If you get a puncture, there will usually be a puncture-wallah within a few blocks. Several budget hotels can also arrange bike hire.

Electric Transport As part of the government's antipollution drive, electric buses and tempos (large three-wheelers) operate from the Taj Mahal to Agra Fort and Shilpgram craft village (Rs 4).

FATEHPUR SIKRI

☎ 05619 • pop 29,280

This magnificent fortified ghost city was the capital of the Mughal empire between 1571 and 1585, during the reign of Emperor Akbar. Regarded as the greatest of the Mughals, Akbar was thrust into the position of power at the tender age of thirteen. He expanded the Mughal empire to cover most of northern India.

Although Akbar's campaigns were as bloody as any in the Mughal era – following his victory at Panipat, he is said to have built a tower of his enemies' heads – the great Mughal is best remembered for his tolerance of other religions. A firm believer in the principle of *Sulh-i-Kul* or 'peace for all', Akbar counted Christians and Hindus among his five thousand wives (yes, five thousand!) and went on to invent a philosophy known as Din-i-Ilahi (Faith of God), asserting the common truth in all religions. Akbar also abolished many of the restrictions placed on infidels (nonbelievers), including the vastly unpopular 'pilgrimage tax' on Hindus.

Fatehpur Sikri, the 'Perfect City', was constructed in honour of the Sufi mystic Shaikh Salim Chishti, who Akbar credited with bringing him an heir. The city was designed as a physical expression of Din-i-Ilahi and a community of intellectuals and artists from many different religions was assembled to satisfy the emperor's love of debate.

In fact, the perfect city was Akbar's only folly. Built far from the nearest river, Fatehpur was plagued by water shortages and all the ingenious irrigation systems developed by Akbar's engineers were unable to solve the problem. Fatehpur was abandoned shortly after Akbar's death, along with most of his liberal policies.

The main palace compound and the magnificent Jama Masjid have been brilliantly restored by the Archaeological Survey of India, but perhaps the most interesting part of Fatehpur is the ruined city, which spreads out as far as the eye can see across the surrounding countryside.

Most people visit Fatehpur Sikri as a day trip from Agra (you could spend a day in Fatehpur Sikri and continue on to the world-renowned bird sanctuary at Bharatpur in the evening) but there are several places to stay, and the ruined city is at its most atmospheric at sunset or first thing in the morning. The best viewpoint is from the top of the city walls, a 2km walk to the south. The town which has grown up around Fatehpur has a lively little bazaar and friendly inhabitants and comes alive every year for Eid-ul-Fitr, the festival celebrating the end of Ramadan.

Orientation & Information

The deserted city lies along the top of a ridge, 40km south-west of Agra. The village of Fatehpur Sikri, where you'll find the train and bus station, is just south of the ridge. The grand Buland Gate to the Jama Masjid is at the top of an alley leading up from the main road. If you come by taxi, a Rs 5 fee per car is payable at Agra Gate, the eastern entrance to the village.

The historic enclosure is open from sunrise to sunset and the entry fee is a steep Rs 475 for foreigners and Rs 24.50 for Indians (free on Friday). A video camera permit is Rs 25. Fortunately, there is no charge to visit the spectacular Jama Masjid and the ruined city surrounding the Archaeological Survey area. This is probably the most evocative part of Fatehpur Sikri and is worth a visit even if you don't pay to see the palaces. The function and even the names of many buildings at Fatehpur remain contentious so you may find it useful to hire a guide. Licensed guides cost around Rs 85 and loiter near the ticket office; unlicensed guides solicit tourists outside the Jama Masjid.

Jama Masjid

Fatehpur Sikri's beautiful mosque, known as Dargah Mosque, contains elements of Persian and Hindu design and is said to be a copy of the mosque at Mecca. The main entrance is through the impressive 54m-high **Buland Gate**, the Gate of Victory, constructed to commemorate Akbar's victory in Gujarat, reached by a steep 13m-high flight of stone steps. A Quran inscription inside the archway quotes Jesus saying: 'The world is a bridge, pass over it but build no house upon it. He who hopes for an hour may hope for eternity', which seems highly appropriate considering the fate of the city.

In the northern part of the courtyard is the superb white marble *dargah* or **Shaikh Salim Chishti's tomb**, built in 1570. Just as Akbar came to the saint four centuries ago looking for a son, childless women visit his tomb today. The *jalis* (carved marble lattice screens) are probably the finest examples of such work you'll see anywhere in the country. The saint's grandson, Islam Khan, also has his tomb within the courtyard. The eastern gate of the mosque, known as the **Shahi Darwaza** (King's Gate), was used by Akbar.

Palace of Jodh Bai

North-east of the mosque is the ticket office and entrance to the old city. The first building inside the gate is a palace, commonly but wrongly ascribed to Jodh Bai, Jehangir's Hindu mother and the daughter of the

FATEHPUR SIKRI

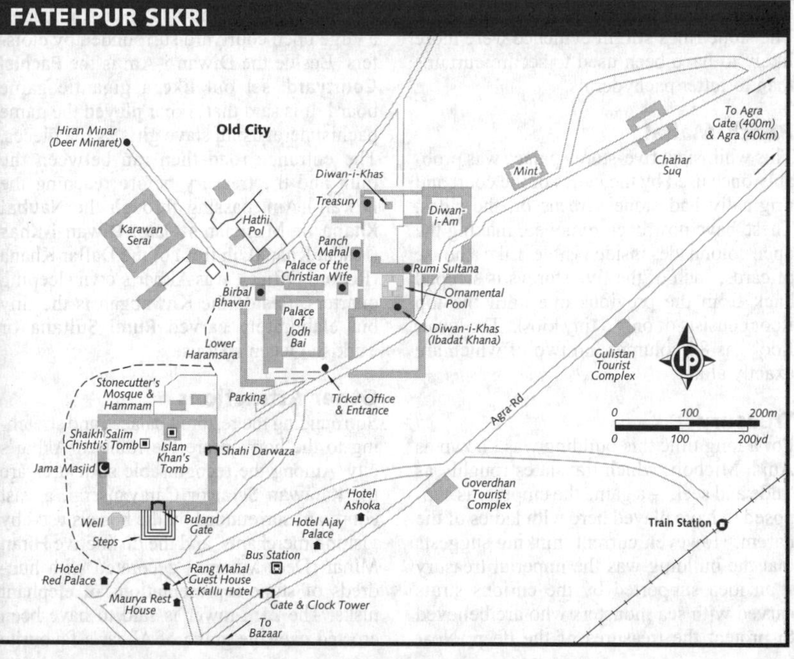

Maharaja of Amber. The architecture is a blend of styles with Hindu columns and Muslim cupolas. The **Hawa Mahal** (Palace of the Winds) is a projecting room whose walls are made entirely of stone latticework. The ladies of the court may have sat inside to keep an unobtrusive eye on events below.

Close to the Jodh Bai Palace, the **Palace of the Christian Wife** was used by Akbar's Goan Christian wife, Maryam, and at one time was gilded throughout – giving it the name the Golden House.

Birbal Bhavan

Thought to have been built either by or for Akbar's favourite Hindu courtier, Raja Birbal, this elegant building provoked Victor Hugo, the 19th century French author, to comment that it was either a very small palace or a very large jewellery box. The palace fronts onto the **Lower Haramsara**, which was once believed to be an enormous stable, with nearly 200 enclosures for elephants, horses and camels. This is now thought to be where the palace maids lived. The stone rings still in evidence were more likely to have been used to secure curtains than to fetter pachyderms.

Panch Mahal

This whimsical five-storey palace was probably once used by the ladies of the court and originally had stone screens on the sides. These have now been removed, making the open colonnades inside visible. Like a house of cards, each of the five storeys is stepped back from the previous one until the top floor consists of only a tiny kiosk. The lower floor has 84 columns, no two of which are exactly alike.

Treasury

For a long time this building was known as Ankh Micholi, which translates roughly as 'hide and seek' – a game the emperor is supposed to have played here with ladies of the harem. However, current thinking suggests that the building was the imperial treasury – an idea supported by the curious struts carved with sea monsters who are believed to protect the treasures of the deep. Near one corner is a small canopied enclosure known as the Astrologer's Seat, where Akbar's Hindu guru may have sat while instructing him.

Diwan-i-Khas

The Hall of Private Audiences, known as the Jewel House, has a fairly plain exterior, but the interior is dominated by a magnificently carved stone column in the centre of the building. The pillar flares to create a flat-topped plinth linked to the four corners of the room by narrow stone bridges, from where Akbar is believed to have debated with scholars of different religious persuasions who stood at the ends of the four bridges. Another theory is that Akbar meted out justice from this stone perch and yet another is that this was where the emperor was weighed at the commencement of the Persian New Year.

Diwan-i-Am

Just inside the north-eastern gates of the deserted city is the Hall of Public Audiences, a large open courtyard surrounded by cloisters. Beside the Diwan-i-Am is the **Pachisi Courtyard**, set out like a gigantic game board. It is said that Akbar played the game pachisi here, using slave girls as the pieces. The entrance road then ran between the mint and the treasury before reaching the Diwan-i-Am, passing through the **Naubat Khana** or Musician's Gate. **Diwan-i-Khas** (Ibadat Khana), in front of the Daftar Khana (Record Office), was Akbar's own sleeping quarters. Beside the Khwabgah is the tiny but elaborately carved **Rumi Sultana** or Turkish Queen's House.

Other Attractions

Surrounding the restored palaces and stretching to the horizon are the ruins of Akbar's city. Among the recognisable structures are the **Karawan Serai** or Caravanserai, a vast courtyard surrounded by the hostels used by visiting merchants, and the distinctive **Hiran Minar** (Deer Minaret) decorated with hundreds of stone representations of elephant tusks. The 21m tower is said to have been erected over the grave of Akbar's favourite elephant and the emperor used the tower as a vantage point to shoot at deer and other game which were driven in front of him.

Near the Karawan Serai, badly defaced elephants still guard the **Hathi Pol**, or Elephant Gate to the palace. To one side is a mysterious well, faced by a series of chambers reached by individual stairways, just one of many attempted solutions to Fatehpur's water problems. Immediately behind the Jama Masjid are the remains of the small Stonecutters' Mosque, which was supposedly erected on the site of Shaikh Salim Chishti's cave. There's also a fine **hammam** (Turkish bath) here. Many more impressive ruins can be found around the Agra Gate, to the east of the modern village.

True Lies

For centuries, Fatehpur Sikri was believed to be an expression of Akbar's philosophy of tolerance for other faiths, but new archaeological evidence has shed doubt on the great Mughal's liberal reputation. In December 1999, extensive Jain ruins, including decapitated idols of the Jain *tirthankars* (great teachers), were found buried below the Mughal city, suggesting that a sophisticated temple culture existed on the site for close to a millennium before Akbar arrived.

Hindu fundamentalists quickly seized upon this as evidence that the liberal emperor was anything but, and there were even calls for Fatehpur to be torn down. However, historians place responsibility for the destruction on the Muslim generals Mohammed Gauri or Iltutmish in the early 12th century. The head of the local Jain Samaj, also a prominent figure in the BJP party, is campaigning for the World Heritage site to be handed over to the Jain community for 'restoration and conservation', presumably of the sort practised at Ayodhya. In February 2000, hundreds of Jain ascetics marched to Fatehpur to make the same demands. Fortunately for Fatehpur, attention has recently shifted to the Taj Mahal following claims that the famous mausoleum was built over the ruins of a Hindu temple.

Places to Stay & Eat

Fatehpur has no shortage of cheap, basic guesthouses. Closest to the Buland Gate is ***Maurya Rest House*** *(☎ 882348)*. There are basic singles/doubles with shared bathroom for Rs 60/90, or Rs 120/150 with private bathroom (free bucket of hot water). It's well run by a friendly family, and food is available in the small, shady courtyard or the rooftop restaurant.

Rang Mahal Guest House *(☎ 883020)* and ***Hotel Red Palace*** *(☎ 882637)*, nearby, offer rooms of a similar standard and price (checkout is 10 am). ***Kallu Hotel*** is a basic restaurant serving thalis for around Rs 30.

The other offerings in town are all near the bus stand. The friendly ***Hotel Ajay Palace*** *(☎ 882950)* is run by the amiable Ajay family and offers just four clean rooms with fan and private bathroom for Rs 100 for a single or double. The restaurant here is excellent.

Hotel Ashoka *(☎ 882964)*, also well run with a rooftop terrace and garden has singles/doubles for Rs 80/100 with bathroom.

Farther from the centre, the ***Goverdhan Tourist Complex*** *(☎ 882643)* is more family oriented, with a large garden and a variety of clean airy rooms. Dorms cost Rs 50, while large rooms with fan and bathroom cost Rs 100/150 and a flat with hot water and TV costs Rs 300.

About 300m towards the Agra Gate, the ***Gulistan Tourist Complex*** *(☎ 882490)* is run by UP Tourism, which explains the slightly institutional feel. Large rooms with fan and bathroom cost Rs 525/575, while similar air-con rooms with phone, TV and fridge are Rs 775/900.

There are plenty of snack and soft-drink vendors around all the entrances to the enclosures. Fatehpur Sikri's speciality is *khataie*, the biscuits you'll see piled high in the bazaar.

Getting There & Away

Tour buses only stop for an hour or so at Fatehpur Sikri, so if you want to spend longer (which is recommended) it's worth catching a bus from Agra's Idgah bus station (Rs 17, 1½ hours). Buses depart every 30 minutes between 5.30 am and 7 pm. There are also eight trains a day to Fatehpur Sikri (Rs 8, one hour) from Agra Fort.

Buses leave Fatehpur Sikri's bus stand for Bharatpur (Rs 10) every hour until 5 pm.

Don't encourage the villagers along the Agra road who force dancing bears to stop passing traffic. Animal welfare groups are making great efforts to save India's bears from this miserable life, which continues because tourists pay to watch the bears perform.

BATESHWAR

Few tourists make it out to this important pilgrimage centre, 70km south-east of Agra. With 101 temples strung out along the banks of the Yamuna River, Bateshwar is essentially one long bathing ghat, with thousands of stone steps leading down to the water's edge. Most of the temples here are devoted to Shiva, but there are also some ancient Jain temples.

During Kartika Purmina (the November full moon) thousands of Jain and Hindu pilgrims flock here to bathe in the river and honour Lord Shiva. Bateshwar is also the site of northern India's largest cattle fair in October/November.

There are several cheap hotels and *dharamsalas* (pilgrims' guesthouses) that cater to tourists, but most are unused to foreign tourists. To get here, take a bus from Agra's Power House bus station to Bah and change to a local bus there. A return taxi from Agra will cost around Rs 650.

MATHURA

☎ 0565 • pop 272,500

Although identified with Lord Krishna today, Mathura was originally a Buddhist monastic centre. The Chinese visitor Fahsien (who visited India from AD 401 to 410) wrote that Mathura had twenty Buddhist monasteries attended by some 3000 monks. Mathura began to decline in the 8th century as Buddhism gave way to Hinduism throughout the north. The Afghan warlord Mahmud of Ghazni finished off the job in 1017, levelling most of the Buddhist and Hindu shrines.

In the 16th century, Hindu scholars identified the town as the birthplace of Krishna and the town's renaissance began, only to be nipped in the bud by the fanatical Aurangzeb. The Mughal emperor flattened the Kesava Deo Temple, which marked the exact spot Krishna was born, and built a mosque in its place, ensuring religious tension for centuries to come. The Afghan Ahmad Shah Abdali finished off what the others began by torching Mathura in 1757.

With such an important religious pedigree, Mathura bounced back, and today is a busy, hectic pilgrimage town. The most interesting part of Mathura lies along the Yamuna River, where there are numerous bathing ghats, an atmospheric bazaar area and several interesting temples. You can barely move in Mathura during Janmashthami, when the Dwarkadheesh Temple is

Braj Bhoomi

Braj Bhoomi, the 'Land of Eternal Love', existed only in the collective consciousness of Hindus until it was rediscovered in the physical world in the area around Mathura, 58km north-west of Agra. Identified from references in early Hindu texts in the 16th century, Mathura (Muttra) is believed to be the birthplace of Krishna, who later revealed himself to be an incarnation of Vishnu. Many formative events in Krishna's life have been mapped to the surrounding countryside: Krishna is believed to have been raised by cowherders in nearby Gokul and Mahaban. As an adolescent, he 'sported' with his *gopis* (milkmaids) in the forest of Vrindavan (Vrindaban). Goverdhan is said to be the site of the hill that Krishna raised on one finger to shelter the people of Braj from Indra's wrath.

Today these towns are important pilgrimage sites for devotees of Krishna and are home to hundreds of temples, bathing ghats and ashrams, including the headquarters of the Hare Krishna movement. The whole area comes alive every year for Holi, the festival of colours, (March) and more significantly at Janmashthami, when Mathura becomes the centre for the nationwide celebration of the birth of Lord Krishna (August/September).

swathed in decorations and thousands of pilgrims and sadhus (holy men) come to give thanks for the birth of Krishna.

Information

The helpful tourist office (☎ 405351) at the old bus stand is open 10 am to 5 pm daily except Sunday. UP Tourism runs a daily 'Brij Brashan' tour visiting Vrindavan, Barsana, Nandgaon and Goverdhan, which departs near the tourist office at 6.30 am and is a real bargain at Rs 60. Note that many temples in the area are closed between about 11 am and 4 pm.

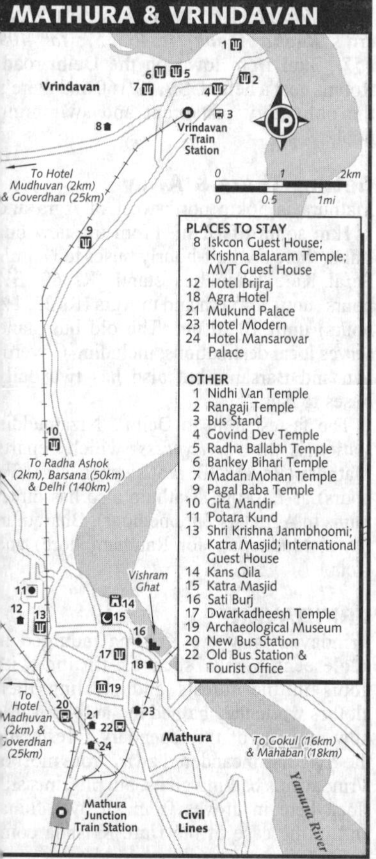

Shri Krishna Janmbhoomi

Among the foundations of the Kesava Deo Temple is a small room designed to look like a prison cell. Here pilgrims file past the stone slab on which Krishna is said to have been born 3500 years ago. He was obliged to make his entry into the world in these undignified surroundings because his parents had been imprisoned by the tyrannical King Kansa, Krishna's uncle.

In fact, this is only an approximation of the site as the original temple now lies buried under Aurangzeb's mosque, the **Katra Masjid**, which looms over the new Hindu temple and has a 24-hour police guard to prevent a repeat of the events at Ayodhya in 1992. Many areas are off-limits and cameras must be deposited at the security checkpoint at the entrance. The temple is open 5 am to noon and 4 to 9 pm (3 to 8 pm in winter).

About 200m from the Shri Krishna Janmbhoomi there's an alternative Krishna birthplace, and nearby is the **Potara Kund**, a tank where baby Krishna's nappies (diapers) are supposed to have been washed.

Yamuna River Attractions

The Yamuna River flows through Mathura and is lined with ghats (riverside steps for bathing). **Vishram Ghat** is the most important bathing ghat where Krishna is said to have rested after killing King Kansa. Shoes must be removed before entering and a donation is expected. You can hire a boat for a spell on the river for Rs 30 for half an hour; turtles are often seen in the water here.

The **Sati Burj**, beside Vishram Ghat, is a four-storey tower built by the son of Behari Mal of Jaipur in 1570 to commemorate his mother's *sati* (self-immolation). Aurangzeb knocked down the upper storeys, but they have since been rebuilt. The surrounding **bazaar** is full of colourful little shops selling items of religious devotion. Along the narrow alleys that lead up towards Shri Krishna Janmbhoomi is an ornate gateway, which leads into the **Dwarkadheesh Temple**, built in 1814 by Seth Gokuldass in honour of who else but Lord Krishna. This is Mathura's most popular temple and forms the centrepiece for the **Janmashthami** celebrations in

August/September. Nearby in a predominantly Muslim area is the ancient **Jama Masjid**, built by Abo-in Nabir Khan in 1661.

The ruined fort, **Kans Qila**, situated on the riverbank, was built by Raja Man Singh of Amber.

Archaeological Museum

The Archaeological Museum is well worth visiting for its superb collection of the Mathura school of sculpture, comprising Buddhist and Jain sculptures from the Kushan (1st to 3rd century) and Gupta (4th to 6th century) periods. This includes a famous and immaculately preserved standing Buddha, attributed to the monk Dinna in around AD 434. The museum is open 10.30 am to 4.30 pm daily except Monday. Entry is free.

Places to Stay & Eat

Mathura's numerous ***dharamsalas*** are useful in an emergency, but they don't see too many foreigners, so the language barrier can be a problem.

International Guest House *(☎ 423888)*, next to Shri Krishna Janmbhoomi, is excellent value offering singles/doubles with shared bathroom for Rs 35/50 and doubles with private bathroom starting at Rs 85, but it also serves as a barracks for soldiers protecting the nearby mosque and is often full. There is a pleasant garden and a cheap vegetarian restaurant.

Nearby is the simple but comfortable ***Hotel Brijraj*** *(☎ 424172)*, offering clean rooms with bathroom starting at Rs 175/200.

Tucked away beside the Yamuna River, ***Agra Hotel*** *(☎ 403318, Bengali Ghat)* gets mixed reports, but the rooms are OK. Rooms with fan and private hot-water bathroom cost Rs 250 to 400, while air-con will set you back Rs 600.

There are a few basic places by the old bus stand, including the ***Hotel Modern*** *(☎ 404747)*, with, frankly, what are old rooms with cold-water bathroom for Rs 125/200. Checkout is 24 hours, Hotel Modern has a bar and nonveg restaurant.

Hotel Mansarovar Palace *(☎ 408686)*, near the State Bank of India, is more upmarket and has slightly ageing fan-cooled rooms with private bathroom and hot water starting at Rs 700/800; Rs 900/1050 for air-con. There's a good restaurant.

Nearby, the new ***Mukund Palace*** *(☎ 410-316, Junction Rd)* is a stylish new, red sandstone building with superior fan-cooled rooms for Rs 500/600 and air-con rooms for Rs 700/800.

Hotel Madhuvan *(☎ 420064, fax 420684)* is a three-star establishment. Rooms start at Rs 1000/1200 and there's a swimming pool, restaurant and bar. It's a Rs 20 cycle-rickshaw ride north-west from the new bus stand.

The top hotel in the area is Best Western's ***Radha Ashok*** *(☎ 405557, fax 409557)*, 3km from town on the Delhi road. Rooms cost a hefty US$140/160 and there's the obligatory restaurant and swimming pool.

Getting There & Away

Mathura is 56km north-west of Agra and 141km south of Delhi. From the new bus stand, there are half-hourly buses to Delhi's Sarai Kale Khan bus stand (Rs 69, 3½ hours) until 1.45 pm and to Agra (Rs 23, 1½ hours) until 10.30 pm. The old bus stand serves local destinations, including Goverdhan and Barsana, but also has two daily buses to Agra.

The fastest train to Delhi's Nizamuddin station is the *Taj Express*, which departs Mathura (Rs 42/213, seat/sleeper class, 2½ hours) at 7.30 pm. Mathura also has direct trains to Agra (Rs 43, one hour), Bharatpur, Sawai Madhopur (for Ranthambhore) and Kota.

VRINDAVAN

Vrindavan is where Krishna indulged in adolescent pranks such as flirting with gopis in the forests and stealing their clothes while they bathed in the river. Little now remains of the legendary forests and the river has meandered away from most of Vrindavan's bathing ghats, but pilgrims still flock here in droves from all over India and in the case of the Hare Krishna community, from all over the world.

Krishna Consciousness

The International Society of Krishna Consciousness (Iskcon; ☎ 446053), more popularly known as the Hare Krishna movement, is based at the incredible white marble Krishna Balaram Temple complex in Vrindavan. The flamboyant use of carving may not be to everyone's taste, but the complex attracts several hundred Westerners every year to attend courses and seminars (call the centre for more details). Iskcon was founded in New York in the 1960s by Swami Prabhupada, who died in 1977 and has his mausoleum in the complex, but has faced considerable controversy in recent years.

Long regarded as a benign institution, Iskcon stunned the world in 1999 by admitting the existence of widespread child abuse at its boarding schools during the 1970s and 1980s. In a damning report commissioned by the organisation, the American sociologist E Burke Rochford exposed a culture of abuse, which he linked to the society's stance on celibacy, marriage and the value of the family unit.

In response to the report, Iskcon has radically shifted its emphasis away from residential centres and revised its policies to ensure better protection for the children in its care. The report highlights a growing concern about new-age religious sects, and several other religious groups have recently faced sexual-abuse allegations.

There are dozens of temples here, from garish modern shrines flanked by giant painted statues to more refined ancient temples. The bulky red sandstone **Govind Dev Temple** is the most impressive building in Vrindavan and architecturally it's one of the most advanced Hindu temples in Northern India. The temple was built in 1590 by Raja Man Singh of Amber in honour of the Divine Cowherd (Krishna) but was cut down a peg or two by the Mughal emperor Aurangzeb, who lopped off the top four floors during one of his demolition sprees.

The **Rangaji Temple** dates from 1851 and is a bizarre mixture of architectural styles, including a Rajput entrance gate, a soaring South Indian *gopuram* (intricate gateway tower) and an Italianate colonnade. At the entrance are two amusing electronic puppet shows telling the stories of the Ramayana and the Mahabharata. Non-Hindus are not allowed in the middle enclosure of the temple where there's a 15m gold-plated pillar.

There are said to be 4000 other temples in Vrindavan, including the truly massive 10-storey **Pagal Baba**, the popular **Bankey Bihari**, **Radha Ballabh** (built in 1626), **Madan Mohan** and the **Nidhi Van**. Vrindavan is also home to several charitable resthouses for widows from the surrounding villages. You may hear them singing devotional songs as you pass some of the ashrams in town.

The Hare Krishna movement has its base in the Krishna Balaram Temple complex (see the boxed text 'Krishna Consciousness' for more information).

Places to Stay & Eat

Many travellers choose to stay at the Iskcon complex, where the ***Iskcon Guest House*** *(☎ 442478)* has clean doubles with private bathroom, bucket hot water and very hard beds for Rs 200. It's also possible to stay in some of Vrindavan's ashrams, such as ***Chitrakoot*** *(☎ 442729)* and ***Sadhna Kunj***, which both charge Rs 100 per night. The ashram ***Chintamani Kunj*** *(☎ 442503)* has slightly plusher doubles for Rs 150 to 175. Ask for directions at Iskcon.

Next door to Iskcon, ***MVT Guest House*** *(☎ 443400)* has a good restaurant and well-equipped rooms for Rs 600 with fan and Rs 850 with air-con.

The restaurant at the Iskcon guesthouse is the best place to eat in this vegetarian-only town. It serves thalis for Rs 40 and other meals for less than Rs 25.

Getting There & Away

Tempos ply the 10km stretch between Mathura and Vrindavan (Rs 5, 25 minutes). You can pick them up at Mathura's new bus stand or on the main road near the Shri Krishna Janmbhoomi temple. These vehicles are packed to capacity so be prepared to carry your luggage on your lap. Autorickshaws are more comfortable but charge around Rs 60 one way.

BARSANA & GOVERDHAN

Krishna's consort Radha was from Barsana, 50km north-west of Mathura. The village is dominated by the huge **Ladli-ji Temple**, sacred to Radha, which sprawls along the ridge. Barsana is an interesting place to be during the festival of **Holi** when local women take the symbolic throwing of coloured powder to the next level and attack the men of nearby Nandgaon with sticks! Buses to Barsana depart from Mathura's new bus stand (Rs 16).

Goverdhan is 25km west of Mathura, on the road to Deeg, and is said to be where Krishna protected the inhabitants of Goverdhan from Indra's wrath (in the form of rain) by holding a hilltop, neatly balanced on top of his finger, over the town for seven days and nights. There are numerous temples around the sacred hill, including the **Har Deva-ji Temple** founded during the reign of Akbar. Mansingh of Jaipur is responsible for the artificial lake known as Mansi Ganga. About 3km from Goverdhan is the impressive temple complex of **Kusum Sarover**, with its vast bathing ghat. Buses to Goverdhan also leave from Mathura's new bus stand (Rs 11).

GOKUL & MAHABAN

Gokul, where Krishna was secretly raised, is 16km south of Mathura, and has numerous crumbling 16th-century temples. Hordes of pilgrims flock here during Krishna's birthday **festival** each July/August. It's best to get to Gokul by autorickshaw. It costs around Rs 160 return, with bargaining, which should include waiting time.

Mahaban, 18km south-east of Mathura, is another location from Krishna's idyllic childhood, though it's just a dusty village today. The ancient Mathura Nath Temple is worth a look. You can get here by bus or rickshaw.

MEERUT

☎ 0121 • pop 980,000

Only 70km north-east of Delhi, this is where the 1857 Uprising broke out, when the British unwisely deposed the last nawab of Lucknow. Meerut was then the largest garrison in northern India and the rebelling soldiers besieged Lucknow and Delhi among other towns before they were finally suppressed by the British. There's little to remember that event by today – just the cemetery near St John's Church, which also has the grave of General Ochterlony, whose monument dominates the Maidan in Kolkata. The **Suraj Khund** is the most interesting Hindu temple in Meerut and there's a **Mughal mausoleum** the Shahpir, near the old Shahpir Gate.

At **Sardhana**, 18km north of Meerut, is the palace of Begum Samru. The begum converted to Catholicism and built the basilica here in 1809, which has an altar of white Jaipur marble and houses her tomb.

There are several hotels in Meerut; the best is ***Hotel Shaleen*** and there's also the cheaper ***Anand Hotel*** – both in the Begum Bridge area. Meerut can be reached by bus from the ISBT Kashmiri Gate bus stand in Delhi (Rs 36, two hours).

ALIGARH

pop 562,330

Formerly known as Koil, this was the site of an important fort as far back as 1194. During the collapse of the Mughal empire the region was fought over by the Afghans Jats, Marathas and Rohillas – first one coming out on top, then another. Renamed Aligarh (High Fort) in 1776, it fell to the British in 1803 despite French support for its ruler Scindia. The **fort** is 3km north of the town, and in its present form dates from 1524.

Aligarh is best known today for the **Aligarh Muslim University**, where the 'seeds of Pakistan were sown'. Muslim students from all over the Islamic world come here to study.

ETAWAH

This town rose to importance during the Mughal period, only to go through the usual series of rapid changes during the turmoil that followed the Mughals' decline. The **Jama Masjid** shows many similarities to the mosques of Jaunpur, and there are **bathing ghats** on the riverbank below the ruined fort.

KANNAUJ

Only a few dismal ruins indicate that this was the mighty Hindu capital of the region in the 7th century AD. It quickly fell into disrepair after Mahmud of Ghazni's raids. This was where Humayun was defeated by Sher Shah in 1540, and forced to temporarily flee India. There's not much to see now – just an **archaeological museum**, a **mosque** and the ruins of the **fort**.

KANPUR

☎ 0512 • pop 2,470,000

Although Lucknow is the capital of Uttar Pradesh, Kanpur is the largest city. It's a major industrial centre that attracts few tourists and has the unfortunate distinction of being one of the world's most polluted cities.

Some of the most tragic events of the 1857 Uprising took place here when the city was known as Cawnpore. General Sir Hugh Wheeler defended a part of the cantonment for almost a month but, with supplies virtually exhausted, he surrendered to Nana Sahib, only to be massacred with most of his party at Sati Chaura Ghat. Over 100 women and children were taken hostage and imprisoned in a small room. Just before relief arrived, they were murdered and their dismembered bodies thrown down a well.

General Neill, their avenger, behaved just as sadistically. Some of the mutineers he captured were made to drink the English blood that still lay in a deep pool in the murder chamber. Before being executed, Hindus were force-fed beef and told they would be buried; Muslims got pork and the promise of cremation.

Things to See & Do

There's not much to see in Kanpur, though you can visit the site of **General Wheeler's entrenchment**, just over 1km from Kanpur Central train station. Nearby is **All Souls' Memorial Church**, which has poignant reminders of the tragedy of the Uprising. There's a large **zoo** at Allen Park, a few kilometres north-west of The Mall.

The main shopping centre, **Navin Market**, is famous for its locally produced cotton goods. Kanpur is a good place to find cheap leather shoes and bags.

Places to Stay & Eat

Kanpur has a string of overpriced hotels along The Mall, which is where you'll probably have to stay since the city's budget hotels, located around the train station, do not accept non-Indians. All the hotels listed here provide room service.

The ***retiring rooms*** at Kanpur Central train station are a useful, cheap option and have certainly improved since travel writers Eric and Wanda Newby spent a sleepless night here on their way down the Ganges in 1963. Dorms cost Rs 100, doubles Rs 250 and air-con doubles Rs 450 for 24 hours.

Meera Inn *(☎ 319972, 37/19 The Mall)* has good air-cooled singles/doubles with bathroom and hot water geyser for Rs 375/475 and air-con rooms for Rs 600/700.

The Attic *(☎ 311691, 15/198 Vikramajit Singh Rd)*, just north of The Mall, is a Raj-era bungalow in a pleasant garden with a good restaurant. Air-con rooms cost Rs 550/650, which for Kanpur is good value. Both places add a 10% 'amenities' charge.

Hotel Landmark *(☎ 317601, fax 315291, 10 Som Datt Plaza, The Mall)* is further up the luxury scale and has been recommended by readers.

Getting There & Away

The Chunniganj bus stand, 3km west of The Mall, services destinations to the west. The Collectorganj bus stand, 300m from the train station, covers points east, and has plenty of buses to Lucknow (Rs 39, two hours).

Kanpur has plenty of train connections to Delhi (Rs 99/520, 2nd/1st class, around six hours) and Kolkata (Rs 284/961, sleeper/1st class, 16 to 25 hours). There are also trains to Mumbai (Rs 326/1103, around 24 hours),

Allahabad (Rs 53/279, 2nd/1st class, three hours), Varanasi (Rs 77/441, seven hours) and Lucknow (Rs 28/173, 1½ hours).

JHANSI

Jhansi is a major transport hub for the north of Madhya Pradesh and is the most popular transit point for Khajuraho. Although it's actually in Uttar Pradesh, Khajuraho is included in the Madhya Pradesh chapter of this book (see that chapter for details).

LUCKNOW

☎ 0522 • pop 1,917,000

Despite its rich cultural associations Lucknow is not a particularly attractive city and it suffers from high levels of pollution. However, the huge crumbling mausoleums of the nawabs and the pock-marked ruins of the Residency, in particular, make it an interesting place to visit.

Lucknow became popular with Western followers of the octogenarian guru, Poonjaji, who died in 1997. If you're interested in visiting his nearby ashram, inquire at the Carlton Hotel.

History

The capital of Uttar Pradesh rose to prominence as the centre of the nawabs of Avadh. These decadent Muslim rulers, also known as the nawabs of Oudh, controlled a region of north-central India for about a century after the decline of the Mughal empire. Most of the interesting monuments in Lucknow date from this period.

The capital of Avadh was moved from Faizabad to Lucknow during the reign of Asad-ud-Daula (r. 1775–97). After Sa'adat Ali Khan (r. 1798–1814), the rest of the Avadh nawabs were uniformly hopeless at running affairs of state. Wajid Ali Shah (r. 1847–56) was so extravagant and indolent that to this day his name is regarded by many in India as synonymous with lavishness. However, the nawabs were great patrons of the arts, especially dance and music, and Lucknow's reputation as a city of culture and gracious living stems from this time.

In 1856 the British annexed Avadh, exiling the incompetent Wajid Ali Shah to a palace in Kolkata with a sizable annual pension. The annexation was one of the sparks that ignited the Indian Uprising in 1857. Lucknow was the scene for some of the most dramatic events of the Uprising. The British residents of the city held out in the Residency for 87 harrowing days, only to be besieged again for a further two months after being relieved.

Orientation

Lucknow is very spread out. The historic monuments are mainly in the north-western part of the old city, near the Gomti River. The narrow alleys of Aminabad form the main shopping area and Hazratganj is the modern, fashionable district where you'll find most of the budget and mid-range hotels.

Information

Tourist information is available at Hotel Gomti from UP Tours (☎ 212659), a branch of UP Tourism. The regional tourist office (☎ 226205) is hidden down an alley off Station Rd. It's open 10 am to 5 pm daily except Sunday, but it's pretty hopeless. There's a useful information booth at Lucknow train station, open 7 am to 6 pm daily. All the offices sell basic maps of the city.

Changing money can be a real hassle – although there are a lot of banks in the city, few seem interested in converting travellers cheques. Don't even bother trying on Saturday morning. The Canara Bank on MG Rd in Hazratganj should be able to help, or try a branch of the State Bank of India in the same area. Alternatively, the jewellery shop at the Carlton Hotel changes money.

Mayfair Travels is the American Express (AmEx) Travel Service representative.

Login Cybercafe, 1A Sapru Marg, upstairs next to Hotel Gomti, has very quick Internet connections for Rs 50 per hour.

The British Council library in Hazratganj is open 10.30 am to 6.30 pm Tuesday to Saturday. Next door is Ram Advani, an excellent bookshop. Universal Booksellers on Mahatma Gandhi (MG) Rd has a vast selection of books and sells a superior street map of Lucknow for Rs 35.

[Continued on page 435]

NORTH INDIA'S PILGRIMAGE SITES

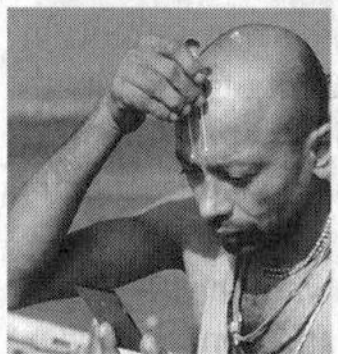

The religious and spiritual heritage of India is one of the richest in the world. With some 800 million Hindus, 18 million Sikhs, 120 million Muslims and devotees of many other religions, spiritual belief and observance underpin the lives of most Indians. Devotional practice is inextricably linked to the physical world in India, and for many, the very landscape, with its myriad religious sites, is a sacred landscape.

North India has the lion's share of sites, attracting many millions of followers to its places of pilgrimage. Here we cover some of the key pilgrimage sites; for important shrines on the Buddhist trail, see the special section 'The Way of the Buddha'.)

Hindu Sites

Most of the sacred sites of Hinduism are in North India. The holiest places bestow immediate blessings upon the Hindu supplicant, which explains why they have become important pilgrimage sites. The journey to the site is also viewed as part of the devotion – walking is considered to be more meritorious than taking public transport, and particularly dedicated sadhus have been known to make their way by onerous methods such as crawling or walking backwards. Once every three years millions of Hindus journey to the Kumbh Mela, which shifts between four locations, three of which are in Uttar Pradesh and one in Maharashtra. It's the largest, and one of the most significant, religious gathering in the world (see the boxed text 'Maha Kumbh Mela (Great Urn Festival)' in the Uttar Pradesh & Uttaranchal chapter).

Inset: A pilgrim applies a tilak (forehead mark worn by devout Hindu men) after bathing at [t]he Maha Kumbh Mela.

[R]**ight:** A devotee bathes at the *sangam* (conflu[en]ce) of the Ganges and Yamuna Rivers at the Maha Kumbh Mela.

BOTH PHOTOGRAPHS BY RICHARD I'ANSON

The number seven has special significance in Hinduism. Especially sacred are seven cities and seven rivers. Also sacred are the four cardinal points, of which Badrinath in Uttaranchal is the north point. In addition, together with Yamunotri, Kedarnath and Gangotri, Badrinath forms one of the Char Dham, which are considered the foremost Hindu pilgrimage sites in the Himalaya (see the Char Dham section in the Uttar Pradesh & Uttaranchal chapter for more information).

The seven sacred cities are Varanasi (associated with Shiva), Haridwar (where the Ganges enters the plains from the Himalaya), Ayodhya (birthplace of Rama), Mathura (birthplace of Krishna), Dwarka (legendary capital of Krishna), Ujjain (one of the sites for the Kumbh Mela) and Kanchipuram (the only sacred city not in North India).

The seven sacred rivers are the Ganges (Ganga), Saraswati (thought to be underground), Yamuna, Indus, Narmada, Godavari and Cauvery; the latter two are in the south. The Ganges is the holiest river; on its banks is Varanasi, the holiest of the seven cities. For a Hindu, there's no better place to visit – and no better place to die, for the Ganges transports the deceased directly to heaven, freeing them from the cycle of reincarnation.

To Hindus the Himalaya is a network of *tirthas* (literally a 'crossing points', or fords); it is a network of sacred nodes where the mundane

The Divine Descent of the Ganges

The prelude to the Ganges falling at Gangotri was the struggle between King Sagar, who slew the demons troubling the earth, and Indra, ruler of the abode of the gods. After dispatching the demons, King Sagar embarked on an aswamedh yagya, an elaborate religiou spritual to proclaim his supremacy. Fearing his own power would be threatened, Indra set out to thwart the upstart king. He stole the king's horse and tethered it to the ashram of the sage Kapil, who was engaged in a deep trance. Sagar's 60,000 sons traced the horse to the ashram, but their noisy arrival disturbed the meditating sage. Kapil opened his eyes and all those upon whom his gaze fell turned to ashes. The sage advised the king's grandson, Anshuman, that the 60,000 brothers could only enter heaven if the Ganges was brought down to earth and the ashes of the incinerated brothers were cleansed in its divine waters.

The task of enticing the goddess Ganga to earth proved too much for Anshuman, but his grandson, Bhagirath, took up the challenge, resolving not to move from the spot until the deed had been accomplished. After several years of deep meditation he was partly rewarded when the Ganges fell earthwards, however, it became tangled in Lord Shiva's matted hair. More intensive meditation on the greatness of Shiva was needed before the god released the waters of the Ganges. (According to another tradition, Shiva allowed the Ganges to fall through his hair, thus sparing the world from the destruction that would have been wrought if it had borne the river's full weight.) The water fell in seven distinct streams, including the Bhagirathi at Gangotri, and the 60,000 brothers finally gained entrance to heaven.

ALL PHOTOGRAPHS BY RICHARD I'ANSON

Pilgrimage occurs on a grand scale at the Maha Khumb Mela (Great Urn Festival): pontoon bridges at the confluence of three sacred rivers (top); a devotee of Hanuman, the monkey god (bottom right); a procession on the main bathing day, Mauni Amavasya (bottom left)

RICHARD I'ANSON

RICHARD I'ANSON

RICHARD I'ANSON

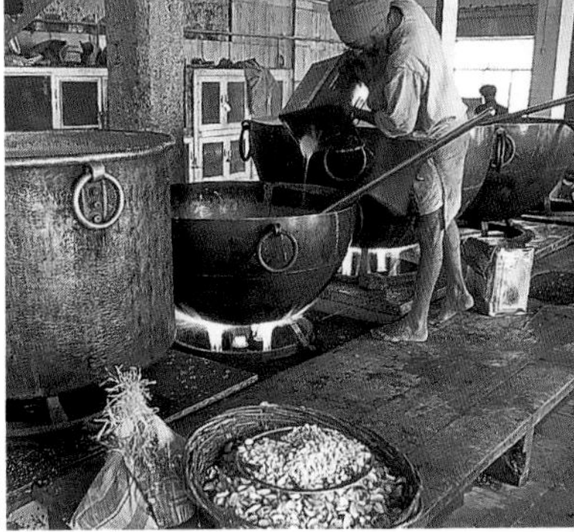

GREG ELMS

The Golden Temple in Amritsar is the most sacred of all Sikh temples (top); statues at a Digambara Jain temple in Kolkata (centre right); food is prepared for the thousands of pilgrims who visit the Golden Temple each day (bottom right); the devout at prayer, Jama Masjid, Delhi (bottom left) world meets the spiritual. A tirtha can be a mountain, *prayag* (river confluence), river source, birthplace of a saint or even the saint himself, but all can be worthy of pilgrimage.

The Himalaya is the mythical home of Shiva, who resides in several mountains, including Kinnaur Kailash and Manimahesh in Himachal Pradesh, and Mt Kailash in Tibet. The sacred Ganges falls from the dreadlocks of Shiva's hair to emerge at Gangotri in Uttaranchal a particularly pure and sacred spot. The true source of the river is a demanding nine-hour trek from Gangotri, at Gaumukh (3890m), negotiable in summer only. The source of the Yamuna, India's second-holiest river, at Yamunotri, is another pure tirtha.

There are many other holy sites that form a Himalayan pilgrimage circuit. There are 12 *jyoti linga,* or 'rays' of light, that are sacred to Shaivites. In the Himalaya these include Baijnath in Himachal Pradesh and Jageshwar in Kumaon. According to Hindu texts there are also 51 *shakti pirthas,* or seats of the goddess, where various parts of Sati's body fell after her charred body was dismembered by Vishnu. Sati's tongue fell to earth at Jawalamukhi, in Kangra, her right temple fell along the Indus River in Ladakh, her eye formed Nainital and her right palm landed at Lake Mansarovar, in Tibet.

In Uttaranchal, Panch Kedar marks the five sites where parts of Shiva's body emerged from the earth in the form of a bull after he plunged into the earth to escape the Pandavas. His hump appeared at Kedarnath, his hand at Tunganath, his face at Rudranath, his middle at Madmaheshwar and his hair at Kalpeshwar – together they form a powerful pilgrim circuit.

Sikh Sites

Around 18 million Sikhs live in India; most hail from Punjab, which is the site of the premier shrine of Sikhism – the Golden Temple in Amritsar. It is the goal of many Sikhs worldwide to visit the Golden Temple and offer obeisance, which will usually involve the donating of sweet,

RICHARD I'ANSON

Right: Women and men pray together inside the Golden Temple at Amritsar.

doughy *prasad* to the temple attendants. Even for non-Sikhs, the temple is a breathtaking site, especially when the (reputed) 100kg of pure gold on the dome of the Hari Mandir glows in the post-sunrise or pre-sunset light. Up close, the Hari Mandir is impressive, with its Taj Mahal–style *pietra dura,* or inlaid marble.

Jain Sites

Gujarat is home to two sites of prime importance to India's three million Jains. Shatrunjaya, at Palitana, is one of the holiest pilgrimage sites. It comprises a stunning hilltop complex of 863 temples, most dating from the 16th century. Shatrunjaya (Place of Victory) is believed to have been visited by Adinath, the first Jain tirthankara ('crossing-maker', or teacher). The site is accessible via a hot, 1½-hour ascent up 3000 steps. Near Junagadh, Girnar Hill is where Neminath, the 22nd tirthankara, is believed to have died, and it's a pilgrimage site for Hindus as well as Jains. The temples are reached after a climb up 10,000 steps.

Just over the border in Rajasthan are the Dilwara temples at Mt Abu. Dating from 1031, they feature exquisite marble carvings. Devotion for Jains takes the forms of prayer and offering, which are made at temples.

Islamic Sites

For Muslims, the only *haj* (pilgrimage) is to Mecca, something every Muslim aspires to do at least once in their life. However, Islam in India also has sites – mainly mystic Sufi in nature – to which devotees journey at particular times of the year. Three key sites are the mausoleum of Rauza Sharif, at Sirhind in Punjab, visited in August; the mausoluem at Ajmer in Rajasthan, visited by pilgrims from all over the subcontinent and South-East, Asia especially during Ramadan; and the shrine of Sufi saint Nizam-ud-din Chisthi in Delhi, which is one of the capital's most important devotional sites.

RICHARD I'ANSON

Left: India's largest mosque, the Jama Masjid in Delhi. Islam recommends that Muslims pray in congregation. On Fridays, Islam's holy day, the faithful pray in the sacred and social environment of a mosque.

[Continued from page 430]

Bara Imambara

The Bara or Great Imambara (an *imambara* is the tomb of a Shi'ia Muslim holy man) was built in 1784 by Asat-ud-Daula as a famine relief project. The central hall of the Imambara, at 50m long and 15m high, is one of the largest vaulted galleries in the world. An external stairway leads to an upper floor laid out as an amazing labyrinth known as the **bhulbhulaiya**; a guide may be useful since the dark passages stop abruptly at openings, which drop straight to the courtyard below. Guides claim that tunnels extend as far as Jaipur, Delhi and Mumbai! The labyrinth entry fee of Rs 12 includes entry to a picture gallery.

There's a mosque with two tall minarets in the courtyard complex but non-Muslims are not allowed in. To the right of this is a 'bottomless' well. The Imambara complex is open from sunrise to sunset.

Beside the Bara Imambara, and also built by Asat-ud-Daula, is the imposing **Rumi Darwaza**, a replica of an entrance gate built in Istanbul. 'Rumi' (relating to Rome) is the term Muslims applied to Istanbul when it was still Byzantium, the capital of the eastern Roman Empire.

Lakshman Tila, the high ground on the southern bank of the Gomti River nearby, was the original site of the town, which became known as Lucknau in the 15th century. Aurangzeb's mosque now stands on this site.

Hussainabad Imambara

Also known as the Chhota, or Small Imambara, this was built by Mohammed Ali Shah in 1837 as his own mausoleum. Thousands of labourers worked on the project to gain famine relief. The large courtyard encloses a raised rectangular tank with small imitations of the Taj Mahal on each side. One of them is the tomb of Mohammed Ali Shah's daughter, the other is that of her husband. The main building of the imambara, topped by a golden dome, contains the tombs of Ali Shah and his mother. The nawab's silver-covered throne, other paraphernalia of state and lots of tacky chandeliers are stored here. It's open from sunrise to sunset.

The decaying **watchtower** opposite the Hussainabad Imambara is known as Satkhanda, or the Seven Storey Tower, but it actually has four storeys because construction was abandoned when Ali Shah died in 1840. A 67m-high defunct **clock tower**, reputedly the tallest in India, overlooks the Hussainabad Tank nearby. A *baradari,* or **summer house**, built by Ali Shah, fronts onto the tank. It houses portraits of the nawabs of Avadh.

West of the Hussainabad Imambara is the **Jama Masjid**, which was started by Mohammed Ali Shah and completed after his death.

British Residency

Built in 1800 for the British Resident, this group of buildings became the stage for the most dramatic events of the 1857 Uprising – the Siege of Lucknow. The red-brick ruins are peaceful nowadays, surrounded by lawns and flowerbeds, but thousands died during the months-long siege.

The Residency has been maintained as it was at the time of the final relief, and the shattered walls are still scarred by cannon shot. Even since Independence, little has changed. The only major work done on the place was the unveiling of an **Indian Martyrs' Memorial** directly opposite.

There's a **model room** in the main Residency building which is worth visiting to get your bearings from the rather tatty model. Downstairs you can see the cellars where many of the women and children lived throughout the siege. The **cemetery** at the nearby ruined church has the graves of 2000 men, women and children, including that of Sir Henry Lawrence, 'who tried to do his duty' according to the famous inscription on his weathered gravestone.

The Residency is open from sunrise to sunset, but the model room is open only from 10 am to 5 pm. Entry is Rs 250 for foreigners.

Other Attractions

The plain **Shah Najaf Imambara**, opposite the Carlton Hotel, is the tomb of Ghazi-ud-din Haidar, who died in 1827. The interior

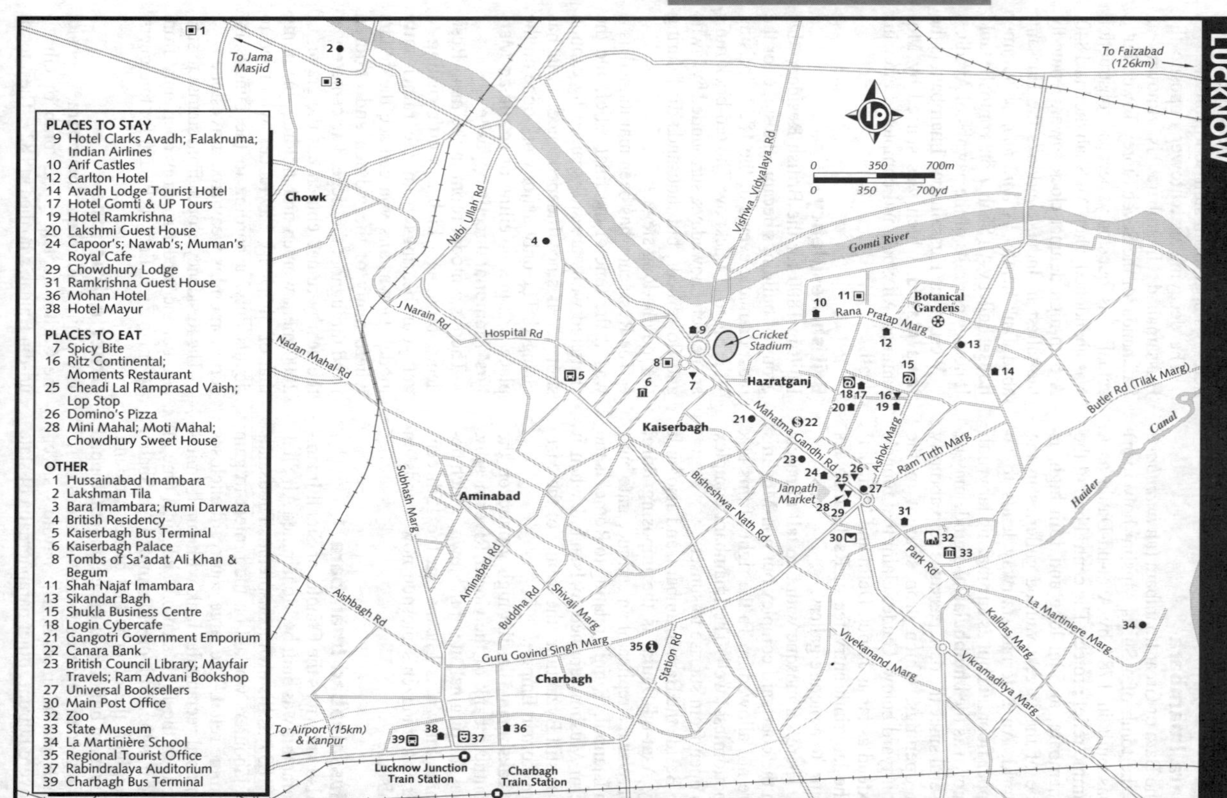
LUCKNOW
PLACES TO STAY
9 Hotel Clarks Avadh; Falaknuma; Indian Airlines
10 Arif Castles
12 Carlton Hotel
14 Avadh Lodge Tourist Hotel
17 Hotel Gomti & UP Tours
19 Hotel Ramkrishna
20 Lakshmi Guest House
24 Capoor's; Nawab's; Muman's Royal Cafe
29 Chowdhury Lodge
31 Ramkrishna Guest House
36 Mohan Hotel
38 Hotel Mayur
PLACES TO EAT
7 Spicy Bite
16 Ritz Continental; Moments Restaurant
25 Cheadi Lal Ramprasad Vaish; Lop Stop
26 Domino's Pizza
28 Mini Mahal; Moti Mahal; Chowdhury Sweet House
OTHER
1 Hussainabad Imambara
2 Lakshman Tila
3 Bara Imambara; Rumi Darwaza
4 British Residency
5 Kaiserbagh Bus Terminal
6 Kaiserbagh Palace
8 Tombs of Sa'adat Ali Khan & Begum
11 Shah Najaf Imambara
13 Sikandar Bagh
15 Shukla Business Centre
18 Login Cybercafe
21 Gangotri Government Emporium
22 Canara Bank
23 British Council Library; Mayfair Travels; Ram Advani Bookshop
27 Universal Booksellers
30 Main Post Office
32 Zoo
33 State Museum
34 La Martinière School
35 Regional Tourist Office
37 Rabindralaya Auditorium
39 Charbagh Bus Terminal
To Jama Masjid
To Faizabad (126km)
To Airport (15km) & Kanpur
0 350 700m
0 350 700yd
Chowk
Nabi Ullah Rd
Vishwa Vidyalaya Rd
Gomti River
J Narain Rd
Hospital Rd
Nadan Mahal Rd
Botanical Gardens
Rana Pratap Marg
Cricket Stadium
Hazratganj
Kaiserbagh
Mahatma Gandhi Rd
Ashok Marg
Butler Rd (Tilak Marg)
Canal
Ram Tirth Marg
Haider
Janpath Market
Bisheshwar Nath Rd
Subhash Marg
Aminabad
Aminabad Rd
Buddha Rd
Shivaji Marg
Aishbagh Rd
Park Rd
La Martiniere Marg
Kalidas Marg
Vikramaditya Marg
Vivekanand Marg
Guru Govind Singh Marg
Station Rd
Charbagh
Lucknow Junction Train Station
Charbagh Train Station

The Siege of Lucknow

The Uprising of 1857 is known to some as the 1857 Mutiny and to others as the First War of Independence, or the First Freedom Struggle.

Upon the outbreak of the Uprising the British inhabitants of the city all took refuge with Sir Henry Lawrence in the Residency. In total there were 2994 people crammed into the Residency's grounds: 740 British soldiers, 700 pro-British Indian troops, 130 British and Indian officers, 150 European volunteers, 27 noncombatant European men, 237 women, 260 children, 50 La Martinière schoolboys and 700 Indian servants. The Residency was technically indefensible, but those seeking shelter expected relief to arrive in a matter of days.

In fact, it was 87 days before a small force under Sir Henry Havelock broke through the besiegers to the remaining half-starved defenders. But once Havelock and his troops were within the Residency, the siege immediately recommenced. It continued unabated from 25 September to 17 November, when relief finally arrived with Sir Colin Campbell. Only 980 of the original inhabitants survived the ordeal. Many who did not die from bullet wounds succumbed to cholera, typhoid or smallpox.

The published accounts of the siege of Lucknow combine tales of derring-do with traces of domestic comedy wrung from the British contingent's struggle to maintain a stiff upper lip in the face of adversity.

Several accounts were written by women, some of whom at first seemed more troubled by the shortage of good domestic help than by being surrounded by tens of thousands of affronted, angry and bloodthirsty mutineers. This changed during the drawn-out months of the siege, by the end of which they were said to be able to judge the weight of shot being fired into the compound better than the men.

is used to store garish chandeliers and *tazia*, elaborate creations of wood, bamboo and silver paper, which are carried through the streets during the Muharram Festival. The imambara is open from sunrise to sunset.

Sikandar Bagh, the scene of pitched battles in 1857, is a partially fortified garden with a modest gateway bearing the nawabs' fish emblem. The **botanical gardens**, home of the National Botanical Research Institute, are nearby.

The stately **tombs** of Sa'adat Ali Khan and his wife, the begum, are close to the remnants of **Kaiserbagh Palace** on the south-eastern edge of the large double roundabout near the cricket stadium. Cannons mounted on the tombs during the siege of Lucknow were effective in delaying Havelock from relieving the Residency.

The dusty Lucknow **zoo** in the Banarsi Bagh is open 8 am to 5 pm (6.30 pm in summer) daily except Monday; entry costs Rs 10. Within the zoo is the **state museum**, which contains an impressive collection of stone sculptures, especially from the Mathura school (1st to 6th centuries). It's open 10.30 am to 4.30 pm daily except Monday, and entry is Rs 2. There is an additional fee of Rs 15 for your camera if you want to take a few snaps. Don't miss the British-era statues (of Queen Victoria and others) that have been dumped in a garden around the back.

La Martinière School, on the eastern edge of the city, was designed by the Frenchman Major-General Claude Martin as a palatial home. His architectural abilities were, to say the least, a little confused – Gothic gargoyles were piled merrily atop Corinthian columns to produce a finished product that a British marquess sarcastically pronounced to be inspired by a wedding cake. Martin died in 1800 before his home could be completed, but left the money and instructions that it should become a school. It duly became one of India's premier private schools (the school in Rudyard Kipling's story *Kim* is modelled on La Martinière). The school can be visited with permission from the principal (☎ 223863).

Organised Tours

UP Tours (☎ 212659) runs worthwhile half-day sightseeing tours of Lucknow (Rs 75, reserve ahead). Tours pick up people from the train station (at 8.30 am) and various hotels, including the Hotel Gomti next door.

Special Events

The spirit of the nawabs returns during the **Lucknow Mahotsava** between late November and early December. During the 10-day festival of nostalgia there are processions, plays, *kathak* dancing (an energetic style of traditional dancing, performed in striking costumes), *ghazal* (melancholic Urdu songs derived from poetry) and sitar recitals, kite flying and *tonga* (two-wheeled horse-drawn carriage) races.

Lucknow is a good place to see the **Shi'ia Muharram** celebrations (dates vary from year to year) as it has been the principal Indian Shi'ia city since the nawabs arrived. The activity during Muharram, which centres on the Bara Imambara, can get intense as penitents scourge themselves with whips; keep a low profile.

Places to Stay – Budget

Most travellers head for the Hazratganj area. Rooms mentioned here have private bathroom.

Chowdhury Lodge *(☎ 221911, 273135, 3 Vidhan Sabha Marg)*, down an alley opposite the main post office near the Capitol Cinema, has singles/doubles, some without windows, starting at Rs 125/170 and air-cooled rooms for Rs 200/250. The lodge has 24-hour checkout and charges extra for bedding and buckets of hot water.

Hotel Ramkrishna *(☎ 280099, 17/2 Ashok Marg)* is a standard Indian hotel with clean air-cooled singles/doubles/triples with hot water for Rs 180/230/350 and air-con rooms for Rs 620. The cheaper rooms are a bit grubby. Checkout is 24 hours.

Ramkrishna Guest House *(☎ 238363, 4A Park Rd)* has fairly good air-cooled doubles for Rs 340 and air-con doubles with TV for Rs 575. The rooms are on the small side, and avoid those at the front as they can be pretty noisy. The guesthouse is handy for the zoo.

Avadh Lodge Tourist Hotel *(☎ 282861, 1 Ram Mohan Rai Marg)*, near Sikandar Bagh, was closed for repairs at the time of research so expect prices to have increased. Varied singles/doubles/triples with hot water were Rs 200/300/375.

Lakshmi Guest House *(☎ 228661, 5 Shahnajaf Rd)* has singles/doubles with hot water and TV for Rs 350/450, Rs 450/550 with air-cooler and Rs 550/650 with air-con.

There are a few options in the noisy area near the train stations. The best option is ***Hotel Mayur*** *(☎ 451824, Subhash Marg)*, which has rooms with a TV and private bathroom with hot water geyser and squat toilet for Rs 275/350.

The Lucknow Junction ***retiring rooms*** offer dorms (Rs 50), doubles (Rs 250) and air-con rooms (Rs 450) for a 24-hour period.

Mohan Hotel *(☎ 635642, 635797, Buddha Rd)* is fine but generally overpriced. Rooms with air-con start at Rs 450/600. It's better value for three people in a double room – Rs 150 per extra person.

Places to Stay – Mid-Range & Top End

Carlton Hotel *(☎ 224021, fax 229793, Rana Pratap Marg)* was once a palace and is still an impressive building with a musty air of decaying elegance. Large singles/doubles with character cost Rs 600/700, or Rs 900/1200 with air-con and TV. You can shut out the noisy sounds of the city in this place, and extensive gardens make it a relaxing place to stay.

Capoor's *(☎ 223958, MG Rd)* is a long-established hotel in the heart of Hazratganj. The hotel was closed at the time of research due to the death of the owner.

Hotel Gomti *(☎ 220624, 6 Sapru Marg)* is a UP Tourism operation with overpriced but good air-cooled rooms with TV for Rs 550/650 and air-con rooms for Rs 875/975. The hotel has a restaurant, coffee shop and a popular bar.

Arif Castles *(☎ 211313, ⓔ arifind@lw1.vsnl.net.in, 4 Rana Pratap Marg)* is a modern hotel with small but pleasant rooms starting at Rs 900/1000.

Hotel Clarks Avadh *(☎ 216500, fax 216507, 8 MG Rd)* has rooms with good views and luxury fittings from Rs 3700/4000. There is also a restaurant, coffee shop and bar.

Places to Eat

The refined palates of the nawabs have left Lucknow with a reputation for rich Mughlai cuisine. The city is famous for its wide range of kebabs and *dum pukht* – the 'art' of steam pressure cooking, in which meat and vegetables are cooked in a sealed clay pot. Huge *rumali roti* (paper-thin chapatis) are served in many small Muslim restaurants in the old city. They are served folded up and should be eaten with a goat or lamb curry such as *bhuna ghosht* or roghan josh. The popular dessert *kulfi faluda* (ice cream with cornflour noodles) is served in several places in Aminabad. The sweet orange-coloured rice dish known as *zarda* is also popular. In the hot months of May and June, Lucknow has some of the world's finest mangoes, particularly the wonderful *dashhari* variety grown in the village of Malihabad, west of the city.

Hazratganj's MG Rd is lined with restaurants, snack bars and Western-style fast-food joints.

Nawab's, in Capoor's, serves decent veg/nonveg fare starting at Rs 45, and has live Indian music in the evenings. The *khas* dishes have a good, rich sauce.

Muman's Royal Cafe has veg/nonveg Indian and Chinese food, prompt service, good live music and a civilised ambience. Snacks start at Rs 25, and nonvegetarian mains are around Rs 65. The excellent *chaat* (snack) ***stall*** outside does a roaring trade in tasty snacks costing only Rs 15.

Cheadi Lal Ramprasad Vaish *(MG Rd)* has great coffee, juices and ice cream, which are consumed by customers standing on the pavement outside. It's poorly marked, but next to the Lop Stop fast-food joint.

Domino's Pizza *(MG Rd)* has made an appearance and has the usual Western-style pizzas.

Mini Mahal, nearby, has a good selection of Indian sweets and pastries, and Chinese fast food. ***Moti Mahal*** next door is similar, but has Indian food.

Also close by, ***Chowdhury Sweet House*** is an atmospheric place for coffee or tea.

Ritz Continental *(Sapru Marg)* is a fairly upmarket vegetarian restaurant, serving good snacks (starting at Rs 16), Indian food (mains around Rs 40), Chinese food and pizzas (Rs 38 to 50). The restaurant has diner-like booths.

Next door, ***Moments Restaurant*** is inexpensive, and good for kebabs and chicken.

Spicy Bite, in the Tulsi Theatre building, is rated highly by locals. Acceptable pizzas start at Rs 50 and burgers are around Rs 35, though it mostly specialises in Chinese and South Indian food.

Falaknuma, in Hotel Clarks Avadh, is one of the best places to try Lucknow cuisine. Main courses are expensive but the food is good and the restaurant has great views across the city.

Entertainment

Lucknow has a strong tradition in the performing arts. The ***Rabindralaya Auditorium*** *(☎ 455670)*, opposite the train stations, hosts classical music, dance and theatrical performances.

The extensive grassed gardens at the Carlton Hotel are a perfect spot for drinks on a warm night. It isn't cheap – a large bottle of Black Label beer is Rs 80 – but the setting definitely makes it worth the splurge, with the floodlit Carlton Hotel (a former palace) in the background.

Some restaurants have live Indian music in the evening – see ***Nawab's*** under Places to Eat earlier.

Shopping

The bazaars of Aminabad and Chowk are interesting to wander through, even if you are not buying. In the narrow lanes of Aminabad you can buy *attar* – pure essential oils extracted from flowers in the traditional manner. In the chowk, you'll find a bird-sellers' district known as Nakkhas – pigeon-keeping and cockfighting have been popular in Lucknow for centuries, since the time of the nawabs.

The Gangotri Government Emporium in Hazratganj sells local handicrafts, including the hand-woven embroidered cloth known as *chikan* for which Lucknow is famous.

Getting There & Away

Air The airport is 14km from town. Indian Airlines (☎ 220927) has an office at the Hotel Clarks Avadh. There are daily flights to Delhi (US$90), and flights to Patna (US$ 100) and Kolkata (US$155) four times weekly.

Sahara India Airlines (☎ 377675) has daily flights to Delhi (US$90) and Mumbai (US$250). Jet Airways (☎ 202026) also has flights to Delhi and Mumbai.

Bus There are two bus stations – Charbagh, near the train stations, and Kaiserbagh. From Charbagh there are regular departures to Kanpur (Rs 39, two hours) and Allahabad (Rs 86, five hours), and early-morning and evening buses to Varanasi (Rs 120, 8½ hours) and Agra (Rs 105, 10 hours). From Kaiserbagh there are buses to Delhi (Rs 207, 12 hours), Gorakhpur (Rs 112, 7½ hours) and Faizabad (Rs 55, three hours).

Train The two main stations, Charbagh and Lucknow Junction, are side by side; Northern Railway trains run to both, North Eastern Railway trains only to the latter. Essentially, Charbagh handles all trains between New Delhi and Kolkata, while Lucknow Junction handles many of the trains heading to cities in the south.

The *Shatabdi Express* runs between Lucknow and Delhi (Rs 640, chair class, 6½ hours) via Kanpur (Rs 210, 1½ hours). There are also plenty of regular expresses to both Delhi (Rs 107/588, 2nd/1st class, eight to nine hours) and Kolkata (Rs 270/914, sleeper/1st class, around 23 hours).

Other express trains (fares in 2nd/1st class) from Lucknow include Allahabad (Rs 36/321, four hours), Faizabad (Rs 43/226, three hours), Gorakhpur (Rs 70/368, five to six hours) and Varanasi (Rs 73/384, five to six hours).

Trains also go to Mumbai (Rs 331/1119, sleeper/1st class, 27 hours) and Agra (Rs 143/222/751, 2nd/sleeper/1st class, five to six hours).

Getting Around

To/From the Airport Amausi airport is 15km south-west of Lucknow. Taxis charge around Rs 220 for the trip; if you don't have much baggage catch a tempo from Charbagh train station for Rs 8.

Local Transport There are autorickshaws at the train station – to Hazratganj will cost about Rs 35. Tempos run along fixed routes, connecting Charbagh train station with the main post office (Hazratganj), Sikandar Bagh, Kaiserbagh (for the bus station) and Chowk (for the imambaras). Most journeys cost around Rs 4.

The best way to get around is on the back of a cycle-rickshaw, a pleasant way to cruise the manic streets around the centre. A cycle-rickshaw between the train stations and Hazratganj costs locals Rs 5 but foreigners can expect to pay Rs 10 to 15. From Hazratganj to the imambaras costs Rs 20; sightseeing is around Rs 25 per hour but you'll need to bargain.

ALLAHABAD

☎ 0532 • pop 2,000,000

This city is 135km west of Varanasi at the confluence of two of India's most important rivers: the Ganges and the Yamuna (Jumna). The mythical Sarasvati River, the River of Enlightenment, is also believed to join them here. The confluence, known as the *sangam*, is considered to have great soul-cleansing powers and all pious Hindus hope to bathe here at least once in their lifetime. Hundreds of thousands bathe here every January/February in the Magh Mela, and once every 12 years the Maha Kumbh Mela, the world's largest gathering of pilgrims, draws millions to the confluence for a holy dip.

Allahabad has a fort built by Akbar, overlooking the confluence of the rivers. Allahabad also has the Nehru family home, Anand Bhavan. Not many foreign travellers pause in this friendly city but it's a worthwhile stop, especially if you're partial to Indian-style espressos and sidewalk cafes.

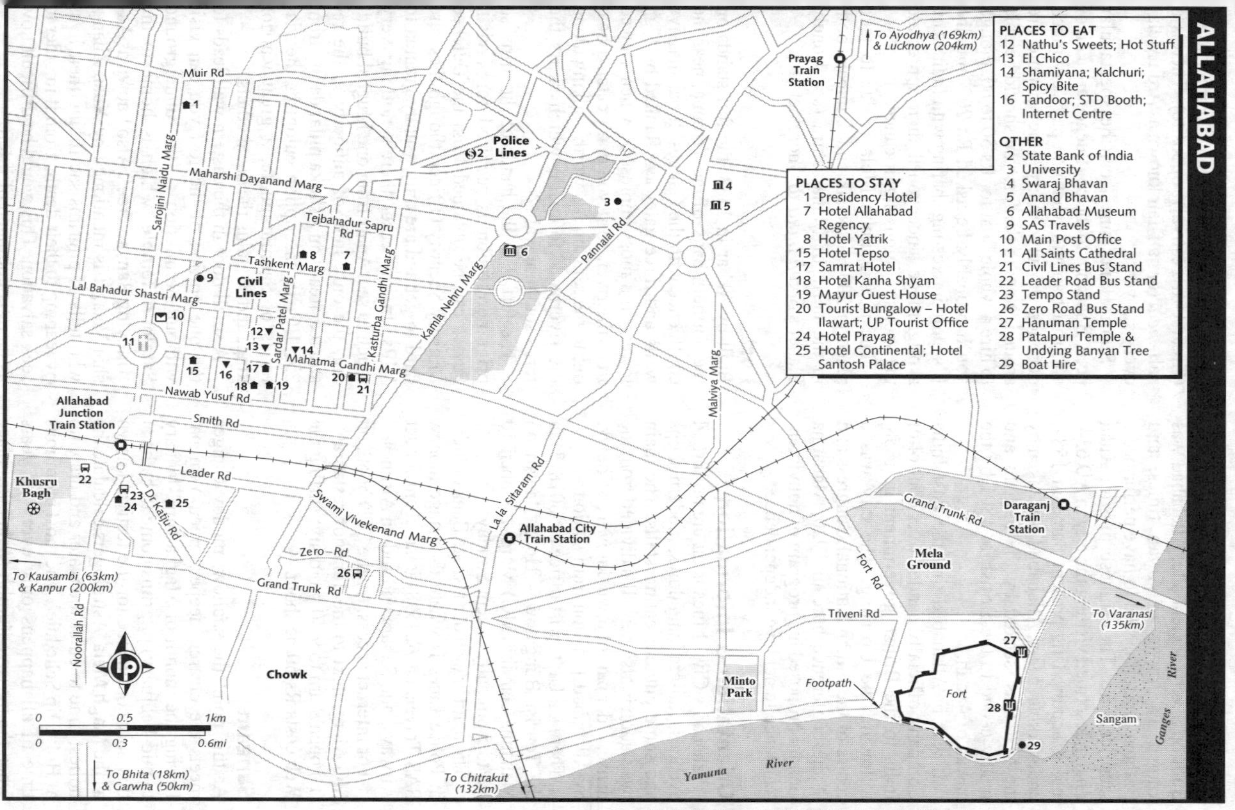
ALLAHABAD
PLACES TO STAY
1 Presidency Hotel
7 Hotel Allahabad Regency
8 Hotel Yatrik
15 Hotel Tepso
17 Samrat Hotel
18 Hotel Kanha Shyam
19 Mayur Guest House
20 Tourist Bungalow – Hotel Ilawart; UP Tourist Office
24 Hotel Prayag
25 Hotel Continental; Hotel Santosh Palace
PLACES TO EAT
12 Nathu's Sweets; Hot Stuff
13 El Chico
14 Shamiyana; Kalchuri; Spicy Bite
16 Tandoor; STD Booth; Internet Centre
OTHER
2 State Bank of India
3 University
4 Swaraj Bhavan
5 Anand Bhavan
6 Allahabad Museum
9 SAS Travels
10 Main Post Office
11 All Saints Cathedral
21 Civil Lines Bus Stand
22 Leader Road Bus Stand
23 Tempo Stand
26 Zero Road Bus Stand
27 Hanuman Temple
28 Patalpuri Temple & Undying Banyan Tree
29 Boat Hire
To Ayodhya (169km) & Lucknow (204km)
Prayag Train Station
Police Lines
Civil Lines
Muir Rd
Maharshi Dayanand Marg
Sarojini Naidu Marg
Tejbahadur Sapru Rd
Tashkent Marg
Kasturba Gandhi Marg
Kamla Nehru Marg
Pannalal Rd
Malviya Marg
Mahatma Gandhi Marg
Sardar Patel Marg
Nawab Yusuf Rd
Lal Bahadur Shastri Marg
Smith Rd
Leader Rd
Dr Katju Rd
Noorallah Rd
La la Sitaram Rd
Swami Vivekenand Marg
Zero Rd
Grand Trunk Rd
Allahabad Junction Train Station
Allahabad City Train Station
Daraganj Train Station
Khusru Bagh
Chowk
Minto Park
Mela Ground
Fort Rd
Triveni Rd
Fort
Footpath
Sangam
Ganges River
Yamuna River
To Varanasi (135km)
To Chitrakut (132km)
To Kausambi (63km) & Kanpur (200km)
To Bhita (18km) & Garwha (50km)
0 0.5 1km
0 0.3 0.6mi

UTTAR PRADESH & UTTARANCHAL

History

Built on a very ancient site, Allahabad was known as Prayag in Aryan times, and Brahma himself is said to have performed a sacrifice here. The Chinese pilgrim Xuan Zhang described visiting the city in AD 634, and it acquired its present name in 1584, under Akbar. Later, Allahabad was taken by the Marathas, sacked by the Pathans and finally ceded to the British in 1801 by the nawab of Avadh.

It was in Allahabad that the East India Company officially handed over control of India to the British government in 1858, following the Uprising. The city was a centre of the Indian National Congress and at the conference here in 1920, Mahatma Gandhi proposed his program of nonviolent resistance to achieve independence.

Orientation & Information

Allahabad's Civil Lines is an area of broad avenues, Raj-era bungalows, modern shops and some outdoor eating stalls. The main bus station is also here. It's divided from the dense, older part of town, known as Chowk, by Allahabad Junction train station.

There's a UP tourist office (☎ 601873) in the Tourist Bungalow – Hotel Ilawart on Mahatma Gandhi (MG) Marg. It's open 10 am to 5 pm daily except Sunday.

The main branch of the State Bank of India in Police Lines is where to change money. SAS Travels (☎ 623598) is an agent for Jet Airways, and Sahara and Indian Airlines.

For Internet access, try the STD booth on MG Marg, next to the Tandoor restaurant. It's open 9 am to 9.30 pm daily; surfing the Web costs Rs 60 per hour.

Sangam

At this point the shallow, muddy Ganges meets the clearer, deeper, green Yamuna. During the month of Magha (mid-January to mid-February) pilgrims come to bathe at this holy confluence for the festival known as the **Magh Mela**. Astrologers calculate the holiest time to enter the water and draw up a 'Holy Dip Schedule'. The most propitious time of all happens only every 12 years when the massive **Kumbh Mela** takes place (see the boxed text 'Maha Kumbh Mela (Great Urn Festival)' opposite). There's a half-*mela* (or half-fair known as Ardh Mela) every six years.

Sunrise and sunset can be spectacular here. Boats out to the confluence are a bit of a tourist trap and what you pay very much depends on how many other people are around. Next to the fort you should be able to hire a whole boat for Rs 50 to 60, though you'll probably be asked Rs 200 initially. It's more interesting sharing with Indians on a pilgrimage since you'll then appreciate the spot's religious significance.

The next Kumbh Mela is due to take place in 2004 at Nasik and Trimbak, both in the north of Maharashtra (see Lonely Planet's *South India* for more details).

Fort

Built by Akbar in 1583, the fort stands on the northern bank of the Yamuna, near the confluence with the Ganges. It has massive walls and three gateways flanked by high towers. It's most impressive when viewed from the river, so if you don't catch a boat out to the sangam it's worth walking along the riverbank footpath, which skirts the fort's southern wall.

The fort is in the hands of the army so prior permission is required for a visit. Passes can be obtained from the Defence Ministry Security Officer, though these are hard to get and are only usually granted to VIPs. In any case, there's nothing very much to see. Apart from one Mughal building, the only item of antiquity in the restricted area is an **Ashoka pillar** dating from 232 BC. Its inscription eulogises the victories of Samudragupta, a great warrior king, and contains the usual edicts.

A small door in the eastern wall leads to the one portion of the fort you can visit without permission – the underground **Patalpuri Temple**, which is home to the '**Undying Banyan Tree**'. Also known as Akshai Veta, it is mentioned by Xuan Zhang, who tells of pilgrims sacrificing their lives by leaping to their deaths from it in order to seek salvation. This would be difficult now as there is not much of it left.

Maha Kumbh Mela (Great Urn Festival)

Around the time of the creation of the universe, the gods and the demons churned up the oceans in search of an urn of *amrit*, the nectar of life that could bestow immortality. The urn was retrieved from the raging seas by demons, but during a great aerial battle was grasped by Vishnu and flown to safety. During the flight Vishnu either rested in four places or spilled four drops of the precious *amrit*, and in so doing created four sacred sites.

This famous battle is celebrated once every three years (on a rotating schedule) with a great festival that draws millions of pilgrims from different religions from across the world to the banks of the holy rivers of the Godavari in Naski, the Shipra in Ujjain, the Ganges in Haridwar and the confluence of the Ganges, Yamuna and the mythical Saraswati in Allahabad. The biggest and most auspicious of the four festivals is the Maha Kumbh Mela, or Great Urn Festival, at Allahabad. Here a drop of *amrit* fell into the water at the confluence of the rivers and the devout believe that bathing during the festival will cleanse and purify the soul, washing away the sins of this and all other lifetimes.

Given that it only comes around every 12 years the Maha Kumbh Mela has always been big. The 2001 mela was even bigger than usual as it was the twelfth event in a series of 12 and coincided with a very auspicious planetary alignment not seen for 144 years. It was also the first Kumbh Mela of the Christian new millennium.

I planned my visit to the Maha Kumbh Mela 12 years ago, when I realised that I'd been in India for the last one but didn't know about it. It was definitely worth waiting for. Seventy million people turned up over the 44 days of the festival. On the main bathing day, known as Mauni Amavasya, or the New Moon of the Saints, authorities estimated that 30 million people bathed in the holy waters, making it the largest gathering of humanity ever. It was truly an incredible event to be part of.

The high point of Mauni Amavasya was the daylong procession. Starting at the astrologically perfect time of 4.02 am the groups of sadhus, swamis and gurus left their camps in a grand procession to the bathing area. Surrounded by attendants and fierce looking minders, the leaders rode high on tractor-pulled trailers or on the roofs of small trucks adorned with garlands of golden marigolds. Following on foot were the devotees, chanting, waving flags, beating drums, blowing horns and singing, filling the air with religious fever.

The atmosphere gained intensity as the eye-catching *nagars*, or naked sadhus, approached. Taking a vow of poverty and chastity, the nagars pledged to wander naked around India for the rest of their lives. In the mela camps many nagars were very accessible and I was often invited to talk and share a cup of chai. Thousands of ascetics, their bodies smeared with ash, led the holy dip on bathing days. The police moved in ahead of the procession clearing everyone from the route. Photographers were especially targeted and pushed back behind the fences. 'No photos!' was the instruction shouted, and rocks were thrown at anyone who put a camera to their eye. When the nagars appeared, several of them undermined the previously shouted instruction by playing up for the photographers. Their presence generated an incredible energy, and as they passed by I felt that I had witnessed something very special, an age-old event that is well and truly alive at the beginning of the 21st century.

The Kumbh Mela certainly lived up to expectations. It was India to the max.

Richard I'Anson

The popular **Hanuman temple**, open to non-Hindus, is unusual because the Hanuman idol is reclining rather than upright. It's said that each year during the floods the Ganges rises to touch the feet of the sleeping Hanuman before receding.

Anand Bhavan

This shrine to the Nehru family must be the best-kept museum in the country, indicating the high regard in which this famous dynasty is held in India. The family home was donated to the Indian government by Indira

Gandhi in 1970. The exhibits in the house show how this well-off family became involved in the struggle for Indian independence and produced four generations of astute politicians: Motilal Nehru, Jawaharlal Nehru, Indira Gandhi and Rajiv Gandhi.

Visitors walk around the verandahs of the two-storey mansion looking through glass panels into the rooms. You can see Nehru's bedroom and study, the room where Mahatma Gandhi used to stay during his visits and Indira Gandhi's room, as well as many personal items connected with the Nehru family. A quick look at the extensive bookshelves (full of Marx and Lenin) indicate where India's post-Independence faith in socialism sprang from. The house is open 9.30 am to 5 pm daily, except Monday and holidays. It's free to see the ground floor but costs Rs 5 to go upstairs. Last entry is at 4.30 pm, and no tickets are sold from 12.45 to 1.30 pm.

In the manicured garden is an outbuilding housing a pictorial display of Jawaharlal Nehru's life. A **planetarium**, built in the grounds in 1979, has hourly shows between 11 am and 4 pm; tickets cost Rs 10.

Next door is **Swaraj Bhavan**, where Motilal Nehru lived until 1930 and where Indira Gandhi was born. It houses a museum featuring dimly lit rooms and an audio-visual presentation, 'The Story of Independence'. Unfortunately, the commentary is only in Hindi. It is open 11 am to 1 pm and 2 to 5 pm daily except Monday; entry costs Rs 5.

Other Attractions

Close to the Allahabad Junction train station is **Khusru Bagh**, a scrappy walled garden which contains the tomb of Prince Khusru, son of Jehangir, who sought to wrest power from his father and was executed by his brother Shah Jahan. Nearby is the unoccupied tomb intended for his sister and the tomb of his Rajput mother, who was said to have poisoned herself in despair at Khusru's opposition to his father.

All Saints Cathedral was designed by Sir William Emerson, the architect of the Victoria Memorial in Kolkata. Its brass memorial plaques show that even for the sons and daughters of the Raj, life was not all high teas and pink gins. The inscriptions morbidly record the causes of death: 'died of blood poisoning', 'died in a polo accident' and, probably even more likely today, 'died in a motor accident on the road to Nainital'. It is open 8 to 10 am and has services in English on Sunday.

Allahabad Museum has galleries devoted to local archaeological finds, including terracotta figurines from Kausambi. It also has natural history exhibits, an art gallery and a large room of artefacts donated by the Nehru family. In the latter are all sorts of wonderful and ridiculous items presented to Nehru while he was prime minister. The museum is open 10.15 am to 4.30 pm daily except Monday and holidays. Entry is a hefty Rs 100. Not far away, opposite the university, is the house where Rudyard Kipling lived, but it is not open to the public.

Minto Park, near the Yamuna, is where Lord Canning read out the declaration by which Britain took over control of India from the East India Company in 1858. The **Nag Basuki Temple** is mentioned in the writings of the Puranas and is on the bank of the Ganges, north of the railway bridge.

Places to Stay

Paying guest accommodation, which enables travellers to stay with a local Indian family is possible in Allahabad (as well as Agra and Varanasi). Rates start at Rs 150 to 500 per night, depending on the type of accommodation. Meals (Indian) are generally included for an extra Rs 30. Contact UP Tourism in Allahabad for details.

Places to Stay – Budget

Budget hotels can be found in the peaceful Civil Lines area though many are immediately south of Allahabad Junction train station. Rooms have private bathroom unless otherwise stated.

The ***retiring rooms*** at Allahabad Junction train station cost Rs 135 for a double and Rs 50 in a dorm. Rates are for 24 hours; the tariff is roughly two-thirds this if you stay less than 12 hours.

The ***Tourist Bungalow – Hotel Ilawart*** *(☎ 601440, fax 611374, 35 MG Marg)* is a clean UP Tourism operation set back from the road in a well-tended garden and has a restaurant. Dorms are overpriced at Rs 100 and spacious air-cooled singles/doubles are Rs 300/400; air-con rooms go for Rs 650/800. The rooms are not bad value if you can put up with the noise that filters through from the adjacent bus stand.

The friendly, pokey ***Mayur Guest House*** *(☎ 420250, 10 Sardar Patel Marg)*, just off MG Marg, has smallish air-cooled rooms, hot water geyser and TV for Rs 265/345 and air-con rooms for Rs 475/600.

Hotel Tepso *(☎ 623635, MG Marg)* has a dilapidated reception area but the rooms are very clean, reasonably quiet and cost Rs 275/400.

Hotel Prayag *(☎ 656416, fax 655596, 73 Noorullah Rd)*, south of Allahabad Junction train station, is a typical good budget hotel. It has rooms (most with TV) from Rs 150/185 to 475/525 with air-con.

There are numerous places to stay in a similar price bracket along Dr Katju Rd, the next street east, including ***Hotel Continental*** *(☎ 652629)*, which operates on the 24-hour checkout system. Rooms start at Rs 140/260. ***Hotel Santosh Palace*** *(☎ 654773, fax 609791, 100 Dr Katju Rd)* offers a generally higher standard. Modern spacious rooms with TV and air-cooler start at Rs 220/300, or Rs 600/700 with air-con. The cheaper rooms have squat toilets.

Places to Stay – Mid-Range & Top End

There is less to choose from in this range, although the hotels available are a decent standard. All the mid-range and top-end hotels are in the Civil Lines area.

Samrat Hotel *(☎ 420780, fax 420785)* in an alley off MG Marg, has clean singles/doubles with TV for Rs 500/700 with air-cooler and Rs 900/1000 with air-con. Samrat is looking pretty tired these days and although the rooms have a certain charm, it's a bit overpriced.

Hotel Allahabad Regency *(☎ 601519, ⓔ tglalld@hotmail.com, 16 Tashkent Marg)* is a tranquil two-star place with air-con rooms starting at Rs 1050/1250, including breakfast. It has a nice pool (open April to September), a garden and gym.

Hotel Yatrik *(☎ 601713, fax 601434, 33 Sardar Patel Marg)* is a smart, modern establishment. Air-con rooms are of a good standard and cost Rs 1100/1300. It has a lovely garden and a good pool (open late April to September). Checkout is 24 hours.

The ***Presidency Hotel*** *(☎ 623308, fax 623897, Sarojini Naidu Marg)* is in a quiet residential area a little north of Civil Lines. Modern, neat, air-con rooms start at Rs 875/950, however the bathrooms are not so good. It also has a garden, and a pool (open March to October).

The classiest hotel is the modern, four-star, high-rise ***Hotel Kanha Shyam*** *(☎ 420 281, fax 622164, ⓔ info@kanhashyam.com)* just off MG Marg. Prices start at Rs 1550/1750 and there's a health club, coffee shop, restaurant and bar.

Places to Eat

Outdoor eating is all the rage in Allahabad. Many semipermanent stalls set up tables and chairs on the footpath of MG Marg in the evening, making it a popular, atmospheric and cheap area to eat. There's a good sidewalk ***coffee stall*** in front of Hotel Tepso, one of many in the area boasting an espresso machine.

Shamiyana is one of the few established food stalls on MG Marg open all day. It dishes up excellent half-full-plate chow mein for Rs 18/32 and OK *masala dosa* (lentil pancake) for Rs 16. A little farther east, ***Kalchuri*** and neighbouring ***Spicy Bite*** are stalls serving cheap and tasty veg/nonveg and Chinese food.

There's nothing much to distinguish between Allahabad's handful of proper restaurants, which try to cover every possible base by offering veg/nonveg Indian, Chinese and continental fare. They're rather bland compared to the outdoor stalls, and none serve alcohol. ***El Chico*** *(MG Marg)* is arguably the best of these, though meals are not cheap at Rs 60 to 130. At the time of research it was being renovated. The ***potato***

UTTAR PRADESH & UTTARANCHAL

chaat stand directly in front of El Chico serves fantastic snacks for Rs 5.

Tandoor *(MG Marg)* focuses mainly on Indian food, although it does pizzas as well; half a tandoori chicken is Rs 70 and a vegetarian pizza is Rs 60.

Nathu's Sweets *(18B Sardar Patel Marg)* is a vegetarian place with pizza, South Indian dishes and a wide selection of sweets downstairs. A few doors along is ***Hot Stuff***, a Western-style, fast-food joint with pizzas starting at Rs 55, burgers, Indian and Chinese food, and a good range of ice cream.

There are many basic restaurants in the old town, plus several ***dhaba*** (snack) places close to the train station along Dr Katju Rd. The bar in the ***Tourist Bungalow*** in Civil Lines is a cosy place to sink a beer.

Getting There & Away

Air At the time of research there were no flights to Allahabad, though some services may operate during the Kumbh Mela and other festivals.

Bus From the Civil Lines bus stand, beside the Tourist Bungalow, there are regular buses to Varanasi (Rs 55, three hours), Lucknow (Rs 74/105 ordinary/deluxe, five hours), Faizabad (Rs 72, five hours) and Gorakhpur (Rs 119, 9½ hours), via Jaunpur. There are four buses to Sonauli (Rs 158, 13 hours) if you're heading to Nepal.

Train The main train station is Allahabad Junction, in the centre of the city. There are connections to Varanasi (Rs 41/365, 2nd/2nd air-con class, three hours) and Lucknow (Rs 61/321, 2nd/1st class, four hours). There are also expresses to Delhi (Rs 204/688, sleeper/1st class, 10 hours), Kolkata (Rs 242/819, 15 hours) and Mumbai (Rs 326/1512, sleeper/2nd air-con class, 24 hours).

Allahabad is a good place from which to travel to Khajuraho, since there are numerous express trains to Satna (Rs 104/448/784, sleeper/2nd/1st class, 3½ hours). The *Patna-Kurla Express* leaves at 8.30 am, leaving plenty of time to catch a bus from Satna to Khajuraho (four hours).

Getting Around

There are plenty of cycle-rickshaws for hire but few autorickshaws. Use the back exit at Allahabad Junction train station to reach Civil Lines bus stand. A cycle-rickshaw from the train station to Civil Lines costs no more than Rs 5, by cycle-rickshaw from train station to fort costs Rs 20 and Rs 10 from MG Marg to Anand Bhavan. Tempos go from Allahabad Junction train station to Daraganj train station, which is 800m north of the fort.

AROUND ALLAHABAD

Bhita

Excavations at this site on the Yamuna River, 18km south of Allahabad, have revealed the remains of an ancient fortified city. Layers of occupation dating from the Gupta period (AD 320–510) back to the Mauryan period (321–184 BC) and perhaps even earlier have been uncovered. There's a museum with stone and metal seals, coins and terracotta statues. It's best to get here by taxi from Allahabad.

Garwha

The ruined temples in this walled enclosure are about 50km south-west of Allahabad, 8km from Shankargarh – the last 3km have to be completed on foot.

The major temple has 16 beautifully carved stone pillars, and inscriptions reveal that the temples date back to the Gupta period at the very least. Some of the better sculptures from Garwha are now on display in the state museum in Lucknow. Transport connections to Shankargarh are not good, so consider hiring a taxi in Allahabad.

Kausambi

This ancient Buddhist centre, once known as Kosam, is 63km south-west of Allahabad on the way to Chitrakut. It was the capital of King Udaya, a contemporary of the Buddha, and the Enlightened One is said to have preached several sermons here. There's a huge **fortress** near the village, which contains the broken remains of an **Ashoka pillar**, minus any pre-Gupta period inscriptions. Buses depart irregularly from Allahabad's Leader Rd bus stand.

Chitrakut

It was here that Brahma, Vishnu and Shiva are believed to have been 'born' and taken on their incarnations, which makes this town a popular Hindu pilgrimage place. **Bathing ghats** line the Mandakini River and there are over 30 temples. UP Tourism has a ***Tourist Bungalow*** *(☎ 22219)* here, with ordinary singles/doubles for Rs 150/175, and there are a number of other cheap hotels and basic restaurants. The town is close to the border with Madhya Pradesh, 132km from Allahabad and 195km from Khajuraho. Buses depart from Allahabad's Zero Rd bus stand.

FAIZABAD

☎ 05278 • pop 350,000

Faizabad was once the capital of Avadh but rapidly declined after the death of Bahu Begum, the wife of Nawab Shuja-ud-Daula. Most of the Islamic buildings in Faizabad were built at her behest, and her mausoleum is said to be the finest of its type in Uttar Pradesh. Her husband also has an impressive mausoleum. There are three large mosques in the chowk area and pleasant gardens in Gupta Park, where the temple from which Rama is supposed to have disappeared stands. The town makes a convenient base for visiting nearby Ayodhya.

The CyberCafe is just up the road from the Hotel Krishna Palace.

Places to Stay & Eat

There are a couple of good hotels in the Civil Lines area, about 1.5km west of the chowk, but both are on the main Lucknow-Gorakhpur road so avoid the front rooms. If your luggage isn't too heavy you can walk to the hotels from the bus stand, which is on the same road; the train station is a Rs 5 cycle-rickshaw ride away.

Hotel Shane-Avadh *(☎ 23586)* is a clean, efficiently run place with a lift. Singles/doubles with bathroom with hot water start at Rs 150/175 and air-con rooms with TV are Rs 550/650. Its ***Mezban restaurant*** turns out decent veg/nonveg and Chinese fare in big portions (starting at Rs 35), and coffee so frothy you could mistake it for a cappuccino if you've been in India long enough.

Hotel Tirupati *(☎ 23231)*, next door, is also good value and has helpful staff. Rooms with private bathroom, hot water and TV start at Rs 135/175, or Rs 550/650 with air-con. It has a rather small but grand restaurant, with a similar range to the Mezban. Snacks start from about Rs 20 and vegetarian mains are around Rs 40.

Abha Hotel *(☎ 22550)* is the best of several places on a side street near the Majestic Cinema in the chowk area. It has good-size rooms with TV and large, clean, private bathrooms starting at Rs 160/200, and a veg/nonveg restaurant. It's a Rs 10 cycle-rickshaw ride from the train station and Rs 8 from the bus stand. There were renovations going on at the time of research.

Hotel Krishna Palace *(☎ 21367, fax 21371)*, a few minutes' walk from the train station, is Faizabad's top hotel, though there's no lift. It has a range of modern, comfortable rooms starting at Rs 550/650 with fan. The ***Caveri Restaurant*** serves good Indian, Chinese and continental food.

Getting There & Away

Faizabad has fairly good train connections, including express trains to Lucknow (Rs 39/205, 2nd/1st class, three hours) and Varanasi (Rs 54/284, four to six hours).

There are numerous buses from the quiet bus stand on the Lucknow-Gorakhpur road, 750m west of Hotel Shane-Avadh. Connections include Gorakhpur (Rs 62, four hours), Lucknow (Rs 55, three hours), Allahabad (Rs 71, five hours), Sonauli (Rs 94) and Ayodhya (Rs 10). Tempos to Ayodhya (Rs 8) depart from the main road, about 80m north of the clock tower in the chowk area.

AYODHYA

pop 75,000

Ayodhya, 6km from Faizabad, is one of Hinduism's seven holy cities. It's a major pilgrimage centre since it is not only the birthplace of Rama, but is also connected with many events in the Ramayana. Unfortunately, its name has become synonymous with rising Hindu fanaticism since the fateful day on 6 December 1992 when a Hindu mob destroyed a mosque they believed had been built on the site of a temple marking Rama's birthplace. The event sent shock waves throughout India and threatened the nation's secular framework.

The Atharvaveda described Ayodhya as 'a city built by gods and being as prosperous as paradise itself', although today it's just a small, dusty town with an amazing abundance of temples and monkeys. It sees few foreigners, and anyone intending to visit should keep an eye on the latest developments in the temple-mosque saga. Give the town a wide berth during festivals. Be particularly careful on the 6 December anniversary of civil unrest.

Babri Masjid/Ram Janam Bhumi

The **Babri Masjid** was constructed by the Mughals in the 15th century on what was reputed to be the site of Rama's birth. The mosque was little used and was eventually closed to Muslims by the civil authorities and limited Hindu *puja*, or offerings of respect, were permitted inside.

By 1990, Rama had been appropriated by Hindu fundamentalists to justify their calls for a Hindu India. Their plans to build a temple to Rama (the Ram Mandir) in place of the mosque led to outbreaks of violence between local Hindus and Muslims. A fragile court order called for the maintenance of

Ayodhya – Playing with Religious Fire

Eight years on from the 'storming of the temple', the Ayodhya issue remained potentially explosive and is still a very sensitive topic of conversation. Any event in India with the capacity to divide along religious lines has the potential for nasty repercussions.

This should be more obvious to India's political players than anyone else. India's politicians, however, are quickly learning how to best use this issue to their political advantage. Instead of playing it down, they seem to go out of their way to stir things up.

In late 2000 India's prime minister, Atal Bihari Vajpayee, asserted that the Ram temple issue was a 'nationalist movement' and that 'there was unfinished business'. This statement from the prime minister (who theoretically should represent all factions) surprised and outraged members from his own Bharatiya Janata Party (BJP), their alliance partners and the opposition. There seemed no reason to purposely agitate the population with such provocative remarks.

Headlines in the country's major newspapers condemned the comments and opposition members of parliament called for clarification. A few days later, with his back against the wall, the PM stated that the building of a Ram Mandir would only be possible 'should the (Allahabad) court give a verdict' or following 'a dialogue between Hindus and Muslims'.

So, why the contentious remarks in the first place? One explanation is that it was the PM losing his cool after days of attack from the opposition Congress Party and Samajwadi Party (SP), who were calling for the resignation of three government ministers. These ministers have been charged by authorities as 'being collaterally responsible' for the demolition of the Babri Masjid. Others say the prime minister's real intentions have now become apparent after these remarks.

Whatever the case, it is undeniable that the BJP's constituency is made up of a large section of Hindus who support the building of a Ram Mandir. The BJP went from two to 161 seats between 1984 and 1996, riding the wave of public outcry over the Ram Mandir saga; building the temple also forms part of their current agenda (subject to the court's findings or an agreement between Hindus and Muslims).

The opposition Congress Party also believes it can gain mileage out of the issue. With the Muslim vote crucial in Uttar Pradesh it hopes to embarrass the BJP's alliance partners, who are already shirking from this latest development.

Tinkering with this issue is perilous and the party that pushes it too far may just bring bad karma on their chances of re-election. Keep an eye out for the latest developments, which are covered in detail in most major newspapers.

the status quo and armed guards surrounded the mosque and attempted to keep the two communities apart.

In late 1992, a Hindu mob stormed the site and destroyed the Babri Masjid, erecting a small Hindu shrine known as **Ram Janam Bhumi** (also known as Ram Janmabhoomi). This sparked riots across India and caused unrest in neighbouring Muslim countries.

The government, which owns the site, has promised to build a temple here if it is decided a temple was here before the mosque. In late 1994 the Indian High Court wisely refused to adjudicate on the issue, and the matter moved on to the Allahabad High Court. In 2001 a final resolution had yet to be reached, though orders were still in force which required the union government to maintain the status quo as it existed on 7 January 1993.

There is a massive security presence at the temple/mosque site, since it's the country's most volatile flash point. You will be thoroughly (and rather over-zealously) searched. Cameras are prohibited, and you cannot safely deposit them. In fact you can't take any bags in with you – even pens are taken away. Make sure you carry your passport.

Although the palpable tension in the air makes a visit memorable, as a tourist spectacle it's eminently forgettable; all you see is a small shrine protected by a tent-like structure. The site is open daily. The exact hours change periodically; at the time of research they were 8 am to 1 pm and 3 to 5 pm.

From Faizabad, take the small road that turns left off the main Faizabad-Ayodhya road next to the Hanumangadhi (Hanuman temple). If you arrive by tempo, ask the driver to drop you at the Hanuman temple, from where it's about a 10-minute walk.

Other Attractions

The **Hanumangadhi** is dedicated to Hanuman, who is believed to have lived in a cave here while guarding the Janam Bhumi. It was built within the thick white walls of a fortress. There are good views from the ramparts, and real monkeys scampering around the Hanuman images. There are more than 100 other temples in Ayodhya, including the **Kanak Mandir** and several **Jain shrines**.

Places to Stay & Eat

The UP ***Tourist Bungalow*** *(☎ 05278-32435)*, also known locally as the Saket Hotel, is near the train station and is the only acceptable place to stay in Ayodhya. It's a peaceful place and some rooms have good balconies. Clean singles/doubles with private bathroom start at Rs 175/200, air-con rooms are Rs 450/500 and a bed in the dorm costs Rs 60. There's a lacklustre vegetarian restaurant and a tourist office.

Getting There & Away

There are regular tempos shuttling along the main road between Ayodhya and Faizabad for Rs 8, or you can take a bus for Rs 4. Ayodhya bus station is about 300m from the Hanumangadhi in the direction of Faizabad.

SHRAVASTI

Not far from the Rapti River or the border with Nepal in the north-east of the state, Shravasti is a city founded by a mythological king called Sravast. From the 6th century BC, Shravasti became capital of the Kosala Kingdom and was an affluent trading centre, as well as an important Buddhist site – many of the Buddha's earliest sermons were delivered here.

The extensive ruins of this ancient city and Jetavana Monastery were rediscovered by General Cunningham in 1863 and are near the villages of Saheth and Maheth. At its peak there were temples, meditation halls, baths, a hospital and a large library.

Shravasti is best remembered as the place where the Buddha defeated the other doctrines. On his wanderings the Buddha was challenged many times to a 'contest of miracles' by leaders of six other philosophical schools. Eventually he accepted and a great hall was built for the event.

After the other leaders had taken their seats the Buddha came in flying through the air and proceeded to shoot forth fire and water from his body. He then performed the miracle of sitting on a 1000-petalled lotus and multiplying himself a million times. His opponents were completely defeated and the Buddha continued to perform miracles for the next seven days.

Ashoka was an early pilgrim and left a couple of pillars and stupas at the site when he passed through, although the present ruins show traces of the Guptas. Today, remains of monasteries and stupas have been excavated and there are lots of stone sculptures and other findings from the site at the state museum in Lucknow.

There are three relatively new Buddhist temples near the site and this may be your best chance to find a bed; they usually offer accommodation to pilgrims so it may depend on how busy they are.

The site can be reached from Gonda, 50km north-west of Ayodhya. The nearest train station is Gainjahwa, on the Gonda-Naugarh-Gorakhpur loop. The nearest large town is 20km away at Balrampur.

VARANASI

☎ 0542 • pop 2 million

Varanasi, the city of Shiva on the bank of the sacred Ganges, is one of the holiest places in India. Hindu pilgrims come to bathe in the river's waters, a ritual that washes away all sins. The city is an auspicious place to die, since expiring here ensures release from the cycle of rebirths and an instant passport to heaven. It's a magical city where the most intimate rituals of life and death take place in public on the city's famous ghats (steps leading down to the river). It's this accessibility to the practices of an ancient religious tradition that captivates so many visitors.

Being used to catering for pilgrims and now tourists, Varanasi has an abundance of hotels, restaurants, and facilities to suit all budgets. Many people who come for a couple of days spend a lot longer in the city, not because there is a lot to do, but because it's a fascinating place to just 'hang out', particularly for backpackers.

The old city is a fascinating warren of alleyways and narrow lanes filled with tiny shops and street vendors trying to flog anything from cheap trinkets to the famous 'Benares silk' – getting lost is a prerequisite for a good exploration. Varanasi is recklessly crowded, and controlling waste has become a major problem, with the Ganges suffering from extreme levels of pollution.

In the past, the city has been known as Kashi and Benares, but its present name is a restoration of an ancient name meaning the city between two rivers – the Varuna and Assi.

History

Varanasi has been a centre of learning and civilisation for over 2000 years, and claims to be one of the oldest living cities in the world. Mark Twain obviously thought it looked the part when he dropped by on a lecture tour, since he told the world that 'Benares is older than history, older than

Drowning in Conservatism

Given Varanasi's importance to Hinduism, it's no surprise to learn that the city has an element of entrenched religious conservatism. In January 2000 Canadian-Indian film director, Deepa Mehta, and her crew discovered the ferocity of this conservatism when violated.

They were in town shooting a film called *Water*. The third piece in a trilogy which includes the equally controversial films *Fire* and *Earth*, *Water* is the story about the predicament of Indian widows (there are over 30 million in India today); many turn to prostitution in order to survive.

After shooting one scene, director and crew were practically run out of the city by enraged crowds who believed the subject of the film was the product of Western decadence.

In fact it appears that the volatile reaction to the film was a carefully orchestrated political stunt. A distorted copy of the script was leaked to journalists to stir up trouble – and it worked. Blazing headlines followed around the country and the film was condemned. Local politicians jumping on the conservative bandwagon were quick to denounce the film and support the backlash from hardliners.

Filming continued in the state of Madhya Pradesh where Mehta was offered sanctuary by the chief minister, who was happy to admit that his invitation was motivated politically and not because of his interest in film making.

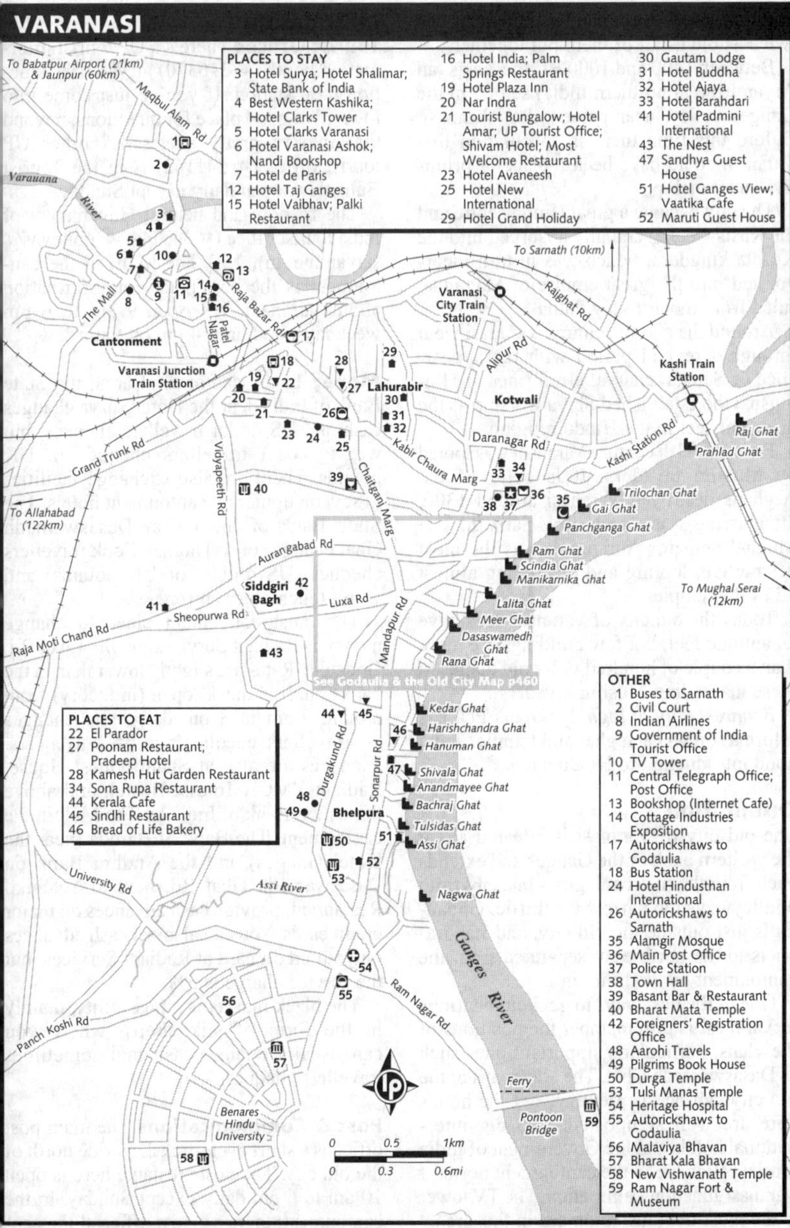
VARANASI
PLACES TO STAY
3 Hotel Surya; Hotel Shalimar; State Bank of India
4 Best Western Kashika; Hotel Clarks Tower
5 Hotel Clarks Varanasi
6 Hotel Varanasi Ashok; Nandi Bookshop
7 Hotel de Paris
12 Hotel Taj Ganges
15 Hotel Vaibhav; Palki Restaurant
16 Hotel India; Palm Springs Restaurant
19 Hotel Plaza Inn
20 Nar Indra
21 Tourist Bungalow; Hotel Amar; UP Tourist Office; Shivam Hotel; Most Welcome Restaurant
23 Hotel Avaneesh
25 Hotel New International
29 Hotel Grand Holiday
30 Gautam Lodge
31 Hotel Buddha
32 Hotel Ajaya
33 Hotel Barahdari
41 Hotel Padmini International
43 The Nest
47 Sandhya Guest House
51 Hotel Ganges View; Vaatika Cafe
52 Maruti Guest House
PLACES TO EAT
22 El Parador
27 Poonam Restaurant; Pradeep Hotel
28 Kamesh Hut Garden Restaurant
34 Sona Rupa Restaurant
44 Kerala Cafe
45 Sindhi Restaurant
46 Bread of Life Bakery
OTHER
1 Buses to Sarnath
2 Civil Court
8 Indian Airlines
9 Government of India Tourist Office
10 TV Tower
11 Central Telegraph Office; Post Office
13 Bookshop (Internet Cafe)
14 Cottage Industries Exposition
17 Autorickshaws to Godaulia
18 Bus Station
24 Hotel Hindusthan International
26 Autorickshaws to Sarnath
35 Alamgir Mosque
36 Main Post Office
37 Police Station
38 Town Hall
39 Basant Bar & Restaurant
40 Bharat Mata Temple
42 Foreigners' Registration Office
48 Aarohi Travels
49 Pilgrims Book House
50 Durga Temple
53 Tulsi Manas Temple
54 Heritage Hospital
55 Autorickshaws to Godaulia
56 Malaviya Bhavan
57 Bharat Kala Bhavan
58 New Vishwanath Temple
59 Ram Nagar Fort & Museum
To Babatpur Airport (21km) & Jaunpur (60km)
Maqbul Alam Rd
Varauana River
The Mall
Raja Bazar Rd
Patel Nagar
Cantonment
Varanasi Junction Train Station
To Sarnath (10km)
Varanasi City Train Station
Rajghat Rd
Alipur Rd
Kashi Train Station
Lahurabir
Kotwali
Daranagar Rd
Kashi Station Rd
Raj Ghat
Prahlad Ghat
Kabir Chaura Marg
Grand Trunk Rd
Vidyapeeth Rd
Chaitganj Marg
To Allahabad (122km)
Trilochan Ghat
Gai Ghat
Panchganga Ghat
Ram Ghat
Scindia Ghat
Manikarnika Ghat
Aurangabad Rd
Siddgiri Bagh
Luxa Rd
Sheopurwa Rd
Raja Moti Chand Rd
Mandapur Rd
Lalita Ghat
Meer Ghat
Dasaswamedh Ghat
Rana Ghat
To Mughal Serai (12km)
See Godaulia & the Old City Map p460
Kedar Ghat
Harishchandra Ghat
Hanuman Ghat
Durgakund Rd
Sonarpur Rd
Shivala Ghat
Anandmayee Ghat
Bachraj Ghat
Tulsidas Ghat
Assi Ghat
Bhelpura
University Rd
Assi River
Nagwa Ghat
Ganges River
Ram Nagar Rd
Panch Koshi Rd
Benares Hindu University
Ferry
Pontoon Bridge
0 0.5 1km
0 0.3 0.6mi

tradition, older even than legend, and looks twice as old as all of them put together'.

Between 1400 and 1000 BC the Kasis (an Aryan tribe in northern India) settled in the Ganges valley, near present-day Varanasi. Before this time there is speculation that Varanasi could have been a place of primitive sun worship.

The city became a great Hindu centre and the Kasis were eventually absorbed into the Kosala kingdom, which was in turn incorporated into the great empire of Magadha, ruled from modern-day Patna.

Around the eighth century, Varanasi went through a revival period with the appearance of Sankaracharya, a reformer of Hinduism who established Shiva worship as the principal sect in the Hindu religion.

From the 11th century Varanasi was looted by Muslim invaders. It is believed the Afghans destroyed Varanasi around 1300, after laying waste to nearby Sarnath. The Mughal emperor Aurangzeb was the most destructive, looting and destroying almost all of the temples.

Today the old city of Varanasi does have an antique feel, but few buildings are more than a couple of hundred years old thanks to these marauding Muslim invaders.

Benares: City of Light by Diana Eck has information on each ghat and temple, and a good introduction to Hinduism.

Orientation

The old city of Varanasi is situated along the western bank of the Ganges and extends back from the riverbank ghats in a labyrinth of alleyways too narrow for traffic. Godaulia is just outside the old city, and Lahurabir is to the north-east, separated from the cantonment by the train line.

One of the best ways to get your bearings in Varanasi is to remember the positions of the ghats, particularly important ones such as Dasaswamedh Ghat. The alleyways of the old city can be disorienting, but the hotels here are well signposted. The big international hotels and the Government of India tourist office are in the cantonment north of Varanasi Junction train station. The TV tower is the most obvious landmark in this area.

Information

Tourist Offices There's a UP tourist information booth (☎ 346370) at Varanasi Junction train station. If you've just come into town it's a good place for directions, beyond that they're pretty useless. Another UP tourist office (☎ 341162) is in the Tourist Bungalow, open daily except Sunday.

The friendly and helpful Government of India tourist office (☎ 343744, ⓔ goitovns@satyam.net.in), 15B The Mall, in the cantonment is the best place for information about Varanasi. It's open 9 am to 6 pm weekdays, and until 4 pm on Saturday.

Money In the cantonment area, the State Bank of India near the Hotel Surya changes cash and US dollar travellers cheques, but won't accept travellers cheques in UK pounds. There are also exchange facilities in several upmarket cantonment hotels. The State Bank of India near Dasaswamedh Ghat changes only Thomas Cook travellers cheques (US dollars or UK pounds) and won't touch other currencies.

The most convenient place to change money is Radiant Services, on the Luxa Rd, Godaulia. Rates are slightly lower than in the banks but it is quick, open (in theory) from around 9 am to 8 pm daily, and changes all travellers cheques and 36 currencies. Branches are also at Shanti Guest House, Radiant YMCA Tourist Hostel, and above the Union Bank of India on The Mall in the cantonment. The Bank of Baroda (near the Hotel Ganges) and the Andhra Bank on Dasaswamedh Ghat Rd, next to Yelchiko Restaurant, provide cash advances on major credit cards. You can also get cash advances on your credit card at Radiant Services, but the service charge is 5%.

The black market is a possibility, mainly in the form of silk shops, where you can usually change cash and sometimes travellers cheques.

Post & Communications The main post office is a short cycle-rickshaw ride north of the old city. The poste restante here is open 10 am to 6 pm daily except Sunday. In the cantonment, there's a post office at the cenral telegraph office (CTO). You can make nternational and STD calls from the CTO 24 hours a day.

Lots of places have Internet access, but only a few use service providers based in Varanasi, so it can be expensive. The rate is around Rs 50 to 70 per hour outside of the old city in a place that uses a local service provider and Rs 2 per minute if the service provider is based in Lucknow. Rates can drop after 7 pm. Two places to try are a bookshop, near Hotel Taj Ganges on Raja Bazar Rd (which has four terminals), and Aarohi Travels, on Durgakund Rd, if you're further south. In the old city rates can be as low as Rs 30 per hour. A good place is an Internet centre in a private call booth, just near Dasaswamedh Ghat. There are six terminals and connections are quick. Another good place is Fontac Computer, behind the Garden Restaurant in Godaulia.

Visa Extensions The Foreigners' Registration Office (☎ 351968) is in Srinagar Colony, Siddgiri Bagh, Sigra. Head west along Luxa Rd away from the river and turn right just before the Theosophical Society on the left. Follow this road until it ends at a T-junction; the office is 50m to the right.

Travel Agencies Aarohi Travels (☎ 312 729, ⓔ arohivns@satyam.net.in), 74–5, 2nd floor, Dharm Sangh Complex, Durgakund Rd, has been recommended by travellers. They provide all the usual services, such as helping out with train booking, reservations and travel arrangements in the Varanasi area.

Bookshops The Universal Book Company in Godaulia is an excellent bookshop. Pilgrims Book House, just off Durgakund Rd, is great for books on spirituality, yoga, Buddhism and Hinduism; it's open daily. The Nandi Bookshop in the Hotel Varanasi Ashok has lots of old and unusual titles.

Medical Services & Emergency The Heritage Hospital (☎ 313977) is close to the main gate of Benares Hindu University. Medical supplies are available all over the city through pharmacies. There is a group of small pharmacies just before the entrance to Benares University.

The closest police station (☎ 330653) to the old city is between the town hall and the main post office.

Dangers & Annoyances Persistent touts and predatory rickshaw-wallahs are the main hassles for most travellers. Use common sense and keep a close eye on your valuables, particularly in crowded areas such as the old city and down at the ghats.

Unfortunately Varanasi does have a darker side. There is a very small criminal element operating mainly at the major entry points to the city (ie, the airport, train station and bus station), members of which offer information to tourists about hotels, taxis etc. When you arrive in Varanasi catch a taxi/rickshaw to the hotel of your choosing on your own or with friends. Don't listen to people who try to lead you to a different hotel or offer you services as a 'guide'. Especially ignore nonsense from autorickshaw drivers about 'your hotel' being closed, full or burnt down. Be firm.

It has been unofficially estimated that two or three travellers go missing in the city every three or four months, but for some reason this doesn't seem to get much press coverage. Three Japanese tourists disappeared in November 2000; according to an official tour guide they were last seen with a boatman down at the ghats.

There are plenty of drugs in the city and, particularly down at the ghats, you'll get plenty of 'hushed' offers – you can pick up just about anything. If you're not interested just ignore these whispers – be very careful if you do go down this path (which we don't recommend), as these guys may have other ideas for extracting your money than just selling you some grass.

Only do boat trips in groups, stay alert and ignore any other services offered by boatmen. If you want a guide, use authorised guides from the Government of India tourist office or one of the bigger hotels.

The old city is also said to be potentially dangerous after dark, and many hotels in this area lock their doors at 10 or 11 pm.

Ghats

Varanasi's principal attraction is the long string of ghats that line the western bank of the Ganges. Most are used for bathing but there are also several 'burning ghats' where bodies are cremated. The best time to visit the ghats is at dawn when the river is bathed in a magical light and pilgrims come to perform puja to the rising sun.

There are around 100 ghats in Varanasi, but Dasaswamedh Ghat is probably the most convenient starting point. A short boat trip from Dasaswamedh to Manikarnika Ghat can be an interesting introduction to the river (see River Trips later in this section). Alternatively, if the water level is low, you can simply walk from one ghat to the next. This way you're among the throng of people who come to the edge of the Ganges not only for a ritual bath, but to do yoga, offer blessings, buy paan, sell flowers, get a massage, play cricket, have a swim, get a shave, and improve their karma by giving money to beggars.

The city extends from Raj Ghat, near the major road and rail bridge, to Assi Ghat, near the university. The **Assi Ghat** is one of the five special ghats that pilgrims are supposed to bathe at in sequence during the ritual route called Panchatirthi Yatra. The order is Assi, Dasaswamedh, Adi Keshava, Panchganga and finally Manikarnika.

Much of the **Tulsidas Ghat** has fallen down towards the river. The **Bachraj Ghat** is Jain and there are three riverbank Jain temples. Many of the ghats are owned by maharajas or other princely rulers, such as the very fine **Shivala Ghat** owned by the maharaja of Varanasi. The **Dandi Ghat** is the ghat of ascetics known as Dandi Panths, nearby is the very popular **Hanuman Ghat**.

The **Harishchandra** or Smashan Ghat is a secondary burning ghat. It's one of the oldest ghats in the city. Above it, the crowded **Kedar Ghat** is a shrine popular with Bengalis and South Indians. **Mansarowar Ghat** was built by Raja Man Singh of Amber and named after the Tibetan lake at the foot of Mt Kailash, Shiva's Himalayan home. **Someswar** or Lord of the Moon Ghat is said to be able to heal diseases. The **Munshi Ghat** is very picturesque, while **Ahalya Bai's Ghat** is named after the female Maratha ruler of Indore.

The name of **Dasaswamedh Ghat** indicates that Brahma sacrificed *medh* (10) *das* (horses) *aswa* (here). Conveniently central, it's one of the most important and busiest ghats and therefore is a good place to linger and soak up the atmosphere, as long as you don't mind being pestered by people wanting to read your palm. Note its statues and the shrine of Sitala, goddess of smallpox.

Raja Man Singh's **Man Mandir Ghat** was built in 1600 but was poorly restored in the 19th century. The northern corner of the ghat has a fine stone balcony and Raja Jai Singh of Jaipur erected one of his unusual observatories on this ghat in 1710.

The **Meer Ghat** leads to the Nepali Temple, which has erotic sculptures. The **Jalsain Ghat**, where cremations take place, virtually adjoins **Manikarnika Ghat**, one of the oldest and most sacred in Varanasi. Manikarnika is the main burning ghat and one of the most auspicious places that a Hindu can be cremated. Bodies are handled by outcasts known as *doms*, and they are carried through the alleyways of the old city to the holy Ganges on a bamboo stretcher swathed in cloth. The corpse is doused in the Ganges prior to cremation. You'll see huge piles of firewood stacked along the top of the ghat, each log carefully weighed on giant scales so that the price of cremation can be calculated. There are no problems watching cremations, since at Manikarnika death is simply business as usual, but don't take photos and keep your camera well hidden.

Above the steps here is a tank known as the **Manikarnika Well**; Parvati is said to have dropped her earring here and Shiva dug the tank to recover it, filling the depression with his sweat. The **Charanpaduka**, a slab of stone between the well and the ghat, bears footprints made by Vishnu. Privileged VIPs are cremated at the Charanpaduka. There is also a temple dedicated to Ganesh on the ghat.

Dattatreya Ghat bears the footprint of the Brahmin saint of that name in a small temple nearby. **Scindia Ghat** was originally built in 1830 but was so huge and magnificent hat it collapsed into the river and had to be ebuilt. The **Ram Ghat** was built by the raja of Jaipur. The **Panchganga Ghat**, as its name ndicates, is where five rivers are supposed o meet. Dominating the ghat is Aurangzeb's maller mosque, also known as the **Alamgir Mosque**, which he built on the site of a large Vishnu temple erected by the Maratha chieftain Beni Madhav Rao Scindia. The **Gai Ghat** has a figure of a cow made of stone upon it. The **Trilochan Ghat** has two turrets emerging from the river, and the water between them is especially holy. **Raj Ghat** was he ferry pier until the road and rail bridge vas completed here.

Vishwanath Temple

The Vishwanath Temple, or Golden Temple, is the most sacred temple in Varanasi and is dedicated to Vishveswara – Shiva as lord of the universe. The current temple was built in 1776 by Ahalya Bai of Indore, and the 800kg of gold plating on the towers, which gives the temple its colloquial name, was provided by Maharaja Ranjit Singh of Lahore some 50 years later. It's located in the narrow alleys of the old city. Non-Hindus are not allowed into the temple but can view it from the upper floor of a silk shop across the street.

There has been a succession of Shiva temples in the vicinity for at least the past 1500 years, but they were routinely destroyed by successive waves of Muslim invaders. Aurangzeb continued this tradition, knocking down the previous temple and building his **Great Mosque** over it. Armed guards protect the mosque since the BJP has declared that, after Ayodhya, the mosques at Varanasi and Mathura are its

Hindu Rituals on the Ganges

A boat ride on the Ganges at sunrise reveals thousands of devout Hindus – pilgrims, sadhus and residents alike – making their way down to the ghats and into the holy waters. Waist-high in water they face the rising sun muttering prayers and performing a complex series of Hindu rituals.

Although individual worship differs between different castes and sects of Hinduism, they are all paying tribute to the Ganges or 'Great Mother', a living Goddess, which provides a passage to reach Pitriloka, the World of the Ancestors. You'll see offerings such as grains and garlands of marigolds or pink lotuses being tossed into the river, which twinkles in the early morning light with the many tiny oil lamps bobbing lazily on its currents.

Bathing is an integral part of worship. Hindus will take the water of the river in their hands and allow it to trickle through their fingers, letting it rejoin the Great Mother. This is a form of offering to their ancestors and the gods. They may also take a ritual drink and even pour the water into a brass or copper container, which they later tuck under their arm as they head off to the temple.

There are many mysterious rites performed at the Ganges. Some involve the bather splashing water with both hands towards the sun as a form of salute. Others will scoop up water in the palms of their hands and pour it over their heads, or hold their breath and submerge themselves for several seconds – this absolves the body from the defilement of sins.

There are also rites involving the sacred *upavita* or Brahminical thread. The thread is swapped between the right and left shoulders and water is taken from the sacred river and allowed to trickle out of the hand between the thumb and forefinger and fall over the neck.

Many bathers count the beads on their rosaries, while muttering a cryptic prayer – others wash their bodies with ashes from sacrificial fires and put the mark of Shiva or Vishnu on their foreheads; a vertical mark for Vishnu and a horizontal one for Shiva.

Brahmin priests mutter the holiest of *mantras* (sacred prayers) – an age-old sun invocation that can be translated as '*Let us adore the light of the Divine Sun. May it enlighten our minds.*' In Hindu folklore a mystic significance has been attached to it as a mantra designed specifically for the Supreme Soul: Brahman.

next targets. Be discreet if taking photographs in this area as the soldiers sometimes disapprove.

Next to the Vishwanath Temple is the **Gyan Kupor Well** (Well of Knowledge). The faithful believe drinking its water leads to a higher spiritual plane, though they are prevented from doing so by both tradition and a strong security screen. The well is said to contain the Shiva lingam removed from the previous temple and hidden to protect it from Aurangzeb.

Durga Temple

The Durga Temple, on Durgakund Rd, is commonly known as the Monkey Temple due to the many frisky monkeys that have made it their home. About 2km south of the old city, this small temple was built in the 18th century by a Bengali maharani and is stained red with ochre. It's in North Indiar Nagara style with a multitiered *sikharc* (corn-cob shaped spire). Durga is the 'terrible' form of Shiva's consort Parvati, so a festivals there are often sacrifices of goats Non-Hindus can enter the courtyard but no the inner sanctum.

Tulsi Manas Temple

Only 150m south of the Durga Temple is the modern marble sikhara-style Tulsi Manas Temple, built in 1964. Its two-tier walls are engraved with verses and scenes from the Ram Charit Manas, the Hindi version of the Ramayana. Its author, the poet Tulsi Das lived here while writing it.

You can watch figures performing scene from Hindu mythology on the second floo for Rs 1. The temple is open 6 to 11.30 am and 3 to 9 pm.

Hindu Rituals on the Ganges

Brahmins perform rituals known as *pranayama* or 'the exercise of breathing', which involves a sequence of inhaling and exhaling through the left and right nostrils; the worshipper then holds their breath for as long as possible by using his fingers to clamp both nostrils. The hands are an integral part of this procedure – the right hand is covered with a cloth or plunged into a red bag. Symbolic gestures are also made with the hands to represent the 10 incarnations of Vishnu and hypnotic recitations of mantras are muttered continuously.

These complex ceremonies form part of a Brahmin's *sandhya* – a spiritual exercise designed to free the soul from earthly sin. Rituals and mantras must be performed in an exact sequence and without blemish; any error in the order of the ritual or pronunciation of prayer will result in the perpetrator being cursed by misfortune. This is why bathers, absorbed in perfecting their devotions, often seem oblivious to the hoards of snap-happy tourists floating past in boats.

Of course not every bather follows these complex rituals performed by the pious Brahmins. Every sect and caste are represented among the multitude of bathers and many are simple peasants who are on a pilgrimage and may perform a version of the sandhya peculiar to their caste. Or they may mutter a mantra that has been prescribed to them by a Brahmin who has been acting as their spiritual guide.

For Hindus, death in Varanasi means an instant passport to Shiva's Himalayan Paradise on Mount Kailasa. Old people will come to Varanasi and spend their last days fervently performing the Brahmin rituals. If not lucky enough to die in the holy city then relatives will bring their dead for cremation, or just their ashes – to have one's ashes scattered on the holy river assures a Hindu of salvation.

Without the sacred waters of the Ganges, the deceased will suffer in limbo and haunt their ancestors on Earth; the waters of the Ganges are referred to as *amrita*, or 'nectar of immortality'. Sometimes a family who can't afford the firewood required for cremation will release a half-burned corpse into the river, and this has become a macabre but fairly common sight for visitors.

At different times of the year, particularly during festivals, it is possible to observe many variances on these rituals. During some festivals in Varanasi boats full of the faithful can be heard crying *Ganga Mata Ki Jai* or 'Victory to Mother Ganga!'

Benares Hindu University

Varanasi has long been a centre of learning and that tradition is continued today at the Benares Hindu University (BHU), built in 1917. It was founded by the great nationalist Pandit Malaviya as a centre for education in Indian art, music, culture and philosophy, and for the study of Sanskrit.

The lovely, green campus covers 5 sq km and houses the Bharat Kala Bhavan, which has a fine collection of miniature paintings, sculptures from the 1st to 15th centuries and old photographs of Varanasi. It's open 11 am to 4 pm daily except Sunday (7.30 am to 12.30 pm May to June). To visit all sections costs Rs 40 (Rs 10 for Indians). BHU is a 20-minute walk or a short rickshaw ride from the Durga Temple.

New Vishwanath Temple

It's about a 30-minute walk from the gates of the university to the New Vishwanath Temple, which was planned by Pandit Malviya and built by the wealthy Birla family of industrialists. Pandit Malaviya wished to see Hinduism revived without its caste distinctions and prejudices – accordingly, unlike many temples in Varanasi, this temple is open to all, irrespective of caste or religion. The interior has a Shiva lingam (phallic symbol) and verses from Hindu scriptures inscribed on the walls. The temple is supposed to be a replica of the earlier Vishwanath Temple destroyed by Aurangzeb. It's open from 4 am to noon and 1 to 9 pm. From Godaulia it costs around Rs 20 by cycle-rickshaw or Rs 35 by autorickshaw to reach the temple.

Ram Nagar Fort & Museum

On the opposite bank of the river, this 17th-century fort is the home of the former maharaja of Benares. It looks most impressive from the river, though the decrepit planking of the pontoon bridge you cross to reach it is something of a distraction. During the monsoon, access is by ferry. The interesting museum here contains old silver and brocade palanquins for the ladies of the court, gold-plated elephant howdahs (seats for carrying people on an elephant's back), an astrological clock, macabre elephant traps and an armoury of swords and old guns. The fort is open 9 am to noon and 2 to 5 pm daily; entry is Rs 7.

Bharat Mata Temple

Dedicated to 'Mother India', this unadorned temple has a marble relief map of India instead of the usual images of gods and goddesses. The map is said to be perfectly in scale, both vertically and horizontally. It's open 7 am to 5 pm daily; entry is free though there is a camera/video camera fee of Rs 10/20. The temple was opened by Mahatma Gandhi.

River Trips

A boat ride on the Ganges has become one of the must-dos of a visit to Varanasi, but be prepared to see the odd corpse floating down the river. It's customary to do the trip early in the morning when the light is particularly inspiring. Even if you're not staying near the river, it's easy to organise a boat for sunrise as rickshaw-wallahs are keen to get a pre-dawn rendezvous arranged for the trip to the river. Get the rickshaw-wallah to take you to a large ghat such as Dasaswamedh, since there will be a number of boats to choose from. Travellers have reported being taken to smaller ghats where there was only one boat, placing them in a poor bargaining position.

The government rate for hiring a boat capable of holding up to four people is supposedly set at Rs 50 per hour; for a boat that can seat up to 15 people it's Rs 75 per hour. You'll undoubtedly have to remind boatmen of these rates since tourists frequently pay much more. Be sure to agree on a price before getting into a boat.

Steam Baths & Massage

The Hotel Surya offers steam baths for just Rs 50, and body massages for Rs 150. You can get a vigorous head, neck and back massage at Dasaswamedh Ghat which will cost about Rs 10.

Swimming

If the sight of pilgrims bathing in the Ganges makes you want to have a splash yourself,

Helping the Great Mother to Breathe Again

The Ganges River, or Great Mother as it is known to Hindus, provides millions of Indians with an important link to their spirituality. Around 60,000 people go down to the ghats to take a holy dip every day along a 7km area of the river (see the boxed text 'Hindu Rituals on the Ganges' earlier in this chapter). Along this same stretch, 30 sewers are continuously discharging into the river.

The Ganges River is so heavily polluted at the end of Varanasi that the water is septic – no dissolved oxygen exists. The statistics get worse. Samples from the river show the water has 1.5 million faecal coliform bacteria per 100 millilitres of water. In water that is safe for bathing and swimming this figure should be less than 500!

The problem extends much further beyond Varanasi – 400 million people live along the basin of the Ganges River. The pollution levels mean that waterborne diseases run rampant among many villages using water from the river.

The battle to clean the river has intensified in recent years. A nonprofit initiative, the Sankat Mochan Foundation, is dedicated to cleaning the Ganges River. Between 1986 and 1993 there was enough lobbying to see the government invest about US$25 million to set up three sewage treatment plants and an electric crematorium.

Unfortunately, there have been many problems with the plants, which are very power intensive; Varanasi regularly has long blackout periods. In addition the operation of the plants causes a build up of pollution in nearby villages and is also the cause of sewage backing up throughout Varanasi. This sewage then flows out into bathing areas, out through manhole covers and into the streets. The consequences for health are disastrous.

A plan for a better sewage treatment system, which has lower costs and is far more effective than the current system has been developed by the foundation. The plan has not yet been accepted by the government, but the signs are good.

Education is the key to effect real change, and this has been recognised. In 1998 the Swatcha Ganga Environmental Education Centre was established at Tulsi Ghat. The centre runs environmental education courses with schools, local villages, pilgrims and boatmen. Changes have started to creep in, albeit slowly – in some cases Brahmin priests have persuaded pilgrims to bury their relatives by the side of the river instead of cremating them.

Visitors who wish to make a contribution, financially or through voluntary work efforts, should contact Professor Veer Bhadra Mishra at the Sankat Mochan Foundation (☎ 313884, fax 314278, ⓔ vbmganga@satyam.net.in), Tulsi Ghat, Varanasi.

the following hotels permit nonguests to use their pools: Hotel Varanasi Ashok (Rs 150), Hotel Hindusthan International (Rs 200), and Hotel Clarks Varanasi (Rs 200). Clarks has the best pool.

Courses

Arts & Culture Studies Jnana-Pravaha (☎ 366326, fax 366971, ⓔ jpvns@satyam.net.in) is south of Samne Ghat and is a centre for culture studies in Varanasi. They run a number of short courses including Indian culture, art, music and philosophy. It's worth getting in touch with them in advance to see what they have coming up.

Language Bhasha Bharati (☎ 32044… ⓔ bhasha_bharati@hotmail.com), Ck 19/… Thatheri Bazar, has language courses fo… those interested in learning Hindi. Basi… courses are 30 hours and these are designe… for travellers – the emphasis is on speakin… and listening, not reading and writing. Th… course can be done in a week or it can b… done over a longer period of time (you ca… have a one-hour lesson every day for … month).

Music Triveni Music Centre (☎ 452266… D24/38 Pandey Ghat, Dasaswamedh Rd, ha… been recommended for tuition in classic…

ndian music. It teaches a range of instruments including the sitar and tabla. Lessons by professionals such as Sri Monilal Hazra and Sri Nandlal Mishra run for 1 to 1½ hours and cost about Rs 50. It's also possible to buy a Sitar here (see Shopping later in this section).

Aarohi Travels (☎ 312729, ⓔ arohivns@satyam.net.in), 74–5, 2nd floor, Dharm Sangh Complex, Durgakund Rd, can organise music tuition in Indian classical and folk music. Lessons are generally between Rs 50 and Rs 100 for 1 to 1½ hours.

Yoga & Hindu Philosophy We've heard good things from travellers about the International Yoga Clinic & Meditation Centre (☎ 327139), D16/19 Man-Mandir, Dasaswamedh, near Meer Ghat. Yoga classes are for one hour and cost Rs 100 per person, less if you are in a group. For the less committed, the Shanti Guest House runs morning and evening yoga classes, which cost about Rs 60.

The Malaviya Bhavan (☎ 310291, fax 312059) at Benares Hindu University offers courses in yoga and Hindu philosophy, such as a four-week certificate course or a four-month part-time diploma.

The Government of India tourist office also recommends Vipsana (☎ 346644) at C-27/273, Indian Press Colony, Maldahiya; and Vagyoga Kundalini Meditation Centre (☎ 311706), B3/131 A, Shivala.

Organised Tours

Government guides hired via the Government of India tourist office cost Rs 255/380 for a half/full day, or you can pay more to include road and/or boat transport. Three-hour tours of the old city by foot, Sarnath by rickshaw or the river by boat cost Rs 300 each. (The entry fee to the ruins at Sarnath costs extra.) You can choose from their set itineraries or construct your own.

Special Events

It is only fitting that Varanasi, one of the holiest places in North India, should have a plethora of festivals on the calendar. They are not all religious based celebrations (although many are) and you'll find some very fine classical music events, which feature top Indian musicians.

If you're lucky enough to witness one of these celebrations it will greatly enhance your experience of the holy city, so keep festival dates in mind when planning your visit. The festivals marked on the regional map at the start of this chapter are by no means exhaustive and only point out some of the bigger celebrations in Varanasi (see also Public Holidays & Special Events in the Facts for the Visitor chapter for India-wide festivals).

Places to Stay

There are three main accommodation areas in Varanasi: the old city, Lahurabir and the cantonment. Wherever you intend to stay in Varanasi, be firm when giving instructions to your rickshaw-wallah when you first arrive (see Dangers & Annoyances earlier in this section). For places in the old city, it's better to just ask the rickshaw-wallah for Dasaswamedh Ghat and walk to the hotel from there, since rickshaws won't be able to negotiate the alleyways anyway.

Contact the Government of India tourist office or the UP tourist office about Varanasi's paying guest accommodation, which enables you to stay with a local family. ***The Nest*** *(☎ 360137, ⓔ goitovns@satyam.net.in, B21/122 A2, Kamachha)*, near Baijnath Mandir (an old Shiva temple), is one of the cheapest of such places and charges Rs 60/125 for singles/doubles. If you have your own bed roll it's only Rs 15 per night.

Note that most hotels drop their rates by up to 50% in the low season (April to July).

Places to Stay – Budget & Mid-Range

Godaulia & the Old City The old city is the place to look for budget hotels if you don't mind living in cramped conditions. It is certainly the city's most atmospheric area and there are several good lodges right on the river with superb views along the ghats. Nearly all the hotels have rooftop terraces to relax on. However, there are very few options above the budget level. Monkeys scampering along the rooftops of the riverside places can be entertaining, but also a nuisance.

Vishnu Rest House *(☎ 450206, Panday Ghat)* is a popular riverside place with terraces offering great views. Fine singles with shared/private bathroom start at Rs 60/70 and dorms are Rs 40. Doubles start at Rs 120. Bucket hot water is free. Don't confuse it with the Real Vishnu Guest House or various other similarly named lodges that deliberately try to feed off this place's success. Phone ahead as it's generally full.

Puja Guest House *(Lalita Ghat)* is a reasonable option close to the action. It's just behind the Nepali temple and has great views from its 24-hour roof terrace restaurant as well as live music most evenings. Good doubles are Rs 200, and there's bucket hot water.

Alka Hotel *(☎ 328445, ⓔ hotelalka@hotmail.com)* is slightly more upmarket than other riverside places in the area. There's constant hot water, a pleasant terrace restaurant, and some rooms have TVs. Singles/doubles with shared bathroom star at Rs 120/200. Air-con rooms with a bal cony cost Rs 750.

Scindhia Guest House *(☎ 32031 Scindia Ghat)*, a little way north, has clea rooms, some with superb river views. Room with shared bathroom cost Rs 100/150, dou bles with private bathroom with hot water, balcony and air-cooler go for Rs 350. Th management is not keen on drug use.

You don't need a river view to enjoy th old city and many travellers prefer th places in the alleys set back from the ghats

Yogi Lodge *(☎ 392588, ⓔ yogilodge@ yahoo.com, Kalika Gali)* has long been favourite with budget travellers and it's effi ciently run by a friendly family. Dorms star at Rs 50, and small rooms with shared bath room start at Rs 80/100. Sheets and blanket are Rs 5. Like many other popular hotels i the old city, its success has spawned count less similarly named, inferior places.

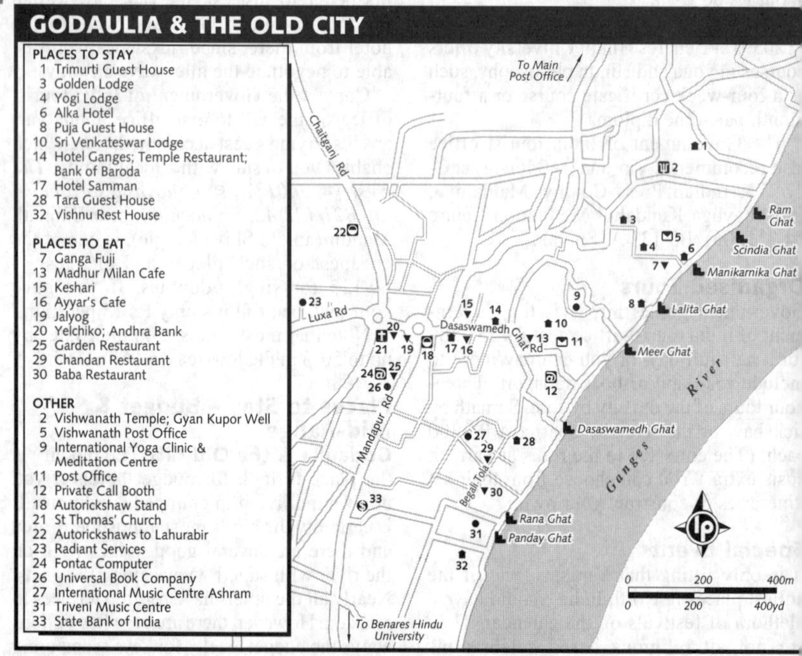

Close by, ***Golden Lodge*** *(☎ 328788)* is a quiet place with basic rooms for Rs 50/100 with shared bathroom (hot water) or Rs 80/120 with private bathroom. It sells a good selection of ice cream.

Sri Venkateswar Lodge *(☎ 392357, ⓔ venlodge@satyam.net.in)*, behind the Shiva temple on Dasaswamedh Ghat Rd, is a quiet place with rooms around a courtyard. It charges Rs 70/110 with shared hot-water bathroom and prices start at Rs 175 for doubles with private bathroom. Rooms are clean and air-cooled; the management is helpful.

The popular ***Trimurti Guest House*** *(☎ 393554)*, near the Vishwanath Temple, has dorms for Rs 30, singles/doubles with shared bathroom for Rs 50/80 and doubles with private hot-water bathroom for Rs 120.

Recommended by readers, ***Om House Lodge*** *(☎ 392728)* is in a small street also near the Vishwanath Temple. Apparently it's very friendly and the owners are helpful in providing bus, train and airline information. A dorm bed is only Rs 25, singles/doubles Rs 40/80.

Shanti Guest House *(☎ 392568, ⓔ info@visitvaranasi.com)* is just off an alleyway leading to Manikarnika Ghat. It's very popular and has a 24-hour rooftop restaurant with great views of the old city and river. Spartan rooms with shared bathroom start from a mere Rs 40/60. Rooms with private bathroom and only lukewarm water start at Rs 100/125. Unfortunately, the place has few outward facing windows and the slightest noise reverberates through the building.

Tara Guest House *(☎ 450769, Sonarpura)*, south of Dasaswamedh Ghat, is a new basic place that gets mainly Japanese travellers. Rooms with shared bathroom start at Rs 50/100. It's a peaceful spot and the manager is very keen on good hygiene.

There are a couple of decent choices on Dasaswamedh Ghat Rd in Godaulia. They're a bit more spacious than those in the alleyways of the old city, but try to avoid rooms that front onto the noisy main road.

Hotel Samman *(☎ 392241)* is good value and often full. Basic but fine rooms with private bathroom start at Rs 100/150. Bucket hot water is free and checkout is 24 hours.

Hotel Ganges *(☎ 321097, ⓔ bhataksun@yahoo.com)* has variable rooms with private bathroom ranging from Rs 175/225 to 400/500 with air-con. Add 5% service charge. There are pool tables and table tennis.

Bhelpura This area is by the river, midway between the old town and the university.

Sandhya Guest House *(☎ 313292, Sonarpur Rd)* is a few minutes' walk from Shivala Ghat. It's run by a friendly, helpful manager and has an eating area on the roof where you can chow down on home-made soups and brown bread. Clean rooms with shared bathroom cost Rs 80/100 and with private bathroom Rs 100/130.

Maruti Guest House *(☎ 312261, Assi Rd)* is a friendly, family-run place with rooms starting at just Rs 50/80, or Rs 200 with private bathroom. Interesting conversation is provided by the owner, a doctor who gives free yoga and meditation lessons. It can be hard to spot – it's upstairs next to the 'Dr Maruti, Yoga & Meditation' sign.

Hotel Ganges View *(☎ 313218, fax 367495)* is a stylish, cultured place overlooking Assi Ghat. There are lots of paintings and ornaments on display, and excellent vegetarian meals are available in the evening. Doubles start at Rs 450.

Lahurabir & Chetganj While these areas offer nothing of particular interest, they may be to your liking if you want to keep out of the crush of the old city, or need to be close to transport options.

Hotel Ajaya *(☎ 207763, Kabir Chaura Marg)* is good value. It has clean, pleasant singles/doubles with private bathroom and colour TV for Rs 150/250 and air-con rooms for Rs 450/500. Checkout is 24 hours.

Hotel Buddha *(☎ 343686, ⓔ hotel_buddha@satyam.net.in)* is one of the best budget hotels in the area. It's behind the Hotel Ajaya, off the main street, so it's quieter. The rooms are a little plain, but they're mostly spacious with high ceilings. Singles/doubles with private bathroom with hot water start at Rs 170/250. There are also a few tiny rooms with shared bathroom for Rs 90/130.

Gautam Lodge *(☎ 206239)* is an amiable place with spacious rooms, just around the corner from Hotel Buddha. Rooms with clean, private bathroom start at Rs 350/450. Air-con rooms are Rs 550/650.

Hotel Grand Holiday *(☎ 203792, Narain Villa)* is in a quiet residential street, and has variable rooms with private hot-water bathroom starting at Rs 250, or Rs 500 with air-con. There are also dorms for Rs 75. The best thing about this place is the garden and the friendly, family atmosphere. Checkout is 24 hours. Call ahead for free pick-up.

Hotel Barahdari *(☎ 330040, ⓔ baradari@lw1.vsnl.net.in)* is east of Lahurabir, not far from the main post office and within walking distance of the ghats. It's a bit overpriced, but well run by a friendly Jain family and has a vegetarian restaurant and a peaceful garden. Comfortable, smallish, air-cooled rooms with private hot-water bathroom and TV cost Rs 425/475, or Rs 625/700 with air-con.

Hotel Avaneesh *(☎ 350730, Station Rd)* is a modern place offering small but comfortable air-con rooms with balcony and TV starting at Rs 450/550.

Along the road is ***Hotel New International*** *(☎/fax 350805)* with a range of rooms starting at Rs 350/450 with TV and other facilities. The rooms that have balconies are only good if you enjoy traffic noise and fumes.

Hotel Padmini International *(☎ 220079, fax 220972, Sigra Rd)* is OK, if a little out of the way. It has good rooms with private bathroom, hot water and TV for Rs 475/550, or Rs 650/775 with air-con. There is running hot water in the morning and evening.

Train Station Area There are lots of cheap hotels close to Varanasi Junction train station if you need to be close to transport options. Most supply bucket hot water during the cool season.

Nar Indra *(☎ 343586)* is one of several hotels lining the noisy Grand Trunk Rd, right outside the train station. Clean, simple singles/doubles with TV cost Rs 200/250 with shared bathroom, Rs 225/275 with private bathroom and Rs 325/375 with air-con. Checkout is 24 hours.

Tourist Bungalow *(☎ 343413, Parade Kothi)*, just off the Grand Trunk Rd, is quite popular since it has a pleasant garden. Dorms cost Rs 75, rooms with private bathroom go for Rs 200/250 and air-con rooms are Rs 550/650. Some cheaper rooms have squat toilets.

Shivam Hotel *(☎ 348412)*, next to the Tourist Bungalow, is an excellent new place with squeaky-clean rooms, smiling staff and modern facilities. Rooms start at Rs 275/375, or Rs 500/650 with air-con.

Across the road is ***Hotel Plaza Inn*** *(☎ 348210, fax 340504)*, with comfortable good-value rooms that have all the amenities. Rooms start at Rs 500/600 with fan.

The other places in this street are very basic, but at least at ***Hotel Amar*** *(☎ 343509)* there's hot water (Rs 5 a bucket) and all rooms have a TV, although the rooms are rather dark and smelly. Singles are Rs 100 to 200 and doubles are Rs 175 to 300; the more expensive rooms have private bathroom and are air-cooled.

Cantonment Area This area, on the northern side of Varanasi Junction station, contains a sprinkling of budget hotels and most of the city's upmarket accommodation. It's the place to retreat to when the claustrophobia of the old city gets to you.

Hotel Surya *(☎ 343014, fax 348330, ⓔ Suria@lw1.vsnl.net.in, The Mall)* is a great place to stay if you need to wind down from the rigours of being on the road. The hotel is set around a pleasant garden and has singles/doubles with private bathroom and constant hot water for Rs 250/350, or Rs 500/650 with air-con.

Hotel Shalimar *(☎ 346227)*, next door, is of a similar standard but lacks the garden. The rooms for Rs 250/350 are fine, but the air-con rooms for Rs 600/700 aren't such good value, despite having colour TV.

There's a group of hotels on Patel Nagar, the street that runs north from the train station into the cantonment. ***Hotel Vaibhav*** *(☎ 345056, fax 346466, 56 Patel Nagar)* is clean, well run and has a bar and a good restaurant. Comfortable rooms with private bathroom, constant hot water and TV cos

Rs 400/500. Air-con rooms are Rs 600/700. Rooms in the new wing (starting at Rs '50/850) are very pleasant.

Hotel India *(☎ 342912, fax 348327, 59 Patel Nagar)* feels slightly more upmarket. Air-con rooms with bathtubs start at Rs 550/ 550 and rise to Rs 950/1250 in the semiluxurious modern wing. A suite is Rs 3000. The hotel has an excellent restaurant, a cellar bar and a scrappy rooftop eating area.

Places to Stay – Top End

Nearly all the top-end hotels are in the cantonment.

Hotel Clarks Varanasi *(☎ 348501, fax 348186, The Mall)* is the oldest hotel in the city. It dates back to the British era, though it now has a large modern extension. It boasts the usual range of facilities plus a good swimming pool. Air-con rooms cost US$80/90.

Hotel Taj Ganges *(☎ 345100, fax 348 067, Nadesar Palace)* is equally upmarket and has the most luxurious doubles in town, costing from US$125. It has a swimming pool, tennis court, jogging track and other amenities.

Best Western Kashika *(☎ 348091, fax 348685, The Mall)*, formerly Hotel Ideal Tops, near Clarks, is a modern hotel with well-appointed air-con singles/doubles for US$45/70. ***Hotel Clarks Tower*** *(☎ 348250, fax 348685, ⓔ clarkvns@satyam.net.in, The Mall)*, formerly Hotel Ideal Palace, is next door and is another swish place. Rooms start at US$80/90.

The ***Hotel Varanasi Ashok*** *(☎ 346020, fax 348089, The Mall)*, on the other side of Clarks, is a four-star establishment; air-con rooms with balcony cost Rs 1600/2500 (Rs 1400/2000 from April to September). It has a swimming pool, restaurant, bar and a quiet atmosphere.

Hotel de Paris *(☎ 346601, fax 348520, 15 The Mall)* is in a large rambling building set in a spacious garden. This old-fashioned three-star place is a little run-down. Huge, simple rooms with big windows and (usually) air-con, but no TV, are perhaps overpriced at US$25/35.

Hotel Hindusthan International *(☎ 351 484, fax 350931, Maldahiya)* is the only luxury hotel outside the cantonment. It's a modern four-star concrete block in the centre of the city offering air-con rooms for US$45/80. Facilities include a swimming pool and a massage centre, however it's not good value compared to other places in this category.

Places to Eat

Godaulia & the Old City The food in the old city is pretty uninspiring and standards of hygiene are not all that they might be. Cafes offer a standard travellers' menu consisting of Western breakfasts and snacks that mostly involve giving their jaffle machine a serious work out. Indian food tends to be oily and there are plenty of restaurants where no matter what you order, every dish that comes out of the kitchen looks exactly the same. On the other hand, Varanasi is well known for its sweets and high-quality paan. The alleyways of the old city are full of shops offering ample opportunity to indulge in either. Places here are not supposed to serve alcohol, though one or two serve beer – it's served discreetly in a teapot! If you arrive during mango season, try the locally grown variety known as Langda Aam.

Ganga Fuji, not far from the Vishwanath Temple, is a snug place offering Western breakfasts and Indian, Chinese and Japanese meals for between Rs 25 and 40, including nonveg. There's live classical Indian music in the evenings, starting at 7 pm.

Garden Restaurant *(Mandapur Rd)* is a relaxing little rooftop eatery with the usual travellers menu. It also has veg/nonveg Indian food for between Rs 25 and Rs 60, though portions are quite small. Breakfast starts at Rs 15.

There are a number of eateries along Dasaswamedh Ghat Rd offering Indian food.

Yelchiko by the main roundabout in Godaulia is a basement restaurant serving standard Indian, Chinese and continental fare for between Rs 25 and Rs 55. The food is merely adequate, but you can get special 'tea' here for Rs 75.

Next door, ***Jalyog*** has *kachauri* (Indian-style breakfasts of puris and vegetables). It's small, simple, and the entry sign is mainly in Hindi. Samosas are only Rs 2.

Ayyar's Cafe *(Dasaswamedh Ghat Rd)* is a modest vegetarian eatery serving good masala dosas for less than Rs 18, and full thalis for Rs 30.

Keshari, down a small alley opposite, is a clean, popular vegetarian restaurant providing an extensive menu. Main dishes are around Rs 35 to 60.

Temple Restaurant in the Hotel Ganges offers a first-floor view of the hustle and bustle of Dasaswamedh Ghat Rd. It serves good veg/nonveg Indian fare, Chinese food and Western breakfasts. Main dishes (which are 'very pleasing' according to the menu) are between Rs 30 and Rs 70.

A little way east is ***Madhur Milan Cafe***, a small but busy vegetarian restaurant with cheap dosas, samosas and thalis.

Traveller-style restaurants on Begali Tola, an alley south of Dasaswamedh Ghat Rd, include ***Chandan Restaurant***, a small eatery with an extensive menu (meals cost Rs 35 or less), and ***Baba Restaurant***, where you can chow down on a veg/nonveg thali for Rs 25/75.

Bhelpura Beside the Lalita Cinema is ***Sindhi Restaurant*** which prepares a range of good Indian vegetarian food for under Rs 40.

Even more popular is the ***Kerala Cafe*** *(Mandapur Rd)*, across the junction, which mostly specialises in dosas for only Rs 12 to 18. Their masala dosa is apparently the best in the city.

Bread of Life Bakery *(Sonarpur Rd)* is a haven for Western-style breads and biscuits. It also has a restaurant section with tuna burgers for Rs 65, plus breakfasts and baked potatoes. It's open 8 am to 9 pm (restaurant is closed from 3 to 6 pm).

Vaatika Cafe, next to the Hotel Ganges View and overlooking Assi Ghat, serves reasonable versions of pizza and spaghetti dishes for Rs 35 to 50.

Lahurabir & Train Station There are several places to choose from in these areas. In addition to the places listed here, the ***restaurants*** in the hotels Buddha, Shivam and Plaza Inn are worth visiting (see Places to Stay, earlier).

Most Welcome Restaurant, near the Tourist Bungalow, is a cute little eatery with cheap veg/nonveg fare and Western breakfasts (between Rs 15 and Rs 40). It's a great spot – the service is attentive and lashings of food are served with a smile.

Fairly close by is ***El Parador***, with an eclectic menu offering Greek, Mexican and Italian dishes, and a relaxed 'traveller' ambience. However, reports on the food are mixed, and it's pricey, with starters costing around Rs 35 and mains Rs 90 to 100.

Poonam Restaurant, in the Pradeep Hotel, Jagatganj, has good service and decent Indian, Chinese and continental dishes. There is also a very pleasant rooftop restaurant for hotel guests. Mains start at Rs 75/100 for veg/nonveg.

Around the corner is the ***Kamesh Hut Garden Restaurant***. It has a pleasant garden setting and excellent food for the price. Indian, Chinese and continental dishes start at Rs 25 for vegetarian and Rs 45 for nonveg.

Opposite the main post office is ***Sona Rupa Restaurant***, serving vegetarian dishes. The dosas for around Rs 20 are popular. There's also a bakery on site. It can be hard to spot – it's downstairs and has a green door.

Cantonment Area Hotel restaurants are the best bet in this area. ***Canton Restaurant*** at the Hotel Surya serves good veg/nonveg fare, Western stand-bys and, despite its name, more Indian than Chinese dishes. The restaurant overlooks the hotel garden and a lazy breakfast on the lawn makes a great start to the day. Mains are between Rs 4[illegible] and Rs 80; beer is a tad pricey at Rs 80.

Palm Springs in the Hotel India has excellent Indian cuisine. Dishes cost around Rs 100 but they're worth it. If you can order the Huggy Buggy without laughing you should win a prize. ***Palki Restaurant*** in the next-door Hotel Vaibhav is equally good.

Hotel Clarks and Hotel Taj Ganges are the places to go if you want to dine in style. Each has a choice of ***restaurants***.

Entertainment

Varanasi is not renowned for its nightlife. About the only choice, other than the cinema howing Bollywood fare, are the Indian clas-ical music recitals. These are mostly held t music teaching centres (and cost about ₹s 50), such as at the ***International Music Centre Ashram***, south of Dasaswamedh Ghat Rd (between 7 and 9 pm on Wednesday nd Saturday) and the ***Triveni Music Centre***, ear Panday Ghat (between 8 and 10.30 pm n Monday and Thursday). Major classical oncerts are also occasionally held at ***Nagari Natak Mandali***. Check the *Pioneer* news-aper for details. ***Ganga Fuji*** restaurant (see Places to Eat, earlier) also has music in the venings.

Bars are few and far between in Varanasi. You could try the ***Basant Bar & Restaurant*** *(Chaitganj Marg)*. A bottle of beer starts at bout Rs 65. Otherwise, try one of the big otels.

For a completely different option, a boat ide on the Ganges just before sunset is a great way to start the evening (see River Trips earlier in this section). It is also perfect for a bit of hassle-free people-watching, particularly if you're cruising by Dasaswamedh Ghat.

Shopping

Varanasi is famous throughout India for silk brocades and beautiful 'Benares saris'. However, there are lots of rip-off merchants and commission people at work. Invitations to 'come to my home for tea' will inevitably mean to somebody's silk showroom, where you will be pressured into buying things. See the UP Tourism city map (free from the tourist offices) for addresses of government emporiums and 'recognised' souvenir shops.

There's a market west of the main post office where the makers of silk brocades sell directly to local shops. You can get cheaper silk brocade in this area than in the big stores

Benares Silk

Varanasi is famous throughout India for its silk – taking time out to buy handicrafts or garments, or to do a bit of 'window shopping', is a great way to spend an afternoon.

Locals boast that the city's silk tradition dates as far back as 600 BC, at which time spice and ivory were also main industries of the city. Both the spice and ivory industries have since diminished, but the silk industry is thriving, and Varanasi's silk (Benares silk) is still considered to be unique.

Silk is not simply a commodity in the city, it holds a greater significance due to its use in religious rituals. Varanasi, the 'holy city', has been a place of worship for centuries and this may, in part, explain the abundance of silk throughout much of its history.

Although silk can be bought elsewhere in India, it is the specific weaving and design of the local artists that sets Varanasi silk apart. Varanasi crafts people are best known for their *kinkab* (brocade work). This product is a result of combining silk with fine metal thread during the weaving process. A traditional sari or shawl from Varanasi usually comes in the form of a single coloured fabric with gold and silver motifs and patterns woven into it.

The smaller or more intricate the design, the more skill required in the weaving process. Once upon a time crafts people used pure gold and silver, and although this practice is not so common any longer, many Indian families would have an older member who still possesses fabric with gold or silver designs spun into it.

There are plenty of places to buy silk for whatever purpose you may have in mind. If you are game, you may want to visit the Saree Satti of Kunj Gali for a unique experience. Here you will be able to bargain for silk and brocade saris auctioned off on the street. The market is mostly for wholesalers, but individual buyers are more than welcome.

Many stores also operate as tailors and will make a garment up to your specific design. Wherever you decide to go, if you are buying, be aware that you'll need to bargain – and hard. If time allows, your best option is to visit two or three shops and compare quality and price.

Justine Vaisutis

in the chowk area, but you must be careful about the quality. Mixtures of silk and cotton can look very like pure silk to the untrained eye. Pilikothi, a Muslim area north-east of the main post office, also has good silk.

It's difficult to give an idea of price as silk is worth whatever the shopkeeper can get for it, but as a very rough guide; silk may cost from Rs 150 to 600 per metre; you can expect a discount of at least 20% off this if you are making multiple purchases. It costs about Rs 125 to 140 for a tailor to whip you up a long sleeve shirt or knee-length dress.

You can buy musical instruments at the Triveni Music Centre (see under Courses earlier). A sitar can cost from Rs 5000 to 30,000. Check the type of wood the sitar is made from as it may change shape in a different climate, destroying the sound of the instrument.

Varanasi is also renowned for its ingenious toys and expensive Bhadohi carpets. There's a range of local and national products in the fixed-price Cottage Industries Exposition in the cantonment, opposite the Hotel Taj Ganges. The prices are high but a visit will give you an idea of the relative costs of various items.

Getting There & Away

Air Varanasi is on the popular daily tourist shuttle route linking Khajuraho (US$80), Agra (US$105) and Delhi (US$125). There are also daily Indian Airlines flights to Mumbai (US$235). The Indian Airlines office (☎ 345959) is in the cantonment near Hotel de Paris. Office hours are 10 am to 1 pm and 2 to 5 pm.

Sahara Airlines (☎ 343094) has four flights a week to Mumbai and Lucknow and three flights a week to Delhi.

To/From Nepal Indian Airlines has a daily flight to Kathmandu (US$72 plus US$4 tax), but it can be difficult getting a seat. If you're under 30, you'll get 20% off this price.

Bus Varanasi's bus station is a few hundred metres north-east of Varanasi Junction train station. It's a fairly sleepy depot and there's no timetable information in English. Buses lined up on the street out front are mostly faster, private buses. There are frequent ex press buses to Jaunpur (Rs 26, 1½ hours Allahabad (Rs 54, three hours), Luckno (Rs 120, 8½ hours), Faizabad (Rs 94, seve hours) and Gorakhpur (Rs 95, seven hours

Buses to Khajuraho leave from the othe side of the station and cost Rs 165. Buse also leave from here to Bodhgaya (Rs 91 Buses to Sarnath (Rs 4) leave from just nort of the cantonment.

To/From Nepal There are regular ordinar buses from Varanasi's bus station to Sonau (Rs 120, 10 hours). Plenty of travel agen and lodges offer 'through' tickets to Kat mandu and Pokhara (Rs 400). The bu leaves Varanasi at 8.30 am and include breakfast, an overnight stop in spartan ac commodation in Sonauli and a change c buses at the border. Doing it yourself is n only cheaper but gives you a choice c accommodation and buses at the border.

Train Varanasi Junction (also known a Varanasi Cantonment) is the main train sta tion. There is a separate reservation centr building on the left as you approach the sta tion, but foreign tourist quota tickets mu be purchased at the Foreign Tourist Assis tance Bureau by the UP Tourism informa tion booth in the main station building. Th office is open between 8 am and 8 pm dai except Sunday.

Not all trains between Delhi and Kolka stop at Varanasi Junction but most halt Mughal Serai, 12km south of Varanasi. Th is a 45-minute ride by bus (Rs 5), temp (Rs 10) or autorickshaw (Rs 70) along congested stretch of the Grand Trunk R You can make reservations at Varana Junction train station for trains leaving fro Mughal Serai.

Travellers should keep a close eye c their baggage while on trains heading Varanasi. The tourist information booth Varanasi Junction reckons hardly a day go by without a traveller arriving on the pla form without their backpack.

To/From Nepal It's not worth catchir a train to the border since the line fro

Major Trains from Varanasi

destination	train No & name	departures	distance (km)	duration (hrs)	fare (Rs)
Chennai	6040 *Ganga Kaveri Exp*	5.45 pm V	2144	41	262/1913 *
Delhi	2301 or 2305 *Rajdhani Exp*	2.35 am MS	764	9	–/1073 *
	2381 *Poorva Exp*	8.00 pm V	792	12	151/1088 *
	4257 *Kashi Vishwanath Exp*	2.10 pm V	792	17	151/1088 *
Gorakhpur	5003 *Chauri Exp*	12.00 am V	231	5	61/470 *
Gwalior	1108 *Bundelkhand Exp*	1.30 pm V	679	9	135/972 *
Kolkata	2382 *Poorva Exp*	5.00 am V	678	11	135/972 *
	3010 *Doon Exp*	4.15 pm V	678	15	135/972 *
Lucknow	4227 *Varuna Exp*	5.10 am V	302	5	77/– *
Mumbai	1094 *Mahanagri Exp*	11.30 am V	1509	22	221/1592 *
New Jalpaiguri	5622 *NE Exp*	6.35 pm MS	848	16	158/1138 *
Patna	3484 *Farrakka Exp*	3.20 pm V	228	6	61/470 *
Puri	8476 *Neelachal Exp*	8.10 pm V	1061	23	186/1340 *
Satna	5218 *Tilak Exp*	11.30 pm V	236	7	62/477 *

All trains run daily except:
6040 *Ganga Kaveri* only Mon/Wed
2382 *Poorva* only Mon/Tue/Fri
2381 *Poorva* only Wed/Thu/Sun
2301 *Rajdhani* only Mon/Tue/Thu/Fri/Sat
2305 *Rajdhani* only Wed/Sun
8476 *Neelachal* only Mon/Wed/Sat

Train station abbreviations: V – Varanasi Junction, MS – Mughal Serai
*2nd class/2-tier air-con

orakhpur to Sunauli is metre gauge, though ou could catch an express train to Gorakhur and pick up a bus to Sunauli from there.

ar If you can't get on the plane to Nepal nd don't want to experience the long bus ourney, travel agents can arrange a car for oout Rs 4.25 per kilometre; the 620km to athmandu should take about 12 hours.

etting Around

o/From the Airport Babatpur Airport is 2km north-west of the city. A bus to the irport (Rs 30, around 45 minutes) runs om the Hotel Vaibhav in the cantonment at 0.30 am and 2.30 pm, via the Government f India tourist office and the Indian Airlines ffice. If you bargain hard you should get an itorickshaw to the airport for around Rs 20 to 150. In the opposite direction, rickiaw-wallahs may charge much less since ey assume they'll pick up a commission at e hotel where they drop you. Taxis will try to charge well over Rs 200 to the airport, from the airport to the city will cost upwards of Rs 210, depending on your destination.

Bus Local buses are very crowded unless you can get on at the starting point. They cost Rs 2 to 5, but they're irregular and you need to be aware of pickpockets. A useful bus goes from Varanasi Junction train station to Lanka, which is close to Benares Hindu University.

Taxi & Autorickshaw For 'private' trips by taxi or autorickshaw you'll have to agree a price since they do not have meters. You'll have a hard time trying to get a decent rate, but there are prepaid booths on the south side of Varanasi Junction train station. In theory, the booths should be staffed 24 hours. However, since their introduction several years ago they have not been overly successful and are rarely staffed, so expect to pay over and above these prices.

Some of the displayed prepaid taxi rates from there are: Dasaswamedh Ghat (Rs 50), Assi Ghat (Rs 64), Benares Hindu University or Sarnath (Rs 78), Mughal Serai (Rs 136).

Some prepaid autorickshaw rates are: Godaulia (Rs 25), Benares Hindu University (Rs 30), Sarnath (Rs 40) and Mughal Serai (Rs 70).

Share-Autorickshaw & Tempo These operate along set routes with fixed prices (Rs 3 to 5). They can be the best way to get around the city cheaply, although not when you have hefty baggage. From the stand outside the northern entrance of Varanasi Junction train station it's Rs 5 to the cantonment TV tower. There's a stand outside the southern entrance for destinations including Lahurabir (Rs 5). Be warned, they may try to charge tourists at least double these rates.

Cycle-Rickshaw It won't take long walking the streets before you start to perceive yourself as transport bait for every cycle-rickshaw-wallah. Figures quoted for trips usually start at five times the price instead of just double, and some rickshaw-wallahs in the cantonment are cheeky enough to quote prices in US dollars. In theory, a trip between the train station and Godaulia should cost about Rs 10; from the cantonment hotels to Godaulia should be around Rs 15 and to Lahurabir around Rs 10. However, these prices are what Indians would pay, and it is generally accepted locally that foreigners should pay more. Unless you want to spend half your visit haggling, expect to pay double these rates.

KAIMOOR WILDLIFE SANCTUARY

A peaceful spot about 100km south of Varanasi, this sanctuary boasts tigers, panthers, sambar and spotted deer. There are also waterfalls and ancient cave paintings in the area. The place to stay (if you can afford it) is ***The Tent Retreat*** *(☎ 0542-511880 for bookings)*; their office is in Varanasi, near Hotel Surya. They offer all-inclusive packages for about US$47 per night which include all meals and jeep/camel or cycle safaris in the sanctuary; bird watching and fishing are also possible if you're inter ested. Accommodation is in luxury tents. I you don't have your own car ask them i they can organise transport from Varanas

SARNATH

☎ 0542

The Buddha came to this hamlet, 10kr north-east of Varanasi, to preach his mes sage of the 'middle way' to nirvana after h achieved enlightenment at Bodhgaya. Late the great Buddhist emperor Ashoka erecte magnificent stupas and monasteries here.

Sarnath was at its peak when the indefati gable Chinese traveller Fahsien visited th site early in the 5th century AD. When Xua Zhang, another Chinese traveller, droppe by in AD 640, Sarnath had 1500 priests, stupa nearly 100m high, Ashoka's migh stone pillar and many other wonders. Th city was known as the Deer Park, after th Buddha's famous first sermon, *The Sermo in the Deer Park*.

Soon after, Buddhism went into declin and when Muslim invaders destroyed an desecrated the city's buildings, Sarnath be came little more than a shell. It was not unt 1835 when British archaeologists started ex cavations that Sarnath regained some of i past glory. It's now a major Buddhist centr

Most of Sarnath's monuments are set i landscaped gardens, making it a pleasar place to spend half a day. The entry fee fc the gardens is US$5 (Rs 230) and you mu pay an extra Rs 25 if you want to use yo video camera.

During the **Buddha Purnima Festival** i May/June, Sarnath celebrates the birth c the Buddha with a big fair and a processio Although you may be able to arrange to sta in some of Sarnath's monasteries, you'd b better off going to Bodhgaya or Dharamsa if you're interested in studying Buddhisr

Dhamekh Stupa

This 34m stupa dominates the site and is be lieved to mark the spot where the Buddh preached his famous sermon. In its preser form it dates from around AD 500 but wa probably rebuilt a number of times. Th geometrical and floral patterns on the stup are typical of the Gupta period, but excavations have revealed brickwork from the Mauryan period – around 200 BC. Originally there was a second stupa, Dharmarajika Stupa, but this was reduced to rubble by 19th-century treasure seekers.

The nearby **Jain Temple**, built in 1824, is thought to mark the birthplace of the 11th Jain tirthankar, Shreyanshnath.

Main Shrine & Ashoka Pillar

Ashoka is said to have meditated in the building known as the 'main shrine'. The foundations are all that can now be seen, and to its north are the extensive ruins of the monasteries.

Standing in front of the main shrine are the remains of Ashoka's Pillar. At one time this stood over 20m high, but the capital is now in the Archaeological Museum, significantly shortening the column. An edict issued by Ashoka is engraved on the remaining portion of the column.

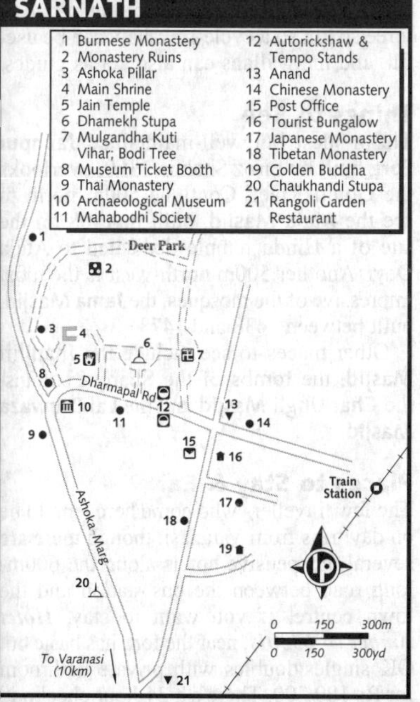

Archaeological Museum

The main attraction at this excellent museum is the superb capital from the Ashokan pillar. It has the Ashokan symbol of four back-to-back lions, which has been adopted as the state emblem of modern India. Below this are representations of a lion, elephant, horse and bull. The lion represents bravery, the elephant symbolises the dream the Buddha's mother had before his birth, and the horse recalls that the Buddha left his home on horseback in search of enlightenment.

Other finds include figures and sculptures from Sarnath's Mauryan, Kushana and Gupta periods. Among them is the (very fine) earliest Buddha image found at Sarnath and many images of Hindu gods dating from the 9th to 12th centuries. The museum is open 10 am to 5 pm daily except Friday; entry is Rs 2. Buy tickets from the booth across the road.

Mulgandha Kuti Vihar

This modern Mahabodhi Society temple has a series of frescoes by the Japanese artist Kosetsu Nosi in the interior. A bodhi tree growing here was transplanted in 1931 from the tree in Anuradhapura, Sri Lanka, which in turn is said to be an offspring of the original tree under which the Buddha attained enlightenment. There's a group of statues here showing the Buddha giving his first sermon to his five disciples. The temple houses relics of the Buddha, which were uncovered in various places. The temple is closed between 11.30 am and 1.30 pm.

Other Attractions

You can visit the modern temples in the Thai, Chinese, Tibetan, Burmese and Japanese monasteries.

The **Chaukhandi Stupa** dates from the Gupta period. It marks the place where the Buddha met the five ascetics who had earlier rejected him when gave up the path of self-mortification; these five became the Buddha's first disciples. The ruins of the stupa are on a high knoll. There's a good view from the Mughal tower, which was built by Akbar.

North of the Mulgandha Kuti Vihar is the **deer park**, where the deer inmates are joined by some Indian birds and waterfowl.

Organised Tours

The UP Tourist Bungalow run six-day 'Buddhist Circuit' tours of important Buddhist sites in Uttar Pradesh and Nepal. Tours include, Varanasi, Kushinagar, Lumbini, Shravasti, Allahabad and Sarnath. The cost is Rs 9000, including meals, guides, entrance fees, transport in an air-con coach and accommodation; there is a minimum requirement of two people.

In summer they also offer a range of one-day sightseeing tours, including Varanasi or Lucknow for Rs 400, which include one meal, a guide and transport.

Places to Stay & Eat

The UP ***Tourist Bungalow*** *(☎ 586965)* has singles/doubles with private bathroom for Rs 250/300, or Rs 450/550 with air-con. The bathrooms are clean (some have bucket hot water) and there's also a basic dorm (Rs 70), and a restaurant serving the standard tourist bungalow fare.

Behind the Japanese temple, the ***Golden Buddah*** *(☎ 587933)* has a beautiful garden and well-kept rooms. There is a bookshop with a range of Buddhist texts and they can organise lectures by Tibetan scholars. Doubles/triples with private bathroom and hot water geyser are Rs 350/450. There are also some dorm beds available.

Anand is a small, inexpensive restaurant serving Indian and Chinese food. ***Rangoli Garden Restaurant*** is a larger place with inside or garden seating. Indian meals start at Rs 45 for vegetarian and Rs 100 for nonveg.

Getting There & Away

Most visitors come here on day trips from Varanasi. An autorickshaw for the 20-minute journey costs Rs 40 (prepaid rate). Local buses depart frequently from the south side of Varanasi Junction train station (Rs 4, 45 minutes); they call at the Civil Court (Rs 3) in the cantonment but they'll be full by then. Only a few local trains stop at Sarnath.

JAUNPUR

☎ 05452 • pop 160,000

This bustling town, 58km north-west of Varanasi, sees few travellers but is of interest to architectural historians for its mosques, which are built in a fascinating style that is part Islamic, part Hindu and part Jain.

History

Founded by Firoz Shah Tughlaq in 1360 on an ancient site, Jaunpur became the capital of the independent Muslim Sharqui kingdom. The most impressive mosques were constructed between 1394 and 1478. They were built on the ruins of Hindu, Buddhist and Jain temples and shrines, and are notable for their odd mixture of architectural styles, their two-storey arcades and large gateways, and their unusual minarets. Jaunpur was sacked by Sikander Lodi, who left only the mosques undamaged. The Mughals took over in 1530.

Orientation & Information

The bus stand is south of the Gomti River, an Rs 8 cycle-rickshaw ride from the 16th-century stone Akbari Bridge, which crosses to the northern part of town where most of the mosques and the train station are located. The sights are spread out over two or three sq km so a cycle-rickshaw can be useful, and the wallahs can also act as guides.

Things to See

The modest but well-maintained **Jaunpur Fort**, built by Firoz Shah in 1360, overlooks the Gomti River. Continue 500m north to see the **Atala Masjid**, built in 1408 on the site of a Hindu temple dedicated to Atala Devi. Another 500m north-west is the most impressive of the mosques, the **Jama Masjid**, built between 1438 and 1478.

Other places to see include the **Jhanjhri Masjid**, the **tombs** of the Sharqui sultans, the **Char Ungli Masjid** and the **Lal Darwaza Masjid**.

Places to Stay & Eat

The few travellers who come here tend to be on day trips from Varanasi, though there are several inexpensive hotels along the 600m-long road between the bus station and the town centre. If you want to stay, ***Hotel Amber*** *(☎ 63201)*, near the fort, has basic but OK singles/doubles with private bathroom for Rs 100/200. There's a 24-hour checkout.

Getting There & Away

There are regular buses to and from Varanasi (Rs 26, 1½ hours). A few express trains connect Jaunpur Junction with Varanasi (Rs 25/173, 2nd/1st class, 1½ hours), Faizabad (Rs 42/221, three hours) and Lucknow (Rs 61/321, six hours).

GORAKHPUR

☎ 0551 • pop 575,000

Most travellers happily pass straight through Gorakhpur on their way to or from Nepal. This is hardly surprising since the city is infamous for its annual plagues of flies and mosquitoes and even the local tourist office candidly tells visitors 'there are no sights in Gorakhpur'. The city is, however, the headquarters of the North Eastern Railway and is a useful train junction.

Gorakhpur is named after the sage, Yogi Gorakhnath. The **Gorakhnath Temple** is a couple of kilometres north-west of the city centre and is worth visiting if you have time to fill in between transport connections. The city is home to well-known Hindu religious publishers Geeta Press. A visit to their office will result in a pile of invaluable English-language books being offered to you with titles such as 'How to lead a household life'. These make excellent presents to friends back home with a sense of humour.

Information

Tourist offices are at the train station and on Park Rd (☎ 335450). They're open 10 am to 5 pm daily except Sunday and give out a useful map of Gorakhpur and Kushinagar. The State Bank of India on Bank Rd exchanges only cash and AmEx travellers cheques (in US dollars or UK pounds only).

There is a group of Internet centres down an alley off Cinema Rd, around the corner from Hotel President. Among them, the Internet Club is the best. Connections are fast and cost Rs 35 per hour. It's open from 6 am to midnight.

Places to Stay

The best places to stay in Gorakhpur are in the central Golghar district, close to the few decent restaurants in the city, but none are particularly inspiring and all have bucket hot water. Checkout is typically 24 hours. It costs about Rs 10 to reach them by cycle-rickshaw from the train station.

Hotel Yark-Inn *(☎ 338233)* has a range of rooms with private bathroom and (usually) TV. Singles/doubles cost Rs 120/200, up to Rs 500 for a large air-con double.

Hotel Marina *(☎ 337630)* has clean rooms starting at Rs 170/195 with bathroom and black-and-white TV, and air-con doubles starting at Rs 500. Cheaper rooms tend to be on the small, dark side and have squat toilets.

Hotel President *(☎ 337654)*, in front of Hotel Marina, has a lift but is a bit on the expensive side. It has clean, tiled doubles for Rs 350 with fan, private bathroom and TV or Rs 550 with air-con.

The hotels opposite the train station are the closest to the bus stand – handy for those early buses to Sonauli. Unfortunately, the area can be so noisy that you may not need to set your alarm.

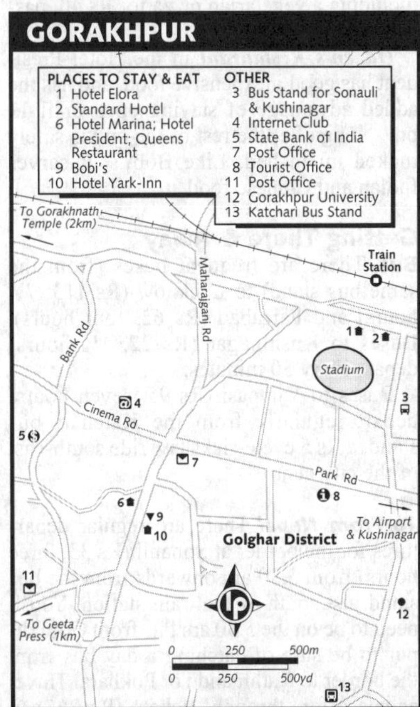

Friendly ***Hotel Elora*** *(☎ 200647)* is the best of this bunch. Rooms at the back have balconies overlooking a large playing field and are sheltered from the worst of the noise. Rooms start at Rs 110/150 with private bathroom and TV and Rs 300/400 for air-con.

Standard Hotel *(☎ 201439)* has pleasant singles/doubles/triples with private bathroom (squat toilet) and TV for Rs 175/225/300. The mosquito nets over the beds are useful, but they make sleeping hot from late March onwards.

The ***retiring rooms*** at the train station cost Rs 90/140 with private bathroom, and Rs 175/300 with air-con. Dorms are Rs 50.

Places to Eat

There aren't many places in Gorakhpur catering to visitors so you could do worse than try the small ***outdoor eateries*** near the train station.

The busy ***Bobi's*** at the Ambar Hotel in the city centre has decent veg/nonveg fare, including a vegetarian pizza for Rs 40, pastries and ice cream.

Queen's Restaurant in the Hotel President has good inexpensive food, and has the added advantage of staying open until 11 pm – long after the rest of the city is safely tucked up in bed. Like Bobi's, it serves Indian and Chinese food.

Getting There & Away

Bus There are frequent buses (from the same bus stand) to Lucknow (Rs 113, 7½ hours) and Faizabad (Rs 62, four hours). Buses to Kushinagar (Rs 22, 1½ hours) depart every 30 minutes.

Buses to Varanasi (Rs 95, seven hours) depart regularly from the Katchari bus stand, a Rs 5 cycle-rickshaw ride south-east of the city centre.

To/From Nepal There are regular departures for the border at Sonauli (Rs 33, three hours) from 5.30 am onwards from the bus stand just south of the train station. You'll need to be on the 5.30 am bus from Gorakhpur to be sure of catching a day bus from the border to Kathmandu or Pokhara. Travel agents offer 'through' tickets (Rs 265) to Kathmandu or Pokhara though you still have to change buses at the border. Doing it yourself is cheaper and gives you a choice of buses at the border.

Train Gorakhpur has direct train connections with Varanasi (Rs 62/326, 2nd/1st class, five hours), Lucknow (Rs 70/368, five to six hours), Delhi (Rs 231/793, sleeper/1st class, 15 hours), Kolkata (Rs 248/840, 18 to 22 hours) and Mumbai (Rs 366/1278, 30 to 34 hours, 1690km).

There are also metre-gauge trains to Nautanwa, which is 8km short of the border at Sonauli. It's much faster and more convenient to get to Sonauli by bus.

KUSHINAGAR

☎ 05564

Kushinagar is a peaceful, green town and makes a great respite from the chaotic larger towns in north-east Uttar Pradesh. It's a good place to kick back and take a break from the road for a day or two.

The town is a popular pilgrimage spot for Buddhists and pilgrims pass through in large numbers. The Buddha is reputed to have breathed his last words, 'Decay is inherent in all component things' and expired at Kushinagar. Similar to Bodhgaya in Bihar (but on a much smaller scale) a lot of countries with large Buddhist populations have built copies of the temples or monasteries here, usually in the representative architectural style of that country.

The site was excavated in 1861 by General Cunningham and later excavations by the Archaeological Survey of India confirmed that a monastic tradition prospered here for many years. Remains of 10 different monasteries that flourished between the 4th and 10th centuries AD have been discovered.

The tourist office opposite the Myanmar monastery is helpful; it's open 10 am to 5 pm Monday to Saturday, and sometimes Sunday.

Things to See

Sights include the remains of the Buddha's brick **cremation stupa** and the reclining

Buddha figure in the **Mahaparinirvana Temple**, which was extensively rebuilt by the Burmese in 1927. There are also other stupas that have been erected by passing pilgrims and the ruins of at least four monasteries. Not far away is the **Mathakuar Shrine** where an image of the Buddha was recovered during excavations and it is believed marks the site where Lord Buddha gave his last sermon.

About 1km away is the **Ramabhar stupa** which marks the spot where the Buddha was cremated.

Built by the Atago Isshin World Buddhist Cultural Association, the **Japanese Temple** has a huge circular chamber that houses a golden image of the Buddha. There are many other temples in town and numerous Buddhist monasteries.

Passing of the Buddha

Disciples of the Buddha were keen for him to go to Shravasti or Rajgir (both great cities at this time) for his passing, which he knew was imminent. However, the Buddha decided to go to Kushinagar and told his disciples that in an earlier life he had been a king and ruled from a magnificent city called Kushavati (present-day Kushinagar).

During this last journey the Buddha is said to have eaten a meal of contaminated meat – according to Buddhist folklore all Buddhas eat a meal containing meat just before their earthly time is over.

Not far from Kushinagar the Buddha rested near a village, where a passing nobleman came to talk to him. Impressed by his teachings the nobleman offered the Buddha some gold cloth. However, it is said that its radiance was diminished by the Enlightened One's complexion, which became astoundingly brilliant just before his passing and just before enlightenment.

Legend has it that on the death of the Buddha in Kushinagar, the earth shook, stars shot from the heavens and the skies erupted with fire. After cremation took place, relics from the Buddha's teeth, bones and burial shrouds remained. At this time eight countries made up present-day India and representatives from these countries came forth to claim some of the relics. Today the relics can be found in various stupas strewn across Asia.

Places to Stay & Eat

Budget accommodation, either by donation or for a set fee, is provided at the Chinese, Myanmar, Thai and Tibetan monasteries. Please respect the facilities in these places so they will continue to provide accommodation for travellers.

The ***International Cultural Guest House*** *(☎ 72164)*, opposite the Buddhist Centre, is simple, has 18 rooms and charges Rs 100 for bare, clean doubles. This place is fairly popular so you might want to try for a room early in the day.

Pathik Nivas *(☎ 71038)*, the UP Tourist Bungalow, is in a quiet, spacious garden setting and has good but overpriced singles/doubles with private bathroom with hot water starting at Rs 500/600 to 1100/1400 (with air-con). Its pricey restaurant charges Rs 30 for a bottle of water.

Lotus Nikko Hotel *(☎/fax 71139)* is a three-star establishment popular with Japanese visitors touring India's Buddhist sites. Huge rooms are US$90 per person, including three meals a day. In the cheaper annexe, simple four-bed rooms cost Rs 4500 and include one meal. It boasts a Japanese restaurant and a Japanese bathhouse.

Yama Kwality Cafe, by the Chinese temple, provides inexpensive veg/nonveg fare.

Getting There & Away

Kushinagar is 55km east of Gorakhpur and there are frequent buses (Rs 24, 1½ hours) between the two towns (the last at around 6 pm). The Kushinagar bus stand is several kilometres from the temples and monasteries, so get off/on by the Kushinagar Police Post, and walk down the southwards turn-off for the temples.

SONAULI

☎ 05522

This sleepy village straddling the Nepali border is little more than a bus stop, a couple of hotels, a few shops and a 24-hour border crossing. There's a much greater range of facilities on the Nepali side, where the atmosphere is decidedly more upbeat. Local Indians and Nepali are free to wander back and forth between the two parts of Sonauli (without going through any formalities), others need a passport. Foreigners, however, must officially exit one country and acquire the requisite visa for the other.

The Nepali border crossing is actually called Belhiya but everyone refers to it as Sunauli (with a 'u'). Nepali visas are available 24 hours (so they claim!) from the immigration office and take 10 minutes to process. Visas cost US$30 for 60 days, payable in US dollars cash only.

The easy-to-miss Indian immigration checkpoint is on the right-hand side of the road heading towards Nepal, about 200m from the border crossing.

The State Bank of India in Sonauli does not change money, but there are numerous foreign exchange offices on the Nepali side offering competitive rates. Note that you can pay for bus tickets and just about anything else in Indian rupees on the Nepali side of the border.

Places to Stay & Eat

Hotel Niranjana *(☎ 38201)*, one of UP Tourism's establishments, is a clean and friendly place with a garden 600m from the border. It has singles/doubles with bathroom, hot water and air-cooler for Rs 275/350, air-con rooms with TV for Rs 450/500 and dorms for Rs 50. The restaurant serves unexciting but acceptable fare.

Baba Lodge & Restaurant *(☎ 38366)*, by the bus stand, is very friendly and has doubles for Rs 150/250 with shared/private bathroom. Dorms cost Rs 40. Prices are negotiable so try bargaining. The restaurant serves cheap veg/nonveg food.

Sanju Lodge *(☎ 38355)* is around the corner from the Indian immigration post. It's fairly rudimentary but has pleasant common areas; a hard bed in a clean but crowded dorm costs only Rs 30. Singles/doubles cost Rs 60/90 with shared bathroom and Rs 140/170 with private bathroom and hot water.

There are several good, cheap hotels, plenty of open-air restaurants and a sudden blitz of beer advertisements on the Nepali side of the border, where most travellers prefer to stay.

Getting There & Away

Bus Buses to Indian cities depart from the Sonauli bus stand on the edge of town, about 800m from the border crossing. There are plenty of buses to and from Gorakhpur (Rs 33, three hours) and direct buses to Varanasi (Rs 140, 10 hours) and Delhi (Rs 358, 24 hours), via Lucknow (12 hours).

If you're entering India at Sonauli, be wary of touts offering onward combined bus/rail tickets, since these are not 100% reliable. It's easy enough to arrange onward train travel yourself at the Gorakhpur or Varanasi train stations.

To/From Nepal Private buses (paid for in Nepali rupees; NRs) leave from the Nepali side of the border for Kathmandu (NRs 240, nine hours) or Pokhara (NRs 230, nine hours), roughly every hour between 6 am and 1 pm and 4 and 8 pm. Travelling during the day is preferable – at night it not only takes longer, you also miss the great views on the journey. You should get a ticket in advance; there's a booking office at the Nepali bus stand. Travel agents on either side of the border also sell bus tickets, or can arrange a taxi (about NRs 850, six hours).

Government 'Sajha' buses leave for Kathmandu from Bhairawa, 4km north of Sonauli, at 6.45 and 8 am, and at 6.30 and 7 pm. They're very popular as they're cheap (around Nep Rs 185) and bookings should be made a day in advance. Tickets are sold from a kiosk near the Hotel Yeti in Bhairawa, on the main road from Sonauli. A cycle-rickshaw from the border to Bhairawa costs only Nep Rs 3. There are no government buses to Pokhara.

Numerous buses ply the 22km stretch between Bhairawa and Lumbini, the birthplace of the Buddha. They depart from the bus stand, which is about 1km north of the Hotel Yeti.

Uttaranchal

Formerly northern Uttar Pradesh, the new state of Uttaranchal came into being on 9 November 2000, formed from the regions of Garhwal and Kumaon (known collectively as Uttarakhand, the Land of the North). The new state is a region of rolling hills and snow-covered mountains, divided by some of Hinduism's most sacred rivers. Most significant is the River Ganges, which rises at Gaumukh in the far north, and winds its way down to the plains via the pilgrimage centre of Rishikesh and Haridwar, which marks the official spot where the Ganges leaves the Himalaya and enters the plains.

As in nearby Himachal Pradesh, the Himalaya is surrounded by extensive foothills, which are home to many popular hill stations, including Nainital and Mussoorie. Garhwal, the western portion of the state, is more visited than Kumaon to the east, but both regions see more Indian pilgrims than foreign visitors, and most of these stick to strictly defined *yatra* (pilgrimage trails).

Most important among the many pilgrimage routes that wind through the Uttaranchal

Himalaya are the Char Dham, which mark the spiritual sources of the Yamuna, Bhagirathi (Ganges), Mandakini and Alaknanada Rivers. In recent years the government has relaxed many of the restrictions on foreigners in the politically sensitive area close to the Tibetan Border and new areas for trekking are opening up all the time.

Closer to the plains, many visitors head for Corbett and Rajaji National Parks, which are home respectively to some of India's rare wild tigers and elephants. Yoga fans have been coming to Rishikesh to attend meditation classes since the 1960s. A few visitors also pass through en route to Nepal, via the little-used border crossing from Banbassa to the western Nepali town of Mahendrenagar.

Except in budget hotels, you can expect a 10% tax to be added to your bill throughout Uttaranchal. Most hotels drop their rates by up to a third from August to March.

History

The idea of carving a new state out of overpopulated Uttar Pradesh existed almost since partition, but it wasn't until the election of a Hindu-nationalist BJP government in Delhi that the movement began to gain ground. The main factor that tipped the balance in Uttaranchal's favour was the allocation of government jobs and places in educational institutions to members of 'backward' castes in the 1990s. Recognising a political opportunity, the BJP championed the cause of the impoverished but predominantly high-caste Hindu population of Uttaranchal, promising to create a new mountain state and a whole new set of government jobs in the process.

After years of negotiations, the state was formally declared, with its capital in Dehra Dun. However, the transfer of power to the new state government is likely to take several years. For now, some roles will continue to be governed from Lucknow until the relevant departments are established in Uttaranchal. From a tourist perspective, the most disruptive event is likely to be the creation of a new state bus company, scheduled for 2001.

The region of Uttarakhand was originally home to the Kuninda people, an Aryan group who practised a primitive version of Shaivism and lived a seminomadic existence, herding livestock and trading salt across the Himalaya to neighbouring Tibet. Many of their shrines have been incorporated in modern Hindu mythology. Over the centuries, various dynasties dominated the area, including the Guptas, Katyuri and Chand rajas, all of whom perpetuated the Brahminical order. Finally, the British stepped in briefly to repulse the invading Gorkhas, creating many replicas of England in the hills in the years before partition.

Tourist Offices

UP Tourism still organises some package tours to the region, but the bulk of the responsibility for tourism has been handed over to the excellently organised Garhwal Mandal Vikas Nigam (GMVN) and Kumaon Mandal Vikas Nigam (KMVN), which manage a network of tourist bungalows throughout the region. UP Tourism represents both organisations in Ahmedabad, Mumbai and Kolkata (see Tourist Offices under Uttar Pradesh for contact details).

The GMVN and the KMVN have the following offices.

Dehra Dun GMVN (☎ 0135-747898, fax 744 408) 74/1 Rapur Rd, Dehra Dun, GMVN
Delhi GMVN & KMVN (☎ 011-3350481 fax 3327713) 36 Janpath
Jaipur GMVN & KMVN (☎ 0141-378892) Government Hostel, MI Rd
Lucknow GMVN (☎ 0522-207844) Flats 4–7, RF Bahadur Marg
Lucknow KMVN (☎ 0522-239434) 2 Gopai Khera, Sarojini Marg
Nainital KMVN (☎/fax 05942-36374) Sukhatal, Mallital
Rishikesh GMVN (☎ 0135-430799, fax 430372) Lakshman Jhula Rd, Muni-ki-Reti. There is a Trekking & Mountaineering division (☎ 431793, fax 430372) next door.

Internet Resources

The following sites are a good place to start.

GMVN Official site for organised tours around the Garhwal region of Uttaranchal. www.gmvn.com.

KMVN A useful site for all your organised tour needs around the Kumaon region of Uttaranchal.
www.kmvn.com
Uttar Pradesh Gateway Site Continues to provide excellent detailed coverage of both Uttar Pradesh and Uttaranchal.
www.upportal.com/uttaranchal/tourism
Uttaranchal Gateway Site Describing itself as 'community on Web', this is a friendly and useful site focusing on the north of the state.
www.garhwali.com

Dangers & Annoyances

Trekking at high altitude involves serious and potentially lethal risks. See under Health and under Activites in the Facts for the Visitor chapter for more information on safe trekking at altitude.

DEHRA DUN

☎ 0135 • pop 424,500

Now the capital of Uttaranchal, this old centre of the Raj is in the broad Doon Valley between the Siwaliks and the front range of the Himalaya and forms a stepping stone to the hill station of Mussoorie, 34km farther up the valley. Although it's an historic town, Dehra Dun is probably best known for the institutions the British left behind, most notably the huge Forest Research Institute (FRI) in the north-east of town. Other important institutions include the Indian Military Academy, the Wildlife Institute of India and the Survey of India (responsible for mapping the nation). Also in Dehra Dun is the prestigious Doon School, India's most exclusive private school, where Rajiv Gandhi was educated.

The town is well served by buses and trains and many tourists just whistle through on their way from Haridwar or Rishikesh to Himachal Pradesh or north to the Garhwal Himalaya. However, there are several things to see here, including the Rai Ram Darbar, built by Aurangzeb in 1687; Dehra Dun exudes a pleasant air of prosperity.

As the biggest town in Garhwal, it's good to stock up on essentials for trekking in the hills; almost anything can be found in Paltan Bazaar north of the train station. Conservation organisations have offices here where you may be able to volunteer (see Volunteer Work in the Facts for the Visitor chapter).

Orientation

Most of Dehra Dun's restaurants and places to stay are strung out along Rajpur Rd, which runs north from the clock tower, the unofficial centre of Dehra Dun. The train station and bus stand are just south of the clock tower near the intersection of Gandhi and Haridwar Rds. The Ram Rai Darbar is tucked away in the maze-like Paltan Bazaar, west of Gandhi Rd, just north of the train station.

Information

Tourist Offices The useful Uttaranchal Tourism office (☎ 653217), the first of its kind, is at the Hotel Drona (now a government hostel), near the Delhi bus stand on Gandhi Rd. It's open 10 am to 5 pm daily except Sunday. The headquarters of the GMVN (see Tourist Offices earlier in this section) keeps the same hours, but mainly deals with administration.

Money The State Bank of India is upstairs in the Windlass Shopping Complex near the clock tower, but can only exchange cash (in US dollars or UK pounds). The Central Bank, Astley Hall area, on Rajpur Rd, can exchange Visa and other travellers cheques in US dollars and UK pounds.

Post & Communication The main post office is near the clock tower on Rajpur Rd. Within the compound at the Motel Himshri on Rajpur Rd are several good Internet cafes, which all charge around Rs 60 per hour.

Warning – Keep Cashed Up

There is nowhere to change money in the region of Garhwal other than at Rishikesh, Haridwar, Dehra Dun and Mussoorie. If you plan to head north to the Char Dham or other areas in the Himalaya, change all the money you will need (and then some) at one of these towns! Otherwise, you may be forced to try and change cash with unscrupulous moneychangers or even pilgrims at hugely unfavourable rates.

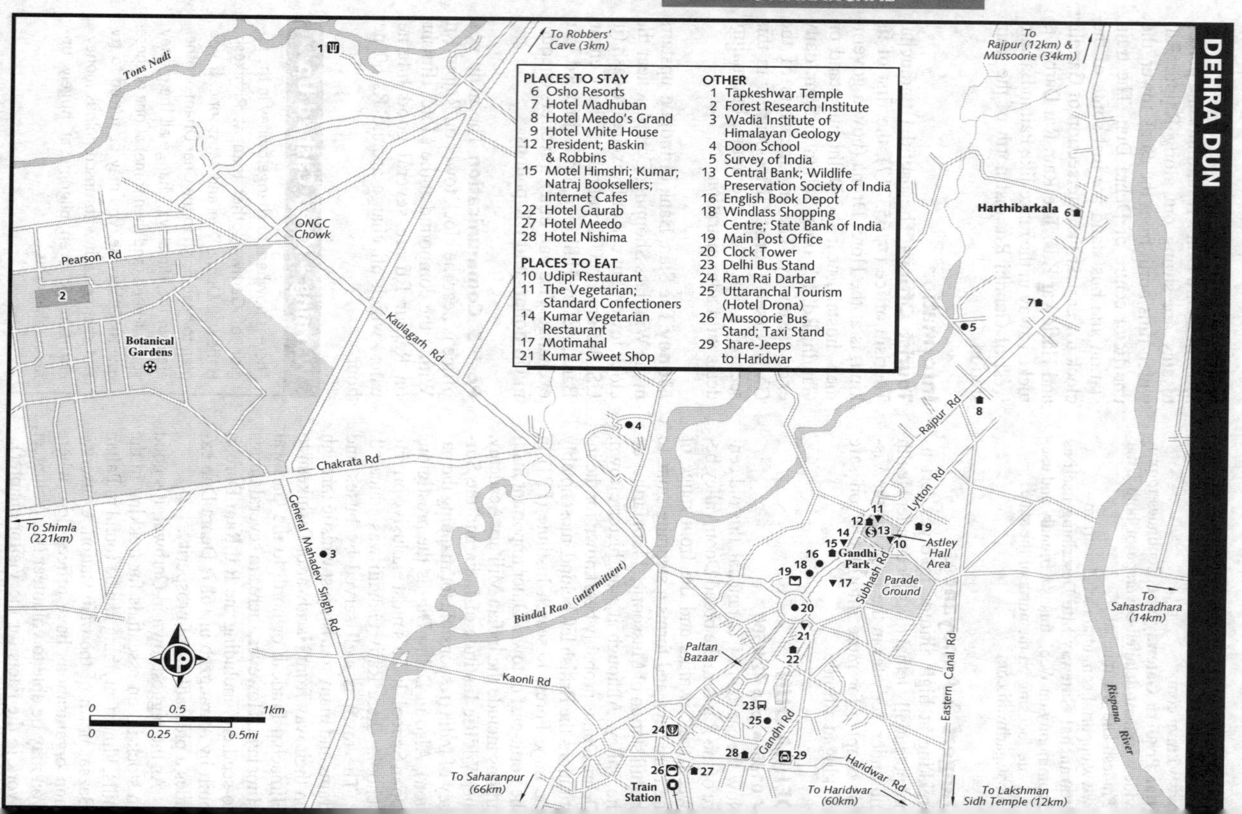
DEHRA DUN
UTTAR PRADESH & UTTARANCHAL
PLACES TO STAY
6 Osho Resorts
7 Hotel Madhuban
8 Hotel Meedo's Grand
9 Hotel White House
12 President; Baskin & Robbins
15 Motel Himshri; Kumar; Natraj Booksellers; Internet Cafes
22 Hotel Gaurab
27 Hotel Meedo
28 Hotel Nishima
PLACES TO EAT
10 Udipi Restaurant
11 The Vegetarian; Standard Confectioners
14 Kumar Vegetarian Restaurant
17 Motimahal
21 Kumar Sweet Shop
OTHER
1 Tapkeshwar Temple
2 Forest Research Institute
3 Wadia Institute of Himalayan Geology
4 Doon School
5 Survey of India
13 Central Bank; Wildlife Preservation Society of India
16 English Book Depot
18 Windlass Shopping Centre; State Bank of India
19 Main Post Office
20 Clock Tower
23 Delhi Bus Stand
24 Ram Rai Darbar
25 Uttaranchal Tourism (Hotel Drona)
26 Mussoorie Bus Stand; Taxi Stand
29 Share-Jeeps to Haridwar
To Robbers' Cave (3km)
To Rajpur (12km) & Mussoorie (34km)
Tons Nadi
Harthibarkala
ONGC Chowk
Pearson Rd
Botanical Gardens
Kaulagarh Rd
Rajpur Rd
Lytton Rd
Chakrata Rd
To Shimla (221km)
General Mahadev Singh Rd
Bindal Rao (intermittent)
Gandhi Park
Subhash Rd
Astley Hall Area
Parade Ground
To Sahastradhara (14km)
Paltan Bazaar
Kaonli Rd
Eastern Canal Rd
Rispana River
Gandhi Rd
Haridwar Rd
To Saharanpur (66km)
Train Station
To Haridwar (60km)
To Lakshman Sidh Temple (12km)
0 0.5 1km
0 0.25 0.5mi

Bookshops Natraj Booksellers, at 17 Rajpur Rd, next to the Motel Himshri, has an extensive selection of books on environmental issues, with particular emphasis on the Indian Himalaya. There's also a hefty selection of Penguin titles. Around the corner at 15 Rajpur Rd, the English Book Depot also has an excellent range.

The Survey of India (☎ 747051) has its headquarters off Rajpur Rd, 2.5km from the clock tower, and there's a shop selling many maps of Indian towns and regions (plus some poor trekking maps with questionable distances). It's open 9 am to 4.30 pm weekdays.

Ram Rai Darbar

Tucked away in the streets of the Paltan Bazaar is the mausoleum of Ram Rai, errant son of the seventh Sikh Guru Har Rai. Groomed from birth to be the eighth Sikh guru, Ram Rai disgraced himself by performing tricks for the Mughal emperor Aurangzeb. Har Rai declared him unfit to become the eighth guru and excommunicated him from the Sikh faith.

Uncharacteristically, Aurangzeb, who was not known for his tolerance of other religions, took pity on Ram Rai and awarded him an estate on the present site of Dehra Dun in 1675. Gobind Singh was declared the eighth guru, but Rai Ram picked up a sizable following and established his own religious order, the Udasi sect. The sect became so popular that first a village, then a town and finally a city grew up on the site.

Upon Ram Rai's death – he was murdered by his servants – Aurangzeb ordered a mausoleum to be built to the saint's memory, using the same architects who built Jehangir's tomb in Lahore. The resulting structure follows broadly Mughal lines – the mausoleum is in the centre, topped by an onion dome and four minarets – but there are curious asymmetric ponds in the formal gardens and four smaller shrines surround the main building, reflecting elements of Gurdwara architecture. The interior of the mausoleum is covered in fine frescoes of flowers and animals, and in the central chamber is the bed of Ram Rai, kept in a state of eternal readiness by devotees of the Udasi sect.

Forest Research Institute

Established by the British early in the 20th century, the FRI is now reputedly one of the finest institutes of forest sciences in the world and houses an excellent museum. It's set in large botanical gardens, with the Himalaya providing a spectacular backdrop.

The institute is open 9 am to 4 pm daily except Sunday and entry is free. To get here take a tempo (also known as vikrams) on Route 1 or 2 from the parade ground on Subhash Rd (one block east of the clock tower).

Other Attractions

The **Wadia Institute of Himalayan Geology** has a museum with fossils and minerals from around the nation. It's open 9 am to 4 pm weekdays. Take the same tempo as for the FRI.

Tapkeshwar Temple is dedicated to Shiva. It's set beside a pretty little river in a damp cave, where water constantly drips onto the lingam. A small donation is asked. The cave is reached by a long set of steps leading down to the river, with several small shrines along the way. The large Tapkeshwar Mahadev Mela is held here on Shivaratri day (usually in March).

Other places to visit include the **Lakshman Sidh Temple**, the cold springs at **Sahastradhara** (14km south of Dehra Dun) and the **Robbers' Cave**, a popular picnic spot 8km from Dehra Dun. Take a local bus to Anarwala and walk the remaining 1.5km.

On the way to Mussoorie there are several Tibetan Buddhist gompas and colleges. About 12km north of Dehra Dun is **Rajpur**, which is home to a large Tibetan community and the pretty Shakya Centre Gompa. You can get here by tempo.

Organised Tours

For organised trekking tours and advice, try Garhwal Tours & Trekking (☎ 627769) 151 Araghar Rd.

Places to Stay

Close to the train and bus stations, ***Hotel Nishima*** *(☎ 626640)* is a simple budget place with adequate singles/doubles for Rs 150/200.

Right by the train station, the simple ***Hotel Meedo*** *(☎ 627088, Haridwar Rd)* is a large place; rooms with private bathroom start at Rs 150/250. The rooms at the back are quieter.

Hotel White House *(☎ 652765, Lytton Rd)* behind Astley Hall is a nice old villa (if a little run down) set in a quiet garden. There is a pleasant patio where you can take tea, and rooms start at Rs 195/285; air-coolers or heaters are available for Rs 60 a day. Some of the rooms are enormous.

Hotel Gaurab *(☎ 654215, Gandhi Rd)* is a grand new hotel. Pleasant rooms start at Rs 350/450, while air-con rooms go for Rs 670/770. The restaurant here is also good.

Motel Himshri *(☎ 653880, fax 650177, 17 Rajpur Rd)* is well-located with ordinary rooms starting at Rs 325/395. Larger deluxe rooms cost Rs 525/625 (with air-con).

Hotel Meedo's Grand *(☎ 747171, 28 Rajpur Rd)*, 3km from the train station, has comfortable rooms with TV starting at Rs 500/600. There's a restaurant and bar.

The ***President*** *(☎ 657082, fax 658883)* at Astley Hall is a charming and tastefully decorated establishment. All rooms have air-con and TV; rates start at Rs 1100/1300. The hotel has a restaurant, bar and coffee shop.

Osho Resorts *(☎ 749544, fax 748535, 111 Rajpur Rd)* is a curious retreat belonging to the organisation of the late guru Osho. There's a good vegetarian restaurant and a variety of decent rooms with fan and bathroom starting at Rs 390/490 (Rs 790/990 with air-con); there are free video shows of Osho's commentaries.

The most lavish hotel in Dehra Dun is the ***Hotel Madhuban*** *(☎ 749990, fax 746496, 97 Rajpur Rd)* on the way out of town. The hotel is part of the Best Western chain and there's a minigolf course and a very good (and very expensive) restaurant. Air-con rooms start at Rs 1700/2500, with all creature comforts.

Places to Eat

If you've come from one of the pilgrimage towns and are craving meat, head for ***Kumar*** *(Rajpur Rd)*. This upmarket place serves excellent chicken and mutton dishes for around Rs 75, and gives huge portions. Vegetarians should make for the similarly excellent ***Kumar Vegetarian Restaurant*** a few doors down, which serves great stuffed roti (flat bread from the tandoor oven).

Motimahal *(Rajpur Rd)* is one of the best in a string of eateries on the opposite side of the road. It serves good vegetarian and non-veg dishes in a pleasant environment.

Udipi Restaurant *(Lytton Rd)* is a good South Indian place with air-con; masala dosas cost Rs 80.

The Vegetarian by the Hotel President dishes up inexpensive (Rs 30 and under) but tasty meals.

Standard Confectioners near The Vegetarian restaurant is one of several good bakeries in Dehra Dun.

Dehra Dun is known for its excellent sweet shops. Probably the most popular is the ***Kumar Sweet Shop*** near the clock tower, which has a huge range of sticky sweet things for only a few rupees and great kulfi (Indian ice cream).

For 21 flavours of ice cream, the American chain ***Baskin & Robbins*** has a branch near Astley Hall.

Getting There & Away

Bus The Delhi bus stand, beside the Hotel Drona, services destinations on the plains. There are hourly deluxe buses (Rs 202, seven hours) to Delhi from 6.15 am to 1.15 pm. Ordinary buses (Rs 120) also leave hourly until 10.30 pm. There are half-hourly buses to Rishikesh (Rs 20, two hours) until 7.30 pm, hourly buses to Chandigarh (Rs 95, seven hours) and buses to Lucknow (Rs 235, 11 hours) at 1.30 and 6.30 pm.

Dehra Dun is also well connected to Himachal Pradesh. A bus leaves for Dharamsala (Rs 220, 11 hours) at 12.30 pm and for Manali (Rs 250, 13 hours) via Kullu (Rs 215, 11½ hours). Buses to Shimla (Rs 130, 10 hours), via Nahan and Paonta Sahib, leave at 6, 8 and 10 am and 11 pm. Buses for Nainital (Rs 180 to 200, 10 hours) in Kumaon leave every few hours from 5.30 am to 8 pm. For Ramnagar, Corbett National Park (Rs 135), there are buses at 4.30, 6.15 and 7.30 am.

Buses for destinations in Garhwal leave from the Mussoorie bus stand near the train station. There are half-hourly buses to Mussoorie (Rs 22, 1½ hours) from 6 am to 8 pm; make sure you ask if the bus is going to the Library or Masonic Lodge bus stand as it's quite a walk between the two. Buses for Uttarkashi (Rs 125, eight hours) leave at 6, 8.30 and 10.30 am. In season, there are at least four morning buses to Hanuman Chatti via Mussoorie for Yamunotri (Rs 100).

Train Services to Dehra Dun, the terminus of the Northern Railway, include the speedy *Shatabdi Express*, which leaves Delhi at 7 am daily and reaches Haridwar at 11.20 am and Dehra Dun at 12.40 pm. The return trip leaves Dehra Dun at 5 pm (Haridwar at 6.10 pm) reaching Delhi at 10.40 pm. The fare is Rs 495 for a chair car seat.

The *Mussoorie Express* is an overnight train service from Delhi to Dehra Dun. It leaves Old Delhi station at 10.15 pm, arriving at Haridwar at 6 am and Dehra Dun at 8 am. On the return journey, it leaves Dehra Dun at 9.15 pm, Haridwar at 11 pm, arriving at Old Delhi at 7 am. The fare is Rs 146/451 in sleeper/first class.

There are also useful services to Varanasi (Rs 268/475, sleeper/first class, 14½ hours) at 6.15 pm, Amritsar (Rs 104/475, 14½ hours) at 7.20 pm and Kolkata (Rs 366/1218, 30 hours) at 8.30 pm.

Taxi Share-taxis for Mussoorie leave until about 6 pm from a stand in front of the train station on Haridwar Rd (Rs 70, 1½ hours). For Rishikesh and Haridwar, you can pick up share-jeeps a block east of the Hotel Prince on Haridwar Rd. Taxis leave when full until about 9 pm and charge Rs 20 to Rishikesh and Rs 30 to Haridwar.

Reserve taxis can be hired from opposite the Delhi bus stand for destinations including Rishikesh or Mussoorie (Rs 350), Haridwar (Rs 450), Delhi (Rs 1325), Uttarkashi (Rs 1500) and Hanuman Chatti (Rs 2300).

Getting Around

Six-seater tempos belch diesel fumes all over the city, but are a cheap way to get around. Routes 1 and 2 run from the parade ground on Subhash Rd (east of the clock tower) to Astley Hall and on to the FRI, returning along Rajpur Rd. The starting fare is Rs 4. Autorickshaws refuse to charge less than Rs 25 to anywhere.

MUSSOORIE

☎ 0135 • pop 35,000

Perched above Dehra Dun at an altitude of 2000m, the hill station of Mussoorie was established by the British in 1823. With the nearest railhead just 34km away, it became hugely popular as a summer retreat for the 'Raj set' in Delhi and picked up a reputation as *the* place to have an affair. The ghost of this time lives on in several splendid old hotels and summer palaces, though the ballrooms have fallen silent and the hotels are slowly crumbling.

The crowds from Delhi still storm Mussoorie every summer, but these days most of the visitors are young Indian honeymooners. More than 100 hotels compete for the lucrative honeymoon trade and dozens of photographers stalk Gun Hill, Mussoorie's highest point, offering romantic portraits against a backdrop of Himalayan peaks.

Mussoorie is at its best in the low season, when the crowds and room rates are at their lowest. Many travellers come here to stay in one of the old Raj-era palaces and there are good walks along the mountain ridges. Low-season room rates are very reasonable, but many visitors find Mussoorie prohibitively expensive in the high season (May to July).

Orientation

Mussoorie consists of two settlements: Gandhi Chowk and Kulri Bazaar, which are joined by the road known as The Mall. It's a pleasant 2km walk between the two. Buses from Dehra Dun go to either Gandhi Chowk (Library bus stand) or Kulri Bazaar (Masonic Lodge bus stand), so make sure you get the right bus, as The Mall is closed to traffic during the high season.

Information

In the high season, you can roller-skate at the skating rink for Rs 65 including skate hire.

Tourist Offices There's a UP tourist office (☎ 632863) towards the Kulri Bazaar end of The Mall, near the ropeway station and a GMVN booth (☎ 631281) at the Library bus stand in Gandhi Chowk; both are open 10 am to 5 pm daily except Sunday.

Money The State Bank of India at Kulri Bazaar will exchange AmEx travellers cheques (in US dollars only), and Thomas Cook and MasterCard travellers cheques (in US dollars or UK pounds only). The only place it may be possible to change Visa travellers cheques is at Trek Himalaya Tours.

Post & Communications The post office is on the Upper Mall in Kulri Bazaar and there are numerous ISD/STD phone offices in Mussoorie.

In the arcade beneath the Rice Bowl restaurant, the Mouse Trap Internet cafe charges Rs 100 per hour; it's open till 8 pm.

Bookshops There is a good selection of books and maps (including Penguin titles) at Cambridge Booksellers and Chander Book Depot at Kulri Bazaar.

Gun Hill

Gun Hill is Mussoorie's highest point; the British used to fire a gun here at noon daily to announce their presence to the surrounding countryside. At the top are a few dhabas and numerous photographer's stalls offering portraits in sequined Garhwali costumes for around Rs 50. There are distant views of several Himalayan peaks including Bandarpunch (6316m).

A ropeway runs up to Gun Hill from 10 am to 6 pm daily (open later in the high season) for Rs 30, or you can walk up the steep path.

Walks

The walks around Mussoorie offer great views. **Camel's Back Rd** was built as a promenade and passes a rock formation that looks like a camel – hence the name. You can rent ponies or cycle-rickshaws (Rs 120/80). Another good walk takes you down to Happy Valley and the **Tibetan Refugee Centre** where there's a temple and a small shop selling hand-knitted sweaters. An enjoyable longer walk (5km) takes you through Landour Bazaar to **Childers Lodge** (Lal Tibba), an impressive lookout point,

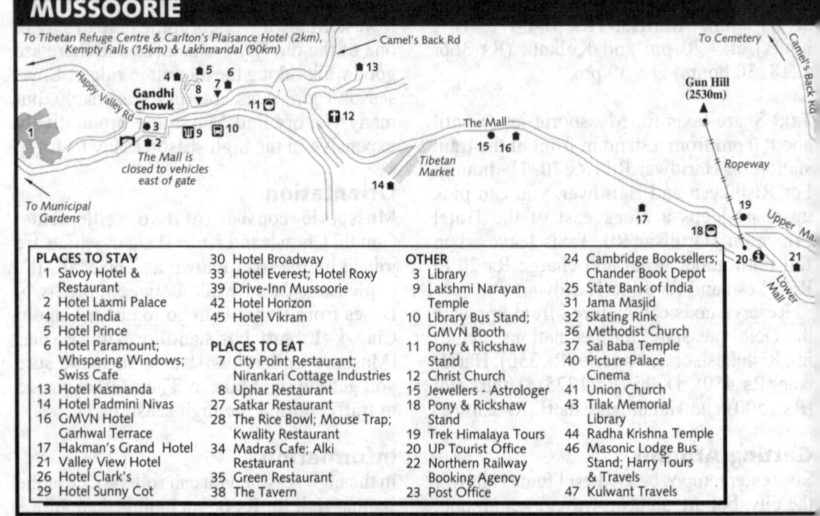

and Sisters' Bazaar. There are decaying Raj-era cemeteries in Landour Bazaar and on the Camel's Back Rd.

Language Courses

The Landour Language School (☎ 631487, fax 631917) in the attractively forested Landour area has introductory courses in Hindi, with most classes held in an old Methodist church. The school is open between 9 February and 11 December. Private lessons cost Rs 70 an hour and group lessons Rs 45 an hour. Contact the principal, Mr Chitranjan Datt, Landour Language School, Landour, Mussoorie, 248179.

The nearby ***Hotel Dev Dar Woods** (☎ 632 644)* offers discounts to students at the school (rates start at Rs 350 per night with breakfast).

Organised Tours

The GMVN runs half-day tours to the touristy Kempty Falls (Rs 50, three hours) at 10 am and 1 pm. Full-day tours to Kempty, Mussoorie Lake, the picnic site at Dhanolti (with good Himalayan views) and the Surkunda Devi Temple (also with good views) cost Rs 130 and leave at 10 am.

A respected trek operator is Trek Himalaya Tours (☎ 630491, fax 631302) Upper Mall, which can arrange treks in the Garhwal area, and jeep safaris to Kinnaur and Spiti, in Himachal Pradesh, and Ladakh (permits included).

Harry Tours & Travels (☎ 631747) and Kulwant Travels (☎ 632717) at the Masonic Lodge bus stand can also organise treks, as well as book air and train tickets and long-haul taxis.

Places to Stay

Mussoorie is probably the most expensive hill station to visit, though prices vary enormously according to the season. The rates quoted are for the high season (or rather honeymoon season) from May to July. All hotels in Mussoorie drop their rates by up to 60% at all other times. You can also expect to pay high season rates during the Christmas week and the Hindu festivals of Dussehra and Diwali.

The porters at the bus stands will often double as touts, and hotels will charge you double for your room to cover their commission.

Places to Stay – Budget

There a few budget places dotted around Mussoorie, but most places drop their rates to budget levels out of season. A double at any of the following hotels will cost around Rs 200 from August to April.

Kulri Bazaar Downhill from Kulri Bazaar in the alley beside the Tilak Memorial Library, ***Hotel Vikram** (☎ 632551)* has doubles starting at Rs 400 to 500. It's a quiet place with decent rooms and great views over the Doon Valley.

***Hotel Sunny Cot** (☎ 632789)* is a friendly family-run hotel on a hilltop with clean doubles for Rs 850. Take the alley leading uphill, just east of the Hotel Clark's on the way to the bus stand.

On The Mall near the State Bank, the ***Valley View Hotel** (☎ 632324)* is a well-managed place with friendly staff. Clean rooms go for Rs 600 to 800 and there is a nonveg dining hall.

Away from the centre on the road leading past the skating rink, ***Hotel Broadway*** *(☎ 632243)* is a friendly, well-kept place with some very pleasant views, and is deservedly popular. Doubles start at Rs 250 or there are a few singles with shared bathroom for Rs 150.

Nearby are ***Hotel Everest*** *(☎ 632954)* and ***Roxy Hotel*** *(☎ 632741)*, which share the same building, opposite the skating rink, and offer ageing but inexpensive rooms starting at Rs 400.

Gandhi Chowk The well-located ***Hotel Paramount*** *(☎ 632352)*, right on The Mall, has a variety of small but comfortable rooms from Rs 600 to 1500. Better rooms have views and balconies.

Hotel Laxmi Palace *(☎ 632774)* is a new place with clean, pleasant rooms and reliable hot water. The path down to the hotel is next to the arch on Gandhi Chowk. Doubles cost Rs 900.

Reached via the alley behind the City Point and Uphar restaurants, the friendly ***Hotel India*** *(☎ 632359)* has simple doubles with private bathroom for Rs 600. Nearby, ***Hotel Prince*** *(☎ 632674)* has a great balcony, but somewhat neglected rooms, starting at Rs 800.

About midway between Gandhi Chowk and Kulri Bazaar is the fading ***GVMN Hotel Garhwal Terrace*** *(☎ 632682)* with overpriced doubles for Rs 1300 (Rs 650 in the low season) but better-value dorms for Rs 130 (Rs 70).

Places to Stay – Mid-Range & Top End

Most of Mussoorie's more expensive hotels are converted palaces or relics from the Raj, and all offer TV, hot showers and carpets.

Kulri Bazaar ***Hotel Clark's*** *(☎ 632393)* has plenty of Raj-era character and boasts a billiard room with a full-size table. The well-maintained doubles are bright and spacious and cost Rs 850 to 1700.

Hakman's Grand Hotel *(☎ 632159)* is a great place for Raj-era nostalgia buffs. There's even a ballroom, which once played host to stiffly formal British dances. Large dark rooms, which may not be to everyone's taste, start at Rs 750.

Hotel Horizon *(☎ 632899)* is a very good small hotel with thick pile carpets, marble bathrooms, satellite TV and views across the valley. Doubles cost Rs 1400; there's a 40% discount in the low season.

Right in the middle of the action, the ***Drive-in-Mussoorie*** *(☎ 631226, fax 632555)* offers luxurious rooms with black marble bathrooms (which have their own telephone!) and all mod-cons. Rates start at Rs 1450 for a deluxe double.

The splendid ***Hotel Raghushree*** *(☎ 632 287)* is another former palace with luxurious rooms for Rs 2000 (Rs 1000 from July to October). The hotel is closed from October to March.

Gandhi Chowk ***Hotel Kasmanda*** *(☎ 632 424, fax 630007)*, uphill from Christ Church, was formerly a palace of the maharaja of Kasmanda. It has been beautifully maintained. There are hectares of gardens and the rooms are decorated with pictures of tiger hunts and old lithographs. Rooms rates start at Rs 1400.

Carlton's Plaisance Hotel *(☎ 632800)* is a wonderful old place surrounded by peaceful lawns about 2km from Gandhi Chowk on Happy Valley Rd. Everest conqueror Sir Edmund Hillary left a letter of recommendation. Doubles are a little expensive at Rs 1500 to 2500.

Hotel Padmini Nivas *(☎ 631093, fax 632793)*, 600m east of the library, belonged to the maharaja of Rajpipla. The attractive rooms are warmed by the sun and ooze old-world charm. Doubles start at Rs 900, while well-appointed suites start at Rs 1650.

Savoy Hotel *(☎ 632010, fax 632001)* is a vast British place covered with ivy and replete with faded touches of the Raj, including deer heads eaten down to the bone. Fittingly, it's said to have a resident ghost, one Lady Gore Ormsby, whose death allegedly provided inspiration for Agatha Christie's first novel *The Mysterious Affair at Styles*. Singles/doubles with three meals start at Rs 1395/2995.

Places to Eat

Most of the better hotels have their own restaurants, and there are lots of good-value eating places in the Kulri Bazaar area. In the low season, restaurants generally close by 10 pm.

Kulri Bazaar ***Madras Cafe*** is one of several vegetarian places in Kulri Bazaar. It specialises in South Indian food, with the menu featuring 24 different types of dosa (Rs 10 to 30), plus plenty of *paneer* (cheese) options. Other good vegetarian choices include ***Alki Restaurant*** and ***Green Restaurant***, which both offer main dishes for around Rs 40.

The Tavern, uphill from the Picture Palace cinema specialises in Mughlai (nonveg) and Chinese cuisine and serves up some excellent dishes from the tandoor oven. Main dishes start at Rs 70. There's often live music in the high season, but the restaurant closes down for the winter.

Kwality Restaurant in the heart of Kulri Bazaar has reasonable food but a spartan canteen atmosphere. Nonveg dishes are around Rs 50, with most vegetarian dishes under Rs 40.

Downhill from the Hotel Clark's, ***The Rice Bowl*** is a justly popular Tibetan restaurant that also rustles up Chinese and Thai dishes. The steamed mutton momos (dumplings) are excellent (Rs 22 to 28).

Nearby, ***Satkar Restaurant*** serves up good coffee and Indian vegetarian and nonveg food in a pleasant old-fashioned dining room. Most dishes cost Rs 40 to 65.

Gandhi Chowk Close to the library, ***City Point*** and ***Uphar Restaurant*** are well presented and serve good vegetarian and nonveg Indian standards.

Near the Hotel Paramount, ***Whispering Windows*** is an ageing ballroom that serves up OK Indian food at tables looking out on to the promenade. Dishes such as biryani cost around Rs 65. During the high season there's ballroom dancing to recorded music on the tiled floor.

Swiss Cafe next to the Hotel Paramount has Chinese and Indian food, as well as a selection of muffins and Danish pastries during the high season.

If you book ahead, you can take a meal at the atmospheric ***Savoy Hotel***, but only during the high season. You may be rewarded with a glimpse of the ghost of Lady Gore Ormsby (who probably expired at the sight of the bill).

Shopping

There are several places in town selling Raj-era antiques and handicrafts, including *pashmina* (goat wool) shawls and assorted knick-knacks from Kashmir and Tibet. Nirankari Cottage Industries, at the library end of The Mall, and Jewellers-Astrologer near the Hotel Garhwal Terrace are worth browsing.

Getting There & Away

Bus Numerous buses leave from the Mussoorie bus stand (next to the train station) in Dehra Dun for Mussoorie (Rs 22, 1½ hours) between 6.30 am and 8.30 pm. These go either to the Library bus stand (Gandhi Chowk) or Masonic Lodge bus stand (Kulri Bazaar).

Buses to Dehra Dun (Rs 22) leave half-hourly to hourly from the Library and Masonic Lodge bus stands. For Delhi, there's a deluxe overnight service (Rs 172) from the library at 8.30 pm, and an ordinary express overnight service (Rs 139) from the Masonic Lodge stand at 8.30 pm.

Several daily buses to Hanuman Chatti (for Yamunotri; Rs 90, seven hours) originate in Dehra Dun and collect passengers in Mussoorie mid-morning at the Library bus stand. For Uttarkashi and Gangotri, it's possible to take a bus to Tehri and change (the Tehri bus stand is a steep 45-minute walk towards Landour Bazaar), but you're probably better off going back down to Dehra Dun.

Train The Northern Railway booking agency (☎ 632846), at the Kulri Bazaar end of The Mall, has a small quota of tickets out of Dehra Dun, but need 24 hours notice for bookings. It's open 8 to 11 am and noon to 5 pm Monday to Saturday and 8 am to 2 pm Sunday.

Taxi There are taxi stands at both bus stands offering identical rates to popular destinations in Garhwal and Kumaon. Destinations include Sister's Bazaar (Rs 150 one way); Dehra Dun (Rs 350); Rishikesh (Rs 700); Haridwar (Rs 800); Uttarkashi, for Gangotri (Rs 1700); and Hanuman Chatti (Rs 3000).

Getting Around

The Mall is closed to traffic for most of the year, so to traverse the 2km between Kulri Bazaar and the Library area, you can either walk, rent a pony (officially Rs 20 per kilometre), or take a cycle-rickshaw. Expect to pay about Rs 20 to 25 from the ropeway to Gandhi Chowk.

AROUND MUSSOORIE

Har-ki-Dun Valley Trek

Far above Mussoorie at an altitude of 3566m is the wonderfully remote Har-ki-Dun, a high altitude meadow crisscrossed by glacial streams and surrounded by pristine forests and snowy peaks. The area is preserved as Govind Wildlife Sanctuary and National Park and foreigners are now charged Rs 350 to enter the region for up to three days (Rs 175 for subsequent days).

The trail begins at Sankri (Saur), accessible by a single early morning bus from Dehra Dun, where there's a ***GMVN Tourist Rest House*** with dorms for Rs 120 and doubles for Rs 360. Local share-jeeps run up to Taluka (12km) from where you follow a tributary of the Tons River for 12km through forests to Osla. Another ***GMVN Tourist Rest House*** here has dorms for Rs 120 and doubles for Rs 300. It's a further 14km to Har-ki-Dun where you can camp and spend a day or two exploring the Swargarohini Range. Possible extensions include the Jaundhar Glacier (8km) and the remote Ruinsara Tal (26km), reached via the trail that branches off between Har-ki-Dun and Osla.

Other Attractions

The most popular sight around Mussoorie is **Kempty Falls**, 15km north-west, which can be quite impressive but draws huge crowds. The same crowds normally continue to nearby **Mist Lake** where you can hire pedal boats, and **Mussoorie Lake** which offers similar facilities.

More peaceful is the trip up to **Dhanoltri**, a lovely picnic spot set among deodar forests 25.5km north-east of Mussoorie. There are great Himalayan views from the ridge. About 10km farther north is **Surkunda Devi temple**, at a height of 3030m. The temple is a 2km hike from the road, and affords panoramic views of the Himalaya.

Altogether more interesting and remote is **Lakhmandal**, 75km beyond Kempty Falls. This ancient temple complex features interesting statues and a stone sikhara-style temple dedicated, like most mountain shrines, to Lord Shiva. A return trip by taxi from Mussoorie costs Rs 1500, or there are occasional buses from the Mussoorie bus stand in Dehra Dun.

HARIDWAR

☎ 0133 • pop 230,000

Propitiously located at the point where the Ganges emerges from the Himalaya to begin its slow progress across the plains, Haridwar is one of the most sacred cities in India for Hindus. Pilgrims flock here all year to ceremonially bathe in the River Ganges, which at this point is clean and very cold. The most interesting part of town is Har-ki-Pairi, the town's main bathing ghat, which is surrounded by a maze of shops selling religious paraphernalia. At dusk, the river comes alive with flickering flames as floating offerings are released onto the Ganges.

Haridwar means Gateway to the Gods and is much more important than nearby Rishikesh within the spiritual architecture of India. There are numerous ashrams here where yoga study is possible, but these are mainly geared to locals and most only accept long-stays and have extremely strict rules regarding silence and prayer.

Orientation

Haridwar's main street is Railway Rd which runs parallel to the Ganges Canal and changes its name to Upper Rd north of the turn off to the Laltarao Bridge toward Rishikesh. At the south-west end of Railway Rd are the tourist office, bus and train

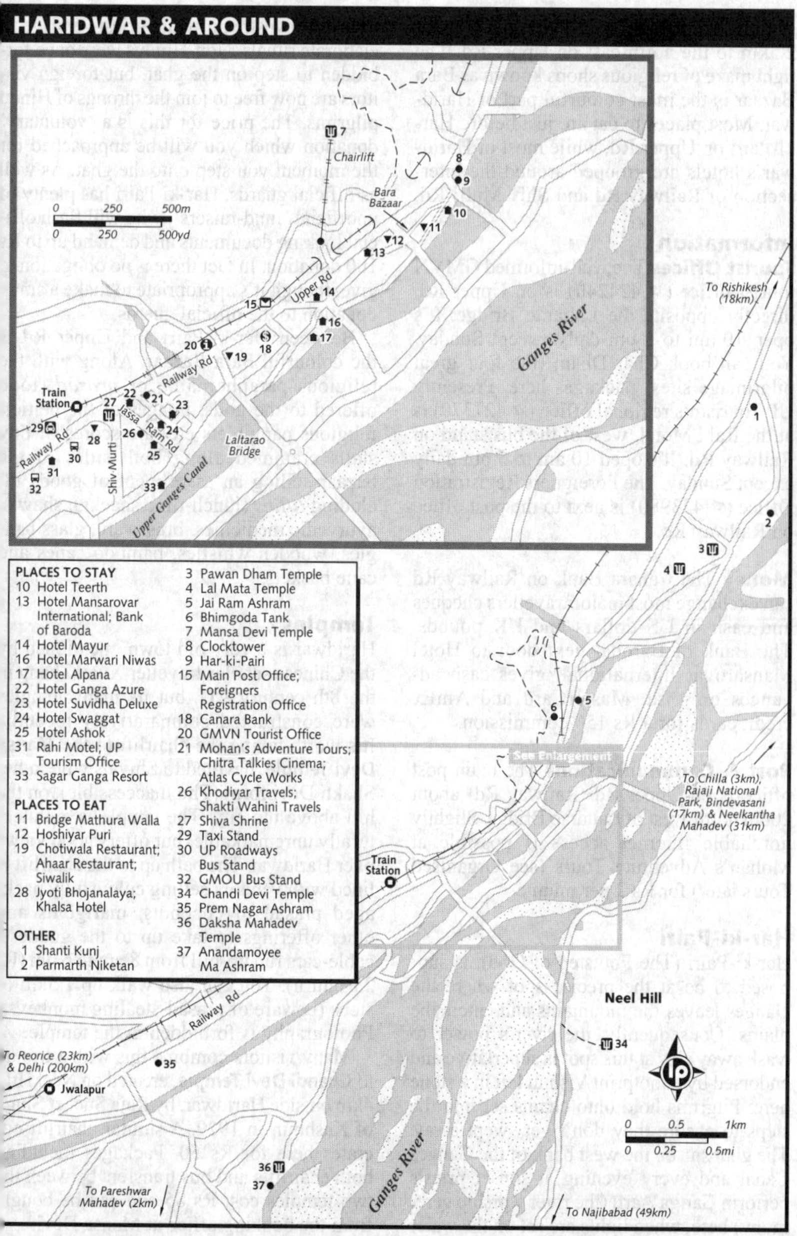

HARIDWAR & AROUND

PLACES TO STAY
10 Hotel Teerth
13 Hotel Mansarovar International; Bank of Baroda
14 Hotel Mayur
16 Hotel Marwari Niwas
17 Hotel Alpana
22 Hotel Ganga Azure
23 Hotel Suvidha Deluxe
24 Hotel Swaggat
25 Hotel Ashok
31 Rahi Motel; UP Tourism Office
33 Sagar Ganga Resort

PLACES TO EAT
11 Bridge Mathura Walla
12 Hoshiyar Puri
19 Chotiwala Restaurant; Ahaar Restaurant; Siwalik
28 Jyoti Bhojanalaya; Khalsa Hotel

OTHER
1 Shanti Kunj
2 Parmarth Niketan
3 Pawan Dham Temple
4 Lal Mata Temple
5 Jai Ram Ashram
6 Bhimgoda Tank
7 Mansa Devi Temple
8 Clocktower
9 Har-ki-Pairi
15 Main Post Office; Foreigners Registration Office
18 Canara Bank
20 GMVN Tourist Office
21 Mohan's Adventure Tours; Chitra Talkies Cinema; Atlas Cycle Works
26 Khodiyar Travels; Shakti Wahini Travels
27 Shiva Shrine
29 Taxi Stand
30 UP Roadways Bus Stand
32 GMOU Bus Stand
34 Chandi Devi Temple
35 Prem Nagar Ashram
36 Daksha Mahadev Temple
37 Anandamoyee Ma Ashram

stations, while the Har-ki-Pairi ghat is about 2.5km to the north-east on Upper Rd. The tight maze of religious shops known as Bara Bazaar is the most colourful part of Haridwar. Most places to eat are just before Har-ki-Pairi on Upper Rd, while most of Haridwar's hotels are grouped around the intersection of Railway Rd and Shiv Mutri Rd.

Information

Tourist Offices The well-informed GMVN tourist office (☎ 424240) is on Upper Rd, directly opposite the Laltarao Bridge. It's open 10 am to 5 pm daily except Sunday. You can book Char Dham (the four great pilgrimage sites) packages here. Presently UP Tourism's regional office (☎ 427370) is at the Rahi Motel, west of the bus stand on Railway Rd. It's open 10 am to 5 pm daily except Sunday. The Foreigners Registration Office (☎ 423980) is next to the post office on Railway Rd.

Money The Canara Bank on Railway Rd can exchange most major travellers cheques and cash in US dollars and UK pounds. The Bank of Baroda, next door to Hotel Mansarovar International, gives cash advances on Visa, MasterCard and AmEx credit cards for a Rs 150 commission.

Post & Communications The main post office is on Upper Rd (Railway Rd) about 200m north-west of Laltarao Bridge. Slightly unreliable Internet access is possible at Mohan's Adventure Tours (see Organised Tours later) for Rs 2 per minute.

Har-ki-Pairi

Har-ki-Pairi (The Footstep of God), is supposed to be at the precise spot where the Ganges leaves the mountains and enters the plains. Consequently, the river's power to wash away sins at this spot is superlative and endorsed by a footprint Vishnu left in a stone here. Pilgrims hold onto chains set into the steps to ensure they don't get swept away. The ghat sits on the west bank of the Ganges Canal and every evening at sunset priests perform **Ganga Aarti** (the river worship ceremony) here, when lights are set on the water to drift downstream while priests engage in elaborate rituals. Non-Hindus were once forbidden to step on the ghat, but foreign visitors are now free to join the throngs of Hindu pilgrims. The price for this is a 'voluntary' donation which you will be approached for the moment you step onto the ghat. As well as official guards, Har-ki-Pairi has plenty of unofficial 'fund-raisers', who will flash official looking documents and demand up to Rs 100 donation. In fact there is no obligation to give, though it's appropriate to make a small donation to the official guards.

Between Har-ki-Pairi and Upper Rd is the colourful **Bara Bazaar**. Along with the religious paraphernalia, or *prasad* (food offered to the gods, images of the deities, religious pamphlets etc) are scores of tiny stalls crammed along both sides of the bazaar selling an assortment of goods including *tiffins* (lunch-time snacks), shawls, ayurvedic medicines, brassware, glass bangles, wooden whistles, bamboo canes and cane baskets.

Temples

Haridwar is a very old town, mentioned by the Chinese scholar/traveller Xuan Zhang in the 8th century AD, but its many temples were constructed comparatively recently. It's worth taking the chairlift to the **Mansa Devi Temple**, devoted to Shiva's wife in her Shakti Devi form (The Inaccessible), on the hill above the city. The temple is architecturally unremarkable, but offers good views over Haridwar. The path up to the chairlift is lined with vendors selling colourfully packaged prasad of coconuts, marigolds and other offerings to take up to the goddess. cable-cars run up-hill from 8 am to 6 pm (Rs 25 return). You can also walk up 1.5km of steps (beware of prasad-stealing monkeys). Photography is forbidden in the temple.

Many visitors combine this with a trip up to **Chandi Devi Temple**, erected on Neel Hill 4km outside Haridwar, by Raja Suchet Singh of Kashmir, in 1929. A similar chairlift operates here for Rs 50. Packages including both chairlifts and bus transfers between the two temples cost Rs 85 and can be bought from the booking office at Mansa Devi.

About 4km south of Haridwar is the brand new **Pareshwar Mahadev Temple**. The temple, which was inaugurated by the late former president of India, Gyani Zail Singh, houses a sacred lingam reputedly made of mercury.

The **Daksha Mahadev Temple** (also known as Shri Dakheswar) is 2km from the centre on the riverbank at Khankhal. Daksha, father of Shiva's first wife Sati, refused to invite Shiva to a family sacrifice on this spot and the enraged Sati immolated herself in protest. Opposite this temple is the **Anandamoyee Ma Ashram** which, since the death of this female Bengali guru, has become an enormous mausoleum. Indira Gandhi was a regular visitor.

Other temples and buildings of note include the **Bhimgoda Tank**, about 1km to the north of Har-ki-Pairi. The tank is said to have been formed by a blow from Bhima's knee (Bhima is the brother of Hanuman). About 150m farther north, on the Rishikesh road, is the **Jai Ram Ashram**, which features pristine white sculptures of the gods and demons battling for the waters of humanity and electronic displays from the Hindu epics. Off the main road and up a track about 1km farther north is the **Pawan Dham Temple**, which is famed for its fantastic glass and mirrorwork and its elaborately garbed idols.

About 1km further along this road, on the left, is the extraordinary **Lal Mata Temple**, a perfect replica of the Vaishno Devi Temple in Kashmir, right down to the artificial hill on which the replica is situated. Also here is a perpetually frozen ice lingam, a replica of that in the Amarnath Cave in Kashmir. Tempos run north from the barrier on Upper Rd, just beyond the Har-ki-Pairi.

Yoga Courses

Haridwar is a major centre for yoga study with dozens of ashrams, but most offer extremely formal tuition, with very strict rules regarding discipline, silence and attendance at prayer. Most travellers prefer to take the softer options available in Rishikesh, which place less emphasis on austerity. Yoga centres and ashrams in Haridwar include:

Maha Prabhu Yoga & Natural Medicine Centre (☎ 425602) Kankhal
Parmarth Niketan (☎ 427099) Swami Shukdevanand Marg
Prem Naga Ashram (☎ 426345) Jwalapur Haridwar Rd
Shanti Kunj (☎ 426403) north of Har-ki-Pairi
Yogadham (☎ 424961) Arya Nagar

Organised Tours

The GMVN offers day tours, which sprint around Mussoorie, Kempty Falls, Sahastradhara and Rishikesh for Rs 200. The GMVN is also the principal agent for Char Dham tours, which take in the four main pilgrimage sites of Yamunotri, Gangotri, Kedarnath and Badrinath, but are generally crowded with noisy Indian pilgrim groups and are not the best way to appreciate the scenery or temples. To cover all four temples takes up to eleven days, with accommodation provided in GMVN tourist bungalows, and costs Rs 5916. Tours run from May to November.

Every travel agent in town will also try to book you on a Char Dham trip, with packages covering one, two, three or four of the temples by coach or pricey share-jeeps. Most also offer day trips to Rishikesh (Rs 60) and Dehra Dun and Mussoorie (Rs 110) and expensive package tours to Rajaji National Park. On Jassa Ram Rd, Shakti Wahini Travels (☎ 427002) and Khodiyar Travels (☎ 423560) are both long-established outfits. The undisputed Rajaji expert is Mohan's Adventure Tours (☎ 420910), by the Chitra Talkies cinema on Railway Rd, offers day tours led by veteran guide Sanjeev Metha for Rs 1600 per day, including all fees.

Special Events

Every twelve years Haridwar is the site of the **Kumbh Mela** festival. Believed to be the world's largest religious gathering, the mela attracts millions of pilgrims, including ascetics from Hinduism's remote monastic orders. The mela takes place every three years, consecutively at Allahabad, Nasik, Ujjain and Haridwar, and is next due to take place in Haridwar in 2010. Allahabad was the setting for the 2001 Kumbh Mela (see the boxed text 'Maha Kumbh Mela' earlier in this chapter).

The **Ardh Khumb** (next due in 2004) also attracts huge numbers of pilgrims. During interval years, pilgrims usually still gather from January to February for **Magh Mela**.

Places to Stay

Seasonal rates apply in Haridwar, which means that most places are fairly expensive from May to July, and a veritable bargain from August to April. January and February also see large numbers of pilgrims. Rates given are for the high season and exclude the 10% luxury tax; you can expect these rates to drop by 30% to 50% at other times.

Hotel Mayur *(☎ 427586, Upper Rd)*, near the chairlift, has basic singles/doubles for Rs 170/220 in the low season, and Rs 300/500 in the high season (May to July). Rooms have private bathrooms, fans and geysers; those at the front are larger.

Hotel Marwari Niwas *(☎ 427759, Subzi Mandi)* is down the lane beside the Mayur. Air-cooled doubles are Rs 250, and rooms with air-con are Rs 450. Rooms are set around a well, and all have running hot water and satellite TV. Room service is available.

Hotel Mansarovar International *(☎ 426 501, Upper Rd)*, towards Har-ki-Pairi, is relatively new. The rooms are a little plain for the money at Rs 500/600 (Rs 800/900 with air-con). There's a good restaurant, the Swagat, and major credit cards are accepted.

Hotel Teerth *(☎ 425311)*, in the heart of Bara Bazaar, is set right on the river, with great views over Har-ki-Pairi. Doubles with fan/air-con cost Rs 900/1200. All rooms have balconies facing the river, the staff are friendly and helpful and there's a restaurant.

Just south in the Baba Bazaar, the swish ***Hotel Alpana*** *(☎ 4245667)* has central air-con and offers immaculate doubles with TV and bathroom starting at Rs 1100 (Rs 500 in the low season).

There is a large cluster of fairly cheap hotels close to the train and bus stations in the area known as Shiv Mutri (near the roundabout with the Shiva shrine). Standards are variable in these places and all are a little pricey in summer but good value in winter.

Hotel Ashok *(☎ 426469, Jassa Ram Rd)* is a long-established place in the alley beside the Chitra Cinema. Budget singles with colc shower cost Rs 150/110 in the high/low season, while doubles with hot shower cos Rs 350/220 (Rs 475/250 with TV).

On the same road, the ***Hotel Swagga*** *(☎ 421581, fax 426553, Jassa Ram Rd)* is one of the better Shiv Mutri hotels. Clea modern doubles with TV and private bath room start at Rs 495/995 with fan/air-con In winter, the starting price for rooms drops to a very reasonable Rs 200.

Around the corner, ***Hotel Suvidha Delux*** *(☎ 427023, fax 629033)* has higher standards than some of its more expensive neighbours. Good singles/doubles with hot wate and TV start at Rs 500/600 with fan and R 800/950 with air-con.

Back on Railway Rd, ***Ganga Azur*** *(☎ 420938)* is modern and well maintained with fan-cooled rooms for Rs 500 (bucke hot water) and a range of air-con room starting at Rs 1000 with carpet, TV and ho water. There's also an air-con restaurant.

Rahi Motel *(☎ 426430)* is handy for th bus stand and train station, but in a quiet location, and also houses the UP Tourism of fice. Air-cooled doubles are Rs 600 (Rs 90 with air-con) and you may be able to swin a Rs 100 discount for a single. Beds in th small dorms cost Rs 50. All rooms hav colour TV and there's a restaurant.

Sagar Ganga Resort *(☎ 422115)* is lovely lodge in the style of Indo–Art Decc which once belonged to the King of Nepal right on the river. Doubles cost Rs 750, an an enormous deluxe double costs Rs 125 There's a lovely colonial-style dining roor overlooking the Ganges.

Places to Eat

As a holy pilgrimage place, alcohol an meat are strictly prohibited and you won find any of either in Haridwar. There is, nc surprisingly, a good selection of vegetaria restaurants.

On Upper Rd, near Har-ki-Pairi, ***Hoshyar Puri*** has been serving thalis for over 5 years, and they're still good value. The are plenty of paneer options and a goo choice of special thali, all with tasty dha and *kheer* (rice pud).

Right by the ghats are numerous fast-food *puri houses* offering meals of puri with various vegetarian curries for Rs 10 or less.

Bridge Mathura Walla sweet shop in the heart of the Bara Bazaar has a range of sticky temptations for under Rs 10 including *ras malai* (a milk-based sweet served in a banana leaf plate, floating in sugar syrup and sprinkled with pistachio nuts).

There are a few places opposite the GMVN tourist office including ***Ahaar Restaurant***, with good Punjabi dishes and a popular ice cream parlour; ***Chotiwala***, a long-established South Indian place with good dosas; and ***Siwalik***, a multicuisine restaurant specialising in Gujarati dishes, which start at Rs 65.

There are some superior *bhojanayalas* (vegetarian dhabas) across from the train station. Best are ***Jyoti Bhojanalaya*** and ***Khalsa Hotel*** which offer vegetarian standards such as *aloo gobi* (cauliflower and potato curry) and filling vegetarian thalis for Rs 20 to 40.

Getting There & Away

Bus The UP Roadways bus stand (☎ 427 037) is at the south-western end of Railway Rd. Buses leave every 30 minutes for Rishikesh (Rs 14, one hour) and Dehra Dun (Rs 26, 1½ to two hours). For Mussoorie, you'll need to change at Dehra Dun. There are ordinary bus services every 30 minutes up to 1 pm to Delhi (Rs 95, eight hours), and services to Agra (Rs 149, 12 hours) every two hours or so from 5.40 am to 9 pm.

For Kumaon, there are several morning buses to Nainital (Rs 135, seven hours) between 5.30 and 9.30 am, and night buses at .30 and 9.30 pm. Buses to Almora (Rs 171, 0 hours) leave at 5, 6.30 and 7.30 am and pm and to Ranikhet (Rs 150, nine hours) t 6.30 am and 4.30 pm.

Himachal Road Transport Company buses to Shimla (Rs 179, 14 hours) leave at 6 and 8.30 am and 5, 7, 8.30 and 10 pm. For Dharamsala (Rs 227, 15 hours), a single bus leaves at 2.30 pm. You can book seats at the blue booth across from the UP Roadways inquiry booth. Haryana Roadways has buses to Chandigarh (Rs 95, 10 hours), while Rajasthan State Road Transport has regular buses to Jaipur (Rs 207, 12 hours); the superdeluxe service (Rs 368) leaves at 5 pm.

Heading towards the Char Dham pilgrimage sites, there are UP Roadways buses to Uttarkashi (Rs 118, 10 hours) at 3.30, 6.20, 8.30 and 9.30 am. From April to October, direct buses to Hanuman Chatti (for Yamunotri), Gangotri, Badrinath and Kedarnath are run by the Garhwal Motor Owners' Union (GMOU; ☎ 426886) near the Rahi Motel. Buses to Badrinath (Rs 200, 15 hours) via Joshimath leave every few hours from 3.30 am to 2.30 pm; buses to Kedarnath (Rs 150, 10 hours) leave at 5, 5.30 and 8.30 am and 12.30 pm; buses to Hanuman Chatti (Rs 190, 10 hours) leave at 3 and 4.30 am and a lone bus leaves for Gangotri (Rs 175, eight hours) at 5 am.

GMOU also has buses to Chilla (for Rajaji National Park) every few hours between 4 am and 1.30 pm (Rs 5). The last return trip leaves Chilla at 5.30 pm.

Train See Getting There & Away under Dehra Dun earlier for details of trains between Haridwar and Delhi. Haridwar also has express trains to Kolkata (Rs 363/1592, sleeper/two-tier, 35 hours), Mumbai (Rs 380/1673, 40 hours), Varanasi (Rs 262/1149, 20 hours) and Lucknow (Rs 194/821, 11 hours). The most convenient train for Varanasi is the 6.15 pm *Varanasi Express*, which arrives at 6.15 pm the next day.

Taxi & Tempo The somewhat pricey Haridwar Taxi Union (☎ 427338), open 24 hours, is directly opposite the bus stand. Posted rates are as follows:

Chilla (for Rajaji National Park)	Rs 410
Dehra Dun	Rs 510
Delhi	Rs 1510
Gangotri	Rs 2810
Hanuman Chatti (for Yamunotri)	Rs 2810
Mussoorie	Rs 860
Nainital	Rs 2510
Rishikesh	Rs 330
Uttarkashi	Rs 1510

Shared Ambassador taxis to Delhi depart from near the train station and charge Rs 150 per seat.

Shared tempos run between Haridwar and Rishikesh all day, charging Rs 15 for the hour-long bumpy ride. Drivers solicit for business near Laltarao Bridge.

Getting Around

You can get from the train station or UP Roadways bus stand to Har-ki-Pairi by cycle-rickshaw for Rs 15. Don't be tricked into taking an autorickshaw as motor vehicles are prohibited from Upper Rd.

Low-tech rattle-you-senseless bicycles can be hired from Atlas Cycle Works, Railway Rd for an absurdly cheap Rs 1.50 per hour.

RAJAJI NATIONAL PARK

This beautiful park, covering 820 sq km in the forested foothills east of Haridwar, is best known for its wild elephants, numbering around 445 in all. Unfortunately, their future is in question since human competition for land has severed their traditional migration route, which once stretched from here to Corbett National Park. Plans for a 'migration corridor' got as far as the construction of large 'elephant-ducts' under the Chilla-Rishikesh road, but have since floundered in bureaucracy. Elephants are also threatened by the presence of Gujar Adivasis (people) in the reserve. This semi-nomadic tribal group keep vast herds of water buffalo and strip the trees for fodder to feed their animals.

As well as elephants, the park contains some rarely seen tigers and leopards, chital (spotted deer), sambar (India's largest species of deer), wild boars, sloth bears, barking deer, porcupines, jungle fowls, hornbills and pythons. However, most visitors report seeing little wildlife of any kind.

About a kilometre beyond the entry gate is a *machaan* (hide), previously used by hunters, but now a vantage point from where visitors can unobtrusively view the park's inhabitants.

The (rather unattractive) village of Chilla, 13km east of Haridwar, is the only area that currently has an infrastructure in place for visitors. Elephant rides are offered in the morning and at dusk and cost Rs 100 (Rs 50 for Indians) and offer your best chance of seeing wildlife. These can be arranged at the Forest Ranger's office, close to the tourist bungalow at Chilla, where you also pay your entry fee.

Information

The park is open from mid-November to mid-June and the entry fee is Rs 350 for up to three days (Rs 30 for Indians), and Rs 175 for each additional day (Rs 20). Entry into the park is not permitted between sunset and sunrise. Fees are Rs 50 for a camera, and a staggering Rs 2500 for a video camera!

Places to Stay

The ***Tourist Bungalow*** *(☎ 01832-66697)* at Chilla is run by the GMVN. Fan-cooled doubles range from Rs 590 to 720, while air-con rooms are Rs 1040. Dorms cost Rs 130 and 'jungle huts' Rs 650.

Nine ***Forest Rest Houses*** are dotted around the park. Double rates at Beribara, Ranipur, Kansrao, Kunnao, Phandowala, Satyanarain and Asarodi are all Rs 225; at Motichur and Chilla, rates are Rs 450. Except at Chilla, you'll need to bring your own food. For bookings contact the Director (☎ 621669), Rajaji National Park office, 5/1 Ansari Marg, Dehra Dun.

Getting There & Away

Buses to Chilla (Rs 5) leave the GMOU in Haridwar every few hours from 4 am to 1.30 pm. The last return trip leaves Chilla at 5.30 pm. Taxis charge Rs 410 return (although ensure that the driver knows how much time you plan to spend at the park).

To walk to Chilla from Haridwar, cross the Laltarao Bridge and walk to the roundabout, then turn left onto the Rishikesh road. Turn right before the cable bridge over the Ganges and then left on the far side of the dam, where a short walk will bring you to a small artificial lake where migratory birds, including Siberian cranes, and elephants are often seen (although you should be wary of wild elephants at dusk). The road flanking the lake leads to Chilla 5km farther on.

AROUND RAJAJI NATIONAL PARK

Situated 14km north-east of Chilla is the small village of **Bindevasani**, a popular picnic spot in the hills above the park. There are good views from the Durga temple above the village, which look out over the sangam of the Bindedhara and Nildhara Rivers. Local buses come here from Haridwar or Chilla.

About 14km north of Bindevasani is **Neelkantha Mahadev**, with its gaudy South Indian–style temple dedicated to Shiva. From Nilkantha, it is possible to continue to **Lakshman Jhula** (see under Rishikesh following), the suspension bridge that traverses the Ganges to the north-east of Rishikesh. The trail follows the original pilgrim trail, which affords magnificent forest scenery – be wary of wild elephants, especially at dusk.

RISHIKESH

☎ 0135 • pop 82,000

In spite of its claim to being the 'Yoga Capital of the World', Rishikesh is a quieter and more easy-going place than Haridwar. The setting on the banks of the Ganges surrounded by hills on three sides, is perfectly conducive to meditation, and the main areas for yoga study are far from the noisy centre of town. The holy Ganges is almost clear here (unlike at Varanasi!) and many travellers join the sadhus for a dip in the morning. In the evening, the wind blows down the valley from the Himalaya, setting temple bells ringing and adding to the contemplative atmosphere.

Although it's less authentic than Haridwar, Rishikesh is still a great place to stay and study yoga, meditation and other aspects of Hinduism, or just to unwind from the rigours of travel. The yoga movement really took off here in the 1960s when the Beatles came here to find their guru, the Maharishi Mahesh Yogi. For Indian pilgrims, Rishikesh is most important as the starting point for the Char Dham pilgrimage to Yamunotri, Gangotri, Kedarnath and Badrinath.

Orientation

The downtown area of Rishikesh is on the west bank of the Ganges, with a busy bazaar, banks and the post office and several mid-range hotels. The main and yatra bus stands are here, but most people stay further north in the much more attractive pilgrim centres on the east bank of the Ganges River.

Haridwar Rd, later Lakshman Jhula Rd, runs north from the centre, passing several temples and the GMVN tourist office and trekking centre. Just beyond is Shivanand Jhula, the suspension bridge that crosses the Ganges to Swarg Ashram, the bigger of Rishikesh's two religious communities. This side of the river is blissfully free from traffic and abounds with yoga ashrams, cheap guesthouses and travellers cafes. Farther north on the same side of the river, accessible by the Lakshman Jhula, is the smaller settlement of Lakshman Jhula, with more temples, guesthouses and ashrams.

Information

Tourist Offices For now, you can find some local information at the UP tourist office (☎ 430209) on Train Station Rd. It is open 10 am to 5 pm daily except Sunday. The helpful GMVN tourist office (☎ 430-799, fax 430372) is on Lakshman Jhula Rd in the area known as Muni-ki-Reti. It's open 10 am to 5 pm daily except Sunday. Next door is the GMVN Trekking & Mountaineering division (☎ 431793, fax 430372). For Char Dham inquires call ☎ 431783.

Money The State Bank of India is next to Inderlok Hotel on Ghat Rd and exchanges Thomas Cook, Citicorp and AmEx travellers cheques in US dollars, UK pounds, Deutschemarks, Yen and French Francs. The Bank of Baroda and Indian Overseas Bank, both on Dehra Dun Rd towards the Yatra bus stand, can exchange most travellers cheques in US dollars or UK pounds. These days, numerous jewellers in Swarg Ashram and Lakshman Jhula can exchange cash, travellers cheques and even give cash advances on credit cards. Jaipur Gems in Lakshman Jhula is trustworthy and offers decent rates.

Post & Communications The post office is near the Triveni Ghat on Ghat Rd. For Internet access, try Blue Hills Travels or the

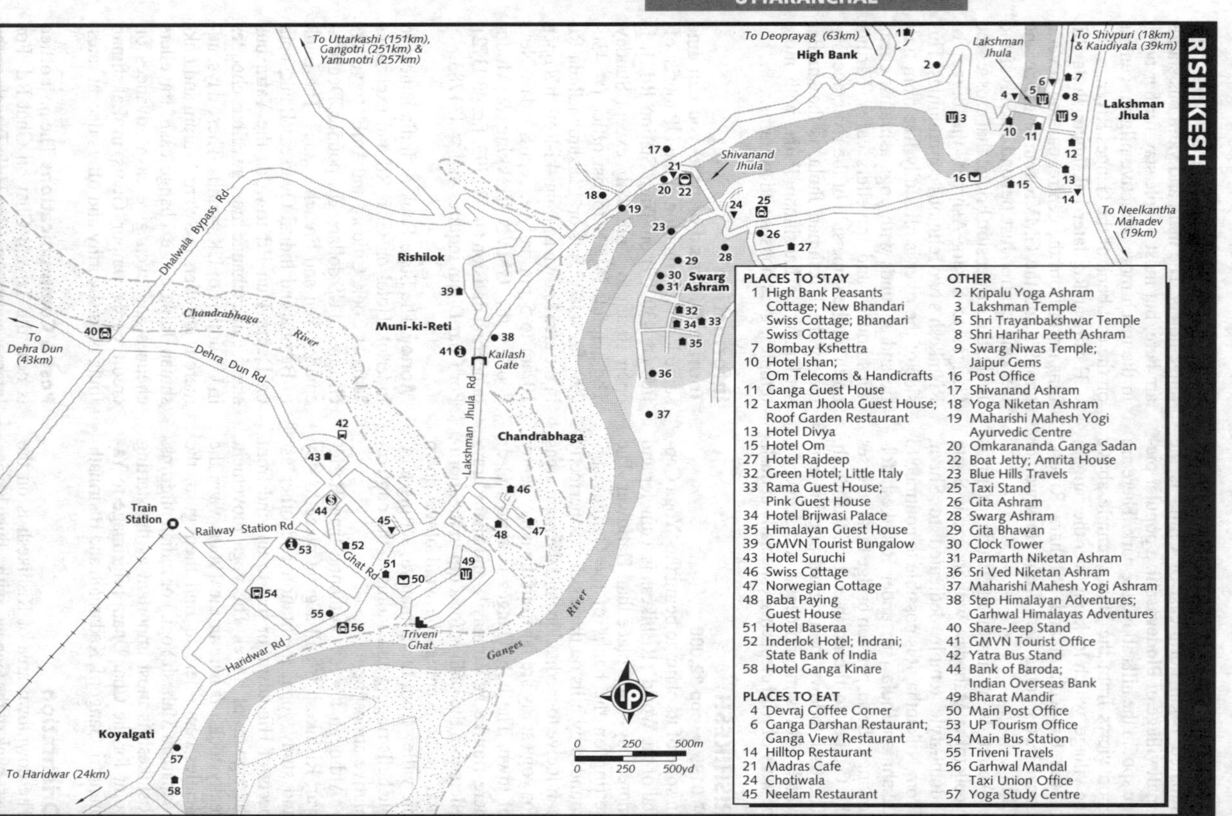
RISHIKESH
PLACES TO STAY
1 High Bank Peasants Cottage; New Bhandari Swiss Cottage; Bhandari Swiss Cottage
7 Bombay Kshettra
10 Hotel Ishan; Om Telecoms & Handicrafts
11 Ganga Guest House
12 Laxman Jhoola Guest House; Roof Garden Restaurant
13 Hotel Divya
15 Hotel Om
27 Hotel Rajdeep
32 Green Hotel; Little Italy
33 Rama Guest House; Pink Guest House
34 Hotel Brijwasi Palace
35 Himalayan Guest House
39 GMVN Tourist Bungalow
43 Hotel Suruchi
46 Swiss Cottage
47 Norwegian Cottage
48 Baba Paying Guest House
51 Hotel Baseraa
52 Inderlok Hotel; Indrani; State Bank of India
58 Hotel Ganga Kinare
PLACES TO EAT
4 Devraj Coffee Corner
6 Ganga Darshan Restaurant; Ganga View Restaurant
14 Hilltop Restaurant
21 Madras Cafe
24 Chotiwala
45 Neelam Restaurant
OTHER
2 Kripalu Yoga Ashram
3 Lakshman Temple
5 Shri Trayanbakshwar Temple
8 Shri Harihar Peeth Ashram
9 Swarg Niwas Temple; Jaipur Gems
16 Post Office
17 Shivanand Ashram
18 Yoga Niketan Ashram
19 Maharishi Mahesh Yogi Ayurvedic Centre
20 Omkarananda Ganga Sadan
22 Boat Jetty; Amrita House
23 Blue Hills Travels
25 Taxi Stand
26 Gita Ashram
28 Swarg Ashram
29 Gita Bhawan
30 Clock Tower
31 Parmarth Niketan Ashram
36 Sri Ved Niketan Ashram
37 Maharishi Mahesh Yogi Ashram
38 Step Himalayan Adventures; Garhwal Himalayas Adventures
40 Share-Jeep Stand
41 GMVN Tourist Office
42 Yatra Bus Stand
44 Bank of Baroda; Indian Overseas Bank
49 Bharat Mandir
50 Main Post Office
53 UP Tourism Office
54 Main Bus Station
55 Triveni Travels
56 Garhwal Mandal Taxi Union Office
57 Yoga Study Centre
To Uttarkashi (151km), Gangotri (251km) & Yamunotri (257km)
To Deoprayag (63km)
High Bank
Lakshman Jhula
To Shivpuri (18km) & Kaudiyala (39km)
Lakshman Jhula
Shivanand Jhula
To Neelkantha Mahadev (19km)
Dhalwala Bypass Rd
Rishilok
Swarg Ashram
Chandrabhaga River
Muni-ki-Reti
To Dehra Dun (43km)
Dehra Dun Rd
Kailash Gate
Lakshman Jhula Rd
Chandrabhaga
Train Station
Railway Station Rd
Ghat Rd
Haridwar Rd
Triveni Ghat
Ganges River
Koyalgati
To Haridwar (24km)
0 250 500m
0 250 500yd

Green Hotel in Swarg Ashram or Om Telecoms & Handicrafts and the Hotel Divya in Lakshman Jhula. All charge around Rs 60 per hour and short, sharp messages are the order of the day as the connections fail constantly.

Things to See

The definitive image of Rishikesh has to be the view across the **Lakshman Jhula suspension bridge**, built in 1929, which looks towards the huge 13-storey temples of **Swarg Niwas** and **Shri Trayanbakshwar** (built by the organisation of the guru Kailashanand). Both are vivid orange constructions tapering to narrow turrets, with dozens of shrines on each level to the various deities of the Hindu pantheon. Being 13-storeys high, both temples offer excellent views over the river (there isn't any particular significance to the number 13 – it just seem to be the height you build temples in Rishikesh!).

Pilgrims take Ganga water to offer at the **Neelkantha Mahadev temple** (17km), a four-hour walk from Lakshman Jhula on the east bank. Neelkanth (Blue Throat) is another name for Lord Shiva. In legend, Shiva drank the poison churned up from the sea by the gods and demons; he did this to protect the world, turning his throat this peculiar hue in the process. There are good views but it's a hot and tiring walk, so many less austere pilgrims take the bus or hire a taxi (Rs 500 return).

In downtown Rishikesh, the **Triveni Ghat** is an interesting place to be at dawn, when people make offerings of milk to the river and feed the surprisingly large fish. After sunset, priests set floating lamps on the water in the Ganga Aarti ceremony. Nearby is the **Bharat Mandir**, the oldest temple here.

Swarg Ashram is home to many vast yoga ashrams, which are worth a visit even if you aren't studying (see Meditation & Yoga Courses).

Trekking

The GMVN Trekking & Mountaineering division (see under Information earlier) is next to the tourist office and offers a variety of high- and low-altitude treks to rugged and challenging spots throughout the Garhwal Himalaya, as well as assorted Char Dham packages. You can hire tents, backpacks, sleeping bags and cooking equipment at very reasonable rates. For all-inclusive trekking packages, rates start at Rs 2200 per day (minimum three persons) with porters, guides, meals, tent or rest house accommodation and transportation to the trailheads. If you want to make your own itinerary, it's Rs 600 per day for a guide and Rs 250 to 550 for a porter. Possible summer destinations include Har-ki-Dun (nine days), Rup Kund (10 days) and the Valley of the Flowers (8 days, July and August only).

In the vicinity of the GMVN are various private operators who offer similar trekking trips and Char Dham expeditions. Reliable operators include Step Himalayan Adventures (☎ 432581, fax 431558) and Garhwal Himalayas Adventures (☎ 433478, fax 431654).

Rafting & Wildlife Safaris

Blue Hills Travels (☎ 31865) in Swarg Ashram is the most popular rafting operator with travellers; a day's rafting on the Ganges near Shivpuri, 18km from Rishikesh costs Rs 300. GMVN Rafting Resort (☎ 01378-62911) in Kaudiyala offers similar packages for Rs 350 per 'patch' (12km stretch) of the Ganges. A minimum of six people is required for trips and two patches can be rafted in a day. Lodging is available for Rs 350 to 500 a double. You can book at the GMVN tourist office. Step Himalayan Adventures and Garhwal Himalayas Adventures (see Trekking above) can also organise rafting for Rs 350 to 450, as well as wildlife safaris to nearby Rajaji National Park.

Meditation & Yoga Courses

There are many ashrams offering courses in meditation, yoga and Hindu philosophy. Some of the more reputable ashrams are included here, but ask around and you'll probably hear of others that are just as good. See the boxed text 'Yoga' for more information on the types of tuition available.

It's a pleasant 2km walk along the east bank from Lakshman Jhula to Swarg Ashram,

Yoga

The most commonly practised form of yoga is the hatha system, which uses a series of body positions, breathing exercises and movements to increase physical and mental health. The main techniques of hatha yoga are *asanas* (fixed body positions), *kriyas* (movements designed to increase circulation) and *mudras* (exercises designed to promote secretions from the major endocrine glands). The goal of hatha is to cleanse and purge all the body organs.

Also important to hatha are the breathing exercises of pranayama yoga. Physical exercises are used to relax the lungs in order to achieve higher mental states required for meditation. The peak of yoga practise involves the arousal and control of the kundalini shakti, a vital force believed to lie dormant in the conus medullaris at the base of the spine.

The classes on offer in Rishikesh usually involve basic hatha techniques and pranayama exercises. Most centres offer a choice of day-by-day tuition or long-term residential study, but many foreigners report difficulties in finding one that satisfies them. Some have extremely rigid rules, some only accept people for long-term study, and some see foreigners as the source of a quick buck. It's worth going to a few lectures at different ashrams before you commit to a course.

passing numerous private retreats in the woods. As its name suggests, Swarg Ashram is home to many vast yoga ashrams; most have private Ayurvedic pharmacies (with remedies that claim to cure everything from gout to stuttering) and murals and statues depicting scenes from the epics. The most flamboyant are Parmarth Niketan Ashram, which features a ghat topped by a sculpted arch, nearby Gita Bhawan and Swarg Ashram itself, with many religious paintings and attractive gardens.

Gita Ashram (☎ 431998) East of Swarg Ashram, this extensive place offers classes in hatha yoga at 7.30 and 9.15 am and 4 and 5.30 pm. Classes are by donation; inquire at the gatehouse for more information.

Kripalu Yoga Ashram (☎ 430599) This ashram is popular with Europeans, it is a five-minute walk uphill from Lakshman Jhula on the road to Rishikesh. There are ten-day courses (Rs 1000) in hatha yoga with daily classes at 10 am and 4 pm. Additional classes after this time cost Rs 50 per day. Accommodation at this relaxed centre costs from Rs 90/150 to 100/175 for a single/double.

Omkarananda Ganga Sadan (☎ 431473) On Lakshman Jhula Rd, close to the western end of Shivanand Jhula, this offers daily hatha yoga classes during the summer season at 7 am and 4 pm. Registration costs Rs 25, and a small fee is levied per class. Comfortable rooms are available for Rs 175 to 250, all with hot water shower. Call ahead to check the current schedule as the tutors are sometimes away on seminars etc.

Parmarth Niketan Ashram (☎ 434301) Close to the eastern end of Shivanand Jhula, this is lavishly decorated and has a private ghat with some impressive sculptures on the river bank. Daily classes in the hatha form of yoga start at 7.30 am and 3.30 pm (classes are by donation). There's also a popular ganga aarti ceremony on the riverside every evening at 5 pm.

Shivanand Ashram (☎ 430040) This was founded by Swami Shivananda and is under the auspices of the Divine Life Society. The ashram is on the west side of Lakshman Jhula Rd, opposite the Shivanand Jhula. There are lectures, discussion and meditation and yoga classes daily, with courses from three days to two months (all free). It is possible to stay at the ashram (for a limited period, by donation) but two month's notice is required; write to the Divine Life Society, PO Shivanandanagar, 249192, District Tehri, Garhwal, Uttar Pradesh.

Shri Harihar Peeth Ashram (☎ 431182) Close to the eastern end of the Lakshman Jhula suspension bridge, this peaceful old complex offers daily hatha yoga classes at 7 am and 5 pm for Rs 50 per class. People studying here can stay in simple rooms with shared bathroom for Rs 50.

Sri Ved Niketan Ashram (☎ 430279) At the southern end of Swarg Ashram, this is housed in a vast orange and turquoise edifice. On offer are two-week or one-month courses in hatha yoga, with the opportunity to study other disciplines such as raja, karma and kundalini yoga. Classes take place at 8 am, 6.30 and 9 pm daily except Sunday and cost Rs 100 per day. Accommodation is available in large but very spartan singles/doubles with hard beds for Rs 60/150 with private bathroom (bucket hot water) and

Rs 50/120 with shared bathroom. There is a common kitchen and smoking is prohibited. The ashram has very strict rules of conduct.

Yoga Niketan Ashram (☎ 430227) Close to Shivanand, this place is reached along a path leading up from Lakshman Jhula Rd. It is set in lovely gardens high above the Ganges. Classes on meditation and the pranayama form of hatha yoga are held throughout the year, although you must stay for a minimum of 15 days. The cost is Rs 225 per day, including basic accommodation. It's possible to extend tuition to advanced levels for an additional fee.

Yoga Study Centre (☎ 431196) South of Rishikesh on the Haridwar Rd, this well-regarded centre at Koyalgati runs three-week courses in the iyengar form of hatha yoga during February, April and September. Payment is by donation and accommodation can be arranged.

Organised Tours

As the principal leaping-off point for the hugely auspicious Char Dham, Rishikesh is well equipped with travel agents offering package tours to the temples. The biggest and most reliable operator is the GMVN (see Tourist Offices earlier), which has a huge range of packages covering one, two, three or all four temples. Itineraries range from four to 10 days. The full Char Dham takes 10 days and costs Rs 5800 (Rs 8645 by taxi), while just Badrinath and Kedarnath costs Rs 3300 by bus (Rs 5222 by taxi) and takes six days. Prices include shared accommodation in GMVN rest houses, but not meals. In winter, skiing packages to Auli near Joshimath can also be arranged.

Special Events

The **International Yoga Festival**, arranged by UP Tourism, is held annually in February. Yoga and meditation masters from around India converge on Rishikesh at this time and there are also events at Haridwar and other pilgrimage cities across India. Seven-day packages including meals, accommodation, transport from your hotel to venues, lectures and air-con deluxe coaches between Delhi and Rishikesh cost US$40/60 a single/double in ashram accommodation and US$60/100 in hotel accommodation. Bookings should be made at least two months in advance to the Director (☎ 0552-228349, fax 221776), UP Tourism, Chitrahar Bldg, 3 Naval Kishor Rd, Lucknow. Exact dates change from year to year.

Places to Stay

Swarg Ashram Area Centred around the huge Swarg Ashram on the east bank of the Ganges, this is the main centre for both pilgrims and travellers.

The long-running ***Green Hotel*** *(☎ 431 242)* is down a lane off the riverside path and has very clean downstairs doubles for Rs 125 (bucket hot water) and more spacious upstairs doubles with running hot water for Rs 250. The restaurant serves great pizzas.

On the alley parallel to the riverside path, ***Hotel Brijwasi Palace*** *(☎ 435181)* is a large modern place with a garden and perfectly adequate singles/doubles for Rs 100/120 with bucket hot water. There are yoga classes at 10 am and 4 pm for Rs 50.

In the same maze of alleys, the ***Himalayan Guest House*** *(☎ 435507)* is popular but fairly basic, with plain rooms for Rs 80 or Rs 120 upstairs with bathrooms. Yoga meditation sessions take place at 8 am and 4.30 pm.

Nearby, ***Rama Guest House*** and ***Pink Guest House*** have tiny spartan rooms starting at Rs 40, which is about right for what you get.

Hotel Rajdeep *(☎ 432826, fax 433109)* is north of the bridge, on the lane that leads uphill from the taxi stand. Standard rooms cost Rs 125/200 with bucket hot water, or there are better doubles with hot water for Rs 350, or Rs 925 with air-con. There's a travel desk and occasional yoga classes.

High Bank This small enclave on the west bank, high above the Ganges, has several peaceful retreats. Take the road to the left, 1km before Lakshman Jhula.

The family run ***High Bank Peasants Cottage*** *(☎ 431167)*, set in beautiful flower gardens, has a friendly communal atmosphere. Singles/doubles start at Rs 300/350 with bathroom (free bucket hot water), and the balcony has wicker chairs where you can sit and contemplate the Ganges. Discounts are offered for stays of over a week.

Also here is the well-run ***New Bhandari Swiss Cottage*** *(☎ 431322)*, with large, pleasant rooms for Rs 100 with cold shower, or Rs 150 to 250 with hot water. There's a cafe, an Internet cafe, a quiet garden for relaxing and great views from the balcony.

Similar rooms at similar prices are offered by the less atmospheric ***Bhandari Swiss Cottage*** *(☎ 432676)* opposite.

Lakshman Jhula Many long term residents now feel that Swarg Ashram is too commercial and have pulled back to this quieter settlement farther north. The best choices are all on the east bank.

Just north of the bridge, ***Bombay Kshettra*** is an atmospheric, colourful old building with rooms ranging from Rs 80 to 100, depending on the size, all with shared bathroom, and set around a pleasant courtyard.

Right beside the bridge is the ***Ganga Guest House*** *(☎ 435422)* with rather tired rooms for Rs 100 with cold shower.

The popular ***Hotel Divya*** *(☎ 434938)* is a well-run modern place uphill from the road, with simple but clean rooms for Rs 150 with a view or Rs 100 at the back. All rooms have hot-water bathroom and there's an Internet cafe and restaurant.

In the same area is the ***Laxman Jhoola Guest House*** *(☎ 435720)* which has spartan but tidy rooms with bathroom for Rs 100/150, as well as the friendly ***Roof Garden Restaurant***.

At the southern end of the village, ***Hotel Om*** *(☎ 433272)* offers a range of clean rooms with private hot water bathrooms from Rs 150 to 250.

At the other end of the bridge, ***Hotel Ishan*** *(☎ 433271)* has a range of clean rooms with bathroom for Rs 100 to 125.

Chandrabhaga There are some very basic options in this Indian neighbourhood just north of the Chandrabhaga River. Tucked away in the maze of alleys (ask for directions), the ***Swiss Cottage*** is run by a disciple of Swami Shivananda and caters to long-term yoga students. Spartan rooms are Rs 60. Nearby, the similar ***Norwegian Cottage*** also charges Rs 60.

Nearby, ***Baba Paying Guest House*** *(☎ 433339)* is a massage centre with a few simple singles/doubles for Rs 100/200. Relaxing massage costs Rs 150 for 30 minutes and tuition is available. Motorcycles can also be hired here.

Downtown Rishikesh Most of Rishikesh's mid-range options are in the noisy market area.

Inderlok Hotel *(☎ 430555, Ghat Rd)* has standard singles/doubles for Rs 600/700 and air-con rooms for Rs 900/1000, all with TV, carpets, hot water and telephone.

On the far side of Haridwar Rd, ***Hotel Baseraa*** *(☎ 430720, fax 430888, Ghat Rd)* is better than most, with neat, well-kept rooms for Rs 350/350 with fan and Rs 850/950 with air-con. All rooms have TV and hot water.

Hotel Suruchi *(☎ 432269)*, beside the Yatra bus stand, is a cheap and cheerful option. Doubles start at Rs 150 with cold shower and Rs 250 with running hot water.

GMVN Tourist Bungalow *(☎ 430373)*, north of the centre over the train tracks, is set in lovely grounds and offers rooms at Rs 140/180 with cold shower, starting at Rs 340/420 with hot shower and at Rs 620/840 with air-con. There's also a small dorm for Rs 70 per head, and a good restaurant.

The most upmarket option in Rishikesh is ***Hotel Ganga Kinare*** *(☎ 431658, fax 435 243, 16 Virbhadra Rd)*, about 2km south of the centre. It's a peaceful place with a restaurant, its own ghat and a quiet terrace where yoga and meditation classes are held. Well-appointed doubles start at Rs 1650 with all the luxuries you would expect.

Wolves in Sadhus' Clothing

Travellers should be cautious of befriending sadhus and chillum-smokers at Rishikesh and other religious centres. While many sadhus are on genuine spiritual journeys, the orange robes have been used as a disguise by fugitives from the law since medieval times. At least 10 travellers are known to have been murdered by criminals posing as sadhus since 1995.

Places to Eat

Rishikesh is a holy pilgrimage town, and is therefore strictly vegetarian.

Indrani at the Inderlok Hotel has a good range of Chinese cuisine (Cantonese and Manchurian), as well as specials such as *rajmah* – seasoned kidney beans (Rs 30).

Neelam Restaurant, run by the helpful Mr Singh, is a clean and friendly Italian-cum-Indian restaurant in a small lane just off Haridwar Rd. It's popular with Westerners looking for dishes such as macaroni (Rs 30), pizza and spaghetti, as well as Indian fare.

Madras Cafe, on the west side of Shivanand Jhula, has a good range of dosas and other South Indian treats for Rs 20 to 30. It also has decent coffee.

Down by the boat jetty, the ***Amrita House*** is another Italian-Indian place with excellent spaghetti and pizzas, made with home-made buffalo cheese. There are books to read and a great range of breakfasts.

Chotiwala, near the eastern end of Shivanand Jhula in Swarg Ashram, is worth a visit just for the gentlemen made up as the Chotiwala from the company's logo, who sit in thrones in front of the restaurant. Filling thalis range from Rs 35 to 70 and there's a good range of Kwality ice cream.

The ***Little Italy*** restaurant at the Green Hotel serves excellent pizzas and other Western dishes as well as Indian standards. Most dishes are around Rs 50.

Perched above the bridge in Lakshman Jhula, ***Devraj Coffee Corner*** has great views over the 13-storey-high temples, good coffee and a wide range of tasty baked goods and snack meals, plus a well-stocked bookshop.

Just north of the bridge on the east bank are the ***Ganga Darshan Restaurant*** and ***Ganga View Restaurant***, which offer similar menus of Indian and Chinese standards and thalis for around Rs 30.

Up on the hill above Lakshman Jhula is the more upmarket ***Hilltop Restaurant*** with a fine range of Chinese, Indian, Tibetan and Italian dishes ranging from Rs 35 to 60.

Shopping

Rishikesh is a good place to pick up a *rudraksh mala*, the strings of beads used in puja offerings made from the nuts of the rudraksh tree. Prices start at around Rs 100, with beads of the smaller nuts commanding higher prices.

Most ashrams boast their own Ayurvedic pharmacies, which sell various cures and restoratives made from herbs collected from the Himalaya. The Maharishi Mahesh Yogi Ayurvedic Centre, on Lakshman Jhula Rd is well-regarded.

Getting There & Away

Bus From the main bus station (☎ 430066), just off Haridwar Rd at the west end of town, there are buses to Haridwar (Rs 14, one hour) every 30 minutes from 4.30 am to 10.30 pm, continuing on to Delhi (Rs 112, seven hours). There are also half-hourly buses to Dehra Dun (Rs 19, 1½ hours) between 5.30 am and 7.30 pm. There's one bus at 8.15 am to Ramnagar (Rs 99, seven hours) which continues to Nainital (Rs 135, 11 hours) in Uttaranchal. Both Dehra Dun and Haridwar have connections to Shimla and Dharamsala.

Buses for the Char Dham roadheads are run by the GMOU (☎ 430076) and Tehri-Garhwal Motor Owners Union (TGMOU; ☎ 430344) and leave from the Yatra bus stand, behind Dehra Dun Rd. Schedules are fairly informal, but most buses leave early in the morning, between 3 and 7 am. There are several daily buses to Uttarkashi (Rs 92, seven hours), Kedarnath (Rs 127, 12 hours), Badrinath (Rs 152, 10 hours) and Joshimath (Rs 142, eight hours), and one or two buses to Gangotri (Rs 155, 10 hours) and Hanuman Chatti (Rs 159, eight hours). Outside of the pilgrimage season (April to October) buses only run to Joshimath and Uttarkashi.

Train Bookings can be made at the train station (☎ 434167) from 8 am to 6 pm daily (until 2 pm Sunday). The station has a small allocation of seats for Haridwar. There are trains to Haridwar (Rs 5, one hour) at 6.40 and 7.45 am and 2.20, 3.15 and 6.35 pm. The 6.40 am service continues to Delhi (Rs 146 in sleeper class) arriving at 5.20 pm. The 6.35 pm train connects with the *Mussoorie Express* for Delhi.

Local Transport The main office for the Garhwal Mandal Taxi Union (☎ 430413) is on Haridwar Rd, just over Ghat Rd. Official rates for the Char Dham are Rs 9500, or for Badrinath and Kedarnath only, Rs 5500.

The following are official low-season reserve taxi rates; expect to pay 20% to 50% more during summer:

Dehra Dun	Rs 450
Delhi	Rs 1500
Haridwar	Rs 350
Mussoorie	Rs 700
Ramnagar (for Corbett National Park)	Rs 1800
Ranikhet	Rs 2200
Uttarkashi (for Gangotri)	Rs 1000

You can flag down share-jeeps for Dehra Dun anywhere along the Dehra Dun Rd. The cost to Dehra Dun is Rs 20. You may be able to get a share-taxi to Haridwar from the main bus stand (Rs 20). An alternative (and less comfortable) proposition is to pick up a shared tempo anywhere along the Haridwar Rd (Rs 15).

Share-jeeps to Uttarkashi (Rs 120, five hours) and Joshimath (Rs 200, eight hours) leave from the corner of Dehra Dun Rd and Dhalwala Bypass Rd. There's no timetable as such – share-jeeps leave when full (or to be more accurate, when overloaded) between 8 am and 2 pm.

Getting Around

Tempos run from Ghat Rd junction up to Shivanand Jhula (Rs 4) and Lakshman Jhula (Rs 6; but may try to give you a 'specials trip' for Rs 40). Taxis charge Rs 40/60 for the same trips.

Shivanand Jhula is a pedestrian-only bridge, so you'll have to lump your backpack across if you're planning to stay on the east side of the Ganges in the Swarg Ashram area. On the east bank of the river, a seat in a share-jeep between Lakshman Jhula and Shivanand Jhula costs Rs 4 (or Rs 40 for the whole jeep).

For Rs 4 you can cross the river to Swarg Ashram between 8 am and 5.30 pm by boat (particularly auspicious). Motorcycles can be hired from the Baba Paying Guest House (☎ 433339) in Chandrabhaga.

RISHIKESH TO THE CHAR DHAM

If you are heading north to the Char Dham, there are some interesting stops in the hills around Rishikesh. Great views can be had from the modern temple of **Kunjapuri**, about 18km north of Rishikesh. It's a 6km walk from Hindolakhal (45 minutes by bus from Rishikesh), which lies on the bus route to Uttarkashi.

About 70km from Rishikesh on the way to Kedarnath, the pretty town of **Deoprayag** sits at the confluence of the Alaknanda and Bhagirathi Rivers and marks the beginning of the true Ganges. Deoprayag is well served by share-jeeps and buses and there are several ancient temples and ghats at the auspicious spot where the two rivers meet, including the sikhara-style Raghunath and Shiv temples.

About 27km north of Deoprayag, the modern temple of **Chandrabadani** is perched on a hilltop and offers great views of the Himalaya. It's a 2km hike to the peak from Jamnikhal on the Deoprayag-Tehri road (take any Tehri bus or share-jeep).

Tehri itself is an important transport hub, but the town is fairly uninspiring and is due to vanish under the floodwaters created by the new Tehri dam in 2004. Its role will be taken over by the deeply unattractive planned city of **New Tehri**, 24km south. Buses and share-jeeps run from Tehri to Mussoorie, Rishikesh, Uttarkashi, Gangotri and east to Srinagar and Rudraprayag.

North of Deoprayag, **Srinagar** was the capital of Garhwal until it was gifted to the British in 1815 as payment for driving the Ghurka invaders back to Nepal. On the day of Vaikunth Chaturdashi (November) childless couples make an all night vigil at the ancient Kamleshwar Temple to pray for children. The ***GMVN Tourist Rest House*** *(☎ 01388-52199)* near the bus stand has dorms for Rs 70 and doubles from Rs 330. Many buses on the yatra route stop here overnight, heading off early in the morning to Kedarnath and Badrinath (you may need to change at Rudraprayag).

GARHWAL HIMALAYA

The far north of Uttaranchal is best known as the home of the Char Dham, the most important pilgrimage destination in the Hindu religion. Thousands of pilgrims undertake the auspicious circuit of the Char Dham every year, some on foot and some by luxury coach, palanquin and rented ponies. While the temples are fascinating and the locations spectacular, there are more impressive (and peaceful!) treks in the region. Nature lovers may be interested in the isolated Har-ki-Dun Valley (3566m) near the border with Himachal Pradesh, or the stunning Valley of Flowers, high above Joshimath. The region also boasts some spectacular high altitude lakes, including Dodi Tal (between Hanuman Chatti and Uttarkashi), Kedar Tal (high above Gangotri) and Hem Kund near Joshimath.

The best time to trek is either in the pre-monsoon period (mid-May to the end of June), or the post-monsoon season (mid-September to mid-October). In July and August the region is subject to heavy rainfall, though this is the best time to appreciate the rich variety of wildflowers in the Valley of the Flowers or the nearby *bugyals* (high alpine meadows).

The GMVN Trekking & Mountaineering division in Rishikesh can arrange organised treks to these and other destinations in Garhwal for around Rs 2200 per day all-inclusive, and they also offer guides, porters and equipment hire. More information on trekking in Garhwal is given in Lonely Planet's *Trekking in the Indian Himalaya*.

Uttarkashi

☎ 01374 • elevation 1158m

The pleasant town of Uttarkashi is 155km from Rishikesh on the bank of the Bhagirathi (Ganges) and is an important pilgrimage stop on the way north to the Char Dham. There are numerous temples here, the most significant being the **Vishwanatha Temple**, sacred to Shiva (though this should be obvious from the massive iron trident!). Also here is the Nehru Institute of Mountaineering, where Bachhendri Pal, the first Indian woman to climb to the summit of Mt Everest, was trained. On the day of **Makar Sakranti**, which usually falls in January, Uttarkashi hosts a colourful fair, when deities are borne aloft into the town on palanquins from outlying villages.

Treks in the immediate area include the lake of Dodi Tal (see Dodi Tal Trek below), from where you can continue to Hanuman Chatti, and peaceful Nachiketa Tal.

Information There's a small tourist office (☎ 22290) on the main road and the town market is a good place to stock up on supplies for trekking farther north. Numerous graduates from the Institute of Mountaineering offer their services as guides, charging between Rs 200 and 500 per day. All-inclusive treks can be organised by Mount Support (☎ 22419), a short walk north of the bus stand.

Places to Stay & Eat The Divisional Forest Officer in Uttarkashi can arrange accommodation in ***Forest Rest Houses*** in the hills but many were damaged by the earthquake of 1991.

Accommodation in Uttarkashi includes a ***GMVN Tourist Rest House*** *(☎ 22271)* with dorms for Rs 70 and doubles from Rs 240 to 660, and ***Hotel Hanslok*** *(☎ 22290)* in the main bazaar, with basic doubles with bathroom for Rs 80. Nearby, ***Hotel Bhadari*** *(☎ 22203)* is basic but clean with doubles starting at Rs 200.

While in town, try the local speciality, Bhagirathi River trout in chilli sauce, served up by vendors around the bus stand.

Getting There & Away Buses depart early in the morning for Gangotri (Rs 80), Hanuman Chatti (Rs 50), Rishikesh (Rs 92) and Dehra Dun (Rs 125). There are also frequent morning share-jeeps to Rishikesh (Rs 120). To get to Kedarnath or Badrinath, you'll have to change at Srinagar or Ghansali, which are both served by buses and share-jeeps.

Dodi Tal Trek

The trek begins at Kalyani, a 13km bus or taxi ride from Uttarkashi, from where it's an easy 7km along a well-defined trail to the village of Agoda, which has a basic ***tourist bungalow***. The second day climbs for 16km through attractive forests of oak, pine,

Share-Jeeps

A vast network of share-jeep routes criss-crosses Garhwal and Kumaon, linking towns and villages to important road junctions. If you can't go where you want directly, you should be able to leap-frog across to your destination from transport hub to transport hub in the relative comfort of a Tata Sumo or Maruti share-jeep. Share-jeeps usually solicit for customers on the highway in the direction of the next town or transport hub and leave when full (or overfull), charging just a little more than the equivalent bus ride.

deodar and rhododendron before reaching scenic Dodi Tal, where there is basic accommodation. If you want to continue on to Hanuman Chatti, it's a short steep ascent to the Darwa Pass (4150m) before the trail levels out for the long haul to Seema (17km), where you must camp out. The final day involves a 12km walk to Hanuman Chatti but it's downhill all the way. From Hanuman Chatti you can pick up buses to Dehra Dun or Uttarkashi.

The Char Dham

Just as Muslims make the *haj* pilgrimage to Mecca, many devout Hindus make the pilgrimage to the Char Dham once in their lifetime in hope of achieving paradise. The four ancient temples on the Char Dham circuit mark the spiritual sources of the four sacred rivers of Hinduism, the Yamuna (Yamunotri), the Ganges (Gangotri), the Mandakini (Kedarnath) and the Alaknanda (Badrinath). All of Char Dham's temples boast spectacular mountain settings, but have been rebuilt many times over the years and the sheer-number of pilgrims in peak season can be quite overbearing. The yatra business is well-developed with luxury coaches, ponies and even palanquins on hand to make sure that anyone with the will (and the means) can make it around the four shrines. The plus side of this is that there is a well-established network of rest houses and dhabas to provide shelter and food to hungry trekkers.

The number of pilgrims dies down dramatically once you leave the main yatra circuit, and there are numerous side treks that include ancient shrines such as the Panch Kedar, the beautiful Valley of Flowers and the high altitude lakes of Kedar Tal and Hem Kund. These are serious treks however, and are best attempted with an experienced guide. Most temples and rest houses are closed over the winter, should you think of making a rash winter expedition.

The pilgrimage season runs approximately from May to October, but the exact dates are declared by the priests each year.

During the high season, regular buses run to and between the Char Dham shrines, but most services leave early in the morning. Schedules are erratic so you should check the current bus times when you arrive. Fortunately there are share-jeeps connecting most settlements in the hills, which run until the afternoon.

For the yatra without the hassle, the GMVN organises 11-day Char Dham packages from Delhi during the peak season, including transport and accommodation in GMVN rest houses but not meals. See Tourist Offices at the start of the Uttaranchal section for a list of GMVN offices.

Yamunotri Yamunotri is the source of the Yamuna River, the second-most sacred river in India after the Ganges. This was once the source of the Sarasvati River, one of the cradles of early Indian civilisation, before geological upheavals diverted its course. The river emerges from a frozen lake of ice and glaciers on the Kalinda Parvat mountain at an altitude of 4421m, 1km beyond the temple. The temple itself isn't particularly attractive, though there are several hot springs where the priests warm themselves on a marble platform and cook potatoes in the scalding water to offer as prasad. However, the walk up the valley is spectacular.

Buses go as far as Hanuman Chatti from Dehra Dun or Rishikesh, although you may have to change buses at Barkot. From Hanuman Chatti, it's 13km to Yamunotri. Accommodation is provided at Yamunotri in the form of basic ***dharamsalas*** and a ***Touris***

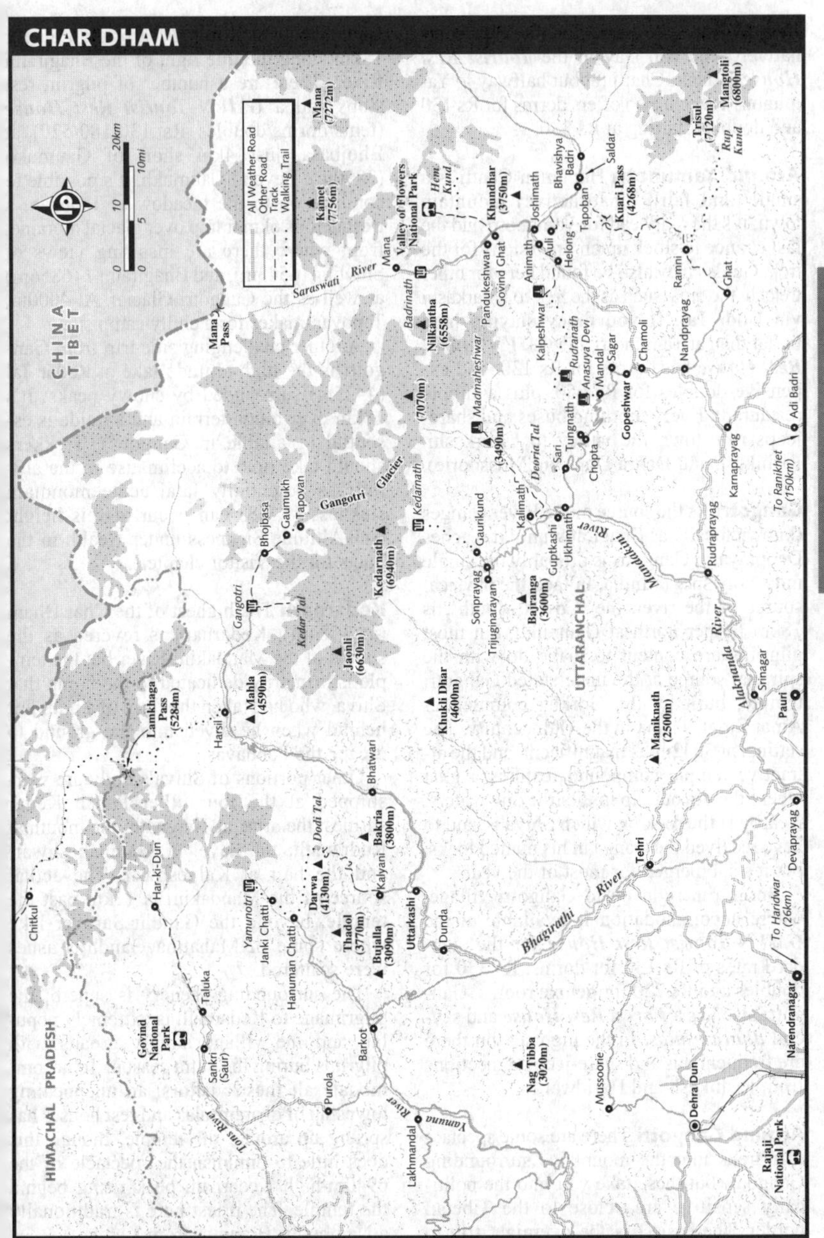
CHAR DHAM
CHINA
TIBET
HIMACHAL PRADESH
UTTARANCHAL
0 10 20km
0 5 10mi
All Weather Road
Other Road
Track
Walking Trail
Mana (7272m)
Kamet (7756m)
Valley of Flowers National Park
Hem Kund
Mana
Saraswati River
Mana Pass
Badrinath
Nilkantha (6558m)
Khundhar (3750m)
Govind Ghat
Pandukeshwar
Joshimath
Animath
Auli
Helong
Tapoban
Bhavishya Badri
Saldar
Kuari Pass (4268m)
Trisul (7120m)
Mangtoli (6800m)
Rup Kund
Ramni
Ghat
Nandprayag
Chamoli
Kalpeshwar
Rudranath
Anasuya Devi
Mandal
Sagar
Gopeshwar
Chopta
Tungnath
Sari
Deoria Tal
Madmaheshwar
(3490m)
(7070m)
Gangotri Glacier
Tapovan
Gaumukh
Bhojbasa
Gangotri
Kedar Tal
Kedarnath
Kedarnath (6940m)
Jaonli (6630m)
Gaurikund
Sonprayag
Trijuginarayan
Kalimath
Guptkashi
Ukhimath
Mandakini River
Bajranga (3600m)
Karnaprayag
Adi Badri
To Ranikhet (150km)
Rudraprayag
Alaknanda River
Srinagar
Pauri
Khukli Dhar (4600m)
Maniknath (2500m)
Devaprayag
To Haridwar (26km)
Narendranagar
Rajaji National Park
Dehra Dun
Mussoorie
Nag Tibba (3020m)
Tehri
Bhagirathi River
Harsil
Mahla (4590m)
Lamkhaga Pass (5284m)
Chitkul
Har-ki-Dun
Taluka
Govind National Park
Sankri (Saur)
Purola
Tons River
Barkot
Yamuna River
Lakhmandal
Hanuman Chatti
Janki Chatti
Yamunotri
Thadol (3770m)
Bujalla (3090m)
Darwa (4130m)
Dodi Tal
Kalyani
Bakria (3800m)
Bhatwari
Uttarkashi
Dunda

Rest House with dorms for Rs 130. Alternatively you can stay in the ***Tourist Rest House*** in Janki Chatti (about halfway to Yamunotri), which also offers dorms for Rs 130 and doubles starting at Rs 330.

Around Yamunotri Hanuman Chatti is a small (and fairly unattractive) mountain town; it's the roadhead for Yamunotri and the last chance to stock up on provisions for the trek. Guides may also be found here for other treks in the area, such as the trek to Uttarkashi via Dodi Tal. If you fancy staying here rather than at Yamunotri, the ***GMVN Tourist Rest House*** has dorms for Rs 130, and expensive doubles for Rs 650, plus a simple restaurant. Every morning buses and share-jeeps run down the valley to Uttarkashi, Rishikesh and Dehra Dun (via Mussoorie).

Gangotri As the source of the River Ganges (known locally as Bhagirathi until it reaches Deoprayag), Gangotri is probably the single most holy spot in India. In fact, the physical source of the river, the 'Cow's Mouth', is 18km farther north at Gaumukh, but most pilgrims are content to make do with the spiritual source at the understated Gangotri temple, built by the Gorkha commander Amar Singh Thapa in the 18th century. The setting, at 3042m, is magnificent, and the attractive temple compound features a ghat where the devout dip in the freezing waters. Nearby is the rock on which Shiva is said to have received the Ganga in his matted locks, but it's submerged for most of the year.

Buses run right up to Gangotri village, where accommodation is available at the ***GMVN Tourist Rest House*** for the standard rates of Rs 130 for dorms, Rs 330 for doubles and Rs 720 for deluxe rooms. Gangotri also has a ***Forest Rest House*** and several ***dharamsalas***. In the high season there are frequent bus and share-jeep connections from Rishikesh and Haridwar.

Around Gangotri There are some spectacular treks into the mountains surrounding Gangotri, but these take you into the politically sensitive area close to the Tibetan border. The easiest is the overnight trip to Gaumukh, which follows a bridle trail for 18km along the true right of the Bhagirathi River. There are a number of pilgrim rest stops and a ***GMVN Tourist Rest House*** (tents/dorms/doubles Rs 130/180/520) at Bhojbasa, just 4km short of Gaumukh (3890m). Beyond Gaumukh, it's possible to continue on to the meadow at Tapovan, a treacherous 6km tramp over glacial moraine, from where there are inspiring views of Shivling (6543m), and Bhagirathi 1 (6856m) as well as the Gangotri Glacier. At 4000m, Tapovan makes for a chilly camp site.

Another challenging side trip from Gangotri is the high-altitude lake at **Kedar Tal** (4425m) surrounded by snowy peaks. It's 18km over tough terrain and a guide is essential (available in Gangotri). Trekkers should take time to acclimatise to the altitude as potentially fatal acute mountain sickness (AMS) can occur at this height (see Altitude Sickness under Health in the Facts for the Visitor chapter).

Kedarnath The highest of the Char Dham (at 3584m), Kedarnath is revered as the source of the Mandakini River but the temple is primarily dedicated to the hump that Shiva, who had taken the form of a bull, left behind when he dived into the ground to escape the Pandavas.

Other portions of Shiva's body are worshipped at the four other Panch Kedar shrines: the arms at Tungnath; the mouth at Rudranath; the navel at Madmaheshwar; and the hair at Kalpeshwar. The actual source of the Mandakini is 12km past the temple, beyond the Gandhi Sarover lake where some of Mahatma Gandhi's ashes were scattered.

The surrounding scenery is superb; the pilgrimage to Kedarnath is extremely popular, and the village simply groans with pilgrims during the yatra season. To accommodate all these visitors, an unappealing township of dharamsalas and rest houses has sprung up around the temple, though this does little to diminish the spectacle of the 6940m-high Kedarnath peak rising behind the temple. The priest here is traditionally a Nambudiri Brahmin from Kerala.

The temple itself is very attractive, with a tall stone sikhara-style tower fronted by an antechamber reminiscent of a European church. Kedarnath contains one of the 12 *jyoti linga*, a source of divine power or *shakti*. The original structure dates from the 8th century and was built by guru Shankara, who died shortly after and is buried behind the shrine (look for the peculiar statue of a fist holding a staff). The site is so auspicious that pilgrims used to throw themselves from one of the cliffs behind the temple in the hope of instantly attaining *moksha* (liberation), until the British stamped out the practice in the 19th century.

Accommodation is available at the ***GMVN Tourist Rest House*** *(☎ 01364-6210)* which has the usual dorms for Rs 130 and doubles starting at Rs 260. If it's full you can usually find a bed at one of the ***ashrams*** or ***dharamsalas*** between the temple and the bridge. There are plenty of inexpensive dhabas catering to the hordes.

Buses from Rishikesh to Kedarnath only run as far as **Gauri Kund**, from where it's a steep 14km trek past an endless column of dhabas and chai (spicy milk tea) stands to the temple. Ponies (which can be rented for the trip for a steep Rs 400 each way) have stripped the trail of all vegetation and it can be treacherously slippery after rain. Gauri Kund also has a ***GMVN Tourist Rest House*** with cheap dorms and expensive doubles.

A convoy of share-jeeps and buses leaves in the morning bound for Rishikesh and Rudraprayag, for connections to Joshimath and Kumaon. A few early morning buses and share-jeeps run to Badrinath, passing many of the trailheads for the Panch Kedar and other shrines. Alternatively, you can take local services down to Guptkashi or Chamoli and change there.

Around Kedarnath For those who prefer their spiritualism without the commercialism, there are dozens of smaller shrines between Kedarnath and Badrinath with similarly spectacular locations and none of the crowds.

Shrines Closest to Kedarnath is the ancient Shaivite shrine of **Trijuginarayan**, a 14km trek from Sonprayag, 5km south of Gauri Kund. An eternal flame burns on the spot where Shiva and Parvati are said to have been married. All southbound buses from Kedarnath pass through Sonprayag.

About 32km south of Gauri Kund on the Kedarnath–Badrinath road is **Guptkashi**, famed for its painted stone sikhara-style Vishwanath and Ardhnareshwar temples. Guptkashi has a ***GMVN Tourist Rest House*** with dorms for Rs 130 and doubles for Rs 520. It is also the starting point for the 36km trek to Madmaheshwar, the most remote of the Panch Kedar pilgrimage trail (see following).

About 12km further east, beyond the turn-off to Rudraprayag is **Ukimath**, the winter seat of Lord Kedarnath. When Kedarnath is closed by snows, the idol is worshipped here and there are imposing stone sikhara temples to Shiva, Parvati, Usha and Annirud-dha. Buses and share-jeeps to Badrinath pass through Ukimath and there's a ***GMVN Tourist Rest House*** with the usual dorms for Rs 130 and doubles starting at Rs 330.

Lakes For a break from temples, the gorgeous lake of **Deoria Tal** is an easy 2km hike from Sari, 14km east of Ukimath on the Kedarnath-Badrinath route. There are stunning views of the Himalaya, including mighty Chaukhamba (7138m) but you'll need to camp if you want to stay overnight.

Panch Kedar After leaping into the ground in the form of a bull at Kedarnath, Shiva is said to have reappeared, in pieces, at various sites in the surrounding hills. Along with Kedarnath these auspicious sites are commemorated by ancient Shivaree shrines and are collectively known as the Panch (Five) Kedar. Buses and share-jeeps between Kedarnath and Badrinath pass many of the trailheads.

A 36km trek north of Guptkashi is the splendidly remote shrine of **Madmaheshwar**, which marks the spot where Shiva's navel and stomach reappeared. This is the most peaceful of the Panch Kedar shrines and the hike to the temple passes through an area of outstanding natural beauty. There are a few basic dharamsalas at Kalimath (10km above Guptkashi) and Madmaheshwar itself. Buses and share-jeeps run as far as Kalimath.

Tungnath is where Shiva's arms appeared and is perched at 3680m with magnificent views over the surrounding hills. It's a steep 3km walk through rhododendron forests from the village of Chopta, 43km east of Guptkashi, which has a few basic places to stay.

The shrine at **Rudranath** marks where Shiva's face and mouth reappeared and is reached by a challenging 20km trek from Sagar, 34km east of Chopta on the Kedarnath-Badrinath route. The trail passes through peaceful bugyals, which are carpeted with flowers in the summer. On clear days, the views are breathtaking. It's also possible to walk here via the ancient **Anasuya Devi** temple. Rudranath is a 6km walk from Mandal, 9km west of Sagar on the main road.

The trail continues from Rudranath to **Kalpeshwar**, the most easterly of the Panch Kedar, but it's an exhausting 23km trek. Easier is the approach from Helong, 10km east of Kalpeshwar and 14km from Joshimath on the road to Chamoli. The temple sits beside a pretty waterfall and represents the spot where Shiva's hair is said to have appeared. All buses to Badrinath pass through Helong.

Badrinath Named for Lord Vishnu (also known as Badrinath), the third of the Char Dham represents the source of the Alaknanda River and boasts a spectacular setting in the shadow of snow-topped Nilkantha (6558m). However, the uncontrolled construction of hotels and dharamsalas to accommodate the tens of thousands of pilgrims who come here every year has eroded some of Badrinath's charm. People are believed to have worshipped here since around 1500 BC, and the shrine has changed denomination several times over the years. The vividly colourful temple here was founded by the guru Shankara in the 8th century, but the current structure is much more recent. As at Kedarnath, the priest of Badrinath is a Nambudiri Brahmin from Kerala.

Pure Priests

Much of the credit for the revival of Hinduism in the 8th century goes to the guru Shankara who established the shrines at Kedarnath and Badrinath. Although Hindu in origin, both these sacred sites were taken over by Buddhist worshippers when Ashoka brought the 'middle way' to the hills. Shankara was eager to purge the sacred sites of any Buddhist associations and searched across India for untainted priests to take over as custodians. He eventually settled on the Nambudiri caste of Brahmins, who came from the tip of Kerala, far beyond the spread of the Buddhist empire, and were therefore least likely to have been corrupted by Buddhist ideas.

Surrounding the temple is a colourful religious **market** selling prasad and religious trinkets, and the old village of Badrinath with its slate-roofed houses is a short walk south. Several places in town will video your trip to the temple and edit in religious images and music for a negotiable fee.

Mana, an ancient Buddhist village 4km beyond Badrinath, is an interesting detour but may be off-limits to foreigners – ask about the current situation when you arrive. Some travellers have been allowed to walk as far as **Vasudhara Falls**, 4km beyond Mana, where the Alaknanda is said to fall from heaven. Devotees of Vishnu also visit the other four Panch Badri temples dotted around Badrinath.

The GMVN has the large ***Devlok Hotel*** *(☎ 01381-2212)* and a smaller ***Tourist Rest House*** with rooms from Rs 260 to 850 and dorms for Rs 50. You'll need to speak to the Badrinath Temple Committee on the east bank of the Alaknanda for permission to stay in one of their many ***dharamsalas***. There are some posh restaurants on the east bank, plus the usual assortment of dhabas.

In the high season, there are plenty of morning share-jeeps and buses to Rishikesh and Haridwar, a few early morning buses to Kedarnath and numerous share-jeeps and buses on the Kedarnath-Badrinath route.

Around Badrinath In the hills around Badrinath are several other interesting shrines, including the Panch Badri group (of which Badrinath is one). Sacred to Vishnu, the other four Panch Badri are Yogdhyan Badri, Bhavishya Badri, Adi Badri and Vriddha Badri. The legend goes that Vishnu was chastised by a *rishi* (sage) for having his feet massaged and fled to the hills above Joshimath to meditate for several years, living off *badri* (berries) he found in the woods. His wife, Lakshmi, finally tracked him down and persuaded him to come down from the hills, but not before he had decreed that the area should be reserved for meditation rather than worldly pleasures.

The closest shrine to Badrinath is the squat sikhara temple of **Yogdhyan Badri**, 24km from Badrinath at Pandukeshwar on the main road south, which also boasts impressive views.

There's another ancient temple 2km farther down the valley at Gopeshwar, the headquarters of Chamoli district. Gopeshwar is well served by share-jeeps and local buses and has several places to stay including a ***GMVN Tourist Rest House*** *(☎ 01372-52488)* with doubles starting at Rs 280 and dorms for Rs 80.

About 20km south-east of Joshimath is Saldar, from where it's a 6km walk to the ancient stone **Bhavishya Badri** or 'Future Badri' temple, hidden away in dense forests near the Dhauliganga River. There are hot sulphurous springs at **Tapoban**, 4km south of Saldar, which marks the start of the Kuari Pass trek.

The ancient Vishnu temple of **Birdha Badri**, which predates Badrinath by several centuries, is 7km south of Joshimath at Animath. All southbound buses from Joshimath pass through the village.

Far from the other Panch Badri, **Adi Badri** consists of 16 stone temples dating to the sixth century. Adi Badri is 18km below Karnaprayag on the road to Ranikhet. The best place to stay in the area is **Karnaprayag**, which has a ***GMVN Tourist Rest House*** *(☎ 01372-44348)* with good-value rooms starting at Rs 170 and dorms for Rs 70. There are several interesting temples here and Karnaprayag is an important transport hub for share-jeeps and buses heading east to Gwaldam and Kumaon.

Joshimath This important administrative town (elevation 1845m) is the gateway to the dham (one of the holiest pilgrimage places) of Badrinath, and is where the guru Shankara meditated under a mulberry tree and received his celestial instructions to revive Hinduism and establish the Char Dham shrines. The town is perched high above the confluence of the Saraswati and Dhauliganga Rivers and has some interesting temples including the brightly painted Narsingh Temple, dedicated to Vishnu in his lion form.

The small tourist office (☎ 01389-22181) no longer hires out trekking gear; for this you'll have to go to the ski resort at Auli (see following). Private trekking companies include Nanda Devi Mountain Travel (☎ 01389-22170) and Garhwal Adventure Sports (☎ 01389-22288), both in the Hotel Nanda Devi on the main bazaar in Joshimath.

As an alternative to staying in Auli, there are two ***GMVN Tourist Rest Houses*** in Joshimath. The *new* rest house *(☎ 01389-22226)* is the better of the two, with dorms for Rs 130 and doubles starting at Rs 460. The slightly neglected *old* rest house *(☎ 01389-22118)* has dorms for Rs 1390 and doubles starting at Rs 260. Private hotels include ***Shailja*** *(☎ 01389-22208)* and ***Kamet*** *(☎ 01389-22155)*, with spartan but cheap rooms.

The Thin Arm of Vishnu

Devotees of Lord Vishnu believe that one arm of the Vishnu idol, enshrined in the Narsingh Temple in Joshimath, is growing progressively thinner and will one day shatter, ushering in the *kali-yuga*, or Evil Times, predicted in the Vedic texts. At this time, the mountains of Jai and Vijay will collapse at Vishnukashi, blocking the way to Badrinath, and a new temple will rise from the ground at Bhavishya Badri near Tapoban, fulfilling the prophesy that this site will become the future Badrinath.

UTTAR PRADESH & UTTARANCHAL

Buses and share-jeeps charge around Rs 25 from Joshimath to Badrinath (three hours). Heading down the valley, there are morning buses to Rishikesh (Rs 142, 10 hours), Haridwar (Rs 170) and Gauri Kund (Rs 110).

Auli Just 13km from Joshimath by road, and easily reached by bus or share-jeep from Rishikesh, Auli is India's premier ski resort, managed by the GMVN. The resort boasts 5km-long slopes, which drop from an altitude of 3049m to 2519m and there's a 500m chairlift running beside the main slope (Rs 50 per trip). The upper and lower slopes are linked by a 800m chairlift imported from France.

Open from January to March, Auli is usually assured of good snow, and a convenient 3.9km-long cable car links Joshimath to the resort for Rs 250 return.

The GMVN resort hires out skis and boots (Rs 175/225 for a half/full day, Rs 125/175 for children), gloves (Rs 100) and goggles (Rs 30). It's up to you to bring a hat and some suitably warm clothing. Daily lessons cost Rs 100/150 per child/adult, which must be some of the cheapest skiing in the world.

Out of season, Auli is still worth a visit for the impressive treks in the area.

Places to Stay Accommodation is provided in the comfortable ***GMVN Tourist Rest House*** *(☎ 01389-23208)* for Rs 900 a double, or Rs 70 in dorms. Seven/14-day ski packages, including all meals, lodging, equipment, hire, ski lifts and lessons, are offered for Rs 4000/8000. To book, write in advance to the General Manager (☎ 0135-746817, fax 744408), GMVN, 74/1 Rajpur Rd, Dehra Dun, UP.

Kuari Pass Trek

Also known as the Curzon Trail (though Lord Curzon's party abandoned their attempt on the pass following an attack of wild bees), the trek over the Kuari Pass (4268m) offers stunning views of Dunagiri (7066m) and Chaukhamba 1 (7138m). The trailhead is at Auli, reached by bus or cable-car from Joshimath, but you can also shave 11km from the journey by taking a local bus from Joshimath to Tapoban, which has hot springs.

Various routes ascend to the pass (21–4km) and continue on the far side to Ghat (47km, four days), from where you can take a bus or share-jeep to Nandprayag on the Rishikesh to Joshimath road.

Nandprayag has a ***GMVN Tourist Rest House*** *(☎ 01372-51215)* with dorms for Rs 70 and doubles for Rs 330. It's also possible to continue on from Ghat to Gwaldam on the border with Kumaon, via the sinister lake of Rup Kund (see Rup Kund Trek following). The Kuari Pass is a camping-only trek, so it's best attempted with a guide, available in Joshimath.

Rup Kund Trek

Set beneath the towering summit of Trisul (7120m), the spooky lake of Rup Kund is known as the 'mystery lake' because of the many human and equine skeletons found here. The grisly remains are believed to belong to a pilgrim train that got caught in heavy snowfall around 600 years ago. Every 12 years, thousands of pilgrims make an arduous trek to Rup Kund as part of the Raj Jay Yatra from Nauti Village, near Karnaprayag, carrying a golden idol of the goddess Nanda Devi on a silver palanquin, and the procession is traditionally led by a four-horned ram.

The roadhead for the trek is Ghat, which can be reached by bus or share-jeep from Nandprayag on the Rishikesh-Joshimath road. The poorly defined trail branches off the Kuari Pass route at Ramni, 10km above Ghat, from where the lake can be reached in four days. The descent to Gwaldam on the far side also takes at least four days, but there are ***Tourist Rest Houses*** at Wan, Mandoli and Debal, with dorms for Rs 70.

Gwaldam also has a ***GMVN Tourist Rest House*** *(☎ 01372-84744)* with dorms for Rs 80 and doubles from Rs 260. From here you can continue by share-jeep or bus to Kausani, Bageshwar and Almora in Kumaon though you may need to change at Garur. Alternatively, return to Garhwal via Karnaprayag on the Rishikesh-Joshimath road.

Valley of Flowers National Park

Discovery of the legendary Valley of the Flowers is attributed to British mountaineer

Frank Smythe in the 1930s, though Garhwalians have known about its beauty for centuries. During the summer months (mid-June to mid-September) the valley is carpeted with an astonishing variety of wildflowers. The valley is cradled by snow-clad peaks including Nilgiri Parbat (6474m) and divided by the Pushpawati stream, which is fed by numerous rivulets and waterfalls.

Trekkers and livestock have taken their toll on the park in the past (by picking, walking on or eating the flowers) so access to the national park has been restricted to daylight hours and camping is prohibited. Fortunately, there is accommodation available at the ***GMVN Tourist Rest House*** in Ghangaria, 4km below the valley, which has the usual dorms for Rs 130 and pricey doubles for Rs 590.

Access to the park is via Govind Ghat, served by local buses from Joshimath. The 13km trail to Ghangaria is well defined and follows the pretty gorge of the Laxman Ganga. An interesting detour is the trek to the lake at **Hem Kund** – identified as the spot where the Sikh guru Gobind Singh meditated in a former life, which he described in some detail in the Sikh holy book, the Guru Granth Sahib. Hem Kund has a spectacular setting, surrounded by seven snow-capped peaks, but the construction of a modernist gurdwara detracts from the natural beauty. The trail to Hem Kund branches off the Valley of Flowers route 3km beyond Ghangaria, from where it's 6km to the lake.

KUMAON HIMALAYA

The summit of Nanda Devi (7816m), the highest peak wholly in India, is recognised as the border between Garhwal and Kumaon. The area to the east is one of the least visited parts of the Indian Himalaya and offers a multitude of treks for the adventurous traveller, including the Pindari and Milam Glaciers, nestled up against the Tibetan border. Descending into the foothills, you'll find the wonderfully untouched Gomti and Sarju river valleys, home to the peaceful hill stations of Ranikhet, Almora and Nainital. Corbett National Park – the birthplace of Project Tiger and Kumaon's most famous attraction – sits right on the edge of the plains, while Banbassa in the far east of the state is an entry point for Nepal. Few travellers make it farther north to Pithoragarh district, which boasts yet more ancient temples.

The best season for trekking, as in Garhwal, is either in the pre-monsoon period (mid-May to the end of June), or the post-monsoon season (mid-September to mid-October). However, there is comparatively little provision for trekkers in Kumaon so camping gear and guides are essential. If you are organising your own expedition, guides can be hired at many trailheads for around Rs 300 per day. Kumaon is a sensitive border area and several treks are off-limits to foreigners, including the trek to Nanda Devi Base Camp and the pilgrimage to Mt Kailash across the border in Tibet.

The KMVN offices in Delhi and Nainital can organise all-inclusive trekking packages to the Pindari Glacier (Rs 2640, six days) and Milam Glacier (Rs 3660, eight days). Also on offer are week-long rafting expeditions on the Sarju and Kali Ganga Rivers, originating in Delhi – see Tourist Offices at the start of this section for a list of KMVN offices.

Corbett Tiger Reserve

☎ 05947

Corbett Tiger Reserve was established in 1936 as India's first national park by the legendary tiger-hunter, Jim Corbett, who put Kumaon on the map with his book *The Man-Eaters of Kumaon*. Held in awe by local villagers for shooting tigers who had developed a taste for human flesh, the British hunter was nevertheless one of the first people in India to realise that tiger numbers were declining. With the help of UP governor Sir Johns Hewett, Corbett was instrumental in setting up the Hailey National Park, which was renamed Corbett National Park in 1957. With the inclusion of the Sonanadi Wildlife Sanctuary to the west, the park now covers 1318 sq km, which may grow further if the planned migration corridor to nearby Rajaji National Park is ever completed.

The reserve Jim Corbett established was the starting point for the India-wide Project Tiger program in 1973, inspiring the creation of 22 other reserves. However, sighting one of Corbett's 92 tigers is down to chance as the animals are neither baited or tracked. If you really *must* see a tiger, your best chance is to come late in the season (April to mid-June) and stay in the park for several days.

Few visitors leave disappointed, though, as the park is home to a wide variety of other wildlife and has a beautiful location in the foothills of the Himalaya on the Ramganga River. More commonly seen wildlife include wild elephants, langur monkeys (black face, long tail), rhesus macaques, peacocks, chital (spotted deer), sambar, hog deer and barking deer. There are also mugger crocodiles, gharials (thin-snouted, fish-eating crocodiles often spotted from High Bank), monitor lizards, wild boars, leopards and jackals. Since the creation of the Ramganga Reservoir on the Ramganga River, large numbers of waterfowl have been attracted here. The best time of year for sightings is from mid-December to the end of March.

At Dhikala there's a library where interesting wildlife **films** are shown (free) in the evenings. During the day you can sit in one of Dhikala's **observation towers** to watch unobtrusively for animals. The **elephant rides** at Dhikala at sunrise and sunset are not to be missed and cost Rs 100 each (minimum of four people) for about two hours. Elephant rides are also available at Bijrani, where there's an interpretation centre and restaurant, and from the lodges at Khinnanauli.

Jeeps can be hired at Ramnagar and will cost about Rs 600 for a one-way drop to Dhikala, or Rs 450 to 500 for a half-day **safari** to Bijrani, plus guide and car charges (see Permits & Fees). Book through any hotel or deal directly with a driver.

No walking or trekking is allowed in the park at any time (introduced after a British ornithologist was killed by a tigress in 1985).

CORBETT TIGER RESERVE

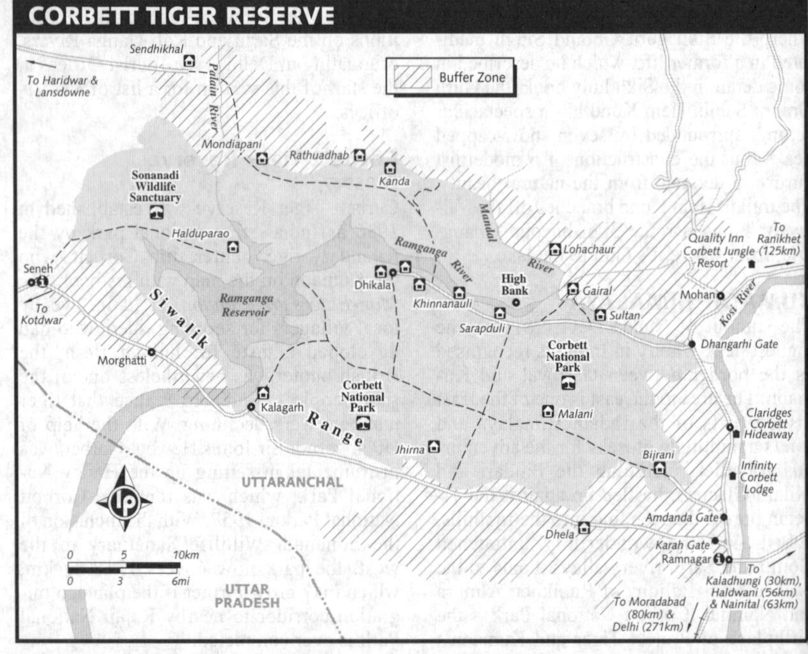

The gates are closed at sunset and no night driving is permitted. When leaving the park, visitors must obtain a clearance certificate, which should be shown at the exit gate.

The national park is open from mid-November to mid-June but much of the wildlife goes into hiding during the crowded weekends. It's a good idea to bring mosquito repellent, mineral water and binoculars.

Orientation & Information

The main reception centre is at Ramnagar (☎ 51489, fax 51376), outside the park on its south-eastern perimeter, and there is a second reception centre at Kotdwar (☎ 01382-24823), on the south-western edge of the park. Both centres are open daily, including holidays, 8.30 am to 1 pm and 3 to 5 pm. Ramnagar is the nearest railhead and has several hotels and tour agents.

Permits & Fees Permits are normally bought at Dhangarhi Gate (for Dhikala) or Amdanda Gate (for day trips to Bijrani). To stay at Dhikala you must first make an accommodation reservation at the park reception centre at Ramnagar. You will then receive a booking chit, which you must show at Dhangarhi Gate.

Foreigners pay an entry fee of Rs 350 for a stay of up to three days, then Rs 175 per day (Indians pay Rs 30 and Rs 20). There's no charge to use a camera but the video camera fee is a whacking Rs 5000 (Rs 2500 for Indians).

To take a car to Bijrani costs Rs 100, and you'll have to hire a (compulsory) guide for Rs 75 (for up to four hours; additional hours cost Rs 20). An officially registered guide is required for all excursions, whether driving or walking. If you hire a jeep you will have to pay these charges yourself. The guide fees at Dhikala are Rs 100 and Rs 20 per additional hour.

With the entrance fee, a jeep ride in and out and even the most basic accommodation, you are probably looking at around US$40 for a two day visit (though you can do it cheaper by sharing the jeep ride or by hitching).

Organised Tours UP Tourism in Delhi runs two/three-night fixed-departure tours to Dhikala from Delhi for Rs 3000/3500, including transport, accommodation, entrance fees, guide and one elephant ride.

The park reception centre in Ramnagar offers day trips by bus to Dhikala for Rs 1000, and Bijrani for Rs 600, including the entrance

Man-Eaters

GREG HERRMAN

Although the words 'man-eating tiger' seem to fit together effortlessly, these ferocious cats only turn to human prey as a last resort. Most of the man-eaters dispatched by Jim Corbett were old or infirm and no longer able to chase after such elusive prey as sambar and chital. The most common cause of injury among the man-eaters of Kumaon was found to be porcupine quills which had embedded in the tigers' paws and become infected. Rural farmers were particularly at risk from these hungry and desperate animals as they ventured into the jungle to collect fire wood at dusk, when tigers are at their most active.

Despite their formidable reputation, tigers have historically been less of a threat to human life than leopards, which pounce on unwary travellers from the trees. The Rudraprayag leopard, eventually shot by Jim Corbett, is thought to have killed 125 people in the area around Rudraprayag between 1918 and 1926.

Of course, the risk posed to humans by big cats is as nothing compared to the risk posed to big cats by humans. Back in the days when Corbett Tiger Reserve was a shooting block, it wasn't uncommon for 10 or 20 tigers to be killed in a single shoot, particularly during the hunting extravaganzas laid on for visiting politicians and royalty.

fee. This is the only way to visit Dhikala on a day trip. Buses leave the reception centre at 8.30 am.

Places to Stay & Eat Dhikala, 51km north-west of Ramnagar inside the reserve, is the main accommodation centre and where most travellers stay, but it is only open to overnight guests, or as part of a tour booked through the reception centre at Ramnagar. Day trippers are restricted to the Bijrani visitors centre closer to the edge of the reserve.

Most people choose to stay at Dhikala, Bijrani or Khinnanauli, where elephant rides are available. Rest houses are also available at various locations around the reserve, but your chances of spotting wildlife will be reduced to sightings from the rest houses themselves, as venturing into the reserve on foot is prohibited.

Dhikala, Bijrani & Khinnanauli There are several choices at Dhikala, but all charge higher rates for foreign visitors (Indians pay one-third of the following rates).

The ***Log Huts*** have a very basic dorms (like three-tier train sleepers!) for Rs 100. The ***Tourist Hutment*** has better-value triples (Rs 500). An extra charge (Rs 25) is made for mattresses and sheets in both these places. More comfortable are the ***Cabins*** and the rooms at the ***Forest Rest House***, which all cost Rs 900 and come with private bathroom. All three places can be booked at the reception centre at Ramnagar.

Through a slightly perverse ruling, doubles at the ***Old Forest Rest House*** (Rs 1500) in Dhikala must be booked through the Chief Conservator of Forests in Dehra Dun (☎ 0135-745779), while the seven ***annexe rooms*** (Rs 900), must be booked through the KMVN in Delhi (☎ 011-3350481).

Dhikala has two ***restaurants***, one run by KMVN, and another by a private operator.

The ***rest house*** at Khinnanauli is reached via the Dhangarhi Gate and costs Rs 1500 per room (Rs 100 extra to use the generator). The ***rest house*** at Bijrani, in the south-eastern corner of the reserve, has singles/doubles for Rs 500/900 and meals are available; access is via the Amdanda Gate.

Ramnagar The ***KMVN Tourist Bungalow*** (*☎ 51225*), next to the reception centre, has good doubles from Rs 400 to 800. Dorms are Rs 60.

Along the main road in Ramnagar are several basic but clean guesthouses. ***Corbett Guest House*** singles/doubles go for Rs 150/200 with shared hot shower. The ***Govind Guest House*** (*☎ 51614*), farther north, charges Rs 200 to 300 for big clean doubles with fan and semiprivate bathroom.

On the street opposite the bus stand, the friendly ***Hotel Everest*** (*☎ 51099*) has comfortable rooms for Rs 250 to 400 (Rs 200 in the low season). More expensive rooms have TV and air-cooler. Meals can be arranged and there's a nice balcony.

Farther along the same road is the ***Rameshwam Hotel*** (*☎ 52664*) with home-like rooms with bathroom for Rs 300.

On the main road is the ***Corbett Green Valley Restaurant*** with a wide menu of Indian favourites.

Other Areas Inside the Reserve With your own transport and food, there are numerous rest houses dotted throughout the park. Booked through the reception centre in Ramnagar, the ***rest houses*** at Sarapduli and Gairal cost Rs 500/900 a single/double (generator power). The rest house at Sultan has a generator and costs Rs 450.

Rest houses without electricity are available at Mailani, Kanda and Lohachaur (Rs 450) and Dhela, Jhirna and Kalagarh (Rs 300). All these places can be accessed from the Dhangarhi Gate except Mailani, which is accessed from Amdanda Gate.

Booked through the Kotdwar reception centre, the rest houses at Morghatti, Mondiapani, Rathuadhab and Sendhikhal cost Rs 300 per double; rooms at Halduparac cost Rs 450.

For all these rest houses you should bring food and a flashlight.

Outside the Reserve There are several upmarket resorts strung along the Ramnagar-Ranikhet road, all outside the reserve precincts. All offer discounts of around 50% when the park is closed.

RICHARD I'ANSON

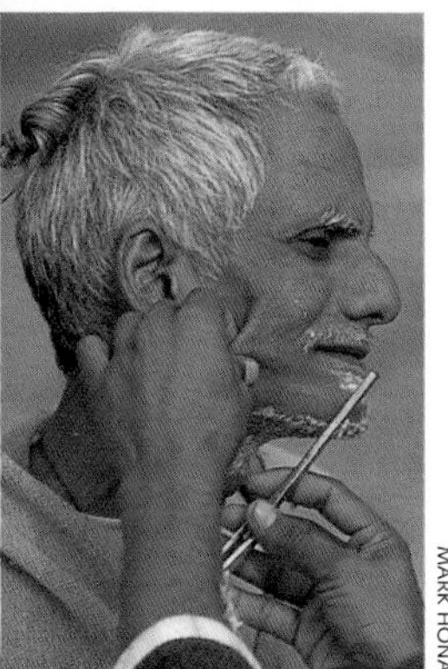
MARK HONAN

PAUL BEINSSEN

RICHARD I'ANSON

Life spills out onto Uttar Pradesh's crowded streets: a souvenir seller expansively displays his wares in Agra (top); a sadhu on his spiritual quest (centre right); children stare straight back at the camera (bottom); a clip round the chin at Dasaswamedh Ghat in Varanasi (centre left)

ALL PHOTOGRAHPS BY GARRY WEARE

Seasons dictate life in Uttaranchal's mountainous north: goats carry supplies to summer grazing pastures around Milam (top left); trekkers strike camp before facing the challenges of Rup Kund Pass (top right); a village in the Har-ki-Dun Valley, free of snow but with glacial streams flowing (bottom)

Formerly known as Tiger Tops, the ***Infinity Corbett Lodge*** *(☎ 51279, fax 85278; in Delhi ☎ 011-6444016)*, 7km from Ramnagar, is a luxurious place with prices to match. Doubles start at US$95 per person, including elephant rides, jeep trips, access to the pool and a wildlife slide show in the evenings. Lower rates apply for Indians.

Claridges Corbett Hideaway *(☎ 51959; in Delhi ☎ 011-3010211)* has accommodation in attractive ochre cottages set in an orchard of mango trees. Air-con doubles cost from US$175, and rates include all meals. Staff can arrange bird-watching and nature-trail excursions, and mountain bikes are available for hire.

The ***Quality Inn Corbett Jungle Resort*** *(☎/fax 51230)*, in the Kumeria Forest Reserve, has attractive cottages high above the river for Rs 3850, including all meals. This place features its own in-house elephant so rides are assured.

Getting There & Away UP Roadways and Delhi Transport Corporation buses for Delhi (Rs 110, seven hours) depart Ramnagar approximately every hour between 5 am and 7.30 pm. For Dehra Dun (via Haridwar; Rs 100), buses leave hourly from 8 am to 1.30 pm. Buses to Nainital (Rs 56, 3½ hours) leave every few hours throughout the day, passing through Kaladungi (Rs 19, one hour).

Various private buses leave from the opposite side of the Corbett Tiger Reserve reception centre for destinations in Kumaon. To Ranikhet (Rs 60, 4½ hours), buses leave every few hours until 2 pm. The 9.30 am service continues to Almora (Rs 97). Regular local buses run up to Haldwani (Rs 17), from where there are share-jeep connections to Nainital, Almora and Ranikhet.

Ramnagar train station is 1.5km south of the reserve reception centre. The nightly *Ranikhet Express* leaves Ramnagar at 9.10 pm, arriving in Delhi (Rs 120 in sleeper class) at 4.30 am. For other destinations, change at Moradabad. It's worth making a reservation before you visit the reserve.

Getting Around Providing you have booked accommodation, you can take the local bus from Ramnagar to Dhikala at 3.30 pm (Rs 150, 2½ hours). The bus returns to Ramnagar at 9.30 am the next day.

Jeeps can usually only be rented at Ramnagar (see under Activities earlier).

Safaris on foot are strictly prohibited. The only other mode of transport is the ubiquitous elephant.

Kaladhungi

Although he spent much of his time in Nainital, Jim Corbett is best associated with his childhood house in Kaladhungi, 26km from Ramnagar towards Nainital on the fringes of the national park. The house has been opened as a museum (Rs 10 entry), and makes an interesting detour from Ramnagar.

During his hunting days, Corbett is said to have shot some 90 tigers at the request of local people after attacks on villagers or cattle, and there are mementos to many of his exploits, including the killing of the Rudraprayag leopard. There are also photographs taken by Corbett after he traded his gun for a camera.

Buses between Ramnagar and Nainital stop in Kaladhungi (Rs 19 from Ramnagar; Rs 37 from Nainital).

Nainital

☎ 05942 • pop 35,7000

At 1938m, this attractive hill station was once the summer capital of Uttar Pradesh and is the largest town in Kumaon. Nainital is very much a green and pleasant land and it immediately appealed to the homesick Brits, who were reminded of the Cumbrian Lake District. Things really took off here when a sugar-trader named Mr Barron had his yacht carried up here in 1840. The Nainital Boat Club, whose wooden clubhouse still graces the edge of the lake, became the fashionable focus of the community. Disaster struck on 16 September 1880 when a major landslide buried 151 people and created the recreation ground now known as the Flats.

The hotels and villas of this popular resort are set around the peaceful Naini lake or *tal*, hence the name. This is certainly one of the most pleasant hill stations to visit and there are many interesting walks through the forests to points with superb views of the Himalaya.

The high season (when Nainital is packed and hotel prices double or triple) corresponds to school holidays. Avoid Christmas and the New Year, mid-April to mid-July and mid-September to the end of October.

Orientation During the high season, The Mall is closed to heavy vehicles and cycle-rickshaws take passengers along the 1.5km Mall between Tallital (Lake's Foot), at its southern end, and Mallital (Lake's Head), to the north-west. The bus stand is in Tallital. Hotels and guesthouses are found in Tallital, along the entire length of The Mall and in the Mallital area. Most of the top-end hotels are 10 to 15 minutes' walk to the west of Mallital in the area known as Sukhatal.

Information There is a post office near the bus stand in Tallital and the main post office is in Mallital. The State Bank of India and Bank of Baroda in Mallital exchange all major travellers cheques. The friendly UP Tourism office (☎ 35337) is towards the Mallital end of The Mall.

Among the many travel agencies, Hina Tours (☎ 35860), Anamika Travels (☎ 35186) and Darshan Travels (☎ 35035), all on The Mall, are reliable operators. Parvat Tours (☎ 35656), at the Tallital end of The Mall, is run by the KMVN (see Organised Tours later in this section).

Naini Lake This attractive lake is said to be one of the emerald green eyes of Shiva's wife, Sati (*naina* is Sanskrit for eye). Sati is said to have immolated herself at Haridwar after her father failed to invite Shiva to a family sacrifice. The grieving Shiva gathered the charred remains in his arms and began a cosmic dance that threatened to destroy the world. To terminate the dance, Vishnu chopped up the body into pieces and scattered the remains across India. The modern Naina Devi Temple at the northern end of the lake is built on the precise spot where the eye is believed to have fallen.

Boat operators will take you on a circuit of the lake for Rs 80 in a rowboat or you can hire a small yacht by the hour from the Nainital Boat Club (Rs 60). Alternatively, you can join the small flotilla of pedal boats on the lake and make your way around under your own steam (Rs 80 per hour).

Snow View A chairlift (ropeway), officially called the 'Aerial Express', takes you up to the popular Snow View at 2270m, from which there are excellent Himalayan views, dominated by Nanda Devi (7816m). The lift is open 10.30 am to 4 pm and costs Rs 30/50 one way/return (valid for one hour). At the Mallital end of The Mall, near The Flats, beautifully groomed horses and mountain ponies are available for hire to Snow View and back for Rs 75, offering a pleasant alternative to the steep 2km walk.

At the top there are powerful binoculars (Rs 5) for a close-up view of Nanda Devi (7816m), which was once the highest mountain in the British empire, and a small marble temple dedicated to Dev Mundi. From Snow View you can walk west to the main road and continue to Kilbury, another popular picnic spot and viewpoint. You can also walk from Snow View to China Peak.

A walk up to Snow View can take in the tiny **Gadhan Kunkyop Ling Gompa** of the Gelukpa order (of which the Dalai Lama is the spiritual leader). Take the road uphill from the Hotel City Heart, from where a path branches off towards the gompa (the colourful prayer flags are visible from the road).

Walks There are several other good walks in the area with views of the snow-capped mountains to the north. **China Peak** (pronounced 'Cheena'), also known as Naini Peak, is the highest point in the area (2610m) and can be reached either from Snow View or from Mallital (5km).

A 4km walk west of the lake brings you to **Dorothy's Seat** (2292m), known as Tiffin Top, where a Mr Kellet built a seat in memory of his wife killed in a plane crash. From here there is a lovely 1km walk to **Land's End** (2118m) through a forest of oak, deodar and pine forest. Early morning you may see jungle fowl or goral (mountain goats) and there are fine views out over the lake at Khurpatal.

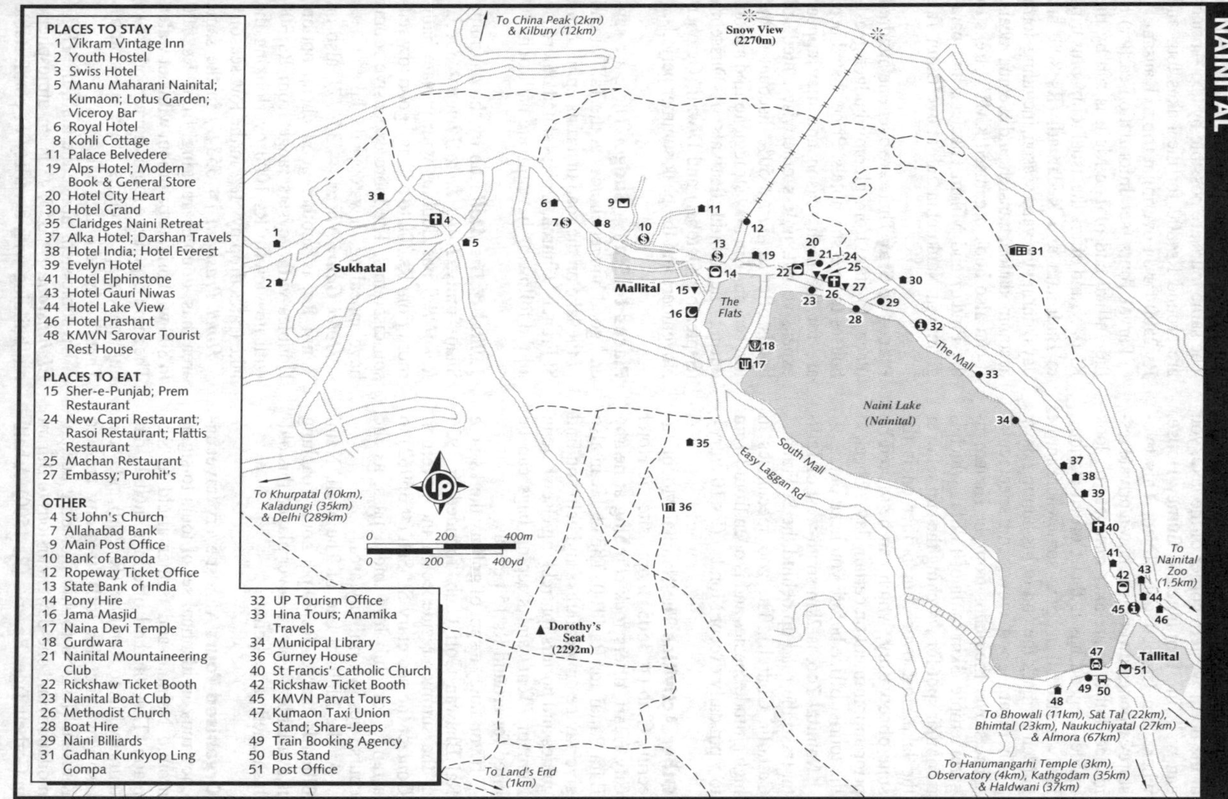
NAINITAL
PLACES TO STAY
1 Vikram Vintage Inn
2 Youth Hostel
3 Swiss Hotel
5 Manu Maharani Nainital; Kumaon; Lotus Garden; Viceroy Bar
6 Royal Hotel
8 Kohli Cottage
11 Palace Belvedere
19 Alps Hotel; Modern Book & General Store
20 Hotel City Heart
30 Hotel Grand
35 Claridges Naini Retreat
37 Alka Hotel; Darshan Travels
38 Hotel India; Hotel Everest
39 Evelyn Hotel
41 Hotel Elphinstone
43 Hotel Gauri Niwas
44 Hotel Lake View
46 Hotel Prashant
48 KMVN Sarovar Tourist Rest House
PLACES TO EAT
15 Sher-e-Punjab; Prem Restaurant
24 New Capri Restaurant; Rasoi Restaurant; Flattis Restaurant
25 Machan Restaurant
27 Embassy; Purohit's
OTHER
4 St John's Church
7 Allahabad Bank
9 Main Post Office
10 Bank of Baroda
12 Ropeway Ticket Office
13 State Bank of India
14 Pony Hire
16 Jama Masjid
17 Naina Devi Temple
18 Gurdwara
21 Nainital Mountaineering Club
22 Rickshaw Ticket Booth
23 Nainital Boat Club
26 Methodist Church
28 Boat Hire
29 Naini Billiards
31 Gadhan Kunkyop Ling Gompa
32 UP Tourism Office
33 Hina Tours; Anamika Travels
34 Municipal Library
36 Gurney House
40 St Francis' Catholic Church
42 Rickshaw Ticket Booth
45 KMVN Parvat Tours
47 Kumaon Taxi Union Stand; Share-Jeeps
49 Train Booking Agency
50 Bus Stand
51 Post Office
To China Peak (2km) & Kilbury (12km)
Snow View (2270m)
Sukhatal
Mallital
The Flats
Naini Lake (Nainital)
The Mall
South Mall
Easy Laggan Rd
Dorothy's Seat (2292m)
Tallital
To Khurpatal (10km), Kaladungi (35km) & Delhi (289km)
To Land's End (1km)
To Nainital Zoo (1.5km)
To Bhowali (11km), Sat Tal (22km), Bhimtal (23km), Naukuchiyatal (27km) & Almora (67km)
To Hanumangarhi Temple (3km), Observatory (4km), Kathgodam (35km) & Haldwani (37km)
0 200 400m
0 200 400yd

UTTAR PRADESH & UTTARANCHAL

From the Jama Masjid (Friday Mosque), at the north-western corner of the lake, you can walk in 30 minutes to **Gurney House**, where Jim Corbett once lived. This two-storey wooden dwelling is now a private residence, but the caretaker may let you look inside. Legend has it that Corbett symbolically buried all his guns somewhere in the garden to mark the end of his hunting days.

There are good views and spectacular sunsets over the plains from the Hanumangarhi temple, 3km south of Tallital, which is a popular spot for watching the sun set over the lake. Just over 1km farther on is the state **observatory**, which can be visited by prior appointment on certain days. Check at the tourist office before you head out.

Nainital Zoo, is 2km south-west of Tallital (take the road up behind the St Francis' Catholic Church). The zoo specialises in high altitude species and is open from 10 am to 5 pm daily except Monday (Rs 10 entry).

Other Activities The Nainital Mountaineering Club (☎ 35051), opposite the Hotel City Heart, offers **rock climbing** at nearby Bara Pattar for Rs 1100. The club can also give advice on local treks and help you find guides and porters for trekking elsewhere in Kumaon. Tents and sleeping bags can be hired for around Rs 15 per day.

If you fancy a spot of **golf** try the 18-hole Raj Bhawan Golf Club, founded in 1926 at the summer residence of the governor. Contact the secretary SL Sah (☎ 36962) to arrange for club hire and a pass, as the course lies in a military area.

At the Mallital end of The Mall, Naini **Billiards** charges Rs 40 per hour. Coaching is available if you've never played this old-fashioned game before.

Organised Tours Almost every travel agency runs an identical set of tours to sights around Nainital and farther afield in Kumaon. The standard offerings include day tours by bus to Ranikhet (Rs 200) and Mukteshwar Lake (Rs 150), two-day trips to Kausani (Rs 350 to 450 including accommodation) and one-day excursions to Bijrani in Corbett Tiger Reserve (Rs 1500). A half-day tour of the local lakes will cost Rs 100. The same tours are possible by taxi – prices are around Rs 800 for the Lakes tour and Rs 2500 for an overnight trip to Kausani.

Parvat Tours (see Information earlier) at the Tallital end of The Mall, is run by the KMVN, and offers the usual tours, plus trips to Badrinath and Kedarnath (Rs 800, six days) during the yatra season, including dorm accommodation, transfers and evening meals. It can also book organised KMVN treks to the Pindari and Milam Glaciers, and paragliding at Naukuchia Tal, above Bhim Tal.

Places to Stay There are over one hundred places to stay, from gloomy budget guesthouses to five-star hotels. Prices listed here are for the high season and may appear expensive but, unless otherwise stated, all hotels offer *at least* a 50% discount in the low season. You may struggle to find a room during the Hindu festivals of Dussehra (September/October) and Diwali (October/November) and the peak summer periods.

Places to Stay – Budget There are several good budget choices at the Tallital end of the lake on the road that runs uphill from St Francis' Church. Unless stated otherwise all the following have private bathrooms.

Tallital & The Mall Run by the charming Shah family, ***Hotel Lake View*** *(☎ 35632, Ramji Rd)* has doubles with private bathroom from Rs 300 to 550 and good low season discounts. The more expensive rooms have appealing views over the lake.

Hotel Gauri Niwas *(☎ 36617)*, also on Ramji Rd, is another good cheap option. Doubles with geysers range from Rs 300 with no view to Rs 1000 overlooking the lake (rates drop by 50% in the low season).

Hotel Prashant *(☎ 35347)* in the same area has doubles ranging from Rs 700 to 800 with private bathroom with hot water. The more expensive rooms have good views but the cheaper rooms are a bit shabby. There's a good dining hall.

Up some steps above the mall, the ***Hotel Elphinstone*** *(☎ 35534)* is an atmospheric old building with a variety of comfortable rooms from Rs 300 to 800. Rooms are bright and airy (with hot water) and there's a pleasant dining hall.

Dorms are available at ***KMVN Sarovar Tourist Rest House*** (see under Mid-Range to Top End later).

Mallital & Sukhatal An excellent choice in the heart of Mallital, ***Kohli Cottage*** *(☎ 36 368)* has doubles for Rs 300, Rs 400 and Rs 500, with private bathroom (24-hour hot water) and TV. Rooms are light, airy and clean and the manager is friendly and helpful. There are lovely views from the roof terrace.

Alps Hotel *(☎ 35317)* is a rather creaky centenarian, but has enormous doubles with basic private bathroom for Rs 200 to 300. There's a lovely old broad balcony for watching the promenaders on The Mall.

The ***Youth Hostel*** *(☎ 36353)* is set in a peaceful wooded location, but it's a long haul from anywhere else in town. The compensation is the prices – dorms (with lockers) cost Rs 22 for members, Rs 42 for nonmembers. Hot water is available in the mornings and filling vegetarian meals are available in the dining hall.

Places to Stay – Mid-Range & Top End

Unless otherwise stated the following listings have private bathroom.

Tallital & The Mall The ***KMVN Sarovar Tourist Rest House*** *(☎ 35570)* is close to the bus stand. Doubles range from Rs 450 to 900 depending on the season, but the dorm is good value year round, from Rs 40 to 80.

The large ***Evelyn Hotel*** *(☎ 35457)* is one of several Victorian-looking hotels right on The Mall. All these places proudly announce that there is 'no climb' and charge high rates for the privilege, typically Rs 600 to 1200 for doubles with a view. Other choices include the nearby ***Hotel India*** *(☎ 3517)* and the more expensive ***Hotel Everest*** *(☎ 36648)*, both with very similar facilities.

The swish ***Alka Hotel*** *(☎ 35220)*, stands out from the other places on the mall and has a fine restaurant. Rooms aren't bad for the money at Rs 1100 to 2000, though the low-season discount is only 30%.

Mallital & Sukhatal Sukhatal has the bulk of the top-end places.

The ***Hotel Grand*** *(☎ 35406, fax 37057)* in Mallital is only open from April to November, but it's the closest Raj-era place to the lake. Doubles cost Rs 1500 downstairs or Rs 1800 upstairs (with good lake views). There's a pleasant veranda sitting area where you can gaze out over the lake.

Hotel City Heart *(☎ 35228)*, is a good mid-range choice, just uphill from the lake. The high spirited owner is friendly; spotless doubles are good value, with prices ranging from Rs 700 to 1400 in the high season (Rs 250 to 700 at other times). Cheaper rooms have no views, but you can always watch the sun sink behind the hills from the roof terrace.

The ***Royal Hotel*** *(☎/fax 35357)* near the Allahabad Bank, is housed in a charismatic old building bedecked with hunting trophies and other Raj-era relics. Doubles with TV and fireplaces (wood is Rs 7 per bundle) cost from Rs 1000 to 1400.

Palace Belvedere *(☎ 35082, fax 35493)* was formerly the palace of the raja of Awagarh. Take the road that leads up behind the Bank of Baroda. Doubles start at Rs 1500 and some of the rooms have very good lake views. There are also good views over the lake from the wicker chairs on the shady veranda. There's a 30% low season discount and credit cards are accepted.

For comfort and peace and quiet, ***Claridges Naini Retreat*** *(☎ 35105, fax 35103)* is on the hillside high above Mallital and has luxury doubles for Rs 3000 (Rs 3800 half-board).

Swiss Hotel *(☎ 36013, fax 35493)* consists of two old Raj-era buildings about 15 minutes' walk above Mallital. There's a wonderfully evocative dining room and spacious rooms (some with garden views), prices start at Rs 1800 a double.

Farther along the same road, ***Vikram Vintage Inn*** *(☎/fax 36177)* is a very stylish option with luxurious singles/doubles for Rs 1650/3000, including breakfast.

Nainital's top hotel is the ***Manu Maharani Nainital*** *(☎ 37341, fax 37350, Grasmere Estate)*, also in Sukhatal. Rooms are splendidly appointed and most have lake views; rates start at Rs 3300 per night. The restaurants are excellent.

Places to Eat There's a wide range of eating establishments along the length of The Mall, and all of the top-end hotels have their own restaurants (visitors welcome).

Sher-e-Punjab and ***Prem Restaurant*** are cheap but good dhaba-style places in a small cul-de-sac in Mallital's main bazaar, which serve the usual vegetarian standards.

New Capri Restaurant, at the Mallital end of The Mall, has Indian, Chinese and continental cuisine. It's popular and often full at lunch time. Nonveg dishes are around Rs 50. Next door are the similarly popular ***Rasoi*** (vegetarian) and ***Flattis*** (nonveg).

The popular ***Machan Restaurant***, nearby, serves excellent soups (Rs 25 to 35) and a broad range of Indian, Chinese and European dishes for around Rs 55.

Embassy is considered one of the best restaurants by locals and serves filling Indian staples and good value sizzlers from around Rs 65. ***Purohit's***, next door, serves vegetarian South Indian cuisine, including cheap thalis.

The ***restaurant*** at the Alka Hotel serves up good Gujarati food in a sophisticated setting. Expect to pay around Rs 150 for a meal.

There are two restaurants at the Manu Maharani Nainital Hotel: the multicuisine ***Kumaon***, and the ***Lotus Garden***, serving Chinese cuisine. The Kumaon serves great European dishes and good Indian food for around Rs 140. The impressive buffet breakfast (Rs 150) features all the European favourites. Also here is the ***Viceroy Bar***.

Getting There & Away Transport links aren't as good as you might expect as Nainital is off the main highway.

Bus Ordinary buses to Delhi (Rs 142, nine hours) leave from the Tallital bus stand at 7, 8.30 and 9 am and 6, 6.30, 7 and 7.30 pm. To Dehra Dun, ordinary buses (Rs 159, 10 hours) leave at 5.30, 6 and 7 am and 4.30 pm, and there's a deluxe service (Rs 231) at 8 pm. Ordinary buses to Haridwar (Rs 133, eight hours) depart every 30 minutes from 5 to 7.30 am, and at 4.30 pm. There's also a semi-deluxe service at 8 pm (Rs 170). There's a single direct bus to Rishikesh (Rs 150, nine hours) at 5 am and a single daily service to Pithoragarh (Rs 115, nine hours) at 7 am.

To Ramnagar (Rs 56, 3½ hours), buses leave at 7 am and 8.30 am, but you're much better off taking a bus to Haldwani, the regional transport hub, and changing to a local bus for Ramnagar there. Buses to Haldwani leave Tallital every 15 minutes (Rs 22, 1½ hours). Haldwani also has regular buses to Delhi and the Nepali border crossing at Banbassa. You can pick up the train to Delhi from either Haldwani or Kathgodam a few kilometres north.

Heading north, there are 7 am buses to Almora (Rs 42, three hours) and Kausani (Rs 70, five hours) and 12.30 and 2.30 pm buses to Ranikhet (Rs 39, three hours). A faster alternative is to take a bus to Bhowali (Rs 8, 20 minutes) at the junction of the Ranikhet and Almora roads, from where there are buses onto Almora, Ranikhet and Kausani about every 30 minutes. Buses to Bhowali leave Tallital every half hour. Bhowali also has frequent services to Bageshwar (Rs 129, five hours), where you can pick up share-jeeps and buses to Gwaldam (for destinations in Garhwal) and Song (for the Pindari Glacier trek). A single direct bus to Song leaves Bhowali at 6 am.

Many private agencies offer overnight deluxe coaches (two-by-two seating) to Delhi (Rs 250/350, deluxe/air-con) and Haridwar (Rs 250).

Train Kathgodam (35km south) is the nearest train station, but Haldwani, one stop earlier, is the major transport hub in the region. The train booking agency near the bus stand in Tallital has a quota for trains to Delhi, Moradabad and Kolkata. The *Ranikhet Express* departs Old Delhi station at 10.45 pm, arriving into Haldwani at 5.50 am and Kathgodam at 6.10 am. The return trip leaves Kathgodam at 8.45 pm and Haldwani at 9 pm, arriving at Old Delhi station at 4.45 am. (Rs 129/550, sleeper/two-tier). The office is open 9 am to noon, and 2 to 5 pm Monday to Saturday; 9 am to 2 pm Sunday.

Taxi & Share-Jeep A reserve taxi from the bus stand in Tallital will charge Rs 700 to Ramnagar, Rs 650 to Almora or Ranikhet and Rs 1200 to Kausani.

Share-jeeps leave from the bus stand when full and go to Bhowali (Rs 8), Kathgodam and Haldwani (Rs 40).

Getting Around The official rate for a rickshaw from Tallital to Mallital is Rs 4; tickets can only be purchased at the booths at either end of The Mall and rickshaws cannot be flagged down anywhere else.

Around Nainital

The Nainital region is famed for its many lakes. Closest to Nainital is the delightful **Khurpa Tal**, a 10km walk from Mallital (local buses also run there). This tranquil lake is set at an elevation of 1635m and is surrounded by green terraced fields. About 22km east of Nainital is the group of peaceful lakes known as **Sattal** (Seven Lakes), surrounded by woodland, where you can hire row boats. You can get here by bus or share-jeep.

Bhim Tal, 23km from Nainital, is a large lake with an island, which attracts crowds of day-trippers from Nainital. Rowboats can be hired (Rs 80 per 30 minutes) and there is a small restaurant on the island. Fishing permits can be obtained from the Fisheries Office in the bazaar at the west end of Bhim Tal.

There are several hotels here; the KMVN ***Tourist Reception Centre*** *(☎ 47005)* has dorms starting at Rs 60 and doubles from Rs 400 to 900 (Rs 200 to 450 in the low season). There are several daily private and public buses from Nainital (Rs 16, one hour) or you can do the trip by share-jeep via Bhowali.

About 4km north-east is **Naukuchiya Tal** (Lake of Nine Corners), which is more laid-back than Bhim Tal but also has boating facilities. There are a few upmarket resorts and the peaceful lakeside ***KMVN Tourist Reception Centre*** *(☎ 47138)* with dorms for Rs 60 and doubles from Rs 450 to 950 (Rs 225 to 525 in the low season). The lake is well served by buses.

Ranikhet

☎ 05966

North of Nainital and at an altitude of 1829m, Ranikhet is a peaceful hill station established as a barracks and still home to the Kumaon Regiment. There are good views of the Himalaya from the village, which has several places to stay, but all of the old Raj-era hotels are all about 3km distant, on the far side of the cantonment.

There are several good walks, including the **Jhula Devi Temple** (1km south of West View Hotel) and the orchards at **Chaubatia** (3km farther on). The tourist office (☎ 20227) is by the UP Roadways bus stand. The State Bank of India, on the road up to the cantonment, can change most travellers cheques in US dollars or UK pounds, but there's a US$100 limit per day.

Places to Stay & Eat There are several hotels in Sadar Bazaar between the bus stands, all offering basic rooms with squat toilet. ***Hotel Rajdeep*** *(☎ 20017)* is the best of the cheap places, with a wide range of clean rooms from Rs 100 to 300, and a communal sitting area. The ***Hotel Tourist*** next door has simple rooms for Rs 80 to 100 and a nice balcony, while things are more basic at the ***Everest Hotel***, where singles/doubles go for Rs 100/150.

Across the road, the large ***Moon Hotel*** *(☎ 20382)* has slightly overpriced rooms from Rs 650 to 1650, all with TV.

Near the UP Roadways bus stand, ***Parwati Inn*** *(☎ 20325)* is a modern complex with good rooms starting at Rs 500 (less 40% in the low season), and a restaurant and cinema.

There are three old Raj-era places in a tranquil location on the west side of the cantonment. The ***Hotel Meghdoot*** *(☎ 20475)* charges start at Rs 450/650 for clean singles/doubles with hot water and it has a good restaurant.

Across the road, ***Norton's Hotel*** *(☎ 20377)* has a homelike atmosphere and a cheery living room. Comfortable rooms with hot water cost Rs 300 to 400.

West View Hotel *(☎ 20261)* is another former Raj establishment. Large rooms with fireplaces start at Rs 1500 (Rs 800 in the low season). There's afternoon tea, and croquet on the lawn.

The ***Mayur Restaurant*** opposite the bus stand offers a good choice of Indian dishes.

Getting There & Away UP Roadways and KMOU have separate bus stations at opposite ends of town. UP Roadways has buses to Delhi at 4, 4.30 and 5 pm (Rs 168, 12 hours), and to Haridwar at 8.30 am and 3 pm (Rs 146 or Rs 175, 10 hours). There are half-hourly buses to Haldwani and Kathgodam (Rs 58), which pass through Bhowali, where you can take a bus or share-jeep to Nainital. Direct buses to Nainital leave at 8 and 10.30 am; KMOU has a bus at 11.30 am.

Both companies have buses to Almora (Rs 34, two hours) and Kausani (Rs 34, two hours) every few hours until 3 pm. Buses to Ramnagar also leave every few hours until 2.30 pm (Rs 60, four hours). Just as useful are share-jeeps, which leave when full for Almora (Rs 30), Haldwani (Rs 60) and Dwarahat (Rs 30).

Hina Tours and Travel operates deluxe overnight buses to Delhi (Rs 225) and Haridwar (Rs 260) at 6 pm. During the yatra season, a bus to Badrinath (Rs 550) leaves at 5 am. You can pick up the train to Delhi from Haldwani or Kathgodam; the train booking office at the bus stand has a tiny quota of tickets.

RANIKHET

PLACES TO STAY & EAT
2 Moon Hotel
3 Mayur Restaurant
7 Parwati Inn
8 Hotel Rajdeep; Hotel Tourist
9 Everest Hotel
16 Hotel Meghdoot
17 Norton's Hotel
18 West View Hotel

OTHER
1 Taxi Stand
4 Share-Jeep Stand
5 UP Roadways Bus Stand; Train Booking Agency
6 UP Tourism Office
10 State Bank of India
11 Hina Tours & Travel
12 KMOU Bus Stand; Share-Jeep Stand
13 Catholic Church
14 Main Post Office
15 Kumaon Lodge (Officers' Mess)

Dwarahat

About 32km north of Ranikhet this historic town is the former capital of the Katyuri Rajas. This pleasant hill town is worth a detour for its 12th century temples, which feature particularly fine carving. Every April, Dwarahat holds the Syalde-Bhikhauti fair, which attracts revellers from all over Kumaon. You can get here by bus or share-jeep from Ranikhet.

Almora

☎ 05962 • pop 53,507

At an altitude of 1650m, this picturesque hill town was established as a summer capital by the Chand rajas of Kumaon in 1560, predating the British summer capital tradition by several hundred years. The stone Nanda Devi Temple, reached through the colourful Lalal Bazaar area, is the only relic from the Chand days, but there are several stone houses and colonial-era buildings in town. Images from surrounding temples are paraded up to **Nanda Devi** in September accompanied by the usual festival shenanigans.

Information There is a small and informal UP tourist office (☎ 30180) near the Hotel Savoy. The State Bank of India only exchanges AmEx travellers cheques in US dollars or UK pounds, but may change other travellers cheques in a dire emergency.

For treks locally or to the Pindari or Milam Glaciers try High Adventure (☎ 32277), Discover Himalaya (☎ 31470), or Ridge & Trek (☎ 22492) on The Mall. All charge around Rs 1000 per day with guides, porters, food and accommodation. The Divisional Forest Office on The Mall (☎ 33753) can book forest resthouses in the hills.

Things to See Like Ranikhet and Kausani, Almora offers good views of the mountains and great walks, including the 8km trek up to the **Kasar Devi Temple** where Swami Vivekananda came to meditate. There are impressive sunsets from **Bright End Corner**, 2.5km south-west of the town centre. The small **Pt GB Pant Museum** in town has displays on local temples and archaeology.

Places to Stay & Eat Most of the places to stay are spread out along The Mall and all offer significant reductions in the low season.

Right in the centre, the vast ***Hotel Shikhar*** *(☎ 30253)* has well-maintained rooms to suit all budgets, but the atmosphere is a little impersonal. Budget rooms start at Rs 150/200 with shared/private bathroom with hot water; better rooms with TV start at Rs 600.

In the Lal Bazaar area, ***Hotel Shyam*** *(☎ 35467)* has clean, cosy doubles starting at Rs 500 and dorms for Rs 50. The communal balconies upstairs have great views.

Opposite the State Bank of India, the ***Hotel Konark*** *(☎ 31217)* has spotless doubles from Rs 300 to 450 with private bathroom and hot water.

The ***Kailas Hotel*** *(☎ 30624)* is colourful and slightly new-age; most travellers seem to enjoy the eccentricities of the guesthouse itself and its elderly proprietors, Mr and Mrs Shah, and there are tasty home-cooked meals and excellent herbal teas. There are rooms starting at Rs 75/125 in summer, and dorms for Rs 40. Only the doubles have private bathrooms.

A five-minute walk east of the centre, the ***Hotel Surmool*** *(☎ 22860)* has friendly staff and good-value rooms with private bathroom and geyser starting at Rs 300/400 a single/double (Rs 450/500 with TV and geyser); dorms are Rs 150. The ***Sunrise Restaurant*** here is also good value.

On the hill behind the Surmool, the peaceful ***Hotel Savoy*** *(☎ 30329, Upper Mall Rd)* has decent rooms with hot shower for Rs 400 or Rs 500 for upstairs rooms on the balcony. Prices drop by 30% in low season.

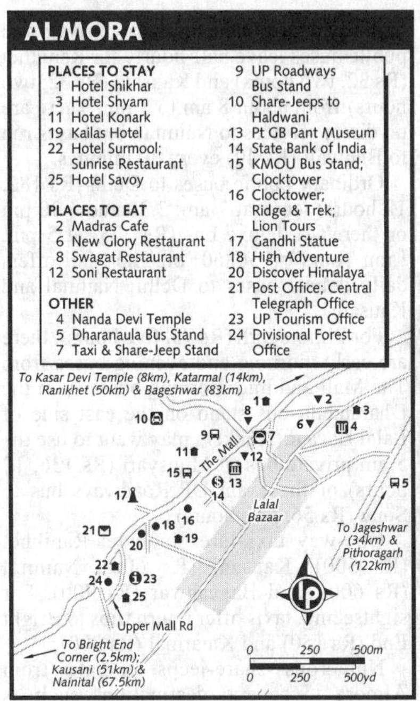

Just before the Hotel Shikhar, stairs lead down to the ***Swagat Restaurant***. There's an extensive vegetarian menu and a good range of sweet milky Indian deserts.

The gloomy ***Madras Cafe***, in the Lalal Bazaar area is a no-frills, reasonably priced vegetarian restaurant with main dishes under Rs 25. The ***New Glory Restaurant***, opposite, is a better vegetarian option with a broad menu, but look out for the low ceilings.

Back on The Mall, the popular Sikh-run ***Soni Restaurant*** offers both vegetarian and nonveg options in a slightly fast-food environment.

Almora's regional delicacy is *ball mithai* (fudge coated in sugar balls), which can be bought from any of the ***sweet shops*** on the main road.

Getting There & Away The KMOU and UP Roadways bus stands are both on The Mall (UP Roadways buses stop on the highway opposite the museum). Private and public buses leave half-hourly for Ranikhet (Rs 32, two hours) and Kausani (Rs 32, two hours) from about 8 am to 3 pm. There are no direct services to Nainital, but buses run to Bhowali (Rs 40) every 30 minutes.

Ordinary public buses to Delhi (Rs 182, 12 hours) leave at 7 am, 3.30 and 4.30 pm or there's a deluxe bus (Rs 225) at 5 pm. Lion Tours (☎ 30860) on The Mall offers daily deluxe buses to Delhi, Nainital and Kausani.

For Pithoragarh (Rs 73, five hours), there are early morning and evening buses from The Mall and mid-morning buses from the Dharanaula bus stand on the east side of Lalal Bazaar. Trekkers may want to use the 5 am private bus to Munsyari (Rs 136, 12 hours) or the 5 am UP Roadways bus to Song (Rs 56, five hours).

One-way taxi fares include: Ranikhet (Rs 500); Kausani (Rs 600); Nainital (Rs 600); and Bageshwar (Rs 700). For sightseeing, taxis offer return trips to Bright End (Rs 150) and Katarmal (Rs 300).

Numerous share-jeeps operate from Almora to several destinations such as Ranikhet (Rs 35), Kausani (Rs 40), Bageshwar (Rs 60), Haldwani (for trains to Delhi, Rs 70) and Gwaldam (for connections to Garhwal, Rs 70).

Around Almora

The hills around Almora are dotted with ancient temples; the 800-year-old Surya (Sun) Temple at **Katarmal** (12km to Kosi and then a 2km walk west) is worth a look. Although damaged, the huge temple is still impressive and is surrounded by 34 smaller shrines. Buses between Almora and Ranikhet stop in Kosi.

About 38km north-east of Almora in a forest of deodars is the huge temple complex of **Jageshwar**, which dates back to the 7th century AD. There are a staggering 124 temples here, from waist-high linga shrines, to vast sikhara-style temples. The doorway to the main **Jageshwar Temple** is flanked by beautifully carved figures representing the Ganges and Yamuna Rivers. The other important structure here is the **Mrityunjaya Temple**. The complex is a 4km walk through the forest from the village of old Jageshwar, where there's a ***KMVN Tourist Rest House*** with doubles starting at Rs 300 and dorms for Rs 60. The ***Forest Rest House*** here can be booked with the Divisional Forest Office in Almora (Rs 250).

There's a noon bus from Almora to Jageshwar, or you can take a Pithoragarh-bound bus to Artola and walk (or hitch) 3km north. Taxis charge Rs 600 for a return trip from Almora.

Kausani

☎ 05962 • elevation 1890m

There are even closer views of the Himalaya from the cluster of hotels along the ridge at Kausani, 51km north of Almora. The most easily identifiable peak is Trisul (7120m), shaped like a trident. It's a peaceful spot, and was home to the poet GB Pant, who is commemorated by a small museum above the bus stand. Gandhi stayed at the Anasakti Ashram here in 1929 and was inspired to write *Anasakti Yoga*.

Places to Stay & Eat The ***Uttarakhand Tourist Lodge*** *(☎ 45012)*, at the top of the stairs leading up from the bus stand, has basic doubles with private bathroom starting at Rs 400 in the high season and Rs 100 in the low season. For TV/hot water you'll pay an extra Rs 250/1400. All rooms face the snows; mountain-biking tours depart from here in the high season.

Up on the ridge, close to the ashram, ***Hotel Prashant*** *(☎ 45037)* is a popular cheapie – rates make up for the lack of a view. In the high season, rooms cost Rs 400 to 750; in the low season they're Rs 175 to 300.

Nearby are the ***Hotel Dak Bangla*** *(☎ 45074)*, offering large rooms with views starting at Rs 250/950 in the low/high season, and the upmarket ***Krishna Mount View*** *(☎ 45008)*, with nice gardens, great views and the excellent ***Vaibhav restaurant***; plush doubles with TV start at Rs 1025 in the high season (30% less at other times).

Other mid-range options include the ***Sun 'n' Snow Inn*** *(☎ 45010)* and ***Hotel Jeetu***

(☎ *45023)*, farther along the ridge, and the ***Hotel Sagar*** (☎ *45018)*, halfway between the ridge and the village.

KMVN Tourist Rest House (☎ *45006)* is a couple of kilometres beyond the village. It's very good value and has doubles from Rs 200 to 800 with great views, balconies and hot water. There are dorms for Rs 60.

Anasakti Ashram has accommodation by donation, but you are required to attend prayers; smoking, meat and alcohol are prohibited.

By the Sagar Hotel are several very similar restaurants, including the ***Hill Queen***, ***Ashoka*** and ***Sunrise***, all serving Indian and Chinese food.

Getting There & Away Buses to Almora (Rs 32, 2½ hours) pass through town approximately every hour between 7 am and 3 pm, continuing to Nainital (Rs 70, six hours). Share-jeeps to Almora charge Rs 50. There are buses to Ranikhet (Rs 42, four hours) at 6 and 9 am and 2 pm. There are also several buses to Bageshwar (Rs 23, 1½ hours), via Baijnath. A bus leaves between 7 and 8 am for Karnaprayag in Garhwal (Rs 56, three hours).

The nearest share-jeep hub is Garur, 10km downhill (Rs 10, 15 minutes), from where there are regular connections to Gwaldam (Rs 20), and Bageshwar (Rs 15). Taxis charge Rs 600 to Almora or Bageshwar and Rs 650 to Ranikhet.

Baijnath

This peaceful village, 19km north of Kausani and 23km west of Bageshwar, is famous for its 12th century sikhara-style temples. The main group (known collectively as Baijnath Temple) is devoted to Shiva and has a lovely location shaded by trees on the edge of the Gomti River. There are several other Shaivites shrines in the old village, a ten-minute walk north of Baijnath, and at Kot-ki-Mai, 3km west.

The only place to stay is the ***KMVN Tourist Rest House*** (☎ *05962-24101)* with doubles for Rs 200 and dorms for Rs 50. From Kausani, you can either take a Bageshwar bus or change to a Bageshwar share-jeep at Garur. Taxis charge Rs 250 return with an hour waiting time.

Bageshwar

This pleasant pilgrimage town is situated at the confluence of the Gomti and Sarju Rivers, 41km from Kausani and 78km from Almora. The town is renowned for its ancient stone **Bagnath Temple**, which is devoted to Shiva and houses some impressive carvings; there are some interesting ghats and bazaar backstreets nearby. The smaller **Baneshwar Mahadev** temple opposite also dates from the 12th century. On Makar Sankranti (14th January) Bageshwar hosts the colourful **Uttarayani Fair**, which attracts thousands of Hindu bathers.

Places to Stay There are several decent places to stay. Right by the bus stand, the ***Hotel Annpurna*** (☎ *22109)* has a nice riverside terrace and simple rooms for Rs 175 (Rs 240 with TV and geyser). Farther along the main road are the ***Hotel Rajdoot*** (☎ *22146)*, with slightly gloomy singles/doubles with private bathroom for Rs 100/175, and the ***Hotel Siddhartha*** (☎ *22114)* with good value rooms with geyser and TV for Rs 250 a double.

Getting There & Away There are several daily buses to Almora (Rs 55, three hours) and Ranikhet (Rs 65, three hours) via Kausani (Rs 23, 1½ hours). Buses leave hourly until 10.30 pm for Bhowali (Rs 139, six hours) and Haldwani (Rs 155, 7½ hours). Share-jeeps and buses run up to Gwaldam (Rs 30, two hours) for connections on to Garhwal.

For the Pindari Glacier, there's a 7 am bus to Song. For the Milam Glacier take the 9 am bus to Munsyari, or change at Thal.

It's also possible to reach all these destinations, in several stages, by share-jeep; Garur (Rs 15, 30 minutes) is the hub for share-jeeps to Kausani and on to Almora and Ranikhet.

Pindari Glacier Trek

Song, 36km north of Bageshwar, is the starting point for the trek to the Pindari Glacier on the southern rim of the Nanda Devi National Park. The trail passes through truly virgin country and offers wonderful views of Nanda Kot (6860m) and Nanda Khat (6611m). The return trip takes six days (a 100km round trip), but you can also include the Kafni Glacier (add two days) or continue west to Gwaldam (add two days). The standard route is from Song to Dhakri Khal (10km), Dhakri to Khati (9km), Khati to Dwali (11km); Dwali to Phurkiya (8km) and Phurkiya to Zero Point at the foot of the glacier. There are KMVN ***bungalows*** (offering bare floors with no bedding for Rs 50 a night) at Dhakri, Khati, Dwali and Phurkiya.

There are buses to Song from Bhowali and Bageshwar, or you can take a local bus to Bharari and change to a share-jeep there.

Pithoragarh

☎ 05964 • pop 42,113

Situated at 1815m, Pithoragarh is the main town of a region that borders both Tibet and Nepal and has several Chand-era temples and an old fort. The town is in a small valley called 'Little Kashmir' and there are plenty of picturesque walks in the area, including the rewarding climb up to **Chandak** (7km) for views of the Pithoragarh Valley and the Panchchuli (Five Chimneys) massif.

The district magistrate's office (☎ 22202) is the place to enquire about inner-line permits for the sensitive area around Nanda Devi.

There's a tourist office (☎ 25527) and a ***KMVN rest house*** *(☎ 25434)*, with doubles for Rs 350 and dorms for Rs 50. There are several other reasonable hotels, including the central ***Uttranchal Deep*** and ***Samrat***.

Several buses leave for Almora (Rs 73, five hours) between 4.30 am and 10 am. There also regular buses to Haldwani, Delhi and Tanakpur (the railhead, 151km south), where you can take a local bus to the Nepali border crossing at Banbassa. Buses and share-jeeps run north to Munsyari, the trailhead for the Milam Glacier.

Milam Glacier Trek

This challenging trek passes through magnificent rugged country to the east of Nanda Devi (7820m), following the gorge of the Gori Ganga River. The trailhead is the spectacularly located village of Munsyari, accessible by bus from Almora or Pithoragarh. Accommodation is mostly limited to camping and the trek is best attempted with a guide (available in Munsyari).

The standard route (many variations are possible) runs from Munsyari to Lilam (16km); Lilam to Bogdwar (14km); Bogdwar to Railkot (12km); Railkot to Milam village (20km, gentle ascent); and finally Milam village to the glacier (5km each way). This is a politically sensitive area, and you'll need to show your passport and register with the Indo-Tibet Border Police (ITBP) at Milam, who may not let you proceed any further. If you are allowed to continue to the glacier, there are amazing views of the peaks of Rishi Pahar (6992m), Hardeol (7151m) and Trishuli (7074m) to the north-west.

Munsyari has a ***KMVN Rest House*** *(☎ 059612-2339)* with rooms starting at Rs 450 and dorms for Rs 60. There is a daily bus from Almora to Munsyari and several trips from Pithoragarh but you can also do the trip in several hops by share-jeep.

Banbassa

Banbassa is the closest Indian village to the Nepali border crossing of Mahendrenagar. The border crossing is conveniently close to Delhi, but it's certainly not the most convenient way to enter Nepal. The time you save on the Indian side of the border is cancelled out by the arduous journey on to Pokhara or Kathmandu. Of course, some travellers choose the crossing for just this reason, taking time to explore western Nepal on the way.

Getting There & Away Between 7 am and 9 pm, there are hourly buses from Delhi's Anand Vihar bus stand to Tanakpur which stop in Banbassa (Rs 138, 10 hours). From Almora, you're best off taking a bus or share-jeep to Haldwani and picking up one of the frequent buses to Banbassa (Rs 42, three hours). Buses between Pithoragarh and Bareilly also stop in Banbassa.

From Banbassa, you can catch a rickshaw for the 3km to the border and across to Mahendrenagar. Visas valid for 21 days can be obtained at the border (US$30, two passport photos required), but only between 9 am and 4 pm. Moneychangers loiter around the border offering to exchange your dollars or Indian rupees for Nepali rupees. If you already have a visa, crossing should be no problem between 7 am and 7 pm.

On the Nepali side, regular buses will take you the 6km to Mahendrenagar's old bus stand, from where a few daily buses leave for Kathmandu at around 2 pm (a gruelling 24-hour trip). It's much more enjoyable to break the journey at Nepalganj (served by frequent buses from the new bus stand, eight hours) and travel on to Kathmandu (16 hours) or Pokhara (night buses, 15 hours) from there. This is really a dry-season-only route as the road on from Mahendrenagar is prone to flooding in the monsoon.

Around Banbassa

Most people come to Banbassa to enter Nepal, but there are a few other things to see in Udham Singh Nagar district (named in honour of the Sikh freedom fighter who assassinated Lieutenant Governor O'Dwyer in London in 1940 in revenge for the Jallianwala Bagh massacre of 1919).

The pilgrimage centre of **Nanak Matta**, 29km south-west of Banbassa, is home to a huge Sikh gurdwara sacred to the Guru Nanak. It's a tranquil spot and you can stay at the gurdwara for a small donation. Buses between Haldwani and Tanakpur pass through hourly.

About 88km north of Banbassa on the bus route from Tanakpur to Pithoragarh, **Champawat** was the capital of the Chand Rajas until 1560 and is famous for its ancient and profusely carved stone temples. There are ***KMVN rest houses*** in both Champawat and Nanak Matta, with dorms for Rs 40 and doubles starting at Rs 300.

UTTAR PRADESH & UTTARANCHAL

Bihar & Jharkhand

In November 2000, after years of lobbying by Adivasi (tribal) interests, Bihar was split into two states. The new state, Jharkhand, is comprised of 18 mineral-rich southern districts. This is not good news for Bihar, which will be even worse off without its more prosperous south.

It had been argued for a long time that the southern region was culturally and historically different from the rest of Bihar, but it was not until the 1990s that the movement for a new state really gathered momentum.

There have been some teething problems with the creation of Jharkhand, including a petition in Patna's High Court from members of the legislative council, challenging the validity of the new state. Such issues will probably take a while to sort out, but travellers should notice few real changes when moving around the area of former Bihar.

Despite having areas of great beauty and historic religious links, Bihar is India's poorest state and is notorious for political uprisings. Both Bihar and Jharkhand are well known for Naxalite bandit activity, and Ranchi, the capital of Jharkhand, regularly has curfews to combat law-and-order problems.

Historically, Bihar has been closely linked with the life of the Buddha. The Buddhist (or Lotus) Circuit is a pilgrim's trail following in the footsteps of the Buddha, primarily in Bihar where he spent most of his time. See the special section 'The Way of the Buddha' for more information on the Buddha's life and the Lotus Circuit.

Today, the Buddha's predictions continue to come true: the rivers periodically flood; per capita income is meagre; the literacy rate is one of the lowest in the country; and Bihar is considered to have the most widespread government corruption. Strikes and demonstrations are the order of the day and 'feud and fire' take the form of outbreaks of inter-caste warfare and violence – dacoity (armed robbery) is still widespread.

Bihar & Jharkhand at a Glance

Population: 109.8 million
Area: 173,877 sq km
Capital: Patna (Bihar), Ranchi (Jharkhand)
Main Language: Hindi
When to Go: Oct to Mar

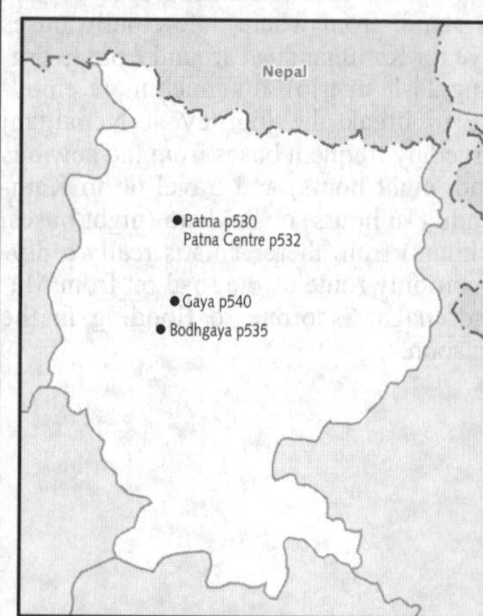

- Seek enlightenment under the sacred Bodhi Tree at Bodhgaya
- Explore Patna Museum, a little oasis of knowledge and artefacts
- Enjoy the quiet of the ruins at Nalanda University, an ancient seat of learning
- Relax just after the monsoon at one of the many beautiful waterfalls in the area around Ranchi
- Check out everything from chickens to elephants at Sonepur Fair, India's largest livestock fair

Because of the lawlessness, political instability and lack of tourism infrastructure, few travellers spend much time in Bihar or Jharkhand. This is a pity because there is so

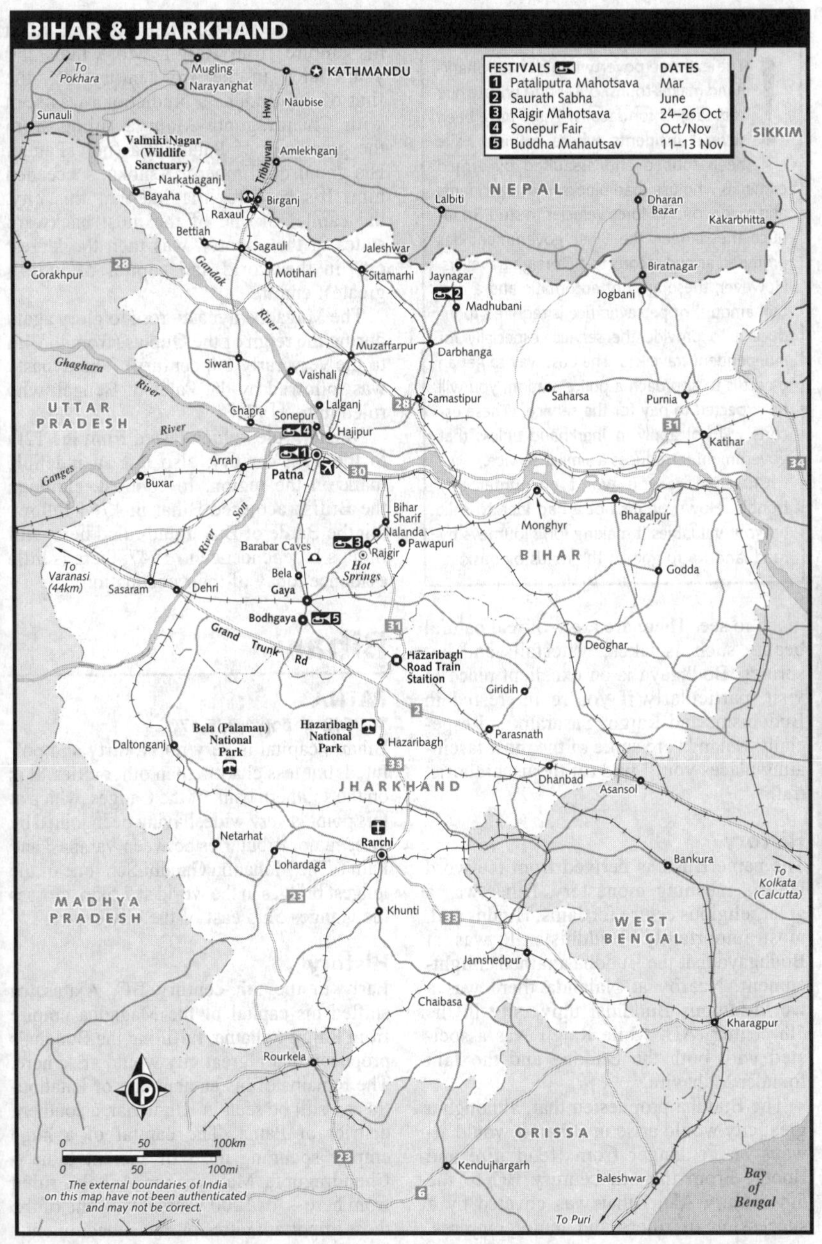
BIHAR & JHARKHAND
FESTIVALS
DATES
1 Pataliputra Mahotsava Mar
2 Saurath Sabha June
3 Rajgir Mahotsava 24–26 Oct
4 Sonepur Fair Oct/Nov
5 Buddha Mahautsav 11–13 Nov
To Pokhara
Mugling
Narayanghat
KATHMANDU
Naubise
Tribhuvan Hwy
Sunauli
Valmiki Nagar (Wildlife Sanctuary)
Amlekhganj
Narkatiaganj
Bayaha
Birganj
Raxaul
Bettiah
Sagauli
Lalbiti
NEPAL
Dharan Bazar
Kakarbhitta
SIKKIM
Gorakhpur
Gandak River
Motihari
Jaleshwar
Sitamarhi
Jaynagar
Madhubani
Biratnagar
Jogbani
Muzaffarpur
Darbhanga
Ghaghara River
Siwan
Vaishali
Saharsa
Purnia
UTTAR PRADESH
Chapra
Lalganj
Samastipur
Sonepur
Hajipur
Katihar
River
Arrah
Patna
Ganges
Buxar
Son River
Monghyr
Bhagalpur
Bihar Sharif
Nalanda
Barabar Caves
Rajgir
Pawapuri
BIHAR
To Varanasi (44km)
Hot Springs
Bela
Gaya
Godda
Sasaram
Dehri
Bodhgaya
Grand Trunk Rd
Deoghar
Hazaribagh Road Train Staition
Giridih
Parasnath
Bela (Palamau) National Park
Hazaribagh National Park
Hazaribagh
Daltonganj
Dhanbad
Asansol
JHARKHAND
Netarhat
Ranchi
Lohardaga
Bankura
To Kolkata (Calcutta)
MADHYA PRADESH
Khunti
WEST BENGAL
Jamshedpur
Chaibasa
Kharagpur
Rourkela
ORISSA
Kendujhargarh
Baleshwar
Bay of Bengal
To Puri
28
30
31
34
2
33
23
6
0 50 100km
0 50 100mi
The external boundaries of India on this map have not been authenticated and may not be correct.

Warning

The extreme poverty in Bihar and Jharkhand makes tourist buses and private hire cars targets for dacoits. There have been several incidents where tourists have been robbed and assaulted by armed criminals who use road blocks, mock accidents and road works to force vehicles to stop. To reduce the danger, the Bihar government has promised armed escorts to all foreign travellers. However, these are not automatic and a certain amount of perseverance is required to induce it to provide the service, especially for independent travellers. The best way to get an escort is to approach a police station; you will be expected to pay for the service. (These escorts will not apply in Jharkhand unless that government introduces a similar service.)

Chances are you won't encounter any trouble. However, it's not a bad idea to split up your valuables if making long journeys by road, and try to get off the roads by dusk.

much to see. There are areas of real natural beauty such as lakes, waterfalls and hot springs. Bodhgaya is an excellent place to visit, particularly if you're interested in Buddhism; and Rajgir, Sasaram and especially Nalanda are some of the most fascinating places you'll find off the usual tourist trail.

History

The name Bihar is derived from the word *vihara*, meaning monastery. Bihar was a great religious centre for Jains, Hindus and, most importantly, Buddhists. It was at Bodhgaya that the Buddha attained enlightenment. Nearby at Nalanda there was a world-famous Buddhist university in the 5th century AD, while Rajgir was associated with both the Buddha and the Jain founder Mahavira.

The Buddha prophesied that, although a great city would arise in Bihar, it would always be in danger from 'feud, fire and flood'. From the 6th century BC to the 5th century AD, Bihar was coveted by a succession of rulers and major empires. Ajatsatru, the second Magadha king, ruled his empire from Rajgir. More than 250 years later, in the 3rd century BC, the first of the Buddha's predictions was seen with Chandragupta Maurya ruling from the great city of Pataliputra (now Patna). His grandson, Emperor Ashoka, succeeded him. It's hard to imagine that this city, the capital of one of the most backward states in the country, was then the largest city in the world and capital of India's greatest empire.

The Magadha dynasty rose to glory again during the reign of the Guptas (from the 4th to the very early 6th century). The dynasty was followed by the Palas of Bengal, who ruled until 1197.

Muslim rule, which lasted from the 12th to the 17th century, also left an indelible mark on the region. In contrast, although the British acquired Bihar in 1764 following the Battle of Buxar and ruled here until India's Independence in 1947, there is little evidence today of their occupation.

Bihar

PATNA

☎ 0612 • pop 1,285,470

Bihar's capital is very noisy, dirty and polluted, but less chaotic than other cities. It is on the southern bank of the Ganges, which at this point is very wide, having been joined by three major tributaries between Varanasi and Patna. The Mahatma Gandhi Seti, one of the longest bridges in the world at 7.5km, crosses the Ganges 5km east of the city centre.

History

Early in the 5th century BC, Ajatasatru shifted his capital of the Magadha empire from Rajgir to Patna, fulfilling the Buddha's prophecy that a great city would arise here. The remains of his ancient city of Pataliputra can still be seen in Kumrahar, a southern district of Patna. The capital of a huge empire spanning most of ancient India – Chandragupta Maurya and Ashoka ruled from here – for 1000 years it was one of the most important cities on the subcontinent.

Renamed Azimabad, the city regained its political importance in the mid-16th century AD when Sher Shah made it his capital after defeating Humayun. In 1764, after the Battle of Buxar, it passed to the British.

Orientation

The city stretches along the southern bank of the Ganges for about 15km. The hotels, main train station (Patna Junction) and airport are in the western half of Patna, known as Bankipur, while the older and more traditional area is to the east, in Patna City. The 'hub' of the new Patna is at Gandhi Maidan. The main market area is Ashok Raj Path, which starts from Gandhi Maidan.

Fraser and Exhibition Rds have officially had their names changed to Muzharul Haque Path and Braj Kishore Path respectively, and Boring Rd has become Jal Prakash Rd, but everyone still uses the old names. Gardiner Rd however, is now nearly always referred to as Birchand Patel Path.

Information

Tourist Offices The Bihar State Tourist Office (BSTO; ☎ 210219, fax 236218) is in spacious new premises on the corner of Dak Bungalow and Fraser Rds, upstairs next to the Silveroak Bar & Restaurant. There are also counters at Patna Junction train station and the airport, but don't expect much from them. There's a Government of India tourist office (☎ 345776) inconveniently located south of the railway line on old Bypass Rd.

Money Trade Wings, on the 1st floor behind the Maurya Patna hotel, is a good place to change foreign currency and travellers cheques, or to get credit card cash advances. It's open from 11.30 am to 5.30 pm Monday to Friday.

The State Bank of India at Gandhi Maidan is also good for changing money, if a little slow, and has an ATM.

Post & Communications There are plenty of Internet centres to choose from on Fraser Rd. Yahoo Internet Cafe (Rs 35 per hour) on the corner of Dak Bungalow and Fraser Rds is friendly and has fast connections.

There is another place to check your email, next to Hotel Samrat International, on Fraser Rd. Near the Satkar International Hotel also on Fraser Rd is a photo developing studio.

Travel Agencies Target Travel Agency (☎ 228771), upstairs from Trade Wings, is an efficient, friendly outfit worth checking out if you need to book a flight. It should also be able to help with booking train tickets, which, given the state of Patna Junction train station, could be useful.

Bookshops There are a couple of reasonable bookshops on Fraser Rd near the Satkar International Hotel, and a British Library (☎ 224198) on Bank Rd.

Patna Museum

This excellent, albeit somewhat dog-eared, museum contains badly labelled metal and stone sculptures dating back to the Maurya and Gupta periods, terracotta figures and archaeological finds from sites in Bihar such as Nalanda. It also houses the world's longest fossilised tree – 16m and 200 million years old. Stuffed wildlife includes the usual (tiger, deer) and the unusual (a kid with three ears and eight legs). There is a fine collection of Chinese paintings and *thangkas* (Tibetan cloth paintings), but unfortunately this collection is frequently closed. The museum is open from 10.30 am to 4.30 pm Tuesday to Sunday. Entry costs Rs 2, and you need to ask permission before taking photos.

Kumrahar Excavations

The remains of Pataliputra, as well as the ancient capital of the rulers Ajatasatru (491–459 BC), Chandragupta (321–297 BC) and Ashoka (274–237 BC), have been uncovered in Kumrahar, south of Patna. A few large pillars from the assembly hall, dating back to the Mauryan period, and the foundations of the brick Buddhist monastery known as Anand Bihar are all that remain. There's a small display of clay figures and wooden beams that were discovered here.

The Kumrahar excavations are fairly esoteric and are likely to attract only those with

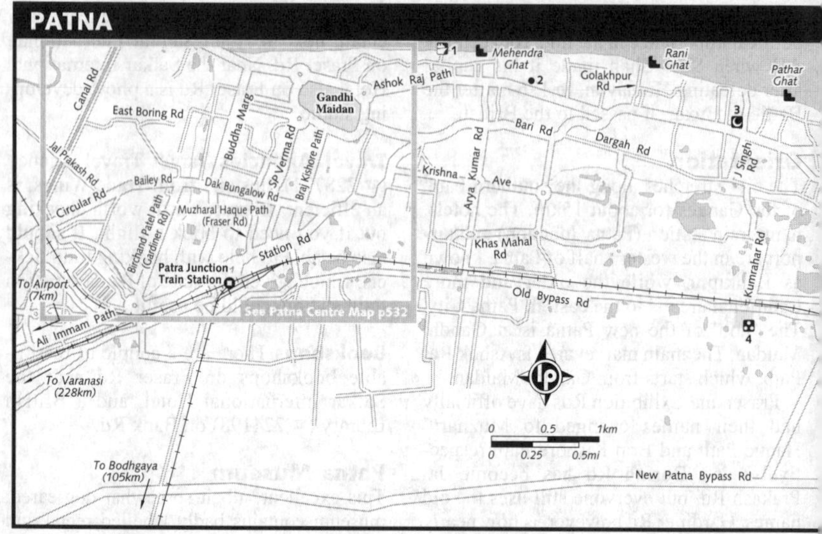

a keen interest in archaeology and India's ancient history. They are set in a pleasant park and are open from 9 am to 5 pm Tuesday to Sunday. Entry costs a hefty US$5 (Rs 230) for foreigners and a mere Rs 5 for Indians.

Har Mandir

At the eastern end of the city, in the Chowk area of old Patna, stands one of the holiest Sikh shrines. Built of white marble by Ranjit Singh, the Viceroy of Lahore, it marks the place where Gobind Singh, the 10th and last of the Sikh gurus, was born in 1660.

You must be barefoot within the temple precincts and your head must be covered. You can borrow cloth for this purpose at the entrance.

Qila House

Built on the foundations of Sher Shah's fort, Qila House (☎ 642354), also known as Jalan Museum, contains an impressive private collection of antiques, including a dinner service that once belonged to George III, Marie Antoinette's Sèvres porcelain, Napoleon's four-poster bed, Chinese jade and Mughal silver filigree. Phone ahead for permission to visit.

Khuda Baksh Oriental Library

Founded in 1900, this library has a renowned collection of very rare Arabic and Persian manuscripts, Mughal and Rajput paintings, and oddities such as the Quran inscribed in a book only 25mm wide. The library also contains the only books to survive the sacking of the Moorish University of Cordoba in Spain. It's open Monday to Friday and has free entry.

Other Attractions

Non-Hindus are welcome at the modern **Mahavir Mandir**, dedicated to the popular god Hanuman. At night this place is lit up in garish pink and green neon – you can't possibly miss it as you leave Patna Junction train station.

The heavily decorated, domed **Sher Shahi Mosque**, built by the Afghan ruler Sher Shah in 1545, is the oldest mosque in Patna. Other mosques include the squat **Pathar ki Masjid** and the riverside **madrassa**.

Organised Tours

BSTO sometimes operates a day trip that includes Patna, Rajgir, Nalanda and Pawapuri for Rs 125.

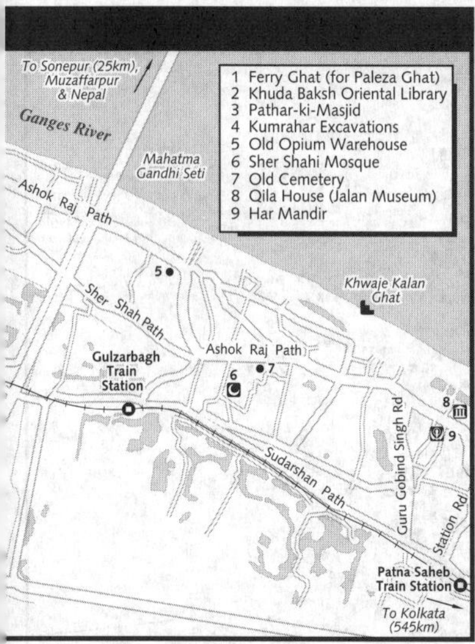

Special Events

Every March Patna comes alive with the **Pataliputra Mahotsava** featuring parades, sports, dancing and music. The festival celebrates the past when Patna (then called Pataliputra) was a great city.

Places to Stay – Budget

A lot of the cheaper hotels are tucked away in lanes off Fraser Rd. Many of Patna's cheaper hotels are being upgraded to mid-range places so the pickings these days, or at least at the time of research, are slim.

Youth Hostel *(SP Verma Rd)* south of the Maurya Patna, has clean, spartan dorms and rooms. It only accepts members (although you'll probably be able to convince them otherwise if they're not busy). Dorms/doubles are Rs 20/40.

Hotel Parker, at the northern end of Fraser Rd, is reasonable but rather dark and very basic. Rooms with private bathroom are Rs 60/70 a single/double.

Hotel Amar *(☎ 224157)* is down the lane opposite the Hotel Samrat International. Rooms with private bathroom cost Rs 125/160. It's the most pleasant of all the places off Fraser Rd.

Kautilya Vihar Tourist Bungalow *(☎ 225 411, R-Block, Birchand Patel Path)* is in a noisy spot, but it's clean and has private bathrooms with hot water, at least in theory. Dorm beds are Rs 75 and double rooms start at Rs 350.

Places to Stay – Mid-Range

Standards are relatively high in this range. All have private bathroom and hot water.

Hotel President *(☎ 220600)* is on the side street off Fraser Rd, which leads to the museum. Its location makes it a bit quieter than most. It has rooms starting at Rs 350/400, or Rs 600/700 with air-con.

Rajasthan Hotel *(☎ 225102, ⓔ hotelrajasthan@hotmail.com, Fraser Rd)* is scruffy but friendly. Standard double rooms with bucket hot water are Rs 500, or Rs 800 with air-con. The hotel also has room service until 10.30 pm.

Satkar International Hotel *(☎ 220551, fax 220556, Fraser Rd)* is pretty good value. Clean rooms with constant hot water cost Rs 570/800; there is also a lift.

Hotel Yash Krishna *(☎ 23984, Fraser Rd)* has a lift, running hot water and room service. Rooms start at Rs 300/350 and rooms with air-con are Rs 525/600.

Hotel Vijay Shree *(☎ 685312, Exhibition Rd)* used to be Hotel Swayam Sidhi. It has had a tasteful makeover and is excellent value. Air-con rooms with TV and constant hot water are Rs 550/650.

Hotel Republic *(☎ 655021, Exhibition Rd)* is newly renovated and has a range of tariffs starting at Rs 500/600 for a room with a fan.

Places to Stay – Top End

Maurya Patna *(☎ 222061, fax 222069)* overlooks Gandhi Maidan and is Patna's top hotel. You can count on the usual mod cons, including a pool. Rooms start at Rs 1900/2500 with breakfast. ***Hotel Pataliputra Ashok*** *(☎ 226270, Birchand Patel Path)* is similar at Rs 1600/2000.

Hotel Chanakya *(☎ 220590, fax 220598, ⓔ chanakya@gias101.vsnl.net.in)* is an air-conditioned three-star place that charges Rs 1700/2300.

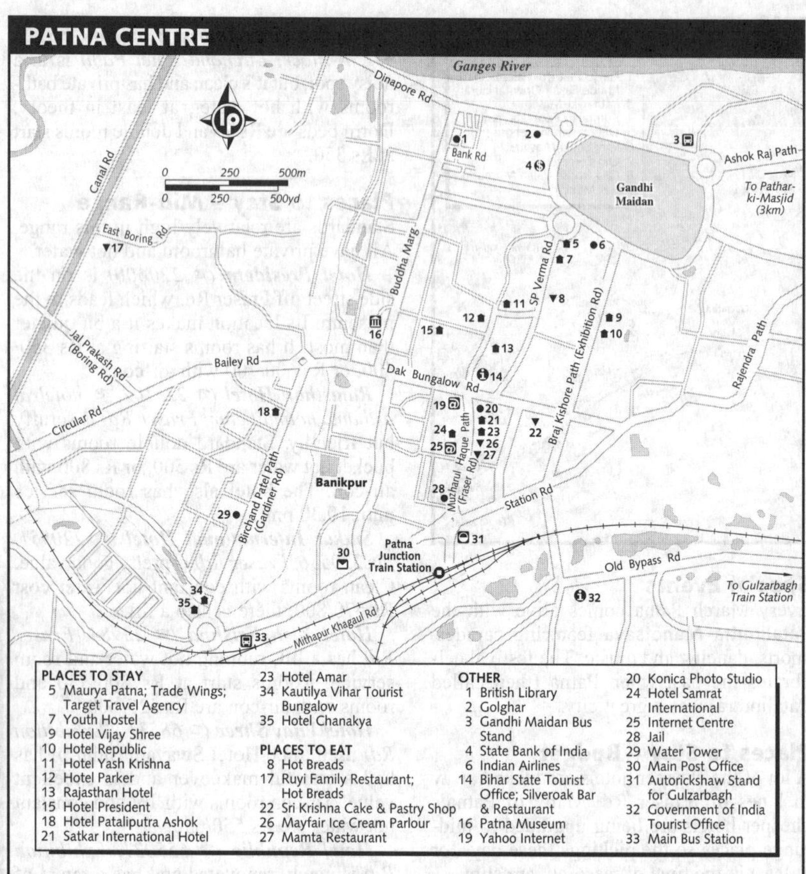

Places to Eat

Bustling Fraser Rd is the best place to chow down.

Mayfair Ice Cream Parlour is a clean and very popular place with good *masala dosas* (curried vegetables inside a pancake) and other snacks, as well as 16-odd ice-cream flavours.

Mamta Restaurant, next door, is an intimate place for dinner. There's a fish tank with the biggest goldfish you'll ever see – fortunately fish isn't on the menu. Main courses start at around Rs 50 and beer is more expensive at Rs 65.

Rajasthan Hotel, not far from the Ashoka, has a good vegetarian restaurant. It's not cheap, but the food is excellent and it has a good range of ice cream.

Sri Krishna Cake & Pastry Shop, on Dak Bungalow Rd, is a good place to pick up lunch. A couple of sandwiches and a drink will cost about Rs 40. It also does pizzas and lots of tempting pastries.

Silveroak Bar & Restaurant, in the building also housing the BSTO on Fraser Rd, near the Ashoka Restaurant, serves Indian and Chinese meals. It is clean, comfortable and affordable.

Hot Breads sells excellent freshly baked breads, pastries and cakes and has two outlets: one on SP Verma Rd and one, which also sells ice cream, on East Boring Rd.

Ruyi Family Restaurant, next to Hot Breads on East Boring Rd, is the only restaurant in Bihar specialising in Chinese cuisine. Although it's quite expensive, it is well decorated, clean, friendly, nonsmoking and the service is first class.

Getting There & Away

Air Indian Airlines (☎ 226433) has two daily flights between Patna and Delhi (US$145); four weekly flights to Kolkata (Calcutta; US$100); and daily flights to Ranchi (US$70). A daily flight connects Patna with Lucknow (US$100); you can book tickets at the Indian Airlines office near Gandhi Maidan. Sahara Air has one flight a day to Varanasi (US$85) and Delhi. Necon Air flies four times a week between Kathmandu and Patna (US$75, plus Rs 50 airport tax).

Bus The main bus station is at Harding Park, west of Patna Junction train station. It's a large place with departure gates spread out along the road. The fare varies according to the speed of the service. Buses from Gate 7 include:

destination	fare (Rs)	duration (hrs)
Gaya	50	4
Rajgir	50	3
Ranchi	142	9
Sasaram	70	6
Siliguri	175	12

The Gandhi Maidan bus stand is used by government buses going to many places in Bihar. There are night buses to Ranchi and a deluxe bus to Siliguri (Rs 165, daily).

To/From Nepal Buses for Raxaul, on the Nepali border, go from the main bus station (Rs 100, seven hours, Gate 6). There are hourly morning departures and less-frequent afternoon services. A deluxe night bus also leaves the Gandhi Maidan bus stand (Rs 110, seven hours) at 10 pm. Buses from Birganj (on the Nepali side of the border) to Kathmandu cost about Rs 82 (Nep Rs 114).

Train The train booking office at Patna Junction is a joke – it's absolutely chaotic. If time is short, you might be better off paying a small commission to a tour company to buy tickets for you.

The fastest trains on the Kolkata to Delhi line take 12 hours to Delhi (Rs 324/926 in 2nd/1st class, 992km) and seven hours to Kolkata (Rs 202/640, 545km). There are a number of direct trains daily to Gaya (Rs 35/173, two hours, 92km); Varanasi (Rs 115/346, five hours, 228km); Ranchi (Rs 168/524, 10 hours, 591km); and Mumbai (Bombay; Rs 397/1310, 36 hours, 1660km).

If you're heading to Darjeeling or the north-eastern region, the fast *North East Express* from Delhi leaves Patna at 10.20 pm, arriving in New Jalpaiguri (the main train station 5km south of Siliguri) at 9.40 am (Rs 132/951, 2nd class/2nd air-con class, 636km).

There are no direct trains from Patna to the border town of Raxaul (you have to change at Muzaffarpur) so buses are faster.

Getting Around

To/From the Airport The airport is 7km west of the city centre. There is a massive free-for-all for immigration and customs, and the security staff appear to double as porters. Indian Airlines runs a bus service from its office by the Gandhi Maidan; cycle-rickshaws cost approximately Rs 60 and taxis should charge about Rs 130.

Autorickshaw Shared autorickshaws shuttle back and forth between Patna Junction train station and Gulzarbagh (Rs 5). The other main route is from Patna Junction train station to Gandhi Maidan bus stand (Rs 3).

SONEPUR

Sonepur Fair, a two-week cattle fair, is held in October/November here. It takes place around the full moon of Kartika Purnima, the most auspicious time to bathe at the confluence of the Ganges and Gandak

Mithila Paintings

Bihar's unique and most famous folk art is its Mithila or Madhubani paintings. Traditionally, wives from Madhubani and surrounding villages in the Mithila district started creating strong line drawings on the walls of their homes from the day of their marriage. Using pigments from natural products such as spices, minerals, charcoal and vegetable matter, the women painted local deities and scenes from mythology. Special events and aspects of everyday life were often incorporated with the images of gods and goddesses.

These paintings, both in black and white and strong primary colours, are now being professionally produced on paper, canvas and textiles for commercial purposes.

Examples of the original wall paintings can still be seen in homes around Madhubani (approximately 160km north-east of Patna, five to six hours by bus) and in the Bihar government tourist village huts at the Sonepur Fair.

Each June, the Saurath Sabha is held in a mango grove in Saurath village. It is a unique gathering of Mithila Brahmins from all over India, who come for the biggest marriage market in the country. Parents of marriageable children come armed with horoscopes in the hope of negotiating suitable marriages for their offspring.

SIMON BORG

Rivers. Four times the size of Pushkar's Camel Fair, it's probably the largest animal fair in Asia. Not only cattle are traded here – at Haathi Bazaar, elephants change hands for anything from Rs 10,000 to 100,000, depending on their age and condition. If you're considering purchasing an alternative form of transport, Mark Shand's *Travels on my Elephant* is essential reading for anyone who fancies themself as a modern-day mahout (elephant trainer).

The Bihar State Tourist Development Corporation (BSTDC) runs a tourist village during the fair. Double cottages cost Rs 500 (no single rates) and beds in the 20-bed dorm cost Rs 77. There are also temporary huts decorated with Mithila paintings, the cost of which varies with demand. For bookings contact BSTDC (☎ 0612-225411) in Patna.

VAISHALI

As long ago as the 6th century BC, Vaishali was the capital of a republic. Mahavira, one of the Jain founders was born here, and the Buddha preached his last sermon here. There's little to see – an **Ashoka pillar** (with its lion capital intact), a few dilapidated **stupas** (one contains one-eighth of the Buddha's ashes) and a small **museum**. Admission to these ruins costs US$5 (Rs 230) for foreigners.

An inexpensive ***BSTDC Tourist Youth Hostel & Tourist Bungalow*** has singles/doubles for Rs 150/180; single rooms have shared bathroom and double rooms have private bathroom.

There are guided tours from Patna or buses from Lalganj and Muzaffarpur.

MUZAFFARPUR

Apart from being a bus transit point en route to the Nepal border, Muzaffarpur is a poverty-stricken, agriculturally backward area of limited interest.

If you have to stay the night, ***Hotel Deepak*** has reasonable food and spartan single rooms for Rs 100. There are better air-con doubles which cost Rs 450.

Hotel Elite near the train station on Saraiya Gunj has double rooms for Rs 400.

Useful train connections include Gorakhpur (Rs 73/384, 2nd/1st class, seven hours, 293km) and Narkatiaganj (Rs 47, 2nd class, 3½ hours, 160km).

RAXAUL

Raxaul is virtually a twin town with Birganj, just across the border in Nepal. Both are crowded and dirty. Cycle-rickshaws take 20 minutes (Rs 20) from the border (open 4 am to midnight) to the bus stand in Birganj. Visas are available at the border for US$30. Be warned that US currency *only* is accepted as payment for visas.

Neither Raxaul or Birganj are places to hang around, but if you're stuck ***Hotel Kaveri*** has singles/doubles for Rs 100/120.

Hotel Ajanta is better. It's down a side road near the bus stand and charges Rs 80/100 for a room with shared bath.

Getting There & Away

There are several buses a day from Raxaul to Patna (Rs 100, seven hours). Beware of touts selling combined bus/train tickets: it's much more reliable to organise things yourself.

From Birganj morning and evening buses to Kathmandu take around 12 hours (Rs 95); Pokhara buses take 10 hours (Rs 75). Most Kathmandu buses take the much longer road via Narayanghat and Mugling, rather than the dramatically scenic Tribhuvan Highway via Naubise.

BODHGAYA

☎ 0631

For the traveller, Bodhgaya is probably the most interesting of all the holy sites associated with the life of the Buddha, being much more of a working Buddhist centre than an archaeological site. It's also the most important Buddhist pilgrimage place in the world.

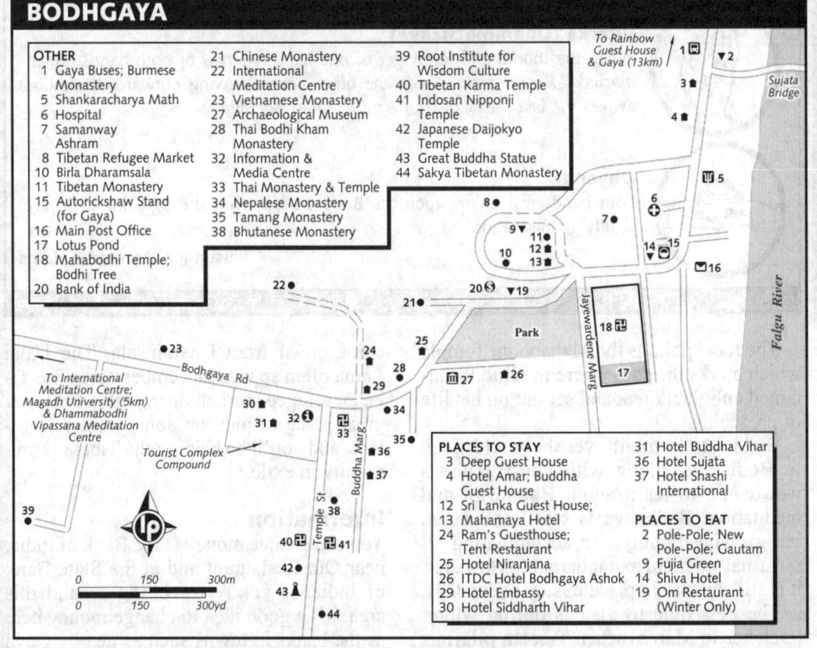

Sculptural Symbolism

Buddha images throughout India are, for the most part, sculptured according to strict rules found in Buddhist art texts from the 3rd century AD. However, the tradition leaves room for innovation, allowing the various 'schools' of Buddhist art to distinguish themselves.

Most Buddha figures wear a simple long robe that appears to be transparent – the body is usually clearly visible underneath. In some earlier sculptures his hair is shown coiled.

Indian Buddha figures in all Indian religious sculpture, whatever the faith, can be distinguished from those of other countries by their body type – broad shoulders and chest, slim waist and a slight pot belly.

One aspect of the Buddhist tradition that almost never varies is the *asana* (posture) and *mudra* (hand position) of Buddha images. There are four basic postures and positions: standing, sitting, walking and reclining.

Abhaya

One or both hands extend forward, palms out, fingers pointing upward, to symbolise the Buddha's offer of protection. This mudra is most commonly seen in conjunction with standing or walking Buddhas.

Bhumisparsa

In this classic mudra the right hand touches the ground, known as earth touching, while the left rests in the lap. During the Buddha's legendary meditation under the Bodhi Tree, Mara, the Lord of Death, tried to interrupt by invoking a series of distractions. The Buddha's response was to touch the earth, thus calling on nature to witness his resolve to stay in the one place until he had gained enlightenment.

Vitarka (Dhammachakka)

When the thumb and forefinger of one hand *(vitarka)* or both hands *(dhammachakka)* form a circle with the other fingers curving outward, the mudra evokes the first public discourse on Buddhist doctrine.

Dhyana

Both hands rest palms upon the Buddha's lap, with the right hand on top, signifying meditation.

Illustrations by Martin Harris

The focal point is the Mahabodhi Temple which marks the spot where the Buddha attained enlightenment and set out on his life of preaching.

Buddhists from all over the world flock to Bodhgaya, along with non-Buddhists who come to learn about Buddhism and meditation. Bodhgaya is small and quiet, but growing rapidly and accumulating all the usual 'tourism' paraphernalia. However, it is still a pleasant place to stay a few days.

The best time to visit is during winter (October to March) when Tibetan pilgrims come down from Dharamsala. The Dalai Lama often spends December here. The Tibetan refugee market, open at this time, is a great place to pick up some winter woollens, and you'll be helping the Tibetan community in exile.

Information

You can change money at the Bank of India, near Om Restaurant and at the State Bank of India. If you're travelling around this area, it's a good idea to change money here as the banks in towns such as nearby Gaya don't have a foreign exchange service. The tourist complex on the corner of Bodhgaya Rd and Temple St consists of two hotels, a restaurant, gardens and an 'Information & Media Centre' which is little more than a fancy building open from 10 am to 5 pm daily, except Sunday; it is less than helpful. There is a post office on the Gaya road, just south of the hospital.

There were no email facilities at the time of research, but this will change – have a look around the Mahabodhi Temple area.

Mahabodhi Temple

Standing adjacent to a descendent of the original Bodhi Tree under which the Buddha meditated on the excesses of life and formulated his philosophy of a balanced approach to it, this temple is a place of pilgrimage for all Buddhists.

A sapling from the original Bodhi Tree was carried to Anuradhapura in Sri Lanka by Sanghamitta (the Emperor Ashoka's daughter). That tree now flourishes there and, in turn, a cutting from it was carried back to Bodhgaya when the original tree died. A red sandstone slab under the tree is said to be the Vajrasan, or diamond throne, on which the Buddha sat.

The Mahabodhi Temple stands on the site of a temple erected by Ashoka in the 3rd century BC. Topped by a 50m pyramidal spire, the ornate structure houses a large gilded image of the Buddha. The current temple was restored in the 11th century, and again in 1882. The stone railing (around 184–172 BC) around the temple, parts of which still stand, is considered to be from the Sunga period. The carved and sculptured railing has been restored, although parts of it now stand in the museum in Kolkata and in the Victoria and Albert Museum in London. Stone stupas, erected by visiting pilgrims, dot the temple courtyard.

There is a great sense of peace and serenity within the temple compound. Pilgrims and visitors from all walks of life and religions come here to worship or just admire. Entry to the temple grounds, which are open from 6 am to noon and 2 to 6.30 pm, is free, but there is a Rs 10/200 charge for cameras/video cameras. A relaxing way to finish the day is a stroll in the evening around the perimeter of the temple compound, threading your way through monks from all over the world, while soaking up the ambience of this sacred place.

TAMSIN WILSON

The Buddha meditating under the Bodhi Tree

For more information on Buddhism and the Buddha's life, see the special section 'The Way of the Buddha' earlier in this book.

Monasteries

Most countries with a large Buddhist population have a temple or monastery here, usually built in a representative architectural style. Thus the Thai temple looks very much like the colourful wats you see in Thailand. The Tibetan Karma temple and monastery were built in 1934 and contain a large prayer wheel.

The Burmese, who led the campaign to restore the Mahabodhi Temple in the 19th century, built their present monastery in 1936. The Japanese temple (Indosan Nipponji) has a very beautiful image of the Buddha brought from Japan; across the road is the Daijokyo Temple. There are also Chinese, Sri Lankan, Bhutanese, Vietnamese, Nepalese, Korean, Taiwanese and Bangladeshi monasteries. The Tai Bodhi Kham Monastery was built by Buddhist tribes from Assam and Arunachal Pradesh.

Voluntary Work

If you're interested in working on social development projects in the area, contact Mr Dwarko Sundrani at the Samanway Ashram in Bodhgaya. This is a good place for doing voluntary work (during which time you'll also be taught Indian beliefs and ways of life) or to just make a donation.

The ashram works mainly with children from the lowest castes, performing thousands of eye operations every year; as a volunteer you can work with the children. There is also a dairy and agriculture farm that requires voluntary labour. At the time of research there were eight foreigners working here including Japanese, Australians and Danes. Ask for directions near the Mahabodhi Temple, as the ashram can be difficult to locate.

Sujata Charitable Society (☎ 400463) is run by Mr Sunil Kumar Sinha, the enthusiastic manager of Deep Guest House. He has opened a school which provides education to illiterate children and adults for free. He also plans to make free medical services available for people in Bihar. Volunteers are welcome, as are donations.

Other Attractions

The **archaeological museum** (open from 10 am to 5 pm Saturday to Thursday) has a small collection of Buddha figures and pillars found in the area. The Hindu **Shankaracharya Math** has a temple, and there's a sculpture gallery in the grounds. Across the river are the **Dungeshwari** and **Suraya Temples.**

The 25m-high **Great Buddha Statue** in the Japanese Kamakura style was unveiled by the Dalai Lama in 1989. A Maitreya Buddha statue over 100m high is being built in Bodhgaya as a symbol of world peace.

Meditation & Buddhism Courses

Courses and retreats take place in winter, mainly from October to early February.

Some of the most accessible courses (excellent for beginners) are run by the Root Institute for Wisdom Culture (☎ 400714, ⓔ rootinst@nda.vsnl.net.in). It runs basic eight-day meditation courses for Rs 2600 (this includes meals and accommodation). Courses include meditation teachings, and discussion about adherence to the Buddhist lay vows; retreats are also held in a peaceful location on the edge of Bodhgaya.

Travellers who have spent some time here seem impressed, not only with the courses but by the way the institute is working to put something back into the local community with agricultural, educational and health projects.

Courses are also run by the International Meditation Centre (☎ 400707) near the Magadh University (5km from Bodhgaya), and another centre closer to town. These courses are far more informal and students can start and finish any time they choose.

Meditation courses are also offered at the Burmese and Tibetan monasteries, and at the Dhammabodhi Vipassana Meditation Centre (☎ 400437). Dhammabodhi is a bit out of town in a very peaceful location near Magadh University. It runs 10-day courses during most of the year. It has a far stricter regime than the International Meditation Centre and you must stay for the full 10 days if you sign up – no exceptions. There are lots of books on meditation for sale.

The annual insight meditation *(vipassana)* and spiritual inquiry retreats, which have places for 130 people, take place from 7 to 15 January, 15 to 23 January, and 23 January to 4 February at the Thai Bodhi Karu Monastery. For information and bookings write to Gaia House (☎ 01626-333613), West Ogwell, Near Newton Abbot, Devon TQ12 6EN, UK or (from mid-October) you can contact the Thai Monastery, c/o Burmese Monastery (fax 400848) in Bodhgaya. There are often cancellations, so if you just turn up on the day there's a good chance you'll get a spot.

Other courses are sometimes advertised on the noticeboard at Om Restaurant.

Special Events

Buddha Mahautsav (11 to 13 November) is a very popular festival in Bodhgaya with locals from nearby villages turning up for the celebrations. There is a huge stage showing traditional singing, dancing and performances. There is also an art show with portraits on display from local students.

Places to Stay – Budget

Prices given here are for the low season; note that they increase substantially in the high season (December to March).

Rainbow Guest House *(☎ 400308)* is the first hotel, on the right-hand side of the road, coming into town from Gaya. It's a new spot and is good value. Dorms are Rs 30 and double rooms are Rs 150/250 without/with fan. All rooms have squat toilets.

Deep Guest House *(☎ 400463)* on the road to Gaya and next to the Burmese Monastery comes highly recommended, with friendly and helpful staff. The shared bathrooms are tiled, clean and have copious amounts of hot water. Doubles cost Rs 200 with shared bathroom and Rs 300 with private bathroom.

Hotel Amar *(☎ 400462)*, close by on the same road, is a basic little place with squat toilets. Doubles cost around Rs 100.

Buddha Guest House *(☎ 400934)*, next to Amar, is also basic but clean and has a good view from the rooftop. Double rooms with fan, hot water and squat toilet are Rs 150; dorms are Rs 50.

Sri Lanka Guest House *(☎ 400742)*, a Mahabodhi Society place, is popular and well run. It accepts donations of around Rs 80 for rooms with private bathroom.

Ram's Guesthouse *(☎ 400644)*, behind Hotel Embassy, is a friendly family-run place. Double rooms with private bathroom and hot-water geyser are Rs 200. Doubles with clean, shared bathrooms are Rs 150.

Tourist bungalows No 1 and No 2 are next door to each other and are also known by more imaginative names. ***Hotel Buddha Vihar*** *(☎ 400445)* has very comfortable dorm accommodation. Beds with shared/private bathroom are Rs 50/75. ***Hotel Siddharth Vihar*** *(☎ 400445)* offers excellent compact doubles with TV and private bathroom for Rs 200.

If you're planning a longer stay or don't mind roughing it a bit, behaving in a dignified manner and abiding by some simple rules, it's possible to stay at a monastery. ***Burmese Monastery*** (popular with Westerners for its study courses), ***Bhutanese Monastery*** and ***Tibetan Monastery*** all take guests for around Rs 50 a night.

Places to Stay – Mid-Range & Top End

The continuing spate of hotel building in this range ensures competitive prices and plenty of rooms. All singles/doubles have private bathroom.

Hotel Niranjana *(☎ 400475, Bodhgaya Rd)* has good doubles with private bathroom and TV, although the bathrooms are a bit grotty for the price. Non air-con rooms are Rs 600/900.

Hotel Embassy *(☎ 400711, Bodhgaya Rd)* with its rooftop seating, passes the white-glove test. Rooms with TV and private bathroom are Rs 500/800.

ITDC Hotel Bodhgaya Ashok *(☎ 400700/790, fax 400788)*, near the archaeological museum, has singles/doubles for Rs 1000/1500, or Rs 1600/2400 with air-con. Overpriced dorm beds are Rs 400.

Hotel Sujata *(☎ 400761/481, ⓔ hotel_sujata@yahoo.com, Buddha Marg)* is an upmarket place with 24-hour room service, foreign exchange and restaurant. There is a Japanese-style bathroom and prayer hall. Rooms cost Rs 1895/2295.

Hotel Shashi International *(☎ 400459, fax 400483, Buddha Marg)*, next door, has a restaurant serving Chinese and Thai cuisine. Small but spotless rooms are Rs 1000/1200.

Mahamaya Hotel *(☎ 400221, ⓔ htl_mahamaya@hotmail.com)*, close to the Mahabodhi Temple, is a luxurious place in a very central spot. This large hotel with its impressive marble lobby has internal courtyards and comfortable, spacious rooms starting at Rs 1400/2000. You may get a discount if it's quiet.

Places to Eat

The standard of food here is pretty low out of season and surprisingly high during winter, when the pilgrims arrive.

The cuisine at ***Shiva Hotel*** is varied and includes Japanese, Indian and continental.

A mushroom chow mein ins Rs 40, chilli chicken is Rs 75 and burgers are Rs 35. The service is pleasantly friendly and fast.

Ram's Guesthouse has a cheap tent restaurant with a good selection of Sri Lankan, Japanese, Chinese, Tibetan and Western food.

Other tent restaurants which offer great value include ***Pole-Pole***, ***New Pole-Pole*** and ***Gautam***, which is opposite the Burmese Monastery. All are popular and have varied menus, over-worked jaffle machines and good tape collections. Gautam also has a bakery in winter.

There are also several Tibetan-run restaurants behind the Tibetan Monastery. Most operate in tents and only open during winter, but there are some perennial places which you can try. ***Om Restaurant***, near the Bank of India, is well established, and is a popular meeting place. It has a particularly good breakfast menu and does good Tibetan and Japanese food as well. ***Fujia Green***, opposite the Tibetan refugee market, serves Tibetan and Chinese grub year-round.

Getting There & Away

Bodhgaya is 13km from Gaya, and shared autorickshaws shuttle back and forth between the two. They're phenomenally overloaded: up to 15 people (plus animals, goods and so on) travel on a vehicle intended for three! The fare is Rs 8 (or starts at Rs 50 for the entire autorickshaw, but you'll probably pay closer to Rs 100).

There are frequent buses to Gaya (Rs 5) that are also very crowded. They leave regularly from outside the Burmese Monastery and near the tent restaurants.

GAYA

☎ 0631

Gaya is about 100km south of Patna. Just as nearby Bodhgaya is a major centre for Buddhist pilgrims, Gaya is a centre for Hindu pilgrims. Vishnu is said to have given Gaya the power to absolve sinners. Pilgrims offer *pindas* (funeral cakes) at the ghats along the river here, and perform a lengthy circuit of the holy places around Gaya, to free their ancestors from bondage to the earth.

There's a BSTO at the train station. The nearest place to exchange money is in Bodhgaya, at the Bank of India and the State Bank of India.

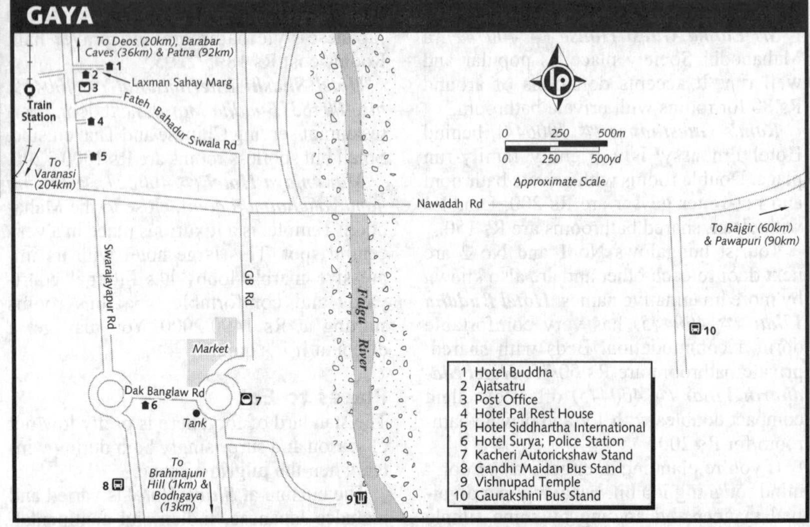

Things to See & Do

In the crowded central part of the old town, the *sikhara* (spired) **Vishnupad Temple** was constructed in 1787 on the banks of the Falgu River by Queen Ahalya Bai of Indore. Inside the temple the 40cm 'footprint' of Vishnu is imprinted in solid rock and surrounded by a silver-plated basin. Note that non-Hindus are not permitted to enter.

During the monsoon, the river carries a great deal of water here but it dries up completely in winter. You can see cremations taking place on the riverbanks.

A flight of 1000 stone steps leads to **Brahmajuni Hill**, 1km south-west of Vishnupad Temple. There's a good view over the town from the top. Gaya also has a small **archaeological museum** (open Tuesday to Sunday).

Places to Stay & Eat

There are many options around the station; most are spartan but OK for a short pause.

Hotel Buddha *(☎ 423428)* is down the lane opposite the train station. There is a roof garden, and reasonable singles/doubles with private bathroom are Rs 150/200.

Hotel Pal Rest House *(☎ 436753)*, set back from the road, is quiet and cheap. Rooms with private bathroom cost Rs 100/135; singles with shared bathroom are a mere Rs 70.

At ***Ajatsatru*** *(☎ 434584)* rooms vary greatly: some are small, some dark, some have balconies and some are spacious and light. Doubles with fan and TV are Rs 300 or Rs 600 with air-con. All rooms have hot-water geyser and private bathroom.

Hotel Surya *(☎ 424004)*, adjacent to the police station is a Rs 5 cycle-rickshaw ride from the train station. It has doubles for Rs 150 with private bathroom, or Rs 200 with hot-water geyser and air-cooler.

Hotel Siddhartha International *(☎ 436 243, fax 436368)* is overpriced and caters to upmarket pilgrims. Rooms cost US$45/60, although there are cheaper rooms for Rs 995/1400. Breakfast/dinner is US$6/9.

All over Bihar you will see stalls selling the popular puff-pastry sweet known as *khaja*, which originated in a village between Gaya and Rajgir. Catch them as they come out of the oil – the flies are as partial to them as the Biharis are.

Getting There & Away

Buses to Patna (Rs 45, four hours) and Ranchi (Rs 75 to 120, seven hours) leave from Gandhi Maidan bus stand. Buses to Rajgir (Rs 35, three hours) leave from Gaurakshini bus stand, across the river.

Gaya is on the main Delhi-Kolkata railway line and there are direct trains to Delhi (Rs 174/310, 2nd class/2nd-class sleeper, 29 hours); Kolkata (Rs 104/199/571, 2nd class/2nd-class sleeper/1st class, 7½ hours); Varanasi (Rs 61/115/346, 2nd class/2nd-class sleeper/1st class, 2½ hours); Puri (Rs 156/282, 2nd class/2nd-class sleeper, 20½ hours); and Patna (Rs 31/198, 2nd-class/1st class, 2½ hours).

Autorickshaws from the train station to Bodhgaya (13km) should cost Rs 50 but they'll probably try for twice as much. From the Kacheri stand, a 25-minute walk from the train station, shared autorickshaws cost Rs 8, plus Rs 4 for a backpack. Local buses start at Rs 5.

Getting Around

From the train station it's Rs 10/15 by cycle-rickshaw to the Kacheri autorickshaw stand (for Bodhgaya) or the Gaurakshini bus stand (for Rajgir).

AROUND GAYA

At Deos, 20km to the north of Gaya, is a **temple of Surya**, the sun god.

Barabar Caves (200 BC) are 36km north of Gaya. These are the 'Marabar' caves of EM Forster's *A Passage to India*. They are considered to be the earliest Buddhist rock-cut caves in existence, and have been occupied by numerous religious sects. Hewn from granite, the interior of the caves are designed to look like they're made from wood and have very smooth enamel-like surfaces, typical of the Ashokan era. Two of the caves contain Ashokan inscriptions.

In the Barabar hills there are four caves that have seven chambers; collectively they are referred to as **Satgarva**. In this group the Loma Rishi Cave is the most impressive with its sculpted lattice screens, exhibiting a very early example of Buddhist chaitya arch-style. About 1km away in the Nagarjuni hills are another three caves, of which the Gopika Cave is the largest.

Although well worth visiting, it is advisable not to travel to the Barabar Caves on your own or after dusk. Visit a police station and organise an armed guard if possible as the caves are in the very heart of Naxalite bandit country.

The basic ***Barabar Siddhnath Rest House*** *(☎ 06322-6364)* is the only place to stay – there are no fixed rates.

To get to Barabar take the train to Bela (Rs 15, 2nd class), grab a tonga (Rs 20) from there for 10km of potholes and it is then an arduous 5km walk to the two groups of caves.

SASARAM

Sasaram is a chaotic dust bowl on the Grand Trunk Rd, the famous Indian highway built

The Bandit Queen

The story of Phoolan Devi (the Bandit Queen), one of India's most notorious dacoits (bandits) and infamous champion of lower-caste women, is an intriguing and revealing tale about a remarkable woman. It also presents a rare portal into the realities of India's entrenched caste system. An understanding of Phoolan's life, together with a look at caste conflict in Bihar today, will give you a stronger grasp of the forces constantly tearing at the fabric of Bihar society. Nowhere are the problems with the caste system more apparent than in Bihar, where intercaste warfare claims many lives each year.

Phoolan Devi was born to a poor, lower-caste family in rural Bihar. Throughout her life, beginning when she was 'sold' into marriage as an 11-year-old, she was subject to severe oppression, including beatings, rape and abuse from upper-caste landowners and even her husband.

After abandoning her marriage she returned home to her village (an act that was, until then, unheard of from a lower-caste woman, who is thought of as nothing without her husband). In her village she was a target of torment from upper-caste boys and was treated as a disgraced member of her community.

Eventually she got mixed up in banditry, until ultimately she led her own gang (only one of three female dacoit leaders in Indian history), terrorising the hated upper castes. During this time her gang committed one of the most nefarious massacres in India's modern-day history.

The St Valentine's Day massacre occurred in the hamlet of Behmai in Uttar Pradesh in 1981. The bandit gang led by Phoolan intended originally to rob the upper-caste villagers, but when she got there she recognised the village as the home of two men who, some years earlier, had raped her and killed her lover. On Phoolan's orders the young men of the village were rounded up by her gang and the bandits opened fire, killing about 20 and injuring several others.

The massacre prompted a large-scale hunt for Phoolan, although she managed to elude authorities for a couple of years. Becoming desperate, Indira Gandhi's government instructed the police to offer her a deal; and in 1983 Phoolan surrendered herself and her gang to authorities on a stage before a crowd of about 8000 people, who had come to see their vigilante liberator. Her surrender made headlines throughout the country.

Phoolan Devi then spent 11 years in jail without trial, before being pardoned in 1994 by Mulayam Singh Yadav, the then newly elected chief minister of Uttar Pradesh who ordered all charges against her to be dropped. The chief minister was also from one of India's lower castes.

The story of Phoolan Devi was translated into a film called *The Bandit Queen*, by Indian filmmaker Shekar Kapur. The film created great controversy when released in 1995 as it claimed to be a true life account of the woman dacoit, yet Kapur had never met the Bandit Queen, and seemingly made little effort to verify events in the film that were passed off as factual.

by Sher Shah in the mid-16th century (see the boxed text 'The Grand Trunk Road' later in this chapter). The impressive **mausoleum of Sher Shah**, who died in 1545, is worth seeing. Built of red sandstone and standing in the middle of a large artificial pond, it's particularly striking in the warm light of sunset. The 46m-high dome has a 22m span, which is 4m wider than the dome of the Taj Mahal. There's also the **tomb of Hassan Khan** (Sher Shah's father) and several other Muslim monuments; entry is US$5 (Rs 230) for all.

Shershah Tourist Lodge is the best place to stay. Turn left onto the Grand Trunk Rd at the train station and it's by the second petrol station, a 15-minute walk away. Doubles are Rs 110, or Rs 160/370 with private bathroom/air-con. Dorm beds cost Rs 50.

There are frequent buses for Patna (Rs 75, five hours). For Varanasi and Gaya it's better to take a train. There are two

The Bandit Queen

Phoolan herself reacted angrily to the narrow view the film took of her life, claiming it to be a fictional account that overlooks the issues surrounding herself and her family – such as land ownership and the injustices of the caste system – that led to her acts of banditry.

Critics have said the film is one violent rape scene after another; certainly it's a brutal portrayal of her life and the atrocities she endured. This is summed up succinctly in the film when the viewer is told that women can be beaten, in the same manner as drums, animals and lower castes.

These days Phoolan Devi is in politics, after being elected to India's Lok Sabha (Lower House) in 1996. She was thrust into the parliament on the back of popular support from the lower castes, who make up 85% of voters, in her electorate of Mirzapur in Uttar Pradesh. In the elections of 1999 she was re-elected, retaining a comfortable lead. She remains a popular cult figure. Her acts of banditry in the 1970s and 1980s have become the stuff of legend and she is still seen as a symbol of empowerment for the lower caste.

India's Bandit Queen by Mala Sen is the biography of Phoolan Devi, detailing her fight against the caste system in rural India.

Caste Conflict in Bihar

The Hindu caste system is a complex, ingrained hierarchy based on ancient mythical beliefs, which still dominates life in rural India. See Society & Conduct in the Facts about North India chapter at the beginning of this book for more information.

The manifestation of this caste system is nowhere more stark than in Bihar where intercaste warfare is rife. In 2000, animosity and killings from long-running feuds between different castes in Bihar was on the increase with a death toll of more than 120 by mid-year.

In one such incident, members of the landowning Bhumihar caste, which make up in effect a private army, slaughtered 34 people (including women and children). Most of the victims were members of the Yadavas, a middle caste, whose leaders have been successful in politics, ruling Bihar. Some Dalits, previously known as 'untouchables', were also included in the killing spree.

Some battles can be accounted for by long-running conflicts between the upper-caste Bhumihars and the Naxalites, who fight in the name of the landless lower castes. Their confrontations usually lead to tit-for-tat atrocities. However, worryingly, new versions of the caste war have become apparent. Recent killings are the result of gang wars, which occur over business contracts such as transport. In May 2000, 11 lower-caste labourers were slaughtered by a gang of Yadavs. The motivation for the killing was apparently a dispute over rights to quarry sand from a riverbed.

Why doesn't the government of Bihar do something to stop it? Unfortunately, government ministers have strong links with gangs and killings; members of both government and opposition parties have been linked to gang members. The government is reluctant to 'tread on its own toes'. The caste system is far too entrenched in Bihar society for it not to be a powerful influence on the political landscape.

direct trains from Varanasi, but it's possible to take a local bus from Varanasi train station to Mughal Serai (Rs 8, 17km), from where there are frequent trains to Sasaram (Rs 23, three hours).

There are some Muslim tombs a short distance from Sasaram at **Maner**. At **Dehri**, 17km east of Sasaram, the railway and the Grand Trunk Rd cross the Son River, on a 3km-long bridge. The hill fort of **Rohtas** is 38km from here.

NALANDA

☎ 061194

Founded in the 5th century BC, Nalanda was one of the world's great universities and an important Buddhist centre until its sacking by the Afghans in the 12th century. When Chinese scholar and traveller Xuan Zhang visited between AD 685 and AD 762, 10,000 monks and students resided here.

A credit to the curators, the site is peaceful, clean, well maintained and perfumed with the scent of roses and shrubs. Allow at least half a day for wandering around as the ruins are extensive. The site is open from 7.30 am to 5 pm in winter and admission is US$5 (Rs 230) for foreigners. Just outside the entrance are souvenir stands with the usual tacky assortment, cold-drink stalls – useful on a hot day – and plenty of guides offering their services.

The extensive brick-built remains include the **Great Stupa**, with steps, terraces and a few intact votive stupas around it, and the monks' cells. An **archaeological museum**, open from 10 am to 4 pm Saturday to Thursday (Rs 2), houses the Nalanda University seal, sculptures and other remains found on the site. Pilgrims venerate Buddha figures in spite of signs saying 'Do not offer anything to the objects in the museum'! Guidebooks cost Rs 4.

The **Xuan Zang Memorial Hall** was recently built as a peace pagoda by the Chinese. Xuan Zhang spent five years here as both student and teacher.

There's also an international centre for the study of Buddhism, established in 1951.

Most people stay in Rajgir and visit on day trips, but you can stay at the Burmese, Japanese or Jain ***dharamsalas*** (pilgrims' resthouses) at Nalanda as well as the ***PWD Rest House***. A bed at these places costs about Rs 50.

Getting There & Away

Ridiculously crowded shared Trekkers (jeeps) cost Rs 8 from Rajgir to Nalanda village, from there it's Rs 8 for the 10-minute ride on a shared tonga to the university site. Take another jeep (Rs 5) from Nalanda village to Bihar Sharif, north of Nalanda, for buses to Patna (Rs 28, 3½ hours).

RAJGIR

☎ 06119

Rajgir, 12km south of Nalanda, is a minor Indian holiday centre. In winter, visitors are drawn by the hot springs and healthy climate. Rajgir is where the Buddha tamed a ferocious elephant that was set upon him by Devadatta, a former follower who became jealous of the Buddhist order.

These days Rajgir is a very significant pilgrimage site because the Buddha spent 12 years here, and the first Buddhist council after the Buddha attained nirvana was convened here.

Rajgir is also an important place for Jains, as Mahavira spent some time in Rajgir and the hills are topped with Digambara (the 'sky-clad' Jain sect) shrines. A mention in the Mahabharata also ensures that there is a good supply of Hindu pilgrims.

This was the capital of the Magadha empire until Ajatasatru moved to Pataliputra (Patna) in the 5th century BC.

Orientation & Information

The main road with the train station, bus stand and a number of hotels is about 500m west of town. There's a tourist complex by the hot springs, about 1km south of town along the main road.

Things to See

Most people rent a tonga for half a day to see the sites, as they're spread out over several kilometres. This costs about Rs 60 but, with the brutal way these horses are treated, you might prefer to take a taxi.

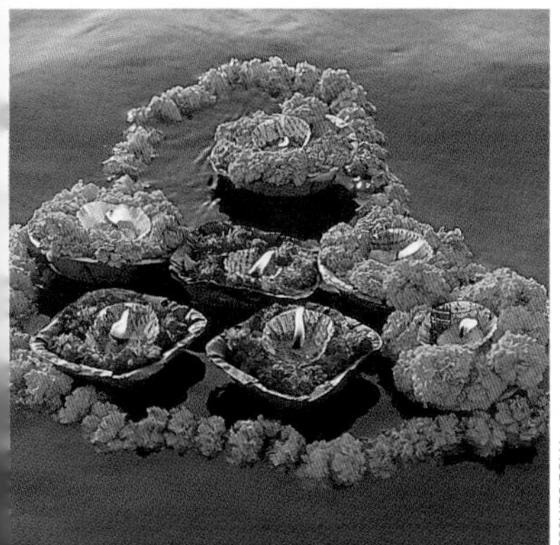

PAUL BEINSSEN

SARA-JANE CLELAND

SARA-JANE CLELAND

SARA-JANE CLELAND

Beliefs may differ but observance has many similarities: Buddhist pilgrims visit the Mahabodhi Temple (top right) in Bodhgaya, and offer incense to the Buddha (centre left); Hindu followers at the Shiva Temple (bottom) in Bihar, and an offering of saffron-coloured marigolds on the Ganges (top left)

RICHARD I'ANSON

GREG ELMS

RICHARD I'ANSON

RICHARD I'ANSON

The rush and roar of Kolkata's hectic streets: religious offerings are conveyed across town (top left); Imperial time meets Indian time outside New Market (right); a family celebrates the new year at Kalighat Temple (bottom left); taking a break with fresh coconut juice near New Market (centre left)

Main sites include parts of the ruined city, caves and places associated with Ajatasatru and his father Bhimbisara, who he imprisoned and murdered. The **Jeevak Amravan** monastery, which was a favourite retreat of the Buddha's, has been excavated in recent times.

Vulture's Peak, around 10km from the train station, is where the Buddha delivered many sermons after his enlightenment and two particularly important sutras: the Lotus Sutra and the Prajnaparamita (Perfection of Wisdom Sutra, which is claimed contains the core of his teachings).

The pink building by the crowded hot springs is the **Lakshmi Narayan Temple**.

There's also a Burmese temple, an interesting **Jain exhibition** (Rs 10) and a modern Japanese temple. On the top of Ratnagiri Hill, 3km south of the hot springs, is the **Japanese Shanti Stupa**, reached by a chairlift (open from 8.15 am to 5 pm daily; Rs 20 return).

Special Events

The **Rajgir Mahotsava** (Indian Classical Performing Arts Festival) is held from 24 to 26 October every year. The festival includes performances of folk dance, ballet, opera, devotional song and instrumental music.

Places to Stay & Eat

High-season (October to March) rates are given here, but up to 50% discount applies out of season or if occupancy is low.

Hotel Anand *(☎ 55030)*, near the bus stand, is one of the cheaper places. Gloomy singles/doubles with squat toilet and no hot water cost Rs 75/150. The Jain restaurant is strictly vegan – no eggs, onions or garlic.

Hotel Siddharth *(☎ 55216)*, south of town near the hot springs, has a pleasant walled courtyard, and is known for its excellent food and friendly staff. Rooms are Rs 250/450 with private bathroom.

Hotel Rajgir *(☎ 55266)*, an old-fashioned Indian-style hotel with a garden, has basic rooms with bathroom which are a staggering Rs 210/310 plus Rs 5 for bucket hot water.

The BSTDC has three properties in Rajgir. The all-dorm ***Ajatshatru*** *(☎ 55027)* is clean and has squat toilets; a bed costs Rs 50. ***Gautam*** *(☎ 55273)* has dorm beds for Rs 50 and double rooms with TV and balcony for Rs 321/535 without/with air-con. ***Tathagat Vihar*** *(☎ 55176)* has double rooms with flushing squat toilet for Rs 300 or Rs 600 with air-con.

Hotel Centaur Hokke *(☎ 55245)*, 3km west of the hot springs, is Rajgir's top hotel. Although it looks a bit like a prison from the outside, it's a very pleasant, Japanese-designed place with an in-house shared bathhouse and temple. Japanese or Western style singles/doubles are US$86/124 (meals are an extra US$43 per person per day).

Getting There & Away

The nearest useful train station is at Gaya; see that section earlier for fare information. There are regular buses to Gaya (Rs 35, three hours) and Pawapuri. For Nalanda take a shared jeep for Rs 8.

PAWAPURI

Mahavira, the final tirthankar and founder of Jainism, died and was cremated here in about 500 BC. It is said the demand for his sacred ashes was so great that a large amount of soil was removed around the funeral pyre, creating the lotus-filled tank. A marble temple, the **Jalmandir**, was later built in the middle of the tank and is now a major pilgrimage spot for Jains. You can get here by bus from Rajgir or Bihar Sharif.

Jharkhand

An area known as Jharkhand (Jhar means forests and Khand means hilly land) has existed in India for many years – long before the movement for an autonomous region began. The Mughals invaded this area of India in the 14th and 17th centuries and their maps show Jharkhand covering parts of Bihar and Madhya Pradesh.

Demands for autonomy in the Jharkhand region can largely be attributed to groups representing Adivasi interests. The area has a large population of tribal people who have long felt that their needs have been disregarded by the Bihar government.

The movement for a separate Jharkhand state can be traced back to 1915 when the first pan-tribal organisation (Chotanagpur Unnati Samaj) was established. By 1950, this evolved into the Jharkhand Party, which claimed 32 seats in the Bihar Assembly following the first general election. The Jharkhand Party became the largest opposition party; it renewed calls for a separate state, including submitting a petition to the newly created State Reorganisation Commission, which came into being in 1953.

In the two decades that followed, the movement lost seats and impetus. This was turned around in the 1980s, with the Indian government setting up a committee on Jharkhand matters. The latter's recommendations led to the creation of the Jharkhand Area Autonomous Council in August 1995 – an important step in the creation of the new state.

Finally, with the agreement of most major political parties and the seal of approval from the national government, a dream for many became reality in November 2000, with the birth of Jharkhand state. Ceremonies were accompanied by wild celebrations in Ranchi, as the populace, delirious with anticipation of a better deal, celebrated self-rule.

RANCHI

☎ 0651

At 652m, Ranchi doesn't really deserve its title of hill station, especially since it has now lost most of its tree cover. In British times it was Bihar's summer capital and it is now capital of the new state of Jharkhand.

An interesting thing to see here is the **Jagannath Temple**, a small version of the great Jagannath Temple at Puri. It's 6km southwest of Ranchi and visitors are welcome.

There are several hills around Ranchi with sunset views over the rocky landscape. There's also a Tribal Research Institute in Ranchi with a **museum of anthropology**.

There are many beautiful waterfalls in the area, the most spectacular, especially at the end of the monsoon, are the **Hundru Falls** 45km north-east of Ranchi.

The same distance away to the northwest is **Macluskiganj**, an almost deserted hill station, once a holiday haven for Anglo-Indians. There's not a lot to see, but there are some pleasant walks through woods, gardens and orchards and some of the old, albeit dilapidated, Victorian buildings.

Places to Stay & Eat

There are many hotels around the bus stand. All have private bathroom unless stated.

The Grand Trunk Road

India's Grand Trunk Road (GTR) runs the breadth of the country, from the Pakistan border near Amritsar to Kolkata (Calcutta). It is by far the busiest road in the country and Rudyard Kipling described it as a 'river of life'; many of the events in his novel *Kim* take place along it.

Unfortunately, the road has been in a long period of decline with little maintenance since the 17th century when it was lined with *khayaban* trees and became known among European travellers as the 'Long Walk'. The only significant realignment of the road was under the British, when the East India Company sought a more direct route between Kolkata and Varanasi. This route – the one that exists today – was completed in 1838 and is still a vital part of the Indian road network.

Nowadays the GTR, especially the stretch crossing Bihar and Jharkhand, often descends into bone-shattering potholes and narrow sections that are more loose gravel and ditches than road. This causes considerable transport problems; you'll probably see more than one abandoned truck overturned, with its cargo sprawled along the roadside.

However, the GTR still provides a vivid picture of Indians on the move: oil tankers from Assam; Tata trucks from Punjab; garish and battered buses, all with horns blaring; barefoot sadhus on a Ganga pilgrimage; farmers steering overloaded ox-carts; wayward cows; schoolkids on bicycles; and women on foot. Sit at a roadside *dhaba* (snack bar) and observe the passing parade, but be warned: you'll probably also suffer industrial deafness from the racket.

Hotel Konark *(☎ 307840)*, the best small place, is friendly with clean singles/doubles starting at Rs 150/175 and a good restaurant.

Hotel Paradise, with rooms at Rs 120/200, is another good place.

Tourist Bungalow Birsa Vihar *(☎ 314 826)* has dorms with shared bathroom for Rs 60 and double economy/deluxe air-con rooms for Rs 200/500.

Hotel Yuvraj *(☎ 300403)* is a 15-minute walk from the station with singles/doubles from Rs 350/450.

Hotel Yuvraj Palace *(☎ 500326)*, Ranchi's best hotel, nearby, is centrally air-conditioned with rooms starting at Rs 1200/1800.

Getting There & Away

Ranchi has good air, bus and train connections. There are buses to Gaya (Rs 75 to 120, seven hours), Hazaribagh (Rs 35, three hours) and Netarhat (Rs 52, four hours). A direct bus to Puri takes 15 hours.

The train station is 500m from the bus stand and there are daily trains to Patna (Rs 95/499, 2nd/1st class); Gaya (Rs 123/415, 2nd/1st class); and Delhi (Rs 326/1512, sleeper/two-tier air-con sleeper).

HAZARIBAGH

☎ 06546 • elevation 615m

This pleasant leafy town is situated 107km north of Ranchi. About the only reason for coming here would be to visit **Hazaribagh National Park**, 19km to the north.

Hotel Upkar *(☎ 2246)* is the best hotel in Hazaribagh, and good value with singles/doubles for Rs 175/300.

The train station, Hazaribagh Rd, is 67km away. Private minibuses to Gaya (Rs 50, four hours) leave from the bus terminal.

BELA NATIONAL PARK

Known as both Palamau and Bela, this park, 140km north-west of Ranchi, is part of Project Tiger and is one of the best places to see wild elephants. Gain permission to enter the park from the district forest officer in Bela. Although there are *machaans* (observation towers) for viewing the animals, wildlife is sparse since the government drove a major road through the area. Worse still, the World Bank is pumping funds into the construction of Kotku Dam, which will ensure the best forests in the park will need gills to survive.

Jeep safaris can be organised in Bela, the park's access point. Expect to pay around Rs 8 to 10 per kilometre for spins around the park's 250 sq km. There are also tree-top and ground-level hideaways where you can watch the animals without being seen.

Accommodation is mostly in Bela, but you can stay farther afield in Daltonganj (24km away). In Bela, the ***Forest Rest House*** or ***Tourist Lodge*** (built as an ITDC hotel) are OK places to stay for around Rs 200.

Bela is accessible by road from Ranchi and Gaya (both Rs 50, four to five hours).

Unfortunately, it is the same old bandit warning story – before going into the area it is imperative to seek security advice from locals, other travellers or local police.

PARASNATH

☎ 0653232

Just inside the Jharkhand state boundary with West Bengal, and north of the Grand Trunk Rd, Parasnath is the railhead for Sikayi, the major Jain pilgrimage centre in the east of India (Madhuban is the main town). Sikayi, at 1450m, is the highest point in Jharkhand and, like so many other pilgrimage centres, it is reached by a stiff climb on foot. Rich pilgrims from Kolkata are carried up in palanquins by porters.

The 24 temples, representing the Jain tirthankars, are at an altitude of 1366m. Parasnath, the 23rd tirthankar, achieved nirvana here 100 years after his birth. An internationally famous yoga school at Munger (☎ 06344-22430, fax 20169), known variously as the Bihar Yoga School, the University of Yoga and the Bihar Yog Vidyalaya, runs courses here.

There are a number of ***dharamsalas*** in Sikayi, which are strictly vegan and, like those in Bodhgaya, with strict rules of conduct. A ***tourist bungalow***, built by the BSTDC and given to the Jain community at Madhuban, has no fixed rate.

Trains run to Patna and Kolkata, and Maruti vans and minibuses run between the train station and Madhuban.

Kolkata (Calcutta)

For many, contemporary Kolkata (formerly Calcutta) still conjures up hideous images of interminable squalor – a skewed reputation largely built on antiquated stereotypes regurgitated by the (mainly Western) media. For first-time travellers to India, Kolkata, with its mass of humanity, crumbling buildings and frenetic streets, may well come across as a desperate and even ugly place. But after spending time in India's other major cities, it's plain to see that modern-day Kolkata has been unfairly stigmatised.

Get to know Kolkata and you'll see why it has long been acknowledged as the cultural capital of India. Although it may have some of the country's finest visual remnants of British colonial architecture, it undeniably possesses a distinct Bengali soul. Kolkata is referred to as India's friendliest metropolis. Bengali humour is renowned and the Bengalis, so ready to raise arms against political wrongdoings, are also the poets and artists of India. Kolkata was the birthplace and home of many famous people including the inimitable Bengali poet, novelist and painter Rabindranath Tagore, novelist William Thackeray and actress Merle Oberon, who appeared in various films including *The Scarlet Pimpernel*. The house she lived in is on Lindsay St near New Market.

Kolkata has certainly had its share of problems. It has been plagued by chronic labour unrest resulting in a decline in productivity. Massive trade union rallies frequently block traffic in the city centre for hours at a time and the port has been silting up, limiting the size of ships that can use it. The Marxist government of West Bengal has received a lot of criticism over Kolkata's chaos, but as it has rightly pointed out, apparent neglect and mismanagement of the city has been accompanied by considerable improvement in the rural environment. Threats of flood or famine in the countryside no longer send hordes of refugees converging on the city as in the past.

Kolkata at a Glance

Population: 14 million
Area: 18,733 sq km
Main Language: Bengali
Telephone Area Code: 033
Best Time to Go: Nov to Mar

China
Tibet
Bhutan
Nepal
Bangladesh
Kolkata p552
BBD Bagh (Dalhousie Square) p559
Chowringhee p566
Bay of Bengal

- Soak up the city's vibrant Bengali culture at a museum, gallery, coffee house or drama performance
- Explore the historical collections of the Victoria Memorial, one of India's most telling remnants of the British Raj
- Stroll through the 'lungs', the Maidan of modern Kolkata, in the early morning or late afternoon as people exercise their dogs, power walk, do yoga or catch up with friends
- Witness the fascinating spectacle of the mighty Howrah Bridge set against the ethereal expanse of the Hooghly River
- Kick back at the Botanical Gardens, a serene slice of Kolkata that features a spectacular 200-year-old banyan tree

As personal wealth has grown in Kolkata, so too has the number of fume-belching cars jostling for space on the already clogged streets. For the visitor, road travel can be a nail-biting experience, as drivers weave through the ferocious traffic, constantly swerving to avoid local buses travelling at breakneck speed. Indeed, a drawback of sightseeing in Kolkata is the amount of time simply spent stuck in traffic jams – be mentally prepared. Sunday is best, as the roads are generally less congested (by Kolkata standards anyway). The traffic police, decked out in their crisp white uniforms and armed with shiny silver whistles, really have their work cut out for them. Some of these tenacious fellows are downright determined to control the tumultuous traffic, wildly throwing their arms about as they obstreperously threaten law-breaking drivers with hefty fines. Others have more of a 'go-with-the-flow approach', as if resigned to the fact that their chances of completely controlling the impatient mechanical monsters around them are about as likely as starring in a Bollywood blockbuster.

The incredible contrasts and tenacity of this effervescent metropolis have enticed many to wax lyrical about Kolkata. Some good books include Geoffrey Moorhouse's classic 1971 study *Calcutta*, and VS Naipaul's *India – A Million Mutinies Now*, which has some engaging chapters on Kolkata. The interesting *10 Walks in Calcutta*, by Prosenjit Das Gupta, is a light paperback offering cultural, historical and contemporary insights into the city via 10 short (two- to four-hour) walking 'packages', complete with maps. If you want a taste of the acclaimed Rabindranath Tagore's works, get hold of *Selected Short Stories*. And, of course, there is an array of books about Mother Teresa – see Women under Books in the Facts for the Visitor chapter. Dominique Lapierre's *City of Joy* (love it or detest it) is curiously still *de rigueur* reading among many travellers and is thus stocked at most bookshops. The film version of this novel, starring Patrick Swayze, was shot in Kolkata in the early 1990s at a purpose-built slum (!). It's hardly surprising that the film copped a lot of flak from the state government, which felt it was yet another condescending and exaggerated Western depiction of the city's poverty.

HISTORY

Kolkata isn't an ancient city like Delhi, with its impressive relics of the past. In fact, it's largely a British creation: It dates back only some 300 years and was the capital of British India until the beginning of the 20th century.

In 1686 the British abandoned Hooghly, their trading post 38km up the Hooghly River from present-day Kolkata, and moved downriver to three small villages – Sutanati, Govindpur and Kalikata. Job Charnock, an English merchant who later married an Indian widow he dissuaded from committing *sati* (suicide by immolation), was the leader of the British merchants who made this move. At first the post was not a great success and was abandoned on a number of occasions, but in 1696 a fort was laid out near present-day BBD Bagh (Dalhousie Square), and in 1698, the grandson of the Mughal ruler Aurangzeb gave the British official permission to occupy the villages.

Kolkata then grew steadily until 1756, when Siraj-ud-daula, the nawab of Murshidabad, attacked the town. Most of the British inhabitants escaped, but those captured were packed into an underground cellar where, during the night, most of them suffocated in what became known as the Black Hole of Calcutta.

Early in 1757, the British, under Clive of India, retook Kolkata and made peace with the nawab. Later the same year, however, Siraj-ud-daula sided with the French and was defeated at the Battle of Plassey (now Palashi), a turning point in British-Indian history. A much stronger fort was built in Kolkata and the town became the capital of British India.

Much of Kolkata's most enduring development took place between 1780 and 1820. Later in the 19th century, Bengal became an important centre in the struggle for Indian independence, and this was a major reason for the decision to transfer the capital to

Delhi in 1911. Loss of political power did not alter Kolkata's economic strength, and the city continued to prosper until after WWII.

Partition affected Kolkata more than any other major Indian city. Bengal and Punjab were the two areas of India with mixed Hindu and Muslim populations and the dividing line was drawn through them. The result in Bengal was that Kolkata, the jute-producing and export centre of India, became a city without a hinterland, while across the border in East Pakistan (now Bangladesh), jute (a plant fibre used to make sacking and mats) was grown without a centre to process or export it. Furthermore, West Bengal and Kolkata were disrupted by tens of thousands of refugees fleeing from East Bengal, although fortunately without the communal violence and bloodshed that Partition brought to Punjab.

The massive influx of refugees, combined with India's own postwar population explosion, led to Kolkata becoming an international urban horror story. The work of Mother Teresa's Kolkata mission focused worldwide attention on the city's festering problems. In 1971, the India-Pakistan conflict and the creation of Bangladesh led to another flood of refugees, and Kolkata's already chaotic condition further deteriorated.

ORIENTATION

Kolkata sprawls north-south along the eastern bank of the Hooghly River, which divides it from Howrah on the western bank. The parts of Kolkata of most interest to travellers are south of the bridge in the areas around BBD Bagh and Chowringhee. BBD Bagh, formerly Dalhousie Square, is the hub of the central business district (CBD). South of BBD Bagh is the open expanse of the Maidan, and east from here is the area known as Chowringhee. Here you'll find most of the lower-priced hotels, as well as many of the restaurants, banks and airline

Calcutta Becomes Kolkata

In late December 2000, the Indian government officially agreed to the West Bengal government's proposal to restore Calcutta's traditional name, Kolkata. From 1 January 2001, government offices began using Kolkata on their letterheads, and newspapers now refer to the city by its new name. The city is also in the process of changing street signs, maps and anything that bears the old name. The two other major Indian hubs that have changed names in a nationalistic move to reclaim their pre-colonial heritage are Mumbai (Bombay) and Chennai (Madras).

Although the city has now reverted to its pre-colonial name, city officials have recently decided to reinstall statues of some of India's former British rulers, which were unceremoniously dumped in dusty warehouses in the late 1970s in a bid to eradicate any lingering memories of British colonialism. The uprooting of the colonial statues was instigated by the United Front government of the late '70s, which promptly removed 37 statues of erstwhile English lords, viceroys and noblemen that stood in the Maidan, the city's heartland. Some of the statues were placed in the Victoria Memorial and elsewhere. One statue, that of the Earl of Auckland, was sent to New Zealand at the request of that country's government! This nationalist move attracted criticism from many, who believed it robbed the city of its inherent cultural charm. The government attempted to allay the anger by quickly placing statues of great Indian statesmen, such as Gandhi and Nehru, on the sites formerly occupied by the British statues, but this ignited even more outrage because of the shoddy craftsmanship of the Indian statues.

The current move to reinstall the former British statues is designed to restore a prominent part of the city's heritage, even if it was colonial. A committee is in the process of deciding where exactly the discarded statues should be placed – no easy task considering that many potential sites are now occupied by statues of Indian personalities. Some of the British statues seeking a home include those of Lord Mayo, Lord Napier, Lord Curzon, Lord Canning and even King George V.

offices. Sudder St runs off Chowringhee Rd and is the core of the city's travellers' (especially budget travellers') scene. Farther south down Chowringhee Rd, which runs alongside the eastern edge of the Maidan, is Park St, with more-upmarket restaurants and shops.

Street Names

The renaming of city streets, particularly those with Raj-era connotations, can make getting around slightly confusing. While many street signs still display the old names, some maps show new ones. Taxi- and rickshaw-wallahs largely still go by the old (familiar) names; in this chapter's maps, we have provided the new name, with the old name in brackets. However, in the text, the most commonly used name has been used. For instance, most people still know Jawaharlal Nehru Rd as Chowringhee Rd, so that's what we've gone with.

Adding to the confusion, in a bid to alleviate traffic problems, Kolkata has adopted 'timed' one-way streets, which flow in different directions depending on the time of day. For example, in morning rush hour a street might flow east to west, in the afternoon rush hour it will flow west to east, and in the middle of the day it might take two-way traffic!

Some Renamed Roads

old name	new name
Baker Rd	Kanai Bhattacharya Rd
Ballygunge Rd	Gurusday Rd
Bowbazar St	Bepin Behary Ganguly
Buckland Rd	Bankim Ch Rd
Central Ave	Chittaranjan Ave
Chowringhee Rd	Jawaharlal Nehru Rd
Cotton St	Gopabandhu Ave
Free School St	Mirza Ghalib St
Harrington St	Ho Chi Minh Sarani
Harrison Rd	Mahatma Gandhi Rd (MG Rd)
Hastings St	K Sankar (KS) Roy Rd
Kyd St	Dr M Ishaque Rd
Lansdowne Rd	Sarat Bose Rd
Lindsay St	Nellie Sengupta Sarani
Lower Chitpur Rd	Rabindra Sarani
Lower Circular Rd	Acharya Jagadish Chandra (AJC) Bose Rd
Machuabazar St	Madan Mohan St & Keshab Sen St
Mirzapore St	Surya Sen St
Theatre Rd	Shakespeare Sarani
Wellesley St	Rafi Ahmed Kidwai Rd
Wellington St	Nirmal Chunder St

INFORMATION

Tourist Offices

The helpful Government of India tourist office (☎ 2825813), 4 Shakespeare Sarani in Chowringhee, disseminates information about Kolkata as well as other destinations in India. The office has a couple of touch-screen computers enabling you to navigate your way through general tourist information, including local taxi rates and places to see in Kolkata. The office is open 9 am to 6 pm Monday to Friday and until 1 pm on weekends.

The West Bengal Tourism Centre (☎ 248 8271), 3/2 BBD Bagh (on the opposite side to the main post office), is open from 10.30 am to 4 pm Monday to Friday, 10.30 am to 1 pm Saturday, and 7 am to noon on Sunday. It doesn't have as many brochures as the Government of India tourist office and can get awfully busy at times. This is the place to make reservations for the string of West Bengal Tourism Development Corporation (WBTDC) hotels scattered throughout the entire state.

Both the state and national tourist offices have counters at the airport (☎ 5118299), and the West Bengal Tourism Centre has an office at Howrah train station (☎ 6602518) that is open 7 am to 1 pm daily. Both tourist offices can arrange a guide for sightseeing: The official rates for a half/full day are Rs 255/380 for one to four people, Rs 380/505 for five to 15 people, and Rs 505/825 for 16 to 35 people. If you intend to hire a guide for several days, it's a good idea to meet several before making a final decision, as enthusiasm and knowledge can vary quite considerably.

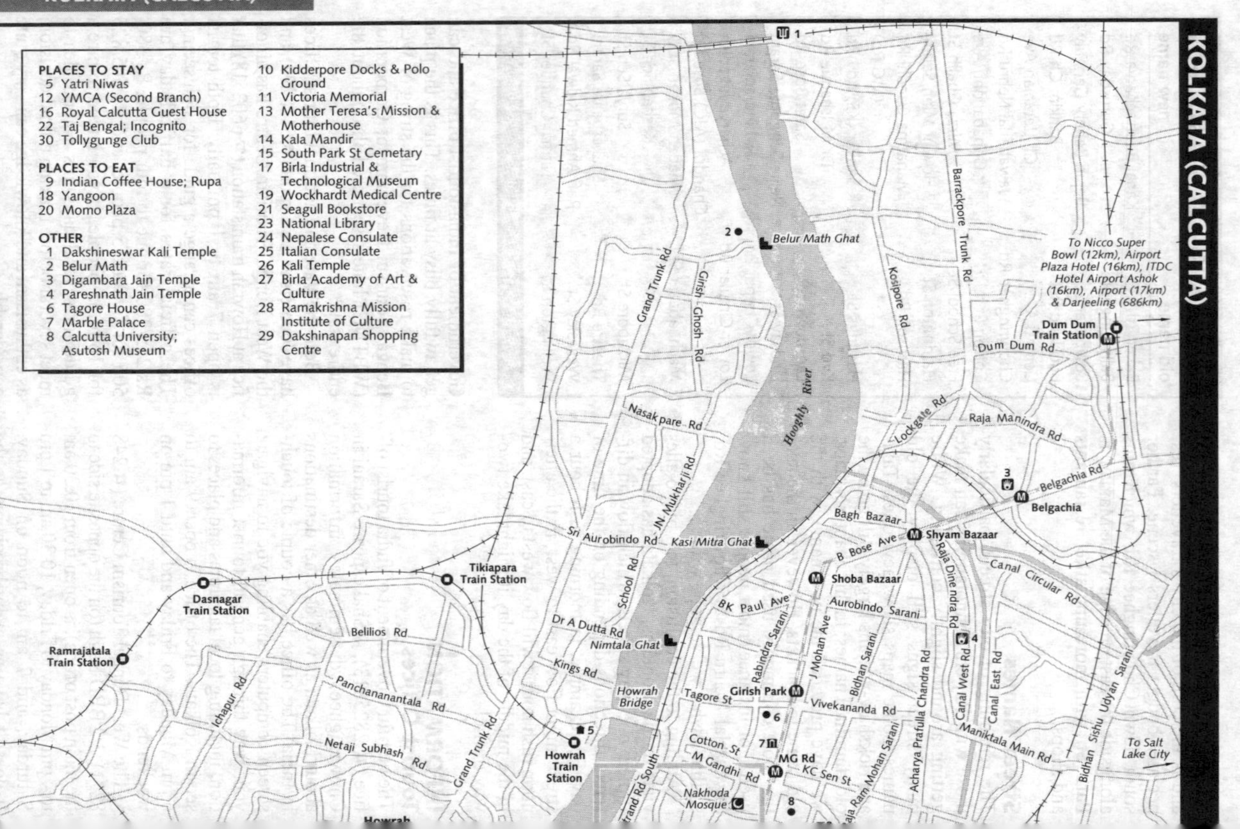

KOLKATA (CALCUTTA)
PLACES TO STAY
5 Yatri Niwas
12 YMCA (Second Branch)
16 Royal Calcutta Guest House
22 Taj Bengal; Incognito
30 Tollygunge Club
PLACES TO EAT
9 Indian Coffee House; Rupa
18 Yangoon
20 Momo Plaza
OTHER
1 Dakshineswar Kali Temple
2 Belur Math
3 Digambara Jain Temple
4 Pareshnath Jain Temple
6 Tagore House
7 Marble Palace
8 Calcutta University; Asutosh Museum
10 Kidderpore Docks & Polo Ground
11 Victoria Memorial
13 Mother Teresa's Mission & Motherhouse
14 Kala Mandir
15 South Park St Cemetary
17 Birla Industrial & Technological Museum
19 Wockhardt Medical Centre
21 Seagull Bookstore
23 National Library
24 Nepalese Consulate
25 Italian Consulate
26 Kali Temple
27 Birla Academy of Art & Culture
28 Ramakrishna Mission Institute of Culture
29 Dakshinapan Shopping Centre
To Nicco Super Bowl (12km), Airport Plaza Hotel (16km), ITDC Hotel Airport Ashok (16km), Airport (17km) & Darjeeling (686km)
Dum Dum Train Station
Dum Dum Rd
Barrackpore Trunk Rd
Kosipore Rd
Belur Math Ghat
Hooghly River
Grand Trunk Rd
Girish Ghosh Rd
Nasak pare Rd
JN Mukharji Rd
Lockgate Rd
Raja Manindra Rd
Belgachia Rd
Belgachia
Bagh Bazaar
B Bose Ave
Shyam Bazaar
Sri Aurobindo Rd
Kasi Mitra Ghat
Canal Circular Rd
Raja Dinendra Rd
Shoba Bazaar
Tikiapara Train Station
Dasnagar Train Station
Ramrajatala Train Station
School Rd
BK Paul Ave
Aurobindo Sarani
Dr A Dutta Rd
Nimtala Ghat
Belilios Rd
Kings Rd
Howrah Bridge
Rabindra Sarani
J Mohan Ave
Bidhan Sarani
Acharya Prafulla Chandra Rd
Canal West Rd
Canal East Rd
Bidhan Sishu Udyan Sarani
Ichapur Rd
Panchananantala Rd
Tagore St
Girish Park
Vivekananda Rd
Maniktala Main Rd
To Salt Lake City
Netaji Subhash Rd
Howrah Train Station
Grand Rd South
Cotton St
M Gandhi Rd
MG Rd
KC Sen St
Raja Ram Mohan Sarani
Nakhoda Mosque

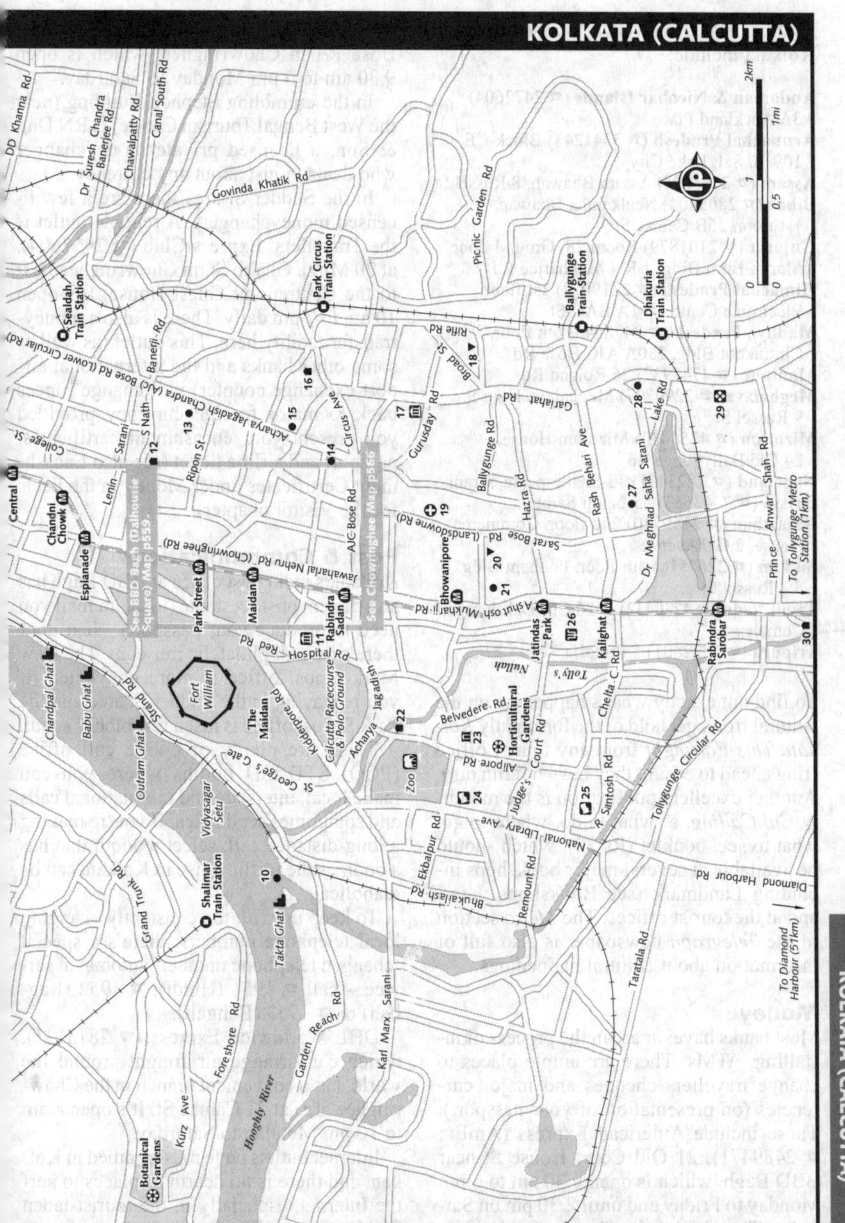

KOLKATA (CALCUTTA)

Other states that have tourist offices in Kolkata include:

Andaman & Nicobar Islands (☎ 2472604) 3A Auckland Place
Arunachal Pradesh (☎ 3341243) Block-CE, 109/10 Salt Lake City
Assam (☎ 2295094) Assam Bhawan, 8 Russel St
Bihar (☎ 2803304) Neelkantha Bhawan, 1st floor, 26B Camac St
Gujarat (☎ 2101879) Room 28, Ground floor, Martin Burn Bldg, 1 RN Mukharjee Rd
Himachal Pradesh (☎ 2219072) 1st floor, Electronic Centre, 1-1A BAC St
Madhya Pradesh (☎ 2478543) 6th floor, Chitrakoot Bldg, 230A AJC Bose Rd
Manipur (☎ 4747937) 26 Roland Rd
Meghalaya (☎ 2290797) Meghalaya House, 9 Russel St
Mizoram (☎ 4756430) Mizoram House, 24 Old Ballygunge Rd
Nagaland (☎ 2823491) 13 Shakespeare Sarani
Orissa (☎ 2443653) 55 Lenin Sarani
Rajasthan (☎ 2159740) 2nd floor, Commerce House, 2 GC Avenue
Sikkim (☎ 2267516) 4th floor, Poonam Bldg, 5/2 Russel St
Tamil Nadu (☎ 4720432) G-26 CIT Dakshinapan Complex
Tripura (☎ 2822801) 1 Pretoria St

To find out exactly what's happening on the cultural front, get hold of the fortnightly *Kolkata This Fortnight* from any tourist office (ring ahead to ensure they have not run out). Another excellent publication is the monthly *Cal Calling*, a 'what to do, where to go, what to see' booklet (Rs 20), which should be available at several major bookshops including Landmark (see Bookshops, later) and at the tourist offices. The *Metro* section of the *Telegraph* newspaper is also full of information about cultural happenings.

Money

Most banks have, or are in the process of installing, ATMs. There are ample places to change travellers cheques and major currencies (on presentation of your passport). These include American Express (AmEx; ☎ 2489471), 21 Old Court House St near BBD Bagh, which is open 9.30 am to 6 pm Monday to Friday and until 2.30 pm on Saturday. There's also the Thomas Cook office (☎ 2803907), Chitrakoot Bldg, 230 AJC Bose Rd in Chowringhee, which is open 9.30 am to 6 pm Monday to Saturday.

In the crumbling Stephen Building (near the West Bengal Tourism Centre) is RN Dutt & Son, a licensed private moneychanger who deals in just about any currency.

In the Sudder St area there are a few licensed moneychangers. A reliable outlet is the Travellers' Express Club (☎ 2457604), at 20 Mirza Ghalib St, in Chowringhee next to the Centrepoint Guest House. It's open 10 am to 7 pm daily. There is also a money-transfer facility here. This outlet (as well as some other banks and the international airport exchange counter) will change rupees back to major foreign currency provided you present your encashment certificates, passport and airline ticket (see also Encashment Certificates under Money in the Facts for the Visitor chapter).

Post & Communications

Kolkata's main post office at BBD Bagh has an efficient poste restante (to claim mail you need to produce your passport). Next door there's a small philatelic museum. The New Market post office is more convenient if you're staying in the Sudder St area and the Park St post office is just a few blocks south.

There are plenty of public call office (PCO) STD/ISD booths where you can make local, interstate and international calls and sometimes send faxes. If you're making a long-distance call, select a booth that has a door, as the traffic noise in Kolkata can be diabolical.

To keep up with the constantly changing local telephone numbers, there's a special 'changed telephone number' automated service – call ☎ 1951 (Hindi), ☎ 1952 (English) or ☎ 1953 (Bengali).

DHL Worldwide Express (☎ 2813131), which can arrange air freight around the world, has a convenient branch in the Chowringhee area at 21 Camac St. It's open 8 am to 10 pm Monday to Saturday.

Internet outlets have mushroomed in Kolkata and there is no dearth of places to surf the Internet, especially in the tourist-laden Sudder St area. The usual charge is around

Rs 40 per hour (some impose a minimum of 15 minutes for Rs 10). To print a page costs around Rs 5. As more and more places crop up, expect charges to drop over time.

Netfreaks is at 2/1 Sudder St (near the Salvation Army Guest House) and is a cool, calm place to tap out emails to friends back home. There is a minimum of 15 minutes (Rs 10). It costs Rs 40 per hour, but long-term stayers should consider the special deal of 10 hours for Rs 300 (expires after one month).

The British Council has a library (☎ 282 5944) at 5 Shakespeare Sarani and charges Rs 30 for half an hour (minimum) for non-members, or Rs 15 for members. The Cyber Empire Internet Cafe, in the New Empire Cinema complex near New Market, charges Rs 20 for 15 minutes, or Rs 50 per hour.

Visa Extensions

The Foreigners' Registration Office (☎ 247 3301) is at 237A AJC Bose Rd, Chowringhee, and is open 10 am to 5 pm Monday to Friday. However, it does not issue extensions unless you have an exceptionally good reason.

Travel Agencies

Travellers' Express Club (☎ 2457604) at 20 Mirza Ghalib St offers competitive prices on domestic and international airline tickets and is reliable. The helpful manager can also arrange specialist tours of India's Buddhist sites (see its Web site at www.nirvana-tours.com for details). Kuka Travels (☎ 226 0496), on the 1st floor of the Tourist Inn building on Sudder St, deals in domestic flight bookings.

Rail tickets can be purchased (for a commission) from several outlets in the Sudder St area. However, some travellers have reported overcharging and shoddy service, so shop around. To avoid being hoodwinked, go to the tourist railway booking office at Fairlie Place (see Train later in this chapter) – but be prepared to wait.

Photography

If you need passport photos, a good option is North East Color Photos (☎ 2492098), near the corner of Sudder St and the small road directly opposite the Salvation Army Guest House. It charges Rs 50 for the standard four mug shots (including negatives), but you'll have to come back later in the day to collect them. To develop 36 colour prints costs Rs 18, plus Rs 3.50 per print. Although you can also have slide film developed here, the most reputable place for this is Bourne & Shepherd (☎ 2281658), 141 SN Banerjee Rd (not far from the Sudder St area), which prides itself as being 'the oldest photographic studio in the world'. Bourne & Shepherd charges Rs 120 (cardboard mounts) or Rs 160 (plastic mounts) to develop 36 slides.

Bookshops

Kolkata has some brilliant bookshops and many around the Sudder St area sell a selection of interesting second-hand books. The main bookshop area is along College St, opposite the Calcutta University east of BBD Bagh. In the same building as the Indian Coffee House here, Rupa has a decent range including its own publications. Newman's is one of Kolkata's oldest bookshops – it's in the same block as the Great Eastern Hotel just south of BBD Bagh.

In the Chowringhee area, Cambridge Book & Stationery Company at 20D Park St is a good, small bookshop. A bit farther along Park St towards Chowringhee Rd, the swanky Oxford Book Shop is much larger and has plenty of well-stocked shelves and well-dressed browsers. The small and delightfully unpretentious Classic Books, at 10 Middleton St, has a reasonably good collection, and the owner, Bharat, is a mine of information. Bookland is a modest street-front bookstall at the eastern end of Sudder St (opposite the Khwaja restaurant). Run by a friendly fellow, it sells new and second-hand books in various languages, and will buy them back for 50% of what you paid. There are other similar small swap 'n' sell places nearby on Mirza Ghalib St.

Landmark is on the 3rd floor of the modern Emami Shoppers City complex at 3 Lord Sinha Rd. This is a large, commercial-flavoured place with a wide range of books, cards, stationery and music. Go down to the 2nd-floor Starlit Cafe for some refreshing organic ice cream (Rs 15 per scoop).

The well-kept Seagull Bookstore, at 31A Shyama Prasad Mukherjee Rd (near the Indira Cinema and opposite the Bhowanipore police station), is a real treasure trove. It even publishes its own titles and sometimes hosts author talks.

Libraries & Cultural Centres

The British Council (☎ 2825944) on Shakespeare Sarani offers a full lending and reference library, plus an electronic media centre with Internet access (see Post & Communications). Membership is Rs 600 per year or Rs 100 per month. Photocopying costs Rs 1 per sheet. There is a garden cafe that serves light meals and nonalcoholic drinks. The library is open 11 am to 7 pm Tuesday to Saturday.

Medical Services & Emergency

It's best to contact your country's embassy if you're in serious trouble (see Embassies & Consulates in the Facts for the Visitor chapter). For an ambulance call ☎ 102, for fire call ☎ 101 and for the police call ☎ 100.

Vital Medical Services (☎ 2825664), 6 Ho Chi Minh Sarani in Chowringhee, is open 9.30 am to 5.30 pm. Wockhardt Medical Centre (☎ 4754320, 4754096) at 2/7 Sarat Bose (Lansdowne) Rd, south of Chowringhee, is open 8 am to 8 pm. Alternatively, medical queries should be directed to any of the large hospitals. Some of the mid-range and all of the top-end hotels usually have reputable doctors on call.

CHOWRINGHEE AREA

Indian Museum

This museum, built in the mid-1870s, is a fine colonial building housing an impressive collection. The entrance hall is dominated by an original Mauryan Lion Capital, India's national symbol, and the archaeological gallery houses the Barhut Gateway (2nd century BC), a massive structure decorated with a bas-relief depicting the life of the Buddha. It has the best collection of Pala-dynasty statues in the country and the art collection has many fine pieces from Orissan and other temples. It also has superb examples of Buddhist Gandharan art – an interesting meeting between Greek artistry and Buddhist ideals that produced Buddha images and other sculptures of great beauty. The art and textile galleries are worth a look. Unfortunately, the natural history collection, while vast, is disintegrating, and the exhibits are coated in dust. The museum is on the corner of Sudder St and Chowringhee Rd and is open 10 am to 5 pm Tuesday to Sunday. It closes half an hour earlier between December and February. Entry is Rs 10 for Indians and a whopping Rs 150 for foreigners. There's also a camera fee (Rs 25).

Asiatic Society

Founded on 15 February 1784, at the instigation of scholar and visionary Sir William Jones, the Asiatic Society was formed to preserve the science, civilisation and culture of India. The society established the first modern-style museum in Asia in 1814 in Kolkata, but because of a chronic lack of space and facilities, most of the priceless exhibits were transferred to the Indian Museum on its completion in 1875. However, a small collection of valuable art and antiquities was retained and is now on display at the society's museum in Park St. Among the fabulous collection of paintings, *thangkas* (Tibetan cloth paintings), botanical specimens and other objects, the Barhut Ashokan Rock Edict (circa 250 BC, from Orissa) is unquestionably the most important piece, representing India's most famous and revered emperor and his conversion to Buddhism. Of great interest to scholars is the library, which contains over 200,000 books, journals and manuscripts of rare antiquity.

Library hours are 8 am to 7 pm Monday to Friday and until 6 pm on Saturday. Entry is free. The museum is open 8 am to 7 pm Monday to Friday. A small but informative quarterly publication, *The Asiatic Society*, is sold at the society's offices (Rs 100).

MP Birla Planetarium

This planetarium (☎ 2231516), near the Government of India tourist office, is one of

Rabindranath Tagore

MARTIN HARRIS

Born in Kolkata, the brilliant and prolific Rabindranath Tagore is affectionately dubbed the grand master of Bengali culture and is particularly renowned around the world for his romantic poetry. This legendary poet, novelist, playwright and artist was born on 7 May 1861 and was the youngest of 14 children. His father, Debendranath Tagore, was a respected Sanskrit scholar and the leader of the Brahmo Samaj (a Hindu reform movement). Rabindranath's early education was undertaken at home in a vibrant environment of cultural and intellectual activity. He was barely seven years old when he wrote his very first poem and his first book of poems was published when he was just 17. Rabindranath Tagore was sent to study in England in 1878, but he stayed there for just under 1½ years, finding the lessons too mundane. On his return to India, he spent most of his time writing not only poems, but also short stories and even novels. He wed Mrinalini Devi in 1883.

From the early 1890s, a number of Tagore's works were published, many of which revolved around Bengal's traditional village lifestyles. He was particularly inspired to write about the hardships faced by those living in rural poverty, after he was sent to manage several of his father's properties in Bengali villages. Tagore was deeply affected by the poverty around him, and *Galpa Guccha*, published in 1912, is a true reflection of daily life in Bengal's rural regions.

In 1901, Tagore founded a school in Shantiniketan (see the West Bengal chapter), which aimed to amalgamate positive aspects of Indian and Western educational styles. It later developed into the Visvabharati University with an emphasis on humanity's relationship with nature.

Between 1902 and 1907, Tagore tragically lost his wife, son and daughter, and some say that his intense sadness translated into some of his most poignant writings, particularly *Gitanjali*. It was this very compilation of poetic prose, published in Bengali in 1910 and translated into English by Tagore himself in 1912, which won Tagore the Nobel prize for literature in 1913. He was credited with introducing India's historical and cultural magnificence to the modern world. In 1915 Tagore was awarded a knighthood by the British, but he surrendered it in 1919 as a protest against the Amritsar massacre, during which British troops killed hundreds of unarmed protestors. Tagore wrote a letter to the viceroy stating that: 'The disproportionate severity of the punishment inflicted upon the unfortunate people and the method of carrying it out, we are convinced, are without parallel in the history of civilised governments and these are the reasons which have painfully compelled me to ask your Excellency to relieve me of my title.'

Tagore, a passionate nationalist, went on to write the lyrics of India's national anthem, *Jana Gana Mana*. This anthem was originally written in Bengali, but was adopted by the Constituent Assembly in its Hindi version as the country's national anthem on 24 January 1950. The anthem consists of five stanzas. The first stanza translates as: 'Thou art the ruler of the minds of all people, dispenser of India's destiny'.

Rabindranath Tagore continued to write and had 21 works published between 1916 and 1941. Over his lifetime he wrote more than 1000 poems, almost two dozen plays, eight novels, nine volumes of short stories and over 2000 songs. He also wrote a plethora of prose on various issues ranging from religion to politics. In the latter years of his life, he gave public lectures around India and across the world, including China, Japan, Europe and the USA, always attracting large audiences. Tagore passed away in Kolkata on 7 August 1941. To this day he remains a cherished national icon.

the largest in the world. For Rs 10 you'll get a much better view of the stars in here than you'll get through the polluted atmosphere outside. There are shows in English at 1.30 pm and 6.30 pm every day, but as these times may change, check in advance.

St Paul's Cathedral

Built between 1839 and 1847, St Paul's Cathedral stands at the southern end of the Maidan on Cathedral Rd, just east of the Victoria Memorial. The steeple fell during an earthquake in 1897 and, following further damage in a 1934 quake, was redesigned and rebuilt. Inside, there's some impressive stained glass, including the great west window by Sir Edward Burne-Jones. It's open to visitors 9 am to noon and 3 to 6 pm daily. There are Sunday services in English at 7.30 am, 8.30 am and 6 pm. A Bengali service starts at 10.30 am.

Academy of Fine Arts

The Academy of Fine Arts, on Cathedral Rd, has a permanent exhibition and runs an artists' studio. The academy is open 3 to 8 pm daily except Monday. Entry is free.

Nehru Children's Museum

The small Nehru Children's Museum, 94/1 Chowringhee Rd, has models depicting the Hindu epics, the Ramayana and the Mahabharata. It's open 11 am to 6.30 pm Wednesday to Sunday and 3 to 6.30 pm Tuesday; admission is Rs 5.

BBD BAGH AREA

BBD Bagh (Dalhousie Square)

When Kolkata was the administrative centre of British India, BBD (Binoy Badal Dinesh) Bagh was the centre of power. On the north side stands the huge **Writers' Building**, dating from 1880 (when clerical workers were known as writers). The East India Company's writers have now been replaced by modern-day West Bengal state government employees, and this is where the quintuplicate forms, carbon copies and red ink originate.

Until it was abandoned in 1757, the original Fort William stood on the site of the present-day post office. It stretched from there down to the river, which has since changed its course. Brass markers by the post office indicate where the fort walls used to be.

Kolkata's renowned **'black hole'** stood at the north-eastern corner of the post office, but since Independence all indications of its position have been removed. The black hole was actually a tiny guardroom in the fort, and according to the British version of the story, 146 people were forced into it on that fateful night when the city fell to Siraj-ud-daula. Next morning, only 23 were still alive. Historians now suggest the numbers of prisoners and fatalities were exaggerated in a propaganda exercise; there were probably only half as many incarcerated and half as many deaths. Whatever the numbers, death by suffocation on a humid Kolkata night must have been a horrific way to go.

For stamp enthusiasts, there's a small **philatelic museum** near the main post office on BBD Bagh.

Millennium Park

Superbly positioned right on the banks of the Hooghly River (on Strand Rd South, directly opposite the Shipping Corporation of India building) and with a terrific view of Howrah Bridge, this park is a glorious place to kick back and observe life on the river. It's especially beautiful at sunset (although it can get busy at this time). It has a children's playground and a kiosk. The park is open 1 to 8 pm daily (last tickets sold at 7.30 pm). Admission is Rs 5.

St John's Church

A little south of BBD Bagh is this crumbling church, which dates from 1787. The overgrown, tranquil graveyard here has a number of interesting monuments, including the octagonal mausoleum of Job Charnock, founder of Kolkata, who died in the early 1690s. Admiral Watson, who supported Clive in retaking Kolkata from Siraj-ud-daula, is also buried here. The obelisk commemorating the 'black hole' was moved from near the main post office to a corner of this graveyard.

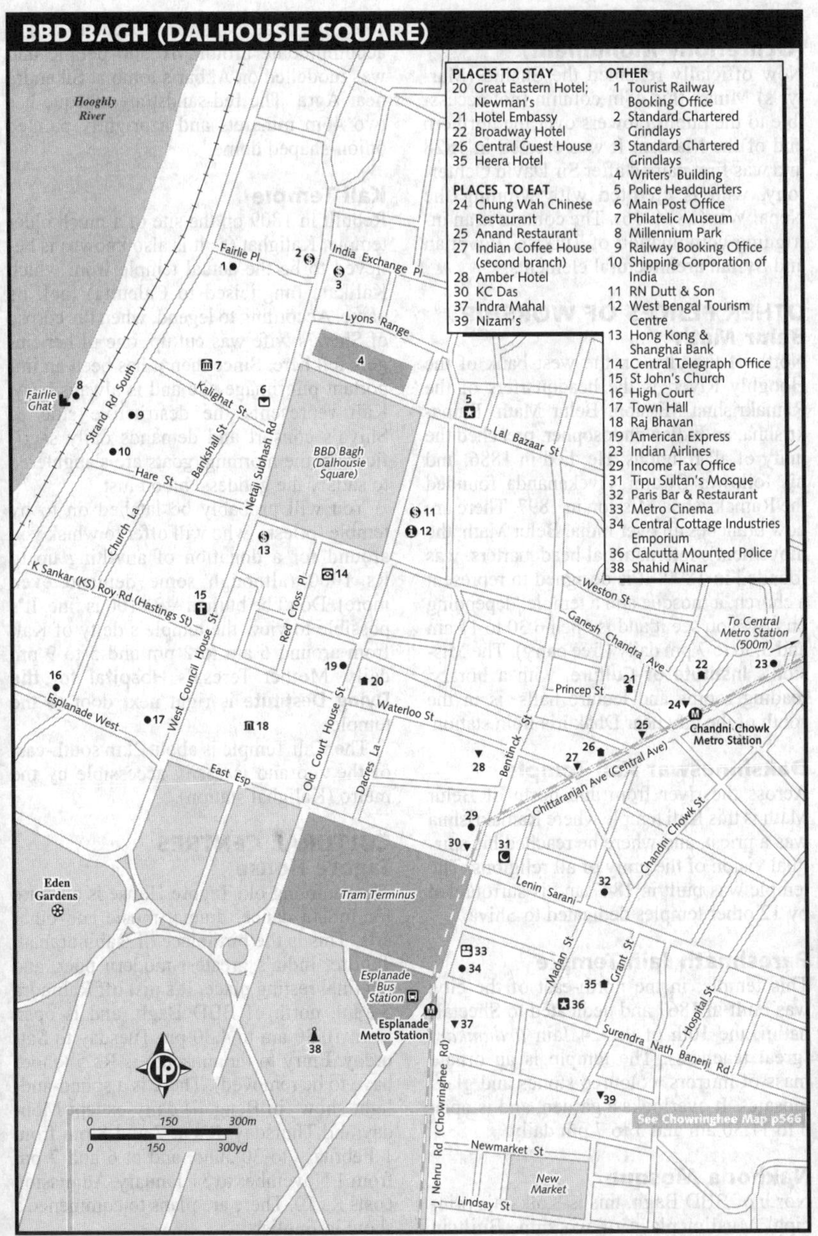
BBD BAGH (DALHOUSIE SQUARE)
PLACES TO STAY
20 Great Eastern Hotel; Newman's
21 Hotel Embassy
22 Broadway Hotel
26 Central Guest House
35 Heera Hotel
PLACES TO EAT
24 Chung Wah Chinese Restaurant
25 Anand Restaurant
27 Indian Coffee House (second branch)
28 Amber Hotel
30 KC Das
37 Indra Mahal
39 Nizam's
OTHER
1 Tourist Railway Booking Office
2 Standard Chartered Grindlays
3 Standard Chartered Grindlays
4 Writers' Building
5 Police Headquarters
6 Main Post Office
7 Philatelic Museum
8 Millennium Park
9 Railway Booking Office
10 Shipping Corporation of India
11 RN Dutt & Son
12 West Bengal Tourism Centre
13 Hong Kong & Shanghai Bank
14 Central Telegraph Office
15 St John's Church
16 High Court
17 Town Hall
18 Raj Bhavan
19 American Express
23 Indian Airlines
29 Income Tax Office
31 Tipu Sultan's Mosque
32 Paris Bar & Restaurant
33 Metro Cinema
34 Central Cottage Industries Emporium
36 Calcutta Mounted Police
38 Shahid Minar
Hooghly River
Fairlie Pl
India Exchange Pl
Lyons Range
Fairlie Ghat
Strand Rd South
Kalighat St
Bankshall St
Netaji Subhash Rd
BBD Bagh (Dalhousie Square)
Hare St
Church La
K Sankar (KS) Roy Rd (Hastings St)
West Council House St
Red Cross Pl
Old Court House St
Dacres La
Esplanade West
Waterloo St
East Esp
Lal Bazaar St
Weston St
Ganesh Chandra Ave
To Central Metro Station (500m)
Princep St
Bentinck St
Chandni Chowk Metro Station
Chittaranjan Ave (Central Ave)
Chandni Chowk St
Lenin Sarani
Eden Gardens
Tram Terminus
Esplanade Bus Station
Esplanade Metro Station
Madan St
Grant St
Hospital St
Surendra Nath Banerji Rd
J Nehru Rd (Chowringhee Rd)
See Chowringhee Map p566
Newmarket St
New Market
Lindsay St
0 150 300m
0 150 300yd

Shahid Minar (Ochterlony Monument)

Now officially renamed the Shahid (Martyr's) Minar, this 48m column (not accessible to the public) towers over the northern end of the Maidan. It was erected in 1828 and was first named after Sir David Ochterlony, who is credited with winning the Nepal War (1814–16). The column is an intriguing combination of Turkish, Egyptian and Syrian architectural elements.

OTHER PLACES OF WORSHIP

Belur Math

North of the city, on the west bank of the Hooghly River, is the headquarters of the Ramakrishna Mission, Belur Math. Ramakrishna, an Indian philosopher, preached the unity of all religions. He died in 1886, and his follower Swami Vivekananda founded the Ramakrishna Mission in 1897. There are now branches all over India. Belur Math, the movement's international headquarters, was founded in 1899. It is designed to represent a church, a mosque and a temple, depending on how you see it and is open 6.30 to 11 am and 3.30 to 7 pm daily (free entry). The Mission's **Institute of Culture**, with a library, reading rooms and lecture halls, is in the south of the city near Dhakuria train station.

Dakshineswar Kali Temple

Across the river from and north of Belur Math is this Kali temple where Ramakrishna was a priest, and where he reached his spiritual vision of the unity of all religions. The temple was built in 1847 and is surrounded by 12 other temples dedicated to Shiva.

Pareshnath Jain Temple

This temple, in the north-east of the city, was built in 1867 and dedicated to Sheetalnathji, the 10th of the 24 Jain *tirthankars* (great teachers). The temple is an ornate mass of mirrors, coloured stones and glass mosaics. It overlooks a garden, and is open 6 to 11.30 am and 3 to 7 pm daily.

Nakhoda Mosque

North of BBD Bagh, this is Kolkata's principal Muslim place of worship. Built in 1926, the huge Nakhoda Mosque is said to accommodate around 10,000 people and was modelled on Akbar's tomb at Sikandra near Agra. The red-sandstone mosque has two 46m minarets and a brightly painted onion-shaped dome.

Kali Temple

Rebuilt in 1809 on the site of a much older temple, Kalighat (as it is also known) is believed to be the actual temple from which Kalikata (anglicised to Calcutta) took its name. According to legend, when the corpse of Shiva's wife was cut up, one of her fingers fell here. Since then it has been an important pilgrimage site and is always busy. Kali represents the destructive side of Shiva's consort and demands daily sacrifices. In the morning, goats are slaughtered to satisfy the goddess' blood lust.

You will probably be latched on to by temple 'priests' who will offer to whisk you around for a donation of anything up to Rs 1000 (although some demand even more). Don't be bullied – Rs 100 is fine. It's possible to view the temple's deity of Kali from around 6 am to 2 pm and 5 to 9 pm daily. Mother Teresa's **Hospital for the Dying Destitute** is right next door to the temple.

The Kali Temple is about 2km south-east of the zoo and is easily accessible by the metro (Kalighat station).

CULTURAL CENTRES

Tagore House

The rambling old Tagore House is a centre for Indian dance, drama, music and other arts. This is the birthplace of Rabindranath Tagore, India's greatest modern poet, and his final resting place. It's just off Rabindra Sarani, north of BBD Bagh, and is open from 10.30 am to 4.30 pm Tuesday to Saturday. Entry to the museum is Rs 5 (shoes have to be removed). There is a sound-and-light show (in Bengali) daily except Monday and Thursday. It's at 7 and 8 pm from 1 February to 30 June, and at 6 and 7 pm from 1 November to 31 January. Admission costs Rs 10. There are plans to commence a show in English.

Mother Teresa

The late Mother Teresa, the 'Saint of the Gutters', came to epitomise selflessness because of her dedication to the destitute, the suffering and the dying. Born Agnes Gonxha Bojaxhiu in Serbia in 1910 to Albanian parents, she joined the Irish Order of Loreto nuns in 1929 and was sent to Darjeeling as a teacher. Moving to a school in Kolkata in 1937, she was horrified at the number of poor people who perished on the streets of the city because there was nowhere else for them to go. She began to feel that behind the secure walls of the nunnery she was too far removed from the people she wanted to help.

Mother Teresa formed a new order, the Missionaries of Charity, in 1950. Among the order's vows is the promise 'to give wholehearted and free service to the poorest of the poor'. This vow was put into action with the setting up of several homes including Nirmal Hriday (for the dying), Shanti Nagar (for lepers) and Nirmala Shishu Bhavan (a children's home). There are now homes in many other places around the world. In 1979 her work achieved world recognition when she was awarded the Nobel Peace Prize.

For all her saintliness, Mother Teresa was not without her critics. Feminist Germaine Greer, for example, accused her of being a religious imperialist, although anyone who has spent some time with the nuns and seen them at work could hardly call them Bible-bashing evangelists. Mother Teresa herself said that hers was contemplative work. Her inspiration was spiritual and Christian and was put into practice mainly by ministering to physical needs; she never sought to convert anyone. There have also been an increasing number of recent allegations that the mission adheres to antiquated healthcare systems that compromise the quality of health care, and that it lacks financial accountability.

Early in 1997 Mother Teresa resigned her position at the Missionaries because of bad health, and named Sister Nirmala as her replacement. On 5 September 1997, a few days after her 87th birthday, and the day of Diana, Princess of Wales' funeral, Mother Teresa went to join her God. Not one to tolerate the restrictions of a hospital, she died surrounded by the sisters in her beloved Motherhouse in Kolkata. For one week her body lay in a glass case, draped with the Indian flag, in St Thomas' Church. Thousands of people, from the poor of Kolkata to dignitaries from around the world, came to pay their last respects. The government honoured Mother Teresa with a state funeral and her coffin was carried on a gun carriage that once bore the bodies of India's greatest statesmen, Mahatma Gandhi and Jawaharlal Nehru. The funeral service was attended by around 12,000 people.

Mother Teresa's coffin now rests in the Motherhouse; its only embellishment is a small marble tombstone inscribed with her name and Christ's instruction 'Love one another as I have loved you'.

PARKS & GARDENS
Botanical Gardens

The extensive Botanical Gardens, on the west bank of the Hooghly River, stretch for over 1km along the river and occupy 109 hectares. The gardens were originally founded in 1786 and administered by Colonel Kyd. It was from these gardens that the tea now grown in Assam and Darjeeling was first developed. The prime attraction is the 200-year-old **banyan tree**, claimed to have the second-largest canopy in the world (the largest is in Andhra Pradesh). It covers an area of nearly 400m in circumference and continues to flourish despite having its central trunk removed in 1925 because of fungal damage. The **palm house** in the centre of the gardens is also worth a look.

The gardens (open from sunrise to sunset) are a wonderful haven from the clamour of the city, although they can get very crowded on Sunday. You can get there by ferry from Babu Ghat, but this runs on a 'casual basis' at sporadic times.

The Maidan & Fort William

After the events of 1756, when Siraj-ud-daula sacked the town, the British set out to replace the original Fort William, in the Maidan, with a massive and impregnable new fort. First they 'cleared out' the inhabitants of the village of Govindpur and in 1758 laid the foundations of a fort. By the time it was completed in 1781, the fort had cost the awesome total, for those days, of £2 million. Around the fort a huge expanse of jungle was destroyed to give the cannons a clear line of fire, but as is common, the fort has never fired a single shot in aggression.

The fort is still in use today and visitors are only allowed inside with special permission, which is rarely granted. Even the trenches and deep fortifications surrounding the fort's massive walls seem to be out-of-bounds.

The area cleared around Fort William became the Maidan, the 'lungs' of modern Kolkata. This huge, green expanse stretches 3km north to south and is over 1km wide. The stream known as Tolly's Nullah is to the south, and here you'll find a racecourse and the Victoria Memorial. In the northern section of the Maidan is Eden Gardens, while Raj Bhavan (Old Government House) overlooks it from the north.

Within the gardens are cricket and football fields, ponds, trees and even musical fountains. Cows graze, political discussions are held and people stroll across the grounds or come for early morning yoga/meditation sessions.

Eden Gardens

At the northern corner of the Maidan are the small and pleasantly laid out Eden Gardens. A tiny Burmese pagoda was brought here from Prome, Myanmar (Burma), in 1856; it's set in a small lake and is extraordinarily picturesque. The gardens were named after the sister of Lord Auckland, a former governor general. **Calcutta Cricket Ground (Ranji Stadium)**, where international matches are held, is also within the gardens – these grounds have a terrific atmosphere and it's well worth trying to see a match if there's one on during your visit. Call the Cricket Association of Bengal on ☎ 248 1528 (see also Spectator Sports in the Facts for the Visitor chapter).

Near the gardens you can take a pleasant walk along the banks of the **Hooghly River**. Ferries run across the river from several ghats and there are plenty of boat operators around offering to take you out on the water for a short cruise. There are no fixed prices for these cruises but expect to pay around Rs 80 per hour per boat.

In the corner of the gardens near Raj Bhavan, where a diagonal pathway joins the road and opposite the statue of Rash Behari Bose, there is a colony of small, virtually tame rats that live in burrows. They may not be obvious at first – just scatter some food to entice them out of their cosy underground abode.

Zoo & Horticultural Gardens

South of the Maidan is Kolkata's 16-hectare zoo, which was opened in 1875. Some animals are displayed in near-natural environments, while others are not so blessed. It is open from 9 am to 5 pm daily except Thursday (Rs 5).

Just south of the zoo on Alipore Rd are the pleasant and quiet Horticultural Gardens. They're open 6 to 10 am and 1 to 5 pm daily (free entry).

OTHER MUSEUMS & GALLERIES

Asutosh Museum at Calcutta University has a collection of objects with an emphasis on Bengali folk art. It's open 11 am to 5 pm Monday to Friday and entry is free.

At 19A Gurusday Rd is the **Birla Industrial & Technological Museum**, open 10 am to 5.30 pm daily (Rs 7). The philanthropic (and very wealthy) Birla family has also provided the **Birla Academy of Art & Culture** at 109 Southern Ave, which is open 4 to 8 pm daily except Monday (Rs 2). It has a good collection of sculpture and modern art. Also in the same area of Ballygunge is the **Cima Gallery** at Sunny Towers, 43 Ashutesh Chowdhauri Ave. The gallery displays contemporary art and is open 11 am to 7 pm daily except Sunday (free entry). Check out the Web site at www.cimaartindia.com for more details.

Victoria Memorial

At the southern end of the Maidan stands the Victoria Memorial, possibly the most awesome reminder of the Raj to be found in India. This huge white-marble museum houses a vast collection of memorabilia from the days of the British empire. There are portraits, statues and busts of almost all the main participants in British-Indian history. Scenes from military conflicts and the events of the Indian Uprising of 1857 are illustrated. There are some superb watercolours of Indian landscapes and buildings that were executed by travelling Victorian artists. There's also a piano that was played by Queen Victoria as a young girl and a huge painting depicting King Edward VII entering Jaipur in a regal procession in 1876. French guns captured at the Battle of Plassey are on show along with the black stone throne of the nawab defeated by Clive.

The **Calcutta Gallery**, opened in 1992, exhibits many early pictures of Kolkata as well as relics from the Raj, such as pistols. Upstairs is the **National Leaders Gallery** which displays portraits of various political and social leaders of India, including Tagore. There is a model of Fort William and there are various historical documents, including some pertaining to the Indian struggle for independence.

The memorial is open 10 am to 3.30 pm daily except Monday (until 4.30 pm in summer). Entry costs Rs 2; photography is not permitted inside.

Informative sound-and-light shows are held at 6.15 pm (Bengali) and 7.15 pm (English) from October to February. During these months, tickets can be bought from noon to 7.30 pm. From March to June, the show takes place at 6.45 pm (Bengali) and 7.45 pm (English); the ticket counter is open 12.30 to 8 pm. Tickets cost Rs 10/20 for children/adults.

OTHER ATTRACTIONS

Howrah Bridge

Until 1943, the Hooghly River was crossed by a pontoon bridge that opened to let river traffic through. To alleviate fears that the building of a new bridge would affect river currents and cause silting problems, the Howrah Bridge was constructed to cross the river in a single 450m span – there are no pylons at all on the riverbed.

This amazing feat of engineering, also known as Rabindra Setu, is similar in size to Australia's Sydney Harbour Bridge, but with a daily stream of some 100,000 vehicles and pedestrians too numerous to count, it is easily the busiest bridge in the world. It's intriguing to stand at one end of the bridge at morning rush hour and watch the procession of buses, lumbering bullock carts, push carts, bicycles and cars. During rush hour it can take 45 minutes to get across. The ferries running from in front of Howrah train station are a more convenient way to cross the river and also give you a good view of the bridge. However, if you are not too encumbered, walking is often the easiest way of crossing.

A second bridge, the Vidyasagar Setu, a Golden Gate Bridge lookalike, 2km downriver, was completed in 1994. Although it was supposed to relieve the crush on the old Howrah Bridge, the new bridge is now almost as chaotic itself.

Marble Palace

This private mansion on Muktaram Babu St, a narrow lane off J Mohan Ave, was built in 1835 by a Bengali zamindar (feudal landowner). The palace houses an incongruous collection of curios standing alongside significant statues and paintings (including works of Rubens and Sir Joshua Reynolds). There's a private zoo here too, but the inhabitants are only slightly more animated than the marble lions gracing the palace lawns. It's open 10 am to 4 pm daily except Monday and Thursday. Entry is free with a permit from the Government of India tourist office (for contact details and opening hours of the office, see Information earlier in this chapter).

South Park Street Cemetery

This peaceful cemetery is an evocative reminder of Kolkata's colonial past and is definitely worth a visit. Well maintained and set under shady trees, there are some incredible tombs with poignant epitaphs (especially the children's). The more famous occupants include Colonel Kyd, founder of the Botanical Gardens, and Rose Aylmer, remembered only because her unfortunate death was supposed to have been caused by an addiction to pineapples! The cemetery really transports you to another era and is a very interesting place to wander around at leisure.

Opening hours are 7.30 to 10.30 am and 3 to 4.30 pm weekdays and 7.30 to 10.30 am on Saturday. Entry is free. A booklet (Rs 40) about the cemetery is available on site.

Other British Buildings

Raj Bhavan, the old British Government House, built between 1799 and 1805 at the northern end of the Maidan, is now occupied by the governor of West Bengal and entry is restricted. Near the Raj Bhavan is the Doric-style **town hall**, and next to that the **High Court**, which was copied from the Staadhaus at Ypres, Belgium, and completed in 1872. It has a 55m tower.

Just south of the zoo on Alipore Rd is the **National Library**, the biggest in India, which is housed in Belvedere House, the former residence of the lieutenant-governor of Bengal.

MEDITATION

Vyakti Vikas Kendra (☎ 4631018, e aritra@vsnl.com) offers meditation courses. The basic course is a minimum of six days and costs about Rs 800.

At the time of writing, the manager of the Travellers' Express Club (see Travel Agencies earlier in this chapter) was planning to offer Buddhist meditation sessions with a Burmese monk.

SWIMMING

If you fancy a cool dip, unfortunately there are few options unless you stay at an upmarket hotel. The only hotels that allow nonguests to use their pool are the Hotel Hindustan International and the ITDC Hotel Airport Ashok (see Places to Stay). Both charge Rs 350 per person (free for hotel guests), which includes a towel; the Hindustan's pool is better. You can splash around in the Tollygunge Club's two pools (see Places to Stay) only if you are staying there, or are a club member or guest of a club member.

HORSE RIDING

The Tollygunge Club has horses and ponies that can be hired by club members and their guests (Rs 75 per hour) to use on the bridleway around the perimeter of the club.

GOLF

The magnificent Royal Calcutta Golf Club at the Tollygunge Club is the oldest golf club in the world outside Great Britain. Established in 1829, the club was originally near the airport, but moved to Tollygunge in 1910. The title 'Royal' was conferred upon it by King George V and Queen Mary in 1911.

The fee is Rs 150 per round – but you can only play if you are staying at the club or are a club member or guest of a club member.

ORGANISED TOURS

The Government of India tourist office operates a full-day sightseeing tour for Rs 100, departing at 8 am daily (except Monday) from its office in Chowringhee and returning at around 5 pm. It includes Belur Math, the Dakshineswar Kali Temple, Victoria Memorial, Indian Museum and more.

The West Bengal Tourism Centre at BBD Bagh offers a similar tour, also for Rs 100. This office can also arrange tours during the city's largest festival, **Durga Puja** (in October), which include a boat cruise down the Hooghly River to see the immersion of idols of the goddess Durga (for whom the festival is held) – prices are available only on application.

This office runs trips to the Sunderbans Wildlife Sanctuary several times per week from October to March – see Sunderbans Wildlife Sanctuary in the West Bengal chapter for more information.

Walking Tours

Interesting and informative walking tours of BBD Bagh and north Kolkata (including areas off the tourist circuit) are conducted by architect and conservationist Manish Chakraborti. They leave from the Great Eastern Hotel and cover historic buildings, heritage sites and general history. The cost is Rs 350 per person and the tour takes about two hours. For more information contact Footsteps (☎ 3375757, fax 3553188, ⓔ ashmon@cal2.vsnl.net.in), AA171A Salt Lake, Kolkata 700064.

Other Tours

A tour run by Kali Travel Home (☎/fax 5587980, ⓔ refresh@cal2.vsnl.net.in) operates a two-week **Kolkata Food & Culture Tour**, includes various cultural excursions, all meals and Bengali cooking lessons by local women in their homes. It costs US$65 per person per day for groups of five; 15% extra per person for smaller groups. Shorter cooking courses, lasting about three hours, are also available (US$13 per person). Advance bookings are essential.

The same people offer an **Impressions of Kolkata Tour**, which may appeal to those who wish to sketch, video, photograph or write about Kolkata. Tailor-made tours of West Bengal and eastern India can also be arranged. For more details contact David Rowe or Martyn Brown at Kali Travel Home.

SPECIAL EVENTS

Dates for fairs and festivals often vary from year to year depending on the lunar calendar – for exact dates and happenings it's best to contact the West Bengal Tourism Centre (see Information earlier in this chapter). As many festivals in Kolkata are actually held throughout the state, these are discussed in the West Bengal chapter.

For 10 days in late January/early February the largest **book fair** in Asia is held on the Maidan. The entry fee is nominal and a 10% discount applies to all books bought.

The **Dover Lane Music Conference**, held in January, celebrates Indian classical music. It was first held in 1952 and has become a major event on India's cultural calendar.

Helping Out

Kolkata has long attracted volunteers from India and beyond. There are various charity organisations in the city, ranging from the well-known Missionaries of Charity (see the boxed text 'Mother Teresa' earlier in this chapter) to the lesser-known Calcutta Society for the Prevention of Cruelty to Animals (CSPCA). If you're interested in helping out in Kolkata (or other parts of West Bengal), see Volunteer Work in the Facts for the Visitor chapter at the beginning of this book.

During the festival of **Durga Puja** in October, idols of the goddess Durga are ceremonially immersed in the Hooghly River. It is a time of much festivity in Kolkata.

The **National Theatre Festival**, which is held from 16 to 25 December, hosts theatre performances from India and neighbouring countries.

Various other touring exhibitions occasionally take place on the Maidan (mainly during the cooler winter months) – inquire at the West Bengal Tourism Centre.

PLACES TO STAY

Budget and mid-range accommodation in Kolkata is decidedly lacklustre, with most hungry for a lick of paint and general sprucing up. The service at many places is also pretty unenthusiastic. Many places have spartan rooms with rock-hard mattresses and pillows and a cell-like atmosphere due to the small or nonexistent windows. If you're planning a long stay here (as a volunteer for instance), you may like to bring along photos of your pet pooch and other loved ones to cheer up your home away from home (and cover particularly soiled parts of the wall). Colourful Indian bedspreads and fabrics also do wonders in brightening dreary rooms and are available in Kolkata at modest prices.

The din of traffic and dogs barking at night can be diabolical at some places, so request a quiet room (earplugs are recommended). Note that most budget and mid-range places lock their gates after around

CHOWRINGHEE

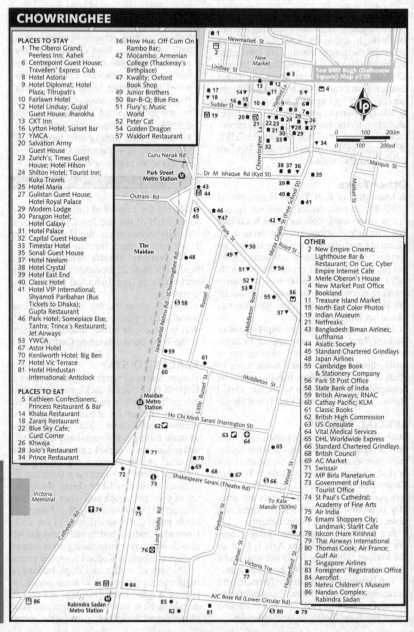

PLACES TO STAY
1 The Oberoi Grand; Peerless Inn; Aaheli
6 Centrepoint Guest House; Travellers' Express Club
8 Hotel Astoria
9 Hotel Diplomat; Hotel Plaza; Titrupati's
10 Fairlawn Hotel
12 Hotel Lindsay; Gujral Guest House; Jharokha
13 CKT Inn
16 Lytton Hotel; Sunset Bar
17 YMCA
20 Salvation Army Guest House
23 Zurich's; Times Guest House; Hotel Hilson
24 Shilton Hotel; Tourist Inn; Kuka Travels
25 Hotel Maria
27 Gulistan Guest House; Hotel Royal Palace
29 Modern Lodge
30 Paragon Hotel; Hotel Galaxy
31 Hotel Palace
32 Capital Guest House
33 Timestar Hotel
35 Sonali Guest House
37 Hotel Neelam
38 Hotel Crystal
39 Hotel East End
40 Classic Hotel
41 Hotel VIP International; Shyamoli Paribahan (Bus Tickets to Dhaka); Gupta Restaurant
46 Park Hotel; Someplace Else; Tantra; Trinca's Restaurant; Jet Airways
53 YWCA
67 Astor Hotel
70 Kenilworth Hotel; Big Ben
77 Hotel Vic Terrace
81 Hotel Hindustan International; Anticlock

PLACES TO EAT
5 Kathleen Confectioners; Princess Restaurant & Bar
14 Khalsa Restaurant
18 Zaranj Restaurant
22 Blue Sky Cafe; Curd Corner
26 Khwaja
28 JoJo's Restaurant
34 Prince Restaurant
36 How Hua; Off Cum On Rambo Bar;
42 Mocambo; Armenian College (Thackeray's Birthplace)
47 Kwality; Oxford Book Shop
49 Junior Brothers
50 Bar-B-Q; Blue Fox
51 Flury's; Music World
52 Peter Cat
54 Golden Dragon
57 Waldorf Restaurant

OTHER
2 New Empire Cinema; Lighthouse Bar & Restaurant; On Cue; Cyber Empire Internet Cafe
3 Merle Oberon's House
4 New Market Post Office
7 Bookland
11 Treasure Island Market
15 North East Color Photos
19 Indian Museum
21 Netfreaks
43 Bangladesh Biman Airlines; Lufthansa
44 Asiatic Society
45 Standard Chartered Grindlays
48 Japan Airlines
55 Cambridge Book & Stationery Company
56 Park St Post Office
58 State Bank of India
59 British Airways; RNAC
60 Cathay Pacific; KLM
61 Classic Books
62 British High Commission
63 US Consulate
64 Vital Medical Services
65 DHL Worldwide Express
66 Standard Chartered Grindlays
68 British Council
69 AC Market
71 Swissair
72 MP Birla Planetarium
73 Government of India Tourist Office
74 St Paul's Cathedral; Academy of Fine Arts
75 Air India
76 Emami Shoppers City; Landmark; Starlit Cafe
78 Iskcon (Hare Krishna)
79 Thai Airways International
80 Thomas Cook; Air France; Gulf Air
82 Singapore Airlines
83 Foreigners' Registration Office
84 Aeroflot
85 Nehru Children's Museum
86 Nandan Complex; Rabindra Sadan

See BBD Bagh (Dalhousie Square) Map p559

11 pm, so if you're going to get back late, let the appropriate person at the hotel know in advance.

To stay with an Indian family, contact the Government of India tourist office (see Information earlier in this chapter), which can arrange guesthouse accommodation (ranging from around Rs 200 to 2000 per night). These guesthouses can be a pleasant alternative to the commercial hotels and may be particularly suitable for long-term stayers. Some of these places offer home-cooked meals (at extra cost) and provide you with an opportunity to get to know a local family. Keep in mind that some paying guesthouses are far better than others, so check out several places (and families) before deciding.

Most hotels whack an extra 10% service tax on their advertised room rates; air-con rooms attract 10% luxury tax on top of that (taxes have not been included in the prices given in this chapter). Checkout at most hotels is at noon and discounts are usually offered in the low season (around April to late September).

For quick reference, the following places to stay have been listed under the name of the area map on which they appear in this chapter.

PLACES TO STAY – BUDGET

Chowringhee Area

Sudder St is the budget travellers' hang-out and rooms here can fill up fast, especially during the tourist season in winter. Being a tourist hotbed, there's a fair bit of the 'yes have a look! change money! buy something!' from the touts and others, but it's not as bad as Agra or parts of Rajasthan…yet. That said, the number of beggars in the Sudder St area has risen in line with tourist numbers. Your money will probably go to better use at one of Kolkata's charitable institutions, but if you still want to give something, food offerings are best (packets should be opened to prevent them being resold on the black market). A recent 'scam' in Sudder St is for female beggars to ask you to buy milk for their baby. Sadly, this seemingly laudable request is a ploy – once you have handed over the milk, most of these women simply dash round the corner to resell it for cash.

> **Safety Alert**
>
> Many of Kolkata's budget and mid-range hotels have installed sturdy 'safety' gates across the entrance to the hotel or, worse, on each individual floor. Locked at night with a padlock, they are designed to keep out undesirables. Unfortunately, they also keep the guests in – not good in case of fire.
>
> Although the management will undoubtedly kick up a big fuss and say you can always ring reception if you should need to get out ('There's always someone on duty'), you can insist on being given a copy of the key. Alternatively, you can insist on the gates being left unlocked and have a *chowkidar* (night watchman) sleep on each floor. If you are really concerned, try to get a ground-floor room that has a window big enough to get through in case of an emergency.

The ***Salvation Army Guest House*** *(☎ 245 0599, 2 Sudder St)* has long been popular with volunteers working for Mother Teresa's mission. It's a mellow, well-kept place, with dorm beds for Rs 65 and doubles with private bathroom from Rs 200 to 700. There's also a laid-back living area. If you want to stay here it's wise to book in advance to avoid disappointment.

Hotel Maria *(☎ 2450860, 5/1 Sudder St)* is another favourite among travellers, with an equally relaxed atmosphere and a strict 'no drugs, no alcohol' policy. Basic singles/doubles go for Rs 150/200 with shared bathroom, Rs 200/250 with private bathroom. If you're strapped for cash, there are dorm beds for Rs 70.

Hotel Hilson *(☎ 2173896, fax 2463999, 4 Sudder St)* has singles with shared bathroom for Rs 150, doubles with private bathroom starting at Rs 350 and four-bed rooms for Rs 500. Some rooms are musty – choose carefully.

Times Guest House *(☎ 2451796, 3 Sudder St)*, near Zurich's restaurant, is a flophouse – only worth considering if other places on Sudder St are full. Dishevelled doubles with private bathroom are Rs 250, but the owner claims that he will renovate in the near future so let us know if things have improved.

Shilton Hotel *(☎ 2451512, 5A Sudder St)* has rooms with private bathroom for Rs 220/300. Some rooms are rather gloomy (the norm rather than the exception in Kolkata's budget accommodation), but otherwise OK.

Tourist Inn *(☎ 2450134, 4/1 Sudder St)*, on the 2nd floor, is a small, decent place which has singles/doubles with shared bathroom for Rs 100/200, and four-bed rooms with private bathroom for Rs 400. This is run by the same people as Kuka Travels, down on the 1st floor (see Travel Agencies earlier in this chapter).

Paragon Hotel *(☎ 2442445, 2 Stuart Lane)*, just off Sudder St, gets mixed reviews from travellers. A dorm bed is Rs 60, small rooms with shared bathroom are Rs 130/140, and doubles with private bathroom start at Rs 250.

Hotel Galaxy *(☎ 2464565, ⓔ juvena@vsnl.com, 3 Stuart Lane)*, next door, is unpretentious with just four rooms starting at Rs 400, all with private bathroom.

The nearby ***Timestar Hotel*** *(☎ 2450028)* is particularly popular with Japanese travellers and is a bit quieter than other hotels in this area, making it easier to get some shuteye. Small rooms with private bathroom are Rs 175/250.

Modern Lodge *(☎ 2444960, 1 Stuart Lane)* is also popular, especially with long-term visitors. Singles/doubles with shared bathroom are Rs 70/90, and doubles with private bathroom range from Rs 120 to 240.

Hotel Palace *(☎ 2446214, 13 Chowringhee Lane)*, just off Sudder St, is a bit of a warren of a place but not a bad choice in a city low on quality budget accommodation. There are rooms for Rs 200/300 with private bathroom. Request a room with a window.

Capital Guest House *(☎ 2450598, 11B Chowringhee Lane)*, nearby, is in a quiet courtyard away from the noise of Sudder St. Doubles with private bathroom range from Rs 300 to 350. Singles/doubles with shared bathroom go for Rs 150/200. Although some of the bathrooms here could be better, the rooms are acceptable.

Gujral Guest House *(☎ 2440620, fax 2455109, 8B Lindsay St)* is just north of Sudder St in the same building as the Hotel Lindsay, but off to the side on the 2nd floor. It has reasonable (if somewhat musty and dark) offerings at Rs 250/450 with private bathroom. With shared bathroom they are Rs 200/270. Air-con rooms cost Rs 850/950.

Centrepoint Guest House *(☎ 2448184, fax 2442867, 20 Mirza Ghalib St)* is a bustling place with dorm beds for Rs 75 and tiny rooms with private bathroom for Rs 250/300. It's right next door to the Travellers' Express Club, where you can change money and make domestic and international flight bookings.

Gulistan Guest House *(☎ 2260963, 30F Mirza Ghalib St)*, opposite the fire station and up a flight of stairs, is a popular choice with volunteers. The rooms (Rs 200/400 with private bathroom) are cleaner than many other cheapies in this area, although the service is nothing to rave about. In the same building is ***Hotel Royal Palace*** *(☎ 2455168)* which is similar in price and standard.

Sonali Guest House *(☎ 2451844)*, farther south on Mirza Ghalib St, has rooms with private bathroom for Rs 150/350. It gets variable reviews from travellers, but it is no worse than any other budget place.

Classic Hotel *(☎ 2297390)*, down an alley just off Mirza Ghalib St, has singles with shared bathroom for Rs 150. Doubles with private bathroom are Rs 260. Hot water is by the bucket (free) and the rooms are pretty good value.

Hotel East End *(☎ 2298921, 9/1 Dr M Ishaque Rd)* is nearby, and although the rooms are rather dull, it's run by friendly folk. Rooms with private bathroom start at Rs 250/350.

Hotel Neelam *(☎ 2269198, 11 Dr M Ishaque Rd)* has ordinary but good-sized rooms with private bathroom starting at Rs 175/300. Larger doubles cost Rs 400.

The gloomy ***YMCA*** *(☎ 2492192, 25 Chowringhee Rd)* is a rambling building and not great value. Drab rooms with private bathroom cost upwards of Rs 370/540. All accommodation includes early morning tea, breakfast and dinner. There's a second ***YMCA*** *(☎ 2443814, 42 Surendra Nath Banerji Rd)* with simple rooms starting at 250 per double with private bathroom.

YWCA *(☎ 2297033, 1 Middleton Row)* is a much better choice and you'll have no hassles here whatsoever. Despite the name, it accepts women *and* men. Tidy rooms are Rs 300/500 with shared bathroom, or Rs 550/750 with private bathroom. Rates include all meals.

BBD Bagh Area

There is a paucity of respectable budget accommodation in this part of town.

Central Guest House *(☎ 2374876)* is a good choice in a city starved of quality budget hotels. Singles/doubles with private bathroom go for Rs 200/275. The hotel (which is on the 2nd floor) fronts on to Chittaranjan (CR) Ave, but the entrance is around the corner at 18 Prafulla Sarkar St.

Elsewhere

Yatri Niwas *(☎ 6601742)*, in the new building next door to Howrah train station, accepts only transit train/air passengers. It has dorm beds for Rs 75 and doubles with private bathroom for Rs 250, or Rs 450 with air-con. You can only stay here if you have a train or air ticket, and then only for two nights (one extra night on application). There are also ***retiring rooms*** at the Howrah and Sealdah train stations (Rs 50 per bed), but these are nothing fancy and several travellers have complained about them.

For transit air passengers, moderately priced rooms are available at the airport (ask anyone official-looking at the airport to point you in the right direction).

If you want to stay near the airport but are low on cash, try the small ***Airport Plaza Hotel*** *(Tarun Sengupta Sarani, No 1 Airport Gate)*. The rooms are basic, but cheap at Rs 150/250 a single/double with private bathroom (all with squat toilet). Try to have a look at a few rooms before deciding, as some are superior to others.

PLACES TO STAY – MID-RANGE

Kolkata's mid-range hotels are certainly nothing flash, but most come with private phone (many with free local calls), cable TV and room service (or a restaurant delivery option – pay the hotel staff member about Rs 10 to take your order and pick up your food).

All mid-range places listed here have private bathrooms and air-con unless otherwise indicated.

Chowringhee Area

Hotel Diplomat *(☎ 2468434, 10 Sudder St)* is a mid-range hotel that also has a smattering of budget rooms. You'll pay Rs 150/200 for singles/doubles with shared bathroom (Rs 200/225 with private bathroom). The air-con rooms (Rs 495) are much more salubrious and worth splashing out on if you can afford to. Next door is the less impressive ***Hotel Plaza*** *(☎ 2446411, fax 2468434)*, with windowless doubles for Rs 400, or Rs 475 with air-con.

Hotel Astoria *(☎ 2451514, fax 2448589, ⓔ astoria@hotmail.com, 6/2 & 6/3 Sudder St)* looks seductively snazzy from the outside, but once you pass reception things take a turn for the worse. Many rooms are remarkably spacious, but rather scruffy, and the corridors could be cleaner. Rooms cost Rs 600/850.

Hotel Lindsay *(☎ 2452237, fax 2450310, 8A Lindsay St)* offers small rooms for a hefty Rs 800/950, or Rs 1200/1400 with air-con.

The centrally air-conditioned ***CKT Inn*** *(☎ 2448246, fax 2440047, 12A Lindsay St)* is a small, cordial place with respectable rooms for Rs 825/1100. It is often full, so advance reservations are a good idea. The only drawback of this place is that if there is a heavy smoker in the room next door, the air-conditioning rudely blows the smoke into your room.

Hotel VIP International *(☎ 2290345, fax 2293715, ⓔ hvipcal@mantraonline.com, 51 Mirza Ghalib St)* lacks panache, but the rooms (Rs 1295 to 1695 a double) are comfortable enough in comparison to other mid-range hotels in Kolkata.

Hotel Crystal *(☎ 2266400)* is close to the action of Dr M Ishaque Rd, but the standards have dropped over recent years according to many travellers. Doubles cost Rs 500, or Rs 800 with air-con.

Astor Hotel *(☎ 2829917, fax 2827430, ⓔ astor@cal3.vsnl.net.in, 15 Shakespeare Sarani),* with sloppy rooms, is a bit disappointing considering the price tag of Rs 1100/1300. It's an option if all other places are booked out.

Hotel Vic Terrace *(☎ 2408788, fax 2404063, 1B Victoria Terrace)*, opposite Industry House, charges upwards of Rs 870/970. Although some of the cheaper rooms are cramped, they are modern and tidy and the staff are obliging. This hotel has had good reviews from travellers.

BBD Bagh Area

Hotel Embassy *(☎ 2379040, fax 2373288, 27 Princep St)* is an old, no-frills place with singles/doubles for Rs 400/500; with air-con they go for Rs 500/600.

Broadway Hotel *(☎ 2363930, fax 236 4151, ⓔ broadway@vsnl.com, 27A Ganesh Chandra Ave)* is more popular, with a range of reasonably well-maintained rooms starting at Rs 340/440. There are also some cheaper rooms with shared bathroom which go for Rs 285/400.

Heera Hotel *(☎ 2280663, fax 2280171, 28 Grant St)*, north of New Market, would have to have the world's smallest lift! Although the reception area is more glamorous than the rooms, it's not a bad choice. The rate is Rs 475/550, or Rs 700/825 with air-con.

Elsewhere

Royal Calcutta Guest House *(☎ 2800377, fax 2404823, 124 Karaya Rd)* is away from the central district (look for the preschool sign), but is delightfully homey and particularly good for long-term stays. There are just six spacious doubles, which are arranged in pairs with a common lounge and kitchen in between. Singles/doubles cost Rs 500/600, or Rs 750/850 with air-con. Car hire can be arranged and the owners seem friendly and helpful.

PLACES TO STAY – TOP END

If you are cashed up and seeking some serious pampering, there are two hotels that stand out from the rest: The Oberoi Grand and the Taj Bengal. The Park Hotel is also quite ritzy, but other hotels in the top-end category lack the same 'wow' factor.

Keep in mind that the prices provided here do not include tax (expect to add at least 20% tax to the following room rates).

Chowringhee Area

The renowned ***Fairlawn Hotel*** *(☎ 2451510, fax 2441835, ⓔ fairlawn@cal.vsnl.net.in, 13A Sudder St)* is a slice of Kolkata where the Raj still prospers, albeit in a decidedly eccentric fashion which you may find quaintly amusing or downright irritating. Although atmospheric, the service here can be abrupt to the point of rudeness. Edmund Smith and his Armenian wife, Violet, still run the hotel more than 50 years after Independence. There's a lush courtyard garden and the interior is crammed with memorabilia, chintz and prewar furnishings. Some bathrooms have deep baths standing on ball-and-claw feet. A single/double room costs US$50/60, including three meals (set menu).

Lytton Hotel *(☎ 2491872, fax 2491747, ⓔ lytton@giascl01.vsnl.net.in, 14 Sudder St)* has a sterile ambience, but is adequately luxurious and friendlier than the nearby Fairlawn Hotel. The cheapest accommodation costs Rs 1600/2200, but if you can afford it opt for the super deluxe rooms (Rs 2200/2700) which have more flair. There are two restaurants and a bar (see Entertainment later in the chapter).

The Oberoi Grand *(☎ 2492323, fax 2491217, ⓔ fo@oberoi-cal.com, 15 Chowringhee Rd)* has long been acknowledged as Kolkata's finest hotel and indeed is one of the jewels in the Oberoi crown. Tasteful and immaculate rooms start at US$225/250 and have all the mod-cons you would expect of a word-class hotel. There are three fine restaurants, an outdoor pool (residents only) and more.

Peerless Inn *(☎ 2280301, fax 2286650, ⓔ peerinn@giascl01.vsnl.net.in, 12 Chowringhee Rd),* near the Oberoi, is rather low on atmosphere, but some rooms boast magnificent city views and the staff are pleasant. Good rooms start at Rs 2625/3250. The Aaheli Bengali restaurant receives positive reviews (see Places to Eat).

Park Hotel *(☎ 2493121, fax 2497343, ⓔ resv.cal@theparkhotels.com, 17 Park St)* is a relatively large property, but has the ambience of a boutique hotel. Swish rooms start at US$225/250 and there are several good restaurants, an indoor pool (residents only) and other five-star facilities.

Kenilworth Hotel *(☎ 2828394, fax 282 5136, 1–2 Little Russel St)* has old and new wings, but gets mixed reviews from travellers. Basic rates are US$100/110 in the new wing, and US$140 (doubles only) in the old wing.

Hotel Hindustan International *(☎ 247 2394, fax 2472824, 235 AJC Bose Rd)* is quite popular and has a health club, shopping arcade, restaurants, bars and a swimming pool (open to nonguests for Rs 350 per person). Attractive rooms start at US$150/165.

BBD Bagh Area

Great Eastern Hotel *(☎ 2482311, fax 2480289, ⓔ geh@vsnl.com, 1–3 Old Court House St)* is a rambling old Raj-style hotel, originally named The Auckland when it was built in 1840. It's not nearly as grandiose as other top-end hotels, but is atmospheric, laid-back and cheaper than other top-end places. There are some budget rooms for Rs 660/825; more luxurious and spacious air-con rooms cost upwards of Rs 1375/1980 (some are bigger and better than others so try to look at a few first).

Elsewhere

The well-known ***Tollygunge Club*** *(☎ 473 2316, fax 4731903)* is set on 44 hectares on the southern edge of Kolkata. It has a sensational golf course (see Golf earlier in this chapter), and although it's looking a little faded around the edges these days, it's still a good place to get an idea of how the other half frolicked in the days of the Raj. For decades it was run by Englishman Bob Wright, who now lives in retirement on the property. Today, 'Tolly' is the playground of the city's elite. As well as the championship golf course, there are indoor and outdoor pools, grass and clay tennis courts, squash courts, a croquet lawn, a billiard room, badminton and table-tennis facilities, and a stable of horses. As a foreign visitor, as long as you telephone, fax or write in advance (120 DP Sasmal Rd, Kolkata 700033), you may stay here and have temporary membership allowing you to use the facilities.

Although this club oozes old-world charm, quite a few travellers have complained about the lackadaisical service and mediocre, run-down rooms. The cheapest rooms are in 'Hastings' (Rs 1150/1250 a single/double). The 'Grandstand' cottages go for Rs 2200/2400 and have small sitting areas overlooking the lush golf course. Most rooms in Tolly Towers or Tolly Terrace are similarly priced.

Taj Bengal *(☎ 2233939, fax 2231766, ⓔ tbhfo.cal@tajhotels.com)*, at the southern end of the Maidan, scores top marks for its slick service and impeccable interior. It has all the luxuries of a deluxe hotel, including a pool (residents only), several restaurants, a coffee shop (see Places to Eat) and a business centre. Suitably sumptuous singles/doubles start at US$215/245; rates shoot up to US$625 for the Presidential Suite.

The government-operated ***ITDC Hotel Airport Ashok*** *(☎ 5119111, fax 5119137, ⓔ airpotel@cal.vsnl.net.in)* is poor value for money and presumably manages to stay in business because of its proximity to the airport (1km away), which makes it a convenient stopover for transit passengers. Overpriced rooms start at Rs 4500/5500 and facilities include a nondescript swimming pool (open to nonguests for Rs 350). On the plus side, the 24-hour coffee shop is a relaxing place to kill time over a cup of chai (Rs 40) or a toasted sandwich (Rs 80) while waiting for your flight (nonguests are welcome).

PLACES TO EAT

Fish (fried or curried) and rice are the focus of Bengali cuisine, but surprisingly, there are few restaurants in this teeming metropolis that whip up the real stuff. If you are lucky enough to be invited to a Bengali home, that's where you'll indulge in authentic, flavoursome Bengali fare at its best.

Bengali sweet specialities include *misthi dhoi* (curd sweetened with palm sugar) and *rasgulla* (sweet cream-cheese balls flavoured with rose water), which can be found at virtually all sweet shops.

'Indianised' Chinese food is particularly popular with Kolkatans and you'll find at least several Chinese dishes tacked on to most menus. Chilli chicken seems to be the red-hot favourite. For those with money to burn, fine dining in swish surroundings is available at the top-end hotels (see Places to Stay).

Kolkata has a number of street stalls (many setting up in the early evening) that sell all sorts of goodies. If you do eat here, not only can you get a darn cheap feed, you can also ensure food is freshly cooked in front of you.

Many non-air-con restaurants levy an 8% to 12% tax on menu prices, while those with air-con generally charge between 15% and 17% (taxes have not been included in the prices quoted in this chapter).

Chowringhee Area

Most budget eateries, especially on tourist-laden Sudder St, offer the usual have-a-go-at-anything menu and stay open throughout the day for breakfast, lunch, dinner and snacks. Although the food and service can be a bit of a hit-and-miss affair, they're reasonably cheap and are ideal places to strike up conversation with other travellers (sometimes unavoidable considering how tightly packed the tables are!).

Sudder Street Area The small ***Blue Sky Cafe***, on the corner of Sudder St and Chowringhee Lane, has long been a travellers' hang-out, but nowadays it has just as many detractors as fans. The menu is as jam-packed as the tables, offering everything from spaghetti fantasia (Rs 65), to various porridge concoctions (around Rs 20). It also offers Indian food such as chicken curry (Rs 30), which is good washed down with a glass of papaya lassi (Rs 16). ***Curd Corner***, next door on Sudder St, is a no-frills little place that whips up some of the best curd and lassis in town at nominal prices.

Zurich's, close by, is not as buzzing as the Blue Sky Cafe, but does get much rosier reports from travellers. Small and friendly, it serves Indian, Western and Chinese cuisine, including pizzas (around Rs 35) and apple pancakes (Rs 18).

Titrupati's, across the street from Zurich's, is a tiny but busy street stall much patronised by volunteers for its cheap, wholesome preparations (Rs 10 to 25 per hearty feed). You may have to queue at lunch time.

Khwaja is a tad more expensive than other cheapies in this area, but it's a rejuvenating retreat from the furore of the streets – an ideal place to kick back with a book (plenty available at Bookland, directly opposite), or to scribble letters to friends back home. The soothing hot lemon (Rs 8) is a godsend for sore throats, and the cooks also do a good job of omelettes. The chicken steak sizzler (Rs 69) is particularly satiating and the mashed potato (Rs 18) is perfect for tender tummies.

Khalsa Restaurant, just off Sudder St, looks pretty ordinary, but the food is satisfying and the service is speedy. On top of that, it's blissfully cheap; veg curry is a mere Rs 10.

JoJo's Restaurant, a popular little spot with travellers and locals, is down the lane opposite the Hotel Astoria. Although a tad gloomy inside, it's tidy and friendly with a varied menu including tasty egg curry (Rs 20). Anyone who can order the jelly belly (Rs 21) with a straight face should be awarded a special prize.

The large ***Zaranj Restaurant*** on Sudder St has wider menu choices but the bill hits harder. Nonetheless, it's recommended for a minor splurge with some innovative North-Western Frontier dishes such as *gobi Peshawari* (cauliflower sauteed with spices and topped with roasted cumin seeds and mint leaves; Rs 150).

Jharokha, just north of Sudder St, is a rooftop indoor/outdoor restaurant 10 floors above the Hotel Lindsay. It's worth visiting purely for its tremendous panoramic views over Kolkata. The food and interior are more upmarket than in other places in this area – try the fish masala (Rs 65) or *palak paneer* (soft, unfermented cheese in a spicy gravy of pureed spinach; Rs 50). If that will break the bank, lick some ice cream (Rs 30) while admiring the view.

Aaheli is at the Peerless Inn, a couple of blocks north of Sudder St. According to Kolkatans, it's the best place to feast on authentic Bengali food. To sample various Bengali dishes, order the veg Aahelir Bhoj (Rs 225) or, for carnivores, the nonveg Aahelir Mahaabhoj (Rs 275). For cheaper Bengali food, there's Suruchi, on Elliot Rd (by the Mallik Bazaar bus stop), which is only open for lunch. Although the food is not as exceptional as it once was, it's still not bad; a vegetarian *thali* (all-you-can-eat meal) is Rs 29.

Mirza Ghalib Street Near the Hotel VIP International, ***Gupta Restaurant*** is a welcome escape from the hubbub outside and offers a tempting mix of Indian and Chinese food. Offal lovers can indulge in dishes such as brain masala (Rs 44); for those who think offal is awful, there's vegetable korma (Rs 50), ginger fish (Rs 74) and plenty more.

Mocambo has an old-world ambience and flaunts some curious Indian and continental creations, such as Greek drunken prawns (Rs 140). Other goodies include risotto with chicken liver (Rs 80), rogan josh (Rs 70), roast chicken (Rs 90), and good old-fashioned creme caramel (Rs 45).

Princess Restaurant & Bar is a relaxing place to dine. It does some particularly good chicken dishes, including chicken tikka (Rs 75) and honey chicken (Rs 75), as well as some vegetarian specialities such as spicy potato curry, *dum aloo* (Rs 50).

How Hua, a popular Chinese eatery, is another great escape from the tumultuous streets. The sweet-and-sour wantons (Rs 52 for 10 pieces) are recommended by the chef and deservedly so. Decent Chinese food is also available at the ***Golden Dragon***.

Prince Restaurant, a noisy streetfront place on the corner of Mirza Ghalib and Marquis Sts, is certainly nothing fancy as far as decor goes, but is worth visiting for a cheap chow down. It specialises in Bengali fish preparations (ranging from Rs 20 to 40) and you can scoop up the gravy with a stack of piping hot rotis for just Rs 2.50 each.

Kathleen Confectioners proudly showcases its sugar-laden Western cakes, many of which are decorated with colourful iced artwork. Although it may claim to be the best in town, the cakes are no match for those that grandma used to bake. The Black Forest cake (Rs 13 per slice) is probably the pick of the over-creamy batch. There's another, small outlet on AJC Bose Rd.

Park Street Area Ritzy Park St has a string of appealing eateries which are quite upmarket but won't totally decimate your cash stash.

Bar-B-Q is one of the most popular Chinese and Indian restaurants in this area and there is usually a queue after 7.30 pm. The service is good and the atmosphere buzzes. Fried chicken wings are Rs 60 and vegetable fried rice is Rs 55.

Next door is the ***Blue Fox***, a pleasant multicuisine restaurant featuring several Thai specialities such as *mee krob* (Thai crispy noodles; Rs 135). Other options include asparagus soup (Rs 65), Russian salad (Rs 60) and fish tikka (Rs 100).

Waldorf Restaurant has a Chinese emphasis but also turns a hand to Thai food. If you need a tofu fix, there are various dishes to choose from (Rs 60 to 70). On the other hand, if it's underwater creatures you feel like sinking your teeth into, the seafood sizzler (Rs 175) is bound to please.

Junior Brothers churns out standard Indian fare, but is less pricey than other Park St places.

Kwality is a roomy restaurant with a seductive selection, such as piquant prawn curry (Rs 95). If you would prefer something cooler, perhaps you could opt for a grilled chicken sandwich (Rs 34) followed by a chocolate sundae (Rs 57).

Trinca's Restaurant, near the Park Hotel building, has a band each night from 8 pm if you feel like something more than just a meal out. For eats, the green-peas masala (Rs 65) and tandoori chicken (Rs 72 for half a bird) are good. Light snacks such as chutney sandwiches (Rs 35) are also available.

Peter Cat, just off Park St on Middleton Row, is a dimly lit, mellow bar-restaurant which is perfect for a frosty beverage over warm conversation. A bottle of Kingfisher beer is Rs 68. If you're feeling frazzled, a tequila (Rs 52 a shot) may hit the spot, or maybe the 'Gentle Murderer' (Rs 48) is more your poison. If alcohol is not your thing, see if you can resist the chocolate castle ice cream (Rs 46).

Flury's, nearby back on Park St, is a lively cafe-style spot which makes an invigorating tea 'n' treat break in between shopping. It has savoury and sweet offerings, ranging from cheese croissants (Rs 39) to nut sundaes (Rs 48). The service can be sluggish.

The ***Hare Krishna Bakery*** is a teeny-weeny corner place (next door to the Anokhi shop), just south of Park St. This snug little veg bakehouse sells satiating takeaway snacks as well as brown bread and small bags of homemade cookies. The pizza slab (Rs 25) is particularly pleasing.

BBD Bagh Area

Chung Wah Chinese Restaurant *(Chittaranjan Ave)*, with private wooden booths, looks like something out of Shanghai in the 1930s. The fried chilli chicken (Rs 55) is a favourite among locals. There's another branch around the corner.

Anand Restaurant *(Chittaranjan Ave)* is a very popular and reasonably priced vegetarian restaurant with some especially good South Indian specialities such as *dosas* (lentil-flour pancakes).

Amber Hotel *(11 Waterloo St)* is right in the centre of town in the narrow street that runs by the Great Eastern Hotel. Although the food is tasty enough, it does not get the standing ovation it once did. The chicken *saag* (green vegetables; Rs 69) is truly sublime.

Nizam's, just north of New Market, serves good-value mutton and chicken rolls, kebabs and other fast food with Muslim influences. It can get busy at lunch time so be prepared to queue.

You can buy Indian and Bengali sweets at various 'sweeteries' in Kolkata, including ***Indra Mahal*** *(Chowringhee Rd)*, and ***KC Das*** *(Lenin Sarani)* near the corner of Bentinck St; the latter gets glowing reviews from locals and travellers alike.

Elsewhere

The ***Indian Coffee House***, near the Calcutta University, was once the meeting place of the city's intellectuals. Nowadays it's popular with young undergraduates for its coffee and moderately priced snacks. There's a second (more central) branch in the BBD Bagh area.

Yangoon *(☎ 4401442, 7D Swinhoe St)*, near Southpoint School, is an unpretentious little place that cooks up authentic Burmese food. The *ohn no khawshwe* (rice noodles with chicken in a spicy sauce made with coconut milk; Rs 55) is positively divine and shouldn't be missed. Yangoon is open only for dinner (closed Thursday) – call for reservations.

For real *momos* (dumplings), make a beeline for ***Momo Plaza*** *(2A Suburban Hospital Rd)*, south of Chowringhee. This modest, no-nonsense eatery has perfected the art of momo-making. A plate of five steamed chicken momos is a reasonable Rs 30.

To hobnob with Kolkata's yuppies, cruise over to the swish cafe-style ***Aqua Java*** *(79 Shambhu Nath Pandit St)*, near the PG Hospital. The coffee concoctions are particularly innovative; a Black Forest cappuccino is Rs 65. For something more familiar, try the cafe latte (Rs 35). There's a billiard table upstairs (Rs 50 per game) if you're pressed for conversation.

If you're sick of scrimping and want a minor budget-breaking luxury fix, spruce yourself up a bit and seek out a suitable top-end hotel coffee shop (most are open 24 hours and welcome nonguests). One possibility is the coffee shop at the ***Taj Bengal*** (see Places to Stay): For a full-on splurge, there's lobster (Rs 1000), or Norwegian pink salmon with mango and lime sauce (Rs 650); for a minor splurge there are pizzas (Rs 225) and dosas (Rs 125). If that will still break the bank, share a banana split (Rs 125) with a friend, or ask for several straws with your chocolate milkshake (Rs 90) or iced tea (Rs 60).

ENTERTAINMENT

Pubs & Bars

Most hotel watering holes are open to nonguests but be warned that although the drinks may quench your thirst, too many beverages will suck your wallet dry.

On Sudder St, the Lytton Hotel's intimate, dimly lit ***Sunset Bar*** charges Rs 80 for a bottle of beer and Rs 90 for a shot of cognac. The open-air forecourt of the ***Fairlawn Hotel***, also on Sudder St, usually attracts an interesting crowd.

The more upmarket ***Someplace Else*** *(Park St)*, a pub at the Park Hotel, has a live band every night from 8 pm. The Kenilworth Hotel's ***Big Ben*** *(Little Russel St)* is also a hip place to meet for a drink.

The somewhat seedy ***Paris Bar & Restaurant***, south of BBD Bagh near Lenin Sarani, is a curious combination of Indian pub and nightclub. This large, dark cavern of a place has a casual atmosphere, but single women should be prepared to be ogled. Open 11 am to 11 pm daily, it has live bands and sells some knockout beers such as Thunderbolt and Haward's Turbo 5000 (each is Rs 65 per bottle), as well as the usual spirits including velvety Old Monk rum (Rs 40 per peg). Snacks are also available; *paneer pakora* (curd cheese fritter) is Rs 41. If the Paris is too much of a scene, try the more conservative (but duller) ***Lighthouse Bar & Restaurant*** in the New Empire Cinema complex near New Market. Here, a bottle of beer is Rs 65 and masala peanuts are Rs 40. ***Off Cum On Rambo Bar*** (!) on Mirza Ghalib St is an absolute dive – probably best avoided by women on their own – but it does sell beer till late.

Discos

Some of the top-end hotels have pumping discos, but if you're not a hotel guest or member there's a hefty door charge (ranging from Rs 200 to 400 per couple). Solo shakers will need to find a friend of the opposite sex, as most discos have a 'couples only' policy. If you want to rub shoulders with the young generation of Kolkata's high society, these hotel discos are the place to hang out, although there's obviously no guarantee that you'll be welcomed into the various cliques.

At the time of writing, the 'in' place was ***Tantra*** at the Park Hotel. Other recommended options include ***Incognito*** at the Taj Bengal and ***Anticlock*** at the Hotel Hindustan International; the latter is open only to hotel guests.

Dance & Theatre

Kolkata is renowned for its film, poetry, music, art and dance. Current programs are listed in various publications, including the *Metro* section of the *Telegraph* newspaper and *Kolkata This Fortnight* (see Information earlier in this chapter).

A dance-drama performance, a Bengali poetry reading or a similar event takes place on most nights at the ***Rabindra Sadan*** *(☎ 2239936, Cathedral Rd)*.

There are sometimes drama, music or dance performances in English at the ***Kala Mandir*** *(☎ 2479086, 48 Shakespeare Sarani)*, and musical programs (mainly Bengali) at the ***Sisir Mancha*** *(☎ 2239917, 1/1 AJC Bose Rd)*. The Government of India tourist office (see Information earlier) holds Indian regional dance performances by the Academy of Oriental Dance at its Shakespeare Sarani premises. These take place at 5.30 pm weekdays and tickets cost Rs 100 for a 45-minute show.

Cinemas

Foreign films and retrospectives are screened at the cinema in the ***Nandan*** complex near Cathedral Rd; some Chowringhee cinemas show recent-release US blockbusters (check local newspapers). And of course there is no dearth of cinemas showing the latest Bollywood blockbusters.

Billiards

If you're a bit of a pool shark, ***On Cue***, near the New Empire Cinema complex, has 10 billiard tables and is open from 11 am to around 9 pm daily. It charges Rs 30 per game (Rs 40 for the two full-sized tables) and you can synchronise shots to the beat of Western pop.

Ten-Pin Bowling

Although rather inconveniently located out at Nicco Park (about 12km from the city centre), the modern ***Nicco Super Bowl*** *(☎ 3578101)* boasts six good bowling alleys. You can also play billiards, but it's daylight robbery at Rs 40 for a mere 15 minutes (two people) – go to On Cue instead (see Billiards earlier). There's a fast-food joint serving the usual array of deliciously sinful junk food.

This complex is open noon to 10 pm daily and there's an entry fee of Rs 25 per person. To bowl costs Rs 75 per person per game (20 bowls) from noon to 3 pm weekdays, or Rs 100 after 3 pm. On weekends the charge is Rs 125. To get here by taxi from Sudder St will set you back about Rs 100 (one way) – share with others to split the cost.

SHOPPING

Kolkata's local specialities are terracotta ware and hand-woven cotton and silk saris. There are lots of interesting shops (including the Central Cottage Industries Emporium) lining Chowringhee Rd selling everything from handicrafts to carpets. The shops along the entrance arcade to The Oberoi Grand hotel are worth a browse but are not as entertaining as Chowringhee's amazing variety of pavement vendors. Kolkata's administration has been trying to whisk street hawkers away to (as yet unbuilt) underground markets in an attempt to clear the footpaths, but the unionised street merchants have so far resisted attempts to uproot them.

New Market, formerly Hogg Market, is probably Kolkata's premier place for bargain shopping. Here you can find a little of almost everything, and it is worth an hour or so just wandering around. Other markets include the Treasure Island Market (between Sudder St and New Market), and the AC Market on Shakespeare Sarani, which specialises in imported foodstuffs. There is a good, reasonably cheap street market (mainly clothes) along Lenin Sarani in the evenings. For designer products, there are upmarket boutiques around Park, Camac and Russel Sts.

The top-end hotels usually have an enticing arcade or two, stocked with high-quality goods and high prices to match. The city's modern shopping complexes (such as Emami) are cheaper.

The Dakshinapan Shopping Centre is rather inconveniently located out on Gariahat Rd way south of Chowringhee (near the Dhakuria flyover), but it has various Indian state government emporiums (fixed prices) which sell some terrific regional fare.

For a wide range of Indian and Western music, go to Music World at 18G Park St (next to Flury's), which has some particularly good regional Indian CDs.

The Rabindra Sadan (Sarani) area sells an array of traditional Indian musical instruments at competitive prices. It's a good idea to shop around before making a purchase, just to get an idea of quality and costs.

GETTING THERE & AWAY

For details on air and land travel to neighbouring countries such as Bangladesh, see the Getting There & Away chapter at the beginning of this book. There is now a direct bus service between Kolkata and Dhaka; you can purchase tickets from Shyamoli Paribahan (☎ 2290345, fax 2293715) at 51 Mirza Ghalib St (Free School St; near the Hotel VIP International) in Kolkata. At the time of writing, buses departed from the International Bus Depot out at Salt Lake (double-check in case a more convenient departure point has since commenced).

Air

Most airline offices are around Chowringhee.

Aeroflot (☎ 2829831) 58 Chowringhee Rd
Air France (☎ 2408646) Chitrakoot Bldg, 230A AJC Bose Rd
Air India (☎ 2822356) 50 Chowringhee Rd
Bangladesh Biman Airlines (☎ 2292844) 30C Chowringhee Rd

KOLKATA (CALCUTTA)

British Airways (☎ 2883451) 41 Chowringhee Rd; enter from Middleton St
Cathay Pacific (☎ 2403312/211) 1 Middleton St
Gulf Air (☎ 2477783/5576) Chitrakoot Bldg, 230A AJC Bose Rd
Indian Airlines (☎ 2364433) 39 Chittaranjan Ave
Japan Airlines (☎ 2468370/1) 35A Chowringhee Rd
Jet Airways (☎ 2292227/2660) 18D Park St
KLM – Royal Dutch Airlines (☎ 2403151) 1 Middleton St
Lufthansa (☎ 2299365) 30A/B Chowringhee Rd
Royal Nepal Airlines (☎ 2888549) 41 Chowringhee Rd; enter from Middleton St
Singapore Airlines (☎ 2809898/8586) 1 Lee Rd; off AJC Bose Rd
Swissair (☎ 2884643) 46C Chowringhee Rd
Thai Airways International (☎ 2801630/5) 229 AJC Bose Rd

Kolkata is good for competitive airfares to other parts of Asia, Europe and the US east coast. To hunt down the hottest deals, speak to fellow travellers and check frequently with agencies and airlines (see Air in the Getting There & Away chapter for some international fares from Kolkata).

Kolkata's Indian Airlines office is open 24 hours daily. There's a tourist counter (open 9 am to 7 pm daily) that rarely has a queue. As well as its domestic routes (see the boxed text 'Flights from Kolkata'), Indian Airlines flies several international routes. These include Dhaka (Rs 2410, four times weekly), Bangkok (Rs 5825, six times weekly) and Kathmandu (US$96, five times weekly). These fares are for one-way travel; departure tax is an extra Rs 150.

Bus

It's generally quicker and more comfortable to travel to and from Kolkata by train, though there are several useful bus routes to other towns in West Bengal. Apart from Bihar, Jharkhand and Orissa, there are very limited bus services to other states.

The only buses that travellers use with any regularity are those from Kolkata to

Flights from Kolkata

This table lists only domestic Indian Airlines flights. Jet Airways currently flies only to Bagdogra, Bangalore, Chennai, Guwahati, Hyderabad, Imphal, Jorhat and Mumbai; it offers the same fares as Indian Airlines on these routes.

destination	duration (hrs)	frequency (per week)	fare (US$)
Agartala	¾	12	50
Ahmedabad	2½	6	230
Aizawl	1	3	90
Bagdogra	1	6	80
Bangalore	2½	14	265
Chennai	2	14	220
Delhi	2	21	200
Dibrugarh	1½	4	95
Dimapur	2¼	4	90
Guwahati	1¼	19	70
Imphal	1	9	80
Jaipur	2¼	6	220
Jorhat	1¼	4	90
Lucknow	2¼	7	155
Mumbai	2¼	35	230
Patna	1	7	100
Silchar	1	6	75
Tezpur	1¼	2	80

Siliguri and New Jalpaiguri (for Darjeeling). The 'Rocket Service' (!) costs Rs 152 and leaves Kolkata at 6, 7 and 8 pm daily, arriving the next morning (but travelling by train or air is still preferable). There's an air-con bus (Rs 440) that leaves Kolkata at 7 pm and arrives at Siliguri at around 7 am the next morning.

Buses generally depart from the Esplanade bus station area at the northern end of the Maidan, near Chowringhee Rd, but there are a number of private companies that have their own stands. Buses to and from the south generally use the bus stand at Babu Ghat near Fort William.

Train

Kolkata has two major train stations, both of them frenetic. Howrah, on the west bank of the Hooghly River, handles most trains into the city, but trains going north to Darjeeling or the north-eastern region leave from Sealdah station on the eastern side of the Hooghly. Beware of pickpockets at both stations. At Howrah station, Platforms 1 to 16 are in the old main building; Platforms 17 to 22 are in the new annexe next door. A fair price for porters is about Rs 25 per bag. If they demand much more, pick up your own bag and the fee tumbles down.

The tourist railway booking office is on the 1st floor at 6 Fairlie Place near BBD Bagh. It's fully computerised and has a tourist quota, but be prepared to queue. It's open 8 am to 1 pm and 1.30 to 8 pm Monday to Saturday, and 8 am to 2 pm Sunday. There's another booking office nearby, at 14 Strand Rd South, where you can buy advance tickets on routes into and out of Delhi, Chennai and Mumbai. Get a form and join the correct queue; the tourist quota isn't accessible from this office. Bookings can be made up to 60 days before departure for all trains other than the *Shatabdi Express*, for which bookings only open 15 days prior to departure.

Both these offices can attract long queues and the staff at the Fairlie Place office demand to see encashment certificates (obtained whenever you change foreign currency) if you pay in rupees. There are other computerised booking offices that may be better for buying advance tickets out of Kolkata. The office at Tollygunge metro station is easy to get to and is rarely very

Major Trains from Kolkata

destination	train No & name	departures	distance (km)	duration (hrs)	fare (Rs) 3rd/2nd air-con
Agra	2307 *Jodhpur Exp*	11.30 am H	1420	20¾	277/874
Ahmedabad	8034 *Ahmedabad Exp*	8.20 pm H	2090	41¼	428/1424
Ajmer	2315 *Ananaya Exp*	12.40 pm S	1760	32	420/1250
Amritsar	3005 *Amritsar Exp*	7.20 pm H	1829	38½	365/1235
Chennai	2841 *Coromandel Exp*	1.15 pm H	1636	28	406/1117
Delhi	2301 *Rajdhani Exp*	5 pm H	1441	17	1500/2470
	2303 *Poorva Exp*	9.15 am H	1441	24	383/1080
	2313 *Rajdhani Exp*	4.45 pm S	1441	17	1500/2470
Guwahati	5959 *Kamrup Exp*	3.35 pm H	991	25	290/806
Jodhpur	2307 *Jodhpur Exp*	11.30 pm H	1975	35	474/1240
Mumbai VT	2860 *Geetanjali Exp*	12.40 pm H	1960	33	433/1194
New Jalpaiguri	3143 *Darjeeling Mail*	7.15 pm S	573	12½	210/565
Patna	3231 *Danapur Exp*	9.05 pm H	545	11	202/555
Puri	8007 *Puri Exp*	9.45 pm H	500	10¾	206/565
Tirupati	7479 *Tirupati Exp*	11.30 pm H	1650	16½	377/889
Varanasi	3009 *Doon Exp*	10.15 pm H	670	12	230/787

Train station abbreviations: H – Howrah, S – Sealdah

busy. Alternatively, for a fee (about Rs 40), agents in and around Sudder St can buy tickets for you, often at short notice. But beware of some small-fry travel agents who promise the best train class, but actually give you a ticket on an inferior train or class. Only leave a small deposit, if any, and check the tickets before paying.

Boat

From Kolkata, you can take a boat to Port Blair in the Andaman Islands. However, foreigners do need a permit to visit. The 30-day maximum permit (which can sometimes be extended to 45 days) allows you to stay in the capital, Port Blair, with short-term visits to other areas. You apply for a (free) permit on arrival at Port Blair or get one beforehand from the Foreigners' Registration Office (☎ 2473301) at 237A AJC Bose Rd, Chowringhee. On arrival at Port Blair, ship passengers must immediately report to the deputy superintendent of police in Aberdeen Bazaar. If you fail to do this you could encounter problems when departing, since it will be difficult to prove that you have not been on the island longer than 30 days.

There are usually two to four sailings a month between Port Blair and Kolkata on vessels operated by the Shipping Corporation of India (SCI; ☎ 2842354), 13 Strand Rd South, near BBD Bagh. Contact SCI for the latest information on the schedules. It's best to arrange a return ticket when purchasing your outward ticket.

The length of the trip varies with the weather. On a good crossing, it takes 56 hours from Kolkata. The categories of accommodation include deluxe cabin (Rs 4140, two berths per cabin), 1st-class cabin (Rs 3420, usually two berths), 2nd-class A cabin (Rs 2700, four to six berths) and 2nd-class B cabin (Rs 2070, similar to A but smaller). Some ships have an air-con dorm with beds for Rs 1449. Food (thalis for breakfast, lunch and dinner) costs around Rs 120 per day. Almost everyone complains about the food so you may wish to bring something (fruit in particular) to supplement this.

GETTING AROUND

To/From the Airport

The airport (domestic and international terminals) is 17km north-east of the city centre. A public minibus runs from BBD Bagh to the airport for Rs 10. The metro line to Dum Dum stops 5km short of the airport; a bus from there will cost about Rs 5 (although there are plans to extend this route all the way to the airport which will be far more convenient – check the current situation).

If you want to take a taxi from the airport, it's cheaper and more reliable to go to the prepaid taxi booth (after you clear customs) where you'll be assigned one. It costs about Rs 160 to Sudder St.

Although the airport is now officially called the Netaji Subhas Chandra Basu International Airport (the domestic terminal is here too), taxi drivers still commonly refer to it as Dum Dum. It was named Dum Dum airport because this was the site of the Dum Dum Barracks, where the explosive dum-dum bullet, banned after the Boer War, was once made.

Bus

Local buses are passenger-crammed, mechanical monsters that travel at frightening speed – pedestrians beware! Fares start at just Rs 2. There is also a private minibus service, which is even faster (fares start at Rs 2.25).

Never risk crossing the road if a bus is heading your way, as there is a growing number of pedestrian fatalities caused by speeding buses in Kolkata each year. During our visit, 20 pedestrians standing on the curb were mowed down by a bus which was travelling too fast around a corner and completely lost control.

Tram

Kolkata's public tram service injects character into the city, even though the trams are like sardine tins in rush hour. Although they're pollution-free there's been ongoing pressure to abolish them because they are a major cause of traffic jams. Tram enthusiasts, including a sister society in Melbourne,

Australia, have campaigned to save the trams and they've succeeded – for now. Fares start at Rs 1.75.

Metro

Kolkata boasts India's first underground railway system. The southern sector, from Chandni Chowk to Tollygunge station, and the northern sector to the west of BBD Bagh are most useful. There are two stations near Sudder St: to the north (almost opposite The Oberoi Grand hotel) and to the south (opposite Dr M Ishaque Rd).

The metro is clean and efficient, although still terribly crowded during peak hours (from approximately 9 to 11 am and 5 to 7 pm Monday to Saturday). Trains run from 8.15 am to 10 pm Monday to Saturday, and 3 to 9.15 pm on Sunday. Tickets range from Rs 3 (one sector) to Rs 7 (to the end of the line).

Taxi

You'll see two types of taxis in Kolkata: the yellow ones have permits to travel all over Kolkata and West Bengal, while the black-and-yellow taxis are restricted to Kolkata.

For all taxi trips (other than those negotiated) add 20% to the reading on the meter. Meters are inevitably outdated, so it's best to see the fare conversion chart, which every driver should carry. Officially, taxi fares start at Rs 12 and go up by Rs 0.50 increments, but that can be more theory than practice. Not all drivers are willing to use the meter so you may have to firmly insist or choose another driver. Frustrating as it is, there are plenty of taxis, so shop around for a metered ride or a reasonable negotiated price. For a half/full day of sightseeing expect to pay around Rs 500/800. If you would like to hire a taxi for several days of sightseeing, make sure you negotiate a package deal. Most drivers will be prepared to offer a discounted rate, especially for a minimum of one week's hire – Rs 750 per day is reasonable but you may even be able to barter this down a little more.

Outside Howrah station there's a prepaid taxi rank, and from here it will cost you Rs 40 to Sudder St, although there may be a queue so be prepared to wait. There's also a prepaid booth at the airport (see To/From the Airport earlier in this section).

Rickshaws in Kolkata

Hand-pulled rickshaws still exist as tourist curiosities or historical oddities in very small numbers in several cities around the world. Only in Kolkata are hand-pulled rickshaws still in everyday use as real transport.

Although Kolkata has the last remaining hand-pulled rickshaws it did not have the first, even in India. The first Indian rickshaws made their appearance in 1880 in the Himalayan hill station of Shimla, a hot-season retreat for officials of the British Raj. This was the same year rickshaws were first seen in Singapore. It was a further 20 years before the first rickshaws appeared in Kolkata and then only for conveying goods. The first Kolkata rickshaws were not only owned by Chinese residents, they were pulled by Chinese immigrants. The Chinese workers have long disappeared but even today Kolkata's rickshaw pullers are mainly outsiders from the neighbouring, and even more poverty-stricken, state of Bihar.

It was 1914 before rickshaws were finally allowed to carry passengers but through the 1920s and 1930s the city's rickshaw fleet expanded rapidly, even though by that time rickshaw numbers were declining in other cities. In 1939 the city authorities decreed an absolute maximum of 6000 licences, but after WWII the rickshaw population continued to grow. The combination of poverty, congestion and a ban on cycle-rickshaws in the city centre encouraged hand-pulled rickshaw numbers to reach 30,000 to 50,000 in the late 1980s. In his bestselling novel, *City of Joy*, Dominique Lapierre estimated that Kolkata's 100,000 rickshaw pullers handled one million passengers a day and covered a greater distance than the entire Indian Airlines fleet of Boeing and Airbus aircraft.

Tony Wheeler, *Chasing Rickshaws*

Rickshaw

Kolkata is the last real bastion of the human-powered rickshaw. The city's rickshaw-wallahs rejected the new-fangled cycle-rickshaws when they were introduced elsewhere in India. After all, who could afford a bicycle? Many can't even afford to buy their own rickshaw and have to rent from someone who takes the lion's share of the fares.

You may find it morally unacceptable to have a man pulling you around in a carriage. The only compensation is that they would not have a job if people didn't use them, and as a tourist, you naturally pay more than the locals. Kolkata's administration has long wanted to completely ban the rickshaws, as part of a short-sighted traffic-management plan that equates slow-moving transport with slow-moving traffic. As it is, Kolkata's narrow lanes and poor drainage mean that, aside from walking, jumping in a rickshaw is often the only way to get somewhere. Anyway, this sort of rickshaw (as well as autorickshaws) is already restricted to small parts of central Kolkata. Across the river in Howrah or in the suburbs, there are autorickshaws and cycle-rickshaws.

A short ride in a cycle-rickshaw costs around Rs 10; a trip from Sudder St to the Motherhouse costs about Rs 25. A tip is heartily appreciated.

Ferry

The ferries can be a quicker and more pleasant way to get across the river than the congested Howrah Bridge. From Howrah to Chandpal Ghat or Fairlie Ghat there are several crossings an hour between 8 am and 8 pm. Ferries to the Botanical Gardens go from Chandpal Ghat or Babu Ghat, but they are a 'casual' service on negotiation and not at any designated times. The fares are minimal (Rs 3 to 5).

West Bengal

The cradle of Indian renaissance and the national freedom movement, Bengal has long been considered by many as the cultural centre of India. After Partition, the state was split into East and West Bengal. East Bengal eventually became Bangladesh and West Bengal became a state of India with Kolkata (Calcutta) as its capital. The state is long and narrow, running from the delta of the Ganges River system in the Bay of Bengal to the south, up through the Ganges plain, to the heights of the Himalaya and Darjeeling in the north.

A land of aesthetes and political activists, West Bengal is rightly famous for its many eminent writers, poets, artists, spiritualists, social reformers, economists, freedom fighters and revolutionaries.

South of Kolkata on the Bay of Bengal is the area known as the Sunderbans, one of the largest deltas in the world, and home to the elusive royal Bengal tiger. To the north lie the flourishing mango plantations and jute fields of the fertile river plains. Farther north again in the Himalayan foothills are the world-famous Darjeeling tea plantations.

Everywhere you look you will find historic sites and some interesting aspect of Bengali culture. Yet foreign tourists have been slow to visit the ruined mosques of Malda, the palaces of Murshidabad, the living arts museum and Visvabharati University in Shantiniketan, the temples of Vishnupur or even the Sunderbans Wildlife Sanctuary. If you do venture into the area, the friendly Bengalis will make you feel all the more welcome for being an exception to the rule.

Several railway sabotage cases in northern Bengal in early 2000, which resulted in some near misses of passenger trains, did little to help tourism. Officials were quick to point the finger at Pakistan, but these allegations have not been proven. Although there were no subsequent sabotage cases, if you're still concerned, check out the situation locally.

West Bengal at a Glance

Population: 74.5 million
Area: 87,853 sq km
Capital: Kolkata (Calcutta)
Main Language: Bengali
When to Go: Oct to Mar

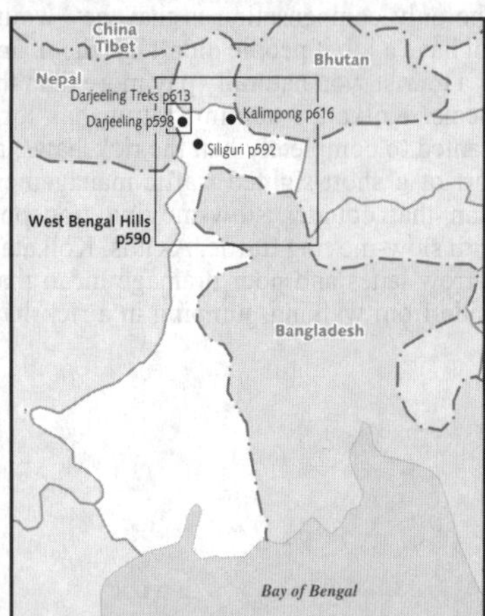

- Visit the popular hill station of Darjeeling, replete with gompas, nearby tea plantations and awesome views of the mighty Kanchenjunga
- Search for the prolific but elusive tigers at the picturesque, World Heritage-listed Sunderbans Wildlife Sanctuary
- Experience the vibrant mix of statewide festivals, from the quaint folk fair of Paush Mela to the wildly exuberant Durga Puja celebrations

To put a halt to illegal immigration and smuggling between India and Bangladesh, the West Bengali government was at the time of research planning to construct a fence-like barrier (around 900km long) between the two countries.

History

Referred to as Vanga in the Mahabharata, this area has a long history that predates the rise of the Aryans of India. It was part of the Mauryan empire in the 3rd century before being overrun by the Guptas. For three centuries from around the 9th century AD, the Pala dynasty controlled a large area based in Bengal and including parts of Orissa, Bihar and modern-day Bangladesh.

Bengal was brought under Muslim control by Qutb-ud-din, first of the sultans of Delhi, at the end of the 12th century. Following the death of the Mughal leader Aurangzeb in 1707, Bengal became an independent Muslim state.

Britain had established a trading post in Kolkata in 1698, which quickly prospered. Sensing rich pickings, Siraj-ud-daula, the nawab of Bengal, came down from his capital at Murshidabad and easily took Kolkata in 1756. Clive defeated him the following year at the Battle of Plassey, helped by the treachery of Siraj-ud-daula's uncle, Mir Jafar, who commanded the greater part of the nawab's army. He was rewarded by succeeding his nephew, but after the Battle of Buxar in 1764 the British took full control of Bengal. For entertaining background reading on this period as seen through the eyes of a modern-day traveller, Peter Holt's book *In Clive's Footsteps* is recommended. The author is the great-grandson five times removed of Clive.

Planning

Foreigners need a permit to visit Sunderbans Wildlife Sanctuary; permits are issued on the spot on presentation of your passport at the West Bengal Tourism Centre in Kolkata (☎ 2488271), 3/2 BBD Bagh, open from 10.30 am to 4 pm Monday to Friday, 10.30 am to 1 pm Saturday, and 7 am to noon Sunday. There is currently no charge for permits.

State government (West Bengal Tourism Development Corporation; WBTDC) hotels are scattered throughout the state and reservations for all of these can also be made at the West Bengal Tourism Centre in Kolkata. These state-run hotels vary vastly in quality, but most are pretty ordinary with humdrum rooms and lacklustre service. However, most offer good food and are satisfactory for a night or two.

Special Events

State-wide festivals celebrated in West Bengal include the **Naba Barshq**, the Bengali New Year, celebrated in mid-April, and the **Durga Puja** festival, the largest Bengali festival, held in October in honour of the goddess Durga. There are also local festivals held on Sagar Island and in Shantiniketan, Mahesh and Siliguri.

South of Kolkata

DOWN THE HOOGHLY

The Hooghly River is very difficult to navigate due to constantly shifting shoals and sandbanks. River pilots have to stay in touch with it to keep track of its frequent course changes. When the Howrah Bridge was built, it was feared it would affect the river's flow patterns.

Tides rise and fall over 3.5m at Kolkata and there is a bore, 2m high, during rising tides. As a result of this and the silting up of the Hooghly, Kolkata is losing its importance as a port.

Falta, 43km downriver, was the site of a Dutch factory. The British retreated here in 1756 when Kolkata was captured by Siraj-ud-daula. It's also from here that Clive recaptured Kolkata. Below Falta the Damodar River joins the Hooghly.

The Rupnarain River also joins the Hooghly nearby, and a little up this river is **Tamluk**, which was an important Buddhist centre over 1000 years ago. The James & Mary Shoal, the most dangerous on the Hooghly, is just above the point where the Rupnarain River enters (its name comes from a ship wrecked here in 1694). Birdlife is abundant in areas south of Kolkata, so bring along your binoculars.

There is a catamaran service between Kolkata and Haldia (south of Kolkata) which operates on weekdays only. It leaves Kolkata at 7.45 am, returning at 5.30 pm. The one-way fare is US$9/23 for economy/1st class.

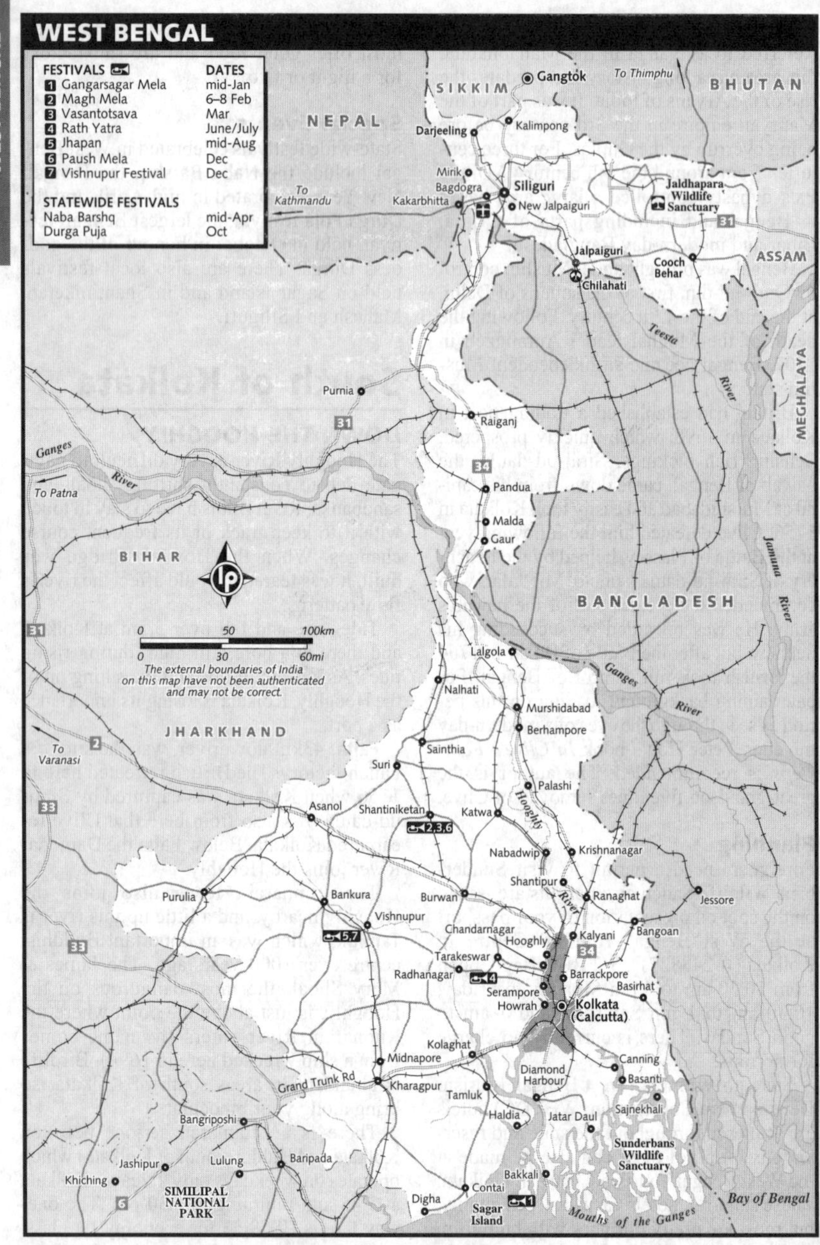
WEST BENGAL
FESTIVALS
DATES
1 Gangarsagar Mela mid-Jan
2 Magh Mela 6–8 Feb
3 Vasantotsava Mar
4 Rath Yatra June/July
5 Jhapan mid-Aug
6 Paush Mela Dec
7 Vishnupur Festival Dec
STATEWIDE FESTIVALS
Naba Barshq mid-Apr
Durga Puja Oct
The external boundaries of India on this map have not been authenticated and may not be correct.
0 50 100km
0 30 60mi
NEPAL
SIKKIM
BHUTAN
ASSAM
MEGHALAYA
BIHAR
JHARKHAND
BANGLADESH
Gangtok
To Thimphu
Darjeeling
Kalimpong
Mirik
Bagdogra
Siliguri
To Kathmandu
Kakarbhitta
New Jalpaiguri
Jaldhapara Wildlife Sanctuary
Jalpaiguri
Chilahati
Cooch Behar
Teesta
River
Purnia
Raiganj
Ganges
River
To Patna
Pandua
Malda
Gaur
Jamuna
River
Lalgola
Ganges
River
Nalhati
Murshidabad
Berhampore
To Varanasi
Sainthia
Suri
Palashi
Hooghly
Asanol
Shantiniketan
2,3,6
Katwa
Nabadwip
Krishnanagar
Shantipur
Purulia
Bankura
Burwan
Ranaghat
River
Jessore
Vishnupur
5,7
Chandarnagar
Hooghly
Kalyani
Bangoan
Tarakeswar
Radhanagar
4
Barrackpore
Basirhat
Serampore
Howrah
Kolkata (Calcutta)
Kolaghat
Midnapore
Canning
Grand Trunk Rd
Kharagpur
Diamond Harbour
Basanti
Tamluk
Sajnekhali
Bangriposhi
Haldia
Jatar Daul
Sunderbans Wildlife Sanctuary
Lulung
Baripada
Jashipur
Khiching
Bakkali
SIMILIPAL NATIONAL PARK
Contai
Digha
Sagar Island
1
Bay of Bengal
Mouths of the Ganges
31
34
33
2
6

DIAMOND HARBOUR

A resort 51km south of Kolkata by road, Diamond Harbour is at the point where the Hooghly turns south and flows into the open sea. Launches run from here to Sagar Island (Sagardwip). From Diamond Harbour you can visit the **crocodile breeding centre** at Bhagabatpur – catch a bus to Namkhana (Rs 15, 1½ hours) and then hire a boat to Bhagabatpur.

Places to Stay

The ***Sagarika Tourist Lodge*** *(☎/fax 03174-917455246)* has acceptable air-con doubles with bathroom for Rs 650.

Getting There & Away

There are several daily buses from Kolkata to Diamond Harbour. These cost Rs 20 and take 1½ hours.

SAGAR ISLAND (SAGARDWIP)

Accessible by bus and ferry from Diamond Harbour, Sagar Island, which is at the mouth of the Hooghly River, is considered to be the point where the Ganges joins the sea. The Gangarsagar Mela takes place on the island, held on the occasion of Maker Sankrati (mid-January). The festival attracts hundreds of thousands of Hindu pilgrims who come to visit the Kapil Muni Temple and bathe at the confluence of the Ganges and the Bay of Bengal.

Cheap lodgings are possible at various ***ashrams*** and at the ***youth hostel*** (book through Youth Services India in Kolkata on ☎ 033-2480626).

DIGHA

Close to the border with Orissa, 185km south-west of Kolkata on the Bay of Bengal, Digha is another self-styled 'Brighton of the East'. The 7km beach is very wide, but if a beach holiday is what you want, continue south to Puri or Gopalpur-on-Sea. The **Chandaneshwar Shiva Temple** is just across the border in Orissa, 8km from Digha.

Places to Stay

Digha has a range of accommodation options, including a ***WBTDC Tourist Lodge*** *(☎ 03220-66255, fax 66256)*, which has ordinary doubles from Rs 275. If you're on a shoestring budget, there are dorm beds for Rs 80.

Getting There & Away

There are several daily buses between Kolkata and Digha (Rs 60, about six hours).

BAKKALI

Sometimes referred to as Fraserganj, the beach resort of Bakkali, 132km from Kolkata, is not as busy as Digha and is not as striking. However it does boast some wonderful birdlife. From Bakkali you can get boats to the small island of **Jambu Dwip** to the south-west.

Places to Stay

The ***WBTDC Bakkali Tourist Lodge*** *(☎ 03210-25260)* is probably your best bet in Bakkali. It has standard doubles for Rs 300 and cheaper dorm beds for Rs 80.

Getting There & Away

Buses from Kolkata to Bakkali take about two hours; there are several bus services each day (Rs 40).

SUNDERBANS WILDLIFE SANCTUARY

The innumerable mouths of the Ganges form the world's largest delta, and part of this vast mangrove swamp is a wildlife reserve that extends into Bangladesh (2585 sq km). The sanctuary is designated a World Heritage site and, as part of Project Tiger, has one of the largest tiger populations of any parks worldwide. Tourist agencies capitalise on this fact, but in reality, few visitors get even a glimpse of one of the shy tigers (estimated to number just under 300 in 2000) that remain well hidden in the sanctuary. Be prepared not to see a big cat, and you won't leave disappointed.

The tigers may be tourist shy, but they are partial to human flesh, killing a number of villagers each year. They generally stalk along the narrow channels that crisscross the estuarine forest. Since tigers are less likely to attack if they suspect they are being watched, fishermen and honey collectors have taken to wearing masks cleverly painted with human faces on the back of their heads.

Winter and spring are the best times to visit the wildlife sanctuary, which is also home to spotted deer, wild pigs, monkeys and various bird species. The whole area is wonderfully peaceful after teeming Kolkata, and even if you don't catch sight of a tiger, you'll see lots of other fascinating sights.

At the **Sajnekhali visitors centre** there's a shark pond, a turtle hatchery and an interesting Mangrove Interpretation Centre. From here **boats** are available for excursions through the mangroves. Trips cost around Rs 800 per person for the whole day, or Rs 400 for four hours; you need a guide and boat permits. There are watchtowers at several points around the park.

South of the Sunderbans are **Lothian** and **Halliday Islands**, reached from Namkhana (three hours by bus from Kolkata).

Permission is required to visit Sunderbans Wildlife Sanctuary (see Planning earlier in this chapter). There's also a small entry fee to visit the reserve, payable at Sajnekhali.

Organised Tours

From October to March, the West Bengal Tourism Centre (WBTC) organises weekly boat tours that include food and accommodation. It costs Rs 1200 per person for one night and Rs 1500 for two nights. If you're expecting 'adventure at every corner', as one brochure suggests, forget it. One traveller described his trip as 'More like a totally uneventful three-day picnic on the water.' Nonetheless, picnics can be fun too.

Places to Stay & Eat

Sajnekhali Tourist Lodge *(☎ 03219-52560)*, at Sajnekhali, has reasonably good doubles from Rs 525 and dorm beds for a whopping Rs 200 (but these rates do include one major meal and breakfast).

Getting There & Away

Travelling independently is more complicated than taking the WBTC boat tour, but is good for exploring the area at leisure – you could hire a guide from the WBTC in Kolkata (Rs 500 per day plus food and accommodation for any overnight stays). If you plan on visiting Sunderbans Wildlife Sanctuary independently, ask the tourism centre about the current travel conditions, as some roads can become inaccessible after foul weather. From Kolkata (Babu Ghat) it's quickest to get a bus to Basanti or Sonakhali (Rs 30, about three hours). Continuing from Basanti or Sonakhali the next step is a boat to Gosava (Rs 10, 1¼ hours). From Gosava get a cycle-rickshaw for the 45-minute ride to Pakhirala (Rs 20), then a boat across the river to Sajnekhali.

There's also a direct boat (Rs 9) leaving Basanti for Sajnekhali at 3.30 pm. A private boat to Sajnekhali costs Rs 400 from Basanti.

North of Kolkata

SERAMPORE & BARRACKPORE

On the Hooghly River, 25km north of Kolkata, is Serampore, which was a Danish centre until Denmark's holdings in India were transferred to the East India Company in 1845. The old Danish church and cemetery still stand. The missionaries Ward, Marshman and Carey operated from here in the early 19th century.

Across the river is Barrackpore. A few dilapidated buildings are all that is left of the East India Company's cantonment here. There is also a memorial to Gandhi by the river.

Just three kilometres from Serampore, **Mahesh** has a very old Jagannath temple. The Mahesh Rath Yatra (Car Festival), when the pulling of Lord Jagannath's chariot is enacted, takes place here each June/July.

CHANDARNAGAR

Also known as Chandernagore, this was one of the French enclaves in India that was handed over at the same time as Pondicherry in 1951. On the banks of the Hooghly, 39km north of Kolkata, it has several crumbling buildings dating from the French era. The first French settlers arrived here in 1673 and the place later became an important trading post, although it was taken by the British during conflicts with the French.

Buses from Kolkata to Chandarnagar take two hours (Rs 10).

HOOGHLY & SATGAON

The historic town of Hooghly is 41km from Kolkata and was an important trading port long before Kolkata rose to prominence. In 1537 the Portuguese set up a factory here; before that time Satgaon, 10km farther north, had been the main port of Bengal but was abandoned because the river silted up. There are still a few traces of Satgaon's former grandeur, including a ruined mosque. After a lengthy siege, the Portuguese were expelled from Hooghly in 1632 by Shah Jahan, but were allowed to return a year later. The British East India Company also established a factory here in 1651. The *imambara* (tomb), built in 1836, has a gateway flanked by lofty minarets and is the main sight.

A kilometre or so south of Hooghly, **Chinsura** was exchanged by the Dutch for the British-held Indonesian island of Sumatra in 1825. There is a fort and the Dutch cemetery, with many old tombs, 1km to the west.

A couple of kilometres north of Hooghly, **Bandel** has a Portuguese church and monastery built in 1599. Destroyed by Shah Jahan in 1640, they were later rebuilt. Just 4km north of Bandel is **Bansberia** where the Vasudev Temple, with interesting terracotta wall carvings, and the Hanseswari Temple can be found.

There are buses from Kolkata to Chinsura, Bandel and Bansberia (Rs 8, two hours).

VISHNUPUR

This town of terracotta temples flourished as the capital of the Malla kings from the 16th to the early 19th centuries. The Mallas were great patrons of the arts.

Since there is no stone found in the area, the traditional construction material for important buildings was brick. The facades of the dozen or so temples here are covered with ornate terracotta tiles depicting lively scenes from the Hindu epics. The main temples are the highly decorated Jor Bangla, the large Madan Mohan, the pyramidal Ras Mancha and the Shyam Rai.

Vishnupur is in Bankura district, famous for its **pottery** (particularly the stylised Bankura horse) and **silk**. In the markets here you can also find metalwork, tussar silk and Baluchari saris, *ganjifa* (circular playing cards for a game long forgotten) and conch jewellery.

In August, the **Jhapan Festival** draws snake charmers to honour the goddess Manasa, who is the central figure of snake worship. In December, there is the Vishnupur festival of local handicrafts and music.

The ***Vishnupur Tourist Lodge*** *(☎ 03244-52013)*, not far from the train station, offers dorm beds for Rs 80 and average doubles which start at Rs 300.

There are daily buses from Kolkata to Vishnupur (Rs 66, six hours).

JAIRAMBATI & KAMARPUKUR

Ramakrishna was born in Kamarpukur, 143km north-west of Kolkata, and there is a Ramakrishna Mission ashram here. Ramakrishna was a 19th-century Hindu saint who did much to rejuvenate Hinduism when it was going through a period of decline during British rule. Jairambati, 5km away, is another important point for Ramakrishna devotees.

SHANTINIKETAN

The town of Shantiniketan is 3km from Bolpur, a major transport hub in the region.

The brilliant poet, writer, artist and nationalist Rabindranath Tagore (1861–1941) founded a school here in 1901. It later developed into the Visvabharati University with an emphasis on humanity's relationship with nature. Tagore went on to win the Nobel Prize for Literature in 1913, and is credited with introducing India's historical and cultural greatness to the modern world. In 1915 Tagore was awarded a knighthood by the British, but he surrendered it in 1919 as a protest against the Amritsar massacre. See also the boxed text 'Rabindranath Tagore' in the Kolkata chapter.

Amartya Sen, the Nobel Prize for Economics winner in 1998, was educated here.

Shantiniketan is a very peaceful place and worth a visit if you have an interest in art, culture, the humanities and the life and works of Tagore. Points of interest to visitors include the museum and art gallery within the Uttarayan complex where Tagore lived. Of particular prominence are the Shantiniketan Murals, mural paintings that were developed in this town. Seagull Books publishes the magnificently illustrated *The Shantiniketan Murals* by Jayanta Chakrabarti, R Siva Kumar & Arun K Nag (Rs 750), which you can purchase at the Seagull Bookstore in Kolkata (see Bookshops in the Kolkata chapter).

There are several annual **festivals** held at Shantiniketan, such as the spring Vasantotsava festival in March and the Paush Mela festival in December, which features folk music, dance, singing and theatre.

Places to Stay

If you're planning a long stay here, a cheap option may be the ***university guesthouses*** *(☎ 03463-52751)*.

The ***WBTDC Shantiniketan Tourist Lodge*** *(☎ 03463-52699, fax 52398)* has doubles for Rs 275 and dorm beds for Rs 80.

For something far more upmarket, there's the ***Chhuti Holiday Resort*** *(☎ 03463-52692; in Kolkata ☎ 033-2208307)*, with singles/doubles starting at Rs 700/850.

Getting There & Away

There are rail connections between Shantiniketan and other parts of West Bengal, however at the time of writing the trains were not functioning; check with the tourist office in Kolkata for schedules.

NABADWIP & MAYAPUR

Nabadwip (also known as Nawadip), 114km from Kolkata, is an important Hare Krishna pilgrimage centre, attracting throngs of devotees to its many temples. It is also an ancient centre of Sanskrit culture. The last Hindu king of Bengal, Lakshman Sen, moved his capital here from Gaur.

Across the river from Nabadwip, Mayapur is a centre for the International Society for Krishna Consciousness (Iskcon) movement. There's a large temple and moderately priced accommodation is available at the ***Iskcon Guest House*** (for bookings call ☎ 033-4634959 in Kolkata). Iskcon runs a bus tour from Kolkata during winter (Rs 250) – for more details contact Iskcon (☎ 033-2476075), 3C Albert Rd, Kolkata.

PALASHI (PLASSEY)

In 1757 Clive defeated Siraj-ud-daula and his French supporters at Palashi (previously Plassey), a turning point in British influence in India. Palashi is 172km north of Kolkata and there's essentially nothing to see here apart from the 15m-high memorial a few kilometres west.

MURSHIDABAD

When Siraj-ud-daula was nawab of Bengal, Murshidabad was his capital, and it was here that he was assassinated after the defeat at Palashi. Murshidabad was also the major trading town between inland India and the port of Kolkata, 221km south. Today it's an insignificant but peaceful town on the banks of the Bhagirathi River, offering a chance to see rural Bengali life.

Cycle-rickshaw-wallahs offer you guided tours of all the sites of Murshidabad for around Rs 80 for a half-day. This is a good idea as everything is fairly spread out.

Hazarduari

The classical-style Hazarduari (Palace of a Thousand Doors) was built for the nawabs in 1837. In the renovated throne room a vast chandelier, a gift from Queen Victoria, is suspended above the nawab's silver throne. In the armoury downstairs is a cannon used at Palashi. The palace is open from 10.30 am to 4.30 pm daily except Friday; entry costs Rs 2. The library houses at least 10,000 books, 3000 manuscripts and a collection of magnificently illuminated Qurans. Though closed to the public, you can get permission to view or use the collection from the Assistant Superintending Archaeologist, Archaeological Survey of India, Hazarduari Palace Museum, Murshidabad (inquire at your hotel or at the palace).

Other Attractions

Across the grass from the palace is the deteriorating **Great Imambara**. Murshid Quli Khan, who moved the capital here in 1705, is buried beside the impressive ruins of the **Katra Mosque**. Siraj-ud-daula was assassinated at the **Nimak Haram Deohri** (Traitor's Gate). The Jain **Parswanath Temple** is at Kathgola, and south of the train station there's the **Moti Jhil**, or Pearl Lake, a fine place to view the sunset. It's worth taking a boat across the river to visit Siraj's **tomb** at Khusbagh, the Garden of Happiness.

Places to Stay

In Murshidabad, the pick of the bunch is the tranquil ***Hotel Manjusha*** *(☎ 03482-70321)*, ideally located on the banks of the river, not far from the palace. The rooms downstairs cost Rs 125/200 a single/double with private bathroom (most with squat toilet), but it's worth paying a bit more for the better rooms upstairs that cost Rs 250 (doubles only) and have sit-down flush toilets and balconies sporting splendid lake views. The owner is an enthusiastic chap who will be able to fill you in on what to see and do in this area.

Getting There & Away

There are several trains a day between Kolkata and Murshidabad (about Rs 52, six hours). A bus from Kolkata to Murshidabad costs around the same. There are also bus connections to other destinations in the state including Malda and Siliguri. Autorickshaws, taxis and buses regularly whiz the distance between Murshidabad and Berhampore (a share-rickshaw costs Rs 5 per person).

BERHAMPORE

Eleven kilometres south of Murshidabad, Berhampore is a notable centre for silk production. In the old bazaar area of Khagra there are some dilapidated mansions, once belonging to European traders.

Places to Stay

In Berhampore, the best place to stay is the ***Hotel Samrat*** *(☎ 03482-51147, 51725, NH-34 Panchanantala)*, which has dorm beds for Rs 50 and good-sized, tidy singles/doubles with private bathroom which start at Rs 100/125. Make sure you request a room with minimal traffic noise as the roar of early-morning trucks is not a particularly pleasant wake-up call.

Getting There & Away

Several daily trains travel between Kolkata and Berhampore (Rs 52, six hours). A bus from Kolkata to Berhampore is around the same price. There are also bus connections to other destinations in the state including Malda and Siliguri.

West Bengal Hills

MALDA

About 349km north of Kolkata, Malda (formerly known as English Bazaar) is the base for visiting the ruined cities of Gaur and Pandua (see those sections following), although it's now also renowned for its large Fajli mangoes.

English Bazaar, also transliterated as Ingraj Bazaar, is now a suburb of Malda. An English factory was established here in 1771. **Old Malda** is nearby, at the junction of the Kalindi and Mahananda Rivers. It was once an important port for the former Muslim capital of Pandua.

Places to Stay & Eat

The modest but pleasant ***Hotel Purbanchal*** *(☎ 03512-66183)* is the best value for money in town. Good singles/doubles with private bathroom range from Rs 200/250 to Rs 550/800. There's a decent restaurant serving hearty mutton curry (Rs 40), chicken stew (Rs 45) and plenty more.

If all the rooms at Hotel Purbanchal are full, there's the less impressive ***Malda Tourist Lodge*** *(☎ 03512-66123)*, which is rather worn and weary, but is acceptable for a night (check for frogs in the bathroom). Tired-looking rooms with private bathroom start at Rs 267/330 and meals are available in the dining hall.

The ***retiring rooms*** at the train station cost Rs 50 for a dorm bed and Rs 250/400 for air-con rooms with private bathroom.

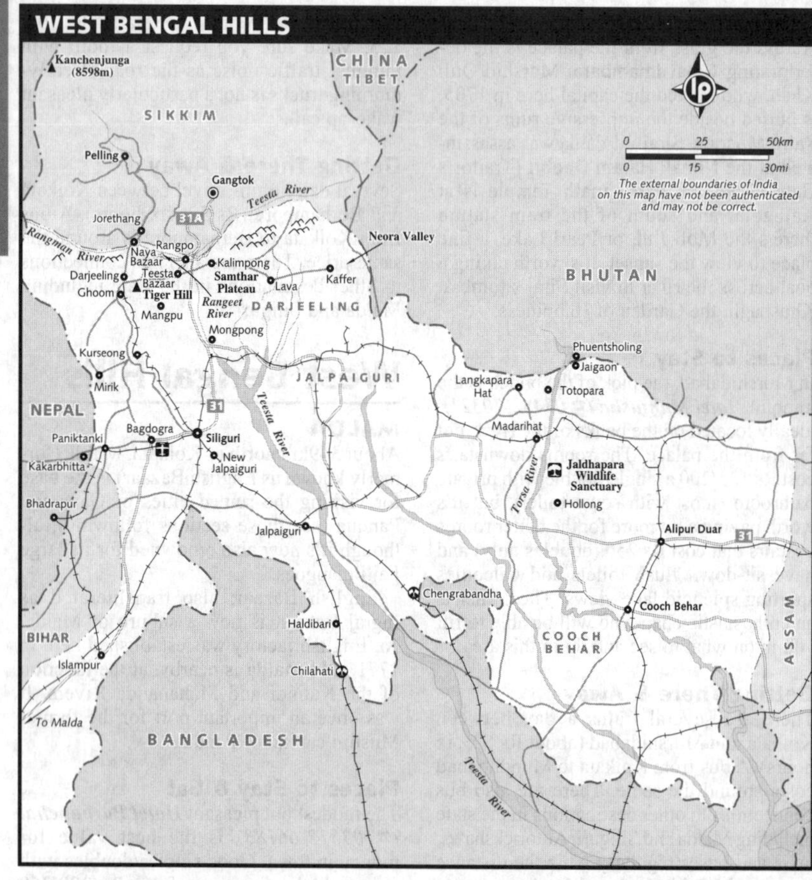

Getting There & Away

Malda is on the main railway line to Kolkata (Rs 148, 2nd-class sleeper, seven hours) and New Jalpaiguri (Rs 120, 2nd-class sleeper, five hours). There are buses to Siliguri (Rs 90, six hours) for Darjeeling, Berhampore or Murshidabad (Rs 35, three hours) and Kolkata (Rs 117, eight hours).

GAUR

Twelve kilometres south of Malda, near the border with Bangladesh, Gaur was first the capital of the Buddhist Pala dynasty, then the seat of the Hindu Sena dynasty, and finally the capital of the Muslim nawabs. The ruins of the extensive fortifications and several large mosques are all that remain. (There are also some ruins on the other side of the ill-defined border). Most impressive are the **Bara Sona Mosque** and the nearby brick **Dakhil Darwajah** built in 1425. The **Qadam Rasul Mosque** enshrines a footprint of Mohammed, but it looks as if he was wearing flip flops at the time! Fath Khan's tomb is nearby and a sign says that he 'vomited blood and died on this spot'. There are still some colourful enamelled tiles on the **Gumti Gate** and **Lattan Mosque** but few left on the **Firoz Minar**.

The monuments are very spread out and are not all easy to find. Some determined cycle-rickshaw-wallahs offer half-day trips from Malda for Rs 80 (return). Taxis cost about Rs 400 (return) and include Pandua.

PANDUA

For a time Gaur alternated with Pandua as the seat of power. The main sites in the area are at Adina, 2km north of the village of Pandua. The principal place of interest is the vast **Adina Mosque**, built by Sikander Shah in the 14th century. Built over a Hindu temple, traces of which are still evident, it was one of the largest mosques in India but is now in ruins. Nearby is the **Eklakhi mausoleum**, so called because it cost Rs 1 lakh (Rs 100,000) to build. There are also several smaller mosques.

Getting There & Away

Pandua is on the main highway (National Highway 34), 18km north of Malda, and there are many buses that can drop you here for a nominal cost. Adina is to the north of Pandua, right by the highway.

SILIGURI & NEW JALPAIGURI

☎ 0353

Siliguri lies 8km north of the main railway junction of New Jalpaiguri (known throughout the district as NJP), though there's effectively no break between the two places. This crowded sprawl is the jumping-off point for Darjeeling, Kalimpong, Sikkim, the states in the north-east, eastern Nepal and Bhutan. For most travellers, Siliguri is essentially just an overnight transit point and for this reason the hotels can fill up fast.

Orientation

The towns of Siliguri and New Jalpaiguri basically have just one north-south main road – Hill Cart Rd (also less commonly known as Tenzing Norgay Rd). It's about 3km from NJP train station to Siliguri train station, and a further 4km from there to Siliguri Junction train station, behind the Tenzing Norgay central bus terminal. You can catch the toy train (if it's running) from the NJP train station. Bagdogra, 12km west of Siliguri, is the airport serving this northern region.

Information

Tourist Offices The West Bengal tourist office (☎ 511974), Hill Cart Rd, is open from 10.30 am to 5 pm weekdays. The staff are not particularly enthusiastic, so you may have to push for information. It's possible to book accommodation in the Jaldhapara Wildlife Sanctuary (see later in this chapter), as well as arrange tours to Sikkim and Bhutan here. There are also tourist counters at the airport and train stations.

Money There is a counter at the Delhi Hotel (see Places to Stay following) which changes travellers cheques and major currencies. It's open from 7 am to 9 pm daily and is pretty efficient. The State Bank of India exchanges American Express travellers cheques in US dollars and pounds sterling only. It's open from 10 am to 2 pm weekdays and until noon Saturday.

Email & Internet Access There were few places to surf the Internet in Siliguri at the time of research. One fairly central place is Biswadeep Communication, near the TSA Guest House, not far from the Tenzing Norgay bus terminal on Hill Cart Rd. It charges Rs 15 to send an email, Rs 15 to print a page and Rs 60 for 30 minutes of Internet use.

Permits Permits for Sikkim are available from Sikkim Tourism (☎ 432646) at the Sikkim Nationalised Transport (SNT) office, diagonally opposite the bus terminal. Sikkim Tourism is open from 10 am to 4 pm Monday to Saturday.

Places to Stay & Eat

There are dozens of hotels in town, many opposite the Tenzing Norgay central bus terminal on Hill Cart Rd (also known as Tenzing Norgay Rd). The budget hotels are generally friendlier and better value for money than those in Kolkata, and most have a noon checkout. The best places to eat are in the hotels, although you can get some cheap snacks on the footpath stalls and street-fronting restaurants in town – make sure the food is freshly cooked rather than reheated (to avoid nasty tummy upsets).

Rooms attract a 10% service charge plus another 10% if they're air-con (taxes are not included here).

The ***Siliguri Lodge*** *(☎ 533290, Hill Cart Rd)* has well-kept singles/doubles with shared bathroom for Rs 100/140. Rooms with private bathroom start at Rs 200 a double. A four-bed room with/without bathroom is Rs 350/200.

About 1km to the north on Hill Cart Rd is the ***WBTDC Mainak Tourist Lodge*** *(☎ 430986)*. Rooms are a little dark, but otherwise not too bad. Doubles range from Rs 500 to 1000 and there is a good restaurant here.

The no-frills but friendly Tibetan-run ***Hotel Chancellor*** *(☎ 432360)*, at the corner of Sevoke and Hill Cart Rds, has tiny, basic rooms with private bathroom (some with squat toilet). Rooms start at Rs 110/220. Be warned that the front rooms can cop a fair bit of traffic noise. There's no restaurant, but meals can be arranged.

The ***Hotel Vinayak*** *(☎ 431130, fax 531067, LM Moulik Complex, Hill Cart Rd)* is a good mid-range choice that also has some budget rooms. Rooms (doubles only) have private bathroom and range from Rs 350 to 950. Good food is available at the restaurant.

Friendly ***Hotel Rajdarbar*** *(☎ 534316, Hill Cart Rd)* has acceptable rooms with bathroom from Rs 275/350 and a generous 1 pm checkout. There's a nice little restaurant; fish masala costs Rs 40.

The calm ***Hotel Blue Star*** *(☎ 431550, 53 Hill Cart Rd)* is a splendid budget choice – cheerful and clean. Rooms with private bathroom cost from Rs 250/350. The restaurant serves Indian, continental and Chinese fare.

Opposite the Tenzing Norgay central bus terminal on Hill Cart Rd is the ***Hotel Mount View*** *(☎ 425919)* which has good-sized rooms, many with a fairyfloss pink paint job. Singles range from Rs 175 to 300, and doubles from Rs 250 to 400. It's quite a good choice, but you might have to get management to change the sheets and shake the TV to make it work. Tasty food is available at the plain-looking little restaurant. For more culinary variety, pop next door to the pleasant and efficient ***Khana Khazana*** restaurant, which has an assortment of Indian and Western food including some refreshing ice creams.

Hotel Heritage *(☎ 532510)*, nearby, has comfortable if somewhat drab doubles starting at Rs 400. Many rooms are carpeted, making them rather musty.

If strapped for cash, cheap possibilities in this area include the ***Delhi Hotel*** *(☎ 522 918)*, with OK rooms which start at Rs 100/

SILIGURI

To Darjeeling (80km)
National Hwy 31
To Hotel Marina, Bagdogra Airport (12km) & Kolkata (600km)
Siliguri Junction
Hill Cart (Tenzing Norgay) Rd
Mahananda River
To Hotel Cindrella (6km) & Kalimpong (70km)
Sevoke Rd
Bidhan Rd
Hospital Rd
Siliguri Town Train Station
To Kolkata (600km)
To Jalpaiguri (40km) & Haldibari (55km)
New Jalpaiguri (NJP) Train Station
0 0.5 1km
0 0.3 0.6mi
Approximate Scale

PLACES TO STAY & EAT
1 Hotel Sinclairs
2 WBTDC Mainak Tourist Lodge; Indian Airlines
5 Hotel Mount View; Khana Khazana; Hotel Heritage; Hotel Hindustan; TSA Guest House; Delhi Hotel; Biswadeep Communication
6 Siliguri Lodge
8 Hotel Rajdarbar
9 Hotel Air View Palace
12 Hotel Blue Star
14 Hotel Vinayak; Jet Airways
15 Hotel Chancellor
18 Hotel Holydon; Hotel Baydanath

OTHER
3 Assam Tourist Office
4 Tenzing Norgay Central Bus Terminal; Share Jeeps
7 Sikkim Nationalised Transport (SNT) Terminal; Sikkim Tourism
10 Share-Jeep Stand
11 State Bank of India
13 Taxi Stand
16 Main Post Office
17 Train Booking Office

150 with private bathroom (all with squat toilet); the ***Hotel Hindustan*** *(☎ 526571)* which has doubles with private bathroom (squat toilet) from Rs 250; and the similarly priced but slightly less impressive ***TSA Guest House*** *(☎/fax 432893)*.

The ***Hotel Air View Palace*** *(☎ 431542, 538337, Hill Cart Rd)* has clean doubles with private bathroom (some with squat toilet) starting at Rs 200/250, as well as a very good restaurant.

The three-star ***Hotel Sinclairs*** *(☎ 522674, fax 432743)*, 2km north of Tenzing Norgay central bus terminal, is a little faded around the edges these days but is certainly comfortable enough. Doubles cost Rs 1210. There's a foreign-exchange facility, swimming pool, bar and restaurant.

A better choice is the ***Hotel Cindrella*** *(☎ 547136, fax 430615, e cindrella@dte.vsnl.net.in, 3rd Mile, Sevoke Rd)*, which although lacking panache is away from the hustle and bustle (about 6km from the town centre). Facilities include a swimming pool, health club, money-exchange facility and travel desk. Rooms (all with air-con) start at Rs 2100/2300. The Web site at www.cindrellahotels.com is worth a look.

If you've got a flight to catch, an option near the airport is ***Hotel Marina*** *(☎ 551371)*, which has doubles with private bathroom for Rs 350. It's relatively quiet, has a restaurant, and provides free 'bed tea'. Rooms here can fill up mighty fast, so book ahead if possible. A taxi to/from the airport costs about Rs 100 (one way).

There are two good places near the NJP train station: ***Hotel Holydon*** *(☎ 564062)* has rooms with shared bathroom for Rs 100/160 and Rs 200/250 with private bathroom; next door is the similarly priced ***Hotel Baydanath***. Request a quiet room at both places.

Shopping

Siliguri is known for its caneware, and you'll find everything from letter racks to lounge suites. Though bulky, caneware is light and is easily shipped home.

The town also offers a reasonably good range of clothing, from the cheap and cheerful in the markets (and next to the taxi and bus stands), to designer label creations on Hill Cart Rd. Tailors and material vendors abound in the area around NJP train station, so even if you are not spending long in town before heading for the hills, you can have clothes made to measure at rock-bottom prices and pick them up on your return to the plains. Make sure you settle on a price before leaving your clothes to be tailored, to avoid an unpleasant scene when you come back to collect them.

Getting There & Away

Air Bagdogra airport is 12km west of Siliguri. The Indian Airlines office (☎ 431509) is in the grounds of the WBTDC Mainak Tourist Lodge (see Places to Stay earlier). It's open from 10 am to 1 pm and 2 to 5.30 pm daily. Indian Airlines has two flights a week between Siliguri (Bagdogra) and Kolkata (US$80, 55 mins) or Delhi (US$185, four hours), and two a week to Guwahati (US$50, 50 mins). Not all the flights to Delhi are direct, some backtrack to Guwahati first.

Jet Airways (☎ 435876) services the same destinations as Indian Airlines for the same fares, but the flight schedules are variable. The Jet Airways office (up a flight of stairs) is next to Hotel Vinayak (see Places to Stay earlier) and is open from 9 am to 6.30 pm daily.

Bus Most North Bengal State Transport Corporation (NBSTC) buses leave from the Tenzing Norgay central bus terminal. Private buses with services to hill regions (such as Darjeeling and Gangtok) also have counters at the terminal. Note that if you are travelling to Jorethang in West Sikkim, you will require a trekking permit (see the Permits section in the Sikkim chapter for details).

NBSTC buses for Darjeeling (Rs 45, three hours) depart hourly between 6.30 am and 3 pm. There's a bus at 7 am for Kalimpong (Rs 45, three hours), and frequent services for Mirik (Rs 25, 2½ hours). There are private buses to Kolkata, which leave at 6, 7 and 8 pm daily and cost Rs 210.

The 'Rocket' services to Kolkata also leave at 6, 7 and 8 pm (Rs 177, 12 hours). Other destinations include Malda (Rs 90, six hours), Berhampore (Rs 130, eight hours) and Patna (Rs 170, 12 hours). The bus to Patna leaves from a stand near the Tenzing Norgay central bus terminal.

For Guwahati in Assam, there's a NBSTC Rocket service from Tenzing Norgay central bus terminal at 5 pm (Rs 175, 12 hours).

SNT buses to Gangtok (Rs 60, five hours) leave the SNT terminal every hour between 7 am and 2 pm. There's also a deluxe bus, the *Sikkim Queen*, at 8 am and 1 pm (Rs 100).

To/From Nepal Local buses leave from in front of the Tenzing Norgay central bus terminal for Paniktanki (Rs 12, one hour), which is opposite the Nepali border town of Kakarbhitta. See the Darjeeling Getting There & Away section later in this chapter for more details.

Train The *Darjeeling Mail* leaves Sealdah (Kolkata) at 7.15 pm (12 hours, 570km). Tickets cost Rs 210/600 in 2nd/1st class. In the other direction the train leaves NJP train station at 7.20 pm, reaching Sealdah at around 8.30 am.

The *North East Express* is the fastest train to Delhi (33 hours, 1628km). It departs from NJP at 5.25 pm, travelling via Patna (16 hours, 636km). In the other direction this train continues to Guwahati (10 hours, 423km).

There's a train booking office at the junction of Hospital and Bidhan Rds. It's open from 8 am to 8 pm Monday to Saturday and until 2 pm on Sunday.

To/From Bangladesh For Bangladesh you can take a train from NJP to Haldibari, the Indian border checkpoint (Rs 20, two hours). From here it's a 7km walk along a disused train line to the Bangladesh border point at Chilahati, where there's a train station. See also the Land section in the introductory Getting There & Away chapter.

Toy Train Tickets for the toy train from Siliguri/New Jalpaiguri to Darjeeling can be purchased from NJP, Siliguri or Siliguri Junction train stations. As there are no advance reservations, it may be easier during the busy high season (from May to mid-July) to pick up tickets at NJP, where the train originates. When in operation, a daily service leaves at 8.30 am (also sometimes at 7.15 am during high season). The journey by steam engine takes an interminable nine hours to cover the 80km up to the hill station, or four hours to Kurseong, 30km short of Darjeeling (for more details see the Darjeeling Getting There & Away section).

Taxi & Jeep The fastest and most comfortable way of getting around the hills is by share-jeep. There are a number of taxi stands, including one on Sevoke Rd and one outside the Tenzing Norgay central bus terminal, where you can get share jeeps to destinations in the West Bengal Hills and Sikkim including Darjeeling (Rs 50, 2½ hours), Kalimpong (Rs 60, 2½ hours), Kurseong (Rs 30, two hours) and Gangtok (Rs 100, 4½ hours). Jeeps to Gangtok leave from the taxi stand opposite Sikkim Nationalised Transport.

Posted rates for a private taxi are: Darjeeling, Rs 750; Kalimpong, Rs 750; Mirik, Rs 500; Gangtok, Rs 1200; Malda, Rs 2000; Kolkata, Rs 6000; and Guwahati, Rs 4500. If you want to retain the car and driver, it will cost more (negotiate this with driver).

Getting Around

From the Tenzing Norgay central bus terminal on Hill Cart Rd to NJP train station a taxi/autorickshaw will cost about Rs 150/75. A cycle-rickshaw costs about Rs 20 for the 45-minute trip from NJP to Siliguri Junction, or Rs 20 to Tenzing Norgay bus terminal. There are infrequent bus services along this route (Rs 4).

A taxi between the Bagdogra airport and Siliguri costs about Rs 250. Alternatively, take a taxi to Bagdogra bazaar (Rs 100, 3km), and get a local bus from there into Siliguri (Rs 4, 9km).

JALDHAPARA WILDLIFE SANCTUARY

Although most visitors are keen to head for the hills after the commotion of Siliguri, it's worth making the 135km trip east to this rarely visited sanctuary. It protects 100 sq km of lush forests and grasslands, is cut by the wide Torsa River and is a refuge for the Indian one-horned rhinoceros *(Rhinoceros unicornis)*, which has come under serious threat from poachers.

The best time to visit is from mid-October to May, particularly in March to April when wild animals are attracted by the growth of new grasses. The sanctuary is closed during the monsoon (around 15 July to 15 October). Apart from about 35 rhinos, other animals found in the park environs include tigers (rarely seen), wild elephants and various deer. You can take elephant safaris from Hollong, inside the park. These trips cost Rs 70/140/65 for Indians/foreigners/students. The park entry fee is Rs 10/50 for Indians/foreigners and Rs 25 per vehicle. To use a still/video camera costs Rs 5/75.

The West Bengal tourist office (☎ 511 974) in Siliguri on Hill Cart Rd can organise tours to Jaldhapara – they leave the tourist office at noon on Saturday and return at 5 pm next day (Rs 1100/1575, Indians/foreigners, including an elephant ride, transport, accommodation and all meals).

Places to Stay & Eat

Within the park itself is the ***Hollong Forest Lodge*** with doubles for Indians/foreigners for Rs 425/850, plus a compulsory Rs 110/160 per person for breakfast, dinner and bed tea. Outside the park precincts at Madarihat is the ***Jaldhapara Tourist Lodge*** *(☎ 03563-62230)* where doubles start at Rs 525. Both of these places must be booked in advance through the West Bengal tourist office in Siliguri (☎ 511974), or at the West Bengal Tourism Centre in Kolkata.

Getting There & Away

From the Tenzing Norgay central bus terminal in Siliguri, buses ply the route to Madarihat, 9km from Jaldhapara (Rs 40, three hours). From here, a taxi to Hollong, inside the park, is Rs 250. To hire a taxi from Siliguri to Jaldhapara will cost about Rs 1200. The *Intercity Express* train leaves Siliguri at 6 am daily and arrives at Madarihat at about 9.30 am (Rs 35); it also leaves Siliguri at 5 pm and arrives at 8.30 pm. There are also deluxe/air-con buses for Rs 200/400 from Kolkata to Siliguri that take about 14 hours.

MIRIK

☎ 0354 • elevation 1767m

Promoted as a 'new' or 'minor' hill station, Mirik is about 50km from both Siliguri and Darjeeling. It is still fairly pristine and far less commercial than Darjeeling and other heavily publicised hill stations, making it a much more serene place to stay. There are some beautiful walks in this area, many of which are virtually devoid of *humanus touristicus*, which is itself a real attraction.

The artificial lake is the main attraction at Mirik (vendors on the bridge sell bread so you can feed the ravenous fish); there's a 3.5km path that meanders around it. The main tourist area lies to the south of the lake, in the area known as Krishnanagar.

While this is certainly a pretty spot surrounded by tea estates, orange orchards and cardamom plantations (the views from the top of the hill are stunning), ambitious plans to 'develop' the area for tourism threaten the tranquil ambience. Hopefully Mirik won't become a mini Darjeeling.

At the time of research there was nowhere to change foreign currency in Mirik, so come with enough rupees.

Things to See & Do

Perched high above the town is the small, brightly coloured **Bokar Gompa**. On the western side of the lake, about a 10-minute walk from the taxi stand and set among banana trees, are three small **Hindu temples** sacred to Hanuman, Kalamata (Durga as the Mother of Time) and Shiva.

Two/four-seater **boats** can be hired on the eastern side of the lake for Rs 30/40 for 30 minutes. A good way to see the sights is by **pony ride**. Half-day hire (three hours) costs between Rs 300 and Rs 400; a half/full round of the lake costs Rs 20/40; or it is Rs 60 to the Mirik (Swiss) Cottages (see Places to Stay & Eat following) at the top of the hill.

Mirik to Kurseong Day Trek

If you do not have time for a longer trek, or just want a taste of Himalayan village life in the West Bengal Hills, the trek from Mirik to Kurseong (seven to eight hours) may be your cup of tea.

A guide is essential because of the myriad trails in the last part of the walk. Guides can be arranged at the Mirik Tourist Lodge. Guides can also be arranged through the Darjeeling Gorkha Hill Council (DGHC) office or a trekking agency in Darjeeling.

The trail starts at the Genesis English School just past the Mirik Tourist Lodge. Heading out of town you will pass a number of schools. One kilometre from Mirik there are good views of Kanchenjunga. Continuing, you will pass through a number of small villages, stands of pine and bamboo, and orange groves, finally entering Murmah Tea Estate.

Walk through the tea estate, heading downhill, roughly following the ropeway (used to carry tea and supplies to and from the estate). A few villages later you will reach the river. Only ford the river if the water level is low, and only with an experienced guide: It is better to cross the bridge that is visible 1km upstream and then backtrack.

After crossing the river, head up the tributary for 500m, then up the steep hill on the right-hand side. Stop for a 'Darjeeling' chai and biscuits in the village of Khomara atop the hill. From the teahouse you have excellent views back across the valley you have just traversed.

There are two main routes to Kurseong from here. The right-hand track is shorter but takes you through less villages. We took the left-hand trail. Again, you walk through a number of tea estates interspersed with villages and pockets of forest. From the Singell Tea Estate follow the jeep track, taking short cuts when you can, and you will emerge on the main Darjeeling to Kurseong road. Turn right for Kurseong (roughly 1km away) or left for Darjeeling. You may be lucky and catch a jeep or minibus to Kurseong or even back to Darjeeling.

Martin Bradshaw

Places to Stay & Eat

Places to stay in Mirik are homey and unpretentious, which is what makes them so appealing. There are places to eat in the hotels and also in the centre.

Down a small lane opposite the State Bank of India is the quaint ***Lodge Ashirvad*** *(☎ 43272)*. Downstairs doubles with shared bathroom are Rs 130; upstairs doubles with private bathroom start at Rs 200. There are separate kitchen facilities for self-caterers.

Lodge Panchashil *(☎ 43284)* is delightfully down-to-earth, with small but cheerful singles/doubles with bathroom (some with squat toilets) for Rs 120/150, doubles for Rs 150 and triples for Rs 200. The manager is friendly, and there's a good rooftop terrace.

Hotel Mhelung *(☎ 43300, Samendu Complex)* is also beautifully homey and all rooms have polished timber floors. Rooms range from Rs 450 to 800.

Hotel Jagdeet *(☎ 43359)*, on the main road, is more upmarket than other places and has comfortable doubles with bathroom from Rs 650 to 1600; a family room is Rs 1200 (maximum eight people).

Slightly further afield, but within easy walking distance of the lake, is the ***Mirik Tourist Lodge*** *(☎ 42237)* which underwent renovation at the time of writing. Doubles with bathroom are expected to cost Rs 550.

Also undergoing vigorous renovation was the ***Mirik (Swiss) Cottages*** *(☎ 43612)*, which consists of 12 hilltop two-storey cottages affording glorious views of the township and surrounding countryside including Kanchenjunga. Rates are pegged at around Rs 1500 per cottage (each can accommodate four people).

Getting There & Away

Buses to Darjeeling leave frequently each day (Rs 30, three hours), and there are buses to Siliguri (Rs 25, 2½ hours). Tickets can be purchased from the wooden shack next to the Restaurant Liberty, near the lake shore.

There are no share taxis to Darjeeling. A private taxi to Darjeeling or Siliguri will cost about Rs 650.

KURSEONG

Kurseong (1458m) is 51km north of Siliguri and 30km south of Darjeeling. The name is said to be derived from the Lepcha word, *kurson-rip*, a reference to the small white orchid prolific in this area. It has a peaceful atmosphere and, like Mirik, is not nearly as commercial as tourist-laden Darjeeling. There are several good **walks** in the area, including one to Eagle's Crag that affords splendid views down over the Teesta River and the southern plains, and a four-hour walk along the ridge and through unspoilt forest to Ghoom.

The ***Kurseong Tourist Lodge*** *(☎ 0354-44409)* has large rooms for Rs 600 a double. Meals are also available here.

There are buses to Darjeeling (Rs 30, 2½ hours) and Siliguri (Rs 30, 2½ hours). The toy train from Siliguri to Kurseong takes about four hours (when it is running).

DARJEELING

☎ 0354 • pop 83,000

Straddling a ridge at 2134m and surrounded by tea plantations, Darjeeling has been a popular hill station since the British established it as a rest and recreation centre for their troops in the mid-19th century. Indians and foreigners still come here in droves to escape the heat, humidity and hassle of the North Indian plain, and to explore Buddhist monasteries, visit tea plantations, ride on a cable car, hunt for bargains in handicraft shops and arrange short hikes, longer treks or rafting trips. You get an indication of how popular Darjeeling is from the 100 or so hotels recognised by the tourist office, and the scores of others that don't come up to their requirements or that haven't even applied for status.

In Darjeeling, you'll find yourself surrounded by mountain people from all over the eastern Himalaya who have come to work or trade, or – in the case of many Tibetans – seek refuge. Mother Teresa spent her early years as a nun here with the sisters at Loreto Convent; and writer and naturalist Gerald Durrell was educated at the prestigious St Joseph's School at North Point.

The peak (tourist) seasons – from mid-March to the end of May, and mid-September to mid-November – are when organised tours are more likely to be available and accommodation prices are higher. For mountain views, the best time to visit is mid-September to mid-December. During the monsoon (June to September), clouds obscure the mountains and the rain is often so heavy that whole sections of the road are washed away, but the town is rarely cut off for more than a few days at a time.

Christmas is a delightful time. Christmas trees, decorations, open fires and strolling carol singers are the norm for several days, all contributing to the feel of a European or North American Christmas. There is something rather poignant about hearing *Silent Night*, among other popular carols, sung in Nepali and played on local instruments.

History

Until the beginning of the 18th century, the area between the present borders of Sikkim and the plains of Bengal, including Darjeeling and Kalimpong, belonged to the rajas (kings) of Sikkim. In 1706, Kalimpong was lost to the Bhutanese, and the remainder was wrested from them by the Gurkhas who invaded Sikkim from Nepal in 1780.

The annexations by the Gurkhas, however, brought them into conflict with the British East India Company. A series of battles were fought between the two parties, eventually leading to the defeat of the Gurkhas and the ceding of all the land they had taken from the Sikkimese to the British East India Company. Part of this territory was restored to the rajas of Sikkim, and the country's sovereignty guaranteed by the British, in return for British control over any disputes that arose with neighbouring states.

One dispute in 1828 led to the dispatch of two British officers to the area, and during their fact-finding tour they spent some time at Darjeeling. (It was then called Dorje Ling, meaning Place of the Thunderbolt, after the lama who founded the monastery that once stood on Observatory Hill.) The officers

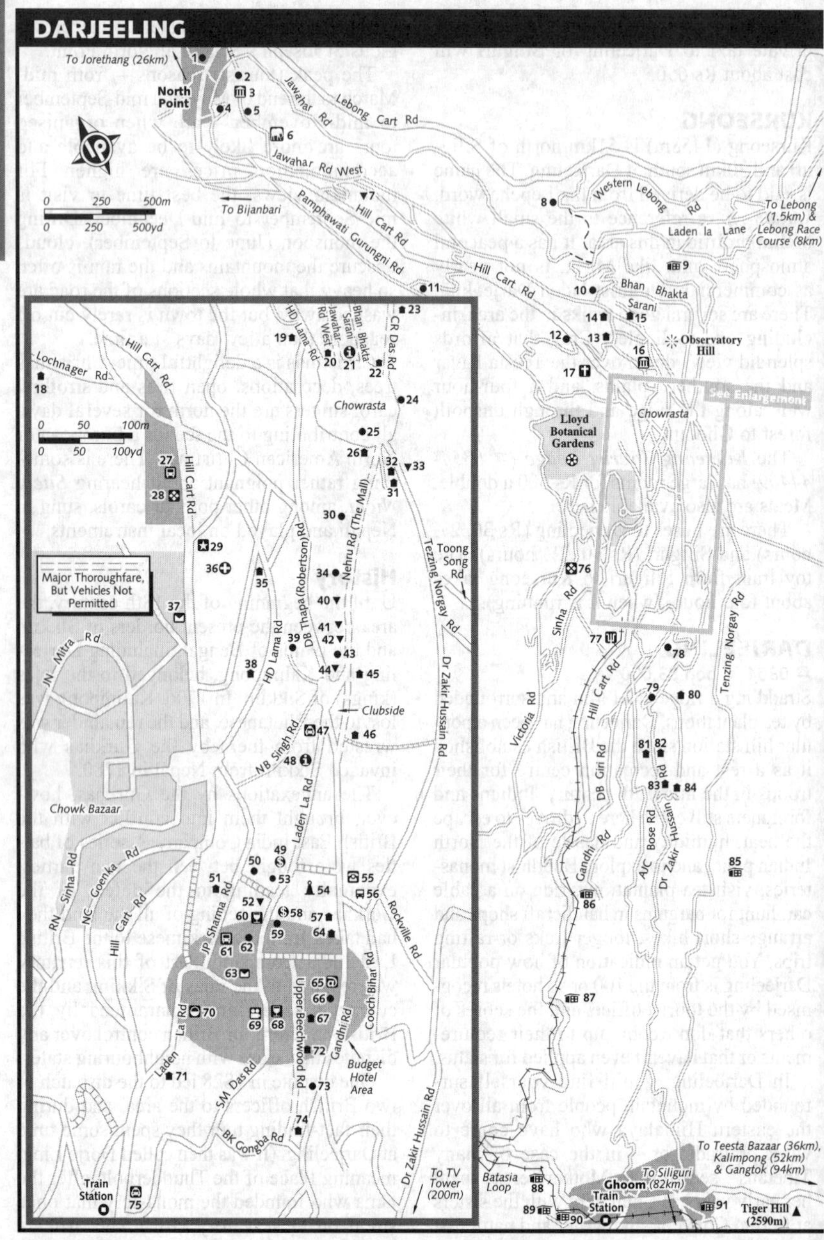
DARJEELING
To Jorethang (26km)
North Point
Jawahar Rd
Lebong Cart Rd
Jawahar Rd West
To Bijanbari
Hill Cart Rd
Pamphawati Gurungni Rd
Western Lebong Rd
To Lebong (1.5km) & Lebong Race Course (8km)
Laden la Lane
Bhan Bhakta Sarani
Observatory Hill
See Enlargement
Chowrasta
Lloyd Botanical Gardens
Sinha Rd
Victoria Rd
Tenzing Norgay Rd
DB Giri Rd
Gandhi Rd
AJC Bose Rd
Dr Zakir Hussain Rd
To Teesta Bazaar (36km), Kalimpong (52km) & Gangtok (94km)
To Siliguri (82km)
Ghoom
Train Station
Batasia Loop
Tiger Hill (2590m)
0 250 500m
0 250 500yd
Lochnager Rd
HD Lama Rd
Jawahar Rd West
Bhan Bhakta Sarani
CR Das Rd
Chowrasta
0 50 100m
0 50 100yd
Nehru Rd (The Mall)
DB Thapa (Robertson) Rd
Toong Song Rd
Tenzing Norgay Rd
Dr Zakir Hussain Rd
Major Thoroughfare, But Vehicles Not Permitted
IN Mitra Rd
Laden La Rd
Clubside
NB Singh Rd
Chowk Bazaar
RN Sinha Rd
NC Goenka Rd
JP Sharma Rd
Rockville Rd
Cooch Bihar Rd
Upper Beechwood Rd
Gandhi Rd
Budget Hotel Area
Laden La Rd
SM Das Rd
BK Gongba Rd
To TV Tower (200m)
Train Station

PLACES TO STAY
13 Maple Tourist Lodge
14 Mayfair Hill Resort
15 Darjeeling Tourist Lodge; Darjeeling Gymkhana Club
18 Hotel New Garden
19 New Elgin
20 Hotel Alice Villa
22 Windamere Hotel
23 Classic Guest House
26 Pineridge Hotel; Pineridge Travels
31 Main (Old) Bellevue Hotel
32 Bellevue Hotel; Tourist Bureau; Indian Airlines Office
35 Mohit Hotel; Moneychanger
38 Hotel Seven Seventeen; Moneychanger; Tibetan Medical & Astro Institute
45 The Darjeeling Club (The Planters); D&DMA Nursing Home
46 Hotel Dekeling; Kunga Restaurant
51 Hotel Tshering Denzongpa; Rhythm Internet Cafe
57 Hotel Springburn
64 Hotel Fairmont
67 Hotel Pagoda
71 Hotel Red Rose; Cyber Cafe
72 Hotel Shamrock
74 Hotel Hemadrie
80 Tower View Lodge & Restaurant
81 Triveni Guest House & Restaurant
82 Aliment Hotel & Restaurant
83 Tenzing Norgay Youth Hostel
84 Andy's Guest House

PLACES TO EAT
7 Hot Stimulating Cafe
33 Stardust Restaurant; Police Assistance Booth
40 Glenary's Restaurant, Bakery & Bar
41 Frank Ross Cafe
42 Hasty Tasty
44 Keventer's Snack Bar
52 Park Restaurant; Hayden Hall; Third Eye

OTHER
1 St Joseph's School
2 Darjeeling Rangeet Valley Ropeway Station
3 Himalayan Mountaineering Institute
4 Snow Leopard Breeding Centre
5 Himalayan Nature Interpetation Centre
6 Padmaja Naidu Himalayan Zoological Park
8 Tibetan Refugee Self-Help Centre
9 Bhutia Busty Gompa
10 Raj Bhavan (Government House)
11 Happy Valley Tea Estate
12 Office of the District Magistrate
16 Bengal Natural History Museum
17 Loreto Convent & Catholic Church
21 DGHC Tourism Office
24 Pony Stand
25 Oxford Book & Stationery Company
27 Chowk Bazaar Bus/Jeep Station
28 Old Super Market Complex; Kasturi Tours & Travels Office; Diamond Treks Tours & Travels Office
29 Police Station
30 Souvenir Shops
34 Das Studios
36 Sadar Hospital
37 Post Office
39 Manjushree Centre of Tibetan Culture
43 Trek-Mate Tours Office
47 Clubside Taxi Stand; Pool Cafe; Juniper Tours & Travels Office
48 Tourist Assistance Booth
49 Standard Chartered Grindlays Bank
50 Clubside Tours & Travels Office
53 Foreigners' Registration Office
54 Clock Tower
55 Telegraph Office
56 Jeep/Taxi Stand (to Siliguri)
58 State Bank of India
59 Samsara Tours, Travels & Treks Office
60 Golden Dragon Restaurant & Bar
61 Darjeeling Motor Service Co (Buses to Sikkim)
62 Nathmull's Tea Rooms (Merchants)
63 Head Post Office
65 Compuset Centre
66 Himalayan Travels Office
68 Joey's Pub
69 Rink Cinema; Video Parlours
70 Darjeeling Transport Corp (Jeeps to Gangtok)
73 Tibetan Refugee Self-Help Centre (Head Office)
75 Taxi Stand (for Ghoom)
76 DGHC Lowis Jubilee Complex
77 Dhirdham Mandir; Maa Singha Mandir
78 Nepali Girls' Social Service Centre
79 TV Tower
85 Aloobari Gompa
86 Samdrub Dargye Choling Gompa
87 Thupten Sangag Choling Gompa
88 Samten Choling Gompa
89 Yiga Choling Gompa
90 Sakya Choling Gompa
91 Phin Choling Gompa

were quick to appreciate Darjeeling's value as a site for a sanatorium and hill station, and as the key to a pass into Nepal and Tibet.

When the British arrived in Darjeeling, it was almost completely forested and virtually uninhabited. Development was rapid and by 1840 a sanatorium, hotel, roads and houses had been built. By 1857, Darjeeling had a population of about 10,000.

The population increase was due mainly to the recruitment of Nepali labourers to work the tea plantations established in the early 1840s. Even today, the vast majority of people speak Nepali as a first language, and the name 'Darjeeling' continues to be synonymous with tea.

The immigration of Nepali-speakers (mainly Gurkhas) into the mountainous areas of West Bengal eventually led to political problems, including the call for the separate state of Gorkhaland in the mid-1980s. Resentment had been growing among the Gurkhas over what they felt was discrimination against them by the government of West Bengal. For example, their language was not recognised by the Indian constitution and government jobs were only open to those who could speak Bengali. In 1986 (and to a lesser extent in the late 1990s), riots were orchestrated by the Gurkha National Liberation Front (GNLF) in Darjeeling.

A compromise was hammered out in late 1988 whereby the GNLF and the new Darjeeling Gorkha Hill Council (DGHC) were given a large measure of autonomy from the state government. However, the GNLF's reluctance to promote secession led to the formation of the breakaway Gorkhaland Liberation Organisation (GLO) in 1990.

In late 2000, the local media reported the official formation of an armed group linked to the GLO in Darjeeling and Kalimpong. No other details were available at the time of research, but it would be prudent to read local newspapers to determine if this or any other similar group is carrying out any violent activities in the region.

Orientation

Darjeeling sprawls over a west-facing ridge, spilling down the hillside in a complicated series of interconnecting roads and flights of steps. The town centre is Chowrasta, with the statue of Bhanu Bhakta Agharya, a Nepali poet, at the upper (north-eastern) end. From Chowrasta, a series of paths head north and north-east, and Nehru Rd (still generally referred to as The Mall) heads south-west and joins Laden La and Gandhi Rds at a junction called Clubside.

The main road through the lower (north-western) part of town is Hill Cart Rd, which links Ghoom with Darjeeling and passes the Darjeeling train station and the Chowk Bazaar bus/jeep station. Confusingly, Hill Cart Rd is also sometimes called Tenzing Norgay Rd, despite this also being the name of a long road to the south-east.

Information

Tourist Offices The Tourist Bureau (☎ 54 050), run by the West Bengal government, is below the Bellevue Hotel at Chowrasta. Staff are helpful and can offer up-to-date pamphlets and a map of Darjeeling. It is open from 10 am to 4.30 pm weekdays. In the peak season, useful tourist booths are also opened up around town, including at Clubside.

The DGHC Tourism Office (☎ 54214, ⓔ dghctourism@hotmail.com) is virtually opposite Hotel Alice Villa, and is accessible from either HD Lama Rd or Jawahar Rd West. Open from 8 am to 6 pm daily, it's the place to arrange an organised tour, a rafting trip or (maybe) a bus to the airport, but staff are not very helpful. The DGHC also has a tourist counter (☎ 0353-450714) at the Bagdogra airport near Siliguri, and at the train station in Darjeeling; the Web site at www.darjeelingtourism.com may be useful.

Another handy private site is at www.darjnet.com which has information about Darjeeling and Kalimpong.

Money The Standard Chartered Grindlays Bank (SCB Grindlays) and the State Bank of India (SBI) are both on Laden La Rd, and are open from 10 am to 3 pm weekdays. Incredibly, SCB Grindlays does not change cash; it *only* changes travellers cheques (of most major currencies and brands), and charges an outrageous Rs 200 fee per transaction. It also offers cash advances against Visa Card, with no commission.

The SBI only changes cash in US dollars and pounds sterling, and travellers cheques issued by American Express (in US dollars) and Thomas Cook (in US dollars and in pounds sterling). The commission rate is only Rs 20 for amounts of less than Rs 5000 and Rs 25 for amounts of more than Rs 5000.

The moneychangers at both Hotel Seven Seventeen on HD Lama Rd and at Pineridge Travels (at the Pineridge Hotel) at Chowrasta change major currencies in cash and travellers cheques.

Post & Communications The Head Post Office on Laden La Rd has poste restante. A smaller post office is located in the Chowk Bazaar market.

Internet centres are springing up all over Darjeeling, but most centres only have two or three computers (so demand often exceeds supply) and connections in this part of India are notoriously slow and unreliable.

The following Internet centres charge about Rs 1.25 per minute: Cyber Cafe, in the Hotel Red Rose on Laden La Rd, is always crowded with waiting customers; Compuset Centre, on Gandhi Rd, has several computers and starts charging when a connection to Hotmail (or whatever) is made; and Rhythm Internet Cafe, near Hotel Tshering Denzongpa on JP Sharma Rd, has great Western music in the background.

Trekking & Travel Agencies There is a plethora of travel agencies in Darjeeling, and can arrange personalised local tours (see Organised Tours later in this section), and some can arrange treks, rafting trips and other interesting activities. A few of the more reliable agencies include the following:

Clubside Tours & Travels (☎ 54646, ⓔ clubside@dte.vsnl.net.in) JP Sharma Rd. Arranges treks and tours in northern Bengal, Sikkim and Assam, and specialises in wildlife tours in the north-eastern states.

Diamond Treks, Tours & Travels (☎ 53467) Old Super Market Complex, Hill Cart Rd. Has been operating for many years, and can arrange treks in Sikkim and luxury buses to Nepal.

Himalayan Travels (☎ 55405, ⓔ kkgurung@cal.vsnl.net.in) 18 Gandhi Rd. Also has many years experience arranging treks and mountaineering expeditions in Darjeeling and Sikkim.

Juniper Tours & Travels (☎ 52095, fax 52625) Clubside. One of several nearby agencies that offers a range of local and regional tours.

Kasturi Tours & Travels (☎ 53468, fax 54430) Old Super Market Complex, Hill Cart Rd. Organises tours to Kathmandu, Gangtok and Bhutan, and luxury buses to Nepal.

Samsara Tours, Travels & Treks (☎ 56370, ⓔ samsara@dte.vsnl.net.in) Laden La Rd. This very helpful and knowledgeable agency can also book rafting trips and may offer treks in the future.

Trek-Mate Tours (☎ 74092, ⓔ odyssey@dte.vsnl.net.in) Singalila Arcade, Nehru Rd. Offers budget-priced treks around Sikkim, Nepal and Darjeeling.

Anyone can hire trekking gear from Tenzing Norgay Youth Hostel (see Places to Stay – Budget later in this section), subject to a deposit to cover the value of the articles borrowed (the deposit is returned, less hire charges, on return of the equipment). The DGHC Lowis Jubilee Complex, on Dr SK Pal Rd, also rents out trekking equipment – ie, sleeping bags and day-pack – at good prices. Some travel agencies, such as Trek-Mate Tours, rent equipment to customers, and some of the budget hotels around the TV Tower area do the same for guests.

Photography Several photographic shops along Nehru Rd sell print and slide film, and can reliably and cheaply process print film (but not slide film) within 24 hours. These shops also stock compact discs of Western, Indian and Nepali music, and sell gifts and souvenirs, such as photographic prints. Das Studios is probably the best.

Bookshops The Oxford Book & Stationery Company at Chowrasta is unquestionably the best bookshop in Darjeeling. Open until late into the evening (so there's plenty of time for browsing), it sells a comprehensive selection of books about, and maps of, Tibet, Nepal, Sikkim, Bhutan and the Himalaya.

Emergency There are several well-stocked pharmacies along Nehru Rd. D&DMA Nursing Home (☎ 54327), next to The Darjeeling Club at Clubside, is the best private hospital. The public Sadar Hospital (☎ 54 218) is down some steps from HD Lama Rd. An alternative is the Tibetan Medical & Astro Institute, under Hotel Seven Seventeen on HD Lama Rd. It's open from 9 am to noon and 2 to 4 pm weekdays.

The police station (☎ 52193) is on Hill Cart Rd, and there's a Police Assistance Booth near Stardust Restaurant at Chowrasta.

Other useful emergency numbers are Fire Brigade ☎ 52121 and Ambulance ☎ 52131.

Permits If you're entering western Sikkim from Darjeeling, you'll need a permit (see the Sikkim chapter for details), which can be obtained in Darjeeling. Firstly, visit the Office of the District Magistrate (ODM) on Hill Cart Rd. If walking, take Bishop Eric Benjamin Rd from Chowrasta and veer left at the fork (the right-hand road goes to the museum). At the Maple Tourist Lodge, keep zigzagging down and to the left along Kuchery Rd. When you first see Hill Cart Rd, walk straight ahead (don't turn left) and look for the large blue 'Office of the District Magistrate' sign. Alternatively, take a share-taxi from the Chowk Bazaar bus/jeep station.

At the ODM, find the entrance (at the back of the main building), go upstairs and look for the 'Sikkim Permit' sign. At the counter, which is open from 11 am to 1 pm and 2.30 to 4 pm weekdays, fill out a form and get it stamped. Then traipse back up to the Foreigners' Registration Office on Laden La Rd, which is open from 10 am to 5.30 pm daily, and get the form stamped again. Finally, return to the ODM, where your permit can be obtained while you wait. The paperwork takes about 15 minutes; the walking back and forth, about 45 minutes.

Tea Plantations

Tea is, of course, Darjeeling's most famous export. From its 80 gardens, employing over 40,000 people, the region produces the bulk of West Bengal's crop – almost a quarter of India's total. About 80% of Darjeeling tea is exported; the domestic market is quite small. Darjeeling tea is mild, and most Indians prefer the bracing jolt afforded by the stronger teas produced in Assam.

The most convenient tea plantation is the Happy Valley Tea Estate. Here, tea is still produced by the 'orthodox' method rather than the 'curling, tearing and crushing' method used on the plains. However, it is only worth visiting when plucking and processing is in progress (April to November). The estate is open 8 am to noon and 1 to 4.30 pm daily except Sunday. An employee will whisk you around the factory and then demand an outrageous sum for his trouble; about Rs 20 per person is appropriate. The turn-off to the estate is about 500m down past the ODM, look out for the green sign.

Tiger Hill

The highest spot in the area (2590m) is Tiger Hill, 11km from Darjeeling near Ghoom. The hill affords magnificent dawn views over Kanchenjunga and other eastern Himalayan peaks – but only if it's not cloudy. It can be very cold and very crowded at the top, but coffee is available.

Every day in, um, 'peak' season, a convoy of battered jeeps leaves Darjeeling at about 4.30 am for the 'sunrise trip' to Tiger Hill. Tickets for these trips (usually with a detour to Batasia Loop on the way back) can be purchased at the DGHC Tourism Office, or from one of the abundant travel agencies around town. It's also easy enough to jump on a jeep going to Tiger Hill from along Gandhi or Laden La Rds between 4 and 4.30 am.

Anyone for Tea?

Although the region offers the right climatic conditions for producing fine tea bushes, the final result depends on a complex drying process. After picking, the fresh green leaves are placed 15cm to 25cm deep in a 'withering trough' where the moisture content is reduced from between 70% and 80% to between 30% and 40% using high-velocity fans. The withered leaves are then rolled and pressed to break the cell walls and express their juices onto the surface of the leaves. Normally, two rollings at different pressures are undertaken, and in between rolls the leaves are sifted to separate the coarse from the fine. The leaves, coated with their juices, are then allowed to ferment on racks in a high-humidity room, a process which develops their characteristic aroma and flavour. This fermentation must be controlled carefully since either over- or under-fermentation will ruin the tea. This process is stopped by passing the leaves through a dry air chamber at round 120°C on a conveyer belt to further reduce the moisture content to around 2% to 3%. The last process is the sorting of the tea into grades. In order of value they are Golden Flowery Orange Pekoe (unbroken leaves), Golden Broken Orange Pekoe, Orange Fannings and Dust (the last three consisting of broken leaves).

In the last few years, modern agricultural practices have improved the viability of the Darjeeling tea estates. The tea plantations were one of the first agricultural enterprises to use clonal plants in their replanting schemes, although most of the tea trees are at least 100 years old and nearing the end of their useful or even natural lives. The ageing plants and deteriorating soil causes grave concerns, because tea not only earns the country valuable export revenue but also provides much employment in the area. With the collapse of the USSR, the Darjeeling tea planters lost their best customers and had to look for new markets. Some have simply switched to growing cardamom, which is more profitable.

Despite the difficulties, tea from some estates in the Darjeeling region is of very high quality: the highest price ever paid for tea is US$220 per kg, for tea from the local Castleton Estate.

Margaret's Hope estate on the road to Kurseong produces the tea that eventually finds its way to Buckingham Palace. The estate's name came about from a rather sad story: An English tea planter took his daughter to England to be educated, but she was not happy there. Her one wish was to return to Darjeeling and the mountains, but she died before she could ever return. In her memory, her father named his property Margaret's Hope.

This allows you to check possible cloud cover (by seeing if the stars are out) before deciding to go. A one-way/return trip costs about Rs 45/60.

The early start and discomfort are compensated for by the spectacular vision of a 250km stretch of the Himalayan massifs, with, from left to right, Lhotse (8501m) flanked by Everest (8848m) and Makalu (8475m), then an apparent gap before the craggy Kokang (5505m), flanked by Janu (7710m), Rathong (6630m), the apparently flat summit of Kabru (7338m), Kanchenjunga (8598m), Pandim (6691m), Simvo (6811m) and the cone-like Siniolchu (5780m).

Some people take the jeep one way to Tiger Hill and then walk back to Darjeeling. However, to avoid the awful traffic along the main road it's better to walk back as far as Batasia Loop, and visit a few gompas along the way, and then catch a bus or jeep to Darjeeling. See the boxed text 'Trekking & Hiking Around Darjeeling' later in this section for more information.

To avoid the early start from Darjeeling, stay at the ***Tourist Lodge***. It offers reasonable dorm beds for Rs 100 per person, including breakfast and an evening meal.

Mountain Views

At 8598m, Kanchenjunga is the world's third-highest mountain, and the biggest in India. The name 'Kanchenjunga' is derived from the Tibetan words for Big Five-peaked Snow Fortress or Big Five-peaked Treasury of the Snow (depending on who you ask). Some of the best spots around Darjeeling for views of Kanchenjunga and other mountains (if it's not cloudy or foggy), apart from Tiger Hill, are the several lookouts along Bhanu Bhakta Sarani, Observatory Hill (though some views are blocked by trees) and the roof of Keventer's Snack Bar at Clubside.

Observatory Hill

This place is sacred to both Hindus and Buddhists. Hindus visit **Mahakala Mandir**, dedicated to Mahakala (see Bhutia Busty Gompa following) and located in a small cave down some stairs from the hill. Buddhists believe Mahakala was an incarnation of Padmasambhava, who established Buddhism in Tibet under the Nyingmapa order; the hill was also once the site of the Dorje Ling monastery (from which Darjeeling got its name).

The multicoloured prayer flags double as trapezes for monkeys which can be aggressive. The steps leading to the hill are not entirely obvious; they start about 300m on the left along Bhan Bhakta Sarani from Chowrasta.

Gompas

Bhutia Busty Gompa This very colourful monastery, with Kanchenjunga providing a spectacular backdrop, was originally a branch of the Nyingmapa order's Phodong Gompa in Sikkim, before it was transferred to Darjeeling in 1879. (The shrine here originally stood on Observatory Hill.) The gompa houses a library of Buddhist texts, including an original copy of the *Tibetan Book of the Dead*, and a fine mural depicting Mahakala, a wrathful Tantric deity with its roots in the Hindu god, Mahakali. You will, however, need permission from the caretaker to see the mural.

Follow CR Das Rd for about 800m from Chowrasta, and then head down to the right at the fork in the road; the monastery comes into view within a few hundred metres.

Yiga Choling Gompa This is probably the most famous monastery in the region. Although originally built in 1875 by a Mongolian lama for the Gelukpa order, it now also houses lamas of the Nyingmapa order. The gompa enshrines an image of the Maitreya Buddha (Future Buddha), which has a Western posture (seated with hands on his knees rather than in the traditional lotus position) and has blue eyes. (Buddhists believe the next Buddha will appear in the West, hence these Western manifestations.) The gompa also houses a very fine image of Mahakala.

Foreigners are allowed to enter the shrine and take photographs, but a small donation is customary. As Ghoom is often swathed in mists, and the monastery is old and dark, the gompa is sometimes affectionately called the 'Gloom Monastery'.

The gompa is below Hill Cart Rd and the Ghoom train station. From Darjeeling, take a shared jeep or the toy train, or visit the gompa on the way back from Tiger Hill (see the Tiger Hill section earlier).

Other Gompas There are three other gompas in Ghoom: the very large, but relatively uninteresting, **Samten Choling Gompa** (Gelukpa order) with its 8m-high stupa dedicated to Lama Anagarika Govinda; the smaller **Sakya Choling Gompa** (Sakyapa order), which has a small institute for the study of Buddhist philosophy; and the little-known **Phin Choling Gompa**.

About halfway between Ghoom and Darjeeling is **Thupten Sangag Choling Gompa** (Drukpa sect), inaugurated by the Dalai Lama in 1992. Westerners interested in Tibetan Buddhism often study here. Closer to Darjeeling, and along the same road, is the opulent **Samdrub Dargye Choling Gompa**, established in 1964. It is presided over by the second Kaloo Rinpoche.

Aloobari Gompa, along Tenzing Norgay Rd, also welcomes visitors. The monks – who are from the Yolmo sect – often sell Tibetan and Sikkimese handicrafts and religious objects (usually hand bells). If the monastery is closed, ask someone at the cottage next door to let you in.

Padmaja Naidu Himalayan Zoological Park

This zoo was established in 1958 to study, conserve and preserve Himalayan fauna. It houses India's only collection of (massive) Siberian tigers, some rare species including Himalayan black bears, and red pandas and Tibetan wolves (the zoo has had great success in breeding these last two). Compared with other zoos in India, the animals are reasonably well cared for by dedicated keepers.

Inside the park is the **Himalayan Nature Interpretation Centre**. This tacky indoor sound-and-light show can be avoided. Tickets to this cost an extra Rs 5.

The zoo is a pleasant 30-minute walk down from Chowrasta along Jawahar Rd West; alternatively, take a share-taxi from the Chowk Bazaar bus/jeep station. The zoo is open from 8 am to 4.30 pm daily except Thursday. Entry is Rs 5 and an extra Rs 5/200 for still/video cameras.

Tenzing Norgay

Tenzing Norgay, who conquered Everest with Edmund Hillary in 1953, lived in Darjeeling, and was the director of the Himalayan Mountaineering Institute for many years. He died in 1986, but the climbing tradition of the Tenzings lives on: his eldest daughter, Pem Pen, was a climber of some note; his son, Jamling, climbed Everest in 1996; and his granddaughter climbed it a year later.

Himalayan Mountaineering Institute (HMI)

India's most prestigious mountaineering institute was founded in 1954. It boasts the **Mountaineering Museum**, with a collection of historic mountaineering equipment, specimens of Himalayan flora and fauna and a relief model of the Himalaya showing the principal peaks. There is also a display of badges and pins of mountaineering clubs around the world, and examples of the traditional dress of hill tribes of the Himalaya.

Next door, the very interesting **Everest Museum** traces the history of attempts on the highest peak, with photographs and biographies of all the 'summiteers'.

The HMI is located within (and only accessible through) the zoo, and has the same opening hours and admission fees. Next to the museums, there are a few ***chai stalls*** and a souvenir shop, and above it stands the **Tenzing Samadhi** statue.

Snow Leopard Breeding Centre

The snow leopards *(Panthera uncia)* were originally housed in the zoo but, due to the disturbance of visitors and the proximity of other animals, breeding was largely unsuccessful. Pairs of these rare and beautiful animals are now housed in a large separate enclosure, and this has made all the difference. However, most visitors may just be

Fight for Survival

The beautiful snow leopards can be found across the entire Indian Himalaya, from Kashmir in the west to Bhutan to the east; to the north, they're found in Tibet, Central Asia and the Altai mountains in Mongolia. Due to the inaccessibility of the terrain and the high altitudes of their habitats (reaching over 3600m), it's almost impossible to be accurate about the number of snow leopards in the wild, but it's estimated to be between 4000 and 5000. The snow leopard is a highly endangered and protected species, but tragically the smuggling of leopard pelts continues.

In captivity, snow leopards live approximately 14 years. Females have two breeding cycles per year, but are more likely to conceive in the winter cycle. The gestation period is from 92 to 100 days, and there are usually two cubs per litter, although this can be up to five in the wild.

While it is distressing to see these magnificent animals in cages, it's a sad fact that programs, such as the Snow Leopard Breeding Centre in Darjeeling, significantly enhance the snow leopard's prospects for survival as a species. This project commenced in 1986 with two leopards brought from Switzerland.

The International Snow Leopard Trust, which controls all breeding programs, was founded in the early 1970s. For further information contact The Conservation Education Director (☎ 206-632 2421, fax 632 3967, ⓔ islt@serv.net), International Snow Leopard Trust, 4649 Sunnyside Ave Nth, Seattle, Washington 98103, USA.

disappointed. Though you can get a lot closer to the leopards' cages, the centre is little more than an extension of the zoo.

The centre is a further 10 minutes' walk along Jawahar Rd West from the entrance to the zoo. Otherwise, take a shared taxi from the Chowk Bazaar bus/jeep station and ask to be dropped off at the access road, which is not signposted along Hill Cart Rd. The centre is open from 8 am to 4 pm daily except Thursday. Tickets cost Rs 10.

Darjeeling Rangeet Valley Ropeway

India's first 'ropeway' or cable car (☎ 70231) connects North Point with Tukvar village, about 1.2km across the Rangeet Valley. It's an exhilarating ride, although a little scary if windy and pointless if the clouds or fog are thick. The return trip (including insurance) costs Rs 55, and takes about 50 minutes. The ropeway operates from about 10 am to 5 pm daily.

You can get off at Tukvar, but there's nothing more than a few simple ***cafes*** and ***bars***. The starting point is about 15 minutes' walk along Hill Cart Rd from the zoo, or you can take a shared jeep to North Point from the Chowk Bazaar bus/jeep station.

Tibetan Refugee Self-Help Centre

This centre was established in 1959 to help rehabilitate Tibetan refugees who fled from Tibet with the Dalai Lama following the Chinese invasion.

It now comprises a home for the aged, as well as an orphanage, a school, a clinic (☎ 53122), a **gompa** and **craft workshops** that produce carpets, woodcarvings, leatherwork and wool items. The handicrafts, as well as Tibetan souvenirs and jewellery, are available for sale in the **showroom** (☎ 52552). Prices are similar to those in the souvenir shops at Chowrasta and along Nehru Rd, but the proceeds go straight back to the Tibetan community.

Visitors can wander around at leisure through the workshops. The shops with weaving or dyeing and woodcarving are particularly interesting, and the people are friendly and welcoming. As the centre is self-funded, and a registered charity, donations are always welcome (see also Volunteer Work later in this section). It's open during daylight hours Monday to Saturday.

The centre is not easy to find, however. From Chowrasta, walk down CR Das Rd for about 800m until you come to a fork. The road to the left is signposted to the centre, but this steep vehicle road is about 4km long. If you take the road to the right at the fork, past the Bhutia Busty Gompa and keep heading downhill, it's shorter (about 1.2km) – but ask for directions along the way, and look out for the huge sign on the roof of the centre. Alternatively, take a chartered or share-taxi to the turn-off along Lebong Cart Rd.

Other Attractions

Built in 1939, **Dhirdham Mandir** is the most conspicuous Hindu temple in Darjeeling, and was modelled on the famous Pashupatinath Temple in Kathmandu. It's easy to find, just below the train station. Nearby is the tiny **Maa Singha Mandir**, presided over by a *mataji* (female priest) and sacred to the goddess Durga.

If you're travelling on the toy train, or walking back from Tiger Hill (see the Tiger Hill section earlier), look out for the **war memorial** at the incredible **Batasia Loop** along the track. It's open during daylight hours daily and entry is Rs 2.

Within walking distance of Tiger Hill near Ghoom, **Senchal Lake** is the (somewhat erratic!) source of Darjeeling's water supply. It's a particularly scenic area, popular with Indian holiday-makers, and boasts a small golf course.

The unimpressive **Bengal Natural History Museum** was established in 1903. It offers a dilapidated collection of Himalayan and Bengali fauna, and an incongruous replica of a crocodile. It's open from 10 am to 4 pm daily except Thursday; entry costs Rs 5. From Chowrasta, walk along Bishop Eric Benjamin Rd for two minutes, and take the lane to the right at the fork.

Lloyd Botanical Gardens contain an impressive representation of Himalayan plants and flowers, including orchids. The gardens are open between 6 am and 5 pm daily, the glasshouse between 8 am and 5 pm. Follow the signs along Lochnager Rd from the Chowk Bazaar bus/jeep station. Admission is free.

White-Water Rafting

Teesta Bazaar is the centre for rafting along the Rangeet and Teesta Rivers. Although only about 16km from Kalimpong, most travellers organise trips from Darjeeling. The rapids are graded from Grade II to Grade IV, and the best time for rafting is from September to November and March to June.

Himalayan River Journey (☎ 53969, e jdriverjourney@rediffmail.com) has rafting trips from Rs 1200 for one hour to Rs 2100 for 4½ hours, including transport from Darjeeling, food, equipment and a guide. Longer trips are available on demand. Bookings can also be made at Samsara Tours, Travels & Treks (see Trekking & Travel Agencies earlier in this section for contact details, and see also Around Kalimpong later in this chapter for more information on tours).

Other Activities

Membership of the Darjeeling Gymkhana Club (☎ 54341), below the Darjeeling Tourist Lodge along Jawahar Rd West, costs Rs 30/250 per day/week and Rs 400/600 per fortnight/month. The activities here are not equestrian, however. (The word 'gymkhana' actually derives from the Hindi *gend-khana*, or 'ball house'.) Games on offer – at an extra cost – include tennis, squash, badminton, roller-skating, table tennis and billiards. Ring the club to find out which games are available and when, or check the notice board in the foyer.

The grand Darjeeling Club (also called The Planters), at Clubside, offers temporary membership to visitors for Rs 50 per day. This allows free access to the billiard room, bar and library.

From near the Indian Airlines office at Chowrasta, pony rides are available along any path without vehicles, eg, Jawahar Rd West as far as the zoo. The usual charge is a negotiable Rs 60 per hour. A pony can also be hired for longer treks from about Rs 250 per day (plus the cost of the pony-wallah).

Lebong Race Course is reputed to be the smallest racecourse in the world (437m long). Horse races and other activities are held here from May to June and October to November; ask either of the two tourist offices for details. It's about 8km north-east of Chowrasta; charter a taxi or jeep.

The DGHC, and several agencies (including those listed earlier under Trekking & Travel Agencies), offer 'adventure tours', eg, mountain biking and rock climbing, in their brochures, but these places are not generally well set up for 'adventure tourism'. For rock climbing, contact the experts – the Himalayan Mountaineering Institute (see that section earlier in the chapter) – about courses, expeditions and equipment hire.

Courses

Tibetan-language courses for beginners (three to six months) are conducted at the Manjushree Centre of Tibetan Culture (☎ 56714), 8 Burdwan Rd. The centre can also arrange Buddhist study courses for groups of six or more.

You can study traditional Tibetan woodcarving at the Tibetan Refugee Self-Help Centre; contact its head office (☎ 52346) at 65 Gandhi Rd.

Volunteer Work

The Nepali Girls' Social Service Centre (☎ 2985), on Gandhi Rd, undertakes projects to protect the environment, and to promote the empowerment of women, child survival and development. Volunteers are welcome on an informal basis to teach English, art or music. Contact the centre for details.

Hayden Hall (ⓔ hayden@cal.vsnl.net.in) at 42 Laden La Rd, near the Park Restaurant, is a Christian-based organisation that can arrange volunteer work in medicine, teaching, handicrafts and counselling, but volunteers must be prepared to commit themselves for at least six months.

The Tibetan Refugee Self-Help Centre has openings for volunteer teachers (of children and adults), medical staff and geriatric and childcare workers. For more information, contact its head office (☎ 52346) at 65 Gandhi Rd.

Organised Tours

All travel agencies offer the same sort of organised local tours as the DGHC, but unless you can get enough passengers together to share the cost the agencies will often suggest you go on a DGHC tour – and the DGHC needs a minimum number before any tour can start. If there's not enough demand for a half-day local tour, the DGHC can arrange a taxi for Rs 350 per vehicle.

The DGHC's half-day 'local sightseeing tour' (Rs 50 per person) includes the zoo, Himalayan Mountaineering Institute and Tibetan Refugee Self-Help Centre, but these places can be easily visited independently, and on foot. The DGHC's day trip (Rs 100) to Mirik is worthwhile, because going there on your own by public transport will cost about the same, and take longer.

In the peak season, the DGHC offers a 'Tiger Hill Tour' (see the Tiger Hill section earlier in this chapter), which also fits in a quick trip to the Samten Choling Gompa and Batasia Loop.

Special Events

Surprisingly, Darjeeling has no specific festivals worth mentioning. The New Year for the Sikkimese (December/January), Lepchas and Bhutias (January) and Tibetans (February/March) is celebrated enthusiastically, often at the major gompas. The five-day **Tihar Festival** is celebrated by Nepalis in late October or early November.

Places to Stay

Only a limited selection of the massive number of hotels in Darjeeling is listed below. Prices vary widely according to the season. Those listed are for the peak tourist season – in the low season prices drop by about 50%. A lot of hotels don't offer single rates, and the 10% 'service charge' often added to the tariff is arbitrary and negotiable. Many places, particularly in the top-end range, offer an 'American Plan' including all meals, but this is never worthwhile (unless you're staying in a remote hotel), because there are plenty of good cheap restaurants around town.

Darjeeling suffers from chronic power and water shortages, and not all hotels have backup generators or permanent hot water. If there's a television in the room, make sure it has cable, which offers more variety (and English-language options) than local TV; and if heating is promised, find out what type (see the boxed text 'Carbon Monoxide Poisoning' under Dangers & Annoyances in the Facts for the Visitor chapter) and make sure it works.

Touts & Porters

Accommodation touts are paid up to 30% commission for finding guests, and you will ultimately pay for this if you use them. However, saying 'no' doesn't always work because they often follow new arrivals to their chosen hotel and then demand a commission from the manager on the basis that the touts brought you there. If you are followed, be sure to inform the manager immediately that the tout was in no way responsible for your choice of hotel.

Porters also often accost new arrivals at the train station, the Chowk Bazaar jeep/bus station and at other jeep stops around lower Darjeeling. They *are* useful, however, if you have heavy baggage, or are not confident about finding your preferred hotel, especially in the dark or during inclement weather. Also, the myriad confusing and steep stairways can be daunting at first, so a porter is handy. Expect to pay about Rs 20 for someone to carry your luggage.

Places to Stay – Budget

Near the TV Tower along Dr Zakir Hussain Rd there are four places which cater mostly to backpackers. The area is a little inconvenient, and is sometimes hard to find at night, but it's clean and quiet. All places (except the youth hostel) boast a book exchange, Internet centre and a good, cheap restaurant. The best way to reach the TV Tower is to walk up Rockville Rd from opposite the Clock Tower, head left behind the Telegraph Office and then up to Dr Zakir Hussain Rd.

Tenzing Norgay Youth Hostel is perched on a ridge and undoubtedly has some of the best views in Darjeeling. (There's no need to go to Tiger Hill to watch the sunrise on Kanchenjunga – just wander out onto the balcony.) It's reasonably clean, if a little characterless, and is good value with dorm beds for Rs 40 per person (membership of an international youth hostel organisation is not required). It has an informative and helpful travellers' comment book, and the staff can help with trekking information and equipment.

Triveni Guest House *(☎ 53878)* is basic, but very popular and friendly. Clean singles/doubles cost Rs 90/120 with shared bathroom; doubles (no singles) with private bathroom are Rs 130.

Aliment Hotel *(☎ 55068)* has clean rooms with shared bathroom (and squat toilet) for Rs 70/150, and doubles with spotless private bathroom (and hot water) for Rs 200.

Tower View Lodge *(☎ 54452, ⓔ compuset@cal.vsnl.net.in)*, just down from the TV Tower, is simple but is excellent value – so it's often full of long-term guests. Singles range from Rs 80 to 100, and doubles from Rs 100 to 150 – all have private toilet, but the showers (with hot water) are shared. Dorm beds cost Rs 40 per person. Visitors must stay at least two nights.

Along Upper Beechwood Rd, there are two charming, but very basic, choices. Neither have more than a handful of rooms, however, and they are not geared up for lots of travellers. ***Hotel Pagoda*** *(☎ 53498)* charges a bargain Rs 80/100 for tiny but clean rooms with shared bathroom; and next door ***Hotel Shamrock*** charges Rs 80/180 for similar facilities.

Hotel Hemadrie *(☎ 52967, ⓔ prashantpips@hotmail.com, 4 Gandhi Rd)*, is a little inconvenient and noisy, has been recommended by readers. All rooms have cable TV and private bathroom (with squat toilet), and are very good value from Rs 165/275. Better doubles start at Rs 385.

Other unexciting and noisy budget hotels costing about Rs 100/150 for basic rooms, often with private bathroom (cold water), can be found along the steps up from near Hotel Dekeling at Clubside, along the steps between Laden La and Gandhi Rds which lead to Upper Beechwood Rd, and around the train station.

The best of a bad lot around the Chowk Bazaar bus/jeep station is ***Hotel New Garden*** *(Lochnager Rd)*, down the quiet access road to the botanical gardens. A clean room with three beds and a rudimentary private bathroom costs Rs 200.

Places to Stay – Mid-Range

All rooms in the places listed below have private bathrooms (unless stated otherwise) with hot water (often mornings only).

Andy's Guest House *(☎ 53125, ⓔ mgurung@dte.vsnl.net.in, 102 Dr Zakir Hussain Rd)* continues to get rave reviews from readers. All rooms are airy and spotlessly clean, and range from Rs 150/200 to 250/300. The owners are very friendly and helpful.

Hotel Tshering Denzongpa *(☎ 56061, JP Sharma Rd)* is a friendly, Sherpa-run place with rooms from Rs 350/600 and doubles with shared bathroom for Rs 250. The more expensive rooms have better views. It's often full.

Hotel Springburn *(☎ 52054, Gandhi Rd)* has some character. The doubles for Rs 385 are large, clean and come with cable TV, but the bathrooms have squat toilets and the hot water is erratic. The rooms at the back have views of Kanchenjunga.

Bellevue Hotel *(☎ 54075)* is a charming old place at Chowrasta. Large, comfortable doubles range from Rs 440 to 660, but this place is noisy because of the wooden floors and walls. For long-term guests, there are huge, but rather characterless, rooms (some with kitchens) at the back. Guests can enjoy the rooftop terrace, private Buddhist prayer room and cafe with excellent views over Chowrasta.

Main (Old) Bellevue Hotel *(☎ 54178)* also has a great position at Chowrasta, and is constantly recommended by readers for its friendly staff. The Raj-era building at the back has large, musty doubles for Rs 400, and the newer wing has better rooms with great views for Rs 500.

Pineridge Hotel *(☎ 54074, Nehru Rd)* is a huge, rambling place with loads of character. All rooms are nicely furnished, including fireplaces and cable TV, and some have bay windows. Rooms range from Rs 400/550 to 600/700 for larger rooms with views. The negotiable off-season discounts are particularly attractive.

Hotel Alice Villa *(☎ 54181, HD Lama Rd)* has charming doubles in the original building for Rs 825 or Rs 935 including breakfast and dinner. The rooms in the new annexe are disappointing, but are cheaper at Rs 715 without meals and Rs 880 with two meals. All rooms have cable TV. The negotiable rates in the off-season make this excellent value.

The Darjeeling Club *(☎/fax 54348, Clubside)*, also known as The Planters, is a real ghost of the Raj era. Large but musty doubles with a fireplace cost from Rs 660 to 1320; the superb 'suite' is Rs 2200.

Hotel Dekeling *(☎ 54159, ⓔ dekeling@dte.vsnl.net.in, Clubside)* is popular and friendly, but is a little pricey. The double rooms, located mostly around convivial communal lounge areas, are small but quaint, and range from Rs 660 with shared bathroom to Rs 1210 with better views and private bathroom.

Hotel Fairmont *(☎ 53646, fax 53647, 10 Gandhi Rd)* offers very comfortable rooms with great views, cable TV and a phone. It's particularly good value at Rs 1155/1650 for doubles/triples.

Hotel Seven Seventeen *(☎ 55099, HD Lama Rd)* is probably the best of several similar hotels along HD Lama Rd. It's run by a welcoming Tibetan family, and offers four-star service and facilities at two-star prices. The comfortable singles/doubles/triples with cable TV are good value at Rs 880/1100/1430; it's slightly more for rooms with views.

Hotel Red Rose *(☎ 56062, ⓔ hotelredrose@yahoo.com, 37 Laden La Rd)* is convenient and popular, but is overpriced and very noisy. The well-furnished doubles come with phone and cable TV, and cost from Rs 770 to 1210. Several other similarly priced mid-range places are dotted along the same road.

Classic Guest House *(☎ 54106, CR Das Rd)*, just down from Chowrasta, is a delightful place, although a little expensive. It offers charming decor, great views and friendly service. Doubles with cable TV and balcony cost Rs 1000. It's popular, so book ahead.

Maple Tourist Lodge *(☎ 52813, Kuchery Rd)*, run by the West Bengal tourist department, is in a quiet location and surprisingly good value. Rooms with shared (spotless) bathroom with hot water cost Rs 315/473.

It's often full, so book ahead. See under Permits earlier in this section for details about getting to the lodge on foot from Chowrasta.

Darjeeling Tourist Lodge *(☎ 54411, Jawahar Rd West)* is above the Darjeeling Gymkhana Club. Most rooms are overpriced, but the doubles in the old annexe for Rs 400 are good value.

Places to Stay – Top End

Most top-end hotels only offer an 'American Plan', with breakfast, lunch and dinner included, so the prices quoted here are for the American Plan.

New Elgin *(☎ 54114, ⓔ newelgin@cal.vsnl.net.in)*, off HD Lama Rd, retains its colonial ambience. Most of the elegantly furnished rooms boast marble bathrooms and have open fires, and the lovely gardens are a perfect place to relax and enjoy afternoon tea. Singles/doubles cost US$92/99.

Above Chowrasta, ***Windamere Hotel*** *(☎ 54041, ⓔ windamere@vsnl.com)*, is an institution among Raj relic aficionados, with Tibetan maids in starched frilly aprons and high tea served in the drawing room. The rooms are cosy and comfortable, and TVs are conspicuously (and deliberately) absent. Rates start from US$103/137.

Mayfair Hill Resort *(☎ 56376, ⓔ mayfair@cal2.vsnl.net.in)* is along Jawahar Rd West and opposite the Raj Bhavan (Government House). Originally a maharaja's summer palace, it's been extensively renovated so its origins are no longer apparent. It does, however, offer luxury in beautiful surroundings and fabulous views. Rooms and cottages are comparatively good value for Rs 3500/4500/5500 for singles/doubles/triples.

Places to Eat

Below is a small sample of the many fine places to eat in Darjeeling.

Keventer's Snack Bar *(Clubside)* has a deli on the ground floor selling uncooked sausages, cheese, ham and other goods. The range of meals at the small restaurant upstairs is limited, but it's ideal for a cooked breakfast. The service is slow, but this gives you time to enjoy the magnificent views.

Hasty Tasty *(Nehru Rd)* specialises in South Indian vegetarian snacks and meals, such as *dosas* (pancakes). It's popular with Indian tourists, which is always a good sign.

Frank Ross Cafe *(Nehru Rd)* is also strictly vegetarian. It offers a decent range of pizzas (from Rs 40), burgers, South Indian snacks and even Mexican nachos (Rs 35).

Glenary's *(Nehru Rd)* has a classy restaurant and bar upstairs with a limited range of Indian, Chinese and continental dishes from Rs 50. The ***bakery*** underneath sells excellent pastries, cakes and chocolates, and is a wonderful place to enjoy a cup of Darjeeling's finest chai.

Stardust Restaurant is the best value at Chowrasta, and the views from the tables outside are staggering. Vegetarian (only) meals start from Rs 30, but inexplicably this place does not serve tea.

Park Restaurant, near Hayden Hall on Laden La Rd, is probably the best place for a splurge. The service is excellent, the decor is charming and the meals (from Rs 50) are not as expensive as you'd imagine.

Kunga Restaurant, under Hotel Dekeling at Clubside, is small but very popular. It offers a huge range of authentic Tibetan and Chinese cuisine, including 36 varieties of soup (!), as well as decent pizzas. The servings are huge, for example, a plate of steamed *momos* (dumplings), which costs Rs 30, is probably large enough for two people.

Opposite the Head Post Office on Laden La Rd, a number of tiny, cheap ***Tibetan restaurants*** serve simple, traditional cuisine; and, opposite Hotel Seven Seventeen on HD Lama Rd, several small ***Indian eateries*** serve excellent samosas and other snacks.

Hot Stimulating Cafe *(Jawahar Rd West)*, perched over the mountain side on the road down to the zoo, offers beautiful views over the hills and valleys. The Nepali owners make tasty and cheap food (such as momos), and serve excellent chai and coffee.

For a spot of afternoon tea with a colonial atmosphere, try the ***Windamere Hotel*** at Chowrasta, although it's not great value (it costs Rs 200 per person for tea, sandwiches and scones). The ***New Elgin*** is just as good, but cheaper.

Entertainment

Golden Dragon Restaurant & Bar *(Laden La Rd)*, with its rainbow-painted walls and seedy 1920s ambience, is one of several similar dens where the beer, rather than the limited menu, is the main attraction. Decent restaurants that serve beer and other alcoholic drinks include the upstairs restaurant at ***Glenary's*** *(Nehru Rd)* and ***Park Restaurant*** *(Laden La Rd)*. The cosy bar at ***Hotel Seven Seventeen*** *(HD Lama Rd)* is pleasantly well lit, and has reasonable prices.

The best place to meet other travellers is undoubtedly ***Joey's Pub*** *(SM Das Rd)*. It has friendly staff and Western music, and can even rustle up some 'continental cuisine' (such as baked beans on toast!), but the drinks are expensive.

The ***Rink Cinema***, on SM Das Rd, shows mainly Indian films in Hindi. Nearby, several dingy video parlours show sleazy and violent films. ***Pool Cafe***, above the Juniper Tours & Travels office at Clubside, is a great place to while away some time; pool tables cost Rs 100 per hour.

Shopping

Souvenirs Most souvenirs shops are at Chowrasta and along Nehru Rd. They sell *thangkas* (rectangular Tibetan religious cloth paintings), brass statues, religious objects, jewellery, woodcarvings and carpets, but if you're looking for bargains, shop judiciously and be prepared to spend plenty of time looking. Thangkas in particular may look impressive at first sight, but you'll find little care has been taken over the finer detail in the cheaper ones. One reputable merchant is Habeeb Mullick & Sons at Chowrasta, established in the 1890s. Another is Nepal Curio House in the Pineridge Hotel complex on Nehru Rd. Next door, Kalimpong Art Gallery specialises in Nepali pastel paintings, jewellery and *khukuri* (traditional Gurkha knives).

Other great souvenirs are photographic prints of Kanchenjunga and nearby mountains, and of other places around Darjeeling, which cost from Rs 150 to 495. These are available from photographic shops along Nehru Rd, such as Das Studios.

Chowk Bazaar is huge, chaotic and fascinating, although it is not the best place for souvenirs, except loose-leaf tea, spices and incense.

Tibetan Carpets One of the best places for Tibetan carpets is Hayden Hall on Laden La Rd. This women's cooperative sells *casemillon* (wool and synthetic mix) shawls, woollen hats, socks and mufflers. Virtually next door, Third Eye is an all-women enterprise which gives free training to female weavers and guarantees work at the end of their training. Shipping of carpets can be arranged.

Darjeeling Tea Tea is a popular souvenir. First Flush Super Fine Tippy Golden Flowery Orange Pekoe 1 has a forgettable name, but an unforgettable taste. To test the quality, take a small handful in your closed fist, breathe on it through your fingers, open your hand and smell the aromas released. At least it'll look as if you know what you're doing even if you don't have a clue! Avoid the tea in fancy boxes, because it's usually blended and packaged in Kolkata. A good supplier is Nathmull's Tea Rooms along Laden La Rd. Cheaper tea is available from stalls in Chowk Bazaar; it's sold loose, but can be packaged.

Getting There & Away

Air The nearest airport is 90km away at Bagdogra, about 12km from Siliguri. Refer to Getting There & Away in the Siliguri & New Jalpaiguri section earlier in his chapter for details about flights to/from Bagdogra.

The two agents for Jet Airways in Darjeeling are Clubside Tours & Travels (☎ 54646, ⓔ clubside@dte.vsnl.net.in) on JP Sharma Rd, and Pineridge Travels (☎ 53912, ⓔ pineridge@dte.vsnl.net.in) at Chowrasta. The Indian Airlines office (☎ 54230) is under the Bellevue Hotel at Chowrasta. These offices are open Monday to Saturday.

Clubside, Pineridge and some of the other companies listed under Trekking & Travel Agencies earlier in this section sell tickets for flights on Nepali airlines, eg, from Bhadrapur (just over the border in Nepal) to Kathmandu.

Trekking & Hiking Around Darjeeling

Trekking around Darjeeling (and Kalimpong) is best from March to mid-June and late September to early December. The clearest mountain views are in October and November, and although it's cold and snowy in December and January, most treks can be undertaken during the winter months. From late March to late May, there is much haze and clouds, but the rhododendrons are in full bloom.

Camping equipment – sleeping bags (usually needed even if you're using trekkers huts), day-packs and cooking gear – can be hired from a few places in Darjeeling (see Trekking & Travel Agencies). The Darjeeling Gorkha Hill Country (DGHC) has trekkers huts with dorm beds (Rs 25 per person) at Sandakphu, Phalut, Rimbik, Tonglu, Gairibas, Shirikhola, Gorkhey and Ramam, so a tent is not necessary here. Try to book beds in advance at the DGHC office in Darjeeling (or Kalimpong). However, there are 20 to 30 beds in each hut so you're likely to get a bed even if you just turn up.

Basic meals are available in some villages, such as Gairibas and Rimbik, and at some trekkers huts, but bring your own food and bottled water, or use purification tablets. And take out all your rubbish!

Guides (about Rs 250 per day) and porters (about Rs 150 per day) are not necessary, but are available in Darjeeling and most villages along the way. Treks can also be arranged with most agencies listed earlier in this chapter, and with the DGHC. It's a good idea to read the travellers' comments books at the Tenzing Norgay Youth Hostel, and at other nearby budget hotels in Darjeeling.

Singalila Range

The most popular trekking area is around the Singalila Range near the border with Nepal. Below is a brief description of one route between Mana Bhanjang (Maneybhanjang) and Phalut.

At the Chowk Bazaar jeep/bus station in Darjeeling, ask for the direct morning bus (1½ hours), or a share-jeep, to Mana Bhanjang. Alternatively, get a jeep or bus to Sukia Pokhri, and another to Mana Bhanjang (or walk 4km), where there is basic accommodation. From Mana Bhanjang (2150m), the obvious 11km trail passes a series of small settlements to Tonglu (3070m).

On the second day, continue 9km through (flat) bamboo forests to Gairibas (2621m), from where it's a gradual 4km ascent to Kali Pokahari (2930m). From this lake, it's 2.5km uphill and then 1.5km downhill to Bikhay Bhanjang (3350m), and another 4km uphill to Sandakphu (3636m). This is the highest spot in the region and perfect for viewing the eastern Himalaya; to the north is an impressive selection of peaks, including the Kanchenjunga massif (8598m), the world's third highest peak. From Sandakphu, the 21km trail is spectacular, and relatively easy, along the ridge to Phalut (3600m), via Sabarkum (3536m). Alternatively, return to Darjeeling (29km) from Sandakphu, via Bikhay Bhanjang, through rhododendron and conifer forest to the road head at Rimbik.

If continuing to trek from Phalut, the fourth day is a steep 15km descent to Ramam (2560m), via Gorkhey (3100m). From Ramam, it's a pretty and easy 19km trek to Rimbik (2286m). From Rimbik there is a morning bus to Darjeeling (four to five hours), or ask around for a shared jeep.

Stage 1	Mana Bhanjang to Tonglu	(4–5 hours)
Stage 2	Tonglu to Sandakphu, via Gairibas, Kali Pokahari & Bikhay Bhanjang	(6–7 hours)
Stage 3	Sandakphu to Phalut	(6–7 hours)
Stage 4	Phalut to Ramam	(4–5 hours)
Stage 5	Ramam to Rimbik	(4–5 hours)

Short Hikes

Shorter hikes are possible between Mirik and Kurseong (see the boxed text 'Mirik to Kurseong Day Trek' earlier in this chapter); around Samthar Plateau (see that section later in this chapter); and from Lava or Kaffer. The walk between Darjeeling and Ghoom (about 8km), or between Darjeeling and Tiger Hill (about 11km), is popular, but is better *downhill* from Darjeeling. The main thoroughfare, Hill Cart Rd, goes past several interesting gompas and Batasia Loop, but the traffic is appalling; walk along the quieter Tenzing Norgay or Dr Zakir Hussain Rds.

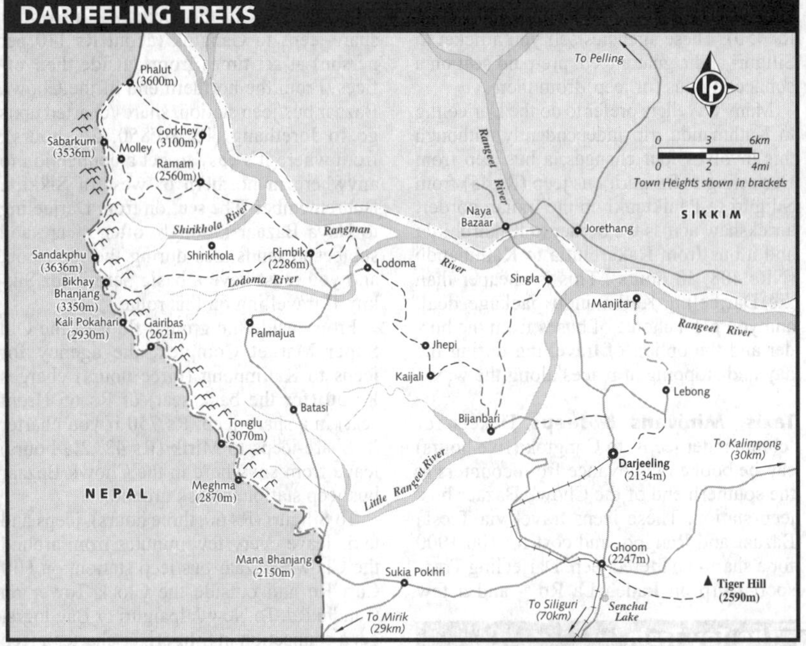

Bus From the Chowk Bazaar bus/jeep station, public buses go to Kalimpong (Rs 42, 3½ hours) at 8 am; to Mirik (Rs 30, three hours) every 30 minutes from 8 am to 3.15 pm; and to Siliguri (about Rs 45, three hours) every 30 minutes during the day. Tickets can be bought from counters along the ground floor of the Old Super Market Complex on Hill Cart Rd, but only buses to Gangtok and Kalimpong can be booked in advance.

No buses travel between Darjeeling and Jorethang, Pelling or anywhere else in Sikkim (except Gangtok). To get to western Sikkim, first take a share-jeep to Jorethang (see Taxis, Minivans & Jeeps following). From the bus/jeep station, a public bus leaves every day at 7.30 am for Gangtok (Rs 80, six to seven hours). The SNT agent is the Darjeeling Motor Service Co (☎ 52101), 31 Laden La Rd; the SNT bus to Gangtok leaves opposite the office every day at 12.30 pm.

Several travel agencies around the Old Super Market Complex on Hill Cart Rd, eg, Kasturi Tours & Travels and Diamond Treks, Tours & Travels, offer daily buses to Guwahati (Assam), via Siliguri, for Rs 285 to 320. Samsara Tours, Travels & Treks on Laden La Rd sells tickets for 'luxury' overnight buses to places all over northern India and Kolkata from Siliguri. However, before buying a long-distance bus ticket from Darjeeling, determine the number and length of connections, because *all* long-distance bus services start/finish in Siliguri.

To/From Nepal It's important to note that foreigners can only cross the border into Nepal at Kakarbhitta (not at Pasupati), so make sure your bus goes through the correct border crossing. The nearest Nepali consulate is in Kolkata, but visas are available at Kakarbhitta for US$30 (and must be paid for in cash).

A number of travel agencies (see Trekking & Travel Agencies earlier in this section) sell tickets for the daily buses that run between Darjeeling and Kathmandu (about Rs 450). These agencies sell you a ticket to Siliguri and a guaranteed, pre-paid seat on a connecting bus (or jeep) from there.

Many travellers prefer to do the Darjeeling to Kathmandu trip independently, although this involves four changes: a bus/jeep from Darjeeling to Siliguri; bus/jeep (Rs 45) from Siliguri to Paniktanki on the Indian border; a rickshaw across the border to Kakarbhitta; and a bus from Kakarbhitta to Kathmandu (NRs 408, 13 hours). This is cheaper than the Darjeeling-Kathmandu package deal, and you get a choice of buses from the border and the option of travelling during the day and stopping at places along the way.

Taxis, Minivans & Jeeps Tickets for 'commander jeeps' to Gangtok (five hours) can be booked in advance from counters at the southern end of the Chowk Bazaar bus/jeep station. These jeeps travel via Teesta Bazaar and Rangpo, and cost Rs 100/1000 for a share-/chartered jeep. Darjeeling Transport Corp on Laden La Rd – and a few other agencies in the vicinity – also offer share-jeeps to Gangtok (about Rs 110 per person) at set times from outside their offices. From the northern end of the Chowk Bazaar bus/jeep station, share-/charted taxis go to Jorethang (Rs 80/850, 2½ hours), from where it's easy to get a connection to anywhere in northern or western Sikkim. But remember: The section from Darjeeling to Naya Bazaar is tough, often steep, and subject to landslides during the monsoon, and you must have a basic permit for Sikkim if travelling on this route.

From inside the ground floor of the Old Super Market Complex, the agency for jeeps to Kalimpong (three hours) charges Rs 50 (for the back seat) or Rs 65 (front seat) in a share-jeep; Rs 750 if you charter it. Share-jeeps to Mirik (Rs 42, 2½ hours) leave from anywhere in the Chowk Bazaar bus/jeep station, so ask around.

To Siliguri (Rs 60, three hours), jeeps and taxis leave every few minutes from around the Chowk Bazaar bus/jeep station, on Hill Cart Rd and outside the Clock Tower on Gandhi Rd. To New Jalpaiguri or Bagdogra, get a connection in Siliguri, or charter a jeep or taxi from Darjeeling for about Rs 650.

Train The nearest major train station is at New Jalpaiguri (NJP), near Siliguri (see Getting There & Away in the Siliguri & New Jalpaiguri section earlier in this chapter for details). Tickets – mostly 2nd-class sleepers only – can be bought for major services out of NJP at the Computerised Reservations Counter (☎ 52555) at the Darjeeling train station between 8 am and 2 pm daily.

Toy Train The charming toy train has three different services, but note that wet weather causes landslides and services can be cancelled for months. Also, timetables change, so check the schedules at the stations for current details. No advance tickets are available on any service to NJP or Kurseong; tickets are available from one hour before departure. The fares for ordinary/1st class from Darjeeling are Rs 3/45 to Ghoom, Rs 10/90 to Kurseong, Rs 19/172 to Siliguri and Rs 22/202 to NJP.

The Toy Train

To avoid the exorbitant cost of road transportation along Hill Cart Rd, construction of a railway line to Darjeeling began in 1879 at Siliguri, and took only two years to reach Darjeeling. These days, the 'toy train' starts at New Jalpaiguri and chugs along the plains to Sukna, before puffing its way uphill for a total of 87.48km to Darjeeling.

This train line boasts the world's highest railway station (Ghoom; 2222m) for a steam locomotive. Train buffs may also like to know that the line crosses the main road, Hill Cart Rd, 177 times; and there are over 500 bridges, four complete loops and six incredible 'Z-shaped' curves along which the train must go very slowly uphill *backwards*.

Enthusiasts from around the world continue to ensure the survival of this unprofitable service, which now enjoys World Heritage status – only the second train line (after Austria) to receive this honour.

A train leaves Darjeeling for NJP every day at 9.10 am, and stops at Ghoom (9.56 am), Kurseong (noon), Siliguri (4.40 pm) and NJP (5.20 pm). It leaves NJP at 9 am, and stops at Siliguri (9.23 am), Kurseong (12.56 pm), Ghoom (2.57 pm) and Darjeeling (3.30 pm).

A local service departs Darjeeling every day at 3 pm for Ghoom (3.26 pm), and continues on to Kurseong (5.30 pm). In the other direction, it leaves Kurseong at 6.40 am and stops at Ghoom (8.31 am) on the way to Darjeeling (9.10 am).

A special tourist 'joy ride' departs daily at 10.30 am for a two-hour return trip to Ghoom, via Batasia Loop. Tickets are limited to about 25, so book one day in advance, if possible (Rs 200).

Getting Around

The DGHC tourist office runs a bus to the Bagdogra airport (Rs 65 per person) if there are 12 or more passengers (which is rare) – and at a time that suits the majority. If the bus doesn't leave Darjeeling, it won't be at Bagdogra airport for the return trip.

So, the alternatives from the airport to Darjeeling are either a pre-paid taxi to Siliguri bus station, and then a bus/jeep to Darjeeling; or charter (or ask around about sharing) a pre-paid taxi, which costs from Rs 690 (2½ hours) to Rs 1150 (five hours, for the scenic route via Mirik). Chartered and share-taxi fares are a little cheaper outside the airport, and from Darjeeling to the airport.

Share-taxis to anywhere north of the city centre, eg, North Point, leave from the northern end of the Chowk Bazaar bus/jeep station.

KALIMPONG

☎ 03552 • pop 46,500 • elevation 1250m

Although still relatively small, Kalimpong is a bustling and rapidly expanding bazaar town set among the rolling foothills and deep valleys of the Himalaya. It was part of the lands belonging to the rajas of Sikkim until the beginning of the 18th century, when it was taken from them by the Bhutanese.

In the 19th century, Kalimpong passed into the hands of the British and thus became part of West Bengal. It became a centre for Scottish missionary activity, particularly by the Jesuits, in the late 19th century, and Dr Graham's orphanage and school is still running today. Until the outbreak of the China-India war in 1962, Kalimpong was one of the most important centres of India-Tibet commerce, with mule trains passing over the 3300m Japen La (pass) into Tibet.

The main local crops are ginger and cardamom. Kalimpong division was once densely forested, but widespread tree felling has left large areas denuded. Some areas of forests remain, however, including the left bank of the Teesta River, around Lava and along the border with Bhutan.

Kalimpong is quieter (with far less Indian and foreign tourists), cheaper, warmer, smaller and flatter than Darjeeling, but is not as pretty and has fewer attractions.

Refer to History in the Darjeeling section earlier in this chapter about the possible activities of the Gorkhaland Liberation Organisation (GLO).

Orientation & Information

Main Rd is also known as SDB Giri Rd – the two names are used interchangeably by locals. The latter is not to be confused with the separate DB Giri Rd!

Staff at DGHC Tourist Reception Centre (☎ 57992), on DB Giri Rd, can't be too bothered with lots of questions from visitors, but they can arrange rafting trips and offer a left-luggage service. The office is open from about 9 am to about 5 pm daily. The private Web site at www.kalimpong.org has useful information.

The State Bank of India and Central Bank of India, both along Main (SDB Giri) Rd, are not interested in changing money. Mid-range and top-end hotels can usually change money for guests.

The Odyssey Internet Cafe, upstairs in the shopping complex on the corner of Main (SDB Giri) and Rishi Rds, is the best place to send and receive email. It charges a reasonable Rs 1 per minute.

There is nowhere in Kalimpong to obtain permits for Sikkim, but free two-day extendable permits are available at the border at Rangpo (see the Sikkim chapter for details). Otherwise, get a permit in Darjeeling (see Permits earlier in this chapter).

Kashi Nath & Sons Booksellers, on DB Giri Rd, sells current newspapers and books and maps of the eastern Himalaya, but the selection is better at the newsagency along the southern end of Main (SDB Giri) Rd.

Some of the regional forest resthouses, such as those at Lava and Kaffer (see the Around Kalimpong section later in this chapter), can be booked in advance at the Forest Development Corporation (☎ 55783), next to the Nature Interpretation Centre on Rinkingpong Rd.

Zong Dog Palri Fo-Brang Gompa

Kalimpong's largest monastery was built on top of the spectacular Durpin Hill (1372m). In 1976, the gompa was consecrated by the Dalai Lama, who donated a rare 108-volume edition of The Kangyur to the library. The gompa also boasts impressive wall paintings in the prayer room, which has a ceiling embellished with large mandalas (circular

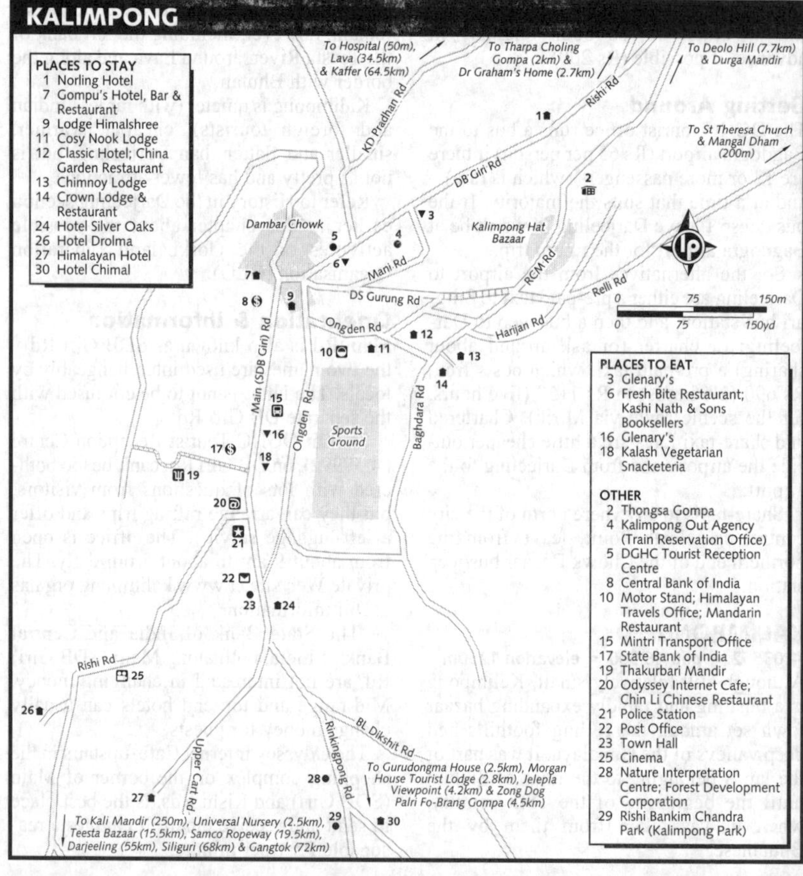

images depicting the universe). Close to the ceiling are images of the 25 disciples of Padmasambhava, the founder of the Nyingmapa order, each inhabiting a cave and engaged in different miraculous feats, such as flying through the sun's rays and bringing the dead back to life. Suspended from the ceiling are magnificent thangkas.

In an upstairs room is an intricate wooden model of the palace of Guru Rinpoche, including tiny figures of lamas blowing *radungs* (long-stemmed Tibetan horns) and statues of Padmasambhava and Avalokiteshvara. There is also a three-dimensional mandala, one of only three in the world.

The monastery is about 5km south of the town centre, and is only accessible by chartered jeep. There are wonderful views from the **Jelepla Viewpoint**, about 300m below the gompa (it's not signposted; look for the steps).

Nearby, the DGHC's ***traditional tea house*** offers fine tea and meals, and exceptional vistas. This area is a military camp, but visitors are free to walk and drive around.

Other Gompas, Temples & Churches

Built in 1937, **Tharpa Choling Gompa** belongs to the Gelukpa order, which is led by the Dalai Lama. It's atop Tripai Hill, a 45-minute walk (uphill) from town; head up Tripai Rd, turn right at KD Pradhan Rd and take the path to the right just before the Milk Collection and Extension Wing Building.

Lower down the hill, **Thongsa Gompa** (Bhutanese Monastery) is the oldest monastery in the area, founded in 1692. However, the present building isn't so old: The original structure was destroyed by the Gurkhas during their rampage across Sikkim before the arrival of the British. Visitors are welcome.

Mangal Dham, along Relli Rd, is a large and majestic temple, completed in 1993 and dedicated to Krishna. It is notable for the contemporary architecture featuring white marble, and the large central sanctum with colourful scenes from the life of Krishna. It was closed at the time of research, but is going to reopen.

Thakurbari Mandir was originally built over 100 years ago, but the newer section is only 20 years old. It's accessible along a laneway beside the State Bank of India.

The Mary Mother of God Catholic Church along Relli Rd boasts the highly unusual **St Theresa Church**, built completely in the style of a Buddhist monastery. The cross at the top is the only indication of its different religious purpose.

Dr Graham's Home

This orphanage and school was built in 1900 by a Scottish missionary, JA Graham, to educate the children of tea garden workers, and it now boasts over 1300 students. The **chapel** above the school dates from 1925, and features fine stained-glass windows (if the caretaker is around, he will open it for you).

Visitors are also welcome to visit the fine school building. Some bring a picnic lunch to eat in the grounds, which encompass 193 hectares.

The complex is about 3km up the *very* steep KD Pradhan Rd. It's really only accessible by chartered taxi or jeep, but it's a charming walk back to town.

Other Attractions

Kalimpong produces about 80% of India's gladioli, and is an important orchid-growing area (flowers are exported from here to many cities in northern India). The best time to see gladioli is from March to April, while orchids are at their best from December to February.

Universal Nursery is one of the more extensive nurseries in the region, but like most others it's more interested in serious customers than curious tourists. It's along Rishi Rd, about 3km from the town centre.

Deolo Hill (1704m) is surrounded by two reservoirs which provide water to the town. It offers fine views over Kalimpong and Sikkim on a clear day, and there's a ***chai stall*** at the end of the road. The small Hindu **Durga Mandir** is a short walk south-east from the hill. Deolo is about 8km from town along a steep, windy road. It is accessible by chartered taxi/jeep, and is a one-hour walk from Dr Graham's Home (but you will need to ask for a lot of directions).

The **Nature Interpretation Centre**, run by the Soil Conservation Division of the Ministry of the Environment & Forests, consists of a number of well-organised dioramas depicting the effects of human activity on the environment. It's an easy walk from the town centre along Rinkingpong Rd, and is open from 10 am to 1.30 pm and 2 to 4 pm daily except Thursday. Admission is free.

About 100m farther up the hill is the small but serene **Rishi Bankim Chandra Park** (also known as Kalimpong Park).

Organised Tours

Unlike Darjeeling, all of Kalimpong's attractions are accessible by road, and many are within walking distance of the town centre. The tourist office offers a half-day '11 point' sightseeing tour for Rs 400 per vehicle if there's enough demand (which is rare). This sort of tour can easily be arranged for about Rs 350 per vehicle through your hotel or a jeep agency at the Motor Stand, such as Himalayan Travels (☎ 55023).

Gurudongma Tours & Travels (☎ 55204) at Gurudongma House (see Places to Stay following) organises all sorts of fascinating tours around Kalimpong, Darjeeling, Sikkim and the north-eastern states, including trekking, rafting, mountain-biking and fishing. The Web site at www.adventuresikkim.com has more details.

Places to Stay – Budget & Mid-Range

***Gompu's Hotel** (☎ 55818, Main Rd)* has pleasantly rustic singles/doubles for Rs 150/250 with private bathroom (and a free bucket of hot water). However, it's in a noisy area, and the wooden floors seem to creak constantly.

***Lodge Himalshree** (☎ 55070, Ongden Rd)* is a small place on the top floor of a tall building. The rooms are plain but clean and good value at Rs 120/180 with shared bathroom.

Nearby, ***Cosy Nook Lodge** (Ongden Rd)* is more noisy than cosy, but it's not bad value for Rs 150/200/350 for singles/doubles/triples with private bathroom.

***Classic Hotel** (☎ 56335)* is in a quiet cul-de-sac around the corner from the Motor Stand. The rooms are small, but some have good views, and it is reasonable value for Rs 150/250 for a single/double with private bathroom (cold water).

The best two places in the town centre are adjacent in a quiet area, just off Baghdara Rd. ***Crown Lodge** (☎ 55846)* is good value for Rs 200/350 with private bathroom (erratic hot water) and cable TV. ***Chimnoy Lodge** (☎ 56264)* has tiny singles for Rs 150 and better doubles from Rs 250 to 300 (depending on the view) with cable TV – all rooms have private bathroom, with squat toilet and cold water. The helpful owner can organise tours and transport.

***Norling Hotel** (☎ 57354, DB Giri Rd)* is run by a friendly Tibetan family. Clean rooms with private bathroom (hot water and squat toilet), cable TV and views cost Rs 250/350/450 for singles/doubles/triples, but the road is noisy at times.

***Hotel Drolma** (☎ 55968, fax 55290, Rishi Rd)* is a renovated bungalow, which still exudes some old-fashioned charm, set in lovely gardens. The rooms around the communal TV lounge are unexciting, however, and a little pricey – doubles with private bathroom (hot water) range from Rs 620 to 825, and triples start at Rs 962. The separate cluster of small 'economy' doubles for Rs 275 are good value, but they all have a shared bathroom. This hotel has friendly staff who keep the whole place spotlessly clean.

***Hotel Chimal** (☎ 55776, Rinkingpong Rd)* has a quiet countryside atmosphere, but is a little inconvenient and the rooms need renovation. The 'standard' rooms with a private bathroom for Rs 220/330 are OK, but the 'deluxe' rooms for Rs 330/550, with hot water, cable TV and excellent views, are good value.

Places to Stay – Top End

All places listed here offer rooms with private bathroom (and hot water).

***Gurudongma House** (☎ 55204, ⓔ rags@dte.vsnl.net.in)* is a delightful place, lost among the hilltops about 3km south of the town centre. The charming singles/doubles cost Rs 1320/1760; more including breakfast or three meals. It's often recommended by readers, but book ahead because it only has a small number of rooms.

The West Bengal tourist department runs several old colonial bungalows with pleasant gardens and views, but they can be a hassle to reach. ***Morgan House Tourist Lodge*** *(☎ 55384)*, about 3.3km from the town centre, has enchanting rooms from Rs 770/1430, including three meals.

A beautiful old place surrounded by superb gardens with views of Kanchenjunga, ***Himalayan Hotel*** *(☎ 54043, ⓔ windamere@vsnl.com, Upper Cart Rd)* is Rs 1430/2200, the rates are reasonable considering the location and luxury, but cost a lot more including all meals.

Hotel Silver Oaks *(☎ 55296, fax 55368, Rinkingpong Rd)*, once the home of a British family, is now a pretty hotel with delightful gardens. The rooms cost US$92/99, and are spacious, bright, well furnished and offer views of the valley or Kanchenjunga.

Places to Eat

Kalimpong cheese is a local speciality introduced by the Jesuits who established a dairy here. The dairy has since closed, but cheese is still produced in the area. Kalimpong lollipops are another speciality introduced by the sweet-toothed Jesuits. Both are available at the shops around Dambar Chowk.

Glenary's (which is deservedly popular in Darjeeling) has two bakeries in Kalimpong – one on DB Giri Rd and another on Main (SDB Giri) Rd. Both serve pastries, cakes, burgers and small pizzas, and have informal eating areas inside.

Kalash Vegetarian Snacketeria *(Main Rd)* offers all sorts of meals and snacks, from pizzas to momos, but it's probably best to stick with what it does best: South Indian dosas and hearty *thalis* (all-you-can-eat meals) which cost about Rs 35.

Gompu's Bar & Restaurant, in the hotel of the same name at Dambar Chowk, serves tasty meals, including breakfast, and is also a cheap and cheerful bar.

Crown Restaurant, next to the Crown Lodge off Baghdara Rd, has good service, pleasant decor and hearty meals which start at Rs 40.

For authentic Chinese food, try ***Mandarin Restaurant*** at the Motor Stand; ***Chin Li Chinese Restaurant***, on the ground floor of the shopping complex at the corner of Main (SDB Giri) and Rishi Rds; or the classy ***China Garden Restaurant***, in the hotel of the same name near the Motor Stand and the Classic Hotel.

Fresh Bite Restaurant, above Kashi Nath & Sons Booksellers on DB Giri Rd, is a cosy place. The range of meals is impressive, the service is friendly and the prices are good.

Shopping

The Kalimpong Hat Bazaar market along Harijan Rd is held on Wednesday and Saturday, and is a great place to watch locals from nearby villages, often dressed in traditional gear. Dambar Chowk is home to several souvenir shops with authentic Tibetan jewellery and handicrafts. The very friendly Bhutia Shop, next to the DGHC Tourist Reception Centre, stocks traditional Bhutia crafts, such as woodcarvings, pastel paintings and embroidered bags.

(Dambar Chowk, originally known as Maharani Chowk, was adorned with a huge bronze statue of Queen Victoria. Her statue was replaced by another of a local leader of the Gorkha League, Dambar Singh, but the plaque remains declaring him to be 'Queen Victoria, Empress of India'!)

Getting There & Away

Air The nearest airport is at Bagdogra, near Siliguri (see the Siliguri & New Jalpaiguri section earlier in this chapter for more information).

Bus, Taxi & Jeep All long-distance buses and jeeps leave from the Motor Stand. Taxis and jeeps can be chartered for local trips from along Main (SDB Giri) Rd.

To Siliguri (Rs 45, three hours), buses leave every 30 minutes or so from one of the agencies around the Motor Stand. A share-jeep to Siliguri costs Rs 40 (for the back seat) or Rs 50 (front seat); or about Rs 500 to charter a jeep. The road to Siliguri follows the Teesta River after the bridge, so it's much cheaper and quicker than going via Darjeeling.

To Gangtok, via Rangpo, several agencies offer two or three buses each (Rs 55, three to four hours) every morning, which can (and should) be booked in advance. A chartered share-jeep to Gangtok costs Rs 70/700 (three hours).

Jeeps leave regularly for Darjeeling (three hours), and cost Rs 50 (back seat) or Rs 65 (front); about Rs 700 if chartered. A bus also leaves for Darjeeling at about 8 am (Rs 42, 3½ hours).

From the Himalayan Travels office at the Motor Stand, there is a daily service to Kakarbhitta at 7.30 am (Rs 65, five hours) on the border with Nepal, but jeeps are more frequent (Rs 70/700).

Himalayan Travels, and Mintri Transport (☎ 55744) on Main (SDB Giri) Rd, provide buses to Bagdogra airport (Rs 120, three hours) at about 7 am. Mintri Transport can also book regional flights, including around Nepal.

To/From Bhutan See the Land section of the main Getting There & Away chapter for details on travel to Bhutan.

Train It's possible to make bookings for all train journeys originating from New Jalpaiguri station at the Kalimpong Out Agency (☎ 55643) on Mani Rd (walk up the steps behind the building with the relevant sign along DS Gurung Rd). The agency only has a small quota of tickets – mostly 2nd-class sleepers – and is open from 10 am to 1 pm and 4 to 5 pm daily.

AROUND KALIMPONG

Teesta Bazaar

About 16km from Kalimpong where the road divides towards Darjeeling and Siliguri, Teesta Bazaar is becoming a centre for white-water rafting (see White-Water Rafting in the Darjeeling section earlier in this chapter).

The DGHC arranges trips from its office (☎ 09252-68261) in Chitrey Wayside Inn, about 1.5km up from Teesta Bazaar along the road to Gangtok and Kalimpong. It charges from Rs 350 (1½ hours) to Rs 650 (three hours), including equipment and guide, but not food or transport. Bookings can also be made at the DGHC tourist offices in Darjeeling and Kalimpong.

Chitrey Wayside Inn (*☎ 09252-68261*) offers dorm beds for Rs 80 per person, and pleasant doubles with private bathroom for Rs 365. It also has a restaurant.

Teesta Bazaar is approximately two hours from Darjeeling; take any bus or share-jeep (Rs 40) to Kalimpong.

Lava & Kaffer

About 35km east of Kalimpong, Lava (at an altitude of 2353m) is a small village with a Kagyupa **gompa** and a bustling, energetic **market** on Tuesday.

Kaffer (at 1555m), also known locally as Lolegaon, is about 30km farther east. From nearby Jhandidara, the views of Kanchenjunga and other mountains are as good as those from Tiger Hill, near Darjeeling. Kaffer is also the base for organised treks through the Neora Valley, near the border with Bhutan.

The ***forest resthouses*** at Lava and Kaffer offer comfortable doubles with bathroom (and hot water in buckets) for Rs 450, and dorm beds for Rs 50 per person. Book at the Forest Development Corporation (see under Information in the Kalimpong section earlier).

Dafay Munal Tourist Lodge – also known as the Kaffer Tourist Lodge – at Kaffer is run by the DGHC. It charges Rs 450 for doubles with bathroom and cable TV. Dorms are usually available for Rs 50 per person.

Himalayan Travels at the Motor Stand in Kalimpong has two buses a day (8 am and 1 pm) to Kaffer (Rs 35, four hours), via Lava (Rs 21, 2½ hours).

Samco Ropeway

Thrill seekers should head for the Samthar Agriculture Marketing Co-operative (Samco) ropeway (chairlift), installed as part of an aid program to help villagers, and their produce, travel about 1.5km across, and some 40m above, the Teesta and Relli Rivers. At the other end, it's possible to walk around Samthar Plateau (see section following). However, if the idea of dangling from a piece of wire doesn't entice, give this a miss – it is most definitely not for vertigo sufferers!

The ropeway operates from about 8 am to 4 pm daily, but usually not on Sunday. It's 20km from Kalimpong, along the main Siliguri-Gangtok road at a place known locally as 27th Mile. From Kalimpong, catch any bus/jeep towards Siliguri (about Rs 23, one hour).

Samthar Plateau

This gorgeous area offers awesome mountain views, traditional villages and forests – all ideal for short hikes.

Farm House is run by Gurudongma House (Web site www.adventuresikkim.com/samtharfarmhouse.html) in Kalimpong, and is a luxurious place in the midst of the forest. It offers packages, including accommodation, meals, hiking and transport, from US$75/110 a day for singles/doubles. Camping may also be available.

The occasional shared jeep (Rs 65, three hours) makes the journey from Kalimpong; alternatively, use the Samco Ropeway.

Sikkim

For many years, Sikkim was regarded as one of the last Himalayan 'Shangri-las' because of its remoteness, spectacular mountain terrain, varied flora and fauna, and ancient Buddhist *gompas* (monasteries). It was never easy to visit and, even now, you need a permit to enter Sikkim – although this is easy to obtain (see the Permits section later in this chapter).

To ease potential resentment against the central government, India spends relatively large sums of money to subsidise Sikkim's road building, electricity supply, water supply and agricultural and industrial development. Much of this activity is also no doubt motivated by India's fear of Chinese military designs on Sikkim. Consequently, the state is more affluent than West Bengal, and being a tax-free zone no doubt helps further.

History

The region was originally home to the Lepchas, a tribal people thought to have migrated from the hills of Assam, or possibly even from South-East Asia, around the 13th century. The Lepchas were peaceful forest foragers and small-crop cultivators who worshipped nature spirits.

Tibetans began migrating to Sikkim during the 15th century to escape religious strife between various Buddhist orders. In Tibet, the Gelukpa order (of which the Dalai Lama is the head) gradually gained the upper hand. The Nyingmapa order was introduced in Sikkim by three Tibetan lamas (priests), Lhatsun Chempo, Kathok Rikzin Chempo and Ngadak Sempa Chempo. These lamas consecrated the first *chogyal* (king), Phuntsog Namgyal, at Yuksom, which became the capital of the kingdom (it was later moved to Rabdentse, near Pelling). In the face of waves of Tibetan migrants (known as Bhutias), the Lepchas retreated to remote regions.

When the kingdom of Sikkim was founded, the country included the area encompassed by the present state as well as

Sikkim at a Glance

Population: 507,000
Area: 7096 sq km
Capital: Gangtok
Main Language: Nepali
When to Go: Mar to late May; mid-Oct to mid-Dec

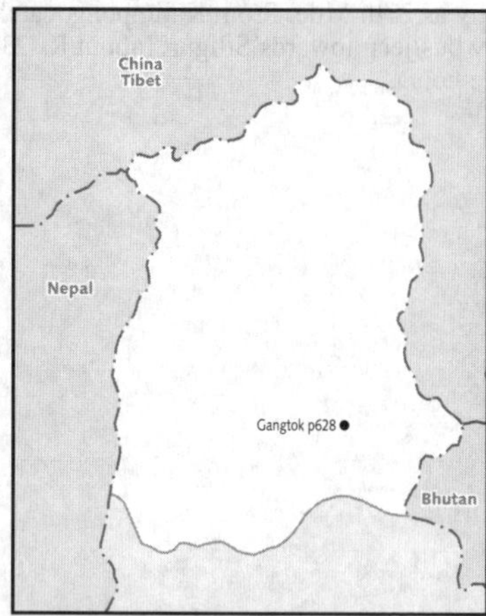

- Visit the monks at Rumtek Dharma Chakra Centre near Gangtok
- Walk the very accessible route from Pelling to Pemayangtse Gompa, one of the state's most important monasteries
- Take a wonderful journey through the Kanchenjunga National Park with a Yuksom-Dzongri-Goecha La trek
- Enjoy the wonderfully peaceful atmosphere at Sangachoeling Gompa, the second-oldest gompa in Sikkim
- Take a walk or ride on a yak along the shores of the sacred Tsomgo (Changu) Lake
- Learn about Buddhism at the Namgyal Institute of Tibetology in Gangtok

part of eastern Nepal, the Chumbi Valley (Tibet), Ha Valley (Bhutan) and the terai foothills down to the plains of India, including Darjeeling and Kalimpong. Much of this territory was later lost during wars with Bhutan and the Gurkhas from Nepal.

In 1835, the British, seeking a hill station as a rest and recreation centre for their troops and officials, persuaded the chogyal to cede the Darjeeling area in return for an annual stipend. Tibet objected to this transfer of territory, regarding Sikkim as a vassal state – also Darjeeling's rapid growth as a trade centre began to make a considerable impact on the fortunes of Sikkim's leading lamas and merchants.

Tensions rose and, in 1849, the British annexed the entire area between the present Sikkim border and the Ganges plains, and withdrew the chogyal's stipend. Further British interference lead to the declaration of a protectorate over Sikkim in 1861 and the delineation of its borders. Tibet, however, continued to regard these actions as illegal and, in 1886, invaded Sikkim to reassert its authority. The attack was soon repulsed by the British, who sent a punitive military expedition to Lhasa in 1888.

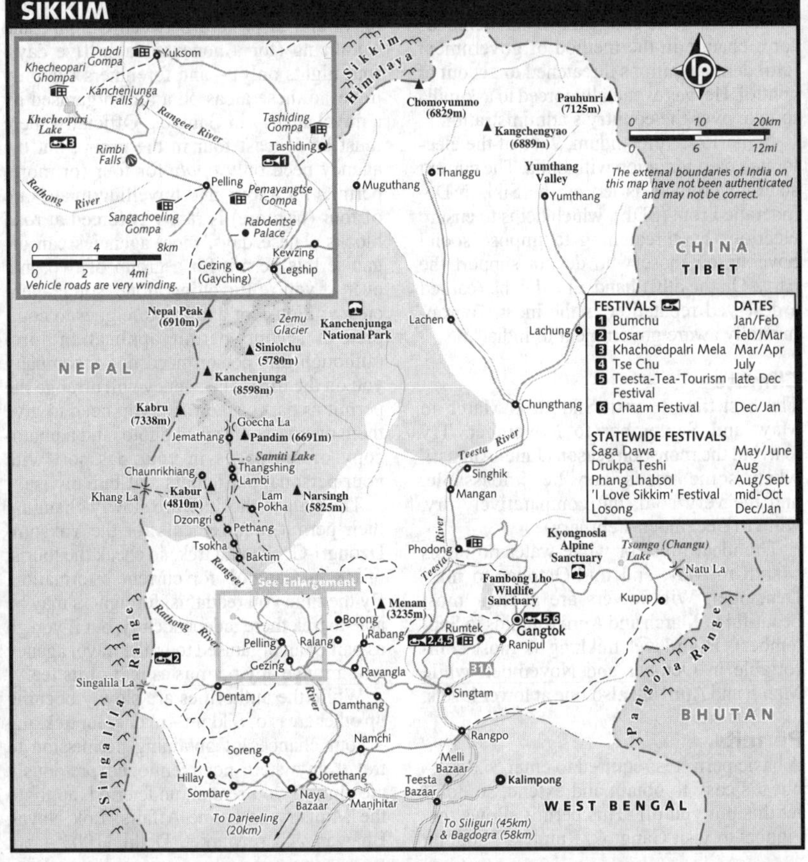

The British treaties with Sikkim passed to India at Independence. Demands within Sikkim for a democratic form of government as opposed to rule by the chogyal were growing. The Indian government supported these moves as it didn't want to be seen to be propping up an autocratic regime while doing its best to sweep away the last traces of princely rule in India itself.

The last chogyal, Palden Thondup Namgyal, came to the throne in 1963, but struggled to live up to the revered memory of his father, Tashi Namgyal. The Nepali population in Sikkim pushed for a greater say in government, and impoverished Nepali farmers began attacking the larger landowning monasteries. The chogyal resisted demands for a change in the method of government until demonstrations threatened to get out of control. He was eventually forced to ask India to take over the country's administration.

In the 1975 referendum, 97% of the electorate voted for union with India. The current state government is led by the Sikkim Democratic Front (SDF), which helps to ensure elections by threatening to impose social boycotts on those who do not support the party. On the other hand, the SDF has earned a deserved reputation as the most environmentally aware government in India.

Climate

The best time to visit Sikkim is March to May, and September to November. Try to avoid the monsoon season (June–August), when some roads can be impassable, and the very cold, but comparatively dry, winter (December–February).

The ideal time for white-water rafting is March to May, and mid-October to mid-December. Wildflowers are at their most beautiful in March and April (orchids in September). High-level trekking is most comfortable in October and November, while March and April are also fine at lower levels.

Permits

A basic permit is required to enter Sikkim – but it's easy to obtain and extend, so don't let this put you off. This permit allows foreigners to visit Gangtok, Rumtek, Phodong and Pemayangtse (which includes Pelling, Legship and Gezing). Although it doesn't say so on the permit, foreigners can also visit any town along the main roads between these four places, and the border towns of Rangpo and Jorethang.

A special endorsement on this permit (or one's visa) allows foreigners to also visit Khecheopari Lake, Singhik, Yuksom and Tashiding, and anywhere on the way to, or near, these places. This endorsement can be obtained from the tourist office in Gangtok in a minute or two without a fee or photo.

Because of military sensitivities, foreigners need an additional special permit to visit Tsomgo (Changu) Lake (valid for one day only) and anywhere between Singhik and Yumthang (for a nonextendable five days/four nights only) – and foreigners can only travel to these areas on a tour organised by a travel agency in Gangtok. Officially, there must be at least four in the group, but the agency need only *apply* for four (or more) permits for a tour, and travelling in a group of four (or more) is rarely enforced at road blocks. These days, most agencies can organise this permit for a group of two, and even if you're travelling alone, some agencies will look for another foreigner to complete a second permit application form (although this person need not accompany you on the trip). The agency will arrange the permit as part of their fee; you need to give them one passport-sized photo, and a photocopy of the pages in your passport with your personal particulars and Indian visa.

The state authorities are slowly changing their permit requirements for the Yuksom-Dzongri-Goecha La trek, so check the tourist office in Gangtok for current information. By the time you read this, foreigners may be able to trek there independently, but if you go as part of an organised tour, the travel agency will arrange any permits as part of its fee.

While the authorities are slowly opening up other areas of Sikkim – mainly for trekking – your chances of obtaining permission to travel anywhere not mentioned previously are slim. If you remain undeterred, apply to the Ministry of Home Affairs, Lok Nayak Bhawan, Khan Market, Delhi 11003 – but each application will take at least three visits and a month or more of waiting and frustration. If all else fails, try for a permit at the Home Office in Gangtok.

There are two entry points to Sikkim: Jorethang (if travelling to/from Pelling) and Rangpo (if travelling to/from Gangtok). If coming through Jorethang, you must have a permit (or endorsed visa – see later in this section) obtained beforehand. If travelling via Rangpo, you can get a (free) two-day permit at the border; the permit must be extended within two days at Gangtok (see Permit Extensions following).

Basic permits (ie, for Gangtok, Rumtek, Phodong and Pemayangtse) are easy to obtain in India. You must fill out a form specifying your intended date of entry to Sikkim. (Note that you cannot enter Sikkim *before* this date.) You also have to provide one passport-sized photo, and possibly a photocopy of your passport pages with your personal details and Indian visa. There is no fee, and the permit is often available within one or two hours.

Permits are normally valid for 15 days from the specified date of entry. Note that re-entry into Sikkim within three months is not possible, even if you leave Sikkim before your 15-day permit expires.

Basic permits can be obtained from any of the following places:

Foreigners' Registration Offices Delhi and Kolkata (Calcutta) (see the relevant chapters for more details)
New Sikkim House (☎ 011-6116346) 14 Panchseel Marg, Chanakyapuri, Delhi
Office of the District Magistrate Hill Cart Rd, Darjeeling (see the West Bengal chapter for more details)
Sikkim Tourist Information Centres (☎ 0353-432646) SNT Colony, Hill Cart Rd, Siliguri (☎ 033-2468983) 4C Poonam Bldg, 5/2 Russell St, Kolkata

When you apply for your Indian visa overseas, you can also ask for the visa to be endorsed with permission to travel to Gangtok, Rumtek, Phodong and Pemayangtse. An entry date to Sikkim is normally not specified on your visa (which is an advantage), but Indian embassies/consulates overseas charge an extra fee (up to US$30) for travel to Sikkim.

Basic permits (or endorsed visas) are checked, and your passport is stamped, when entering and leaving Sikkim, and usually on the Yuksom-Dzongri-Goecha La trek – but probably nowhere else in Sikkim.

Permit Extensions Within two days of expiry, a basic permit can be extended, by an extra 15 days, twice (ie, 45 days is the maximum time allowed in Sikkim). Firstly, fill out an application form at Tashi Ling (Home Office), just off Bhanu Path in Gangtok. (Ignore the sign at the gate 'Tourists cannot enter from 10 am to 4 pm weekdays', which are the official opening hours.) Then stroll down to the Foreigners' Registration Office on Kazi Rd (open 10 am to 4 pm Monday to Friday and 10 am to 2 pm Saturday and Sunday). The whole process takes about 30 minutes.

National Parks Access to Kanchenjunga National Park – other than the Yuksom-Dzongri-Goecha La trek – is generally only permitted to mountaineering expeditions, or experienced trekking parties using the services of a recognised travel agency. Most of the travel agencies listed in the Gangtok section later in this chapter can assist; otherwise, apply for a permit at your local Indian embassy/consulate, or the Ministry of Home Affairs, Grih Mantralaya, Delhi 11003. Permission is also required from the Chief Wildlife Warden (☎ 23191), Forest Department, Deorali, Gangtok, Sikkim, 737102.

Mountaineering expeditions interested in climbing peaks over 6000m need to obtain clearance at least six months in advance from the Indian Mountaineering Foundation (☎ 011-4671211, fax 6883412), Benito Juarez Rd, Anand Niketan, Delhi 110021. Some peaks are still off limits because they are regarded as sacred or located in sensitive military areas. For religious reasons, climbers are not permitted to climb to the top of Kanchenjunga – they must stop 10m short of the summit.

Permits are also currently required to visit Fambong Lho Wildlife Sanctuary and

Kyongnosla Alpine Sanctuary. These are available from the Divisional Forest Officer (☎ 23191), Wildlife Circle, Forest Department, Deorali, Gangtok, Sikkim 737102.

Special Events

Sikkim hosts a number of statewide festivals:

Losong December/January. Celebrates Sikkimese New Year.
Saga Dawa May/June. Features processions to celebrate the Buddha's birth.
Drukpa Teshi August. Celebrates the Buddha's first teaching.
Phang Lhabsol August/September. Features Sikkimese dances devoted to Kanchenjunga.
'I Love Sikkim' Festival Mid-October. Features music, dance and food.

For information about other festivals held in Sikkim, see under Gangtok, Enchey Gompa, Rumtek, Pemayangtse Gompa, Khecheopari Lake and Tashiding.

SIKKIM

East Sikkim

GANGTOK

☎ 03592 • pop 90,000

The capital of Sikkim, Gangtok (which means 'hilltop') sprawls down the west side of a long ridge flanking the Ranipul River. The scenery is spectacular, especially from the area known as 'the ridge', and many points in the city offer excellent views of the entire Kanchenjunga range.

Gangtok only became the capital of Sikkim in the mid-19th century. It has undergone a rapid and rather unattractive modernisation in recent years, but it's still a pleasant place with good facilities for visitors. In late December, Gangtok co-hosts (with Rumtek) the **Teesta-Tea-Tourism Festival**, featuring music, food and flowers.

Information

Tourist Offices The Sikkim Tourist Information Centre (☎ 22064), at the northern end of MG Marg, should be the first point of call for all visitors. The notice board is a mine of information, and staff can advise on permits and festival dates. It's open 8 am to 6 pm daily March to May and October to December, and 10 am to 4 pm the rest of the year.

Money Some mid-range and top-end hotels can change money for clients, but the best place is the State Bank of India, on MG Marg; open 10 am to 2 pm and 2.30 to 4 pm Monday to Friday and 10 am to 1 pm Saturday. It changes US dollars and pounds sterling in Thomas Cook and American Express (AmEx) travellers cheques, and cash in US dollars, pounds sterling, French francs, Swiss francs and Japanese yen. It does not provide cash advances with any credit card.

Post & Communications The main post office along PS Rd has a poste restante. There is no shortage of public call offices (PCOs) for local and long-distance telephone calls around the streets.

Access at the many Internet centres is reliable, and the standard rate is about Rs 1 per minute. The best three are Gokul, in an arcade off MG Marg; the trendy Sip 'n' Surf, at the top of the steps along Lal Market Rd; and Logon.com, farther along MG Marg.

Trekking & Travel Agencies Some attractions, eg, Tsomgo (Changu) Lake and areas such as northern Sikkim, can only be visited through a travel agency (see the Permits section earlier in this chapter). Some agencies can also offer tours specialising in bird-watching, mountain-climbing, rafting and mountain-biking. Equipment hire (sleeping bags etc) is available from some operators.

Following is a short list of some reliable operators; there are dozens more which are probably just as good.

Blue Sky Treks & Travels (☎ 25113, ⓔ skar@cal2.vsnl.net.in) Tibet Rd. Offers several interesting budget-priced treks, and runs lodges in northern Sikkim.
Potala Tours & Travels (☎ 24434, ⓔ potala@dte.vsnl.net.in) PS Rd. One of several adjacent agencies, it offers the usual range of tours (including rafting) and treks at reasonable prices.
Sikkim Tours & Travels (☎ 22188, ⓔ sikkimtours@sikkim.org) Church Rd. An impressive and friendly outfit which also organises photography and bird-watching tours.

Siniolchu Tours & Travels (☎ 25569, ⓔ siniolchu@dte.vsnl.net.in) PS Rd. Offers a wide range of treks, and cultural and mountain-biking tours. Web site: www.sikkiminfo.com/siniolchu

Tashila Tours & Travels (☎ 22979, ⓔ tashilatt@hotmail.com) 31A National Highway. Can arrange rafting and special-interest tours. Web site: www.sikkiminfo.com/tashila

Wisdom Tours & Travels (☎ 20824, ⓔ baichungb@hotmail.com) Next to the tourist office on MG Marg. Friendly, convenient and competent. Web site: www.wisdomtravels.com

Yak & Yeti Travels (☎/fax 24643, ⓔ yakyeti@dte.vsnl.net.in) Hotel Superview Himalchuli, 31A National Highway. Informative and good value, it specialises in mountain-climbing.

Bookshops Good Books, at the end of an arcade off MG Marg, and Jainco Booksellers at 31A National Highway, offer an impressive range of books and maps about Sikkim.

Emergency In case of an emergency, contact the police on ☎ 22033 or the STNM hospital on ☎ 22944.

Enchey Gompa

This monastery is worth a visit, particularly when religious mask dances are performed during the **Chaam Festival** in December/January. A fairly recent construction, built in 1909, it's now home to about 100 monks from the Nyingmapa order.

The prayer hall is completely covered with exquisite paintings, and the roof is supported by four intricately carved pillars. At the *chwashyam* (altar) end of the prayer hall is a large Buddha; on the right is Padmasambhava and, on the left, is Avalokiteshvara. On the left wall, near the chwashyam and behind the glass cabinet, is an image of Dorje Phurba. The *dorje* (thunderbolt) and *phurba* (ritual dagger) are important tantric ritual instruments; Dorje is the wild-eyed male part of the image and Phurba, the female, is locked in his embrace.

The gompa sits on a spectacular ridge, with views across Gangtok and as far as Kanchenjunga. It's near the unmissable telecommunications tower, a steep 2km walk north-east from the city centre.

Namgyal Institute of Tibetology

Established in 1958 and built in traditional Tibetan style, this unique institute promotes research into Mahayana Buddhism and the language and traditions of Tibet. It has one of the world's largest collections of books and rare manuscripts on Mahayana Buddhism, many religious works of art and a collection of finely embroidered silk *thangkas* (Tibetan cloth religious paintings). It also houses relics of monks from the time of Ashoka, examples of Lepcha script, masks, and ceremonial and sacred objects such as a *kapali* (bowl made from a human skull) and *varku* (flute made from a thigh bone).

The institute also sells religious arts and crafts, and books about Buddhism. It's open 10 am to 4 pm Monday to Friday and every second Saturday; entry costs Rs 5. As a sacred place, footwear should be removed before entering the main building. It is an easy walk down 31A National Highway, and accessible by share-taxi, share-jeep and van.

Do-Drul Chorten & Gompa

The gold apex of this huge white chorten, surrounded by prayer flags, is visible from many points in Gangtok. Next to the chorten is a gompa for young lamas with a shrine containing huge images of Padmasambhava and his manifestation, Guru Snang–Sid Zilzon. While the gompa is relatively unimpressive, the chorten is spectacular and the whole area is wonderfully serene. It's about 500m above the Namgyal Institute of Tibetology.

Parks & Gardens

Surrounding the Namgyal Institute of Tibetology, and enclosed by a peaceful forest, is the unimpressive **Orchid Sanctuary**, which features some of the 454 species of orchid found in Sikkim.

Along Jawharlal Nehru Marg, the small **Flower Exhibition Centre** features orchids and bonsai, among other plants. It's open 10 am to 6 pm daily from April to June and September to late November. Just above the exhibition centre, the small but pretty **Ridge Park** is one of many tranquil places in the area known as The Ridge. The new **City**

SIKKIM

Millennium Garden, between 31A National Highway and Bhanu Path, is another pleasant spot.

Tsuk-La-Khang (Royal Chapel) & Palace

The Royal Chapel is the repository of a large collection of scriptures. It's a beautiful and impressive building, and its interior is covered with murals. Lavishly decorated altars hold images of the Buddha, Bodhisattvas and Tantric deities, and there are also plenty of fine woodcarvings.

Normally, the chapel is closed to the public; the only time it's definitely open to visitors is during **Losar**, the Tibetan New Year in February/March.

The nearby palace is also rarely open to the public.

Activities

For something special (on a clear day), Sikkim Helicopter Service offers flights over West Sikkim (Rs 3250 per person, one hour); Yumthang (Rs 3750, 70 minutes); Kanchenjunga (Rs 5000, 1½ hours); and joyrides around Gangtok (Rs 1200, 20 minutes). See Getting There & Away later in this section for contact details.

Rafting trips down the Teesta River can be organised with several travel agencies, such as Tashila and Potala. These are good value: about Rs 350/600/900 per person for a 1/2/3½ hour trip, including equipment and guide, but not transport. A minimum number of about six is required.

Organised Tours

Any of the travel agencies listed earlier can arrange customised local tours. These agencies, as well as local taxi drivers, also offer three types of 'official' tours: 'three point tours', including Ganesh Tok and Tashi view points (for Rs 300 per vehicle); 'five point tours', including Enchey Gompa, Flower Exhibition Centre and Namgyal Institute (Rs 420); and 'seven point tours' (basically the same as the 'five point tour' plus Rumtek) for Rs 600.

Unless you can get a group of four or five people together, these tours are way over-

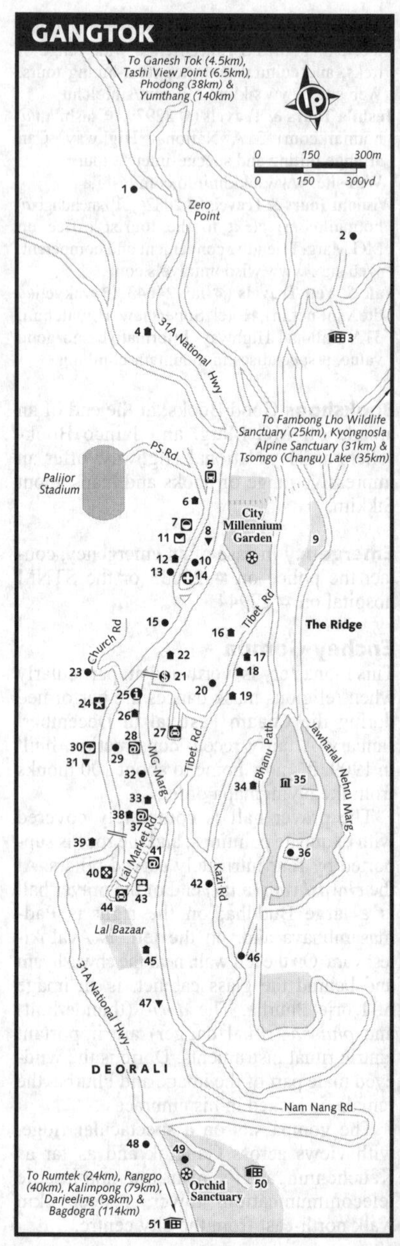

GANGTOK

PLACES TO STAY
4 Hotel Superview Himalchuli; Yak & Yeti Travels
6 Hotel Lha Khar
12 Hotel Tibet; Charitrust Tibetan Handicraft Emporium
16 Hotel Sonam Delek; Oyster Bar & Restaurant
17 Hotel Heritage
18 Modern Central Lodge
19 Hotel Lhakpa
22 Gangtok Lodge
26 Green Hotel; Silk Route Tours & Travels
33 Hotel Golden Pagoda
34 Hotel Pomra
38 Hotel Orchid; Orchid Cafe
39 Hotel Central
45 Hotel Tashi Delek

PLACES TO EAT
8 Cafe Tibet
31 Hotel Hungry Jack; Tripti's
47 Oberoi's Barbique Restaurant

OTHER
1 Directorate of Handicrafts & Handlooms
2 Telecommunications Tower
3 Enchey Gompa
5 SNT Bus Station; Railway Reservation Counter
7 Jeep Station
9 Flower Exhibition Centre; Ridge Park
10 Siniolchu Tours & Travels; Potala Tours & Travels
11 Main Post Office
13 Tibetan Souvenir & Handicrafts Stores
14 STNM Hospital
15 Jainco Booksellers
20 Blue Sky Treks & Travels
21 State Bank of India
23 Sikkim Tours & Travels
24 Police Station
25 Sikkim Tourist Information Centre; Blue Sheep Fast Food Centre; Blue Sheep Fast Food Restaurant; Wisdom Tours & Travels
27 Old Children's Park Taxi Station
28 Gokul (Internet Centre); RNC Enterprises; Parivar Restaurant; Khan Khazana
29 Tashila Tours & Travels
30 Private Bus & Taxi Station
32 Good Books; Rural Artisans' Marketing Centre
35 Palace
36 Tsuk-La-Khang (Royal Chapel)
37 Sip 'n' Surf
40 Supermarket Complex
41 Logon.com
42 Foreigners' Registration Office
43 Denzong Cinema
44 Lal Bazaar Taxi Stand
46 Tashi Ling (Home Office)
48 Forest Department Office
49 Namgyal Institute of Tibetology; Orchid Sanctuary
50 Do-Drul Chorten & Gompa
51 Guru Lhakhang Gompa

priced; and most attractions are within walking distance or easily accessible by chartered or share-taxi, share-jeep and van.

Places to Stay

In winter, it's important to inquire about the reliability and cost of hot water and heating. Few places have single rooms, and there's often no discount for single occupancy of a double room. A lot of mid-range and top-end hotels offer rates including meals, but these are not good value because there are plenty of good, cheap restaurants in Gangtok.

Low-season discounts (January to March, and July to August) vary between 15% and 30%. High-season rates are listed here.

Places to Stay – Budget

Modern Central Lodge *(☎ 24670, Tibet Rd)* is popular and well set up for backpackers. Unexciting but clean singles/doubles with shared bathroom cost Rs 100/180; doubles with private bathroom (and hot water) are Rs 250. A dorm bed (eight in a room) with shared bathroom costs only Rs 40 per person.

Plenty of hotels with decent rooms for about Rs 200/250 are dotted along the middle section of Tibet Rd. ***Hotel Lhakpa*** *(☎ 23002)* offers doubles (no singles) with private bathroom (cold water and squat toilets) for Rs 250. ***Hotel Heritage*** *(☎ 22701, e nirmal-mist@hotmail.com)* boasts some imaginative decor. Pleasant rooms with private bathroom (and hot water) cost a negotiable Rs 250/300; Rs 325/400 with cable TV. It also offers dorm beds for Rs 150 per person.

Green Hotel *(☎ 25057, e greenhot@dte.vsnl.net.in, MG Marg)* is comfortable and good value. It charges from Rs 150 for tiny singles to Rs 250 for larger doubles; better doubles with cable TV cost Rs 350. All come with private bathroom (with erratic hot water), and prices are negotiable.

Hotel Lha Khar *(☎ 25708, PS Rd)* is one of several budget places near the main post office, and is convenient to the SNT bus station. This pleasant, quiet hotel has basic, but spotless, rooms for Rs 200/300 with private bathroom (hot water) and cable TV.

SIKKIM

Hotel Orchid *(☎ 23151, 31A National Highway)* is another reasonable option, but the rooms with outside windows face the noisy road and the rooms without windows are gloomy. It is good value and clean. Rooms with shared bathroom cost Rs 100/200; and doubles (no singles) with private bathroom are Rs 300.

Hotel Pomra *(☎ 26648, Bhanu Path)* has been recommended by readers, mainly because it's in a quiet area. Clean rooms (some with views) cost Rs 250/370, and the dorm beds for Rs 80 are good value.

Places to Stay – Mid-Range

All places listed following have private bathrooms (with continuous hot water) and cable TV.

Gangtok Lodge *(☎ 27319, ⓔ moderntreks@hotmail.com, MG Marg)* is very friendly and central – but noisy. Standard doubles cost Rs 300, and very nice 'special' rooms (with lovely bathrooms) are Rs 800. Single rates are not available, however, hefty discounts (of about 30%) are offered most of the time.

Hotel Sonam Delek *(☎ 22566, ⓔ sonam.delek@gokulnet.com, Tibet Rd)* is pleasant and offers great views. The double rooms are bright and airy (most are quiet), and range from Rs 550 to 800 for the 'super deluxe' (ie, with the best views).

Hotel Superview Himalchuli *(☎/fax 24643, ⓔ himalchuli@usa.net, 31A National Highway)* is in a more pleasant area, and boasts excellent views and helpful staff. Dorm beds cost Rs 75 per person; small 'standard' doubles are unremarkable, but adequate for Rs 375; and spacious, well-furnished 'deluxe' rooms cost Rs 675/775 for doubles/triples.

Hotel Golden Pagoda *(☎ 26928, ⓔ goldenpagoda@hotmail.com, MG Marg)* is almost a top-end hotel with mid-range prices. It's central, but the rooms are smallish. Singles/doubles (some of which have great views) start at Rs 495/875.

Places to Stay – Top End

Top-end hotels add a 10% service charge (included in the rates given here).

Hotel Tashi Delek *(☎ 22991, ⓔ tashidelek@sikkim.org, MG Marg)* has luxurious suites (Rs 4500) with awesome mountain views. The less-expensive singles/doubles (Rs 2500/2700) are comfortable, but the views of the grimy walls of neighbouring hotels are disappointing.

Hotel Tibet *(☎ 22523, fax 26233, PS Rd)* is comfortable, popular and friendly. (You'll be welcomed by a doorman in full traditional Tibetan dress!) The cheaper rooms (starting at Rs 1012/1320) have no views, but the more expensive ones (starting at Rs 1265/1760) are well furnished, with traditional Tibetan decor, and have wonderful views.

Hotel Central *(☎ 22105, ⓔ hotel_central@hotmail.com, 31A National Highway)* has been recommended by readers. It's friendly and convenient, but noisy, and offers very comfortable rooms for Rs 990/1430.

Places to Eat

Some of the best places to eat are in the hotels listed previously. ***Modern Central Lodge***, ***Hotel Lhakpa***, ***Hotel Lha Khar*** and ***Green Hotel*** have popular restaurants offering cheap and tasty meals – usually Tibetan, Chinese and Indian – with some Western alternatives such as pancakes.

Oyster Bar & Restaurant, at Hotel Sonam Delek on Tibet Rd, is a bit more upmarket, and offers continental dishes, such as French toast, pizza and pancakes, as well as Chinese, Indian and Tibetan cuisine.

Hotel Golden Pagoda *(MG Marg)* has a rooftop vegetarian restaurant with lovely views and reasonable prices. It is open at 8 am for breakfast.

Hotel Hungry Jack *(31A National Highway)* has quick service, tasty meals and a reliable supply of cold beer. Underneath, ***Tripti's*** is the best bakery in town.

Cafe Tibet *(31A National Highway)* is popular with local youth for sickly cakes, burgers, pizzas and milkshakes. ***Orchid Cafe***, underneath Hotel Orchid on 31A National Highway, is similar.

Oberoi's Barbique Restaurant *(MG Marg)* is informal, clean and modern, and great for Western snacks, such as club sandwiches, as well as Indian and Chinese meals.

Blue Sheep Fast Food Centre, next to the tourist office on MG Marg, does adequate burgers, while ***Blue Sheep Restaurant***, upstairs, is classy and good value.

Parivar Restaurant, downstairs from Gokul on MG Marg, is good for vegetarian food; and ***Khan Khazana***, at the back of the same arcade, has excellent service and delicious vegetarian food, including pizzas.

Entertainment

Numerous seedy little bars are dotted around town. All offer cheap prices (eg, a large bottle of tasty Dansberg beer costs about Rs 35), but finding a cold 'un is not always easy. More inviting places for a drink are ***Hotel Hungry Jack*** and ***Blue Sheep Restaurant*** (see Places to Eat). Full-moon and new-moon days are 'dry' days in Sikkim, but some bars still serve alcohol. For something different, try a mug of *chang*, known locally as *tongba* (fermented millet beer), from a shop in Lal Bazaar.

Denzong Cinema, at Lal Bazaar, shows popular Indian films (in Hindi) for Rs 15/30 for front/upper circle seats.

Shopping

The Directorate of Handicrafts & Handlooms at Zero Point sells hand-woven carpets, blankets and shawls, patterned decorative paper, and beautifully carved Choktse tables. It's open 9.30 am to 12.30 pm and 1 to 3 pm daily (except Sunday). It also hosts several craft fairs throughout the tourist season.

Many shops sell Tibetan handicrafts, especially along PS Rd, such as the Charitrust Tibetan Handicraft Emporium (beneath Hotel Tibet), where profits are used to fund education programs for Tibetan children. The Rural Artisans' Marketing Centre, on MG Marg, sells Tibetan carpets, among other things, and profits also help fund local development projects.

Lal Bazaar is also worth a visit, and is the place to try tough *churpi* (yak cheese). It's open daily, but especially lively on Sunday.

Getting There & Away

Air The nearest airport is at Bagdogra, near Siliguri – see Getting There & Away under Siliguri & New Jalpaiguri in the West Bengal chapter for details.

Sikkim Helicopter Service offers a daily flight between the Bagdogra airport and a helipad, 6km north of Gangtok (Rs 1500, 30 minutes). It leaves Gangtok at 11 am and returns from the airport at 2.45 pm. Book at RNC Enterprises (☎ 28652), upstairs on MG Marg, which is also the Jet Airways agency. The Indian Airlines agency is Silk Route Tours & Travels (☎ 23354), above Green Hotel on MG Marg.

Bus Sikkim Nationalised Transport (SNT), the main bus operator to/from Gangtok, offers plenty of decrepit buses from its well-organised bus station on PS Rd. The booking office is open 9 am to noon and 1 to 2 pm daily.

SNT has several buses a day to Siliguri (Rs 55, five hours); one a day to Darjeeling (Rs 83, six to seven hours) at 7 am, and to Kalimpong (Rs 55, three to four hours) at 1 pm. Within Sikkim, SNT buses go to Rumtek (Rs 17, 1½ hours) at 4 pm; Mangan (Rs 25, 2½ hours), via Phodong, at 8 am; Singhik (Rs 75, four hours) at 1.30 pm; and Jorethang at 7 am (Rs 55, four hours). SNT buses also leave for Pelling (Rs 70, 5½ hours) at 7 am, via Ravangla, Legship (for connections to Tashiding and Yuksom) and Gezing.

Private buses operate from the private bus and taxi station on 31A National Highway to Siliguri (about every 30 minutes in the morning), and to Darjeeling and Kalimpong at least twice a day. These cost a little more than the SNT buses, but are faster and more comfortable. Tickets can be booked in advance at the station.

Train The Passenger Computerised Railway Service reservation counter (☎ 22014), at the SNT bus station, has a meagre allocation of tickets for services from New Jalpaiguri, near Siliguri. It's open 8 am to 2 pm daily.

Share-Taxi & Share-Jeep Faster and more frequent than buses, share-taxis and share-jeeps are potentially more dangerous and not necessarily as comfortable if you're sitting in the back of a share-jeep.

From the private bus and taxi station on 31A National Highway, share-jeeps regularly depart in the morning to Siliguri (Rs 90, four hours), Darjeeling (Rs 100, five hours), Kalimpong (Rs 65, three hours), Bagdogra (Rs 120, four hours) and Kakarbhitta (Rs 120, five hours) on the border with Nepal. These jeeps can often be booked in advance.

From the Old Children's Park taxi station, many share-jeeps go to Jorethang (Rs 70, three hours); two a day go to Gezing (Rs 95, 4½ hours), and on to Pelling (Rs 130, five hours), via Ravangla (Rs 60, three hours) at 7 am and 12.30 pm; and several a day go to Rangpo (Rs 35, two hours) and Mangan, via Phodong (Rs 40, two hours). Most can be booked in advance from a shed at the back of the station.

From Lal Bazaar, share-jeeps go to regional villages such as Rumtek (Rs 20, one hour).

Getting Around

Taxis, jeeps and vans can be chartered from jeep/taxi stations for trips around Gangtok – eg, a trip across town costs about Rs 50. The rates for chartered taxis to tourist sites are officially fixed, and extortionate – but actually negotiable. Share-taxis, jeeps and vans stop at designated 'taxi stops' along 31A National Highway; from the city centre to Namgyal Institute or Zero Point costs Rs 5.

AROUND GANGTOK

Rumtek

In Rumtek village, on the other side of the valley from Gangtok, is the **Rumtek Dharma Chakra Centre**. It is the seat of the Gyalwa Karmapa, the head of the Kagyupa order of Tibetan Buddhism.

Since 1992, there has been a bitter dispute between two factions, led respectively by Samar Rinpoche and Situ Rinpoche, over the successor to the 16th Gyalwa Karmapa (who died in 1981). The Dalai Lama chose Situ Rinpoche after performing the Kalachakra (Wheel of Time) ceremony in 1993. However, both are still struggling for power – evidenced by the armed soldiers in the vicinity.

The main **gompa** was built recently by the 16th Gyalwa Karmapa, in strict accordance with the traditional designs of his monastery in Tibet. The prayer room enshrines an enormous statue of the Buddha, completely painted in gold. Hundreds of tiny Buddhas kept in glass-fronted holes nearby represent the number of Buddhas who will come to the world. The walls are richly embellished with paintings, including those of Tibetan and Indian scholars, but the murals are not as refined as some of the older gompas in Sikkim. Visitors are welcome to sit in on prayer and chanting sessions.

In the vestibule to the prayer room there are four **paintings** depicting the Great Kings of the four cardinal directions, who guard the universe and the heavens from demons. When facing the prayer hall from left to right they are: Yulkhor Srung (with a white face and playing a stringed instrument) – the King of the East; Namthose (the antithesis of the King of the East, with a blue face, fangs, bulging eyes and drawing a sword from a scabbard) – the King of the North; Chenmizang (blood-red face, with a serpent coiled around his arm, and holding a stupa in his hand) – the King of the West; and Yulkhor Srung (yellow face, holding a rat and banner) – the King of the South.

Behind the prayer hall is the **Great Golden Reliquary Stupa** of the 16th Gyalwa Karmapa. Around the walls are statues of him and his 15 predecessors, and in front of the stupa paper prayer wheels constantly rotate through heat generated by butter lamps. Numerous richly embroidered thangkas are suspended from the ceiling.

Opposite the stupa, is the lavishly decorated **Karma Shri Nalanda Institute**, where monks study advanced Buddhist philosophy.

The centre hosts many religious festivals, including **Tse Chu** in July which features Buddhist dancing, and it celebrates the Tibetan New Year, **Losar**, in February/March. It's open 8 am to 5 pm daily in summer and 10 am to 5 pm daily in winter. A small booklet/map (Rs 20) about the centre is available at the entrance. Visitors must register at the main gate to the village on arrival.

In late December, Rumtek co-hosts (with Gangtok) the **Teesta-Tea-Tourism Festival** which features music, food and flowers. About 3km past the main gate to Rumtek, and through another gate to the left, is an interesting, but far smaller, **gompa**, which was restored in 1983.

Places to Stay & Eat The *Sungay Guest House (☎ 03592-52221, ⓔ dechen@dte.vsnl.net.in)* is an obvious, friendly place surrounded by a pretty garden. It offers basic doubles, some with balconies and views, and private bathroom (with hot water) for a bargain Rs 150. Doubles with private bathroom (cold water) and no views are Rs 100. The staff also serve basic Tibetan and Western meals for guests.

Sangay Hotel (☎ 03592-52238) is down some steps on a corner near the Rumtek Dharma Chakra Centre. Tiny, basic but clean singles/doubles with shared bathroom cost only Rs 50/100.

Hotel Kunga Delek, at the entrance to the Rumtek Dharma Chakra Centre, is run by the centre itself. The double rooms are ordinary, and comparatively overpriced for Rs 100/150 without/with private bathroom.

A few *stalls* along the road to the Centre sells chai, *momos* (steamed dough parcels of vegetables or meat) and other snacks.

Getting There & Away Rumtek is only 26km from Gangtok. The official rate for a chartered jeep/taxi is a ridiculous Rs 240/400 one way/return, but bargaining down to a more reasonable Rs 300 return is not hard. Share-jeeps occasionally leave Lal Bazaar (Rs 20, one hour), and an SNT bus leaves for Rumtek daily from Gangtok at 4 pm (Rs 17, 1½ hours).

It's a pleasant 14km hike (downhill) from Rumtek to the turn-off along the highway, from where it's easy to get a ride for the 12km (uphill) to Gangtok. However, don't expect too much public transport after 3 pm.

Tashi View Point & Ganesh Tok

From Tashi View Point, 8km north of central Gangtok, there are great views of Kanchenjunga (8598m), as well as Siniolchu (5780m). From Tashi, it's possible to walk (about one hour) to Ganesh Tok, another popular lookout. A combined trip to both by taxi from Gangtok costs about Rs 200 return, including about 30 minutes' waiting time. They are also included in local sightseeing tours (see Organised Tours under Gangtok earlier in this chapter).

Fambong Lho Wildlife Sanctuary

This 52-sq-km sanctuary is home to a variety of animals, including barking deers, Himalayan black bears and red pandas, and birdlife, such as laughing thrushes and Nepalese tree creepers. These creatures can be admired from along the 23km path between Golitar and Sang Tsokha inside the sanctuary, or from watchtowers at Alubari, Tinjurey and Sang Tsokha.

SIKKIM

Fambong Lho is open from October to April. Permits are currently required (but easy to obtain) from the Forest Department in Deorali, Gangtok (see National Parks under Permits earlier in this chapter for details) – although the department may drop permit requirements in the future. Entry costs Rs 5, plus Rs 50/250 per day for a still/video camera.

Basic accommodation (about Rs 100 per person) is available at the ***log houses*** in Golitar and Tumin, but bring your own food and water. Book at the Forest Department in Deorali, Gangtok.

The sanctuary is 25km from Gangtok. It's not accessible by public transport, so the only alternative is a chartered jeep or an organised tour. Most agencies listed under Trekking & Travel Agencies in the Gangtok section earlier in this chapter can arrange tours.

Tsomgo (Changu) Lake

Sacred to the local Buddhists, Tsomgo Lake (also called Changu Lake) is perched about 3752m above sea level (about 1250m higher than Gangtok), 37km to the north-east.

It's a great day trip, but don't bother if the weather in Gangtok is cloudy or foggy because it will probably be a peasouper at the lake and the views will be very disappointing. Most of the lake is frozen from

December until about mid-May, but it's still worth seeing if the weather is clear.

Around the lake, there are a few short **walking trails**, **yak rides**, plenty of ***stalls*** selling hot tea/coffee and momos, and the ***Alpine Lodge*** which serves the same sort of food and drink undercover. There are bizarre plans to build an artificial lake nearby for boating and fishing – activities which are not allowed at Tsomgo because it's sacred.

Currently, foreigners can only visit the lake on a day trip organised by a travel agency in Gangtok (see the Permits section earlier in this chapter). The standard charge for foreigners is outrageous: US$10 (or the rupee equivalent) per person in a jeep with two to four people; US$8 per person for a jeep with six or more; and (if possible) US$15 to US$20 for a jeep with one person. If foreigners are eventually allowed to visit the lake independently, a chartered jeep (1½ hours one way) from Lal Bazaar will cost about Rs 700 return, or Rs 130 per person in a share-jeep, including waiting time. No-one (foreign or Indian) is allowed to visit the lake in a private vehicle, and there is no bus service.

Kyongnosla Alpine Sanctuary

This 31-sq-km sanctuary is home to red pandas and musk deers, as well as pheasants, kites and vultures. It also boasts several waterfalls and wonderful blooms of rhododendrons (best from May to August).

Permits are required (but easy to obtain) from the Forest Department in Deorali, Gangtok. There are basic ***log huts*** (about Rs 100 per person) at Kyongnosla and Namnang Lakha; book at the Forest Department. The sanctuary is along the road between Gangtok and Tsomgo Lake, but only accessible by chartered jeep or on a tour organised by one of the travel agencies listed in the Gangtok section earlier in this chapter.

North Sikkim

More of this region is opening to foreigners, but during the monsoons (June – August) the roads are often cut off by landslides.

PHODONG

The main attraction of Phodong is **Phodong Gompa** which belongs to the same order as Rumtek, but is much smaller and less ornate. It's a fairly recent structure, although the original gompa was founded, like Rumtek, in 1740. It has about 60 friendly monks, who are always happy to show visitors around.

The gompa shelters an image of the 9th Karmapa, Wang Chok Dorje, who is believed to have founded the gompa. The chwashyam is covered with ornate woodcarvings of two entwined dragons. Murals depict ranks of previous karmapas and, on the right wall (when facing the chwashyam), is the gompa's protective deity, Mahakala. On the back wall is a depiction of Padmasambhava. The ceiling is supported by six large wooden pillars and has beautiful carved cornices.

Behind the chwashyam is the Nagpo Chenpo meditation room, which features disturbing murals of various demonic deities dismembering miscreants in the bowels of hell. Access is prohibited, however, when monks are meditating inside this room.

Labrang Gompa, 1.2km farther up the road (and visible from Phodong Gompa), was established in 1844 and belongs to the Nyingmapa order.

Places to Stay & Eat

There are a couple of basic places to stay in Phodong village. ***Hotel Northway*** has clean singles/doubles (some with good views) and shared bathroom for Rs 50/100. ***Hotel Yak & Yeti***, about 100m farther down the road, has bright, airy and clean doubles (no singles) for a negotiable Rs 120/150 without/with private bathroom. Both places can rustle up some basic meals, and even some cold beer.

Getting There & Away

Phodong village straddles the main Gangtok-Mangan road, 38km north of the capital. The road (1.2km) to the gompa is unsigned but obvious, and starts about 1.5km south of the village. At the time of research, some of the Gangtok-Mangan road could only be crossed by jeep, so Phodong was not accessible by bus. Share-jeeps from Gangtok to Mangan travel via the gompa turn-off and village (Rs 40, two hours); to avoid the back seat, buy a fare for Mangan (Rs 60).

YUMTHANG VALLEY

Yumthang Valley, situated 140km north of Gangtok at an elevation of 3564m, is now open to foreigners. You can travel as far as Singhik with an endorsement of the basic permit, but between Singhik and Yumthang village you need to join an organised tour (see the Permits section earlier in this chapter). Trekking is not allowed in this area.

There is budget accommodation in Singhik, Chungthang and Lachung. A SNT bus usually leaves Gangtok for Singhik (Rs 75, four hours) at 1.30 pm. Otherwise, take a share-jeep to Mangan and another to Singhik or beyond.

South Sikkim

Most travellers rush through this region while going between Gangtok and Pelling, but the district headquarters of Ravangla is a pleasant base and stopover, and Jorethang is the border town with several places to stay if necessary.

RAVANGLA

☎ 03595

Ravangla has an awesome location facing the Kanchenjunga range. The town is at the junction of the highway between Gangtok and Pelling (ie, Kewzing Rd) and Main Bazaar Rd which goes through the town. At the junction is the jeep stand and Tourist Information Centre.

A 15-minute walk (follow the road to Gangtok, and then to Namchi) from the jeep stand is the **Kunphenling Tibetan Settlement**, where you can buy authentic handmade carpets and other handicrafts. Flags at the end of Main Bazaar Rd indicate steps to the small but friendly **Mani Chokharling Gompa**.

Places to Stay & Eat

Any hotel facing the mountains will initially ask an outrageous price, but negotiation is always possible. All places listed here have a private bathroom (with hot water), unless otherwise stated; and all have a ***restaurant***.

Hotel 10zing *(☎ 60705)*, at the jeep stand, has spartan but clean singles/doubles for Rs 150/250, some with cable TV – but there are rooms with a view.

Hotel Kanchenjunga, up the hill from the jeep stand and behind the State Bank of India, has large and quiet doubles (no singles) for Rs 200.

Hotel Meanamla *(☎ 60666, ⓔ meanamla@hotmail.com)*, along the highway about 100m up from the jeep stand, has poor 'standard' doubles with shared bathroom for Rs 495, but pleasant 'deluxe' doubles start at Rs 660 with cable TV and views.

Hotel Babyla, up from Meanmala, is one of several dreary places on the wrong side of Kewzing Rd (for the views). It has grimy doubles with shared bathroom for Rs 150.

Getting There & Away

From the jeep stand, share-jeeps go to Siliguri (Rs 40, four hours) and Legship (Rs 32, two hours). For Gangtok or Pelling, wait near the jeep stand for a share-jeep or SNT bus to drive past.

AROUND RAVANGLA

The **hot sulphur springs** at Ralang and Borong are open from December to February. The former is accessible on foot (one hour downhill) from the revered **Karma Rabtenling Gompa** in Ralang village; and above the gompa is the huge and new **Palchen Choeling Gompa**. Borong springs are a 45-minute walk downhill from Borong village. From Ravangla, Ralang village is 13km, and Borong village is 20km, and both can be reached by chartered or share-jeep.

JORETHANG

☎ 03595

There is no need to stay at the border town of Jorethang, because Darjeeling is only 26km to the south and Pelling 53km to the north, but it's a pleasant place.

A short, steep walk up some steps opposite the SNT bus station leads to a tiny

SIKKIM

gompa. The prayer room shelters images of Sakyamuni Buddha flanked by Akalokiteshvara on the Buddha's left and Padmasambhava on his right.

Several cheap places to stay and eat are located opposite the bus station. ***Hotel Namgyal*** *(☎ 57263)*, next to the station towards the river, is the best: decent singles/doubles, with private bathroom (and a huge bath) and cable TV cost Rs 150/300.

SNT buses go to Gangtok (Rs 55, four hours) at 7 am and 1.30 pm; to Siliguri (Rs 56, four hours) at 9 am; and to Pelling (Rs 35, three hours) at 9.30 am and 1 pm. Share-jeeps leave regularly (when full) from outside Hotel Namgyal to Darjeeling (Rs 80, 2½ hours); Gangtok (Rs 70, three hours); and Siliguri (Rs 80, 3½ hours). Jeeps leave less often to Yuksom (Rs 90, four hours), via Legship and Tashiding (Rs 75, 2½ hours); and to Pelling (Rs 60, three hours), via Gezing (Rs 35, 2½ hours).

West Sikkim

The roads in this region are mostly sealed between Jorethang and Pelling, but to Tashiding and Yuksom some of the roads are unsealed and subject to landslides.

GEZING (GAYSHING)

☎ 03595

Public transport between Gangtok and Pelling often bypasses the unexciting village of Gezing, but you may have to wait there for a connecting jeep or bus. Gezing is at its best on **market day** (Sunday). The Central Bank of India, down a laneway behind the town square, *may* (or may not) change cash and travellers cheques.

Hotel Attri *(☎ 50602)*, 100m uphill from the town square, has large, clean and quiet singles/doubles, with private bathroom (and hot water) for Rs 385/495.

SNT buses to Gangtok (Rs 54, 4½ hours) leave at 9 am and 1 pm; and about every hour to Jorethang and Siliguri in the morning.

Share-jeeps to Pelling (Rs 15, 15 minutes) leave every 15 to 20 minutes. There are also regular jeeps to Gangtok (Rs 95, 4½ hours), via Jorethang or Ravangla, every 30 minutes in the morning; several at about 7 am daily to Siliguri (Rs 95, four hours); and one per day to Tashiding (Rs 50, two hours) at 1 pm, and to Yuksom (Rs 70, three hours) at 12.30 pm.

PELLING

☎ 03593

The tiny village of Pelling is little more than a string of hotels, but it's a charming and popular place to relax and organise day trips and hikes. It's perched high on a ridge with great views of Kanchenjunga (8598m), which appears to be smaller than the distinctive flat-topped Kabru (7338m) to its left. To the right of Kanchenjunga is the pyramid-shaped Pandim (6691m). The massive bulk dominating the foreground to the right is Narsingh (5825m).

Orientation & Information

Along the road from Gezing is 'Upper Pelling', with a handful of better hotels, the Sikkim Tourist Centre, post office, jeep/bus stand and several restaurants. The road continues up about 250m to an area known as 'the helipad' (actually a football field), with a group of mid-range hotels. Another road at the jeep/bus stand winds down past 'Middle Pelling' and 'Lower Pelling', where there's a bunch of unexciting and inconvenient hotels, and eventually on to Yuksom.

Surprisingly for a place with about 50 hotels, there's nowhere to change money (so try in Gezing), send an email or even buy a newspaper.

Pemayangtse Gompa

Pemayangtse (Perfect Sublime Lotus) was founded in 1705, and is one of the state's most important gompas. Reconstructed several times after earthquakes, it belongs to the Nyingmapa order.

The monastery is a three-storey structure filled with wall paintings and sculptures. In an upstairs hall, elaborately carved cornices frame the ceiling which is supported by brightly painted beams. On the top floor is **Zandog Palri**, an amazing seven-tiered painted wooden model of the abode of

Padmasambhava, complete with rainbows, angels and an array of Buddhas and Bodhisattvas. The model – all seven tiers – was built singlehandedly by the late Dungzin Rinpoche in five years.

Pemayangtse is a 30-minute walk downhill from Upper Pelling, and well signposted from the road to Gezing. In February/March, the gompa celebrates **Losar**, Tibetan New Year, with a big festival.

Sangachoeling Gompa

A 45-minute walk south-west from The Helipad is Sangachoeling Gompa, the second-oldest gompa in Sikkim (first built in 1697). The monastery belongs to the Nyingmapa order, and is one of the few gompas in Sikkim to admit women as nuns. It shelters fine images of Padmasambhava and the Buddha, and the walls are completely covered in murals, although the colours are more muted than usual.

An upstairs room enshrines some less-ornate images, as well as cloth-bound sacred texts. In a small room at the back are some of the original clay statues, some of which still retain fragments of colour. Beside the gompa is a **Buddhist cremation ground** used by Bhutia and Lepcha villagers.

The gompa is in a majestic position, and a wonderful spot to watch the sun rise.

Other Attractions

The ruins of **Rabdentse Palace**, in Sikkim's former capital, is an interesting place to explore, and the views are superb. Walk about 30 minutes farther down towards Gezing from the turn-off to Pemayangtse Gompa, turn left at the 'Archaeological Survey of India' sign, walk across the archery field and look for the start to the 2km track. It's fairly easy to then find your way downhill from the ruins to the Gezing-Pelling road.

The road from Pelling to Yuksom passes the pretty **Rimbi Falls**, about 10km from Pelling.

Organised Tours

Most hotels sell tickets for organised tours, eg, to Rimbi and Kanchenjunga waterfalls and Khecheopari Lake (Rs 100 per person), or to other waterfalls, Pemayangtse Gompa and a few villages (Rs 75); or a combined day trip (starting at Rs 150).

A day trip to Rimbi Falls, Khecheopari Lake, Yuksom and Tashiding will cost about Rs 1200 per jeep (with nine passengers); book at Simvo Tours & Travels (☎ 58342), just down from the jeep/bus stand.

Places to Stay & Eat

All places listed here are in Upper Pelling and, unless stated otherwise, have a private bathroom (with hot water). There is a massive oversupply of hotels throughout Pelling, so negotiation is possible.

Hotel Kabur *(☎ 50685)* is the first place you see as you come from Gezing. It has plain singles/doubles for Rs 150/300. The quaint ***restaurant*** has great views, but not everything on the menu is always available. Nearby, there are several other ***hotels*** for about the same price.

Sikkim Tourist Centre *(☎ 50788)* is a few doors farther down. The rooms (all doubles) are smallish, and cost from Rs 550 to 660 (with better views), but they don't have TV. The ***restaurant*** on the top floor has good service, tasty meals and wonderful views.

Hotel Garuda *(☎ 50614)*, at the jeep/bus stand, is a popular travellers' haunt. Dorm beds (four to a room) cost Rs 50 per person. Ordinary rooms with shared bathroom start at Rs 60/100, and better rooms with private bathroom and cable TV start at Rs 150/200. The ***restaurant*** offers a huge range of Western, Indian, Tibetan and Sikkimese meals.

Hotel Phamrong *(☎ 58218)*, next to Hotel Garuda, is a popular mid-range option. Comfortable rooms with cable TV and views start from a negotiable Rs 550/660.

Ladakh Guesthouse is a rustic Sikkimese house just down from the Garuda. It only has five rooms, all with shared bathroom. At Rs 100 per double, and Rs 50 per dorm bed, not surprisingly it's often full.

Sister Guest House *(☎ 50569)* is a quaint, family-run place along the road to Lower Pelling just below the Garuda. Clean doubles with shared bathroom cost Rs 190. Next door, ***Alpine Restaurant*** is a cosy place run by a friendly Tibetan family. The servings are large, and prices very reasonable.

Hotel Mt Pandim (☎ *50756*), along the road leading up to Pemayangtse Gompa, is a government-run place which has seen better days. Rooms (most with views) start at Rs 550/650, and there's a restaurant and bar.

Getting There & Away

Public transport is infrequent, so if nothing is available go to Gezing (9km downhill), and take a share-jeep or bus from there. Always check the current transport schedules from Pelling with hotel staff.

A SNT bus leaves Pelling for Jorethang (Rs 35, three hours) at 7 am. Another SNT bus leaves Pelling at 3.30 pm and goes past the turn-off (Rs 25, 1½ hours) to Khecheopari Lake.

Simvo Tours & Travels, just down from the jeep/bus stand, has share-jeeps to Siliguri at 6 am (Rs 110, four hours) and 8.30 am (Rs 150), via Jorethang or Ravangla; to Kalimpong (Rs 110, three hours), via Jorethang, at 6 am; and to Gangtok (Rs 130, five hours) at 6 am and 12.30 pm. If there's enough demand, a jeep will leave for Darjeeling (Rs 170, five hours) – otherwise get a connection in Jorethang. Full fares are demanded for partial rides, and advance bookings are essential.

Share-jeeps to Gezing (Rs 15, 15 minutes) leave every 15 to 20 minutes. Share-jeeps between Gezing and Yuksom come through Pelling about every 30 minutes between about 6.30 and 9 am, but these are often full. To Yuksom and Tashiding, it's sometimes easier to start from Gezing, or hitch a ride from Legship.

KHECHEOPARI LAKE

This small and serene lake (pronounced 'catch a perry') is situated in a depression surrounded by prayer flags and forested hills. It's a very holy place, so swimming and smoking is not allowed. The lake is about a five-minute walk from the end of the road, and about 1.5km above it is the small Khecheopari Gompa. In March/April, the lake hosts the Butter Lamp Floating Festival, **Khachoedpalri Mela**.

Khecheopari Trekkers' Hut, about 200m before the end of the road, offers clean, but very basic, dorm beds (Rs 30 per person) and rooms (Rs 60 per person). Simple Tibetan and Western meals are available for guests. It's also a good source of hiking information.

At the lake, the unsigned ***Pilgrims' Hut*** offers spotless dorm beds for Rs 40 per person – and some rooms only have two dorm beds. It also offers meals for guests. A ***chai stall*** nearby serves drinks and momos.

By road, the lake is about 27km from Pelling; the hiking trail is shorter, but much steeper (see Trekking in Sikkim for details). The daily SNT bus from Pelling only goes as far as the turn-off (11km) up to the lake. Share-jeeps leave the lake from about 6 am and stop at Pelling and Gezing. From Pelling directly to the lake, ask around about a share-jeep, join an organised (morning) tour from Pelling (Rs 75 per person) or charter a jeep (about Rs 500 one way).

TASHIDING

This friendly village is quite popular with trekkers, but is worth visiting anyway for the astonishing setting and superb monastery. Founded in 1716, **Tashiding Gompa** is Sikkim's most sacred monastery, and is perched majestically atop a hill, a steep 45-minute walk from Tashiding village. The gompa belongs to the Nyingmapa order, but is much less ostentatious than Pemayangtse.

A large Buddhist festival, **Bumchu**, is held here in January/February. During the festival, a pot of holy water is opened by the lamas, who tell the future of the coming year from the water.

As you enter the gompa, the building on the right surrounded by prayer wheels houses the sacred *bhumpa* (water vessel) used in the festival. The main prayer hall enshrines an image of the Buddha flanked by four Bodhisattvas on either side. At the south end of the ridge, beyond the prayer hall and on a lower terrace, are numerous **chortens**.

Hotel Blue Bird, halfway up the village street, is a very basic but welcoming place with dorm beds starting at Rs 25 per person.

and doubles with shared bathroom starting at Rs 50. ***Mt Siniolchu Guest House***, at the end of the main street, has better doubles with shared bathroom for Rs 100.

The SNT bus does not currently reach Yuksom, so the only way to get there is by share-jeep. Most leave Yuksom between 6 and 8 am; several travel daily to/from Gezing, via Pelling; to Jorethang; to Yuksom, when there's enough demand; and to Gangtok once daily.

YUKSOM

Yuksom is where the north-western road stops, and is the trailhead for anyone trekking to Dzongri or Goecha La. Police usually check permits along these trekking routes, so don't try setting off on any route without one.

This peaceful village is where the three lamas of the Nyingmapa order arrived to establish Buddhism in Sikkim, and where the coronation of the first chogyal of Sikkim took place. **Norbugang Chorten**, at the end of a track which branches to the left just before Kathok Lake, was built to commemorate this.

Dubdi Gompa was the first capital of Sikkim. Built in 1701, it's one of the oldest gompas in Sikkim. No monks are now based there, but a caretaker (check with your hotel for his whereabouts) will open it up. The gompa is a 45-minute steep walk uphill from Yuksom – go past the hospital to the end of the driveable road, and then past three disused prayer wheels. After crossing a bridge, take the track to the right.

Khangchendzonga Conservation Committee, next to Hotel Wild Orchid, is an essential stop for anyone hiking/trekking in the area. It can provide excellent advice, organise guides and porters (if required) and rent equipment (gas stoves especially). It also plans to open a trekking agency in the future.

Places to Stay & Eat

The following hotels are based around the village square. ***Hotel Wild Orchid*** has clean singles/doubles with shared bathroom for Rs 75/100. ***Hotel Dzongrila*** has basic doubles for Rs 150, as well as good food, beer and chang. ***Hotel Demazong*** is a clean, well-run place with dorm beds starting at Rs 60 per person, and doubles starting at Rs 150/200 without/with private bathroom. ***Gupta Restaurant*** offers tasty samosas and other Indian snacks.

Hotel Tashi Gang is unmissable on a hill above the village. The well-furnished rooms have fine views, cable TV and private bathroom (with hot water), and are worth a splurge for Rs 710/990 for singles/doubles. The 'deluxe' rooms for Rs 990/1260, however, are not worth the extra. It also boasts a charming ***restaurant*** and bar.

Getting There & Away

Several share-jeeps go to Gezing, via Pelling, between about 5 and 7 am every morning; and about four to five jeeps go to Jorethang, via Tashiding, from about 6 am.

About 10km from Yuksom on the road to Pelling, the spectacular **Kanchenjunga Falls** is a popular stopoff.

TREKKING IN SIKKIM

While the authorities are continuing to open up more of Sikkim to trekking, new areas (especially those near an international border) are only likely to be accessible on an organised tour.

The best places for current information about trekking regions and permits, and to arrange guides/porters for possible independent trekking in the future, are (in order of usefulness): the Khangchendzonga Conservation Committee (KCC) in Yuksom; the Sikkim Tourist Centre in Pelling, the Trekkers' Hut at Khecheopari Lake, and the tourist office in Gangtok. There is nowhere in Sikkim for independent trekkers to hire the complete range of equipment yet (but trekking agencies should have tents, cooking gear etc for customers). Some gear is available for rent at the KCC, however.

More detailed information about the treks mentioned in this section, and the many others around Sikkim, is included in the useful *Sikkim, A Guide & Handbook* by Rajesh Verma, and available in Kolkata, Darjeeling and Gangtok.

SIKKIM

Pelling to Legship

This trek links some interesting villages and attractions in West Sikkim. You don't need a special additional permit, but you must get your basic permit endorsed in Gangtok to allow you to visit Khecheopari Lake and Tashiding.

The first stage takes you from Pelling to Khecheopari Lake along the main roads. For the second stage, the short cut to Yuksom heads downhill for about one hour, and then for the last two, ascends gradually into Yuksom. The short cut is confusing, so ask for advice at the lake before you start and whenever you meet anyone en route.

From Yuksom to Tashiding, follow the road, taking some of the obvious short cuts. Then it's an easy two- to three-hour walk along the road to Legship. Bring snacks because there's not much on offer along the way, and always check with locals for the best short cuts. To save the long uphill walk back (six hours) to Pelling from Legship, jump on a bus or share-jeep.

stage	route	duration (hrs)
1	Pelling to Khecheopari Lake	5–6
2	Khecheopari Lake to Yuksom	3
3	Yuksom to Tashiding	5–6
4	Tashiding to Legship	2–3

Yuksom Circuit via Dzongri and Goecha La

This is the most popular trek in Sikkim, and offers superb views of Kanchenjunga. To start this trek, your basic permit must be endorsed for Yuksom, and to do the trek you must *currently* be in an organised group of at least four. However, this rule may be relaxed or even waived in the future (see Permits earlier in this chapter).

Even if independent trekking is allowed, inexperienced trekkers may wish to join an organised tour anyway. Most of the travel agencies mentioned in the Gangtok section earlier can arrange a tour from US$30 to US$60 per person per day, including food, yaks and porters.

There are ***trekkers' huts*** at Baktim, Tsokha, Dzongri, Thangshing and Samiti Lake, and these are the best bet if it's cold. At the height of the trekking season, there's sometimes not enough space in the huts so your travel/trekking agency will need to provide tents. And it's *imperative* not to trek too high too quickly. (See the Health section in the Facts for the Visitor chapter for advice about altitude sickness.)

From Yuksom (1630m), the trail follows the Rathong Valley through unspoilt forests to Baktim (2740m), from where there's a steep ascent to Tsokha (3050m). Above Tsokha, the trail enters magnificent rhododendron forests to an intermediary ***camp site*** at Pethang (3760m). It's a good idea to either bring tents and spend a night at Pethang, or spend two nights at Tsokha, to acclimatise.

The next stage brings you to Dzongri (4025m). From Dablakang, 200m above Dzongri, there are excellent mountain views. If spending more than one night at Dzongri to further acclimatise (recommended), walk up to Dzongri La (4550m) – four hours return – for more great mountain views.

From Dzongri, the trail drops steeply down to the river where there's a ***trekkers' hut***; then follow the river to Thangshing (3840m). The final stop is at Samiti Lake (4200m), from which an early-morning assault is possible to the head-spinning Goecha La (4940m) for the best views of Kanchenjunga. Then it's down to Thangshing for the night, and back to Yuksom two days later.

stage	route	duration (hrs)
1	Yuksom to Tsokha, via Baktim	6–7
2	Tsokha to Pethang	2–3
3	Acclimatisation day	
4	Pethang to Dzongri	2–3
5	Dzongri to Samiti Lake, via Thansing	6–7
6	Samiti Lake to Goecha La & down to Thangsing	8–9
7	Thangshing to Tsokha	6–7
8	Tsokha to Yuksom	5–6

North-Eastern Region

The north-eastern region is the most varied yet least visited part of India. Before Independence this beautiful area of rolling forested hills and lush green fields was known as Assam province, but it has since been gradually broken up into seven separate states. Nowadays, the state of Assam consists mostly of the plains around the Brahmaputra and Barak Rivers, while the other states (excluding Tripura) occupy the hills.

The north-east is the country's chief tribal area, with many different languages and dialects; in Arunachal Pradesh alone over 50 distinct languages are spoken. These Adivasis or tribal people have many similarities to the hill tribes, who live across an arc that stretches from the eastern end of the Himalaya through Myanmar (Burma) and Thailand into Laos.

India has always been touchy about the north-east, although the permit requirement for foreign tourists visiting Assam, Meghalaya and Tripura was lifted in 1995. Encompassing a sensitive border zone where India meets Bhutan, Tibet (China), Myanmar and Bangladesh, the region is remote, and only the narrow Siliguri corridor connects it to the rest of India.

As well as the perceived threat from their neighbours, most of the north-east states have been – and continue to be – wracked by insurgencies and ethnic violence. The reasons for this unrest include a feeling of neglect from the central government; poor transport links and a lack of industrial development are two issues. Very little of the oil wealth from Assam, for example, has found its way back to the state, and the whole region remains overwhelmingly agricultural.

Also of concern to the indigenous population is the inflow of 'foreigners' into the region. The poverty in crowded Bangladesh, and the oppression of that country's Hindu minority, has created a never-ending flow of Bangladeshis to the north-east. This has been so great that migrants now outnumber the indigenous population in Tripura. There

North-Eastern Region at a Glance

ARUNACHAL PRADESH
Pop: 1.1 million
Area: 83,743 sq km
Capital: Itanagar

ASSAM
Pop: 26.6 million
Area: 78,438 sq km
Capital: Dispur

MIZORAM
Pop: 891,058
Area: 21,081 sq km
Capital: Aizawl

MANIPUR
Pop: 2.4 million
Area: 22,327 sq km
Capital: Imphal

NAGALAND
Pop: 2 million
Area: 16,579 sq km
Capital: Kohima

MEGHALAYA
Pop: 2.3 million
Area: 22,429 sq km
Capital: Shillong

TRIPURA
Pop: 3.2 million
Area: 10,486 sq km
Capital: Agartala

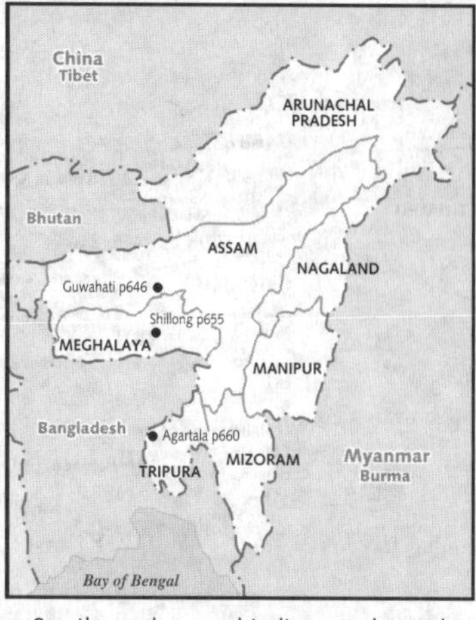

- See the endangered Indian one-horned rhino in Assam's Kaziranga National Park
- Visit Assam's Hindu Vaishnavaite Monasteries, on the world's largest river island
- Splash around the pseudo-Scottish hill station of Shillong in Meghalaya
- Wander around Tripura's Neermahal, a water palace for thousands of birds

has also been a significant migration of Nepalis to the hill states; despite the lack of shared borders, this is a migratory flow seen in many parts of North India and Bhutan.

Matters have been complicated by the demands of various ethnic minorities within the states. In Assam, for example, the Bodos are demanding a homeland separate from the rest of the state. In Manipur, there is bitter fighting between rival tribes, especially the Kukis and Nagas. In some states, such as Tripura, insurgency has simply become a way of life, with good money to be made from kidnapping and extortion. Several hundred local people die each year in the north-east as a result of the troubles, and the situation continues.

Permits

Permits are no longer required for Assam, Meghalaya or Tripura, but make sure you check that it's safe to travel in these areas before heading off (see the boxed text 'Warning' opposite).

Foreigners may be issued a permit for independent travel in Arunachal Pradesh and Nagaland, but most visitors go on an organised tour anyway because it's easier and safer.

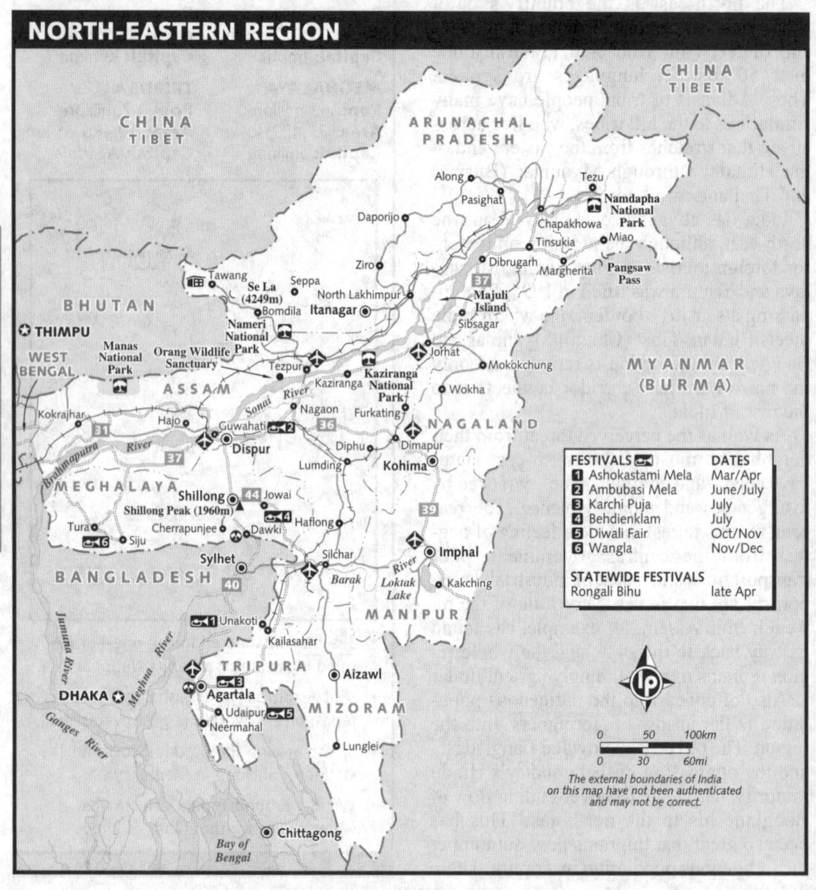

Warning

Due to constant rebel activity and ethnic violence, you are strongly advised to check the current situation before visiting the north-eastern region, especially Manipur and Nagaland. Don't underestimate the potential danger: At the time of research, large-scale massacres of locals were a weekly occurrence in all states (except Arunachal Pradesh), and over 100 police officers had been killed in this part of India in the last 12 months.

The best – and, sometimes, only – way to know which areas are currently dangerous to visit is to read regional daily English-language newspapers, such as the *Sentinel*, the *Assam Tribune* and the *Northeast Daily*.

A day or two after a massacre, a 12-hour daytime bandh (strike) is inevitably called by at least one regional political group as a protest. All shops, offices and restaurants usually close during a bandh, and all public transport around, and originating from, the area with the bandh ceases – but hotels, hotel restaurants and all interstate transport to the area continues to function.

To ensure that the bandh is effective, members (often fanatical) of the group(s) usually roam the streets, but under the observation of many policemen and soldiers. If possible, avoid any area where a bandh is taking place (they are detailed in advance in local English-language newspapers), or at least stay in your hotel.

To gain access to Mizoram and Manipur, foreigners must travel in a group of four on a tour organised by an approved travel agent. If your patience knows no bounds and you want to try your luck getting into these two states without joining an organised tour, you will need either a very good excuse for visiting or friends in *very* high places. It is worth contacting someone at the relevant state government office for advice before applying for a permit; a letter from such an office will significantly improve your chances.

Foreigners need a Restricted Area Permit (sometimes called a Protected Area Permit) for Arunachal Pradesh. This will be arranged by your travel agent if you're on an organised tour. If travelling independently, apply at one of the following places:

- the state government offices (bhavans) listed in the relevant sections later in this chapter – certainly the best option
- the Ministry of Home Affairs, Foreigners' Division, Lok Nayak Bhavan, Khan Market, Delhi – where you can expect a bureaucratic nightmare
- a major Foreigners' Registration Office, eg, Chennai (Madras), Mumbai (Bombay) and Kolkata (Calcutta)
- the embassy/consulate where you applied for an Indian visa

Permits are usually valid for 10 days and are normally extendable, and you need separate permits for each state. Allow at least three weeks for each permit to be issued. Even in the states that openly accept tourism, red tape is alive and well; if travelling by air, you'll be checked in (and out) by the police at the airport.

See the Warning & Permits information later in this chapter for more details about permits for each state.

Because of the difficulty of obtaining permits for the north-eastern region, and the potential problems of safety in the area, many travellers choose to join an organised tour. Several reliable operators offering tours around the north-east are based in Darjeeling and Kalimpong (West Bengal), Guwahati (Assam) and Gangtok (Sikkim) – refer to those chapters or sections for details.

Assam

The largest and most accessible of the north-east states, Assam grows about 60% of India's tea and produces a large proportion of oil. The main attractions of the state are Kaziranga National Park, home of India's rare one-horned rhinoceros, and the remarkable Majuli Island.

History

Early Assamese history includes some semi-mythical Hindu rulers such as the great Narakasura, mentioned in the Mahabharata, who ruled from Pragjyotishpura (modern-day Guwahati). Branches of Hinduism based on *shakti* (creative energies perceived as female deities) worship and mystic-erotic Tantric cults are thought to have emerged in Assam, and these traditions continue at temples in Guwahati.

The Chinese traveller Hiuen Tsang visited the court of King Bhaskar Barman in AD 640. In the 13th century, the Ahoms, a Shan tribe from Myanmar, conquered Assam, adopted Hinduism and established a dynasty that lasted until 1826. The Ahoms also repulsed some 17 invasions by the Mughals, thereby allowing Assam's Hindu culture to blossom in relative peace. The dynasty reached its peak under Rudra Singha (r. 1696–1714), who built trade links with Tibet and was renowned as a military strategist.

In the late 16th century, Sankardeva the philosopher-saint began a Vaishnavaite movement that rejected the Hindu caste system and the rituals of Tantric Hinduism. Instead, a Hinduism based on community prayer was spread by *satras* (Vaishnavaite monasteries), such as those on Majuli Island, which became centres for arts such as dance, manuscript painting and music. The monks also played a major role in reclaiming the wetlands of the Brahmaputra for rice cultivation.

The Ahom dynasty gradually declined until a Burmese invasion from 1817 to 1822 that killed one in every three people. The British then drove out the Burmese and annexed the Ahom kingdom.

The British developed the tea industry, but found the locals unwilling to be labourers, and so by 1900, hundreds of thousands of Adivasis from Bihar and Orissa (the 'tea tribes' of today) had been contracted to work on the plantations.

In the lead-up to Independence it took delicate manoeuvring, and the separation of the Muslim-majority Sylhet district, to stop the then-large Assam province joining East Pakistan (now Bangladesh) rather than staying in India. After Independence, old rivalries (between peoples from the hills and plains, Hindus and Muslims, and Adivasi and non-Adivasi peoples), intensified and Assam province gradually separated into seven states in 1972.

Warnings & Permits

Since the mid-1970s, Assam has been subject to the militant actions of numerous groups. The United Liberation Front of Asom (ULFA), based primarily in Bangladesh and Bhutan, is pledged to the independence of Assam through armed struggle. Its military wing enjoyed a great deal of initial success and kept the Indian army on the run for many years. Unwilling to countenance the loss of Assam, the Indian government mounted a series of massive military operations to flush out the guerrillas. Operation Rhino had some success in 1991, but the ULFA regrouped and the violence continued.

In late 2000, the ULFA increased its rebel activities in upper (north-east) Assam, especially near Dibrugarh, to include for the first time the wholesale massacre of non-Assamese villagers. The ULFA's activities are currently widespread enough to affect the stability of all states in the north-east region.

The Bodo minority is campaigning for a separate state stretching along the border with Bhutan. Several militant groups, such as the Bodo Liberation Tiger Force (BLTF) and the National Democratic Front of Bodoland (NDFB), are operating in the north-west areas of Assam.

Other active rebel groups include the Karbi National Volunteers; the Muslim United Liberation Tigers of Assam (Multa); and the Assam Tiger Forces, a new group that may be linked to the ULFA and seeks the expulsion of all non-Assamese people from the state. The Indian and Assamese governments continue to offer all sorts of amnesties for these and other rebel groups, but with limited success.

It's imperative to understand that travelling by train anywhere in upper Assam is potentially dangerous because of the activities of armed dacoits (bandits).

No permits are required for travel to anywhere within Assam. The major Assam government offices are on Baba Kharak Singh Marg, Delhi (☎ 011-3343961), and 8 Russel St, Kolkata (☎ 033-298331).

GUWAHATI

☎ 0361 • pop 580,000

Alongside the impressively wide Brahmaputra River is Guwahati, once known as Pragjyotishpura ('The Light of the East'). It has long been the region's most important city, and is now the service centre for the oil and tea industries. There is a certain amount of tension at times in the city, mostly between the indigenous Assamese and Bangladeshi migrants, but foreigners are not targeted.

Guwahati is sprawling and ugly, but as the gateway to Assam and the north-eastern region most travellers spend a few days here. The city is split into two on either side of the river. Most places of interest and use to visitors are in the southern section, simply known as Guwahati, while the northern section is called Uttar Guwahati. The state government is actually based in Dispur, a drab town about 8km to the south-east.

Information

Assam Tourism (☎ 544475, ⓔ astdcorp@gw1.dot.net.in) is based at the Tourist Lodge on Station Rd. It isn't particularly helpful, but sells a useful map (Rs 25) of the city. There's also a small tourism counter at the train station. The Government of India tourist office (☎ 547407) is on the corner of B Barua & GS Rds.

Standard Chartered Grindlays Bank on GN Bordoloi Rd, and the State Bank of India on MG Rd, change cash and travellers cheques. Stock up here on rupees before heading to anywhere else in the north-east.

There are a few Internet centres along MN Rd, such as NE Communication (which also has a pool table), Nick Computers, just up from the Ananda Lodge, and Cyberzone on B Barua Rd. The standard fee is about Rs 50 per hour.

Modern Book Depot, on HB Rd, has a wide range of books on the region.

For emergencies, contact the Guwahati Medical College (GMC) Hospital (☎ 562-521), off GS Rd about 5km south of the city centre, or the police station (☎ 555650) on HB Rd.

Temples

Umananda Mandir The most interesting thing about this Shiva temple is its location, on Peacock Island in the middle of the river. Ferries and boats regularly leave Kachari and Umananda Ghats near MG Rd between 7 am and 5 pm every day; the exact departure points vary according to the tides. A return trip costs about Rs 10.

Navagrah Mandir On Chitrachal Hill to the north-east of the city centre, Navagrah Mandir (Temple of the Nine Planets) has long been known as a centre of astrology and astronomy. The nine planets are represented by nine linga (phallic symbols) inside the main temple.

Kamakhya Mandir The best-known temple is Kamakhya Mandir on Nilachal Hill, about 8km west of the city. It is the centre for Shakti worship and Tantric Hinduism – worshippers believe that when Shiva sorrowfully carried away the corpse of his first wife, Shakti, her body disintegrated and her *yoni* (part of the female genitalia) fell there.

Although rebuilt in 1665, after being destroyed by Muslim invaders, the temple's origins are much older. It was probably an ancient sacrificial site used by the Khasi people, and daily goat sacrifices are still part of worship. The temple attracts pilgrims from all over India, especially during **Ambubasi Mela**, a celebration of the end of the earth's menstrual cycle (June or July). **Rongali Bihu** is another festival held across Assam at the end of April to celebrate the start of harvest.

Non-Hindus are usually allowed into the inner sanctum, but no photographs are permitted. Inside it's dark and quite eerie, and the floor is often sticky with the blood of sacrificial goats.

To reach the temple, take bus No 15 from along AT Rd (eg, at Paltan Bazaar), or charter an autorickshaw.

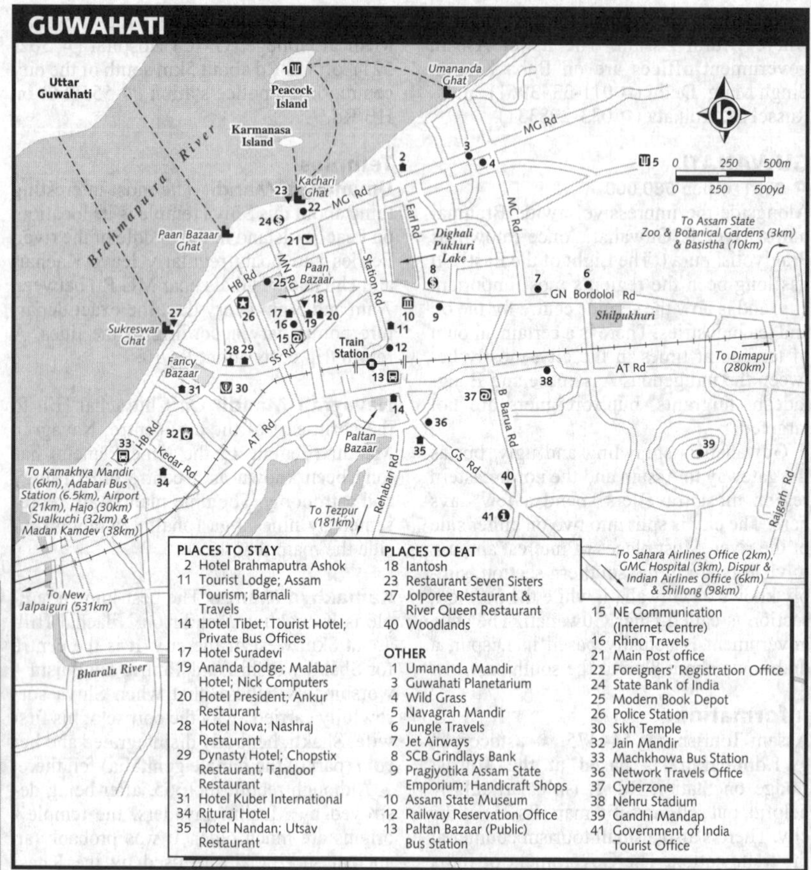

Assam State Museum

This large archaeological, ethnographic and natural history museum on GN Bordoloi Rd is well worth a visit. Particularly interesting are the 'walk-through' reconstructed village, the displays of local arts and crafts (weavings and musical instruments) and the explanations about the various tribal groups around Assam, such as the Karbi, Bodo, Rabha and Miri.

The museum is open from 10 am to 4.15 pm (to 5 pm in summer) daily except Monday. Tickets cost Rs 5; still/video cameras are an extra Rs 10/250.

Assam State Zoo & Botanical Gardens

The combined zoo and botanical gardens are spacious and well managed, with tigers, leopards and Assam's famous Indian one-horned rhinos – plus the African two-horned variety. It's about 5km south-east of the city centre, and is open from 8 am to 4 pm, daily except Friday. A combined ticket costs Rs 5; still/video cameras are an extra Rs 5/250.

Other Attractions

If you are running out of things to see and do, you could go on a boat ride along the green and unappealing **Dighali Pukhuri Lake**, virtually opposite the museum; visit the **Guwahati Planetarium**, on MG Rd, which has shows every day on the hour between 11 am and 7 pm; or enjoy the views, and see the memorabilia about the great man, at **Gandhi Mandap** on Sarania Hill, accessible by autorickshaw.

A popular picnic spot with small temples and a waterfall is **Basistha**, where the *rishi* (sage) Basistha once lived. It's about 12km from central Guwahati, and is accessible by one of the numerous city buses going west along GN Bordoloi Rd.

Organised Tours

As the gateway to the north-east, Guwahati is one of the best places to organise a tour around Assam and the other states. Some of the more reliable agencies are the following:

Barnali Travels (☎ 544475) in the Tourist Lodge on Station Rd. Associated with the Assam tourism office, this agency offers day trips (Rs 150 per person) to the local temples, zoo and museum; day trips to Hajo and Sualkuchi (Rs 250) and Shillong (Rs 250); and two-day trips to Kaziranga (see Kaziranga National Park later in this chapter). If, as often is the case, there aren't enough passengers for a bus trip, staff can arrange a taxi for the day for Rs 500.

Jungle Travels (☎ 520890, ⓔ jtxgau@gw1.vsnl.net.in) GN Bordoloi Rd. This is an impressive outfit that offers rafting, trekking, fishing and 'jungle safaris' around all major regional national parks. It also offers all sorts of other interesting trips around the north-east.

Rhino Travels (☎ 540666) MN Rd. Rhino offers a range of tours around Assam and the north-east, but office staff seem fairly disinterested.

Wild Grass (☎ 546827, fax 541186) Baruah Bhawan, 107 MC Rd. This helpful and knowledgeable agency, runs an excellent resort at Kaziranga National Park, and tours to neighbouring states.

Places to Stay

There is a dire lack of decent budget hotels in Guwahati, and government taxes and service charges of up to 30% (which have been included in the prices quoted in this section) make accommodation fairly expensive anywhere in Assam. All places listed in this section have rooms with private bathroom and fan, unless stated otherwise.

Places to Stay – Budget

The hotels near the corner of GS and AT Rds in Paltan Bazaar are convenient for the private bus offices, public bus station and train station, but you won't get much sleep. ***Hotel Tibet*** *(☎ 539600, AT Rd)* is one of the better options because it's friendly and clean. Singles/doubles cost Rs 150/250; it is more with cable TV.

Tourist Hotel *(☎ 566882, AT Rd)* has a huge number of rooms for about the same price as Hotel Tibet.

Ananda Lodge *(☎ 544832, MN Rd)* is nothing special, but is friendly. Very small singles with a portable fan (if you're lucky) cost from Rs 60 to 95 with shared bathroom, but it's often full and staff are sometimes reluctant to accept foreigners.

Tourist Lodge *(☎ 544475, Station Rd)*, run by Assam Tourism and close to the train station, was previously the only decent budget option. Clean and comfortable rooms used to cost Rs 170/210, but prices subsequently increased to a ridiculous Rs 324/383. Hopefully sense will prevail, and the rates will go down and/or the rooms will be improved considerably.

Hotel Suradevi *(☎ 545050, MN Rd)* is a large place with dormitory beds for Rs 60 per person; basic, clean rooms for Rs 85/120 with shared bathroom; and Rs 95/150/195 for singles/doubles/triples with private bathroom. It's good value, which is why it's often full. Also, the managers may baulk at letting foreigners stay.

Hotel Kuber International *(☎ 520807, HB Rd)* is a little run-down but is otherwise fine. Rooms cost Rs 200/300, or Rs 325/425 with air-con.

Rituraj Hotel *(☎ 522495, Kedar Rd)* has unexciting rooms for Rs 281/375 and is in an inconvenient location.

Places to Stay – Mid-Range & Top End

All places listed below include cable TV and private bathrooms with hot water.

Hotel Nova *(☎ 523464, SS Rd)* is convenient, clean and comfortable, and has helpful and pleasant staff. Small-sized rooms cost Rs 845/858.

Hotel President *(☎ 544979, e presihot@gw1.dot.net.in, SS Rd)* is of the same standard as Nova Hotel, and has rooms starting at Rs 676/780.

Hotel Nandan *(☎ 540855, e nandan@gw1.dot.net.in, GS Rd)* is another comfortable and convenient three-star place. Rooms start at Rs 813/1235.

Hotel Brahmaputra Ashok *(☎ 541064, e brahmaputra@satyam.net.in, MG Rd)* has a great location right by the river. Rooms are large and airy, and some have wonderful river views. Rooms start at Rs 2000/3250.

Dynasty Hotel *(☎ 510499, fax 522112, SS Rd)* is a favourite with businesspeople. The comfortable rooms have air-con and start at Rs 1950/2600.

Places to Eat

Freshwater fish from the Brahmaputra River feature in most local menus, and is very tasty and often cheap (from Rs 15 to 30). The most common varieties are known locally as rahu, elish, puthi and chital.

Malabar Hotel *(MN Rd)*, near Ananda Lodge, specialises in South Indian vegetarian fare, and is cheap and convenient.

Woodlands *(GS Rd)* is a well-known South Indian vegetarian restaurant, with filling thalis (all-you-can-eat plates) for about Rs 50. The food, and heavenly air-con, is worth the trip out to Woodlands.

Hotel restaurants are generally the best places to eat: ***Nashraj Restaurant*** in Hotel Nova serves tasty, but expensive, Indian and Chinese cuisine; Dynasty Hotel is home to the upmarket ***Chopstix*** (Chinese) and ***Tandoor*** (Indian) restaurants; and ***Ankur Restaurant***, in Hotel President, is pricey (starting at Rs 60 per dish), but the food is excellent and worth a splurge.

Iantosh *(GN Bordoloi Rd)* is a clean, friendly and informal eatery that offers the usual range of Chinese and Indian meals, as well as tasty burgers, fries and milkshakes at reasonable prices.

Restaurant Seven Sisters, at Kachari Ghat off MG Rd, is a 'floating restaurant' permanently moored along the Brahmaputra. It offers welcome breezes and views of the islands, and the prices are surprisingly reasonable – about Rs 50 for a hearty meal. ***Jolporee Restaurant*** and ***River Queen Restaurant***, both at Sukreswar Ghat off MG Rd, are similar.

Shopping

Several places along GN Bordoloi Rd, such as Pragjyotika Assam State Emporium, sell Assam's *muga* silk, as well as other fabrics and handicrafts. The bazaars are fascinating and chaotic places to shop.

Getting There & Away

Air Indian Airlines (☎ 264425), on GS Rd in Dispur, has daily flights between Guwahati and Kolkata for US$70 one way, and several each week to/from Delhi (US$220), Agartala (US$45), Aizawl (US$55) and Imphal (US$50).

Jet Airways (☎ 520202), on GN Bordoloi Rd, has daily flights to/from Kolkata (S$70), and regular flights to/from Delhi (US$210), Imphal (US$50) and Bagdogra (US$50). Sahara Airlines (☎ 266667), 3.5km south of the city along GS Rd, has daily flights to/from Delhi (US$210) and Dibrugarh (US$55).

For a quick and exhilarating alternative try Meghalaya Helicopter Service, which has flights to Shillong (Rs 625, 30 minutes) every day, and to Tura (Rs 1325, one hour), in the Garo Hills of Meghalaya, three times a week. Book at the airport office (☎ 840311).

Silks of Assam

Of the several silks available in Assam, the most famous is the unique *muga* silk, which is naturally a golden colour and is not dyed. Many Assamese women have a loom at home upon which they weave magnificent lengths of silk. Adivasi, or tribal, women are renowned for producing colourful silk clothes.

Sualkuchi (see Northern Assam later) is the best place at which to observe muga, *endi* (used for making winter clothes) and *pat* silks being made, and to buy something. Prices are lower here than in Guwahati (around Rs 350 per metre for muga and Rs 170 per metre for pat).

NORTH-EASTERN REGION

Bus The well-organised Paltan Bazaar (public) bus station is at the southern exit of the train station on AT Rd. Most offices for the quicker and more comfortable private buses are near the corner of AT and GS Rds – the most reliable companies include Blue Inn, Green Valley and Blue Hill. Network Travels has an impressive, um, 'network' of bus routes; its office is farther down GS Rd.

Private and public buses go to Shillong (about Rs 50, 3½ hours) every few minutes between 6 am and 5 pm. Buses leave regularly for Dimapur (Rs 100, seven hours), Kohima (Rs 145, nine hours) and Imphal (Rs 232, 13 hours), and travel overnight to Siliguri (Rs 250, 13 hours), Bomdila (Rs 220, 18 hours), Agartala (Rs 300, 25 hours) and Itanagar (Rs 175, 12 hours).

Within Assam, private and public buses depart frequently for Tezpur (Rs 75, six hours), Kaziranga village (Rs 95, six hours), Jorhat (Rs 110, seven to eight hours), Haflong (Rs 180, nine to 10 hours), Sibsagar (Rs 145, eight to nine hours) and Silchar (Rs 215, 12 hours).

There are regular services to regional towns from the Machkhowa and Adabari bus stations.

Train Between Guwahati and Kolkata (993 km, 24 hours) there are several trains each day; tickets cost about Rs 270/914/1253 for 2nd class/1st class/air-con. The Guwahati-Kolkata trains run daily – some of them start or finish in Chennai – and cost Rs 472/1823/2213 from Guwahati. Most trains heading south and west stop at New Jalpaiguri (422km, eight hours), near Siliguri, for which the fare is Rs 154/520/713.

The *Rajdhani Express* travels between Guwahati and New Delhi three times a week (Rs 143/402/1876). The *BP Mail* and *Kamrup Express* travel daily to Lower Haflong (Rs 111/373/535), sometimes detouring through Dimapur (Rs 100/336/508) in Nagaland, but foreigners are not allowed to disembark there without a permit. The line from Lumding to Silchar is metre gauge (Rs 212/473/653 from Guwahati).

The reservation office is along Station Rd (☎ 520560).

Getting Around

Lok-Priya Gopinath Bordoloi airport is 23km south-west of Guwahati. Rhino Travels offers a daily bus from its office on MN Rd to the airport at 10 am; it returns from the airport at 1 pm (Rs 30 one way). Otherwise, get a share-taxi to the airport from outside Hotel Nandan on GS Rd (Rs 70 per person). Share-taxis are very easy to arrange from the airport.

Along the Brahmaputra River, there are frequent ferries and boats (Rs 2 one way) from Paan Bazaar and Sukreswar Ghats along MG Rd to Uttar Guwahati. One-hour boat cruises (Rs 50 per person) leave from Sukreswar Ghat on the hour between 4 and 8 pm daily.

There is no shortage of autorickshaws, cycle-rickshaws and taxis, and the bus service is a cheap and reasonably easy way to get around.

AROUND GUWAHATI

On the northern bank of the Brahmaputra, **Hajo** is an important pilgrimage centre for Hindus, Buddhists and Muslims. While some Buddhists believe that the Buddha attained nirvana here, the Hindus worship at the Hayagriba-Madhava Mandir, and for Muslims, Pao-Mecca Mosque is considered to have one-quarter of the holiness of the Great Mosque at Mecca. Buses regularly link Machkhowa bus station in Guwahati with Hajo (Rs 15, 1¼ hours).

Sualkuchi is a famous silk-weaving centre (see the boxed text 'Silks of Assam' opposite). It is easily accessible from the Machkhowa bus station in Guwahati, and is about 2km south of Hajo.

Madan Kamdev, about 40km north-east of Guwahati and 5km south-west of Baihata Chariali, has some archaeological ruins that mystify the experts. Catch a bus from the Adabari bus station in Guwahati.

Manas National Park (360 sq km) is part of Project Tiger, but is also home to langurs, elephants, rhinos and buffalos. However, Manas is currently too dangerous to visit because of the continuing activities of Bodo rebels in the area. Contact the local tourist office for current information, and to book the lodges at Barpeta, Bansbari and Mathanguri inside the park (☎ 03666-32749).

TEZPUR

☎ 3712

Tezpur, meaning 'City of Blood' after a mythical war, is a centre for the regional tea industry. The town still retains a colonial atmosphere, and it's a pleasant place to stay.

Tezpur boasts several ancient temples, including **Mahabhairava Mandir**, as well as ancient Gupta sculptures at the ruins of the 6th-century **Da-Parbatia Mandir**, 5km west of Tezpur.

In **Chitralekha Udyan** (also known as Cole Park), in the middle of Tezpur, there are 9th-century sculptures and excavated sections of the palace belonging to the former king, Banasura. The lake in the park has **boat trips**, and there's a snack bar. At sunset, the views of the Brahmaputra River are superb from **Agnigarh Hill**.

Places to Stay & Eat

***Tourist Lodge** (☎ 21016)* is a pleasant place opposite the lake. Comfortable singles/doubles cost Rs 210/260 with private bathroom and mosquito net. This place is often full so book ahead. The tourist office is attached.

***Hotel Meghdoot** (☎ 20714, Cemetery Rd)* has rooms with shared bathroom for Rs 90/110, and doubles with private bathroom starting at Rs 180. Some rooms have no outside windows, and can be a bit gloomy.

***Hotel Luit** (☎ 22083)* has a large number and variety of rooms, all with cable TV and private bathroom. The rooms in the 'old wing' for Rs 192/275 are OK, and are virtually the same as the overpriced 'new' doubles for Rs 330.

Gabharu Restaurant, in Hotel Luit, is overpriced and the food is nothing special. ***D'Oasis Restaurant & Bar** (Jonaki Rd)*, on the other side of the tank from Hotel Luit, is better.

Getting There & Away

Indian Airlines (☎ 22083), in Hotel Luit, has several flights a week between Saloni airport, 16km from Tezpur, and Kolkata (US$80), often via Dimapur (US$35).

Since Tezpur is on a branch line, buses are more useful than trains. Buses frequently depart for Guwahati (Rs 75, six hours), Jorhat (Rs 60, four hours) and Kaziranga village (Rs 32, two hours), and there are several daily buses to Itanagar (Rs 100, six hours) and Tawang (Rs 185, 24 hours). Buses leave from the ASTC or CM Market bus stations; tickets can be booked at numerous agencies around town.

ORANG WILDLIFE SANCTUARY

The 72-sq-km Orang Wildlife Sanctuary east of Tezpur is less developed than Kaziranga National Park (see that section following), and has less prolific wildlife, but is safer and more accessible than Manas National Park, north-east of Guwahati. The sanctuary boasts small numbers of one-horned rhinos, barking deer and tigers, and plenty of birdlife.

The ***forest resthouses*** inside the park at Silbori and Satsimlu can be booked through the Western Assam Wildlife Division office (☎ 22289) in Tezpur, but it's an easy enough to day trip from Tezpur (32km one way) by chartered taxi.

NAMERI NATIONAL PARK

This 212-sq-km national park protects forest and wetlands along the Bharali River, as well as endangered birdlife and species such as the Assam reefed turtle (once thought to be extinct in the area), tigers and elephants (over 200 at last count). Nameri became a wildlife sanctuary in 1985, and was given status as a national park as recently as 1998. The park is open from 1 November to 31 March.

At Potasali, 3km from the park entrance, ***Eco Camp** (☎ 03714-44246, ⓔ ripman@gw1.vsnl.net.in)* offers 'eco-friendly' fishing (ie, tag the fish and throw them back), bird-watching, rafting, hiking (with an armed guard!), boat trips and elephant rides. It also offers accommodation in tents and dorm beds; contact the camp for current rates.

Tourist Lodge, at Bhalukpong on the border with Arunachal Pradesh, charges Rs 270/325 for singles/doubles with private bathroom.

The park entrance is 35km north of Tezpur, and is best reached by chartered vehicle from Tezpur as public transport is unreliable.

KAZIRANGA NATIONAL PARK

The 430-sq-km Kaziranga National Park is famous as one of the last habitats of the Indian one-horned rhino (see the boxed text 'The Great Indian Rhino'). It has an official rhino population (of various species, including the rare one-horned rhino) of over 1500, although in 1904 they were on the verge of extinction.

Kaziranga, which became a 'game sanctuary' in 1916 and a national park in 1974, also has gaurs (Indian bison), deer, elephants, tigers and bears. There is also prolific birdlife, best between December and January, including ibises, pelicans, eagles and storks; the best way to see the wildlife is on an (expensive) elephant ride.

The forest reserve at Panbari, 12km north-west from Kaziranga village, features rare species of gibbons, and has abundant birdlife. It can be visited with permission from the tourist information centre.

Information

The park is open from 1 November to 30 April. Inside the park, the tourist information centre (☎ 036776-62423) at Bonani Lodge is where you must register, and where you can book accommodation, jeeps and elephant rides.

Entry costs Rs 175. Other charges include Rs 150 per day to bring in a vehicle; Rs 175/525 per day for a still/video camera; and Rs 525 for a one-hour elephant ride. A 25% discount off these fees (except the elephant ride) is usually provided if you spend more than three days in the park. Jeeps are available from the main gate near Kaziranga village, or from the Bonani Lodge and Aranya Lodge, for at least Rs 50 per person per hour (depending on the number of passengers).

Places to Stay & Eat

All accommodation listed below (except Wild Grass Resort) offers rooms with fan and private bathroom; rooms with air-con cost about Rs 100 extra. All rooms, except those at Aranya Lodge and Wild Grass Resort, should be booked in advance at the tourist information centre at Bonani Lodge.

Bonoshree Lodge charges Rs 150/210 in the off-season/peak season for singles and Rs 200/260 for doubles; meals can be preordered with staff.

Bonani Lodge charges Rs 250/350 for singles and Rs 310/410 for doubles, and has a ***restaurant***.

Kunjaban Lodge has dorm beds for Rs 25 per person without linen and Rs 50 per person with linen. Basic ***meals*** can be ordered.

The Great Indian Rhino

Assam is famous for the rare great Indian one-horned rhinoceros *(Rhinoceros unicornis)*. Once widely distributed across the northern floodplains of the subcontinent, the rhino has been consistently killed to make way for tea plantations and villages, so it's now restricted to only a handful of national parks, such as Kaziranga in Assam (where the largest number is found) and Royal Chitwan in Nepal.

These rhinos are now on the Convention on International Trade in Endangered Species of Fauna and Flora (Cites) endangered list because less than 200 individuals remain. Large and formidable, the rhino has few natural predators, but a naturally slow population growth makes them especially vulnerable to illegal poaching. As in Africa, political turmoil has provided a cover for poachers, and there is an ever-present market for rhino products. In India and Nepal, there's little of a rhino's anatomy that is not prized for its aphrodisiac, medicinal or spiritual attributes.

SIMON BORG

Cottages around the park, which have no cooking facilities or restaurant (so bring your own food), cost Rs 650 per double.

Aranya Lodge *(☎ 03376-62429)* is the best of the lodges. The rooms with hot water (not always available) and a balcony cost Rs 250/410 in the off-season/peak season for singles and Rs 350/510 for doubles. The ***Rhino Restaurant*** here is wonderful but is expensive (set meals are Rs 120), and the ***Buffalo Bar*** is also very welcoming.

Wild Grass Resort *(☎ 0361-546827, fax 541186)* is an excellent, 'eco-friendly' private resort, signposted off the main road about 4km east of Kaziranga village. Accommodation is either in luxury tents or a lodge. Doubles (no singles available), with private bathroom, cost Rs 1800, but discounts of 40% are readily available. Its 'Jungle Plan' (Rs 2200 per person per day) includes accommodation, meals and trips into the park by elephant.

Getting There & Away

The nearest airport is at Jorhat (84km away); the nearest train station is at Furkating (75km away).

Buses between Guwahati (Rs 95, six hours) and Jorhat (Rs 45, 2½ hours) go through Kaziranga village (also known as Kohora), from where it's easy to walk or hitch a ride to the park entrance.

If possible, allow at least three nights and four days in Kaziranga, so try to avoid organised tours from Guwahati, because they're too short (two days) and you'll spend most of that time on the bus and only have time for one wildlife drive. Tours are offered by Barnali Travels (see Organised Tours in the Guwahati section for details) for Rs 1440 per person including transport, meals, a guide, park fees, accommodation and an 'elephant safari'. Hotel Paradise in Jorhat can also arrange pricey tours.

UPPER ASSAM

Jorhat

Jorhat is the gateway to Upper Assam, and is a pleasant stopover. Assam Tourism (☎ 0376-321579) is at the Tourist Lodge on MG Rd. The State Bank of India on AT Rd changes cash and travellers cheques.

Along Biman Barua Rd, a laneway at the back of the ASTC bus station on AT Rd, there are several quiet, adjacent hotels. The three listed below have a ***restaurant*** and rooms with fan and private bathroom.

Hotel Dipti *(☎ 0376-323502)* has simple but clean singles/doubles with a mosquito net for Rs 120/200. ***Hotel Dilip*** *(☎ 0376-321610)* offers rooms for Rs 150/200 and Rs 300/500 with air-con, which are good value. ***Hotel Paradise*** *(☎ 0376-321521)* is the best, and has large, comfortable rooms with cable TV for Rs 375/500.

Tourist Lodge *(☎ 0376-321579, MG Rd)* is a comfortable alternative for Rs 210/260 with private bathroom, fan, mosquito net and balcony.

Indian Airlines (☎ 0376-320011) and Jet Airways (☎ 0376-325652) – both based in Hotel Paradise – fly twice a week to/from Kolkata (US$90). Jet Airways also goes to Imphal (US$80).

Long-distance buses to Guwahati (Rs 110, seven to eight hours), Sibsagar (Rs 18, 1½ hours), Tezpur (Rs 60, four hours) and Kaziranga village (Rs 45, 2½ hours) leave from the ASTC bus station; local buses depart from the public bus station on the corner of AT and MG Rds. Trains are less convenient because Jorhat is on a branch line.

Majuli Island

In the midst of the mighty Brahmaputra River, Majuli is famous as the world's biggest (albeit rapidly eroding) river island at 886 sq km. However, it's more interesting for its 22 *satras*, important Hindu Vaishnavaite monasteries, which also function as centres for Assamese arts.

The institution of the satra was founded in the 15th century by the Assamese poet, composer and philosopher Sankardeva. At the Majuli satras, Vishnu is worshipped through dance dramas re-enacting the stories of the Mahabharata, performed with music and poetry. Sankardeva saw Vishnu as the pre-eminent deity without form – a concept that marks Assamese Hinduism apart from the other traditions.

The main satras are at Kamalabari (the centre for learning), Garamur (home of ancient weapons), Shamaguri (famed for mask-making), Auniati (with interesting jewellery and handicrafts), Dakhinpat (which hosts major festivals) and Bengenaati (with its centre of dance and arts). All are several kilometres apart, but are accessible from Garamur, the main town, for about Rs 300 per day by autorickshaw and Rs 600 per day by taxi. They are listed on a map and brochure available from the tourist office in Jorhat.

It's possible to stay at some satras, but you should make a donation. ***Circuit House*** *(☎ 03775-74439)*, near Garamur, has prices which start at Rs 100 per person for simple but clean rooms with bathroom. Alternatively, ask about staying with a village family.

Getting There & Away From Jorhat, ramshackle buses leave regularly from the public bus station to Nimati Ghat (Rs 12, 1¼ hours), from where ferries leave at 10 am and 3 and 4 pm for Kamalabari on Majuli (Rs 5). The ferries depart Kamalabari for Nimati Ghat at 8 and 9 am and 2 pm, but check current schedules with the tourist office in Jorhat. Motorboats (Rs 15 per person) travel more regularly between Nimati Ghat and Kamalabari, from where there's public transport to Garamur.

Sibsagar

Sibsagar was the ancient capital of the Ahom dynasty, which ruled Assam for over 600 years. It's now an important centre for the tea and oil industries. The area's tea gardens employ the 'tea tribes', including the Santhals and Oraons, who were brought here from central India by the British.

The town is dominated by **Sibsagar Tank**, a huge artificial lake created in 1734. Beside the tank stand three temples, including **Shivadol Mandir**, possibly the tallest Shiva temple in India at 33m.

A number of other temples are accessible by bus or chartered taxi from Sibsagar. About 6km west of the town centre are the ruins of the seven-storey palace known as **Talatal Ghar**, which dates from the 18th-century, and the nearby two-storey **Rang Ghar**.

About 13km to the east of Sibsagar is **Gargaon Palace**, the ruins of another 18th-century Ahom palace. Tombs of the Ahom kings lie at the 13th-century capital of **Charaideo**, about 28km east of Sibsagar.

Tourist Lodge *(☎ 03772-21814)*, by the tank in Sibsagar, has comfortable singles/doubles with private bathroom for Rs 210/260; Assam Tourism (☎ 03772-22394) is also based there.

Kareng Hotel *(☎ 03772-22713, Temple Rd)* is pretty good value for Rs 90/150 with shared bathroom, and has a reasonable ***restaurant***.

Hotel Brindavan *(☎ 03772-22974, AT Rd)* has air-con doubles with private bathroom starting at Rs 600.

Simaluguri, the mainline train station, is 16km from Sibsagar. Buses are more convenient, and leave regularly for Guwahati (Rs 145, eight to nine hours) and Jorhat (Rs 18, 1½ hours).

SOUTHERN ASSAM

Assam's southern finger links the Brahmaputra and Barak Valleys with the multitribal North Cachar Hill District in between. The state extends down as far as Tripura and Mizoram, and also has borders with Bangladesh and Manipur.

Haflong

Assam's only hill station is a friendly town based around the pretty **Haflong Lake**. The area is best known for **Jatinga** village (9km south of Haflong), where flocks of birds are said to 'commit suicide' between August and November. (Actually, migrating birds passing by are attracted to lights set up by the villagers, and the birds land and end up in the villagers' cooking pots.)

Tourist Lodge *(☎ 03673-2468)* in Haflong has decent singles/doubles with private bathroom for Rs 210/260.

Hotel Elite, just above the market, is the best place to stay (and eat). Doubles with private bathroom start at Rs 220.

At least two buses a day link Haflong with Silchar (Rs 60, four hours). From the station at Lower Haflong, two trains a day travel to/from Silchar and Guwahati.

Silchar

Silchar, on the Barak River in the far south of the state, is a significant transport hub. If you need to spend the night, ***Tourist Lodge*** *(Park Rd)* has singles/doubles with private bathroom for Rs 210/260. Silchar is linked to Kolkata (US$75), via Imphal, most days by Indian Airlines. Several buses a day travel to Agartala, Aizawl, Shillong and Guwahati, and two trains a day ride along the metre gauge up to lower Haflong.

Meghalaya

Created in 1972, Meghalaya ('The Abode of Clouds') is the home of the Khasi, Jaintia and Garo tribespeople, noted for their matrilineal society (ie, property and wealth are passed through the female rather than male line). Great stone monoliths erected to the old tribal kings can be found in the Khasi and Jaintia Hills, as well as sacred forest groves.

The gently rolling hills of Meghalaya are noted for growing fruit and betel nut, which locals enjoy immensely. The state – and in particular its capital, Shillong – is one of the wettest places on earth, with about 1150cm (nearly 40 feet) of rain falling each year in some places. So come prepared.

History

Khasi and Jaintia tribes are closely related and are thought to have originally emigrated from South-East Asia, while the Garo came from Tibet. The Khasi and Jaintia trace their descent back to the Ri Hinniew Trep (Seven Families) and are collectively known as 'Hynniewtrep'. According to legend, there were 16 families, nine in heaven and seven on earth, connected by a golden vine ladder, but the link was severed when sin poisoned the earth.

The Garo – or, as they often refer to themselves, the Achik – traditionally practice shifting *jhurning* (slash-and-burn agriculture), although in recent years population pressure has encouraged a change to rice cultivation. In the forested Garo Hills, men would stand guard in treetop *borangs* (watchtowers).

Warring chiefs ruled the area before the arrival of the British, who established control by the 1820s by playing the tribes off against each other. Shillong's gentle rainy climate made it a favoured retreat from the plains for British tea planters and administrators of the region. Missionaries were permitted to work among the tribes, and nowadays more than half the population of Meghalaya is Christian. The state separated from Assam in 1972, and has been a political and economic backwater ever since.

Warnings & Permits

Meghalaya is comparatively safe from rebel activity. However, ethnic violence occasionally flares up in the south-west near the border of Bangladesh, so ask around before travelling to Tura and the Garo Hills. One group based near Shillong is the Achik National Volunteer Council, which strives for a 'Greater Garoland', but is currently ineffectual.

No permit is required for travel anywhere in the state. The major Meghalaya government offices are at 9–10 Russel St, Kolkata (☎ 033-2290797), and 9 Aurangzeb Rd, Delhi (☎ 011-3014417).

Special Events

Behdienklam is a religious festival held in the Jaintia Hills in July, during monsoon.

Wangla is a music festival held in the Garo Hills in November or December (see the Around Meghalaya section later in this chapter).

SHILLONG

☎ 0364 • pop 260,000 • elevation 1496m

From 1874 until 1972, the hill station of Shillong was the capital of Assam, and was known as the 'Scotland of the East'. Surrounded by pine trees and veiled in clouds, it's understandable why Shillong reminded the Brits so much of home, and at its high altitude, it provided a welcome relief from the heat of the plains. The colonists built a championship golf course (the world's wettest) and a polo ground, and soon the surrounding hills were dotted with neat Victorian bungalows and churches.

These days, central Shillong is often congested with traffic, and a multitude of ugly concrete buildings have sprung up. However, it's still a very charming place, with pleasant walks in the area, and enchanting markets that attract tribespeople from outlying villages. There is some underlying communal and religious tension that sometimes turns nasty during Hindu and Islamic festivals, but foreigners are not targeted.

Information

The Meghalaya Tourism office (☎ 226220), opposite the MTC bus station, is open from 7.30 am to 5 pm daily (until 11 am on Sunday). It can't help much, but it is the place for booking organised tours (see Organised Tours later in this section). If you really need some help, contact the tourism department head office (☎ 224933) in the Orchid Hotel on Polo Rd, about 2km north of Police Bazaar. The Government of India tourist office (☎ 225632) is on GS Rd.

Cash and travellers cheques can be changed at the State Bank of India which is on Kacheri Rd.

Internet facilities are available at Aryans Dotcom on Police Bazaar Rd and Cyberzone on GS Rd. The standard rate is about Rs 40 per hour.

Parks & Waterfalls

As expected in a place with so much rain, there are numerous waterfalls and pretty spots in and around Shillong (see also the Around Meghalaya section later in this chapter).

The attractive **Ward's Lake**, named after Sir William Ward, the chief commissioner, was the focus of European settlement. Apparently, the lake's construction was initiated by a bored Khasi prisoner who had requested any kind of work to get him out of his cell. He was told to dig holes and then fill them in again, but when he hit a spring in this spot the civic engineer decided that

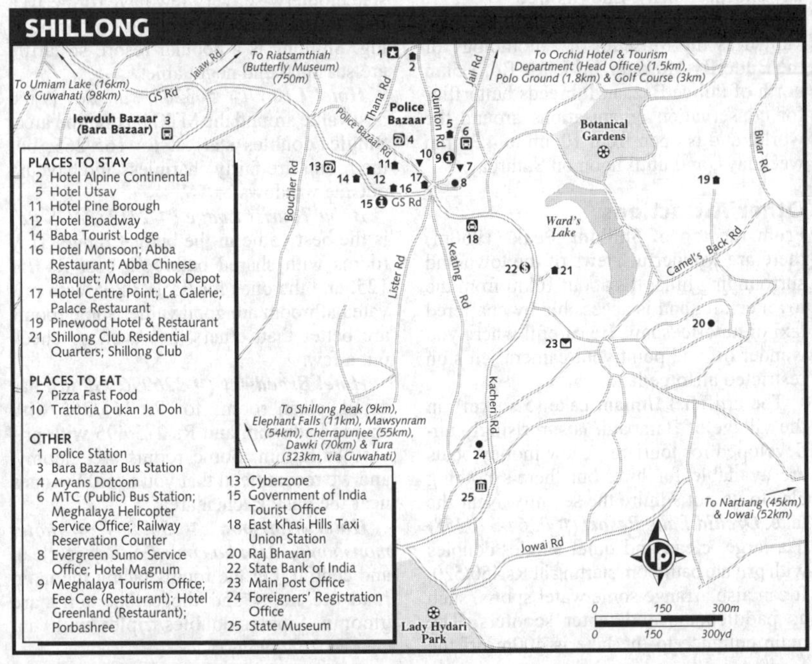

a lake and gardens should be created. Entry to the surrounding park is Rs 15, and 20-minute **boat rides** cost Rs 60 per four-person boat. The **Botanical Gardens** are a few minutes' walk farther north. Both the lake and the gardens are open daylight hours every day.

The spectacular **Elephant Falls** are 12km by autorickshaw or chartered taxi from central Shillong, and is about 120 steps down from the car park. There is no charge to see the falls.

The immaculate **Lady Hydari Park** is popular, particularly with young local couples, and features a minizoo. It's open daily except Monday, and tickets cost Rs 2.

Museums

The unimpressive **State Museum** on Kacheri Rd provides dusty coverage to the flora, fauna, culture and anthropology of the state, but does have some interesting sculptures. It's open from 10.30 am to 4.30 pm every day except Sunday. Entry is free.

More interesting is **Riatsamthiah**, also known as the Museum of Entomology or the Butterfly Museum, on Jaiaw Rd, 1.5km north of Police Bazaar. It breeds butterflies for conservation organisations around the world, and is open from 10 am to 4.30 pm weekdays, and until noon on Saturday.

Other Attractions

From the top of **Shillong Peak** (1960m) there are wonderful views of the town and surrounding hills. It's about 10km from the town centre, and is accessible by chartered taxi or autorickshaw. Be careful where you wander off and point your camera – it's on restricted airforce land.

The artificial **Umiam Lake** (5 sq km), in the village of Barapani, is surprisingly undeveloped for tourism. A few motley boats are available for hire, but there's nothing else to do but admire the serenity. Near the lake, ***Orchid Lake Resort** (☎ 0364-570258)* has large, clean and quiet singles/doubles with private bathroom starting at Rs 450/520. It can also arrange some water sports, such as paddleboats and water scooters. The main entrance to the lake is 400m off the road to Guwahati (17km from Shillong), and is accessible by any bus or jeep along that road.

Organised Tours

Despite all sorts of advertisements and promises, travel agencies only bother arranging local tours if you can find other passengers to share the cost. To see a few sights quickly, charter a taxi with the East Khasi Hills Taxi Union (see Getting Around later in this section); or, better still, jump on a tour organised by the tourist office. These tours leave daily at 8 am for Cherrapunjee (Rs 100 per person, eight hours); and at 8.30 am (Rs 80, six hours) for places such as Umiam Lake and Elephant Falls. Book tickets the day before or from 7.30 am on the same day.

Places to Stay

All places listed below offer rooms with private bathroom and cable TV, unless stated otherwise; very few have (or need) a fan, and none bother with air-con or heating. Shillong is a popular resort, so tariffs are seasonal and negotiable.

***Hotel Utsav** (☎ 503268, Jail Rd)* is the best value around the MTC bus station area. Singles/doubles start at Rs 165/265, but the rooms are fairly charmless and have no outside windows or TV.

***Baba Tourist Lodge** (☎ 211285, GS Rd)* is the best value in the budget range. Tiny rooms with shared bathroom cost Rs 75/125, and the ones for Rs 182/265 with private bathroom are good value. Some rooms are better than others, however, so check out a few.

***Hotel Broadway** (☎ 226996, GS Rd)* has small, clean rooms for Rs 165/265 with shared bathroom and Rs 275/495 with private bathroom. Some rooms are gloomy, and we recommend that you avoid the ones near the busy kitchen area.

***Hotel Monsoon** (☎ 500064, e hotelmonsoon@123india.com, GS Rd)* is clean and central, but the rooms facing the main road are noisy and those that don't are gloomy. Singles/doubles/triples with fan cost Rs 265/495/605.

Hotel Pine Borough *(☎ 220698, Police Bazaar Rd)* is probably the best value, and is surprisingly quiet despite its central location. Small but clean and comfortable rooms cost from Rs 198 to 275 for singles, and about Rs 330 for doubles.

Hotel Centre Point *(☎ 225210, fax 225239, GS Rd)* is a central landmark in Police Bazaar. The rooms are comfortable and bright, and some boast pleasant views, but it's overpriced at Rs 605/715.

Shillong Club Residential Quarters *(☎ 226938, ⓔ shillongclublitd_resi@123india.com, Kacheri Rd)* boasts some real colonial charm. The rooms are large, comfortable and quiet, and cost Rs 478/565. The tariff includes temporary membership of the Shillong Club next door. It's worth a splurge, and you should book ahead.

Hotel Alpine Continental *(☎ 223617 ⓔ alpineshillong@hotmail.com)*, on the corner of Thana and Quinton Rds, is a classy place and is excellent value. Very comfortable rooms with hot water – but most with views of the building next door – cost Rs 708/828.

Pinewood Hotel *(☎ 223116, fax 224176)*, just off Camel's Back Rd, is a wonderful Raj-era place built in the early 20th century and set in attractive grounds. The rooms have high ceilings, large comfortable beds and open fireplaces and cost from Rs 660/990 to 2400/3000 for the 'Presidential Room'.

Places to Eat

Some of the best restaurants are in the hotels. ***La Galerie***, in the Hotel Centre Point building, is a classy place with tasty Indian and Chinese cuisine, and marvellous views. In the same building, ***Palace Restaurant*** is an informal eatery serving Indian fast food such as samosas (pastry triangles stuffed with vegetables) and *dosas* (filled pancakes).

Trattoria Dukan Ja Doh *(Police Bazaar Rd)*, opposite the entrance to Hotel Pine Borough, is a simple cafe, and is the best place to try authentic Khasi fare.

Abba Restaurant *(GS Rd)*, under Hotel Monsoon, is a tiny place serving cheap Chinese and Tibetan meals. At the back of an adjacent arcade is probably Shillong's finest restaurant, the classy ***Abba Chinese Banquet***. Meals cost around Rs 60, and the service is excellent.

Eee Cee *(Jail Rd)*, next to the tourist office, is popular for cheap Chinese and Indian dishes, and pastries. Above it, ***Hotel Greenland*** is one of the better places for a cheap and tasty curry; fish curry is a speciality and costs Rs 25.

Pizza Fast Food *(Jail Rd)* does what the name suggests, and does it quite well, with pizzas costing Rs 50.

The restaurant in ***Pinewood Hotel*** still serves the sort of meals that must have been offered to crusty Scottish tea planters 75 years ago, and orders are still taken by the 'butler'. Book a table in advance.

Shopping

For handicrafts, try Porbashree, the emporium next to the tourist office on Jail Rd. Also, near the corner of Police Bazaar and Kacheri Rds, several shops sell finely woven baskets in all sizes.

The most interesting market takes place in Iewduh Bazaar (usually called Bara Bazaar) on Iewduh, which is the first day of the eight-day Khasi week. Khasi and Jaintia villagers – mostly women – come from all over eastern Meghalaya to buy and sell produce at the market, and Khasi food is sold at stalls. Ask the Meghalaya tourist office for current details.

Getting There & Away

The nearest airport and train station are at Guwahati (Assam). Meghalaya Helicopter Service has flights to Guwahati (Rs 625, 30 minutes), and joy rides around Shillong for Rs 400 per person. The office (☎ 223200) is at the MTC bus station, where there is also a computerised railway reservation counter.

Between Shillong and Guwahati (3½ hours), public MTC buses run at least every hour (Rs 50), as do more comfortable private buses (Rs 60). To Guwahati, share-taxis from Police Bazaar cost Rs 125 per person or Rs 625 per vehicle, and crowded share-jeeps leave from the Evergreen Sumo Service office near Hotel Magnum in Police Bazaar (Rs 90).

MTC and the private companies also offer overnight buses to Silchar (Rs 105, eight hours), Dimapur (Rs 175, 15 hours) and Agartala (Rs 250, 21 hours).

Private bus companies, such as Green Valley Travels, Network Travels and Assam Valley Tours, have small offices near the corner of Police Bazaar and GS Rds. Private buses usually leave from the Bara Bazaar bus station, but those that leave before about 9 am often depart from the corner of Police Bazaar and GS Rds. Local buses depart from the Bara Bazaar bus station.

To/From Bangladesh Refer to the Land section in the Getting There & Away chapter for information about crossing the border to/from Bangladesh, via Dawki.

Getting Around

Shillong is too steep for cycle-rickshaws and too wet for autorickshaws, so the only private transport is the ubiquitous black-and-yellow taxis. These can be chartered for Rs 120 per hour, and a negotiable Rs 900 per day. Share-taxis to local areas leave from outside the East Khasi Hills Taxi Union station on Kacheri Rd. A share-taxi or chartered taxi to the airport near Guwahati costs Rs 180/900. Jeeps can also be chartered for local tours from the Evergreen Sumo Service office at Police Bazaar.

AROUND MEGHALAYA

There continues to be communal violence in the Garo Hills, so check the current situation before travelling in the area. In the Garo Hills, **Wangla** is a four-day festival of music held in November/December to celebrate the end of harvest.

Nohkalikai Falls (also known as Nohsngithiang Falls) at **Cherrapunjee** village (also known as Sohra), 56km south of Shillong, are magnificent falls, reputed to be the fourth-highest in the world. The village is the centre for the Khasi people, where you'll find traditional houses built with curved walls and a sturdy arching roof to withstand the frequent storms. Buses leave from the Bara Bazaar bus station; otherwise, visit the village on an organised tour (see Shillong).

Mawsynram, which recently took the title of the wettest place on earth from Cherrapunjee, is 55km from Shillong and close to Cherrapunjee. About 1.5 km before the village is Mawjymbuin Cave, which features a giant stalagmite worshipped as a Shiva lingam (phallic symbol) by Hindu pilgrims.

In the Jaintia Hills, near the pleasant market town of Jowai, is **Krem Um Lawan**, India's longest cave (6.5km). At **Nartiang**, about 12km north of Jowai, lies the atmospheric remnants of the ancient capital of the Jaintia kingdom, including the 500-year-old Temple of Durga. Jowai is accessible by bus from Bara Bazaar.

Around Siju, 50km from the district capital of Tura, are numerous deep limestone **caves**, including several near **Naphak Lake**.

Orchid Lodge, 3km east of Tura, has comfortable singles/doubles with fan, cable TV and private bathroom for Rs 232/300, and dormitory beds for Rs 65 per person. Contact the Meghalaya tourism office in Shillong for bookings.

Buses from Shillong to Tura (Rs 140, 12 hours) go via Guwahati, but share-jeeps and chartered jeeps can use the rough, direct road between Shillong and Tura. Meghalaya Helicopter Service offers flights from Guwahati to Tura three times a week (Rs 1325, one hour).

The pristine 220-sq-km **Balpakram National Park**, south of Tura, features the canyon of the Mahadeo River and fauna that includes tigers, elephants, barking deer and gaurs. The park is also known for its medicinal herbs. Balpakram isn't easy to reach, however; the Orchid Lodge near Tura is the best place to organise a visit.

Tripura

Tiny Tripura is the second smallest state in India, and is almost surrounded by Bangladesh. Tribal customs, such as leaving parasols over ponds to commemorate the dead, can still be seen in rural areas, and official visitors to villages have bamboo arches built in their honour. Tripura is renowned for its vast array of caneware products.

Despite the fact that 60% of Tripura is forested, the largest industry is handloom weaving. Although 19 tribes live in the state, the majority of the population is Bengali.

History

Tripura emerged as a distinct entity at the end of the 14th century under the Manikya dynasty, led by former Indo-Mongolian tribal chieftains who adopted Hinduism. The area was also once part of a large Hindu kingdom conquered by the Mughals in 1733. It was eventually taken over by the British in 1808, became a union territory of India in 1949 and a full state in 1972.

Under the British Raj, the maharajas led a self-ruling princely state, although each ruler had to be approved first by the colonial overlords. At Independence, the Regent Maharani led the state into India, while the Sylhet district to the north joined East Pakistan (now Bangladesh). Like the state of West Bengal, the Communist Party of India (Marxist-Leninist) has dominated state politics in recent decades.

Warnings & Permits

Within Tripura, it is safe to travel to and around Agartala, but not in the north and, particularly, the far south where the National Liberation Front of Tripura (NLFT) continues to kill and kidnap indiscriminately. The victims are often Bengalis from Bangladesh, some of whom have sought equally violent retribution through the United Bengali Liberation Front (UBLF). There are also clashes in northern Tripura between the Brus and the Reangs, who have fled from Mizoram. Seek reliable advice before travelling outside of Agartala or Neermahal, or travelling overland to/from the capital.

No permits are required to travel anywhere within Tripura. The major Tripura government offices are at Chanakyapuri, Kautilya Marg, Delhi (☎ 011-3014607) and 1 Pretoria St, Kolkata (☎ 033-2825703).

AGARTALA

☎ 0381 • pop 175,500

Tripura's sleepy capital, Agartala, was moved to its present site in 1850 by Maharaja Radha Krishna Kishore Manikya Bahadur. The city is pleasant enough, and the locals are very welcoming, but there's not a lot to see; it's really only a stopover for anyone travelling to or from Bangladesh.

Information

The helpful Tripura Tourism office (☎ 225-930), in the eastern wing of Ujjayanta Palace, is open from 10 am to 5 pm weekdays; its Web site at www.tripura.nic.in is excellent. Staff can organise tours around Agartala and to Sepahijala Wildlife Sanctuary and the Water Palace of Neermahal, but the chances of getting the minimum passengers required (about six) is remote. The tourist counter (☎ 422393) at the airport is useless. Foreigners arriving and departing by air must register with the police at the airport.

The State Bank of India on HGB Rd does not change money. If you're travelling to/from Bangladesh, use the moneychangers at the border. MediaNet, along Jagannath Bari Rd, offers Internet access for Rs 60 per hour.

The Bangladesh Visa Office (☎ 225260), on Palace Compound Rd, is open from 8.30 am to 4.30 pm weekdays. To obtain a visa, complete an application form, provide two photos and deposit the fee (in US dollars or Indian rupees) into its account at the State Bank of India – the visa office will provide account details. A single-entry visa that is valid for one month costs US$13 for Germans, US$45 for Americans, US$29 for Australians and US$40 for Britons. The whole process can take less than two hours.

Things to See

Built in 1901 by Maharaja Radha Kishore Manikya in a mixed European-Mughal style, **Ujjayanta Palace** is surrounded by 28 hectares of parkland and overlooks two large pools. Because the building now houses the Tripura State Legislative Assembly, it's not open to the public. The grounds, however, are open between 5 and 7 pm to see the 'Musical Fountain'; enter from the main gate.

Nearby, are **Ummaneshwar Mandir** and **Jagannath Mandir**, both painted a striking ochre colour. At **Buddha Vihar**, on Airport

Rd about 8km north of the city, there are Burmese statues of the Buddha.

The small **Tripura Government Museum**, at the roundabout along HGB Rd, is quite interesting. The results of archaeological excavations around the state are on display, as well as rare coins and more recent sculptures. It's open from 10 am to 5 pm daily except Sunday; entry is free.

The former capital, now known as **Old Agartala**, is 5km to the east. **Chaturdasha Devata Mandir** – also known as the 'Temple of Fourteen Deities' – draws thousands of devotees in July for the **Karchi Puja** festival, which is held for seven days and worships 14 goddesses.

Places to Stay

All places listed below offer rooms with private bathroom, unless stated otherwise.

Agartala Rest House *(Motor Stand Rd)* is about as basic as it comes – around Rs 50 for a rudimentary single room with shared bathroom. Several other places of similar standard and price are located nearby.

Moonlight Hotel & Restaurant *(Durga Bari Rd)* is better known as a place to eat, but it also has some basic singles/doubles

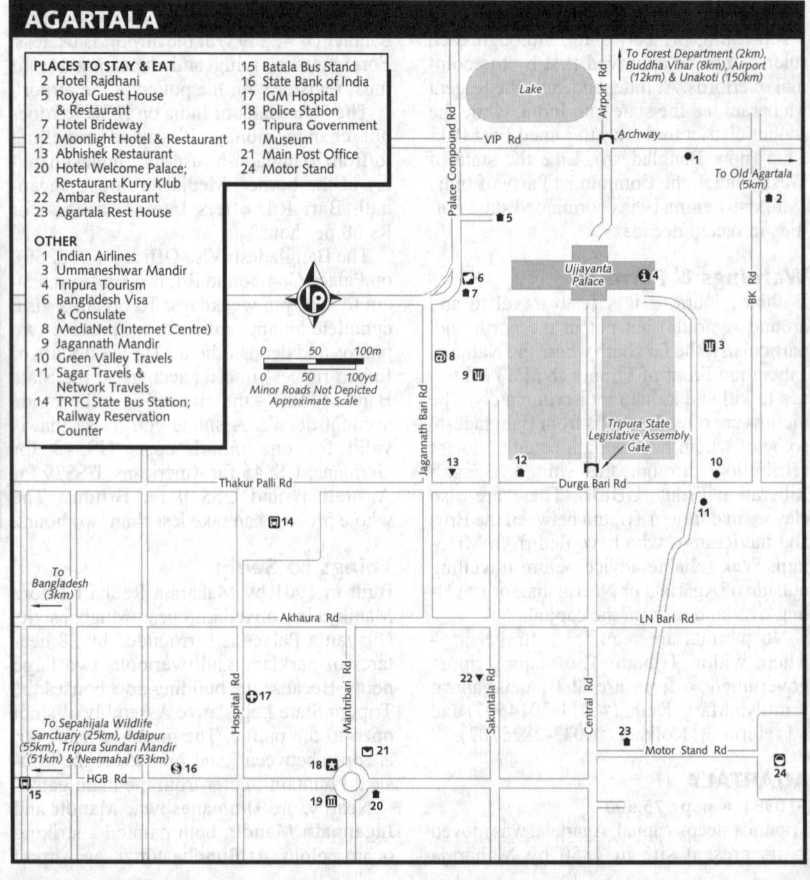

for Rs 80/100 with shared bathroom. The hotel is on a very noisy corner.

Hotel Brideway *(☎ 207298, Palace Compound Rd)* is also in a noisy location. It's not bad value if you crave air-con and cable TV (for Rs 440 per double), but the rooms with fan and mosquito net are overpriced at Rs 275.

Royal Guest House *(☎ 225652)* is just off Palace Compound Rd, but is not signposted. The rooms are unremarkable, but they are clean, quiet and good value. Singles cost from Rs 165 to 275 and doubles are Rs 440; all rooms come with cable TV and fan.

Hotel Rajdhani *(☎ 223387, BK Rd)* is also good value. Singles with a fan start at Rs 187 (but these are rarely available). Large, comfortable doubles with air-cooler (not air-con), fan, hot water and cable TV cost just Rs 330.

Hotel Welcome Palace *(☎ 224940, ⓔ welcome_palace@usa.net, HGB Rd)* is worth a splurge, but you should book ahead. It's new, spotless and central. Rooms start at Rs 220/330 with fan and Rs 440/550 with air-con; all have cable TV.

Places to Eat

Abhishek Restaurant *(Durga Bari Rd)* is the best place in town, and turns into a pretty garden oasis at night. It's a little pricey (vegetarian dishes start at Rs 40), but the food is delicious and the service is efficient.

Ambar Restaurant *(Sakuntala Rd)* is a cheap, simple and friendly eatery. There are several others of similar standard and price nearby.

The best restaurants are in the hotels. ***Restaurant Kurry Klub***, in Hotel Welcome Palace, serves Chinese, Indian and passable Thai food. Despite the uninviting decor, the dining room in the ***Royal Guest House*** is also worth trying.

Getting There & Away

Air Travelling by air is the safest and most direct way to/from Agartala, so flights are often booked out days in advance. Indian Airlines (☎ 225470), on VIP Rd, has at least one flight a day to/from Kolkata (US$50), and three flights a week to/from Guwahati (US$45). Between the city centre and airport (12km), taxis cost about Rs 150 and autorickshaws about Rs 80.

Bus & Share-Jeep Check the current situation before travelling too far from Agartala by public transport.

There are three bus stations in Agartala. From the TRTC station on Thakur Palli Rd, state-run buses go to Guwahati (Rs 300, 25 hours), via Shillong (Rs 250, 21 hours), and to Silchar (Rs 105, 12 hours). The TRTC station also has a computerised railway reservation counter (☎ 225533).

Private buses leave from Batala bus stand, on HGB Rd, and from Motor Stand, on the aptly named Motor Stand Rd. Companies with offices along Durga Bari Rd, such as Green Valley Travels, Sagar Travels and Network Travels, offer comfortable buses to Guwahati, Shillong and Silchar for a little more than the public buses.

Public buses and share-jeeps to local towns leave from Batala bus stand.

To/From Bangladesh For information about crossing the border to/from Bangladesh at Akhaura, near Agartala, refer to the Land section in the introductory Getting There & Away chapter.

AROUND TRIPURA

All of the places mentioned here are accessible by bus or share-jeep from Batala bus stand in Agartala.

Sepahijala Wildlife Sanctuary (18.5 sq km), 25km south of Agartala, has bison, deer and monkeys, and water birds (especially in winter). There is also a minizoo, toy train, elephant rides, orchard garden and boating lake. Entry costs Rs 5.

Nearby, ***Abasarika Forest Bungalow***, set in pleasant gardens near the lake, charges Rs 50 per person for dorm beds and Rs 100 per person in a cottage. For bookings, contact the Forest Department (☎ 223779) on Airport Rd, Agartala, 2km north of Agartala centre.

Some 53km from Agartala, on an island in the middle of Rudrasagar Lake (5 sq km), is Tripura's top attraction is the **Water Palace of Neermahal**. The palace was built in 1930 by Maharaja Bir Bikram Kishore Manikya in a combination of Hindu and Islamic styles, but is now starting to fall into ruin. Still, it is a beautifully peaceful place that attracts migrating birds in winter. The tourist authorities intend to establish a sound-and-light show, incongruous water sports and even a floating restaurant – all of which will no doubt spoil the ambience. On the lake shore, ***Sagarmahal Tourist Lodge*** has doubles with private bathroom for Rs 132/220 without/with air-con, and dorm beds for Rs 50; book at the tourist office in Agartala.

Some 55km south of Agartala, in the centre of the ancient Hindu capital, Udaipur, is the **Jagannath Digthi tank**. On its banks is the ruined **Jagannath Mandir**, a temple which once held the famous Jagannath statue transported from Puri (Orissa) in the 16th century. Nearby are several **temples** to Vishnu, and the ruins of the **old royal palace**.

Tripura Sundari Mandir (also known as Matabari) is 4km from Udaipur. It's the most famous Hindu temple in southern Tripura, and was built on a hilltop in the classic Bengali-hut style in 1501. A large **fair** is held there during Diwali (October/November). ***Matabari Pantha Niwas*** offers dorm beds for Rs 50.

The ancient pilgrimage centre of **Unakoti** is believed to date back to the 8th century. Unakoti means 'one less than a crore' (10 million) and, according to legend, one divinely inspired sculptor carved 9,999,999 images in one day! Several impressively large rock-cut images (possibly the largest bas-relief in India) of Shiva and Ganesh are set into the hills, and there are attractive waterfalls and pools nearby. Many other sculptures are scattered about the region. The cultural fair and pilgrim festival, Ashokastami Mela, is held here every year during March or April. Unakoti is about 150km from Agartala, and 10km from Kailasahar where ***Uttarmegh Tourist Lodge*** has doubles for Rs 130; book at the tourist office in Agartala.

Arunachal Pradesh

Because Arunachal Pradesh borders Bhutan, China and Myanmar, it is politically sensitive and has been off-limits to foreigners until recently. The roads are much better in Arunachal Pradesh than anywhere else in the north-eastern region, a sure indication of the state's strategic importance to the Indian government. However, it is not set up for tourism, so you'll have to change money somewhere else, for example, Guwahati in Assam.

Arunachal Pradesh is the most sparsely populated state in India, with about one million people scattered across 84,000 sq km. The state comprises valleys separated by the ridges of the eastern Himalaya, and about 70% of the land is still forested, although logging companies continue to sacrifice a great deal of this crucial resource.

History

Of all the north-eastern states, Arunachal has the least documented history. The Ahom dynasty in Assam had a policy of not interfering with the hill tribes, except for retaliatory raids. The British continued this policy and after declaring the region off-limits in 1873 ignored the place until the eve of WWII. After Independence, Nehru supported the policies of Verrier Elwin, a British-born anthropologist, to gradually prepare the tribes for the impact of the modern world, and village democracy was introduced in preparation for a statewide legislature.

The region has always acted as a buffer between empires on the plains and the Tibetan plateau, and in recent times between India and China. Development was stepped up after China invaded Tawang in 1962 (Tawang was always in India, but this Buddhist mountain valley had until the late 1940s been claimed by Tibet). China advanced as far as Tezpur in Assam and then withdrew, so India moved quickly to build roads and military bases along the border. From 1954 to 1971, the region was called the North-East Frontier Agency. It became a Union Territory and was renamed Arunachal Pradesh in 1972; it became a state in 1987.

Tribes of Arunachal Pradesh

The Anthropological Survey of India estimates that there are 66 different tribes in the state, although the 1971 census counted 115.

The largest group are the Adi tribes, who live in the centre of the state. The Adi live mostly in villages of bamboo huts raised on stilts. Bamboo weaving is highly developed, and rural Adi often wear cane clothing such as hats and vests.

The Mishmi dominate the area east of the Adi lands, and traditionally live in enormous bamboo and wooden longhouses. Each clan has its own distinctive dress made from cotton, nettle fibre and wood.

Around Ziro, the Apatani cultivate a plateau of 26 sq km with paddy fields. Some women wear traditional *yapinghules* (wooden nose plugs), a custom apparently started to make the Apatani women unattractive to other tribes.

The Singpho are an Early Buddhist tribe who live on the eastern edge of the state. They emigrated from Myanmar (Burma), and use the Thai script. In the far west, around the famous Tawang Gompa, are the Monpa, who follow Tibetan Buddhism.

From 1979 to 1999, the state's forests were increasingly exploited until a court ban on logging came into force in 1997. Since this ban, the state has been in a deep economic slump, which is partly why tourism is being promoted.

Like many of the region's hill tribes, the Arunachalese are increasingly turning to Christianity to build social bonds as the tribal systems of mutual obligation break down in the modern cash economy.

In 1999, the long-serving chief minister was deposed by his own party, but the feared ensuing political instability did not eventuate.

Warnings & Permits

A stable and reasonably effective administration has helped Arunachal Pradesh avoid the ethnic violence of neighbouring states, although there are muted demands for a separate state in the eastern districts.

However, it is a militarily and politically sensitive area, so foreigners (with permits) are only currently allowed to visit Bhalukpong, Bomdila, Seppa and Tawang in the west; Itanagar; the road from Itanagar to Pasighat along the Brahmaputra River or through Ziro, Daporijo and Along; and Namdapha National Park (including Miao).

All foreigners must obtain a Restricted (Prohibited) Area Permit. These can be obtained from the Foreigners' Registration Offices in Delhi and Kolkata, but it's probably quicker and easier at one of the Arunachal Pradesh government offices: 109 CE-Block, Sector 1, Salt Lake City, Kolkata (☎ 033-3589865), opposite the Salt Lake telephone exchange; or Kautilya Marg, Chanakyapuri, Delhi (☎ 011-3013915). You need to provide four passport-sized photos, and four photocopies of the passport pages with your personal details and Indian visa.

The Arunachal Pradesh government charges foreigners US$50 per day just to be in the state. (The government, however, may relent in the future, and reduce this to an acceptable one-off fee of US$50.) The state government offices also have to wait for approval from the Home Secretary in Itanagar and the Ministry of Home Affairs in Delhi. Once final approval is granted, the total fees must be paid upfront to the state government offices in either US dollars or the rupee equivalent. Permits are theoretically for 10 days, although if you pay for 15 days you're likely to get a 15-day permit. Extensions are possible in Itanagar, but are problematic and very time consuming.

In reality, individuals are still unlikely to get permits, so the best way to visit the state is on an organised tour. Travel agencies (eg, in Kolkata, Guwahati and Darjeeling) charge about US$150 per day (including the current daily fee), and will arrange the permit for you. If you do get a permit for independent travel, the checkpoints along the various roads entering the state may detain you for as long as three hours while they fill in registration forms. You will also probably be required to register with the authorities in each town you stay in – either the district magistrate's office or the local magistrate. If so, you'll probably be obliged to stay in the local government bungalow. However, you should be allowed to stay in any hotel of your choice in Itanagar (and its sister town Naharlagun, 12 km away), Tawang, Ziro, Pasighat and Bomdila.

Getting Around

Helicopters are a quick and exhilarating way to travel to more remote places such as Ziro, Along, Pasighat and Daporijo, and between Guwahati and Naharlagun. Schedules and prices are available from the Meghalaya Helicopter Service offices in Shillong and Guwahati (see those sections in this chapter for contact details).

ITANAGAR

☎ 0360 • pop 17,700

Itanagar is not particularly appealing, but it is home to a fascinating cross section of Arunachal's peoples. The sprawling new capital is home to both Adivasis living in traditional houses and the nascent elite living in standard-issue Indian government estates. The nearest tourist office is in Itanagar's sister town, Naharlagun, 12km northeast on the road to Assam, but it offers little except reams of brochures.

Buddha Vihar, on the hill near Hotel Arun Subansiri, serves the local Monpa and Sherdrukpen communities. About 6km from Itanagar, **Ganga Lake** lies at the end of a rugged road and a short, steep track; you'll probably need to charter a jeep to find it. **Jawaharlal Nehru Museum**, near the Secretariat, covers the state's many tribes with dioramas and displays of wood carvings, textiles, musical instruments and headgear. It's open from 10 am to 5 pm Tuesday to Sunday.

NORTH-EASTERN REGION

Places to Stay & Eat

In Ganga Market, ***Hotel Himalaya*** has basic doubles for Rs 150.

Hotel Blue Pine *(☎ 212042)*, on the lane leading down to the ASTC bus station, is good value and has singles/doubles with shared bathroom for Rs 320/535.

Hotel Arun Subansiri *(☎ 212677, Zero Point)* has comfortable singles/doubles/triples for Rs 600/800/900 with private bathroom and cable TV.

In Naharlagun, ***Hotel Arunachal*** *(☎ 0360-244960)* is a large multistorey place with decent rooms with private bathroom and fan for Rs 350/450, and rooms with air-con for Rs 550/750. The ***restaurant*** here is quite good.

Getting There & Away

The nearest airport is 216km away at Tezpur (Assam). Green Valley and Blue Hills have several buses to Tezpur (Rs 100, six hours) and Guwahati (Rs 175, 12 hours).

WESTERN ARUNACHAL PRADESH

The route over the Se La (4249m) (La means 'pass') to Tawang via Bomdila is the most visited area of the state.

At **Tipi**, a few kilometres from the state border with Assam, the **Orchid Research Centre** boasts over 7500 orchids. The best time to visit is in April and May.

About halfway between Tezpur and Tawang, the attractive town of **Bomdila** (2530m) has a couple of **gompas** (Tibetan Buddhist monasteries), and the unusual **Yak Research Centre**. The friendly ***Hotel Siphiyang Phong*** *(☎ 03782-22373)* has comfortable singles/doubles starting at Rs 435/685 with private bathroom. Buses from Guwahati (Rs 220) take about 18 hours.

Seppa, home of the Nishi people, is now open to foreigners, but there is little to see or do there. ***Inspection Bungalow*** is the best place to stay, and costs about Rs 100 per person; book with the magistrate's office in Seppa. The village is accessible on the daily bus (eight hours) from Bhalukpong, via Tipi.

Tawang

Near the border with Bhutan, **Tawang Gompa** is in a superb location at 3400m. Dating from the mid-17th century, it is the most important monastery in the north-east. The sixth Dalai Lama was born here, and it's now home to over 500 lamas (monks) of the Gelukpa order.

The main temple is filled with rich brocades and tapestries, and an 8m-high gilded statue of Sakyamuni (the Historical Buddha). To the left of Sakyamuni are smaller statues, and on the right is a gold and turquoise-covered *chorten* (Tibetan for stupa) the relics of the founding lama. On the main courtyard is the ancient stone and wooden library with a fascinating collection of *thangkas* (Tibetan paintings on cloth), although you may have to seek permission to enter the library. The gompa is on a small hill, about 2km from town.

A **handicrafts centre** is located at the lower end of Tawang, near the hospital.

Tourist Lodge has adequate doubles with private bathroom from Rs 400 to 700. ***Inspection Bungalow***, uphill from the bus station, has basic accommodation for about Rs 100 per bed with shared facilities. ***Hotel Paradise***, in the main market, has doubles from Rs 200 to 500 with private bathroom. A few ***restaurants*** on the main street serve *momos* (dumplings). The local drink is *chang* – a rice beer with melted yak butter (certainly an acquired taste).

Buses from Tezpur, via the Se La (which is often closed for a time during winter), take about 24 hours and cost Rs 185. Infrequent share-jeeps cost a little more, but are far quicker (12 to15 hours).

CENTRAL ARUNACHAL PRADESH

In **Ziro**, home of the Apatani people, is the ***Blue Pine Lodge***, on the edge of the plateau on the left just as the road enters the basin. It has decent singles/doubles with private bathroom for Rs 200/300. ***Circuit House*** has dorm beds for Rs 100 per person; book at the Deputy Commissioner's office. However, there's very little to do in Ziro.

In the overgrown village of **Daporijo**, ***Circuit House*** has dorm beds for Rs 100 per person. **Along**, a quiet town mostly inhabited by the Adi people, also has a ***Circuit House*** (Rs 100 per person). Book either place at the Deputy Commissioner's office (☎ 03782-221).

Pasighat is larger than Along, and the population is also predominantly Adi. Several shops sell locally made handicrafts, such as caneware and shawls. Of the few basic hotels, the best is ***Circuit House***, also known as the Inspection Bungalow, for Rs 100 per person; book at the Deputy Commissioner's office (☎ 03796-22340).

Two or three buses travel every morning in each direction between Itanagar and Pasighat, via Ziro, Daporijo and Along.

EASTERN ARUNACHAL PRADESH

The eastern region of the state is the least visited because only Namdapha National Park is open to foreigners.

Namdapha National Park

This vast and pristine park (1850 sq km), on the border with Myanmar, is under the auspices of Project Tiger, and is home to the four 'big cats': tigers, leopards, clouded leopards and snow leopards. Other creatures include elephants and gibbons, and various types of fish and butterflies. There aren't many treks or trails into the park, because it's mostly wilderness. Entry to the park costs Rs 50.

The ***Forest Rest House*** and ***Tourist Bungalow*** at Deban inside the park are simple but pleasant. Doubles cost Rs 110 with private bathroom. The cooks are good, but you may want to bring extra snacks. Book with the Namdapha National Park Field Director in Miao.

Buses leave from Dibrugarh in Assam for Miao, where you'll have to charter a taxi to and around Namdapha.

Miao, 28km from Deban, is a market town with an ***Inspection Bungalow***. The Tibetan refugee settlement of **Choephelling**, where Tibetan carpets are made and sold, is 3km from Miao on the road to Deban.

Nagaland

South of Arunachal Pradesh and north of Manipur, the remote and hilly state of Nagaland is a fascinating area of tribal villages and stunning scenery.

The main religion in Nagaland is Christianity, and churches are the centre of most communities.

There are 16 Naga tribes, including the Angami, Rengma, Ao, Konyak, Wanchu, Sema and Lotha. Nagaland is the only state with English as opposed to Hindi as the official language, a clear indication of the Naga's rejection of India.

History

The tribes of Nagaland were once headhunters dreaded by the neighbouring Assamese. Naga warriors collected heads during raids and stored them in the *morung*, the boys' dormitory and ceremonial house at the core of traditional Naga villages. The custom was linked to the belief that the soul can only be released when the head is severed, and in the conviction that the gruesome trophies ensure the village harvest.

After first encountering the Nagas in 1832, the British managed to crush them with considerable difficulty in 1879 at the stone-walled village of Khonoma, an event which became a symbol of Naga nationalism. Naga leaders campaigned for outright independence before the British left, but were unwillingly absorbed into India. Almost immediately a rebellion began, which still continues with many factional splits and failed peace deals.

Warnings & Permits

Various rebel groups including the National Socialist Council of Nagaland (Khaplang) – which should not be confused with the National Socialist Council of Nagalim (Isak-Mulivah) – have been waging a war against the state and Indian governments (and among themselves) for many years. Clashes between Indian and Burmese forces along the border are also common.

At the time of research, rumours abounded among tourist authorities and travel agencies about the relaxation of permits and restrictions for foreigners in 2001. However, foreigners still had to apply for a permit and travel in a group of at least four or as a married (not de facto) couple, ie, they didn't need to be part of an organised tour.

Travel around Nagaland is currently restricted to (and around) Kohima, Dimapur, Wokha and Mokokchung. You must register with the police when you visit each of these places, and at Dimapur airport if you arrive by air.

Permit forms are available from Indian embassies and consulates and Foreigners' Registration Offices in major cities (eg, Delhi or Kolkata), but the best options are the Nagaland government offices at 29 Aurangzeb Rd, Delhi (☎ 011-3012296, fax 3794240), or at 11 Shakespeare Sarani, Kolkata (☎ 033-2825247, fax 2823491). A copy of the completed permit form must be sent by you, together with one passport photo, an itinerary and a photocopy of the personal details and Indian visa in your passport, to the Home Commissioner, Government of Nagaland, Kohima 797001 (☎ 0370-270068, fax 270071). The authorities will mail, or even fax, the permit back to you. No fee is required, but allow about two weeks for the process.

KOHIMA

☎ 0370

The capital of Nagaland, Kohima, is where the Japanese advance into India was halted in April 1944. To commemorate this, the well-maintained **Kohima War Cemetery** has been established. Also worthwhile is the **State Museum**, with anthropological displays of the Naga tribes, including statues, jewellery and musical instruments; the tourist-oriented **Kohima Village**; and the **New Market** (also known as the Sales Emporium), opposite the NSTC bus station, which sells local handicrafts. On Aradura Hill, the **Catholic Church** is an impressive landmark and boasts the largest cross in India. The tourist office (☎ 22214) in Kohima is helpful.

Around Kohima, **Khonoma** (20km to the west) has awesome scenery and was the site of a famous battle against the British. Trekking may soon be possible at **Dzukuo Valley**, about 30km south of Kohima.

Yatri Niwas *(☎ 22708)* charges Rs 120/150 for basic but clean singles/doubles with shared bathroom. ***Hotel Pine*** *(☎ 22234)*, at Phoolbari, has a small number of rooms with private bathroom for Rs 220/275 and Rs 300 for doubles with cable TV. ***Hotel***

Japfu *(☎ 22721)* has very comfortable rooms with private bathroom and cable TV starting at Rs 550/770. Most of the hotels have decent restaurants.

The nearest airport and railhead are at Dimapur, two to three hours by road to the north. Buses regularly link Kohima with Imphal and Guwahati; see the Guwahati section for details.

DIMAPUR

☎ 03862

Dimapur is Nagaland's gateway, and is near the border with Assam; it is also Nagaland's commercial centre. In the 13th century, Dimapur was the capital of the Kachari tribal kingdom, and their huge decorative phallic symbols at **Kachari Ruins** can still be seen. The pretty hand-woven shawls for which Nagaland is famous are sold at the Nagaland Handloom & Handicrafts Centre.

About 5km away along the road to Kohima is the colourful **Ruzaphema** village. The **North East Zone Cultural Centre**, with its reasonable museum, is 3km from Dimapur.

Tourist Lodge *(☎ 26355)* offers comfortable singles/doubles with private bathroom for a reasonable Rs 150/220. ***Hotel Saramati*** *(☎ 20560)* has rooms with private bathroom starting at Rs 325/475; more with air-con. ***Hotel Nagi*** *(☎ 21043, Kohima Rd)* has comfortable rooms with private bathroom starting at Rs 180/230; and ***Hotel City Tower*** *(☎ 20173, Circular Rd)* has slightly better rooms starting at Rs 250/350 with private bathroom. Most of the hotels have decent restaurants.

Dimapur is an important transport hub. Indian Airlines (☎ 20114) flies to Kolkata (US$90) several times a week, often via Tezpur (US$35). Buses regularly travel to Kohima, Imphal, Shillong and Guwahati.

MOKOKCHUNG

This pretty town is home to the Ao Naga people. About 17km to the south-west, **Longkhum** is one of several local traditional villages with superb views.

In Mokokchung, there are several hotels, including ***Tourist Lodge***, which has basic singles/doubles with shared bathroom starting at Rs 100/120; and ***Circuit House*** for about the same price. The town is accessible by bus from Wokha and Jorhat in Assam.

WOKHA

Wokha offers spectacular rock-climbing at nearby **Mt Tiyi** (1970m). Singles/doubles with shared bathroom for about Rs 100/150 are available at both ***Tourist Lodge*** and ***Hotel Fab***.

Wokha is about half-way between Kohima and Mokokchung, and is accessible by bus from either, as well as from the railway town of Furkating in Assam.

Mizoram

Mizoram (Hill People's Land) is a finger-like extension in the extreme south-east of the region poking between Myanmar and Bangladesh. It's a picturesque state where the population is predominantly tribal and overwhelmingly Christian. The Mizos boast the second-highest literacy rate in India, and most locals speak some English.

Under the British, the area was known as Lushai Hills, a name that persisted until 1972 when it became a Union Territory.

History

The Mizo people probably settled here some 300 years ago, perhaps from China. Under the British, it was one of the few areas where missionaries were encouraged to operate, and today almost 95% of the Mizo population is Christian. Over 10,000 Mizos have identified themselves as one of the lost tribes of Israel and have converted to Judaism. Social cohesion is boosted by large volunteer groups such as the Young Mizo Association (YMA), which has recruited as much as 60% of the population between the ages of 15 and 25. Buddhist and animist tribes, such as the Chakmas and Reangs, have been discriminated against and even forced out of the state.

A natural crisis called *mautam* was one reason for the Mizo rebellion in 1959. (Every 50 years the great bamboo forests burst into flower, attracting a plague of rats which devours the rice fields and vegetable gardens.) The two-year famine that followed inspired the Mizo National Famine Front to fight for independence against what they regarded as an inept and uncaring Indian administration.

In July 1986, after 20 years of bitter fighting, a peace deal that included statehood was made with the renamed Mizo National Front (MNF). The MNF government lasted one year, but democratically regained power in 1998.

Warnings & Permits

Mizoram had been comparatively peaceful since achieving statehood in 1986, but since the mid-1990s the state and Indian governments have been fighting against the Bru National Liberation Front and the Hmar People's Convention (Democrats). These groups are fairly ineffectual, however, and travelling around Mizoram is comparatively safe.

Foreigners can only obtain a permit for Mizoram if they travel as part of an organised tour of at least four that has been arranged by a recognised travel agent. For more information, contact the Mizoram government offices at Circular Rd, Chanakyapuri, Delhi (☎ 011-3015951), and 24 AT Chowdury Ave, Kolkata (☎ 033-4757034).

AIZAWL

☎ 0389 • pop 160,000 • elevation 1130m

Mizoram's capital clings to the sides of a central ridge, and is home to nearly one-third of the state's population. The staff at Mizoram Tourism (☎ 21227), Chandmary, are helpful.

Bara Bazaar, in the city centre, is interesting; other good places to buy handicrafts are the **Weaving Centre** and **Solomon's Cave**. The small **Mizoram State Museum**, at Babu Tlang, has a fascinating collection of traditional Mizo costumes and implements. The small **zoological gardens** are located in the northern part of town.

Hotel Embassy** (☎ 22570)*, near the tourist office, has singles/doubles with private bathroom for about Rs 250/320, and a decent ***restaurant. ***Tourist Lodge***, farther from the city centre at Chatlang, is similarly priced. ***Hotel Ritz***, in Bara Bazaar, is a little cheaper.

Several times a week, Indian Airlines flies between Guwahati and Aizawl (US$55). There are no railway lines anywhere near Aizawl, so all overland transport to Mizoram is by road through Silchar (Rs 150, six hours) in Tripura.

AROUND MIZORAM

Travelling around the state is comparatively safe, but it is problematic because of infrequent public transport and poor roads.

Luangmual is a small ridge-top village, 7km south from Aizawl. It offers enchanting views, a handicraft centre and budget accommodation at ***Yatri Niwas***. Also reasonably accessible are the pretty twin villages of Bung and Paikhai, about 16km from the capital.

Manipur

Manipur ('Jewelled Land') borders Myanmar, and is inhabited by over two dozen tribes. Manipuri dancing is one of the great classical dance forms, and involves acrobatics on the part of the male dancers and slow graceful movements from the female participants. The favourite sport in the area is polo, which has long been played in this part of India. Agriculture and weaving form the basis of the economy.

History

Manipur has a unique Hindu culture, fostered in the security of the hills. The Hindu tribe of the Imphal Valley, the Meitei, were championed by the poet Rabindranath Tagore for their dances and music. A movement to disown Vaishnavaite Hinduism and the Bengali script grew among the Meitei in the 1960s, looking back 200 years to the time before Hinduism had been adopted.

After a war against the Burmese, Manipur aligned itself with the British and signed the Treaty of Yandabo in 1826, thereby becoming a princely state within the Raj. The maharajas ruled with little interference, but their power began to erode after a popular leader and relative of the royal family embraced communism.

During WWII, most of the state was occupied by the Japanese. The Indian National Army, recruited from Indian prisoners of war, fought against British India, and at Independence the maharaja ceded his state to India.

Warnings & Permits

Violent clashes, particularly between the Naga and Kuki tribes in the south, have continued for many years. These days, an estimated 50 separate guerrilla armies, such as the People's Liberation Army, Manipur People's Army and Kangleipak Communist Party, operate around Manipur. Travelling anywhere outside Imphal is *not* recommended. In any case, foreigners cannot currently travel overland into or out of Manipur: they can only fly to or from Imphal.

Foreigners can only obtain a permit if they travel on an organised tour of at least four people arranged by a recognised travel agency. However, the chances of getting a permit, even on an organised tour, are slim. More information is available from the Manipur government offices at 2 Sardar Patel Marg, Chanakyapuri, Delhi (☎ 011-3013009), and 25 Ashutosh Shastri Rd, Kolkata (☎ 033-3504412).

IMPHAL

☎ 0385 • pop 210,000

Imphal, the capital of Manipur, is surrounded by wooded hills and lakes. The Vaishnavaite **Shri Govindajee Mandir** has two gold domes and often hosts ceremonial dances. Nearby are the ruins of the **Old Palace**. **Khwairamband Bazaar**, also known as Ima Market, is a wonderful place to buy Manipuri wickerwork, basketry and weavings, as well as meat, fruit and vegetables; it is run almost entirely by 2000 to 3000 women. In the middle of Tikendrajit Park is the huge war memorial, **Shaheed Minar**, and the **State Museum**, near the polo ground, is also worth a look.

Imphal has a decent range of accommodation, including the government-run ***Hotel Imphal*** *(☎ 220459)* which charges Rs 250/375 for singles/doubles with private bathroom and air-con. Manipur Tourism is based here.

Indian Airlines (☎ 220999) and Jet Airways (☎ 230835) link Imphal with Kolkata every day (US$80), and both airlines fly regularly to Guwahati (US$50). Jet Airways also flies to Jorhat (US$80), and Indian Airlines flies to Delhi (US$240) and Silchar (US$45). Buses regularly depart Imphal for Kohima, Silchar and Guwahati.

LOKTAK LAKE

Loktak Lake is the largest freshwater lake in the north-east, and much of it falls within the Keibul Lamjao National Park. Large areas of the lake are covered with 'islands' of thick matted weeds. The area is home to local fishing people, prolific birdlife and rare species of wildlife such as *sangai* (dancing deer). Accommodation is available at ***Tourist Home*** on Sendra Island; you can make bookings at the toursit office in Imphal. The lake is accessible by bus from Imphal (48 km).

Rajasthan

Rajasthan, the Land of the Kings, is India at its exotic and colourful best: battle-scarred forts, palaces of breathtaking grandeur and whimsical charm, riotous colours, and a romantic sense of pride and honour.

The state is diagonally divided into the hilly and rugged south-eastern region and the barren north-western Great Thar Desert, which extends across the border into Pakistan. There are plenty of historic cities, incredible fortresses awash with legends, and rare gems of impressionistic beauty such as Udaipur. There are also a number of centres which attract travellers from far and wide, such as Pushkar with its holy lake, and the desert city of Jaisalmer which resembles a fantasy from *The Thousand and One Nights*.

Rajasthan is one of India's prime tourist destinations. Nobody leaves here without priceless memories, a bundle of souvenirs, and an address book full of friends.

Rajasthan at a Glance

Population: 51.5 million
Area: 342,239 sq km
Capital: Jaipur
Main Languages: Hindi, Rajasthani
When to Go: mid-Oct to mid-Mar

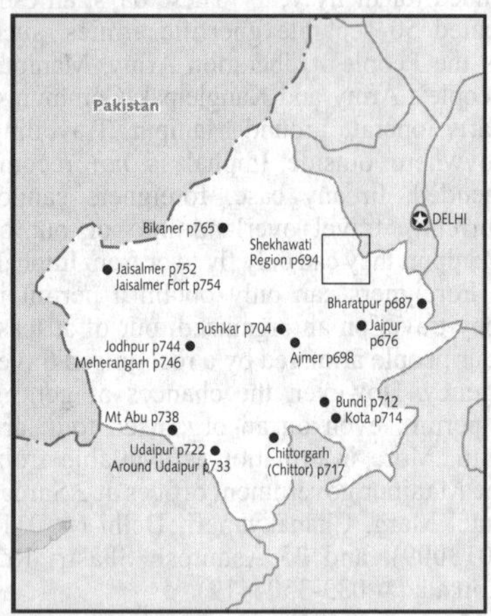

- Lose yourself in the medieval Jaisalmer Fort, rising from a stark desert landscape
- Explore Udaipur, with its whitewashed temples, grand palaces by the lakeside, and the gorgeous Lake Palace Hotel
- Marvel at Jodhpur, the 'blue city' of Rajasthan, overlooked by the mighty Meherangarh
- Relax in Keoladeo Ghana National Park, a World Heritage–listed bird sanctuary
- Enjoy Rajasthan's 'open-air gallery' of Shekhawati, with its scores of ornately painted *havelis*, or mansions
- Wander through the Dilwara temples in the exquisitely sculptured ancient Jain temple complex at Mt Abu

History

This diverse state is the home of the Rajputs, a group of warrior clans who controlled this part of India for 1000 years according to a code of chivalry and honour akin to that of the medieval European knights. While temporary alliances and marriages of convenience were the order of the day, pride and independence were always paramount. The Rajputs were therefore never able to present a united front against a common aggressor. Indeed, much of their energy was spent squabbling among themselves and the resultant weakness eventually led to their becoming vassal states of the Mughal empire. Nevertheless, the Rajputs' bravery and sense of honour were unparalleled.

Rajput warriors would fight against all odds, and when no hope was left, chivalry demanded that *jauhar* (collective sacrifice) take place. In this grim ritual, the women and children committed suicide by immolating themselves on a huge funeral pyre, while the men donned saffron robes and

RAJASTHAN

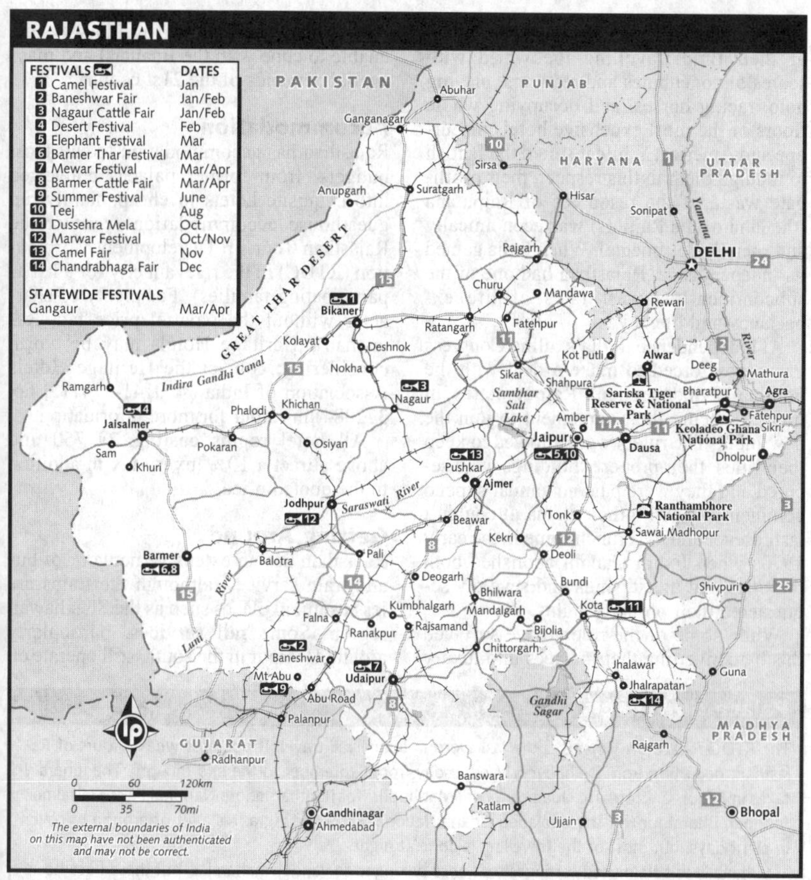

rode out to confront the enemy and certain death. In some of the larger battles, tens of thousands of Rajput warriors lost their lives in this way. This tragic fate befell many forts around the state, with Chittorgarh the most renowned. It's hardly surprising that Akbar persuaded Rajputs to lead his army, nor that subsequent Mughal emperors had such difficulty controlling this part of their empire.

With the decline of the Mughal empire, the Rajputs gradually clawed back their independence through a series of spectacular victories. When the British appeared on the scene and the Raj inexorably expanded, most Rajput states signed articles of alliance with the British which allowed them to continue as independent states, each with its own maharaja (or similarly titled leader), subject to certain political and economic constraints. The British, after all, were not there for humanitarian reasons, but to establish an empire and gain a controlling interest in the economy of the subcontinent in the same way as the Mughals had done.

These alliances proved to be the beginning of the end for the Rajput rulers. Indulgence and extravagance soon replaced chivalry and honour so that by the early

1900s, many of the maharajas spent much of their time travelling the world with scores of concubines and retainers, playing polo, racing horses, and occupying whole floors of the most expensive hotels in Europe and America. While it suited the British to indulge them in this respect, their profligate waste of the resources of Rajputana (the land of the Rajputs) was economically and socially detrimental. When India gained its independence, Rajasthan had one of the subcontinent's lowest rates of life expectancy and literacy.

At Independence, India's ruling Congress Party was forced to make a deal with the nominally independent Rajput states in order to secure their agreement to join the new India. The rulers were allowed to keep their titles, their property holdings were secured and they were paid an annual stipend commensurate with their status. It couldn't last forever and the crunch came in the early 1970s when Indira Gandhi abolished both the titles and the stipends and severely sequestered their property rights.

While some of the rulers have survived this by converting their palaces into luxury hotels, many have fallen by the wayside, unable to cope with the financial and managerial demands of the 21st century.

Accommodation

Rajasthan has accommodation to suit most budgets, from former palaces converted into exquisite hotels to cheap, family-run guesthouse accommodation (contact the Rajasthan Tourism Development Corporation (RTDC) in the relevant city for a list of participating families). For plenty of character without the palatial price tag, Rajasthan's Heritage Hotels may be worth considering; contact the Heritage Hotels Association of India (☎ 0141-374112, fax 372084) in Jaipur for more information.

All hotel rooms costing Rs 750 and above attract a 10% luxury tax in addition to the quoted price.

Getting Around

Rajasthan has an extensive network of bus and train services, although the trains are less useful in places such as the Shekhawati region. Some rail services, particularly around Udaipur in the south, still operate on

Palace on Wheels

The RTDC *Palace on Wheels* is the last word in luxury rail travel. It operates weekly tours of Rajasthan, departing from Delhi every Wednesday from September to the end of April. The itinerary takes in Jaipur, Chittorgarh, Udaipur, Sawai Madhopur (for Ranthambhore National Park), Jaisalmer, Jodhpur, Bharatpur (for the Keoladeo Ghana National Park) and Agra. It's a lot of ground to cover in eight days, but most of the travelling is done at night.

Originally this train used carriages that once belonged to various maharajas, but these became so ancient that new carriages were refurbished to look like the originals. They were also fitted with air-conditioning. The result is a very luxurious mobile hotel and it can be a memorable way to travel if you have limited time and limitless resources. The train comes equipped with two dining cars and a well-stocked bar. Each coach, which is attended by a splendidly costumed captain and attendant, contains four coupes (double or twin share) with bathrooms.

Rates per person per day from October to March are US$260 for triple occupancy (the third person sleeps on a fold-away bed), US$325 for double occupancy and US$460 for single occupancy. In the months of September and April the tariff is lower: US$215/270/370. The cost includes tours, entry fees, accommodation on the train and all meals. It's a very popular service and bookings must be made in advance at the RTDC Tourist Reception Centre (☎ 011-3381884, fax 3382823), Bikaner House, Pandara Rd, New Delhi 110011, or at the RTDC Hotel Swagatam (☎ 0141-202152, fax 201145, ⓔ rtdc@jp1.dot.net.in), Jaipur 302006. For those who can't afford to do it for real, there's a Web site (www.palaceonwheels.net) to show you what you're missing.

the slower metre-gauge system. The conversion to broad gauge is taking place but is a painfully slow process. Please note that all train prices quoted in this chapter do not include the reservation charge of Rs 20/25 levied by Indian Railways on sleeper/three- or two-tier air-con (3A or 2A) berths.

More and more travellers are engaging a private taxi and driver to get around. Costs start at Rs 4 per kilometre, although when calculating the costs that you must also pay for the driver to return to his home base.

Eastern Rajasthan

JAIPUR

☎ 0141 • pop 1.86 million

Jaipur, the vibrant capital of Rajasthan, is popularly known as the 'pink city' for the colour of the buildings in its wonderful old city. This buzzing metropolis is certainly a place of wild contrasts and a feast for the eyes. Vegetable-laden camel carts thread their way through streets jam-packed with cars, motorcycles, rickshaws, bicycles, tempos and pedestrians frantically dodging the incessant traffic. In the midst of it all, traditionally dressed Rajput men sporting bright turbans and swashbuckling moustaches discuss village politics outside restaurants serving spaghetti bolognese and American ice-cream sodas. To cap it off, ramshackle roadside stalls selling *jootis* (traditional Rajasthani shoes) stand beside kitsch shops flogging a mishmash of modern trinkets.

Jaipur has long outstripped the confines of its city wall and is today among the most tumultuous and polluted places in Rajasthan. It can also feel at times as though many of the city's inhabitants are on the lookout for tourists. Despite this, it seldom disappoints the first-time visitor.

History

The city owes its name, its foundation and its careful planning to the great warrior-astronomer Maharaja Jai Singh II (1693–1743). His predecessors enjoyed good relations with the Mughals and Jai Singh was careful to preserve this alliance.

In 1727, with Mughal power on the wane, Jai Singh decided the time was ripe to move down from his somewhat cramped hillside fort at nearby Amber to a new site on the plains. He laid out the city, with its surrounding walls and rectangular blocks, according to principles set down in the *Shilpa-Shastra*, an ancient Hindu treatise on architecture. In 1728, he built the remarkable observatory (Jantar Mantar) that is still one of Jaipur's main attractions.

Orientation

The walled old city, home to most of the city's attractions, is in the north-east of Jaipur; the new parts spread to the south and west. There are three main interconnecting roads in the new part of town: Mirza Ismail Rd (MI Rd), Station Rd and Sansar Chandra Marg. Along or just off these roads are most of the budget and mid-range hotels and restaurants, the main train and bus stations and many of the banks.

Information

Tourist Offices The helpful RTDC Central Office (☎ 202152, fax 201145, ⓔ rtdc@jp1.dot.net.in) is behind the Hotel Swagatam; it's open 10 am to 5 pm every day except Sunday, and a range of literature is available. There are other tourist offices on Platform 1 at the train station (☎ 315714), open 7 am to 6 pm daily; and outside the RTDC Tourist Hotel (☎ 375466). The Government of India tourist office (☎ 372200, ☎ 1323), in the grounds of the Hotel Khasa Kothi, can provide some good, if dated, brochures but is otherwise of limited use. It's open 9 am to 6 pm Monday to Friday and until 4.30 pm on Saturday.

Money Thomas Cook (☎ 360940), on the ground floor of Jaipur Towers on MI Rd, will change most currencies and travellers cheques. It's open 9.30 am to 6 pm daily. Nearby, also on MI Rd, Tata Finance AmEx (☎/fax 364223) is the local representative for American Express (AmEx). The tiny Bank of Rajasthan (☎ 381416) in Rambagh Palace changes money and is conveniently open 7 am to 8 pm daily.

The HDFC Bank on Ashoka Marg has a 24-hour ATM which is the most convenient way to get cash from your Visa, MasterCard and Cirrus. The Andhra Bank (☎ 369906), MI Rd, does cash advances on MasterCard, Visa and JCB (Japanese Credit Bureau) cards. The efficient Central Bank of India (☎ 317419), Anand Building, Sansar Chandra Marg, issues cash advances on MasterCard and Visa (minimum US$100).

Post The main post office (☎ 368740) on MI Rd is quite efficient and there's a man at the entrance who sews up parcels, sealing them with wax. It's open 10 am to 5 pm Monday to Saturday.

DHL Worldwide Express (☎ 362826) is in a lane off MI Rd at C-scheme, G-7A Vinobha Marg. It operates air freight around the world, starting at Rs 3500 for a 10kg box and Rs 5500 for a 'jumbo' 25kg box to Australia (around Rs 500 more for Europe and the USA). Make sure you ask to pay upfront any customs charges for the destination country unless you want the receiver to find a nasty surprise in the mail.

Email & Internet Access Jaipur is awash with places advertising Internet access. Costs vary (from Rs 45 to 180 an hour) as does the quality of the connection; many advertise rates of Rs 1 per minute, but the minimum charge is usually Rs 30. Many are simply in travel agencies or are one-computer operations in hotel lobbies. Among those for whom Internet is their main business, Communicator (☎ 360760, ⓔ pravin@jp1.dot.net.in), on the ground floor of the Jaipur Towers complex on MI Rd, is the cheapest at Rs 45 an hour.

Also good are Web-Struk Cafe (☎ 373333, ⓔ webstruk@ usa.net) in the same building, Cybarea (☎ 379644, ⓔ cybarean@hotmail.com) in Ganpati Plaza, and the Mewar Cyber Cafe & Communication (☎ 204734, ⓔ mewar@jp1.dot.net.in) on Station Rd near the main bus terminal; all charge Rs 60 per hour. The last is open 24 hours.

Photography Two of the best places for photographic supplies and developing are Goyal Colour Lab, on MI Rd next to Lassiwala, and Sentosa Colour Lab (☎ 388748) in Ganpati Plaza. The latter can also develop a roll of 36-exposure slide film, usually within 24 hours, for Rs 300 (including mounting).

Bookshops There's a reasonable range of English-language books as well as magazines and maps at Books Corner (☎ 366323) on MI Rd (near Niro's restaurant) and Ganpati Books (☎ 388762) in the Ganpati Plaza complex; they both sell a small range of Lonely Planet guidebooks. At Books Corner, you can pick up copies of the informative *Jaipur Vision* and *Jaipur City Guide* which contain useful information about the city.

Medical Services & Emergency One place which comes highly recommended by a number of travellers is the Galundia Clinic (☎ 361 040), on MI Rd opposite All India Radio. Dr Chandra Sen runs a highly professional service and is well versed in dealing with travellers' ailments. Importantly, he is also on call 24 hours (mobile ☎ 9829061040) and will visit you in your hotel. He works with most travel insurance companies and a normal consultation costs Rs 300. This should be your first port of call. He has a small number of beds, although should you need to be hospitalised, you may end up at the Sawai Mansingh Hospital (☎ 560291), Sawai Ram Singh Marg, or the Santokba Durlabhji Hospital (☎ 566251), Bhawani Singh Marg.

Emergency numbers are police ☎ 100; fire ☎ 101; and ambulance ☎ 102. For the police, you can also call ☎ 369796.

Old City (Pink City)

In 1876, Maharaja Ram Singh had the entire old city painted pink, traditionally a colour associated with hospitality, to welcome the Prince of Wales (later King Edward VII), a practice which has been maintained. The old city is partially encircled by a crenellated wall with a number of gates – the major gates are Chandpol, Ajmeri and Sanganeri. Broad avenues, over 30m wide, divide the pink city into neat rectangles. In the evening light, the pink and orange buildings have a magical glow which is complemented by the brightly clothed Rajasthanis.

A major landmark in this part of town is the **Iswari Minar Swarga Sal** (Heaven-Piercing Minaret), near the Tripolia Gate. You can climb to the top between 9 am and 4.30 pm for Rs 5 (an additional Rs 10/50 for a camera/video) for great views over the old city. The entrance is around the back – take the alley 50m west of the minaret along Chandpol Bazaar.

The main **bazaars** in the old city include Johari Bazaar, Tripolia Bazaar, Bapu Bazaar and Chandpol Bazaar.

Hawa Mahal Constructed in 1799, the Hawa Mahal, or Palace of the Winds, is one of Jaipur's major landmarks, although it is actually little more than a facade. This five-storey building, which overlooks the main street of the bustling old city, is a stunning example of Rajput artistry with its pink, delicately honeycombed sandstone windows. It was originally built to enable ladies of the royal household to watch the everyday life and processions of the city. You can climb to the top of the Hawa Mahal for a fine view over the city. The palace was built by Maharaja Sawaj Pratap Singh. There's a small **archaeological museum** (closed Friday) on the same site.

Entrance to the Hawa Mahal is from the rear of the building. To get there, go back to the intersection on your left as you face the Hawa Mahal, turn right and then take the first right again through an archway. It's open 9 am to 4.30 pm daily and entry costs Rs 2. A still camera costs Rs 10/30 for Indians/foreigners, and a video camera is Rs 20/70.

KELLI HAMBLET

The sandstone Palace of the Winds is Rajput artistry at its most indulgent.

City Palace Complex In the heart of the old city, the City Palace occupies a large area divided into a series of courtyards, gardens and buildings. The outer wall was built by Jai Singh, but other additions are much more recent, some dating from the start of the 20th century. Today, the palace is a blend of Rajasthani and Mughal architecture. The son of the last maharaja and his family still reside in part of the palace.

Before the palace proper you'll see the **Mubarak Mahal**, or Welcome Palace, which was built in the late 19th century by Maharaja Sawai Madho Singh II as a reception centre for visiting dignitaries. It now forms part of the **Maharaja Sawai Mansingh II Museum**, and contains a collection of royal costumes and superb shawls including Kashmiri *pashmina* (wool shawl). One remarkable exhibit is a set of the voluminous clothing of Sawai Madho Singh I, who was a stately 2m tall and 1.2m wide and weighed 250kg!

Other points of interest include the **Diwan-i-Am**, or Hall of Public Audience, with its intricate decorations and manuscripts in Persian and Sanskrit, the **Diwan-i-Khas**, or Hall of Private Audience, with a marble-paved gallery, and the exquisite **Peacock Gate** in the Chandra Mahal courtyard.

Outside the buildings, you can see enormous silver vessels in which a former maharaja used to take holy Ganges water to England. Being a devout Hindu, he preferred not to risk the English water!

The palace and museum are open between 9.30 am and 4.30 pm daily. Entry is Rs 150 for adults and Rs 80 for children between five and 12 years old. The cost includes entry to Jaigarh (see the Around Jaipur section later in this chapter) and the ticket is valid for two days. Photography is prohibited inside the museums. If you're still interested, the video camera fee is

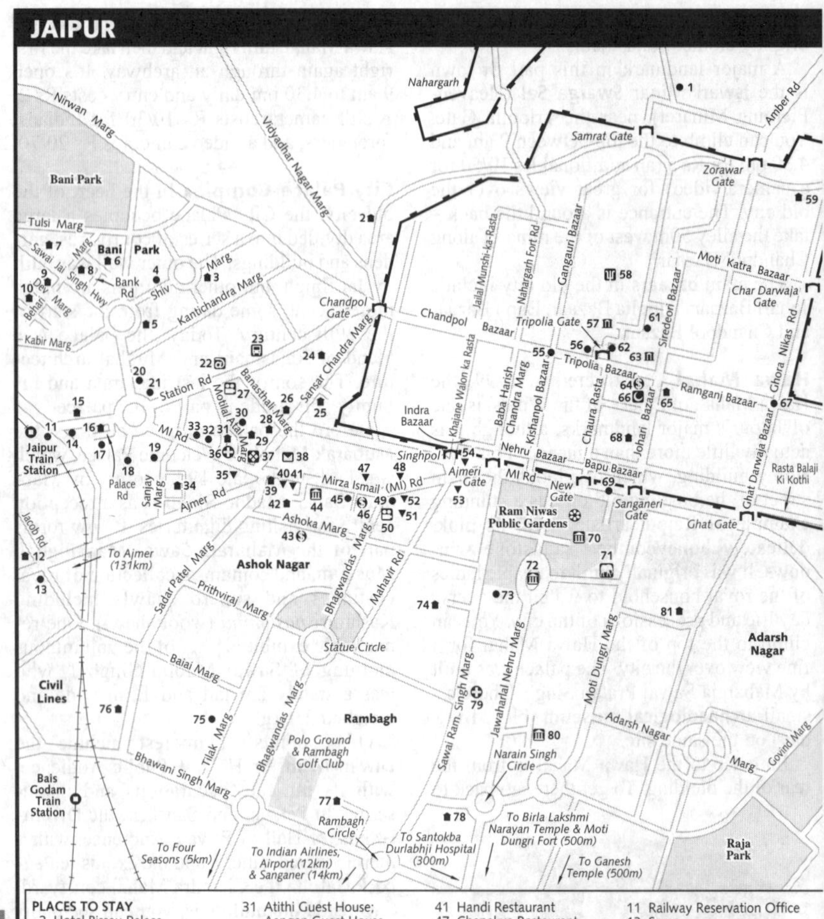

PLACES TO STAY
2 Hotel Bissau Palace
3 Jaipur Inn
5 Hotel Jaipur Ashok
6 Umaid Bhawan Guest House; Sajjan Niwas Guest House
7 Hotel Meghniwas
8 Madhuban; Madhavanand Ashram
9 Shagun Paying Guest House
10 Shahpura House
12 Jai Mahal Palace Hotel
15 RTDC's Hotel Swagatam; RTDC Central office
16 Rajputana Palace Sheraton
24 Alsisar Haveli
25 Hotel Arya Niwas
26 Hotel Mangal
28 Mansingh Hotel; Central Bank of India
29 Karni Niwas
31 Atithi Guest House; Aangan Guest House
34 Hotel Pearl Palace
39 RTDC's Tourist Hotel; Tourist Office; Rajasthali Emporium; Rajasthan Handloom House
42 Evergreen Guest House; Ashiyana Guest House
59 Samode Haveli
65 Hotel Kailash
68 LMB Hotel & Restaurant
74 Hotel Diggi Palace
76 Rajmahal Palace Hotel
77 Rambagh Palace; Bank of Rajasthan; Polo Bar
78 Narain Niwas Palace Hotel
81 Nana-ki-Haveli

PLACES TO EAT
35 Rainbow Restaurant
40 Copper Chimney
41 Handi Restaurant
47 Chanakya Restaurant
48 Lassiwala; Goyal Colour Lab; Charmica
51 Golden Dragon Restaurant; Bake Hut
52 Niro's; Surya Mahal; Natraj Restaurant
53 Mehfil Restaurant
54 Indian Coffee House

OTHER
1 Royal Gaitor
4 Kripal Kumbh (Pottery Store)
11 Railway Reservation Office
13 Soma
14 Bicycle Hire
17 Crown Tours
18 Government of India Tourist Office; Hotel Khasa Kothi
19 RTDC's Hotel Gangaur
11 Railway Reservation Office
13 Soma
14 Bicycle Hire
17 Crown Tours
18 Government of India Tourist Office; Hotel Khasa Kothi
19 RTDC's Hotel Gangaur Palace
20 RTDC's Hotel Teej
21 Sita World Travels
22 Mewar Cyber Cafe & Communication
23 Main Bus Station
27 Polo Victory Cinema
30 Hotel Neelam
32 Jaipur Towers; Thomas Cook; Satyam Travels & Tours; Communicator; Web-Struk Cafe
33 British Airways
36 Galundia Clinic; Chic Chocolate; Tata Finance Amex

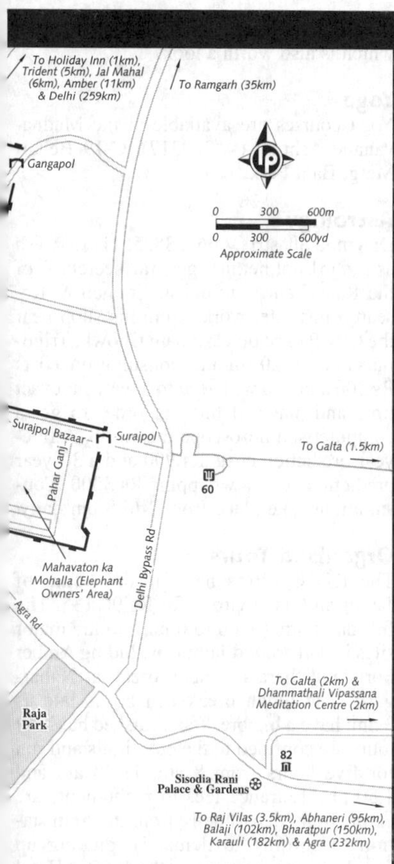

37 Ganpati Plaza; Swaad; Pizza Hut; Celebrations; Baskin 31 Robbins; Rajasthan Travel Service; Cybarea; Ganpati Books; Sentosa Colour Lab
38 Main Post Office
43 HDFC Bank (24-hour ATM)
44 Juneja Art Gallery (Lakshmi Complex)
45 DHL Worldwide Express
46 Andhra Bank
49 Books Corner; Pool Club & Restaurant
50 Raj Mandir Cinema
55 Choti Chaupar (crossroads)
56 Iswari Minar Swarga Sal (Heaven-Piercing Minaret)
57 City Palace & Maharaja Sawai Mansingh II Museum
58 Govind Devji Temple
60 Temple of the Sun God (Monkey Temple)
61 Jantar Mantar (Observatory)
62 Rajasthan Astrological Council & Research Institute
63 Hawa Mahal
64 Bank of Baroda
66 Jama Masjid
67 Ramganj Chaupar (crossroads)
69 Lufthansa; Singapore Airlines
70 Modern Art Gallery
71 Zoo
72 Central Museum (Albert Hall)
73 Maharaja College
75 Anokhi Showroom
79 Sawai Mansingh Hospital
80 Museum of Indology
82 Vidyadharji-ka-Bagh

Rs 100/150 for Indians/foreigners, but the Rs 50 camera fee is inexplicably levied only on Indians. There are guides for hire inside the palace complex for Rs 150.

Jantar Mantar Almost opposite the entrance to the City Palace is the Jantar Mantar, or Observatory, begun by Jai Singh in 1728. Jai Singh's passion for astronomy was even more notable than his prowess as a warrior, and before commencing construction, he sent scholars abroad to study foreign observatories. The Jaipur observatory is the largest and the best preserved of the five he built, and was restored in 1901. Others are in Delhi (the oldest, dating from 1724), Varanasi and Ujjain. The fifth, the Muttra observatory, is gone.

At first glance, Jantar Mantar appears to be just a curious collection of sculptures but in fact each construction has a specific purpose, such as measuring the positions of stars, altitudes and azimuths, and calculating eclipses. The most striking instrument is the sundial with its 27m-high gnomon. The shadow this casts moves up to 4m an hour.

The observatory is open 9 am to 4.30 pm daily and entry is Rs 4 (free on Monday). Photography is Rs 20/50 for Indians/foreigners; Rs 50/100 for video cameras.

Central Museum

This somewhat dusty collection is housed in the architecturally impressive Albert Hall in the Ram Niwas Public Gardens, south of the old city. Exhibits include models of yogis adopting various positions, tribal ware, dioramas depicting Rajasthani dances, and sections on decorative arts, costumes, drawings and musical instruments. The museum is open 10 am to 4.30 pm daily except Friday. Entry is Rs 5/30 for Indians/foreigners (free on Monday). Photography is prohibited.

Nahargarh

Nahargarh, or Tiger Fort, overlooks the city from a sheer ridge to the north, and is floodlit at night. The fort was built in 1734 and extended in 1868. The fort can be reached by an 8km road that runs up through the hills from Jaipur or along a zigzagging 2km footpath. The glorious views fully justify the effort – it's a great place to go for sunset. Entry is Rs 10, and the camera/video fee is Rs 30/70.

There's a small restaurant on the top (with a toilet). You can even stay at the fort (see Places to Stay – Mid-Range).

Royal Gaitor

The **cenotaphs** of the royal family are at Gaitor, just outside the city walls. The cenotaph of Maharaja Jai Singh II is particularly impressive. Entry is free, but there's a charge of Rs 10/20 for a camera/video (Rs 5/10 for Indians).

Other Attractions

The cenotaphs of the maharanis of Jaipur are on Amber Rd, midway between Jaipur and Amber. Nearby is the **Jal Mahal** (Water Palace), in the middle of a lake and reached by a causeway (if they've repaired it).

The Ram Niwas Public Gardens has a **zoo** with unhappy looking animals. It's open 8 am to 5 pm daily except Tuesday; entry is Rs 5. Nearby, an old theatre houses Jaipur's **Modern Art Gallery**, on the 1st floor of the Ravindra Rangmanch Building (closed Sunday; free entry). The excellent **Juneja Art Gallery** (☎ 367448, fax 204237), Lakshmi Complex, MI Rd, has a full program of exhibitions of contemporary art by predominantly Rajasthani artists and is worth a visit.

The rather ramshackle **Museum of Indology** is an extraordinary private collection of folk art objects – there's everything from a map of India painted on a rice grain, to manuscripts (one written by Aurangzeb), tribal ornaments, fossils, old currency notes, clocks and much more. The museum is signposted off J Nehru Marg, south of the Central Museum. It's open 8 am to 6 pm daily. Entry is Rs 40 (including a guide). Cameras and videos are not allowed.

Farther south down J Nehru Marg, looming above the road to the left, is the small fort of **Moti Dungri** (closed to the public). At the foot of this fort is the large marble **Birla Lakshmi Narayan Temple**. There is a small **museum** next to the temple, which is open 6 am to noon and 3 to 9 pm daily (free entry). Nearby is a **Ganesh temple**, which is also worth a look.

Yoga

Yoga courses are available at the Madhavanand Ashram (☎ 200317), C-19 Behari Marg, Bani Park.

Astrology

Dr Vinod Shastri (☎ 663338, 551117, ⓔ vshastri@jp1.dot.net.in), general secretary of the Rajasthan Astrological Council & Research Institute, works from his shop near the City Palace on Chandani Chowk, Tripolia Gate. A 20-minute consultation costs Rs 300 and you will need to have your exact time and place of birth in order to get a computerised horoscope drawn up. A five-year prediction costs Rs 900 and a 30-year prediction costs a whopping Rs 3000. Consultations take place from 2 to 8 pm daily.

Organised Tours

The RTDC offers half/full-day tours of Jaipur and its environs for Rs 90/135. The full-day tours (9 am to 6 pm) do the major sites in and around Jaipur (including Amber Fort) and there's a lunch break at Nahargarh. The lunch break can be as late as 3 pm; have a big breakfast. Rushed half-day tours are confined to the city limits and run for five hours from 8 am, 11.30 am and 1.30 pm. Entrance fees to monuments are extra. Tours depart daily from the train station (according to demand), picking up people along the way at the RTDC Hotel Teej, Hotel Gangaur Palace and RTDC Tourist Hotel. Contact any of the RTDC offices (see Information earlier). Just because it's a government operation, don't imagine yourself immune from prolonged shopping stops at emporiums along the way.

An expensive but more free-wheeling alternative is offered by Rajasthan Travel Service (☎ 365408, fax 376935, ⓔ dilip@datainfosys.net) in Ganpati Plaza. For Rs 750/625, you get an air-con/nonair-con car with driver to take you around all the sights. The service can also arrange night sightseeing tours of the city for Rs 400 including dinner and musical entertainment.

Special Events

Teej, also known as the Festival of Swings (a reference to the flower-bedecked swings which are erected at this time), celebrates the onset of the monsoon and is held in honour of the marriage of Shiva and Parvati. It commences on 11 August 2002, 1 August 2003, and 19 August 2004, and runs for two days.

The **Elephant Festival** is the time to see colourfully adorned elephants parading through the streets, elephant polo and a bizarre tug-of-war between elephants and men. It is held on 28 March 2002, 17 March 2003, and 6 March 2004.

Finally, **Gangaur** in March/April is a statewide festival celebrated with particular excitement in Jaipur. It also celebrates the love between Lord Shiva and Parvati, and colourful parades are the order of the day. Gangaur commences on 15 April 2002, 4 April 2003, and 23 March 2004, and runs for two days.

Places to Stay

Getting to the hotel of your choice in Jaipur can be a headache. Autorickshaw drivers besiege most travellers who arrive by train (less so if you come by bus). A good rule of thumb is to pick the least pushy among them. If you don't want to go to a hotel of their choice, many will either refuse to take you or demand at least double the normal fare. If you do go to their hotel, you'll pay through the nose for accommodation because the manager will be paying them a commission of at least 30% of what you are charged for a bed (and the charge won't go down for subsequent nights). In the absence of much competition, some enterprising rickshaw drivers openly declare their financial interest in getting you to a certain place, which is, if nothing else, refreshingly honest. Ignore the 'ten rupees anywhere in Jaipur' crowd – 'anywhere' means the place of their choice or a sudden increase in price.

To get around this performance, go straight to the prepaid autorickshaw stands which have been set up at both the bus and train stations, where rates are set by the government. Alternatively, some hotels will pick you up if you ring ahead. Most hotels provide Internet access.

If you wish to stay with an Indian family, contact Mr SK Bhanot (☎ 200970), the president of Jaipur's Paying Guest House Scheme, for a list of participating families.

Places to Stay – Budget

Hotel Pearl Palace *(☎ 373700, fax 214415, ⓔ pearlpalaceindia@yahoo.com, Hari Kishan Semani Marg)*, off Sanjay Marg, has an enthusiastic following. Singles/doubles (all with private bathroom, some with balcony) cost Rs 250/350 and upwards. The rooftop area has views over the small Hathroi Fort next door, the food is excellent and cheap (thalis cost Rs 40), and the kitchen is one of the cleanest in India.

Jaipur Inn *(☎ 201121, fax 204796, ⓔ jaipurinn@hotmail.com, B-17 Shiv Marg, Bani Park)* is an old favourite with travellers. Rooms range from cramped and spartan with shared bathroom for Rs 100/200 to better rooms with private bathroom for Rs 350/400. Beds in the dorm cost Rs 80 or you can camp on the lawn (Rs 50) if you have your own tent. Mosquito nets can be hired for Rs 15 per day. Meals are available and the rooftop terrace commands sensational views.

Atithi Guest House *(☎ 378679, fax 379 496, ⓔ tanmay@jp1.dot.net.in, 1 Park House Scheme Rd)*, between MI and Station Rds, is a good budget option. Clean rooms with private bathroom range from Rs 400/450 to 700/750. Despite its central location, the rooms are quiet. Veg meals are available on the pleasant terrace. This is one place rickshaw drivers hate (always a good sign) because the owner won't pay commission.

Aangan Guest House *(☎ 373449, fax 204796, ⓔ aangan25@hotmail.com)*, next door, isn't as good but is a little cheaper. Cells with bathroom start at Rs 175/250.

The friendly ***Karni Niwas*** *(☎ 365433, fax 375034, ⓔ karniniwas@hotmail.com, C-5 Motilal Atal Marg)*, in a lane behind Hotel Neelam, is another good choice. Rooms (all with private bathroom) are attractive with terrace balconies and range from Rs 275/300 up to Rs 650/700 for a room with TV and air-con. The owners will gladly pick you up from the train or bus station. Home-cooked meals are available.

Hotel Arya Niwas *(☎ 372456, fax 361 871, ⓔ aryahotl@jp1.dot.net.in)*, just off Sansar Chandra Marg, is another very popular choice. This large hotel has clean rooms with bathroom starting at Rs 350/450, although some rooms are a little claustrophobic. There's a nice front lawn, a self-service veg restaurant and a laundry service. There are many reasons for staying at this well-run place, although the touts who are drawn to its perimeter are not among them.

Hotel Mangal *(☎ 375126, fax 361236, Sansar Chandra Marg)* has dark, overpriced rooms starting at Rs 325/375, although there's a bar, a kitchen for use by groups and a veg restaurant.

Evergreen Guest House *(☎ 362415, fax 204234, ⓔ evergreen34@hotmail.com)* is just off MI Rd in the area known as Chameliwala Market. It's a good place to meet other backpackers and has a pleasant sheltered garden area. Facilities include a small swimming pool and a restaurant. Large, sometimes clean rooms with private bathroom start at Rs 150/175; stay here for the setting rather than the quality of the rooms.

Ashiyana Guest House *(☎ 375414)* is nearby if you find the Evergreen too much of a scene. Grubby rooms go for Rs 80 (Rs 120 with private bathroom). No meals are available. Next door, ***Hotel Pink Sun*** has a decidedly relaxed approach to privacy and should be avoided by lone female (and possibly other) travellers.

Hotel Diggi Palace *(☎ 373091, fax 370 359, ⓔ diggihtl@datainfosys.net)*, just off Sawai Ram Singh Marg, about 1km south of Ajmeri Gate, is another hang-out popular with budget travellers. Formerly the residence of the *thakur* (similar to a lord or baron) of Diggi, it has a lovely lawn area and relaxing ambience. Reasonable rooms with shared bathroom cost Rs 375/425. Although most leave satisfied, some travellers have found the welcome less than warm.

Hotel Kailash *(☎ 565372)*, opposite the Jama Masjid, is one of the few places to stay within the old city. It's basic and, as you might expect, impossibly noisy. Small rooms cost Rs 160/190 with shared bathroom, Rs 225/260 with private bathroom.

Shagun Paying Guest House *(☎ 205981, Bani Park)* is basic but clean and friendly enough. Rooms cost Rs 250/300. The rustic restaurant in the garden does Chinese and Indian meals.

Sajjan Niwas Guest House *(☎/fax 206029, Bani Park)*, not far away, has spacious, airy rooms starting at Rs 250/300.

RTDC Hotel Swagatam *(☎ 200595)* is handy for the train station and has beds in a musty dorm for Rs 50; it also has luggage storage for Rs 5 per bag. ***RTDC Tourist Hotel*** *(☎ 360238)* must have been grand once but is now dingy and neglected; rooms cost Rs 150/250.

Retiring rooms *(☎ 131)* at the train station are handy if you're catching an early morning train. Rooms are Rs 100/250 with shared bathroom, or Rs 150/300 with private bathroom. Air-con rooms start at Rs 500.

Places to Stay – Mid-Range

The ***Madhuban*** *(☎ 200033, fax 202344, ⓔ madhuban@usa.net, D-237 Behari Marg, Bani Park)* is heartily recommended if you crave a homey ambience with no hassles whatsoever. Singles/doubles range from Rs 440/550 up to Rs 900/1000. The more expensive rooms have fine antique furnishings and even some of the cheaper rooms are elegantly decorated. The Madhuban offers free pick-up from the bus and train stations (ring ahead). There's an indoor restaurant, or you can eat in the pleasant garden where puppet shows are sometimes performed. For dessert, try the delicious Rajasthani *maalpuas* (small, sweet chapati).

Umaid Bhawan Guest House *(☎ 206426, fax 201276, ⓔ umaidbhawan@yahoo.com, D1-2A Bani Park)*, behind the Collectorate, is a family affair with a lovely personalised feel. Good rooms start at Rs 450/550; some of the rooms are enormous. Renovations were underway when we visited which should make this excellent place even better. There's a bar and a lovely swimming pool at the front.

Shahpura House *(☎ 202293, fax 201 494, ⓔ shahpurahouse@usa.net, D-257*

Devi Marg, Bani Park) is a beautifully restored house in a quiet residential street. Prices start at Rs 500 and range up to Rs 2200 for a luxury suite.

Alsisar Haveli *(☎ 368290, fax 364652, ⓔ alsisar@satyam.net.in, Sansar Chandra Marg)* is a gracious 19th-century mansion set in beautiful gardens. Although more pricey than other mid-range places, it's still a marvellous choice, with quaintly furnished rooms for Rs 1550/1850 plus tax; credit cards are not accepted. There's also a swimming pool.

Hotel Meghniwas *(☎ 202034, fax 201420 ⓔ email@meghinwas.com, C-9 Sawai Jai Singh Hwy, Bani Park)* is another excellent choice. Air-con rooms start at Rs 1000/1100. Room Nos 201 and 209 are like mini-apartments – they're ideal for long-term guests (Rs 1650/1750). There's a swimming pool, a lawn area with croquet and a good restaurant. Major credit cards are accepted.

Hotel Bissau Palace *(☎ 304391, fax 304628, ⓔ sanjai@jp1.dot.net.in)*, north of Chandpol, was built by the *rawal* (nobleman) of Bissau. The cheapest rooms cost Rs 990; prices increase according to size, although some rooms have more character than others. There are two restaurants (one on the rooftop with fine views) and a swimming pool.

Narain Niwas Palace Hotel *(☎ 561291, fax 561045, Narain Singh Rd)* was once grand but is a little faded around the edges these days. Rooms are Rs 1925/2395. There's a pool and a nice garden.

Nana-ki-Haveli *(☎ 665502, fax 605481, Fateh Tiba)*, off Moti Dungri Marg, is a friendly place, although the transport yards nearby can make it noisy. Attractive rooms start at Rs 1095/1195.

LMB Hotel *(☎ 565844, fax 562176, ⓔ info@lmbsweets.com, Johari Bazaar)* is right in the heart of the old city, above the well-known restaurant of the same name. Ordinary rooms are Rs 1075/1375.

Nahargarh is a romantic choice, although there's only one double room which costs Rs 500. It's located in one of the fort's parapets, behind the restaurant, and the views over Jaipur from the bed are unparalleled. Reservations should be made at the Tourist Reception Centre (☎ 202152) or you can call the fort direct (☎ 320538).

Places to Stay – Top End

Raj Vilas *(☎ 640101, fax 640202, ⓔ reservations@rajvilas.com, Goner Rd)*, about 8km from the city centre, is the most upmarket hotel in Jaipur, if not Rajasthan. Run by the Oberoi Group, this sophisticated boutique hotel has 71 rooms yet still retains a personal touch. Set in over 12 hectares complete with orchards and fountains, all rooms are immaculate and tastefully decorated. Deluxe singles/doubles are US$260/280, luxury tents are US$300 and villas (each with their own pool) range from US$600 to $1000. Ayurvedic treatments are available in the health centre (Rs 1500 for a full-body massage) and amenities range from a white marble jacuzzi to a fragrant Mughal herb garden.

Rambagh Palace *(☎ 381919, fax 381098, ⓔ rambagh@jp1.dot.net.in, Bhawani Singh Marg)*, once the maharaja of Jaipur's residence, is now a plush and palatial hotel operated by the Taj Group. Standard rooms are US$185/205. The more expensive rooms are decidedly sumptuous – US$775 will get you the Maharaja Suite. If you can't afford to stay, at least treat yourself to an evening drink at the Polo Bar (see Entertainment).

Samode Haveli *(☎ 632407, fax 631397, Gangapol)* is one of the more romantic top-end places to stay. This 200-year-old building was once the town house of the rawal of Samode, who was also prime minister of Jaipur. Elegant rooms cost Rs 1950/2750 (less from May to September). The only problem with staying in the breathtaking deluxe suite (Rs 3950), which is totally covered with original mirrorwork, is that you may no longer feel the need to visit any of the city's palaces. There's also an impressive dining room.

Jai Mahal Palace Hotel *(☎ 223636, fax 220707)* is on the corner of Jacob and Ajmer Rds. Most of the pleasant rooms (US$135/155 plus 20% tax) overlook the property's beautifully manicured Moghul gardens. The building itself is over 250 years old.

Raj Mahal Palace Hotel *(☎ 383260, fax 381887, ⓔ rmp.jaipur@tajhotels.com, Civil Lines)* has spacious, hoary old singles/doubles/triples for US$65/85/100.

Trident *(☎ 670101, fax 670303)* is modern but the rooms (Rs 4000/4500) have some nice touches. All have an electronic safe and individual balconies with great views; ask for one overlooking the Jal Mahal, or Water Palace. There's also a swimming pool.

Holiday Inn *(☎ 672000, fax 672335, ⓔ hjaiin@jp1.dot.net.in)*, north of the old city, lacks the charm of Trident. Rooms cost Rs 2000/3400.

Mansingh Hotel *(☎ 378771, fax 377582, ⓔ mansingh.jaipur@mailcity.com)*, off Sansar Chandra Marg in the centre of town, has rooms starting at Rs 1995/3000 plus tax. Amenities include a pool, a health club and two restaurants and its modern rooms have a little more character than some others in the price range.

Rajputana Palace Sheraton *(☎ 360011, fax 367848)* is between Station and Palace Rds. Run by Welcomgroup, this modern hotel is built around a swimming pool. Standard singles/doubles cost US$130/140, though if you have a spare US$700 you might want to consider the Presidential Suite. There's a coffee shop, a bar, two restaurants, a disco and a health club.

Hotel Jaipur Ashok *(☎ 204491, fax 202099, Bani Park)* is modern, somewhat luxurious and completely devoid of character (Rs 1600/2500).

Places to Eat

Most of the best restaurants are along MI Rd.

Chanakya Restaurant *(☎ 376161)*, on the north side of MI Rd, is highly recommended. It's not as expensive as the decor and livery would suggest and the attentive staff are happy to explain the various pure-veg menu items; continental dishes range from Rs 60 to 150 and most tandoori dishes are under Rs 70. It's worth booking ahead.

Mehfil Restaurant *(☎/fax 367272)*, near Ajmeri Gate, gets good reviews from long-term residents of Jaipur. There's traditional live music every night and the menu includes Indian, Chinese and Italian food. Servings are large and the quality good – expect to pay Rs 150 to 250 for a meal.

Niro's *(☎ 374493)* was established in 1949 and was a long-standing favourite with Indians and Westerners alike. It still fills up fast (book ahead on weekends), although many will tell you that it's trading on past glory. The expensive menu includes veg and nonveg Indian, Chinese and continental food. The nearby ***Surya Mahal*** *(☎ 369840)* is better value and specialises in excellent South Indian food with nothing over Rs 70.

Golden Dragon Restaurant, in a lane off MI Rd near Niro's, does reasonable Chinese food from around Rs 70.

Natraj Restaurant *(☎ 375804)*, near Niro's, is popular for its Indian sweets and spicy nibbles. The North Indian veg food (ranging from Rs 30 to 90) is tasty; the vegetable bomb curry (Rs 70) is a blast. ***Lassiwala***, opposite Niro's, is the place to go for a thick, creamy lassi which will set you back Rs 10/20 for a small/jumbo cup.

Handi Restaurant *(☎ 364839)*, opposite the main post office, is tucked away at the back of the Maya Mansions building. The furnishings are nothing flash, but it offers scrumptious barbecue dishes and specialises in tandoori and Mughlai cuisine at reasonable prices.

Copper Chimney *(☎ 372275)*, nearby, offers veg and nonveg Indian, continental and Chinese food in a pleasant setting. A main veg course ranges from Rs 50 to 100; nonveg costs from Rs 85 to 200. Try the Rajasthani dish *lal maas* (mutton in a thick spicy gravy) for Rs 85. In spite of the restaurant's name, smoking is not permitted.

Swaad *(☎ 360749, Ganpati Plaza, MI Rd)* is recommended for a minor splurge. It has varied Indian, continental and Chinese cuisine; travellers' favourites include *subz malaai kofta-palak* (cottage cheese and herbs in spinach gravy) for Rs 60 and the sizzlers (Rs 95 to 170). Desserts start at Rs 45. In the same complex is the swanky, but less popular, ***Celebrations***, which serves pure-veg food.

Rainbow Restaurant *(MI Rd)*, opposite Ganpati Plaza, offers OK Indian, continental and Chinese for around Rs 40, although nonveg dishes cost considerably more.

Chic Chocolate *(☎ 204138, MI Rd)*, around the corner from the Atithi Guest House, is a clean pastry shop which does excellent cheese toast (Rs 15) and delicious fruit trifles (Rs 16). It also bakes its own bread. ***Bake Hut*** *(☎ 369840)*, close to Niro's, offers a selection of sweet treats including chocolate doughnuts (Rs 9) and little lemon tarts (Rs 11), and can bake birthday cakes to order.

Four Seasons *(D-43A Subhash Marg, C-Scheme)* is miles from anywhere, but the food is great. This multicuisine veg restaurant has moderately priced fare served in pleasant surroundings. A speciality is the *rava dosa* (Rs 35), a ground rice and semolina pancake with coconut, chilli, carrot and onion.

LMB *(Laxmi Mishthan Bhandar, Johari Bazaar)* has quaint 1970s-style decor and waiters in dinner suits and sandals. It has been going strong since 1954, but the food and service are not as good as they once were. Main dishes range from Rs 35 to 80. Out the front, a counter serves snacks and colourful Indian sweets.

Indian Coffee House *(MI Rd)* is rather seedy inside, but good if you are craving a decent cup of coffee.

Jaipur Inn (see Places to Stay – Budget) boasts one of the city's only rooftop restaurants, with superlative views over Jaipur. The Indian veg buffet dinner costs Rs 100 (nonguests should book in advance).

Entertainment

Entertainment in Jaipur is limited, although many hotels put on some sort of evening music, dance or puppet show.

Raj Mandir Cinema *(☎ 379372)*, just off MI Rd, is *the* place to go if you're planning to take in a Hindi film while you're in India. This opulent cinema is a Jaipur tourist attraction in its own right and is usually full, despite its immense size. Bookings can be made one day in advance (from 1 to 2 pm and 4 to 5 pm) at windows 7 and 8 and this is your best chance of securing a seat, but forget it in the early days of a new release. Alternatively, sharpen your elbows and join the queue when the ticket office opens 45 minutes before the curtain goes up. Tickets range from Rs 20 to 60; avoid the cheaper tickets, which are very close to the screen. Sessions are at noon, 3, 6.15 and 9.30 pm.

Rambagh Golf Club *(☎ 384482)*, near the Rambagh Palace, charges US$25 per round, plus US$5 for equipment and Rs 100 for a caddie; left-handers are not catered for. If it's a quiet game of pool you're after, head to the ***Pool Club and Restaurant***, around the corner from the Raj Mandir (Rs 50 an hour).

Polo Bar, at the Rambagh Palace, is Jaipur's most atmospheric watering hole; a large bottle of beer is Rs 165, cocktails are around Rs 250.

Shopping

Jaipur is *the* place to shop until you drop! It has a plethora of handicrafts ranging from grimacing papier-mache puppets to exquisitely carved furniture. You'll have to bargain hard, though – this city is accustomed to tourists with lots of money and little time to spend it. Shops around the tourist traps, such as the City Palace and Hawa Mahal, tend to be more expensive.

Jaipur is especially well known for precious stones, which seem cheaper here than elsewhere in India, and is even better known for semiprecious gems. The best place to start looking is Johari Bazaar, the jewellers' market. There are many shops which offer bargain prices, but you do need to know your gems and be aware that there are plenty of scams operating designed to part travellers from their money, including convincing some people to part with thousands of dollars for (invariably worthless) gems on the promise of a lucrative sale back home. See the boxed text 'Buyer Beware!' in the Facts for the Visitor chapter.

Marble statues, costume jewellery and textile prints are other Jaipur specialities.

The government-run Rajasthali emporium, opposite the main post office, sells an interesting range of handicrafts from around the state and is a good place to get an idea of prices before launching into the bazaar.

Rajasthan Handloom House is upstairs (although it was due to move to opposite Ganpati Plaza when we visited). Another highly recommended place for textiles is the Anokhi showroom, at 2 Tilak Marg, near the Secretariat. It has high-quality products such as block-printed fabrics, tablecloths, bed covers and cosmetic bags. Soma, out at 5 Jacob Rd in Civil Lines, sells similar fare.

Kripal Kumbh, B-18A Shiv Marg in Bani Park, is a great place to see the famous blue pottery. For good-quality jootis, go to Charmica (opposite Natraj restaurant) on MI Rd; a pair costs from Rs 150 to 350.

Many rickshaw-wallahs are right into the commission business and it's almost guaranteed that they'll be getting a hefty cut from any shop they take you to.

Getting There & Away

Air Indian Airlines flies from Jaipur to Delhi (US$55, daily), Mumbai (Bombay; US$155, daily), Udaipur (US$80, daily), Jaisalmer (US$125, three times a week), Jodhpur (US$80, daily) and Kolkata (Calcutta; US$220, daily except Sunday) via Ahmedabad (US$105, three times a week). Jet Airways shadows many of these routes for a similar price.

You can book all domestic flights at a travel agent, such as Satyam Travels & Tours (☎ 378794, fax 375426), on the ground floor of the Jaipur Towers building, Rajasthan Travel Service (☎ 365408, fax 376935) in Ganpati Plaza, and Crown Tours (☎ 363310, fax 371751, ⓔ crown@jp1.dot.net.in) opposite the Rajputana Sheraton; Crown Tours is open Sunday. The Indian Airlines office (☎ 514500) is a little out of town on Tonk Rd, the southern extension of Sawai Ram Singh Marg.

Bus Rajasthan State Transport Corporation (RSTC) buses all leave from the main bus station on Station Rd, picking up passengers at Narain Singh Circle. There is a left-luggage office at the main terminal (Rs 5 per small bag for 24 hours, Rs 10 for larger items), as well as a prepaid autorickshaw stand. The deluxe (essentially nonstop) buses all leave from Platform 3, which is tucked away in the right-hand corner of the bus station. These buses should be booked in advance from the reservation office (☎ 205790) on Platform 3. For other bus inquiries call ☎ 206143.

There are deluxe buses to many destinations: Delhi (Rs 206, 5½ hours); Jodhpur (Rs 161/98 for a day/night bus, seven hours); Kota (Rs 120, five hours); Ajmer (Rs 66, 2½ hours); Udaipur (Rs 201, 10 hours); Bikaner (Rs 168/99, eight hours); Bharatpur (Rs 88, 4½ hours); Bundi (Rs 102, five hours); Mt Abu (Rs 247, 13 hours); Jaisalmer (Rs 288/178, 15 hours); Chittorgarh (Rs 125, seven hours); and Jhunjhunu (Rs 88).

Train The reasonably efficient computerised railway reservation office (☎ 135) is in the building to your right as you exit the main train station. It's open 8 am to 2 pm and 2.15 to 8 pm Monday to Saturday; 8 am to 2 pm

Major Trains from Jaipur

destination	train No & name	departures	distance (km)	duration (hrs)	fare (Rs)
Abu Road	9106 *Ahmedabad Mail*	4.40 am	441	8½	99/154/713 *
Agra	2308 *Howrah Jodhpur Exp*	11.15 pm	310	7¼	77/120/564 *
Bikaner	4737 *Bikaner Exp*	9 pm	517	10	113/176/831 *
Delhi	2015 *Shatabdi Exp*	5.55 pm	308	4¼	495/985 †
Delhi	2414 *Delhi-Jaipur Exp*	4.20 pm	308	5½	77/120/564 *
Jodhpur	2465 *Intercity Exp*	5.30 pm	320	5¼	79/237 ♦
Udaipur	9615 *Chetak Exp*	10.10 pm	431	12¼	96/149/692 *

* general/sleeper/2-tier air-con † chair/executive chair class ♦ general/chair class

RAJASTHAN

Sunday. Join the queue for 'Freedom Fighters and Foreign Tourists' (counter 769). For general railway inquiries call ☎ 131.

Car RTDC charges Rs 4.80 per kilometre with a minimum of 250km; the overnight charge starts at an extra Rs 100. Prices do not include fuel. Private taxis charge a negotiable Rs 4 per kilometre.

Getting Around

To/From the Airport There is currently no scheduled bus service between the airport and the city. An autorickshaw/taxi will cost at least Rs 150/200 for the 15km journey into the city centre.

Autorickshaw There are prepaid autorickshaw stands at the bus and train stations. Rates are fixed by the government, so there's no need to haggle. If you want to hire an autorickshaw for local sightseeing it should cost about Rs 150/300 for a half/full day (including a visit to Amber but not Nahargarh). Prices are often inflated for tourists, so be prepared to bargain. Cycle-rickshaws (known by their riders as 'Indian helicopters') are a cheaper option.

Bicycle Bicycles can be hired from some hotels and most bike shops, including the one to the right as you exit the main train station, opposite the reservation office (Rs 3/20 per hour/day).

AROUND JAIPUR

Amber

About 11km north of Jaipur, on the Delhi-Jaipur road, is Amber, the ancient capital of Jaipur state. Construction of the fort-palace was begun in 1592 by Maharaja Man Singh, the Rajput commander of Akbar's army. It was later extended and completed by the Jai Singhs before the move to Jaipur on the plains below. The fort is a superb example of Rajput architecture, stunningly situated on a hillside overlooking a lake.

You can climb up to the fort from the road in about 10 minutes; cold drinks are available within the palace if the climb is a hot one. A seat in a jeep up to the fort costs Rs 120 return. Riding up on elephants is popular at Rs 400 per elephant return (each can carry up to four people), although the elephant owners would prefer you to walk back down as the steep path is more challenging for the animals going down.

An imposing stairway leads to the **Diwan-i-Am**, or Hall of Public Audience, with rows of columns and latticed galleries above. Steps to the right lead to the small **Kali Temple**.

The maharaja's apartments are on the higher terrace – you enter through a gateway decorated with mosaics and sculptures. The **Jai Mandir**, or Hall of Victory, is noted for its inlaid panels and glittering mirror ceiling. Regrettably, much of this was allowed to deteriorate during the 1970s and 1980s but restoration proceeds. Opposite the Jai Mandir is the **Sukh Niwas**, or Hall of Pleasure, with an ivory-inlaid sandalwood door, and a channel which once carried cooling water running right through the room. From the Jai Mandir you can take in the fine views from the palace ramparts over the lake below.

Amber Palace is open 9 am to 4.30 pm daily and entry costs Rs 50. A camera costs Rs 25, a video camera Rs 100. Guides can be hired at the tourist office (at the fort entrance) for Rs 75/230/380 (1½ hours/half day/full day; maximum four people).

There are frequent buses to Amber from near the Hawa Mahal (Rs 5, 25 minutes).

Jaigarh

The imposing Jaigarh, built in 1726 by Jai Singh, was opened to the public in mid-1983. The fort was never captured and so has survived virtually intact through the centuries. It's within walking distance of Amber and offers a great view over the plains from the Diwa Burj watchtower. The fort, with its water reservoirs, residential areas, puppet theatre and the cannon, Jaya Vana, is open 9 am to 5 pm daily. Entry is Rs 15, plus Rs 50 per car, Rs 25 for a camera and Rs 100 for a video camera.

Galta

The Temple of the Sun God, also known as the Monkey Temple, is 100m above Jaipur to the east, a 2.5km climb from Surajpol. A deep, temple-studded gorge stands behind the temple and there are good views over the surrounding plains.

The Dhammathali Vipassana Meditation Centre (☎ 641520) at Galta runs meditation courses for a donation.

Sisodia Rani Palace & Gardens

Six kilometres from the city on Agra Rd (leave Jaipur by the Ghat Gate), and surrounded by terraced gardens, this palace was built for Maharaja Jai Singh's second wife, the Sisodia princess. The outer walls are decorated with murals depicting hunting scenes and the Krishna legend.

The gardens are open 8 am to 6 pm daily and entry is Rs 1 (no video cameras allowed).

Vidyadharji-ka-Bagh

Vidyadharji-ka-Bagh, a garden built in honour of Jai Singh's chief architect and town planner, Vidyadhar, is near Sisodia Rani Palace on Agra Rd.

The gardens are open 8 am to 6 pm daily and entry is Rs 1 (no video cameras allowed).

Sanganer

This small town, 16km south of Jaipur, is entered through the ruins of two *tripolias*, or triple gateways. In addition to its ruined palace, Sanganer has a group of Jain temples with fine carvings to which entry is restricted. The town is noted for handmade paper and block printing (most shops can be found on, or just off, Stadium Rd). Salim's Paper on Gramodyog Rd is the largest handmade-paper factory in India. Here you can see the paper production process and buy a beautiful range of paper products. For block-printed fabrics, there are a number of shops, including Sakshi, which also has excellent blue pottery (downstairs).

A bus from Jaipur to Sanganer takes 30 minutes and costs Rs 6.

Samode

This small village, nestled among rugged hills about 50km north of Jaipur, is home to the beautiful **Samode Palace** where you can stay. The highlight of the building is the exquisite Diwan-i-Khas, which is covered with original paintings and mirrorwork.

Samode Palace *(☎ 01423-4114, fax 4123, reservations ☎ 0141-632370, fax 631397)* has pleasant doubles costing from Rs 2750 to 3500. Breakfast/lunch/dinner is Rs 250/375/450. Entry to the palace for nonguests is Rs 100 (deducted if you have a set meal). Luxurious tent accommodation is available, from October to April, 3km away at ***Samode Bagh*** (Rs 2400/1950) where there's a lovely garden and pool.

There are four daily direct buses that go from Jaipur's main bus station to Samode (Rs 13.50, 1½ hours).

Ramgarh

This green oasis, about 35km from Jaipur, has a picturesque lake (boating available), an ancient Durga temple, and a polo ground (call Jaipur ☎ 0141-374791 to find out when matches are being played).

Ramgarh Lodge *(☎ 01426-2217, fax 0141-381098)*, a former royal hunting lodge overlooking Ramgarh Lake, is the best place to stay (Rs 1600/2300 a single/double). Alternatively, there's the ***Ramgarh Resort and Polo Complex*** *(☎ 01426-2214, fax 0141-374790)* which has luxurious single/double tents for Rs 1199/2000.

Buses travel daily between Jaipur and Ramgarh (Rs 9, one hour).

Abhaneri

About 95km from Jaipur on the Agra road, this little village has one of Rajasthan's most awesome *baoris* (step-wells). Flanking the baori is a small, crumbling palace, now inhabited by pigeons and bats.

From Jaipur, catch a bus to Sikandra, from where you can hire a jeep for the 10km trip to Abhaneri (Rs 200 return, including a 30-minute stop). Alternatively, from Jaipur get a bus to Gular, from where it's a 5km walk to Abhaneri.

Balaji

The extraordinary Hindu exorcism temple of Balaji is 1.5km off the Jaipur-Agra road, 102km east of Jaipur. The exorcisms are sometimes very violent and many people being exorcised don't hesitate to discuss their experiences. Most exorcisms take place on Tuesday and Saturday (go upstairs). Remove your shoes before entering the temple. Photography is prohibited.

From Jaipur there are numerous local buses to Balaji (Rs 26, 2½ hours).

BHARATPUR

☎ 05644 • pop 1.7 million

Bharatpur is renowned for its World Heritage-listed bird sanctuary, the Keoladeo Ghana National Park, a tranquil haven nestled between Delhi, Agra and Jaipur. This is one bird sanctuary that even nonornithologists should visit.

In the 17th and 18th centuries, the town was an important Jat stronghold. Before the arrival of the Rajputs, the Jats lived in this area and were able to retain a high degree of autonomy, both because of their prowess in battle and because of their chiefs' marriage alliances with Rajput nobility. They successfully opposed the Mughals on more than one occasion and their fort at Bharatpur, constructed in the 18th century, withstood an attack by the British in 1805 and a long siege in 1825. This siege eventually led to the signing of the first treaty of friendship between the Indian states of north-west India and the East India Company.

The town itself, surrounded by a decaying 11km wall, is of little interest. Bring mosquito repellent with you, as the mosquitoes can be bothersome.

Orientation & Information

The Keoladeo Ghana National Park lies 3km to the south of the city centre, and is easily accessed by cycle-rickshaw.

The helpful Tourist Reception Centre (☎ 22542) is opposite the RTDC Hotel Saras, about 700m from the park entrance. It's open from 10 am to 5 pm Monday to Saturday (closed the second Saturday of every month). It sells a moderately useful

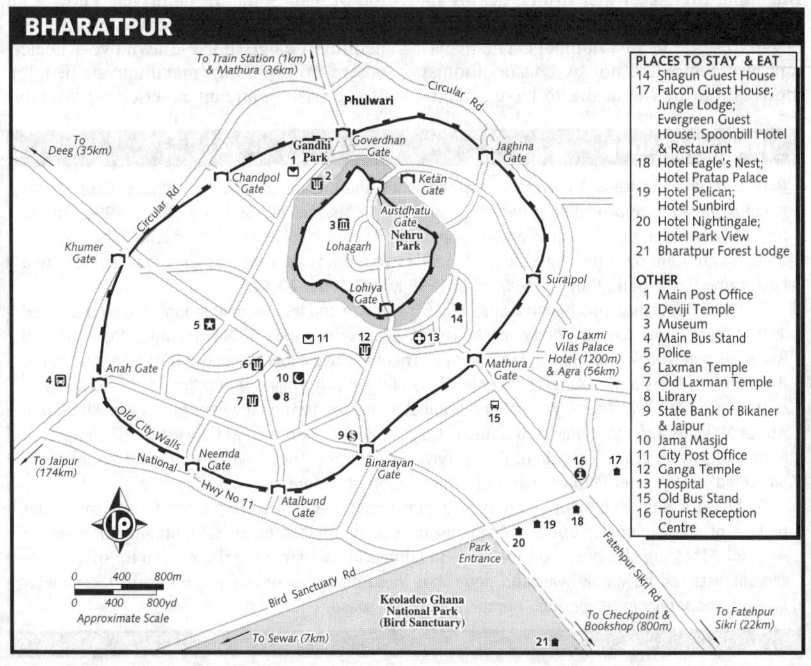

map of Bharatpur (Rs 2) and the handy *Birds of Bharatpur – A Checklist* (Rs 50). A good map of the park is available at the park entrance (included in the ticket price). Books on birdlife are also available at a bookshop inside the park, about 1.5km from the main gate. You can change money at the State Bank of Bikaner & Jaipur, near the Binarayan Gate.

Keoladeo Ghana National Park

According to recent reports, around 354 species of birds have been identified at the beautiful Keoladeo sanctuary, a remarkable figure given that the park only covers 29 sq km. Apart from the Siberian crane, expect to see the Saras crane (the largest bird in the park), herons, egrets, geese, owls, cormorants, kingfishers and even pythons.

The sanctuary was formerly a vast semiarid region, filling with water during the monsoon season only to rapidly dry up afterwards. To prevent this, the maharaja of Bharatpur diverted water from a nearby irrigation canal and, within a few years, birds began to settle in vast numbers. The maharaja was compelled not by conservationist motives, but by the desire to have a ready supply of waterfowl, affording fine shooting (and dining) possibilities. Keoladeo continued to supply the maharajas' tables until as late as 1965. An inscription on a pillar near the small temple in the park is testimony to this slaughter. It reveals that on one day alone, over 5000 ducks were shot.

The best time to visit the sanctuary is from October to late February, when many migratory birds can be seen. The park is open 6 am to 6 pm daily. Entry is Rs 25/200 for Indians/foreigners, which entitles you to only one entrance per day; if you want to spend the day inside the park, get your hotel to provide a packed lunch. There is no still-camera charge, but there's a typically steep Rs 200 video charge.

Only cycle-rickshaws authorised by the government (recognisable by the yellow plate bolted onto the front) are allowed inside the park. Although you don't pay entry fees for the drivers, you'll be up for Rs 30 per hour and the driver will expect a tip on top of that. Some of the drivers know a lot about the birds you'll see and can be very helpful. A *tonga* (horse-drawn two-wheeler) costs Rs 60 per hour (maximum six people). If you wish to hire an experienced ornithol-

Siberian Cranes

Park authorities at Keoladeo were concerned when the endangered Siberian crane *(Grus leucogeranus)* failed to appear during two successive winter seasons in 1994 and '95. In 1996, on the first day of winter, ornithologists around the world heaved a collective sigh of relief when four of these magnificent birds flew into the park, nearly two months after their usual arrival. In 1998, two birds came to the park; they came again in 1999 and October 2000.

The total population of Siberian cranes wintering in Iran and India is only around 15; an estimated 100 of these birds have perished over the last 12 years during their 5000km journey from the Orb River basin in Siberia over inhospitable terrain. There are two other populations of Siberian cranes; the largest winters at the Yangtze River in China and a much smaller group flies to the south coast of Iran's Caspian Sea. The tiny remaining population makes its annual winter journey to Bharatpur. About 30 years ago more than 200 sibes, as they are known, wintered at Keoladeo. The sharp drop in numbers raises grave fears about their survival as a species. They have been termed 'critically endangered' by the International Union of Conservation of Nature.

Tragically, it is not the natural rigours of the long migration which are blamed for the critical depletion of sibe numbers, but the Afghanistan war, with sibes being slaughtered for meat by Afghanis. They are also believed to fall prey to hunters in Pakistan, who shoot them for sport. Conservationists can now only wait and hope that these brave journeyers will return to their winter grounds, hopefully in replenished numbers, in future seasons.

ogist guide, this will cost around Rs 35 (maximum five people) or Rs 75 (more than five people) per hour. Guides can be hired at the park entrance and many hotels are run by qualified guides who charge the same.

An excellent way to see the park is to hire a bicycle (around Rs 20 per day), either at the park entrance or from your hotel. This allows you to easily avoid the bottlenecks which occur at the nesting sites of the larger birds and increases your chances of seeing the kingfishers which are easily frightened away. Try and visit the sanctuary at dawn (the best time to see the birds). The southern reaches of the park are virtually devoid of *humanus touristicus* but in dry years there is little water and even fewer birds. The south-eastern corner of the park is supposedly home to a tiger, and therefore off limits, although its presence is more a matter of legend than hard evidence.

At the main entrance to the park is a small display of photos, stuffed birds, nests and aquatic species found in the park's lakes (free entry). There's a small snack bar about halfway through the park, next to the Keoladeo Temple.

Lohagarh

Lohagarh, or Iron Fort, was built in the early 18th century and took its name from its supposedly impregnable defences. Maharaja Suraj Mahl, the fort's constructor and the founder of Bharatpur, built two towers within the ramparts, the Jawahar Burj and Fateh Burj, to commemorate his victories over the Mughals and the British.

The fort occupies the small artificial island in the centre of Bharatpur, and the three palaces within its precincts are in an advanced state of decay. Entry costs Rs 50. One of the palaces houses a museum exhibiting sculptures, paintings, weapons and dusty animal trophies. The museum is open 10 am to 4.30 pm daily except Friday. Entry is an additional Rs 3 (free on Monday), and Rs 10/20 for a camera/video.

Places to Stay & Eat

The commission system has reared its ugly head in Bharatpur – don't give in to the pressure exerted by touts at the train station or bus stand.

Park Precincts The following places are all within easy walking distance of the main entrance to the bird sanctuary, making them the most popular with travellers.

Spoonbill Hotel & Restaurant *(☎ 23571, fax 29359, e hotelspoonbill@rediffmail.com)*, almost opposite the tourist office, is a popular choice with travellers. It has good singles/doubles with private bathroom for Rs 150/200 and dorm beds for Rs 50. There's also one larger room which is good value at Rs 400/500. This place has a campfire in winter and a resident cow used to produce cheese, yogurt and butter.

Falcon Guest House *(☎ 23815)*, in the same area, is a well-kept and homey place to stay. Good-sized rooms go for Rs 150/200 with bathroom; Rs 400/500 gets you a bigger room with a softer mattress and private balcony. There's a little garden restaurant.

Evergreen Guest House *(☎ 25917)* is a little more basic but is a good cheapie with friendly staff and a cosy restaurant serving delicious home-cooked meals. Rooms cost Rs 100 to 150. The owner is an excellent guide for the park.

Jungle Lodge *(☎ 25622)*, also nearby, has small but comfortable rooms with private bathroom starting at Rs 125/200 and better rooms for Rs 250/300. The owner is a naturalist and there's a lending library and a nice garden.

Hotel Nightingale *(☎ 27022, fax 24351)*, in a eucalyptus grove close to the park entrance, offers tents (available mid-October to mid-February) starting at Rs 80 per person. It also has four simple but clean rooms for Rs 150/200. The restaurant specialises in tandoori meals (half a chicken is Rs 75).

Hotel Park View *(☎ 20802, fax 27800, e bharatpur007@yahoo.com)*, next door, is quite good value, with rooms ranging from a clean dungeon with shared bathroom for Rs 40/60, up to between Rs 80 and 150 for doubles with private bathroom. The restaurant is pleasant; the Rajasthani *aloo deera* (potatoes lightly seasoned with cumin) costs Rs 25 and a chicken curry is Rs 45.

Hotel Pelican *(☎ 24221)*, nearby, has reasonable doubles with private bathroom from Rs 150, up to Rs 400 for an upstairs rooms with a balcony – it's a lot extra to pay for a balcony but it's worth bargaining.

Hotel Pratap Palace *(☎/fax 25093)*, on Bird Sanctuary Rd, has rooms with bathroom for Rs 200/300, and deluxe rooms with satellite TV for Rs 600/700. The restaurant has an a la carte menu but the buffet lunches and dinners are good value at Rs 135.

Hotel Sunbird *(☎ 25701, fax 25265, ⓔ sunbird@jp1.dot.net.in)* is a well-run place where the rooms fill up fast. Decent rooms with private bathroom start at Rs 300/500 including breakfast. Newer rooms out the back (quiet if a little small) cost Rs 550/750. The restaurant has a good menu.

Hotel Eagle's Nest *(☎ 25144, fax 22310)* has large, pleasant rooms with satellite TV for Rs 500/650, or Rs 650/800 with air-con.

Bharatpur Forest Lodge *(☎ 22760, fax 22864)*, run by the Indian Tourism Development Corporation (ITDC), is inside the park, 1km beyond the entrance gate. It's OK but looking a little faded these days. Standard rooms cost Rs 1995/3000. The restaurant is open to nonguests; the buffet lunch or dinner is Rs 250, or you can opt for a light snack.

Bharatpur It's hard to think of a good reason to stay in the town. If you can think of one, ***Shagun Guest House*** *(☎ 29202)*, down a laneway just inside Mathura Gate, is very basic but suitably cheap. Beds start at Rs 50/70 in a primitive grass hut. The owner is a friendly guy and has a wealth of knowledge on the bird park.

Laxmi Vilas Palace Hotel *(☎ 23523, fax 25259)*, Kakaji-ki-Kothi, on the old Agra road, is an upmarket hotel with singles/doubles starting at Rs 1195/1250.

Getting There & Away

Bus There are buses to Agra (Rs 25, 1½ hours), Fatehpur Sikri (Rs 12, one hour), Jaipur (Rs 78, 4½ hours) and Deeg (Rs 15, one hour).

Train The *Janata Express* (9023/4) leaves New Delhi station at 2 pm and arrives in Bharatpur at 6.25 pm (Rs 52/81, general/sleeper class, 175km). It leaves Bharatpur at 8 am, arriving in the capital at 1.10 pm. There are seven trains daily to Sawai Madhopur (Rs 52/81, 182km). These include the *Golden Temple Mail* (2903), which leaves Bharatpur at 1 pm, arriving at 3.35 pm.

Getting Around

Bharatpur has autorickshaws, tongas and cycle-rickshaws. An autorickshaw from the bus stand to the tourist office and most of the hotels should cost around Rs 15.

DEEG

☎ 05641 • pop 41,300

Very few travellers ever make it to Deeg, about 36km north of Bharatpur. This is a pity because this small town with its massive fortifications, stunning palace and busy market is actually more interesting than Bharatpur itself (apart from the bird sanctuary). It's an easy day trip from Bharatpur, Agra or Mathura.

Built by Suraj Mahl in the mid-18th century, Deeg was the second capital of Bharatpur state and the site of a famous battle in which the maharaja's forces successfully withstood a combined Mughal and Maratha army of some 80,000 men. Eight years later, the maharaja even had the temerity to attack the Red Fort in Delhi! The booty he carried off included an entire marble building, which can still be seen.

Deeg's massive walls (up to 28m high) and 12 bastions, some with their cannons still in place, are also worth exploring.

Suraj Mahl's Palace

Suraj Mahl's Palace (Gopal Bhavan) has to be one of India's most beautiful and delicately proportioned buildings. In an excellent state of repair, it was used by the maharajas until the early 1970s and most of the rooms still contain their original furnishings.

Built in a combination of Rajput and Mughal architectural styles, the 18th-century palace fronts on to a tank, the Gopal Sagar, and is flanked by two exquisite pavilions. The tank and palace are surrounded by well-maintained gardens which also contain the Keshav Bhavan, or Summer Pavilion, with its hundreds of fountains. Many of the fountains are still functional but they're usually turned on only for local festivals.

The palace is open 8 am to 5 pm daily and entry is Rs 200.

Places to Stay & Eat

RTDC Motel Deeg *(☎ 21000)*, not far from the bus stand, has just three rooms with private bathroom for Rs 300/400 a single/double. If you have a tent, you can pitch it in the compound for Rs 40 per person (includes use of bathroom). Meals are available; a veg thali is Rs 55.

Getting There & Away

There are frequent buses between Deeg and Alwar; the trip by local/express bus costs Rs 23/30 and takes three/2½ hours. Buses for Bharatpur leave every 30 minutes and the one-hour journey costs Rs 12/15. There is one daily direct bus to Agra (Rs 45).

ALWAR

☎ 0144 • pop 258,600

Alwar was once an important Rajput state. It emerged in the 18th century under Pratap Singh, who pushed back the rulers of Jaipur to the south and the Jats of Bharatpur to the east, and who successfully resisted the Marathas. It was one of the first Rajput states to ally itself with the fledgling British empire, although British interference in Alwar's internal affairs ensured that this partnership was not always amicable.

The Tourist Reception Centre (☎ 21868) is not far from the train station and is open 10 am to 1.30 pm and 2 to 5 pm Monday to Saturday. You can change money at the State Bank of Bikaner & Jaipur, near the bus stand.

Bala Quila

This imposing fort, with its 5km of ramparts, stands 300m above the city. Predating the time of Pratap Singh, it's one of the few forts in Rajasthan built before the rise of the Mughals. Unfortunately, the fort now houses a radio transmitter station and can only be visited with special permission from the superintendent of police (☎ 337453).

Palace Complex

Below the fort sprawls the huge city palace complex, its massive gates and tank lined by a beautifully symmetrical chain of ghats (steps) and pavilions. Today, most of the complex is occupied by government offices, but there's an interesting **government museum** housed in the former city palace (open 10 am to 4.30 pm daily except Friday; entry Rs 3, free on Monday). Photography is prohibited. The museum's exhibits include stunning weapons, royal ivory slippers and old musical instruments.

Places to Stay & Eat

Ankur *(☎ 333025)*, ***New Alankar*** *(☎ 20027)*, ***Atlantic*** *(☎ 21581)*, ***Akash Deep*** *(☎ 22912)* and the ***Ashoka*** *(☎ 21780)* form a cluster of cheap hotels which all face each other around a central courtyard, about 500m east of the bus stand, set back from Manu Marg. The five hotels are each owned by one of five brothers. Without wishing to cause a family dispute, we think the Ashoka seems to be the best of the lot, with singles/doubles with private bathroom for Rs 100/150 (plus Rs 3 for bucket hot water) or Rs 200/250 with geyser.

At ***Hotel Aravali*** *(☎ 332883, fax 332011)*, south of the train station, dorm beds cost Rs 100 and rooms with private bathroom start at Rs 200/250 (request a quiet room). There's a restaurant, a bar and a pool.

RTDC Hotel Meenal (☎ 22852), farther south down Nehru Marg, is a respectable mid-range place, starting at Rs 300/400 for tidy rooms. There's a little dining hall; a veg/nonveg thali costs Rs 55/70.

Alwar Hotel *(☎ 20012, fax 332250, 26 Manu Marg)*, set in a leafy garden, has decent rooms starting at Rs 300/450 with private bathroom. There's a good restaurant.

Narula's, near the Ganesh Talkies, whips up Indian, Chinese and continental cuisine. This pleasant restaurant, which is down a stairway, offers a good choice of dishes, including veg sizzlers (Rs 45) and strawberry milkshakes (Rs 25).

Getting There & Away

From Alwar, there are frequent buses to Sariska (Rs 9/14, local/express, 1½/one hour), Bharatpur (Rs 29/45, five/3½ hours), Deeg (Rs 23/30, three/2½ hours) and Jaipur (Rs 45/61, three/two hours).

The *Shatabdi Express* (2015/6) passes through Alwar daily except Sunday. It departs Alwar for Ajmer (Rs 480/950 chair/executive class, four hours) at 8.34 am and stops at Jaipur along the way (Rs 145/315, two hours). For Delhi, it departs at 7.41 pm (Rs 350/670, 2½ hours). You have to be quick – the train only stops at Alwar for two minutes in either direction.

Getting Around

There are cycle-rickshaws, autorickshaws, tempos and some tongas. A cycle-rickshaw from the train station to the town centre should cost Rs 10. Bicycles can be hired near the train station (Rs 20 per day).

SARISKA TIGER RESERVE & NATIONAL PARK

Located 107km from Jaipur and 200km from Delhi, the park is in a wooded valley surrounded by barren mountains. It covers 800 sq km (including a core area of 498 sq km) and has sambars, spotted deer, wild boars and, above all, tigers. Project Tiger has been in charge of the sanctuary since 1979.

As at Ranthambhore National Park, also in Rajasthan, this park contains ruined temples, as well as a fort and pavilions built by the maharajas of Alwar. The sanctuary can be visited year-round, although during July and August your chance of spotting wildlife is minimal. The best time is between November and June. You'll see most wildlife in the evening, although tiger sightings are becoming more common during the day.

The park is open in winter (October to the end of February) from 7 am to 4 pm, and during the rest of the year from 6.30 am to 5 pm. The best way to visit the park is by jeep and these can be arranged at the Forest Reception Office (☎ 0144-41333) on Jaipur Rd, directly opposite the Hotel Sariska Palace. A diesel/petrol jeep costs Rs 500/600 (maximum five people). There's an entry fee of Rs 125 per jeep and Rs 20/100 for Indians/foreigners. Entry for Indians is free on Tuesday and Saturday (from 8 am to 3 pm), so if you're a foreigner try to avoid visiting on these days as the park can get busy. Using a still camera is free but a video camera will cost you Rs 200. Guides are available for Rs 50 per hour.

Places to Stay & Eat

Hotel Sariska Palace *(☎ 0144-41322, fax 41323)*, near the park entrance, is the imposing former hunting lodge of the maharajas of Alwar. It's a pleasant place to stay with single/double rooms starting at Rs 2000/3000. There's a small lending library and a restaurant (lunch or dinner is Rs 350).

RTDC Hotel Tiger Den *(☎ 0144-41342)* near the Forest Reception Centre is cheaper and has a lovely garden, although the rooms are a bit run-down. Dorm beds are Rs 50, air-cooled singles/doubles with private bathroom are Rs 500/600, and air-con rooms are Rs 700/800. Bring a mosquito net or repellent. A veg thali costs Rs 65.

Getting There & Away

Sariska, 35km from Alwar, is a convenient town from which to approach the sanctuary. Frequent buses travel between Sariska and Alwar (Rs 14, one hour). It takes about three hours to Jaipur (Rs 48). Buses stop at the front of the Forest Reception Office.

SHEKHAWATI REGION

A number of Muslim clans moved into this semidesert region, in the triangular area between Delhi, Jaipur and Bikaner, in the 14th century. The towns that developed became important trading posts on the caravan routes emanating from the ports of Gujarat.

The area is now famous for its beautifully painted *havelis* (see the boxed text opposite) which were constructed by the wealthy merchants of the region. Most of the buildings date from the 18th to early 20th centuries, and the entire area has been dubbed the 'open-air gallery of Rajasthan'. There are also forts, a couple of minor castles, baoris, *chhatris* (small, domed Mughal kiosks, literally 'umbrellas') and a handful of mosques.

Lonely Planet's *Rajasthan* travel guide has a more detailed chapter on Shekhawati. For a full rundown of the history, people, towns and buildings of the area, it's worth investing in a copy of *The Painted Towns of Shekhawati* by Ilay Cooper.

Getting There & Away

Access to the Shekhawati region is easiest from Jaipur or Bikaner. The towns of Sikar (gateway to the region, but with no notable havelis) and Fatehpur are on the main Jaipur-Bikaner road and are served by many buses.

Churu is on the main Delhi-Bikaner railway line, while Sikar, Nawalgarh and Jhunjhunu have daily passenger train links with Jaipur and Delhi.

Getting Around

The Shekhawati region is crisscrossed by narrow bitumen roads. All towns are well served by government or private buses. Local services to smaller towns can get very crowded and riding 'upper class' (on the roof!) is quite acceptable – and often necessary.

If you have a group of four or five people, it's worth hiring a taxi for the day to take you around the area. It's usually easy to arrange in the towns that have accommodation, although finding a driver who speaks English can be a challenge. The official taxi rate is Rs 4 per kilometre.

Ramgarh

The town of Ramgarh, not to be confused with the town of the same name 35km northeast of Jaipur, was founded by the powerful Poddar merchant family in 1791, after they had left the village of Churu following a disagreement with the thakur. It had its heyday in the mid-19th century and was one of the richest towns of the area.

The **Ram Gopal Poddar Chhatri** near the bus stand, and the **Poddar Havelis**, near the

Havelis

According to some locals, the colourful, painted designs of Shekhawati's *havelis* (traditional ornately decorated residences) were conceived as attempts to ward off loneliness, and to bring colour to a landscape dominated by the parched tones of the surrounding desert. A more mundane theory is that the area's wealthy merchants were keen to build mansions on a grand scale to show off their new wealth.

The popular design focused on one or more internal courtyards. This provided security and privacy for the women of the household, as well as offering relief from the fierce heat that grips the area in summer. The main entrance is usually a large wooden gate leading into a small courtyard, which in turn leads into another courtyard. The largest mansions had as many as four courtyards and were up to six storeys high. Having built houses of grand proportions, families then had them decorated with murals. The major themes are Hindu mythology, history, folk tales, eroticism (many now defaced or destroyed) and – one of the most curious themes – foreigners and their modern inventions, such as planes and gramophones.

Originally the colours used in the murals were all ochre-based, but in the 1860s artificial pigments were introduced from Germany. The predominant colours are blue and maroon, but other colours including yellow, green and indigo are also featured.

Few of the havelis are occupied by their owners, who find that the small rural towns in outback Rajasthan have little appeal. Their upkeep is often left to the meagre resources and loving attention of local *chowkidars* (caretakers) and their families. Not all are open to the public; always ask permission before wandering inside. Local custom dictates that shoes should be removed when you enter the inner courtyard of a haveli, and some are forbidden territory for men.

One unfortunate aspect of the tourist trade is beginning to manifest itself here – the desire for antiques. A couple of towns have antique shops chock-a-block with items ripped from the havelis – particularly doors and window frames, but anything that can be carted away is fair game. Investing in these antiques perpetuates this desecration.

Churu Gate, are both worth seeing. This town is also known for its local handicrafts.

Fatehpur

Fatehpur was established in 1451 as a capital for Muslim nawabs but was taken by the Shekhawat Rajputs in the 18th century.

Some of the main havelis of interest are the **Mahavir Prasad Goenka Haveli**, the **Geori Shankar Haveli**, the **Nand Lal Devra Haveli** and the **Harikrishnan Das Sarogi Haveli**.

Near the private bus stand are the remains of a large 17th-century **baori** in a pitiful state of decay.

RTDC Hotel Haveli (☎ *01571-20293*), about 500m south of the bus stand, has dorm beds for Rs 50, and singles/doubles with private bathroom starting at Rs 300/400. There's a dining hall; chicken curry is Rs 50 and a curd lassi is Rs 13.

Mandawa

The compact and busy little market town of Mandawa was settled in the 18th century, and was fortified by the dominant merchant families. Increasingly, travellers are choosing this quiet town as a base for exploring the Shekhawati area.

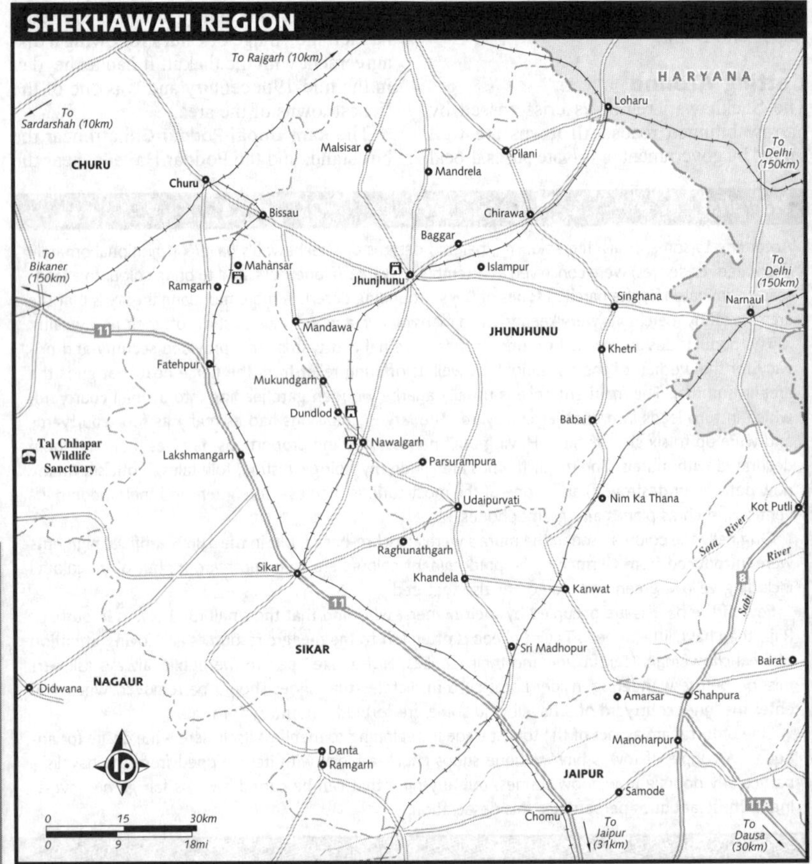

Of the havelis, the **Binsidhar Newatia Haveli** has some curious paintings on its outer eastern wall – a boy using a telephone, and a European woman in a car driven by a chauffeur. The haveli is in the compound of the State Bank of Bikaner & Jaipur. The **Gulab Rai Ladia Haveli** has some defaced erotic images.

Places to Stay & Eat Near the Subhash Chowk bus stand, ***Hotel Heritage Mandawa*** *(☎ 01592-23742, fax 23243)* is an attractive old haveli with clean, split-level singles/doubles with private bathroom starting at Rs 300/400 with progressively larger and more elegant rooms from Rs 700 to 1200. A tasty lunch/dinner is Rs 150/175 (available to nonresidents). There are plans to put a swimming pool in the rear courtyard. The staff have experience in organising traditional weddings for Western couples with help from the family next door who do excellent henna paintings.

Gayatri Niwas is another haveli (142 years old) run by the same owners and will be a good budget choice when renovations are complete. Rooms are expected to cost from Rs 150 to 300.

Hotel Mandawa Haveli *(☎ 01592-23088, ⓔ hotelmandawahaveli@yahoo.com)*, close to Sonathia Gate, is another excellent choice. Located in a lovely 19th-century haveli, rooms around the internal courtyard cost Rs 600/1000 including breakfast. There's also a lovely suite for Rs 1000 without breakfast. Traditional Rajasthani meals are served on the rooftop and there's a small reading room.

Hotel Shekhawati *(☎ 23036)*, 100m south of Hotel Heritage Mandawa, has perfectly reasonable standard/deluxe rooms for Rs 450/800.

Hotel Castle Mandawa *(☎ 01592-23124, fax 23171)* is upmarket and impersonal. Tastefully designed single/double rooms range from Rs 1800/2200 up to Rs 3995 for the Royal Suite. Some rooms have more charm than others, so try to look at a few first. Breakfast/lunch/dinner costs Rs 250/400/450. Pricey barbecues, fire-dancing and camel rides can be arranged.

Dundlod

Dundlod is a tiny village right in the heart of the Shekhawati region. The **fort** here dates back to 1750, though much of it is more recent. The Diwan-i-Khas is still in very good condition and has stained-glass windows.

Other attractions in Dundlod include the **Tuganram Goenka Haveli**, the **Jagathia Haveli** and the **Satyanarayan Temple**.

Dundlod Fort *(☎ 01594-52519; in Jaipur ☎ 0141-211276)* offers good singles/doubles for Rs 1500/1800. Breakfast/lunch/dinner is Rs 150/250/300. Expensive horse, camel and jeep safaris are available, and you can even learn to play camel polo! To organise an exhibition game of camel polo will set you back a cool Rs 30,000.

Nawalgarh

Nawalgarh's **fort**, founded in 1737, houses two banks and some government offices and is of minor interest. There's a good selection of havelis, including the **Aath Havelis**, the **Hem Raj Kulwal Haveli**, the **Bhagton-ki-Haveli** and the **Khedwal Bhavan**. The **Podar Haveli Museum**, built in the 1920s on the eastern side of town, has been magnificently restored with wonderful, vibrant murals and a small collection of Rajasthani wedding costumes and miniature paintings. Entry is Rs 30. The **Morarka Haveli** around the corner is less well preserved but worth a visit (Rs 15).

Places to Stay & Eat Near the Maur Hospital, ***Ramesh Jangid's Tourist Pension*** *(☎ 01594-24060, fax 24061)* offers cheap and cheerful accommodation in a homey atmosphere, with friendly staff who have a wealth of knowledge about Shekawati. Clean singles/doubles with private bathroom (bucket hot water) range from Rs 180/200 to 280/300. Veg meals are available and a thali costs Rs 60. Guided tours and bicycle hire can be arranged.

Apani Dhani *(☎ 01594-22239, fax 24061)*, or Eco Farm, is located on the west side of the main Jaipur road. Rooms (Rs 600/750) are decorated in traditional style and have thatched roofs and mud plaster. Alternative energy is used wherever possible.

Nawal Hotel *(☎ 01594-24148)*, adjacent to the bus stand, has OK rooms for Rs 150/200 with shared bathroom or Rs 200/250 with private bathroom and bucket hot water. There's a nicer room on the roof for Rs 250/300. Dinner or lunch costs Rs 50, breakfast Rs 35. Lone female travellers may feel uncomfortable here.

Roop Niwas Palace *(☎ 01594-22008, fax 23388)*, 1km from the fort, is the most luxurious place to stay. Rooms cost Rs 1150/1300; try to look at a few rooms first as some are much nicer than others. There's a restaurant and a swimming pool.

Parsurampura

Located 20km south-east of Nawalgarh, this little village has among the best-preserved and oldest paintings in Shekhawati. The paintings of the interior of the dome of the **Chhatri of Thakur Sardul Singh** date from the mid-18th century and are worth a look. There is also the **Shamji Sharaf Haveli** and the small **Gopinathji Mandir**, an 18th-century temple constructed by Sardul Singh.

Jhunjhunu

This is one of the largest towns of Shekhawati and is the district headquarters. The town was founded by the Kaimkhani nawabs in the mid-15th century, and stayed under their control until it was taken by the Rajput ruler Sardul Singh in 1730.

It was in Jhunjhunu that the British based their Shekhawati Brigade, a troop raised locally in the 1830s to try to halt the activities of dacoits (bandits), who were largely local petty rulers who had decided it was easier to become wealthy by pinching other people's money than by earning their own.

The Tourist Reception Centre (☎ 01592-32909) is out of the town centre at the Churu bypass, Mandawa Circle. It's open 10 am to 5 pm Monday to Friday and every second Saturday.

Things to See The main item of interest here is the **Khetri Mahal**, a minor palace dating from around 1770. It's one of the most sophisticated buildings in the region, although it's not in the greatest condition. From the top, there are sensational views of the whole town. The **Bihariji Temple** is from a similar period and contains some fine murals; these too have suffered over the years. The **Modi Havelis** and the **Kaniram Narsinghdas Tibrewala Haveli**, both in the main bazaar, are covered with murals.

Places to Stay & Eat The hotel most popular with travellers is ***Hotel Shiv Shekhawati*** *(☎ 01592-32651, fax 38168)*, and deservedly so. Squeaky-clean singles/doubles cost Rs 350/400 with private bathroom, and Rs 600/800 with air-con; the owner is sometimes willing to negotiate. Veg breakfast/lunch/dinner is available for Rs 75/150/150, although a la carte meals are also available. The owner can organise everything from painting classes to camel safaris. This place is east of the town centre.

Hotel Jamuna Resort *(☎ 01592-32871, fax 38168)*, 1km away, has the same owner but only four rooms and there's a swimming pool (which nonguests can use for Rs 50). Rooms start at Rs 700/800, and some are decorated with mirrorwork. The vibrant 'painted room' is Rs 1300/1500. There's a relaxing outdoor dining area also open to nonresidents; a set veg/nonveg meal is Rs 150/200.

In the bus stand area, there are a number of OK choices if you're catching an early bus. ***Hotel Sangam*** *(☎ 01592-32544, fax 33086)* has reasonable rooms with private bathroom (bucket hot water provided) starting at Rs 125/250. Checkout is 24 hours. Almost across the road, the ***Hotel Naveen*** *(☎ 01592-32527)* has depressing, dreary rooms for Rs 125/150 and hot water for Rs 5 per bucket. ***Hotel Neelam*** *(☎ 01592-38415)* is of the same genre with rooms starting at Rs 100/175.

Hotel Shekhawati Heritage *(☎ 01592-35757, fax 33077, ⓔ Shekhawati_Heritage@yahoo.com)*, nearby, is arguably the pick of those in this area. Rooms with geyser hot water start at Rs 400/500, although those for Rs 500/600 are better.

Mahansar

Although this sleepy little village does not have a great selection of painted havelis, it oozes old-world charm. Attractions include the mid-19th-century **Raghunath Temple**, the **Sona-ki-Dukan Haveli** and the **Sahaj Ram Poddar Chhatri**.

Narayan Niwas Castle (☎ 01595-64322), in the old fort, is an authentic castle without the commercial flavour of many of Rajasthan's royal hotels. Singles/doubles start at Rs 700/900 – see a few rooms first, as some are more atmospheric. There are cheaper rooms in a separate portion of the castle.

AJMER

☎ 0145 • pop 493,000

Just over 130km south-west of Jaipur is Ajmer, a burgeoning town on the shore of the Ana Sagar, flanked by barren hills. Historically, Ajmer had considerable strategic importance and was sacked by Mohammed of Ghori on one of his periodic forays from Afghanistan. Later, it became a favourite residence of the Mughals. One of the first contacts between the Mughals and the British occurred in Ajmer, when Sir Thomas Roe met with Jehangir here in 1616.

The city was subsequently taken by the Scindias, and in 1818 it was handed over to the British, becoming one of the few places in Rajasthan controlled directly by the British rather than being part of a princely state. The British chose Ajmer as the site for Mayo College, a prestigious school opened in 1875 exclusively for the Indian princes, but today open to all those who can afford the fees. Ajmer is a major centre for Muslim pilgrims during the fast of Ramadan, and has some impressive Muslim architecture. However, for most travellers Ajmer is essentially just a stepping stone to nearby Pushkar.

Orientation & Information

The main bus stand is close to the RTDC Hotel Khadim in the north-east of town. The train station and most of the hotels are on the east side of town.

The tourist office (☎ 627426) is in the RTDC Hotel Khadim compound and is open 8 am to noon and 3 to 6 pm daily except Sunday. The State Bank of India, opposite the Collectorate, changes travellers cheques and currency. The Bank of Baroda on Prithviraj Marg, opposite the main post office, changes travellers cheques and issues cash advances on MasterCard and Visa.

The Cyber Planet (☎ 628721, ⓔ faakhir moini@usa.net), 100m south of the railway station on Station Rd, has Internet access for Rs 35 per hour. It's open from 11.30 am to 10.30 pm daily except Friday, when it opens at 2.30 pm.

Ana Sagar

This artificial lake was created in the 12th century by damming the River Luni. On its bank is a pleasant park, the **Dault Bagh**, containing a series of marble pavilions erected in 1637 by Shah Jahan. There are fine views from the hill beside the Dault Bagh, particularly just before sunset when the views back towards Ajmer are wonderful. Paddle boats can be hired for Rs 15 per person (minimum of two people). Lifejackets are provided, although if you fall in you're probably in greater danger from the polluted water than from drowning.

The lake tends to dry up if the monsoon is poor, so the city's water supply is taken from **Foy Sagar**, 3km farther up the valley.

Dargah

At the foot of a desolate hill in the old part of town, this is one of India's most important places for Muslim pilgrims. The Dargah is the tomb of a Sufi saint, Khwaja Muin-ud-din Chishti, who came to Ajmer from Persia in 1192. Construction of the shrine was completed by Humayun and the gate was added by the Nizam (the ruler of Hyderabad). Akbar used to make the pilgrimage to the Dargah from Agra once a year.

You must cover your head in certain areas so don't forget to take a scarf or cap – you can buy one at the bazaar leading to the shrine.

As you enter the courtyard remove your shoes at the gateway; a mosque constructed by Akbar is on the right. The large iron cauldrons are for offerings customarily shared by families involved in the shrine's upkeep. In an inner court, there is another mosque built by Shah Jahan. Constructed of white marble, it has 11 arches and a Persian inscription running the full length of the building.

The saint's tomb is in the centre of the second court. It has a marble dome and the actual tomb inside is surrounded by a silver platform. The horseshoes nailed to the shrine doors are offerings from successful horse dealers! Beware of 'guides' pestering for donations around the Dargah using the standard fake donation books or 'visitor registers' – you'll have to pay a generous donation if you sign up.

The tomb attracts hundreds of thousands of pilgrims every year on the anniversary of the saint's death, the Urs, in the seventh month of the lunar calendar (the dates are variable so check with the tourist office). It's an interesting festival, but the crowds can be suffocating. At this time, sufis from all over India converge on Ajmer.

Adhai-din-ka-Jhonpra & Taragarh

Beyond the Dargah, on the very outskirts of town, are the ruins of the Adhai-din-ka-Jhonpra (Two and a Half Days) Mosque. According to legend, its construction, in 1153, took 2½ days, as its name indicates. Others say it was named after a festival lasting 2½ days. It was originally built as a Sanskrit college, but in 1198 Mohammed of

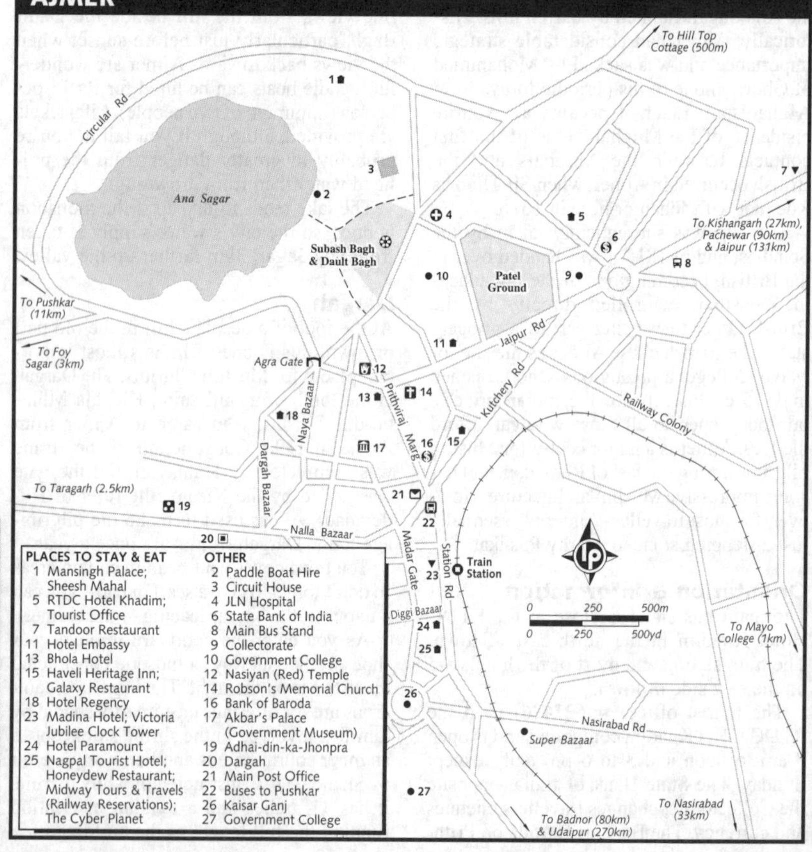

Ghori seized Ajmer and converted the building into a mosque by adding a seven-arched wall in front of the pillared hall.

Although the mosque is now in need of restoration, it is a particularly fine piece of architecture – the pillars are all different and the arched 'screen', with its damaged minarets, is noteworthy.

Three kilometres and a steep 1½ hour climb beyond the mosque, the Taragarh, or Star Fort, commands a superb view over the city (accessible by car). This ancient fort was built by Ajaipal Chauhan, the town's founder. It was the site of much military activity during Mughal times and was later used as a sanatorium by the British.

Akbar's Palace

Back in the city, not far from the main post office, this imposing building was constructed by Akbar in 1570 and today houses the **government museum**, with a limited collection. Items include a collection of stone sculptures, some dating back to the 8th century AD, old weapons and miniature paintings. It's open 10 am to 4.30 pm daily except Friday. Entry is Rs 3 (free on Monday). A camera costs Rs 10/20 for Indians/foreigners; video is Rs 20/50.

Nasiyan (Red) Temple

The Nasiyan Temple (Red Temple) on Prithviraj Marg is a Jain temple built last century and definitely worth checking out. Its double-storey hall contains a fascinating series of large, gilt wooden figures from Jain mythology which depict the Jain concept of the ancient world. The temple is open 8.30 am to 6 pm daily (Rs 3).

Places to Stay

With some notable exceptions, Ajmer's hotels are generally poor value, especially during Pushkar's Camel Fair when hotels in Ajmer can raise their prices considerably.

Haveli Heritage Inn *(☎ 621607)* is arguably the best choice in Ajmer. Set in a 100-year-old haveli, it's a welcoming oasis in the heart of the city. The rooms are large and well maintained (all with private bathroom and air cooler) with lovely high ceilings. There's a pleasant courtyard and a real family atmosphere, complete with home-cooked meals. Rooms range from Rs 300 to 600 depending on the size.

Hill Top Cottage *(☎ 623984, 164 Shastri Nagar)*, behind the shopping centre, is almost as good though farther out of town. Far removed from the crowds and dust, it's another family-run house on an elevated site (the rooftop has panoramic views). Clean singles/doubles with private bathroom go for Rs 350/400, while a two-bed suite costs Rs 600. Meals are sometimes available, failing which the owners can point you to some of the restaurants nearby.

Nagpal Tourist Hotel *(☎ 429503)*, 150m south of the train station on Station Rd, is pretty good value if lacking the character of the other two. Rooms with private bathroom start at Rs 350/450, while those costing Rs 650/900 are very spacious and comfortable. Checkout is 24 hours.

Bhola Hotel *(☎ 432844)*, south-east of Agra Gate, is one of the few habitable budget options with five nondescript rooms for Rs 150/200 with private bathroom (free bucket hot water).

RTDC Hotel Khadim *(☎ 627490, fax 431330)* is near the main bus stand and has rooms with private bathroom starting at Rs 300/400; dorm beds are Rs 50.

Hotel Regency *(☎ 620296)*, close to the Dargarh, is a reasonable choice. Rooms with private bathroom cost Rs 400/450, although the levying of a luxury tax is a tad ambitious. There's a nice veg restaurant, a bar, 24-hour room service and a parking area.

Hotel Embassy *(☎ 623859, ⓔ hotelembassy@satyam.net.in, Jaipur Rd)* is friendly and modern with nice rooms for Rs 450/550.

Hotel Paramount *(☎ 623437, fax 430 166)* is opposite the train station and charges Rs 300/450 for reasonable rooms. It also has Internet access (Rs 50 per hour).

Mansingh Palace *(☎ 425702, fax 425858, ⓔ mansingh.ajmer@mailcity.com, Circular Rd)*, overlooking Ana Sagar, is the only top-end hotel. Far from anywhere but with attractive rooms (Rs 1995/3000) and there's a nice garden at the back. There's a bar and restaurant (see Places to Eat), and a gift shop.

Places to Eat

Bhola Hotel has a good veg restaurant at the top of a seedy staircase. Tasty thalis cost Rs 35, and there's also a variety of other dishes such as *paneer kofta* (curd cheese balls; Rs 40).

Honeydew Restaurant, next to Nagpal Tourist Hotel, has a good selection of veg and nonveg Indian, Chinese and continental food. There are pizzas (Rs 45 to 60), or you could try the brain pakoras (Rs 40). The banana lassi (Rs 20) is refreshing. You can eat indoors or out in the garden. There is a good range of ice creams and you can even take away a 'brick of butterscotch' for Rs 115.

Tandoor Restaurant, a little out of town on Jaipur Rd, offers Indian veg and nonveg fare; a tandoori chicken costs Rs 90.

Sheesh Mahal, at Mansingh Palace, is worth considering for a minor splurge. It serves Indian, Chinese and continental cuisine including chicken tikka masala (Rs 160). Occasional buffets cost Rs 200 (breakfast) or Rs 400 (lunch or dinner).

Madina Hotel is handy if you're waiting for a train (the station is opposite). This simple eatery has cheap veg and nonveg fare.

Galaxy Restaurant, a few doors up from the Haveli Heritage Inn, has a small menu but what they do they do well. There's a nice (air-con) ambience. A half chicken *makhanwala* (butter chicken) costs Rs 80.

Getting There & Away

Bus There are state transport buses from Ajmer to Jaipur every 30 minutes, some nonstop (Rs 51, 2½ hours). The nine-hour trip to Delhi costs Rs 163.

Other destinations in Rajasthan include Jodhpur (Rs 81, 210km), Udaipur (Rs 111, 303km), Bundi (Rs 66, 165km), Bharatpur (Rs 121, 305km), Bikaner (Rs 111, 277km) and Jaisalmer (Rs 140, 490km). Buses also go to Ahmedabad (Rs 211, 526km) and Agra (Rs 152, 388km). The inquiry number is ☎ 431615.

Many of these destinations are also served by private buses – most of the companies have offices on Kutchery Rd.

There are frequent buses from Ajmer to Pushkar (Rs 6, 30 minutes) which leave from the roadside 150m north of the train station at the intersection of Station and Kutchery Rds. If you are arriving in Ajmer by private bus, some drivers will try to convince you that the Pushkar buses leave from the railway crossing – they don't and there are taxi drivers lying in wait.

Train There are no tourist quotas for many trains out of Ajmer so it's worth booking as soon as you have a departure date. Midway Tours & Travels (☎ 628744) will prebook sleeper and upper-class berths for Rs 15/25.

Ajmer is on the Delhi to Mumbai line (via Jaipur and Ahmedabad) and most of the trains on this line stop here. The comfortable *Shatabdi Express* (92016/5) travels daily except Sunday between Ajmer and Delhi (Rs 630/1250, chair/executive class) via Jaipur (Rs 320/615). This train leaves Delhi at 6.15 am and arrives in Ajmer at 12.45 pm. Going in the other direction, it leaves Ajmer at 3.30 pm, arriving in Jaipur at 5.25 pm and Delhi at 10.15 pm.

The *Delhi-Ahmedabad Mail* (9105/6) is another useful train, which departs Ajmer at 8.33 pm and arrives in Delhi at 5.20 am (Rs 99/154/446, general/sleeper/3A class). Heading for Gujarat, the train leaves Ajmer at 7.35 am and arrives in Ahmedabad at 5.20 pm (Rs 107/166/482).

Getting Around

There are plenty of autorickshaws as well as some cycle-rickshaws and tongas. To travel anywhere in town by autorickshaw should cost you around Rs 15.

AROUND AJMER

Kishangarh

Located 27km north-east of Ajmer, the small town of Kishangarh was founded by Kishan Singh in the early 17th century. Kishangarh is famous for its unique style of miniature painting, first produced in the 18th century.

Roopangarh Fort *(☎ 01497-20217, fax 01463-42001)*, about 25km out of town, is a 17th-century fort which has been converted into a hotel by the maharaja and maharani of Kishangarh. Smaller rooms are Rs 750; bigger single/double rooms cost Rs 1190/1700, and a suite is Rs 2500. The rooftop is the place to be at sunset.

The affiliated ***Phool Mahal Palace*** is nearby; rooms start at Rs 900/1150. There's a good restaurant.

PUSHKAR

☎ 0145 • pop 13,500

Pushkar is a bewitching little town despite its somewhat touristy feel these days. It is right on the edge of the desert, only 11km from Ajmer but separated from it by Nag Pahar (Snake Mountain).

This traveller-friendly town clings to the side of the enchanting Pushkar Lake with its many bathing ghats and temples. For Hindus, Pushkar is a very important pilgrimage centre and you'll see plenty of sadhus (individuals on a spiritual search).

Pushkar is perhaps best known for the Camel Fair which takes place here each November. This massive congregation of camels, cattle, livestock traders, pilgrims, tourists and film-makers is one of the planet's most incredible events. If you are anywhere within striking distance at the time, it's an event not to be missed.

Pushkar is a holy place, so alcohol, meat and even eggs are banned.

Information

There is no tourist office in Pushkar (except at the time of the Camel Fair – see the boxed text over the page), but it's easy to find your way around. At the time of writing, the State Bank of Bikaner & Jaipur (open 10 am to 2 pm Monday to Friday, 10 am to noon on Saturday) was only changing travellers cheques (not currency) – the wait can be long and the staff brusque. Every second shop along Sadar Bazaar Rd doubles as a moneychanger, changing both cash and travellers cheques at market rates, but check the commission before handing over your money. On the same road are plenty of places offering Internet services, but connections can be painfully slow.

For quality film processing (prints only), the Rajasthan Colour Lab (which doubles as a bookshop) on Sadar Bazaar charges Rs 5 per photo.

Temples

Pushkar boasts temples, though few are as ancient as you might expect at such an important pilgrimage site, since many were desecrated by Aurangzeb and subsequently rebuilt. The most famous is the **Brahma Temple**, one of the few temples in the world dedicated to this deity. It's marked by a red spire, and over the entrance gateway is the *hans*, or goose symbol, of Brahma, who is said to have personally chosen Pushkar as the site for his temple.

The one-hour trek up to the hilltop **Savitri Temple** overlooking the town is best made early in the morning; the view is magical. The views from the closer **Pap Mochani Temple**, reached by a track behind the Marwar bus stand, are also worth the climb.

Ghats

Numerous ghats run down to the lake, where pilgrims bathe in the sacred waters. If you wish to join in, do so with respect, remembering this is a holy place. Remove your shoes, don't smoke, refrain from kidding around and don't take photographs.

Priests, some genuine, some not, will approach you near the ghats and offer to do a puja (prayer) for which you'll receive a 'Pushkar passport' (a red ribbon around the wrist). More and more travellers are reporting problems with pushy priests (although one traveller did write to tell us that one priest helped to cure his skin cancer). Don't be bullied into giving an exorbitant donation and agree on the price beforehand.

Another 'scam' involves 'priests' giving a traveller a flower. Once you take it, you are then asked to throw it into the holy lake – for a price! To avoid a scene, it's best to not take any flowers offered to you at all.

Massage & Yoga

For reiki, yoga and shiatsu, head to the Honeymoon Hotel, not far from the Marwar bus stand, where reiki master Roshi Hiralal Verma (☎ 773298) is located. Costs depend on the duration and nature of your session.

Women travellers have reported feeling comfortable here.

From October to December, the experienced Sibi George (e sibi80@hotmail.com) runs the Kerala Traditional Ayurvedic Massage Centre near the western end of the lake. He provides massages for a variety of complaints (including asthma and arthritis), full body massages with herbal Ayurvedic oils (Rs 450 for two hours), and courses in Ayurvedic massage. Ten-day courses (four hours a day, minimum of two people) cost US$100. Sibi also does the renowned Ayurvedic treatment known as *panchakarma*, a 28-day cleansing program. This costs Rs 26,000 including accommodation

Camel Fair

The Pushkar Camel Fair is one of India's grand epics. Each year, over 200,000 people flock to Pushkar for the fair, bringing with them some 50,000 camels and cattle for several days of pilgrimage, livestock trading, horse dealing and spirited festivities. The place becomes a flurry of activity with musicians, mystics, comedians, tourists, traders, animals and devotees all converging on this small town. This fair is the only one of its kind in the world and has featured in numerous magazines, travel shows and films. It's truly a feast for the eyes.

The exact date on which the Camel Fair is held depends on the lunar calendar, but in Hindu chronology, it falls on the full moon of Kartik Purnima, when devotees cleanse away their sins by bathing in the holy lake. It commences on 27 November 2001, 16 November 2002, 5 November 2003, and 23 November 2004, and runs for four days. Check in advance as these dates are sometimes subject to change.

It's strongly recommended that you get to the fair several days before the official commencement date in order to see the camel and cattle trading at its peak. The signing of deeds sometimes takes place a full two days before the official commencement date.

Although the place assumes a carnival atmosphere, the Camel Fair is taken very seriously by livestock owners, who come from all over the country with the sole intent of trading. A good camel can fetch tens of thousands of rupees and is a vital source of income for many villagers.

Check with the makeshift RTDC Tourist Information Tents (fair-time only), inside the gate of RTDC Hotel Sarovar and outside the stadium, for a list of events which include cultural performances and fiercely contested camel-judging competitions. They're also the people to see if you want to take a hot-air-balloon ride over Pushkar for Rs 2000, although other travel agents around town can also make the arrangements. It can get noisy at night so if you're a light sleeper, bring earplugs. Carry appropriate allergy medication if you are affected by dust or animal hair.

We heard of one group of travellers who got right into the spirit of the fair, purchasing a camel or two and a luggage cart and setting off from Pushkar, across the desert, heading for Jaisalmer.

RICHARD I'ANSON

and full diet, or Rs 18,000 including a diet diary but excluding accommodation.

Music Lessons

The Saraswati Music School (☎ 773124) is an excellent place to learn classical tabla (drums) and singing. Birju, with over 12 years of experience, charges Rs 100 for one hour or Rs 600 for three days of lessons. It's open from 10 am to 10 pm most days and performances are held from 8 to 9.30 pm on many nights.

Tailors

Pushkar is an excellent place to get some clothes made up. One reliable place which has been recommended by a number of travellers is Navjyoti Tailors (☎ 772589, ⓔ yogeshnavjyoti@hotmail.com), opposite the Lake View (see Places to Stay – Budget). The relaxed yogi can make just about anything you want in one to two days and is very reasonably priced.

Places to Stay

Most hotels in Pushkar are nothing fancy, but they're generally clean and freshly whitewashed. You should ask to see a few rooms before deciding, as many have a cell-like atmosphere owing to the tiny or non-existent windows. At the time of the Camel Fair, when demand for rooms is exceptionally fierce, most hotel tariffs blow sky high. To get the room of your choice at this time, you'll need to book ahead, although there are sometimes rooms to be found.

Places to Stay – Budget

Hotel VK *(☎ 772174)*, at the eastern end of the lake, is a popular cheapie with acceptable singles/doubles with shared bathroom for Rs 75/125. Doubles with private bathroom cost Rs 175. Rs 200 gets you a room with a balcony. There are plans to extend upwards which hopefully won't impinge upon the pleasant rooftop restaurant.

Hotel Venus *(☎ 772323, ⓔ venushotel@yahoo.com)*, on the main thoroughfare nearby, offers doubles with private bathroom for Rs 150. It's set in a shady garden, and there's a popular restaurant upstairs. The same owner runs the ***Venus Holiday Resort***, north of the Hanuman Temple; tidy singles/doubles cost Rs 70/100.

Krishna Guest House *(☎ 772461)* does not quite live up to the manager's claim that it's 'the best guesthouse in the world' but it's still a very pleasant place to stay. There are some very small rooms for Rs 40 and Rs 60 but most cost Rs 80/100 with shared bathroom and Rs 100/150 with private bathroom. It's a lovely old building and there's a nice garden area.

Hotel Om *(☎ 772672)* is similarly good, charging Rs 50/100 with shared bathroom and Rs 100/150 with private bathroom. The rooms are spacious, the owner is relaxed and buffet dinners (Rs 40) are available in the garden.

Bhagwati Guest House *(☎ 772423)*, almost opposite the Ajmer bus stand, is also cheap, with small rooms with shared bathroom for Rs 40/60. Larger singles with shared bathroom cost Rs 50, while rooms with private bathroom go for Rs 60/100. There's a pleasant rooftop restaurant.

Prince Hotel *(☎ 772674)*, north-east of the lake, is quite basic but cheap, friendly and quiet. It has rooms with shared bathroom for Rs 50/80; a double with private bathroom is Rs 100.

Hotel Kanhaia *(☎ 772146)*, also north-east of the lake, has neat doubles for Rs 80 (Rs 100 with private bathroom).

Hotel White House *(☎ 772147, fax 772950)*, north of the lake, is a very appealing place with fine views from the rooftop restaurant. Spotless, airy and air-cooled rooms start at Rs 250, while Rs 350 to 450 gets you progressively larger rooms with balcony. The mango tea (complimentary on arrival) is refreshing and the home-cooked meals are good.

Mayur Guest House *(☎ 772302)*, closer to the lake, is an unpretentious, relaxed place with a number of repeat visitors. Rooms go for Rs 50/70 with shared bathroom; Rs 90/125 with private bathroom.

Rajguru Guest House *(☎ 772879, fax 772102)*, nearby, is quiet and friendly. Some rooms are a little small and have (free) bucket hot water, but the compact garden is

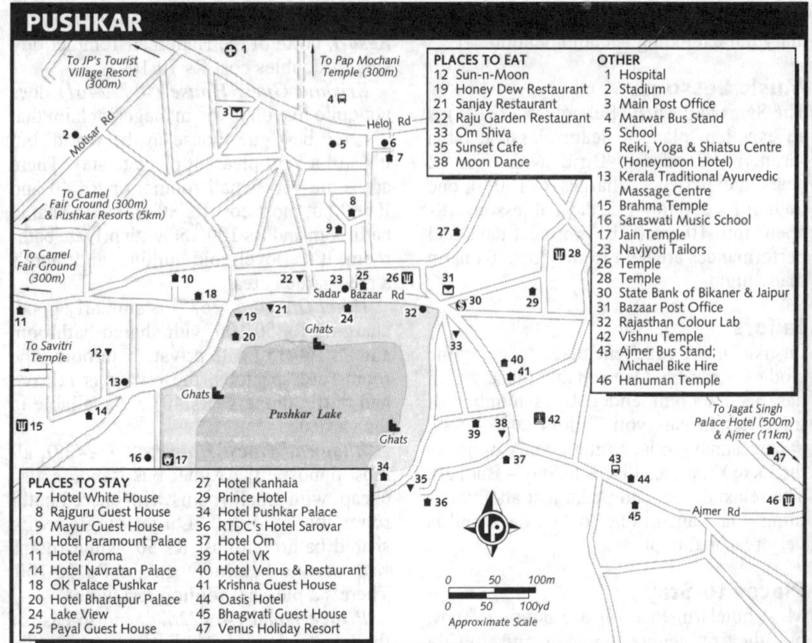

nice and the owner eager to please. Doubles cost Rs 80 (Rs 125 with private bathroom).

Payal Guest House (☎ *772163)*, right in the middle of the main bazaar, is a favourite with travellers. It has rooms starting at Rs 100/150 with shared bathroom, and Rs 150/200 with private bathroom. The courtyard is in the shade of a banana tree. Meals are available.

Lake View *(☎ 772106, fax 772106)*, almost directly across the road, is wonderfully located with superb views over the lake from the roof. Doubles with private bathroom cost from Rs 200 to 300, but some of those with shared bathroom (Rs 150 to 200) have a balcony overlooking the lake. There are also other rooms for Rs 100.

Hotel Paramount Palace *(☎ 772428, fax 772244)* has fine views over the town. Doubles with private bathroom cost Rs 100 to 450 depending on size – the most expensive rooms (Nos 106, 108, 109 and 111) with balconies are particularly good value.

Nearby is the ***OK Palace Pushkar*** *(☎ 772868)* – good if you're suffering a cash crunch. Rooms with shared bathroom go for Rs 40/80, while doubles with private bathroom cost Rs 100. Some rooms have a swing chair.

Hotel Aroma *(☎ 772729, fax 772244)* is a welcoming place and one of the closest to the location of the Camel Fair. Tidy doubles cost Rs 100.

Hotel Navratan Palace *(☎ 772729, fax 772225)*, close to the Brahma Temple, is a good choice with a lovely enclosed garden and swimming pool. Decent rooms start at Rs 150/200.

Hotel Bharatpur Palace *(☎ 772320)* occupies one of the best spots in Pushkar, literally on the upper levels of the western ghats. Prices range from Rs 100 for singles with shared bathroom up to Rs 500 for a double with private bathroom. Room No 5 has a great position (Rs 200) but room No 1 wins the prize for the best place to wake up in the morning and is one of the most romantic choices in Pushkar. Surrounded on three sides by the lake (with doors that open out on each of these sides), it is possible to lie in bed with the doors open and have the lake and ghats laid out before you (with all of the attendant clamour and noise). Even without a private bathroom, it's a bargain at Rs 300 (Rs 2000 during the Camel Fair).

Places to Stay – Mid-Range & Top End

***Hotel Pushkar Palace** (☎ 772001, fax 772226)*, near the lake, once belonged to the maharaja of Kishangarh. It's a popular place to stay, although it has had some mixed reviews in recent years. The cheapest rooms cost Rs 600 (Rs 745 with air-con); better rooms start at Rs 1100 (Rs 1195 with air-con). The most expensive rooms (Rs 1995) have superlative lake views for which you'll pay US$175 during the Camel Fair.

***RTDC Hotel Sarovar** (☎ 772040)* is just along from Hotel Pushkar Palace but approached from a different entrance. Set in its own spacious grounds at the far end of the lake and with a restaurant, it has more character than most RTDC places, although some travellers have complained about the indifferent service. Singles/doubles cost Rs 100/ 200 with shared bathroom, Rs 300/ 400 with private bathroom. Lake-view rooms cost Rs 500/600. There are also dorm beds for Rs 50.

***Oasis Hotel** (☎ 772100, fax 772018)*, near the Ajmer bus stand, seems very anxious to get you in the door but less keen to keep you. It's a big place with large, bare rooms with private bathroom starting at Rs 350/400. There's a restaurant and a swimming pool, although the latter is made less appealing by the number of men who seem to lurk permanently around the entrance and reception area.

***Jagat Singh Palace Hotel** (☎ 772953, fax 772952)*, a little out of the main town area, is one of the most upmarket places in Pushkar, designed like a fort and now a Heritage Hotel. Attractively furnished rooms cost around Rs 1100/1195, and there's a large garden and restaurant.

***Pushkar Resorts** (☎ 772017, fax 772946, e pushkar@pushkarresorts.com)*, 5km out of town, is also suitably luxurious. There are 40 modern cottages which are comfortable but a little lacking in character. All have air-con and TV and cost Rs 1895/2195. There's a dining hall (residents only), a swimming pool and two telescopes for stargazing.

***JP's Tourist Village Resort** (☎ 772067, fax 772026)* is also a little out of town, but is a peaceful place to stay. Comfortable doubles with private bathroom range from Rs 500 to 750. It costs Rs 200 per person to inhabit the treehouse. There's also a swimming pool and a restaurant.

Tourist Village During the Camel Fair, the RTDC and many private operators set up a sea of tents near the *mela* (fair) ground. It can get quite cold at night, so bring something warm to wear. A torch (flashlight) may also be useful. Demand for tents is high so you're strongly advised to book well ahead.

***RTDC Tourist Village** (☎ 772074)* has dormitory tents for US$7 per person, and standard single/double tents with shared bathroom for Rs 4000/4500 including all meals. There are also more upmarket 'Swiss' tents with private bathroom for Rs 5000/ 5500 and deluxe huts for Rs 5500/6000 including meals. These huts are open all year round, and are significantly cheaper outside fair time – Rs 150 to 400. To book, contact RTDC Hotel Swagatam (☎ 0141-202152, fax 201145) in Jaipur; or the RTDC Hotel Sarovar in Pushkar. Full payment must be received 45 days in advance.

Royal Tents, owned by the maharaja of Jodhpur, seem to be the most luxurious tents, but you'll pay for this privilege. They cost US$175/225 with private bathroom (bucket hot water), including all meals. Reservations should be made in advance at the Umaid Bhawan Palace in Jodhpur (☎ 0291-433316, fax 635373).

Royal Desert Camp, farther away from the fairground, is another good option with tents with bath and running showers for US$85/100 and others for US$115/125. There are also some cheaper tents with shared bathroom. The price includes all meals and a 'camel shuttle service' to and from the fair. Book well ahead on ☎ 772957 or through the Hotel Pushkar Palace in Pushkar (☎ 772001, fax 772226).

Places to Eat

Pushkar has plenty of reasonably priced eating places, although hygiene standards are sometimes quite low. Strict vegetarianism that forbids even eggs rather limits the range of ingredients, but the cooks make up for this with imagination. You can get an eggless omelette in some places, while others serve spaghetti bolognaise without meat! In general, steer clear of Western-style dishes which tend to be a disappointment.

Buffet meals are popular, with many places offering all-you-can-eat meals for Rs 35 to 45.

There are a number of places where the view or location is better than the food. Surprisingly, one such place is the ***Hotel Pushkar Palace*** – a great place for a drink at sunset (a mango lassi is Rs 25) but eat elsewhere. Others include the ***Venus Restaurant***, which has a prime vantage point overlooking the main thoroughfare and its fascinating passing parade (the chocolate pancake with banana and honey for Rs 25 isn't bad), and ***Sanjay Restaurant*** which has a great view over the lake.

Sunset Cafe, right on the eastern ghats, has long been a popular hang-out for travellers – a good place to swap stories about Goa, Kathmandu and beyond. This simple cafe offers the usual have-a-go-at-anything menu, including *dosas* (lentil-flour pancakes; Rs 20) and sizzlers (from Rs 50 to 75). There's a German bakery too. The location by the lakeshore is pleasant, especially at sunset.

Om Shiva, near the State Bank of Bikaner & Jaipur, offers reasonably priced and tasty buffets (Rs 45).

Moon Dance is one place that gets consistently good reviews, although its Indian food is surprisingly patchy and the service can be slow. It has tables in a laid-back garden and serves a wide range of food, including high-quality Mexican, Italian and Israeli dishes. A spectacular spinach and mushroom enchilada is Rs 55, a good spinach and mushroom burger Rs 50 and great bruschetta starts at Rs 20. A cup of soothing cinnamon tea is Rs 5. You sit at tables or on cushions and there's also a pool table.

Raju Garden Restaurant serves a mishmash of Western, Chinese and Indian fare. The prices are a little high, but the selection is good. If your tummy is screaming for something simple, try the baked potatoes (Rs 45). Birthday cakes can be ordered here (with advance notice); they range from a meek and modest Rs 65 to a mind-blowing Rs 1000!

Sun-n-Moon, not far from the Brahma Temple, has tables around a bhodi tree, and is a peaceful place to eat. It offers a variety of Western and Indian food such as Kashmiri burgers (Rs 45) and large breakfasts (Rs 55 to 75), and boasts of the 'best apple pie in Pushkar' (Rs 45).

Honey Dew Restaurant, at the western end of Sadar Bazaar, is a cosy place doing reasonable thalis for Rs 25.

Old Complaint – New Name

An unnamed traveller at an unnamed hotel in Rajasthan ate a less-than-hygienic meal, necessitating the all-too-common experience of travellers in India – frequent trips to the toilet. Her travelling companion asked the owner of the hotel for a meal of plain rice. No problem, and indeed, soon after, a waiter appeared at the door of their hotel room, announcing his arrival, straight-faced, with the words, 'I hear that madam is not farting with confidence this evening.'

Anthony Ham

Shopping

Pushkar's main bazaar is a tangle of narrow lanes lined with an assortment of interesting little shops – ideal for picking up gifts for friends back home. Here you'll come across everything from clothing shops catering to styles which were in vogue at the end of the 1960s to Rajasthani turbans, from firecrackers to incense sticks, from statues of

Ganesh to the Bhagavad Gita and the novels of Salman Rushdie. Particularly good buys include costume jewellery, embroidered fabrics, wall-hangings, groovy shoulder bags, Rajasthani puppets and traditional music. You'll have to haggle over prices. There's the usual nonsense about 'last price' quotes that aren't negotiable – take your time and visit a few shops.

There are a number of bookshops in the main bazaar selling a tremendous range of second-hand novels in various languages, and they'll usually buy them back for around 50% of what you pay.

Getting There & Away

Buses depart Ajmer for Pushkar frequently for Rs 6 (although it's only Rs 4 from Pushkar to Ajmer because of the road toll; for cars the toll is Rs 25). Like everything else in Pushkar it all costs a bit more at Camel Fair time.

Travel agencies around town sell tickets for private buses – shop around for the best price. These buses generally leave from Ajmer, but the agents should provide you with free transport to Ajmer in time for the departures. Those that leave from Pushkar generally stop for an hour or more in Ajmer anyway. Be warned that some travellers have reported that a few buses (particularly those via Jodhpur) don't go all the way in spite of promises and involve a change of bus *and* an extra fare. Private buses go to Jaisalmer (Rs 180, 10½ hours), Jodhpur (Rs 100, 5½ hours), Udaipur (Rs 120, eight hours), Delhi (Rs 160, 10½ hours), Jaipur (Rs 80, four hours) and Agra (Rs 160, nine hours) among other destinations.

For around Rs 50, some agents will book rail tickets for services ex-Ajmer (including a free jeep transfer to Ajmer).

Getting Around

Fortunately there are no autorickshaws in the town centre, and it's a breeze to get around on foot. Another good option is to hire a bicycle (Rs 5/25 per hour/day). A wallah can carry your luggage on a hand-drawn cart to or from the bus stand for around Rs 10.

RANTHAMBHORE NATIONAL PARK

☎ 07462

Near the town of Sawai Madhopur, midway between Bharatpur and Kota, Ranthambhore National Park is one of the prime examples of Project Tiger's conservation efforts in Rajasthan. Sadly, it also demonstrates the program's overall failure, for it was in this park that government officials were implicated in the poaching of tigers for the Chinese folk medicine trade. The visit of the then US president Bill Clinton in 2000 led to a rapid growth in the park's popularity, although sadly it also highlighted its problems – Bumbram, the tiger seen by President Clinton, could not be found when the park reopened in October 2000 after the monsoon, leading to fears that the now-famous tiger had been poached. Keen to play down the issue, park authorities denied the reports, but some doubts remained at the time of writing.

According to a 1999 census, the park had a total of 42 tigers (32 adults and 10 cubs). There's a reasonable chance of seeing one, but you should plan on two or three safaris. Even if you don't see a tiger, it's worth the effort for the beautiful scenery alone: In India it's not often you get the chance to visit such a large area of virgin bush. There are also over 250 species of resident and migratory birds.

The park covers some 1334 sq km. A system of lakes and rivers is hemmed in by steep, high crags; Ranthambhore Fort, built in the 10th century, stands on top of one of them. The lower ground alternates between open bushland and fairly dense forest and is peppered with ruined pavilions, chhatris and 'hides' – the area was formerly a hunting preserve of the maharajas.

India's parliament has approved a law to rename the park the Rajiv Gandhi National Park, but implementation of the decision has been put indefinitely on hold.

Orientation & Information

It's 10km from Sawai Madhopur to the first park gate, where you pay the entry fee, and a farther 3km to the main gate and the

Ranthambhore Fort. Accommodation is strung out along the town to the park road.

The helpful Tourist Reception Centre (☎ 20808) is in the grounds of the RTDC Vinayak Tourist Complex. It's open 10 am to 1.30 pm and 2 to 5 pm daily except Sunday. You can change travellers cheques (not currency) at the State Bank of Bikaner & Jaipur, in Sawai Madhopur.

The Project Tiger office (☎ 20223) is 500m from the train station.

The best time to visit the park is between October and April; the park is closed during the monsoon from 1 July to 1 October. The park entry fee for Indians/foreigners is Rs 25/200, plus Rs 100 for a video camera.

Wildlife Safaris

Early morning and late afternoon are generally the best times for spotting wildlife. If you are taking photos, it's worthwhile bringing some 400 ASA or 800 ASA film, as the undergrowth is dense and surprisingly dark in places.

Jeeps are almost impossible to obtain during most of the season. To have any chance you need to book at least *two* months in advance and pay the hire charge (Rs 750) in advance. There are a limited number of jeeps but the main reason why demand outstrips supply is that the authorities wish to restrict the number of motorised vehicles within the park. Assuming you are able to plan your life that far in advance, contact the Project Tiger office or the Tourist Reception Centre, or find a travel agent (or local hotel) to make the booking and payment arrangements. Occupants of jeeps must pay an additional fee of Rs 125 per jeep upon entry to the park.

A seat in a large open-topped truck (called a canter), which can be arranged on arrival, costs Rs 80 per person. Ask for a mini-canter, which feels a little less like (although not entirely unlike) a circus show. To increase your chances of seeing a tiger, contact either the Project Tiger office or the tourist office the day before your safari to ask where the latest sighting took place and then arrange for a canter taking that route. It doesn't always work but it's still worth trying, particularly if your time is short. Bookings can be made through most hotels, the tourist office or the Project Tiger office.

A guide is compulsory and is included in the ticket price for a canter, but will cost an extra Rs 150 if you go by jeep.

In winter (October to February), vehicles leave at 7 am and 2.30 pm; the safari takes three hours. In summer (March to June), they leave at 6.30 am and 3.30 pm. You can book for morning trips between 4 and 5 pm the day before, and for the afternoon safari between 11 am and noon, although many hotels seem able to do it outside these hours.

Places to Stay & Eat

The best places to stay are on Ranthambhore Rd, but 'shoestringers' will find the cheapest (and grimiest and noisiest) lodgings in uninspiring Sawai Madhopur.

Ranthambhore Road The cheapest place along Ranthambhore Rd is ***Hotel Ranthambhore Resort*** *(☎ 21645, fax 21430)*, about 5km from the train station. Simple but clean and decent-sized doubles with bathroom and constant hot water cost Rs 200. ***City Heart Restaurant*** was due to open next door just after we were there, and promised Punjabi, South Indian, Chinese and tandoori cuisine.

Hotel Tiger Safari Resort *(☎ 21137, fax 22391)*, 4km from the station, has good doubles with bathrooms starting at Rs 300.

Ankur Resort *(☎ 20792, fax 23303, ⓔ ankur@ranthambor.com)*, 3km from the station, is a popular choice though a touch overpriced with doubles starting at Rs 600. Deluxe single/double cottages cost Rs 1200/1500 (the doubles have satellite TV).

Hotel Anurag Resort *(☎/fax 20451)*, 100m east, is similar with doubles starting at Rs 500. Dorm beds are Rs 75, and it's possible to camp (in your own tent) for around Rs 100.

Hotel Ranthambhore Regency *(☎ 21176, fax 22299, ⓔ ranthambhoreregency@ranthambor.com)*, nearby, has attractive singles/doubles for Rs 600/800. For Rs 1300/1500 you get an air-con cottage.

RTDC Castle Jhoomar Baori *(☎ 20495)* is a former royal hunting lodge stunningly located on a hillside about 7km from the train station. The rooms are not really luxurious, but they do have character. Standard rooms cost Rs 700/800. A Panther Suite is Rs 900/1100, while a Tiger or Leopard Suite is Rs 1200/1500.

Hammir Wildlife Resort *(☎ 20562, fax 21842)* has rather neglected rooms with private bathroom starting at Rs 600/700, and cottages for Rs 1000.

RTDC Vinayak Tourist Complex *(☎ 213 33)*, farther along the road, has decent rooms for Rs 550/600. There's a nice lawn area and a campfire is lit in the winter.

Sawai Madhopur Lodge *(☎ 20541, fax 20718)*, 3km from the train station, once belonged to the maharaja of Jaipur. Run by the Taj Group, it's suitably luxurious with a pool (open to nonresidents for Rs 300), bar, restaurant, library and lovely gardens. Rooms are Rs 2500/3500, and upmarket tented accommodation (with private bathroom) is Rs 2800 a double.

Sawai Madhopur Large singles/doubles at ***Hotel Chinkara*** *(☎ 20340, 13 Indira Colony, Civil Lines)* cost Rs 125/200 with private bathroom and semiconstant hot water.

Rajeev Resort *(☎ 21413, fax 33138)*, almost next door, is similar with decent rooms with private bathroom for Rs 125/200.

The following places are really only for those for whom price is everything. At each place you'll need to ask the staff to change the sheets.

Vishal Hotel *(☎ 20504)*, in the main bazaar, offers one dank single with shared bathroom for Rs 60 and dingy doubles with private bathroom (free bucket hot water) for Rs 80 to 175. The nearby, rather seedy, ***Hotel Swagat*** *(☎ 20601)* is similarly priced and similarly grubby; the only saving grace is one room on the top floor with a balcony and away from the street for Rs 80/125.

Hotel Pink Palace *(☎ 20722, plot A1, Bal Mandir Colony)* has pretty basic rooms with shared bathroom (free bucket hot water) for Rs 60/100, or with private bathroom for Rs 125/150. For Rs 200/250 you get a sit-down flush toilet, geyser hot water and a satellite TV which sometimes works.

Hotel Mayur *(☎ 20909)*, next door, is equally spartan; rooms start at Rs 80/100.

Shopping

The Dastkar Craft Centre, 3km beyond the park entrance on Ranthambhore Rd, is worth a visit. The handicrafts, all of which are produced by low-caste women in local villages, include bedspreads, clothes and other textile pieces.

Getting There & Away

Bus There are buses to Jaipur (Rs 45, 4½ hours) and Kota (Rs 45, four hours). To reach these destinations via Tonk, go to the small bus stand near the petrol station not far from the overpass. To go via Dausa (on the Jaipur-Bharatpur road), buses leave from the roundabout near the main post office. Travelling to Bharatpur by bus invariably involves a change in Dausa – the train is infinitely preferable.

Train The computerised reservation office is open from 8 am to 8 pm daily except Sunday when it closes at 1.45 pm.

For Delhi, the *Golden Temple Mail* (2903) leaves Sawai Madhopur at 1 pm, arriving in the capital at 7.35 pm (Rs 84/131/378 general/sleeper/3A class). It goes via Bharatpur, arriving at 3.35 pm (Rs 52/81/234). To Kota, there are seven trains daily, the most convenient of which is probably the *Avadh Express* (5063) which leaves Sawai Madhopur at 9.55 am, arriving at 11.35 am (Rs 36/56/183).

Getting Around

Bicycle hire is available outside the train station entrance, and at the eastern end of the main bazaar (around Rs 20 per day).

Southern Rajasthan

BUNDI

☎ 0747 • pop 80,000

Visiting Bundi is like stepping back in time. It's a picturesque, captivating and friendly little town which has more or less retained a medieval atmosphere. Bundi is not a major tourist tramping ground, which is a big part of its charm. In the evening, people throng to the colourful and bustling markets that meander through the town's lanes. In Bundi, unlike many other places in Rajasthan, you're unlikely to be hounded by persistent shopkeepers.

Bundi's Rajput legacy is well preserved in the massive fort, which broods over the town in the narrow valley below, and the imposing palace that stands beneath it. In this palace are the famous Bundi murals. The old city has a number of blue-coloured houses, similar to those found in Jodhpur.

Bundi was the capital of a major princely state during the heyday of the Rajputs. Nearby Kota was part of Bundi, deemed as the land grant of the ruler's eldest son. But in 1624, Kota was made into a separate state at the instigation of the Mughal emperor Jehangir. Although its importance dwindled with the rise of Kota during Mughal times, Bundi kept its independence until its incorporation into the state of Rajasthan in 1947.

Information

Tourist Offices There's a small tourist office (☎ 442697) in the grounds of Circuit House. It's open from 10 am to 1.30 pm and 2 to 5 pm Monday to Saturday. Mukesh Mehta, at the Haveli Braj Bhushanjee (see Places to Stay & Eat), is also a terrific source of information. His Web site (www.kiplingsbundi.com) is worth a look.

Money At the time of research, no banks in Bundi changed money or gave cash advances on credit cards. The small shopfront moneychanger south of the palace changes US dollars for a little less than the market rate but could be useful if you're stuck.

Email & Internet Access Email is available at the Haveli Braj Bhushanjee (see Places to Stay & Eat) or Cyber Dream.

Medical Services If you're feeling a little off colour, you may like to drop in at the Ayurvedic Hospital (☎ 22708) at Balchand Pada (opposite the Haveli Braj Bhushanjee), which prescribes natural plant-based remedies. There are medicines for all sorts of ailments, from upset tummies to arthritis. In winter, the hospital is open from 9 am to 3 pm Monday to Saturday and from 9 to 11 am on Sunday. In summer, it's open from 8 am to 2 pm Monday to Saturday and from 8 to 10 am on Sunday.

Taragarh

The rather neglected Taragarh, or Star Fort, was built in 1354 and is a great place to ramble around at leisure. It is reached by a steep road leading up the hillside to its enormous gateway. Take the path up behind the Chittra Sala, go east along the inside of the ramparts, then left up the steep stone ramp just before the small disused building 200m from the palace. The views over the town and surrounding countryside from the top are magical, especially at sunset. Inside the ramparts are huge reservoirs carved out of solid rock, and the Bhim Burj, the largest of the battlements, on which is mounted a famous cannon. It's just a shame that the national broadcaster, Doordarshan, decided to build an ugly concrete transmission tower right next to the fort.

Bundi Palace

The palace is reached from the north-western end of the bazaar, through a huge wooden gateway and up a steep cobbled ramp. Only one portion of the outer perimeter of the palace, the Chittra Sala, is officially open to the public. If you want to see the renowned **Bundi murals** (found in the Chattra Mahal and Badal Mahal), you could try contacting the secretary of the maharaja of Bundi; talk to your hotel for advice on how best to make an approach. From a distance, the palace looks beautiful when it is illuminated at night and there are splendid views of it from the south side of Nawal Sagar, especially from the bypass road which climbs the small hill.

Baoris & Water Tanks

Bundi has scores of beautiful baoris, some right in the centre of town. The very impressive **Raniji-ki-Baori** is 46m deep and has some superb carving. One of the largest

The Step-Wells of Rajasthan

Building a step-well is lauded in the ancient Hindu scriptures as an act of great merit. Although the distinctions have become blurred, *kund* generally referred to a structural pond, while a *vapi* (also known as a *vav* or *wav*) indicated a water supply reached via a series of steps. Another generic term for step-wells is *baori* (in Gujarati, the word is spelled *baoli*) which usually denotes a connection to a religious community.

In addition to their essential function as a water supply in arid areas, step-wells were frequently attached to temples and shrines, enabling devotees to bathe and purify themselves. Many formed part of a larger complex which included accommodation for weary travellers. The more elaborate baoris have intricate columns and pillars, steps built in artistic configurations, and rest rooms, corridors, galleries and platforms cut into the various levels. The spiritual and life-giving properties of step-wells, and their pivotal role in daily life, meant that many were adorned with carvings and statues of gods and goddesses, with Ganesh, Hanuman, Durga and Mahishasura the most commonly represented deities.

The most impressive step-wells in Rajasthan are the Raniji-ki-Baori in Bundi and the baori at Abhaneri, although most towns and villages have at least one.

of its kind, it was built in 1699 by Rani Nathavatji. The **Nagar Sagar Kund** is a pair of matching step-wells outside the Chogan Gate to the old city, in the centre of town.

Visible from the fort is the artificial lake of **Nawal Sagar**. At its centre is a temple to Varuna, the Aryan god of water. Also worth a look is the **Bhora-ji-ka-Kund**, opposite one of Bundi's oldest Shiva temples, the Abhaynath Temple. This 16th-century tank attracts a variety of birdlife after a good monsoon, including kingfishers and hummingbirds. The **Dhabhai Kund**, not far from the Ranijiki-baori, is another imposing tank.

Other Attractions

Take a stroll through the old city to soak in the medieval ambience of this town. It's worth visiting the colourful **sabzi (vegetable) market** situated between Raniji-ki-Baori and Nagar Sagar Kund.

Bundi's other attractions are all out of town and are difficult to reach without transport. The modern palace, known as the **Phool Sagar Palace**, has a charming artificial tank and gardens, and is several kilometres out of town on the Ajmer road. It was closed to the public at the time of research.

There's another palace, the smaller **Sukh Mahal**, closer to town on the edge of Jait Sagar, where Rudyard Kipling once stayed. The nearby, rather neglected, **Sar Bagh** has a collection of royal cenotaphs, some with beautifully carved statues. **Shikar Burj** is a small former royal hunting lodge and picnic spot on the road that runs along the north side of Jait Sagar, a picturesque lake flanked by hills and strewn with pretty lotus flowers during the monsoon and winter months.

South of town is the stunning **84-Pillared Cenotaph** (Chaurasi Khambon-ki-Chhatri), which is lit up at night. This impressive monument is set among well-maintained gardens, and is certainly worth a look.

About 32km from Bundi at the village of Garardha, you can see some ancient red-coloured **rock paintings**. Found on boulders flanking the river, these are believed to be about 15,000 years old. There are some hunting scenes, a curious depiction of a man riding a huge bird, and some stick figures of people holding hands – apparently how villagers crossed rivers long ago. To make the most of the trip out here, it's best to come with a local guide – contact your hotel.

Places to Stay & Eat

If only Chittorgarh had Bundi's range of accommodation. The commission racket operates in Bundi so don't feel pressured into staying at a place of your taxi or autorickshaw driver's choice.

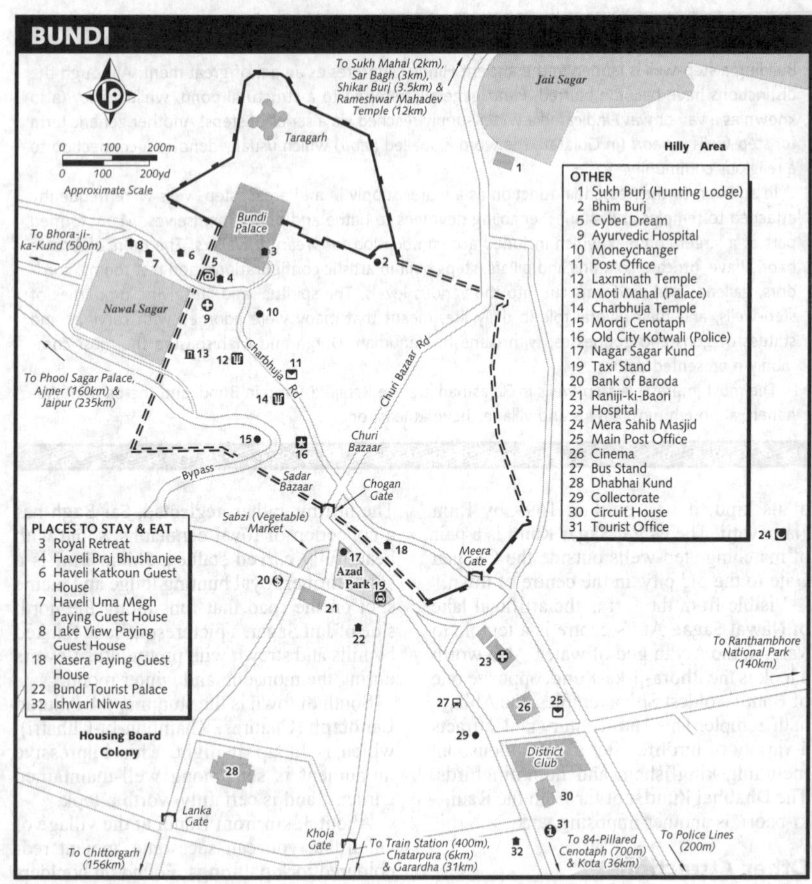

***Haveli Braj Bhushanjee** (☎ 442322, fax 442142, ⓔ res@kiplingsbundi.com)*, opposite the Ayurvedic Hospital just below the palace, is a funky 200-year-old haveli run by the descendants of former prime ministers of Bundi, and has a cosy feel to it. The views from the rooftop terrace are splendid. Attractive rooms with private bathroom range from Rs 350 to 1400; all rooms have geyser hot water and varying degrees of character. Credit cards are accepted, although payment in rupees is preferred. Wholesome, but expensive, set veg meals are Rs 250 – the dining room is very atmospheric. There's also a good shop selling a fascinating array of collectibles. Free pick-ups from the bus stand and train station are available (advance notice appreciated).

***Ishwari Niwas** (☎ 442414, fax 442486, ⓔ in_heritage@timesofindia.com, 1 Civil Lines)*, opposite the tourist office, is within walking distance of the bus stand. It's a graceful old colonial building with high ceilings and a pleasant courtyard. Tidy, well-kept singles/doubles start at Rs 200/250; a suite costs Rs 500. It's excellent value, although the location is not the best. Veg/non-veg lunches and dinners cost Rs 150/175.

***Bundi Tourist Palace** (☎ 442650)*, opposite Azad Park, is pretty basic but clean, friendly and close to the bus stand. Small rooms cost Rs 70/120 with shared bathroom (bucket hot water).

***Kasera Paying Guest House** (☎ 444679, fax 443126, ⓔ kaserapayingguesthouse@usa.net)*, near Chogan Gate in the main bazaar, is another great choice. Set in a delightful old haveli, its cosy doubles (shared bathroom, bucket hot water) cost Rs 250. There's a good roof restaurant – paneer pilau costs Rs 45, fried spinach with Indian cheese is Rs 25 and mango toffee goes for Rs 50.

***Haveli Katkoun Guest House** (☎ 444311, ⓔ raghunandansingh@yahoo.com)*, closer to the palace, charges Rs 150/200 for clean, pleasant rooms with private bathroom, or Rs 200/250 for slightly larger ones. There's also a small garden restaurant here which serves, among other things, good breakfasts, chicken masala (Rs 100) and beer (Rs 80).

***Lake View Paying Guest House** (☎ 442 326, ⓔ lakeviewbundi@yahoo.com)*, not far away, is set in the modest 200-year-old Meghwahanji Haveli. Rooms (mostly with shared bathroom) are good value at Rs 100/150. Some rooms have lake views and Room No 1 (Rs 150) is particularly good. Home-cooked meals are available.

***Haveli Uma Megh Paying Guest House** (☎ 442191)*, almost next door, has a wide range of rooms from small singles with shared bathroom (Rs 75) to a double with bath, sit-down flush toilet and lake view (Rs 350). Some of the cheaper rooms also have a view. There's a nice garden restaurant by the water's edge.

***Royal Retreat** (☎ 444426)*, ideally situated in the palace compound, has rooms set around a quiet open-air courtyard. Prices start at Rs 350/550.

Getting There & Away

Roads to the east and west of Bundi are in an appalling condition making the journey to Chittor and Sawai Madhopur particularly tiring. There are semiregular express buses to Ajmer (Rs 67, five hours), Kota (Rs 15, one hour), Sawai Madhopur (Rs 44, 4½ hours), Udaipur (Rs 122, 8½ hours), Jodhpur (Rs 146, 10 hours), Bikaner (Rs 171, 10 hours), Jaipur (Rs 83, five hours) and Indore in Madhya Pradesh (Rs 147, 12 hours). The nearest train station is at Kota.

Getting Around

Taxis can be hired from the stand near the Raniji-ki-Baori. Autorickshaw drivers will quote around Rs 15 to take you from the bus stand to Bundi Palace. For local sightseeing, expect to pay around Rs 50 per hour for an autorickshaw. Bicycles are an ideal way to get around and can be cheaply rented near the old city *kotwali* (police station) for around Rs 10 per day.

KOTA

☎ 0744 • pop 662,000

Kota is one of Rajasthan's less inspiring cities, although it's still worth a visit for its palaces and gardens. Most travellers prefer to visit Kota on a day trip from Bundi.

Building of the city began in 1264 following the defeat of Koteya, a Bhil chieftain. He was beheaded and on that very spot the foundation stone of the fort was laid. Kota didn't reach its present size until well into the 17th century, when Rao Madho Singh, a son of the ruler of Bundi, was made ruler of Kota by the Mughal emperor Jehangir. Subsequent rulers all added to the fort and palaces, and each also contributed to making Kota a flourishing centre of art and culture. In 1624 Kota became a separate state and it remained so until it was integrated into Rajasthan after Independence.

Today Kota serves as an army headquarters and is also Rajasthan's prime industrial centre, powered by the hydroelectric plants on the Chambal River – the only permanent river in Rajasthan – and a nearby nuclear plant. The polluted cityscape is tempered by the leafy parks scattered throughout the town and an artificial lake with an enchanting palace on a little island in the middle.

Kota is well known for its saris, which are woven at the nearby village of Kaithoon. Known as Kota *doria* saris, they are made of cotton or silk in an assortment of colours, many with delicate golden thread designs.

Orientation & Information

Kota is strung out along the eastern bank of the Chambal River. The train station is well to the north; a number of hotels and the bus stand are in the centre and the Chambal gardens and fort are to the south.

The Tourist Reception Centre (☎ 327695) is in the grounds of the RTDC Hotel Chambal. It's open from 10 am to 5 pm Monday to Saturday. The State Bank of Bikaner & Jaipur at Industrial Estate (opposite Rajasthan Patrika) changes travellers cheques and currency. The State Bank of India changes AmEx travellers cheques, as well as major currencies.

City Palace & Fort

Beside the Kota Barrage, overlooking the Chambal River, the City Palace and fort is one of the largest such complexes in Rajasthan. The palace itself was the former residence of the Kota rulers and used to be the centre of power. Some of its buildings are now occupied by schools. Entry is from the south side through the **Naya Darwaza**, or New Gate.

The **Rao Madho Singh Museum**, in the City Palace, is impressive. It's on the right-hand side of the complex's huge central courtyard and is entered through a gateway topped by elephants. Inside, you'll find weapons, old costumes and some of the best-preserved murals in Rajasthan. The pieces are well displayed and it's an enjoyable place to take in the history of the region. The museum is open from 10 am to 4.30 pm daily except Friday. Entry is Rs 7/50 for Indians/foreigners, Rs 50/75 for a camera/video.

After visiting the museum, wander at leisure around the rest of the complex just to appreciate how magnificent it must have been in its heyday before its all-too-obvious decline. Some of the exterior murals are fading, possibly as a result of Kota's pollution problems.

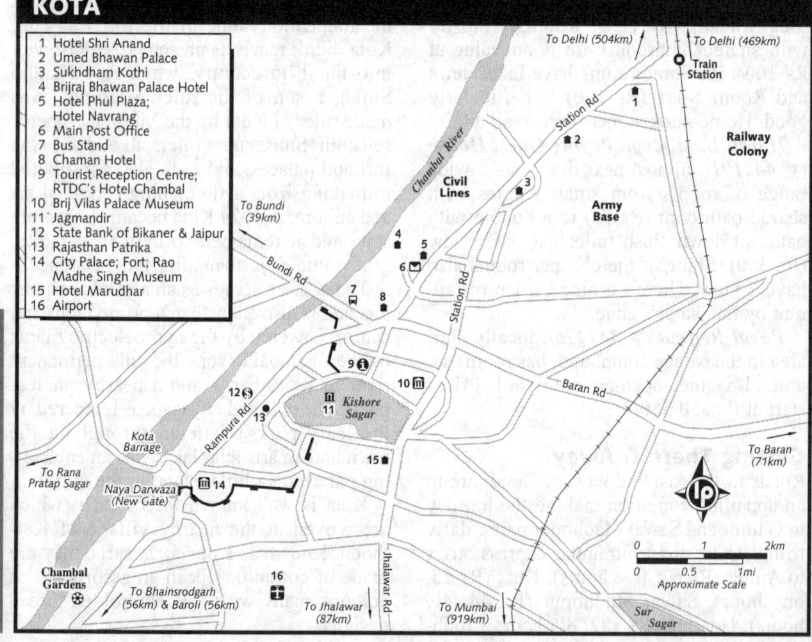

Jagmandir

Between the City Palace and the RTDC Hotel Chambal is the picturesque tank **Kishore Sagar**, constructed in 1346. On a small island in the middle of the tank is the beguiling palace of Jagmandir. Built in 1740 by a maharani of Kota, it's best seen early in the morning but is exquisite at any time. It's not currently open to the public but you can get a closer look by going on a boat (10 am to 5 pm daily except Monday). It costs Rs 60 to hire an entire boat for a 15-minute ride.

Brij Vilas Palace Museum

Near Kishore Sagar, this small museum is not as good as the City Palace Museum. It has a collection of stone idols and other sculptural fragments, mainly from the archaeological sites at Baroli and Jhalawar. There are also some weapons, paintings and old manuscripts. It's open from 10 am to 4.30 pm daily except Friday; entry is Rs 3 (free Mondays). Photography is prohibited.

Gardens

Kota has several well-maintained gardens – a welcome sight in this industrial town. On the banks of the Chambal River, south of the fort, are the **Chambal Gardens**. The centrepiece is a murky pond stocked with crocodiles. Once common all along the river, by the middle of the 20th century, crocodiles had been virtually exterminated through hunting. There are also some rare gharials (thin-snouted fish-eating crocodiles).

Beside the RTDC Hotel Chambal are the **Chhattar Bilas Gardens**, a collection of neglected but impressive royal cenotaphs.

Special Events

The celebration of **Dussehra Mela** to commemorate the victory of Rama over Ravana has a special significance in Kota, where festivities take the form of a large mela, or fair. The festival will commence on 24 October 2001, 13 October 2002, 3 October 2003, and 20 October 2004, and runs for three days.

Places to Stay & Eat

Budget accommodation is limited and lacklustre and mosquitos can be a problem. On the footpath outside the main post office, omelette and ***snack stalls*** set up in the early evening. If you do eat here, select food that has been freshly cooked, not reheated.

Hotel Navrang *(☎ 323294, fax 450044)*, near the main post office, is much better than the exterior suggests. The rooms (some with more character than others) all have private bathroom and are arranged around an inner courtyard. Singles/doubles cost Rs 300/400 with air-cooling, or Rs 650/880 with air-con. There's a reasonably priced veg restaurant.

Hotel Phul Plaza *(☎ 329350, fax 322614)*, next door, offers a range of rooms, all with private bathroom, starting at Rs 275/350. There's also a good veg restaurant with most dishes under Rs 40.

Hotel Shri Anand *(☎ 441157)*, a fairyfloss-pink building 100m along the street opposite the train station, is useful if you're catching an early morning train. The rooms are tiny and could be cleaner, but are cheap at Rs 150/200 with private bathroom and squat toilet. Veg meals are available.

Hotel Marudhar *(☎ 326186, fax 324415, Jhalawar Rd)* is between the fort and Kishore Sagar and is also has painted pink. Small rooms with bathroom cost Rs 225/250, or Rs 350/400 with air-con. This hotel fronts a busy road, so ask for a quiet room.

RTDC Hotel Chambal *(☎ 326527)* at Nayapura, near Kishore Sagar, has bland air-cooled rooms with private bathroom for Rs 300/350, or Rs 500/550 with carpet and air-con. There's a small restaurant; a veg thali is Rs 55 and chicken curry is Rs 60.

Chaman Hotel *(☎ 323377, Station Rd)* is closer to the bus stand. It's one of the cheapest hotels in town, but be prepared for grubby sheets and rooms the size of cupboards. Single female travellers are advised to give this place a miss. Rooms with private bathroom cost Rs 80/120; Rs 150/200 gets you a colour TV and geyser hot water. You can get a veg thali for Rs 30.

The modest ***Brijraj Bhawan Palace Hotel*** *(☎ 450529, fax 450057)*, on an elevated site overlooking the Chambal River, is Kota's most interesting hotel. Named after the current maharaja of Kota, Brijraj Singh (who still lives here), this serene place has attractive rooms for Rs 1050/1450, and a magnificent suite for Rs 1800. Unlike most palaces, this one is more homey than grand. There's a cosy dining room; the set lunch or dinner is Rs 240 (guests only).

Umed Bhawan Palace *(☎ 325262, fax 451110, Station Rd)* is more grandiose than the Brijraj Bhawan Palace, although closer inspection reveals lack of attention to detail. Surrounded by sprawling gardens, this gracious palace has a restaurant, a bar and a billiard room. The cheapest rooms cost Rs 1190/1790. There are also luxury rooms for Rs 1390/2190 and the royal chamber for Rs 1990/2990.

Sukhdham Kothi *(☎ 320081, fax 327781)* has comfortable rooms starting at Rs 735/875. Set in grounds in Civil Lines, this building is over 100 years old. It offers discounts of up to 30% when things are quiet. The set breakfast/lunch/dinner is Rs 110/200/225.

Getting There & Away

There are express buses to Ajmer (Rs 75, six hours), Chittorgarh (Rs 73, six hours), Jaipur (Rs 95, six hours), Udaipur (Rs 90, six hours), Jodhpur (Rs 175, 11 hours) and Bikaner (Rs 175, 12 hours). Buses leave for Bundi every half hour (Rs 15, 50 minutes).

Kota is on the main broad-gauge Mumbai-Delhi line via Sawai Madhopur, so there are plenty of trains to choose from. For Sawai Madhopur, the 108km journey takes around two hours (Rs 36/56/183, general/sleeper/3A class). The 8½-hour trip to Delhi costs Rs 105/163/473 and the 16-hour journey to Mumbai costs Rs 167/259/1203 in general/sleeper/2A class.

Getting Around

Minibuses link the train station and the bus stand (Rs 2). An autorickshaw should cost Rs 15 for this journey. Cycle-rickshaws are a cheaper option.

AROUND KOTA

Baroli

One of Rajasthan's oldest temple complexes is at Baroli, 56km south-west of Kota. Many of these 9th-century temples were vandalised by Muslim armies, but much remains. The best-preserved temple, Ghateshvara Temple, features impressive columns, although some of the figures have been damaged. Many of the sculptures from the temples are displayed in the Brij Vilas Palace Museum in Kota.

There are hourly buses from Kota to Baroli (Rs 15, 1½ hours). These leave from the Gumanpura bus stand, near the petrol pump.

Jhalrapatan

Jhalrapatan (City of Temple Bells), 94km south of Kota, contains the ruins of a huge 10th-century **Surya temple** which has impressive sculptures as well as one of the best-preserved idols of Surya (the sun god) in India. The 12th-century **Shantinath Jain Temple** is also worth visiting, as is the imposing **Gagron Fort**, 10km from nearby Jhalawar, which has a few accommodation options.

Every year Jhalrapatan hosts the **Chandrabhaga Fair**, a cattle fair and a chance for thousands of pilgrims to bathe in the holy Chandrabhaga River. It starts on 18 November 2002, 7 November 2003, and 25 November 2004, and lasts three or four days.

There are semiregular buses between Jhalawar and Kota (Rs 38, 2½ hours)

CHITTORGARH (CHITTOR)

☎ 01472 • pop 87,400

The sprawling hilltop fort of Chittorgarh, also known as Chittor, is one of the most historically significant in Rajasthan and epitomises the whole romantic, doomed ideal of Rajput chivalry. Three times in its long history, Chittor was sacked by a stronger enemy, and on each occasion, the end came in textbook Rajput fashion: Jauhar was declared in the face of impossible odds. The men donned the saffron robes of martyrdom and rode out from the fort to certain death, while the women consigned themselves to the flames on a huge funeral pyre. Honour was always more important than death and Chittor still holds a special place in the hearts of many Rajputs.

Despite the rugged fort's impressive location and colourful history, Chittor is off the main tourist circuit and sees surprisingly few visitors. If you're pressed for time, it's possible to squeeze in a visit to Chittor on a day trip from Udaipur. It's well worth the detour.

History

Chittor's first defeat occurred in 1303 when Ala-ud-din Khilji, the Pathan king of Delhi, besieged the fort in order to capture the beautiful Padmini, wife of the rana of Chittor's uncle. When defeat was inevitable the Rajput noblewomen, including Padmini, committed jauhar and Bhim Singh led the orange-clad noblemen out to their deaths.

In 1535 Bahadur Shah, the sultan of Gujarat, besieged the fort, and once again, the medieval dictates of chivalry determined the outcome. This time, the carnage was immense. It is said that 13,000 Rajput women and 32,000 Rajput warriors died following the declaration of jauhar.

The final sack of Chittor came 33 years later, in 1568, when the Mughal emperor Akbar took the town. The fort was defended heroically, against overwhelming odds. The women performed jauhar, the fort gates were flung open and 8000 orange-robed warriors rode out to their deaths. On this occasion, Maharaja Udai Singh II fled Chittor for Udaipur, where he re-established his capital. In 1616, Jehangir returned Chittor to the Rajputs but there was no resettlement.

Orientation & Information

The fort stands on a 280-hectare site on top of a 180m-high hill, which rises abruptly from the surrounding plain. Until 1568 the town of Chittor was also on the hilltop, within the fort walls, but today's modern town, known as Lower Town, sprawls to the west of the hill. A river separates it from the bus stand, the railway line and the rest of the town.

The Tourist Reception Centre (☎ 41089) is near the train station and is open from 10 am to 1 pm and 2 to 5 pm Monday to Saturday. The State Bank of Bikaner & Jaipur, a short distance north of the main post office, is sometimes reluctant to change money.

Fort

According to legend, Bhim, one of the Pandava heroes of the Mahabharata, is credited with the fort's original construction. All of Chittor's attractions are within the fort. A zigzag ascent of over 1km leads through seven gateways to the main gate on the western side, the **Rampol**.

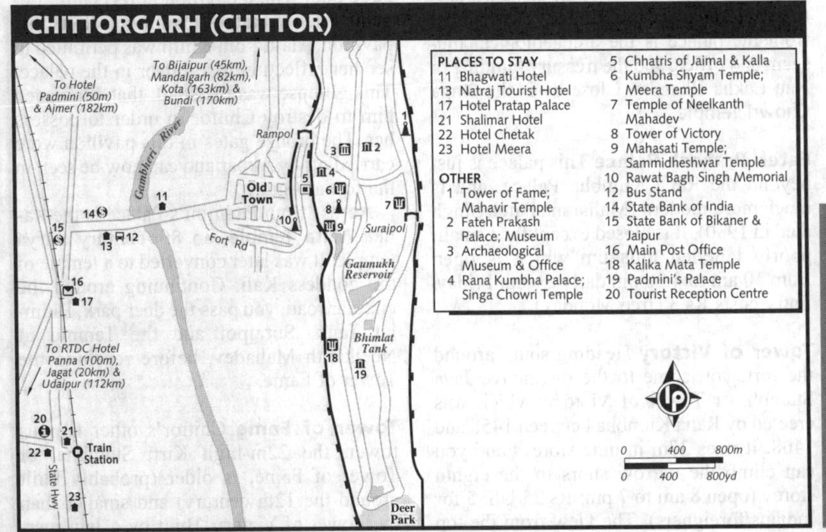

RAJASTHAN

On the climb, you pass two **chhatris**, memorials marking spots where Jaimal and Kalla, heroes of the 1568 siege, fell during the struggle against Akbar. The main gate on the eastern side of the fort is the **Surajpol**. Within the fort, a circular road runs around the ruins and there's a **deer park** at the southern end. From the western end, there are fine views over the town and across the surrounding countryside, as well as a less-than-charming view of the huge cement factory.

Today, the fort of Chittor is a virtually deserted ruin, but impressive reminders of its grandeur still stand. The main sites in the fort can all be seen in half a day (assuming you're not walking), but if you like the atmosphere of ancient sites, then it's definitely worth spending longer as this is a very mellow place. Entry to the fort is free. Guides are available inside the fort, usually at the Rana Kumbha Palace; they charge around Rs 200.

Rana Kumbha Palace After entering the fort and turning right, you come almost immediately to the ruins of this 15th-century palace. It contains elephant and horse stables and a Shiva temple. One of the jauhars is said to have taken place in a vaulted cellar. Across from the palace is the archaeological museum and office, and the treasury building or Nau Lakha Bhandar. Close by is the **Singa Chowri Temple**.

Fateh Prakash Palace This palace is just beyond the Rana Kumbha Palace, and is much more modern (Maharana Fateh Singh died in 1930). It is closed except for a small, poorly labelled **museum** which is open from 10 am to 4.30 pm daily except Friday. Entry costs Rs 3 (free Monday).

Tower of Victory Heading south around the fort, you come to the distinctive Jaya Stambh, or Tower of Victory, which was erected by Rana Kumbha between 1458 and 1468. It rises 37m in nine storeys and you can climb the narrow stairs to the eighth storey (open 8 am to 7 pm; Rs 25/US$5 for Indians/foreigners). The view from the top is good but probably not worth it, especially as the exterior, with its exquisite Hindu sculptures, is most impressive; wandering around the base is free. The dome was damaged by lightning and repaired during the 19th century. Watch your head on the lintels if you do decide to climb!

Close to the tower is the Mahasati, an area where the ranas were cremated during Chittorgarh's period as the Mewar capital. (Mewar is the area encompassing Chittorgarh and Udaipur.) There are many *sati* stones here, commemorating women who burned on their husbands' funeral pyres. The impressive **Sammidheshwar Temple** stands in the same area.

Gaumukh Reservoir Walk down beyond the temple, and at the very edge of the cliff, you'll see this deep tank. A spring feeds the tank from a cow's mouth carved in the cliff, from which the reservoir got its name. The opening here leads to the cave in which Padmini and her compatriots are said to have committed jauhar.

Padmini's Palace Continuing south, you come to Padmini's Palace, built beside a large pool with a pavilion in its centre. Legend relates that as Padmini sat in this pavilion, Ala-ud-din Khilji was permitted to see her reflection in a mirror in the palace. This glimpse was the spark that convinced him to destroy Chittor in order to possess her. The bronze gates in this pavilion were carried off by Akbar and can now be seen in the fort at Agra.

Across from Padmini's Palace is the **Kalika Mata Temple**, an 8th-century Surya temple. It was later converted to a temple of the goddess Kali. Continuing around the circular road, you pass the deer park, Bhimlat Tank, Surajpol and the Temple of Neelkanth Mahadev, before reaching the Tower of Fame.

Tower of Fame Chittor's other famous tower, the 22m-high Kirti Stambha, or Tower of Fame, is older (probably built around the 12th century) and smaller than the Tower of Victory. Built by a Jain merchant, it is dedicated to Adinath, the first *tirthankar* (revered Jain teacher), and is decorated with naked figures of the various tirthankars, thus indicating that it is a *digambara* (sky-clad) monument. A narrow stairway leads through the seven storeys to the top. The door is usually locked, and the gatekeeper will open it for a small tip.

Other Buildings Close to the Rana Kumbha Palace is the **Meera Temple**, built during the reign of Rana Kumbha in the ornate Indo-Aryan style and associated with the mystic-poetess Meerabai. The larger temple in this same compound is the **Kumbha Shyam Temple**, or Temple of Varah.

At the northern tip of the fort is another gate, the **Lokhota Bari**, while at the southern end is a small opening from which criminals and traitors were hurled into the abyss.

Places to Stay & Eat

Hotel standards in Chittor are generally disappointing: Cleanliness and service are below average, many of the cheaper places have miserable bathrooms with squat toilets, all are impossibly noisy, and most are places where lone women will feel uncomfortable. Apart from that, they're fine.

***Shalimar Hotel** (☎ 40842)*, next to the train station, has dull singles/doubles for Rs 125/175 with private bathroom. Hot water is by the bucket (no charge).

***Hotel Chetak** (☎ 41588)*, nearby, is somewhat better, with rooms starting at Rs 150/275 with private bathroom. Deluxe rooms cost Rs 300/400, or Rs 400/500 with air-con. Some rooms are a bit airless. There's a restaurant downstairs serving vegetarian Indian, South Indian and Chinese food. A veg thali costs Rs 35.

***Hotel Meera** (☎ 40266)*, in the same area, is a reasonable option in this town low on hotel talent. Rooms with private bathroom range from Rs 250/325 to 700/800, plus an additional 'government tax' which none of the other hotels seem to know about. The rooms are a tad sterile but most have geyser hot water. Meals are available.

***Natraj Tourist Hotel** (☎ 41009)*, right by the bus stand, is basic, grubby and cheap. Small, dark rooms cost Rs 40/60 with shared bathroom, or Rs 60/100 with private bathroom; but you'll probably have to get the staff to change the sheets. If you want geyser hot water, you pay Rs 125/175. No meals are available.

***Bhagwati Hotel** (☎ 46226)*, just over the river, is only marginally better than the Natraj. Simple rooms with private bathroom and bucket hot water cost Rs 100/150.

***RTDC Hotel Panna** (☎ 41238)* is closer to town (ie, farther away from the fort). Dorm beds are Rs 50, and slapdash rooms with private bathroom start at Rs 150/250. Better air-cooled rooms are Rs 300/400. The hotel has a seedy little bar and a restaurant (the veg/nonveg thali is Rs 45/55).

***Hotel Pratap Palace** (☎/fax 40099)* is one of the most popular places to stay. Air-cooled rooms with private bathroom cost upwards of Rs 550/625. Rooms starting at Rs 850 are slightly better, but overpriced. There's a restaurant near the pleasant garden; a half tandoori chicken costs Rs 100, and *malai kofta* (meat or vegetable balls in a creamy sauce) is Rs 35. Village safaris can be arranged, as can visits to the castle-cum-hotel run by the same owners in Bijaipur (see Around Chittorgarh).

***Hotel Padmini** (☎ 41718, fax 47115)* is a little out of town near the Bearch River, but is the best and quietest place in Chittor. Pleasant air-cooled rooms cost Rs 490/600; nicer but overpriced air-con rooms cost Rs 1000/1200. Some rooms have a balcony, and discounts of up to 15% are available if things are quiet. The veg restaurant serves Punjabi, South Indian and Chinese food; *palak paneer* (soft, unfermented cheese in a spicy gravy of pureed spinach) is Rs 35.

Getting There & Away

Bus Express buses travel to Delhi (Rs 225, 14 hours, one bus daily at 8.45 pm), Ajmer (Rs 75, four hours), Jaipur (Rs 125, eight hours) and Bundi (Rs 68, 4½ hours).

Train The *Jaipur Express* (9770) leaves Chittor at 5.50 am, arriving in Jaipur at 2 pm (Rs 79/123/580, general/sleeper/2A class). The *Ajmer Express* (9672) leaves at an ungodly 3 am (Rs 53/83/426). For Udaipur, the *Chetak Express* (9615) leaves at 6.50 am, arriving at 10.25 am (Rs 36/56/350). Going the other way, it departs at 10 pm and arrives in Delhi at 1.10 pm (Rs 132/205/951). The *Ahmedabad Express* (9943) leaves Chittor at 1.45 pm, arriving in Ahmedabad at 6.35 am (Rs 95/148/684).

Getting Around

Autorickshaws charge around Rs 100 for a trip from the bus station area, around the fort compound, and back again (including waiting time at the various sites). A rickshaw between the bus and train stations should cost around Rs 15.

Bicycles can be rented near the train station (Rs 30 per day) to visit the fort, but as many Indian bikes lack gears, you may have to push the machine to the top. Still, they're great on the top and for the journey back down – check the brakes first!

AROUND CHITTORGARH

In **Bijaipur**, 45km from Chittor, ***Castle Bijaipur*** is a converted 16th-century palace with pleasant rooms from Rs 800/850 to 1350/1500. It's an ideal place to kick back with a good book, do yoga, meditate, walk or do absolutely nothing! The friendly owners can organise horse and jeep safaris to villages such as the nearby Bhil tribal village, or you can see local craftspeople at work in **Bassi** village, 12km from Bijaipur – they specialise in wooden handicrafts. Reservations should be made through the Hotel Pratap Palace in Chittor (☎/fax 01472-40099). There are frequent daily buses from Chittor to Bijaipur (Rs 20, 1½ hours).

On the Bundi to Chittorgarh road, 48km from Bundi, **Menal** is a complex of Shiva temples built in the Gupta period. After a good monsoon, there's an impressive waterfall in this area that's also a big attraction.

A detour between Menal and Bijolia takes you to **Mandalgarh**. It is the third fort of Mewar built by Rana Kumbha – the others are at Chittorgarh and Kumbhalgarh.

One of the oldest towns in Rajasthan, **Nagri** is 17km north of Chittor. Hindu and Buddhist remains from the Mauryan to the Gupta periods have been found here.

UDAIPUR

☎ 0294 • pop 378,000

Possibly no city in Rajasthan is quite as romantic as Udaipur. The French Impressionist painters, let alone the Brothers Grimm, would have loved this place. It's not without justification that Udaipur has been called the Venice of the East, and the old city is a jumble of tangled streets.

Founded in 1568 by Maharaja Udai Singh II following the final sacking of Chittorgarh by the Mughal emperor Akbar, Udaipur rivals any of the world-famous creations of the Mughals with its Rajput love of the whimsical and its superbly crafted elegance. The Lake Palace is certainly the best late example of this unique cultural explosion, but Udaipur is full of palaces, temples and havelis ranging from the modest to the extravagant. It's also proud of its heritage as a centre for the performing arts, painting and crafts.

In common with most Indian cities, Udaipur's urban and industrial sprawl goes beyond the city's original boundaries, and pollution of various kinds can be discouraging. This will be your first impression of Udaipur if you arrive at the train or bus stations. Ignore it and head for the old city where a different world awaits.

The Mewar Festival is a great time to be in town, with the women of Udaipur dressing up in their finest. It commences on 15 April 2002, 4 April 2003, and 23 March 2004, and runs for two days.

Orientation

The old city, bounded by the remains of a city wall, is on the east side of Lake Pichola. The train station and bus stand are both just outside the city wall to the south-east.

Information

Tourist Offices The Tourist Reception Centre (☎ 411535) is in the Fateh Memorial Building near Surajpol, less than a kilometre from the bus stand. The office is open from 10 am to 1.30 pm and 2 to 5 pm Monday to Saturday (closed the second Saturday of every month). A more accessible source of information is *Out & About in Udaipur*, an extremely informative magazine available in most bookshops (Rs 10), or ask at your hotel.

Money You can change money at a number of places including the Vijaya Bank and Thomas Cook, both in the City Palace complex. A couple of hundred metres south-east of Delhi Gate, the Bank of Baroda changes US dollars and British pounds and issues cash advances against Visa, MasterCard and Bobcard (an Indian bank card). It's open 10 am to 2.30 pm Monday to Friday, 10 am to 12.30 pm Saturday. You can also get cash advances on Visa and MasterCard at the Vijaya Bank (open 10 am to 2 pm Monday to Friday, and 10 am to noon Saturday). LKP Forex (☎ 524746), next to the Rang Niwas Palace Hotel on Lake Palace Rd, changes all major (and many 'minor') currencies with a minimum of fuss.

Post & Communications The main post office is directly north of the old city, at Chetak Circle, but the poste restante is at the post office at Shastri Circle. There's also a small post office in the quadrant outside the City Palace Museum. The DHL Worldwide Express office (☎/fax 414388) is at 380 Ashok Nagar, Shree Niketan Building (near Ayer Bridge). It even has a free collection service within Udaipur.

There are loads of places where you can surf the Internet, particularly in the Jagdish Temple area. Expect to pay around Rs 1 per minute. Mewar International (One Stop Shop; ☎ 419810) has the fastest connections (some readers have warned of overcharging on its bus and train bookings).

Dangers & Annoyances If you do have any complaints about rickshaw drivers (note the registration number) or hotels, contact the police on ☎ 413949 (☎ 100 in the case of an emergency) or report it to the Tourist Reception Centre.

Lake Pichola

Placid Lake Pichola was enlarged by Maharaja Udai Singh II after he founded the city. He built a masonry dam, known as the Badipol, and the lake is now 4km in length and 3km wide. Nevertheless, it remains fairly shallow and can dry up in severe droughts. Fortunately, this doesn't happen often. The City Palace extends a considerable distance along the east bank of the lake. North of the palace, you can wander along the lakeshore, where there are some interesting bathing and *dhobi* (laundry) ghats.

Despite being the centrepiece for much of Udaipur's fairytale beauty, there is, inevitably, a downside to this paradise. A close look around the shores of Lake Pichola will reveal a growing collection of rubbish fed primarily by the proliferation of hotels in the area. The lake can also sometimes get choked with water hyacinth.

Out in the lake are two islands – Jagniwas and Jagmandir. **Boat rides**, which leave regularly (10 am to 4 pm) from the City Palace jetty (known as Bansi Ghat), are popular. These cost Rs 100 for half an hour, or Rs 200 for one hour (the latter rate includes a visit to Jagmandir Island). Tickets must be bought at the booth along the road running south of the City Palace, about 100m west of Samor Bagh Restaurant.

Jagniwas Island Jagniwas, the Lake Palace island, is about 1.5 hectares in size. The palace was built by Maharaja Jagat Singh II in 1754 and covers the whole island. Formerly the royal summer palace, today it is the ultimate in luxury hotels, with shady courtyards, lotus ponds and even a small swimming pool shaded by mango trees. Yes, this is the perfect place to fall in love, but casual visitors are not encouraged. Nonguests can only come over for lunch or dinner – and then only if the hotel is not full, which it often is. Bookings are essential and you will not be allowed on the boat unless you pay for your meal at the jetty where your name will be on the list. Hotel launches cross to the island from the City Palace jetty. The Lake Palace, along with the Shiv Niwas Palace and Monsoon Palace in Udaipur, were used as sets in the James Bond movie *Octopussy*.

Jagmandir Island The other island palace, Jagmandir, was commenced by Maharaja

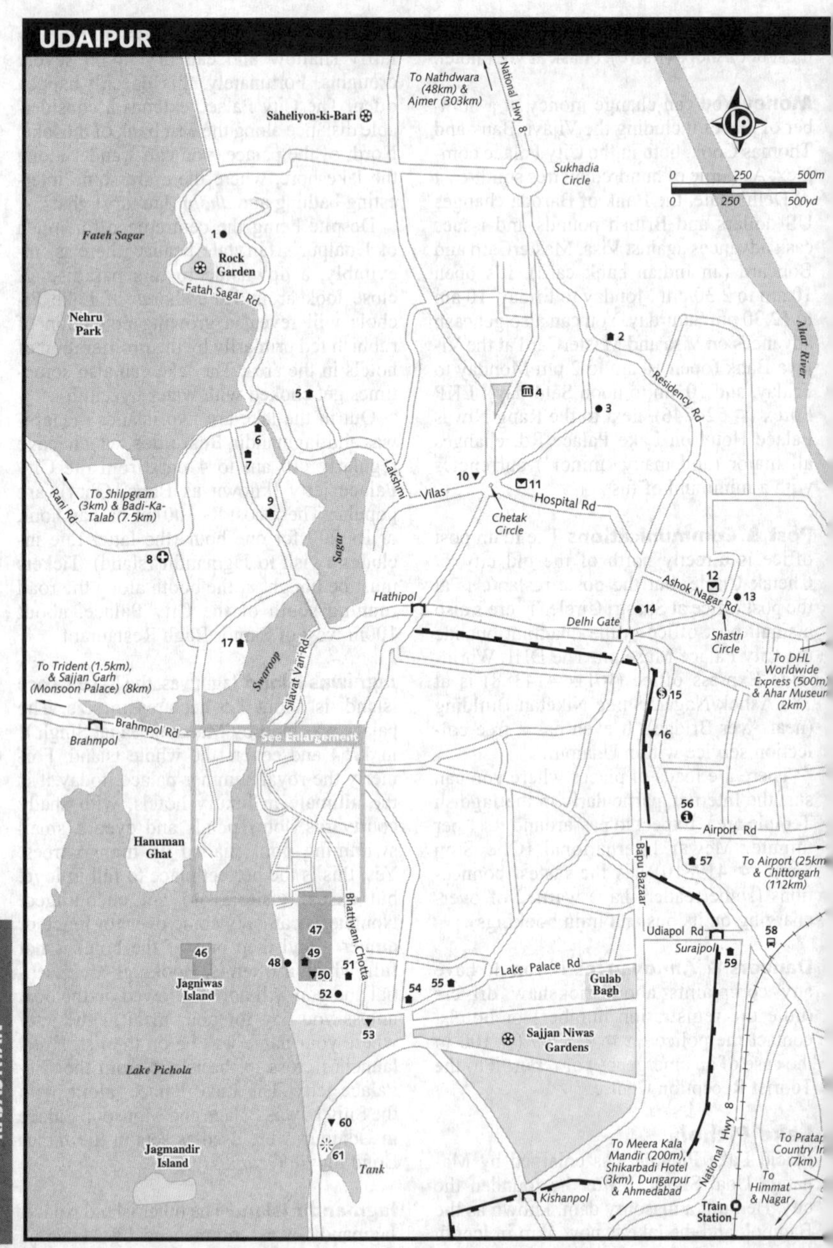
UDAIPUR
To Nathdwara (48km) & Ajmer (303km)
National Hwy 8
Saheliyon-ki-Bari
Sukhadia Circle
0 250 500m
0 250 500yd
Fateh Sagar
Rock Garden
Fatah Sagar Rd
Nehru Park
Ahar River
Residency Rd
Lakshmi Vilas
To Shilpgram (3km) & Badi-Ka-Talab (7.5km)
Rani Rd
Chetak Circle
Hospital Rd
Sagar
Hathipol
Ashok Nagar Rd
Delhi Gate
Shastri Circle
Swaroop
Silavat Vari Rd
To Trident (1.5km), & Sajjan Garh (Monsoon Palace) (8km)
To DHL Worldwide Express (500m) & Ahar Museum (2km)
Brahmpol Rd
Brahmpol
See Enlargement
Airport Rd
Hanuman Ghat
Bapu Bazaar
To Airport (25km) & Chittorgarh (112km)
Bhattiyani Chotta
Udiapol Rd
Surajpol
Lake Palace Rd
Jagniwas Island
Gulab Bagh
Sajjan Niwas Gardens
Lake Pichola
Jagmandir Island
Tank
To Meera Kala Mandir (200m), Shikarbadi Hotel (3km), Dungarpur & Ahmedabad
Kishanpol
National Hwy 8
To Pratap Country Inn (7km)
To Himmat Nagar
Train Station

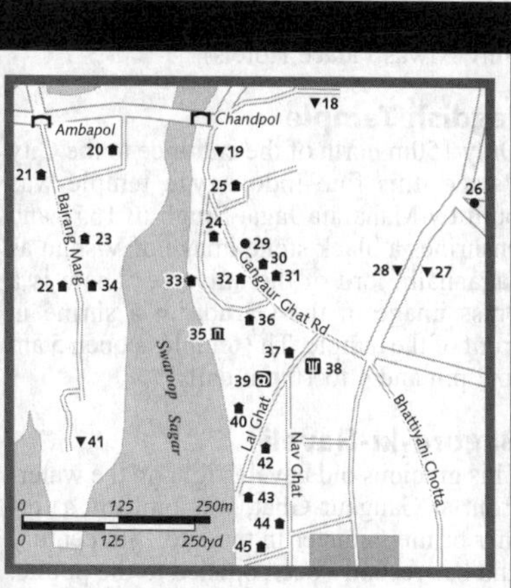

PLACES TO STAY
2 Mewar Inn
5 Laxmi Vilas Palace Hotel
6 Hotel Ram Pratap Palace
7 Hotel Hilltop Palace
9 Pahadi Palace
17 Hotel Natural
20 Dream Heaven Guest House
21 Queen Cafe & Guest House
22 Udai Kothi
23 Hotel Sarovar
24 Hotel Minerwa
25 Nukkad Guest House
30 Anjani Hotel
31 Hotel Badi Haveli; Lehar Paying Guest House; Heera Cycle Store
32 Hotel Gangaur Palace
33 Jheel Guest House
34 Lake Shore Hotel; Lake Pichola Hotel
36 Jag Niwas Guest House
37 Poonam Haveli; Coffee.com
40 Lalghat Guest House; Restaurant Natural View
42 Lake Ghat Guest House; Hotel Caravanserai; Ratan Palace Guest House
43 Kankarwa Haveli; Jagat Niwas Palace Hotel; Hotel Jagat Niwas & Restaurant
44 Shiva Guest House; Hotel Sai-Niwas
45 Lake Corner Soni Paying Guest House
46 Lake Palace Hotel
49 Shiv Niwas Palace Hotel; Fateh Prakash Palace Hotel & Gallery Restaurant
51 Hotel Raj Palace
54 Rang Niwas Palace Hotel; LKP Forex
55 Hotel Mahendra Prakash
57 Apsara Hotel
59 Parn Kulti Hotel

PLACES TO EAT
10 Berry's Restaurant
16 Park View
18 Savage Garden
19 Cafe Edelweiss
27 Anna Restaurant
28 Maxim's Cafe
41 Ambrai
50 Sunset View Terrace
53 Samor Bagh
60 Cafe Hill Park

OTHER
1 Pratap Smarak (Moti Magri)
3 Jet Airways
4 Bhartiya Lok Kala Museum
8 Madan Mohan Malvai Ayurvedic College & Hospital
11 Main Post Office
12 Poste Restante
13 RTDC Hotel Kajri
14 Indian Airlines
15 Bank of Baroda
26 Clock Tower
29 Prem Musical Instruments
35 Bagore-ki-Haveli
38 Jagdish Temple
39 Mewar International
47 City Palace; Museums; Vijaya Bank; Thomas Cook; Heritage Hotels Reservation Office
48 City Palace Jetty (Bansi Ghat)
52 Boat Ride Ticket Office
56 Tourist Reception Centre
58 Bus Stand
61 Sunset Point

Karan Singh, but takes its name from Maharaja Jagat Singh (1628–52) who made a number of additions to it. It is said that the Mughal emperor Shah Jahan derived some of his inspiration for the Taj Mahal from this palace after staying here in 1623–24 while leading a revolt against his father, Jehangir. Flanked by a row of enormous stone elephants, the island has an impressive chhatri carved from grey-blue stone. The view across the lake to the city and its glorious golden palace is a scene of rare beauty.

City Palace & Museums

The imposing City Palace, towering over the lake, is the largest palace complex in Rajasthan. Actually a conglomeration of buildings added by various maharajas, it still manages to retain a surprising uniformity of design. Building was started by Maharaja Udai Singh II, the city's founder. The palace is surmounted by balconies, towers and cupolas and there are fine views over the lake and the city from the upper terraces.

The palace is entered from the northern end through the Baripol (built 1600) and the Tripolia Gate (1725), with its eight carved marble arches. It was once a custom for maharajas to be weighed under the gate and for their weight in gold or silver to be distributed to the populace.

The main part of the palace is now preserved as a museum. It includes the **Mor Chowk** with its beautiful mosaics of peacocks, the favourite Rajasthani bird. The **Manak Mahal** (Ruby Mahal) has glasswork and mirrorwork, while **Krishna Vilas** has a remarkable collection of miniatures (no photography allowed). In the **Bari Mahal**, there is a pleasant central garden. The **Moti Mahal** has beautiful mirrorwork and the **Chini Mahal** is covered in ornamental tiles. There's an armoury section downstairs. More paintings can be seen in the **Zenana Mahal**. There's a large tiger-catching cage near the Zenana Mahal entrance, and a tiny World Wide Fund for Nature shop nearby.

The museum is open 9.30 am to 4.30 pm daily and entry is Rs 35. Enter from the north side (up the hill from the Jagdish Temple) unless you also want to pay the

Rs 75 visitor fee. It costs Rs 75 to take a camera in, and a whopping Rs 300 for a video camera. A guide (Rs 70 for up to five people) is worthwhile; guides for non-Indian languages cost an extra Rs 25.

There's also a **government museum** (entry costs Rs 3, free Monday) within the palace complex. Exhibits include a stuffed kangaroo, a freaky monkey holding a small lamp, and Siamese-twin deer. There's also more serious stuff such as sculptures and paintings. In the large courtyard outside the City Palace Museum are a number of pricey handicraft shops, a money-exchange facility, a kiosk and places to buy film.

The other part of the palace is against the lakeshore and has been partly converted into two luxury hotels: the Shiv Niwas Palace and the Fateh Prakash Palace (see Places to Stay – Top End).

There's a stunning **crystal gallery** at the Fateh Prakash Palace Hotel in the City Palace complex. This rare collection of Osler's crystal was ordered from England by Maharaja Sajjan Singh in 1877. Items include crystal chairs, tables and even beds! It's open 10 am to 1 pm and 3 to 8 pm daily; entry (Rs 250) includes a soft drink, coffee or tea. No photography is allowed.

The Crystal Gallery overlooks the grandiose **durbar hall** with its massive chandeliers and striking portraits of former maharajas of Mewar. Entry is Rs 50 (free for guests of the Fateh Prakash Palace and Shiv Niwas Palace Hotels).

Jagdish Temple

Only 150m north of the entrance to the City Palace, this fine Indo-Aryan temple was built by Maharaja Jagat Singh in 1651 and enshrines a black stone image of Vishnu as Jagannath, lord of the universe. There is a brass image of the Garuda in a shrine in front of the temple. The temple is open 5 am to 2 pm and 4 to 10 pm daily.

Bagore-ki-Haveli

This gracious old haveli, right on the waterfront at Gangaur Ghat, was built by a former prime minister in the late 18th century and has recently been opened to the public. There are more than 100 rooms as well as courtyards, terraces and elegant balconies. The mirrorwork and glasswork are quite lovely, as are the frescoes in the Chambers of the Royal Ladies. It's open 10 am to 5 pm daily and entry is Rs 10.

Fateh Sagar

North of Lake Pichola, this lake is overlooked by a number of hills and is a popular hang-out for young lovers. It was originally built in 1678 by Maharaja Jai Singh, but after heavy rains destroyed the dam, it was reconstructed by Maharaja Fateh Singh. In the middle of the lake is

Durbar Hall

Many Indian palaces have a durbar hall, or hall of audience. Historically, the durbar hall was used by rulers for official occasions such as state banquets and to hold formal or informal meetings. The restored durbar hall in Udaipur is undoubtedly one of the most impressive, with a lavish interior boasting some of the largest chandeliers in India. The walls display royal weapons and striking portraits of former maharajas of Mewar (a most distinguished-looking lot). The illustrious Mewar rulers come from what is believed to be the oldest ruling dynasty in the world, spanning 76 generations.

The foundation stone of the durbar hall was laid in 1909 by Lord Minto, the viceroy of India, during the reign of Maharaja Fateh Singh. As a mark of respect to Lord Minto, it was originally named Minto Hall. The top floor of this hall with its high ceilings is surrounded by viewing galleries, where ladies of the palace could watch in veiled seclusion what was happening below.

Today, the durbar hall in Udaipur is open to visitors. It still has the capacity to hold hundreds of people and can even be hired for special functions, such as conferences or social gatherings – contact the Fateh Prakash Palace Hotel (☎ 528016, fax 528006).

Nehru Park, a garden island with a boat-shaped cafe. You can get there by boat from near the bottom of Moti Magri for Rs 10. An autorickshaw from the old city should cost around Rs 20 (one way).

Bhartiya Lok Kala Museum

This small museum (☎ 529296) is also a foundation for the preservation and promotion of local folk arts. Its exhibits include dolls, masks, musical instruments, paintings and – the high point – puppets. It is open 9 am to 5.30 pm daily; entry is Rs 10, plus Rs 20/50 for a camera/video. Puppet shows are staged daily at 1 and 6 pm (Rs 30).

Saheliyon-ki-Bari

The Saheliyon-ki-Bari, or Garden of the Maids of Honour, is in the north of the city. This ornamental garden, with its fountains, kiosks, marble elephants and delightful lotus pool, is open 9 am to 6 pm daily. Entry is Rs 5, plus Rs 5 to turn the fountains on.

Shilpgram

This crafts village, 3km west of Fateh Sagar, has displays of traditional houses from Rajasthan, Gujarat, Goa and Maharashtra. There are also demonstrations by musicians, dancers and artisans. Although it's much more animated during festival times (usually in early December, but check with the Tourist Reception Centre), there's usually something happening. It is open 11 am to 7 pm daily; entry is Rs 5/10 for Indians/foreigners. Near the site is a swimming pool (Rs 100), open 11 am to 4 pm daily.

A return autorickshaw trip (including a 30-minute stop) between the old city and Shilpgram is Rs 80.

Ahar Museum

About 2km east of Udaipur are the remains of an ancient city. The small collection at the museum here includes some earthen pottery. The museum is open 10 am to 5 pm daily except Friday; entry is Rs 2 (free Monday). No photography is allowed.

Nearby is an impressive cluster of **cenotaphs** of the maharanas of Mewar, which have been recently restored.

Sajjan Garh (Monsoon Palace)

On a distant mountain range, this neglected palace was constructed by Maharaja Sajjan Singh in the late 19th century. It is now owned by the government and is officially closed to the public, but the caretaker has been charging Rs 10 for so long that the fee might as well be official. You also pay Rs 40 per person at the foot of the hill to enter the Sajjan Garh Wildlife Sanctuary, plus Rs 15 for the rickshaw. The main reason to come here is to see the absolutely breathtaking views, particularly at sunset. The palace is illuminated at night and from a distance looks like something out of a fairy tale. The return trip by autorickshaw should cost Rs 180 (including waiting at the site).

Other Attractions

The **Sajjan Niwas Gardens** have pleasant lawns and a zoo – beware of unfriendly dogs here. Beside them is the Rose Garden, or **Gulab Bagh**. **Sunset Point**, not far from Cafe Hill Park, is lovely at sunset (entry Rs 5). There's a musical fountain here, which plays each evening.

Madan Mohan Malvai Ayurvedic College & Hospital at Ambamata Scheme, near Fateh Sagar, prescribes natural medicines and conducts courses in Ayurveda.

Almost 5km beyond Shilpgram is **Badi-ka-Talab**, also referred to as Tiger Lake. This mammoth artificial lake, flanked by hills, is a pleasant picnic spot. Crocodiles apparently lurk in parts of the lake, so swimmers beware!

Music Lessons

Bablu at Prem Musical Instruments (☎ 430 599) has been recommended by a number of travellers for sitar, tabla and flute lessons (around Rs 100 an hour). He also sells and repairs instruments and he can arrange performances.

Organised Tours

Five-hour city tours leave at 8 am daily from the RTDC Hotel Kajri, and cost Rs 73.50 (excluding entry to sites). Depending on demand, afternoon tours (2 to 7 pm) go out to Eklingji, Haldighati and

Nathdwara (see Around Udaipur) and cost Rs 105. Contact the Tourist Reception Centre for details. For information on boat tours, see Lake Pichola earlier in this section.

Places to Stay

The most romantic place to stay is the Lal Ghat area, close to the shores of the lake and west of the Jagdish Temple, where there's a good range of places to suit most budgets. Quieter, and often with even better views, are the handful of excellent hotels and guesthouses just across the water in Hanuman Ghat.

Getting to the accommodation of your choice has been made easier by the police-supervised prepaid autorickshaw stands outside the train and government bus stations. Some unscrupulous operators will still try to take you to the hotel of their choice, but remember, they don't get reimbursed until you hand over the receipt at the end of your journey.

The commission system is in place with a vengeance, so if you get a rickshaw driver who insists that the hotel of your choice has burnt down or suddenly closed, or the owner has died in a freak accident, politely decline his kind offer. Unless your rickshaw is prepaid, ask for the Jagdish Temple when arriving as it's a good place to start looking for accommodation.

Places to Stay – Budget

Lal Ghat Area If you're booking a hotel near Lake Pichola, ask for a lake-facing room (they usually cost a bit more). Most places have fabulous views over the lake and the central location is ideal. If you are staying in this area, actively encourage your hotel to dispose of all rubbish in an environmentally friendly manner to prevent this magnificent place from being spoiled.

Lalghat Guest House *(☎ 525301, fax 418508, 33 Lal Ghat)*, right by the lake, is a mellow place to hang out with other travellers. The rooftop areas (popular for sunbathing) have excellent views over the lake and there's a back terrace which overlooks the ghats. A variety of rooms are available, including dorm beds for Rs 50, small singles/doubles with shared bathroom for Rs 75/100, larger doubles for Rs 150, or rooms with private bathroom for Rs 200/250. The best double room costs Rs 350. All the rooms have fans and mosquito nets. There is a small kitchen for self-caterers.

Hotel Gangaur Palace *(☎ 422303, fax 561121, 3 Gangaur Ghat Rd)* is a terrific choice in this area. It has large, clean doubles with private bathroom starting at Rs 250; Rs 350 gets you a lake-view room. There are also some rooms with shared bathroom for Rs 80/150. Those on the street can be a little noisy. There's a pastry shop near reception which sells croissants (Rs 10), slices of apple pie (Rs 30) and coconut cookies (four for Rs 10).

Hotel Minerwa *(☎ 523471)*, just down the hill, is a friendly place with airy rooms for Rs 125/200 or Rs 350 for a nicer double.

Hotel Badi Haveli *(☎ 412588, Gangaur Ghat Rd)* is also good. Basic rooms start at Rs 150/200; nicer rooms with wall paintings are Rs 200/350. Most rooms have spotless shared bathroom and the ratio of toilets to rooms is high. There's a lovely sheltered and leafy courtyard surrounded by whitewashed walls and the rooftop has spectacular views. The vegetarian restaurant has thalis for Rs 55.

Lehar Paying Guest House *(☎ 417651, 86 Gangaur Ghat Rd)*, next door, has singles with shared bathroom for Rs 80, and rooms with a better view over the town for Rs 100/150. There's a small rooftop restaurant.

Anjani Hotel *(☎ 421770, 77 Gangaur Ghat Rd)* has decent rooms with private bathroom starting at Rs 100/150, although the owners are sometimes willing to bargain if things are quiet. There's a reasonably priced rooftop restaurant.

Lake Ghat Guest House *(☎ 521636, fax 520023)*, across the road from Lalghat Guest House, has OK rooms with private bathroom for Rs 100/150 (some have a balcony), or Rs 200/250 for those higher up. There are splendid views from the summit and a good restaurant.

Jag Niwas Guest House *(☎ 416022, 21 Gangaur Ghat Rd)* is a friendly little place. Clean doubles with private bathroom start at Rs 150, while Rs 300 gets you a lovely room with a sitting area. The rooftop has a veg restaurant.

Lake Corner Soni Paying Guest House, next to the City Palace wall, has rooms for Rs 80/100 with shared bathroom, or Rs 100/125 with private bathroom and squat toilet.

Shiva Guest House *(☎ 421952, 74 Navghat)* is a possibility if you're on a tight budget. Rooms with shared bathroom cost Rs 100/150 – we were quoted the same price for one with private bathroom, so it's worth bargaining.

Jheel Guest House *(☎ 421352, 56 Gangaur Ghat)* is right at the bottom of the hill by the ghat, and is housed in an old haveli. Doubles range from Rs 100 for a basic room at the back up to Rs 450 for a very nice room overlooking the lake in the newer building across the street. Prices are sometimes negotiable.

Nukkad Guest House *(56 Ganesh Ghati)*, run by the friendly Trilok and Kala, has very cheap rooms which aren't bad value. Rooms cost Rs 40/60 with shared bathroom or Rs 80/100 with private bathroom. Meals are available.

Lake Palace Road Area This area is central but farther away from Lake Pichola than the hotels in the Lal Ghat area.

Hotel Mahendra Prakash *(☎ 522993)* has a range of decent doubles with private bathroom ranging from Rs 300 (nice but no windows) up to Rs 1200. The Rs 800 room has a nice balcony with a back view of the City Palace. There's also a sparkling clean swimming pool.

Bus Stand Area This is a very noisy and polluted area, and you'd have to be desperate, totally lacking in imagination or have a (very) early departure to stay here.

Apsara Hotel *(☎ 420400)*, north of the bus stand, has dreary singles/doubles with bleak, cold private bathroom and squat toilet for Rs 100/150. Check that the mosquito wire on the windows is intact.

Parn Kulti Hotel *(☎ 586314, fax 521403)* has somewhat run-down but OK rooms with satellite TV for Rs 300/450.

Hanuman Ghat Directly across the water from Lal Ghat are some excellent choices.

Dream Heaven Guest House *(☎ 431038, 22 Bhim Permashever Marg)* is a fantastic choice. Rs 80 gets you a clean, simple room, some with a view, with private bathroom. Other rooms cost Rs 150, including the appropriately named Room 007 with an unrivalled balcony overlooking the lake and Udaipur at its best. This place has a lovely homey atmosphere and wins our vote for the best rooftop views in town.

Queen Cafe and Guest House *(☎ 430875)* is another brilliant choice. There's a genuine family feel as well as cooking classes, henna painting and Hindi lessons. The two simple rooms with shared bathroom cost Rs 100 to 150 (you can sleep on the roof).

Lake Shore Hotel is a laid-back place which is good if you want to escape from the hustle and bustle. It's fairly basic but OK, with just a few rooms, and a terrace with fine views over the water. Singles/doubles with shared bathroom are Rs 75/150; Rs 350 gets you a larger double with private bathroom and a view over the lake. The best room costs Rs 500.

Elsewhere Farther away from Lake Pichola is ***Hotel Natural*** *(☎ 431979, ⓔ hotelnatural@hotmail.com, 55 Rang Sagar)*, which is good if you want to abscond from the tumult. Basic but fine singles/doubles with private bathroom (bucket hot water) are Rs 100/150; many of them have a shared balcony. There's good veg food, and a slice of cake just like grandma used to bake costs Rs 25.

Pahadi Palace *(☎ 481699, 18 Ambargarh, Swaroop Sagar)*, not far away, has spotlessly clean rooms and is great value for money. Well-kept doubles with private bathroom range from Rs 150 (some at this price have great sunrise views) to Rs 450 for rooms with alcove windows (Rs 600 with air-con). An excellent tandoori chicken costs Rs 90.

Mewar Inn *(☎ 522090, fax 525002, ⓔ mewarinn@hotmail.com, 42 Residency Rd)* is not in a thrilling location, but it's cheap and gets consistently good reports from travellers. Basic rooms with shared bathroom go for a mere Rs 39/49. The rooms with private bathroom range from Rs 79 to 99. A discount is given to YHA members. There's a rooftop veg restaurant, and bicycles can be hired (Rs 20 per day).

Pratap Country Inn *(☎ 583138, fax 583058)* is a serene and secluded country retreat at Titaradi village, about 7km outside Udaipur. It has doubles with private bathroom from Rs 300 to 1200. Horse riding is available (two hours free if you stay here). You can do a 9 am to 6 pm safari (Rs 1200) which takes you up to the Monsoon Palace. It can be tough getting a rickshaw out here (Rs 50), but the hotel can pick you up from Udaipur with advance notice.

Places to Stay – Mid-Range

Lal Ghat Area It's wise to book ahead, as these places (particularly their best rooms) can fill up fast during the tourist season.

Kankarwa Haveli *(☎ 411457, fax 521 403, 26 Lal Ghat)* is a family-run haveli which is a wonderful place to stay. Squeaky-clean doubles range from Rs 400 to 1200; the more expensive rooms overlook Lake Pichola. There's no restaurant, but with prior notice breakfast and dinner can be arranged (veg only). Or you can just pop next door to the Jagat Niwas Palace Hotel for a meal.

Jagat Niwas Palace Hotel *(☎ 420133, fax 520023, ⓔ jagat@jp1.dot.net.in, 25 Lal Ghat)*, on the lakeshore, is a charming converted haveli with pricey rooms for Rs 1250 without view, up to Rs 1895 for a suite with lake view. The rooms for Rs 1400 overlooking the lake are great value. In the same complex is ***Hotel Jagat Niwas*** *(☎ 415547, fax 560414, ⓔ jagatniwas@yahoo.com)*, with rooms for Rs 450 away from the lake up to Rs 1000 for lakeside rooms (Rs 1200 with air-con). It has a great restaurant (see Places to Eat) overlooking the lake.

Poonam Haveli *(☎ 410303, ⓔ poonamhaveli@usa.net, 39 Lal Ghat)* has very nice rooms in need of a bit more furniture from Rs 300/350 to 450/500 for room No 007 with elegant arches.

Hotel Sai-Niwas *(☎ 421586, 75 Navghat Marg)*, just down the hill towards the ghat from the City Palace entrance, is also good. The seven double rooms are imaginatively decorated (even the toilet!) and range from Rs 850 to 1250. There's a cute restaurant which serves Indian and continental food; veg curry is Rs 45, lentil soup is Rs 40.

Ratan Palace Guest House *(☎/fax 561153, 21 Lal Ghat)* offers good double rooms with private bathroom from Rs 250 to 450. The terrace has lake views and meals are available.

Hotel Caravanserai *(☎/fax 521252, 14 Lal Ghat)* is a good choice with well-kept rooms for Rs 1195/1300. The food at the rooftop restaurant is only average, but is compensated for by the lake views and live Indian classical music in the evening.

Lake Palace Road Area An excellent choice is ***Rang Niwas Palace Hotel*** *(☎ 523890, fax 527884, ⓔ rangniwas75@hotmail.com, Lake Palace Rd)*. Set in lovely gardens with a swimming pool, it's a very relaxed hotel with evidence of attention to detail. Attractively furnished singles/doubles with private bathroom start at Rs 550/770; single/double suites are Rs 2200/2500. The only drawback is the tendency to push travellers towards the more expensive rooms.

Hotel Raj Palace *(☎ 410364, fax 410 395, 103 Bhattiyani Chotta)* is another very good place to stay. It has comfortable doubles from Rs 400 to 1200, all with cushioned alcoves. Some of the rooms at the front can be a bit noisy. There's a lush courtyard restaurant which is a great place to chill out with a beer. The restaurant whips up delicious food; the chicken masala is recommended.

Fateh Sagar Area Overlooking the lake, ***Hotel Ram Pratap Palace*** *(☎ 431701, fax 431700, ⓔ rpp_udr@vsnl.com, 5B Alkapuri)* is an elegant modern haveli. It's not fantastic value with air-cooled singles/doubles at the back costing Rs 985/1185; rooms with air-con and lake views go for Rs 1585/1895. There's a good restaurant.

Hanuman Ghat One of Udaipur's best-value hotels is ***Udai Kothi*** *(☎ 432810, fax*

RAJASTHAN

430412, ⓔ *udaikothi@yahoo.com)*. Opened in November 2000, it has stylish, beautifully appointed rooms starting at Rs 750, with most singles/doubles costing Rs 995/1195. Deluxe doubles cost Rs 1295 and suites Rs 1495. Room No 303 (Rs 1495) is undoubtedly the best, with superb views towards the Lal Ghat area and the City Palace from the two cushioned alcoves and the four-poster bed…at least until the honeymoon tent is built on the roof next to the jacuzzi. The hotel also possesses one of the city's most spectacular rooftop terraces. It has 360° views, and you can swim in Udaipur's *only* rooftop swimming pool, or dine well. It's a tremendous place for a splurge.

Lake Pichola Hotel *(☎ 431197, fax 410575)*, directly opposite, also boasts excellent views – especially up on the rooftop terrace. It's a modern building in the traditional style, with rooms for Rs 975/1000. But it's worth paying Rs 1150/1195 to get a deluxe room, with a balcony and lake view. There's a good bar and restaurant.

Hotel Sarovar *(☎ 432801)*, on the same road, is another new place with attractive rooms ranging from Rs 700 to 1450.

Places to Stay – Top End

Trident *(☎ 432200, fax 432211,* ⓔ *reserva tions@tridentudp.com)* is rather out on a limb, beyond Chandpol, but is Udaipur's slickest hotel. Hidden in the hills, this modern property is part of the Oberoi Group and offers smart rooms from US$140 up to US$225. The multicuisine restaurant (non-residents welcome) is excellent and even has frothy cappuccinos. Other amenities include a swimming pool, bar, beauty parlour and health club. Don't miss the wild boar feeding frenzy – a truly awesome sight! The Oberoi Group is planning to open Udai Vilas, an upmarket boutique hotel, in Udaipur (similar to the Raj Vilas in Jaipur) – contact its Delhi corporate office for details on ☎ 011-2914841, fax 2929800.

Laxmi Vilas Palace Hotel *(☎ 529711, fax 526273,* ⓔ *gmlvp@jp1.dot.net.in)* is between Swaroop Sagar and Fateh Sagar, up on the hill. It's a pleasant four-star ITDC place where air-con rooms start at Rs 3300/4000; the Maharani Suite is Rs 9500. There's a bar, restaurant and swimming pool.

Hotel Hilltop Palace *(☎ 432245, fax 432136,* ⓔ *hilltop@ad1.vsnl.net.in)* is atop another hill in the same area. Modern rooms start at Rs 1350/2100 and there's a pool, bar and restaurant. Although the ambience here is somewhat sterile, the rooftop terrace has good 360° views.

Shikarbadi Hotel *(☎ 431701, fax 584 841)* is out of town on the Ahmedabad road. Once a royal hunting lodge, it is set in wilderness and has a swimming pool and relaxing gardens. Attractive rooms cost Rs 1999/3300. A stud farm on the premises offers short horse rides (Rs 250 for 45 minutes) and longer safaris (a half-day safari with breakfast is Rs 1500). Sip tea while you watch the wild boars gorge at 4 pm each day (not far from the pool area). Book at the Heritage Hotels Reservation Office in the City Palace complex (☎ 419023).

Palace Hotels One of the world's most spectacular hotels must be ***Lake Palace Hotel*** *(☎ 528800, fax 528700,* ⓔ *lakepalace .udaipur@tajhotels.com)*, which appears to be floating in the middle of Lake Pichola. It looks like something lifted straight out of a romantic novel and few people would pass up an opportunity to stay here. This swanky white palace has a bar, restaurants (see Places to Eat), a little shopping arcade, open-air courtyards, lotus ponds, and a small swimming pool shaded by mango trees. The cheapest doubles are US$230 (no lake view but they do overlook a lily pond); US$290 gets you a lake view. Sumptuous suites cost US$350 to US$600. Needless to say, you will need to book well in advance.

Part of the City Palace complex, ***Shiv Niwas Palace Hotel*** *(☎ 528016, fax 528006,* ⓔ *sales@udaipur.hrhindia.com)* is another atmospheric palace hotel. The cheapest rooms (US$125 a double) aren't good value. It's much better to get a room around the pool; these start at US$300 a double (room No 16 has fine views over the lake). For a real splurge there are some lavish suites. The Lotus Suite (room No 19, US$600) does not have much of a lake view but it is very romantic – it even has a small fountain near the dreamy four-poster bed! There's a good restaurant (see Places to Eat), bar, holistic health centre and marble pool (open to nonresidents for Rs 300 including a towel). Advance bookings are recommended.

Fateh Prakash Palace Hotel *(☎ 528008/ 528019, fax 528006, ⓔ sales@udaipur .hrhindia.com)*, also in the City Palace complex, was built in the early 1900s during the reign of Maharaja Fateh Singh. The cheapest double rooms are US$125, but these are not in the main palace wing. Far more ornate suites (some with a lake view) cost US$250 to US$300 and are furnished with traditional palace pieces. The intimate Gallery Restaurant (see Places to Eat) has brilliant views across the lake.

Places to Eat

Udaipur has scores of sun-kissed rooftop cafes catering to budget travellers, as well as fine dining at the top-end hotels. Many restaurants also boast terrific lake views. At places offering multicuisine menus, the chefs generally do a better job of Indian food than Western dishes. Some restaurants in Udaipur serve bhang lassi – see the boxed text 'Beware of Those Bhang Lassis!' under Drinks in the Facts for the Visitor chapter.

Many of the budget restaurants try to lure customers by putting on a nightly screening of the James Bond movie *Octopussy*, which was partly filmed in Udaipur. These days, contemporary cult movies are also screened.

Sunset View Terrace, ideally situated on a terrace overlooking Lake Pichola, is *the* place to be at sunset. Located near the Fateh Prakash Palace Hotel in the City Palace complex, this place is worth visiting for the views alone (don't forget your camera). Live Indian classical music is played in the late afternoon. The menu consists mainly of light bites, such as pizza (Rs 125), burgers (Rs 100) and milkshakes (Rs 60).

Ambrai, in the Hanuman Ghat area, is also worth visiting for its superb location and good food. It is a great place to kick back with a cold beer or hot masala tea. The beauty of this outdoor restaurant is that, unlike other places to eat, it sits right at water level. You can get Indian, Chinese and continental cuisine; chicken tikka masala is Rs 100.

Maxim's Cafe, near the Jagdish Temple, is probably the best of the cluster of restaurants in this area. Menu items include paneer tikka (Rs 20) and Rajasthani pizza (Rs 22).

Anna Restaurant, not far away, is also good for a cheap meal. The menu consists of Indian, continental and Chinese food, and includes a selection of cakes (around Rs 30), perfect with a cup of mint tea (Rs 8).

Samor Bagh, at the Lake Palace Rd entrance to the City Palace, has slightly pricey Indian, Chinese and continental food. Its speciality is paneer pasanda (Rs 50). Other menu items include chicken achari (Rs 85) and fish tikka (Rs 80). You can sit in the large 'hut' or in the garden where a nightly puppet and dance show is performed at around 7.30 pm.

Restaurant Natural View, on the rooftop of the Evergreen Guest House, has fine lake views and the food is also good. It serves Indian, Chinese and continental fare; chicken palak is Rs 50, fish curry is Rs 60, aubergine tomato is a bargain Rs 25 and the 'choco cake' (Rs 35) is to die for.

Savage Garden, near Chandpol, is one of the few places that serves freshly ground coffee (Rs 25). The food also gets good reports.

Queen Cafe, in Hanuman Ghat across the water from Lal Ghat, has a wide range of dishes to choose from and the home-cooked Indian food is as good as you'll get anywhere (most dishes are under Rs 50).

Cafe Hill Park, south-west of the Sajjan Niwas Gardens on a hill overlooking Lake Pichola, attracts people for its views rather than its food. This rather ramshackle cafe offers international fare, including cheeseburgers (Rs 35) and chicken curry (Rs 45). Eating outside is more pleasant than indoors.

Park View, one of Udaipur's oldest restaurants, is opposite a small park in the main part of town, but there's absolutely no view. This dimly lit place is particularly good for its North Indian cuisine and is often packed with middle-class Indian families. A fish tandoori is Rs 80 and chicken curry is Rs 55. It does the simple things well, such as cream of chicken soup and cheese naan.

Berry's Restaurant, at Chetak Circle, has a sterile feel to it but cooks up pretty good Indian food and is quite popular with the locals. The butter chicken is a hot seller (Rs 95 for half a bird) and there are also sizzlers (from Rs 85 to 135).

Of the German bakeries that have sprung up around town, ***Cafe Edelweiss***, near Chandpol, and ***Coffee.com***, next to the Poonam Haveli hotel, are probably the best.

Hotel Natural (☎ *431979)* has a menu offering a mishmash of veg Indian, Chinese, Mexican, Tibetan and Italian food – steamed momos with cheese sauce cost Rs 40. It also bakes birthday cakes for around Rs 100 – call ahead to place your order.

Next to the Shilpgram crafts village site, 3km west of Fateh Sagar, the ***Shilpi Restaurant*** serves up good Indian, continental and Chinese food. Not far away is the rather less impressive ***Woodland Restaurant***.

Udai Kothi (see Places to Stay – Mid-Range) is hard to beat for views and value for money. The glorious terrace has fantastic views, the service is attentive and the food is excellent – the paneer tikka (Rs 75), the chicken tikka (Rs 120) and 'fish a la Udai Kothi' (Rs 125) are especially good.

Hotel Jagat Niwas (☎ *415547)* has an absolutely delightful restaurant with superlative lake views – great for a minor splurge. Its Western dishes are a little pricey, but the Indian food is very reasonable; palak paneer is Rs 50. The fish dishes are particularly good. It's wise to book ahead (especially for dinner), as this place can fill up in a flash.

Shiv Niwas Palace Hotel (☎ *528016)* is highly recommended for a dose of pampering and is most captivating in the evening. There's seating indoors or in the pleasant open-air courtyard by the pool. The Indian food is best – try the *aloo chutneywale* (potatoes stuffed with Indian cottage cheese in a mango and mint chutney) for Rs 90. Indian classical music is performed each evening by the poolside, creating a magical ambience. Nonresidents are welcome (though you probably won't get past the gate without paying the Rs 75 visitor fee); it's wise to book ahead, especially for dinner.

Gallery Restaurant, at the Fateh Prakash Palace Hotel, serves a set continental lunch/dinner for Rs 550/650. Although the food here is nothing to write home about, this elegant little restaurant has beguiling views across Lake Pichola. For a really romantic evening, come here at sunset for a drink, then enjoy the live Indian classical music while you dine. For something more moneybelt-friendly, there's an afternoon tea served daily between 3 and 5 pm. A 'full cream tea' costs Rs 150, homemade biscuits and cakes cost Rs 100 and a pot of chocolate served with whipped cream is Rs 65.

Lake Palace Hotel is, of course, the ultimate dining experience, although there's no guarantee – getting a table is usually only possible when the hotel is not full. The sumptuous buffet dinner costs Rs 750 (including the boat crossing), and before your meal you can take a drink at the sophisticated bar. A bottle of wine with your meal will cost around Rs 1000 (plus a whopping 60% tax). Make sure you go on an empty stomach. Reservations are essential, and reasonably tidy dress is expected. For something different, ask about the hotel's tiny ***floating pontoon*** on Lake Pichola, which arranges lunch or dinner for US$40 (maximum four people). If you don't want a waiter hanging around, you can request a cordless phone to be left in case you need anything. Wear something warm if you are dining at night in the winter.

Entertainment

Before dinner, treat yourself to a drink at the Shiv Niwas Palace Hotel's plush poolside ***Paanera Bar***, which has soft sofas to sink into. If it's been a tough day, there's tequila (Rs 180 a shot), or if you're in the mood, go wild on a bottle of bubbly – the Moet costs a cool Rs 5000!

Meera Kala Mandir (☎ *583176, Sector 11, Hiran Magari)*, near the Paras Cinema, has one-hour Rajasthani folk dance and music performances daily except Sunday at 7 pm from August to April. It costs Rs 60 per person. An autorickshaw from the City Palace area costs Rs 25. Closer to town, there are similar performances most nights at the Bagore-ki-Haveli on Gangaur Ghat.

Many hotels stage their own entertainment for guests – usually puppet shows or Rajasthani music or dance performances.

Shopping

Udaipur has oodles of little shops selling a jumble of things, from funky Western clothing to traditional antique jewellery. The town is popular for its local crafts, particularly miniature paintings in the Rajput-Mughal style, and is a good place to buy leather-bound books and handmade paper. There's a good cluster of shops selling these near the Jagdish Temple. Be prepared to bargain hard, as most places have ridiculously inflated prices for tourists. The bookshops stock a good range of titles, although the prices they offer for resale may not be quite what you're used to elsewhere.

Getting There & Away

Air The Indian Airlines office (☎ 410999, fax 410248) at Delhi Gate is open 10 am to 1 pm and 2 to 5 pm Monday to Saturday, and 10 am to 2 pm Sunday. Indian Airlines operates daily flights to Delhi (US$105) via Jodhpur (US$80) and Jaipur (US$85). There is also a daily flight to Mumbai (US$125). Jet Airways (☎ 561105, fax 561106), in the Blue Circle Business Centre near the main post office, has daily flights to Delhi via Jaipur and to Mumbai every day except Saturday for the same price as Indian Airlines.

Bus Destinations served by RSTC buses include Jaipur (Rs 153/226, deluxe/ordinary, nine hours), Ajmer (Rs 111/163, six hours), Jodhpur (Rs 115/146, seven hours), Chittorgarh (Rs 43/61, three hours) and Delhi (Rs 275/404, 14 hours).

There are quite a few private bus companies which operate to Ahmedabad (Rs 100, six hours), Mumbai (Rs 300, 16 hours), Delhi (Rs 250, 14 hours), Indore (Rs 200, 10 hours) and Mt Abu (Rs 90, five hours). For Jaisalmer (Rs 200), you'll probably have to change buses in Jodhpur (Rs 90, six hours).

Train Lines into Udaipur are currently metre gauge only, but are scheduled to be converted to broad gauge – nobody is really sure when this will happen. It's quicker in most cases to catch a bus.

The *Chetak Express* (9616) departs at 6.10 pm and arrives in Delhi (Rs 145/225/1044 general/sleeper/2A class) 19 hours later. It goes via Chittorgarh (Rs 35/55/348, arrives 9.40 pm), Ajmer (Rs 77/120/564, 2.15 am) and Jaipur (Rs 99/154/713, 5.45 am). The *Ahmedabad Express* (9943) costs Rs 73/114/543 and departs at 9.15 pm, arriving in the Gujarati capital at 6.35 am.

Taxi Many drivers will show you a list of 'official' rates to places like Mt Abu, Chittorgarh and Jodhpur. Shop around (Rs 4 per kilometre is a good starting point), as you can often barter for better rates. For travel out of town, remember that taxis generally charge return fares even if you're only going one way.

Getting Around

To/From the Airport The airport is 25km from the city; there's no airport bus. An autorickshaw or taxi will cost at least Rs 180/220.

Autorickshaw These are unmetered so you should agree on a fare before setting off. There are prepaid autorickshaw stands at both the main bus stand and the train station. Otherwise, the standard fare for tourists anywhere within the city appears to be around Rs 20. It costs Rs 180 to hire an autorickshaw for half a day of local sightseeing.

Bicycle & Motorbike You can hire bicycles all over town for around Rs 25 per day. Heera Cycle Store (☎ 523525), near the Hotel Badi Haveli in the old city, rents out bicycles/mopeds/motorcycles for Rs 25/150/300 per day.

AROUND UDAIPUR

Eklingji

The interesting village of Eklingji – a short bus ride (22km) north of Udaipur – has a number of ancient temples. The **Shiva temple** in the village itself was originally built in 734, although its present form dates from the rule of Maharaja Raimal (1473–1509). The walled complex has an elaborately pillared hall under a large pyramidal roof and features a four-faced Shiva image of black marble. The temple is open daily at odd hours – 4.15 to 6.45 am, 10.30 am to 1.30 pm and 5.15 to 7.45 pm (check at the Tourist Reception Centre in Udaipur for current timings). Photography is not allowed. The temple gets very crowded on Monday (an auspicious day for devotees).

Places to Stay & Eat At Lake Bagela in Nagda, ***Heritage Resorts*** *(☎ 0294-440382, fax 527549)* is set in lovely grounds. It offers doubles for Rs 1850 including dinner or breakfast, and a suite for Rs 3200. There's a restaurant (nonguests are welcome) which charges Rs 300 for the buffet lunch or dinner. It has a small pool, and horse rides for Rs 50. Boats can also be hired.

AROUND UDAIPUR

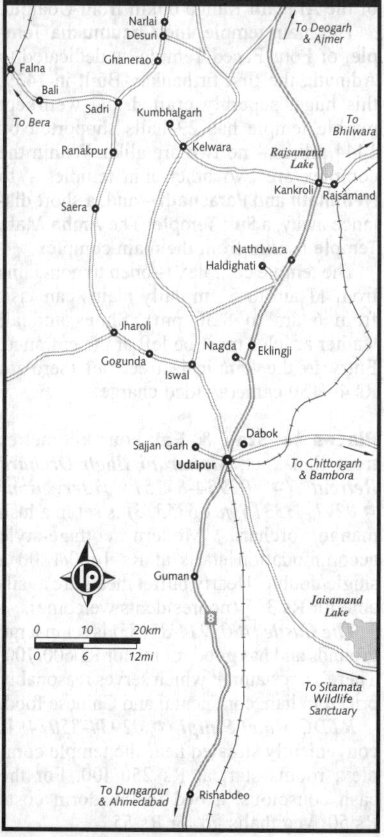

Getting There & Away Local buses run from Udaipur to Eklingji every hour from 5 am to 9 pm (Rs 16, 40 minutes).

Haldighati

This site, 40km north of Udaipur, is where Maharaja Pratap defied the superior Mughal forces of Akbar in 1576. The site is a battlefield and the only thing to see is the small chhatri to the warrior's horse, Chetak, a few kilometres away. Although badly wounded and exhausted, this brave horse carried Maharaja Pratap to safety before collapsing and dying. It is for this loyalty and courage that Chetak is honoured. The site has a beautiful courtyard in a peaceful setting.

Nathdwara

The important 18th-century Vishnu temple of **Sri Nathji** stands here, 48km north of Udaipur, and it's an important shrine for Vaishnavites. The black stone Vishnu image was brought here from Mathura in 1669 to protect it from Aurangzeb's destructive impulses. According to legend, when an attempt was later made to move the image, the getaway vehicle, a wagon, sank into the ground up to the axles, indicating that the image preferred to stay where it was!

Attendants treat the image like a delicate child, getting it up in the morning, washing it, putting its clothes on, offering it specially prepared meals, putting it down to sleep. It's a very popular pilgrimage site, and the temple opens and closes around the image's daily routine. It is very crowded around 4.30 to 5 pm when Vishnu rises after a siesta. The temple's timings in the morning are from 5.30 to 6 am, 7.30 to 8 am, 9.30 to 10 am, and 11.30 am to noon. Afternoon timings are from 3.30 to 4 pm, 4.30 to 5 pm and 6.30 to 7 pm. Check that these timings have not changed.

Nathdwara is also well known for its *pichwai* paintings, which are bright with rather static images, usually on hand-spun fabric.

Places to Stay & Eat Considering it's an RTDC establishment, ***RTDC Hotel Gokul*** *(☎ 02953-30917)* is surprisingly good. It's set in quiet gardens and air-cooled single/double rooms are Rs 300/400, dorm beds are Rs 50. A family room (four people) costs Rs 600. There's also a bar and a restaurant.

Getting There & Away There are frequent daily RSTC buses from Udaipur to Nathdwara (Rs 20, 1½ hours).

Kumbhalgarh

Eighty-four kilometres north of Udaipur, this is the most important fort in the Mewar region after Chittorgarh. It's a secluded place, built by Maharaja Kumbha in the 15th century, and owing to its inaccessibility on top of the Aravalli range at 1100m, it was taken only once in its history. Even then, it took the combined armies of the Mughal emperor Akbar and those of Amber and Marwar to breach its defences. It was here that the rulers of Mewar retreated in times of danger. The walls of the fort stretch some 36km and enclose many temples, palaces, gardens and water storage facilities.

There's also a big **wildlife sanctuary** here, known for its wolves. The scarcity of waterholes between March and June makes this the best time to see animals. Other wildlife includes *chowsingha* (four-horned antelope), leopards and sloth bears. You need permission to enter the reserve from the forest department in nearby Kelwara, or from the deputy chief wildlife warden in Udaipur (☎ 0294-421361).

Places to Stay & Eat By far the best place to stay is ***Aodhi Hotel*** *(☎ 02954-4222, reservations ☎ 0294-528016, fax 528006)*. Singles/doubles in this blissfully tranquil hotel cost Rs 1995/3300. There's a bar, a restaurant (open to nonresidents) and a pool. Horse and jeep safaris can be arranged. This is a wonderful place to rejuvenate yourself.

Nearby is ***Kumbhalgarh Fort Hotel*** (☎ 02954-42372, fax 525106) where rooms start at Rs 1195/2395.

Hotel Ratnadeep *(☎ 02954-42217)* in nearby Kelwara is a bit farther away from the fort, but has cheaper doubles with private bathroom (most with squat toilets) starting at Rs 400; dorm beds cost Rs 100.

Getting There & Away There are several daily RSTC buses from Udaipur (Rs 30, 3½ hours) and one express bus each morning (Rs 38, 2½ hours).

Ranakpur

One of the biggest and most important Jain temples in India, the extremely beautiful Ranakpur complex is well worth seeing. It is tucked away in a remote and quiet valley of the Aravalli Range 60km from Udaipur.

The main temple, the **Chaumukha Temple**, or Four-Faced Temple, is dedicated to Adinath, the first tirthankar. Built in 1439, this huge, superbly crafted and well-kept marble temple has 29 halls supported by 1444 pillars – no two are alike. Within the complex are two other Jain temples – to **Neminath** and **Parasnath** – and, a short distance away, a **Sun Temple**. The **Amba Mata Temple** is 1km from the main complex.

The temple complex is open to non-Jains from 11 am to 5 pm daily (Jains can visit from 6 am to 8.30 pm). Shoes and all leather articles must be left at the entrance. Entry to the temple is free, but there's a Rs 40/150 camera/video charge.

Places to Stay & Eat Four kilometres from Ranakpur, ***Maharani Bagh Orchard Retreat*** *(☎ 02934-85151, reservations ☎ 0291-433316, fax 635373)* is set in a lush mango orchard. Modern cottage-style accommodation starts at Rs 1600/1800 a single/double. Hearty buffet meals are available for Rs 355 (nonresidents welcome).

The Castle *(☎ 02934-85133)* is set in large grounds and has good rooms for Rs 600/700. There's a restaurant which serves reasonably priced Indian, continental and Chinese food.

RTDC Hotel Shilpi *(☎ 02934-85074)* is conveniently situated near the temple complex; rooms start at Rs 250/400. For the cash conscious, a bed in the dorm costs Rs 50. Veg thalis go for Rs 55.

Roopam Restaurant *(☎ 02934-3921)* has a few nice rooms for Rs 550/650. The restaurant offers a buffet (Rs 150) or a la carte dining (Rs 35 to 60 for a main dish). A bottle of beer is Rs 80.

Getting There & Away From Udaipur there are four deluxe buses daily (Rs 35, three hours); at the time of research these were departing at 5.30 am, 3 pm, 10 pm and 10.30 pm). Hiring a private taxi should cost around Rs 500 including waiting time – expensive but it allows you to better appreciate the beautiful scenery en route and you could combine it with a detour to Kumbhalgarh. Ranakpur is 39km from Falna Junction on the Ajmer–Mt Abu rail and road routes.

Deogarh

The attractive little town of Deogarh (pronounced dev-gar), or 'Castle of the Gods', is 135km north of Udaipur. Surrounded by lakes, hills and rugged countryside, it's an ideal place to take a break from the rigours of travelling in India. Deogarh has lots of pleasant walks and is known for its school of miniature painting. While here, you should visit **Anjaneshwar Mahadev**, a small cave temple dedicated to Lord Shiva. It's believed to be around 2000 years old. From the top of this hill there are good views of the countryside.

The delightful ***Deogarh Castle*** *(☎ 02904-52777, fax 52555, ⓔ deogarh@infosys.net)* is a family-run hotel where appealing double rooms start at Rs 2500; a suite costs Rs 3995. This well-managed castle has a good restaurant – request the rarely found *palak-ka-halwa*, a dessert made from spinach which sounds awful, looks awful, but tastes great (kind of like semiburnt toffee). The hotel offers a 2½-hour 'rural ramble' jeep excursion for Rs 500 per person, including refreshments. Bird-watching, trekking and picnic outings can be arranged. Bicycles are for hire for Rs 150 per person per day and horse rides (Rs 400 for two to three hours) can be arranged.

There's a deluxe bus from Udaipur (Rs 60, three hours) and there are train connections to Udaipur.

Bera

About 145km from Udaipur, Bera is a good place for spotting leopards and other wildlife. The best times for wildlife spotting are from 6 to 10 am and 4 to 8 pm.

Leopards Lair *(☎/fax 02933-43479)* has comfortable modern cottages for Rs 4000/4500 a single/double – the price includes all meals and two wildlife safaris.

Rishabdeo

A 15th-century Jain temple of Lord Rishabdeo is here, about 65km south of Udaipur. Rishabdeo is a reincarnation of Mahavir, the 24th and last of the Jain prophets, who founded Jainism around 500 BC and is also worshipped as a reincarnation of Vishnu. The temple, which is a pilgrimage centre, has the Lord's image, some beautiful carvings and two large black stone elephants at the temple's entrance. A short walk through a lane lined with small shops leads you there.

There are irregular buses to Rishabdeo from Udaipur (Rs 45, 3½ hours).

Jaisamand Lake

Located 48km south-east of Udaipur, this stunningly located artificial lake, created by damming the Gomti River, was built by Maharaja Jai Singh in the 17th century. It's one of the largest artificial lakes in Asia, and there are beautiful marble chhatris around the embankment. The summer palaces of the Udaipur queens are also here and there's a wildlife sanctuary nearby.

Jaisamand Island Resort *(☎ 02906-2222, reservations ☎ 0294-415100, fax 523898, ⓔ resort@adl.vsnl.net.in)* is a modern hotel in a secluded position 20 minutes by boat across the lake. Rooms start at Rs 1800/2700 and discounts are often available. There's also a tatty ***Tourist Bungalow***.

There are frequent RSTC buses from Udaipur (Rs 17, 1½ hours).

Sitamata Wildlife Sanctuary

Located 65km south-east of Udaipur, this wildlife sanctuary covers 423 sq km of mainly deciduous forest. If you're in search of picturesque countryside, peace and plenty of fresh air, this place is ideal.

Teekhi Magri Resort (☎ *0141-212235*), 22km from the village of Dhamotar (160km from Udaipur), is a secluded jungle retreat with simple accommodation. There are just three basic clay-brick cottages which cost Rs 1100 a double (lighting is by lantern). The jungle surrounding the cottages is home to a variety of wildlife, including leopards (look for paw prints in the morning). Meals are available. In the winter, it can get very cold at night. Bookings are essential.

Fort Dhariyawad (☎ *02950-20050*), also in the Sitamata sanctuary area, 120km from Udaipur, has comfortable double rooms for Rs 1100. The set breakfast/lunch/dinner is Rs 175/250/350. Horse and jeep safaris to places of interest in the area can be arranged, as can tented accommodation for the Baneshwar Fair (see Baneshwar later).

There are RSTC buses from Udaipur to Dhariyawad (Rs 31, four hours).

Dungarpur

Situated about 110km south of Udaipur, Dungarpur, the City of Hills, was founded in the 13th century. Between 9 am and 4 pm daily, you can visit the old palace, **Juna Mahal**, after obtaining a ticket (Rs 100) from the Udai Bilas Palace. Built between the 13th and 18th centuries, this crumbling seven-storey palace is filled with old frescoes and paintings. The Aam Khas, or main living room, has impressive mirrorwork and glass inlays. The former royal hunting lodge, on a nearby hilltop, has sensational views over the town's many temples.

The beautiful **Deo Somnath Temple**, about 25km out of town, dates back to the 12th century.

Places to Stay & Eat At the budget end, *Hotel Pratibha Palace* (☎ *02964-30775, Shastri Colony*) has tiny rooms with private

Adivasis of Rajasthan

Tribal, or Adivasi, groups were the original inhabitants of the area now called Rajasthan. Many were forced into the Aravalli Range by the rise to power of the Aryans.

Bhils

The Bhils, the largest of the Adivasi communities, traditionally inhabited the south-eastern corner of the state around Udaipur, Chittorgarh and Dungarpur. Legend has it that the Bhils were fine archers and their name can be traced to the Tamil word *vil*, meaning bow. Bhil bowmen are mentioned in both the Mahabharata and the Ramayana. They were highly regarded as warriors, and the Rajput rulers relied heavily on them to thwart the invading Marathas and Mughals. The British formed a Mewar Bhil Corps in the 1820s in recognition of the Bhils' martial tradition.

Although originally food gatherers, the Bhils these days have taken up small-scale agriculture, or have abandoned the land altogether and taken up city residence and employment. The literacy rate of the Bhils, particularly the women, used to be one of the lowest of any group in the country which made them prime targets for exploitation and bonded labour. This trend is now being reversed, and the fortunes of the Bhils are slowly improving. Several Bhils, including one Bhil woman, have even entered state parliament, becoming members of the Legislative Assembly.

Those Bhils who can afford it engage in polygamy. Marriages of love, as opposed to arranged ones, are condoned.

The Baneshwar Fair is a Bhil festival held near Dungarpur, and large numbers gather for several days of singing, dancing and worship. (For dates, see the Baneshwar section.) Holi is another important time for the Bhils. Witchcraft, magic and superstition are deeply rooted aspects of Bhil culture.

Minas

The Minas are the second-largest, and most widely dispersed, Adivasi group in the state. They live in the regions of Shekhawati and eastern Rajasthan. Scholars still disagree as to whether the Minas bathroom (squat toilet, bucket hot water) from Rs 50/100 to Rs 150/250. No meals are available but there are several cheap *dhabas* (snack bars) nearby.

Udai Bilas Palace *(☎ 02964-30808, fax 31008)* is an 18th-century palace which has partly been converted into a hotel by the maharaja of Dungarpur. It features the intricately carved Ek Thambia Mahal (One-Pillared Palace). Singles/doubles here cost Rs 1450/1900 and many rooms are decorated in Art Deco style (some have private balcony with lake views). Suites cost Rs 2600 – suite No 5 has an awesome old shower. Meals are taken at the long dining room table, with stuffed beasts watching over you – note the exquisite ceiling made from Burmese teak.

Getting There & Away Frequent RSTC buses travel to Dungarpur from Udaipur (Rs 35, three hours). There's also a slow train between Dungarpur and Udaipur (Rs 35/55 general/sleeper class, five hours).

Baneshwar

Baneshwar is at the confluence of three holy rivers: the Mahi, Som and Jakham. In January/February the week-long **Baneshwar Fair** is held at the Baneshwar Temple, about 80km from Dungarpur. It attracts thousands of Bhil Adivasis. It starts on 23 February 2002, 12 February 2003 and 1 February 2004.

Tents with private bathroom (Rs 5500 a double including all meals) can be arranged through Fort Dhariyawad (see Sitamata Wildlife Sanctuary earlier).

MT ABU

☎ 02974 • pop 18,600 • elevation 1200m

Mt Abu, in the far south of the state, close to the Gujarat border, is Rajasthan's only hill

Adivasis of Rajasthan

are indigenous, or whether they migrated to the region from Central Asia. The name Mina is derived from *meen*, or fish – the Minas claim descent from the fish incarnation of Vishnu. Originally they were a ruling tribe, but their downfall was a long, drawn-out affair, beginning with the Rajputs and completed when the British government declared them a criminal tribe in 1924.

Following Independence, this ignominious status was officially lifted. However, their culture was by this time more or less destroyed, and they have been given protection as a Scheduled Tribe. With the withdrawal of the Criminal Tribes Act, the Minas took to agriculture. As is the case with the Bhils, the literacy rate among the Minas was very low, but is improving.

Other Adivasi Groups

The Gaduliya Lohars were originally martial Rajput Adivasis, but these days are nomadic blacksmiths. Their traditional territory was Mewar (Udaipur) and they fought with the maharaja against the Mughals. With typical Rajput chivalry, they made a vow to the maharaja that they would only enter his fort at Chittorgarh after he had overcome the Mughals. As he died without achieving this, the clan was forced to become nomadic. When Nehru was in power he led a group of Gaduliya Lohars into Chittorgarh, with the hope that they would then resettle in their former lands, but they preferred to remain nomadic.

The Garasias are a small Rajput Adivasi group found in the Abu Road area of southern Rajasthan. Their marriage ceremony is curious in that the couple elope, and a sum of money is paid to the father of the bride. If the marriage fails, the bride returns home, with a small sum of money to give to her father. Widows are not entitled to a share of their husband's property, and so generally remarry.

The Sahariyas, thought to be of Bhil origin, live in the areas of Kota, Dungarpur and Sawai Madhopur. They are one of the least educated Adivasi groups in the country, with a literacy rate of only 5% and, as unskilled labourers, have been cruelly exploited. All members of the clan are considered to be related so marriages are arranged beyond the tribe.

station. It's a pleasant hot-season retreat from the plains of both Rajasthan and Gujarat. Mt Abu's pace is easy-going, although the place can get impossibly crowded with people and traffic during the summer months.

Mt Abu has a number of important temples, particularly the breathtaking Dilwara group of Jain temples. An important pilgrimage centre for Jains boasting some of the finest marble carvings in all of Rajasthan, if not India. Like other hill stations, Mt Abu has its own lake, which is the centre of activity.

If for some strange reason you are travelling through Rajasthan in the middle of the year, Mt Abu hosts the Summer Festival, which is dedicated to the classical and folk music of Rajasthan. It takes place from 1 June to 3 June each year.

Orientation & Information

Mt Abu is on a hilly plateau about 22km long by 6km wide, 27km from the nearest train station (Abu Road). The main part of the town extends along the road in from Abu Road, down to Nakki Lake.

The Tourist Reception Centre (☎ 43151) is around the corner from the private bus stand and is open 10 am to 1.30 pm and

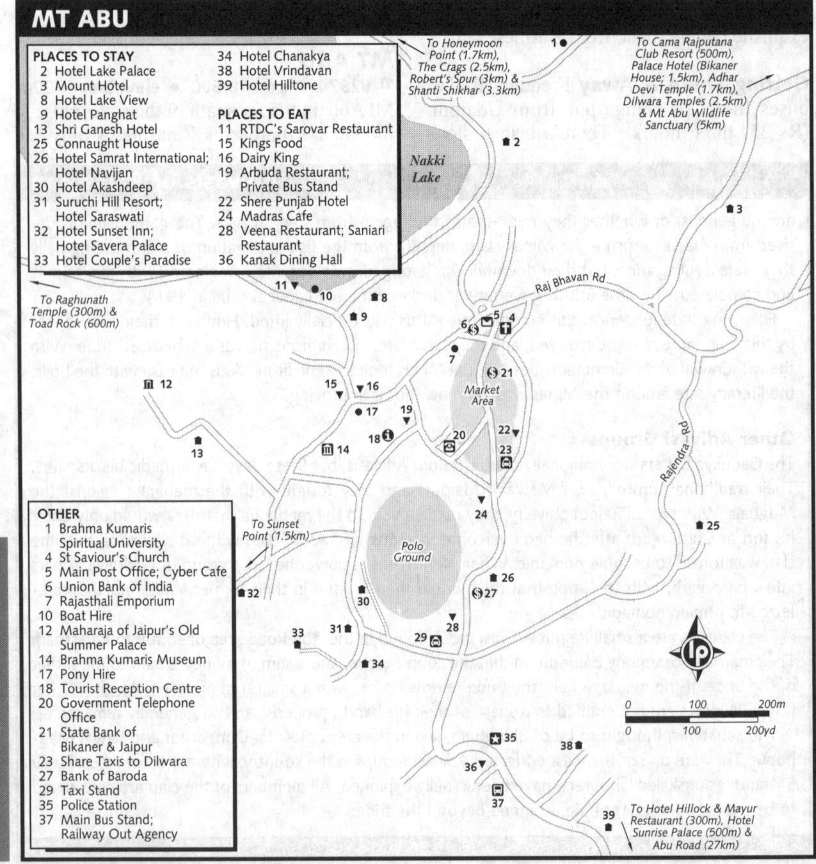

2 to 5 pm Monday to Saturday. Money can be changed at the State Bank of Bikaner & Jaipur and the Union Bank of India.

Nakki Lake

Nakki Lake is a big attraction with tourists. The lake takes its name from the legend that it was scooped out by a god using only his nails, or *nakh*. It's a pleasant stroll around the lake – look for the strange **rock formations**. The best known, Toad Rock, looks just like a toad about to hop into the lake. Others, like Nun Rock, Nandi Rock or Camel Rock, require more imagination. The 14th-century **Raghunath temple** stands beside the lake. You can hire your own boat (Rs 50 for 30 minutes in a two-seater paddle boat).

Viewpoints

Of the various viewpoints around town, **Sunset Point** is the most popular and a great place to catch the setting sun. Other popular spots include **Honeymoon Point**, which also offers a view of the sunset, **The Crags** and **Robert's Spur**. You can follow the white arrows along a path up to the summit of **Shanti Shikhar**, west of Adhar Devi Temple, where there are panoramic views.

For a good view over the lake, the best point is probably the terrace of the maharaja of Jaipur's former **summer palace**. No-one seems to mind if you climb up here for the view and a photo.

Adhar Devi Temple

Three kilometres north of town, some 365 steps lead to this Durga temple built in a natural cleft in the rock. You have to stoop to get through the low entrance to the temple. There are fine views over Mt Abu from up here.

Dilwara Temples

These remarkable temples are Mt Abu's main attraction and among the finest examples of Jain architecture in India. The complex includes two temples in which the art of carving marble reached unsurpassed heights.

The older of the temples is the **Vimal Vasahi**, built in 1031 and dedicated to the first tirthankar, Adinath. The central shrine has an image of Adinath, while around the courtyard are 52 identical cells, each with a Buddha-like cross-legged image. Forty-eight elegantly carved pillars form the entrance to the courtyard. In front of the temple stands the **House of Elephants**, with figures of elephants marching in procession to the temple entrance.

The later **Tejpal Temple** is dedicated to Neminath, the 22nd tirthankar. It was built in 1230 by the brothers Tejpal and Vastupal who were, like Vimal, ministers in the government of the ruler of Gujarat. Although the Tejpal Temple is important as an extremely old and complete example of a Jain temple, its most notable feature is the brilliant intricacy and delicacy of the marble carving. The carving is so fine that, in places, the marble becomes almost transparent. In particular, the lotus flower that hangs from the centre of the dome is an astonishing piece of work. It's difficult to believe that this huge lace-like filigree actually started as a solid block of marble. The temple employs several full-time stone carvers to maintain and restore the work. There are three other temples in the enclosure, but they all pale beside the Tejpal and the Vimal Vasahi.

Celebrations are held here each June as part of Mt Abu's Summer Festival, although some festivities take place after the main festival is over (dates vary according to the lunar calendar).

The complex is open from noon to 6 pm (Jains can visit from sunrise to sunset). Photography is not allowed. As at other Jain temples, all articles of leather (belts as well as shoes) have to be left at the entrance (Rs 1). You can stroll out to Dilwara from the town in less than an hour, or take a share-taxi (see Getting Around).

Brahma Kumaris

The Brahma Kumaris teach that all religions lead to God and so are equally valid, and the principles of each should be studied. The university's stated aim is the establishment of universal peace through 'the impartation of spiritual knowledge and training of easy raja yoga meditation'. There are over 4500 branches in 70 countries around the world.

You can attend an introductory course (seven lessons) while you're in Mt Abu; this would take a minimum of three days. There's no charge – the organisation is entirely supported by donations.

There's a museum in the town outlining the university's teachings and offering meditation sessions. It's open 8 am to 8 pm daily; entry is free.

Organised Tours

RTDC has five-hour tours of all the main sites, leaving from the main bus stand at 8.30 am and 1.30 pm (later in summer). The tours cost Rs 36 plus all entry and camera fees. The afternoon tour finishes at Sunset Point. Reservations can be made at the inquiries counter of the main bus stand (☎ 43434) or the Tourist Reception Centre.

Places to Stay

There is an explosion of hotels in Mt Abu. The high season is from mid-April to mid-November and prices rise considerably during this period. During Diwali (October/November), rooms are virtually unobtainable without advance booking and the tariffs are simply ridiculous. As Mt Abu's charm is its tranquility, it's a good time to stay away.

In the low season (with the exception of Christmas and New Year), discounts of up to 50% are available and mid-range accommodation can be an absolute bargain. The hotels usually have an ungenerous 9 am checkout time.

At all times of the year there are plenty of touts working the bus and taxi stands. In the low season you can safely ignore them; at peak times they can save you a lot of legwork as they'll know exactly where the last available room is.

Places to Stay – Budget

***Shri Ganesh Hotel** (☎ 37292, ⓔ s_ganesh@datainfosys.net)*, up the hill towards the maharaja of Jaipur's old summer palace, is popular with travellers and deservedly so. It's in a quiet location, the management are friendly and the rooms are good value, starting at Rs 100; most rooms (with 24-hour hot water) cost Rs 150/175. The sitting area on the roof, complete with swing chair, is a great place to relax. There's a laundry service, Internet access (Rs 100 an hour) and a kitchen for use by guests. The restaurant serves good home-cooking at reasonable prices (a veg thali costs Rs 40).

***Hotel Lake View** (☎ 38659)* overlooks picturesque Nakki Lake. The views are magnificent, especially from the upper floors. Singles/doubles with private bathroom are decent value in low season starting at Rs 100/200; we were quoted Rs 2000/2500 during Diwali which is brazenly outrageous. Hot water is available between 7 and 11 am.

***Hotel Panghat** (☎ 38886)*, nearby, is also reasonable value, ranging from Rs 125 for a small room up to Rs 200 for a larger one. Prices double in high season. All rooms have private bathroom and bucket hot water (7 to 10 am); the cheaper ones can be a little claustrophobic.

***Hotel Couple's Paradise** (☎ 43504)*, about 300m west of the taxi stand in Akshay Colony, is open only to couples and families and is terrific value. The tidy rooms with private bathroom (and constant hot water) cost Rs 150 and the ones at the front have private balconies. It's within walking distance of the town centre but is nice and quiet. During Diwali, expect to pay Rs 650.

***Hotel Saraswati** (☎ 38887, fax 38337)*, nearby, is good value. There are well-kept doubles with private bathroom and 24-hour hot water for Rs 100, and a range of other rooms from Rs 150 to 300. The veg restaurant serves tasty Gujarati thalis (Rs 40).

Retiring rooms at the Abu Road train station, 27km down the hill, are convenient if you're catching an early morning train. They go for Rs 120 a double; a veg thali is Rs 40.

Places to Stay – Mid-Range

***Hotel Lake Palace** (☎ 37154, fax 38817, ⓔ savshanti@hotmail.com)* is a friendly place across from the lake with singles/doubles/triples for Rs 800/900/1100 in high season; bargain hard in the low season and you should be able to get the same rooms for Rs 450/550/660. Most rooms have semi-

RAJASTHAN

private terrace areas overlooking the lake and are better than the exterior suggests.

Mount Hotel *(☎ 43150)* is a homey place in a tranquil location along the road to the Dilwara Temples. The rooms are a bit worn and weary. Doubles range from Rs 400 to 600. Vegetarian meals (Rs 90) are available with advance notice. The owner can organise horse safaris.

Hotel Chanakya *(☎ 38154)* charges Rs 600 in the low season for a comfortable double with bathroom and hot water between 7 and 10 am. Larger doubles are Rs 700.

Suruchi Hill Resort *(☎ 43577, fax 38573)*, in the same area, has nice doubles which are nonetheless a little overpriced at Rs 800. Facilities include luggage storage, a back-up generator and a parking area.

Hotel Savera Palace *(☎ 43354, fax 38817, ⓔ savshanti@hotmail.com)*, on the western edge of Mt Abu, has singles/doubles for Rs 440/550 in low season or Rs 800/900 at peak times. Air-con costs an extra Rs 300. There's a swimming pool and a reasonable Punjabi and Gujarati restaurant.

Hotel Sunset Inn *(☎ 43194, fax 43515)*, almost next door, is a modern hotel with good rooms for Rs 990/1100 including all taxes. This is one of the few places in Mt Abu not to raise its rates seasonally which makes it good value at peak periods. You can book by calling the reservations number in Ahmedabad (☎ 079-6403906, fax 6469876). The restaurant serves satisfying meals.

Hotel Akashdeep *(☎ 38670)* is in a quiet location overlooking the polo ground with doubles for Rs 500. Deluxe doubles cost Rs 750. All rooms have colour TV and constant hot water.

Hotel Samrat International *(☎ 43153)* and ***Hotel Navijan*** *(☎ 43173)*, on the main road, are actually the same hotel. Attractive, spacious rooms are available for Rs 650 in low season. Some have a sofa, a large sheltered balcony with rocking chair overlooking the polo ground and 24-hour hot water – great value in a central location.

Hotel Vrindavan *(☎ 43147)*, near the main bus stand, is a bit cheaper than other places in this category. Acceptable rooms range from Rs 300 to 700 in the low season.

Places to Stay – Top End

Palace Hotel (Bikaner House) *(☎ 43121, fax 38674)*, not far from the Dilwara temples, is the most atmospheric hotel in Mt Abu. It's a charming place to chill out, replete with shady gardens, a private lake, tennis courts and a restaurant (see Places to Eat). This was once the summer residence of the maharaja of Bikaner. The cheapest singles/doubles are a reasonable Rs 1200/1550 and Visa and MasterCard are accepted.

Hotel Hillock *(☎ 38463, fax 38467, ⓔ hillock.mtabu@POP3.gtsl.co.in)*, on the main road into town, is a stylish place in spite of the unattractive exterior. The staff are more welcoming than at many top-end places and the rooms are beautifully appointed. Standard rooms cost Rs 1590 and are excellent value, particularly in 'non season' when 50% discounts are available. Deluxe rooms cost Rs 2490. There's a pool, a cosy bar, an elegant restaurant and a children's playground. Checkout is at noon and major credit cards are accepted.

Hotel Hilltone *(☎ 38391, fax 38395, ⓔ hilltone@jp1.dot.net.in)*, off the main road a little closer to town, has a swimming pool, restaurant, bar and sauna. It's a modern place with comfortable singles/doubles for Rs 1290/1500 and lovely deluxe rooms for Rs 1790/1990; cottages built into the rock cost Rs 3190. Visa, MasterCard and AmEx are accepted. Small discounts are available in the low season.

Hotel Sunrise Palace *(☎ 43573, fax 38775, ⓔ sunrisepalace@gnahd.global.net.in)*, on a hill in the south of town, is a nice old building. Its family rooms are huge with high ceilings and good value at Rs 1450, although the standard rooms (Rs 650) and the deluxe rooms (Rs 850) are generally airless and cramped.

Connaught House *(☎ 38560, reservations ☎ 011-6561875, ⓔ welcom@ndf.vsnl.net.in)*, just east of the town, has an English cottage feel and is a pleasant place to stay. Owned by the maharaja of Jodhpur, it's set in its own pleasant gardens – the perfect place to sit back with a good book. The rooms in the old building are Rs 1400/1750 and have more character than those in the new wing. Breakfast (Rs 150), lunch and dinner (Rs 250) are available. Major credit cards are accepted.

Cama Rajputana Club Resort *(☎ 38205, fax 38412)*, off the road to the Dilwara temples, is a large, luxurious place with doubles from a paltry Rs 4800. If you stay for three nights, the third night is free; it'd want to be.

Places to Eat

Kanak Dining Hall, near the main bus stand, is popular. The all-you-can-eat Gujarati thalis are perhaps the best in Mt Abu (Rs 45); there's seating indoors and outdoors.

Veena Restaurant *(☎ 43448)* is farther up the hill, next to the junction at the bottom end of the polo ground. Its Gujarati thalis (Rs 40) are also excellent. ***Saniari Restaurant*** next door claims to do espresso coffee.

Shere Punjab Hotel, in the bazaar area, has reasonably priced Punjabi and Chinese food. The restaurant takes delight in its brain preparations (brain curry is Rs 35). There are also some more conventional dishes.

Madras Cafe *(☎ 43294)*, also in this area, is a pure veg place with an assortment of Indian and Western fare. There are even Jain pizzas (no garlic, onion or cheese) for Rs 35. The outdoor tables are a good place to watch the world go by.

Arbuda Restaurant, near the entrance to the private bus stand, has a pleasant dining room with easy Indian music. It specialises in reasonably priced Gujarati food.

Kings Food, on the road leading down to the lake, has the usual have-a-go-at-anything menu and is good for cheap Chinese, Punjabi and South Indian food. ***Dairy King***, opposite, does a good range of ice creams for around Rs 30.

RTDC Sarovar Restaurant is right on the water's edge. The food is nothing special (snacks and South Indian for Rs 40 and below) but it's a pleasant place from which to view the lake; the effect is diminished somewhat by the Hindi rock music blaring from loudspeakers. There are pool tables inside which can be used for Rs 50 per hour.

Palace Hotel (Bikaner House) is the best place to go for a special meal. The set lunch or dinner costs Rs 235 (veg) or Rs 295 (non-veg). It's a good idea to make an advance reservation. The ***Mayur Restaurant*** at the Hotel Hillock is also good for a splurge.

Getting There & Away

As you enter Mt Abu, there's a toll gate where bus and car passengers are charged Rs 5 each, plus Rs 5 per car. If you're travelling by bus, this is an irksome hold-up, as you have to wait until the collector painstakingly gathers the toll from each and every passenger (keep small change handy).

Bus From 6 am onwards, regular buses make the 27km climb from Abu Road station up to Mt Abu (Rs 13/15 for express/local buses, one hour). They leave from outside the main bus stand, next to the ticket booth. Some RSTC buses go all the way to Mt Abu, while others terminate at Abu Road.

The bus schedule from Mt Abu is extensive (inquiries ☎ 43434), and for many destinations you will find a direct bus faster and more convenient than going down to Abu Road station and waiting for a train. Deluxe buses go to Jaipur (Rs 201, 11 hours), Ajmer (Rs 152, eight hours), Udaipur (Rs 75, five hours), Jodhpur (Rs 121, eight hours), Ahmedabad (Rs 85, six hours), Jaisalmer (Rs 176, 12 hours) and Delhi (Rs 305, 15 hours). Buses belonging to private bus companies leave, not surprisingly, from the private bus stand for these and other destinations.

Train Abu Road, the railhead for Mt Abu, is on the broad-gauge line between Delhi and Mumbai via Ahmedabad. In Mt Abu there's a Railway Out Agency (☎ 38697) near the main bus stand (opposite the police station) which has quotas on most of the express trains out of Abu Road. It's open 10 am to 1 pm and 2 to 4 pm daily (only until noon on Sunday).

From Abu Road, the *Ahmedabad Mail* (9106) leaves at 1.05 pm and reaches Ahmedabad at 5.20 pm (Rs 52/81/234 general/sleeper/3A class). Going the other way, it leaves Abu Road at 1.20 pm, arriving in Jaipur at 11.25 pm (Rs 99/154/446) and

Delhi at 5.20 am (Rs 147/228/662). For Bhuj and the rest of the Kathiawar peninsula in Gujarat, change trains at Palanpur, 53km south of Abu Road.

Taxi A taxi, which you can share with up to five people, costs about Rs 200 from Abu Road. Some taxi drivers claim that this amount gets you only as far as the bus stand and ask an extra fee (as much as Rs 50) to take you to your hotel. To hire a jeep for local sightseeing costs around Rs 70/600 per hour/day.

Getting Around

Buses from the bus stand go to the various sites in Mt Abu, but it takes a little planning to get out and back without too much hanging around; it may be easier to take the five-hour tour (see Organised Tours earlier in this section). For Dilwara it's easier to take a share-taxi, which leave when full from opposite the Madras Cafe in the centre of town; it's Rs 4 per person or Rs 30 all to yourself.

There are no autorickshaws in Mt Abu, but it's relatively easy to get around on foot. Porters with trolleys can be hired for a small charge to transport luggage – weary travellers can even be transported on the trolley!

AROUND MT ABU

Achalgarh

The Shiva temple of **Achaleshwar Mahandeva**, 11km north of Mt Abu, has a number of interesting features, including a toe of Shiva, a brass Nandi and, where the Shiva lingam would normally be, a deep hole said to extend all the way to the underworld.

Outside, by the car park, three stone buffaloes stand around a tank while the figure of a king shoots at them with a bow and arrows. A legend states that the tank was once filled with ghee, but demons in the form of buffaloes came down and polluted the ghee – until the king shot them.

Guru Shikhar

At the end of the plateau, 15km from Mt Abu, is Guru Shikhar, the highest point in Rajasthan at 1721m. A road goes almost all the way to the summit. At the top is the **Atri Rishi Temple**, complete with a priest and good views all around.

Mt Abu Wildlife Sanctuary

This 290-sq-km sanctuary, 5.5km north-east of Mt Abu, is home to panthers, sambars, foxes, wild boars and bears. It's open 8 am to 5 pm daily. Entry is Rs 5/40 for Indians/foreigners. Vehicle entry is Rs 125, or Rs 15 for a motorcycle.

Gaumukh Temple

Down on the Abu Road side of Mt Abu, a small stream flows from the mouth of a marble cow, giving the shrine its name. There is also a marble figure of Nandi, Shiva's vehicle. The tank here, **Agni Kund**, is said to be the site of the sacrificial fire made by the sage Vasishta, from which four of the great Rajput clans were born. An image of Vasishta is flanked by figures of Rama and Krishna.

Western Rajasthan

JODHPUR

☎ 0291 • pop 795,000

Jodhpur is at the edge of the Great Thar Desert and is the largest city in Rajasthan after Jaipur. The city is dominated by a massive fort, Meherangarh, topping a sheer rocky ridge right in the middle of the town. From the fort, you can clearly see where the old city ends and the new begins; the view over the blue buildings of the old city is one of Rajasthan's most spectacular sights. Back at ground level, it's fascinating to wander around the jumble of winding streets in the old city, which is surrounded by a 10km-long wall (built about a century after the city was founded) and out of which eight gates lead. Part of the film *Rudyard Kipling's Jungle Book*, starring Sam Neill and John Cleese, was shot in Jodhpur, and yes, it was from here that those baggy-tight horse-riding trousers, jodhpurs, took their name.

Jodhpur was founded in 1459 by Rao Jodha, a chief of the Rajput clan known as the Rathores. His descendants ruled not only Jodhpur, but also other Rajput princely states. The Rathore kingdom was once known as Marwar, the Land of Death.

Every year Jodhpur hosts the Marwar Festival to celebrate the heroes of Rajasthan in music and dance. It commences on 31 October 2001, 19 October 2002, 8 October 2003, and 26 October 2004, and runs for two days.

Orientation

The Tourist Reception Centre, train stations and bus stand are outside the old city. High Court Rd runs from the Raika Bagh train station, past the Umaid gardens, and round beside the city wall towards the main station.

Information

Tourist Offices The Tourist Reception Centre (☎ 545083, ☎ 1364) is in the RTDC Hotel Ghoomar compound and is open 7 am to 8 pm Monday to Saturday.

There's a helpful International Tourists Bureau (☎ 439052) at the main train station which provides information and has comfortable armchairs, a shower and a toilet. It stays open until the 11.15 pm train to Jaisalmer departs.

Money The State Bank of India (High Court Rd branch, north-east of Umaid gar-

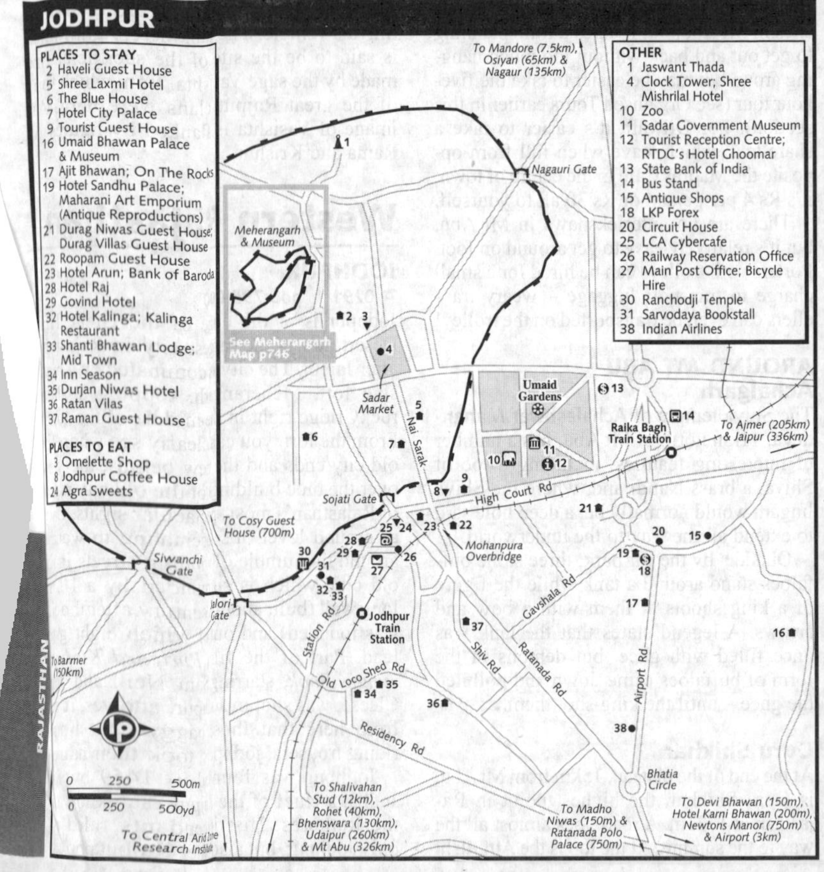

dens) changes currency and travellers cheques. The Bank of Baroda, near Hotel Arun, changes travellers cheques and, at the time of writing, issued cash advances against Visa and MasterCard. Reliable private operators changing a wider range of currencies include LKP Forex (☎ 512532), opposite Circuit House.

Email & Internet Access LCA Cybercafe (☎ 617825), in a lane opposite the Sojati Gate (same building as Lucky Bal Niketan), is arguably the cheapest Internet place in the centre of town (Rs 30 an hour) and connections generally aren't bad. There are numerous other places scattered around town.

Meherangarh

Still run by the maharaja of Jodhpur, Meherangarh, the Majestic Fort, is just that. Sprawled across a 125m-high hill, this is the most formidable fort in fort-studded Rajasthan. A winding road leads up to the entrance from the city, 5km below. The second gate is scarred by cannonball hits, indicating this was a fort that earned its keep. The gates, of which there are seven, include the **Jayapol**, built by Maharaja Man Singh in 1806 following his victory over the armies of Jaipur and Bikaner, and the **Fatehpol**, or Victory Gate, erected by Maharaja Ajit Singh to commemorate his defeat of the Mughals.

The final gate is the **Lohapol**, or Iron Gate, beside which are 15 hand prints, the sati (self-immolation) marks of Maharaja Man Singh's widows who threw themselves upon his funeral pyre in 1843. They still attract devotional attention and are usually covered in red powder.

Inside the fort is a series of courtyards and palaces. The **palace apartments** have evocative names such as the Sukh Mahal, or Pleasure Palace, and the Phool Mahal, or Flower Palace. They house a splendid collection of the trappings of Indian royalty, including an amazing collection of elephant howdahs (used when the maharajas rode their elephants in glittering procession through their capitals), miniature paintings from a variety of schools, and the inevitable Rajput armoury, palanquins, furniture and costumes.

At the southern end of the fort, old cannons look out from the ramparts over the sheer drop to the old town beneath. You can clearly hear voices and city sounds swept up by the air currents from the houses far below. The views from these ramparts are nothing less than magical. The **Chamunda Devi Temple**, dedicated to Durga, stands at this end of the fort.

The fort is open 9 am to 1 pm and 2 to 5 pm daily. Entry costs Rs 10/50 for Indians/foreigners and there's a Rs 50/100 camera/video charge. Guides are available for around Rs 100. For weary travellers, an elevator will take you right up to the top of the fort for Rs 10. There is an **astrologer**, Mr Sharma, at the fort (☎ 548790 ext 39 or mobile ☎ 9828032261) who has over 30 years' experience. He charges Rs 150/300 for a 15/30-minute consultation, and is available 9 am to 1 pm and 2 to 5 pm daily.

Jaswant Thada

This white marble memorial to Maharaja Jaswant Singh II, just off the fort road, is a short distance from the fort. The cenotaph, which was built in 1899, was followed by the royal crematorium and three other cenotaphs which stand nearby. There is some beautiful marble *jali* work (latticework) and there are fine views from the terrace in front of the cenotaph. Entry is Rs 5/10 for Indians/foreigners.

Clock Tower & Markets

The clock tower is a popular landmark in the old city. The vibrant Sardar Market is close to the tower, and narrow alleys lead from here to bazaars selling vegetables, spices, Indian sweets, textiles, silver and handicrafts. It's a great place to ramble around at leisure.

Umaid Bhawan Palace & Museum

Built of marble and pink sandstone, this immense palace is also known as the Chhittar Palace because of the local Chhittar sandstone used. Begun in 1929, it was designed by the president of the British Royal Institute of Architects for Maharaja Umaid Singh, and took 15 years to complete. It is

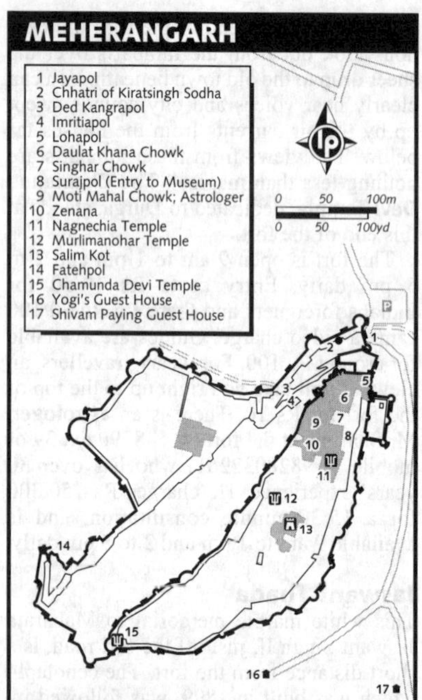

unusual in that it was built so close to independence at a time when such extravagances were decidedly *de rigueur*.

Maharaja Umaid Singh died in 1947; his successor still lives in part of the building. The rest has been turned into a hotel – and what a hotel! (See Places to Stay – Top End.)

The **museum** is worth a visit. An opulent array of items belonging to the maharaja is displayed – weapons, antique clocks, dainty crockery, and hunting trophies. Attendants will ensure you don't stray into the hotel, where they let you know you don't belong. Entry is Rs 10/40 for Indians/foreigners.

Umaid Gardens & Sadar Government Museum

The gardens contain the government museum, the library and the zoo. The museum's unlabelled exhibits include moth-eaten stuffed animals, old weapons and sculptures. It's open from 10 am to 4.30 pm daily except Friday; entry costs Rs 1/3 for students/adults.

Organised Tours & Village Safaris

For those with a tight schedule, the Tourist Reception Centre conducts tours of Jodhpur from 9 am to 1 pm and 2 to 6 pm daily (Rs 85 per person plus entry fees). These take in the Umaid Bhawan Palace, Meherangarh, Jaswant Thada and Mandore gardens (see Around Jodhpur).

Jodhpur is known for its interesting 'village safaris'. You can visit villages of the Bishnoi, a people whose belief in the sanctity of the environment and the need to protect trees and animals dates from the 15th century. Just about every hotel can organise these excursions, but typically, the quality varies. Recommended places include the Madho Niwas (☎ 434486), Durag Niwas (☎ 510692) and Durag Villas (☎ 512298) Guest Houses. Most charge around Rs 400 for the day including transport and lunch. The Govind Hotel (☎ 622758) has a sliding scale from Rs 375 per person (including lunch and mineral water) for the minimum two people, down to Rs 275 if there are five – good value if you can get a group together.

For horse safaris, contact Shalivahan Stud & Stables (☎ 740842), Basni Baghela, Pali Rd (12km south of Jodhpur).

Places to Stay – Budget

Most places advertise wonderful fort views but only a few deliver. Some of the best options are in the old city.

Haveli Guest House *(☎ 614615)* is inside the walled city at Makrana Mohalla. It's excellent value for money. Doubles with private bathroom range from Rs 200 up to 800. The rooftop veg restaurant (meals around Rs 80) boasts stunning views of the fort, Jaswant Thada and the old city. The rooms at the front were being refurbished when we visited and will have great views and some period furnishings (around Rs 400 to 500).

Shivam Paying Guest House *(☎ 610688, e shivamgh@hotmail.com)*, not far from the clock tower, is one place to go if you want a traditional family atmosphere. Rooms cost Rs 150 (Rs 200 with private bathroom). You'll have no hassles at all here.

The Blue House *(☎/fax 621396, e bluehouse36@hotmail.com)*, in the heart of the old city, is also good. The atmospheric rooms range from Rs 200 for a small double to Rs 600 for a larger room with semiprivate terrace. Internet access and home-cooked meals are available.

Yogi's Guest House *(☎ 643436, fax 619808)*, at the base of the fort walls, is another good choice, with a homey atmosphere. Set in the 500-year-old Rajpurohitji-ki-Haveli, the rooms are simple but clean. Those with shared bathroom cost Rs 100 to 150; those with private bathroom and constant hot water go for Rs 250 to 350 depending on the size. There are good views from the roof. This place, which has been recommended by many travellers, is well signposted off the lanes leading to the fort.

Cosy Guest House *(☎ 612066, Novechokiya Rd, Brahm Puri, Chuna-ki-Choki)*, formerly known as Joshi's Blue House, is an atmospheric little place in the old city. This blue-coloured house is also said to be 500 years old and is authentic (don't expect modern gadgets). Simple singles/doubles with shared bathroom start at Rs 90/150 (free bucket hot water). Go to the rooftop for a fine view.

Tourist Guest House *(☎ 541235, ⓔ udaibedi@hotmail.com)* is a great choice outside the old city on High Court Rd – a welcoming family atmosphere with rooms to match. Standard rooms cost Rs 150/250 with private bathroom. There's an elegant, spacious room at the front which is great value at Rs 300, and will remain so even after the private bathroom (under construction when we visited) is finished and the price rises.

Raman Guest House *(☎ 513980)*, opposite Kesar Bagh on Shiv Rd, is also known for its friendly family and is an increasingly popular place to stay. Rooms range from Rs 150/200 up to Rs 450.

Govind Hotel *(☎ 622758, ⓔ govindhotel2000@yahoo.com)*, opposite the railway reservation office, is just five minutes' walk from the train station – great if you've got an early morning train departure. This is a very traveller-friendly place with basic but cheap and clean rooms. Dorm beds go for Rs 60, rooms with private bathroom for Rs 200/250 (bucket hot water), and a double with constant hot water for Rs 300. The rooftop restaurant has wonderful views of the palace and fort.

Hotel Raj *(☎ 628447)*, almost opposite the train station, has cramped rooms for Rs 150/250 with squat toilet and free bucket hot water.

Shanti Bhawan Lodge *(☎ 621689, fax 639211, ⓔ shantib@nda.vsnl.net.in)*, in the street opposite the train station, has single cells for Rs 70, rooms with shared bathroom for Rs 100/150, and doubles with private bathroom from Rs 175 to 250. The rooms are generally spacious, a tad grubby and come with bucket hot water.

Madho Niwas (Bhenswara House) (*☎ 512486, fax 512086, New Airport Rd, Ratanada*) is a pleasant place to stay with a quiet lawn area. Doubles with private bathroom start at Rs 300 and range up to Rs 500. Meals are available; the Marwari-style barbecued chicken with a squeeze of lemon is delicious.

Durag Niwas Guest House *(☎ 510692, 1 Old Public Park)* is a family-run place with doubles from Rs 200 to 250, and an enormous room for Rs 500 where you could conceivably sleep up to eight people.

Durag Villas Guest House *(☎ 512298)*, next door, is good value. Rooms with private bathroom start at Rs 150/200; nicer rooms go for Rs 250/300. It's a quiet, relaxed place.

Roopam Guest House *(☎ 627374, 7 Jagannath Building, Mohanpura Overbridge)* has one room with shared bathroom for Rs 200/250, and three rooms with private bathroom for Rs 400/500.

Shree Laxmi Hotel *(☎ 547047)*, south of the clock tower on Nai Sarak, has rooms which, thankfully, are 'fully equipped with furniture'. They're OK, with a balcony and TV for Rs 150/250.

Hotel Arun *(☎ 620238, fax 436019, ⓔ arvind@bom7.vsnl.net.in)*, opposite Sojati Gate, has clean rooms for Rs 210/310 (satellite TV Rs 10 extra) though they're a bit soulless. There's a pricey dorm (Rs 80) and a handy half-day facility – if you stay less than 12 hours, the cost is 30% less.

Places to Stay – Mid-Range

Ratan Vilas *(☎/fax 614418, Old Loco Shed Rd, Ratanada)* is a lovely, quiet family villa set in a nice garden. Comfortable, well-appointed doubles cost Rs 750 to 950 and there's a suite for Rs 1500. Delicious banquet-style meals are available; if you're keen, cooking classes are available. Horse safaris can be arranged on request.

Devi Bhawan *(☎ 511067, fax 512215, e devibhawan@satyamonline.com, 1 Ratanada Area)* is highly recommended and great value for money. This green oasis has fresh singles/doubles for Rs 700/750, and cottages for Rs 850. There's a good restaurant and the garden is one of the best in Jodhpur.

Durjan Niwas Hotel *(☎ 649546, fax 616991)*, off Old Loco Shed Rd, has elegant, quiet rooms for Rs 1195/1500, but will usually negotiate if things are quiet.

Newtons Manor *(☎ 430686, fax 610603, e info@newtonsmanor.com, 86 Jawahar Colony, Ratanada)* has a nice atmosphere, although some readers have found the welcome less than warm and the location far from ideal. There are just five rooms and prices start at Rs 1095. Scrumptious home-cooked meals are also available here.

Hotel Kalinga *(☎ 627338, fax 627314, e kalingahotel@satyam.net.in)* is convenient if you want to be close to the main train station. Dull but comfortable and spacious rooms start at Rs 490/700, or Rs 540/800 including continental breakfast. Check-out is 24 hours.

Hotel Sandhu Palace *(☎ 510154, fax 510674, e sandhupalace@yahoo.com)*, opposite Circuit House, is a nice, quiet place with pleasant air-cooled rooms starting at Rs 350/450 and air-con rooms starting at Rs 800/900. All major credit cards are accepted and cars (with driver) can be rented for Rs 1000 for eight hours.

Hotel City Palace *(☎ 649911, fax 639033, 32 Nai Sarak)* has comfortable rooms for Rs 990/1190, or Rs 1040/1290 with breakfast. The upper rooms at the back have good views over the old city.

Ajit Bhawan *(☎ 511410, fax 510674, e abhawan@del3.vsnl.net.in, Airport Rd)* has long been popular with travellers. Behind the gracious main heritage building there is a series of attractively furnished stone cottages arranged around a delightful garden for Rs 1895/2295. There's a restaurant, a sensational swimming pool (Rs 250 for nonguests) and a gift shop. Other services include babysitting (Rs 100 an hour), Internet access and a wonderful collection of vintage cars that can be rented for a small fortune – the 1939 Chevrolet convertible costs Rs 2400/4000 for a half/full day.

Hotel Karni Bhawan *(☎ 432220, fax 433495, Palace Rd)* is a modern place with traditional touches, set in well-manicured gardens and with a pool. Comfortable rooms start at Rs 1175/1425 (the rooms in the new building are best). The restaurant is excellent and you can eat indoors or under the stars.

Inn Season *(☎/fax 616400)*, just off Old Loco Shed Rd east of the railway line, is a homey place with well-kept rooms starting at Rs 1200. Check out the funky old German record player with an equally funky collection of records, including Louis Armstrong and Ella Fitzgerald.

Places to Stay – Top End

Umaid Bhawan Palace *(☎ 433316, fax 635373)* is *the* place to stay if you have a passion for pure luxury. This very elegant palace has an indoor swimming pool, a tennis court, a billiard room, lush lawns and several restaurants (see Places to Eat). Standard singles/doubles cost US$165/185, and suites range from US$325 to US$750 for the Maharani Suite. If you can possibly afford it, opt for a suite, as the cheaper rooms are suitably comfortable, but hardly palatial.

Ratanada Polo Palace *(☎ 431910, fax 433118, Residency Rd)* is set in its own spacious grounds, but is a little lacking in character. It has a pool, a restaurant and rooms for Rs 1800/2400.

Places to Eat

While you're in Jodhpur, try a glass of *makhania* lassi, a filling saffron-flavoured variety of that most refreshing of drinks.

Shree Mishrilal Hotel, at the clock tower, is nothing fancy to look at, but whips up the best lassis in town. A delicious glass of creamy special makhania lassi is Rs 10.

Agra Sweets, opposite Sojati Gate, also sells good lassis (Rs 10), as well as tasty Jodhpur desserts such as *mawa ladoo* (Rs 5) and the baklava-like *mawa kachori* (Rs 9).

The ***Omelette Shop***, just through the gate behind the clock tower on the northern side of the square, claims to go through 1000 eggs a day. It's a small place and it's usually packed with locals. Two spicy boiled eggs cost Rs 5; a two-egg omelette with chilli, coriander and four pieces of bread is a bargain Rs 12.

Kalinga Restaurant, at the hotel of the same name near the train station, is a pleasant place to eat. It has tasty veg and nonveg Indian, Chinese and continental food; chicken curry is Rs 65. It's open 7 am to 10.30 pm daily. ***Mid Town***, nearby, is a bit overpriced but not bad. Most mains cost between Rs 40 and 65 and there are some Rajasthani specialities such as *chakki-ka-sagh* (wheat sponge cooked in rich gravy, a speciality of Jodhpur; Rs 55) and Rajasthani thalis (Rs 60).

Jodhpur Coffee House serves filtered coffee for Rs 9 and 'cold coffee' for Rs 15/30 without/with ice cream. It also offers thalis for Rs 28 which includes ice cream for dessert.

On the Rocks, next to the Ajit Bhawan hotel, is very popular, especially with locals. It serves tasty Indian cuisine outdoors; mushroom kebabs are Rs 55 and a half/full tandoori is Rs 100/160. The service can be sluggish, especially when it's busy. In the same compound, there's a ***bar*** and an excellent ***bakery*** (pastries cost Rs 15). The compound is open 12.30 to 3 pm and 7 to 11 pm.

Umaid Bhawan Palace has four restaurants, including the very grand ***Marwar Hall*** (the buffet here is lacklustre). Overlooking the back lawn is ***The Pillars***, a breezy informal eatery recommended for a light bite; the ***Risala***, which is more upmarket; and ***Kebab Konner***, an open-air restaurant which specialises in moderately priced barbecued Indian food (dinner only). Or, you may like to have a drop of amber fluid at the ***Trophy Bar***.

The ***refreshment room*** on the 1st floor of the main train station isn't bad. There's veg and nonveg food to munch on while waiting for your train; a veg/nonveg thali is just Rs 16/22.

Shopping

The usual Rajasthani handicrafts are available here, but Jodhpur specialises in antiques. The greatest number of antique shops is in the streets east and west of Circuit House. These shops are well known to Western antique dealers who come here with wallets stuffed with plastic cards. As a result, you'll be hard pressed to find any bargains. The trade in antique architectural fixtures is contributing to the desecration of India's cultural heritage; Lonely Planet recommends that travellers do not support this trade. Many places also sell cheaper replicas based on original antique designs.

Getting There & Away

Air Indian Airlines (☎ 510757) is south of the centre on Airport Rd (open 10 am to 1.15 pm and 2 to 4.30 pm daily). Daily flights depart for Delhi (US$105) via Jaipur (US$85) at 7.20 pm and for Mumbai (US$150) via Udaipur (US$65) at 8.30 am. Jet Airways (☎ 625094) also flies to Delhi (via Jaipur) and Mumbai (via Udaipur).

Bus RSTC buses depart regularly throughout the day from the bus stand for, among other places, Jaisalmer (Rs 92, five hours), Udaipur (Rs 105, eight hours), Jaipur (Rs 130, seven hours), Ajmer (Rs 82, four hours), Bikaner (Rs 101, five hours), Delhi (Rs 220, 12½ hours) and Ahmedabad (Rs 170, 10 hours). The Roadways inquiry number is ☎ 544686.

Private bus companies have offices opposite the train station and in the street leading to Ranchodji Temple.

Train The computerised reservation office is on Station Rd, between the train station and Sojati Gate. There's a tourist quota (Window 788). The office is open 8 am to 8 pm Monday to Saturday and 8 am to 1.45 pm Sunday.

The *Jodhpur-Jaisalmer Express* (4810) leaves at 11.15 pm, arriving in Jaisalmer around 5.30 am (Rs 82/130, general/sleeper class). The *Mandore Express* (2462) leaves Jodhpur at 7.30 pm, arriving in Delhi at 6.15 am (Rs 131/204/590, general/sleeper/3A class). For Jaipur, the *Intercity Express* (2466) leaves at 5.45 am, arriving at 10.35 am (Rs 104/162/749).

Getting Around

To/From the Airport The airport is only 5km from the city centre. The trip costs about Rs 50/110 in an autorickshaw/taxi.

Taxi & Autorickshaw There's a taxi stand near the main train station. Most autorickshaw journeys should cost less than Rs 25.

AROUND JODHPUR

Mandore

Situated 9km north of Jodhpur, Mandore was the capital of Marwar before the foundation of Jodhpur. Today, its extensive **gardens** with high rock terraces make it a popular local attraction. The gardens also contain the cenotaphs of Jodhpur rulers, including the soaring memorial to Maharaja Dhiraj Ajit Singh.

The **Hall of Heroes** contains 15 figures carved out of a rock wall. The brightly painted figures represent Hindu deities and local heroes on horseback. The Shrine of 33 Crore Gods is painted with figures of deities and spirits (33 crore equals 330 million).

Mandore Guest House *(☎ 0291-545620, fax 546959)* has delightful accommodation in a leafy garden. Singles/doubles with private bathroom cost Rs 350/500.

Bhenswara

Ravla Bhenswara *(☎ 02978-22080; in Jodhpur ☎/fax 0291-434486)* is a simple rural manor that is perfect if you want some respite from the rigours of travelling in India. Located 130km south of Jodhpur, it has a homey appeal. The quaint singles/doubles start at Rs 800/950. There's a pool, and village safaris are available. Don't miss the evening parakeet invasion at nearby Madho Bagh.

Rohet

Rohet Garh *(☎ 02936-68231)* is a heritage hotel in this small village, 40km south of Jodhpur, where Bruce Chatwin wrote *The Songlines* and William Dalrymple began *City of Djinns*. Good rooms start at Rs 1100/1700, meals are available and there's a fantastic swimming pool.

Osiyan

The ancient Great Thar Desert town of Osiyan, 65km north of Jodhpur, was a great trading centre between the 8th and 12th centuries when it was dominated by the Jains. The wealth of Osiyan's medieval inhabitants allowed them to build lavish and exquisitely sculptured temples, most of which have withstood the ravages of time. The sculptural detail on the Osiyan temples rivals that of the Hoysala temples of Karnataka and the Sun Temple of Konark in Orissa.

The Camel Camp *(☎/fax 0291-437023)* offers a range of tented accommodation atop a secluded sand dune overlooking Osiyan. Double-occupancy tents with shared bathroom are Rs 300. More luxurious tents with private bathroom (and shower) are also available. There's a breezy bar with views of the temples, and camel safaris can be arranged. Advance bookings are essential.

For cheaper accommodation, Bhanu Prakash Sharma, a Brahmin priest, runs a very basic ***guesthouse*** *(☎ 02922-74232)* for Rs 200 per room (maximum five people).

There are regular buses from Jodhpur to Osiyan (Rs 20, 1½ hours).

Nagaur

About 135km north-east of Jodhpur, Nagaur has the historic **Ahhichatragarh**, an ancient fort which is currently being restored (entry costs Rs 5/15 for Indians/foreigners, plus Rs 25/50 for a camera/video). Nagaur also sports a smaller version of Pushkar's Camel Fair: The **Nagaur Cattle Fair** in January/ February attracts thousands of rural people from far and wide. It commences on 19 February 2002 and 8 February 2003, and runs for four days.

Luxurious ***royal tents*** *(☎ 0291-433316, fax 635373)* are available for US$175/225 a single/double at fair time. They must be booked in advance.

RTDC Kurjan Nagaur has good rooms for Rs 250/300 with private bathroom (US$40/53 during the fair).

Hotel Mahaveer International *(☎ 01582-43158)* has rooms costing from Rs 250/350 with geyser hot water and colour TV to Rs 725 for a double with air-con. You could also try the ***Hotel Bhaskar*** *(☎ 01582-22100)*, where rooms start at Rs 100/250.

JAISALMER

☎ 02992 • pop 48,000

Jaisalmer is a place that should exist only in the imagination. Nothing else in India is remotely similar to this enchanting city, which has been dubbed the 'golden city' because of the honey colour imparted to its stone ramparts by the setting sun. The vision of the massive fort thrusting heavenwards out of the barren deserts is unforgettable, and the magic doesn't diminish as you approach its walls and bastions, and lose yourself in its labyrinthine streets and bazaars. The fort, which resembles a gigantic sandcastle and is like something out of *The Thousand and One Nights*, is home to several thousand people.

Jaisalmer's popularity has come at a cost. A major concern is that the poor plumbing and open drains have saturated the foundations, causing subsidence and collapse in buildings. The old open drains were created to take a limited amount of water and waste, and cannot cope with the pressure being placed upon them today. There has even been talk of closing all hotels within the fort walls. Tourists can do their bit by disposing of rubbish properly and encouraging hoteliers to do so as well. For more information on the initiatives being taken to preserve Jaisalmer, contact Jaisalmer Conservation Initiative (☎ 011-4631818, fax 4611290), 71 Lodi Estate, New Delhi 110 003, or the British-registered charity Jaisalmer in Jeopardy (☎/fax 020-7460 8592, ⓔ jaisalmer@lineone.net), 20E Redcliffe Gardens, London SW10 9EX.

Jaisalmer hosts the Desert Festival in February each year. It commences on 25 February 2002, 14 February 2003, and 4 February 2004, and runs for two days. It can be a little contrived but it's colourful enough and it does give you the chance to try your hand at turban-tying competitions.

History

Most historians place the foundation of the city and fort at around 1156, when the Bhatti Rajput ruler Jaisala moved the city from the former capital of Lodhruva, 15km to the north-west. Subsequent history has been derived from the tales and songs of the bards.

In the centuries that followed, Jaisalmer's strategic position on the camel-train routes between India and Central Asia brought it great wealth. The merchants and townspeople built magnificent houses and mansions, all exquisitely carved from wood and golden sandstone.

The rise of sea trade and the port of Mumbai saw the decline of Jaisalmer. Partition and the cutting of the trade routes through to Pakistan seemingly sealed the city's fate, and water shortages could have pronounced the death sentence. However, the 1965 and 1971 India-Pakistan Wars revealed Jaisalmer's strategic importance.

Today, tourism rivals the military base as the pillar of the city's economy. The presence of the Border Security Force hardly impinges at all on the life of the old city and only the occasional sound of war planes ever disturbs the tranquility of this desert gem.

While Jaisalmer largely escaped direct conquest by the Muslim rulers of Delhi, it did experience its share of sieges and sackings with the inevitable Rajput jauhar being declared in the face of certain defeat. There is perhaps no other city in which you can more easily conjure up the spirit of those times.

Orientation

The massive fort rises above the city and is entered via the First Fort Gate. Within the fort walls is a warren of narrow, paved streets complete with Jain temples and the old palace of the former ruler – although you may think yourself lost at times, it's small enough that you'll find your way eventually.

The main market, Bhatia Market, and most of the city's attractions and important

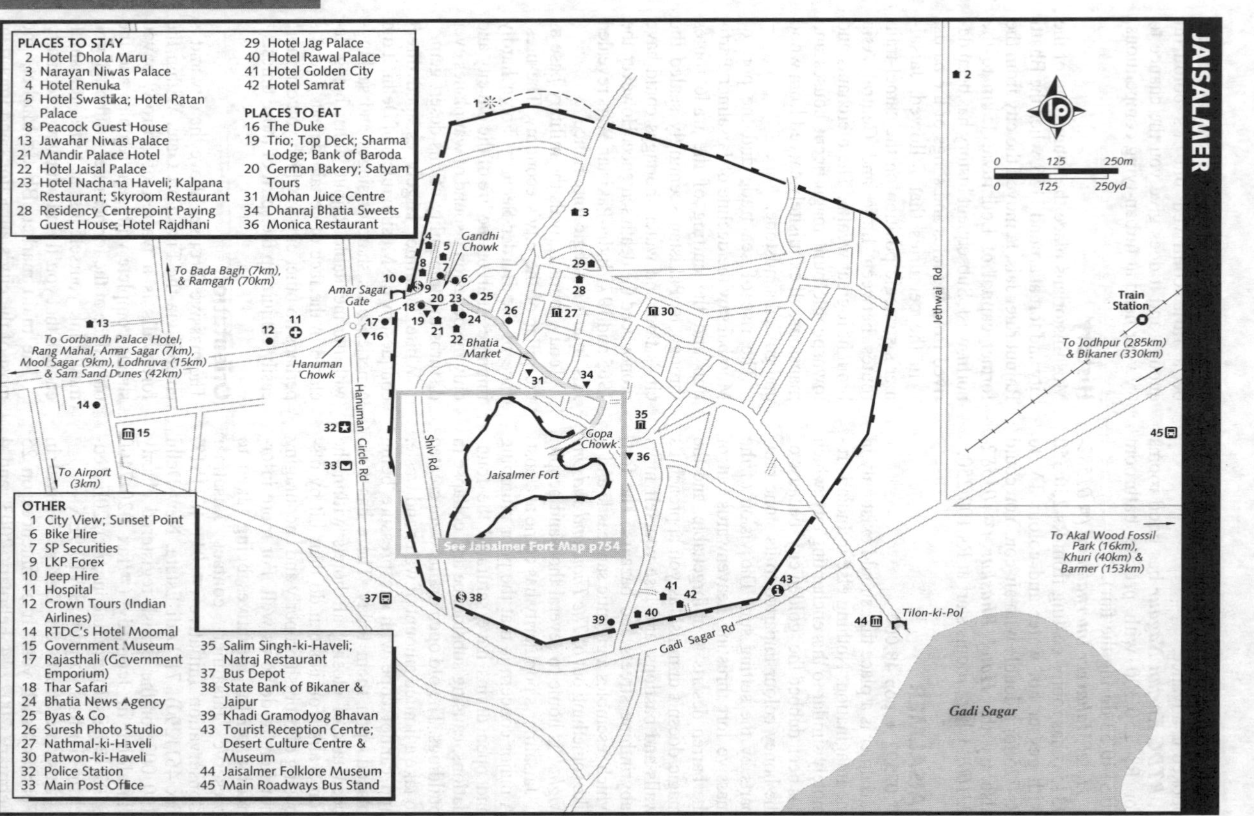
JAISALMER
RAJASTHAN
PLACES TO STAY
2 Hotel Dhola Maru
3 Narayan Niwas Palace
4 Hotel Renuka
5 Hotel Swastika; Hotel Ratan Palace
8 Peacock Guest House
13 Jawahar Niwas Palace
21 Mandir Palace Hotel
22 Hotel Jaisal Palace
23 Hotel Nachana Haveli; Kalpana Restaurant; Skyroom Restaurant
28 Residency Centrepoint Paying Guest House; Hotel Rajdhani
29 Hotel Jag Palace
40 Hotel Rawal Palace
41 Hotel Golden City
42 Hotel Samrat
PLACES TO EAT
16 The Duke
19 Trio; Top Deck; Sharma Lodge; Bank of Baroda
20 German Bakery; Satyam Tours
31 Mohan Juice Centre
34 Dhanraj Bhatia Sweets
36 Monica Restaurant
OTHER
1 City View; Sunset Point
6 Bike Hire
7 SP Securities
9 LKP Forex
10 Jeep Hire
11 Hospital
12 Crown Tours (Indian Airlines)
14 RTDC's Hotel Moomal
15 Government Museum
17 Rajasthali (Government Emporium)
18 Thar Safari
24 Bhatia News Agency
25 Byas & Co
26 Suresh Photo Studio
27 Nathmal-ki-Haveli
30 Patwon-ki-Haveli
32 Police Station
33 Main Post Office
35 Salim Singh-ki-Haveli; Natraj Restaurant
37 Bus Depot
38 State Bank of Bikaner & Jaipur
39 Khadi Gramodyog Bhavan
43 Tourist Reception Centre; Desert Culture Centre & Museum
44 Jaisalmer Folklore Museum
45 Main Roadways Bus Stand
0 125 250m
0 125 250yd
Train Station
To Jodhpur (285km) & Bikaner (330km)
Jethwai Rd
To Akal Wood Fossil Park (16km), Khuri (40km) & Barmer (153km)
Tilon-ki-Pol
Gadi Sagar
Gadi Sagar Rd
Gopa Chowk
Jaisalmer Fort
See Jaisalmer Fort Map p754
Shiv Rd
Hanuman Circle Rd
Hanuman Chowk
Bhatia Market
Gandhi Chowk
Amar Sagar Gate
To Bada Bagh (7km), & Ramgarh (70km)
To Gorbandh Palace Hotel, Rang Mahal, Amar Sagar (7km), Mool Sagar (9km), Lodhruva (15km) & Sam Sand Dunes (42km)
To Airport (3km)

offices surround the fort to the north. This old part of town was itself once completely surrounded by an extensive wall, much of which has sadly been torn down in recent years for building material.

Information

Tourist Offices The Tourist Reception Centre (☎ 52406) is on Gadi Sagar Rd, about 2km south-east of the First Fort Gate. It's open from 7 am to 8 pm daily except Sunday.

Money The Bank of Baroda at Gandhi Chowk changes travellers cheques and issues cash advances on Visa, MasterCard and Bobcard for the usual 1% commission plus Rs 100. The State Bank of Bikaner & Jaipur, south of the fort, changes travellers cheques and major currencies. The more professional and reliable private moneychangers include LKP Forex (☎ 53679) and SP Securities; both have offices on Gandhi Chowk.

Post & Communications The main post office is on Hanuman Circle Rd, just west of the fort. Inside the fort is a small post office which only sells stamps; it's open from 10 am to 3 pm Monday to Saturday.

From no Internet places just a few years ago, Jaisalmer now has dozens of places where you can surf the net, both inside and outside the fort. All charge Rs 1 per minute and connections vary from instant to painfully slow – morning and late evening are your best chance of seeing your inbox within the hour.

Bookshops Postcards and day-old newspapers can be bought at the well-stocked Bhatia News Agency, in Bhatia Market. It has an excellent selection of new books (especially novels), as well as some second-hand books (in English, French, German, Spanish and several other languages) which can be either bought or swapped.

Photography In Bhatia Market (opposite the Bhatia News Agency) is Byas & Co (☎ 51884), where you can buy fresh slide film (Rs 220) and print film (Rs 90). Print developing costs Rs 15, plus Rs 3/4 per small/medium print. It usually takes three hours. The place sells Video 8 cassettes (Rs 250), Mini Digital Video cassettes (Rs 750) and batteries. Suresh Photo Studio, 50m to the east, is similar, but also sells a good range of large black-and-white prints of Jaisalmer from the early 20th century.

Jaisalmer Fort

Jaisalmer Fort is the essence of Jaisalmer and the most alive of any museum, fort or palace you're likely to visit in India. There are homes and hotels hidden in the laneways, and shops and stalls swaddled in the kaleidoscopic mirrors and embroideries of brilliant Rajasthani cloth.

Built in 1156 by the Rajput ruler Jaisala, and reinforced by subsequent rulers, the fort crowns the 80m-high Trikuta Hill. Over the centuries it was the focus of a number of battles between the Bhattis, the Mughals of Delhi and the Rathores of Jodhpur. About a quarter of the old city's population resides within the fort walls, which have 99 bastions around their circumference.

The fort is entered through a forbidding series of massive gates leading to a large courtyard, which was used to review troops, hear petitions and present extravagant entertainment for important visitors. The former maharaja's seven-storey **palace** or Rajmahal fronts onto this square. Part of the palace is open to the public. Note particularly the sculptured pavilion-type balcony on the eastern wall. Here drummers raised the alarm when the fort was under siege. Although there's not much to see inside, the 360° views from the summit are spectacular. It's open from 8 am to 5 pm daily in summer (from 9 am in winter), and entry costs Rs 10, plus Rs 20/50 for a camera/video.

Jain Temples Within the fort walls are seven beautifully carved Jain temples built between the 12th and 15th centuries, including very fine temples dedicated to Rikhabdev and Sambhavanth. They are all connected by a series of corridors and walkways. Only two are open to non-Jains, from 7 am to noon. Entry is Rs 10 and the camera/video fee is Rs 50/100.

Laxminath Temple This Hindu temple, in the centre of the fort, is simpler than the Jain temples, although there are some interesting paintings in the drum of the dome. Devotees offer grain which is distributed before the temple. There is a repousse silver architrave around the entrance to the inner sanctum, and a heavily garlanded image enshrined within.

Havelis

Jaisalmer's finely sculptured sandstone havelis, which were built by wealthy Jaisalmer merchants, are among the most exquisite in Rajasthan.

Patwon-ki-Haveli This most elaborate and magnificent of all the Jaisalmer havelis stands in a narrow lane. It was built between 1800 and 1860 by five Jain brothers who made their fortunes in trading jewellery and fine brocades. Although it's more impressive from the outside, the view back towards the fort from the roof is magnificent. Entry is Rs 2.

Salim Singh-ki-Haveli This private haveli was built about 300 years ago and part of it is still occupied. Salim Singh was the prime minister when Jaisalmer was the capital of a princely state, and his mansion has a beautifully arched roof with superb carved brackets in the form of peacocks. The stone elephants in front of the haveli are traditionally erected in front of the homes of prime ministers. Entry to the haveli costs Rs 15, and it's open from 8 am to 6 pm daily.

Nathmal-ki-Haveli This beautiful late-19th-century haveli was also a prime minister's house. The left and right wings of the building were carved by brothers; they are very similar, but not identical. Yellow sandstone elephants guard the building diligently, and even the front door is a work of art.

Gadi Sagar

This tranquil tank, south of the city walls, once provided the city's water supply, and is surrounded by many small temples and shrines. A wide variety of waterfowl flock here in winter.

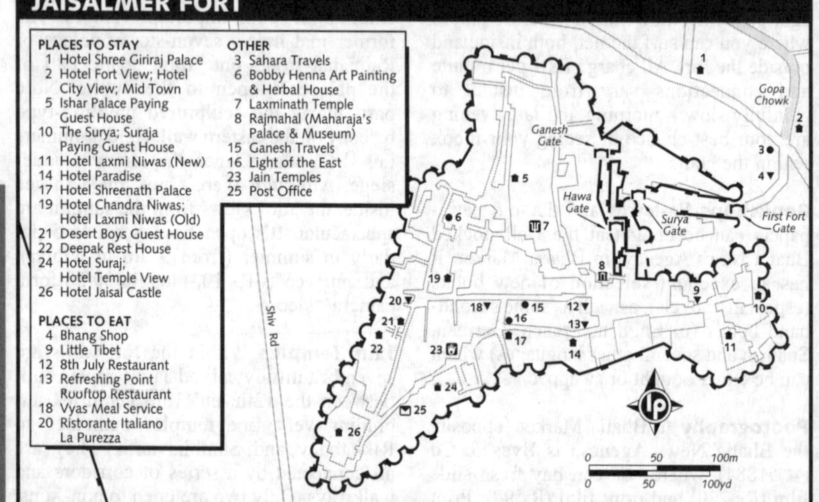

The yellow sandstone gateway arching across the road down to the tank is the **Tilon-ki-Pol**, and is said to have been built by a famous prostitute, Tilon. When she offered to pay to have this gateway constructed, the maharaja refused permission on the grounds that he would have to pass under it to go down to the tank, and he felt that this would be beneath his dignity. While he was away, she built the gate anyway, adding a Krishna temple on top so that the king could not tear it down.

Museums

Next to the Tourist Reception Centre is the **Desert Culture Centre & Museum**, which has textiles, old coins, fossils and traditional Rajasthani instruments, among other things. The museum's aim is to preserve Rajasthan's cultural heritage and to conduct research on local history.

The museum is open from 10 am to 7.30 pm every day and there's a puppet show from 6.30 to 7.30 pm nightly (Rs 30). Entry is Rs 5/10 for Indians/foreigners, which includes entry to the **Jaisalmer Folklore Museum** located on the road leading down to the lake (open from 9 am to 7 pm daily). The hill near this museum is a tremendous place to soak up the sunset.

Close to the RTDC Hotel Moomal is the small **government museum**, which has a limited but well-captioned collection of fossils, some of which date back to the Jurassic era (160 to 180 million years ago). The museum is open 10 am to 4.30 pm daily except Friday. Entry costs Rs 3 (Rs 1 for students), free on Monday. Photography is not permitted.

Henna Painting & Ayurvedic Massage

Bobby Henna Art Painting and Herbal House (☎ 54468) is located in the fort. Because it is run by women, female travellers will feel comfortable here. This welcoming place charges Rs 50 to 100 for henna painting, Rs 250 for a full body massage with oil, and – perfect after a few days on a camel – Rs 300 for a full body Ayurvedic massage (including facial) with 32 herbs.

Arrival in Jaisalmer

You realise that Jaisalmer is a tourist hot spot long before you arrive. Hotel and camel safari touts may even approach you in Bikaner or Jodhpur. If travelling by bus you will usually find the number of passengers suddenly increases about an hour before arrival with touts knowing that they have a captive audience.

In the past few years, the local authorities have introduced policies designed to keep the touts at bay. Most carriages on the overnight train carry at least a couple of soldiers to try to ensure you get a good night's sleep and they also patrol the railway platforms in Jodhpur with varying degrees of vigilance. Perhaps the most surreal experience is stumbling out of the train in the predawn light to find a small army of hotel owners kept behind a barricade about 20m from the station exit, holding up their signs and champing at the bit. Once you cross that line, you're on your own.

Don't believe *anyone* who offers to take you 'anywhere you like' for just a few rupees, and take with a grain of salt claims that the hotel you want to stay in is 'full', 'closed', 'no good any more' or has suffered some other inglorious fate. If the hotel of your choice has a representative waiting for you, by all means accept the free ride. Alternatively, take a rickshaw and hope you get an honest one (they do exist) – pay no more than Rs 30.

Organised Tours

Few travellers visit Jaisalmer without taking a camel safari into the desert. For details, see the boxed text 'Camel Safaris Around Jaisalmer' later in this chapter.

The Tourist Reception Centre offers a morning city sightseeing tour which leaves from its office around 8 am (Rs 75 per person, minimum four people). It also runs daily sunset tours to the Sam sand dunes (Rs 120 per person) which leave at 3 pm and return after sunset. On request, the tours to Sam may stop at Kanoi, 5km before the dunes, from where it's possible to get a camel to the dunes in time for sunset (for about Rs 50).

Places to Stay

Staying at one of the hotels within the fort itself is the most romantic choice, but there are equally good hotels outside the fort walls. Motorised traffic is not permitted in the narrow lanes beyond the main square at most times, which means you'll have to lug your backpack anywhere farther into the maze – a five-minute walk at most. Many hotels have an ungenerous 9 am checkout time.

Unfortunately, many hotels are into the high-pressure selling of camel safaris. Some places can get quite ugly if you book a safari through someone else. Not only will they refuse to hold your baggage, they'll actually evict you from the hotel! Before you check in, make it clear that you will only stay if you don't have to do a safari – if they hassle you, simply move on.

If there's a festival on, prices skyrocket and accommodation of any kind can be hard to get. Many places offer low-season discounts between April and August – but you'd be crazy to come here during this time, as Jaisalmer becomes hellishly hot.

Places to Stay – Budget

Town Area There are three excellent choices in the small street running north of Gandhi Chowk.

Hotel Renuka *(☎ 52757)* is a good-value family-run place. Singles/doubles with shared bathroom cost Rs 80/100, with private bathroom Rs 130/150. The best room, with a balcony, costs Rs 180/200. There's a roof terrace here with great fort views and a rooftop restaurant. The same family runs ***Hotel Ratan Palace*** *(☎ 53615)*, closer to Gandhi Chowk on the same street. Larger, newer rooms cost between Rs 250 and Rs 350.

Hotel Swastika *(☎ 52483)* gets good reports from travellers and deservedly so. It has simple, well-kept rooms with shared bathroom for Rs 90/150 and a range of other rooms including a larger room for Rs 220/250 with private bathroom.

Peacock Guest House *(☎ 50039)*, on the same street, gets mixed reviews from travellers but it's definitely cheap. Basic rooms with shared bathroom cost Rs 40/60. There's also a gloomy dorm with beds for Rs 30.

Hotel Golden City *(☎/fax 51664, ⓔ khangazi@hotmail.com)*, south of the fort entrance just off Gadi Sagar Rd, is a laid-back place which has a real travellers' feel to it. Simple, clean rooms with shared bathroom start at just Rs 40/50; those with private bathroom cost Rs 55/110. There's a pleasant, reasonably priced rooftop restaurant.

Hotel Samrat *(☎ 51498)*, in the same area, is another bargain, with a very clean single cell for Rs 30 and larger rooms with private bathroom for Rs 60/90. A dorm bed is a mere Rs 10 – possibly the cheapest bed in Rajasthan.

Hotel Rawal Palace *(☎ 51966)* has tidy, spacious rooms for Rs 150/200 with private bathroom, balcony and TV.

Hotel Fort View *(☎ 52214)*, close to the entrance to the fort, has rooms starting at Rs 60/80 with private bathroom (some of the rooms are tiny). The best room costs Rs 300/350 and has a fort view. There's a popular restaurant on the top floor.

Hotel City View *(☎ 52804)*, next door, has dusty rooms for Rs 80 a double, while Rs 120/150 gets you a room with a balcony looking towards the fort. You should have no hassles here.

Hotel Shree Giriraj Palace *(☎ 52268)* is a little bit farther west, just off Bhatia Market. This cheap and cheerful place has rooms for Rs 100/120 with shared bathroom, or Rs 150/200 with private bathroom and bucket hot water.

Residency Centrepoint Paying Guest House *(☎/fax 52883)*, near the Patwon-ki-Haveli, has five clean and spacious doubles with private bathroom for Rs 200. Room No 101 has a lovely antique balcony and nice internal fittings. This friendly, family-run place serves good home-cooked meals on the rooftop with superb views of the fort. ***Hotel Rajdhani*** *(☎ 52746)*, next door, and ***Hotel Jag Palace*** *(☎ 50438)*, opposite, aren't as good but are cheaper.

Fort In the western part of the fort, ***Deepak Rest House*** *(☎ 52665, fax 52070)* is a popular place. Most rooms are different with singles/doubles starting at Rs 40/80. Rooms with a view and a balcony (room Nos 8, 14,

17 and 21) cost Rs 200/250. The best is room No 9 (Rs 300/350) which is, not surprisingly, often occupied. The hotel is actually part of the fort wall, so the views from some rooms are stunning, as are those from the rooftop. A bed in the dorm is Rs 25. The rooftop veg restaurant has a good range of dishes.

***Hotel Paradise** (☎ 52674)* is popular with travellers. It's a kind of haveli, with 23 rooms arranged around a leafy courtyard, and has excellent views of the palace from the roof where Rajasthani musicians entertain you in the evening. Rooms with shared bathroom are Rs 150/200, and doubles with private bathroom cost from Rs 350 to 650. Breakfast is the only meal available.

***Ishar Palace Paying Guest House** (☎ 53062)* is near Laxminath Temple. Rooms are spartan but quite clean. A top-floor double with private bathroom and bamboo roof costs Rs 100. A bed in the dorm costs Rs 50. This was the home of a 19th-century prime minister, Ishar Singh, as evidenced by the statues of elephants before the building. You can even stay in his modest but atmospheric room with the balcony from which he used to address supplicants (Rs 150/200). There's also a nearby annexe which can house five people for Rs 50 per person – ideal for families.

***Hotel Chandra Niwas** (☎ 53277)* is a friendly place to stay with just a handful of well-maintained double rooms, which range from Rs 150 with shared bathroom to Rs 250 with private bathroom.

***Hotel Laxmi Niwas (old)** (☎ 52758)*, at the end of the same lane, has very small rooms with shared bathroom for Rs 50/100 (the shared shower is a bit primitive, and the toilet is tiny), and doubles for Rs 125 and 150 on the upper floor. The same owner runs ***Hotel Laxmi Niwas (new)** (☎ 52758)* in the south-east corner of the fort where well-kept rooms with shared bathroom start at Rs 200/300.

***Hotel Temple View** (☎ 52832)* is a simple guesthouse with small but decent doubles for Rs 100 and Rs 200 with shared bathroom, or Rs 250 and Rs 300 with private bathroom. The roof has a terrific view of the Jain temples right next door.

***The Surya** (☎ 50647)* is tucked away in the south-eastern corner of the fort and is a lovely, quiet, family place. Doubles, all with shared bathroom, start at Rs 100, while the room for Rs 270 has great east-facing views. There's a cute little restaurant with loads of charm.

Places to Stay – Mid-Range

Town Area The charming ***Hotel Nachana Haveli** (☎ 51910, Gandhi Chowk)* is a 280-year-old haveli that has been converted into a hotel. The character-filled singles/doubles have lovely high ceilings and are set around a courtyard. Comfortable air-cooled rooms are Rs 750/900, and deluxe air-cooled rooms are Rs 1100/1350. Meals are available with advance notice.

***Hotel Jaisal Palace** (☎ 52717, fax 50257)*, nearby, is a clean and well-run place with smallish rooms starting at Rs 700/850. Those on the south side have balconies facing the fort, or go up to the swing chair on the roof terrace to soak up the view.

***Mandir Palace Hotel** (☎ 52788, fax 51677, Gandhi Chowk)*, just inside the town walls, is a royal palace; the former royal family still lives in part of it. The intricate stone latticework is exquisite and all rooms ooze an old-world charm with antique furniture and fittings – check out a few to see which suits your taste. Air-cooled rooms start at Rs 850/1350 and deluxe air-con suites are Rs 1250/2000.

Fort Close to the Jain temples, ***Hotel Shreenath Palace** (☎ 52907)* is a family-run establishment in a beautiful old haveli. The rooms are rich in atmosphere, with little alcoves and balconies, and some have magnificent sunset views over the temple. Rooms (all doubles) cost Rs 350 with shared bathroom and free bucket hot water. Room No 4 is particularly nice, but all are great value.

***Hotel Suraj** (☎ 51623)*, nearby, is another atmospheric old haveli which features fine sculptures on the facade and good views from the roof. Each single/double is different, and they all have a private bathroom with hot shower and start at Rs 300/350. The enormous room No 1 has antique pillars throughout and a lovely decaying grandeur about it (Rs 600/650). Room No 3 (Rs 500/550) is smaller but has a lovely balcony with good views of the Jain Temples.

Suraja Paying Guest House (☎ *50617*), in the far south-east of the fort, has doubles starting at Rs 400, while some of those for Rs 450 to 600 have lovely, cushioned alcove windows high in the fort wall.

Hotel Jaisal Castle (☎ *52362, fax 52101,* e *narayan@jp1.vsnl.net.in*) is another restored haveli, in the south-west corner of the fort. Its biggest attraction is its position, high on the ramparts overlooking the desert. The cheapest rooms are Rs 700/850, and both veg and nonveg meals are available.

Desert Boys Guest House (☎ *53091,* e *desert_p@yahoo.com*), not far away, has doubles from Rs 250 to 750. All have private sitting rooms and are comfortable and tastefully decorated.

Places to Stay – Top End

Rang Mahal (☎ *50907, fax 51305*), about 2.5km west of the fort, is a dramatic building with impressive singles/doubles starting at Rs 1500/1850. The deluxe suites, at Rs 3800, are divine.

Gorbandh Palace Hotel (☎ *51511, fax 52749*), nearby, is another upmarket modern hotel with traditional design elements. Constructed of local sandstone, the friezes around the hotel were sculptured by local artisans. Rooms cost 1999/3300 and a deluxe suite is Rs 5500. There's a coffee shop, bar, restaurant, travel desk and superb pool (open to nonresidents for Rs 200).

Jawahar Niwas Palace (☎ *52208, fax 52288,* e *jawaharniwaspalace@yahoo.com*), about 1km west of the fort, is a stunning sandstone palace, standing rather forlornly in its own sandy grounds. Elegant, spacious rooms cost Rs 2000/2750. Those upstairs at the front have the best fort views. Set lunch/dinner is Rs 400/450.

Narayan Niwas Palace (☎ *52408, fax 52101,* e *narayan@jp1.vsnl.net.in*), north of the fort, gets mixed reviews from travellers. Overpriced singles/doubles here cost Rs 1500/2500. Suites are Rs 2650. There's a rather gloomy indoor swimming pool.

Hotel Dhola Maru (☎ *52863, fax 53124, Jethwai Rd*), to the north-east of the walled city, is a few kilometres from the fort entrance. It's a popular choice and although the location is not great, this is compensated for by the comfortable rooms. Air-con rooms are Rs 1300/2000. There's an extraordinary little bar, which has incorporated tree roots into its decor, and a restaurant.

Places to Eat

Town Area We hear lots of good things from travellers about ***Monica Restaurant***, near the fort gate. There's an extensive menu with Indian (including Rajasthani), continental and Chinese food. To taste authentic local specialities, try the Rajasthani thali (Rs 70). Ginger chicken (Rs 50) and potato peas curry (Rs 38) also aren't bad.

Natraj Restaurant is a few minutes' walk down from the Monica and is a good place to eat. Chicken masala is Rs 65, paneer kofta is Rs 55, and a beer will set you back Rs 80. For sweet tooths, apple pie and fried ice cream (Rs 35 each) feature on the dessert list. The open-air top floor has a nice view of the Salim Singh-ki-Haveli next door.

Mid Town (*Gopa Chowk*), outside the fort, cooks up vegetarian food. A Rajasthani special thali is Rs 50, and most main courses are under Rs 60. A Dutch apple pie is Rs 60. The food is OK, but nothing to rave about.

Trio, near the Amar Sagar Gate, is worth a try. This long-running Indian and continental restaurant is pricier than its neighbours, but the food is excellent, and musicians play in the evening. The *saagwala* mutton (mutton with creamed spinach) for Rs 90 is delicious. There's even mashed potato (Rs 35) – ideal for tender tummies. The nonveg tandoori thali is good.

Skyroom Restaurant has a somewhat limited menu, but pretty good fort views. Half a tandoori chicken is Rs 80, a banana pancake is Rs 35 and a bottle of beer is Rs 80. Breakfasts cost Rs 50 to 70.

Kalpana Restaurant, in the same area, is nothing special when it comes to the food, but it's a good place just to watch the world go by while sipping on a banana lassi

(Rs 15) or snacking on a toasted chicken sandwich (Rs 30).

Top Deck, also in this area, has reasonably priced Indian, Chinese and continental cuisine. Options include chicken wings (Rs 55), egg curry (Rs 25) and sizzlers (Rs 60). Its fruit lassi (Rs 15) is refreshing.

Sharma Lodge (signboard in Hindi) is a very simple eatery located beneath the Top Deck. It has a filling Indian thali for Rs 25.

German Bakery is a small, simple place near Satyam Tours at Gandhi Chowk. Items on offer include croissants (Rs 10), peanut cookies (Rs 10) and various cakes (Rs 25 per slice).

Gorbandh Palace Hotel (see Places to Stay – Top End) is open to nonresidents and you can opt for buffet or a la carte dining. The all-you-can-eat buffet costs Rs 250/400/500 for breakfast/lunch/dinner. There's a dimly lit bar.

Mohan Juice Centre *(Bhatia Market)* sells an assortment of interesting lassis, such as apple lassi (Rs 12), honey lassi (Rs 13) and even chocolate lassi (Rs 10). A glass of fresh orange juice is Rs 15.

Bhang Shop, outside the First Fort Gate, not far from Sahara Travels, is a government-authorised bhang shop! Medium/strong lassis are Rs 30/35 per glass. Bhang cookies, cakes and candy can be baked with advance notice and the shop specialises in packing supplies for camel safaris. Bhang does not agree with everyone – see the boxed text 'Beware of Those Bhang Lassis!' under Drinks in the Facts for the Visitor chapter for more details.

Dhanraj Bhatia Sweets *(Sadar Bazaar, Bhatia Market)* has been churning out traditional sweet treats for the past 10 generations. It is renowned in Jaisalmer and beyond, for its local speciality sweets, such as *ghotua* and *panchadhari ladoos* (Rs 4.50 each). This simple little shop is worth visiting just to watch the sweetmakers ply their trade.

The Duke, beside Hanuman Chowk, whips up interesting dishes such as a tandoori thali (Rs 175) which contains tandoori chicken, chicken tikka, vegetable kebab, paneer tikka, butter naan and poppadoms. The mixed fruit lassi (Rs 25) is positively divine.

Fort Two of Jaisalmer's best restaurants are inside the fort. ***Little Tibet***, just east of the main square, has a cosy dining area, friendly service and large servings. The menu is extensive with hearty soups (pumpkin and garlic costs Rs 25), a large plate of momos for Rs 40 and good enchiladas for around Rs 50. It's often full so get there early or be prepared to wait.

Ristorante Italiano La Purezza, near the Desert Boys Guest House, serves excellent authentic pasta dishes for Rs 70 to 100 – if you've been travelling in Rajasthan for a while you'll appreciate what a treat this is. The bruschetta is also good (Rs 15 to 30) and it does tiramisu (Rs 45), as well as espresso coffee and cappucino! It's a brilliant place from which to watch the sunset. The service is also good.

Vyas Meal Service, near the Jain temples, is a good place to eat home-made food. This family-run veg restaurant offers traditional cuisine from western Rajasthan. It serves wholesome thalis and also brews a jolly good masala tea. If you have a penchant for it, you can buy a packet of this tea for Rs 30 (it makes 30 cups).

8th July Restaurant and ***Refreshing Point Rooftop Restaurant***, both above the main square in the fort, are good places to watch the passing human and bovine traffic, but the food is variable. Refreshing Point is a small German bakery selling goodies such as choco-banana croissants (Rs 20) and cheesecake (Rs 35 per slice).

Shopping

Jaisalmer is famous for embroidery, Rajasthani mirrorwork, rugs, blankets, old stonework, antiques and anything to do with camels. Tie-dye and other fabrics are made at the Khadi Gramodyog Bhavan (Seemagram), at Dhibba Para, not far from the fort. There's a Rajasthali handicraft emporium just outside Amar Sagar Gate. It's a good place to get an idea of prices.

On the laneway leading up to the Jain temples within the fort is Light of the East, which sells crystals and rare mineral specimens including zeolite, which can fetch up to Rs 5000 depending on the quality.

Camel Safaris Around Jaisalmer

Exploring the desert around Jaisalmer by camel safari is undoubtedly the most evocative way to sample desert life. If you follow a few simple precautions before setting out, you might just find it a highlight of your time in India. October to February is the best time to do a safari.

Before Setting Out

Competition between safari organisers is cut-throat and standards vary considerably. None of the hotels have their own camels – these are all independently owned – so the hoteliers and the travel agents are, with one notable exception (see Ganesh Travels under Safari Agents later), just go-betweens.

Hotel owners typically pay the camel drivers around Rs 150 per camel per day to hire them, so if you're offered a safari at Rs 200 or even Rs 250 per day, this leaves only a small margin for food and the agent's profit. It's obvious that you can't possibly expect three reasonable meals a day on these margins, but this is frequently what is promised. As a result, a lot of travellers feel they've been ripped off when the food isn't what was offered. Beware of operators who claim to offer (and charge for) three-day safaris when in actual fact you return after breakfast on the third day – hardly value for money.

Another precaution suggested by the tourist office is to ask your booking agent for the camel or jeep driver's identity card and note down the registration number (written in red). If they can't produce one, you may want to look elsewhere.

The realistic minimum price for a basic safari is about Rs 350 per person per day. For this you can expect a breakfast of porridge, tea and toast, and a lunch and dinner of rice, dhal and chapatis – pretty unexciting stuff. Blankets are also supplied. You must sometimes bring your own mineral water. Of course, you can pay more for greater levels of comfort – tents, stretcher beds, better food, beer etc.

However much you decide to spend, make sure you know exactly what is being provided and make sure it's there before you leave Jaisalmer. Ensure you know where you're going to be taken. Attempting to get a refund for services not provided is a waste of time. Take care of your possessions, particularly on the return journey. A recent scam involves the drivers suggesting that you walk to some nearby ruins while they stay with the camels and keep an eye on your bags. The police station in Jaisalmer receives numerous reports of items missing from luggage but seems unwilling to help. Nonetheless, any complaints you do have should be reported, either to the superintendent of police (☎ 52233) or to the Tourist Reception Centre (☎ 52406).

If you're on your own it's worth getting a group of at least four people together before looking for a safari. Organisers will make up groups but four days is a long time to spend with people you might not get on with. Usually each person is assigned their own camel, but check this as some agencies might try to save money by hiring fewer camels, meaning you'll find yourself sharing your camel with a camel driver or cook, which is not nearly as much fun.

What to Take

Take something comfortable to sit on – many travellers fail to do this and come back with very sore legs or backsides or both! One traveller wrote to suggest that women wear nylon underwear. Women should also consider wearing a sports bra, as the trotting momentum of the camels can cause some discomfort after even just a few hours. A wide-brimmed hat (or Rajput-style turban), long trousers, toilet paper, sun cream and a personal water bottle (with a strap so you can secure it easily) are also recommended. It can get very cold at night, so if you have a sleeping bag take it along even if you're told that lots of blankets will be supplied.

Camel Safaris Around Jaisalmer

Safari Agents

Several independent camel safari agents (not linked to any hotels) have been recommended. Ganesh Travels (☎ 50138), inside the fort, is wholly owned by former and current camel drivers and gets consistently good reviews from travellers. Sahara Travels (☎ 52609), by the First Fort Gate, is run by Mr Bissa, alias Mr Desert or India's Marlboro Man – the rugged model in the Jaisalmer cigarette ads. At both places, standard tours cost Rs 350 a day for two to four days (you get your own camel).

Remember that no place is perfect and recommendations here ought not be a substitute for doing your own research to see what suits your particular needs and budget. In the past, Lonely Planet has recommended Satyam Tours (☎ 50773) and Thar Safari (☎/fax 52722), both on Gandhi Chowk. These still get overwhelmingly positive reports, although not everyone has found that their safari lived up to expectations. Of the hotels, Hotel Renuka runs good safaris and Hotel Paradise offers 'happy camels', a claim we were unable to verify.

Whoever you book your safari through, insist that all rubbish is carried back to Jaisalmer, and not left at the Sam sand dunes or in remote villages where the wind will carry it across the desert.

Out on the Trail

The desert is surprisingly well populated and sprinkled with ruins. You often come across tiny fields of millet, girls picking berries or boys herding flocks of sheep or goats. The flocks are usually fitted with tinkling neck bells and, in the desert silence, it's music to the ears. Unfortunately the same cannot be said for the noises emitted by the notoriously flatulent camels!

Camping out at night, huddling around a tiny fire beneath the stars and listening to the camel drivers' yarns can be quite romantic. The camel drivers will expect a tip or gift at the end of the trip. Don't neglect to give one.

The reins are fastened to the camel's nose peg, so the animals are easily steered. At resting points, the camels are completely unsaddled and hobbled. They limp away to browse on nearby shrubs while the camel drivers brew sweet chai or prepare food. The whole crew rests in the shade of thorn trees by a tank or well.

Most safaris last three to four days, and if you want to get to the most interesting places, this is a bare minimum unless a significant jeep component is included. The usual circuit takes in such places as Amar Sagar, Lodhruva, Mool Sagar, Bada Bagh and Sam, as well as various abandoned villages along the way. It's not possible to ride by camel to the Sam sand dunes in one day; in 1½ days you could get a jeep to Sam, stay there overnight, and take a camel from there to either Kuldahra (then a jeep back to Jaisalmer) or Kanoi (and catch a jeep from there to Jaisalmer). If you're really pressed for time, you could opt for a half-day camel safari (which involves jeep transfers).

In 2½ days you could travel by camel to Lodhruva, spend the second night at the Sam sand dunes, and return the following day to Jaisalmer by jeep. If you have more time, obviously you can travel at a more leisurely pace through these regions and forgo the jeep component.

MARTIN HARRIS

Getting There & Away

Air Indian Airlines, through its subsidiary Alliance Air, has three flights a week from Jaisalmer to Delhi (US$155) via Udaipur (US$100) and Jaipur (US$125). The agents for Indian Airlines are Crown Tours (☎/fax 51912, ⓔ crown@jp1.dot.net.in), about 350m west of Amar Sagar Gate.

Bus The main Roadways bus stand (☎ 51541) is some distance from the centre of town, near the train station. Fortunately, all buses depart from a bus depot just behind the Hotel Neeraj, which is more conveniently located.

To Jodhpur there are frequent deluxe buses (Rs 92, 5½ hours). Several daily direct deluxe buses run to Bikaner (Rs 130, seven hours) and Ajmer (Rs 140, 9½ hours).

You can book luxury buses through most of the travel agencies. Destinations include Bikaner (Rs 130), Jaipur (Rs 175), Jodhpur (Rs 80) and Udaipur (Rs 150). Be aware that most private buses (except those going to Bikaner) require a change of bus at Jodhpur. Some travellers have found themselves in Jodhpur with an onward ticket no-one will honour so make sure you clarify exactly what you're getting for your money.

Train The reservation office at the train station is open 8 am to 8 pm daily. The *Jodhpur Express* leaves Jaisalmer at 10.25 pm daily, arriving in Jodhpur at 5.30 am (Rs 82/130, general/sleeper class). The *Jaisalmer Express* leaves Jodhpur at 11.15 pm and arrives in Jaisalmer at 5.30 am. A daily passenger train also travels in each direction.

Getting Around

Autorickshaw The drivers can be rapacious here, so bargain hard. An autorickshaw to Gadi Sagar costs about Rs 15 one way from the fort entrance. From the fort to the airport costs Rs 30. If you're going to the station at night, ask the hotel whether it has a jeep going to meet arriving passengers; there's usually a small fee (around Rs 20).

Bicycle A good way to get around is by bicycle. There are a number of hire places, including one at Gandhi Chowk directly opposite the Skyroom Restaurant (Rs 3/20 per hour/day).

Jeep It's possible to hire jeeps from the stand on Gandhi Chowk. To Khuri or the Sam sand dunes expect to pay Rs 300 return with a one-hour stop. For Lodhruva, you'll pay Rs 150 return with a one-hour stop. To cut the cost, find other people to share with (maximum of five people per jeep).

AROUND JAISALMER

About 7km north of Jaisalmer, **Bada Bagh** is a fertile oasis with a huge old dam. Above the gardens are royal **chhatris** with beautifully carved ceilings and equestrian statues of former rulers. In recent years some have fallen into disrepair, but they are currently being restored. Entry is Rs 10.

The once pleasant formal garden of **Amar Sagar**, 7km north-west of Jaisalmer, has now fallen into ruin. According to locals, the stepwells around the seasonal lake were built by prostitutes. Nearby is a finely carved Jain temple. Entry to the temple is free, but it costs Rs 25/50 for a camera/video.

Farther out beyond Amar Sagar, 15km north-west of Jaisalmer, are the deserted ruins of Lodhruva, which was the ancient capital before the move to Jaisalmer in 1156. The Jain temples, rebuilt in the late 1970s, are the only reminders of the city's former magnificence. The main temple enshrines an image of Parasnath, the 23rd tirthankar. The temple has its own resident cobra; seeing it is considered very auspicious. Entry to the temple is free but there's a camera/video charge of Rs 40/70.

Situated 9km west of Jaisalmer, **Mool Sagar** is another pleasant, but rather neglected, small garden and tank. It belongs to the royal family of Jaisalmer. Entry is Rs 5.

Sam Sand Dunes

A desert national park has been established in the Great Thar Desert near Sam village. One of the most popular excursions is to the sand dunes on the edge of the park, 42km from Jaisalmer along a very good sealed road (maintained by the Indian army).

This is Jaisalmer's nearest real Sahara-like desert. It's best to be here at sunrise or sunset, and many camel safaris spend a night at the dunes. This place has become a massive tourist attraction, so don't set your heart on a solitary desert sunset experience. Nonetheless, it is still quite a magical place, and it's possible to frame pictures of solitary camels against lonely dunes.

One tragic consequence of the increasing number of visitors to the dunes is the debris and rubbish lying at their base.

Visitors are charged Rs 2 to visit the dunes.

RTDC Hotel Sam Dhani has eight good double rooms with private bathroom for Rs 300, and dorm beds for Rs 50. There is currently no power, but lanterns are provided. Veg meals are available. Bookings can be made through the RTDC Hotel Moomal (☎ 02992-52392) in Jaisalmer.

There are three daily buses to Sam from Jaisalmer (Rs 15, 1½ hours) and the RTDC runs evening tours to Sam (see Organised Tours in the Jaisalmer section earlier).

Khuri

Khuri is a small village 40km south-west of Jaisalmer, with its own desert sand dunes. It has far less tourist hype (at least for now) than the Sam sand dunes, and is becoming increasingly popular for camel and jeep safaris. It's a peaceful place with houses of mud and straw decorated with patterns like those on Persian carpets. There are, thankfully, no craftshop-lined streets or banana pancake restaurants. The attraction out here is the desert solitude and the brilliant star-studded night sky.

Places to Stay & Eat Places to stay in Khuri are pretty basic with charpoys and bucket hot water. All provide meals and most can arrange camel safaris. Accommodation is limited and you won't get any bargains; basically you're paying for the peace and quiet rather than the facilities, which are minimal.

Khuri Guest House is on the left of the main road as you enter the village. It has conventional singles/doubles with shared bathroom for a reasonable Rs 75/100. Huts with shared bathroom are Rs 100/125; a double with private bathroom is Rs 300.

Mama's Guest House is actually clusters of thatched huts. The cheapest costs a rather hefty Rs 350 per night with shared bathroom, which includes meals and bucket hot water. These cost Rs 200 in the low season, but would be hellishly hot. The huts are set in a semicircle around a campfire. There is a group of better-thatched huts for Rs 450 each, while top-of-the-range huts are Rs 750, and include an electric fan. It's also possible (but not nearly so romantic!) to stay in a conventional room for Rs 300 with shared bathroom.

Sodha Guest House has doubles with shared bathroom for Rs 150. Lunch or dinner is Rs 100 per person.

Gangaur Guest House has huts for Rs 150 to 300. Lunch or dinner is Rs 150.

Getting There & Away There are several buses daily to Khuri from Jaisalmer (Rs 14, two hours).

Akal Wood Fossil Park

About 3km off the road to Barmer, 16km from Jaisalmer, are the fossilised remains of a 180-million-year-old forest. To the untrained eye it's not very interesting. Entry to the park is Rs 5/20 for Indians/foreigners, plus Rs 10 per vehicle. Guides (Rs 50) are sometimes available. The park is open from 8 am to 1 pm and 2 to 5 pm daily.

Barmer

Barmer is a centre for woodcarving, carpets, embroidery, block printing and other handicrafts, and its products are famous throughout Rajasthan. The small shops in the colourful Sadar Bazaar are a good place to start looking and you may also come across some of the artisans at work out the back. There are two annual fairs in Barmer: the **Barmer Thar Festival** in early March and the **Barmer Cattle Fair** (held at nearby Tilwara) in March/April. For details, contact the Tourist Reception Centre in Jaisalmer.

RTDC Khartal *(☎ 02982-22956)* has four neat singles/doubles with bathroom for

Rs 300/400. Other options include the ***Hotel Krishna** (☎ 02982-20785)*, with rooms starting at Rs 100/200 (with shared bathroom) and the cheaper ***Kailash Sarover Hotel** (☎ 02982-20730)*.

From Barmer there are frequent express buses to Jaisalmer and Jodhpur.

Pokaran

At the junction of the Jaisalmer, Jodhpur and Bikaner roads, 110km from Jaisalmer, the **Pokaran Fort** rises from the desert and shelters a tangle of narrow streets lined by balconied houses. It's worth a look, especially as a stop at Pokaran breaks the long journey between Jodhpur and Jaisalmer. The fort is open 7 am to 7 pm daily. Entry is Rs 20; a camera or video is Rs 10.

It was in Pokaran in May 1998 that India detonated five nuclear devices.

Accommodation in town is lacklustre. ***RTDC Motel Godavan** (☎ 02994-22275)* conveniently rents out rooms with private bathroom for six hours (Rs 200), or for the night (Rs 300).

Frequent RSTC buses to Jaisalmer take about 2½ hours and cost Rs 30.

Khichan

This small village lies a few kilometres from the large town of Phalodi, between Jodhpur and Jaisalmer. It has not yet been listed as a wildlife sanctuary, but is a must for bird lovers. From late August/early September to the end of March, it is possible to witness the spectacular sight of hundreds of demoiselle cranes descending on the fields around the village.

BIKANER

☎ 0151 • pop 510,000

This desert town, with its superb fort, is located in the north of Rajasthan and is becoming increasingly popular among travellers keen to extract themselves from the tourist hype of Jaisalmer. Bikaner, though lacking Jaisalmer's charm, has some wonderful Jain temples and an atmospheric old city. It's also a good base for camel safaris and for visiting the extraordinary Karni Mata Temple, 30km to the south, where thousands of holy rats are worshipped (see the boxed text 'The Temple of Rats' at the end of this chapter).

Bikaner was founded in 1488 by Rao Bika, a descendant of Jodha, the founder of Jodhpur. Like many others in Rajasthan, the old city is surrounded by a high crenellated wall, and like Jaisalmer, it was once an important staging post on the great caravan trade routes. The Ganga Canal, built between 1925 and 1927, irrigates a large area of previously arid land around Bikaner.

Orientation

The old city is encircled by a 7km-long city wall with five entrance gates, constructed in the 18th century. The fort and palace are outside the city walls to the north-east.

Information

Tourist Offices The well-organised Tourist Reception Centre (☎ 544125) is in the grounds of RTDC Hotel Dhola Maru. It can provide lists of local doctors, as well as detailed bus and train timetables. It has a small number of brochures and maps. It's open 10 am to 5 pm daily except Sunday.

Money US dollars and UK pounds (cash and travellers cheques) are changed at State Bank of Bikaner & Jaipur (near Thar Hotel; open noon to 4 pm Monday to Friday), and its public park branch (near Junagarh; open 10 am to 2 pm Monday to Friday). Bank of Baroda, opposite the train station on the 1st floor, changes travellers cheques only. At the time of writing, no banks in Bikaner gave cash advances on credit cards.

Email & Internet Access Access is available at Net Yuppies (☎ 540560), which is behind Natraj off Kem Rd (Rs 65 per hour, open 9.30 am to 10.30 pm); Cyber City (☎ 529076), in the east of town, which serves reasonable fast food (Rs 75 per hour); and New Horizons, off Station Rd. An increasing number of hotels have Internet access.

Junagarh

Constructed between 1588 and 1593 by Raja Rai Singh, a general in the army of the

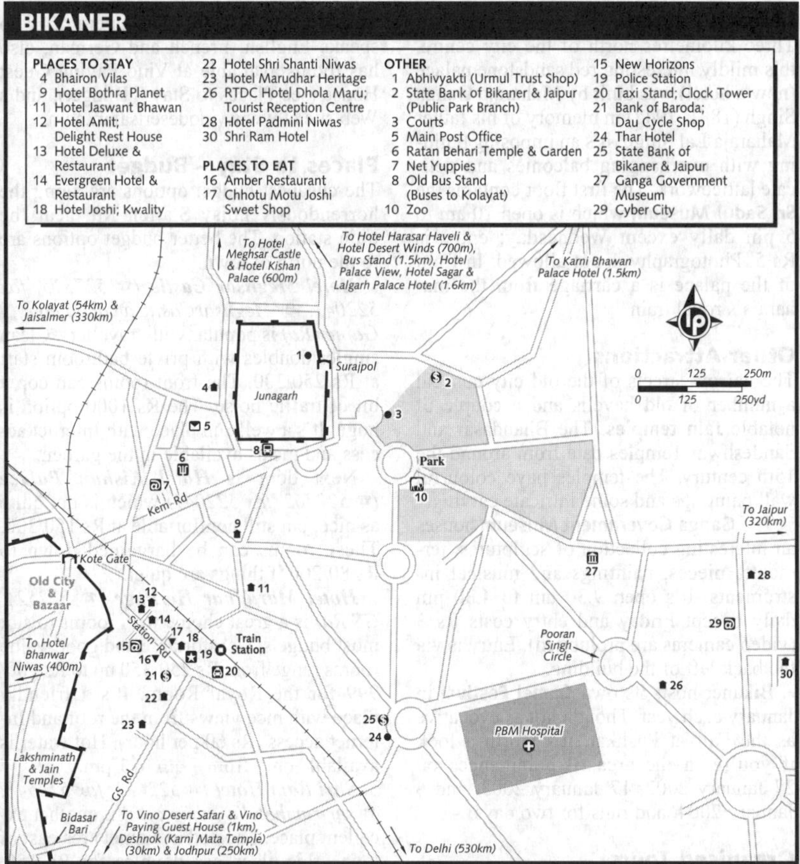

Mughal emperor Akbar, this most impressive fort has a 986m-long wall with 37 bastions, a moat and two entrances. The Surajpol, or Sun Gate, is the main entrance to the fort. The palaces within the fort are on the southern side and make a picturesque ensemble of courtyards, balconies, kiosks, towers and windows. A major feature of this fort and its palaces is the magnificent stone carving. The interiors are among the most exquisite in Rajasthan.

Highlights include the Diwan-i-Khas; the Phool Mahal (Flower Palace), which is decorated with paintings and carved marble panels; and the Hawa Mahal, Badal Mahal and Anup Mahal. Also of interest is the old WWI biplane, one of only two such models in the world.

The fort is open 10 am to 5 pm daily; the ticket office closes at 4.30 pm. Entry is Rs 10/50 for Indians/foreigners and there's a camera/video charge of Rs 30/100. A compulsory guide is included in the ticket price. The guide will usually keep foreigners aside at the conclusion of the tour to show them some of the closed rooms – a hefty tip is expected. It costs an extra Rs 25 to visit the museum and Rs 20 for the camera.

Lalgarh Palace

Three kilometres north of the city centre, this mildly interesting red sandstone palace (now a hotel) was built by Maharaja Ganga Singh (1881–1942) in memory of his father Maharaja Lal Singh. It's an imposing building with overhanging balconies and delicate latticework. The first floor contains the **Sri Sadul Museum** which is open 10 am to 5 pm daily except Wednesday; entry is Rs 5. Photography is not allowed. In front of the palace is a carriage from the maharaja's royal train.

Other Attractions

The narrow streets of the old city conceal a number of old havelis and a couple of notable **Jain temples**. The Bhandasar and Sandeshwar Temples date from around the 15th century. The temples have colourful wall paintings and some intricate carving.

The **Ganga Government Museum** houses an interesting collection of sculptures, terracotta pieces, paintings and musical instruments. It's open 9.30 am to 4.30 pm daily except Friday and entry costs Rs 3 (video cameras are prohibited). Entry is via the back left of the building.

Bikaner hosts its own **Camel Festival** in January each year. Though not as evocative as the Fair at Pushkar, it's worth a look if you're in the area. It commences on 27 January 2002, 17 January 2003, and 6 January 2004, and runs for two days.

Organised Tours

The Tourist Reception Centre can arrange English-speaking guides which cost Rs 75 for two hours.

If you wanted to take a camel safari in Jaisalmer but didn't because it was too much of a scene, Bikaner is an excellent alternative. One good operator is Vino Desert Safari (☎ 204445, ⓔ vino_desertsafari@yahoo.com), opposite the Gopeshwar Temple. There are at least eight different camel treks available (some of which visit Khichan, home of the demoiselle cranes), ranging from two to seven days' duration. Costs are from Rs 400 per person per day (minimum of six people and only for shorter treks), up to Rs 800. The operator, who speaks English, French and German, also has rooms available at Vino Paying Guest House (see Places to Stay – Budget), and a Web site at www.vinodesertsafari.com.

RAJASTHAN

Places to Stay – Budget

The cheapest budget options are along the horrendously noisy Station Rd, near the train station. The better budget options are to the north of town.

Hotel Meghsar Castle *(☎ 527315, fax 522041, ⓔ MeghsarCastle@yahoo.com, 9 Gajner Rd)* is popular with travellers. Clean singles/doubles with privte bathroom start at Rs 250/300. The front rooms can cop a bit of traffic noise. The Rs 1000 option is huge. It's a well-run place with Internet access and meals available in the garden.

Next door is ***Hotel Kishan Palace*** *(☎ 527762, fax 522041)* which is not quite as nice, but still comfortable at Rs 150/300. These rooms can be bargained down to Rs 80/200 if things are quiet.

Hotel Marudhar Heritage *(☎ 522524, GS Rd)* is a great choice with rooms to suit most budgets. Comfortable and good-value rooms range from Rs 250/350 up to Rs 900/999 for the Royal Room. It's a friendly place with nice views from the roof and Internet access (Rs 60 per hour). Hot water is available only from 7 am to 1 pm.

Shri Ram Hotel *(☎ 522651, fax 522548, ⓔ shriramhotel@yahoo.com)* is another excellent place. Located in a quiet area east of town, this place has doubles for Rs 150, 250 and 400 depending on the size. All are spotless and have satellite TV. There's a real family atmosphere.

Vino Paying Guest House *(☎ 270445, ⓔ vino_desertsafari@yahoo.com)*, south of town, is another homey place. There are a small number of rooms available from Rs 125 to 350. If you enjoy the cooking (which most travellers do), the operators run cooking classes and can also adorn you with henna painting.

Hotel Harasar Haveli *(☎ 209891, fax 525150, ⓔ harasar_haveli@yahoo.com)*, near the Karni Singh Stadium, is a great place to stay, with very clean rooms starting at Rs 150/200 and better deluxe rooms for Rs 300/400. It's almost worth staying in this lovely haveli for the rooftop area with its swing chairs and attractive restaurant.

Hotel Desert Winds *(☎ 542202)*, next door, has simple rooms with private bathroom starting at Rs 175/225.

Evergreen Hotel *(☎ 542061)*, on Station Rd, is not a bad choice, although some of the rooms can be noisy. Singles/doubles/triples with private bathroom cost Rs 125/175/200. Hot water is by the bucket (Rs 5).

Nearby, ***Hotel Deluxe*** *(☎ 528127)* has bare, basic and usually clean rooms starting at Rs 100/150.

Delight Rest House *(☎ 542313)* is a dingy flophouse which is cleaned occasionally – it's the place to go if you're short on rupees. Rooms cost Rs 75/95 with shared bathroom or Rs 100/130 with private bucket shower. ***Hotel Amit*** *(☎ 544451)* is cleaner with cramped rooms for Rs 125/150.

Hotel Shri Shanti Niwas *(☎ 542320, fax 524231)* is on GS Rd, which leads out from the train station. Basic but quite clean rooms are Rs 115/165.

RTDC Hotel Dhola Maru *(☎ 529621)*, 1km east of the city centre, has dorms costing Rs 50.

Places to Stay – Mid-Range

Bhairon Vilas *(☎/fax 544751, ⓔ hbhairon@rediffmail.com)*, opposite the main post office, is the funkiest place to stay in Bikaner with an equally funky manager. Quaint doubles start at Rs 500. Single room No 109 is noisy but filled with character and has great views of the fort (Rs 700). There's also an enormous double for Rs 1000. Meals are available with advance notice in the dining room or on the rooftop.

Hotel Palace View *(☎ 543625, fax 522741)*, near Lalgarh Palace, is a good option. Clean singles/doubles are Rs 750/850, and smaller rooms are Rs 400/500.

Nearby is the pink ***Hotel Sagar*** *(☎ 520 677)*, with cottages starting at Rs 800 and plusher rooms with furnishings a little over the top starting at Rs 1000/1175.

Hotel Padmini Niwas *(☎ 522794, 148 Sadul Ganj)* has clean, pleasant rooms from Rs 325/400 up to Rs 500/750 with air-con. The restaurant is quite good and the small lawn area is very nice.

Hotel Joshi *(☎ 527700, fax 521213)*, near the train station, is a real step up in quality compared with other hotels on this street. Air-cooled rooms start at Rs 300/375 and there's a veg restaurant here. Good ice cream is available next door at Kwality.

Hotel Jaswant Bhawan *(☎/fax 521834)* is a pleasant place to stay – handy for the train station without the noise of Station Rd. Attractive doubles cost Rs 400 and Internet access is available.

Hotel Bothra Planet *(☎/fax 544501, ⓔ info@bothraplanet.com)*, nearby, is modern and comfortable if a tad sterile. Rooms with satellite TV go for Rs 500/600. There's a restaurant, some rooms have a bathtub and major credit cards are accepted.

Places to Stay – Top End

Hotel Bhanwar Niwas *(☎ 529323, fax 200880)*, in the Rampuri Haveli, near the kotwali in the old city, is an excellent choice. This attractive pink sandstone building has enormous, opulent singles/doubles around the internal courtyard for Rs 1999/3200. In the foyer is a stunning blue 1928 Buick with a silver horn in the shape of a dragon. Prices drop by 30% from May to July.

Lalgarh Palace Hotel *(☎ 540201, fax 522253)*, 3km north of the city centre, is part of the maharaja's modern palace and has well-appointed rooms for US$43/85 (US$40/70 from 15 April to 15 September). There's a bar, restaurant, billiard room, indoor pool, resident astrologer (Rs 600 per consultation) and masseur (Rs 150 for half an hour).

Karni Bhawan Palace Hotel *(☎ 524701, fax 522408)*, in Gandhi Colony, near the Lalgarh Palace Hotel, is ugly but peaceful and comfortable. Art Deco-style rooms cost Rs 1999/3300; a huge suite is Rs 5500. Good meals are available.

Places to Eat

Bikaner is noted for the spicy snacks known as *namkin*, sold in the shops along Station Rd, among other places.

Deluxe Restaurant, at the hotel of the same name on Station Rd, features a limited selection of cheap veg South Indian and Chinese dishes, all under Rs 40. There's an extensive ice-cream menu. The ***Evergreen Restaurant*** next door is similar.

Amber Restaurant, diagonally opposite the Deluxe, is popular for veg fare. Paneer korma costs Rs 42, a South Indian dosa Rs 26 and cheese toast Rs 22.

Hotel Bhanwar Niwas welcomes non-guests (with advance reservations) to its vegetarian dining hall. The set breakfast/lunch/dinner is Rs 150/300/325, or you can just come here for a drink in the courtyard.

Lalgarh Palace Hotel is good for a treat; the set breakfast/lunch/dinner costs US$8/10/12, or you can opt for a la carte dining.

Chhotu Motu Joshi Sweet Shop on Station Rd is Bikaner's most loved sweet stop, with an assortment of Indian treats. Prices vary but Rs 100 per kilogram is a good guide.

Shopping

On the right-hand side as you enter the fort is a small craft shop, Abhivyakti, run by the Urmul Trust. It was temporarily closed at the time of research but was expected to re-open soon. Items sold here are made by people from surrounding villages and proceeds go directly to improve health and education projects in these villages. You can browse here without the usual constant hassles to buy.

Getting There & Away

Bus The bus stand is 3km north of the city centre, almost opposite the road leading to the Lalgarh Palace Hotel. If your bus is coming from the south, ask the driver to let you out closer to the town centre. There are express buses to Udaipur (Rs 180, 10 hours, 10.30 am), Ajmer (Rs 88, five hours), Jaipur (via Fatehpur and Sikar; Rs 115, seven hours), Jodhpur (Rs 85, 5½ hours), Jaisalmer (Rs 110, eight hours), Agra (Rs 199, 11 hours, 5 am) and Delhi (Rs 137, 11 hours) via Jhunjhunu (Rs 75).

Train To Jaipur, there's the *Jaipur-Bikaner Express* (4737/8), which departs at 8.30 pm (Rs 113/176/831, general/sleeper/2A class, 11 hours) or the *Intercity Express* (2468/7) which leaves Bikaner at 3 pm and arrives in Jaipur at 9.15 pm (Rs 113/348, general/chair class). The *Ranakpur Express* (4707) leaves for Jodhpur at 9.35 am (Rs 70/109/525, general/sleeper/2A class, 5½ hours). To Delhi (Sarai Rohilla station), the *Sarai Rohilla Express* (4790) leaves Bikaner at 8.30 am and arrives in the capital at 7 pm (Rs 104/162/749).

Getting Around

An autorickshaw from the train station to the palace should cost Rs 15, but you'll probably be asked for more. Bicycles can be hired at the Dau Cycle Shop, opposite the police station on Station Rd (Rs 2/10 per hour/day for an old bike, Rs 3/15 for a new one).

AROUND BIKANER

Devi Kund

Eight kilometres east of Bikaner, this is the site of the royal chhatris of many of the Bika dynasty rulers. The white marble chhatri of Maharaja Surat Singh is very imposing.

Gajner Wildlife Sanctuary

The lake and forested hills of this reserve, 32km from Bikaner on the Jaisalmer road, are inhabited by wildfowl and a number of deer and antelopes. Imperial sand grouse migrate here in winter. The reserve is only accessible by Gajner Palace Hotel vehicles (Rs 1100 per jeep, maximum six people).

Gajner Palace Hotel (*☎ 01534-55065, fax 55060; reservations ☎ 0151-524701, fax 522408*) is the former royal winter palace and is ideally situated on the banks of a lake. It's an impressive building made of red sandstone and is set in serene surroundings. Deluxe singles/doubles are Rs 1999/3300 (the Gulab Niwas garden rooms are best). Old-fashioned suites (all with a lake view) are in the main palace and cost Rs 5500.

Kolayat

This small temple town set around a lake, around 54km south of Bikaner, is occasionally referred to as a mini Pushkar. It lacks the vibrant character of Pushkar, but is far

ANDREW LUBRAN

RICHARD I'ANSON

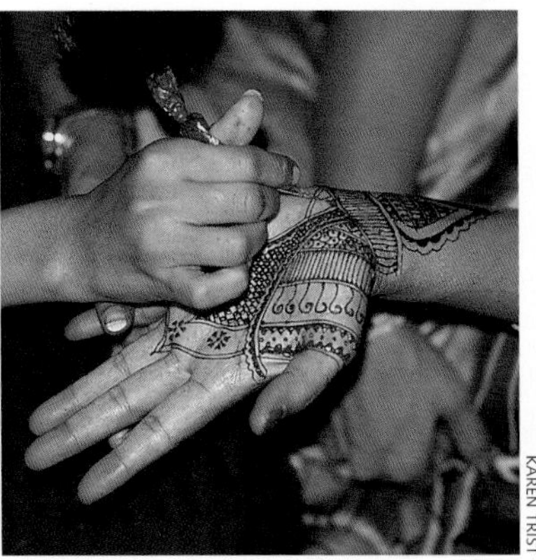
KAREN TRIST

JOHN HAY

The colours of Rajasthan are in sharp contrast to the desert sands: a camel-back safari near Jaisalmer (top); villagers in their festive finery (centre left); elaborate *mehndi* (henna) decorations for a bride (centre right); exquisite Islamic motifs feature on the arches of Samode Palace, near Jaipur (bottom)

TROY FLOWER

CHRISTOPHER HOWE

RICHARD I'ANSON

RICHARD I'ANSON

From forts overlooking cities to the cool quiet of palace interiors and the bustle of its streets, Rajasthan is stunning in all its splendour: the blue city of Jodhpur (top left); an ornately carved window arch (top right); the monumental Amber Fort (bottom); the state capital, Jaipur (centre left)

The Temple of Rats

The Karni Mata Temple at Deshnok is one of India's more disconcerting and fascinating temples. According to legend, Karni Mata, a 14th-century incarnation of Durga, asked the god of death, Yama, to restore to life the son of a grieving storyteller. When Yama refused, Karni Mata reincarnated all dead storytellers as rats, in order to deprive Yama of human souls. The rats were later incarnated as human beings.

The thousands of holy rodents, known as *kabas*, are not for the squeamish. Once you've admired the silver doors and marble carvings donated by Maharaja Ganga Singh, you plunge into the rats' domain, hoping that some will scamper over your feet – most auspicious. Keep your eyes peeled for a rare white rat – it's considered good fortune if you spot one. Eating *prasad* (a holy food offering) that has been salivated over by these holy rats is also claimed by believers to bring good luck, but most travellers are willing to take their word for it.

The temple is an important pilgrimage site and what may seem unusual to Western eyes is devoutly believed by pilgrims – this isn't a sideshow but a place of worship.

The temple is open 4 am to 10 pm daily and there's a charge of Rs 20/50 for a camera/video. Don't forget to remove your shoes.

less touristy. There's a fair here around the same time as the Pushkar Camel Fair (minus the camels and cattle, but with plenty of sadhus). There are many *dharamsalas* (pilgrims' lodgings) in Kolayat, but most won't accept tourists. One place worth trying is the ***Bhaheti Dharamsala***, located right on the main ghat. Simple rooms with shared bathroom cost Rs 100.

Every morning at 8.40 am, a special railbus heads for Kolayat from Bikaner. It costs Rs 11 one way and takes two hours. Buses (Rs 15, one hour) leave much more frequently throughout the day from Bikaner's bus stand or the old bus stand, next to the fort walls.

Deshnok

A visit to Deshnok's fascinating **Karni Mata Temple**, 30km south of Bikaner, is almost worth the trip to Bikaner on its own (see the boxed text above).

There are at least two buses every hour from Bikaner bus stand to Deshnok (Rs 10, 40 minutes). A slow rickshaw from the train station can be arranged for Rs 100 return, but Rs 150 is more common. A taxi (Rs 250) is better and safer.

RAJASTHAN

Gujarat

The west coast state of Gujarat is not one of India's busiest tourist destinations and although it is quite easy to slot Gujarat in between a visit to Mumbai (Bombay) and the cities of Rajasthan, few people pause to explore this interesting state.

Gujarat has always been a major centre for the Jains, and some of its most interesting sights are Jain temple centres such as those at Palitana and at Girnar Hill, near Junagadh. The Jains are an influential and energetic group and, as a result, Gujarat is one of India's wealthier and most industrialised states. Gujarat is also the former home of a surprisingly large proportion of India's emigrants: around 40% of the Indians in the New York area are Gujaratis and the common Gujarati surname 'Patel' has come to be commonly identified as Indian.

Apart from its Jain temples, Gujarat's major attractions include the last Asiatic lions (in the Gir Forest) and the fascinating Indo-Saracenic architecture of Ahmedabad. For more hedonistic pleasures, there are the pristine beaches of Diu, off Gujarat's southern coast.

Geographically, Gujarat can be divided into three areas. The eastern (mainland) region includes the major cities of Ahmedabad, Surat and Vadodara (formerly Baroda). The Gulf of Cambay divides the mainland strip from the flat, often barren, plains of the Kathiawar peninsula, also known as Saurashtra. The Gulf of Kutch (Kachchh) separates Saurashtra from Kutch, which is virtually an island, cut off from the rest of Gujarat to the east and Pakistan to the north by the low-lying *ranns* (deserts) of Kutch.

In January 2001, Gujarat shot to prominence for all the wrong reasons due to a massive earthquake that caused widespread destruction in the Kutch district and farther afield (see the boxed text 'The Day the Earth Shook', later in this chapter, and Dangers & Annoyances in the Facts for the Visitor chapter).

Gujarat at a Glance

Population: 50.6 million
Area: 196,024 sq km
Capital: Gandhinagar
Main Language: Gujarati
When to Go: Oct to Mar

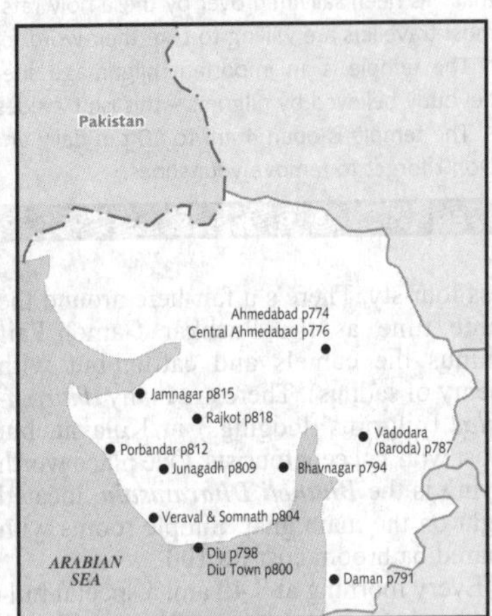

- Kick back in Diu, an easy-going little seaside town with a ramshackle fort
- Visit Sasan Gir Wildlife Sanctuary, home to the last remaining population of Asiatic lion
- Marvel at the fascinating Indo-Saracenic architecture in Ahmedabad
- Climb to the magnificent hilltop temple enclosures of Palitana and Junagadh

History

If you want to go far beyond history into the realm of Hindu legend, then Gujarat's great Temple of Somnath was actually there to witness the creation of the universe. Along Gujarat's south coast are the sites where many of the great events in Krishna's life took place.

Warning

As a result of the earthquake that hit Gujarat in January 2001, some of the information contained in this chapter may be subject to change. We visited Gujarat just prior to the quake and we have since contacted many hotels, restaurants and other sites in order to establish which were affected. Apart from the Kutch district, which was hardest hit, the impact upon tourist infrastructure has been minimal. Nonetheless, many towns throughout Gujarat were affected.

The damage in Ahmedabad was significant; some reports put the number of buildings that collapsed or were seriously damaged at over 300. Damage was, however, largely confined to the newly built residential high-rises in the outlying suburbs. The old city and central Ahmedabad area escaped largely unscathed. Eight out of 53 of Ahmedabad's historical monuments sustained some damage, including the Bhadra Fort, Teen Darwaja, Jama Masjid and Raj Babri Mosque (see individual entries in the Ahmedabad section for further details). Understandably, these are scheduled to be repaired only after many residential buildings have been reconstructed and the residents rehabilitated. In the meantime, some of these monuments have been cordoned off, and access may be restricted until such time as the structures are determined to be safe for visitors.

Some damage was also reported in Rajkot, Jamnagar, Junagadh and Surat, although many of the problems were on the outskirts of these towns, which remain, thankfully, free of large-scale damage. The Little Rann of Kutch was, due to its low population density, spared great loss of life, although damage was reported in the town of Dhrangadhra. Transport links, primarily those which connect the Kutch districts with the rest of the state, were seriously affected and access to many of these routes is likely to remain restricted for some time. Most rail services elsewhere throughout the state were restored within weeks of the disaster.

On firmer historic footing, Lothal was the site of a Harappan or Indus Valley civilisation over 4000 years ago. The main sites of this ancient culture are now in Pakistan, but it is thought that Lothal may have survived the great cities of the Sindh by as much as 500 years. Gujarat featured in the exploits of the mighty Buddhist emperor, Ashoka, and his rock edicts can be seen near Junagadh.

Later, Gujarat suffered Muslim incursions from Mahmud of Ghazni and subsequent Mughal rulers, and was a battlefield between the Mughals and the Marathas. It was also an early point of contact with the West, and the first British commercial outpost was established at Surat. Daman and Diu survived as Portuguese enclaves within the borders of Gujarat until 1961.

Saurashtra was never incorporated into British India, but survived in the form of more than 200 princely states right up to Independence. In 1956, they were amalgamated into the state of Mumbai but in 1960, Mumbai was in turn split, on linguistic grounds, into Maharashtra and Gujarat.

Gujarat also had close ties with the father of modern India, Mahatma Gandhi.

Gandhi's concern for India's tribal communities is reflected in increasing efforts to recognise the state's linguistic and cultural diversity. In 2000, in a number of districts around Surat, Year 8 tribal students were for the first time able to answer examination questions framed in their indigenous Tadpati language – an experiment that many hope will spread to other districts.

The Bhasha Research and Publication Centre (☎ 0265-331190) also publishes a bimonthly periodical, *Dhol*, that uses the Devanagari script in publishing articles in ten tribal languages, and special issues in a number of other dialects, thereby preserving languages under threat from urban migration and the push towards uniform Gujarati. These laudable efforts must also, however, be viewed against the backdrop of the displacement of Adivasis as a result of the decision to proceed with the massive Narmada Dam (see the boxed text 'The Dam Debate' in the Facts about North India chapter).

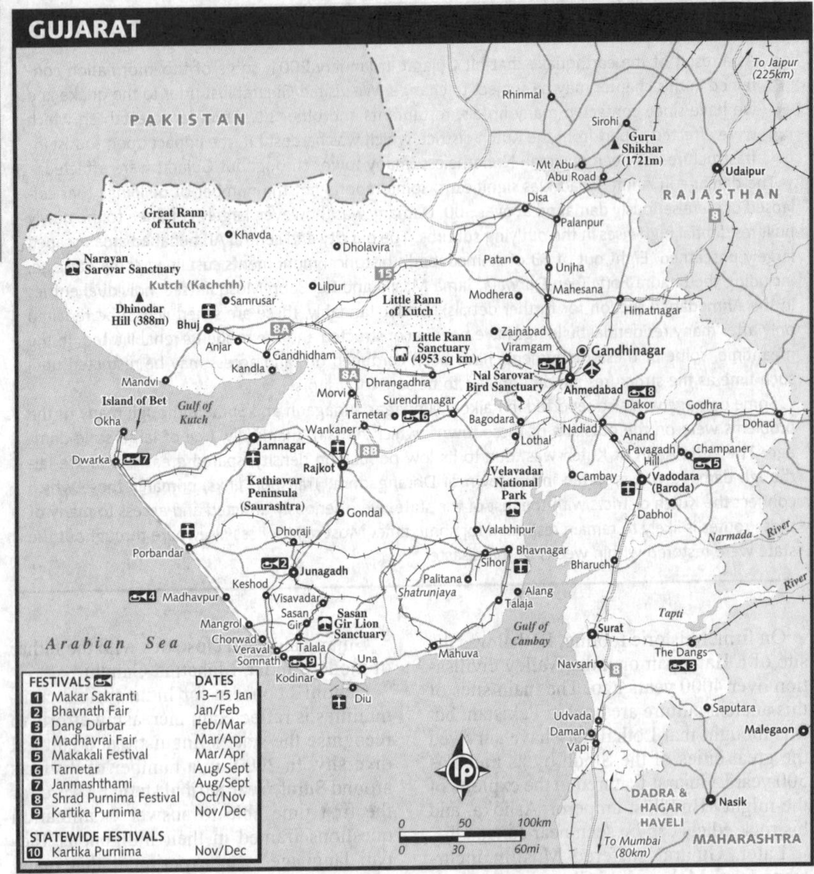

Accommodation

Although Gujarat does not have Rajasthan's selection of palace hotels, it does have a growing number of heritage hotels. Contact the Heritage Hotels Association in Ahmedabad (☎ 079-5506590, fax 4642545) for a full list. Except in the very cheapest hotels, you can expect that a 15% luxury tax will be added to your accommodation bill. In top-end places this soars to 30%.

Getting Around

Most of the medium sized towns in Gujarat are well-served by Indian Railways. State Transport Corporation (STC) buses are generally pretty battered, but they are reliable and regular to all but the smallest villages. The road between Ahmedabad and Mumbai (via Vadodara and Surat) is a major trucking route and one of the most congested in the country, while many of the roads in Saurashtra are narrow and potholed.

Please note that none of the train prices quoted in this chapter include the Rs 20/25 reservation charge levied by Indian Railways on sleeper or three- or two-tier air-con (3A or 2A) berths so you should include this in your budget.

Gujarat – by Rail & in Style

If you want to explore Gujarat quickly and in luxury, you should consider *The Royal Orient*, a special tourist train service that visits various Gujarati and Rajasthani destinations. Run by the Tourism Corporation of Gujarat and Indian Railways, it's a similar concept to the luxurious RTDC *Palace on Wheels* train that tours Rajasthan.

The eight-day trip leaves Delhi on Wednesday and travels to Chittorgarh, Udaipur, Junagadh, Veraval, Sasan Gir, Delwada, Palitana, Sarkhej, Ahmedabad and Jaipur.

Rates per person per day are US$175 in a three-berth cabin; US$200 in a two-berth. Children between five and 12 years are charged half price (free for kids under five), and all fares are reduced by 25% in April and September. Prices include tours, entry fees, accommodation on the train plus all meals. Bookings must be made in advance at HK House, Ashram Rd, Ahmedabad (☎ 079-6589172, fax 6582183, ⓔ ahmedabad@gujarattourism.com), or via India-specialist travel agencies worldwide.

Eastern Gujarat

AHMEDABAD

☎ 079 • pop 5.68 million

Gujarat's principal city is Ahmedabad (also known as Amdavad), one of India's major industrial cities. It been called the 'Manchester of the East' due to its textile industries and smokestacks. It's a noisy and polluted city, and visitors in the hot season should bear in mind the derisive title given to Ahmedabad by the Mughal emperor, Jehangir: Gardabad, the City of Dust. Relief Rd gets our vote as one of the most polluted, congested and thoroughly chaotic strips of barely controlled mayhem in the country.

Nevertheless, this infrequently visited city has a number of attractions for travellers including some excellent museums and Sabarmati (Gandhi's) Ashram. It is also one of the best places to study the blend of Hindu and Islamic architectural styles known as Indo-Saracenic.

If you're arriving from Rajasthan, you'll enjoy the fact that few of the smiles and greetings have an ulterior motive.

Makar Sakranti (13 to 15 January) is the time to see an extravaganza of kite flying in what has become an international festival.

History

Over the centuries, Ahmedabad has had periods of grandeur, each one followed by decline. It was founded in 1411 by Ahmed Shah (from whom the city takes its name) and in the 17th century was thought to be one of the finest cities in India. In 1615, the noted English ambassador Sir Thomas Roe judged it 'a goodly city, as large as London', but by the 18th century its influence had waned. Its industrial strength once again raised the city to prominence, and from 1915 it became famous as the site of Gandhi's ashram.

Orientation

The city of Ahmedabad straddles the Sabarmati River, which dries to a mere trickle in the hot season. On the eastern bank, two main roads – Mahatma Gandhi and Relief Rds – run east from the river to the train station, about 3km away. The busy road flanking the western bank of the Sabarmati is known universally as Ashram Rd. This is the main road to the Sabarmati Ashram. The airport is off to the north-east of the city. Virtually all the old city walls have been demolished, but some of the gates remain.

Information

Tourist Offices The helpful state tourist office, Gujarat Tourism (☎ 6589172, fax 6582183, ⓔ ahmedabad@gujarattourism.com), is in a laneway just off Ashram Rd, across the river from the town centre. Ask rickshaw drivers for HK House or the BATA showroom (a more commonly known landmark). Opening hours are from 10.30 am to 1.30 pm and 2 to 6 pm (closed Sunday and

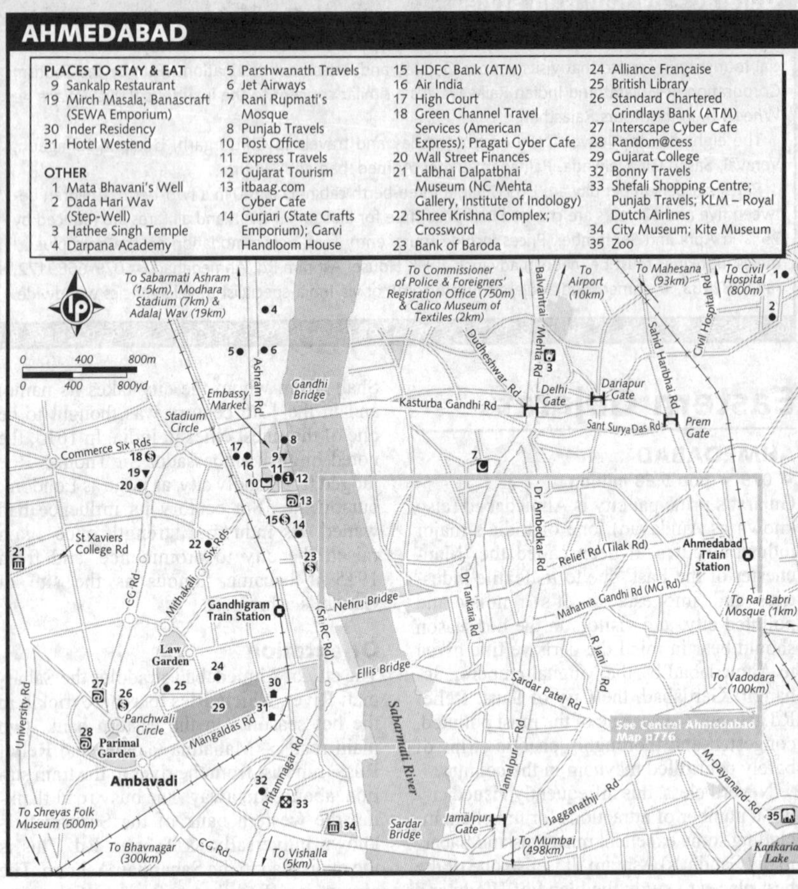

the second and fourth Saturday in the month). If you're there between 11 am and 1 pm Monday to Friday, ask for Professor H Pradhan, the Senior Tourist Officer, who is particularly friendly and a mine of information.

The office has good brochures and maps of Ahmedabad and the Gujarat state, and can also arrange car hire and tours. Tours might be worthwhile if your time in Gujarat is limited. Fast-paced five-day tours to Saurashtra cost Rs 2100; those to northern Gujarat/southern Rajasthan cost Rs 2300. The quoted prices include all transportation, accommodation and guide fees.

Check the office's excellent Web site at www.gujarattourism.com.

Money The State Bank of India branch (1st floor) near Lal Darwaja (the local bus stand) and the Bank of Baroda, at the west end of Relief Rd, have moneychanging facilities. For quicker service, try either Green Channel Travel Services (☎ 6560489; the local representative for American Express) or Wall Street Finances (☎ 6426682), both on

CG Rd, close to Mirch Masala Restaurant. The Bank of Baroda on Ashram Rd can give cash advances on Visa cards, while the HDFC ATM on Ashram Rd services Visa, MasterCard and Cirrus.

Post & Communications The main post office is central, just off Relief Rd. The central telegraph office is just south of Sidi Saiyad's Mosque.

The best Internet connections are found at Interscape Cyber Cafe (☎ 6404131, fax 640 4134, ⓔ espey@interscapeworld.com), which is open 24 hours. It's on the 1st floor of the large white building, opposite the Standard Chartered Grindlays Bank on Panchwati Circle; it charges Rs 30 per hour. Other good options include itbaag.com Cyber Cafe (☎ 6585873, ⓔ itbaag@itbaag.com), close to the tourist office (Rs 25 per hour), and Random@ccess on Ambawadi Rd. The cheapest cafe is Pragati Cyber Cafe, signed above the street as Dat@net Cyber Cafe (☎ 6567569), which charges Rs 20 an hour. On the east side of the river, try the private telephone office(☎ 5507498), 20m north of the Advance Cinema on the opposite side of the road (Rs 60).

Bookshops Crossword, in the Shree Krishna complex at Mithakali Six Rds, has books plus CDs, maps and a coffee shop. It's open 10.30 am to 8.30 pm daily.

Libraries & Cultural Centres The British Library (☎ 6560693), at Bhaikaka Hall, west of the river, has a good selection of books and British newspapers. It's open 11 am to 7 pm Tuesday to Saturday. About 400m east is the Alliance Française (☎ 6401551, ⓔ afad@ad1.vsnl.net.in). The centre has information on French films, which are sometimes screened in the city.

The Darpana Academy (☎ 6445189), about 1km north of Gujarat Tourism on Ashram Rd, has regular cultural programs.

Medical Services & Emergency The Civil Hospital (☎ 2123721) is around 2.5km north of the train station. The ambulance number is ☎ 102.

Bhadra Fort & Teen Darwaja

Bhadra Fort, on MG Rd, was built by the city's founder, Ahmed Shah, in 1411 and later named after the goddess Bhadra, an incarnation of Kali. It now houses government offices, where you can ask for access to the roof for views of the surrounding streets. There is a post office in the former Palace of Azam Khan, within the fort. Some of the bastions inside the fort fell during the 2001 earthquake although the overall structure remains intact. To the east of the fort stands the Teen Darwaja (triple gateway), from which sultans watched processions from the palace to the Jama Masjid. At least one of the balconies collapsed during the tremors.

Mosques & Mausoleums

The **Jama Masjid**, built in 1423 by Ahmed Shah, is beside Mahatma Gandhi Rd, to the east of the Teen Darwaja. Although 260 columns support the roof, the two 'shaking' minarets (see under Sidi Bashir Mosque later) lost half their height in the great earthquake of 1819, and another tremor in 1957 completed their demolition. Sadly, the earthquake of 2001 also took its toll with significant cracks appearing in the domes and pillars. Much of the mosque was built using items salvaged from demolished Hindu and Jain temples. It is said that a large black slab by the main arch is actually the base of a Jain idol, buried upside down for the Muslim faithful to tread on.

The **Tomb of Ahmed Shah** stands just outside the east gate of the Jama Masjid. It was built shortly after his death in 1442. His son and grandson also have their cenotaphs in this tomb. Women are not allowed into the central chamber. Across the street on a raised platform is the tomb of his queens, now a market and in very poor shape compared to his own tomb.

Dating from 1414, **Ahmed Shah's Mosque** was one of the earliest mosques in the city and was probably built on the site of a Hindu temple. It is to the south-west of the Bhadra Fort. The front of the mosque is now a garden.

Sidi Saiyad's Mosque is close to the river end of Relief Rd. It was constructed in 1573

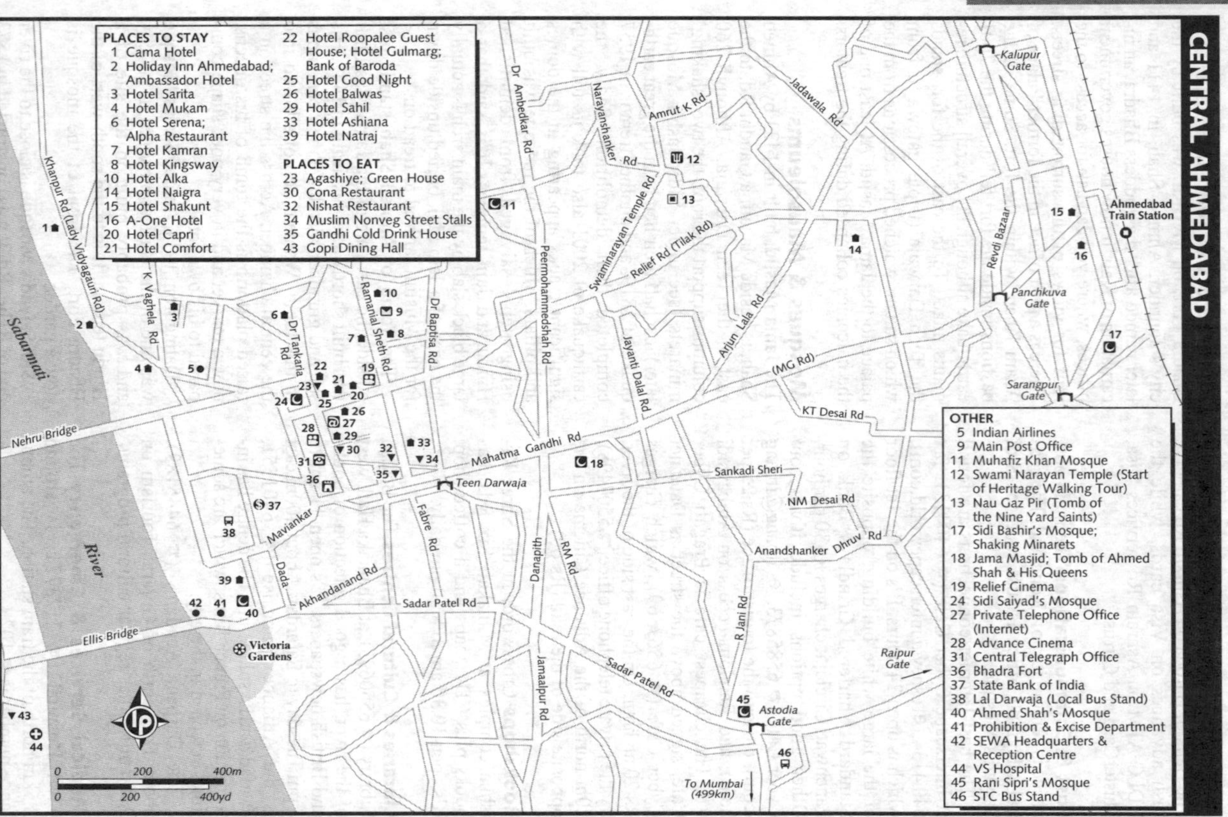
GUJARAT
CENTRAL AHMEDABAD
PLACES TO STAY
1 Cama Hotel
2 Holiday Inn Ahmedabad; Ambassador Hotel
3 Hotel Sarita
4 Hotel Mukam
6 Hotel Serena; Alpha Restaurant
7 Hotel Kamran
8 Hotel Kingsway
10 Hotel Alka
14 Hotel Naigra
15 Hotel Shakunt
16 A-One Hotel
20 Hotel Capri
21 Hotel Comfort
22 Hotel Roopalee Guest House; Hotel Gulmarg; Bank of Baroda
25 Hotel Good Night
26 Hotel Balwas
29 Hotel Sahil
33 Hotel Ashiana
39 Hotel Natraj
PLACES TO EAT
23 Agashiye; Green House
30 Cona Restaurant
32 Nishat Restaurant
34 Muslim Nonveg Street Stalls
35 Gandhi Cold Drink House
43 Gopi Dining Hall
OTHER
5 Indian Airlines
9 Main Post Office
11 Muhafiz Khan Mosque
12 Swami Narayan Temple (Start of Heritage Walking Tour)
13 Nau Gaz Pir (Tomb of the Nine Yard Saints)
17 Sidi Bashir's Mosque; Shaking Minarets
18 Jama Masjid; Tomb of Ahmed Shah & His Queens
19 Relief Cinema
24 Sidi Saiyad's Mosque
27 Private Telephone Office (Internet)
28 Advance Cinema
31 Central Telegraph Office
36 Bhadra Fort
37 State Bank of India
38 Lal Darwaja (Local Bus Stand)
40 Ahmed Shah's Mosque
41 Prohibition & Excise Department
42 SEWA Headquarters & Reception Centre
44 VS Hospital
45 Rani Sipri's Mosque
46 STC Bus Stand
Kalupur Gate
Ahmedabad Train Station
Jadawala Rd
Amrut K Rd
Narayanshanker Rd
Dr Ambedkar Rd
Swaminarayan Temple Rd
Relief Rd (Tilak Rd)
Revdi Bazaar
Panchkuva Gate
Sarangpur Gate
Arjun Lala Rd
(MG Rd)
KT Desai Rd
Peermohammedshah Rd
Jayanti Dalal Rd
Dr Baptisa Rd
Ramanial Sheth Rd
Dr Tankaria Rd
K Vaghela Rd
Khanpur Rd (Lady Vidyagauri Rd)
Sabarmati
Nehru Bridge
Mahatma Gandhi Rd
Teen Darwaja
Sankadi Sheri
NM Desai Rd
Anandshanker Dhruv Rd
Mavlankar
Fabre Rd
Danapith
RM Rd
Dada
Akhandanand Rd
Sadar Patel Rd
River
Ellis Bridge
Victoria Gardens
Jamaalpur Rd
R Jani Rd
Raipur Gate
Astodia Gate
To Mumbai (499km)
0 200 400m
0 200 400yd

by Sidi Saiyad, a slave of the ruler Ahmed Shah, and has beautiful carved stone windows depicting the intricate intertwining of the branches of a tree. These can be viewed from outside (women can't enter).

A little north of the city centre, **Rani Rupmati's Mosque** was built between 1430 and 1440 and named after the sultan's Hindu wife. The minarets were partially brought down by the great earthquake of 1819. Note the way the dome is elevated to allow light in around its base. As with so many of Ahmedabad's early mosques, this one displays elements of both Hindu and Islamic design.

The small **Rani Sipri's Mosque**, southeast of the city, is also known as the Masjid-e-Nagira (Jewel of a Mosque) because of its extremely graceful and well-executed design. Its slender minarets again blend Hindu and Islamic styles. The mosque is said to have been commissioned in 1514 by a wife of Sultan Mahmud Begada after he put their son to death for some minor misdemeanour, and she is in fact buried here.

Just south of the train station, outside the Sarangpur Gate, the **Sidi Bashir Mosque** is famed for its **shaking minarets**, or *jhulta minars*. It was believed that they were built to shake in order to protect against earthquake damage.

This theory didn't save the shaking minarets of the **Raj Babri Mosque**, southeast of the train station in the suburb of Gomtipur. One was partially dismantled by an inquisitive Englishman in an unsuccessful attempt to find out how it worked. They were rebuilt only to collapse again in January 2001, when the tremors proved too much. Undaunted, the city authorities are planning to rebuild.

A little to the north of the train station, minarets are all that remain of a mosque destroyed in a battle between the Mughals and Marathas in 1753.

Temples

Just outside the Delhi Gate, to the north of the old city, the **Hathee Singh Temple**, like so many Jain temples, is made of white marble. Built in 1848, it is dedicated to Dharamanath, the 15th *tirthankar* (Jain teacher).

For a complete change, you could plunge into the narrow streets of the old part of town and seek out the brightly-painted, wood-carved **Swami Narayan Temple**. Enclosed in a large courtyard, it dates from 1850. To the south of this Hindu temple are the nine tombs known as the Nau Gaz Pir (Nine Yard Saints).

Baolis

Baolis (*wavs*; step-wells) are strange constructions, unique to northern India, and **Dada Hari Wav** is one of the best. Built in 1501 by a woman of Sultan Begara's harem, it has a series of steps leading down to lower platforms terminating at a small, octagonal well. The depths of the well are cool, even on the hottest day, and it must once have been quite beautiful. Today, it is completely neglected and often bone dry, but it's a fascinatingly eerie place with galleries above the well and a small portico at ground level.

The best time to visit and photograph the well is between 10 and 11 am; at other times the sun does not penetrate to the various levels. Entry is free. Behind the well is the equally neglected mosque and *rauza* (tomb) of Dada Hari. The mosque has a tree motif like the one on the windows of Sidi Saiyad's Mosque. Bus No 111 (Rs 2.50) to Asarwa goes nearby.

Mata Bhavani's Well is about 200m north of Dada Hari's. Ask children to show you the way. Thought to be several hundred years older than Dada Hari Wav, it is much less ornate and is now used as a simple Hindu temple.

Museums

The **City Museum** (☎ 6578369), just west of the Sardar Bridge, is a well-organised exhibition of all aspects of Ahmedabad's history with sections on each of the city's religious communities, Gujarati literature and the Independence struggle. There are some fine photos, examples of local contemporary art, as well as beautiful textiles and carvings. This excellent museum is open 11 am to 8 pm Tuesday to Sunday and entrance is free. On the ground floor is the **Kite Museum** (same opening hours and also free).

The **Calico Museum of Textiles** (☎ 786 8172) exhibits antique and modern textiles including rare tapestries, wall hangings and costumes. Also on display are various old weaving machines. The museum is in Sarabhai House, a former *haveli* (ornately decorated traditional mansion), in the Shahi Bagh Gardens. You can only enter on one of the free guided tours that depart at 10.30 am and 2.45 pm. The museum is closed on Wednesday and photography is not allowed. To get there, take bus No 101, 102 or 105 (Rs 3) out through the Delhi Gate. An autorickshaw should cost Rs 30.

The **Lalbhai Dalpatbhai Museum** (☎ 630 6883), on University Rd near Gujarat University, houses a fine collection of stone, marble and wood carvings from around India, bronzes, cloth paintings and coins. Among the sculptures is the oldest known carved image of the god Rama on a sandstone carving from Madhya Pradesh dating from the 6th century AD.

On the same campus is the **NC Mehta Gallery** (☎ 6302463, ext 31) which contains an important collection of illustrated manuscripts and miniatures from all over the country. It is well known for its *Chaurapanchasika* (the Fifty Love Lyrics of a Thief). These are attributed to Vilhana, an 11th-century Kashmiri poet, who was sentenced to hang for loving the king's daughter. Just before his execution, he composed the poems, so impressing the king that he gave his daughter to Vilhana in marriage. There are also some Rajasthani miniatures from the Mewar, Bundi, Kota and Bikaner schools. Both museums are open 10.30 am to 5.30 pm (closed Monday); entry is free. In summer, the hours are sometimes changed to 8 am to 1 pm, so ring before heading out there.

The **Shreyas Folk Museum**, about 2.5km west of the Sabarmati in the suburb of Ambavadi, shows the folk arts and crafts of Gujarat, mainly textiles and clothing. It's open 9 am to noon and 3 to 5 pm Tuesday to Thursday. Take bus No 34 or 200 (Rs 3).

Sabarmati Ashram

About 5km from the centre of town, on the west bank of the Sabarmati River, this ashram (also known as Satyagraha Ashram) was Gandhi's headquarters during the long struggle for Indian Independence. The ashram was founded in 1915 and moved to its current site a few years later. It was from here, on 12 March 1930, that Gandhi set out on his famous Salt March to the Gulf of Cambay in protest against government monopolies over the production and sale of salt, vowing not to return to the ashram until India was free. Handicrafts, handmade paper and spinning wheels are still produced on the site. Gandhi's spartan living quarters are preserved as a small museum and there's an excellent pictorial record of the major events in his life. There's also a bookshop selling books by and about the Mahatma, and the library contains the letter sent by Gandhiji to Hitler on 23 July 1939 asking him to pull back from war.

The ashram is open 8.30 am to 6 pm (7 pm between April and September). Entry is free. There is a sound-and-light show (Rs 5, 65 mins) at 7.00 pm (in Gujarati; daily) and 8.30 pm (in English on Sunday, Wednesday and Friday; in Hindi on other nights). The booking office (☎ 7556073) opens at 2 pm. Bus No 81, 83/1 or 84/1 (Rs 3) will take you there. An autorickshaw will cost about Rs 25.

Kankaria Lake

South-east of the city, this artificial lake, complete with an island summer palace, was constructed in 1451 and has 34 sides, each 60m long. Once frequented by Emperor Jehangir and Empress Nur Jahan, it is now a local picnic spot. There's a huge **zoo** (open 9 am to 5.30 pm; Rs 10) and children's park by the lake, and the Ghattamendal pavilion in the centre houses an **aquarium**. The Balvatika waterpark, with a sauna and a restaurant, should open here by 2001. To get to the lake, take bus No 32, 42, 60, 152 or 153 from the Lal Darwaja (Rs 2.50).

Other Attractions

In many streets there are Jain bird-feeding places known as *parabdis*. The pleasant **Victoria Gardens** are at the east end of the Ellis Bridge. The **Law Gardens** on the west bank are also worth a visit, particularly towards sunset when textile stallholders set up their wares around the edge of the gardens.

Organised Tours

The Municipal Corporation (mobile ☎ 9824 032866) runs Heritage Walking Tours (Rs 25) through the old city every day. They start from the Swami Narayan Temple at 8 am and finish close to the Jama Masjid around 10.30 am. There's no need to book; simply turn up a little before the appointed time. Some travellers have recommended the tours as an excellent way to get a feel for the city. Commentaries are given in English and there's sometimes a brief slide show before commencement. Brochures are available from the Gujarat Tourism office (see Information earlier).

Places to Stay

Lots of cheap hotels are scattered along or close to Relief Rd. The real cheapies are opposite the train station, but most of these are assailed by Ahmedabad's horrendous noise and air pollution and are probably best avoided unless you have a very early morning departure. The area around Sidi Saiyad's Mosque at the western end of Relief Rd is better, although it's still far from serene. Many hotels have 24-hour checkout although some top-end hotels have a stingy 9 am checkout.

Places to Stay – Budget

***A-One Hotel** (☎ 2149823)* is opposite the train station. The owner's claims of 'luxuriously furnished rooms' are decidedly ambitious. Basic singles/doubles go for Rs 90/140 without private bathroom and Rs 175/250 with cold-water shower. The manager dismissed questions about hot water with the words, 'Ahmedabad is a very hot city'. He has a point.

***Hotel Shakunt** (☎ 2144515)*, a few doors away, is a bit cramped but comfortable enough with rooms starting at Rs 200/270.

***Hotel Naigra** (☎ 384977)*, just off Relief Rd, has fairly quiet but cramped rooms that are airless and a little grubby. A single with shared bathroom goes for Rs 100 while rooms with private bathroom cost Rs 160/180. Bucket hot water is available.

***Hotel Roopalee Guest House** (☎ 550 3135, Dr Tankaria Rd)*, near Sidi Saiyad's Mosque, is not a bad choice. Simple, but pleasant and clean, rooms with bucket hot water and TV are Rs 150/200, or there's a dorm for Rs 55. The staff are friendly and a number of travellers have given this place the thumbs up. Across the alley is ***Hotel Gulmarg** (☎ 5507202)*, with a range of rooms starting at Rs 150/250, also with TV and hot water. Note that it's a long climb up to the 5th floor if the lift isn't working – which is often.

***Hotel Ashiana** (☎ 5351114, Ramanlal Sheth Rd)* claims 'well-furnished rooms' which is a gross embellishment; they're actually pretty shabby. Price is the only real virtue here: Rs 125/150 with shared bathroom; Rs 150/175 with toilet and bucket hot water.

***Hotel Natraj** (☎ 5506048)*, near Lal Darwaja, is marginally better. Rooms cost Rs 130/220/300 for a basic single/double/triple with bathroom but no shower; bucket hot water is available in the morning. Some rooms have a balcony overlooking the pleasant gardens of Ahmed Shah's Mosque.

***Hotel Sahil** (☎ 5507351)*, opposite the Advance Cinema near Lal Darwaja, is good value for a few more rupees. Rooms start at Rs 200/270 for a single/double, and for Rs 250/325 you get a deluxe double with fan, satellite TV, private bathroom (geyser hot water) and squat toilet. Some rooms are better than others.

***Hotel Mukam** (☎ 5509080, Khanpur Rd)*, near the Nehru Bridge, is also good value in the upper budget range. Decent rooms with satellite TV start at Rs 275/370, though you'll pay more for air-con.

Places to Stay – Mid-Range

***Hotel Serena** (☎ 5510136, Dr Tankaria Rd)*, not far from Sidi Saiyad's Mosque, is probably the best-value mid-range option. Clean, modern rooms start at Rs 325/450 for a single/double (children below 12 free). There is an excellent restaurant (see Places to Eat).

The cluster of hotels close to the intersection of Relief and Dr Tankaria Rds all have modern, clean and comfortable rooms, although at each the more expensive rooms are better value. Each has a private bathroom, satellite TV and 24-hour hot water. ***Hotel Good Night*** *(☎ 5507181, fax 550 6998)* has somewhat sterile rooms starting at Rs 325/450 or Rs 475/600 with air-con. ***Hotel Capri*** *(☎ 5507143, fax 5506646)*, around the corner, is slightly better but also more expensive (Rs 425/500 and upwards); they accept Visa. ***Hotel Comfort*** *(☎ 550 3014)*, in the same street as the Capri, has some quite nice rooms without air-con for Rs 300/400, although some could do with a window.

Hotel Balwas *(☎ 5507135, fax 5506320)*, across the road, is arguably the nicest of the four. Its deluxe rooms are particularly good value at Rs 450/575 with a balcony; if you can't escape the chaos of Relief Rd, you might as well look down on it for entertainment. Noise is, however, a problem.

Hotel Kingsway *(☎ 5501215, fax 550 5271, Ramanlal Sheth Rd)*, not far from the main post office, costs Rs 450/600 for bare, uninspiring rooms with air-con. The suites aren't bad for Rs 1200/1400.

Hotel Kamran *(☎ 5509586, fax 550 9586)*, almost opposite, is another place where the more expensive rooms are better value. The executive suite is a steal at Rs 800/900; the cheapest rooms are Rs 330/440.

Hotel Alka *(☎ 5500830, fax 5501002)*, north of the post office on the same street, charges Rs 375/475 for standard rooms that are better than the exterior suggests.

Hotel Sarita *(☎ 5501569)* is in a reasonably quiet, residential area close to the Indian Airlines office, just off K Varghela Rd. Largish, fairly modern rooms cost Rs 325/ 375, or Rs 500/550 with air-con.

Ambassador Hotel *(☎ 5502490, fax 5502327, Khanpur Rd)*, near the Sabarmati River, has a range of reasonable rooms starting at Rs 450/550. They provide a courtesy service to/from the airport.

Toran Guest House *(☎ 7559342, Ashram Rd)* is a government-run place opposite the Sabarmati Ashram. Clean rooms cost Rs 325/500, or Rs 525/750 with air-con. Tea and breakfast are included; checkout is 9 am.

Places to Stay – Top End

All of the places listed in this category accept major credit cards.

Holiday Inn Ahmedabad *(☎ 5505505, fax 5505501, Khanpur Rd)* is unbeatable in terms of luxury, provided you don't mind overlooking the shacks along the riverbank. Sumptuous rooms range from Rs 4100/4800 to a dizzying Rs 9000 for a palatial suite. The tariff (which is negotiable) includes a buffet breakfast; among the amenities are an indoor swimming pool, spa, sauna, 24-hour coffee shop and restaurant.

Cama Hotel *(☎ 5505281, fax 5505285, e camahotel@vsnl.com, Khanpur Rd)*, farther north, has large, beautifully appointed rooms starting at Rs 3000/3300, many of which overlook the Sabarmati River and lawn area. A buffet breakfast is included in the price. When you arrive you are greeted with a welcome drink, fruit basket and, if you've paid for one of the more expensive rooms, chocolates. There's a restaurant, coffee shop, pool, bookshop, alcohol shop and courtesy airport service. It charges day rates of Rs 1700/2000 (9 am to 6 pm).

Hotel Westend *(☎ 6466464, fax 646 9990, Mangaldas Rd)*, on the west bank, has some stylish, spacious rooms starting at Rs 1500/1900, but try to get one that doesn't overlook the railway line.

Inder Residency *(☎ 6565222, fax 656 0407)*, almost opposite, is a five-star place with a pool, health club and all the other luxury bells and whistles. Rooms start at Rs 2970/3600.

Places to Eat

The strict vegetarianism of the Jains has contributed to Gujarat's distinctive regional cuisine. Ahmedabad is a good place to sample the Gujarati version of *thali* – the traditional all-you-can-eat vegetarian meal with an even greater variety of dishes than usual, although some can be overpoweringly sweet.

Other popular dishes include *kadhi*, a savoury curry of yogurt, fried puffs and finely chopped vegetables. *Undhyoo* is a winter speciality of potatoes, sweet potatoes, broad beans and aubergines roasted in an earthenware pot, which is buried upside

Permission to Drink, Sir?

Getting a drink in the 'dry' state of Gujarat has become possible. Thirsty foreigners are able to purchase and consume alcohol upon obtaining a permit. Officially, you'll need to present yourself to the Gujarat Tourism counter (☎ 2854095) at Ahmedabad airport or the Prohibition & Excise Department, opposite Victoria Gardens just east of Ellis Bridge. A far easier way to proceed is to go through one of the few hotels with alcohol shops where, upon presentation of your tourist visa, you'll be granted a permit. One hotel that does provide this service for guests and nonguests is the Cama Hotel on Khanpur Rd. If all this seems too much like hard work, head to Diu.

CLINT CURE

down and a fire built on top. *Sev ganthia*, a crunchy, fried chickpea-flour snack, is available from *farsan* (salted snack) stalls. Then there's *khaman dhokla*, a salty, steamed chickpea-flour cake, and *doodhpak*, a thick, sweetened, milk-based dessert with nuts. *Srikhand* is a yogurt dessert spiced with saffron, cardamom, nuts and candied fruit. In summer, *aam rasis* is a popular mango drink.

At the bottom end of the restaurant scale, you can get excellent Muslim (nonveg) street food near Teen Darwaja on Bhathiyar Gali, a small street which runs parallel to Gandhi Rd. ***Food stalls*** set up each evening and for around Rs 25 you can get a good feed. There are halal meat, fish and vegetarian dishes to choose from. To get to this area, you may have to walk through the live poultry market, where prospective chickens are (hopefully) unaware of the fate that lies just a few metres away.

The very basic restaurants opposite are only if you want to wait bum-to-sandal on the footpath for an hour or so with the other hungry patrons.

Nishat Restaurant *(☎ 5507335, Khas Bazaar)*, in the same area, is a friendly place that serves good tandoori dishes for under Rs 40 (save for a full chicken which costs Rs 72). Across the lane, ***Gandhi Cold Drinks House*** is a popular spot with locals for a lassi or ice cream.

Gopi Dining Hall, just off the west end of Ellis Bridge, near the VS Hospital, is one of the most popular thali places. Excellent all-you-can-eat Gujarati thalis are Rs 45 (lunch) or Rs 55 (dinner).

Cona Restaurant, opposite the Advance Cinema, is a good place for cheap vegetarian food.

Sankalp Restaurant *(☎ 6583550)*, off Ashram Rd in the Embassy Market area, is worth a visit. This air-con restaurant boasts one of the longest *dosas* (thin lentil-flour pancakes; Rs 400) in India – 4ft long! The Rs 40 South Indian thalis also make a pleasant change from the sweet Gujarati cuisine.

Alpha Restaurant in the Hotel Serena (see Places to Stay) has prices that are (thankfully) nowhere near as grand as the decor. The food is high quality and the service attentive. A good butter chicken costs Rs 55.

Agashiye *(☎ 5506946, fax 5506535, e vcvl@vsnl.com, Dr Tankaria St)*, opposite Sidi Saiyad's Mosque, is one of Ahmedabad's best dining experiences right in the centre of town. Set atop one of the city's finest mansions (dating from the early 20th century), the lovely terrace area has faultless service and offers daily banquets for both lunch (Rs 135, noon to 2.30 pm) and dinner (Rs 170, 7 to 11 pm). The dinner menu, which changes every day, includes introductory fruit juices, entrees, a multitude of veg main dishes, sweets, and ice cream. It's a great place to sample quality Gujarati cuisine and pretend you're not really in one of India's most congested cities. Get there while you can: sadly, the building is under threat of demolition by the municipal authorities, competing with the owner's plans to set up a Heritage hotel and Internet cafe.

Green House, on the same property at street level in a covered garden, is of a similarly high standard, but it only serves snacks (11 am to 11 pm). The coconut coriander tikka (Rs 35) is a sensation and the pineapple lassis are also good (Rs 35). You'll need to duck for cover whenever they turn the sprinklers on, although in summer it may just add to the attraction.

Vishalla, on the southern edge of town in Vasana, is a 'theme' dining experience that evokes the atmosphere of a Gujarati village. You eat seated on the floor in wooden huts. Within the complex there are craft stalls, a puppet display and a Utensils Museum. Lunch (11 am to 2 pm) costs Rs 125; dinner (7.30 to 11 pm) is Rs 190 and is accompanied by music and dance. The food is a set, veg-only all-you-can-eat meal, though dessert costs extra. Bus No 31 will get you within walking distance; an autorickshaw from the centre of town will cost Rs 30, but expect to pay about Rs 50 for the return trip.

Mirch Masala (CG Rd) also evokes a Gujarati village atmosphere, this time with the aid of colourful murals. Although its a la carte menu is good for dinner (Rs 75 and up), the veg/nonveg lunch specials (Rs 85/125) are brilliant value. For your money, you get a salad, pappadams, five main dishes (if you're on your own it's quite a meal!), ice cream, sweets and as much buttermilk (definitely an acquired taste) as you can drink. It all happens from 12 noon to 3.30 pm and the friendly staff accept Visa and MasterCard. It's something of an Ahmedabad institution so you may have to queue.

Shopping

With its busy modern textile works, it's not surprising that Gujarat offers a number of interesting purchases in this line. Extremely fine, and often extremely expensive, patola silk saris are still made by a handful of master craftspeople in Patan. From Surat comes the *zari*, or gold-thread embroidery work. Surat is also a centre for silk saris. Less opulent, but still beautiful, are the block prints of Ahmedabad.

Jamnagar is famous for its tie-dye work, which you'll see throughout Saurashtra. Brightly coloured embroideries and beadwork are also found in Saurashtra, along with woollen shawls, blankets and rugs.

SEWA

The Self-Employed Women's Association (SEWA) is Gujarat's single largest union, comprising 215,000 members in India; 148,000 of these are in Gujarat alone. Established in 1972, SEWA identifies three types of self-employed workers: hawkers and vendors; home-based workers such as weavers, potters and bidi rollers; and manual labourers and service providers such as agricultural labourers, contract labourers, construction workers, and laundry and domestic workers.

Adhering to a Gandhian philosophy of change through nonviolent means, SEWA aims to enable women to actively participate in the mainstream economy and to attain empowerment and self-reliance through financial autonomy. SEWA assists self-employed workers to organise into unions and cooperatives, so that they can ultimately control the fruits of their own labours. SEWA's focus is on areas such as health and child care, literacy, appropriate housing and self-sufficiency, and the SEWA Academy conducts leadership training courses for its members. SEWA is also active in the campaign for a needs-based minimum wage of Rs 125 per day. Membership costs Rs 5 per annum.

SEWA has also set up a bank, giving many poor women their first access to a savings or lending body, since conventional banks are often unwilling to deal with people of such limited means.

The SEWA Reception Centre (☎ 5506444, fax 5506446, e sewamahila@wilnetonline.net) is at the eastern end of Ellis Bridge, opposite Victoria Gardens. They have a range of literature and visitors are welcome (open 10 am to 8 pm, closed Sunday).

Brass-covered wooden chests are manufactured in Bhavnagar, and Kutch is the centre for exquisite, fine embroidery, often with mirrorwork. Ahmedabad is a good place to look for Gujarati crafts. On Ashram Rd, just to the south of the tourist office, is the Gujarat state crafts emporium, Gurjari (☎ 658 9505). The Garvi Handloom House is around the back. For hand-printed fabrics and other textiles, the Self-Employed Women's Association (SEWA; see the boxed text) has a retail outlet called Banascraft (☎ 405784, ⓔ bdmsa@ad1.vsnl.net.in) at 8 Chandan Complex, above the Mirch Masala restaurant. You can visit the Web site at www.banascraft.org.

Getting There & Away

The Ahmedabad edition of the *Times of India* has up-to-the-minute flight and rail information on page two.

Air Ahmedabad airport has international and domestic services. Many travel agents around town handle domestic and international flight bookings. Two good places are Parshwanath Travels (☎ 7544142, fax 7544144, ⓔ parshtrvl@wilnetonline.net), almost opposite the Jet Airways office on Ashram Rd, and Express Travels (☎ 6588602, fax 6582533, ⓔ express@wilnetonline.net), around the corner from Gujarat Tourism. They accept all major credit cards.

International Air India (☎ 6585644), Premchand House, near the High Court building on Ashram Rd, has flights to New York (five per week) and on to Chicago (twice a week) via Mumbai and London. The one-way/return fare to the USA is Rs 27,000/40,000, while as far as London is Rs 22,000/31,000.

Indian Airlines (☎ 5503061; airport office ☎ 2869233) is just off Relief Rd, not far east of the Nehru Bridge. It has twice-weekly flights to Sharjah (Rs 10,300/18,700 one way/return) and Kuwait (Rs 12,500/22,700), and three flights a week to Muscat (Rs 10,300/18,700). Some of these Indian Airlines flights connect with KLM–Royal Dutch Airlines and British Airways for flights on to Europe.

Domestic Indian Airlines flies regularly from Ahmedabad to Chennai (Madras; US$235) via Mumbai (US$75; connections to Goa twice a week), Delhi (US$120), Kolkata (Calcutta; US$205) and Jaipur (US$95).

Jet Airways (☎ 7543304), Ashram Rd, has daily flights to Mumbai (US$75) and Delhi (US$120).

Bus STC (☎ 2144764) buses travel from the bus stand near Rani Sipri's Mosque to, among other places, Vadodara (Rs 45/52 for standard/semideluxe, 2½ hours), Palitana (Rs 68/77, five hours), Jamnagar (Rs 95/101, eight hours), Bhavnagar (Rs 65/74, four hours) and Rajkot (Rs 122 semideluxe only, 6½ hours).

If you're travelling long distances, private buses are a more expensive but much quicker alternative; many of their offices are just east of the STC bus stand. Punjab Travels (☎ 6589200), Embassy Market, just off Ashram Rd near Gujarat Tourism, has a number of intercity services, including: Ajmer (Rs 220, 13 hours), Aurangabad (Rs 300, 15 hours), Jaipur (Rs 250, 16 hours), Jodhpur (Rs 200, 15 hours), Mt Abu (Rs 140, seven hours) and Udaipur (Rs 100, eight hours). It has another office on Pritamnagar Rd in the Shefali Shopping Centre. Bonny Travels (☎ 6579265), on Pritamnagar Rd, serves Jamnagar (Rs 120) and Rajkot (Rs 90) many times throughout the day.

Train There is a computerised booking office (☎ 135) to the left as you exit Ahmedabad train station. It's open 8 am to 8 pm Monday to Saturday, 8 am to 2 pm Sunday. Window No 6 handles the foreign tourist quota and you could try booking tickets with your credit card at window No 7.

Getting Around

To/From the Airport The airport is 10km north of town; an autorickshaw costs about Rs 90. A cheaper option is a local bus from Lal Darwaja (Rs 5, bus No 102 or 105).

Autorickshaw Most autorickshaw drivers are willing to use the meter (it's the dial by their left knee); make sure they set it to zero

Major Trains from Ahmedabad

destination	train No & name	departures	distance (km)	duration (hrs)	fare (Rs)
Bhavnagar	9910 *Shetrunji Exp*	5.10 pm	299	5½	73/231 ◆
Delhi	9105 *Delhi Mail*	10.00 am	938	19¼	261/761 †
Dwarka	9005 *Saurashtra Mail*	6.15 am	453	10	162/468 †
Gandhidham	9031 *Kutch Exp*	2.00 am	300	6½	114/329 †
Mumbai	2902 *Gujarat Mail*	10.00 pm	492	8¾	166/482 †
Udaipur	9944 *Sarai Rohila Exp*	11.00 pm	297	9	114/329 †
Vadodara (Baroda)	2010 *Shatabdi Exp*	2.45 pm	100	1½	230/455 *

* executive/chair class ◆ general/chair class † sleeper/air-con 3-tier sleeper

at the outset. Travelling from Ahmedabad train station to Sidi Saiyad's mosque costs about Rs 10, though drivers will sometimes quote more, especially from the station.

Local buses depart from Lal Darwaja. Details of the routes, destinations and fares are all posted in Gujarati.

AROUND AHMEDABAD

Sarkhej

The suburb of Sarkhej, 8km south-west of Ahmedabad, is noted for its elegant group of buildings, including the **Mausoleum of Azam & Mu'assam**, built in 1457 by the brothers responsible for Sarkhej's architecture. The architectural style is almost purely Hindu, with little of the Saracenic influence so evident in Ahmedabad.

As you enter Sarkhej, you pass the **Mausoleum of Mahmud Begara** and, beside the tank and connected to his tomb, that of his queen, Rajabai (1461). Also by the tank is the **Tomb of Ahmad Khattu Ganj Buksh**, a renowned Muslim saint and spiritual adviser to Ahmed Shah. The saint is said to have died in 1445 at the age of 111. Next to this tomb is a fine mosque. Like the other buildings, it is notable for the complete absence of arches, a usual feature of Muslim architecture. The palace, with pavilions and a harem, is also around the tank.

The Dutch established a factory in Sarkhej in 1620 to process the indigo that is grown here.

To get to Sarkhej from Ahmedabad, take bus No 31 from Lal Darwaja.

Adalaj Wav

Nineteen kilometres north of Ahmedabad, Adalaj Wav is one of the finest of the Gujarati step-wells, with carvings depicting intricate motifs of flowers and birds. The main corridor has four pavilions and the well is five storeys deep, each decorated with exquisite stone carvings. Built by Queen Rudabai in 1499, it provided a cool and secluded retreat during the hot summer months. The Ahmedabad-Gandhinagar bus will get you within walking distance (ask the conductor where to get off).

Nal Sarovar Bird Sanctuary

Between November and February, this 116-sq-km lake, 60km south-west of Ahmedabad, is home to flocks of indigenous and migratory birds, with as many as 250 bird species passing through the park. Ducks, geese, pelicans and flamingos are best seen early in the morning and in the evening. One visitor had the following advice:

> You can hire a boat on Nal Sarovar with someone to punt you to the areas where the flamingos and pelicans are; but please avoid going too close and try to restrain the boatman from scaring the birds, as this causes them to fly away. One of the main reasons for the decline in population of some birds is excessive human disturbance. If possible, avoid weekends and holidays when it gets quite crowded.
>
> **Krys Kazmierczak, UK**

The sanctuary is most easily visited as a day excursion by taxi from Ahmedabad, as buses are infrequent and there is no convenient accommodation. Call the Conservator of Forests in Gandhinagar (☎ 02712-21951; in Ahmedabad ☎ 912-21951) to see if the Forest Rest House has reopened.

Lothal

About 85km south-west of Ahmedabad, and towards Bhavnagar, this important archaeological site was discovered in 1954. The city that stood here 4500 years ago is clearly related to the Indus Valley cities of Mohenjodaro and Harappa, both in Pakistan. It has the same neatly laid-out street pattern, the same carefully assembled brickwork and the same scientific drainage system.

The name Lothal means 'Mound of the Dead' in Gujarati, as does Mohenjodaro in Sindhi. Excavations have revealed a dockyard; at its peak, this was probably one of the most important ports on the subcontinent. Seals discovered at the site suggest that trade was conducted with the civilisations of Mesopotamia, Egypt and Persia.

The **archaeological museum** at the site displays jewellery, pots and other finds (open 10 am to 5 pm, closed Sunday; Rs 5).

Accommodation is a problem in Lothal, though there is the expensive ***Utelia Palace***, 7km from the archaeological site, by the Bhugavo River.

Lothal is a long day trip from Ahmedabad (at least three hours travel each way). You can reach it by rail, disembarking at Bhurkhi on the Ahmedabad to Bhavnagar railway line, from where you can take a bus.

Modhera

The beautiful and partially ruined **Sun Temple of Modhera** was built by King Bhimdev I in 1026–27, and bears some resemblance to the later, and far better known, Sun Temple of Konark in the state of Orissa, which it predates by some 200 years. Like that temple, it was designed so that the dawn sun shone on the image of Surya, the sun god, at the time of the equinoxes. The main hall and shrine are reached through a pillared porch and the temple exterior is intricately and delicately carved.

As with the Temple of Somnath (see Somnath later in this chapter), this fine temple was ruined by Mahmud of Ghazni. Nonetheless, what remains is still impressive. This is hardly surprising given that the building work was first completed by the Silavat stonemasons, renowned for their ability to turn the hardest stone into delicate carvings.

Within the main grounds, the **Surya Kund** is an extraordinary step-well containing over 100 shrines. Shrines to Ganesh, Vishnu and an incarnation of Shiva surround the tank on three sides, while the main temple completes the rectangle and displays 52 intricately carved pillars that depict scenes from the Ramayana and the Mahabharata. The interior of the temple contains a hall with walls that have 12 niches representing the different manifestations of the sun god in each month. Elsewhere in the complex, there are extensive panels of erotic sculpture.

The temple is open 8 am to 6 pm daily.

Accommodation can pose a real problem here. There are a few cheap resthouses but foreigners often find it difficult to get a bed at them.

Modhera is 102km north-west of Ahmedabad. There are direct buses (Rs 30, 3½ hours), or you can take the train to Mahesana and then catch a bus for the 26km trip to Modhera.

Unjha

A little north of Mahesana, and a base for those visiting the Modhera Temple, the town of Unjha is known for the marriage customs of the Kadwakanbis who live in this region. Marriages occur only once every 11 years and, on that day, every unmarried girl over 40 days old must be wed. If no husband can be found, a proxy wedding takes place and the bride immediately becomes a 'widow'. She later remarries when a suitable husband shows up.

There are a number of private guesthouses at Unjha.

Patan

About 130km north-west of Ahmedabad, this was an ancient Hindu capital before it was sacked by Mahmud of Ghazni in 1024. Now a pale shadow of its former self, it still has more than 100 **Jain temples** and is famous for its beautifully designed patola **silk saris**. There's also the renovated **Rani-ki-Vav**, a step-well which boasts some of Gujarat's finest carvings. Built in 1050, the step-well is the oldest in Gujarat and is remarkably well preserved – a product of the restoration work completed in the 1980s to redress centuries of silting. The waters once provided a natural air-cooling system in its chambers for members of the royal family who sought refuge here from the summer heat. It's very impressive and certainly warrants a visit.

Try looking for cheap accommodation near the bus stand and the train station, although what's on offer is unappealing.

Patan is 25km north-west of Mahesana. Buses from Ahmedabad take 3½ hours and cost Rs 40.

GANDHINAGAR

☎ 912 from Ahmedabad, ☎ 02712 from elsewhere • pop 393,000

Although Ahmedabad became the capital of Gujarat state when the old state of Mumbai was split, a new capital was planned 32km north-east on the west bank of the Sabarmati River. Named Gandhinagar after Gujarat-born Mahatma Gandhi, it is India's second planned city after Chandigarh and, like that city, is laid out in dull, numbered sectors. The secretariat was moved here in 1970.

Gandhinagar's sole tourist sight is the splendid **Akshardham Temple** of the Hindu Swaminarayan sect, constructed out of 6000 tonnes of pink sandstone. It's on Ja Rd in Sector 20.

The ***Youth Hostel*** *(☎ 22364, Sector 16)*, has Rs 50 beds and offers cheap meals.

Hotel Haveli *(☎ 23905, fax 24057, Sector 11)* is more upmarket. Standard/deluxe rooms cost Rs 1600/2000, while a suite will set you back Rs 2500. The restaurant here is good, and checkout is noon.

Getting There & Away

Buses going to Gandhinagar (Rs 10) depart Ahmedabad every 15 minutes from the back north-west corner of Lal Darwaja (the local bus stand) or one of the numerous stops along Ashram Rd.

VADODARA (BARODA)

☎ 0265 • pop 1.86 million

Baroda was the capital of the princely Gaekwad state prior to Independence. Today Vadodara (or Baroda, as it is still generally known) is a pleasant, medium-sized city with some interesting museums and art galleries and a fine park. The city's Fine Arts College attracts students from around the country and abroad.

Orientation & Information

The train station, bus stand and a cluster of cheaper hotels are all on the west side of the Vishwarmurti River, which bisects the city. Tilak Rd connects the station with the main part of town. The state tourist office, Gujarat Tourism (☎ 427489) is on the ground floor of Narmada Bhavan, on Jail Rd. It's open from 10.30 am to 6 pm daily (closed Sunday and the 2nd and 4th Saturday of every month). There's also a municipal tourist office (☎ 794456) opposite the train station, open 9.30 am to 6 pm daily. Not much English is spoken here, but you can pick up the useful *Know Vadodara* booklet (Rs 25). The State Bank of India on Tilak Rd changes money, and the Bank of Baroda on RC Dutt Rd (west of the station) gives Visa cash advances.

Sayaji Bagh

This extensive park, encircled by a mini-railway, is a popular spot for an evening stroll. Within the park are several attractions. The most important is the **Baroda Museum & Art Gallery**, open 10 am to 5 pm daily (Rs 1). The museum has some good Indian statues and carvings, but there are also zoology exhibits and an Egyptian room; the gallery has Mughal miniatures and a mediocre collection of works of European masters. The **planetarium** gives demonstrations at 5 pm (English) and 6 pm (Hindi); it's open Friday to Wednesday and entry costs Rs 5. The small **zoo** is open 9 am to 5 pm Friday to Wednesday (Rs 5). There's also a **health museum** (free).

Maharaja Fateh Singh Museum

South of the centre, this royal art collection includes some copies of European works by

Raphael, Titian and Murillo, and examples of Graeco-Roman, Chinese and Japanese art, and Indian exhibits. The museum, in the palace grounds, is open 10.30 am to 5.30 pm Tuesday to Sunday. Entry costs Rs 10.

Other Attractions

The eclectic **Laxmi Vilas Palace** (☎ 431819) has traces of Rajput, Bengali, Gujarati, Venetian and Gothic architectural styles and a large collection of armour and sculptures. Visit the durbar hall with its ornate Venetian chandeliers, carved cedar ceiling and Italian mosaics. Although not normally open to the public, foreigners can sometimes visit by making an advance booking and paying the Rs 100 entry fee. The **Naulakhi Well**, a fine baoli, is 50m north of the palace. About 5km north of the town centre is the unusual **EME Temple**, a Hindu temple with an aluminium-domed roof.

Organised Tours

The Municipal Tourist Office conducts tours of the city from 2 to 6 pm every Tuesday, Wednesday and Friday (Rs 25; book in advance). Ask at Gujarat Tourism about day trips that include the surrounding region.

Places to Stay – Budget

***Jagdish Hindu Lodge** (☎ 361495, RC Dutt Rd)* is in the Sayaji Gunj district near the train station. It has gloomy rooms arranged around a scruffy courtyard. Singles/doubles with private bathroom cost Rs 70/100.

***Hotel Vikram** (☎ 361918)* is in the same street, but is a small notch upmarket. It offers singles with cold-water private bathrooms for Rs 125 or singles/doubles with air-con for Rs 236/350.

Apsara Hotel, in the next street west, is a well-maintained place with rooms for Rs 180/240 with private bathroom (bucket hot water).

Places to Stay – Mid-Range & Top End

All rooms in this class have colour TV, private bathroom and hot water.

***Ambassador Hotel** (☎ 362726)* is opposite the Apsara. There are some large, quiet rooms starting at Rs 225/336, or Rs 438/538 with air-con.

***Hotel Surya** (☎ 361361)*, opposite, is one of the better value places in town. This friendly hotel offers a courtesy coach to the airport and Internet access for guests.

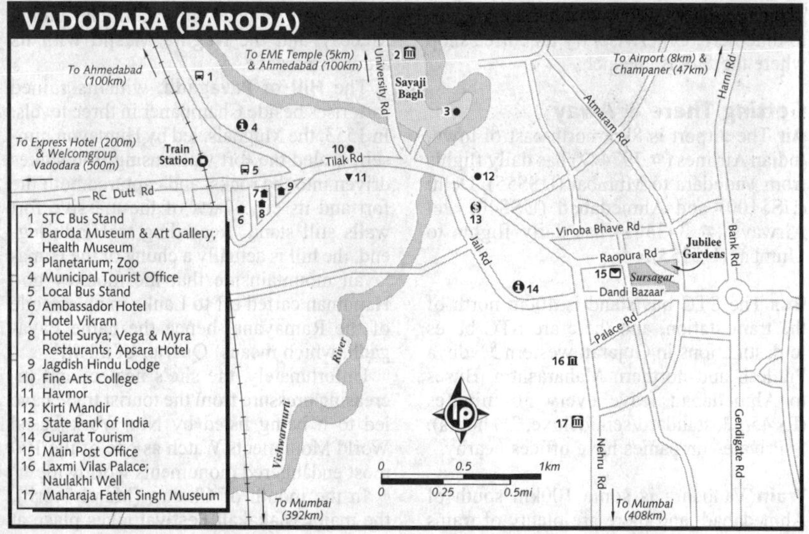

Rooms (including buffet breakfast) go for Rs 475/700, or Rs 700/900 with air-con.

Express Hotel *(☎ 337001, RC Dutt Rd)*, about 1.5km west of the train station, has air-con rooms for Rs 1250/1500 or better executive rooms for Rs 1450/2050. It also has a coffee shop and two restaurants.

Just along the road, ***Welcomgroup Vadodara*** *(☎ 330033, fax 330050)* is the most luxurious hotel in town. Well-appointed rooms start at Rs 2000/3300; all rooms have air-con. There's also a travel counter, swimming pool, 24-hour coffee shop and excellent Indian restaurant.

Places to Eat

Havmor *(Tilak Rd)*, near the river, offers reasonable Indian, continental and Chinese food. Veg/nonveg main courses are Rs 55 to 125. This road also has a number of ice-cream parlours.

Hotel Surya has two restaurants: ***Vega***, where help-yourself buffets cost Rs 75; and ***Myra***, where excellent and filling Gujarati thalis also cost Rs 75.

Ruchika, at the Welcomgroup Vadodara hotel, is recommended for a special treat. It serves scrumptious veg and nonveg Indian cuisine in pleasant surroundings. Be prepared to fork out a couple of hundred rupees to dine here. Otherwise, try its coffee shop where the fare is cheaper.

Getting There & Away

Air The airport is 8km north-east of town. Indian Airlines (☎ 797447) has daily flights from Vadodara to Mumbai (US$55), Delhi (US$100) and Ahmedabad (US$40). Jet Airways (☎ 343441) has daily flights to Mumbai (US$55).

Bus The STC bus stand is 400m north of the train station, and there are STC buses to destinations in Gujarat, western Madhya Pradesh and northern Maharashtra. Buses to Ahmedabad leave every 30 minutes (Rs 45/52, standard/semideluxe, 2½ hours).

Private companies have offices nearby.

Train Vadodara is some 100km south of Ahmedabad, and there are plenty of trains to choose from. The *Ahmedabad Express* (9129) leaves Vadodara at 6.10 pm and arrives in Ahmedabad at 8.40 pm (Rs 34/53, general/sleeper). The *Shatabdi Express* (2009) sets off at 11.35 am and pulls in at 1.20 pm (Rs 230/455, executive chair class). The *Mumbai Express* (2964) departs at 7.20 am and arrives at Bandra station in Mumbai at 1.50 pm (Rs 89/138/401, general/sleeper/3A class).

Between Vadodara and Ahmedabad you pass through **Anand**, noted for its dairy produce. At the station, hordes of vendors selling bottles of cold milk often besiege passing trains.

AROUND VADODARA

Champaner (Pavagadh)

This city, 47km north-east of Vadodara, was taken by Sultan Mahmud Begara in 1484, and he renamed it Muhammadabad.

Among the site's exquisite mosques, the **Jama Masjid**, similar in style to the Jama Masjid of Ahmedabad, is the most impressive. Dating from 1513, it has a wonderful carved entrance, an imposing courtyard surrounded by galleries, lovely archways and slim minarets. Also worth a look are the **Shahr Masjid**, with its rows of pillars, domes and delicate mihrab (niche facing Mecca), and the **Nagina Masjid** with its attractive arcade.

The **Hill of Pavagadh**, with its ruined fort, rises beside Champaner in three levels. In 1553, the Mughals, led by Humayun himself, scaled the fort walls using iron spikes driven into the rocks, and captured both the fort and its city. Parts of the massive fort walls still stand. According to Hindu legend, the hill is actually a chunk of the Himalayan mountainside that the monkey god Hanuman carted off to Lanka in an episode of the Ramayana, hence the name Pavagadh, which means 'Quarter of a Hill'.

Unfortunately, the site's neglect and increasing pressure from the tourist trade have led to it being listed by New York–based World Monuments Watch as one of the 100 most endangered monuments worldwide.

In the month of Chaitra (March/April), the major **Makakali Festival** takes place at the foot of Pavagadh Hill, honouring the goddess Makakali.

Hotel Champaner *(☎ 02676-45641)* is run by Gujarat Tourism. Beds in a four-bed room that doubles as a dorm cost Rs 75 per person, although this room only gets hot water at around 7 am. Nonair-con singles/doubles are Rs 269/400, or Rs 431/591 with air-con.

The trip from Vadodara takes 1½ hours: take one of the frequent buses to Halol then a minibus to Champaner.

Dabhoi

The 13th-century walled town of Dabhoi is 29km south-east of Vadodara (buses leave every 15 minutes from the STC bus stand). A fine example of Hindu military architecture, it is notable for the design of its four gateways – particularly the Hira, or Diamond Gate.

Dakor

Equidistant from Vadodara and Ahmedabad, the Temple of Ranchodrai, sacred to Krishna, is a major centre for the **Shrad Purnima Festival** in October/November. Buses run from Ahmedabad (Rs 26, 2½ hours).

BHARUCH

pop 213,000

This very old town was mentioned in historical records nearly 2000 years ago. It's on the main rail line between Vadodara and Surat, about one hour from each. The **fort** overlooks the wide Narmada River from a hilltop and at its base is the **Jama Masjid**. On the riverbank, east of the city, is the **Temple of Bhrigu Rishi**, from which the city took its name, Bhrigukachba, later shortened to Bharuch. The Narmada River has featured in the news due to the construction of a large dam, the Sardar Sarovar, upstream of Bharuch near the village of Manibeli (see the boxed text 'The Dam Debate' in the Facts about North India chapter).

SURAT

☎ 0261 • pop 2.38 million

Surat stands on the banks of the Tapti River and was once one of western India's major ports and trading towns, although these days there's little reason for travellers to visit.

Parsis first settled in Surat in the 12th century. In 1573 Surat fell to Akbar after a prolonged siege. It then became an important Mughal trading port and also the point of departure for Mecca-bound Muslim pilgrims. Surat soon became a wealthy city. In 1612, the British established a trading factory, followed by the Dutch in 1616 and the French in 1664.

Surat is now a major industrial centre, especially known for the manufacture of textiles and chemicals, and the processing and finishing of diamonds. But the city is probably best known these days as the site of an outbreak of pneumonic plague in 1994; at this time it was rated as the filthiest city in India.

Since then it has apparently transformed itself into India's second-cleanest and healthiest city (after Chandigarh). However, a brief acquaintance with the horrific noise, pollution and chaos of the traffic around the train station will make you question this statistic.

Things to See

Built in 1546 by the Sultan of Gujarat, the **castle** is on the riverbank, beside the Tapti Bridge. Since most of it has been given over to offices it is no longer of great interest, but there is a good view over the city and river from its bastions.

The now very run-down, overgrown and neglected **English cemetery** is just beyond the Kataragama Gate, to the right of the main road. About 500m after the Kataragama Gate, you will find the **Dutch cemetery**. There's the massive mausoleum of Baron Adriaan van Reede, who died in 1691. Adjoining the Dutch cemetery is the **Armenian cemetery**.

Surat has a number of mosques and Jain, Hindu and Parsi temples.

Places to Stay – Budget

Immediately to the left of the train station are various noisy, fairly grotty hotels.

Rupali Guest House *(☎ 423874)* is in the rock-bottom bracket and is very basic. It has dorm beds for Rs 40, singles with shared bathroom for Rs 80 and doubles with private bathroom for Rs 150.

Simla Guest House *(☎ 442339)* is better but still unremarkable. It has singles/doubles with private bathroom for Rs 240/340 and singles with shared bathroom for Rs 120.

Sarvajanik Hotel *(☎ 426159)* is at the top end of this category; rooms with private bathroom cost Rs 190/285.

Places to Stay – Mid-Range & Top End

Rates at the first three hotels, following, include breakfast.

Hotel Central Excellency *(☎ 425325, fax 441271)* is opposite the train station. It has rooms with private bathroom and TV starting at Rs 550/750, or Rs 775/1250 with air-con. There's also a restaurant.

Hotel Yuvraj *(☎ 413001, Station Rd)*, nearby, has rooms with air-con starting at Rs 850/1050. The rooms for Rs 1175/1400 include a chauffeur-driven car for free sightseeing (up to 70 km or seven hours). There is a Gujarati and a multicuisine restaurant.

Embassy Hotel *(☎ 443170, fax 443173, Station Rd)*, next door, is newer and slightly pricier (Rs 990/1200).

Holiday Inn Hotel *(☎ 226565, fax 227294)*, near Bharti Park in Athwa Lines, 6km from the city centre, is Surat's finest hotel. Air-con rooms are Rs 3375/4675. Facilities include a swimming pool, health club, coffee shop and restaurant.

Places to Eat

In winter, try Surat's *paunk*, a curious combination of roasted cereals, or *jowar*, garlic chutney and sugar. *Gharis* are rich sweets made of milk, clarified butter and dried fruits.

Sher-e-Punjab, next to the Hotel Central Excellency, offers good veg/nonveg Punjabi and Chinese dishes from around Rs 30.

Holiday Inn Hotel has a fine restaurant serving delicious (though pricey) Indian food. There's also a coffee shop in this hotel that serves a buffet dinner for Rs 250.

Getting There & Away

Surat is on the main Mumbai to Ahmedabad railway line. The 263km trip to Mumbai takes between 4½ and 6½ hours and costs Rs 67/104 in general/sleeper class. To Ahmedabad, the 229km trip takes around four hours and costs Rs 61/95.

AROUND SURAT

Twenty-nine kilometres south of Surat, **Navsari** has been a headquarters for the Parsi community since the earliest days of their settlement in India. **Udvada**, only 10km north of Vapi, the station for Daman, has the oldest Parsi sacred fire in India. It is said that the fire was brought from Persia to Diu, on the opposite coast of the Gulf of Cambay, in AD 700. **Sanjan**, in the extreme south of the state, is the small port where the Parsis first landed. A pillar marks the spot.

In the week preceding **Holi** (February/March), the Adivasi have a major festival in the forested region called The Dangs, east of Surat near the Maharashtra border – it's known as the **Dang Durbar**.

DAMAN

☎ 02602 • pop 90,000

In the far south of Gujarat is the 56-sq-km enclave of Daman. Along with Diu and Goa, Daman was taken in 1961 from the Portuguese, who had seized Daman in 1531. The Portuguese had been officially ceded the region by Bahadur Shah, the last major Gujarati sultan, in 1559. For a time after reverting to Indian rule, Daman and Diu were governed from Goa but both now constitute the Union Territory of Daman and Diu, which is governed from Delhi. Daman is a laid-back town with a tropical flavour, although its beaches are rather dirty. There's still a lingering Portuguese flavour to the town, with its fine old forts and churches, but it's definitely not a smaller version of Goa.

The streets of Daman are lined with bars selling beer, 'Finest Scotch Whisky – Made in India' and various other spirits such as *feni* (distilled from fermented cashew nuts or coconut milk). You are forbidden to take alcohol out of Daman into Gujarat unless you obtain a permit (see the boxed text 'Permission to Drink, Sir?' under Ahmedabad earlier in the chapter); there are police checks as you leave Daman.

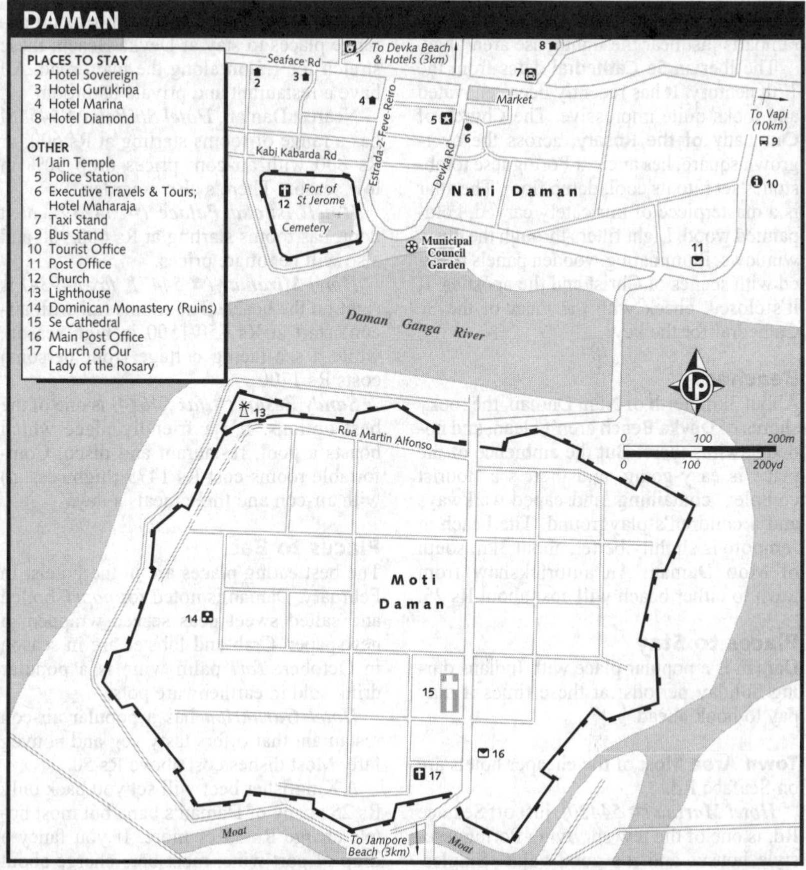

Information

The tourist office (☎ 55104), near the bus stand, is open 9.30 am to 1.30 pm and 2.30 to 6 pm Monday to Friday. No bank, change money, but Executive Travels & Tours, in the arcade below Hotel Maharaja, changes travellers cheques at 50 paisa below the bank rate. The main post office is south of the river in Moti Daman; there's a more convenient branch in Nani Daman near the bridge.

Nani Daman

You can walk around the ramparts of the Nani Daman's **Fort of St Jerome**. They're a good place from which to watch the fish market and small fishing fleet that anchors alongside.

To the north is a **Jain temple**. If you inquire in the temple office, a caretaker should be able to show you around. The walls inside are completely covered with glassed-over 18th-century murals depicting the life of Mahavira, who lived around 500 BC.

Moti Daman

It's quite pleasant to wander through the wide streets within the fortified walls. The place has a sleepy atmosphere, and the views across the river to Nani Daman from the ramparts just near the lighthouse aren't bad.

The Iberian **Se Cathedral** dates from the 17th century. It has recently been renovated and looks quite impressive. The **Church of Our Lady of the Rosary**, across the overgrown square, has ancient Portuguese tombstones set into its cool, damp floor. The altar is a masterpiece of intricately carved, gold-painted wood. Light filters through the dusty windows, illuminating wooden panels painted with scenes of Christ and the apostles. If it's closed, check with the vicar of the Se Cathedral for the key.

Beaches

About 3km north of Nani Daman, the rocky shores of **Devka Beach** aren't clean, and nobody swims there. But the ambience of the place is easy-going, and there's a 'tourist complex' containing landscaped walkways and a children's playground. The beach at **Jampore** is slightly better, about 3km south of Moti Daman. An autorickshaw from town to either beach will cost about Rs 25.

Places to Stay

Daman is a popular place with Indians during holiday periods; at these times it may pay to book ahead.

Town Area Most of the cheaper hotels are on Seaface Rd.

Hotel Marina *(☎ 54420)*, just off Seaface Rd, is one of the few surviving Portuguese-style houses and it's good value. Singles/doubles with bathroom cost Rs 150/175, or Rs 175/200 for deluxe rooms. There's a bar and restaurant downstairs.

Hotel Diamond *(☎ 55135)*, near the taxi stand, is a bit better still. Decent rooms with private bathroom cost Rs 250/400. There's also a bar and restaurant.

Hotel Gurukripa *(☎ 55046, Seaface Rd)* has good, if slightly musty, air-con rooms with TV for Rs 475/575. There's a good restaurant here.

Nearby, ***Hotel Sovereign*** *(☎ 55023, fax 54433, Seaface Rd)* has been extensively renovated and has good air-con rooms for Rs 550/650.

Beach Area There are lots of decent mid-range places to stay at Devka Beach; these stretch for 1.5km along the main road. All have a restaurant and private bathroom.

Nearest Daman, ***Hotel Shilton*** *(☎ 54558)* has a range of rooms starting at Rs 600, or Rs 800 with air-con; prices drop 50% in low season. There's also a garden.

Hotel Ashoka Palace *(☎ 54239)*, next door, has rooms starting at Rs 600/900 and also will negotiate prices.

Hotel Miramar *(☎ 54471, fax 54934)* is right on the beach. The rooms (all with air-con) start at Rs 850/1500 in high season, while a sea-facing cottage (four persons) costs Rs 1700.

Sandy Resort *(☎/fax 54644)* is one of the best options. It's a friendly place which boasts a pool, restaurant and disco. Comfortable rooms cost Rs 1475 (high season) with air-con and three meals a day.

Places to Eat

The best eating places are in the hotels. In February, Daman is noted for *papri*, boiled and salted sweet peas served wrapped in newspaper. Crab and lobster are in season in October. *Tari* palm wine is a popular drink sold in earthenware pots.

Hotel Gurukripa has a popular air-con restaurant that offers tasty veg and nonveg fare. Most dishes cost above Rs 50.

A Kingfisher beer will set you back only Rs 25 at any of Daman's bars, but most hotels charge Rs 35 or more. If you fancy a drop of port wine, most bars charge about Rs 100 a bottle.

Getting There & Away

Vapi station, on the main railway line, is the access point for Daman. Vapi is about 170km from Mumbai and 90km from Surat. It's about 10km from Vapi to Daman. Plenty of share-taxis (Rs 10 per person) wait outside the train station and leave frequently on the 20-minute trip to Daman. Also available are some ramshackle buses (Rs 5).

SAPUTARA

This cool hill resort in the south-east corner of the state sits 1000m high. There is a picturesque lake, attractive gardens, an artists' village and the views from both Valley View Point and Sunset Point are worth the climb. It's a popular base for excursions to **Mahal Bardipara Forest Wildlife Sanctuary** (60km) or the **Gira Waterfalls** (52km) near the town of Waghai. Saputara means 'Abode of Serpents' and there is a sacred snake image on the banks of the River Sarpagana.

Toran Hill Resort *(☎ 02631-37226)* has dorms for Rs 50, cottages starting at Rs 300/450, valley-view doubles starting at Rs 600, and mountain-view rooms for Rs 1650.

State buses run here from Surat.

Saurashtra

The often bleak plains of Saurashtra on the Kathiawar peninsula are generally inhabited by friendly but reserved people. Those in the country are distinctively dressed – the men wear white turbans, pleated jackets (short-waisted and long-sleeved) and jodhpurs (baggy seat and drainpipe legs) and often sport golden stud earrings. The women are nearly as colourful as the women of Rajasthan and wear embroidered backless cholis, which are known by various names but most commonly as *kanjeri*.

The peninsula, which is somewhat off the main tourist routes, took its name from the Kathi tribespeople who used to roam the area at night stealing whatever was not locked into the many *kots* (village forts).

BHAVNAGAR

☎ 0278 • pop 775,000

Founded in 1743, Bhavnagar is an important trading post for cotton goods manufactured in Gujarat. The Bhavnagar lock gate keeps ships afloat in the port at low tide. On the surface, it isn't the most exciting place to visit. It does, however, have an interesting bazaar area with overhanging wooden balconies, countless little shops, lots of local colour and rarely a tourist in sight.

Orientation & Information

Bhavnagar is a sprawling city with distinctly separate old and new sections. The bus stand is in the new part of town and

Gandhi's Gujarat

No other state in India carries with it such a wealth of associations with the Father of the Nation as does Gujarat. It was in the coastal town of Porbandar, on 2 October 1869, that Mohandas K Gandhi was born to Karamchand and Putlibai Gandhi. It is possible to visit the house – now preserved as a monument, the Kirti Mandir, to the origins of Gandhiji – and pause before the exact spot where he came into the world. Gandhi's early schooling took place in Rajkot, at the Albert High School, and the house in which he grew up has also been preserved as a museum, the Kaba Gandhi No Delo. He studied for a brief time in Bhavnagar at the Shamaldas College. His presence in the city is now commemorated with a small collection of memorabilia in the Gandhi Smirti Museum. Upon his return from South Africa, Gandhi renewed his association with Gujarat and founded his ashram in Ahmedabad, thereafter dedicating his life to the practice of satyagraha or nonviolent agitation. It was from here that he launched India along the road to independence, capturing the hearts of the Indian nation, the attention of the world and setting in train the overthrow of one of the world's most powerful empires.

The Mahatma was born and educated in Gujarat.

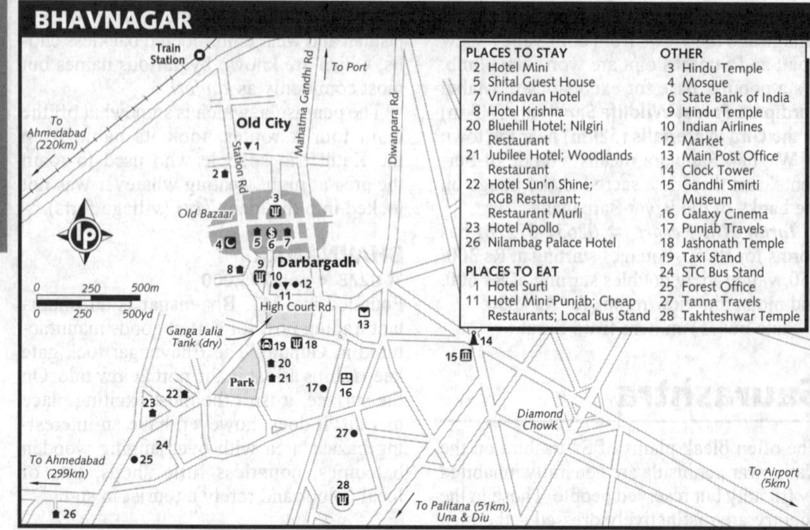

the train station is at the far end of the old town, around 2.5km away.

There are some hotels in the old town, but none around the bus stand. The State Bank of India in the old town changes cash.

Things to See

Takhteshwar Temple sits on a small hill, which is nevertheless high enough to provide good views over the city and out into the Gulf of Cambay. The temple itself is of minor interest.

North-east, by the clock tower, is the **Gandhi Smriti Museum**, which has a moderate collection of Gandhi memorabilia and religious statues (closed Sunday and the second and fourth Saturday in the month; entry is free).

For local colour, wander through the atmospheric shopping streets in the old town, near the State Bank of India.

Places to Stay – Budget

The only cheap hotels in Bhavnagar are in the old bazaar area.

Hotel Mini *(☎ 512915, Station Rd)*, located in the old part of town, close to the train station, is one of the better and friendlier budget hotels. It's clean and quiet with decent-sized singles/doubles for Rs 125/225 with private bathroom (check that the shower nozzle works) or Rs 25 less without a TV. Checkout is 24 hours and they can rustle up breakfasts and thalis.

Shital Guest House *(☎ 428360, Amba Chowk)*, in the middle of the bazaar area, is a good choice. Enter through the rear of the building. Singles with shared bathroom cost Rs 75 while equally basic but clean doubles with private bucket shower (hot water in the mornings) and squat toilet cost Rs 150.

Vrindavan Hotel *(☎ 519149, Darbargadh)*, not far from the Shital, is in a lane just east of the State Bank of India. It's a huge, multistorey place set around a courtyard, with singles/doubles starting at Rs 100/200 or Rs 400/500 with air-con. The rooms are simple and the bathrooms clean. Reception is reached via the stairs on the right as you enter through the main archway.

Hotel Krishna *(☎ 439606)* isn't a bad choice, conveniently between the old and new parts of town. Nonair-con deluxe rooms go for Rs 200/350, while an 'executive' double gets you a dusty bathtub and balcony thrown in. There's also a pricey dorm (Rs 100). There's no restaurant but food can be brought in from a nearby restaurant either by guests or hotel staff.

Places to Stay – Mid-Range & Top End

Hotel Apollo (☎ *425252, fax 412440*), directly opposite the bus stand, is definitely the best mid-price deal. It has very comfortable and spacious rooms with TV for Rs 450/600, or Rs 650/800 with air-con. It also has money-changing facilities (lowish rates) and a good restaurant.

Bluehill Hotel (☎ *426951, fax 427313*), down a quiet road from the taxi stand, has well appointed rooms with air-con starting at Rs 900/1350. There are two veg restaurants and most rooms have nice views over the park.

Jubilee Hotel (☎ *430045*), next door, must have been a nice hotel once but is now very frayed at the edges and lacks even the slightest attention to detail. The rooms, starting at Rs 800/1000, are way overpriced and don't expect everything to work.

Hotel Sun'n Shine (☎ *516131, fax 516130*) has a luxuriant lobby with rooms that mostly live up to this grand entrance. Rooms start at Rs 900/1100 and are pretty good upper-end value. It also has two restaurants, 24-hour room service, Internet access and a health club.

Nilambag Palace Hotel (☎ *424241, fax 428072*), west of the bus stand on the Ahmedabad road, is an interesting place to stay – if you can afford it. This former maharaja's palace is not as swish as some other palace hotels, but it's still luxurious. Rooms are Rs 1990/3500 in the palace or Rs 1200/1800 in the 'royal cottage'. There's also a swimming pool and restaurant.

Places to Eat

There are plenty of choices around town for thalis. ***Hotel Surti***, almost opposite the Hotel Mini, does reasonable ones for Rs 30 while those at ***Hotel Mini*** are also good value (Rs 35). Those at the ***Vrindavan Hotel*** cost Rs 50, while ***Restaurant Murli*** is the place to go if you're happy to pay for the company of besuited waiters (Rs 60).

There are plenty of ***cheap food stalls*** on the northern side of Ganga Jalia tank – the choice is greater when the amusement park is running. One relatively permanent and OK cheapie is ***Hotel Mini-Punjab***.

Of the mid- and upper-range hotels, the ***Nilgiri Restaurant*** in the Bluehills Hotel and the ***RGB Restaurant*** in the Hotel Sun'n Shine are probably the pick, with varied menus, good service and reasonable prices. The veg and nonveg restaurants at the ***Hotel Apollo*** also aren't bad while the ***Woodlands Restaurant*** at the Jubilee Hotel is as lacklustre as the accommodation on offer.

Getting There & Away

Air The Indian Airlines office (☎ 426503) is just north of the Ganga Jalia tank. There are four flights a week to Mumbai (US$75).

Bus STC buses connect Bhavnagar with Ahmedabad and other centres in the region. There are regular departures throughout the day for Una (for Diu; Rs 63, five hours), Palitana (Rs 18, 1½ hours) and half-hourly to Ahmedabad (Rs 65, four hours).

Private bus companies include Punjab Travels (☎ 424582), opposite the Galaxy Cinema, and Tanna Travels (☎ 420477), nearby. Both offer regular deluxe buses to Ahmedabad (Rs 80, four hours) and one daily bus to Mumbai (Rs 300, 13 hours).

Train There are at least three trains to Ahmedabad daily (around 5½ hours). The *Shetrunji Express* (9909) departs at 5.40 am (Rs 73/231, general/chair class), while the *Ahmedabad Express* (9935) and *Link Express* (9947) leave at 3.30 pm and 11.10 pm respectively (Rs 73/384, general/1st class). To Palitana there are three daily trains that cover the 51km in 1½ hours (Rs 10).

Getting Around

An autorickshaw to/from the airport costs around Rs 60.

AROUND BHAVNAGAR

Alang

On the coast between Bhavnagar and Talaja is Alang, India's largest ship-breaking site.

Here supertankers, container ships, warships and other vessels are dismantled – literally by hand – by 20,000 workers day and night. It's an epic, almost Dickensian scene, but sadly one that is almost impossible to see as a tourist.

According to a Gujarat Port Trust Internal memo: 'It has come to our attention that foreign tourists are entering the port for sightseeing/photography on the pretext of an interest in buying ship's fittings'. You could contact the Gujarat Port Trust (☎/fax 0278-563132) for permission, but chances are they'll send you on a paper trail that leads to Gandhinagar via Ahmedabad only to end up back where you started – unless, of course, you're serious about buying a ship. Some travellers have managed to sneak through the gate on a crowded local bus, but more have been hauled off at the gatehouse. It's worth checking with the Port Trust to see whether regulations have changed, although this extraordinary sight is likely to be off-limits for some time to come.

Velavadar National Park

This park, 65km north of Bhavnagar, is well known for its blackbucks, which sport impressive spiralling horns as long as 60cm in mature males. The best time to visit is from October to June. If you want to visit, ask about current regulations at the Forest Office (☎ 0278-428644) or the sanctuary superintendent (☎ 0278-426425) near Bhavnagar's bus stand. The latter is also the number for booking accommodation at the sanctuary's ***Tourist Lodge***, doubles cost about Rs 300.

Getting there by bus from Bhavagnar is possible (change at Valabhipur), but to visit on a day trip you would need to hire a taxi (no more than Rs 700).

PALITANA

☎ 02848 • pop 48,000

The town of Palitana, 51km south-west of Bhavnagar, is little more than a gateway to Shatrunjaya.

Shatrunjaya

Strewn with 863 temples, the hilltop complex of Shatrunjaya (Place of Victory) is one of Jainism's holiest pilgrimage sites. The temples were built over a period of 900 years on a hilltop dedicated entirely to the gods; at dusk, even the priests depart from the temples, leaving them deserted.

Almost all the temples are Jain, and this hill demonstrates their belief that merit is derived from constructing temples. The hilltops are bounded by sturdy walls and the temples are grouped into nine *tunks* (enclosures), each with a central temple surrounded by many minor ones. Some of the earliest temples here were built in the 11th century but were destroyed by Muslims in the 14th and 15th centuries; the current temples date from the 16th century onwards.

The hilltop affords a fine view in all directions; on a clear day you can see the Gulf of Cambay beyond Bhavnagar. The most not able of the temples is dedicated to **Shri Adishwara**, one of the most important Jain tirthankars. Note the frieze of dragons around this temple. Adjacent is the Muslim shrine of **Angar Pir**. Women who want children make offerings of miniature cradles here.

Built in 1618 by a wealthy Jain merchant, the **Chaumukh**, or Four-Faced shrine, has images of Adinath facing out in the four cardinal directions. Other important temples are those dedicated to Kumar Pal, Sampriti Raj and Vimal Shah.

The temples are open from 6.30 am to 5.30 pm. A photography permit can be purchased for Rs 50 just inside the main entrance. (There are two entrances – the main one is reached by taking the left-hand fork as you near the top of the hill and the other by the right-hand fork.) Shoes should be removed at the entrance to the compound, and leather items, including belts and bags, should not be brought onto the site.

A horse cart to the base of the hill costs Rs 20, or you can walk from the Palitana bus stand in about 30 minutes. The heat can be extreme by late morning, so it's a good idea to start early for the ascent. Water (not bottled) can be bought at intervals, and you can buy refreshing curd in pottery bowls outside the temple compound for Rs 10.

The 600m-high ascent from the base of the hill to the summit is 2km, up more than

3000 steps. At a moderate pace, the ascent will take about 1½ hours. You can be carried up the hill in a *doli* (rope chair), which costs from Rs 200 to 700 dependent on comfort (the choice of quite a few affluent and obese pilgrims). The most conspicuous sight on first entering the temple compound is that of exhausted doli bearers resting in the shade.

Places to Stay & Eat

Palitana has scores of *dharamsalas* (pilgrim's guesthouses) but unless you're a Jain, you're unlikely to be allowed to stay at any of them. Gujarat Tourism's ***Hotel Sumeru*** *(☎ 2327, Station Rd)*, 200m towards the train station from the bus stand, is the best. Singles/doubles are Rs 377/538, or Rs 578/807 with air-con, including taxes. Dorm beds are Rs 50. Prices are halved from 15 June to 15 September. Its veg restaurant serves Gujarati thalis (Rs 45) as well as Punjabi and continental dishes.

Hotel Shravak *(☎ 2428)*, opposite the bus stand, has basic singles with shared bathroom for Rs 100 or doubles/triples (with private bathroom) for Rs 200/300. Dorm beds (men only) cost Rs 40. Checkout is 24 hours for rooms, 9.30 am for the dorm.

Across the alley, ***Jagruti Restaurant*** is a wildly busy 24-hour snack place offering *puris* (flat dough that puffs up when deep fried), *sabzi* (curried vegetables), curd, roasted peppers and *ganthia* (varieties of fried dough).

Havmor is a popular ice-cream parlour on the right as you approach the base of Shatrunjaya.

Getting There & Away

Bus STC buses make the 1½-hour trip to/from Bhavnagar every hour (Rs 18). There are also regular departures for Ahmedabad (Rs 68, five hours).

Infrequent buses go to Talaja, where you can switch to a bus to Una or Diu. The total journey takes about six hours; it's a trip from hell, along bumpy village roads in dilapidated old rattletraps.

Train Sleepy Palitana station is only 800m from the bus stand, heading away from Shatrunjaya. It only receives trains to/from Bhavagnar (though they stop at Sihor, which has connections to Ahmedabad). They depart Palitana at 9 am and 6.05 and 8.30 pm, and depart Bhavnagar at 6.30 am and 2.45 and 6.45 pm (Rs 10, 1½ hours).

DIU

☎ 02875 • pop 66,200

Diu is for many the highlight of Gujarat with its relaxed pace of life, decaying Portuguese architecture, huge fort and quiet beaches.

Like Daman and Goa, Diu was a Portuguese colony until it was taken over by India in 1961. Along with Daman, it is still governed from Delhi as a Union Territory rather than as part of Gujarat. The former colony includes the island of Diu, about 13km long by 3km wide, separated from the coast by a narrow channel. There are also two tiny mainland enclaves. One of these, where the village of Ghoghla stands, is the entry point to Diu from Una.

The northern side of the island, facing Gujarat, is tidal marsh and saltpans while the southern coast alternates between limestone cliffs, rocky coves and sandy beaches. The somewhat windswept and arid island is riddled with quarries from which the Portuguese removed vast quantities of limestone to build the fort, city walls, monuments and buildings.

The rocky and sandy interior reaches a maximum height of just 29m and agriculture is limited although there are extensive stands of coconut and other palms. Branching palms (*Hyphaene* species) are very much a feature of the island and were originally introduced from Africa by the Portuguese.

The island's main industry is fishing, followed by booze and salt. Kalpana Distillery at Malala produces rum from sugar cane. Diu Town has many bars where visitors from the 'dry' mainland can enjoy a beer (or stronger IMFL – Indian Made Foreign Liquor).

Diu is a popular hang-out with travellers and you'll probably see more foreigners here than anywhere else in Gujarat. Although the beaches are nothing compared to Goa's, it is still a great place to let your hair down and watch the world drift by.

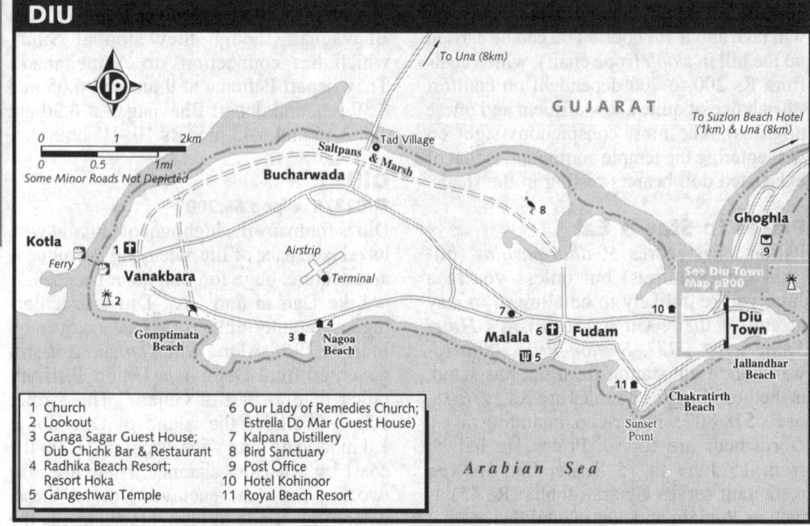

History

Between the 14th and 16th centuries, Diu was an important trading post and naval base from which the Ottoman Turks controlled the shipping routes in the northern part of the Arabian Sea.

Portugal made an unsuccessful attempt to capture the island in 1531, during which Bahadur Shah, the Sultan of Gujarat, was assisted by the Turkish navy. The Portuguese finally secured control in 1535 by taking advantage of a quarrel between the sultan and the Mughal emperor, Humayun.

Under pressure from both the Portuguese and the Mughals, Bahadur concluded a peace treaty with the Portuguese, effectively giving them control over the port at Diu. The treaty was soon cast to the wind and, although both Bahadur Shah and his successor, Sultan Mahmud III, attempted to contest the issue, the peace treaty that was eventually signed in 1539 ceded the island of Diu and the mainland enclave of Ghoghla to Portugal. Soon after the signing of this treaty, the Portuguese began constructing their fort.

The Indian government appears to have an official policy of playing down the Portuguese era. Seven Rajput soldiers and a few civilians were killed in Operation Vijay, which ended Portuguese rule in 1961. After the Indian air force unnecessarily bombed the airstrip and terminal near Nagoa Beach, they remained derelict until the late 1980s. The old church in Diu Fort was also bombed and is now a roofless ruin. It is said that the Portuguese blew up Government House to stop it falling into 'enemy' hands.

Orientation & Information

The tourist office (☎ 52653) is on Bunder Rd, the main road that runs through Diu Town parallel to the waterfront. It has transport information and simple (free) maps. The office is open 9.30 am to 1.30 pm and 2.30 to 6 pm Monday to Saturday.

You can change money at the State Bank of Saurashtra near the town square, but at slightly lower rates than on the mainland. It is reluctant to change large amounts. Many shops around Diu Town also change money. One reliable and efficient place is the grocery store 40m west of the Hotel Alishan where most major currencies (even Australian dollars) can be exchanged.

The main post office overlooks the town square and there's another branch at Ghoghla.

Both Hotel Alishan (Rs 75 per hour; see Places to Stay) and Dee Pee Telecom (Rs 100; opposite the tourist office) have Internet access.

The Jethibai bus stand, for intercity buses, is just outside the city walls, near the bridge to Ghoghla.

Diu Town

Laid-back Diu Town (population 38,500) was the first landing point for the Parsis when they fled from Persia, although they stayed only three years.

The town is sandwiched between the fort to the east and a huge city wall to the west. The main **Zampa Gateway** has carvings of lions, angels and a priest, while just inside the gate is a miniature chapel with an icon, dating from 1702. Just to the south, outside the wall, is the **Zampa Waterfall**, a strange, artificial creation that is lit up at night.

St Paul's is the only church in town still fulfilling its original function; only a tiny Christian population still is living on the island. Though showing signs of neglect, it has fine statues and wooden altars.

Nearby is St Thomas' Church, which houses the **Diu Museum** (open 8 am to 9 pm daily; entry by donation). There's an interesting collection of Catholic statues. If you thought the Hindu pantheon was confusing, take a look at the bewildering collection of Christian saints. There are also some stone remnants of a Jain temple that is thought to have once occupied the site. There is a guesthouse upstairs (see Places to Stay). Ask the caretaker to let you climb to the roof for spectacular views. The third church, **St Francis of Assisi**, has been converted into a hospital.

Unlike Daman, many buildings in Diu show a significant Portuguese influence. The town is a maze of narrow, winding streets and many of the houses are brightly painted. Farther away from this tightly packed residential quarter, the streets turn into meandering and often leafy lanes and it's well worth a couple of hours exploring the area.

In a small park on the esplanade, between the square and the police station, the **Marwar Memorial**, topped by a griffin, commemorates the liberation of the island from the Portuguese.

Completed in 1541, the massive **Portuguese fort** with its double moat (one tidal) must once have been virtually impregnable, but sea erosion and neglect are leading to a slow but inevitable collapse. Piles of cannon balls litter the place and the ramparts have a superb array of cannons; many are in good condition. A small chapel holds engraved tombstone fragments.

The fort, part of which also serves as the island's jail, is open 7 am to 6 pm daily. Entry is free, and photography is allowed.

Around the Island

Fudam Close to Diu Town, the village of Fudam has a huge church, Our Lady of Remedies, that's now used as a guesthouse. A large, old, carved wooden altar with Madonna and child remains inside.

Vanakbara At the extreme west of the island, Vanakbara has a church (Our Lady of Mercy), fort, lighthouse, small bazaar, post office and fishing fleet. This little fishing village is worth a visit – wander through the town to the port area where you can see the locals mending nets and repairing their colourful fishing boats.

Beaches Temple- and fort-satiated travellers used to head to **Nagoa** to catch up on some serious relaxation. Although it's still a pleasant palm-fringed beach and safe for swimming, it's quite busy nowadays, and Western women tend to get unwanted attention from the numerous young Indian men hanging around. **Gomptimata**, to the west, is a sandy beach that is still relatively deserted, and gets big waves. Beaches within easy reach of Diu Town include, from east to west, **Jallandhar**, **Chakratirth** and stunning **Sunset Point**.

Places to Stay

Most hotels offer a discount in the low season, but it's worth bargaining at any time of the year, as places will slash prices by as much as 60% if they are not full. Your chances of success are greater if you're staying for more than a couple of days. Prices given here are for the peak season, which runs roughly from October to June, and, unless stated otherwise, the rooms have a cold-water private bathroom (most of which in Diu are pretty ordinary) with squat toilet. Most places have a noon checkout time.

Diu Town On the west side of town is *Hare Krishna Guest House (☎ 52213)*. This small place has simple singles/doubles/triples for only Rs 75/100/150. Some rooms are better than others; room No 4 on the corner is good.

Hotel Prince (☎ 52765), nearby, charges Rs 300 for a pleasant double. Those on the 2nd floor have good views from the attached balconies.

Nilesh Guest House (☎ 52319, fax 52241), south-east of the Hotel Prince, may be willing to negotiate prices, which is just as well. It has bare and basic doubles with balcony for Rs 100, although they'll start at Rs 200. You can also drag a mattress onto the roof for Rs 50. Lone female travellers may feel uncomfortable here.

Hotel Mozambique (☎ 52223), by the vegetable market, is housed in a lovely old building, although sadly the rooms don't seem to have been renovated (or cleaned) since construction. It's a pity because it's a friendly place and the views from the roof are lovely. Singles/doubles cost Rs 175/200.

Hotel Samrat (☎ 52354), a couple of blocks south of the town square, has very pleasant double rooms with nice private bathrooms, balconies and satellite TV for Rs 350 and singles/doubles with air-con for Rs 500/650. Room service is available. There's a good restaurant and bar, and if the kitchen is not busy, for about Rs 50 the chef will make a meal of fish bought by guests at the fish market.

Super Silver Guest House (☎ 52020), a block south of the vegetable market, is a

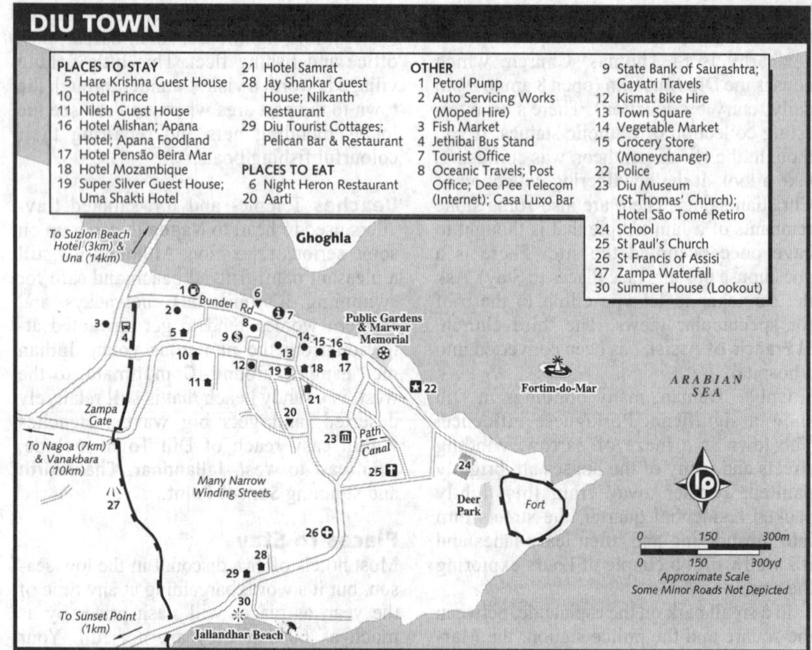

PAUL BEINSSEN

MARK HONAN

MARK HONAN

MARK HONAN

The sights of Gujarat: festival participants impersonate gods at Bhuj (top); a detail of the Muslim mausoleum, Mahabat Maqbara, in Junagadh (centre right); carved figures at Shri Adishwara Temple at Shatrunjaya (centre left); fishing boats at Diu Island, on the Arabian Sea (bottom)

CHRIS MELLOR

MARK DAFFEY

SARA-JANE CLELAND

CHRIS MELLOR

North India's architectural heritage reflects its diverse histories, religions and cultures: the grand fort at Gwalior, Madhya Pradesh (top left); Tibetan-style monasteries in central Sikkim (top right) and western Sikkim (centre left); Chandela-period temples at Khajuraho, Madhya Pradesh (bottom) new place with spotless and spacious rooms (good private bathrooms) for a negotiable Rs 200/300. The owner is eager to please.

***Uma Shakti Hotel** (☎ 52150)*, next door, is another good choice with decent doubles for Rs 200/600 without/with air-con. It's populated by the usual cast of thousands of staff. The terrace garden bar and restaurant on the roof is a lovely place for a meal, beer or breakfast (the cheese omelette for Rs 30 is particularly good).

***Hotel Pensão Beira Mar** (☎ 53031, Bunder Rd)*, midway between the town square and fort, is an old Portuguese villa converted into a semi-upmarket hotel. In previous incarnations it has been known as the Baron's Inn, Hotel Sanman and the totally misleading Fun Club. The staff seems to realise that the comfortable but unspectacular doubles are overpriced at Rs 1000 and will immediately drop to Rs 400 even in high season. Suites start at Rs 1200. There's a rooftop restaurant and bar.

***Apana Hotel** (☎ 52112, fax 52309, Bunder Rd)*, nearby, starts at Rs 550 for reasonable rooms at the back or Rs 650 to 950 for those with views. As they don't seem too willing to negotiate, there's better value to be had elsewhere. They do arrange pick-ups from the airport, and the restaurant is here is one of the town's more atmospheric.

***Hotel Alishan** (☎ 52340, fax 52190, Bunder Rd)*, next door, is better value with decent rooms with TV and balcony. Double rooms with views cost Rs 200/500 in low/high season or Rs 600/800 with air-con. There are cheaper rooms at the back, and a restaurant, bar and Internet access.

Hotel São Tomé Retiro is one of the better choices. Located on the southern fringes of Diu Town, upstairs in St Thomas' Church, its five rooms are atmospheric, large and most have wonderful views. It's a homely, quiet place with the smaller rooms costing Rs 175/200 per night for long/short stays; larger rooms cost Rs 200/300. George D'Souza, the friendly young manager, organises barbecue parties most evenings. The rest of the time, his parents will cook Portuguese and Goan dishes (Rs 75) if you order in the morning.

Jallandhar Beach This is a lovely quiet area in which to stay, just an easy 10-minute walk to Diu Town. The **Summer House** lookout point is a stone's throw away.

***Diu Tourist Cottages** (☎ 52654)* offers pleasant, spacious cottages with double or twin beds for Rs 650/800 without/with air-con. Many rooms have sea views, and its Pelican Bar & Restaurant is not bad, although it's more pleasant to be served the rooms' individual terrace balconies. There are also some pool tables. It's a pretty mellow place. The same family runs the ***Royal Beach Resort** (☎ 52654)* at Sunset Point, charging from around Rs 400 a double.

***Jay Shankar Guest House** (☎ 52420)*, near Diu Tourist Cottages, has doubles from Rs 100 up to Rs 250 (with balcony and sea view); they're good value. They can also help with bus bookings.

Fudam to Nagoa Beach On the road to Fudam is ***Hotel Kohinoor** (☎ 52209, fax 52613)* with attractive, well-equipped villas grouped round a swimming pool and spa. Rooms (all with air-con) cost from Rs 1250 up to Rs 1650 with a bathtub and king-size bed. Suites cost Rs 2500. The hotel also has a good restaurant, a pastry shop, disco and games room.

Estrella Do Mar, at the Fudam church, has double rooms for about Rs 150 with cold water. There's no restaurant, but guests can use the kitchen.

***Ganga Sagar Guest House** (☎ 52249)* is right on Nagoa Beach. Small singles/doubles round a beachside garden cost Rs 100/300 with shared bathroom (bucket hot water) or Rs 500 for a double with private bathroom.

Close by, on the main road, is the ***Resort Hoka** (☎ 53036)*. Doubles go for Rs 350 and the management seems eager to please.

***Radhika Beach Resort** (☎ 52555)*, also in the vicinity, has come highly recommended by a number of travellers. Very comfortable rooms cost Rs 1000/1750, there's a nice swimming pool (guests only) and a good, reasonably priced restaurant.

Ghoghla In the village of Ghoghla on the mainland near a good beach is ***Suzlon***

Beach Hotel *(☎ 52212)*. It is the first building in Diu after you come through the barrier that marks the border with Gujarat. Renovated air-con doubles cost Rs 1400; a suite is Rs 1600. There's also a pleasant restaurant and bar overlooking the sea.

Places to Eat

Beer and drinks are blissfully cheap in Diu – starting at Rs 30 for a large Kingfisher and even a Fosters. Food is rarely anything to write home about, although the fish is good.

Apana Foodland, attached to the Apana Hotel, is probably the pick of the hotel restaurants with a pleasant outdoor setting overlooking the water. They do everything from breakfasts and South Indian (Rs 20 to 30) to Punjabi, Chinese and fish dishes.

Hotel Samrat, ***Uma Shakti Hotel*** and ***Alishan Hotel*** also have good restaurants. The latter does a good fish tandoor (Rs 100).

The ***Nilkanth Restaurant*** in the Jay Shankar Guest House serves good fish dishes; the other offerings are mediocre.

Hotel Pensão Beira Mar is a pleasant spot for a beer on the terrace, although with the name change has gone the former charm. Staff are a little overbearing and the food is surprisingly ordinary.

Night Heron Restaurant, right on the water's edge near the tourist office, is an excellent place for a meal. The staff are friendly and it's very relaxed. Main dishes range from Rs 40 to 80. It's a great choice for breakfast.

Aarti, about 150m south of the vegetable market, is a relaxed travellers' restaurant, with wall hangings and Western music. Pizzas (starting at Rs 50) are excellent and there are usually good fish specialities.

For a drink, ***Casa Luxo Bar***, next to Oceanic Travels, is highly recommended.

One traveller wrote to say that the milkshakes along Bunder Rd were the best in India. We found none living up to that lofty claim but hope you have better luck.

There are a couple of places at Nagoa Beach. ***Ganga Sagar Restaurant*** (beside the basic snack bar) has the usual range of moderately priced Chinese and Indian food. Right next door on the 1st floor, ***Dub-Chichk Bar & Restaurant*** has similar food and it gets sea breezes; Kingfisher is Rs 35. The restaurant at the ***Radhika Beach Resort*** is better and surprisingly reasonably priced.

Gomptimata Beach has no cafes, so bring food with you.

Getting There & Away

Air Jet Airways flies to Mumbai (US$95) at 12.15 pm daily, except Saturday. The Jet Airways agent is Oceanic Travels (☎ 52180), on the town square near the post office.

Bus STC departures from the Jethibai bus stand are usually inconvenient. Buses to Rajkot via Veraval (Rs 30) leave at 4.15 and 5 am and 2.15 pm. For Jamnagar and Ahmedabad it's 6 am, Bhavnagar 7 am and Porbandar 1 pm. There are more civilised and frequent departure times from Una. If you're travelling to Diu and arrive in Una, you have to get yourself the 10km or so to Ghoghla and Diu. Buses depart from the-Una bus stand every 30 minutes between 7.30 am and 8 pm (Rs 9, 40 minutes). Outside these hours, walk 1km to Tower Chowk in Una, from where crowded share-rickshaws go to Ghoghla or Diu for about the same as the bus fare. Private buses currently go from Diu to Mumbai at 10 am (Rs 350, 22 hours) and to Ahmedabad at 7 pm (Rs 150, 10½ hours). Book in advance from Gayatri Travels (☎ 52346).

Train Delwada, between Una and Ghoghla and only about 8km from Diu, is the nearest railhead. A share-autorickshaw from there to Ghoghla costs about Rs 5. There's a direct train at 6 am from Delwada to Veraval (Rs 32/173 for general/3A class, 96km). There is also a daily service to Junagadh (Rs 48/233, 164km) via Sasan Gir.

Getting Around

Share-autorickshaw drivers will demand Rs 100 to Una, and generally want high prices. To travel anywhere within the town of Diu should cost no more than Rs 15. To Nagoa Beach, pay about Rs 30, and to Sunset Point, Rs 20. Share-autorickshaws to Ghoghla cost Rs 3 per person.

Mopeds are ideal for getting around the island – the roads are relatively deserted and in good condition. The going rate per day is Rs 100 for a moped (plus fuel). Motorcycles with leg gears cost Rs 150. Most hotels can arrange mopeds although the quality is variable. Try Kismat (☎ 52971), which also rents bicycles, at the back of the town square, or the friendly Auto Servicing Works (☎ 52824) opposite the petrol pump on Bunder Rd. A deposit of Rs 500 is usually required.

Local buses from Diu Town to Nagoa Beach and Vanakbara leave from the Jethibai bus stand at 7 and 11 am and 4 pm. From Nagoa, buses depart for Diu Town from near the police post, leaving at 1, 5.30 and 7 pm (Rs 4).

VERAVAL

☎ 02876 • pop 135,000

On the south coast of Saurashtra, Veraval was the major seaport for Mecca pilgrims before the rise of Surat. Apart from the port and the outside of the eerie **old Nawab's Palace** in the west of town, there's not a lot to see in Veraval. It still has some importance as one of India's major fishing ports (more than 1000 boats work from here) but the main reason to come here is as a base for a visit to Somnath Temple, 6km to the east.

Wooden dhows of all sizes, from fishing dinghies right up to ocean-going vessels, are still built totally by hand. The largest dhows still make the journey from here to Dubai and other Middle Eastern destinations. It's well worth wandering around the **port** area, although photography is supposedly prohibited. If you're on a bicycle heading for Somnath, you can take a shortcut through the port area.

Information

There's a small Gujarat Tourism counter at the Toran Tourist Bungalow (see Places to Stay) with a few brochures available. For changing money, the State Bank of India will direct you to the State Bank of Saurashtra, who will in turn send you to JP Travels International (☎ 20110) just up the road. They change US dollars and British pounds (cash and travellers cheques) for a lowish exchange rate but no commission.

Places to Stay

There are plenty of hotels along ST Rd between the bus stand and the clock tower. All hotels only have hot water in the morning.

***Chetna Rest House** (☎ 20688)*, directly opposite the bus stand, with all the accompanying noise, has clean, simple singles/doubles for Rs 65/130 with private cold-water bathroom and Rs 55/110 with bucket shower but shared squat toilet. Dorm beds for men are only Rs 35.

***Hotel Satkar** (☎ 20120, fax 43114)*, round the corner, has a phone and TV (check that they work) in most rooms, and the staff is obliging. Rates here start at Rs 100/150 for a cramped room, with larger ones going for Rs 200/300, or Rs 400 for a double with air-con. All rooms have a private bathroom.

***Toran Tourist Bungalow** (☎ 46588)*, not far from the lighthouse, is in a rather inconvenient location but it is quiet and better maintained than most hotels run by Gujarat Tourism. Ordinary/deluxe/air-con singles cost Rs 225/275/425; the corresponding doubles are Rs 350/450/650. The deluxe rooms are very comfy with a balcony complete with swing chair and sunset and ocean views. Checkout is 9 am and the restaurant serves Gujarati and Punjabi food. One downside is the smell from the nearby chemical factory, although if the wind's blowing in the wrong direction, you'll be lucky to escape that anywhere in town.

Hotel Utsav** (☎ 22306)*, up from the bus stand, has pleasant doubles with satellite TV for Rs 350/500 without/with air-con. There are ***retiring rooms in the train station.

Places to Eat

Real Treats advertises continental and Chinese food but delivers only good bottomless Gujarati thalis for Rs 40. The air-con dining area is pleasant. The ***Jalaram Parotha House*** downstairs is also good for a snack.

Fast Food Restaurant, near the clock tower on the road to the station, has simple vegetarian food for around Rs 25.

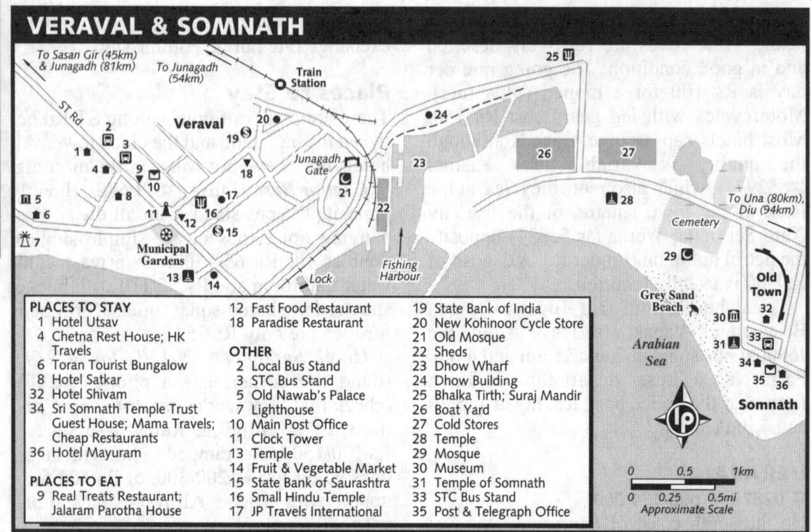

Paradise Restaurant *(☎ 41357)*, almost opposite the State Bank of India, does surprisingly good, reasonably priced Chinese food. It's a friendly place and the won ton soup (Rs 50) is very tasty. There aren't many veg dishes to choose from.

Getting There & Away

Bus STC buses to Junagadh depart from the bus stand half-hourly from 5.45 am (Rs 30, two hours); to Porbandar from 6 am (Rs 43, three hours); and to Rajkot from 6 am (Rs 58, five hours). There are also regular departures for Sasan Gir (Rs 15, 1½ hours) and Ahmedabad (Rs 100, 10 hours). Buses direct to Diu leave at 7.30, 9.30 am and 4.40 pm (Rs 30, three hours). Departures are more frequent if you change at Una.

There are agents for the private bus companies opposite the bus stand, including HK Travels (☎ 21934) who have at least one nightly bus to Ahmedabad (Rs 130/170 for ordinary/sleeper berth).

Train It's a 431km trip from Ahmedabad to Veraval. Fares for the 11½ hour trip are Rs 96/146/504 in general/sleeper/1st class. The *Somnath Mail* (9923) leaves Veraval at 5 pm while the *Girnar Express* (9945) departs at 7.30 pm. The *Rajkot Mail* rolls out at 11.30 am, arriving in Rajkot at 4.50 pm (Rs 52/273 in general/1st class, 186km). There are also trains for Sasan Gir at 10 am and 9.20 pm (Rs 10, 1¼ hours). A daily passenger service to Delwada (for Diu) leaves at 3.50 pm, arriving at 7.55 pm (Rs 16).

The reservation office (☎ 131) is open 8 am to 8 pm Monday to Saturday and 8 am to 2 pm on Sunday.

Getting Around

Bicycles can be hired opposite the gate of the train station from the New Kohinoor Cycle Store for Rs 3/20 per hour/day.

An autorickshaw to Somnath, 6km away, should cost you about Rs 25, although from Veraval they usually ask double that. There are local buses to Somnath for Rs 3.50. The local bus stand is near the long-distance STC stand, on the same road.

SOMNATH

Somnath has a large fair at the full moon of **Kartika Purnima** in November/December, during the statewide festival. Most travellers prefer to stay in Veraval, 6km away, where there are a wider range of accommodation, eating and transport options.

Temple of Somnath

This temple, at Somnath near Veraval and about 80km from Junagadh, has an extremely chequered past. Its earliest history fades into legend – it is said to have originally been built out of gold by Somraj, the moon god, only to be rebuilt by Rawana in silver, then by Krishna in wood and Bhimdev in stone. A description of the temple by Al Biruni, an Arab traveller, was so glowing that it prompted a visit in 1024 by a most unwelcome tourist – Mahmud of Ghazni. At that time, the temple was so wealthy that it had 300 musicians, 500 dancing girls and even 300 barbers just to shave the heads of visiting pilgrims.

Mahmud of Ghazni, whose raids on the riches of India are legendary, descended on Somnath from his Afghan kingdom and, after a two-day battle, took the town and the temple. After looting its fabulous wealth, he destroyed it for good measure. So began a pattern of Muslim destruction and Hindu rebuilding that continued for centuries. The temple was again razed in 1297, 1394 and finally in 1706 by Aurangzeb, the notorious Mughal fundamentalist.

After the 1706 demolition, the temple was not rebuilt until 1950. Outside, opposite the entrance, is a statue of SV Patel (1875–1950), who was responsible for the reconstruction.

The current temple was built to traditional designs on the original site by the sea. It contains one of the 12 sacred Shiva shrines known as *jyoti linga*. Photography is prohibited inside the temple, and you must leave your camera at the hut outside. There is a grey-sand beach outside the temple that is part of the its lonely seaside charm.

Museum

Down the lane from the temple is a museum, open 8.30 am to 12.15 pm and 2.30 to 6 pm (closed Wednesdays and every second and fourth Saturday). There's a small entry fee. Remains of the temple can be seen here as a jumble of old carved stones littering a courtyard. There are pottery shards, a seashell collection and a strange glass case of water bottles containing samples from the Danube, Nile, St Lawrence, Tigris, River Plate and even the Murray in Australia, as well as sea water from Tasmania and New Zealand.

Other Attractions

The town of Somnath is reached from Veraval by the **Junagadh Gate**. This is the very ancient triple gate Mahmud finally broke through to take the town. Close to the second gate is an old **mosque** dating from Mahmud's time.

Halfway between Veraval and Somnath is the **Bhalka Tirth** where Krishna was mistaken for a deer and wounded by an arrow while sleeping in a deerskin. The legendary spot is at the confluence of three rivers. You get to it through the small *sangam* (confluence gate), which is simply known as the Nana, or the Small Gate.

North of this sacred spot is the **Suraj Mandir**, or Temple of the Sun, that Mahmud also had a go at knocking down. This very old temple, with a frieze of lions with elephant trunks around its walls, probably dates from the same time as the original Somnath Temple. Back inside the small gate is a temple that Ahalya Bai of Indore built as a replacement for the Somnath Temple.

Places to Stay & Eat

Don't expect to find too much hot water in Somnath.

Sri Somnath Temple Trust Guest House *(☎ 02876-20212)* is rather dilapidated. Its name is written only in Gujarati. Go to the booking office first, directly opposite the bus stand. The cheaper rooms are a bit dingy and cost Rs 60/100 for a double/triple. The best rooms cost Rs 350, or Rs 550 with air-con. This place is primarily for pilgrims.

Hotel Shivam *(☎ 02876-32899)* is a stone's throw from the temple. Overpriced but otherwise OK doubles cost Rs 400/600 without/with air-con.

Hotel Mayuram *(☎ 02876-31286)*, just down the road heading away from the temple, is marginally better with lighter doubles for Rs 400. Air-con rooms come with three beds and cost Rs 700.

There are dozens of ***cheap restaurants*** between the temple and Hotel Mayuram.

Getting There & Away

Bus Somnath has fewer departures than neighbouring Veraval, but the STC bus stand does service Jamnagar (Rs 72), Porbandar (Rs 48) and Dwarka (Rs 72). There are also daily departures to Diu (Rs 35, 10 am) and Rajkot (Rs 63, 5 pm). Unusually, the timetable is printed in English. Mama Travels (☎ 02876-22286), directly opposite the bus stand, has a 9 pm departure to Ahmedabad (Rs 130, 10 hours).

SASAN GIR WILDLIFE SANCTUARY

This last refuge of the Asiatic lion *(Panthera leo persica)* is 59km from Junagadh via Visavadar. The 1400-sq-km sanctuary was set up to protect the lion and its habitat. Since 1980 numbers have increased from less than 200 to an estimated 325 in May 2000. However, while the lions have been the winners, the local *maaldharis* (herders) have lost valuable grazing land for their cattle. Moves by the Madhya Pradesh government to move 200 lions to the Pulpur Kuno sanctuary in Madhya Pradesh have been indefinitely halted by the Gujarat government, although there are no concrete plans to address the difficulties caused by this competition for scarce resources.

Although the lions seem remarkably tame, in recent years they have reportedly been wandering well outside the limits of the sanctuary in search of easy game – namely calves – which in earlier times was found within the park. One pride even ended up on the beaches of Diu in December 1995, while another responded to the mating calls at Junagadh zoo! The problem is compounded by the declining areas of forest outside the sanctuary, forcing villagers to forage for fuel within the sanctuary precincts, reducing the habitat of the lions.

Apart from lions there are more than 30 other species, including leopards (268 in 1995), hyenas (137), foxes, wild boars and a number of deer and antelope. The deer include the largest Indian antelope (the nilgai), the chinkara gazelle, the chowsingha and the barking deer. You may also see parrots, peacocks, crocodiles and monkeys.

The best time to visit the sanctuary is from December to April; it is closed from 16 June to 15 October, or even later if there has been a heavy monsoon.

Information

The place to go for more information about the park is the Gir Orientation Centre which is next to the Forest Office inside the grounds of the Sinh Sadan Forest Lodge. The centre is very well organised and informative with displays and descriptions of the park's inhabitants, a replica maaldhari hut and by pushing a button you can hear the calls of the lions and other animals. Outside, the Gir Welfare Association sells a range of postcards, books, T-shirts and caps. An aged film about the park is screened at 7 pm daily.

Safaris

The lions are elusive but you'd be unlucky not to see at least one on a safari. If you're determined to spot one, allow for a couple of trips. Understandably, the lions retreat into the undergrowth during Indian holiday periods when convoys of jeeps roar through the park. Morning safaris are generally a better bet than those in the afternoon. Unfortunately, the quality of the local guides is variable and most speak little English.

The Gujarati government has drastically increased the cost of most of the park's services, meaning that a stay at Sasan Gir can be expensive. Before you can go on safari, you must get a permit. These are issued on the spot at the Sinh Sadan Forest Lodge office (see Places to Stay & Eat) and cost Rs 30/US$5 for Indians/foreigners. The permit is valid for the whole day.

Vehicle entry costs Rs 50/US$10 for four hours, plus Rs 50/US$5 for a camera and a ridiculous Rs 2500/US$200 for a non-professional video. The guide's fee for a group is set at Rs 50/US$10, and if your guide's been keen and searched hard then a

The Last Lions in the Wild Outside Africa

In the 19th century, the territory of the Asiatic lion stretched from its current refuge in Gujarat's Gir Forest to as far east as Bihar. Widespread hunting devastated the lion populations, with the last sightings recorded near Delhi in 1834, in Bihar in 1840 and in Rajasthan in 1870. The last lion to die in the Indian wild outside Gujarat's Kathiawar peninsula was recorded in 1884. Why did they survive in Gujarat? They almost didn't. Hunting pushed the Gir lion to the brink of extinction, with as few as twelve remaining in the 1870s. It was not until one of their erstwhile pursuers, the enlightened Nawab of Junagadh, decided to set up a protection zone at the beginning of the 20th century, that the lion began to slowly recover. This zone now survives as the Sasan Gir Wildlife Sanctuary.

Separated from their African counterpart *(Panthera leo leo)* for centuries, the Asiatic lion has developed characteristics found only in the Gir Forest's small population. The mane of *Panthera leo persica* is less luxuriant than those of African lions and doesn't cover the top of the head or ears, while a prominent fold of skin runs the length of the abdomen. Its skin is also slightly lighter in colour. The Gir lions are also purely predators, never feeding off carrion as occurs among lions in Africa – perhaps testament to the fact that, within the sanctuary, ungulate (hoofed) prey is plentiful with few competitors.

tip is certainly appreciated. Jeeps (US$10) can be hired from the lodge office from 6 to 10 am and 3 to 5 pm every day during winter (October to February) with shorter hours from March to June. Although prices are quoted in US dollars, payment is exclusively in rupees.

Private diesel vehicles cannot be used to tour the sanctuary. Whatever else you do, take a jeep and not a minibus. While the latter stick to the main tracks, the jeeps can take the small trails where you're much more likely to come across lions.

Gir Interpretation Zone

Twelve kilometres from Sasan Gir village at Devalia, within the sanctuary precincts, is the **Gir Interpretation Zone**. The 4.12-sq-km zone has a cross section of the wildlife in Gir, so you'd be certain to see a lion here if you've been unlucky in the main sanctuary. The cost to enter the zone, including your jeep, permit and guide, is around Rs 1050 per person, although cheaper minibus minisafaris cost around Rs 590.

To get there from Sasan Gir, vehicles run from the main street for Rs 150. Although your chances of seeing lions here are pretty good, it's all a bit stage-managed and not particularly good value for money as you're only likely to get 30 to 45 minutes looking for wildlife.

Crocodile-Rearing Centre

There are 25 species of reptiles in the sanctuary. A crocodile-rearing centre has been established next to Sinh Sadan Forest Lodge, where hatchlings are reared and then released into their natural habitat. The centre is open to visitors 9 am to 6 pm (free).

Places to Stay & Eat

There are only a few places to stay at Sasan Gir village. It's a good idea to make an advance booking, as rooms can suddenly fill up.

Sinh Sadan Forest Lodge *(☎ 02877-85540)* is a five-minute walk from the train station and is the centre of most of the action. It is, however, outrageously priced at US$30/50 plus tax for a room without/with air-con; Indians pay Rs 500/1000. Even a dorm costs US$5 (Rs 50 for Indians). It's a pleasant place to stay, but it's not that pleasant. Veg meals are available for Indians/foreigners at Rs 70/US$5, nonveg costs Rs 110/US$5, breakfast Rs 40/US$2 and tea or coffee is Rs 7/US$1.

There are a couple of good, cheaper options in town, but officials keen to cash in will push you towards the Sinh Sadan. ***Rajeshri Guest House*** *(☎ 02877-85740)*, opposite the gate to Sinh Sadan, charges Rs 300 for a double with private bathroom during nonholiday periods (Rs 500 during Diwali, in October/November).

Hotel Umang *(☎ 02877-85728)*, signposted off the main road 100m west, is quieter and pretty good value for Rs 500/800 a single/double. There is a dining hall and the manager can arrange jeeps.

Gir Lodge *(☎ 02877-85521, fax 85528)*, down by the river about 200m from the Sinh Sadan Forest Lodge, is a pleasant upmarket hotel operated by the Taj Group, although it's not quite up to the standard of other hotels in the chain. Well-appointed, but not special, rooms, including three meals (but not taxes), cost US$60/110 or US$71/120 with air-con. Checkout is at noon. The restaurant is open to nonguests if things are quiet and you book ahead. They can arrange jeeps for US$25, which may sound like a lot but is possibly worth it if you want one to yourself in peak holiday periods.

The main street of Sasan Gir village is lined with eating stalls, grocery stores and a few restaurants doing not much more than thalis. ***Hotel Gulmohal***, at the western end, is probably the pick with reasonable South Indian and Punjabi food. ***Murlidhar Parotha House*** is more rough-and-ready, but otherwise OK.

Getting There & Away

STC and express buses travel between Junagadh and Veraval via Sasan Gir regularly throughout the day. The 45km trip to Veraval takes 1½ hours (Rs 15). To Junagadh, the 59km trip takes around two hours (Rs 28). Trains run to Veraval (Rs 10, 1¼ hours, 11.54 am and 3.53 pm), to Junagadh (Rs 15, 2½ hours, 5.25pm) and to Delwada (for Diu, Rs 16, three hours, 9.04 am).

JUNAGADH

☎ 0285 • pop 233,000

Junagadh, at the base of the temple-studded Girnar Hill, is the departure point for visits to the Gir Forest. This interesting and unspoilt town has some exotic old buildings and is a fascinating place to explore. Some of the best buildings are in the streets and squares around the Durbar Hall Museum.

The city takes its name from the fort that enclosed the old city (*jirna* means 'old'). Dating from 250 BC, the Ashokan edicts near the town testify to the great antiquity of this site. At the time of Partition, the Nawab of Junagadh opted to take his tiny state into Pakistan, but the inhabitants were predominantly Hindu and the nawab soon found himself in exile.

Information

The best source of information in town is Mr Sorathia, the owner of the Relief Hotel – the unofficial tourist centre. The State Bank of India, near Diwan Chowk, has money-changing facilities (11 am to 2 pm). Other banks are close by and travellers have reported efficient service from the Bank of Baroda next to the local bus stand. Credit cards can't be used in Junagadh.

Junagadh's main post office is inconveniently located south of the city centre at Gandhigram. There's a branch in a small street off MG Rd near the local bus stand. The telegraph office is on Jhalorapa Rd, near Ajanta Talkies. Internet access is available for Rs 30 per hour at Net@Cafe (☎ 628 422, ⓔ netcafe@lovemail.com), downstairs from the Hotel Ashiyana, or Cyber Point (☎ 625655) near Geeta Lodge.

Uperkot Fort

This very old fort stands on the eastern side of Junagadh. It is believed to have been built in 319 BC by Chandragupta, though it has been rebuilt and extended many times over the centuries. In places, the walls are 20m high and an ornate triple gateway forms the entrance to the fort. It's said that the fort was once besieged for a full 12-year period. In all, it was besieged 16 times. It is also said that the fort was abandoned from the 7th to 10th centuries and, when rediscovered, was completely overgrown by jungle. The fort is open 7 am to 6.30 pm daily although you can stay inside until 7 pm; entry is Rs 1.

The **Jama Masjid**, the mosque inside the fort, was built from a demolished Hindu temple. Other points of interest include the **Tomb of Nuri Shah** and two fine baolis known as the **Adi Chadi** and the **Navaghan Kuva**. The Adi Chadi is named after two of the slave girls who used to fetch water from

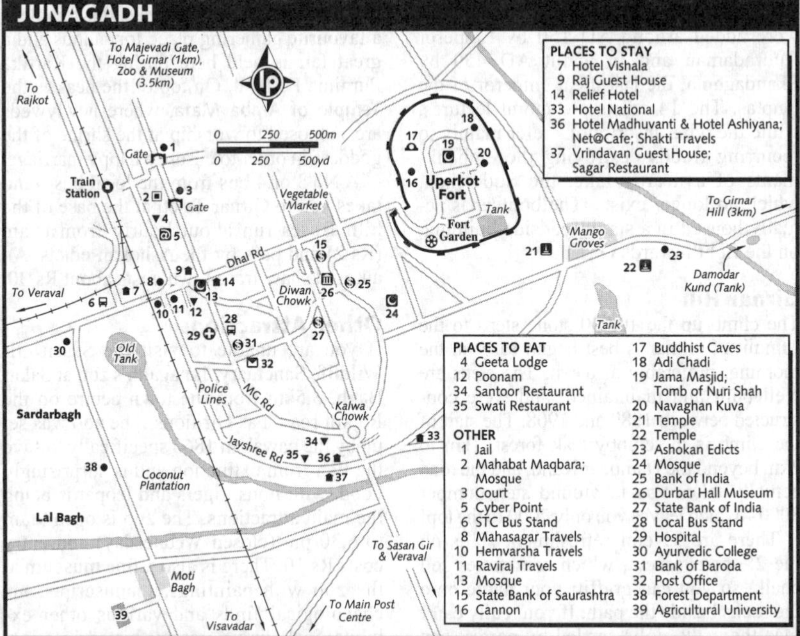

it. The Navaghan Kuva is reached by a magnificent winding staircase cut into the rock.

Cut into the hillside close to the mosque are some ancient **Buddhist caves** which are thought to be at least 1500 years old. These eerie double-storey caves have six pillars with weathered carvings. Entry to the caves costs Rs 5/US$5 for Indians/foreigners. The soft rock on which Junagadh is built encouraged the construction of caves and wells, and there are several others thought to date from the time of Ashoka.

The fort is a popular place with Indian tourists during holiday periods, when you may feel like you're the main exhibit.

Mahabat Maqbara

This stunning mausoleum of one of the nawabs of Junagadh is among the finest examples of intricate Indo-Saracenic architecture in Gujarat, resplendent with silver doors and minarets encircled by spiralling stairways. Completed in 1892, it is generally locked (the outside is more interesting anyway) but you may be able to obtain the keys from the adjacent mosque.

Durbar Hall Museum

This museum has the usual display of weapons and armour from the days of the nawabs, with collections of silver chains and chandeliers, settees and thrones, howdahs and palanquins, and a few cushions and gowns, as well as a huge carpet that was woven in Junagadh's jail. There's a portrait gallery of the nawabs and local petty princes, including photos of the last nawab with his various beloved dogs.

It's open 9 am to 12 noon and 3 to 6 pm daily (closed Monday and the second and fourth Saturday of the month); entry is Rs 5.

Ashokan Edicts

On the way to the Girnar Hill temples, you pass a huge boulder on which Emperor Ashoka inscribed 14 edicts in Pali script around 250 BC. Later Sanskrit inscriptions were added around AD 150 by Emperor Rudradaman and in about AD 450 by Skandagupta, the last great emperor of the Guptas. The 14 edicts are moral lectures, while the other inscriptions refer mainly to recurring floods destroying the embankments of a nearby lake, the Sudershan, which no longer exists. The boulder is actually housed in a small roadside building, on the right towards Girnar.

Girnar Hill

The climb up the 10,000 stone steps to the summit of Girnar is best begun early in the morning, preferably at dawn. The steps are well built and maintained, and were constructed between 1889 and 1908. The start of the climb is in scrubby teak forest, 1km to 2km beyond the Damodar Kund, and the road actually takes you to around step number 3000 – which leaves you only 7000 to the top!

There are several refreshment stalls on the 2½-hour ascent, which sometimes sell chalk, so you can graffiti your name onto the rocks beside the path. If you really can't face the walk, dolis carried by porters can be hired; for these you pay by weight so, before setting off, you suffer the indignity of being weighed on a huge beam scale, just like a sack of grain. From the summit, the views are superb.

The **Bhavnath Fair** is held in the month of Magha (January/February). Folk music and dancing takes place and lots of sadhus converge on town. The first fair was supposed to have been organised by Lord Krishna to honour the Mahabharata hero, Arjuna, who had reached Saurashtra.

Like Palitana, the temple-topped hill is of great significance to the Jains. The sacred tank of **Damodar Kund** marks the start of the climb. The path ascends through a wood to the temples near the summit. Five of them are Jain, including the largest and oldest – the 12th-century **Temple of Neminath**, the 22nd tirthankar. There is a large black image of Neminath in the central shrine and smaller ones around the temple.

The nearby triple **Temple of Mallinath**, the 9th tirthankar, was erected in 1177 by two brothers. During festivals, this temple is a favourite gathering place for sadhus and a great fair is held here during the Kartika Purnima Festival. On top of the peak is the **Temple of Amba Mata**, where newlyweds are supposed to worship at the shrine of the goddess in order to ensure a happy marriage.

A No 3 or 4 bus from the local bus stand takes you to Girnar Taleti at the base of the hill. Buses run about hourly from 6 am (Rs 2) and pass by the Ashokan edicts. An autorickshaw from town costs about Rs 30.

Other Attractions

If you are unable to visit the Sasan Gir Wildlife Sanctuary, Junagadh's **zoo** at Sakar Bagh, 3.5km from the town centre on the Rajkot road, has Gir lions. The zoo was set up by the nawab in 1863 specifically to save the lion from extinction and is surprisingly good, with lions, tigers and leopards being the main attractions. The zoo is open 9 am to 6.30 pm (closed Wednesday) and entry costs Rs 10. There is also a fine **museum** at the zoo with paintings, manuscripts, archaeological finds and various other exhibits, including a natural history section. Its opening hours are the same as for the zoo although the museum is also closed on the second and fourth Saturday of each month. Take a No 6 bus (Rs 2) or a rickshaw (Rs 15) – ask for Sakar Bagh.

The **Ayurvedic College** at Sardarbagh on the western edge of town is housed in one of the former nawab's palaces, and has a small museum devoted to Ayurvedic medicine. The staff are knowledgeable and it's a good place for information on this ancient traditional medicine. The college is open 9 am to 6 pm daily.

Places to Stay

Rooms are equipped with private bathrooms, unless indicated otherwise.

Relief Hotel *(☎ 620280, Dhal Rd)* is a popular hang-out for travellers, and Mr Sorathia is an obliging and knowledgeable host. Singles/doubles cost Rs 125/200, or Rs 500 for air-con doubles. Good meals are available for guests, and include what one Indian newspaper described as 'the best biryani in Gujarat'. There's a secure parking area for those with their own vehicles.

Raj Guest House *(☎ 623961, Dhal Rd)* is less appealing, charging Rs 70/100 for dingy rooms with squat toilets that leave little about the previous occupants' health to the imagination. The Rs 125 doubles at the front are better, with decent views and lots of noise.

Hotel Vishala *(☎ 631599)*, opposite the bus stand, has a range of reasonable rooms starting at Rs 100/150 (bucket hot water). It's on the 3rd floor of an otherwise pitch dark and unoccupied building – pray that the lift is working.

Hotel Girnar *(☎ 621201, Majewadi Darwaja)* is a Gujarat Tourism hotel about 2km out of town. It offers rooms for Rs 225/400, or Rs 425/650 with air-con; prices include tea and breakfast. Most rooms are spacious and have a balcony (try to get one of these). Prices drop 40% from 15 June to 15 September, and the restaurant serves Gujarati thalis for Rs 40.

Retiring rooms at the train station are Rs 50/100; dorm beds are Rs 30.

Vrindavan Guest House *(☎ 622777, Jayshree Rd)* is basic but reasonably welcoming. Small rooms with hot water cost only Rs 70/125.

Opposite are two hotels in the same building. ***Hotel Madhuvanti*** *(☎ 620087, Jayshree Rd)* on the 1st floor has big, clean doubles for a negotiable Rs 300, which is a bit much. There's a pool hall on the same floor. ***Hotel Ashiyana*** *(☎ 620706)* on the 2nd floor has decent rooms with TV starting at Rs 150/250.

Hotel National *(☎ 627891)*, off Kalwa Chowk, ranges from Rs 350 for a double, up to Rs 700 with air-con. The more expensive rooms are comfortable and spacious, although the other rooms (and the service) get decidedly mixed reviews from travellers.

Places to Eat

Junagadh is famous for its fruit, especially *kesar* (mangoes) and *chiku* (sapodilla) which are popular in milkshakes in November and December.

Geeta Lodge, close to the train station, has thalis for Rs 35.

Santoor Restaurant *(☎ 625090, MG Rd)*, has quick service, good veg food (Rs 20 to Rs 40) and good mango fruit shakes (Rs 15). The paneer tikka masala (Rs 35) is particularly tasty. It's a popular place with locals – always a good sign.

Sagar Restaurant *(☎ 623661)* and ***Swati Restaurant*** *(☎ 625296)*, both on Jayshree Rd, are of a similar standard and price to Santoor. It is sometimes necessary to book at the Swati during busy times.

Poonam, down a side road opposite Raj Guest House, is another veg place, with thalis for Rs 25. It's above an STD phone place (the sign is in Gujarati).

Getting There & Away

Bus Just for something different, the timetable at the STC stand is entirely in Gujarati. Buses leave hourly for Rajkot (Rs 35, two hours) and for Sasan Gir (Rs 28, two hours), and there are other regular departures to Porbandar (Rs 42), Veraval (Rs 45), Una (for Diu, Rs 37), Jamnagar (Rs 45) and Ahmedabad (Rs 100).

Various private bus offices are nearby on Dhal Rd, near the rail tracks. Raviraj Travels (☎ 626988), has minibuses to Rajkot every 30 minutes (Rs 25, two hours). Hemvarsha Travels (☎ 620681) with a sign only in Gujarati, has buses going to Ahmedabad (Rs 110) and Mumbai (Rs 300). Shakti Travels (☎ 621913) and Maharsagar Travels (☎ 629919) are also good for help with long-haul travel.

Train The reservation office (☎ 131) is open 8 to 11 am and 3 to 5.30 pm.

The *Girnar Express* departs Junagadh at 9.13 pm, arriving in Ahmedabad at 6.05 am (Rs 88/137/462, general/sleeper/1st class, 377km). Few trains originate in Junagadh but plenty pass through en route to Rajkot (Rs 39/205, general/1st class) and Veraval (Rs 23/173). They rarely stop at the station for longer than a couple of minutes so be prepared for a hasty entry or exit. At 6 am a train leaves for Sasan Gir (Rs 15, 2½ hours) and continues to Delwada (for Una and Diu) arriving at 12.50 pm (Rs 27, general class only).

PORBANDAR

☎ 0286 • pop 189,300

On the south-east coast, midway between Veraval and Dwarka, the modern-day city of Porbandar is chiefly noted as the birthplace of Mahatma Gandhi, beyond which there are few reasons to visit.

In ancient times, the city was called Sudamapuri after Sudama, a compatriot of Krishna, and there was a flourishing trade from here to Africa and the Persian Gulf. The Africa connection is apparent in the number of Indianised blacks, called Siddis, who form a virtually separate caste of Dalits.

Swimming at rocky Chowpatty Beach is not recommended. This beach is used as a local latrine and there is a factory drain outlet by the Hazur Palace.

The State Bank of India, opposite Hotel Flamingo, and the State Bank of Saurashtra, in Manek Chowk, are reluctant to change money for nonaccount holders but may do so if pushed. Otherwise, try Divyaraj Foreign Exchange, south of the Jynbeeli Bridge, or Thankys Tours & Travels on MG Rd (see Getting There & Away later in the section).

Along the coast at Madhavpur near Porbandar, the **Madhavrai Fair** is held in the month of Chaitra (March/April) to celebrate Krishna's elopement with Rukmini.

Kirti Mandir

This memorial to Gandhi was built in 1950. There's a small bookshop and (take the stairs by the entrance) an exhibit of photographs, some with English captions. Next door is Gandhi's actual birthplace – a three-storey, 300-year-old house. A swastika marks the exact spot where the great man was born on 2 October 1869. Entrance is free.

Nehru Planetarium & Bharat Mandir

The doors of the Nehru Planetarium, 2km north of the town centre, celebrate Indian nonalignment, with panels showing Shastri with Kosygin on one side and Nehru with JFK on the other.

The large Bharat Mandir Hall is in a garden directly opposite. On the floor is a huge relief map of India, and the building's pillars are painted with bas-reliefs of more than 100 religious figures and personages from Hindu epics.

Both buildings are open 9 am to noon and 3 to 6 pm daily and entry to each costs

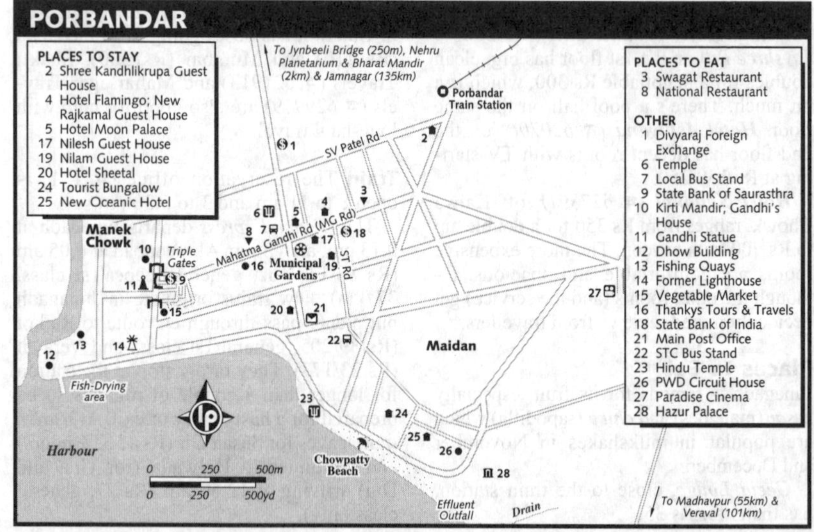

Rs 3. It's worth getting your rickshaw driver to wait as the buildings are down a lonely road populated by stray dogs.

Places to Stay

There isn't a whole lot that is 'new' about the ***New Rajkamal Guest House*** *(☎ 242674, MG Rd)* – it's dirt cheap in every sense and only for real 'shoestringers'. A single with shared bathroom costs Rs 40 while Rs 50/80 will get you a single/double with a grubby private bathroom and bucket cold-water shower.

Nilam Guest House *(☎ 244503, ST Rd)*, has dusty rooms which are a bit on the nose for Rs 80/125 with bucket hot water. Their advertisements for 'single and double bad rooms' are not that wide of the mark.

Nilesh Guest House *(☎ 252200, MG Rd)* has doubles with private bathroom, hot water and TV for Rs 150.

Hotel Flamingo *(☎ 247123, MG Rd)*, opposite, is a friendly place with a good restaurant. Singles/doubles start at Rs 100/150, or Rs 200/250 for better rooms with satellite TV; breakfast is (sometimes) included in the price. Some rooms have a balcony that looks straight into a wall. Checkout is at 10 am.

Hotel Sheetal *(☎ 247596, fax 241821)*, opposite the main post office, is of a slightly better standard. Rooms have TV and hot water and prices start at Rs 150/250, rising to Rs 500 for an air-con double. Prices are likely to increase by Rs 50 to 100 when the renovations are completed. There is 24-hour room service and they can arrange secure parking for those with their own vehicles.

Shree Kandhlikrupa Guest House *(☎ 246 655, SV Patel Rd)*, on the corner near the train station, offers good rooms with cold-water private bathroom for Rs 100/200 or Rs 400 with air-con and balcony. Look for the 'Welcome' sign – the only sign in English.

If you want to be near the sea (while understanding that it's a pretty bleak patch of coastline), Gujarat Tourism's ***Tourist Bungalow*** *(☎ 245476)* is at Chowpatty Beach. The rooms are spacious but run-down and overpriced at Rs 250/350 or Rs 450/600 with air-con. There's also a (men-only) dorm for Rs 50, a restaurant and some helpful tourist brochures available at reception. Almost next door, ***New Oceanic Hotel*** *(☎ 242917, fax 241398)* is similarly priced and a little more friendly, although many rooms have no views.

Hotel Moon Palace *(☎ 241172, fax 243248, ⓔ moonpalace@mail.com, MG Rd)* is the place to go if you're in search of a little more comfort. A few singles are available for Rs 125 though most singles/doubles start at Rs 180/200. The management is decidedly reluctant to give the cheaper rooms to foreigners. Even so, the deluxe suite for Rs 600/700 is good value and as luxurious as you'll get in Porbandar.

Places to Eat

National Restaurant *(MG Rd)* serves only nonveg dishes. It's simple but not bad.

Swagat Restaurant, on the eastern end of MG Rd, is a popular place, with Punjabi food starting at Rs 20.

Hotel Flamingo has a good air-con restaurant which offers a wide range of Punjabi, Chinese and South Indian food; a main dish costs Rs 30 to 60. Nonguests are welcome.

Getting There & Away

Air Gujarat Airways has flights to Mumbai (US$110/Rs 5005, daily except Saturday), although how long they'll continue is anyone's guess. Bookings can be made with Thankys Tours & Travels (☎ 244344, fax 245128, ⓔ thankys@vsnl.com) on MG Rd.

Bus The STC bus stand is a four-minute walk from MG Rd. There are regular services to Dwarka (Rs 52), Jamnagar (Rs 55), Veraval (Rs 50) and Junagadh (Rs 41/52 for local/express bus). The private bus companies have offices on MG Rd, near the Hotel Flamingo.

Train The *Saurasthra Express* (9216) leaves Porbandar at 8 pm nightly and travels to Mumbai (Rs 170/264/1224, general/sleeper/2A class, 23½ hours, 959km), via Rajkot (Rs 59/92/464, 4½ hours) and Ahmedabad (Rs 104/162/749, 10 hours).

Getting Around

An autorickshaw to the airport costs about Rs 30.

DWARKA

☎ 02892 • pop 54,000

On the extreme western tip of the Kathiawar peninsula, Dwarka is one of the four most holy Hindu pilgrimage sites in India and is closely related to the Krishna legend. It was here that Krishna set up his capital after fleeing from Mathura.

Dwarkanath Temple is dedicated to Krishna. Non-Hindus can enter after filling out a form, though the exterior, with its tall five-storey spire supported by 60 columns, is far more interesting than the interior.

Also worth a look are the carvings of **Rukmini Temple**, about 1km to the east, the many pillared **Sabha Mandapa**, reputed to be over 2500 years old, and the **Nageshwar Mandir** with its underground chamber.

Dwarka's **lighthouse** is open to the public between 4 and 6 pm; it affords a beautiful panoramic view (Rs 1) and is a restful place.

Archaeological excavations have revealed five earlier cities at the site. Dwarka is the site of the important **Janmashthami Festival** which falls in August/September and celebrates Krishna's birthday.

A little north of Dwarka, a ferry crosses from Okha to the **Island of Bet**, where Vishnu is said to have slain a demon. There are modern Krishna temples on the island, and a deserted beach on the northern coast. Beware of unfriendly dogs on this island.

Places to Stay & Eat

Most places are willing to negotiate significant discounts except when the town is awash with pilgrims.

Toran Tourist Bungalow *(☎ 34013)*, a state-run place, has dorm beds for Rs 50 and singles/doubles for Rs 200/300.

Meera Hotel *(☎ 34031)*, on the main approach road, has rooms with private bathroom for Rs 100/200, and the dining room does good thalis for Rs 25.

Maruti Guest House *(☎ 34722)*, just a few minutes from Teen Bati Chowk, has rooms for Rs 75/150; some have no windows.

If you don't fancy feeding from the street stalls, nearby ***Shetty's Fast Food*** is one of the cheapest restaurants in town and one waiter at ***Kant Restaurant*** is absolutely convinced that the German philosopher of the same name was a German sadhu.

Getting There & Away

There is a railway line between Dwarka and Jamnagar (Rs 41/365 for general/2A class, 132km), and there are trains to Mumbai (Rs 170/1224, 945km) via Rajkot (Rs 61/470, 207km) as well as to Ahmedabad (Rs 104/ 749, 453km).

STC buses run to all points in Saurashtra and Ahmedabad.

JAMNAGAR

☎ 0288 • pop 635,000

Prior to Independence, the princely state of Jamnagar was ruled by the Jadeja Rajputs. The city was built around the small Ranmal Lake, in the centre of which is a small palace, reached by a causeway.

Jamnagar has a long history of pearl fishing and *bandhani* (a knotting and dyeing process believed to have been used in the area for up to 5000 years). It's a very time-consuming process of tying thousands of tiny knots in a piece of fabric that has first been folded upon itself a number of times. This is then dyed in several stages using different colours. The knots are then pulled apart and the fabric unfolded, to reveal a repeating pattern in a variety of hues. The process is used for saris, shirts, shawls and other items.

Jamnagar is today known for having the only Ayurvedic university in India and a temple listed in the *Guinness Book of Records* (see the Bala Hanuman Temple section later).

The old part of town, known as Chandni Chowk, has a number of delightful and decaying buildings and is a great place to wander around. The centre of the old town is known as Darbar Gadh, a semicircular gathering place where the former maharajas of Nawanagar once held public audiences.

Orientation & Information

The centre of the new part of town, where most places to stay are located, is Teen Batti

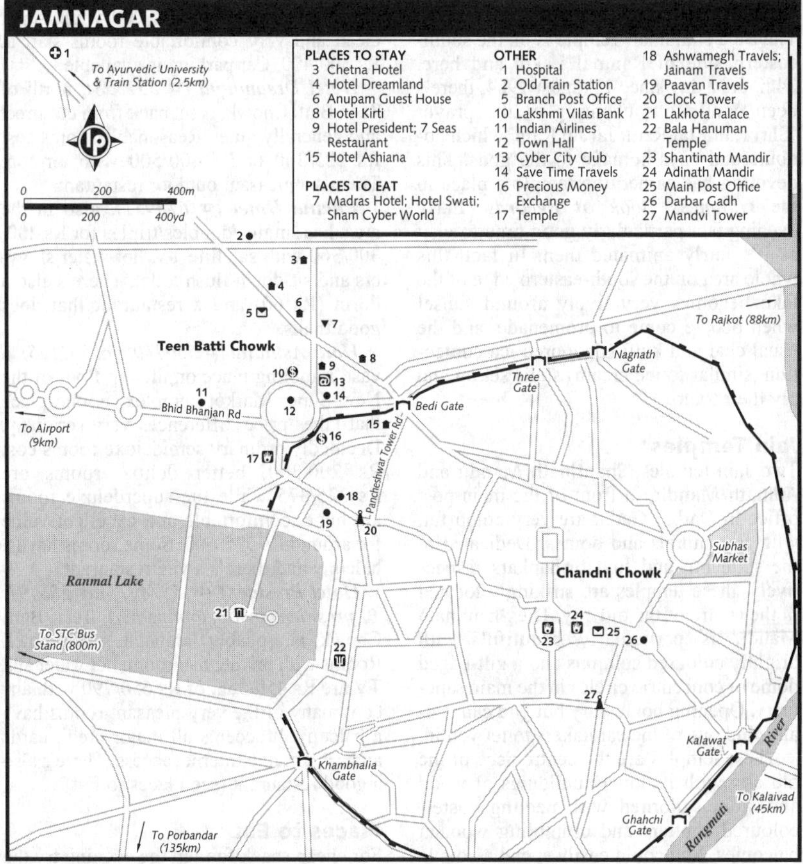

Chowk. The old town is to the south-east. The STC bus stand and the new train station are a long way to the west and north-west respectively.

The Lakshmi Vilas Bank, north of the town hall, is the place to go for foreign exchange, or you could also try Precious Money Exchange farther around the roundabout. The Hotel President will change US dollars, British pounds, euros and deutschmarks, but cash only.

Cyber City Club (signed simply as Cyber Café; ☎ 676772), opposite the town hall, charges Rs 30 an hour, while Sham Cyber World (☎ 672228), on the 1st floor next to the Hotel Swati (see Places to Eat) charges Rs 35. Both are open 9 am to midnight.

Lakhota Palace

This diminutive palace once belonged to the maharaja of Nawanagar. Today it houses a small **museum** with displays from local archaeological sites. The museum is reached by a short causeway from the northern side of Ranmal Lake, and is open 10.30 am to 1 pm and 3 to 5.30 pm daily (closed Wednesday and the second and fourth Saturday in the month). Entry costs Rs 2.

Bala Hanuman Temple

The Bala Hanuman Temple is on the south-eastern side of Ranmal Lake, and here, 24 hours a day since 1 August 1964, there's been continuous chanting of the prayer 'Shri Ram, Jai Ram, Jai Jai Ram' which honours and pays homage to the gods. This devotion has earned the temple a place in the *Guinness Book of Records*. Early evening is a particularly good time to visit as it's fairly animated then. In fact, this whole area on the south-eastern edge of the lake becomes very lively around sunset when people come to promenade, and the usual chai and kulfi (flavoured ice confection, similar to ice cream) stalls set up and ply their trade.

Jain Temples

Two Jain temples, **Shantinath Mandir** and **Adinath Mandir**, in front of the main post office in Darbar Gadh, are very colourful, with fine murals and domes. Dedicated to the sixteenth and first tirthankars respectively, these temples are strikingly located in the centre of the old city. The Shantinath Mandir is particularly beautiful, with brightly coloured columns and a gilt-edged dome of concentric circles in the main sanctuary. Opening hours vary but you can usually find one of the caretakers to let you in.

These temples are the centrepiece of the old city with its lovely buildings of wood and stone, adorned with peeling pastel-coloured shutters and crumbling wooden balconies. You could easily spend a couple of hours exploring the lanes leading out from Chandni Chowk.

Places to Stay

Anupam Guest House *(☎ 675107)*, in Teen Batti Chowk, has grubby, anything but 'semideluxe' singles/doubles for Rs 125/150 with private bathroom containing only a bucket; the shared toilets are awful. Better 'deluxe' rooms go for Rs 150/250 and the manager will negotiate for these rooms. It's a depressing dosshouse, so if you can afford somewhere better, go there.

Hotel Kirti *(☎ 557121)*, off Teen Batti Chowk, is great value. There are a few small, nonair-con singles for Rs 200 while super clean and very comfortable rooms start at Rs 300/400. Car parking is available.

Hotel Dreamland *(☎ 557598)*, north of Teen Batti Chowk, is set back from the street and generally quiet. Reasonable rooms cost Rs 225/300 or Rs 400/500 with air-con. There's a pleasant outdoor restaurant.

Chetna Hotel *(☎ 678951)*, also in the area, has singles/doubles/triples for Rs 200/300/360 with satellite TV, hot water showers and sit-down flush toilet. There's also a dorm (Rs 60) and a restaurant that does good thalis.

Hotel Ashiana *(☎ 559110, fax 551155)*, a vast, rambling place on the top floor of the New Super Market complex, is one place that takes price differences very seriously. Decidedly ordinary semideluxe rooms cost Rs 200/300, better deluxe rooms are Rs 325/375 while the superdeluxe rooms are huge, comfortable and excellent value for around Rs 525/600. Some rooms have a balcony and there's a veg restaurant.

Hotel President *(☎ 557491, fax 558491, ⓔ president@wilnetonline.net)*, Teen Batti Chowk, is arguably Jamnagar's best hotel. Rooms with private bathroom, hot water and TV are Rs 450/560, or Rs 650/790 with air-con; many of the very pleasant rooms have a balcony. It accepts all major credit cards and can arrange Internet access. There's also a good restaurant (see Places to Eat).

Places to Eat

For cheap snack food in the evening try the stalls set up near Bala Hanuman Temple. In the centre of town in the Teen Batti Chowk area, there are plenty of small eating places.

Hotel Swati is a vegetarian place with South Indian (*masala dosas* – curried vegetables inside a thin lentin-flour pancake – cost Rs 30), Jain (the sweet Navratna korma is Rs 40) and Punjabi dishes. It's open 10 am to 3 pm and 5 to 10 pm.

Madras Hotel, nearby, specialises in vegetarian South Indian and Punjabi cuisine, as well as the odd pizza (Rs 40).

7 Seas Restaurant at the Hotel President offers good food, which includes Western choices; veg/nonveg dishes start at Rs 40/60.

Getting There & Away

Air Indian Airlines (☎ 550211) has daily flights to Mumbai (US$95); the office is on Bhid Bhanjan Rd and is open 10.30 am to 6.05 pm daily. Bookings can also be made with Save Time Travels (☎ 553137), between Bedi Gate and the town hall.

Bus STC buses go hourly to Rajkot (Rs 35) and every 30 minutes to Junagadh (Rs 41); other buses go to Dwarka, Porbandar and Ahmedabad.

There are various private bus companies with many in the blocks west of the clock tower. Jainam Travels (☎ 674224) has buses to Mumbai (Rs 350), Ahmedabad (Rs 120), Bhavnagar (Rs 120), and Rajkot (Rs 35). Ashwamegh Travels costs the same with seven daily departures to Ahmedabad and one (2.35 pm) to Mumbai. Paavan Travels (☎ 552002) is also nearby.

Train The *Saurasthra Mail* (9006) is one of many trains which runs between Jamnagar and Ahmedabad (Rs 79/123/356, general/sleeper/3A class, 6½ hours). It also continues on to Mumbai (Rs 157/244/707, 17½ hours). It departs Jamnagar at 2.40 pm daily. There are also trains to Dwarka and Rajkot.

Getting Around

There is no minibus service to the airport, which is a long way out. Autorickshaw drivers demand at least Rs 100. A rickshaw from the bus stand to the Bedi Gate area costs about Rs 10. From Teen Batti Chowk to the new train station, about 4km north of the city centre, expect to pay about Rs 25.

RAJKOT

☎ 0281 • pop 1.17 million

This bustling town was once the capital of the princely state of Saurashtra and is also a former British government headquarters. Mahatma Gandhi spent his early years here and his memory is marked with a statue.

The prestigious Rajkumar College dates back to the 19th century and is regarded as one of the best private schools in the country. It was set up by the British for the sons of nobility (*rajkumar* means 'prince').

Information

Rajkot's helpful tourist office (☎ 234507) is hidden away behind the State Bank of Saurashtra building on Jawahar Rd, almost opposite Galaxy Hotel. It's open 10.30 am to 1.30 pm and 2 to 6 pm Monday to Friday and the first and third Saturday of the month.

The State Bank of India, to the north of the Jubilee Gardens, has money-changing facilities. Entry is from the rear of the building. Some mid-range hotels will also change money although usually only for guests.

For Internet access, head to the Interlink Cyber Cafe (☎ 227237, ⓔ interlinkindia@rajkotonline.com), in a lane opposite the Sarovar Restaurant. One hour costs Rs 30 and it's open 9 am to midnight.

Watson Museum & Library

The Watson Museum & Library in the Jubilee Gardens commemorates Colonel John Watson, Political Agent (Administrator) from 1886–89.

The entrance is flanked by two imperial lions. Among the exhibits are copies of artefacts from Mohenjodaro, 13th-century carvings, temple statues, natural history exhibits and dioramas of local Adivasi costumes and housing styles.

Perhaps the most startling piece is a huge marble statue of Queen Victoria seated on a throne, decidedly not amused. The museum is open 9 am to 1 pm and 2 to 6 pm Tuesday to Thursday; entry costs Rs 2.

Kaba Gandhi No Delo

This is the house where Gandhi grew up, and it now holds a permanent exhibition of Gandhi items. The Mahatma's passion for the handloom is preserved in the form of a small weaving school. It's within the old city on Ghee Kanta Rd, and entry is free. Opening hours are flexible, around 9 am to noon and 3 to 5.30 pm, Monday to Saturday. The surrounding streets of the old city are atmospheric places in which to wander around.

Places to Stay

Rajkot has an excellent selection of mid-range accommodation, although budget travellers are less well-served.

Places to Stay – Budget

Vijay Guest House *(☎ 236550)* north of the bus stand in a lane off Dhebar Rd, is basic but friendly with rooms for Rs 70/130/200 a single/double/triple. All rooms come with private bathroom and bucket hot water.

North-east of the bus stand, ***Jyoti Guest House*** *(☎ 225472, Kanak Rd)* is quiet and good budget value. Basic but clean, spacious doubles cost Rs 150 with private bathroom and sit-down flush toilet. There's also a men-only dorm for Rs 40.

Jayshree Guest House *(☎ 227954, Kanak Rd)*, closer to the bus stand, has few virtues other than location. The rooms without bathroom (Rs 85/130) resemble coffins. Those with private bathroom (Rs 100/160) are slightly better. There's bucket hot water from 6 to 10 am.

Hotel Yash *(☎ 223574, Dhebar Rd)*, a five-minute walk from the bus stand, is newer and has clean, pleasant rooms with TV, telephone and private bathroom, although most have no window. There are two small singles for Rs 195, and a range of other singles/doubles for Rs 245/345 or Rs 345/586 with air-con. There's no restaurant, but the 24-hour room service provides some compensation.

Places to Stay – Mid-Range & Top End

All rooms in this category have satellite TV and noon checkout.

Hotel Samrat International *(☎ 442234, 37 Karanpara Rd)*, south of the bus stand, has well-appointed rooms for the remarkably precise figure of Rs 322.50/483.75 (including tax), or Rs 605/806.25 with air-con. There are more expensive deluxe rooms for Rs 920/1100, although this is one place where even the cheaper rooms are attractive, spacious and excellent value. There's a good veg restaurant here.

Hotel RR Palace *(☎ 241473)*, nearby, also has very pleasant, modern rooms with a touch less character for Rs 250/400, or Rs 400/550 with air-con. The rooms at the front can be a little noisy.

Galaxy Hotel *(☎ 222904, fax 227053, ⓔ galaxyhotel@wilnetonline.net)*, on the 3rd floor of the Galaxy Commercial Centre on Jawahar Rd, is another excellent choice with a classy ambience. Spotless spacious rooms cost Rs 675/1010 with air-con or Rs 440/660 without. The staff are friendly and, although there is no restaurant, they seem to be able to rustle up just about anything through their 24-hour room service. There's a pleasant open terrace area on the roof with swing chairs.

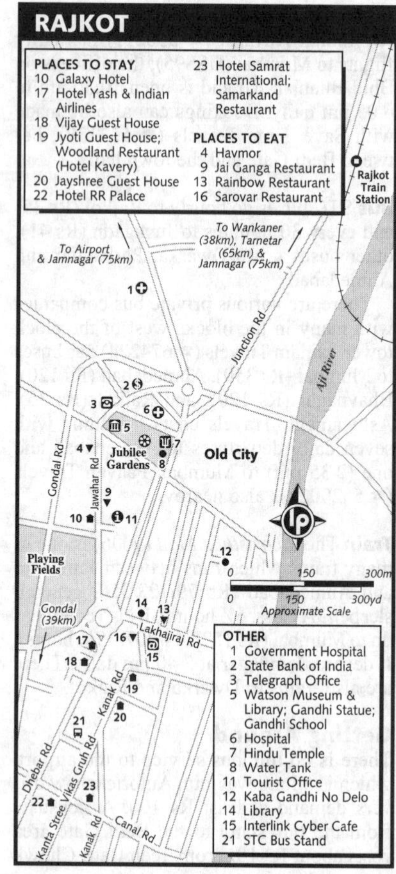

Places to Eat

Rainbow Restaurant *(Lakhajiraj Rd)* is very popular in the evenings and serves tasty and cheap South Indian cuisine. There's an air-con section upstairs. This place has an impressive selection of ice cream: See if you can resist 'Nuts in Love'!

Havmor, near the Jubilee Gardens, serves Indian, Chinese and Western food starting at Rs 40 (veg and nonveg). ***Samarkand Restaurant*** in the Hotel Samrat International is another decent multicuisine place with dishes in the Rs 40 to 70 range.

Jai Ganga, opposite the Galaxy Hotel, and ***Sarovar Restaurant***, north of the bus stand, are similarly good value.

The quality and ambience of the ***Woodland Restaurant*** *(Kanak Rd)* in the Hotel Kavery makes it feel like an upmarket place, but the prices are very reasonable. Vegetarian dishes start at Rs 25; Gujarati thalis are Rs 65.

Getting There & Away

Air Indian Airlines has daily flights between Rajkot and Mumbai (US$75, 5.50 pm departure). The Indian Airlines office (☎ 227916, fax 233329) is on Dhebar Rd.

Bus STC buses (☎ 235025) connect Rajkot with Jamnagar (Rs 35), Junagadh (Rs 35), Porbandar (Rs 60), Veraval (Rs 58) and Ahmedabad (Rs 122).

There are a number of private buses that operate to Ahmedabad, Bhavnagar, Una (for Diu), Mt Abu, Udaipur and Mumbai. These companies' offices are on Kanak Rd, by the bus stand. The road between Rajkot and Bhuj was seriously damaged in the earthquake and transport links to the Kutch region are likely to be difficult for some time to come.

Train There are at least four trains daily between Rajkot and Ahmedabad (Rs 62/97/279, general/sleeper/3A class, around six hours, 246km). Trains also go to/from Jamnagar (Rs 28/44, general/sleeper class, two hours, 75km), Porbandar (Rs 59/464, general/2A, 4½ hours, 221km), and Mumbai (Rs 145/225/653, general/sleeper/3A, 19 hours, 738km). There's a slow metre-gauge service to Veraval (Rs 52/273, general/1st class, 5½ hours, 186 km). For inquiries, call ☎ 443535 or ☎ 131.

Getting Around

A rickshaw to the airport from the city centre costs about Rs 50; to the train station expect to pay Rs 15.

AROUND RAJKOT

Wankaner

This tiny town is about 38km north of Rajkot, and has a striking **palace** (☎ 02828-20000) that looks like something straight out of a fairytale. The palace was built in 1907 and is a curious Graeco-Roman Gothic Indo-Scottish baronial extravagance. As the royal family still lives in the palace, guests are accommodated a couple of kilometres away.

Oasis House is an original Art Deco building complete with indoor swimming pool. While hardly palatial, the rooms are comfortable and meals are taken at the palace with the family. The charge is Rs 1650 per person, including meals.

There are regular buses to Rajkot every half hour, and Wankaner Junction is on the main railway line to Ahmedabad (Rs 57/257, general/3A class, 205km).

Tarnetar

Every year in the month of Bhadra (August/September), the Trineteshwar Temple at Tarnetar, 65km north-east of Rajkot, hosts the three-day **Tarnetar Fair**, which is best known for the different *chhatris* (domed-shaped Mughal kiosk) made specifically for the occasion, and as an opportunity to find a spouse – one of the main functions of the fair is to enable villagers from the Bharwad community to form matrimonial alliances. Prospective candidates are bedecked in their finery, making it an extraordinarily colourful spectacle.

According to legend, Arjuna once danced at this site, and the Ganges River flows into the tank here once a year.

Special state buses go to/from Rajkot during the fair.

Gondal

The town of Gondal, 39km south of Rajkot on the River Gondali, was once the centre of a former prosperous princely state and is still home to impressive buildings. The **Naulakaha Darbargadh palace** (named after the nine lakhs it cost to build) is worth a look.

Riverside Palace *(☎ 02825-20002)* is an interesting place to stay in Gondal. It costs Rs 1975 per person including all meals and local sightseeing. The present royal family still has the maharaja's collection of 30 or so vintage cars, and in the palace railway yard are two royal rail carriages. One of these carriages has been restored to its former glory; sleeping here costs Rs 2200, including meals.

There are regular state buses to Gondal from Rajkot (Rs 12, one hour).

Kutch (Kachchh)

Kutch, the westernmost region of India, is virtually an island; during the monsoon period from May onwards, it really is an island. The Gulf of Kutch divides Kutch (known in the local dialect as Kachchh) from the Kathiawar peninsula. To the north, it is separated from the Sind region of Pakistan by the Great Rann of Kutch. During the dry season, the Rann is a vast expanse of hard, dried mud. Then, with the start of the monsoon in May, it is flooded first by sea water, then by fresh river water. Kutch is also separated from the rest of Gujarat to the east by the Little Rann of Kutch.

The salt in the soil makes this low-lying marsh area almost completely barren. Only on scattered 'islands' above the salt level is there vegetation in the form of coarse grass, which provides fodder for the region's sparse wildlife. These grasslands are under threat from the gando baval plant which is spreading across the Rann at an alarming rate, threatening to destroy fragile ecosystems.

It is believed that the Indus River once flowed through Kutch until a massive earthquake in 1819 altered its course, leaving behind a salt desert. The destructive earthquake in January 2001 similarly altered the fabric of Kachchhi life.

This fascinating, isolated region is populated by several different tribes, including the Jats, Ahirs and Dalits. The Rabaris are the largest group. They are traditionally semi-nomadic; the men spend up to 10 months of the year seeking new grazing pastures with their livestock (sheep, goats or camels), while the women and children stay in the village. Milk and milk products are their main source of income, although Rabari women also excel at embroidery work.

The villages of the Kutch region have long been renowned for their distinctive and high-quality handicrafts (especially exquisite, mirrored embroidery). These handicrafts and the traditional Kachchhi culture that they represent were also preserved by a number of cooperatives aimed at ensuring that the craftspeople received a fair cut of the profits. These included the Kutch Mahila Vikas Sangathan, an organisation comprising 4000 rural women that pays members a dividend of the profits and invests money at village level to meet social needs, Shrujan, the Kala Raksha Trust and Kutchcraft, the local representatives for SEWA (see the boxed text 'SEWA' earlier in the chapter). While the communities that run these organisations have been devastated, you may come across outlets for these groups set up elsewhere in the state of Gujarat to assist the relief effort.

Surrounding as they did the epicentre of the earthquake, many of Kutch's villages were razed by the quake with entire villages wiped off the map. For the foreseeable future, most will be off-limits to travellers. As the region recovers, all requests for permission to visit should be directed to the Office of the District Superintendent of Police (Foreigners Registration Office) in Bhuj.

BHUJ

As the closest major town to the epicentre of the earthquake, Bhuj was reduced to rubble. Around 90% of the town's buildings were either destroyed or rendered uninhabitable and, although the final death toll may never be known, as much as 10% of the city's population of around 150,000 people were killed. A large proportion of the surviving inhabitants fled Bhuj and surrounding districts.

Prior to the earthquake in January 2001, Bhuj was one of the highlights of any visit

The Day the Earth Shook

At around 8.46 am on 26 January 2001, as many of India's Republic Day celebrations were just getting under way, a massive earthquake hit Gujarat. Measuring 7.9 on the Richter scale (in the confused aftermath of the quake, reports of the tremor's magnitude ranged from 6.9 to 8.1) and with its epicentre about 20km north-east of Bhuj, the devastation it wrought was enormous. Apart from Bhuj, the towns of Bhachau (one of the closest towns to the epicentre), Anjar, Surendranagar and countless smaller villages across the Rann of Kutch were destroyed, with few buildings left standing and tens of thousands of lives lost. Farther afield, at least 1000 people were killed in Ahmedabad, up to 100 in Morvi, over 300 in Rajkot, around 100 in Jamnagar, and close to 50 in Surat.

It was a disaster that Gujarat could ill-afford. Like much of western India, the state had been suffering the effects of a crippling drought for two years prior to the quake. As a result of crop failures and scarce water supplies, many traditional farmers and other villagers had already left the land that had been worked by their ancestors for generations. Many had moved to the cities, spawning the satellite suburbs ringing cities like Ahmedabad, putting pressure on strained resources and changing the demographic make-up of the countryside. In the aftermath of the earthquake, as 147 aftershocks (including one which registered 5.9 on the Richter scale two days after the quake) rocked the region between 26 January and 1 February, tens of thousands of Kachchhis were again reported to be leaving Kutch. The task of rebuilding for those who remain is staggering, and the statewide ripples of trauma and social dislocation that will result long after the tremors have ceased can only be guessed at.

The Gujarati government, and to a lesser extent the Indian government, were slated for their slow response to the disaster, and for having contributed to its scale by tolerating the practices of unscrupulous builders. Many locals in Bhuj and Gandhidham blamed the large loss of life upon developers for ignoring local building laws limiting the height of new constructions to two storeys. There were also accusations that some government and nongovernment relief efforts were delivered in a manner which owed much to caste and religious bias, although this was certainly not the norm. The greatest problem in the quake's aftermath was not a shortage of relief materials but rather incompetence in the coordination and distribution of supplies, highlighting official unpreparedness for such a large-scale disaster. This was in spite of the fact that both the Chief Minister of Gujarat and seismological experts had publicly predicted for over a year prior to the quake that Kutch would soon experience a high-intensity earthquake.

As political parties conducted an unseemly squabble for political points, it was the reaction of ordinary Indians which offered the most powerful reasons for hope. As survivors of the quake streamed out of Kutch, many Indians made the reverse journey in an effort to assist relief efforts, even if it meant removing the rubble with their bare hands. Expatriate Kachchhis from around the country (particularly the large community in Mumbai) and members of the sizeable Gujarati community around the world contributed generously to relief efforts. They were joined by expat rescue teams from as far away as Switzerland and Russia, and thousands of volunteers from around the world. The international community, including Pakistan, also contributed millions of dollars in relief aid. In spite of everything, the bravery, resilience and solidarity of the Gujaratis left no-one in any doubt that Gujarat would be rebuilt.

to Gujarat. This old, partially walled city was an intricate maze of streets and alleys with attractive crenellated gateways, old palaces and brightly decorated Hindu temples. It was also the ideal base for exploring the tribal villages of the Kutch region.

It will be a long time before Bhuj and the entire Kutch region will be in a position to handle the arrival of tourists. Its tourist infrastructure was destroyed and the limited resources available in the quake's aftermath will necessarily be dedicated to rebuilding the lives and homes of those who remain.

It is not known which of Bhuj's tourist attractions remained intact. Most of Bhuj's architectural highlights were concentrated in the demolished old city. These once included the beautiful Aina Mahal (Old Palace) with its exquisite Hall of Mirrors and, just outside the city walls, Kachchh Museum dating from 1877 and the oldest museum in Gujarat. Some royal tombs or chhatris south-west of Hamrisar tank were also reduced to rubble. Remarkably, some eyewitness accounts suggested that the distinctive sandstone clock tower of the Prag Mahal (New Palace), right in the heart of the old city, was still standing.

AROUND BHUJ

Gandhidham

The new town of Gandhidham, near Kandla, was established to take refugees from the Sind following Partition. Gandhidham was similarly hard hit by the 2001 earthquake. The town has always contained little of interest to the traveller, although in time it will once again become the railhead for neighbouring Bhuj.

MANDVI

Mandvi was, prior to the earthquake, being promoted as a beach resort and the beach is generally good, long and clean, although, as in many towns along the coast, pollution is an increasing problem. The cleaner sections are away from the wind farm, down by the temple. The town also has a long history of shipbuilding. Mandvi is a pleasant seaside town with friendly people and is a good place to unwind. Remarkably, Mandvi remained relatively unscathed by the earthquake that ravaged Bhuj, a mere 60km to the north-east. Previously Bhuj was the only gateway for Mandvi and with such widespread damage to the region's roads, Mandvi will be difficult to reach for some time to come. That will change if the much talked-about ferry between Mandvi and Jamnagar ever gets underway.

Places to Stay & Eat

If you do make it here, the eccentric but enjoyable ***Rukmavati Guest House*** *(☎ 02834-20558)* is one hotel that is still operating. It's a converted hospital, still with hospital-style beds, and the owner uses the ambulance to conduct tours! Clean singles/doubles are Rs 150/300 (bucket hot water), dorms are a steep Rs 100, and checkout is 24 hours.

You could also try ***Maitri Guest House*** *(☎ 02834-20183, Bunder Rd)*, which has

Dharamanath: The Desolation of Kutch

The legends of Kutch speak of devastation. This is hardly surprising given the barren landscape and the tragic events of recent history.

One such legend speaks of a spiritual warrior named Dharamanath, who journeyed to Kutch in the 12th century to find a tranquil spot in which to practise penance. He settled himself under a tree near Raipur and, while focusing on matters spiritual, depended on the people of Raipur to attend to his material needs. However, the Raipurians were not exactly forthcoming so, in a fit of rage, Dharamanath invoked a curse upon them. The city became desolate and its inhabitants hastily removed themselves to Mandvi. Dharamanath, overcome by remorse, resolved to climb the highest hill he could find, in order to engage in a penance commensurate with his vengeful act. After being rejected by two hills, which refused to carry the burden of his guilt, he climbed *backwards* up a third hill – Dhinodar – and there proceeded to stand on his head...for 12 years. The gods, concerned at this excess, pleaded with Dharamanath to cease his penance. Dharamanath acceded – on condition that wherever his gaze fell, that region should become barren. Casting his gaze before him, the seas receded, leaving a barren, desolate wasteland – the Great Rann of Kutch.

On the highest peak of Dhinodar, a shrine dedicated to Dharamanath contains a red besmeared stone, which allegedly bore the head of the inverted ascetic during his extraordinary act of penance.

Dharamanath founded a community of sadhus at Than, known as the *Kanphata* (split eared), because they had to split open their ears upon joining. This is still done today with a heavy ring.

been recommended by a number of travellers. Clean rooms with private bathroom (hot water) cost Rs 150/200. ***Sahara Guest House*** *(☎ 02834-20272)*, in the town centre, is also good. Rooms for Rs 100/175 come with hot water and TV.

For meals, look out for ***Zorba the Buddha***, in the heart of the city; it's a good place for cheap thalis (Rs 30).

LITTLE RANN OF KUTCH

The Little Rann of Kutch, the barren expanse of 'desert' (actually salt plains) which divides Gujarat's western region of Kutch from the rest of Gujarat, was described by one traveller as 'a striking desert of mud, salt and mirages'.

Before setting out, consider the following traveller's advice:

> The Rann can be treacherously difficult to explore as the desert consists of salt deposited at a time when the area formed part of the delta of the River Indus. This means that rain can quickly turn parts of the desert into a sea of mud, and what to the untrained eye looks like solid ground may in fact be a thin crust of dry silt with soft mud underneath. Hence it is essential to have someone along who is familiar with local conditions.
>
> **Krys Kazmierczak, UK**

The Little Rann of Kurch is home to the last remaining population of khur (Asiatic wild ass) in India. There's also a large bird population, particularly of lesser flamingos; the area is one of the few places in India where the flamingos are known to breed normally. Both are protected in the 4953-sq-km Little Rann sanctuary, which is approached from Dhrangadhra (see the boxed text 'Warning' earlier in this chapter).

The Asiatic wild ass, of which there are about 2100 in the sanctuary, survives off the flat, grass-covered expanses or islands, known as *bets*, which spring up during the monsoon. This remarkable creature is capable of running at an average speed of 24km/h for up to two hours and can even reach speeds of 70km/h over shorter distances.

The small town of **Zainabad**, 105km north-west of Ahmedabad, is very close to the Little Rann of Kutch. Desert Courses (☎/fax 02757-41333 or 079-6752883 in Ahmedabad) is a family-run tour company that organises interesting safari and cultural tours on the Little Rann. Prices are about Rs 1900 per day.

The same family runs ***Camp Zainabad***, offering *kooba* (traditional thatch-roofed huts) with private bathrooms in a peaceful setting. It costs about Rs 1800 per person per night, including breakfast, dinner and unlimited safaris. Advance booking is advised. The self-contained huts are basic but comfortable.

One guide who has come highly recommended by a number of travellers is Devji Bhai Dhamechs, a wildlife photographer based in Dhrangadhra (☎ 02754-50560, fax 50300). You can also stay at his home for Rs 1200 for two nights which includes food and accommodation (advance notice is essential). You could also try the ***Government Rest House***.

Permission is required to enter the sanctuary. Contact the Deputy Conservator of Forests in Dhrangadhra (☎ 02754-23016). The best time to visit the sanctuary is from October to June.

Dhrangadhra is on the Gandhidham to Ahmedabad rail route 170km (3½ hours) from Gandhidham, and 130km (three hours) from Ahmedabad.

To get to Zainabad by road from Ahmedabad, you can take a bus to Dasada, 12km north-east of Zainabad (Rs 28, 2½ hours). From here Desert Courses does free pickups, or there are local buses instead. There are also direct buses from Rajkot. Desert Courses can arrange taxis for approximately Rs 2.50 per kilometre.

Madhya Pradesh & Chhatisgarh

Madhya Pradesh is the geographical heartland of India, but it has recently shrunk in size. After years of lobbying by members of Madhya Pradesh's assembly, the new state of Chhatisgarh came into existence in November 2000, with its capital the city of Raipur.

The movement towards an independent Chhatisgarh can be traced back almost 80 years when it was first argued that the area was culturally and linguistically distinct from Madhya Pradesh. Consisting of the south-eastern corner of the old state, Chhatisgarh is industrially backward, the infrastructure is poor, drought is a major problem and there is little in the way of tourist attractions. The government, however, has promised a focus on education, particularly literacy, to help deal with the many issues facing the new state.

Most of Madhya Pradesh is a high plateau and in summer it can be very dry and hot. Together with Chhatisgarh, it also has the highest percentage of forest in India, sheltering a wide variety of wildlife, including 22% of the world's tiger population. Virtually all phases of Indian history have left their mark on Madhya Pradesh, historically known as Malwa. There are still many pre-Aryan Gond and Bhil Adivasis (tribal people) in the state, but Madhya Pradesh is overwhelmingly Indo-Aryan.

Some of Madhya Pradesh's attractions are remote and isolated: Khajuraho, with its fabulous temples, is a long way from anywhere in the north of the state; Jabalpur, with its marble rocks, is near the centre of the state; Kanha National Park, famous for its tigers, is 160km south-east of Jabalpur.

Most of the state's other attractions are on or near the main Delhi to Mumbai railway line. From Agra (in Uttar Pradesh), just across the state border, you can head south through Gwalior (with its magnificent fort) to Sanchi, Bhopal, Ujjain, Indore and Mandu.

Madhya Pradesh is part of what is known as the Hindi belt, a region of northern India inhabited predominantly by Hindus.

Madhya Pradesh & Chhatisgarh at a Glance

Population: 66.1 million
Area: 443,446 sq km
Capital: Bhopal (Madhya Pradesh) & Raipur (Chhatisgarh)
Main Language: Hindi
When to Go: Sept to Feb

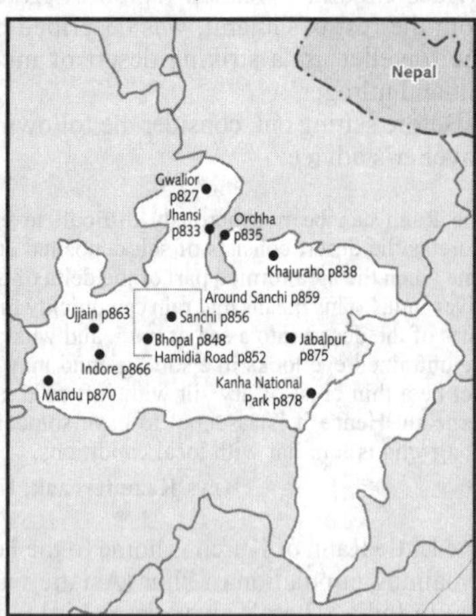

- Admire the exquisite temples in Khajuraho and try not to blush in front of India's visual Kamasutra
- Sleep in a fortified palace on the river island of Orchha and explore the island's magnificent temples
- Prepare for stupa (monument) overdose at Sanchi, whose ancient hilltop structures were built by Emperor Ashoka
- Step 12,000 years back in time in Bhimbetka's caves and marvel at rock paintings depicting prehistoric India
- Be ferried around Kanha and Bandhavgarh National Parks by elephant or by jeep and you may spot that elusive tiger!

History

Signs of human habitation date back 12,000 years with the rock cave paintings at Bhimbetka near Bhopal – excavations have revealed a cultural succession from the late Stone Age. Madhya Pradesh's history, however, can be traced back to the 3rd century BC, when Ashoka, the great Buddhist emperor, controlled the Maurya empire in Malwa. (At Sanchi you can see the Buddhist centre founded by Ashoka, the most important reminder of him in India today.)

The Mauryans were followed by the Sungas and then by the Guptas, before the Huns swept across the state. Around a thousand years ago, the Parmaras ruled in south-west Madhya Pradesh; they're chiefly remembered for Raja Bhoj, who gave his name to the city of Bhopal and also ruled over Indore and Mandu.

From AD 950 to 1050 the Chandelas constructed the fantastic series of temples at Khajuraho in the north of the state.

Between the 12th and 16th centuries, the region saw continuing struggles between Hindu and Muslim rulers and invaders. The fortified city of Mandu in the south-west was frequently the scene for these battles,

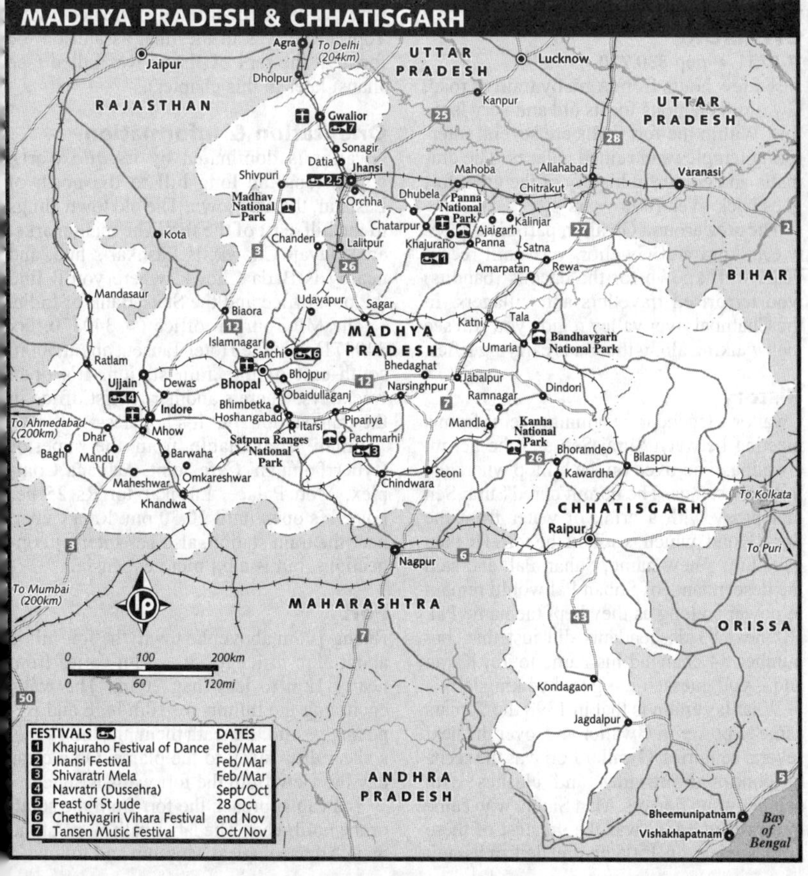

but finally the Mughals overcame Hindu resistance and controlled the region. The Mughals, however, met their fate at the hands of the Marathas who, in turn, fell to the British in the 18th century.

With the States Reorganization Act of 1956, several former states were combined to form Madhya Pradesh. In 2000 the boundaries of Madhya Pradesh changed again (see Chhatisgarh later in this chapter).

Northern Madhya Pradesh

GWALIOR

☎ 0751 • pop 830,720

Just a few hours from Agra by train or road, Gwalior is famous for its old and very large fort. Within the fort walls are several interesting temples and ruined palaces. The dramatic and colourful history of the great fort goes back over 1000 years.

The area around Gwalior, particularly between Agra and Gwalior, was until recent years well known for the dacoits (bandits) who terrorised travellers and villagers. In the Chambal river valley region you still see men walking along the roads carrying rifles.

History

Gwalior's legendary beginning stems from a meeting between Suraj Sen and the hermit Gwalipa, who lived on the hilltop where the fort now stands. The hermit cured Suraj Sen of leprosy with a drink of water from the Suraj Kund, which is still in the fort. He then gave him a new name, Suhan Pal, and said the descendants of Suhan Pal would remain in power so long as they kept the name Pal. His next 83 descendants did just that, but number 84 changed his name to Tej Karan and – you guessed it – goodbye kingdom.

What is certain is that in 1398 the Tomars came to power in Gwalior and, over the next several centuries, Gwalior Fort was the scene of continual intrigues and clashes with neighbouring powers. Man Singh, who came to power in 1486, was the greatest of these Tomar rulers. In 1505 he repelled an assault on the fort by Sikander Lodi of Delhi, but in 1516 the fort was besieged by Ibrahim Lodi. Man Singh died early in the siege, but his son held out for a year. Later the Mughals, under Babur, took the fort and held it until 1754 when the Marathas captured it.

For the next 50 years the fort changed hands on several occasions, including twice to the British. It finally passed into the hands of the Scindias. At the time of the Indian Uprising in 1857, the maharaja remained loyal to the British but his troops didn't, and in mid-1858 the fort was the scene of some of the final, and most dramatic, events of the Uprising. It was near here that the British finally defeated Tantia Topi and it was in the final assault on the fort that the rani of Jhansi was killed (see Jhansi later in this chapter).

Orientation & Information

Gwalior is dominated by its *qila* (fort), which tops the long hill to the north of Lashkar, the new town. The old town clings to the hill, east of the fort. The main market area, Jayaji Chowk, is Lashkar's hub, and nearby is Bada Chowk, where you'll find the post office and the State Bank of India.

The MP Tourism office (☎ 340370, fax 340371) is in the Hotel Tansen, about 500m south-east of the train station. It's open weekdays. There's another tourist office in the train station, but it's hopeless.

Email is available from the superior Cyber Point 'n' Cafe Joint, Ashiana Complex, Moti Palace, Lashkar for Rs 25 per hour. It's open until 10.30 pm. Raja Cyber, near the train station, also has Internet connections, but is a bit more expensive.

Fort

Rising 100m above the town, the fort hill is about 3km in length. Its width varies from nearly 1km to less than 200m. The walls encircling the hilltop are 10m high and imposingly solid. Beneath them, the hill face is a sheer drop away to the plains. On a clear day the view from the fort walls is superb.

You can approach the fort from the south or the north-east. The latter path starts at the State Archaeological Museum and follows a wide, winding slope to the doors of the Man Singh Palace (see North-Eastern Entrance). The southern path, via Urbai Gate, is a long, gradual ascent by road.

An atmospheric sound-and-light show is held every evening at the open-air amphitheatre outside the Man Singh Palace. The English version is at 7.30 pm (the 6.30 pm showing is in Hindi); tickets are Rs 150.

There are several things to see in and around the fort, although most of the enclosed area is simply open space, fields and the grounds occupied by the prestigious private Scindia School.

The fort is open from 8 am to 5 pm daily, and admission is US$5 (Rs 230), plus a Rs 25 video-camera fee.

Jain Sculptures The long ascent on the southern side climbs up through a ravine to Urbai Gate. On the rock faces flanking Gwalior Rd are many impressively large sculptures. Originally cut into the cliff faces in the mid-15th century, they were defaced by Babur's forces in 1527, but later repaired.

The sculptured images are in five main groups and are numbered. In the Arwahi group, image 20 is a 17m-high standing

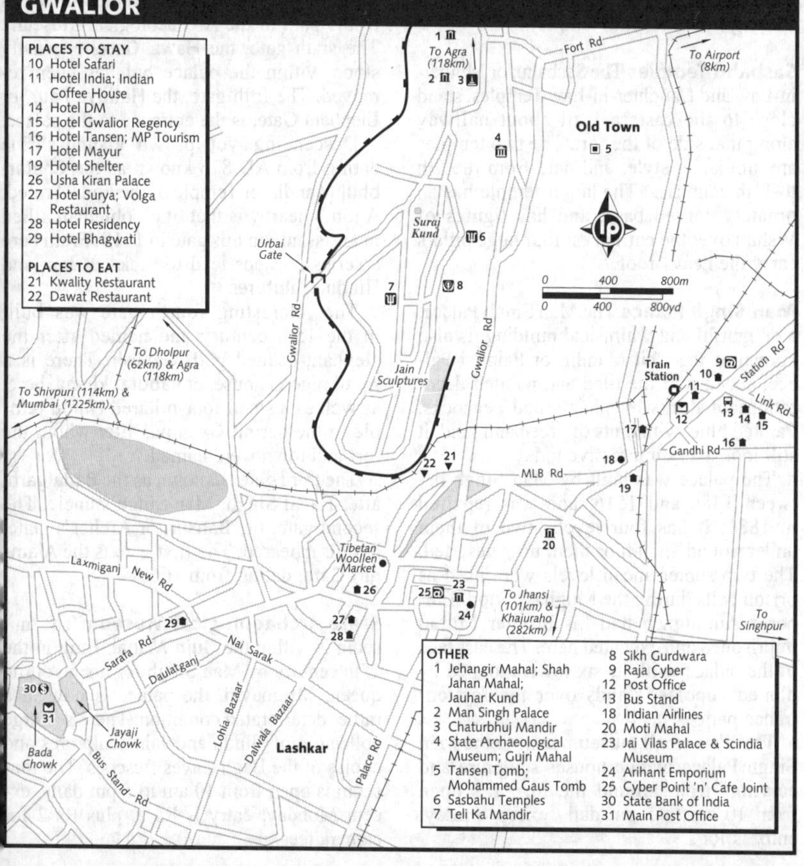

sculpture of Adinath, the first Jain *tirthankar* (teacher), while image 22 is a 10m-high seated figure of Nemnath, the 22nd Jain tirthankar. The south-eastern group is the most important and covers nearly 1km of the cliff face with more than 20 images.

Teli Ka Mandir Dating from about the 9th century, Teli Ka Mandir has since been restored. Its peculiar design incorporates a Dravidian roof with Indo-Aryan decorations (the whole temple is covered with sculptures). A Garuda (the man-bird vehicle of Vishnu) tops the 10m-high doorway.

Between the Teli Ka Mandir and the Sasbahu Temples is an impressive gleaming white **gurdwara** (Sikh temple).

Sasbahu Temples The Sasbahu, or Mother-in-Law and Daughter-in-Law Temples, stand close to the eastern wall about halfway along that side of the fort. The two temples are similar in style, and date from the 9th to 11th centuries. The larger temple has an ornately carved base, and has figures of Vishnu over the entrances; four huge pillars carry the heavy roof.

Man Singh Palace The Man Singh Palace, a delightful and whimsical building, is also known as the Chit Mandir, or Painted Palace, because of the tiled and painted decorations of ducks, elephants and peacocks. Painted blue, with hints of green and gold, it still looks very impressive today.

The palace was built by Man Singh between 1486 and 1516, and was repaired in 1881. It has four levels, two of them underground and all of them now deserted. The two subterranean levels were used as prison cells during the Mughal period. Emperor Aurangzeb had his brother Murad imprisoned and executed here. The east face of the palace, with its six towers topped by domed cupolas, stands over the fort entrance path.

There's a small **museum** next to the Man Singh Palace, which houses sculpture and carvings from around the fort. It's open from 10 am to 5 pm daily except Friday; entry is Rs 2.

Other Palaces There are other palaces clustered within the northern end of the fort walls, though none are as interesting or as well preserved as the Man Singh Palace, including the **Jehangir Mahal** and the **Shah Jahan Mahal**, which has a very large and deep tank, the **Jauhar Kund**. It was here that the Rajput women of the harem committed mass *sati*, or self-immolation, after the raja was defeated in battle in 1232.

The **Karan Palace**, or Kirti Mandir, is a long, narrow two-storey building on the western side of the fort.

North-Eastern Entrance There is a whole series of gates as you descend the worn steps of the path to the Archaeological Museum. The sixth gate, the **Hawa Gate**, originally stood within the palace but has been removed. The fifth gate, the **Hathiya Paur**, or Elephant Gate, is the entrance to the palace.

Descending, you pass a Vishnu shrine dating from AD 876 known as the **Chatarbhuj Mandir**, or Temple of the Four-Armed. A tomb nearby is that of a nobleman killed in an assault on this gate in 1518. From here a series of steps lead to rock-cut Jain and Hindu **sculptures**.

The interesting fourth gate was built in the 15th century and named after the elephant-headed god, Ganesh. There is a small pigeon house, or **kabutar khana**, here, as well as a small four-pillared **Hindu temple** to the hermit Gwalipa, after whom the fort and town were named.

The third gate is known as the **Badalgarh**, after Badal Singh, Man Singh's uncle. The second gate, the **Bansur**, or Archer's Gate, has disappeared. The first gate is the **Alamgiri Gate**, dating from 1660.

State Archaeological Museum The museum is within the **Gujri Mahal**. Built in the 15th century by Man Singh for his favourite queen, Mrignayni, the palace is now in a rather deteriorated condition. There's a large collection of Hindu and Jain sculptures and copies of the Bagh Caves frescoes. The museum is open from 10 am to 5 pm daily, except Monday; entry is Rs 2, plus Rs 2 for camera fees.

Jai Vilas Palace & Scindia Museum

Although the current maharaja still lives in the palace of the Scindia family, 35 rooms are now a museum. This museum is full of the bizarre items Hollywood maharajas are supposed to collect, such as Belgian cut-glass furniture (including a rocking chair), and what looks like half the tiger population of India, all shot, stuffed and moth-eaten. Items in the modes of transport exhibit range from a Rolls Royce on rails to a German bubble car. Then there's a little room full of erotica, including a life-sized marble statue of Leda having her way with a swan. But the *piece de resistance* is a model railway that carried brandy and cigars around the dining table after dinner.

The main palace hall is impressive. The gold paint used around the room is said to weigh 58kg in total, and the two giant chandeliers are incredible. They each hold 248 candles, are 12.5m high and weigh 3.5 tonnes apiece – so heavy that before they were installed, elephants were suspended from the ceiling to check that it could take the weight.

If you go there by autorickshaw, ask for the museum, which is not at the palace entrance. The palace and museum are open 9.30 am to 5.30 pm daily, except Monday. Entry is a ridiculously royal Rs 175, plus a Rs 25/75 camera/video-camera fee.

Old Town

The old town of Gwalior lies to the north and east of the fort. The 1661 **Jama Masjid** is a fine old building, constructed of sandstone quarried from the fort hill. On the eastern side of town is the **tomb of Mohammed Gaus**, a Muslim saint who played a key role in Babur's acquisition of the fort. A good example of early Mughal architecture, it has hexagonal towers at its four corners.

Nearby is the smaller **tomb of Tansen**, a singer much admired by Akbar. Chewing the leaves of the tamarind tree near his grave is supposed to do wonders for your voice. It is a place of pilgrimage for musicians during October/November (see Special Events later), when the tree tends to look unseasonably autumnal, as it is stripped by visiting enthusiasts. To find it, follow Fort Rd from the north-eastern gate for about 15 minutes (on foot) and turn right onto a small road.

Organised Tours

Guides can be hired at the gates of the fort from around Rs 100 for two or three hours, although you can probably bargain them down. Official government-approved guides can be hired from the Arihant Emporium for Rs 255/380 for a half/full-day tour of the city for up to four people.

Special Events

The **Tansen Music Festival** is held around October/November each year and attracts classical musicians and vocalists from all over India. Free performances are usually staged at Tansen's tomb in the old town.

Places to Stay – Budget

Most decent hotels in this range are within walking distance of the train station or bus stand.

Hotel Mayur *(☎ 325559, Padav Rd)* is the best of the cheap places and is in a good location down a quiet alley, just a few minutes' walk across the bridge from the train station. A bed in the roomy, air-cooled dorm (no bunks) costs Rs 55. Spotless air-cooled singles/doubles with private bathroom start starting at Rs 120/150, up to Rs 300/350 with air-con. There is bucket hot water and squat toilets.

Hotel Safari *(☎ 340638, Station Rd)* is above shops on a busy road, but it's not bad value. Reasonably clean fan-cooled rooms with private bathroom (squat toilet) are Rs 135/170; deluxe rooms with TV and hot water are Rs 200/235.

Hotel India *(☎ 341983)*, in front of the train station, is not flash but it's pretty cheap and is convenient for an early morning departure. Rooms start at Rs 160/210 and there is a handy train timetable board in reception.

Hotel DM *(☎ 342083, Link Rd)* is a peaceful, friendly place that is away from the hustle and bustle but close to the bus stand. Rooms with private bathroom are good value at Rs 135/185; bigger rooms with TV are Rs 185/225. There's a restaurant.

Hotel Bhagwati *(☎ 310319)* is one of several cheap but unappealing places near the Jayaji Chowk area. Cell-like singles are Rs 80 and better (but dingy) doubles are Rs 120. All rooms have private bathroom, squat toilets and bucket hot water.

Places to Stay – Mid-Range & Top End

Hotel Tansen *(☎ 340370, fax 340371, 6A Gandhi Rd)*, an MP Tourism place, is pleasantly situated in a shady area about 500m south-east of the train station. Singles/doubles are spacious but not great value at Rs 390/450 (plus Rs 50 for an air-cooler), or Rs 650/750 with air-con. As with a lot of MP Tourism hotels, this place seems to be a breeding ground for mosquitoes. Checkout is at noon and there's a restaurant and bar.

Hotel Residency *(☎ 320743, Inder Ganj, Lashkar)* is an excellent, centrally located and reasonably priced hotel with clean rooms and constant hot water. Good-sized air-cooled rooms start at Rs 275/300.

Hotel Surya *(☎ 331183, fax 310083, Jayendra Ganj, Lashkar)* has plain but comfortable air-cooled rooms for Rs 275/350 and air-con rooms for Rs 375/450.

Hotel Gwalior Regency *(☎ 340670, fax 343520, Link Rd)* has stylish, centrally air-con rooms starting at Rs 750/975. It has a range of facilities, including a health club and swimming pool.

Hotel Shelter *(☎ 326209, Padav Rd)* has 70 rooms and is a comfortable if rather characterless place. Standard rooms with hand-held showers are Rs 450/650; air-con rooms start at Rs 650/850. It also has a bar and a restaurant.

Usha Kiran Palace *(☎ 323993, fax 321103, Jayendra Ganj, Lashkar)* is the town's top hotel. This serene former maharaja's palace with opulent furnishings is great for a splurge. Its huge rooms start at US$65/120.

Places to Eat

The ***Indian Coffee House*** below Hotel India is a good, cheap place, with *masala dosas* (curried vegetables in lentil-flour pancakes) for Rs 15, as well as other vegetarian snacks. It's staffed by the usual attentive waiters in fan-shaped headgear.

Kwality Restaurant is an air-con haven not too far from the southern fort gate (Urbai Gate) on MLB Rd. The food is fresh, the service is good and prices are reasonable, with large vegetarian mains from around Rs 38.

Dawat Restaurant, nearby on the same road, is classier than Kwality Restaurant and has slightly higher prices to match.

Volga Restaurant is at the Hotel Surya. There's nothing Russian about it, but very good Indian food is served.

The restaurant at ***Usha Kiran Palace*** is the place to eat out in style. The Mughlai food is excellent and it occasionally has a buffet as well as a la carte; mains start at around Rs 110.

Shopping

The Arihant Emporium, a government-approved shop, is a good place to start looking for local handicrafts. It specialises in semiprecious silver jewellery. A simple ring may cost Rs 80, a bracelet may be up to Rs 700 and an intricately styled necklace can cost around Rs 10,000. It also specialises in silver carvings, mainly in earth and plant colours. For more atmosphere and better prices have a wander around Jayaji Chowk.

Gwalior is also well known for sandstone carvings of deities and other traditional figures. Statues 2.5m-high can cost around Rs 500,000, while statues just under half a metre may be around Rs 10,000.

A Tibetan Woollen Market operates during the winter months. The products are of high quality and bargaining is definitely required.

Getting There & Away

Air Indian Airlines (☎ 326872), on MLB Rd, has a 'hopping' flight from Delhi through Gwalior (US$70) to Bhopal (US$80), Indore (US$105) and Mumbai (US$160). It flies from Delhi on Monday and Friday, and returns to Delhi via the same route on these days.

Bus From the government bus stand on Link Rd there are regular services to Agra (Rs 56, three hours), Jhansi (Rs 46, three hours) and Shivpuri (Rs 50, 2½ hours), as well as a few departures for Bhopal (Rs 175), Ujjain (Rs 187), Indore (Rs 224) and Jabalpur (Rs 200). There are two buses a day at 7 and 8.30 am to Khajuraho (Rs 129, nine hours), but it's better to take the train to Jhansi and a bus from there.

Train Gwalior is on the main Delhi to Mumbai railway line. The speedy *Shatabdi Express* links Gwalior with Delhi (Rs 495/985 in chair/executive class, 3¼ hours), Agra (Rs 255/505, 1¼ hours), Jhansi (Rs 230/455, one hour) and Bhopal (Rs 545/1110, 4½ hours). If you've got the money but not the time you could use this reliable service for a day trip to Gwalior from Agra.

On other express trains it's five hours to Delhi (Rs 79/415 in 2nd/1st class, 317km), two hours to Agra (Rs 36/189, 118km), 12 hours to Indore (Rs 205/693 in sleeper/1st class, 652km) and 24 hours to Mumbai (Rs 310/1050, 1225km).

Slow passenger trains are useful if you want to get off at Sonagir or Datia on the way to Jhansi, or Dholpur on the way to Agra.

Getting Around

To/From the Airport Autorickshaws plying this 8km route cost approximately Rs 90. A taxi to/from the airport will cost around Rs 200.

Local Transport Gwalior is spread out and congested with traffic, so finding your way around on foot can prove futile. Autorickshaws are plentiful but the meters are just fashion accessories; Rs 10 should cover short trips. A ride from the train station to Bada Chowk, the main square in Lashkar, will cost Rs 20, but you'll have to bargain. The frightening-looking tempos (three-wheeled minivans) are useful and cheap if you can work out where they're going. They run along fixed routes around the city; the fare is Rs 6 from the train station to Bada Chowk.

SHIVPURI

The old summer capital of the Scindias was at Shivpuri, 114km south-west of Gwalior and 94km west of Jhansi. Set in formal gardens, the **chhatris** (tombs) are the main attraction here. With Mughal pavilions and Hindu *sikhara* (temple spires) spires, these beautiful memorials to the Scindia rulers are inlaid with *pietra dura* (inlaid marble), like the Taj Mahal. The chhatri of Madho Rao Scindia faces his mother's chhatri across the tank.

Near Shivpuri, **Madhav National Park** is essentially a deer park (entry Rs 150). On the edge of the park is the Sakhya Sagar lake. Swimming from the old boat club pier here might not be wise as there are crocodiles in the lake.

Most of the accommodation is in MP Tourism lodges, but there are a couple of private options.

Chinkara Motel (☎ *07492-21297*) is MP Tourism's place in Shivpuri. Singles/doubles cost Rs 350/450.

Tourist Village (☎ *07492-23760*) is near Bhadaiya Kund, only a few kilometres from Madhav National Park. It has comfortable rooms in attractive cottages for Rs 390/490, or Rs 590/690 with air-con.

There are frequent buses to/from Gwalior (Rs 50, 2½ hours) and Jhansi (Rs 40, four hours).

DHOLPUR

Between Gwalior and Agra, actually in a part of Rajasthan that separates Madhya Pradesh and Uttar Pradesh, Dholpur was the scene of a pitched battle between Aurangzeb's sons to determine who would succeed him as emperor of the rapidly declining Mughal empire. The **Shergarh Fort** in Dholpur is very old and is now in ruins.

West of Dholpur near Bari is the **Khanpur Mahal**, a pavilioned palace built for Shah Jahan but never occupied.

Slow passenger trains between Agra and Gwalior stop at Dholpur.

CHANDERI

At the time of Mandu's greatest power, Chanderi was an important place, as indicated by the many ruined palaces, caravanserais (inns), mosques and tombs – all in a Pathan style similar to that of Mandu (see that section later in this chapter). The **Koshak Mahal** is a ruined Muslim palace worth a look.

Today the town is chiefly known for its gold brocades and saris. The Chanderi cotton sari is ideal in summer and is made in a variety of sophisticated weaves with subtle hues. The silk and silk-cotton saris show influences of Varanasi weaving, and can range anywhere in price from Rs 400 to 2000. Chanderi silk saris usually have a rich gold border and the more expensive weave will have gold checks with *butis*, or lotus roundels.

Accommodation in the town includes a ***Circuit House*** and the ***Rest House*** near the bus stand.

Chanderi is 33km west of Lalitpur, which is 90km south of Jhansi on the main railway line.

JHANSI

☎ 0517 • pop 456,895

Jhansi, 101km south of Gwalior, is actually just across the border in Uttar Pradesh, but for convenience we've included it here. Although Jhansi has played a colourful role in Indian history, for most visitors it's simply a convenient transit point for those heading to Khajuraho or Orchha (only 18km away).

History

Jhansi was an important centre under Bir Singh Deo around the 17th century. In 1803 the British East India Company gradually assumed control over the state. The last of a string of rajas died in 1853 and the rani, Lakshmibai, was forcibly retired by the British (who had conveniently passed a law letting them take over any princely state under their patronage if the ruler died without a male heir).

The rani was unhappy about her forced retirement and when the Indian Uprising burst into flame four years later, she was at the forefront of the rebellion at Jhansi. The British contingent in Jhansi were all massacred, but the following year the rebel forces were still quarrelling among themselves and the British were able to retake Jhansi. The rani then fled to Gwalior and, in a valiant last stand, she rode out against the British, disguised as a man, and was killed. She has since become a heroine of the Indian Independence movement.

Orientation & Information

The old town is behind the fort, 3km from the train station. The town is quite spread out so you'll need to use autorickshaws to get around.

The Uttar Pradesh and Madhya Pradesh state governments have tourist booths at the train station, though neither of them is particularly good. There's a helpful UP tourist office (☎ 441267), open 10 am to 5 pm weekdays, at the Hotel Veerangana.

The State Bank of India, open 10 am to 4 pm weekdays and to 1 pm Saturday, accepts only American Express (Amex) travellers cheques (in US dollars). Try Hotel Sita or Jhansi Hotel for changing cash.

There's an Internet Centre next to the Hotel Sita. It's well signposted, costs Rs 60 per hour and is open until 11 pm.

Things to See

Once used by the Indian army, **Jhansi Fort** was built in 1613 by Bir Singh Deo of Orchha. Today, there is nothing much to see, apart from the excellent views from the fort ramparts. Guides (about Rs 50) are on hand to show you around and tell you some colourful tales. Watch out for the band of aggressive monkeys. The fort is open from sunrise to sunset daily, entry is US$5 or Rs 230.

Just below the walls as you approach the fort is a bizarre blood-and-guts diorama of the battle in which the rani of Jhansi died.

Rani Mahal, the former palace of Rani Lakshmibai, consists of arched chambers around an open courtyard and was built in the 18th century. The palace is now a museum containing hundreds of 9th to 12th century sculptures. The durbar hall on the 2nd floor features an original painted wood-panelled ceiling. Rani Mahal is open 9.30 am to 5.30 pm daily; entry is Rs 25 (video-camera fees are an extra Rs 25).

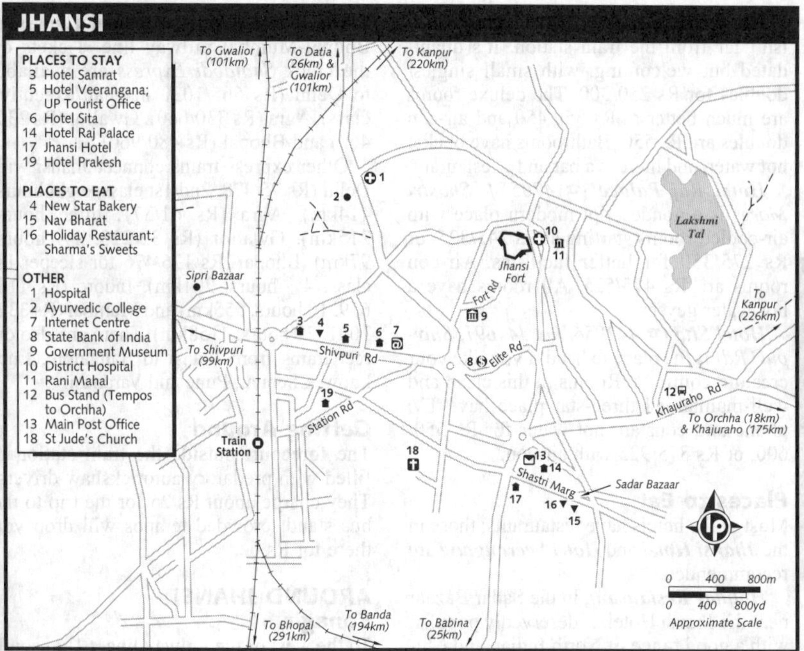

On the road leading up to the fort is the large, but largely empty, **Government Museum**. Its four galleries house an interesting collection of prehistoric tools; terracotta pieces dating from the 4th century BC; and sculptures, costumes and weapons from the Chandela dynasty. It is open from 10.30 am to 4.30 pm daily, except Monday and every second Saturday; entry is Rs 2.

Special Events

The **Jhansi Festival** is a lively arts and cultural event held in February/March. It is a locally organised program of music, arts and dance.

Jhansi is also known for the **Feast of St Jude** on 28 October, when thousands of eager – if not downright desperate – Christian pilgrims converge on St Jude's Church to plead their case to the patron saint of lost causes. The big day is preceded by a 10-day novena. The church is said to contain a relic of St Jude.

Places to Stay

Jhansi has a range of accommodation, much of it strung along Shivpuri Rd.

Hotel Veerangana *(☎ 442402, Shivpuri Rd)* is a UP Tourism place with dorms at Rs 60 and singles/doubles from Rs 200/275, up to Rs 525/600 with air-con (geyser hot water). Although it's a bit run-down, the hotel is a large place with a garden and a good restaurant.

Hotel Samrat *(☎ 444943, Shivpuri Rd)* is pretty good value, with rooms starting at Rs 200/250 with private bathroom (bucket hot water) or Rs 250/275 with air-cooler and TV.

Jhansi Hotel *(☎ 470360, Shastri Marg)* is one of the best in town for old-fashioned charm. It was a hotel in British times and touches of the Raj are still evident. Big, slightly ragged doubles (bucket hot water) with colonial furniture are Rs 475 to 575. The restaurant here is very good, and the bar is open all day.

Hotel Prakash *(☎ 448822, Station Rd)* isn't far from the train station. It's dilapidated but welcoming, with small singles/doubles for Rs 250/300. The deluxe rooms are much better at Rs 350/450 and air-con doubles are Rs 550. Bathrooms have bucket hot water, and there is a bar and a restaurant.

Hotel Raj Palace *(☎ 470554, Shastri Marg)* is a nondescript modern place with air-cooled rooms starting at Rs 245/325, or Rs 275/350 for better facilities. Air-con rooms are Rs 475/525. All rooms have a hot-water geyser.

Hotel Sita *(☎ 442956, fax 444691, Shivpuri Rd)* is the place to head if you like your creature comforts. Rooms in this clean and well-maintained three-star place have TV, phone and constant hot water for Rs 550/600, or Rs 875/925 with air-con.

Places to Eat

Most of the hotels have restaurants; those in the ***Jhansi Hotel*** and ***Hotel Veerangana*** are recommended.

Holiday Restaurant, in the Sadar Bazaar near the Jhansi Hotel, is deservedly popular, with a good range of North Indian and Chinese dishes, and tea served in fine china. Vegetarian dishes are between Rs 20 and Rs 35. Nearby, ***Nav Bharat*** is a creditable second to Holiday Restaurant. Both places have good ice-cream parlours.

New Star Bakery *(Shivpuri Rd)* conjures up excellent sweets, which you can enjoy with a coffee from the espresso machine set up by the road out the front.

Getting There & Away

Bus Deluxe buses to Khajuraho leave from the train station at 5.30 and 11 am (Rs 85, 4½ hours). Local buses to Khajuraho (Rs 75, 5½ hours) leave more frequently from the bus stand east of town. Head to this bus stand for services to many other places including Gwalior (Rs 40, three hours), Shivpuri (Rs 40, four hours) and Datia (Rs 15, one hour). For Kanha National Park, there are buses to Jabalpur (Rs 150). For Orchha, the tempos from here are better. They cost Rs 10 for the 40-minute journey and leave when (very) full. Buses to Orchha cost Rs 8.

Train Jhansi is on the main Delhi-Agra-Bhopal-Mumbai railway line. Tickets on the crack *Shatabdi Express* are available to Delhi (Rs 565/1030 in chair/executive class), Agra (Rs 330/660), Gwalior (Rs 230/460) and Bhopal (Rs 480/960).

Other express trains connect Jhansi with Delhi (Rs 95/478, 2nd/1st class, eight hours, 414km), Agra (Rs 61/371, three hours, 215km), Gwalior (Rs 32/223, 1½ hours, 97km), Bhopal (Rs 176/476 for sleeper/1st class, 4½ hours, 291km), Indore (Rs 116/659, 10 hours, 555km) and Mumbai (Rs 332/1061, 22 hours, 1158km). There are also direct trains from Jhansi to Bangalore, Lucknow, Chennai, Pune and Varanasi.

Getting Around

The forecourt outside the train station is filled with predatory autorickshaw drivers. They charge about Rs 25 for the trip to the bus stand; crowded tempos will drop you there for Rs 6.

AROUND JHANSI

Sonagir

To the west of the railway line, 61km south of Gwalior, a large group of white **Jain temples** is scattered along a hill. It's one of those strange, dream-like apparitions that so often seem simply to materialise in India. Slow trains between Gwalior and Jhansi stop at Sonagir, not far from the temples.

Datia

Only 26km north of Jhansi, Datia makes an interesting side trip. The main attraction is the deserted seven-storey **palace** of Bir Singh Deo, an impressive building with some rooms still containing murals. The town is surrounded by a stone wall and the palace is to the west.

The best way to get there is on one of the frequent buses from Jhansi (Rs 15, one hour), or hop on a passenger train heading towards Gwalior.

ORCHHA

☎ 07680

Once the capital city of the Bundalas, Orchha (Hidden Place) is now just a village, se ımong a wonderful complex of well-›reserved palaces and temples. The main ›alaces were protected inside fortified walls ›n an island in the Betwa River. It's defi-ıitely worth a visit and a lot of travellers are ›eginning to discover Orchha's peaceful ›eauty. Tour groups do it in a couple of ıours but it's a very relaxing place to stay, ınd you can even get a room in part of the ›alace here.

listory

)rchha was founded in 1531 and remained he capital of a powerful Rajput kingdom ıntil 1783, when nearby Tikamgarh became he new capital. Bir Singh Deo ruled from)rchha between 1605 and 1627, and built he Jhansi Fort. A favourite of the Mughal 'rince Salim, he feuded with Akbar and in 602 narrowly escaped the emperor's dis-›leasure; his kingdom was all but ruined by ›kbar's forces. Then in 1605 Prince Salim ›ecame Emperor Jehangir, and for the next 2 years Bir Singh Deo was a powerful fig-re. In 1627, Shah Jahan became emperor nd Bir Singh once again found himself out ›f favour; his attempt at revolt was put own by the 13-year-old Aurangzeb.

Orchha's golden age was during the first alf of the 17th century. When Jehangir vis-ted the city in 1606, a special palace, the ehangir Mahal, was constructed for him. ater, both Shah Jahan and Aurangzeb aided the city.

nformation

'he helpful MP Tourism office is at the Iotel Sheesh Mahal.

Cash and travellers cheques can be hanged at the Canara Bank on the main ›ad; it's open from 10.30 am to 2.30 pm, Ionday to Friday, and to 12.30 pm on Sat-rday. You can only change US$100 or JK£50 here per day.

There were no email facilities at the time f research, but this may change.

Entry to Orchha's sites is Rs 30, making extremely good value in comparison to ıe escalating prices at similar attractions in ıe state. Make sure you hold on to your cket as it includes all the palaces, temples and the museum. It costs an extra Rs 20/50 for camera/video-camera fees and the sites are all open from 9 am to 5 pm.

Palaces

Crossing the bridge over the Betwa River to the fortified island brings you to three 17th-century palaces. The **Jehangir Mahal** is an impressive, rambling complex with good views of the countryside from the upper levels. There's a small **archaeological museum** on the ground floor. The **Raj Mahal & Assembly Hall** nearby has superb murals. Below the Jehangir Mahal is the smaller

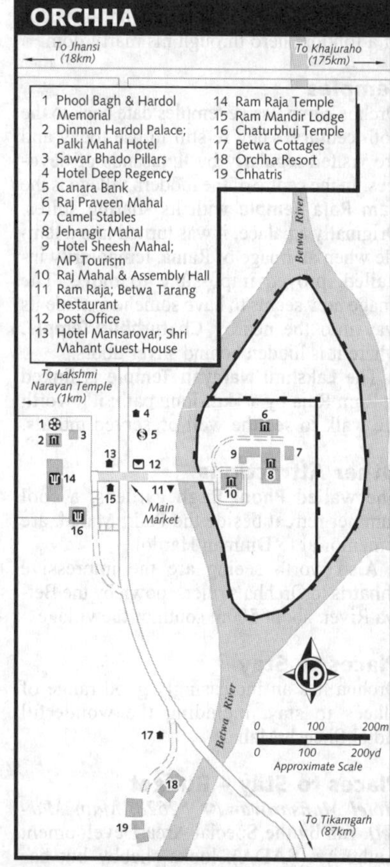

Raj Praveen Mahal, a palace built near a garden. The *hammam* (Turkish baths) and camel stables are nearby. MP Tourism has an excellent personal headset tour; you follow the arrows painted on the floor of the palaces in sync with the commentary. The English narration, sound effects and backing music really bring the empty rooms to life. To hire a headset costs Rs 50, plus a Rs 500 deposit.

On the other side of the village, **Dinman Hardol's Palace** (also called Palki Mahal), next to the Ram Raja Temple, is also interesting. The son of Bir Singh Deo, Dinman Hardol, committed suicide (or was poisoned) to 'prove his innocence' over an affair with his brother's wife, thus achieving the status of a folklore hero through his martyrdom.

Temples

Orchha's impressive temples date back to the 16th century. They're still in use today and are visited regularly by thousands of devotees. In the centre of the modern village is the **Ram Raja Temple** with its soaring spires. Originally a palace, it was turned into a temple when an image of Rama, temporarily installed, proved impossible to move. The image now seems to have somehow made its way into the nearby **Chaturbhuj Temple**, where it is hidden behind silver doors.

The **Lakshmi Narayan Temple** is linked to Ram Raja by a 1km-long path; it's worth the walk to see the well-preserved murals.

Other Attractions

The walled **Phool Bagh** gardens, a cool summer retreat beside the Palki Mahal, are a memorial to Dinman Hardol.

Also worth seeing are the impressive **chhatris** to Orchha's rulers, down by the Betwa River, about 500m south of the village.

Places to Stay

Orchha has an increasingly good range of places to stay, including the wonderful Hotel Sheesh Mahal.

Places to Stay – Budget

Hotel Mansarovar *(☎ 52628, Main Market)*, run by the Special Area Development Authority (SADA), looks shabby but has clean singles/doubles for Rs 50/75 with shared bathroom (squat toilets).

Shri Mahant Guest House *(☎ 52715)* is a newly opened place right next to Hotel Mansarovar. It's possibly the best budget option in Orchha. Spotless rooms with tiled private bathroom (bucket hot water) are Rs 150, Rs 200 or Rs 250 depending on the space you want. Some rooms have squat toilets. It's very friendly and the balcony is an excellent meeting place.

Palki Mahal Hotel, another SADA place (check in at Hotel Mansarovar), is atmospherically set in part of the former palace of Dinman Hardol – though the rooms are anything but palatial. A dorm is Rs 15, or simple doubles with shared bathroom are Rs 90. It's popular with backpackers.

Ram Mandir Lodge *(☎ 52669)*, opposite Mansarovar, has basic but clean doubles with shared bathroom (bucket hot water and squat toilets) starting at Rs 100, and a balcony that overlooks the main street.

Places to Stay – Mid-Range & Top End

Hotel Deep Regency *(☎ 52608)* on the way into town from Jhansi is a good choice if you like big bathrooms. Very clean doubles with fan are Rs 450 and bathrooms have squat and sit-down toilets (bucket hot water). Unfortunately, the extra space used for the bathrooms has been nabbed from the hallways, which are extremely narrow.

MP Tourism runs the following two places in Orchha; both are fairly upmarket.

Betwa Cottages *(☎ 52618)*, in a peaceful location by the river about 500m from the village, is set in a spacious, well-tended garden with good views of the palace. Singles/doubles are Rs 490/590, or Rs 690/790 with air-con.

Hotel Sheesh Mahal *(☎ 52624)*, in a converted wing of the Jehangir Mahal, must be the most romantic place to stay in Madhya Pradesh. The standard rooms, with large bathrooms, colonial furniture and views into the palace courtyard, are Rs 490/590 plus tax. The real luxury is found in the Royal Apartment (Rs 2990), with its own porch and dining area, huge marble bath room and superb views over Orchha, or the equally luxurious room below it (Rs 1990). Book ahead, as the hotel is often full.

Orchha Resort *(☎ 0517-452759 for bookings)* is a swish hotel that's been plonked right in front of the ancient chhatris. The place does nothing for Orchha's character, but if you want ultramodern luxury it costs Rs 1750/2950.

Places to Eat

There are a few restaurants in the village on the road running between the Jehangir Mahal and the market. ***Ram Raja***, near the bridge is vegetarian and pretty good. ***Betwa Tarang Restaurant***, next door, is a bit more upmarket with continental, Chinese and Indian (most curry dishes around Rs 30) cuisine. It's upstairs off the street and has an outdoor area.

For those with a sweet tooth there are lots of ***sweet shops*** opposite Hotel Mansarovar. Some also do good snack food such as samosas.

The restaurant at the ***Hotel Sheesh Mahal*** is the best place to eat in Orchha and is a good spot for breakfast before exploring the palaces. Excellent buffet dinners with traditional entertainment are occasionally held on the upstairs terrace.

Getting There & Away

There are regular buses (Rs 8) and tempos (Rs 10) from the Jhansi bus stand for the 18km journey to Orchha. An autorickshaw will cost around Rs 100.

KHAJURAHO

☎ 07686 • pop 7665

Close behind the Taj and up there with Varanasi, Jaipur and Delhi, the temples of Khajuraho are one of India's major attractions. Once a great Chandela capital, Khajuraho is now a quiet village. In spite of the number of tourists, it's still a mellow place to spend a few days, though the attention from hawkers immediately outside the western temple enclosure can be irritating.

Many visitors come to Khajuraho in March for the spectacular dance festival (see Special Events later in this section).

Khajuraho is on the way from nowhere to nowhere, and while many travellers slot it in between Varanasi and Agra, it involves a lot of slow bus travel over small country roads. If you can afford it, flying is a good alternative.

Orientation

The modern village of Khajuraho is a cluster of hotels, restaurants, shops and stalls near the western group of temples. About 1km east of the bus stand is the old village of Khajuraho (known as Khajuraho Village). Around the old village are the temples of the eastern group and to the south are two further temples.

Information

Tourist Offices The Government of India tourist office (☎ 72347, ⓔ goito@bom6.vsnl.net.in), open from 9.30 am to 6 pm on weekdays, is the best place for information. There's also an office at the airport. The MP Tourism office is hardly worth visiting; it's hidden away at the Chandela Cultural Centre to the north of the modern village.

Money The State Bank of India is the best place to change money (US$200 is the maximum you can change per day). Canara Bank down behind the bus stand is less busy than the State Bank of India. There are a few private moneychangers in the modern village offering lower rates than the banks.

Email & Internet Access Try the Internet Hut near the Archaeological Museum; connections cost Rs 80 per hour. Be warned – power failures in town make connections haphazard. Private telephone booths sometimes provide Internet facilities, but they charge about Rs 120 per hour.

Guides Government of India approved guides are available from tourist offices or at Raja's Cafe and cost Rs 255/380 a half/full day for up to four people. Multilingual guides are an extra Rs 125. MP Tourism also has a novel headset tour of the western group of temples for Rs 50 (plus Rs 500 deposit). The narration is informative and easy to follow.

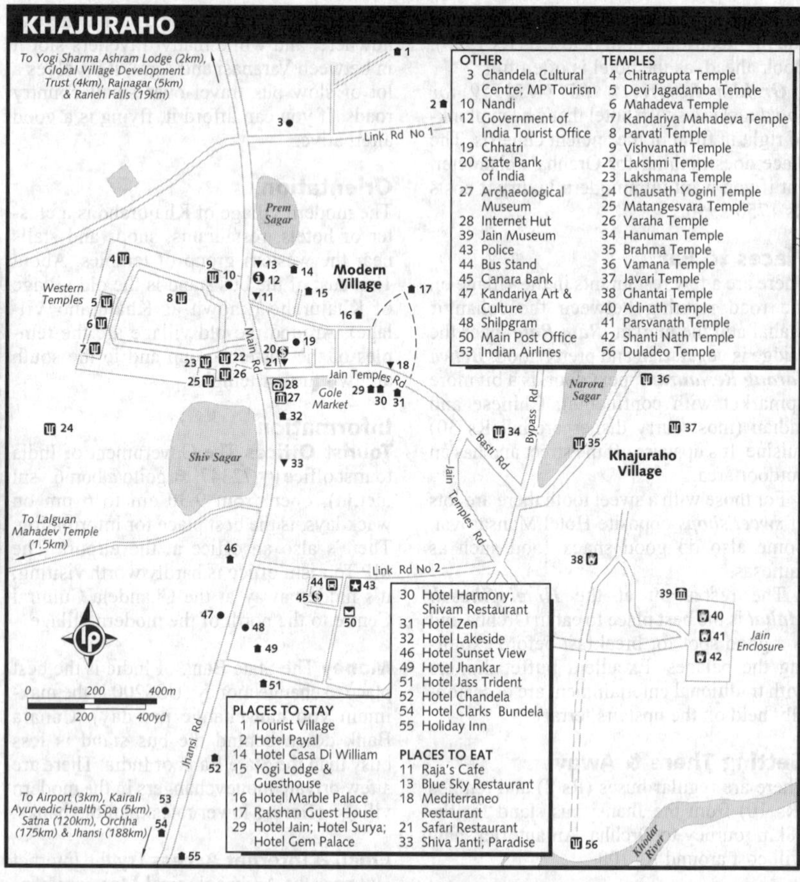

Temples

Khajuraho's temples were built by the Chandelas, a dynasty that survived for five centuries before falling victim to the Mughal onslaught. Most date from one century-long burst of creative genius from AD 950 to 1050. Almost as intriguing as the sheer beauty and size of the temples is the question of why and how they were built here. Khajuraho is a long way from anywhere and was probably just as far off the beaten track a thousand years ago as it is today. There is nothing of great interest or beauty to recommend it as a building site, there is no great population centre here and during the hot season Khajuraho is very hot and dry.

Having chosen such a strange site, how did the Chandelas manage to recruit the labour to turn their awesome dreams into stone? To build so many temples of such monumental size in just 100 years must have required a huge amount of human labour. Whatever their reasons, we can be thankful the Chandelas built Khajuraho where they did. Its very remoteness helped preserve it from the desecration Muslim invaders were only too ready to inflict on 'idolatrous' temples elsewhere in India.

The temples are superb examples of Indo-Aryan architecture, but it's the decorations with which they are so liberally embellished that have made Khajuraho famous. Around the temples are bands of exceedingly artistic stonework showing many aspects of Indian life a millennium ago – gods and goddesses, warriors and musicians, real and mythological animals.

But two elements appear over and over again and in far greater detail than anything else – women and sex. Stone figures of *apsaras*, or celestial maidens, appear on every temple. They pout and pose for all the world like pin-up models posing for the camera. In between are the *mithuna*, erotic figures running through a whole Kamasutra of positions and possibilities.

Western Group The main temples are in the western group; most are contained within a fenced enclosure that is very well maintained as a park. The enclosure is open from sunrise to half an hour before sunset (entry is a steep US$10, or Rs 460). Ask at the ticket office about the excellent Archaeological Survey of India guidebook to Khajuraho. It's often out of stock, but worth buying (Rs 20).

We describe the temples here in a clockwise direction around the loop; those outside of the enclosure are described later in this section.

Varaha Facing the large Lakshmana Temple are the Varaha Temple and the Lakshmi Temple. The former, dedicated to Vishnu's boar incarnation or Varaha avatar, faces the Matangesvara Temple. Inside this small, open shrine is a huge, solid and intricately carved figure of the boar incarnation, dating from around AD 900.

Lakshmana The large Lakshmana Temple is dedicated to Vishnu, although in design it is similar to the Kandariya Mahadev and Vishvanath Temples. It is one of the earliest of the western group of temples, dating from around AD 930 to 950, and is also one of the best preserved, with a full five-part floor plan and four subsidiary shrines. Around the temple are two bands of sculpture instead of the usual three; the lower one has fine figures of apsaras and some erotic scenes. Inside are excellent examples of apsaras acting as supporting brackets.

On the subsidiary shrine at the south-west corner is an image of an architect working with his students; it is thought this may be the temple's designer including himself in the grand plan. Around the base of the temple is a continuous frieze with scenes of battles, hunting and processions. The first metre or two consists of a highly energetic orgy, including one gentleman proving that a horse can be a person's best friend, while a stunned group of women look away in shock.

The temple platform gives you a good view of the Matangesvara Temple (see later in this section).

Kandariya Mahadeva This, the first of the temples on the common platform at the back of the western enclosure is not only the largest, it is also artistically and architecturally superior. Built from AD 1025 to 1050, it represents Chandela art at its finest. Although the four subsidiary shrines that once stood around the main temple are long gone, the central shrine is in superb condition and shows the typical five-part design of Khajuraho's temples.

The main spire is 31m high, and the temple is lavishly carved. The English archaeologist Cunningham counted 226 statues inside the temple and a further 646 outside – 872 in total with most of them nearly 1m high. The statues are carved around the temple in three bands and include gods, goddesses, beautiful women, musicians and, of course, some of the famed erotic groups. The mithuna on the Kandariya Mahadev include some of the most energetic eroticism to be seen at Khajuraho.

Mahadeva This small and mainly ruined temple stands on the same base as the Kandariya Mahadev and Devi Jagadamba Temples. Although small and insignificant compared with its mighty neighbours, it

MADHYA PRADESH & CHHATISGARH

Temple Terminology

The Khajuraho temples follow a fairly consistent and unique design pattern. Understanding the architectural conventions and some of the terms will help you enjoy their unique artistry. Basically, all the temples follow a five- or three-part layout.

You enter the temples through an entrance porch, known as the *ardhamandapa*. Behind this is the *mandapa* or hall. This leads into the main hall, or *mahamandapa*, supported with pillars and with a corridor around it. An *antarala*, or vestibule, then leads into the *garbhagriha*, the inner sanctum, where the image of the god to which the temple is dedicated is displayed. An enclosed corridor, the *pradakshina*, runs around this sanctum. The simpler three-part temples don't have a mandapa or pradakshina, but otherwise follow the same plan as the five-part temples.

Externally, the temples consist of successive waves of higher and higher towers culminating in the soaring *sikhara* or spire, which tops the sanctum. While the lower towers, over the mandapa or mahamandapa, may be pyramid-shaped, the shikhara is taller and curvilinear. The ornate, even baroque design of all these vertical elements is balanced by an equally ornate horizontal element from the bands of sculptures that run around the temples.

The whole temple sits upon a high terrace, known as the *adisthana*. Unlike temples in most other parts of India, these had no enclosing wall but often had four smaller shrines at the corners of the terrace; many of these shrines have now disappeared. The finely carved entrance gate to the temple is a *torana*, and the lesser towers around the main sikhara are known as *urusringas*.

The temples are almost all aligned east to west, with the entrance facing east. Some of the earliest temples were made of granite, or granite and sandstone, but all those from the classic period of Khajuraho's history are made completely of sandstone.

Sculptures & Statues

The sculptures and statues play such an important part in the total design that many have their own terminology:

Apsara Heavenly nymph or beautiful dancing woman.

Mithuna Khajuraho's most famous image, the sensuously carved, erotic figures that have been shocking a variety of people, from Victorian archaeologists to busloads of blue-rinse tourists.

Nayika It's really impossible to tell a nayika from a surasundari (see following), since the only difference is that the surasundari is supposed to be a heavenly creature while a nayika is human.

Salabhanjika Female figure with tree, which together act as supporting brackets in the inner chambers of the temple. Apsaras also perform this bracket function.

Surasundari When a surasundari is dancing she is an apsara. Otherwise she attends the gods and goddesses by carrying flowers, water, ornaments, mirrors or other offerings. She also engages in everyday activities like washing her hair, applying make-up, taking a thorn out of her foot, fondling herself, playing with pets and babies, writing letters, playing musical instruments or posing seductively.

Sardula A mythical beast, part lion, part some other animal or even human. Sardulas usually carry armed men on their backs, and can be seen on many of the temples. They all look like lions but the faces are often different.

houses one of Khajuraho's best sculptures – a fine sardula figure caressing a lion.

Devi Jagadamba The third temple on the common platform is slightly older than the Kandariya Mahadev and of a simpler, three-part design. It was probably originally dedicated to Vishnu, but later dedicated to Parvati and then Kali. Some students believe it may still be a Parvati temple and that the Kali image (or Jagadamba) is actually an image of Parvati, painted black. The sculptures around the temple are again in three bands. Many of the two lower-band images are of Vishnu with sardulas in the inner recesses. But on the third and uppermost band the mithunas again come out to play.

Chitragupta The fourth temple at the back of the western enclosure does not share the common platform with the other three. Similar in design to the Devi Jagadamba, this temple is probably slightly newer and is unique at Khajuraho in being dedicated to Surya, the sun god.

Attempts have obviously been made at restoration, but it is not in as good a condition as the other temples. Nevertheless, it has some very fine sculptures, which include processions, dancing girls, elephant fights and hunting scenes. In the inner sanctum, Surya can be seen driving his chariot and seven horses, while on the central niche in the south facade you can see an 11-headed statue of Vishnu. The central head is that of Vishnu himself; the 10 others are of his incarnations.

Parvati Continuing around the enclosure, you come to the Parvati Temple on your right. The name is probably incorrect since this small and not so interesting temple was originally dedicated to Vishnu and now has an image of Ganga riding on the back of a crocodile.

Vishvanath & Nandi Believed to have been built in AD 1002, this temple has the complete five-part design of the larger Kandariya Mahadev Temple, but two of its four subsidiary shrines still stand. The large image of Shiva's vehicle, the bull Nandi, faces the temple from the other end of the common platform. Steps lead up to this high terrace, flanked by lions on the northern side and elephants on the southern side.

The sculptures around the temple include the usual Khajuraho scenes, but the sculptures of women are particularly notable here. They write letters, fondle a baby, play music and, perhaps more so than at any other temple, languish in provocative poses.

Khajuraho's Erotica

KELLI HAMBLET

The most frequently asked question by visitors to Khajuraho is why all the sex? One theory has it that the erotic posturing was a kind of Kamasutra in stone, a how-to-do-it manual for adolescent Brahmin boys growing up segregated from the world in special temple schools. Another claims that the figures were thought to prevent the temples being struck by lightning, by appeasing the rain god Indra. This old lecher is supposedly a keen voyeur who wouldn't want the source of his pleasure damaged.

Rather more convincing is the explanation that these are Tantric images. According to this sect, gratification of the baser instincts is one way to blot out the evils of the world and achieve final deliverance. *Bhoga* (physical enjoyment) and *yoga* (spiritual exercise) are seen as equally valid in this quest for nirvana. Perhaps the most accurate theory is, however, that the Khajuraho sculptors were simply representing life as it was viewed by their society, including here unhampered sexual expression.

In spite of the fact that modern visitors are drawn as much for reasons of prurience as for cultural appreciation, this is not pornography. Although there are certainly large numbers of erotic images here, many other day-to-day scenes are also shown. The carvings should be seen as a joyous celebration of all aspects of life.

Matangesvara Standing next to the Lakshmana Temple, this temple is not within the fenced enclosure because it is still in everyday use, unlike all the other old Khajuraho temples. It may be the plainest temple here (suggesting that it was one of the first built) but inside it sports a polished lingam (phallic symbol of Shiva), 2.5m high.

Early in the morning, flower-sellers do a brisk trade in garlands for the statue of Ganesh outside. People drape them around the elephant-headed statue, say a prayer and as they walk away the sellers whip the flowers off to resell!

Farther West Standing beyond the tank, some distance from the other western group temples, the ruined temple of **Chausath Yogini** is probably the oldest at Khajuraho, dating from AD 900 or earlier. It is also the only temple constructed entirely of granite and the only one not aligned east to west. Chausath means 64; the temple once had 64 cells for figures of the 64 *yoginis* (female goddess attendants) who attended the goddess Kali. A 65th cell sheltered Kali herself.

A farther 500m west is the **Lalguan Mahadev Temple**, a small, ruined shrine dedicated to Shiva and constructed of granite and sandstone.

Eastern Group The eastern group of temples can be subdivided into two groups. The first is made up of interesting Jain temples in a walled enclosure. The other four temples are scattered through the old village of Khajuraho (as distinct from the modern village near the western temples).

Parsvanath The largest of the Jain temples in a walled enclosure is also one of the finest at Khajuraho. Although it does not approach the western enclosure temples in size, and does not attempt to compete in the sexual-activity stakes, it is notable for the exceptional skill and precision of its construction, and for the beauty of its sculptures. Some of the best-known figures at Khajuraho can be seen here, including the classic figure of a woman removing a thorn from her foot and another of a woman applying eye make-up. Although it was originally dedicated to Adinath, an image of Parsvanath was substituted about a century ago; the temple takes its name from this newer image.

Adinath Adjacent to the Parsvanath Temple, the smaller Adinath Temple has been partially restored over the centuries. It has fine carvings on its three bands of sculptures and, like the Parsvanath Temple, is very similar to the Hindu temples of Khajuraho. Only the striking black image in the inner sanctum indicates that it is Jain rather than Hindu.

Shanti Nath This temple is a relatively modern one built about a century ago, but it contains many components from older temples around Khajuraho. The 4.5m-high statue of Adinath is said to have been sculpted in 1028. Groups of digambara (which means 'sky-clad' or 'naked') Jain pilgrims occasionally stay at the *dharamsala* (pilgrims' lodging) here.

Ghantai Walking from the eastern group of Jain temples towards Khajuraho Village, you come to this small, ruined Jain temple. Only its pillared shell remains, but it is interesting for the delicate columns with their bell-and-chain decoration and for the figure of a Jain goddess astride a Garuda that marks the entrance.

Javari Walk through the village, a typical small Indian settlement, to this temple. Dating from around AD 1075 to 1100, it is dedicated to Vishnu and is a particularly fine example of Khajuraho architecture on a small scale. The exterior has more of Khajuraho's maidens.

Vamana About 200m north-west of the Javari Temple, this temple is dedicated to Vamana, the dwarf incarnation of Vishnu. Slightly older than the Javari Temple, the Vamana Temple stands out in a field all by itself. It's notable for the relatively simple design of its sikhara. The bands of sculpture around the temple are, as usual, very fine with numerous celestial maidens adopting interesting poses.

Brahma & Hanuman Walking west toward Bypass Rd and the modern village you pass a granite and sandstone temple, one of the oldest at Khajuraho. It was actually dedicated to Vishnu and the definition of it as a Brahma temple is incorrect.

Closer to the modern village is a Hanuman temple containing an image of the monkey-headed god. This 2.5m-high statue has on it the oldest inscription here; dating to AD 922.

Southern Group

There are only two temples in the southern group.

Duladeo A dirt track runs to this isolated temple south of the Jain enclosure. This is a later temple, and experts say that at this time the skill of Khajuraho's temple builders had passed its peak and the sculptures are more 'wooden' and 'stereotyped' than on earlier temples. Nevertheless, it's a fine and graceful temple with figures of women in a variety of pin-up poses and a number of mithuna couples.

Chaturbhuja South of the river, about 3km from the old village and a healthy hike down a dirt road, this ruined temple has a fine 3m-high image of Vishnu.

Museums

Close to the western enclosure, the small **Archaeological Museum** has a fine collection of statues and sculptures rescued from around Khajuraho. Admission is a laughable US$10, making it the most overpriced attraction in Madhya Pradesh. Give it a miss unless it's of special interest. It's open from 10 am to 5 pm daily, except Friday.

Outside the Jain enclosure is the **Jain Museum**, a modern circular gallery, filled with statues of the 24 tirthankars. It's open 8 am to 5 pm daily, except Sunday; entry is Rs 2.

Ayurvedic Health Spa

The Kairali Ayurvedic Health Spa (☎ 72 219), opposite the airport, is a great place for a massage if you feel like a splurge. A general whole body massage, including steam bath costs US$25.

Special Events

The **Khajuraho Festival of Dance** is a week-long event held every year in February/March. It attracts the cream of Indian classical dancers who perform amid the temples in the western enclosure. Performances are open-air, with the floodlit temples as a backdrop. MP Tourism's Web site at www.mptourism.com is the best place to find a program.

There is also a relatively new **music festival**, in just its third year. It's held on 28-29 November and should become a regular event on the calendar.

Places to Stay

Khajuraho has a plethora of accommodation. MP Tourism has several hotels, which

An Environmental Initiative

Global Village Development Trust (☎ 74237, 72250, ⓔ globalvillage@indiatimes.com), on Rajnagan Rd in Khajuraho, is a new non-governmental organisation (NGO) committed to saving Khajuraho's fragile environment, which is coming under stress from increasing levels of tourism.

Global Village was born out of a collective frustration at the ineffectiveness of the government to make any real impact on the growing environmental problems in the area. The group is embarking on a local education program in an attempt to help Khajuraho's community fight against plastic waste, diminishing water sources and vehicle pollution.

Importantly it is trying to come up with alternative materials for local households to replace items such as nonbiodegradable plastics, which are having such a negative effect on the environment. For people staying at one of the larger hotels, the Global Village recommends that you request biodegradable products from your hotel.

Contact either Mr Ajay Awasthi or Mr Sharlesh Singh if you're interested in donating to this very worthwhile cause, or if you are interested in doing some voluntary environmental work.

are good value at the height of the season, but overpriced at other times when private hotels reduce their prices. On your arrival at the bus stand you'll be besieged by the usual rickshaw-wallahs offering Rs 5 rides; these are commission agents and you will find bargaining for a room difficult if they take you to a hotel.

The cheapest places are in the centre of the modern village, close to the western group of temples.

Places to Stay – Budget

Yogi Lodge & Guesthouse** (☎ 74158)*, the most popular budget place, has singles/doubles with private bathroom starting at Rs 80/120. More expensive rooms have a hot-water geyser and there is Internet access for Rs 80 per hour. For real tranquillity ask here about ***Yogi Sharma Ashram Lodge, a large house with a garden about 2km north of the modern village. It has bright rooms for Rs 80/120 or a dorm for Rs 40, all with shared bathroom, plus free meditation classes every morning with the Yogi Ramprakash Sharma.

There's a string of very good budget places side by side on Jain Temples Rd. ***Hotel Gem Palace** (☎ 74100)* has small rooms for Rs 100/200, or bigger rooms for Rs 150/250, all with private bathroom and constant hot water. ***Hotel Surya** (☎ 74145)* has a large garden with fruit trees and free yoga classes at dawn. Good rooms with bathroom are Rs 150/200; rooms with balcony are Rs 250/350. ***Hotel Jain** (☎ 72352)* is a family-run place and an old favourite with travellers. There's a range of rooms starting at Rs 80/125 upwards, some with balconies. ***Hotel Harmony** (☎ 74135)* is good value. Comfortable rooms with private bathroom are Rs 200/250. The small walled garden is bright and immaculate.

***Rakshan Guest House** (☎ 74475)* is in its own little space just east of the modern village. Large, very clean doubles cost between Rs 150 and 300. Unfortunately the bathrooms can let this place down. There is also a small restaurant in the garden.

***Hotel Lakeside** (☎ 74120, Main Rd)* has clean rooms set around a central area. Rooms start at Rs 80 for a simple single, and with private bathroom and cooler start at Rs 150/250. You can get a good view of sunrise/sunset from the roof.

***Hotel Sunset View** (☎ 74077, Main Rd)* is lower on the budget scale. It's not the cleanest place around but has good-sized singles/doubles with private bathroom for Rs 80/100 or Rs 150/200. It's in a quiet spot.

MP Tourism's ***Tourist Village** (☎ 74128)* is a somewhat shabby collection of cottages decorated with local carpets and furnishings for Rs 250. It's quiet and north-east of the village.

Places to Stay – Mid-Range

***Hotel Marble Palace** (☎ 74353)* is a private hotel that lives up to its name with its marble floors and winding staircase. Spacious, comfortable singles/doubles with bathtubs are very nice but a little overpriced for Khajuraho at Rs 450/550, and Rs 750 with air-con.

***Hotel Zen** (☎ 74228, fax 72408, Jain Temples Rd)* is a compact, immaculate place with a pleasant courtyard garden. Doubles start at Rs 150, or Rs 350 with bathtub and balcony facing the garden.

***Hotel Casa Di William** (☎ 74244, fax 72252)*, on a side road just past the tourist office, has touches of the Mediterranean with its marble floors and whitewashed railings. Comfortable doubles with constant hot water are Rs 300 for air-cooled and Rs 600 for air-con. There's a good restaurant serving Indian and Italian specialities.

***Hotel Payal** (☎ 74064)*, near Tourist Village, is a dilapidated place with a sprawling garden and singles/doubles for Rs 340/390, or Rs 590/690 with air-con. It's clean and rooms have hot water and TV.

***Hotel Jhankar** (☎ 74063, fax 74194)*, south of the modern village, is MP Tourism's flagship here. Slightly ageing rooms cost Rs 340/390, or Rs 590/690 for air-con, all with bathrooms and constant hot water. There's a restaurant and cold beer is available.

Places to Stay – Top End

Most deluxe hotels attempt to outdo one another and are south of the modern village.

Hotel Jass Trident *(☎ 72344, ⓔ d_bhatial@indiatimes.com)* has rooms for US$44/88 and a certain charm despite its box-like exterior. The hotel's pool is open to non-guests for Rs 150. From August to April there are folk dances (Rs 150). Year-round there is a nightly puppet show, and a sitar and tabla recital (both free).

Hotel Chandela *(☎ 72355, fax 72366, Jhansi Rd)* has air-con rooms with comfortable beds, and bathtubs for US$42/70. Diversions for 'templed-out' guests include tennis, yoga, archery, croquet and badminton. There's a good bookshop, two excellent restaurants and a coffee shop.

Hotel Clarks Bundela *(☎ 72386, fax 72385, Jhansi Rd)*, south of the Hotel Chandela, charges US$45/85 a room and has a swimming pool (open to nonguests for Rs 100). Discounts of up to 50% are available in the low season.

Holiday Inn *(☎ 72301, ⓔ hi.khajuraho@vsnl.com, Jhansi Rd)*, farther south again, has a cavernous lobby, helpful staff, and tastefully furnished rooms for US$40/75. It's probably the most luxurious of the five-star places and has a pool, bar and two restaurants.

Places to Eat

Raja's Cafe *(Main Rd)* has been here about 20 years, and so has the Swiss woman who runs it. The large shady tree makes the restaurant's courtyard a popular gathering spot and there are good views to the temples from the terrace above. Tourist information and guides are also available here.

Blue Sky Restaurant, on the other side of the Government of India tourist office, is a friendly place serving very good Indian, Japanese and Italian food. A vegetarian kofta is Rs 30 and thalis start at Rs 20.

The hole-in-the-wall ***Shivam Restaurant*** *(Jain Temples Rd)*, near Hotel Harmony, has plain thalis for Rs 20 and very good Gujarati thalis for Rs 30.

Safari Restaurant, opposite Internet Hut, is good for reasonably priced breakfasts.

Mediterraneo Restaurant *(Jain Temples Rd)* is one of several popular places specialising in Italian food.

There's a string of decent restaurants on Main Rd with terraces overlooking the small Shiv Sagar – a good place to be in the early evening as the sun sets. ***Shiva Janti*** is a simple place with a good view of the lake. ***Paradise***, nearby, is a bit quieter than most and has a good menu; the management will also whip you up dishes not on the menu. Mango pancakes are Rs 40.

Recommended by readers is ***Gaylord Restaurant***, between the western temple group and the airport.

The top-end hotels all have good restaurants, but expect to pay around Rs 250 per person, excluding drinks.

Entertainment

The ***Sound & Light Show*** at the western temples group every night at 7 pm is excellent. The show (Rs 200) documents the history and culture of Khajuraho.

Kandariya Art & Culture *(☎ 74031)*, on Jhansi Rd, is a private setup with cultural dance shows from India's different states every night, performed in a comfortable indoor theatre. One-hour shows start at 7 and 8.30 pm and cost Rs 250.

Shilpgram *(☎ 42280)*, on the opposite side of the road to Kandariya, is a government operation designed to promote Indian culture. It has classical and folk cultural events on its program (call to see what's coming up). Entry is usually about Rs 100.

The ***Hotel Jass Trident*** hosts various cultural and musical performances. There's also a pool open to nonguests (see Places to Stay – Top End earlier).

Getting There & Away

Air Indian Airlines (☎ 74035) has a daily Delhi-Agra-Khajuraho-Varanasi flight in both directions. It's probably the most popular tourist flight in India and can be booked solid for days by tour groups. It leaves Khajuraho at 5.10 pm on Monday, Wednesday, Friday and Sunday and at 4.10 pm on Tuesday, Thursday and Saturday for Delhi (US$100), Agra (US$80) and Varanasi (US$80). Mumbai via Delhi costs US$275.

Indian Airlines, next to the Hotel Clarks Bundela, is open 10 am to 5 pm daily.

Bus & Train Jhansi (Rs 75/90, ordinary/deluxe, 4½ to six hours) is the nearest train station to Khajuraho on the main Delhi to Mumbai railway line; there are half a dozen buses a day on the popular Jhansi to Khajuraho route. There are also direct Agra-Gwalior buses (Rs 190).

There is no direct route from Varanasi to Khajuraho. Satna is the nearest reliable railhead for travellers from Varanasi and the east. It's on the Mumbai to Allahabad line so there are plenty of connections. There are four buses daily from Satna to Khajuraho (Rs 55, four hours). However, it may not be possible to get from Varanasi to Khajuraho in one day as the last bus from Satna leaves at 2.30 pm. A good option is to take the overnight *Muzaffarpur Lokmanya Tilak Express*, which departs Varanasi at 11.30 pm, and gets you into Satna at 6.30 am.

You can also get to Khajuraho from Varanasi by taking a train to Mahoba (Rs 160, sleeper), 60km north of Khajuraho, then a bus (Rs 35, two hours) from there.

Heading south, there's daily bus at 6 am to Jabalpur (Rs 135, 11 hours), but the train from Satna is more comfortable. Regular buses run to Panna (Rs 21, one hour) via Madla for Panna National Park.

The best place to get bus or train information is Madhur Cold Drinks Stand at the bus stand.

Share-Taxi A taxi can be a good alternative if you find other travellers interested in sharing the cost. As a general guide, it costs about Rs 5/10 per kilometre for nonair-con/air-con. Taxis will take you to Varanasi for Rs 3500, Agra for Rs 4000 and Satna for Rs 1000 (all with air-con).

Getting Around

To/From the Airport Taxis to the airport charge Rs 80 for this short journey; cycle-rickshaws will pedal the 3km for Rs 40.

Local Transport The best way to get around Khajuraho is by bicycle, since it's flat and pleasantly traffic-free. Bicycles cost Rs 20 per day from several places in the modern village.

Cycle-rickshaws are generally a rip-off but it's a long walk to the eastern grou of temples. A cycle-rickshaw should cos around Rs 100 for a half-day trip; make sur this price includes stops at the souther temples and the driver's waiting time.

AROUND KHAJURAHO

Panna National Park

The direct road to Satna passes through thi park (543 sq km) along the Ken River 32km from Khajuraho. It has large areas o unspoilt forest and a variety of wildlife including leopards, *chital* (spotted deer), langur monkeys and sambars. There are abou 22 tigers in the park but since they're no tracked (as at Kanha) you'd be very lucky to spot one.

Entry to the park is Rs 150 (Rs 10 for Indians), plus Rs 25/200 for camera/video camera fees.

Transport within the park is by petrol driven Gypsy 'trucks' only; they can b hired at the park's entrance in Madla, o Khajuraho (see Getting There & Away late in this section for more information).

Cooler months are the best time to visit in summer it can be hotter than a furnace The park is closed from June to October.

Day trips from Khajuraho often also tak in a visit to the **diamond mines** at Majhgawan (41km south-east of Khajuraho) the **Rajgarh Palace**, **Ranah Falls** and th **temples** of Panna town.

Places to Stay On the Ken River, 3km fro the park entrance, ***Giles Tree House*** is th best place to stay. It's literally a platfor built in a tree with a few huts down by th river. Basic huts are Rs 300, rooms are R 500 and rooms by the river with bathroom ar Rs 800. Book at Raja's Cafe in Khajurah

The ***Forest Rest House*** in Madla provides basic accommodation for Rs 275 pe person. It can be booked at the office by th park entrance or through the director i Panna town (☎ 07732-52135). You wil need to bring your own food here. There' another ***Forest Rest House*** (same bookin details) on the opposite side of the park a Hinouta, about 50km from Khajuraho.

Getting There & Away Regular local buses run from Khajuraho to Panna (Rs 15, one hour) via Madla (45 minutes) – get off at Madla for the park.

Day trips (in a six-seater Gypsy only) can be organised in Khajuraho through travel agents or at Raja's Cafe. The whole trip costs around Rs 1500 plus entry and guide fees.

Ajaigarh & Kalinjar Forts

At Ajaigarh, 80km east of Khajuraho, is a large isolated hilltop fort. It was built by the Chandelas when their influence in the area was on the decline. Kalinjar Fort, 25km north (just inside Uttar Pradesh) is much older, built during the Gupta period. It was a stronghold of the Chandelas from the 9th to 15th centuries before being conquered by Akbar in 1569.

The forts can be reached on long day trips from Khajuraho; you can hire a car for around Rs 1500. It's possible to get to Kalinjar by public bus (change at Panna), but not as a day trip. A closer access point is Chitrakut in Uttar Pradesh.

SATNA

☎ 07672

You may find it convenient or necessary to stay here in Satna overnight on your way either to or from Khajuraho. Satna is a fairly unremarkable town that is quite spread out and very noisy around the train station. There's a useful MP Tourism office at the train station.

Places to Stay & Eat

The choice is basically between proximity to the bus stand or the train station. All hotels have free bucket hot water.

Hotel India *(☎ 51012, Rewa Rd)* is a good place behind (east of) the bus stand. Reasonably clean singles/doubles are Rs 95/126 with private bathroom; there's a good cheap restaurant downstairs, part of the Indian Coffee House chain.

Hotel Park *(☎ 23017, Rewa Rd)*, on the other side of the bus stand, is quieter and clean with rooms for Rs 100/160, or Rs 450/500 with air-con. It also has a vegetarian restaurant.

Hotel Chanakya *(☎ 25026, Station Rd)*, about 500m from the train station, has large, tidy rooms with TV for Rs 225/330, or with air-con for Rs 385/495.

Hotel Khajuraho *(☎ 23330)*, behind the road leading from the train station, has good air-cooled rooms with clean private bathrooms for Rs 250/350.

Hotel Savero *(☎ 25231, Rewa Rd)*, close to Hotel Park, sees a lot of tour groups and is a bit more upmarket; it's a clean place and there is constant hot water. Rooms start at Rs 350/450 and Rs 700/850 with air-con. Prices are negotiable when they're not busy.

Saloni Restaurant *(Rewa Rd)* is an air-con vegetarian place opposite the bus stand. There are plenty of ***food stalls*** in the market around the bus stand.

Getting There & Away

Four buses to Khajuraho (Rs 45, four hours) leave from 6.30 am to 2.30 pm.

For Bandhavgarh National Park (see later in this chapter) you can take a bus to tiny Gorsari for tea and samosas with the locals while waiting for the bus from Rewa, which continues to Tala. Otherwise you'll have to take a taxi for around Rs 1000.

There are direct trains from Satna to Varanasi (Rs 123/415 in sleeper/1st class, eight hours, 316km) and Jabalpur (Rs 53/279 in 2nd/1st class, three hours, 189km). Other direct expresses connect with Allahabad, Kolkata (Calcutta), Mumbai and Chennai.

Central Madhya Pradesh

BHOPAL

☎ 0755 • pop 1,278,030

The capital of Madhya Pradesh, Bhopal was built on the site of the 11th century city of Bhojapal. It was founded by the legendary Raja Bhoj who is credited with having constructed the lakes around which the city is built. The present city was laid out by the Afghan chief Dost Mohammed Khan, who was in charge of Bhopal during Aurangzeb's reign, but took advantage of the confusion following Aurangzeb's death in 1707 to carve out his small kingdom.

Today, Bhopal has a multifaceted profile. There is the old city with its crowded marketplaces, huge old mosques, and the palaces of the former begums (women of high rank) who ruled over the city from 1819 to 1926. To the north sprawl the huge industrial suburbs and the slums that these developments in India inevitably give rise to. The new city, with its broad avenues, high-rise offices and leafy residential areas, lies to the south. In the centre of Bhopal are two lakes that, while providing recreational facilities, are also the source of its mosquito plagues.

Bhopal is hardly on every traveller's itinerary, but it has a relaxed feel for a state capital, a number of cultural attractions and is a good base for some excellent excursions.

The city is also famous as the site of the world's worst industrial disaster. See the boxed text, 'The Bhopal Disaster – Curing an Outrage with Neglect', later in this section.

Orientation

Both the train station and central bus stand are within easy walking distance of the main hotel area along Hamidia Rd in Old Bhopal. When arriving by train, leave the station by platform No 4 or 5 to reach Hamidia Rd.

The new part of the city, New Bhopal, which encompasses North TT Nagar, site of most of the major banks and the tourist office, is a long way from either of the transport terminals. Old and New Bhopal are effectively separated by the Upper and Lower Lakes.

Information

Tourist Offices There are helpful and efficient tourist information counters at both the train station and airport. The headquarters of MP Tourism (☎ 778383, fax 774289, ⓔ mail@mptourism.com) is in the Gangotri Complex, 4th floor, North TT Nagar, in New Bhopal; there's a regional tourist office (☎ 553006) at the Hotel Palash. MP

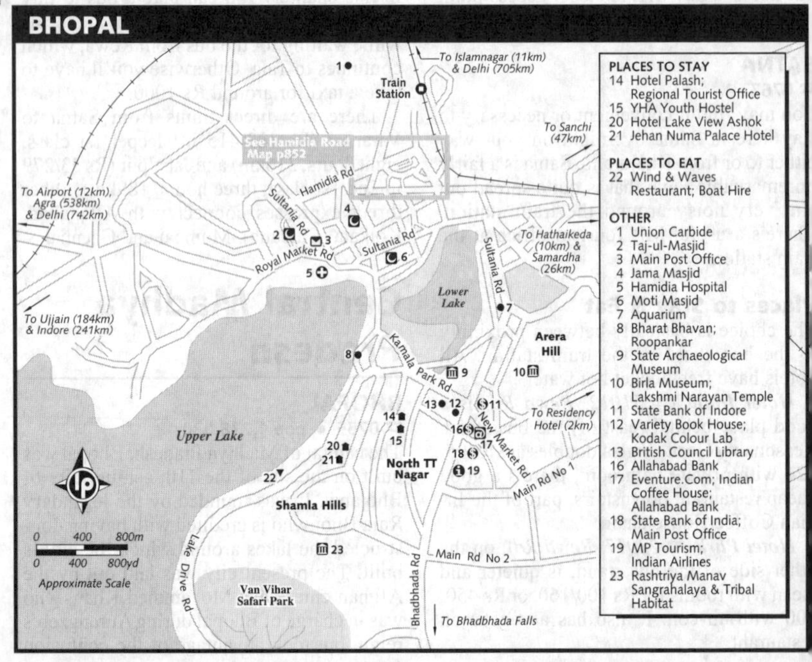

Tourism can book its hotels throughout the state (it's best to book five days in advance). The Web site is at www.mptourism.com.

MP Tourism can also organise a car and driver starting at Rs 4.50 per kilometre or Rs 500 per day.

Money You have to head over to North TT Nagar to change travellers cheques or cash. The State Bank of India (the Rangmahal Talkies Cinema is nearby), the State Bank of Indore (beneath the Hotel Panchanan) or the Allahabad Bank, Bhadbhada Rd, will also make the requisite transactions.

Post & Communications The main post office is on Sultania Rd, Old Bhopal, near the Taj-ul-Masjid.

Computera, on Hamidia Rd not far from the bus stand, has quick Internet connections and charges Rs 40 an hour. If you're in New Bhopal, try Eventure.Com between the Indian Coffee House and the Allahabad Bank. It's a 24-hour place that charges Rs 35 per hour for email during the day and a mere Rs 25 per hour after 11 pm.

Bookshops Near MP Tourism on Bhadbhada Rd in North TT Nagar there are a couple of bookshops with a small English-language range. Variety Book House has the best selection (plus maps), and Books World stocks a lot of second-hand titles.

Cultural Centres The Alliance Française (☎ 466595, ⓔ afbpl@bom.vsnl.net.in) is in Arera Hill. Officially services are for members only, but French visitors who are not members may be able to have a look at their French newspapers and journals.

The British Council Library (☎ 553767), GTB Complex, North TT Nagar, just behind the Variety Book House, has a well-stocked reading room and is open from 11 am to 7 pm Tuesday to Saturday.

Medical Services & Emergency Hamidia Hospital (☎ 511446), Royal Market Rd, in Old Bhopal is the city's best public hospital. There are also many pharmacies around here dispensing medical supplies.

The telephone number for the police is ☎ 100 and ☎ 102 for an ambulance.

Business Hours Shops in New Bhopal close on Monday, and in Old Bhopal on Sunday. Businesses such as airlines and banks close at noon on Saturday and are also closed all day Sunday.

Mosques

The **Taj-ul-Masjid** is one of the largest mosques in India. Construction was started by Shah Jahan Begum (r. 1868–1901) but was never really completed; construction recommenced in 1971. It's a huge pink mosque with two massive white-domed minarets and three white domes over the main building. The entrance to the mosque is not on Sultania Rd, despite the huge staircase here; go around the corner and enter from busy Royal Market Rd. The mosque is closed to non-Muslims on Friday.

The **Jama Masjid**, built in 1837 by Qudsia Begum, is surrounded by the bazaar and has very squat minarets.

The **Moti Masjid** was built in 1860 by Qudsia Begum's daughter, Sikander Jahan Begum. Similar in style to the Jama Masjid in Delhi, it is a smaller mosque with two dark-red minarets crowned by golden spikes.

Lakes

The larger Upper Lake covers 6 sq km and a bridge separates it from the smaller Lower Lake. A veritable flotilla of boats is available for hire on the Upper Lake, including rowboats (Rs 50 for 30 minutes), pedal boats (Rs 60 per hour) and sailboats (Rs 100 per hour; only available in summer). There's a booking office at the bottom of the driveway leading to the Wind & Waves Restaurant.

There's a fairly dull **aquarium** near the Lower Lake. It's open from 3 to 8 pm daily, except Monday; entry is Rs 2.

Lakshmi Narayan Temple & Birla Museum

There are good views over the lakes to Old Bhopal from the Lakshmi Narayan Temple, also known as the Birla Mandir. Beside it on Arera Hill is the excellent Birla Museum,

MADHYA PRADESH & CHHATISGARH

The Bhopal Disaster – Curing an Outrage With Neglect

On the night of 3 December 1984, 40 tonnes of deadly methyl icocyanate, a toxic gas used in the manufacture of pesticides by Union Carbide, a US-based multinational company, leaked out over Bhopal. Carried by the wind, this deadly gas soon enveloped the sleeping city.

Unable to understand the sense of suffocation that overwhelmed them, the barely awake residents of Bhopal ran into the streets, falling by the roadside as they succumbed to the toxic gas. The majority of the 6000 immediate victims were Union Carbide workers and their families living in slums clustered on the perimeters of the factory. Children, elderly people and the disabled, who couldn't outdistance the spreading fumes, were particularly susceptible.

Panic and chaos ensued; officials intent on saving the lives of themselves and their families headed, literally, for the hills, leaving the bulk of the population to fend for themselves. Exact figures of those who perished in the disaster may never be known; local residents claim that the figures quoted by government officials are grossly unrepresentative. To date, the death toll stands at an estimated 16,000 people, and over half a million more have had their health permanently destroyed. Union Carbide's legacy is ongoing: Toxic chemicals dumped and buried during the life of the factory have poisoned water supplies, further threatening the health of Bhopal's residents.

A report prepared by a team of international medical experts that was released on the 10th anniversary of the disaster found that 'a substantial proportion of Bhopal's population' is suffering from 'genuine long-term morbidity', with victims exhibiting symptoms disturbingly similar to those suffered by AIDS victims – a breakdown of the immune system resulting in susceptibility to tuberculosis and respiratory problems. Unfortunately, medical services are inadequate, underfunded and corrupt, exacerbating the suffering of many patients. Since long-term monitoring of health problems was

containing a small but very selective collection of local sculptures dating mainly from the Paramara period. The stone sculptures are mainly of Vishnu, Shiva and their respective consorts and incarnations. The museum is open from 10 am to 5 pm daily, except Monday; entry is Rs 3.

State Archaeological Museum

Near the Lower Lake, this museum contains a small collection of 6th to 10th century Hindu sculptures, bronzes, prehistoric exhibits and copies of cave paintings. It's open 10 am to 5 pm daily, except Monday; entry is free.

Bharat Bhavan

Bharat Bhavan (☎ 540353) is a complex for the verbal, visual and performing arts. It was designed by the well-known Anglo-Indian architect Charles Correa and opened in 1982. It's now regarded as one of the most important centres in the country for the preservation of traditional folk art. As well as the workshops and theatres here, there's the two-part **Roopankar Gallery**. To the right of the entrance is a superb exhibition of tribal folk art paintings, sculptures and carvings produced by previously unknown Adivasi artists. Among the most striking exhibits are the colourful murals depicting animals and village life. Across the central courtyard, the second gallery provides a contrast with some of India's finest contemporary urban photographs and sculptures. Bharat Bhavan is open from 1 to 7pm (2 to 8 pm in winter) daily, except Monday; entry is Rs 5.

Rashtriya Manav Sangrahalaya & Tribal Habitat

This 40-hectare complex in the hills overlooking the Upper Lake is an ambitious attempt to showcase the lives, culture, art and religion of a fraction of India's 450-plus Adivasis. The complex started with **Tribal Habitat (Museum of Man)**, an open-air exhibition of some 25 tribal dwellings in authentic village-like settings. The buildings, from all over India, were constructed using genuine materials by members of the tribes

The Bhopal Disaster – Curing an Outrage With Neglect

abandoned in late 1994, treatment is only symptomatic, and the drugs used are often harmful. Doctors employed in public hospitals often open private clinics, forcing the sick to pay for services they are entitled to free of charge.

Soon after the disaster, the Indian government demanded US$3 billion in compensation, but was persuaded to accept US$470 million or have the case drawn out for at least a decade. All criminal charges were dropped, Union Carbide renounced any liability for the accident, and the money was paid to the government. It was not until seven years after the disaster and after another 2000 people had died that a tiny portion of this money began to trickle down. The compensation funds continue to filter their way through various pockets on the slow flow down to the victims.

Outraged at the grossly inadequate trickle of compensation money slowly coming from the government, organisations of the survivors and relatives of the dead filed a class action in the US courts in late 1999. The suit alleges that Union Carbide and former chairman Warren Anderson committed serious violations of international law and human rights by their 'reckless and depraved indifference to human life'.

Today Bhopal is a pleasant, cosmopolitan city, and residents are understandably reluctant to talk about the horror that suddenly enveloped their lives over a decade ago. Outside the now-closed factory, which lies just north of Hamidia Rd, a memorial statue to the dead is the only testimony to the tragedy of Bhopal. Travellers interested in more information about the recovery of Bhopal can contact the Gas Relief Commission (☎ 573230).

Union Carbide (also operating as Everyday Industries) is a profitable business once more, and batteries produced by this company are available throughout the country.

themselves, many of whom continue to maintain the site. The three newer elements to the park, **Coastal Village** (running along the eastern edge of the lake), **Desert Village** and **Rock Heritage** are designed along similar lines and there are prehistoric rock-art sites scattered around the park. A huge indoor museum and gallery contains Adivasi costumes, jewellery, ornaments, a multimedia display and an information database.

The complex is very much an educational project: there are two visitor information centres, as well as craft and pottery demonstrations, and film shows on Saturday at 4 pm (one hour). Admission to the exhibits and the film are free. The display is open from 11 am to 6.30 pm daily, except Monday. You can walk between the exhibits (there's a sealed road) but it makes for a tiring visit. An autorickshaw costs around Rs 100 to take you up there, including waiting time.

Van Vihar Safari Park

This 445-hectare park is more of a zoo than a safari park, despite the promise of 'natural surroundings'. But if you're in the north during the monsoon, when all the national parks are closed, it's good to know you don't have to completely miss out on tigers, lions, leopards and crocodiles.

The park is open from 7 to 11 am and 3 to 5.30 pm daily, except Friday. Entry is Rs 100 (free for the disabled) and it costs Rs 10/20 for autorickshaw/car entry. A spin around Van Vihar in a rickshaw (from the city centre) should cost around Rs 120.

Places to Stay

Hamidia Rd in Old Bhopal is where most of the city's hotels are clustered. Although it can be difficult to find good cheap accommodation in Bhopal, there are some excellent, reasonably priced mid-range hotels.

Places to Stay – Budget

Most of the following places have rooms with bathrooms.

The ***YHA Youth Hostel*** *(☎ 550899, North TT Nagar)*, near Hotel Palash, is dirt cheap but a bit of a disgrace by YHA standards.

Members pay Rs 20 for a bed in a grimy dorm, or Rs 60 for a double. Nonmembers pay double.

Hotel & Restaurant Ranjit *(☎ 533511, 3 Hamidia Rd, ⓔ ranjit@bom6.vsnl.net.in)* is Bhopal's most popular moderately priced hotel. Very clean air-cooled singles/doubles are Rs 150/200, or Rs 325/375 with air-con.

Hotel Rama International *(☎ 535542, Hamidia Rd)*, nearby, is spacious, if a little shabby. Rooms are Rs 150/200, or Rs 250/300 with air-con.

Hotel Meghdoot *(☎ 713407)* has rather grimy rooms starting at Rs 126/172 or Rs 150/240 for better deluxe rooms. Hot water is by the bucket and there are squat toilets.

Hotel Manjeet *(☎ 536168)*, just off Hamidia Rd near the Ranjit, has smallish but very clean rooms starting at Rs 200/250, better rooms at Rs 250/275 and air-con rooms for Rs 425/465. The management is efficient and the staff friendly.

Places to Stay – Mid-Range

Hotel Sonali *(☎ 533880, fax 510337, Radha Talkies Rd)*, hidden just off busy Hamidia Rd, is possibly Bhopal's best-value hotel. The cheapest rooms are definitely mid-range standard and a bargain at Rs 210/285 for rooms with constant hot water, room service and balcony. There are also deluxe rooms for Rs 250/325 and air-con rooms starting at Rs 450/525.

Hotel Taj *(☎ 533162, 52 Hamidia Rd)* is a big old hotel with a central courtyard. The cheap rooms are looking a bit ragged these days; they cost Rs 200/350 and Rs 600/750 with air-con (plus 20% tax). There is a restaurant, but no bar.

Hotel Shivalik Gold *(☎ 536000, fax 710224, 40 Hamidia Rd)*, behind the Taj, is a worn place with comfortable rooms starting at Rs 250/325, or Rs 450/550 with air-con.

Hotel Ramsons *(☎ 535299)* is in the backstreets off Hamidia Rd. It has friendly staff, but it's gloomy and cavernous compared to its modern neighbours, and reminiscent of the Overlook Hotel from the movie *The Shining* (apart from the management, of course). Big old rooms are Rs 240/310, or Rs 450/550 with air-con.

Hotel Surya *(☎ 741701, Hamidia Rd)* is modern and well run with standard rooms starting at Rs 250/300, air-con at Rs 500/600; it has a good restaurant.

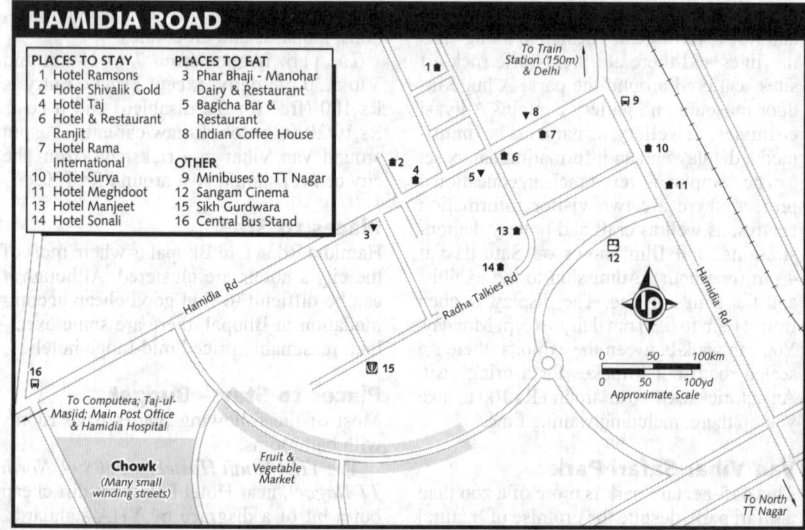

MADHYA PRADESH & CHHATISGARH

Hotel Palash *(☎ 553006, North TT Nagar)*, MP Tourism's hotel, is convenient if you want to stay in the New Market Rd and it's handy for the lake area. Rooms are not cheap, however, starting at Rs 550/650, or Rs 790/890 with air-con.

Places to Stay – Top End

Those who can afford it head for the hills.

Residency Hotel *(☎ 556001, 208 Zone 1, MP Nagar)* is a four-star hotel east of New Bhopal with a swimming pool and health club. Standard rooms are Rs 1140/1490 and deluxe rooms are Rs 1595/1945, plus a whopping 25% tax.

Hotel Lake View Ashok *(☎ 660090, fax 660096, Shamla Hills)* is a well-appointed, three-star hotel with an excellent restaurant. All rooms have private balconies, and there are good views over the lake. Comfortable rooms are Rs 1600/2200, deluxe doubles are Rs 2800.

Jehan Numa Palace Hotel *(☎ 661100, fax 661720)*, only a stone's throw away, was formerly a palace, built in the late 19th century and is Bhopal's stand-out hotel. Rooms start at Rs 2200/2750, or Rs 4300 for deluxe doubles, plus 10% tax; it also has a restaurant and bar.

Places to Eat

The cheapest places to eat are the street stalls surrounding the bus stand and train station. Many of the hotels around Hamidia Rd have good restaurants and bars.

The ***Indian Coffee House*** chain is good and cheap; there are outlets in both Old and New Bhopal. Some of their restaurants have separate areas for women and families.

Hotel & Restaurant Ranjit has an excellent (and well-deserved) reputation. Most dishes on the huge menu (there is even an 'everything' heading!) are around Rs 40; ice-cold beer is Rs 60.

Bagicha Bar & Restaurant, a few doors down, also prepares a good range of food in a quieter, open-air setting. It's set a little way back from the cacophony of Hamidia Rd.

Phar Bhaji – Manohar Dairy & Restaurant *(Hamidia Rd)* has lots of lovely gooey favourites such as *gulab jamun* (sweet rose-flavoured dumplings) as well as an astonishing variety of ice cream. Dosas, *idlis* (South Indian rice dumpling) and vegetarian burgers are also available. This place is very popular with locals.

Kwality Restaurant *(New Market Rd, North TT Nagar)*, opposite the State Bank of Indore, does reasonable fast food, pizzas and Chinese and has an outdoor eating area.

Bread Basket *(Shamla Hills)* at Jehan Numa Palace Hotel has a delicious selection of cakes and other tasties for the sweet tooth, while ***Shahnama Restaurant*** in the same complex is the place for a splurge. It's not cheap, with main dishes starting at Rs 110, but the food is excellent.

Wind & Waves Restaurant *(Lake Drive Rd)* is a (fairly ordinary) snack shop, but you can enjoy a cold drink here (including beer) and there's a fantastic view of the Upper Lake. It's open until 11 pm.

Entertainment

There are pool tables at Eventure.Com (see Post & Communications earlier in this section) and the place is open all night. There are plenty of restaurants and bars along Hamidia Rd, although women are a rare sight in these places.

Shopping

Bhopal's two main shopping areas are the New Market Rd area, in New Bhopal, and the old market area, or *chowk*, in Old Bhopal. While similar items can be found in both markets, prices are much more reasonable in the atmospheric chowk, just off Hamidia Rd near the bus stand. The labyrinthine streets and alleys here make this a fascinating area to wander around – count on getting totally lost. Here you'll find fine gold and silver jewellery, beautifully woven saris and hand-embroidered applique skirts at reasonable prices. Jari shoulder bags are a speciality of Bhopal. They are woven from cotton, and have colourful designs decorating the exterior. These can be purchased in the chowk for about Rs 35.

Mrignayni is the registered trade name for MP state handicraft merchandise, which is mainly textiles and clay or brass sculptures; such items start at about Rs 50 and can cost anything up to Rs 2000 depending on your bargaining prowess. Many retail shops carry Mrignayni products.

Getting There & Away

Air Indian Airlines (☎ 770480) has daily flights to Mumbai (US$130), Indore (US$55) and Delhi (US$120), and two flights weekly to Gwalior (US$80). The office is in North TT Nagar, adjacent to MP Tourism.

Bus From the central bus stand on Hamidia Rd there are numerous daily buses to Sanchi (Rs 15, 1½ hours; via Raisen, Rs 17); Vidisha (Rs 24, 2½ hours); Indore (Rs 78/144 ordinary/deluxe, five to six hours); Ujjain (Rs 78, five hours); Pachmarhi (Rs 91, seven hours) and Jabalpur (Rs 154, 12 hours).

There's an overnight service to Khajuraho which costs about Rs 200, but it is better to go by train to Jhansi and continue by bus from there.

A computerised reservation system operates from 11 am to 8 pm for all deluxe and long-distance ordinary buses.

Train There's an efficient air-con reservation hall on the left as you exit the main terminal, and a separate counter for the *Shatabdi Express* within the terminal building itself. There's a 24-hour left-luggage facility at the train station.

Bhopal is on one of the two main Delhi to Mumbai railway lines. It's the terminus for the daily *Shatabdi Express* from New Delhi. Cheapest fares from Bhopal (air-con chair class) are Rs 480 for Jhansi (three hours), Rs 545 for Gwalior (4¼ hours) and Rs 850 for Delhi (7¾ hours).

Other express trains connect Bhopal with Delhi (Rs 221/746 in sleeper/1st class, 12 hours, 705km), Mumbai (Rs 265/830, 14 hours, 837km), Agra (Rs 174/588, 8½ hours, 506km), Jhansi (Rs 112/378, 4½ hours, 291km) and Ujjain (Rs 53/279 in 2nd/1st class, three hours, 188km). Express trains leave for Sanchi (Rs 21, 2nd class, one hour, 46km) at 8 am and 2.40 pm.

Getting Around

To/From the Airport The airport is 12km from Old Bhopal. Fixed rates operate for both taxis (Rs 180) and autorickshaws (Rs 100).

Local Transport Autorickshaw drivers almost always use their meters (sheer luxury), except at night when you'll have to negotiate the fare. Hopelessly crowded minibuses for North TT Nagar (Rs 2, No 2, 3 or 9) depart about every two minutes from the minibus stand on Hamidia Rd near Hotel Red Sea Plaza. A rickshaw costs about Rs 30.

AROUND BHOPAL

Bhojpur

The legendary Raja Bhoj (1010–53) not only built the lakes at Bhopal but also built another one, estimated at 400 sq km, in Bhojpur, 28km south-east of Madhya Pradesh's capital. History records that the lake was held back by massive earthen dams faced on both sides with huge blocks of sandstone set without mortar.

Unfortunately, the lake no longer exists, having been destroyed by Hoshang Shah, the ruler of Mandu, in a fit of destructive passion in the early 15th century. What does survive here is the huge, partially completed **Bhojeshwar Temple**, which originally overlooked the lake. Dedicated to Shiva, it has some very unusual design features and sports a massive lingam, 2.3m high and 5.3m in circumference. The earthen rampart used to raise stones for the construction of the dome still remains. Nearby is another incomplete monolithic temple, this time a **Jain shrine** containing a colossal statue of Mahavira, over 6m tall.

A few local buses run to Bhojpur from Bhopal's central bus stand, or take any Hoshangabad-bound bus (Rs 12) and get off at the turn-off to Bhojpur from where you should be able to pick up a tempo (Rs 2).

Bhimbetka

Like the Aboriginal rock paintings in the outback of Australia, the cave paintings of the San in the Kalahari Desert in Africa or the Palaeolithic Lascaux Caves of France, the Bhimbetka Caves are a must-see. Among forests of teak and sal in the craggy cliffs of an almost African setting 45km south of Bhopal, some 1000 rock shelters have been discovered. Almost half contain ancient paintings depicting the life and times of the different people who lived here.

Because of the natural red and white pigments used by the painters, the colours have been remarkably well preserved and it's obvious in certain caves that the same surface has been used by different people at different times. There's everything from figures of gaur (wild buffalo), rhinoceros, bears and tigers, to hunting scenes, initiation ceremonies, childbirth, communal dancing and drinking scenes, religious rites and burials.

The extent and archaeological importance of the site was only recently realised and dating is still not complete. The oldest paintings are believed to be up to 12,000 years old, whereas some of the crude, geometric figures probably date from as recently as the medieval period.

The caves themselves are not difficult to find; 15 are accessible and signposted, and linked by a concrete path. A local guide (about Rs 20) can be useful for pointing out some of the more obscure paintings and explaining their significance. The Zoo Rock Shelter is one of the first you come to, and is famous for its variety of animal paintings. Rock shelter No 15 features a huge red bison attacking a helpless stick figure. There's nothing here other than the caves, so bring water with you.

Getting There & Away From Bhopal take any bus to Hoshangabad or Itarsi (Rs 15) via Obaidullaganj, 50 minutes south of Bhopal. Get off 6.5km after Obaidullaganj by the sign pointing right with '3.2' and some Hindi on it (ask the driver). Follow this sign, crossing the railway line for the 3km walk to the hills in front of you. (If you can't find the sign, try asking locals for directions.)

To get back you can flag down a truck or bus on the main road. If you don't fancy the walk, pick up a rickshaw in Obaidullaganj. If you want to visit both Bhimbetka and Bhojpur it's worth springing for a taxi. You can hire a car and driver through MP Tourism in Bhopal for around Rs 500 a day (see Tourist Offices under Bhopal earlier in this section).

Other Attractions

Only 6km from Bhopal, **Neori** has an 11th-century Shiva temple and is a popular picnic spot.

Islamnagar, 11km north of Bhopal on the Berasia Rd, is a hilltop palace built by Dost Mohammed Khan in the 18th century. In the palace's formal gardens, a highly decorated pavilion combines elements of the Afghan rulers' Islamic art and the local Hindus' decorative style. Any Berasia bus will drop you off here.

At **Ashapuri**, 6km north of Bhopal, there are ruined temples and Jain palaces with statues scattered on the ground.

Hathaikheda, 10km out of Bhopal on the Raisen Rd, is a peaceful fishing spot.

Also on the Raisen Rd, **Samardha**, 26km from Bhopal, has forest clearings just begging for a picnic blanket.

Chiklod, 45km out, has a palace in a peaceful sylvan setting.

SANCHI

Beside the main railway line, 46km northeast of Bhopal, a hill rises from the plain. It's topped by some of the oldest and most interesting Buddhist structures in India. This site had no direct connection with the life of the Buddha. It was the great emperor Ashoka, Buddhism's most famous convert, who built the first stupas here in the 3rd century BC, and a great number of stupas and other religious structures were added over the succeeding centuries.

As Buddhism was gradually absorbed back into Hinduism, the site decayed and was eventually completely forgotten. In 1818 a British officer rediscovered the site, and in the following years amateur archaeologists and greedy treasure hunters did immense damage to Sanchi before a proper restoration was begun in 1881. Finally, between 1912 and 1919, the structures were carefully repaired and restored to their present condition by Sir John Marshall.

Sanchi is a very special place and is not to be missed if you're anywhere within striking distance. The site is also a good base for a number of interesting bicycle excursions.

It's possible to take in all that Sanchi has to offer in just two or three hours. However, this is such a peaceful place that it's really worth spending the night here.

Orientation & Information

Sanchi is little more than a small village at the foot of the hill on which the site is located. The site is open daily from dawn to dusk and tickets are available from the ticket office outside the archaeological museum. Entry costs US$10 (Rs 460), which covers both the site and the museum (if you plan on going up for the superb sunrise, you'll need to buy a ticket the day before). It's worth getting a copy of the *Sanchi* guidebook (Rs 12), published by the Archaeological Survey of India. There's also a museum guidebook on sale here.

It's sometimes possible to visit the silkworm farm at the Sericulture Centre. Ask at the MP Travellers' Lodge, next door.

The quickest way up to the site is via the stone steps off to the right of the tarmac road. There's a drink stall by the modern *vihara* (monastery) on Sanchi Hill, and Buddhist publications are for sale in the vihara. Following is a brief description of the buildings at the site.

SANCHI

Train Station

To Vidisha (6km), Udaigiri Caves (14km), Heliodorus Pillar (16km) & Gyaraspur (50km)

Food Stalls & Bike Hire

To Sonari (12km), Raisen (18km), Andher (22km) & Bhopal (46km)

Gate

To Sanchi Village (500m)

Tank

Steps

To Monasteries 45 & 47

0 125 250m

0 125 250yd

PLACES TO STAY & EAT
1 Jaiswal Lodge
2 Sri Lanka Mahabodhi Society Guest House
7 MP Travellers' Lodge
9 MP Tourist Cafeteria
10 PWD Circuit House (VIPs only)

OTHER
3 Bike Hire
4 Mrignayni Emporium
5 Bus Stand
6 Sericulture Centre
8 Health Centre
11 Ticket Office
12 Archaeological Museum
13 Post Office
14 Stupa 2
15 Monastery 51
16 Vihara
17 Stupa 4
18 Stupa 3
19 Temple 31
20 Stupa 5
21 Great Stupa
22 Pillar 10
23 Temple 18
24 Building 43
25 Temple 40

Archaeological Museum

This museum has a small collection of sculpture from the site. The most interesting pieces are the lion capital from the Ashoka pillar, a *yakshi* (maiden) hanging from a mango tree and a beautiful Buddha figure in red sandstone. It's open 10 am to 5 pm daily, except Friday.

Great Stupa

The Great Stupa (or stupa 1, as it is listed at the site) is the main structure on the hill. Originally constructed by Ashoka in the 3rd century BC, it was later enlarged and the original brick stupa enclosed within a stone one. In its present form it stands 16m high and is 37m in diameter. A railing encircles the stupa and there are four entrances through magnificently carved *toranas*, or gateways. These toranas are the finest works of art at Sanchi and among the finest examples of Buddhist art in India.

Walk around the stupa clockwise, as one should around all Buddhist monuments.

The four gateways were erected around 35 BC and had all fallen down at the time of the stupa's restoration. The scenes carved onto the pillars and their triple architraves are mainly tales from the Jatakas, the episodes of the Buddha's various lives. At this stage in Buddhist art the Buddha was never represented directly; his presence was always alluded to through symbols. The lotus stands for his birth, the bo tree represents his enlightenment, the wheel his teachings and the footprint and throne symbolise his presence. Even a stupa itself is a symbol of the Buddha.

The **northern gateway**, topped by a broken 'wheel of law', is the best-preserved torana. Scenes include a monkey offering a bowl of honey to the Buddha, whose presence is indicated by a bo tree. In another panel he ascends a road into the air (again represented by a bo tree) in the Miracle of Sravasti. This is just one of several miraculous feats the Buddha performs on the northern gateway – all of which leave his spectators stunned. Elephants, facing in four directions, support the architraves above the columns, while horses with riders and more elephants fill the gaps between the architraves.

One pillar on the **eastern gateway** includes scenes of the Buddha's entry to nirvana. Across the front of the middle architrave is the Great Departure, where the Buddha (symbolised by a riderless horse) renounces the sensual life and sets out to find enlightenment. Maya's dream of an elephant standing on the moon, which she had when she conceived the Buddha, is also depicted on one of the columns. The figure of a yakshi, hanging out from one of the architraves, is one of the best known images of Sanchi.

The **southern gateway**, the oldest of the gateways, includes scenes of the Buddha's birth and also events from Ashoka's life as a Buddhist. At the rear of the top architrave there is another representation of the Great Departure. As on the western gateway, the tale of the Chhaddanta Jataka features on this gateway.

The **western gateway**, with its architraves supported by pot-bellied dwarfs, has some of the most interesting scenes at the site. The rear face of one of the pillars shows the Buddha undergoing the Temptation of Mara, while demons flee and angels cheer his resistance. The top front architrave shows the Buddha in seven different incarnations, but since he could not, at the time, be represented directly, he appears three times as a stupa and four times as a tree.

The colourful events of the Chhaddanta Jataka are related on the front face of the bottom architrave. In this tale the Buddha, in a lower incarnation, took the form of a six-tusked elephant, but one of his two wives became jealous; she managed to reincarnate as a queen and then arranged to have the six-tusked elephant hunted and killed. The sight of his tusks, sawn off by the hunter, was sufficient for the queen to die of remorse!

Other Stupas

There are many other stupas on the hill, some of them tiny votive ones less than 1m high. Eight were built by Ashoka but only three remain, including the Great Stupa. **Stupa 2**, one of the most interesting of the lesser stupas, is halfway down the hill to the west. If you come up from the town by the main route you can walk back down via stupa 2. There are no gateways to this stupa, but the 'medallions' that decorate the surrounding wall are of great interest. Their design is almost childlike, but full of energy and imagination. Images of flowers, animals and people – some mythological – are found all around the stupa.

Stupa 3 stands north-east of the main stupa and is similar in design, though smaller in size. It has only one gateway and is thought to have been constructed soon after the completion of the Great Stupa. Stupa 3 once contained relics of two important disciples of the Buddha. They were removed and taken to London in 1853, but returned to Sanchi in 1953, and are now housed in the modern vihara.

Pillars

Scattered around the site are pillars and the remains of pillars. The most important is **pillar 10**, which was erected by Ashoka and stands close to the southern entrance to the Great Stupa. Only the base of this beautifully proportioned and executed shaft now stands, but the fine capital can be seen in the museum. The four back-to-back lions that once topped the column are an excellent example of the Graeco-Buddhist art of that era. They now form the state emblem of India and can be seen on every banknote.

Pillar 25, dating from the Sunga period (2nd century BC) and **pillar 35**, dating from the 5th century AD, are not as fine as the earlier Ashoka pillar.

Temples

Immediately south of the Great Stupa is **temple 18**, a *chaitya* (temple hall) that is remarkably similar in style to columned buildings of classical Greece. It dates from around the 7th century AD, but traces of earlier wooden buildings have been discovered beneath it. Beside this temple is the small **temple 17**, also Greek-like in style. The large **temple 40**, slightly south-east of these two temples, in part dates back to the Ashokan period.

Temple 31 was built originally during the 6th or 7th century, but reconstructed during either the 10th or 11th century. This flat-roofed rectangular temple contains a well-executed image of the Buddha. This appears to have been moved here from another temple during the reconstruction of temple 31, as it does not exactly fit the pedestal on which it is mounted.

Monasteries

The earliest monasteries on the site were made of wood and are long gone. The usual site plan consists of a central courtyard surrounded by monastic cells. **Monasteries 45** and **47** stand on the higher, eastern edge of the hilltop. They date from the later period of building, a time of transition from Buddhism to Hinduism, and show strong Hindu elements in their design. There is a good view of the village of Sanchi below and Vidisha in the distance from this side of the hill.

Monastery 51 is partway down the hill on the western side towards stupa 2. Nearby is the **Great Bowl** in which food and offerings were placed for distribution to the monks. It was carved out of a huge boulder. The modern **vihara** on the hill was built to house the returned relics from stupa 3. The design is a poor shadow of the former artistry of Sanchi.

Special Events

In late November each year, the **Chethiyagiri Vihara Festival** attracts hundreds of Buddhist monks and pilgrims to see the relics of two of the Buddha's early disciples, Sari Puttha and Maha Moggallana. The relics, originally discovered in stupa 3 in 1853, are now kept in the vihara and brought out for display during the festival.

Places to Stay & Eat

The ***Sri Lanka Mahabodhi Society Guest House*** *(☎ 07482-62739)* is where the visiting monks stay and is the best budget option in Sanchi. Spartan rooms are in a tranquil garden setting and cost Rs 50 with shared bathroom (cold water only). The ***Jaiswal Lodge*** *(☎ 07482-63908)*, over the road, has five rooms available for Rs 60 each.

MP Tourism runs two places in Sanchi, both with restaurants serving standard fare. ***MP Tourist Cafeteria*** *(☎ 07482-62743)* has clean singles/doubles with private bathroom for Rs 200/290. Rooms have ceiling fans and there's a Rs 50 surcharge to use the air-cooler. ***MP Travellers' Lodge*** *(☎ 07482-62723)*, on the main road to Bhopal near the crossroads, is a better hotel, but it's not as close to the stupas. Singles/doubles cost Rs 250/350, or Rs 350/450 for the deluxe rooms.

The market area around the bus stand has a variety of ***fruit and food stalls***, as well as a couple of basic ***restaurants***.

Getting There & Away

Bus Local buses connect Sanchi with Bhopal (and other towns and villages in the area) about every hour from dawn to dusk, but there are two possible routes. The longer route along the main road goes via Raisen (Rs 17, three hours, 68km). See under Around Sanchi later for more information on Raisen. The shorter route follows the railway line to Bhopal (Rs 15, 1½ hours).

To Vidisha (Rs 5), buses depart from the Sanchi bus stand about every 30 minutes. A rickshaw to Vidisha can be bargained down to about Rs 25.

Train Sanchi is on the main Delhi to Mumbai railway line, 46km north-east of Bhopal.

Slow passenger trains (Rs 10) can take over two hours to get to Bhopal, but there are two express trains each day (Rs 21, one hour). The expresses depart Bhopal at 8 am and 2.40 pm, and depart Sanchi at 10.18 am and 4 pm, so it's possible to visit Sanchi on a day trip.

Bicycle For excursions to places nearby such as Vidisha (6km) and the Udaigiri Caves (14km), you can rent bicycles in Sanchi's market for about Rs 20 a day.

AROUND SANCHI

Buddhist Sites

Within cycling distance of Sanchi are more Buddhist sites, although none are of the scale or as well preserved as those at Sanchi. **Sonari**, 10km south of Sanchi, has eight stupas, two of them important. At **Satdhara**, west of Sanchi on the bank of the Beas River, are two stupas, one 30m in diameter. Another 14km to the south-east is **Andher**, where there are three small but well-preserved stupas. These stupas were all discovered in 1851, after the discovery of Sanchi.

Vidisha

Vidisha was important in Ashoka's time and it was from here that his wife came. Then it was known as Besnagar and was the largest town in the area. The ruins of the 2nd-century BC Brahminic shrine here show traces of lime mortar – the earliest use of cement in India. Finds from the site are displayed in the **museum** near the train station.

From the 6th century AD the city was deserted for three centuries. It was renamed Bhilsa by the Muslims who built the now-ruined Bija Mandal, a mosque constructed from the remains of Hindu temples.

From Sanchi you can reach Vidisha by bicycle (see Udaigiri Caves for rental details), bus (Rs 4, every 30 minutes), train (Rs 15), or rickshaw (Rs 35).

Heliodorus Pillar

Between Vidisha and Udaigiri, 1km north of the Udaigiri Caves turn-off, is this inscribed pillar, known locally as the Khamb Baba pillar. Erected in about 140 BC by Heliodorus, a Greek ambassador to the city from Taxila (now in Pakistan), the pillar celebrates his conversion to Hinduism. It's dedicated to Vishnu and worshipped by local fishers.

Udaigiri Caves

Cut into the sandstone hill, 8km from Vidisha, are about 20 Gupta cave shrines dating from AD 320 to 606; two are Jain, the other 18 are Hindu. In **cave 5** there is a superb image of Vishnu in his boar incarnation. **Cave 7** was cut out for the personal use of King Chandragupta II. **Cave 20** is particularly interesting, with detailed Jain carvings. On the top of the hill are the ruins of a 6th-century Gupta temple.

To reach the caves from Bhopal or Sanchi take a bus or train to Vidisha, and from there take a tonga (horse-drawn carriage) or autorickshaw to the caves. To reach the caves by bicycle from Sanchi, cycle towards Vidisha until you cross the river (after 6km). Turn left 1km farther on (or carry straight on if you want to visit Vidisha first). After 3km you'll reach a junction in the colourful bazaar – turn left again. Another 1km farther is another left

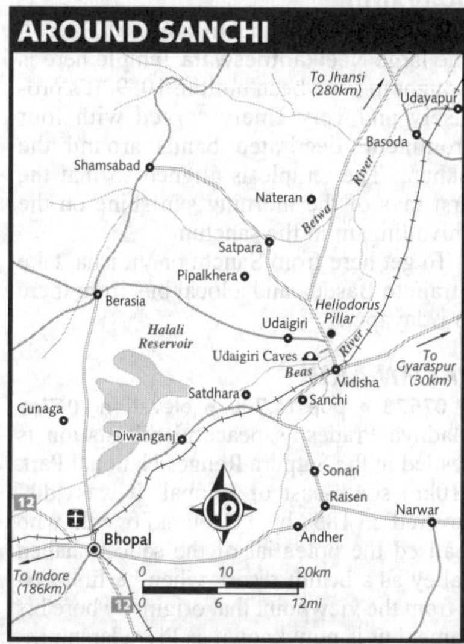

turn. Take this road for the caves (3.5km away) or continue for 1km for the Heliodorus Pillar.

Raisen

On the alternative road to Bhopal, 23km south of Sanchi, the huge and colourful hilltop **fort** of Raisen has temples, cannons, three palaces, 40 wells and a large tank. This Malwa fort was built around AD 1200, and although initially the centre of an independent kingdom, it later came under the control of Mandu. There are also ancient paintings in the caves in this area.

There are local buses to Raisen hourly from Sanchi (Rs 12), and regular departures from Bhopal's central bus stand (Rs 14).

Gyaraspur

There are tanks, temples and a fort dating from the 9th and 10th centuries AD at this town, 51km north-east of Sanchi. The town's name is derived from the big fair that used to be held here in November, sometimes known as Gyaras. From Sanchi you'll have to change buses at Vidisha for the trip to Gyaraspur.

Udayapur

Udayapur is about 65km north of Sanchi. The large **Neelkantheswara Temple** here is thought to have been built in 1059. It's profusely and very finely carved with four prominent, decorated bands around the sikhara. The temple is aligned so that the first rays of the morning sun shine on the Shiva lingam in the sanctum.

To get here from Sanchi or Vidisha, take a train to Basoda and a local bus from there to Udayapur.

PACHMARHI

☎ 07578 • pop 14,700 • elevation 1067m

Madhya Pradesh's peaceful hill station is nestled in the Satpura Ranges National Park 210km south-east of Bhopal. It was 'discovered' in 1857 by a Captain Forsyth, who realised the potential of the saucer-shaped valley as a health resort, when he first saw it from the viewpoint that originally bore his name, but is now known as Priyadarshini.

Although nothing like a Himalayan hill station, Pachmarhi is a very attractive, relaxing place rarely visited by foreign tourists. The area draws quite a few artists, and gurus occasionally hold retreats up here.

There are fine views out over the surrounding red sandstone hills, pools and waterfalls to bathe in, ancient cave paintings and some interesting walks through the sal forests.

Orientation & Information

The bus stand is at the north end of the small village. The main road continues south from here for about 3km to the seven-way junction called Jaistambha, which makes an excellent landmark for walks. Accommodation is spread over a wide area, so you'll need to use a taxi unless you're staying in the village itself.

There is a regional tourist information office (☎ 52100), next to the Hotel Amaltas, that is open weekdays. It can provide brochures, fairly ordinary maps and arrange guides. There are no foreign exchange facilities in Pachmarhi.

There is an Internet centre, which costs Rs 65 per hour; connections are available after 11 am.

Things to See & Do

Built by Captain Forsyth in 1862, **Bison Lodge** was Pachmarhi's first forest lodge and is now a museum covering the history of the area and the flora and fauna of the Satpura region. A free wildlife film is shown in the open-air theatre here at 6 pm nightly, except Monday.

There are a number of interesting short **walks** around Pachmarhi, as well as longer treks for which you'll probably need a guide. A recommended long day walk is to the hilltop shrine of **Chauragarh**, 4km from Mahadeo. You can see the cave paintings at **Mahadeo** on the way.

Jatashankar is a revered cave temple in a gorge less than 2km from the bus stand. The small Shiva shrine is hidden under a huge overhanging rock formation.

Bee Falls are the most accessible of several waterfalls in the district; the drawback is the Rs 100 national park entry fee (Rs 10 for Indians). From the main road about 1km south of Jaistambha a trail leads down to the park entrance, then steps continue down to the falls.

About 2km east of Jaistambha, the **Pandav Caves** are five 1000-year-old rock-cut caves overlooking an attractive garden. Legend has it the Pandavas lived here during their 12-year exile.

Special Events

Every February/March up to 100,000 Shaivite pilgrims, sadhus and Adivasis attend the **Shivaratri Mela** celebrations at Mahadeo Temple, 10km south of Pachmarhi. The festival commemorates Lord Shiva and participants bring symbolic tridents and plant them on top of nearby Chauragarh Hill.

Places to Stay

Most of the accommodation in Pachmarhi is run by MP Tourism or SADA, but there are a few private places in the village. High season is April to July and December to January.

Places to Stay – Budget

***Hotel Pachmarhi** (☎ 52170, Patel Marg)*, in the village, has reasonable singles/doubles with squat toilets starting at Rs 250/350, with a 40% low-season discount.

***Hotel Utkarsh** (☎ 52162)*, a short walk south of the bus stand just off the main road, has doubles with private bathroom and hot-water geyser for Rs 250, or Rs 125 in the low season.

***Holiday Homes** (☎ 52099)* is the MP Tourism budget choice, and a pretty good one. Clean doubles with private bathroom, TV and hot-water geyser are Rs 290. It's about 1km from the bus stand back towards Piparya.

***New Hotel** (☎ 52017, Mahadeo Rd)* is a large place operated by SADA, about 4km from the village. There's a wide range of rooms from Rs 125 to Rs 330 (with TV), and a 25% low-season discount.

***Nandanvan Cottages** (☎ 52018)* are well placed near Jaistambha, and are at the top of the budget range at Rs 470 a double.

Places to Stay – Mid-Range & Top End

The following are MP Tourism places, except Nilamber Cottages which is run by SADA.

***Amaltas** (☎ 52098)* is a rambling old former colonial bungalow. Nondescript doubles with private bathroom are Rs 550, deluxe rooms are Rs 690.

***Satpura Retreat** (☎ 52097)* is another old Raj bungalow, but much more atmospheric with a large veranda, comfortable rooms and vast private bathrooms. It's in a quiet (isolated) location along the Mahadeo road. Standard doubles are Rs 690, but the good rooms are Rs 1390.

***Nilamber Cottages** (☎ 52039)* are excellent. Perched up on a small hill about 3km south of the village, they have great east-west views from the verandas. Doubles with private bathroom, hot-water geyser and TV are worth the Rs 770.

***Rock End Manor** (☎ 52079)*, just below Nilamber Cottages, is the swankiest address in Pachmarhi. It used to be the local maharaja's golf retreat, but has been converted into an elegant heritage hotel. Doubles with panoramic views and all mod cons are Rs 1590, or Rs 1990 with air-con.

Places to Eat

The best places to eat are the hotel restaurants, especially the ***China Bowl*** at Panchavati Huts & Cottages and ***The Club*** at Rock End Manor, but there are a few decent independent places and numerous cheap cafes in the bazaar area around the bus stand.

Mahfil Restaurant is near the bus stand and has cheap dosas and good vegetarian burgers. ***Khalsa Restaurant*** has a pleasant outdoor setting by the lake and a range of good vegetarian and nonvegetarian food.

Getting There & Away

From the bus stand there are four bus services per day to Bhopal (Rs 91, seven hours); the direct MP Tourism minibus leaves for Bohpal at 2.30 pm (Rs 110, five hours). There are departures every couple of hours to Pipariya (Rs 25, 1½ hours).

MADHYA PRADESH & CHHATISGARH

Getting Around

Plenty of jeeps hang around the bus stand looking for passengers to take to Pachmarhi's viewpoints. A half-day trip costs at least Rs 300. The jeeps also operate as the local taxis (Rs 20 for a short trip). Bicycles can be hired from the shop just north of the bazaar. They cost Rs 25 a day and are a good way to get to the various trailheads and viewpoints.

PIPARIYA

Pipariya is the nearest road/rail junction to Pachmarhi, 47km away. If you get stuck here there's the MP Tourism ***Tourist Motel*** *(☎ 07576-22299)* with doubles for Rs 150 (shared bathroom) and a restaurant. It's about 200m from the train station.

Local buses and jeeps leave from the bus stand behind the train station regularly for Pachmarhi. Local buses go to/from Bhopal (Rs 65, six hours).

Western Madhya Pradesh

UJJAIN

☎ 0734 • pop 433,465

Only 56km from Indore, ancient Ujjain is one of India's holiest cities for Hindus. It gets its sanctity from a mythological tale about the churning of the oceans by the gods and demons in search of the nectar of immortality. When the coveted vessel of nectar was finally found, there followed a mad scramble across the skies with the demons pursuing the gods in an attempt to pinch the nectar from them. Four drops were spilt and they fell at Haridwar, Nasik, Ujjain and Prayag (Allahabad).

For non-Hindus, this can be a dull place once you've explored the temples and ghats.

History

Although its origins have been lost in the mists of time, Ujjain, once part of an ancient trade route, is a city with a distinguished history. It was an important city under the rule of Ashoka's father, when it was known as Avantika. Later, Chandragupta II (380–414) ruled from here rather than from his actual capital, Pataliputra. It was at his court that Kalidasa, one of Hinduism's most revered poets, wrote the *Meghdoot*, with its famous lyrical description of the city and its people.

With the passing of the Guptas and the rise of the Parmaras, Ujjain became the centre of a struggle for control of the Malwa region. The last of the Parmaras, Siladitya, was captured by the Muslim sultans of Mandu, and Ujjain thus passed into the hands of Mughal vassals.

An invasion by Altamish in 1234 resulted in the wholesale desecration of many of the temples, but that was halted during the reign of Baz Bahadur of Mandu. Bahadur himself was eventually overthrown by the Mughal emperor, Akbar. Later, under Aurangzeb, grants were provided to fund temple reconstruction.

Following the demise of the Mughals, Maharaja Jai Singh (of Jaipur fame) became the governor of Malwa, and during his rule the observatory and several new temples were constructed at Ujjain. With his passing, Ujjain experienced another period of turmoil at the hands of the Marathas until it was finally taken by the Scindias in 1750. When the Scindia capital was moved to Gwalior in 1810, Ujjain's commercial importance declined rapidly.

Orientation & Information

The railway line divides the city: The old town, including the bazaar and most of the temples and ghats, is north-west of the train line; the new town is to the south-east. The cheap hotels are in front of the train station.

Tourist information is available at the train station, from MP Tourism and at the Hotel Shipra. There's nowhere to change money in Ujjain – Indore and Bhopal are the closest places.

Temples

Mahakaleshwar Mandir The most important temple in Ujjain, the Mahakaleshwar Mandir, is dedicated to Shiva. The temple enshrines one of India's 12 *jyoti linga*: Nat-

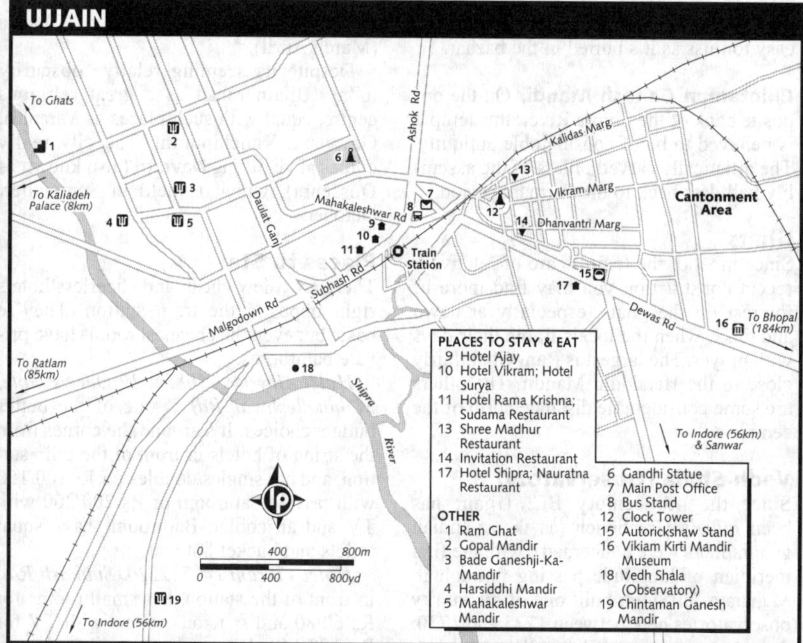

urally occurring lingam believed to derive *shakti* (currents of power) from within themselves as opposed to lingam ritually invested with *mantra-shakti* by the priests.

The myth of the jyoti linga stems from a long dispute for primacy between Brahma and Vishnu. During the dispute, according to legend, the earth split apart to reveal an incandescent column of light. To find the source of this column, Vishnu became a boar and burrowed underground while Brahma took to the sky in the form of an eagle. After a thousand years of fruitless searching, Shiva emerged from the lingam of light and both Brahma and Vishnu acknowledged that he was the greatest of the gods.

The temple was destroyed by Altamish of Delhi in 1235, but was restored by the Scindias in the 19th century. Non-Hindus are welcome to make the busy, jostling round of the many minitemples in this evocative complex, and you may find yourself on the receiving end of a puja (offering).

Above the tank near the Mahakaleshwar Mandir, the large ornate statue of Ganesh here makes **Bade Ganeshji-ka-Mandir** a popular pilgrimage spot.

Harsiddhi Mandir Built during the Maratha period, this temple enshrines a famous image of the goddess Annapurna. The two large pillars adorned with lamps were a special feature of Maratha art and are spectacular when lit at Navratri.

Gopal Mandir The marble-spired Gopal Mandir was built by the queen of Maharaja Daulat Rao Scindia in the 19th century and is a great example of Maratha architecture.

The silver-plated doors of the sanctum have quite a history. They were originally taken from the temple at Somnath in Gujarat to Ghazni in Afghanistan and then to Lahore by Mohammed Shah Abdati. From there they were rescued by Mahadji Scindia and shortly afterwards installed in the temple. This is a large temple but it is easy to miss as it's buried in the bazaar.

Chintaman Ganesh Mandir On the opposite bank of the Shipra River, this temple is believed to be of considerable antiquity. The artistically carved pillars of the assembly hall date back to the Parmara period.

Ghats

Since most of the temples are of relatively recent construction you may find more of interest on the ghats, especially at dawn and dusk, when the locals frame their days with prayer. The largest is Ram Ghat, fairly close to the Harsiddhi Mandir. The others are some considerable distance north of the centre.

Vedh Shala (Observatory)

Since the 4th century BC, Ujjain has been India's Greenwich (as far as Indian geographers were concerned), with the first meridian of longitude passing through it. Maharaja Jai Singh built one of his quirky observatories here between 1725 and 1730. Astrologers can purchase the complete year's astronomical ephemeris in both English and Hindi at the observatory.

Kaliadeh Palace

On an island in the Shipra River, 8km north of town, is the water palace of the Mandu sultans, constructed in 1458. River water is diverted over stone screens in the palace, and the bridge to the island uses carvings from the sun temple that once stood here. The central dome of the palace is a good example of Persian architecture.

With the downfall of Mandu, the palace gradually fell into ruin but was restored, along with the nearby sun temple, by Madhav Rao Scindia in 1920.

Special Events

As a result of the legend surrounding the 'vessel of nectar', Ujjain is one of the sites of the **Maha Kumbh Mela**, which takes place here every 12 years and draws millions to bathe in the Shipra River. The next Kumbh Mela is due in 2004, and begins on the full moon in the month of Chaitra (March/April).

Despite its seeming relative obscurity today, Ujjain ranks as a great religious centre, equal with such places as Varanasi, Gaya and Kanchipuram. The city really comes alive during **Navratri** (also known as Dussehra), which is held in September/October.

Places to Stay

There are a few cheap and cheerless hotels right opposite the train station. They're basic but even the cheapest rooms have private bathrooms.

Hotel Ajay *(☎ 550856, 12 Dewas Gate, Mahakaleshwar Rd)* is one of the better budget choices. It's around the corner from the string of hotels in front of the train station, and has singles/doubles for Rs 100/150 with private bathroom or Rs 200/300 with TV and air-cooler. Bathrooms have squat toilets and bucket hot water.

Hotel Vikram *(☎ 562220, Subhash Rd)*, in front of the station, has small rooms for Rs 60/80 and spacious rooms with TV for Rs 100/140. It's a pretty grubby place – avoid the grotty cells with shared bathrooms. All bathrooms have squat toilets and bucket hot water.

Hotel Surya *(☎ 560747)*, next door, has better rooms for Rs 95/110, or Rs 150/200 with TV. All rooms (theoretically) have constant hot water.

Hotel Rama Krishna *(☎ 557012, Subhash Rd)* charges Rs 125/150, or Rs 240/300 with TV and air-con, and is a bit cleaner than its neighbours.

The ***retiring rooms*** at the train station have dorms for Rs 30, and rooms for Rs 100.

MP Tourism's ***Hotel Shipra*** *(☎ 551495)*, just off Dewas Rd in a very quiet, pleasant setting, has an impressive marble foyer, and extra large rooms. Rooms start at Rs 350/390, and go up to Rs 690/790 with air-con plus tax. The restaurant here is quite good and it has a bar.

Places to Eat

There are a number of places to eat opposite the station.

Sudama Restaurant has good vegetarian dishes for under Rs 35, but the breakfasts are spooky.

Nauratna Restaurant in the Hotel Shipra serves good food. The navratan curry (Rs 45) is good if you like a sweeter curry. Sandwiches are about Rs 25.

Shree Madhur Restaurant *(☎ 456001, 2nd floor, Tower Chowk, Freeganj)* is a clean, airy vegetarian place just off the main circle near the clock tower. Mains are between Rs 20 and Rs 50, and a pizza is Rs 35.

Invitation Restaurant is a rooftop restaurant overlooking the main circle that serves South Indian dishes.

Getting There & Away

Bus There are buses roughly every 20 minutes for the trip to Indore (Rs 24, two hours), which are generally faster than the train. Buses to Bhopal (Rs 78/86, ordinary/deluxe, four hours) go via Dewas. For Mandu you have to change at Indore. An early-morning bus connects Ujjain with Kota in Rajasthan (Rs 100, 256km).

Train The *Malwa Express*, departing at 2.35 pm, is the fastest link with Delhi. It takes 17½ hours (Rs 270/871, sleeper/1st class, 885km), via Bhopal (Rs 104/298, four hours, 184km), Jhansi (Rs 183/577, nine hours, 475km), Gwalior (Rs 210/666, 10½ hours, 572km) and Agra (Rs 234/750, 13 hours, 690km).

The *Narmada Express* connects Ujjain with Indore (Rs 29/173, 2nd/1st class, 2¼ hours) and heads east to Bhopal (Rs 53/279, in 2nd/1st class, three hours, 188km), Jabalpur (Rs 117/615, 12½ hours, 540km) and Bilaspur, Chhatisgarh (Rs 261/882, sleeper/1st class, 25 hours, 929km).

The 5.20 pm *Avantika Express* is the only direct service to Mumbai (Rs 158/268, 2nd/sleeper class, 12 hours). The *Bhopal-Rajkot Express* to Ahmedabad departs at 11 pm and arrives at 8.30 am (Rs 102/179).

Getting Around

Many of Ujjain's sights are a long way from the centre of town so you'll probably use quite a few autorickshaws or the more romantic horse-drawn tongas. There are registration booths at both the bus and train stations that autorickshaw drivers are obliged to use if you request it. The normal system of bargaining should work though – from the train station to the Mahakaleshwar Mandir costs around Rs 10 (Rs 20 for a tonga).

INDORE

☎ 0731 • pop 1,278,690

Indore is not of great interest, but it's a good base for visiting Mandu. The city is a major textile-producing centre and at Pithampur, 35km away, Hindustan Motors, Kinetic Honda, Bajaj Tempo and Eischer all have factories. Indians call Pithampur the Detroit of India, and Indore is its gateway.

Although the city is on an ancient pilgrimage route to Ujjain, nothing much happened here until the 18th century. From 1733, it was ruled by the Holkar dynasty who were firm supporters of the British, even during the Indian Uprising.

Orientation & Information

The old town is on the western side of the railway line; the new town is on the east. If arriving by train, leave the station by platform No 1 for the east side of town and by platform No 4 for the west side.

The tourist office (☎ 528653) is by the Tourist Bungalow at the back of the RN Tagore Natya Griha Hall, RN Tagore Rd. It's open from 10 am to 5 pm.

Cash and travellers cheques can be changed at the main branch of the State Bank of India, near the main post office.

Internet and email facilities are available at Indore Telecom's flash multimedia centre in the central telegraph office in Nehru Park. You have to remove your shoes to enter the spotless air-con room. Rates are very reasonable at Rs 30 per hour. It is open from 10 am to 6 pm daily, except Sunday.

There's a good selection of reading material (including second-hand books) at Badshah Book Shop, in the City Centre shopping complex on Mahatma Gandhi Rd (known locally as MG Rd).

Things to See

In the old town, the multistorey gateway of the **Rajwada**, or Old Palace, looks out onto the palm-lined main square in the crowded streets of the Kajuri Bazaar. A mix of French, Mughal and Maratha styles, the palace has been up in flames three times in its 200-year history. After a very serious conflagration in 1984, it's now not much more than a facade.

On Jawahar Rd, not far from the Rajwada, is the **Kanch Mandir**, or Seth Hukanchand Temple. This Jain temple is very plain externally, but inside is completely mirrored with pictures of sinners being tortured in the afterlife.

The **museum**, near the main post office, has one of the best collections of medieval and pre-medieval Hindu sculpture in Madhya Pradesh. Most are from Hinglajgarh in the Mandasaur district of western Madhya Pradesh, and range from early Gupta to Paramana times. The museum is open from 10 am to 5 pm daily, except Monday; entry is free.

In the south-west of the city, surrounded by gardens, lies the grand **Lal Bagh Palace**, built between 1886 and 1921. It has all the usual over-the-top touches like entrance gates that are replicas of those at Buckingham Palace, a wooden ballroom floor mounted on springs, marble columns, chandeliers, stained-glass windows and stuffed tigers. It's open 10 am to 6 pm daily, except Monday; entry is Rs 2 plus Rs 10/50 for camera/video-camera fees.

The magnificent **Gandhi Hall** (town hall) is open to visitors 10 am to 5 pm daily. Exhibitions are sometimes held here.

The chhatris, or memorial tombs, of former rulers are now neglected and forgotten. They stand in the **Chhatri Bagh**. The cenotaph of Malhar Rao Holkar I, founder of the Holkar dynasty, is the most impressive.

At the western end of MG Rd, the **Bada Ganapati Temple** contains an 8m-high bright-orange statue of Ganesh – reputed to be the world's largest.

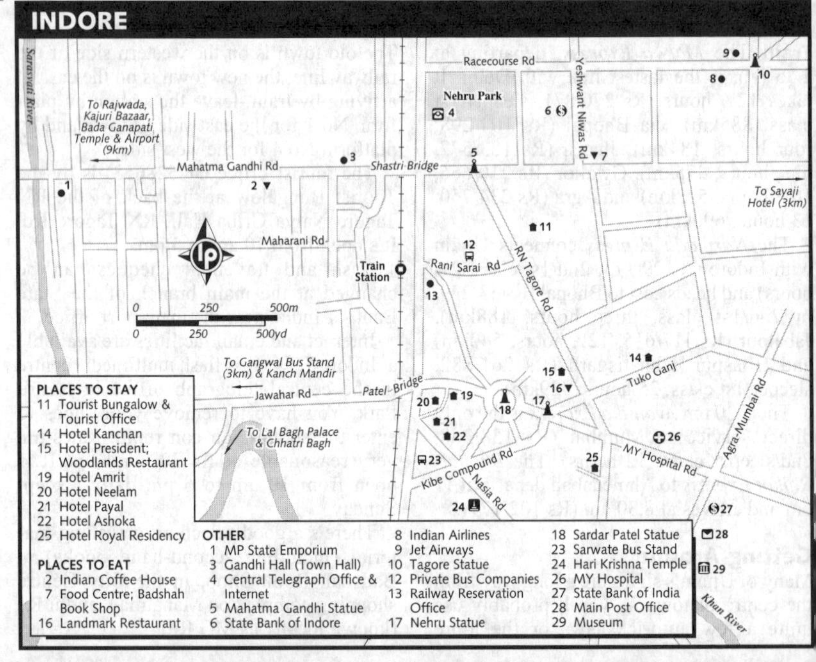

Organised Tours

MP Tourism operates day tours to Mandu from July to September (and outside these months if there are sufficient numbers) for Rs 225, as the monsoon is the high season for local tourists. It's a similar story for tours to Ujjain, Maheshwar and Omkareshwar (Rs 225). These tours include lunch and afternoon tea, and a minimum of 10 people is required.

Places to Stay – Budget

The train station and the Sarwate bus stand are about five minutes' walk apart, and it's in this lively, polluted area that you'll find the budget hotels. The following places have rooms with private bathrooms and 24-hour checkout.

Hotel Ashoka *(☎ 465991, 14 Nasia Rd)* is the closest hotel to the bus stand, which is directly behind it. The cheapest singles/doubles are way up on the 4th floor (no lift), but they are not bad at Rs 150/200 with hot-water geyser. For a shorter walk you pay Rs 185/235.

Hotel Payal *(☎ 478460, Patel Bridge)* is a small place with reasonably priced singles/doubles/triples with TV and air cooler for Rs 200/250/300. Free bucket hot water is available.

Hotel Amrit *(☎ 465876, Patel Bridge)*, near Payal, is not a bad option with cheap singles/doubles starting at Rs 100/150, or Rs 350/450 with TV and air-con.

Hotel Neelam *(☎ 466001, 33/2 Patel Bridge Corner)*, just around the corner from Payal, is a much smarter hotel. Good-value rooms cost Rs 180/230 with TV and hot water. The rooms are spotless but the white-tile decor makes it seem like you're sleeping in someone's bathroom.

Places to Stay – Mid-Range & Top End

Indore has a good selection of comfortable mid-price hotels, as befits a business city of this size.

Tourist Bungalow *(☎ 521818, RN Tagore Rd)* is at the back of the Tagore Natya Griha Hall. Comfortable rooms are Rs 300/350, or Rs 390/490 with air-con.

Hotel Royal Residency *(☎ 764633, 225 RN Tagore Rd)* has well-appointed standard rooms that are good value at Rs 450/600; air-con rooms start at Rs 750/900.

Hotel Kanchan *(☎ 270871, ⓔ kanchan@bom4.vsnl.net.in, Tuko Ganj)* is a small place, and possibly the best value in this range, with clean and comfortable rooms for Rs 400/550; air-con costs Rs 500/700. It has a bar and restaurant.

Hotel Samrat *(☎ 527889, MG Rd)*, large and modern, has comfortable rooms with TV for Rs 400/550, or Rs 650/800 with air-con. The restaurant here has a good reputation and it has a bar. Checkout is available 24 hours.

Hotel President *(☎ 528866, fax 512230, RN Tagore Rd)* describes its lobby as having an 'out of this world look'. The rooms, however, are looking a bit weary these days, although there is a health club and sauna for guests. Rooms start at Rs 875/1075, all with air-con and including breakfast.

Sayaji Hotel *(☎ 552121, fax 553131, Vijay Nagar)*, 4km east of the town centre, is a huge place and Indore's top hotel. It has a swimming pool, bowling alley, tennis and squash courts and health club. Its luxurious rooms start at Rs 1450/1700.

Places to Eat

Indore is famous for its variety of *namkin* (spicy nibbles); Prakash brand is the best. If you're here during one of the festivals watch out for the *bhang gota* (samosas with added zing).

The ***Indian Coffee House*** is always a good, cheap choice. There's a branch on MG Rd, near Gandhi Hall.

Food Centre is a busy cafeteria serving tasty South Indian food in the City Centre shopping complex on MG Rd.

Landmark Restaurant, next to the Hotel President on RN Tagore Rd, is an astonishingly good continental-style place doing things rarely seen in India, such as Waldorf salad and roast lamb. The service is attentive and prices are reasonable.

Most of the top hotels have restaurants and bars. ***Woodlands Restaurant*** at the Hotel President is a good choice, and meals are very reasonably priced.

Shopping

West of the centre, the Kajuri Bazaar is only one of a number of colourful and lively bazaars in the vicinity of the Rajwada (see Things to See earlier). It specialises in gold and silverwork, cloth, leather work and traditional garments.

Getting There & Away

Air Indian Airlines has an office (☎ 431595) on Racecourse Rd. There are daily evening flights to Mumbai (US$90) and daily morning flights to Delhi (US$135), via Bhopal (US$55) and Gwalior (US$105, Monday and Friday only).

Bus There are departures from the Sarwate bus stand every half hour to Ujjain (Rs 27, 1½ hours) and Bhopal (Rs 78/144, ordinary/deluxe, five to six hours). Buses go to Dhar (Rs 28, two hours) at 5, 6, 7.45, 8.30 and 9 am. For Mandu, take a bus to Dhar and another to Mandu from Dhar (Rs 15, 1½ hours).

There are also direct buses to Omkareshwar (Rs 34, three hours), most departing before 11 am. There are two services to Aurangabad (for the Ajanta and Ellora Caves in Maharashtra; covered in Lonely Planet's *South India* and *India* guides) at 5 am and 9.30 pm (Rs 182, 13 hours); the morning service stops at Ajanta but the overnight bus is direct to Aurangabad. There's a daily bus for Mumbai (Rs 244/368, ordinary/deluxe, 16 hours) at 5 and 6.30 am.

From Gangwal bus stand, about 3km west along Jawahar Rd, there are departures to Dhar every 30 minutes.

Train Indore is connected to the main broad-gauge lines between Delhi and Mumbai via Ujjain in the north-west and Bhopal in the north-east. The daily *Malwa Express* leaves Indore at 12.30 pm for Delhi (Rs 287/ 903, sleeper/1st class, 19 hours, 969km), via Ujjain (Rs 29/173, 1½ hours, 80km), Bhopal (Rs 67/352, 5½ hours, 264km), Gwalior (Rs 199/672, 12½ hours, 652km) and Agra (Rs 149/783, 14 hours, 770km). For Mumbai (Rs 284 in sleeper class, 14½ hours, 829km), the *Avantika Express* leaves daily at 3.50 pm and arrives in Mumbai at 6.50 am the next morning.

There is also a metre-gauge line through Indore. Services on this line run from Jaipur in Rajasthan to Indore (Rs 160/22 in 2nd/ sleeper class, 16 hours, 610km), and on to Khandwa and Purna.

Car An alternative to the slow public transport to Mandu, Omkareshwar and Maheshwar is a taxi or hired car and driver. MP Tourism (☎ 528653) can organise a car for Rs 4.50/km (minimum 250km per day). An overnight stay – essential if you want to visit all three places – costs an extra day. You may get a better price from a private taxi outside the bus or train station.

Getting Around

To/From the Airport The airport is 9km from the city. Autorickshaws charge Rs 80 and taxis Rs 250. You may find it is cheaper than this to book your transport from your hotel.

Local Transport Indore's autorickshaws are cheap (most journeys are under Rs 10) and drivers will generally use their meters. Tempos operate along set routes and cost Rs 3 to 5, from point to point. The main stands are in front of the train station and at Gandhi Hall.

AROUND INDORE

Omkareshwar

This island at the confluence of the Narmada and Kaveri Rivers, 73km from Indore, has drawn Hindu pilgrims for centuries on account of its jyoti linga, one of the 12 throughout India, at the Shiva temple of **Shri Omkar Mandhata**. (For an explanation of the myth of the jyoti linga see Mahakaleshwar Mandir under Temples in the Ujjain section earlier in this chapter.)

The temple was constructed from local soft stone that enabled its artisans to achieve a rare degree of detailed work, particularly in the friezes on the upper parts of the structure.

The setting here is stunning. From the village on the banks of the Narmada, the island seems to loom out of the river, crowned by a former palace. A high footbridge connects the village with the island, or you can descend to the ghats and take a motorboat across the Narmada River (Rs 5). The path up to the temple is lined with the usual colourful pilgrim paraphernalia: garlands of marigolds, coconuts, strings of beads and tacky souvenirs. Crowds gather for the puja that is performed in the temple three times a day.

There are other temples on this island including the **Siddhnath**, a good example of early medieval Brahminic architecture, and a cluster of other Hindu and Jain temples. Though damaged by Muslim invaders in the time of Mohammed of Ghazni (11th century), these temples and those on the nearby riverbanks remain essentially intact. The island temples present a very picturesque sight and are well worth visiting.

Places to Stay & Eat Easily the most comfortable place to stay, ***Hotel Aishwarya*** (☎ *07280-71325*) is a concrete block and the only hotel in the village. Clean singles/doubles with private bathroom and bucket hot water are Rs 250/350. The restaurant serves simple, cheap vegetarian food. The hotel is on the other side of the village from the bus stand and is well signposted from the main road.

Holkar Guesthouse is a bit difficult to find; it's the faded yellow building perched on a rocky outcrop with good views across to Omkareshwar Island. Ask for directions in the marketplace. Basic doubles with shared bathroom are Rs 100.

Yatrika Guest House, right near the bus stand, has simple but clean rooms with private bathroom and bucket hot water for Rs 250.

There are ***stalls*** selling basic food around the bus stand.

Getting There & Away There are five direct buses daily to Indore (Rs 35, three hours). There are four direct buses – on atrocious roads – to Maheshwar (Rs 35, 2½ hours), or you can take one of the regular buses to Barwaha and change there.

Maheshwar

Maheshwar was an important cultural and political centre at the dawn of Hindu civilisation and was mentioned in the Ramayana and Mahabharata under its former name of Mahishmati. It languished in obscurity for many centuries until revived by the Holkar queen, Rani Ahilyabai of Indore, in the late 18th century. It's from these times that most of the temples and the fort complex date.

The principal sights are the **fort**, now a museum displaying heirlooms and relics of the Holkar dynasty; the three **ghats** lining the banks of the Narmada River; and the multitiered **temples**, distinguished by their overhanging balconies and intricately worked doorways.

Maheshwar saris are famous throughout the country for their unique weave and beautifully complex patterns. The Rewa Society, inside the fort, runs a **sari-weaving factory** where you can see the weavers at work on handlooms. Saris are on sale here (around Rs 1000 for silk; Rs 500 for cotton), or you can shop around for them in the market.

Maheshwar is easily fitted in between Omkareshwar and Mandu, but the choice of accommodation is slim. ***Akashdeep Rest House***, on the road up to the fort, has very simple doubles with shared bathroom for Rs 50, or try the ***Ahilya Trust Guesthouse***, also near the fort.

There is an afternoon bus from Indore (four hours). Otherwise, regular local buses run to Maheshwar from Barwaha and Dhar, both of which are easily reached by local bus from Indore.

Dhar

Founded by Raja Bhoj, the legendary founder of Bhopal and Mandu, Dhar was the capital of Malwa until Mandu rose to power. There are good views from the ramparts of Dhar's well-preserved **fort**. Dhar also has the large stone **Bhojashala Mosque** with ancient Sanskrit inscriptions, and the adjoining **tomb** of the Muslim saint Kamal Maula.

Dhar is best visited en route to or from Mandu, 33km away.

MANDU

☎ 07292

The extensive and now mainly deserted hilltop fort of Mandu is one of the most evocative sights in central India. It's on an isolated outcrop separated from the tableland to the north by a deep and wide valley, over which a natural causeway runs to the main city gate, known as Alamgir (Delhi) Gate. To the south of Mandu, the land drops steeply away to the plains far below and the view is superb. Deep ravines cut into the sides of the 20-sq-km plateau occupied by the fort.

Although it's possible to make a long day-trip from Indore, Mandu is worth at least a night. In winter, Mandu is quite popular with foreign visitors, but the local tourist season is during the monsoon, when the place turns verdant and the buildings are mirrored in the lakes.

History

Mandu, known as the City of Joy, has had a chequered history. Founded as a fortress and retreat in the 10th century by Raja Bhoj, it was conquered by the Muslim rulers of Delhi in 1304. When the Mughals took Delhi in

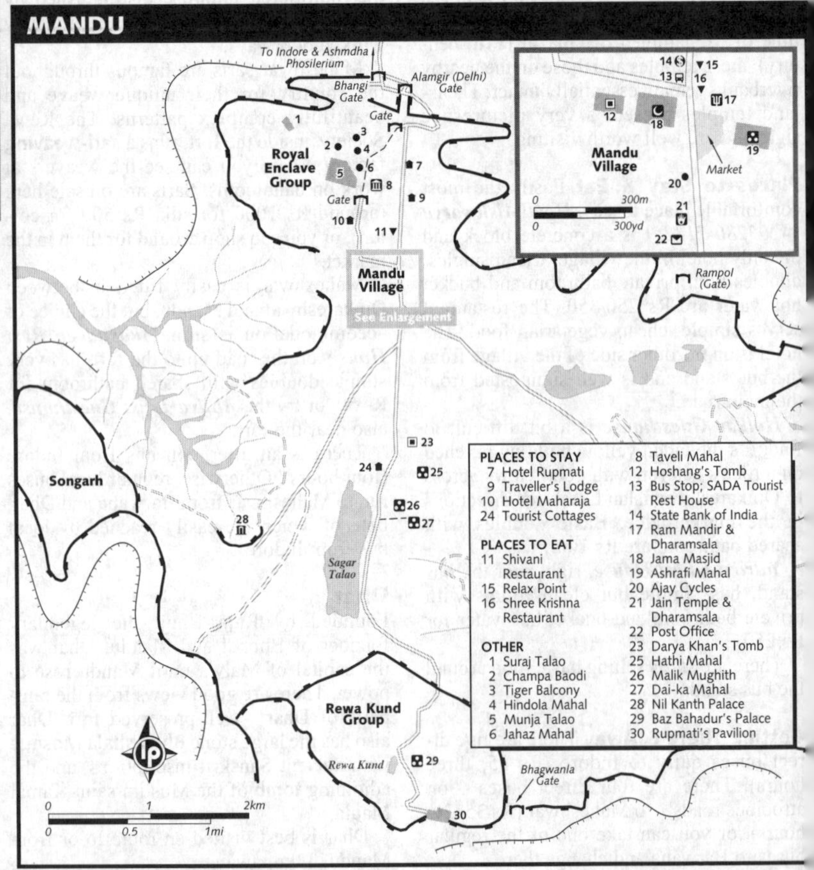

1401, the Afghan Dilawar Khan, Governor of Malwa, set up his own little kingdom and Mandu embarked on its golden age.

Although Dilawar Khan first established Mandu as an independent kingdom, it was his son, Hoshang Shah, who shifted the capital from Dhar to Mandu and raised it to its greatest splendour.

Hoshang's son ruled for only a year before being poisoned by Mohammed Shah, who became king himself and ruled for 33 years. During his reign Mandu was in frequent and often bitter dispute with neighbouring powers.

In 1469, Ghiyas-ud-din, the son of Mohammed Shah, ascended the throne and spent the next 31 years devoting himself to women and song, before being poisoned at the age of 80 by his son, Nasir-ud-din. The son lived only another 10 years before dying, some say of guilt. In turn his son, another Mohammed, had an unhappy reign. Finally, in 1526, Bahadur Shah of Gujarat conquered Mandu.

In 1534 the Mughal Humayun defeated Bahadur Shah, but as soon as Humayun turned his back an officer of the former dynasty took over. Several more changes of fortune eventually led to Baz Bahadur taking power in 1554. In 1561 he fled Mandu rather than face Akbar's advancing troops.

Even after it was added to the Mughal empire by Akbar, Mandu kept a considerable degree of independence, until taken by the Marathas in 1732. The capital of Malwa was shifted back to Dhar, and Mandu became a ghost town. For a ghost town, however, it's very grandiose and impressive, and has one of the best collections of Afghan architecture in India.

Orientation & Information

The buildings of Mandu can be divided into three groups. The Royal Enclave, Mandu's most impressive group of temples, stands on the northern shoulder of the fort, but is only accessible by looping through Mandu Village and entering from the south.

The village is about 2km from the gate and is where most of Mandu's inhabitants live. The buildings here are known as the village group. Continuing on, you'll eventually reach the Rewa Kund group at the extreme south of the fort.

You can get a copy of the Archaeological Survey of India's excellent guidebook *Mandu* for Rs 11 from the Taveli Mahal in the Royal Enclave.

The nearest bank for changing money is in Indore, although a traveller has reported being able to cash a travellers cheque at the State Bank of India, next to the bus stop.

Royal Enclave Group

These are the only temples at Mandu for which you pay admission (US$5 or Rs 230, and Rs 25 in video-camera fees). The enclosure is open sunrise to sunset.

Jahaz Mahal, or the Ship Palace, is probably the most famous building in Mandu. It really is shiplike, being far longer (120m) than it is wide (15m), and the illusion is completed by the two lakes that flank it to the east and west. It was constructed by Ghiyas-ud-din, son of Mohammed Shah, for his harem, reputed to number more than 15,000 maidens. The Jahaz Mahal with its lookouts, arches, cool rooms and beautiful pool was their playground.

Taveli Mahal, just south of the Jahaz Mahal, is now the Archaeological Survey of India's Antiquity Gallery. This small museum is open sunrise to sunset (entry to the Royal Enclave includes this museum). Exhibits include fragments of utensils and vessels found at the site, and some stone images.

Just north of Jahaz Mahal is a churchlike hall known as the **Hindola Mahal**, or Swing Palace, because the inward slope of the walls is supposed to create the impression that the walls are swaying. The wide, sloping ramp at the northern end of the building is said to have been built to enable the ruler to be conveyed upstairs by elephant.

To the west of the first two Royal Enclave structures is **Champa Baodi**, an interesting step-well on the north edge of the tank. Its subterranean levels featured cool wells and bathrooms and it was obviously a popular hot-weather retreat.

Other buildings in the enclave include the 'house and shop' of Gada Shah and the 1405

Mosque of Dilawar Khan, one of the earliest Muslim buildings in Mandu.

Village Group

Jama Masjid Built in 1454, this huge mosque dominates the village of Mandu. It is said to be the finest and largest example of Afghan architecture in India. Construction was commenced by Hoshang Shah, who modelled it on the great Umayyad Mosque in Damascus, Syria. Jama Masjid features an 80-sq-metre courtyard. It's open from 8.30 am to 5.30 pm daily.

Hoshang's Tomb Immediately behind the mosque is the imposing tomb of Hoshang, who died in 1435. Reputed to be India's oldest marble building, the tomb is entered through a domed porch. Light enters the interior through stone jali (carved marble lattice screens), typical of the Hindu influence on the tomb's fine design. It has a double arch and a squat, central dome surrounded by four smaller domes. It is said that Shah Jahan sent his architects to Mandu to study this tomb before they embarked upon the design of the Taj Mahal.

To one side of the tomb enclosure is a long, low colonnade with its width divided into three by rows of pillars. Behind is a long, narrow hall with a typically Muslim barrel-vaulted ceiling, intended as a shelter for visiting pilgrims.

The Perfect Escape

One of the wonderful things about Mandu is the sense of tranquillity, which seems to waft through its ancient palaces. After a few weeks in central India, escaping from the congestion and chaos of the cities is one of the most memorable things about spending a few days in the 'City of Joy'. The palaces are still intact enough to get a sense of Mandu in Dilawar Khan's time, and the echoes of this era resonate loudly through the impressive stone hallways. Fortunately, the flow of tourists has not yet reached the proportions that would rob the place of its magic. Wandering around a roofless, empty palace built for thousands, marvelling at the engineering ingenuity is absorbing and relaxing, particularly late in the day.

Ashrafi Mahal The ruin of this building stands directly across the road from the Jama Masjid. Originally built as a madrasa (religious college), it was later extended by its builder, Mohammed Shah, to become his tomb. The design was simply too ambitious for its builders' abilities and it later collapsed. The seven-storey circular tower of victory, which Mohammed Shah erected, has also fallen. A great stairway still leads up to the entrance to the empty shell of the building.

Jain Temple There are numerous buildings in this modern and ever-developing temple complex. The temples are richly decorated and feature tirthankars in marble, silver and gold, some with glinting jade eyes. Towards the back of the compound is a theme-park style Jain **museum**, which includes a walk-on replica of Shatrunjaya (the hilltop temple complex at Palitana, Gujarat), and a mural of colourful kitsch Jain homilies. One particularly explicit panel shows the terrible consequences of eating meat and drinking: A drunk carnivore lies on the street with dogs peeing on him.

Rewa Kund Group

About 3km south of the village group, past the large Sagar Talao (lake), is the Rewa Kund group.

Baz Bahadur's Palace Baz Bahadur was the last independent ruler of Mandu. His palace, constructed about 1509, is beside the Rewa Kund, and there was a water lift at the northern end of the tank to supply water to the palace. A curious mix of Rajasthani and Mughal styles, it was actually built well before Baz Bahadur came to power.

Rupmati's Pavilion At the very edge of the fort, perched on the hillside overlooking the plains below, is the pavilion of Rupmati. The Malwa legends relate that she was a beautiful Hindu singer, and that Baz

Bahadur persuaded her to leave her home on the plains by building her this pavilion. From its terrace and domed pavilions, Rupmati could gaze down on the Narmada River. The river is now dammed, but once wound across the plains far below.

It's a romantic building, the perfect setting for a fairytale romance – but one with an unhappy ending. Akbar, it is said, was prompted to conquer Mandu partly due to Rupmati's beauty. When Akbar marched on the fort Baz Bahadur fled, leaving Rupmati to poison herself.

For maximum romantic effect come here in the late afternoon to watch the sunset, or at night when the moon is full. Bring a torch (flashlight) as there's no lighting on the road back.

Darya Khan's Tomb & Hathi Mahal

To the east of the road, between the Rewa Kund and the village, are these two buildings. The tomb of Darya Khan was once decorated with intricate patterns of mosaic tiles. The Hathi Mahal, or Elephant Palace, is so named because the pillars supporting the dome are of massive proportions – like elephant legs.

Nil Kanth Palace

This palace, at the end of one of the ravines that cuts into the fort, is actually below the level of the hilltop and is reached by a flight of steps going down the hillside. At one time it was a Shiva shrine, as the name – God with the Blue Throat – suggests. Under the Mughals it became a pleasant water palace with a cascade running down the middle.

At the top of the steps, villagers sell the seeds of the baobab tree; Mandu is one of the few places in India where the baobab is found. The baobab is difficult to miss; it's the tubby grey tree that looks as if it has been planted upside down with its roots in the air.

Ashmdha Phosilerium

Just outside Mandu, on the road from Indore, is Ashmdha Phosilerium; entry is Rs 10. Set on the lip of an impressive gorge, the Phosilerium explains the dinosaur period of Indian history. Unfortunately the place is pretty uninspiring; the large model dinosaurs out the front and some indistinguishable dinosaur remains housed in the Phosilerium are about all you get. The view is the best part, but there are plenty of places in Mandu where you don't have to pay to enjoy it.

Organised Tours

Tours to Mandu are run from Indore (see Organised Tours under Indore earlier in this chapter). Local guides loiter around the bus stand offering their services.

Places to Stay

Hotel Maharaja *(☎ 63288, Jahaz Mahal Rd)*, in a quiet location between Mandu Village and the Royal Enclave, is the best budget option. Basic doubles with private bathroom are Rs 125/200 and bucket hot water is Rs 5. There's a simple restaurant and friendly staff.

Tourist Rest House is a dull SADA place directly opposite the Jama Masjid. Rooms with bathroom are dingy and cost Rs 125; there are squat toilets and bucket hot water.

The following two MP Tourism places should be booked at the tourist office in Indore (☎ 0731-528653) to ensure a bed. ***Traveller's Lodge*** *(☎ 63221)* looks a little dingy compared to the nearby Rupmati, but it's comfortable enough with singles/doubles at Rs 290/390 with bathroom and hot water. ***Tourist Cottages*** *(☎ 63235)* is in a very pleasant location overlooking the Sagar Talao. Rooms cost Rs 350/450, or Rs 750/850 with air-con. Breakfast and dinner are served in the outdoor restaurant and nonguests are welcome.

Hotel Rupmati *(☎ 63270)* is the top hotel in Mandu. Its 10 spacious rooms provide fine views over the gorge from back patios. The modern and comfortable rooms cost Rs 325/400. Air-con doubles are Rs 750. It has a pleasant terrace restaurant.

Places to Eat

The restaurants at Hotel Rupmati and the MP Tourism hotels are the best places to eat, but there are a few cheap independent places in the village. Look out for the green, hard-shelled seed of the baobab tree in the market. The locals love it, but it's a bit like eating sweet-and-sour chalk dust.

Relax Point has drinks and a shop but it doesn't seem to cook food. You may be able to coax a menu out of ***Shree Krishna Restaurant*** next door. We've had reports that the food is good here.

Shivani Restaurant, farther north, serves up good, reasonably priced vegetarian food (between Rs 20 and Rs 45) and breakfasts.

Getting There & Away

There are six daily buses direct from Mandu to Indore (Rs 40, 3½ hours), but coming the other way you must change at Dhar. There's one bus to Maheshwar at 7.30 am (Rs 25, 2½ hours).

For Bhopal, take the 6 am bus to Indore where you can connect with a bus or train to Bhopal. Buses stop near the Jama Masjid in the village.

The alternative is hiring a car and driver; see Getting There & Away under Indore earlier in this chapter.

Getting Around

You can hire bicycles from Ajay Cycles, south of the Jama Masjid, or from the market for Rs 3 an hour or Rs 25 for 24 hours. This is the best way to get around as the sights are quite far apart, and the terrain is relatively flat. This is also a fine area for walking.

There's just one autorickshaw in Mandu, which is available (of course) for a three- to four-hour tour of Mandu's sights (Rs 150). It costs Rs 20 return from the village to Rupmati's Pavilion.

Eastern Madhya Pradesh

JABALPUR

☎ 0761 • pop 1,065,025

Almost due south of Khajuraho and east of Bhopal, the large city of Jabalpur is principally famous today for the gorge on the Narmada River known as the Marble Rocks. It's also the departure point for a visit to the national parks of Kanha (160km) and Bandhavgarh (197km).

History

The original settlement in this area was ancient Tripuri and the rulers of this city, the Hayahaya, are mentioned in the Mahabharata. The city passed successively into Mauryan and then Gupta control until it was taken by the Kalchuri rulers in AD 875. In the 13th century it was overrun by the Gonds and by the early 16th century it had become the powerful state of Gondwana.

Though besieged by Mughal armies from time to time, Gondwana survived until 1789 when it was conquered by the Marathas. Their rule was unpopular, due largely to the increased activities of the thuggees, ritual murderers and bandits from whom the word thug is derived. The Marathas were defeated in 1817 and the thuggees were subdued by the British, who developed the town in the mid-19th century.

Orientation & Information

The Old Bazaar to the north-west is a tangle of streets, which are easy to get lost in. The bus stand is about 4km from the train station, which is near the Civil Lines area of town.

The tourist office (☎ 322111) is at the train station, and is open 7 am to 9 pm daily. You can book MP Tourism accommodation here for Kanha National Park (payment in full required) and Marble Rocks (see these sections later in this chapter for more details).

Money can be changed at the main branch of the State Bank of India (opposite Hotel Rishi Regency) and at Jackson's Hotel.

Internet connections from Jabalpur are slow but cheap during the day. Cyber Estate, near Jackson's Hotel, is open until 9 pm and charges Rs 30 per hour.

Things to See

South of the bazaar, next to the tempo stand, the diverse collection at **Rani Durgavati Museum** is worth a look. The ground floor has 10th- and 11th-century sculptures from temples in the Jabalpur district. Upstairs are letters and photographs relating to Mahatma Gandhi, and a room full of models and photographs depicting the Gond people. It's open from 10 am to 5 pm daily, except Monday; entry is free.

Madan Mahal, a Gond fortress built in 1116, can be found perched on top of a huge boulder en route to Marble Rocks. It's about 5km from Jabalpur, and the tempos going to Marble Rocks will drop you there. The Gonds, who worshipped snakes, lived in this region even before the Aryans arrived, and maintained their independence right up until Mughal times.

Places to Stay – Budget

The cheapest places to stay are almost all near the bus stand, about 3km from the train station. The commission racket for rickshaw-wallahs is alive and well in Jabalpur.

Hotel Mayur *(☎ 310035, Malviya Chowk)* is cheap, clean and close to the bus stand. Economy singles/doubles are Rs 120/220 and the better 'deluxe' rooms are Rs 150/250, all with private bathroom, squat toilets and bucket hot water.

Hotel Vijan Palace *(☎ 310972, 313 Vijan Market)* is a good choice in the heart of the bazaar. Basic rooms with private bathroom are Rs 250/300 and air-con rooms are Rs 500/600. You may get a better price if you try bargaining.

Swayam Hotel *(☎ 325377, Guru Nanak Market)* is grubby but cheap, with decent-size rooms at Rs 65/130. Bathrooms have squat toilets and bucket hot water. ***Hotel Rahul*** *(☎ 325525)*, next door, is only slightly better with rooms at Rs 100/130, or Rs 150/200 with TV and bucket hot water.

Raja Gokul Das Dharmasala, a traditional pilgrim's lodge, is the cheapest place in town, but when busy, foreigners are not accepted. An impressive building from the outside, it has basic rooms (shared bathroom) for Rs 24 per person. It's only five minutes' walk east of the train station.

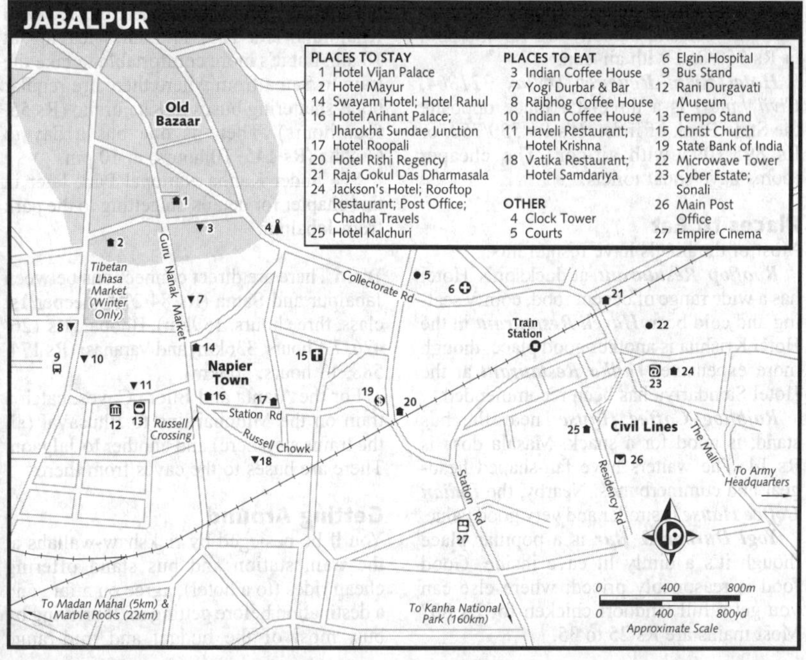

Places to Stay – Mid-Range

Hotel Roopali *(☎ 625566, Station Rd)* is popular and the best of a bunch of places on Station Rd. A range of clean singles/doubles start starting at Rs 300/350, or Rs 600/700 with air-con.

Jackson's Hotel *(☎ 322320, fax 322066, Civil Lines)* must have been the best hotel in town at one time; these days it's a bit shabby, with a large mosquito population, but it's still popular with travellers. Large, well-worn rooms with private bathroom and hot-water shower are Rs 450/500, or Rs 950/1200 with air-con. You can change travellers cheques, and baggage can be left here safely while you visit Kanha National Park. Jackson's is only about a 10-minute walk from the train station.

Hotel Arihant Palace *(☎ 627311, fax 692114, Russell Crossing)* is central and reasonable; rooms with private bathroom (squat toilets) start at Rs 325/400.

Hotel Kalchuri *(☎ 321491, Civil Lines)* is a well-maintained MP Tourism operation close to the train station. Rooms with hot-water geyser and balcony are Rs 450/550, or Rs 750/850 with air-con.

Hotel Rishi Regency *(☎/fax 321804, Civil Lines)* is a three-star place opposite the State Bank of India. It's Rs 550/750, or Rs 895/1095 with air-con. The cheaper rooms have squat toilets.

Places to Eat

Most of the hotels have restaurants.

Rooftop Restaurant at Jackson's Hotel has a wide range of decent food, comfy seating and cold beer. ***Haveli Restaurant*** in the Hotel Krishna is another good place, though more expensive. ***Vatika Restaurant*** at the Hotel Samdariya has been recommended.

Rajbhog Coffee House, near the bus stand, is good for a snack. Masala dosa is Rs 14. The waiters have fan-shaped headgear and cummerbunds. Nearby, the ***Indian Coffee House*** is similar and very good value.

Yogi Durbar & Bar is a popular place though it's a dimly lit cave inside. Good food is reasonably priced; where else can you get a full tandoori chicken for Rs 80? Most mains are Rs 25 to 35.

Jharokha Sundae Junction, next to the Hotel Arihant Palace, is good for ice cream. Try ***Sonali***, next to Jackson's Hotel and Cyber Estate, for mouth-watering sweets.

Shopping

The Tibetan Lhasa Market is open from November to January and is good for woollens. Jackets cost around Rs 400, shawls cost Rs 270 and scarves a mere Rs 50. There are great designs and the shawls in particular are very groovy. Bargaining is possible, particularly if you're making multiple purchases.

Getting There & Away

Bus There are buses to Jabalpur from Allahabad, Khajuraho, Varanasi, Bhopal, Nagpur and other main centres. For overnight journeys the private buses are better as MP state transport buses are mostly in an advanced state of decay. The bus agents are situated near the bus stand (across the road or nearby) and the private buses leave from outside the agent. There's one bus a day to Khajuraho (Rs 125, 11 hours) leaving at 10 am, but it's more comfortable to take the train to Satna from where there are regular bone-shattering buses to Khajuraho (Rs 55, four hours). There is one bus a day to Orchha (Rs 145, 10 hours) at 10 pm.

See under Kanha National Park later in this chapter for details on getting to the park from Jabalpur.

Train There are direct connections between Jabalpur and Satna (Rs 84/279, sleeper/1st class, three hours, 189km), Bhopal (Rs 126/426, 7½ hours, 336km) and Varanasi (Rs 174/588, 13 hours, 505km).

For the Ajanta and Ellora Caves, catch a train on the Mumbai line to Bhusaval (all the trains stop here) and another to Jalgaon. There are buses to the caves from there.

Getting Around

You'll be besieged by rickshaw-wallahs at the train station and bus stand offering cheap rides (to a hotel); agree on a fare and a destination before getting in. If arriving by bus, most of the budget and mid-range hotels are within 10 minutes' walk of the city bus stand.

Tempos trundle around town, but the only time you're likely to use one is to get to Marble Rocks. The tempo stand is near the bus stand (opposite Haveli Restaurant and Hotel Krishna).

AROUND JABALPUR

Marble Rocks

Known locally as Bhedaghat (after the nearby village), this gorge on the Narmada River is 22km west of Jabalpur. The gleaming white (and sometimes pink, brown and black) cliffs rise sheer from the clear water and are a very impressive sight, especially by moonlight. On weekends and full-moon nights the place is invariably packed with local tourists.

The trip up the 2km-long gorge is made in a shared rowboat; it costs Rs 10 per person on a 20-seat boat, or it's possible to rent the whole boat for Rs 210. These go all day every day, October to June, from the jetty at the bottom of the gorge and leave when full. The first 500m is pretty dull, but as you glide upstream with the massive, naturally sculpted marble crags crowding in around you, it's difficult not to be impressed.

A worthwhile 1km walk from the jetty is the **Dhuandhar** or Smoke Cascade Waterfall. Along the way is the **Chausath Yogini** or Madanpur Temple. The circular temple contains damaged ancient images of the 64 yoginis.

Motel Marble Rocks *(☎ 0761-83424)* is a very pleasant MP Tourism place overlooking the foot of the gorge. It has a well-kept garden and an excellent restaurant. The motel is a comfortable ex-colonial bungalow with only four doubles for Rs 450. Bookings can be made at the Jabalpur tourist office. There are plenty of cheap ***cafes*** in the village.

Black and white marble and sandstone sculptures are a speciality of this small town, and because it is primarily an Indian tourist spot, prices are reasonable. Ironically, the marble is actually from Rajasthan but the sculptures, which are mostly Indian devotional figures, are made in the village. As a very rough idea of price, 15cm marble sculptures start at Rs 70, and you can pay about Rs 5000 for a 90cm statue. Smaller objects such as candle holders and ornaments start at Rs 15.

Tempos run to Marble Rocks from the city tempo stand near the museum in Jabalpur for Rs 8.

NARSINGHPUR

Narsinghpur, 84km south-west of Jabalpur, is just a sleepy town but worth a stop if you're interested in the Sleeman trail (see the boxed text below). There's a fascinating account of Sleeman's antithug detective work in Sir Francis Tuker's *The Yellow Scarf*.

Narsingh Mandir is an old temple with a honeycomb of tunnels beneath it. The caretaker may show you the room where Sleeman trapped some of the thuggee leaders.

Thuggees

It was from Narsinghpur in the early 19th century that Colonel Sleeman waged his war against the bizarre Hindu thuggee (from which the word 'thug' is derived) cult, which claimed as many as a million lives over about 500 years. From as early as the 14th century, followers had roamed the main highways of India engaging in the ritual murder of travellers, strangling their victims with a yellow silk scarf in order to please the bloodthirsty goddess Kali.

Bizarre thuggee rites included 'sugar sacrifices' and axe-worshipping ceremonies. They resisted infiltration by using secret signs and developing their own jargon.

It was largely due to Sleeman's efforts that the thuggee cult was wiped out. His campaign during the 1830s was sanctioned by the British governor-general, Lord Bentinck, and saw more than 400 thuggees hanged and about 3000 imprisoned or banished, ensuring the virtual eradication of these scarf-wielding nasties.

MADHYA PRADESH & CHHATISGARH

Lunawat Inn (☎ *07792-30034*) has singles/doubles with private bathroom and TV for Rs 250/450. It's about 100m from the train station (turn right at the exit).

Narsinghpur is on the main Jabalpur to Mumbai/Bhopal rail line, and a handful of express trains stop here.

KANHA NATIONAL PARK

☎ 07649

Kanha, 160km south-east of Jabalpur, is one of India's largest national parks, covering 1945 sq km including a 'core zone' of 940 sq km. The setting for Kipling's *Jungle Book*, it's a beautiful area of sal forest and lightly wooded grassland with many rivers and streams supporting an excellent variety of wildlife. It is also part of the conservation effort known as Project Tiger.

Wildlife was first given limited protection here as early as 1933, but it wasn't until 1955 that the area was declared a national park. A policy of wildlife management over the past 30 years has seen a steady increase in the numbers of tigers and leopards, as well as an increase in sambars, chitals (spotted deer), barasinghas (swamp deer) and gaurs (Indian bison). In the census of 1997, the tiger population numbered 114 and leopards 86.

There's a good chance of sighting tigers, gaurs and herbivores, and this is one of the best places in the state for bird-watching.

When to Go

Kanha National Park is completely closed from 1 July to 31 October, due to the monsoons. Although it's possible to see wildlife throughout the season, sightings increase as the weather gets hotter in March and April and the animals move out of the tree cover in search of water. The hottest months are May and June, when the temperature can reach 42°C in the afternoon. December and January are the coolest months and, although it's warm during the day, as soon as the sun sets the temperature quickly plunges to zero and below.

Orientation & Information

Khatia Village, at the western entrance to Kanha Village, is the best place to base yourself for visits to the park. Kisli, 3km farther in, is the main gate where you pay the entry fee (Rs 200), plus Rs 25/200 for camera/video-camera.

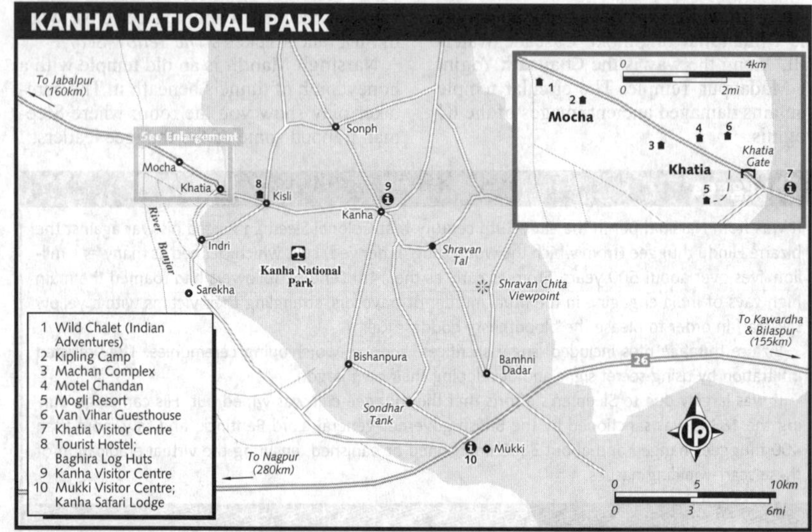

There are no facilities for changing money, but there's a telephone, small shop and petrol pump at Kisli. You'll need fast film (at least 400 ASA) because of low light in the early morning and evening.

The local market at **Sarekha** on Friday draws the colourful Baiga Adivasis, and it is worth going to. A closer market is at **Mocha**, 5km from Khatia, held on Wednesday.

Park gates open from sunrise to noon and 3 pm to sunset from 1 November to 15 February; sunrise to noon and 4 pm to sunset from 16 February to 15 April; and sunrise to 11 am and 5 pm to sunset from 16 April to 30 June. The park is closed during the monsoon from 1 July to 31 October.

Visitor Centres There are three excellent visitor centres at Kanha Village (in the park), Khatia and Mukki with high-standard interpretive displays. The Kanha Village display is the most impressive, with five galleries and a research hall. There's a novel sound-and-light show 'Encounters in the Dark'.

A number of books and postcards are also sold. The centres are open 8 am to noon and 3 to 7.30 pm daily (although these times change depending on the season), and a free outdoor film is shown each evening at the Khatia visitor centre.

Wildlife Safaris

Excursions into the park are made in the early morning and evening; no night driving is allowed. Jeeps can be arranged by most of the accommodation places (which gives you a better chance of splitting the cost with others) and the cost is calculated on a per kilometre basis. Expect to pay around Rs 500 (which can be shared by up to six people), plus Rs 90 for a compulsory guide. Park entry fees are extra but only need to be paid once a day. At the height of the season there may not be enough jeeps to go around, so book as soon as you arrive.

You may need warm clothes for early-morning outings. It is a good idea to choose your safari outfit carefully – a sign in the Khatia visitor centre warns 'Avoid wearing colours that jar. Violators are liable to be prosecuted'!

On the Tiger Trail

Visitors to Kanha National Park might be hoping for the triumph of a chance tiger-spotting, but in reality it's all very well orchestrated.

The tigers are tracked each morning by rangers mounted on trained elephants. They listen for the distinctive warning calls of deer and monkeys that indicate a predator is in the vicinity, then try to pick up the trail of pug marks (footprints). Once a tiger is located, they radio back to the Kanha visitor centre, where most of the jeeps and their passengers are waiting patiently. A flurry of activity then ensues as the jeep drivers race back to a base (eg, Kisli) to pick up a ticket that puts your vehicle in the 'queue' to view the tiger. The jeeps then park some distance from the tiger (which is hopefully still there) and you board an elephant (Rs 300 per person) for the final tramp through the undergrowth to view the tiger. On afternoon excursions sightings are left to chance, but the guides usually have a fair idea where to look.

Places to Stay & Eat

Accommodation is strung out over a distance of about 6.5km (around Khatia) along the road from Jabalpur, so it's important that you get off the bus at the right place. Accommodation ranges from cheap guest-houses to the high-priced lodges operating on all-inclusive 'jungle plans'. Apart from the lodge restaurants, there are a couple of basic *dhabas* (snack and chai shacks) serving vegetarian food, just outside Khatia Gate. Note that accommodation costs 40% to 50% more than the following prices in the high season (April to June).

Khatia 400m from the road, near Khatia Gate, is ***Van Vihar Guesthouse***, the best budget place. Basic doubles with private bathroom (squat toilets and bucket hot water) are Rs 100 per person. It's friendly and the resident family prepares good, cheap food.

Machan Complex is basic, charging Rs 30 for dorms and Rs15 for doubles, all with private bathroom and bucket hot water.

MADHYA PRADESH & CHHATISGARH

There are rather grotty squat toilets. The menu at its restaurant has a handy Hindi language guide on the back.

Motel Chandan *(☎ 77220)* has better doubles with private bathroom for Rs 100 or 250, and large deluxe rooms for Rs 300 that have hot-water geysers. There's a good restaurant here with thalis for Rs 30.

Mogli Resort *(☎ 77228)* is a modern place with little jungle character but clean and comfortable rooms. Excellent air cooled/air-con doubles with private bathroom are Rs 850/1400, and attractive cottages with fan and bathtub are Rs 850. There's also a smaller cottage for Rs 500. The 'jungle plan', which includes all meals and safaris, is the best deal of its type in town.

Wild Chalet *(☎ 77203)*, about 5km from Khatia Gate, is by the river and very peaceful with friendly and knowledgeable staff. Double chalets with private bathroom are US$87 per person (single occupancy is 30% more) including meals and transport into the park (plus two game drives per day). Staff also organise nature trails and bird-watching trips. Book with Indian Adventures (☎ 022-6428244), 257 SV Rd, Bandra, Mumbai 400050, or direct with Wild Chalet (and receive a 10% discount).

Kipling Camp *(☎/fax 77219)* has a certain toffee-nosed charm; it's staffed by enthusiastic Brits. The Kipling Camp can be contacted through the Tollygunge Club (☎ 033-4732316, fax 4731903), 120 DP Sasmal Rd, Kolkata 700033. Make advance bookings; it's not cheap at an all-inclusive Rs 4500 per day (less for three nights or more and there are discounts in the low season). It's also the home of Tara, the central character in Mark Shand's *Travels on My Elephant*.

Kisli & Mukki There's nothing at Kisli apart from the forestry office and two MP Tourism hotels. The ***Tourist Hostel*** has three eight-bed dorms at an overpriced Rs 250 a bed, including all meals (vegetarian only) and hot showers. ***Baghira Log Huts*** has reasonable air-cooled doubles for Rs 690, and a restaurant.

In Mukki, ***Kanha Safari Lodge*** is another MP Tourism place in a pleasant but isolated location 36km south-east of Khatia. It's worth trying if you're coming from Bilaspur or Kawardha, but otherwise you're better off staying in Khatia. Doubles cost Rs 490, or Rs 690 with air-con; it has a restaurant.

Advance bookings can be made at the following MP Tourism offices, but full payment up front is required. Bookings less than five days in advance must be made through the tourist office (☎ 0761-322111) at the train station in Jabalpur.

Bhopal (☎ 0755-778383) Gangotri Complex, 4th floor, North TT Nagar, New Bhopal
Delhi (☎ 011-3341187) 2nd floor, Kanishka Shopping Plaza, 19 Ashoka Rd
Kolkata (☎ 033-2478543) 6th floor, Chitrakoot Bldg, 230A, AJC Bose Rd
Mumbai (☎ 022-2187603) 74 World Trade Centre, Cuffe Parade, Colaba

Getting There & Away

There are state transport buses from the city bus stand in Jabalpur to Khatia Gate (six to seven hours, Rs 50) departing Jabalpur three times daily at 8 and 11 am and 2 pm. The same buses depart from Kisli at around 8 am and 12.30 pm. These buses are crowded and agonisingly slow. There are also some private buses from Jabalpur for around Rs 70.

BANDHAVGARH NATIONAL PARK

This national park is 197km north-east of Jabalpur in the Vindhyan Mountain Range. It's much smaller than Kanha, but claims to have the highest density tiger population in India with between 46 and 52 tigers. There are also 27 leopards.

The park area is 448 sq km, of which 105 sq km is the 'core area'. Bandhavgarh's setting is impressive. It's named after the ancient fort built on 800m-high cliffs. There's a temple at the fort that can be visited by jeep and below it are numerous rock-cut cave shrines.

The core area of the park has a fragile ecology, but it supports a variety of wildlife such as nilgai, wild boar, jackals, gaur, sambar and porcupines, as well as many species of birds. The ramparts of the fort provide a home for vultures, blue rock thrushes and crag martins. Bandhavgarh receives fewer visitors than Kanha and there's a good chance of spotting a tiger here.

Orientation & Information

The village of Tala is the access point for the park and the best place to stay. MP Tourism has an office at the White Tiger Forest Lodge and there's a small visitor centre at the park gate. There's nowhere to change money in Tala.

Like Kanha, entry to the park is restricted to morning and evening visits in hired jeeps, or it's Rs 100 to bring in your own vehicle. The park is closed on Tuesday all year. Entry is Rs 200 (Rs 20 for Indians), plus Rs 25/200 for camera/video-camera fees. Hiring a jeep (seating up to six passengers) costs around Rs 550, including guide. Bandhavgarh is closed from 1 July to 31 October. The telephone area code for Tala is ☎ 07653.

Bhaghela Museum

Attached to the Bandhavgarh Safari Camp in Tala, this museum is part of the private collection of the maharaja of Rewa. As well as the stuffed white tiger, (known as Mohan), there are the usual military and hunting paraphernalia, a carved ivory and silver chess set, and an extravagant swing bench made of Belgian cut glass and silver. It's open 10 am to 3 pm and 5 to 8 pm daily; entry is Rs 5.

Elephant Rides

Unlike at Kanha, elephants are still used for leisurely afternoon rides through the park for Rs 300 per person (maximum of four people) for an hour. Rides can be arranged at the forestry office near the gate on Umaria Rd.

Places to Stay & Eat

Most of the accommodation is along Umaria Rd in Tala.

Tiger Lodge, right where the bus stops, is the cheapest around. Simple doubles with grotty shared bathroom are Rs 150. The ***dhaba*** downstairs does good thalis for Rs 25, as well as basic breakfasts.

Kum Kum Home *(☎ 07653-65324)* is a good budget option. There are four clean doubles with large private bathrooms (hot-water geyser) for Rs 200.

V Patel *(☎ 07653-65323)* is a good choice if you want a bit more comfort at a reasonable price. Set well back from Umaria Rd, it offers pleasant singles/doubles (room only) for Rs 300/400, or US$65/120 including all meals, transport and park fees.

White Tiger Forest Lodge *(☎ 07653-65308)* is a good MP Tourism place (there is an office here), with pleasant cottages overlooking the river where elephants bathe. Rooms with bathroom cost Rs 590/690; rooms set back from the river with air-con are Rs 790/890 (plus 10% tax). Book ahead. There's also a good restaurant and bar.

Bandhavgarh Jungle Lodge *(☎ 07653-65317)* steps right up the price scale, operating on 'jungle plan' where all meals, park fees and safaris are included. It's hidden away near the park entrance; thatched cottages of mud, dung and straw cost US$125 a night. Book through Tiger Resorts (☎ 033-6853760, fax 6865212, ⓔ T-Resorts@indiantiger.com), suite 206, Rakeesh Deep, 11 Commercial Complex, Gulmohar Enclave, Delhi.

Bandhavgarh Safari Camp *(☎ 07653-65307)* is the former palace of the maharaja of Rewa. The spacious old-fashioned rooms have typically cavernous bathrooms. This place also operates on a jungle plan with everything included for US$140 per night.

Getting There & Away

Umaria, 32km away on the Katni to Bilaspur line, is the nearest railhead. Local buses run from there to Tala (Rs 14, one hour). Jeeps are also available from Tala to Umaria if demand is high enough.

From Satna there is an inconvenient bus service via Rewa, although you're probably better off getting a taxi from Satna if there in a group; this should cost about Rs 1100.

Heading west, the only useful train service from Umaria is the *Bilaspur-Indore Express* through Katni, Jabalpur and Bhopal.

Chhatisgarh

The movement for an independent state of Chhatisgarh can be traced back to 1924, when the idea was mooted before the Raipur

Developing Tourism

The new government of Chhatisgarh is keen to exploit the state's tourism potential. At the moment there are few tourist attractions, but the government is keen to develop tourist sites in consultation with the Adivasi population, who make up a large portion of the state's inhabitants. The government plans to develop water sports, as well as places of archaeological and religious significance, to attract visitors. With the abundance of natural forests, national parks are also an obvious target for development.

District Congress. At this time it was argued that the area of Chhatisgarh was historically and culturally different from the rest of Madhya Pradesh. In November 2000, the vision of these early 'Chhatisgarh pioneers' turned into reality with the birth of this new state.

Although the area is poverty-stricken and has major problems with drought, it is also richly endowed with natural resources. There are vast forest reserves: 75% of forest cover in the old boundaries of the state of Madhya Pradesh is now officially in Chhatisgarh. It has rich mineral deposits, including limestone, iron-ore and coal, that historically made up about half of Madhya Pradesh's revenue from mineral resources. Agriculturally, the new state is very productive and has been referred to as 'the rice bowl of India'. Economically, the state is extremely poor because revenue from its resource production has not been ploughed back into the area. However, with such financial potential for earnings, many are optimistic about Chhatisgarh's future. It is also a power surplus state, using only 60% of the power it produces (although most households don't have electricity).

The challenges facing the new government include the building of infrastructure (only about 20% of the population has access to roads), providing education and making clean drinking water available to all households.

BHORAMDEO

At Bhoramdeo, 125km east of Kisli (in Kanha National Park), is a small and interesting 11th-century **Shiva temple** built in the style of the temples of Khajuraho. Carvings cover virtually every external surface, with deities indulging in the usual range of activities, including the familiar sexual acrobatics. The temple is still very much in use today – a cobra lives inside and is fed by the priests. A few kilometres away there are two other temples, the **Mandwa Mahal** and the **Madanmanjari Mahal**, which date from the same period.

KAWARDHA

Well off the tourist trail, 20km south of Bhoramdeo, the ex-maharaja of Kawardha has opened part of his palace to guests.

Palace Kawardha *(☎ 07741-32085, fax 32088)* is a delightfully peaceful place and you're made to feel very welcome here. As far as palaces go it's neither enormous nor particularly old (it was built in 1939), but it does have the touches you'd expect in a maharaja's palace – Italian marble floors, stuffed tigers and ancient English bathroom fittings. It costs US$113 per person (with reductions for stays of more than one night), including all meals, taken with the charming ex-maharaja and his family, and outings in the jeep. Open 1 October to 30 April, reservations must be made in advance.

BILASPUR

☎ 07752 • pop 282,230

Bilaspur is a bustling city in the north of Chhatisgarh. It has no 'attractions' to speak of, but you may find it convenient to stop here if heading from Kanha National Park to Puri in Orissa.

Natraj Hotel *(Link Rd)*, near the bus stand, is well located on the main street, and has singles/doubles starting at Rs 220/270.

Hotel Centrepoint *(☎ 07752-24004, Anand Marg)* is a better quality choice with rooms starting at Rs 300/400, up to Rs 600/650 for air-con.

The bus stand, in the centre of town, has regular departures for Kawardha, Nagpur, Raipur and Mukki (for Kanha National Park).

Bilaspur has rail connections with Jabalpur, Raipur, Bhopal, Sambalpur, Puri, Kolkata and Delhi. The train station is 3km from the town centre.

Language

There is no one 'Indian' language as such. This is part of the reason why English is still widely spoken 50 years after the British left India and why it's still the official language of the judiciary.

Eighteen languages are recognised by the constitution and these fall into two major groups: Indic, or Indo-Aryan, and Dravidian. Additionally, over 1600 minor languages and dialects were listed in the latest census. The scope for misunderstanding can be easily appreciated!

The Indic languages are a branch of the Indo-European group of languages (to which English belongs). The Indic languages were spoken by the Central Asian peoples who invaded what is now India. The Dravidian languages are native to South India, although they have been influenced by Sanskrit and Hindi over the years.

Most of India's languages have their own script, but written English can also be quite common; in some states, such as Gujarat, you'll hardly see a word of it, whereas in Himachal Pradesh virtually everything is in English. For a sample of the different scripts, look at a Rs 5 or larger banknote where 14 languages are represented. As well as Hindi and English there's a list of 12 other languages: from the top, they are Assamese, Bengali, Gujarati, Kannada, Kashmiri, Malayalam, Marathi, Oriya, Punjabi, Sanskrit, Tamil, Telugu and Urdu. (See the boxed text 'North India's Official Languages' on the following page for languages covered in this book.)

Major efforts have been made to promote Hindi as the national language of India and to gradually phase out English. A stumbling block to this plan is that while Hindi is the predominant language in the north, it bears little relation to the Dravidian languages of the south.

For many educated Indians, English is virtually their first language, and for the large number of Indians who speak more than one language, English is often their second tongue. Thus it's very easy to get around India with English, but it's always good to know at least a little of the local language.

Hindi

Hindi is the most important Indian language even though it is only spoken as a mother tongue by about 20% of the population, mainly in the area known as the Hindi-belt, the cow-belt or Bimaru, which includes Bihar, Madhya Pradesh, Rajasthan and Uttar Pradesh. It is the official language of the Indian government and the states listed above, plus Haryana and Himachal Pradesh.

And Indic language, Hindi is written from left to right in Devanagari script. While the script may be unfamiliar, many of the grammatical features will be familiar to English speakers. In this language chapter, masculine and feminine nouns are indicated by (m) or (f) respectively.

For a far more comprehensive guide to Hindi, get a copy of Lonely Planet's *Hindi & Urdu phrasebook*.

Pronunciation

Most of the sounds in Hindi correspond to the Roman letters used to represent them in the transliteration.

Vowels & Diphthongs

It's important to pay close attention to the pronunciation of vowels and especially to their length. A stroke over a vowel (eg, **ā**, **ī**, **ū**) indicates a longer vowel sound. The symbol ~ over a vowel (eg, **ā̃**, **ĩ**, **ī̃**, **ũ**, **ū̃**,) indicates that it should be pronounced through the nose.

a as the 'u' in 'sun'
ā as in 'father'
ai as the 'a' in 'care'

North India's Official Languages

Assamese State language of Assam, spoken by nearly 60% of that state's population. Dates back to the 13th century.
Bengali Spoken by nearly 200 million people (mostly in what is now Bangladesh), and the state language of West Bengal. Developed as a language in the 13th century.
Gujarati An Indic language and the state language of Gujarat.
Hindi An Indic language and the official language of the Indian government and the states of Bihar, Madhya Pradesh, Rajasthan, Uttar Pradesh, Haryana and Himachal Pradesh.
Kashmiri An Indic language written in the Perso-Arabic script. About 55% of the population of Jammu & Kashmir are Kashmiri speakers.
Manipuri An Indic language of the north-eastern region.
Nepali The predominant language of Sikkim, where approximately 75% of the population are ethnic Nepalis.
Punjabi State language of Punjab. An Indic language based on Devanagari (the same script as Hindi), but written in a 16th-century script known as Gurumukhi.
Sanskrit The language of classical India and one of the oldest languages in the world. All the Vedas and classical literature were written in this Indic language.
Sindhi A significant number of Sindhi speakers are found in what is now Pakistan, although the greater number are in India. In Pakistan, the language is written in a Perso-Arabic script, while in India it uses the Devanagari script.
Urdu State language of Jammu & Kashmir; evolved with Hindi, but was adopted by the Muslim population. It is written in the Perso-Arabic script and includes many Persian words.

au as the 'aw' in 'saw'
e as in 'they'
i as in 'sit'
ī as the 'ee' in 'feet'
o as in 'both'
u as in 'put'
ū as the 'oo' in 'fool'

Note that **ai** is pronounced as a diphthong when followed by **ya**, and **au** is pronounced as a diphthong when followed by **va**.

ai as the 'i' in 'high'
au as the 'ou' in 'ouch'

Consonants

Most consonants in the transliterations are pronounced as in English, with the following exceptions:

c as the 'ch' in 'cheese'
g always as in 'gun', never as in 'age'
ḍ pronounced with the tongue curled back towards the roof of the mouth
ṭ pronounced with the tongue further back than in English. Curl the tongue back towards the roof of the mouth.
r slightly trilled
ṛ an 'r' with the tongue placed near the roof of the mouth and flapped quickly down, touching the roof as it moves
q as the 'k' in 'king', but pronounced further back
y as in 'yak'
kh similar to the 'ch' in Scottish *loch*
gh like the 'g' in 'go' but pronounced further back in the throat

Aspirated consonants are pronounced with a breath of air, represented by an h after the consonant (except for **sh**, pronounced as in 'ship', and **kh** and **gh**).

Essentials

Hello.	*namaste/namskār*
Goodbye.	*namaste/namskār*
Yes.	*jī hā̃*
No.	*jī nahī̃*

'Please' is usually conveyed through the polite form of the imperative, or through other expressions. This book uses polite expressions and the polite forms of words.

Thank you.	*shukriyā/dhanyavād*
You're welcome.	*koī bāt nahī̃*
Excuse me/Sorry.	*kshamā kījiye*
Just a minute.	*ek minaṭ rukiye*
How are you?	*āp kaise/ī haĩ?* (m/f)
Fine, and you?	*bas āp sunāiye* (m/f)
What's your name?	*āp kā shubh nām kyā hai?*
My name is ...	*merā snām ... hai*
Where are you from?	*āp kahā̃ ke rehnevāle/kī rehnevālī haĩ?* (m/f)
I'm from ...	*maĩ ... kā rehnevālā/kī rehnevālī hū̃.* (m/f)

Language Difficulties

Do you speak English?	*kyā āp ko angrezī ātī hai?*
Does anyone here speak English?	*kyā kisī ko angrezī ātī hai?*
I understand.	*maĩ samjhā/ī*
I don't understand.	*maĩ nahī̃ samjhā/ī*
Please speak more slowly.	*dhīre dhīre boliye*
Please repeat that.	*ek bār aur kahiye*
Please write it down.	*zarā likh dījiye*

Getting Around

How do we get to ...?	*... kaise jāte haĩ?*

Where is the ...?	*kahā̃ hai ...?*
bus station	*bas aḍḍā*
train station	*(relve) sṭeshan*
road to ...	*... ko jānevālī saṛak*

What time does the ... leave?	*... kitne baje jāyegā/jāyegī?* (m/f)
What time does the ... arrive?	*... kitne baje pahũcegā/pahũcegī?* (m/f)
plane	*havāī jahāz* (m)
boat	*nāv* (f)
bus	*bas* (f)
train	*relgāṛī* (f)

Signs

प्रवेश/अन्दर	**Entrance**
निकार/बाहर	**Exit**
खुला	**Open**
बन्द	**Closed**
अन्दर आना [निषि/मना] है	**No Entry**
धूम्रपान करना [निषि/मना] है	**No Smoking**
निषि	**Prohibited**
गार्म	**Hot**
ठंडा	**Cold**
शोचालय	**Toilets**

When is the ... bus?	*... bas kab jāegī?*
first	*pehlā/pehlī*
next	*aglā/aglī*
last	*ākhirī*

I'd like a ... ticket.	*mujhe ... cāhiye*
a one-way ticket	*ek ek-tarafā ṭikaṭ*
a return ticket	*ek do-tarafā ṭikaṭ*

1st class	*pratham shrēni*
2nd class	*dvitīy shrēni*

Accommodation

Where is the (best/cheapest) hotel?	*sab se (acchā/sastā) hoṭal kahā̃ hai?*
Please write the address.	*zarā us kā patā likh dījiye*
Do you have any rooms available?	*kyā koī kamrā khālī hai?*
Do you a room with a double bed?	*kyā koī ḍabal palang kamrā hai?*

How much for ...?	*... kirāyā kitnā hai?*
one night	*ek din kā*
one week	*ek hafte kā*
two people	*do logõ ke liye*

I'd like a ...	*mujhe ... cāhiye*
single room	*singal kamrā*
double room	*ḍabal kamrā*
room with a bathroom	*ghusalkhānevālā kamrā*

I'd like to share a dorm.	*maĩ ḍorm mẽ ṭheharnā cāhtā/ī hũ* (m/f)
May I see it?	*kyā maĩ kamrā dekh saktā/ī hũ* (m/f)
Is there any other room?	*koī aur kamrā hai?*
Where's the bathroom?	*ghusalkhānā kahā̃ hai?*

bed	*palang*
blanket	*kambāl*
key	*cābī*
pillow	*takiyā*
shower	*shāvar*
toilet paper	*ṭāilet pepar*
towel	*tauliyā*
water (cold/hot)	*pānī (ṭhandā/garam)*
with a window	*khiṛkīvālā*

Around Town

Where's a/the ...	*... kahā̃ hai?*
bank	*baink*
church	*girjāghar*
consulate	*kaũnsal*
embassy	*dūtāvās*
Hindu temple	*mandir*
Jain temple	*jain mandir*
monastery	*maṭh*
mosque	*masjid*
museum	*sangrahālay*
post office	*ḍākkhānā*
public phone	*sārvajanik fon*
public toilet	*shaucālay*
Sikh temple	*gurudvārā*
town square	*cauk*

Is it far from/near here?	*kyā voh yahā̃ se dūr/ nazdīk hai?*

Shopping

Where's the nearest ...?	*sab se qarib ... kah hai?*
barber	*nāī kī dukān*
bookshop	*kitāb kī dukān*
camera shop	*kaimre kī dukān*
chemist/pharmacy	*davāī kī dukān*
clothing store	*kapṛe kī dukān*
general store	*dukān*
market	*bāzār*
tobacconist	*pān kī dukān*
washerman	*dhobī*

Where can I buy ...?	*maĩ ... kah kharīd sakta hũ?*
I'd like to buy ...	*mujhe ... kharidnā hai*
batteries	*baiṭrī*
clothes	*kapṛe*
colour film	*rangin film*
envelope	*lifāfā*
handicrafts	*hāth kī banī cīzẽ*
magazines	*patrikāẽ*
map	*naqshā*
newspaper (in English)	*(angrezī kā) akhbār*
paper	*kāghaz*
razor	*ustarā*
soap	*sābun*
stamp	*ṭikaṭ*
toothpaste	*manjan*
washing powder	*kapṛre dhone kā sābun*

big	*baṛā*
small	*choṭā*
more	*aur*
a little	*thoṛā*
too much/many	*bahut/adhik*
enough	*kāfī*

How much is this?	*is kā dām kyā hai?*
Can you write down the price?	*kāghaz par dām likh dījiye?*
I think it's too expensive.	*yeh bahut mahẽgā/i hai* (m/f)
Can you lower the price?	*is kā dām kam kījiye?*
Do you accept credit cards?	*kyā āp vizā kārḍ vaghairah lete ha?*

Health

Where is a/the ...?	*... kahā̃ hai?*
clinic	*davākhānā*
doctor	*ḍākṭar*
hospital	*aspatāl*

I'm sick.	*maĩ bīmār hũ*
I'm diabetic.	*mujhe madhumeh kī bīmārī hai*
I'm asthmatic.	*mujhe damā hai*
I'm allergic to antibiotics/ penicillin.	*mujhe ainṭībayoṭik/ penisilin se elarjī hai*

antiseptic	*aiṇṭīsepṭik*
antibiotics	*aiṇṭībayoṭik*
asprin	*(esprin) sirdard kī davā*
condoms	*nirodhak*
contraceptives	*garbnirodhak*
diarrhoea	*dast*
medicine	*davā*
nausea	*ghin*
syringe	*sūī*
tampons	*ṭaimpon*

Time & Days

What time is it?	*kitne baje haĩ?/ ṭaim kyā hai?*
It's (ten) o'clock.	*(das) baje haĩ*
half past two	*ḍhāī baje haĩ*
When?	*kab?*
today	*āj*
tomorrow/yesterday	*kal* (while *kal* is used for both, the meaning is made clear by context)
now	*ab*
morning	*saverā/subhā*
noon	*dopahar*
evening	*shām*
night	*rāt*
day	*din*
week	*haftā*
month	*mahīnā*
year	*sāl/baras*
Monday	*somvār*
Tuesday	*mangalvār*
Wednesday	*budhvār*
Thursday	*guruvār/brihaspativār*
Friday	*shukravār*
Saturday	*shanivār*
Sunday	*itvār/ravivār*

Numbers

Whereas we count in tens, hundreds, thousands, millions and billions, the Indian numbering system goes tens, hundreds, thousands, hundred thousands, ten millions. A hundred thousand is a *lākh*, and 10 million is a *crore*. These two words are almost always used in place of their English equivalents.

Emergencies

Help!	*mada kījiye!*
Stop!	*ruko!*
Thief!	*cor!*
Call a doctor!	*ḍākṭar ko bulāo!*
Call an ambulance!	*embulains le ānā!*
Call the police!	*pulis ko bulāo!*
I'm lost.	*maĩ rāstā bhūl gayā/ gayī hū̃* (f/m)
Where is the ...?	*... kahā̃ hai?*
police station	*thānā*
toilet	*g̲husalk̲hānā*
I wish to contact my embassy/ consulate.	*maĩ apne embassy ke sebāt katnā logõ cāhtā/cāhtī hū̃* (f/m)

Once into the thousands, large written numbers have commas every two places, not three.

1	*ek*
2	*do*
3	*tīn*
4	*cār*
5	*pā̃c*
6	*chai*
7	*sāt*
8	*āṭh*
9	*nau*
10	*das*
11	*gyārah*
12	*bara*
13	*terah*
14	*caudah*
15	*pandrah*
16	*solah*
17	*satrah*
18	*aṭṭhārah*
19	*unnīs*
20	*bīs*
21	*ikkīs*
30	*tīs*
40	*cālīs*
50	*pacās*
60	*sāṭh*
70	*sattar*

80	*assī*
90	*nabbe/navve*
100	*sau*
1000	*hazār*
100,000	*ek lākh*
(written 1,00,000)	
10 million	*ek crore*
(written 1,00,00,000)	

Food

breakfast	*nāshtā*
lunch	*din kā khānā*
dinner	*rāt kā khānā*
fork	*kāṭā*
knife	*churī*
glass	*glās*
plate	*pleṭ*
I'm a vegetarian.	*maĩ shākāhārī hũ*
food	*khānā*
bread	*roṭī*
fried bread	*parāṭhā*
tandoori rounds	*nān* or *tandūrī roṭī*
Western-style bread	*ḍabal* (double) *roṭī*
butter	*makkhan*
buttermilk	*chāch*
cheese	*panīr*
chillies	*mirc*
(without chillies)	(*mirc ke binā*)
rice	*cāval*
fried rice	*pulāv*
salt	*namak*
spices	*masāle*
sugar	*cīnī*
yogurt	*dahī*

Vegetables

cabbage	*band gobhī*
capsicum	*shimlā mirc*
eggplant/aubergine	*baĩgan*
lentils	*dāl*
onion	*pyāz*
peas	*maṭar*
potato	*ālū*
pumpkin	*kaddū*
spinach	*pālak*
tomato	*ṭamāṭar*
vegetable	*sabzī/sāg*

Fruit

apple	*seb*
apricot	*khubānī*
banana	*kelā*
fruit	*phal*
grapes	*angūr*
guava	*amrūd*
lemon	*nībū*
mandarin	*santarā*
mango	*ām*
orange	*nārangi*
peach	*ārū*
pear	*naspatī*
papaya	*papītā*

Meat & Poultry

beef	*gāy kā māns*
chicken	*murgh*
fish	*machlī*
goat	*bakrī kā māns*
meat	*māns/gosht*
mutton	*ber kā māns*
pork	*suar kā māns*

Drinks

coffee	*kāfi*
milk	*dūdh*
soft drink	*sauft ḍrink*
(cup of) tea	*cāy*
tea with milk	*dūdhvālī cāy*
tea with sugar	*cīnī ke sāth*
(boiled) water	(*ūblā*) *pānī*
mineral water	*minaral vāṭar*

Glossary

Here, with definitions, are some unfamiliar words and abbreviations you might meet in this book. For definitions of some common food and drink terms, see the separate Food & Drinks section at the end.

General

acha – 'OK' or 'I understand'
acharya – revered teacher; originally a spiritual guide
Adivasi – tribal person
agarbathi – incense
Agni – major deity in the *Vedas*; mediator between humans and the gods; also fire
ahimsa – discipline of nonviolence
AIR – All India Radio, the national broadcaster
air-cooled room – room in guesthouse, hotel or home, generally with a big, noisy water-filled fan built into the wall
Amir – Muslim nobleman
amrit – nectar of life; also baptism
amrita – immortality
Ananda – the *Buddha*'s cousin and personal attendant
ananda – happiness
Ananta – snake on which *Vishnu* reclined
Andhaka – 1000-headed demon, killed by *Shiva*
angrezi – foreigner
anna – 16th of a rupee; no longer legal tender but occasionally referred to in marketplaces
Annapurna – form of *Durga*, worshipped for her power to provide food
apsara – heavenly nymph
Aranyani – Hindu goddess of forests
Ardhanari – *Shiva* in half-male, half-female form
Arishta – *daitya* who, having taken the form of a bull, attacked *Krishna* and was killed by him
Arjuna – *Mahabharata* hero and military commander who married Subhadra, took up arms against and overcame all manner of demons, had the *Bhagavad Gita* related to him by *Krishna*, led Krishna's funeral ceremony at Dwarka and finally retired to the Himalaya
Aryan – Sanskrit word for 'noble'; refers to those who migrated from Persia and settled in northern India
Ashoka – ruler in the 3rd century BC, Buddhism's most famous convert
ashram – spiritual community or retreat
ashrama – system; essentially there are three stages in life recognised under this system: brahmachari, grihastha and sanyasin but this kind of merit is only available to the upper three Hindu castes
attar – essential oil made from flowers and used as a base for perfumes
autorickshaw – small, noisy, three-wheeled, motorised contraption for transporting passengers, livestock etc for short distances; found throughout the country, they are cheaper than taxis
Avalokiteshvara – in *Mahayana* Buddhism, the *Bodhisattva* of compassion; called Kannon in Japan, Kuan Yin in China and Chenrezig in Tibet
avatar – incarnation of a deity, usually *Vishnu*
ayah – children's nurse or nanny
Ayurveda – the ancient and complex science of Indian herbal medicine and healing
azan – Muslim call to prayer

baba – religious master or father; term of respect
babu – a lower level clerical worker (derogatory)
bagh – garden
bahadur – brave or chivalrous; an honorific title
bakhu – the traditional dress of women in Sikkim
baksheesh – tip, bribe or donation
bandh – general strike
banian – T-shirt or undervest
baniya – moneylender
banyan – Indian fig tree

baoli – see *baori*
baori – well, particularly a step-well with landings and galleries; in Gujarat it is more commonly referred to as a baoli
baradari – summer house
bazaar – market area; a market town is also called a bazaar
bearer – rather like a butler
beedi – see *bidi*
begum – Muslim woman of high rank
Bhagavad Gita – Hindu Song of the Divine One; Krishna's lessons to *Arjuna*, the main thrust of which was to emphasise the philosophy of *bhakti*; Bhagavad Gita is part of the *Mahabharata*
Bhairava – the Terrible; refers to the eighth incarnation of *Shiva* in his demonic form
bhajan – devotional song
bhakti – surrendering to the gods; faith
bhang – dried leaves and flowering shoots of the marijuana plant
bhangra – Punjabi disco
Bharat – Hindi for India
Bharata – half-brother of *Rama*; ruled while Rama was in exile
bhavan – house; also spelt 'bhawan'
bheesti – see *bhisti*
bherra – big, important
Bhima – *Mahabharata* hero; he is the brother of *Hanuman* and renowned for his great strength
bhisti – water carrier
bidi – small, hand-rolled cigarette; really just a rolled-up leaf
bindi – forehead mark worn by women
BJP – Bharatiya Janata Party
black money – undeclared and untaxed money
Bodhi Tree – tree under which the *Buddha* sat when he attained enlightenment
Bodhisattva – literally 'one whose essence is perfected wisdom'; in *Early Buddhism*, Bodhisattva refers only to the *Buddha* during the period between his conceiving the intention to strive for Buddhahood and the moment he attained it; in *Mahayana* Buddhism, it refers to one who renounces *nirvana* in order to help others attain it
Bollywood – India's answer to Hollywood; the film industry of Mumbai (Bombay)
Bon – pre-Buddhist animist religion of Tibet
Brahma – Hindu god; worshipped as the creator in the *Trimurti*
brahmachari – chaste student stage of the *ashrama* system
Brahmanism – early form of Hinduism which evolved from Vedism (see *Vedas*); named after *Brahmin* priests and *Brahma*
Brahmin – member of the priest caste, the highest Hindu caste
Buddha – Awakened One; the originator of Buddhism; also regarded by Hindus as the ninth incarnation of *Vishnu*
Buddhism – see *Early Buddhism*
bugyal – high-altitude meadow
bund – embankment or dyke
burkha – one-piece garment used by Muslim women to cover themselves from head to toe
bustee – slum

cantonment – administrative and military area of a Raj-era town
caravanserai – traditional accommodation for camel caravans; also known as serai
caste – one's hereditary station in life
chaam – ritual masked dance performed by some Buddhist monks in *gompas* to celebrate the victory of good over evil and of *Buddhism* over pre-existing religions
chaitya – Sanskrit form of 'cetiya', meaning shrine or object of worship; has come to mean temple, and more specifically, a hall divided into a central nave and two side aisles by a line of columns, with a votive *stupa* at the end
chakra – focus of one's spiritual power; disc-like weapon of *Vishnu*
Chamunda – form of *Durga*; a real terror, armed with a scimitar, noose and mace, and clothed in elephant hide, her mission was to kill the demons Chanda and Munda
chance list – waiting list on Indian Airlines flights
chandra – moon, or the moon as a god
Chandragupta – ruler of India in the 3rd century BC
chappals – sandals
Char Dham – four pilgrimage destinations of Badrinath, Kedarnath, Yamunotri and Gangotri
charas – resin of the marijuana plant; also referred to as 'hashish'

charbagh – literally 'four gardens'; formal Persian garden, divided into quarters
charpoy – Indian rope bed
chedi – see *chaitya*
chela – pupil or follower, as George Harrison was to Ravi Shankar
chhatri – literally 'umbrella'; cenotaph
chikan – embroidered cloth
chillum – pipe of a *hookah*; commonly used to describe the pipes used for smoking *ganja*
chinkara – gazelle
chital – spotted deer
chogyal – king
choli – sari blouse
chomos – Tibetan Buddhist nuns
chorten – Tibetan for *stupa*
choultry – pilgrim's resthouse; also called *dharamsala*
chowk – town square, intersection or marketplace
chowkidar – night watchman or caretaker
chuba – dress worn by Tibetan women
Cong (I) – Congress Party of India; also known as Congress (I)
CPI – Communist Party of India
CPI (M) – Communist Party of India (Marxist)
crore – 10 million, written 1,00,00,000
cutcherry – office or building used for public business

dacoit – bandit (particularly armed bandit) or outlaw
dagoba – see *stupa*
daitya – demon or giant who fought against the gods
Dalit – preferred term for India's *Untouchable* caste; see also *Harijan*
dargah – shrine or place of burial of a Muslim saint
darshan – offering or an audience with someone; viewing of a deity
Dattatreya – *Brahmin* saint who embodied the *Trimurti*
deul – temple sanctuary
devadasi – temple dancer
Devi – *Shiva*'s wife
dhaba – basic restaurant; also snack
dham – holiest pilgrimage places of India
dharamsala – pilgrim's resthouse
dharma – the word used by both Hindus and Buddhists to refer to their respective moral codes of behaviour
dharna – nonviolent protest
dhobi – person who washes clothes
dhobi ghat – place where clothes are washed
dholi – man-carried portable 'chairs'; you may still see some elderly tourists being carried in them
dhoti – like a *lungi*, but the cloth is then pulled up between the legs; worn by men
dhurrie – rug
Digambara – literally 'Sky-Clad'; a Jain sect whose followers demonstrate their disdain for worldly goods by going naked
dikpala – temple guardian
Din-i-Ilahi – Akbar's philosophy asserting the common truth in all religions
diwan – principal officer in a princely state; royal court or council
Diwan-i-Am – hall of public audiences
Diwan-i-Khas – hall of private audiences
dowry – money and goods given by a bride's parents to their son-in-law's family; it's illegal but few arranged marriages (most marriages are arranged) can be made without it
Dravidian – member of one of the original races of India, which were pushed south by the Indo-Europeans and now mixed with them
dukhang – Tibetan prayer hall
dun – valley
dupatta – long scarf often worn with the *salwar* and *kameez*
durbar – royal court; also used to describe a government
Durga – the Inaccessible; a form of *Shiva*'s wife, *Devi*, a beautiful but fierce woman riding a tiger; a major goddess of the Shakti cult
dwarpal – doorkeeper; sculpture beside the doorways to Hindu or Buddhist shrines

Early Buddhism – any of the schools of Buddhism established directly after Buddha's death and before the advent of *Mahayana*; a modern form is the *Theravada* (Teaching of the Elders) practised in Sri Lanka and South-East Asia; Early Buddhism differed from the *Mahayana* in that it did not teach the *Bodhisattva* ideal
elatalam – small hand-held cymbals

election symbols – identifying symbols for the various political parties, used to canvas illiterate voters
Emergency – period in the 1970s during which Indira Gandhi suspended many political rights
Eve-teasing – sexual harassment

fakir – Muslim who has taken a vow of poverty; also applied to a *sadhu* or other Hindu ascetic

gabba – appliqued Kashmiri rug
Ganesh – Hindu god of good fortune; popular elephant-headed son of *Shiva* and *Parvati* he is also known as Ganpati and his vehicle is a rat-like creature
Ganga – Hindu goddess representing the sacred Ganges River; said to flow from the toe of *Vishnu*
ganga aarti – river worship ceremony
ganj – market
ganja – dried flowering tips of the marijuana plant
garh – fort
Garuda – man-bird vehicle of *Vishnu*
gaur – Indian bison
Gayatri – sacred verse of *Rig-Veda*; a *Brahmin* will repeat this mentally twice a day
Gelukpa – an order of Tibetan Buddhism of which the Dalai Lama is the spiritual leader
geyser – hot-water heater usually found in bathrooms
ghat – steps or landing on a river; range of hills, or road up hills
ghazal – Urdu song derived from poetry; sad love theme
giri – hill
GITO – Government of India Tourist Office
GMVN – Garhwal Mandal Vikas Nigam, Garhwal tourist organisation
godmen – commercially minded gurus
gompa – Tibetan Buddhist monastery
Gonds – aboriginal Indian race, now mainly found in the jungles of central India
goonda – ruffian; political parties sometimes employ goondas in gangs
gopi – milkmaid; *Krishna* was fond of them
gumbad – dome on a Muslim tomb or mosque
gurdwara – Sikh temple
guru – teacher or holy person; in Sanskrit literally 'goe' (darkness) and 'roe' (to dispel)
Guru Granth Sahib – Sikh holy book

haj – Muslim pilgrimage to Mecca
haji – Muslim who has made the *haj*
hammam – Turkish bath
Hanuman – Hindu monkey god, prominent in the *Ramayana*, and a follower of *Rama*
Hari – another name for *Vishnu*
Harijan – name (no longer considered acceptable) given by Gandhi to India's *Untouchable* class, meaning 'children of god'
haveli – a traditional, ornately decorated residence, particularly in reference to those found in Rajasthan and Gujarat
hijra – eunuch
Hinayana – see *Early Buddhism*
hookah – water pipe used for smoking *ganja*
howdah – seat for carrying people on an elephant's back
HPTDC – Himachal Pradesh Tourist Development Corporation
hypothecated – Indian equivalent of leased or mortgaged; you may see small signs on taxis or autorickshaws stating that the vehicle is 'hypothecated' to some bank or other

idgah – open enclosure to the west of a town where prayers are offered during the Muslim Eid al-Zuhara festival
ikat – fabric made with thread which is tie-dyed before weaving
imam – Muslim religious leader
imambara – tomb dedicated to a Shi'ia Muslim holy man
Indo-Saracenic – style of colonial architecture that integrated Western designs with Muslim, Hindu and Jain influences
Indra – most important and prestigious of the Vedic gods; god of rain, thunder, lightning and war

jagamohan – assembly hall
Jagannath – Lord of the Universe; a form of *Krishna*
jali – carved marble lattice screen, also used

to refer to the holes or spaces produced through carving timber
janata – literally 'people'; the Janata Party is the People's Party
jataka – tale from *Buddha*'s various lives
jhuggi – shanty settlement; also called *bustee*
ji – honorific that can be added to the end of almost anything; thus 'Babaji', Memji, 'Gandhiji'
JKLF – Jammu & Kashmir Liberation Front
jooti – traditional pointy-toed shoe of Rajasthan
juggernaut – huge, extravagantly decorated temple 'car' dragged through the streets during Hindu festivals
jyoti linga – most important shrines to *Shiva*, of which there are 12; literally phallic symbol of light

kabaddi – traditional game (like tag)
Kailasa – sacred Himalayan mountain; home of *Shiva*
Kali – the Black; terrible form of *Devi* commonly depicted with black skin, dripping with blood, surrounded by snakes and wearing a necklace of skulls
Kama – Hindu god of love
kameez – woman's shirt-like tunic
karma – Hindu-Buddhist principle of retributive justice for past deeds
karmachario – workers
kata – Tibetan prayer shawl, traditionally given to a *lama* when pilgrims are brought into his presence
khadi – homespun cloth; Mahatma Gandhi encouraged people to spin this rather than buy English cloth
Khalistan – Sikh secessionists' name for an independent Punjab
Khalsa – Sikh brotherhood
khan – Muslim honorific title
khur – Asiatic wild ass
kiang – wild ass found in Ladakh
kibla – direction in which Muslims face in prayer, often marked with a niche carved into the mosque wall
kirtan – Sikh hymn-singing
KMVN – Kumaon Mandal Vikas Nigam; Kumaon tourist organisation
kos minar – milestone
kot – fort
kothi – residence, house or mansion
kotwali – police station
Krishna – *Vishnu*'s eighth incarnation, often coloured blue; Krishna revealed the *Bhagavad Gita* to *Arjuna*
Kshatriya – Hindu caste of soldiers or administrators; second in the caste hierarchy
kund – lake or tank; Toda village
kurta – long shirt with either short collar or no collar

la – Tibetan for mountain pass
Lakshmi – *Vishnu*'s consort, Hindu goddess of wealth; she sprang forth from the ocean holding a lotus
lama – Tibetan-Buddhist priest or monk
Laxmi – see *Lakshmi*
lhamo – Tibetan opera
lingam – phallic symbol; symbol of *Shiva*; plural is linga
lok – people
Losar – Tibetan New Year
Losong – Sikkimese New Year
lungi – worn by men, this loose, coloured garment (similar to a sarong) is pleated by the wearer at the waist to fit snugly

machaan – observation tower
madrasa – Islamic college
Mahabharata – Great Hindu Vedic epic poem of the Bharata dynasty; contains approximately 10,000 verses, that describe the battle between the Pandavas and the Kauravas
Mahabodhi Society – founded in 1891 to encourage Buddhist studies
mahal – house or palace
maharaja – great king or princely ruler
maharana – see *maharaja*
maharao – see *maharaja*
maharawal – see *maharaja*
maharani – wife of a princely ruler or a ruler in her own right
mahatma – literally 'great soul'
Mahayana – the 'greater-vehicle' of Buddhism; a later adaptation of the teaching, which lays emphasis on the Bodhisattva ideal, teaching the renunciation of *nirvana* (ultimate peace and cessation of rebirth) in order to help other beings along the way to enlightenment

mahout – elephant rider or master
maidan – open grassed area in a city or a parade ground
Maitreya – *Buddha* of the future
mandal – shrine
mandala – circle; symbol used in Hindu and Buddhist art to symbolise the universe
mandapam – pillared pavilion in front of a temple
mandi – market
mandir – temple
mani stone – stone carved with the Tibetan-Buddhist mantra 'Om mani padme hum', or 'Hail to the jewel in the lotus'
mani walls – Tibetan stone walls with sacred inscriptions
mantra – sacred word or syllable used by Buddhists and Hindus to aid concentration; metrical psalms of praise found in the *Vedas*
Mara – the Buddhist personification of that which obstructs the cultivation of virtue, often depicted with hundreds of arms; also the god of death
Maratha – central Indian people who controlled much of India at various times and fought the *Mughals* and *Rajputs*
marg – major road; meadow
masjid – mosque
mata – mother
mehndi – henna; ornate henna patterns painted on women's hands and feet for important festivals and ceremonies (eg, marriage)
mela – fair
memsahib – married Western women (from 'madam-sahib')
Meru – mythical mountain found in the centre of the earth
mihrab – prayer niche in the wall of a mosque indicating the direction of Mecca; see also *kibla*
mithuna – pairs of men and women; often seen in temple sculpture
Moghul – see *Mughal*
moksha – liberation from *samsara*
monsoon – rainy season
mudra – ritual hand movements used in Hindu religious dancing; gesture of *Buddha* figure
muezzin – one who calls Muslims to prayer from the minaret
Mughal – Muslim dynasty of Indian emperors from Babur to Aurangzeb
mullah – Muslim scholar, teacher or religious leader
mund – village

nadi – river
Naga – mythical serpent-like beings capable of changing into human form
namaz – Muslim prayers
Nandi – bull, vehicle of *Shiva*
nautch girls – dancing girls
nawab – Muslim ruling prince or powerful landowner
Naxalites – ultraleftist political movement begun in Naxal Village, West Bengal, as a peasant rebellion characterised by extreme violence; it still exists in Uttar Pradesh, Bihar and Andhra Pradesh
nilgai – antelope
nirvana – this is the ultimate aim of Buddhists and the final release from the cycle of existence
niwas – house, building

om – sacred invocation representing the absolute essence of the divine principle; for Buddhists, if repeated often enough with complete concentration, it should lead to a state of emptiness

padma – lotus; another name for the Hindu goddess *Lakshmi*
pagoda – see *stupa*
palanquin – box-like enclosure carried on poles on four men's shoulders; the occupant sits inside on a seat
Pali – the language, related to Sanskrit, in which the Buddhist scriptures were recorded; scholars still refer to the original Pali texts
panchayat – village council
pandal – marquee
pandit – expert or wise person; sometimes used to mean a bookworm
Parsi – adherent of the Zoroastrian faith; Persian
Parvati – another form of *Devi*
pashmina – fine wool from a pashmina goat; also a shawl
PCO – public call office from where you

can usually also make interstate and international telephone calls
peepul – fig tree, especially a bo tree
pietra dura – marble inlay used extensively at the Taj Mahal
pinjrapol – animal hospital maintained by Jains
POK – Pakistan Occupied Kashmir
pradesh – state
prasad – food offering used in religious ceremonies
puja – literally 'respect'; offering or prayer
pukka – proper; a Raj-era term
pukka sahib – proper European gentleman
punka – cloth fan, swung by pulling a cord
purdah – custom among some Muslims (also adopted by many Hindus, especially the *Rajputs*) of keeping their women in seclusion
Purnima – full moon; considered to be an auspicious time

Qawwali – Sufi devotional singing
qila – fort
Quran – the holy book of Islam; also spelt Koran

raga – any of several conventional patterns of melody and rhythm that form the basis for freely interpreted compositions
railhead – station or town at the end of a railway line; termination point
raj – rule or sovereignty
raja, rana – king
Rajput – Hindu warrior caste, former rulers of western India
Rama – seventh incarnation of *Vishnu*
Ramayana – the story of *Rama* and Sita and their conflict with Ravana is one of India's best-known legends, retold throughout almost all South-East Asia
rani – female ruler or wife of a king
ranns – deserts
rasa – literally 'flavour'; the unique quality with which a skilled classical dancer imbues a performance
rasta roko – roadblock set up for protest purposes
rath – temple chariot or car used in religious festivals
rawal – nobleman
rickshaw – small, two or three-wheeled passenger vehicle
Rig-Veda – original and longest of the four main *Vedas*, or holy Sanskrit texts
rishi – any poet, philosopher, saint or sage; originally a sage to whom the hymns of the *Vedas* were revealed
Road – railway town which serves as a communication point to a larger town off the line, eg, Mt Abu and Abu Road

sadar – main
sadhu – ascetic, or holy person; one who is trying to achieve enlightenment; usually addressed as 'swamiji' or 'babaji'
sagar – lake, reservoir
sahib – respectful title applied to any gentleman
salwar – loose trousers usually worn with a *kameez*
samadhi – in Hindusim, ecstatic state, sometimes defined as 'ecstasy, trance, communion with God'; in *Buddhism*, concentration; also a place where a holy man has been cremated, usually venerated as a shrine
sambar – deer
samsara – Buddhists and Hindus alike believe earthly life is cyclical; you are born again and again, and the quality of these rebirths is dependent upon your *karma* in previous lives
sangam – meeting of two rivers
sangha – community or order of Buddhist priests
sanyasin – like a *sadhu*; a wandering ascetic who has renounced all worldly things as part of the *ashrama* system
Saraswati – wife of *Brahma*, goddess of speech and learning; usually sits on a white swan, holding a *veena*
Sati – wife of *Shiva*; became a sati ('honourable woman') by immolating herself; although banned more than a century ago, the act of sati is still occasionally performed
satra – Hindu Vaishnavaite monastery and centre for art
satsang – discourse by a *swami* or *guru*
satyagraha – nonviolent protest involving a hunger strike, popularised by Mahatma Gandhi; from Sanskrit, literally meaning 'insistence on truth'

Scheduled Castes – official term used for the *Untouchables* or *Dalits*
serai – accommodation for travellers
shahada – Muslim declaration of faith ('there is no God but Allah; Mohammed is his prophet')
Shaivism – worship of *Shiva*
Shaivite – follower of *Shiva*
shakti – creative energies perceived as female deities; devotees follow the cult of Shaktism
shikara – gondola-like boat used on Srinagar's lakes in Kashmir
shikhar – hunting expedition
shirting – material from which shirts are made
Shiva – Destroyer; also the Creator, in which form he is worshipped as a *lingam*
shola – virgin forest
shree – see *shri*
shri – honorific; these days the Indian equivalent of Mr or Mrs
Shudra – see *Sudra*
sikhara – Hindu temple-spire or temple
singh – literally 'lion'; a surname adopted by *Rajputs* and Sikhs
sitar – Indian stringed instrument
Siva – see *Shiva*
sree – see *shri*
sri – see *shri*
stupa – Buddhist religious monument composed of a solid hemisphere topped by a spire, containing relics of the Buddha; also known as a 'dagoba'
Sudra – caste of labourers
Sufi – Muslim mystic
Surya – the sun; a major deity in the *Vedas*
sutra – string; list of rules expressed in verse
swami – title of respect meaning 'lord of the self'; given to initiated Hindu monks
sweeper – lowest caste servant, who performs the most menial of tasks

tabla – pair of drums
tal – lake
tank – reservoir
tantric Buddhism – Tibetan Buddhism with strong sexual and occult overtones
tempo – noisy, three-wheeler public transport vehicle; bigger than an autorickshaw
thakur – nobleman
thangka – rectangular Tibetan painting on cloth
theertham – temple tank
Theravada – literally 'dwelling'; orthodox form of *Buddhism* practised in Sri Lanka and South-East Asia which is characterised by its adherence to the *Pali* canon
thug – Thuggee; ritual murderers centred in Madhya Pradesh in the last century
tikka – mark devout Hindus put on their foreheads
tilak – forehead mark worn by devout Hindu men
tirthankars – the 24 great Jain teachers
tonga – two-wheeled horse or pony carriage
torana – architrave around a temple entrance
toy train – narrow-gauge railway
Trimurti – triple form; the Hindu triad of *Brahma*, *Shiva* and *Vishnu*
Tripitaka – classic *Theravada* Buddhist scriptures, divided into three categories, hence the name 'Three Baskets'
tripolia – triple gateway
tso – Tibetan for 'lake'
tsuglahkhang – literally 'grand temple'; usually the main hall in a monastery complex

Untouchable – lowest caste or 'casteless', for whom the most menial tasks are reserved; the name derives from the belief that higher castes risk defilement if they touch one; formerly known as *Harijan*, now *Dalit*
Upanishads – esoteric doctrine; ancient texts forming part of the *Vedas*; texts delving into weighty matters such as the nature of the universe and soul

varna – concept of caste
vastu shastra – India's answer to the Chinese art of divine design, feng shui
Vedas – Hindu sacred books; collection of hymns composed in pre-classical Sanskrit during the second millennium BC and divided into four books: *Rig-Veda*, Yajur-Veda, Sama-Veda and Atharva-Veda
veena – stringed instrument
vihara – Buddhist monastery, generally with central court or hall off which open residential cells, usually with a *Buddha* shrine at one end

vikram – large *tempo*
vimana – principal part of Hindu temple
Vishnu – third in the *Trimurti*; Vishnu is the Preserver and Restorer who so far has nine avatars: the fish Matsya; the tortoise Kurma; the wild boar Naraha; Narasimha; Vamana; Parasurama; *Rama*; *Krishna*; and *Buddha*

wallah – man; added onto almost anything, eg, *dhobi*-wallah, taxi-wallah, Delhi-wallah
wavs – step-wells, northern India
wazir – chief minister

yagna – self-mortification
yakshi – maiden
yantra – geometric plan thought to create energy
yatra – pilgrimage
yatri – tourist
yoni – female fertility symbol

zakat – charity or alms, the third 'pillar of Islam'; operates as a form of income tax
zamindar – landowner
zenana – area in an upper-class home where women are secluded; still part of some palaces in India

Food & Drink

The following are some of the more common food and drink terms you will come across in India.

achhar – pickle or marinade
aloo tikka – mashed potato patty, often filled with vegetables or meat
anna, annam – cooked white rice
appam – South Indian rice pancake
arak – liquor distilled from coconut milk, potatoes or rice
areca – see *betel*

barfi – fudge-like sweet made from milk
bati – baked ball of wholemeal flour
besan – chickpea flour
besan gate – spiced *besan* dough steamed and curried in gravy
betel – nut of the betel tree; the leaves and nut are mildly intoxicating and are chewed as a stimulant and digestive in a concoction called *paan*; the betel nut is also called areca nut
bhajia – vegetable fritter
bhang lassi – blend of *lassi* and bhang (a derivative of marijuana)
bhelpuri – thin, crisp fried rounds of dough mixed with puffed rice, fried lentil, lemon juice, chopped onion, herbs and chutney
biryani – fragrant steamed rice with meat or vegetables
bombil – fish dried in the sun and deep-fried to make Bombay Duck
bonda – mashed potato patty
boti – Punjabi dish; spicy, bite-sized boneless lamb

chai – tea (invariably very sweet)
chang – Tibetan rice or millet beer
chapati – unleavened Indian bread
chatni – chutney
cheiku – small brown fruit that looks like a potato, but is sweet
chini – sugar
chota – small, spirit drink measure (as in 'chota peg')
country liquor – locally produced liquor
curd – milk with acid or rennet added to solidify it

dahi – curd
dhaba – hole-in-the-wall restaurant or snack bar; boxed lunches delivered to office workers; snack also
dhal – curried lentil dish; a staple food of India
dhal makhani – black lentils and red kidney beans with cream and butter
dhansak – Parsi dish; meat, usually chicken, with curried lentils and rice
dosa – paper-thin pancakes made from lentil flour
dum pukht – steam-pressure cooking that uses a clay pot

falooda – rose-flavoured Muslim drink made with milk, cream, nuts and vermicelli
faluda – long chickpea-flour noodles
farsan – savoury nibbles
feni – Goan liquor distilled from coconut milk or cashews

ghee – clarified butter
gram – legumes
gulab jamun – deep-fried balls of dough soaked in rose-flavoured syrup
gyarhcee – famous Tibetan hotpot

halal – all permitted foods as dictated by the *Quran*
halwa – soft sweetmeat made with vegetables, cereals, lentils, nuts and fruit
harissa – wheat porridge with lamb

IMFL – Indian Made Foreign Liquor; beer or spirits produced in India

jaggery – hard, brown sugar-like sweetener made from palm sap
jal jeera – refreshing drink made with limewater, cumin, mint and rock salt and sold in earthenware pots by street vendors and in restaurants
jhaal – Bengali dish; curry made with fish, mustard seeds and chillies

kachori – corn and lentil savoury puff
kakori kabab – Lucknow kabab speciality
katori – *thali* bowl/compartment
kachauri – Indian-style breakfast of *puris* and vegetables
khaja – popular Bihari puff-pastry sweet
khataie – biscuits, specialty of Fatehpur Sikri
kheer – North Indian rice pudding
khichdi – heavy rice dish sometimes made with lentils, potatoes and peanut
khoya – reduced milk
korma – curry-like braised dish
kulcha – charcoal-baked bread
kulfi – flavoured (often with pistachio) ice confection, very similar to ice cream
kumbh – pitcher

ladoo – sweetmeat ball made with *gram* flour and semolina
lassi – refreshing yogurt and iced-water drink

malai – cream added for flavour
masala – mix (often spices)
masala dosa – South Indian dish; large lentil-flour crepe *(dosa)* stuffed with potatoes cooked with onions and curry leaves
masala soda – soft drink available at drink stalls
mattar paneer – peas and unfermented cheese in gravy
milk badam – invigorating morning drink made with saffron and almonds
misthi dhoi – Bengali sweet; curd sweetened with *jaggery*
mitha – sweet, eg, mitha *paan*
mithai – sweets
momo – Tibetan fried or steamed dumpling stuffed with vegetables or meat
Mughlai food – food influenced by the Mughals, who ruled the north from the 16th to the 18th century

naan – flat bread
namak – salt
namkin – prepackaged savoury (often spicy) nibbles
nihari – rich goat's broth

paan – *betel* nut and leaves plus chewing additives such as lime
pakora – bite-size piece of vegetable dipped in chickpea-flour batter and deep-fried
palak paneer – unfermented cheese in spinach gravy
paneer – unfermented cheese
pani – water
pappadam – thin, round crisp bread eaten with curries or as a snack
paratha – bread made with *ghee* and cooked on a hotplate
peitha – Agra sweet made from crystallised gourd
pilau – see *pulou*
pinda – funeral cake
poori – see *puri*
pulou – rice cooked in stock and flavoured with spices; known as 'pilau' in the West
puri – flat dough that puffs up when deep-fried; also 'poori'

rabri – milky confectionery
raita – yogurt side dish (usually mildly spiced and sometimes with shredded cucumber, pineapple etc)
ras malai – milk- and sugar-based sweet
rasgulla – sweet, small balls of cream-cheese flavoured with rose-water

reshmi kabab – tender chicken kabab cooked in the *tandoor*
rogan josh – Kashmiri dish; fiery lamb curry
roti – flat unleavened bread cooked on a hotplate

saadha – plain, eg, saadha *paan*
saag – leafy greens
sabzi – vegetables
samosa – deep-fried filled pastries
sev – savoury nibbles
shami – wrapped (kabab)
sheekh – skewered (kabab)
soma – intoxicating drink from plant juice
sonf – aniseed seeds; souf comes with the bill after a meal as a digestive

tandoor – clay oven
tangri – Punjabi chicken drumsticks
thali – traditional South Indian and Gujarati 'all-you-can-eat' meal
thugpa – Tibetan noodle soup
tiffin – snack or meal container often made of stainless steel
tikka – spiced, often-marinated, chunks of chicken, *paneer*, lamb etc, which are sometimes skewered
toddy – alcoholic drink, tapped from palm trees
tongba – Himalayan millet beer
tsampa – Tibetan staple of roast barley flour

vermicelli – thin rice noodles

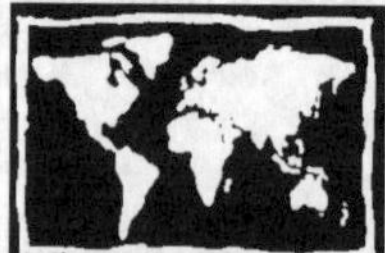

Lonely Planet Guides by Region

Lonely Planet is known worldwide for publishing practical, reliable and no-nonsense travel information in our guides and on our Web site. The Lonely Planet list covers just about every accessible part of the world. Currently there are 16 series: Travel guides, Shoestring guides, Condensed guides, Phrasebooks, Read This First, Healthy Travel, Walking guides, Cycling guides, Watching Wildlife guides, Pisces Diving & Snorkeling guides, City Maps, Road Atlases, Out to Eat, World Food, Journeys travel literature and Pictorials.

AFRICA Africa on a shoestring • Botswana • Cairo • Cairo City Map • Cape Town • Cape Town City Map • East Africa • Egypt • Egyptian Arabic phrasebook • Ethiopia, Eritrea & Djibouti • Ethiopian Amharic phrasebook • The Gambia & Senegal • Healthy Travel Africa • Kenya • Malawi • Morocco • Moroccan Arabic phrasebook • Mozambique • Namibia • Read This First: Africa • South Africa, Lesotho & Swaziland • Southern Africa • Southern Africa Road Atlas • Swahili phrasebook • Tanzania, Zanzibar & Pemba • Trekking in East Africa • Tunisia • Watching Wildlife East Africa • Watching Wildlife Southern Africa • West Africa • World Food Morocco • Zambia • Zimbabwe, Botswana & Namibia
Travel Literature: Mali Blues: Traveling to an African Beat • The Rainbird: A Central African Journey • Songs to an African Sunset: A Zimbabwean Story

AUSTRALIA & THE PACIFIC Aboriginal Australia & the Torres Strait Islands •Auckland • Australia • Australian phrasebook • Australia Road Atlas • Cycling Australia • Cycling New Zealand • Fiji • Fijian phrasebook • Healthy Travel Australia, NZ & the Pacific • Islands of Australia's Great Barrier Reef • Melbourne • Melbourne City Map • Micronesia • New Caledonia • New South Wales • New Zealand • Northern Territory • Outback Australia • Out to Eat – Melbourne • Out to Eat – Sydney • Papua New Guinea • Pidgin phrasebook • Queensland • Rarotonga & the Cook Islands • Samoa • Solomon Islands • South Australia • South Pacific • South Pacific phrasebook • Sydney • Sydney City Map • Sydney Condensed • Tahiti & French Polynesia • Tasmania • Tonga • Tramping in New Zealand • Vanuatu • Victoria • Walking in Australia • Watching Wildlife Australia • Western Australia
Travel Literature: Islands in the Clouds: Travels in the Highlands of New Guinea • Kiwi Tracks: A New Zealand Journey • Sean & David's Long Drive

CENTRAL AMERICA & THE CARIBBEAN Bahamas, Turks & Caicos • Baja California • Belize, Guatemala & Yucatán • Bermuda • Central America on a shoestring • Costa Rica • Costa Rica Spanish phrasebook • Cuba • Cycling Cuba • Dominican Republic & Haiti • Eastern Caribbean • Guatemala • Havana • Healthy Travel Central & South America • Jamaica • Mexico • Mexico City • Panama • Puerto Rico • Read This First: Central & South America • Virgin Islands • World Food Caribbean • World Food Mexico • Yucatán
Travel Literature: Green Dreams: Travels in Central America

EUROPE Amsterdam • Amsterdam City Map • Amsterdam Condensed • Andalucía • Athens • Austria • Baltic States phrasebook • Barcelona • Barcelona City Map • Belgium & Luxembourg • Berlin • Berlin City Map • Britain • British phrasebook • Brussels, Bruges & Antwerp • Brussels City Map • Budapest • Budapest City Map • Canary Islands • Catalunya & the Costa Brava • Central Europe • Central Europe phrasebook • Copenhagen • Corfu & the Ionians • Corsica • Crete • Crete Condensed • Croatia • Cycling Britain • Cycling France • Cyprus • Czech & Slovak Republics • Czech phrasebook • Denmark • Dublin • Dublin City Map • Dublin Condensed • Eastern Europe • Eastern Europe phrasebook • Edinburgh • Edinburgh City Map • England • Estonia, Latvia & Lithuania • Europe on a shoestring • Europe phrasebook • Finland • Florence • Florence City Map • France • Frankfurt City Map • Frankfurt Condensed • French phrasebook • Georgia, Armenia & Azerbaijan • Germany • German phrasebook • Greece • Greek Islands • Greek phrasebook • Hungary • Iceland, Greenland & the Faroe Islands • Ireland • Italian phrasebook • Italy • Kraków • Lisbon • The Loire • London • London City Map • London Condensed • Madrid • Madrid City Map • Malta • Mediterranean Europe • Milan, Turin & Genoa • Moscow • Munich • Netherlands • Normandy • Norway • Out to Eat – London • Out to Eat – Paris • Paris • Paris City Map • Paris Condensed • Poland • Polish phrasebook • Portugal • Portuguese phrasebook • Prague • Prague City Map • Provence & the Côte d'Azur • Read This First: Europe • Rhodes & the Dodecanese • Romania & Moldova • Rome • Rome City Map • Rome Condensed • Russia, Ukraine & Belarus • Russian phrasebook • Scandinavian & Baltic Europe • Scandinavian phrasebook • Scotland • Sicily • Slovenia • South-West France • Spain • Spanish phrasebook • Stockholm • St Petersburg • St Petersburg City Map • Sweden • Switzerland • Tuscany • Ukrainian phrasebook • Venice • Vienna • Wales • Walking in Britain • Walking in France • Walking in Ireland • Walking in Italy • Walking in Scotland • Walking in Spain • Walking in Switzerland • Western Europe • World Food France • World Food Greece • World Food Ireland • World Food Italy • World Food Spain **Travel Literature:** After Yugoslavia • Love and War in the Apennines • The Olive Grove: Travels in Greece • On the Shores of the Mediterranean • Round Ireland in Low Gear • A Small Place in Italy

Lonely Planet Mail Order

Lonely Planet products are distributed worldwide.They are also available by mail order from Lonely Planet, so if you have difficulty finding a title please write to us. North and South American residents should write to 150 Linden St, Oakland, CA 94607, USA; European and African residents should write to 10a Spring Place, London NW5 3BH, UK; and residents of other countries to Locked Bag 1, Footscray, Victoria 3011, Australia.

INDIAN SUBCONTINENT & THE INDIAN OCEAN Bangladesh • Bengali phrasebook • Bhutan • Delhi • Goa • Healthy Travel Asia & India • Hindi & Urdu phrasebook • India • India & Bangladesh City Map • Indian Himalaya • Karakoram Highway • Kathmandu City Map • Kerala • Madagascar • Maldives • Mauritius, Réunion & Seychelles • Mumbai (Bombay) • Nepal • Nepali phrasebook • North India • Pakistan • Rajasthan • Read This First: Asia & India • South India • Sri Lanka • Sri Lanka phrasebook • Tibet • Tibetan phrasebook • Trekking in the Indian Himalaya • Trekking in the Karakoram & Hindukush • Trekking in the Nepal Himalaya • World Food India **Travel Literature:** The Age of Kali: Indian Travels and Encounters • Hello Goodnight: A Life of Goa • In Rajasthan • Maverick in Madagascar • A Season in Heaven: True Tales from the Road to Kathmandu • Shopping for Buddhas • A Short Walk in the Hindu Kush • Slowly Down the Ganges

MIDDLE EAST & CENTRAL ASIA Bahrain, Kuwait & Qatar • Central Asia • Central Asia phrasebook • Dubai • Farsi (Persian) phrasebook • Hebrew phrasebook • Iran • Israel & the Palestinian Territories • Istanbul • Istanbul City Map • Istanbul to Cairo • Istanbul to Kathmandu • Jerusalem • Jerusalem City Map • Jordan • Lebanon • Middle East • Oman & the United Arab Emirates • Syria • Turkey • Turkish phrasebook • World Food Turkey • Yemen **Travel Literature:** Black on Black: Iran Revisited • Breaking Ranks: Turbulent Travels in the Promised Land • The Gates of Damascus • Kingdom of the Film Stars: Journey into Jordan

NORTH AMERICA Alaska • Boston • Boston City Map • Boston Condensed • British Columbia • California & Nevada • California Condensed • Canada • Chicago • Chicago City Map • Chicago Condensed • Florida • Georgia & the Carolinas • Great Lakes • Hawaii • Hiking in Alaska • Hiking in the USA • Honolulu & Oahu City Map • Las Vegas • Los Angeles • Los Angeles City Map • Louisiana & the Deep South • Miami • Miami City Map • Montreal • New England • New Orleans • New Orleans City Map • New York City • New York City City Map • New York City Condensed • New York, New Jersey & Pennsylvania • Oahu • Out to Eat – San Francisco • Pacific Northwest • Rocky Mountains • San Diego & Tijuana • San Francisco • San Francisco City Map • Seattle • Seattle City Map • Southwest • Texas • Toronto • USA • USA phrasebook • Vancouver • Vancouver City Map • Virginia & the Capital Region • Washington, DC • Washington, DC City Map • World Food New Orleans **Travel Literature**: Caught Inside: A Surfer's Year on the California Coast • Drive Thru America

NORTH-EAST ASIA Beijing • Beijing City Map • Cantonese phrasebook • China • Hiking in Japan • Hong Kong & Macau • Hong Kong City Map • Hong Kong Condensed • Japan • Japanese phrasebook • Korea • Korean phrasebook • Kyoto • Mandarin phrasebook • Mongolia • Mongolian phrasebook • Seoul • Shanghai • South-West China • Taiwan • Tokyo • Tokyo Condensed • World Food Hong Kong • World Food Japan **Travel Literature:** In Xanadu: A Quest • Lost Japan

SOUTH AMERICA Argentina, Uruguay & Paraguay • Bolivia • Brazil • Brazilian phrasebook • Buenos Aires • Buenos Aires City Map • Chile & Easter Island • Colombia • Ecuador & the Galapagos Islands • Healthy Travel Central & South America • Latin American Spanish phrasebook • Peru • Quechua phrasebook • Read This First: Central & South America • Rio de Janeiro • Rio de Janeiro City Map • Santiago de Chile • South America on a shoestring • Trekking in the Patagonian Andes • Venezuela **Travel Literature**: Full Circle: A South American Journey

SOUTH-EAST ASIA Bali & Lombok • Bangkok • Bangkok City Map • Burmese phrasebook • Cambodia • Cycling Vietnam, Laos & Cambodia • East Timor phrasebook • Hanoi • Healthy Travel Asia & India • Hill Tribes phrasebook • Ho Chi Minh City (Saigon) • Indonesia • Indonesian phrasebook • Indonesia's Eastern Islands • Java • Lao phrasebook • Laos • Malay phrasebook • Malaysia, Singapore & Brunei • Myanmar (Burma) • Philippines • Pilipino (Tagalog) phrasebook • Read This First: Asia & India • Singapore • Singapore City Map • South-East Asia on a shoestring • South-East Asia phrasebook • Thailand • Thailand's Islands & Beaches • Thailand, Vietnam, Laos & Cambodia Road Atlas • Thai phrasebook • Vietnam • Vietnamese phrasebook • World Food Indonesia • World Food Thailand • World Food Vietnam

ALSO AVAILABLE: Antarctica • The Arctic • The Blue Man: Tales of Travel, Love and Coffee • Brief Encounters: Stories of Love, Sex & Travel • Buddhist Stupas in Asia: The Shape of Perfection • Chasing Rickshaws • The Last Grain Race • Lonely Planet ... On the Edge: Adventurous Escapades from Around the World • Lonely Planet Unpacked • Lonely Planet Unpacked Again • Not the Only Planet: Science Fiction Travel Stories • Ports of Call: A Journey by Sea • Sacred India • Travel Photography: A Guide to Taking Better Pictures • Travel with Children • Tuvalu: Portrait of an Island Nation

lonely planet
South India

lonely planet
Delhi
Includes the Taj Mahal & the forts of Jaipur

lonely planet
HINDI & URDU
PHRASEBOOK

lonely planet
Rajasthan
Includes chapters on Agra, Delhi & Mumbai

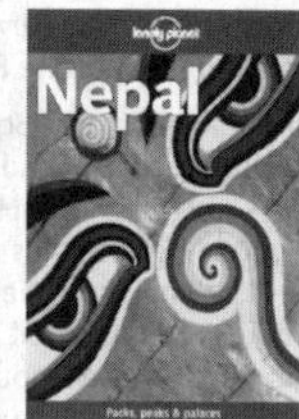
lonely planet
Nepal
Packs, peaks & palaces

lonely planet
healthy travel
Asia & India

lonely planet
Indian Himalaya
Experience the Abode of the Gods

lonely planet walking guide
Trekking in the Indian Himalaya

World Food
INDIA

lonely planet
Read This First:
ASIA & INDIA

lonely planet
İstanbul to Kathmandu

lonely planet
India

Index

Abbreviations

B&J – Bihar & Jharkhand
Del – Delhi
HP – Himachal Pradesh
J&K – Jammu & Kashmir
Kol – Kolkata (Calcutta)
L&Z – Ladakh & Zanskar
MP&C – Madhya Pradesh & Chhatisgarh
NER – north-eastern region
NP – National Park
P&H – Punjab & Haryana
Raj – Rajasthan
Sik – Sikkim
UP&U – Uttar Pradesh & Uttaranchal
WB – West Bengal
WS – Wildlife Sanctuary

Text

Bold indicates maps.

C

D

Bold indicates maps.

Bold indicates maps.

Bold indicates maps.

Bold indicates maps.

Bold indicates maps.

Boxed Text

MAP LEGEND

CITY ROUTES

Freeway — Freeway
Highway — Primary Road
Road — Secondary Road
Street — Street
Lane — Lane
Roadblocks
Unsealed Road
One-Way Street
Pedestrian Street
Stepped Street
Tunnel
Footbridge

REGIONAL ROUTES

Tollway, Freeway
Primary Road
Secondary Road
Minor Road

BOUNDARIES

International
State
Disputed
Fortified Wall

TRANSPORT ROUTES & STATIONS

Train
Metro
Tramway
Bus Route
Monorail
Cable Car, Chairlift
Ferry
Path in Park
Walking Trail
Walking Tour

HYDROGRAPHY

River, Creek
Canal
Lake, Tank
Dry Lake, Salt Lake
Spring, Rapids
Waterfalls

AREA FEATURES

Building
Park, Garden
National Park
Market
Beach
Campus
Cemetery
Urban

MAP SYMBOLS

CAPITAL — National Capital
CAPITAL — State Capital
City — City, Large Town
Town — Town
Village — Village
Place to Stay
Place to Eat
Point of Interest
Airfield, Airport
Bank
Bird Sanctuary
Border Crossing
Buddhist Temple
Bus Terminal, Sfop
Camping Ground
Cathedral, Church
Cave
Cinema
Embassy, Consulate
Festival
Fort
Fountain
Gate
Ghat
Golf Course
Gompa
Hindu Temple
Hospital
Internet Cafe
Islamic Shrine
Jain Temple
Lighthouse
Lookout
Monument
Mosque
Mountain, Hill
Mountain Range
Museum, Gallery
Parking Area
Pass
Petrol/Gas Station
Police Station
Post Office
Pub, Bar
Ruins
Shopping Centre
Sikh Temple
Ski Field
Stately Home, Haveli
Stupa
Swimming Pool
Taxi
Transport (General)
Telephone
Temple
Theatre
Toilet
Tomb
Tourist Information
Zoo

Note: not all symbols displayed above appear in this book

LONELY PLANET OFFICES

Australia
Locked Bag 1, Footscray, Victoria 3011
☎ 03 8379 8000 fax 03 8379 8111
email: talk2us@lonelyplanet.com.au

USA
150 Linden St, Oakland, CA 94607
☎ 510 893 8555 TOLL FREE: 800 275 8555
fax 510 893 8572
email: info@lonelyplanet.com

UK
10a Spring Place, London NW5 3BH
☎ 020 7428 4800 fax 020 7428 4828
email: go@lonelyplanet.co.uk

France
1 rue du Dahomey, 75011 Paris
☎ 01 55 25 33 00 fax 01 55 25 33 01
email: bip@lonelyplanet.fr
www.lonelyplanet.fr

World Wide Web: www.lonelyplanet.com *or* AOL keyword: lp
Lonely Planet Images: lpi@lonelyplanet.com.au